THE ROAMER'S GUIDE
UNITED STATES EDITION

A Complete Guide to America's Parks, Forests, National Landmarks,
Scenic Byways, and Beyond…

by
Chris Hanscom

The Roamer's Guide: United States Edition
© 2025 Chris Hanscom

All rights reserved. No part of this book may be reproduced, stored
in a retrieval system, or transmitted in any form or by any means—
electronic, mechanical, photocopying, recording,
or otherwise—without prior written permission from the publisher.

ISBN: 979-8-218-78084-5
First Edition, 2025
First Printing: December 2025
Second Printing: January 2026
Printed in the United States of America

Edited and designed by Roamwell Press
Published by Roamwell Press
https://roamwellpress.com/

*For the explorers, wanderers, and daydreamers
who find their peace in the wild places of America,
and for **my one** who shares the journey*

Table of Contents

Alabama	1
Alaska	8
Arizona	19
Arkansas	28
California	36
Colorado	61
Connecticut	72
Delaware	89
Florida	93
Georgia	112
Hawaii	121
Idaho	130
Illinois	139
Indiana	147
Iowa	156
Kansas	165
Kentucky	171
Louisiana	181
Maine	186
Maryland	194
Massachusetts	205
Michigan	215
Minnesota	225
Mississippi	235
Missouri	242
Montana	251
Nebraska	261
Nevada	266
New Hampshire	272
New Jersey	280
New Mexico	287
New York	296
North Carolina	315
North Dakota	327
Ohio	332
Oklahoma	346
Oregon	353
Pennsylvania	366
Rhode Island	385
South Carolina	389
South Dakota	398
Tennessee	407
Texas	419
Utah	431
Vermont	441
Virginia	453
Washington	465
West Virginia	481
Wisconsin	489
Wyoming	498

"To roam is to discover our true self."

UNITED STATES EDITION

Alabama

Alabama's landscapes invite exploration, with a rich collection of state parks, national forests, a beloved national park, and remarkable natural landmarks. From rolling Appalachian foothills and dense pine forests to coastal marshes and thundering waterfalls, Alabama offers diverse outdoor adventures.

📅 Peak Season
March–May and October–November bring Alabama's most comfortable weather. Spring offers mild days ideal for hiking, while fall delivers cooler air, colorful landscapes, and lively festivals.

📅 Offseason Months
December–February is mild and quieter, great for those seeking fewer crowds. July–August is hot and humid, making outdoor activities less comfortable, though Gulf Coast beaches stay popular.

🍃 Scenery & Nature Timing
Wildflowers brighten forests and hills in spring, while fall foliage colors the Appalachian foothills. Along the Gulf Coast, summer brings sea turtle nesting and bird migrations, and winter draws waterfowl.draws migratory waterfowl.

✨ Special
Alabama features the glowing "dismalites" of Dismals Canyon, the cascades of Little River Canyon and Noccalula Falls, and vast cave systems like Cathedral Caverns. The state's varied landscapes also include the Mobile-Tensaw Delta wetlands, Appalachian foothills, and Gulf Coast dunes.

ALABAMA

State Parks

☐ ▢ ♡ **Bladon Springs State Park:** Located in the rural town of Bladon Springs, Alabama, this park is known for its serene ambiance and four mineral springs that have been cherished since the 1800s for their purported healing properties. The park also has a quaint museum that delves into the area's history and natural wonders, offering a quiet retreat for nature lovers and history enthusiasts alike.

☐ ▢ ♡ **Brierfield Ironworks Historical State Park:** Situated in Brierfield, Alabama, this park preserves the remains of a Confederate ironworks facility that was vital to the South during the Civil War. Visitors can explore historical structures, including the iron furnace, while hiking through the park's wooded trails. The on-site museum offers exhibits on the region's industrial history and the significance of the ironworks in Alabama's economy.

☐ ▢ ♡ **Blue Springs State Park:** Nestled in the small town of Clio, Alabama, Blue Springs State Park is famed for its crystal-clear spring, which creates a beautiful blue-tinted pool. The spring is a popular spot for swimming and snorkeling, offering a refreshing and scenic experience in the heart of the Alabama countryside. The park is also home to a variety of wildlife, making it a peaceful destination for nature lovers.

☐ ▢ ♡ **Buck's Pocket State Park:** Tucked away in Grove Oak, Alabama, Buck's Pocket State Park is a hidden gem for outdoor adventurers. The park offers rugged hiking trails that lead to breathtaking vistas, ideal for capturing the beauty of Alabama's wilderness. With its secluded atmosphere, the park is perfect for camping, birdwatching, and immersing yourself in the tranquility of nature.

☐ ▢ ♡ **Cathedral Caverns State Park:** Located in Woodville, Alabama, Cathedral Caverns State Park is a stunning underground wonder. The park's cave system features awe-inspiring formations, including stalactites, stalagmites, and massive columns that tower over visitors. Guided cave tours take guests through the dark, cool tunnels, offering a fascinating glimpse into Alabama's geological history.

☐ ▢ ♡ **Cheaha State Park:** Situated in Delta, Alabama, Cheaha State Park sits atop the state's highest peak, offering sweeping views of the surrounding Appalachian Mountains. Visitors can enjoy a variety of outdoor activities, from hiking the challenging trails to camping under the stars. The panoramic vistas, especially at sunrise and sunset, make it a must-see destination for nature lovers and photographers.

☐ ▢ ♡ **Chewacla State Park:** Located in Auburn, Alabama, Chewacla State Park is known for its picturesque 26-acre lake, ideal for fishing, boating, and paddleboarding. The park offers a variety of outdoor experiences, including hiking and biking trails, scenic picnic areas, and camping facilities. The park's beautiful waterfall adds to the park's charm, creating a peaceful atmosphere for relaxation.

☐ ▢ ♡ **Chickasaw State Park:** Situated in Chickasaw, Alabama, this park is a lovely spot for outdoor activities and relaxation. It features a scenic lake for fishing and boating, as well as a sandy beach for swimming and sunbathing. The park also offers hiking trails, picnic areas, and campgrounds, making it an excellent choice for families and nature enthusiasts alike.

☐ ▢ ♡ **DeSoto State Park:** Located in Fort Payne, Alabama, DeSoto State Park is home to the stunning DeSoto Falls, which cascades over 100 feet in a breathtaking display of natural beauty. The park offers an array of outdoor activities, including hiking, fishing, and camping. The park's diverse wildlife and scenic trails make it a popular destination for nature lovers and photographers.

☐ ▢ ♡ **Frank Jackson State Park:** Situated in Opp, Alabama, Frank Jackson State Park is known for its serene 1,000-acre lake, perfect for fishing, boating, and swimming. The park also features a beautiful golf course, making it a great destination for both water and land-based recreation. Its tranquil atmosphere is perfect for those seeking a relaxing escape in nature.

☐ ▢ ♡ **Gulf State Park:** Located in Gulf Shores, Alabama, Gulf State Park is a coastal paradise featuring 2.5 miles of pristine white-sand beaches along the Gulf of Mexico. The park offers a variety of outdoor activities, including hiking and biking along scenic trails, fishing from the pier, and enjoying the beach. With its wide range of accommodations, including campsites and rental cottages, it's a top spot for a beach getaway.

☐ ▢ ♡ **Historic Blakeley State Park:** This park in Spanish Fort, Alabama, offers visitors a glimpse into the past with its preserved Civil War battlefield. The park features the remains of the historic Blakeley Fort, which played a significant role during the Battle of Mobile Bay. The park also has hiking trails, birdwatching opportunities, and a museum that highlights the area's rich Civil War history.

UNITED STATES EDITION

ALABAMA

☐ 🔖 ♡ **Joe Wheeler State Park:** Located on the Tennessee River in Rogersville, Alabama, Joe Wheeler State Park offers a picturesque setting for outdoor recreation. Visitors can enjoy fishing, boating, and hiking along the river, with scenic views and abundant wildlife. The park also features a golf course and comfortable accommodations, making it a perfect spot for a weekend getaway.

☐ 🔖 ♡ **Lake Guntersville State Park:** Nestled in the Appalachian foothills, Lake Guntersville State Park offers panoramic views of the 69,000-acre Lake Guntersville. The park features world-class fishing, boating, and hiking opportunities, as well as comfortable camping and cabin facilities. Its diverse habitats make it an ideal destination for wildlife watching and outdoor activities.

☐ 🔖 ♡ **Lake Lurleen State Park:** Located near Tuscaloosa, Alabama, Lake Lurleen State Park offers a beautiful, peaceful setting for outdoor activities. The park's 250-acre lake is perfect for fishing, boating, and swimming. With a variety of hiking trails, picnic areas, and camping facilities, it's a great location for a weekend escape or family outing.

☐ 🔖 ♡ **Lakepoint Resort State Park:** Located in Eufaula, Alabama, this large state park features a stunning 1,200-acre lake, ideal for fishing, boating, and swimming. The park offers a full-service resort with lakeside cabins, lodges, and a restaurant. Guests can also enjoy the park's hiking trails, golf course, and scenic picnic areas, making it an excellent destination for a relaxing getaway.

☐ 🔖 ♡ **Meaher State Park:** Situated on the shores of Mobile Bay, Meaher State Park in Spanish Fort, Alabama, offers a quiet retreat for fishing, hiking, and wildlife viewing. The park's large freshwater lake is ideal for boaters and anglers. Its proximity tho Mobile makes it a perfect spot for visitors looking to explore the natural beauty of the Gulf Coast.

☐ 🔖 ♡ **Monte Sano State Park:** Located in Huntsville, Alabama, Monte Sano State Park is known for its breathtaking views of the surrounding mountains and the Tennessee Valley. The park offers a variety of hiking and mountain biking trails, as well as scenic overlooks and camping sites. It's a popular spot for outdoor enthusiasts seeking a tranquil escape into nature.

☐ 🔖 ♡ **Oak Mountain State Park:** Situated in Pelham, Alabama, Oak Mountain is the state's largest park, featuring a wide range of outdoor activities. Visitors can enjoy miles of hiking, biking, and equestrian trails, as well as fishing in the park's lakes. The park also boasts a golf course, beach areas, and family-friendly campsites, making it a year-round destination for outdoor fun.

☐ 🔖 ♡ **Paul M. Grist State Park:** This park in Selma, Alabama, offers a peaceful, scenic environment for outdoor recreation. The park features a serene lake for fishing and boating, as well as hiking trails for exploring the surrounding forests. It's a perfect destination for those seeking a quiet and relaxing outdoor experience.

☐ 🔖 ♡ **Rickwood Caverns State Park:** Located in Warrior, Alabama, Rickwood Caverns is a unique park featuring an impressive limestone cave system. Guided tours take visitors through the cave's stunning formations, including stalactites and stalagmites. The park also offers a refreshing pool, hiking trails, and picnic areas for a fun and educational visit.

☐ 🔖 ♡ **Roland Cooper State Park:** Situated in Camden, Alabama, Roland Cooper State Park offers a tranquil setting with a scenic lake for fishing, boating, and swimming. The park also features hiking trails, picnic areas, and camping facilities, making it a perfect destination for a peaceful getaway.

☐ 🔖 ♡ **Tannehill Ironworks Historical State Park:** Located in McCalla, Alabama, Tannehill Ironworks Historical State Park offers visitors the chance to explore the remnants of a 19th-century ironworks that played a significant role in Alabama's industrial history. The park features a museum, historical exhibits, hiking trails, and picnic areas for a fascinating and enjoyable experience.

☐ 🔖 ♡ **Wind Creek State Park:** Situated on the shores of Lake Martin in Alexander City, Alabama, Wind Creek State Park offers a serene escape for fishing, boating, and hiking. With its beautiful lake views and excellent camping facilities, it's a popular spot for outdoor enthusiasts looking to enjoy the natural beauty of central Alabama.

ALABAMA

National Parks

Birmingham Civil Rights National Monument: This monument preserves key landmarks of the Civil Rights Movement in Birmingham, including the 16th Street Baptist Church, Kelly Ingram Park, and the Birmingham Civil Rights Institute. Together, these sites honor the struggle for racial equality, highlighting the city's central role in shaping justice and freedom in America.

Freedom Riders National Monument: Spanning Anniston and Birmingham, this monument honors the Freedom Riders of 1961 who challenged segregation on interstate buses. It preserves sites like the Anniston bus burning, symbolizing the bravery and sacrifice of those who risked their lives. The monument celebrates their courage and the continuing fight for civil rights and equality.

Horseshoe Bend National Military Park: This park preserves the 1814 Battle of Horseshoe Bend, a decisive moment in the Creek War that shaped the history of the Southeast. Trails and interpretive markers guide visitors through the battlefield, where Native American resistance and U.S. forces clashed. The site offers insight into early American conflicts and their lasting impact.

Little River Canyon National Preserve: Nestled in northeast Alabama, this preserve protects the rugged beauty of Little River Canyon. Visitors can hike scenic trails, fish along pristine waters, or drive the rim for sweeping canyon views. The preserve safeguards unique geology and ecosystems, providing a haven for diverse wildlife and outdoor adventures in a dramatic setting.

Natchez Trace National Scenic Trail: Following the historic Natchez Trace across three states, this trail highlights paths once traveled by Native Americans and settlers. Offering hiking, cycling, and horseback riding, the route crosses wetlands, forests, and rolling hills. It provides both recreation and a living connection to the cultural and historical roots of the early South.

Natchez Trace Parkway: Stretching 444 miles from Natchez, Mississippi, to Nashville, Tennessee, this parkway offers a scenic drive through history. Visitors encounter ancient mounds, Civil War sites, and remnants of pioneer settlements. With trails, campgrounds, and stunning countryside vistas, the route blends natural beauty with centuries of American heritage.

Russell Cave National Monument: Located in northern Alabama, this monument protects an archaeological treasure that reveals over 10,000 years of human history. The cave was once home to Native American groups who left behind tools, pottery, and cultural artifacts. A visitor center and trails bring to life the prehistoric cultures that shaped the region's deep past.

Tuskegee Airmen National Historic Site: This site commemorates the Tuskegee Airmen, African American pilots who broke barriers in World War II. Visitors explore the historic airfield and museum, which highlight their skill, courage, and the challenges they overcame. The site honors their role in advancing both military success and civil rights in the United States.

Tuskegee Institute National Historic Site: Established by Booker T. Washington in 1881, Tuskegee Institute became a beacon of African American education and empowerment. The site preserves the historic campus, including Washington's home and the George Washington Carver Museum. Visitors learn about the legacy of teaching, innovation, and leadership that shaped generations.

ALABAMA

State & National Forests

☐ ▯ ♡ **Bankhead National Forest:** Spanning 181,230 acres in northwest Alabama, Bankhead is known for its rugged terrain, waterfalls, and the Sipsey Wilderness, Alabama's only designated wilderness area. Visitors can explore limestone bluffs, hike the Sipsey Fork trail, and enjoy camping, fishing, and wildlife observation in a scenic natural environment.

☐ ▯ ♡ **Conecuh National Forest:** Located in southern Alabama, Conecuh National Forest covers 83,000 acres of longleaf pine ecosystems. The forest is home to diverse wildlife and offers outdoor activities like hiking, camping, fishing, and birdwatching. The 20-mile Conecuh Trail offers a scenic hiking experience through the heart of the forest.

☐ ▯ ♡ **Crawford State Forest:** Situated in Mobile County, this 80-acre forest is primarily used for timber production and educational purposes. It serves as a demonstration area for sustainable forestry practices and is managed by the Alabama Forestry Commission. Visitors can explore the forest for educational programs and quiet nature walks.

☐ ▯ ♡ **Geneva State Forest:** Spanning 7,120 acres in Geneva County, this forest was established during the 1930s. It focuses on timber production and wildlife management while providing recreational opportunities like hunting, fishing, and hiking. The forest also serves as a vital habitat for various species, offering outdoor enthusiasts a peaceful retreat.

☐ ▯ ♡ **Hauss State Forest:** Located in Escambia County, Hauss State Forest covers 319 acres and focuses on timber production, wildlife management, and forestry education. Managed by the Alabama Forestry Commission, it offers limited recreational opportunities, including hunting, making it an important site for sustainable forestry practices.

☐ ▯ ♡ **Johnson-Gjerstad State Forest:** This 1,000-acre forest in Clarke County focuses on timber production, wildlife habitat, and education. The forest offers hiking trails and is managed by the Alabama Forestry Commission. It is an example of responsible forest management and supports sustainable forestry practices while providing opportunities for outdoor activities.

☐ ▯ ♡ **Little River State Forest:** Situated in Escambia and Monroe counties, Little River State Forest is 2,100 acres of scenic woodland established in the 1930s. The forest offers visitors opportunities for hiking, wildlife viewing, and picnicking. It's also a site of historical significance, having been developed by the Civilian Conservation Corps during the Great Depression.

☐ ▯ ♡ **Macon State Forest:** This 190-acre forest in Macon County is managed by the Alabama Forestry Commission. It focuses on timber production and provides opportunities for wildlife management and education. The forest offers outdoor activities, including disabled hunting, in a serene environment that promotes sustainable forestry practices.

☐ ▯ ♡ **Talladega National Forest:** Covering 392,000 acres in central Alabama, this forest is divided into three districts: Talladega, Oakmulgee, and Shoal Creek. It offers activities such as hiking, camping, fishing, and wildlife viewing. The forest is home to Cheaha State Park, which features the highest point in Alabama with stunning views and outdoor recreation.

☐ ▯ ♡ **Tuskegee National Forest:** At 11,252 acres, Tuskegee National Forest is the smallest national forest in the U.S. Located in Macon County, it offers hiking, birdwatching, and wildlife observation. Visitors can enjoy quiet, natural surroundings and explore the park's educational programs, which focus on reforestation and conservation.

☐ ▯ ♡ **Weogufka State Forest:** Located in Coosa County, Weogufka State Forest spans 240 acres. It focuses on timber production and wildlife management. The forest offers outdoor activities such as hunting and is managed by the Alabama Forestry Commission, which ensures sustainable land use and conservation efforts.

ALABAMA

National Scenic Byways & All-American Roads

☐ 🔖 ♡ **Appalachian Highlands Scenic Byway:** Winding through northeast Alabama, this byway showcases the foothills of the Appalachians with forested ridges, waterfalls, and rural valleys. Historic towns and mountain overlooks enrich the route. Recognized nationally for its natural beauty, it highlights the state's dramatic highland landscapes.

☐ 🔖 ♡ **Lookout Mountain Parkway:** Extending from Gadsden into Georgia and Tennessee, this route reveals waterfalls, mountain overlooks, and cultural attractions like Noccalula Falls. It's a celebrated fall-color drive and offers recreational access to parks and preserves. The byway blends natural wonder with Appalachian heritage.

☐ 🔖 ♡ **Natchez Trace Parkway:** Running from Natchez, Mississippi to Nashville, Tennessee, the Parkway passes through northwest Alabama. It follows a historic Native American and pioneer travel corridor. Scenic woodlands, archaeological sites, and cultural landmarks highlight this iconic, slow-paced journey through the Deep South's natural and historic heart.

☐ 🔖 ♡ **Selma to Montgomery National Historic Trail/ Byway:** This route along US 80 commemorates the 1965 Voting Rights March. The Edmund Pettus Bridge, interpretive centers, and civil rights landmarks make it one of the nation's most important heritage corridors. Recognized for its global cultural significance, it blends rolling countryside with powerful history.

State Scenic Byways

☐ 🔖 ♡ **Alabama's Coastal Connection Scenic Byway:** Stretching along the Gulf Coast, this byway links Dauphin Island, Gulf Shores, and Orange Beach. Travelers experience sandy beaches, maritime forests, and historic forts. Wildlife refuges and estuaries teem with birds, while seafood towns and coastal culture highlight the blend of nature, heritage, and recreation along Alabama's shoreline.

☐ 🔖 ♡ **Appalachian Highlands Scenic Byway:** Running 80 miles through northeast Alabama, this route winds from Gadsden to Fort Payne. The byway climbs ridges and valleys of the Appalachian foothills, with sweeping mountain views, waterfalls, and small historic towns. Scenic parks like Little River Canyon National Preserve showcase the natural drama of the highlands.

☐ 🔖 ♡ **Barbour County Governor's Trail Scenic Byway:** Centered on historic Eufaula, this byway highlights antebellum architecture, Civil War heritage, and rolling Black Belt landscapes. It links government sites and preserved historic districts, blending political history with the charm of rural Alabama's towns and countryside.

☐ 🔖 ♡ **Black Belt Nature and Heritage Trail Scenic Byway:** Crossing Alabama's fertile Black Belt, this byway highlights rich cultural traditions and diverse ecosystems. Visitors encounter birding trails, historic churches, and small towns shaped by agriculture and civil rights history. It's a unique blend of natural beauty and deep cultural storytelling.

☐ 🔖 ♡ **Cahaba River Scenic Byway:** Following the Cahaba River near Centreville, this corridor showcases Alabama's longest free-flowing river. Known for rare wildflowers like the Cahaba lily, it also features rich birdlife, fishing, and forested banks. Historic structures and quiet rural landscapes complete this ecological and cultural treasure.

☐ 🔖 ♡ **Lookout Mountain Parkway Scenic Byway:** Extending from Gadsden to Chattanooga, this byway passes through rolling mountains, waterfalls, and overlooks across northeast Alabama. Attractions include Noccalula Falls and DeSoto State Park. Known for autumn color and sweeping ridge-top views, it offers both outdoor adventure and cultural heritage stops.

☐ 🔖 ♡ **Selma to Montgomery March Byway:** Following US 80, this route commemorates the 1965 Voting Rights March led by Martin Luther King Jr. Historic sites include the Edmund Pettus Bridge and interpretive centers. The byway links rolling countryside with one of the most important civil rights journeys in American history.

☐ 🔖 ♡ **Tennessee–Tombigbee Waterway Scenic Byway:** This western Alabama route follows the Tennessee–Tombigbee River system. Forested bluffs, wetlands, and rural communities line the corridor. With recreation areas, historic towns, and abundant wildlife, it highlights both natural beauty and the economic importance of the waterway.

UNITED STATES EDITION

ALABAMA

National Natural Landmarks

Beaverdam Creek Swamp: One of the rarest inland tupelo gum swamps in the Southeast, this site was named a National Natural Landmark for preserving a wetland ecosystem once widespread across Alabama. Its unique conditions support specialized plants and animals, offering scientists a vital place to study wetland biodiversity and ecological processes.
GPS: 34.6250, -86.8269

Cathedral Caverns: Famous for Goliath, one of the world's largest stalagmites, Cathedral Caverns earned National Natural Landmark status for its vast chambers and remarkable mineral formations. The cave illustrates speleogenesis in action, allowing study of subterranean processes such as mineral deposition and the shaping of limestone systems.
GPS: 34.5733, -86.2222

Dismals Canyon: Designated a National Natural Landmark for its rare glowing insects called dismalites, Dismals Canyon also preserves sandstone cliffs, waterfalls, and rich biodiversity. The canyon's unique habitats support species found nowhere else, blending ecological value with scenic beauty in one of Alabama's most distinctive landscapes.
GPS: 34.3253, -87.7817

Mobile–Tensaw River Bottomlands: Spanning 260,000 acres, this delta is the second largest in the U.S. and was recognized as a National Natural Landmark for its unparalleled biodiversity. Cypress–tupelo swamps and waterways sustain rare and endangered species, while serving as a living laboratory for research into delta ecosystems and wetland dynamics.
GPS: 30.7542, -87.9422

Newsome Sinks Karst Area: This site stands out as a National Natural Landmark for its extensive karst terrain, which includes more than 40 caves and over 50,000 feet of mapped passages. The formations reveal how water shapes underground landscapes, providing scientists with one of Alabama's best natural laboratories for studying cave geology and hydrology.
GPS: 34.4408, -86.5972

Red Mountain Expressway Cut: By slicing through Red Mountain, highway construction revealed one of the state's best geologic cross-sections, leading to its National Natural Landmark status. Layers of rock trace Alabama's deep past, preserving mineral deposits and fossils that document hundreds of millions of years of geologic history.
GPS: 33.4956, -86.7883

Shelta Cave: Shelta Cave was declared a National Natural Landmark for its exceptional cave ecosystem, home to rare and endemic species first identified here. Once a popular dance hall, it is now managed for research and conservation by the National Speleological Society, highlighting both its cultural and biological significance.
GPS: 34.7536, -86.6104

ALASKA

Alaska's vast and wild terrain is unmatched, with national parks, expansive national forests, numerous state parks, and stunning natural landmarks. Towering glaciers, remote tundra, majestic mountains, and pristine waterways create endless opportunities for adventure in the Last Frontier.

📅 Peak Season
June–August is Alaska's most popular travel window, with long daylight hours, mild temperatures, and full access to parks, trails, and cruises. These months are best for outdoor adventures, wildlife viewing, and scenic exploration.

📅 Offseason Months
September–May brings colder conditions and fewer services. Winter offers northern lights, snow sports, and quiet landscapes. Early spring and late fall remain off-peak with reduced tourist activity but unique beauty.

🍃 Scenery & Nature Timing
Summer delivers wildflowers, salmon runs, and whale migrations, while fall brings tundra colors and clear mountain views. Winter highlights snow-covered forests and aurora displays, with spring marking wildlife awakening.

✨ Special
Alaska showcases the midnight sun and aurora borealis, massive glaciers like Mendenhall and Exit, and fjords such as Kenai and Glacier Bay. Towering peaks including Denali dominate the Interior, while vast tundra, boreal forests, and coastal wetlands highlight the state's extreme diversity.

ALASKA

State Parks

☐ ▯ ♡ **Afognak Island State Park:** A remote coastal wilderness on Kodiak Island, Afognak Island State Park features dense spruce and alder forests, rugged fjords, and abundant salmon streams. Ideal for backcountry camping, wildlife viewing (especially Kodiak bears, elk, sea otters), and sport fishing. Accessible only by boat or floatplane, this park offers solitude and rugged Alaskan coastline adventures.

☐ ▯ ♡ **Chilkat State Park:** Nestled near Haines in Southeast Alaska, Chilkat State Park offers sweeping views of the Chilkat Inlet, Rainbow Glacier, and the towering Coast Mountains. The park is a prime spot for wildlife viewing, with frequent sightings of bald eagles, seals, and brown bears. Visitors enjoy hiking rugged trails, fishing in rich salmon waters, and experiencing the beauty of Alaska's Inside Passage.

☐ ▯ ♡ **Chugach State Park:** One of the largest state parks in the U.S., Chugach State Park encompasses over 495,000 acres of rugged mountains, glacial valleys, and pristine wilderness just outside of Anchorage. It's an outdoor enthusiast's paradise, offering hiking, skiing, snowboarding, and world-class wildlife viewing, including moose, black bears, and bald eagles.

☐ ▯ ♡ **Denali State Park:** A jewel in Alaska's wilderness, Denali State Park offers stunning views of the iconic Denali Mountain (formerly known as Mount McKinley). Visitors can enjoy a variety of activities, such as hiking, camping, fishing, and wildlife viewing, while taking in the breathtaking vistas of the Alaska Range.

☐ ▯ ♡ **Kachemak Bay State Park:** Located on the Kenai Peninsula, Kachemak Bay is a popular destination for those looking to explore Alaska's coastal wilderness. Known for its dramatic fjords, lush forests, and abundant marine life, the park offers kayaking, hiking, and wildlife viewing, including otters, sea lions, and numerous bird species.

☐ ▯ ♡ **Point Bridget State Park:** About 40 miles north of Juneau, this 2,850-acre park features coastal meadows, rocky beaches, and spruce rainforest overlooking Lynn Canal and the Chilkat Mountains. Trails lead to wildflower fields, cliffs, and marine views where whales, seals, and sea lions are often spotted. Rustic cabins and campsites provide a quiet wilderness retreat blending ocean and forest.

☐ ▯ ♡ **Shuyak Island State Park:** Located off Kodiak Island, Shuyak Island State Park protects over 100,000 acres of rainforest, sandy beaches, estuaries, and ancient Sitka spruce. Accessible only by boat or floatplane, it offers bear-viewing, kayaking, sportfishing, rustic cabins, and multi-day paddling routes. Ideal for wilderness enthusiasts seeking remote coastal forest immersion.

☐ ▯ ♡ **Wood-Tikchik State Park:** Situated in southwestern Alaska, Wood-Tikchik is the largest state park in the U.S., encompassing a stunning mix of alpine mountains, deep lakes, and vast tundra. Known for its remote beauty and rich biodiversity, the park offers premier opportunities for fishing, paddling, wildlife viewing, and solitude in one of the most pristine wilderness areas in North America.

National Parks

 ☐ ▯ ♡ **Alagnak Wild River:** Flowing through southwest Alaska, this wild river is surrounded by volcanic mountains and tundra. Known for abundant salmon runs and thriving bear populations, it's a premier destination for fishing, rafting, and kayaking. Remote and pristine, the river corridor offers a rare wilderness experience where solitude, wildlife, and rugged scenery define the adventure.

 ☐ ▯ ♡ **Aniakchak National Monument:** Set in Alaska's remote southwest, this monument showcases dramatic volcanic landscapes, including the vast Aniakchak Caldera. Rugged terrain, explosive geologic history, and traces of ancient human use make it a rare and wild destination. Visitors encounter solitude, wildlife, and opportunities for backcountry hiking, fishing, and exploring volcanic wonders.

ALASKA

 **Aniakchak National Preserve:** Protecting the same volcanic region as the monument, this preserve adds sweeping wilderness with rivers, tundra, and mountains. Caribou, bears, and wolves thrive here, offering exceptional wildlife viewing. Visitors explore the rugged backcountry through rafting, fishing, and hiking, immersed in the remote beauty and stark volcanic character of the Alaskan landscape.

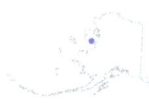 **Bering Land Bridge National Preserve:** Located on the Seward Peninsula, this preserve protects a vital remnant of the ancient land bridge that once linked Asia and North America. Today, it features tundra, wetlands, hot springs, and archaeological sites. Wildlife abounds, and visitors can explore this vast wilderness while connecting with the story of human migration.

 **Cape Krusenstern National Monument:** Stretching along Alaska's northwest coast, this monument preserves a unique series of beach ridges recording 5,000 years of human history. Visitors hike along the Chukchi Sea shoreline, explore ancient Inupiat sites, and enjoy birdwatching in a remote coastal setting. Its mix of cultural heritage and natural beauty make it truly remarkable.

 **Denali National Park & Preserve:** Home to North America's highest peak, Denali rises above six million acres of untamed wilderness. Glaciers, tundra, and boreal forests shelter bears, moose, caribou, and wolves. Visitors experience rugged beauty through hiking, camping, and wildlife viewing, with awe-inspiring views of the Alaska Range and the towering mountain at its heart.

 **Gates of the Arctic National Park & Preserve:** Above the Arctic Circle, this park preserves pure wilderness: rugged mountains, glacier valleys, and wild rivers. With no roads or trails, it offers unmatched solitude and adventure. Visitors hike, raft, and camp in pristine landscapes, sharing the environment with caribou herds and wildlife in one of the last truly untouched places on Earth.

 **Glacier Bay National Park & Preserve:** Famed for towering glaciers and icy fjords, this park protects one of the world's great marine and coastal landscapes. Visitors witness glaciers calving into the sea, kayak among icebergs, and watch whales, seals, and seabirds. Its breathtaking mix of mountains, forests, and marine life makes it a highlight of the Inside Passage.

 **Katmai National Park & Preserve:** Best known for Brooks Falls, where brown bears fish for salmon, Katmai also features dramatic volcanic landscapes like the Valley of Ten Thousand Smokes. Visitors explore rugged terrain, hike wild backcountry, fish world-class waters, and observe incredible wildlife. It's a striking blend of natural power, wilderness adventure, and unforgettable bear encounters.

 **Kenai Fjords National Park:** Along Alaska's southern coast, this park showcases massive glaciers, fjords, and abundant marine wildlife. Visitors take boat tours into Resurrection Bay, kayak among icebergs, and hike the Harding Icefield Trail. From breaching whales to calving tidewater glaciers, Kenai Fjords offers an up-close view of Alaska's wild coastal landscapes and ecosystems.

  Klondike Gold Rush National Historical Park: Centered in Skagway, this park tells the story of the 1897–1898 gold rush. Visitors explore historic buildings, walk the bustling streets once filled with prospectors, and hike the legendary Chilkoot Trail. Preserved artifacts and structures highlight the hardships and determination of those who sought fortune in the Yukon wilderness.

 **Kobuk Valley National Park:** Renowned for its vast sand dunes, the largest in the Arctic, Kobuk Valley also protects wild rivers, boreal forest, and tundra. Visitors can witness caribou migrations, hike remote dunes, and paddle the Kobuk River. Archaeological sites connect people to thousands of years of human history in this rugged and isolated Alaskan wilderness.

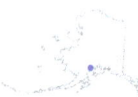 **Lake Clark National Park & Preserve:** This park offers a dazzling variety of landscapes: towering volcanoes, glaciers, wild rivers, and the turquoise waters of Lake Clark. Bears fish along salmon streams, while moose and wolves roam forests and tundra. Popular for fishing, kayaking, and backcountry hiking, Lake Clark remains one of Alaska's most beautiful yet remote destinations.

UNITED STATES EDITION

ALASKA

 ☐ 🔖 ♡ **Noatak National Preserve:** Protecting the wild Noatak River, this preserve offers one of the world's largest untouched mountain river basins. It supports vast caribou herds, grizzlies, and migratory birds. Visitors raft, hike, and camp in solitude across an immense Arctic wilderness, experiencing a landscape that remains virtually unchanged by modern development or roads.

 ☐ 🔖 ♡ **Sitka National Historical Park:** Preserving Tlingit and Russian history, this park is Alaska's oldest federally protected site. Visitors explore scenic coastal trails lined with towering totem poles, tour the Russian Bishop's House, and learn about cultural clashes and resilience. The blend of forest, shoreline, and history offers a unique cultural and natural experience.

 ☐ 🔖 ♡ **Wrangell–St. Elias National Park & Preserve:** The largest national park in the U.S., it encompasses soaring peaks, vast glaciers, and endless wilderness. Visitors explore the historic Kennecott copper mine, hike wild valleys, and climb some of North America's tallest mountains. Its unmatched scale and raw beauty create a breathtaking showcase of Alaska's rugged grandeur.

 ☐ 🔖 ♡ **Yukon–Charley Rivers National Preserve:** Protecting 115 miles of the Yukon River and the wild Charley River, this preserve blends remote natural beauty with gold rush history. Visitors raft, fish, and camp along river corridors once traveled by prospectors. Wildlife thrives here, and the rugged setting offers both adventure and insight into Alaska's historic frontier.

State Recreational Areas/Sites

 ☐ 🔖 ♡ **Anchor River State Recreation Area:** A coastal park on the Kenai Peninsula where Anchor River meets Cook Inlet, offering salmon and steelhead fishing, beach walks, and estuary exploration. Wildlife sightings include otters, eagles, and shorebirds. With picnic sites, easy paddling, and shoreline trails, it's an accessible spot near Homer for family outings, birdwatching, and classic Cook Inlet scenery.

 ☐ 🔖 ♡ **Birch Lake State Recreation Site:** Just south of Fairbanks, this lakeside park sits among spruce forest and lily-pad-covered waters. Visitors enjoy swimming, boating, fishing, and paddling in summer, with ice-fishing in winter. It offers tent sites, a cabin, boat launch, and picnic shelters. Close to town yet quiet and natural, it provides a convenient wilderness retreat for both locals and travelers.

 ☐ 🔖 ♡ **Blueberry Lake State Recreation Site:** This remote Interior Alaska site centers on a spruce-fringed lake, ideal for trout fishing, paddling, berry picking, and rustic camping. Basic amenities keep it wild and peaceful, perfect for sunrise views, quiet hikes, and solitude. Off a gravel road, it offers a true off-grid northern experience for campers seeking remoteness and backcountry immersion.

 ☐ 🔖 ♡ **Caines Head State Recreation Area:** Accessible only by boat or a rugged coastal trail from Seward, this park features WWII fort ruins, hidden beaches, and remote campsites. Trails climb to historic cannon batteries and alpine ridges overlooking Resurrection Bay. Sea otters, eagles, and sea lions frequent the area, making it a favorite for hikers and history buffs seeking Alaska's wild coastline.

☐ 🔖 ♡ **Captain Cook State Recreation Area:** At the northern tip of the Kenai Peninsula near Nikiski, this coastal park offers lake paddling, beachcombing, picnicking, and camping with sweeping views of Cook Inlet and volcanic peaks. Trails connect forests to shorelines, ideal for wildlife watching, half-day canoe trips, and enjoying dramatic sunsets along Alaska's rugged coastal frontier.

☐ 🔖 ♡ **Chena Pump Wayside State Recreation Site:** A small riverside park west of Fairbanks, this wayside offers boat access, fishing, picnic shelters, and peaceful views of the Chena River. In summer, anglers cast for grayling and salmon; in winter, it's a local ice-fishing spot. With easy road access, it serves as a convenient outdoor stop for both day-use visitors and nearby residents.

☐ 🔖 ♡ **Chena River State Recreation Area:** Stretching east of Fairbanks, this expansive park protects 250,000 acres of river corridor with campgrounds, cabins, trails, and boat launches. Popular for fishing, canoeing, hiking, and wildlife viewing, it also provides access to nearby hot springs. Its mix of mountains, rivers, and forests offers a quintessential Interior Alaska wilderness experience.

☐ 🔖 ♡ **Chilkoot Lake State Recreation Site:** Near Haines, this glacier-fed lake is framed by towering Sitka spruce and rugged peaks. The park offers a boat launch, fishing access, picnic areas, and trails. In summer, sockeye salmon draw bears and eagles, making it a hotspot for wildlife viewing. Kayakers and anglers flock here for its serene waters, scenery, and vibrant natural ecosystems.

ALASKA

☐ 🔖 ♡ **Clam Gulch State Recreation Area:** Famous for razor-clam beaches, this Kenai Peninsula park also offers camping, cabins, beachcombing, and panoramic views of Cook Inlet's volcanoes. At low tide, families explore tidepools, while anglers and paddlers take to the surf. Picnic areas, fire rings, and beach trails make it a versatile destination for both coastal adventure and family recreation.

☐ 🔖 ♡ **Clearwater State Recreation Site:** Located in Interior Alaska near Delta Junction, this peaceful riverside site features spruce-lined campsites, picnic tables, and firepits. Its clear, spring-fed waters attract paddlers, anglers, and birdwatchers. Trails wind through berry patches and tundra, offering wildlife viewing. A quiet, low-traffic alternative for visitors seeking fishing, camping, and seclusion.

☐ 🔖 ♡ **Crooked Creek State Recreation Site:** Located near Soldotna, this riverside park provides prized salmon fishing on a Kenai tributary. Anglers target king, silver, and red salmon from shore or campsite. With picnic tables, firepits, and simple camping, it offers a convenient base for fishing trips. Trails along the riverbank highlight wildlife and connect visitors to Alaska's salmon runs.

☐ 🔖 ♡ **Deep Creek State Recreation Area:** On the southern Kenai Peninsula near Ninilchik, this coastal park features campgrounds, a boat launch, and salmon fishing access. Popular for razor clams, beach walks, and Cook Inlet views, it also offers picnicking and birdwatching. Families camp here to enjoy both marine and river recreation in a scenic seaside setting with volcano vistas.

☐ 🔖 ♡ **Delta State Recreation Site:** Conveniently located along the Richardson Highway between Tok and Fairbanks, this riverside park offers camping, a public-use cabin, boat launch, and trails. Anglers fish for grayling and salmon, while travelers pause for rest and views of surrounding uplands. Its mix of river access, forests, and amenities make it a favored Interior stopover.

☐ 🔖 ♡ **Diamond Creek State Recreation Area:** Near Ninilchik on the Kenai Peninsula, this rustic site provides campsites, forested picnic spots, and access to Cook Inlet fishing streams. Trails lead to the beach and riverbanks, popular with anglers and campers. Its simple facilities and wooded setting make it a low-key base for exploring salmon waters and coastal hiking.

☐ 🔖 ♡ **Donnelly Creek State Recreation Site:** South of Delta Junction along the braided Delta River, this park offers camping, a public-use cabin, and river access for fishing grayling and salmon. Gravel bars provide space for boating and wildlife viewing. With short trails and mountain backdrops, it's a scenic and quiet Interior spot for outdoor recreation.

☐ 🔖 ♡ **Dry Creek State Recreation Site:** A small, rustic day-use area in Interior Alaska, this site provides picnic shelters, firepits, and access to fishing and riverside walks. Surrounded by spruce forest, it's a peaceful retreat for anglers and families seeking a quiet creekside stop. Its simplicity makes it appealing for low-impact outdoor enjoyment.

☐ 🔖 ♡ **Eagle Trail State Recreation Site:** Located along the Richardson Highway, this compact park provides picnic tables, campsites, and creekside access. Known for bald eagle sightings and seasonal fishing, it offers shoreline walks and forested surroundings. A convenient pull-off, it serves both locals and travelers as a relaxing outdoor pause in the Interior.

☐ 🔖 ♡ **Eveline State Recreation Site:** A small roadside stop on the Kenai Peninsula, Eveline offers lake access with campsites, a boat ramp, and fishing opportunities. Picnic areas and short trails encourage family outings. Though modest in size, its easy access and calm waters make it a handy stopover for anglers, paddlers, and local recreation.

☐ 🔖 ♡ **Fielding Lake State Recreation Site:** North of Glennallen, this alpine lake park provides camping, a boat launch, cabins, and picnic shelters. Anglers target trout and northern pike, while trails allow hiking, skiing, and snowmobiling in winter. Its mountain scenery, year-round access, and quiet setting make it a versatile Interior getaway.

☐ 🔖 ♡ **Finger Lake State Recreation Site:** Located in the Mat-Su Valley near Palmer, this freshwater lake park features camping, picnic shelters, and trails. It's stocked for fishing and offers boating, paddling, and winter Nordic skiing. With year-round appeal, it's a community hub where locals and visitors enjoy easy lake access, recreation, and scenic beauty.

ALASKA

☐ 🔖 ♡ **Hanson Memorial State Recreation Site:** A small, heritage-oriented park in Interior Alaska, this site provides picnic tables, shoreline access, and seasonal fishing. Surrounded by forested trails, it offers a reflective, family-friendly setting. Its modest facilities and natural character make it a quaint stop for quiet outdoor enjoyment and local remembrance.

☐ 🔖 ♡ **Harding Lake State Recreation Site:** South of Fairbanks, this popular lake park offers a sandy beach, boating, fishing, and RV and tent camping. Group sites, cabins, playgrounds, and trails add family appeal. In winter, visitors enjoy cross-country skiing and snowmobiling. With year-round recreation, it's one of Interior Alaska's most developed lakefront parks.

☐ 🔖 ♡ **Johnson Lake State Recreation Area:** Near Soldotna, this Kenai Peninsula lake park offers a campground, boat launch, fishing pier, and picnic shelters. Forested trails loop the lake, making it ideal for hiking, paddling, and family camping. Its calm waters and well-maintained facilities make it a weekend favorite for anglers and outdoor enthusiasts.

☐ 🔖 ♡ **Kasilof River State Recreation Site:** Situated along the Sterling Highway, this riverside site provides access to Kasilof River salmon runs. Anglers target kings from shore, while a boat launch and picnic areas serve visitors. Its forested setting and easy road access make it a reliable base for fishing trips and casual day use along the Kenai.

☐ 🔖 ♡ **Lake Aleknagik State Recreation Site:** At the gateway to Wood-Tikchik State Park in southwest Alaska, this site offers camping, boat access, and fishing. Salmon and trout draws anglers worldwide, while paddlers explore pristine waters backed by mountains. Rustic facilities, picnic areas, and wildlife viewing make it a key hub for remote wilderness recreation.

☐ 🔖 ♡ **Lake Louise State Recreation Area:** Nestled in boreal forest, this glacially-fed lake park offers camping, fishing, boating, hiking, and salmonberry picking. Its quiet setting and limited development provide a serene retreat for anglers, paddlers, and families seeking solitude. With scenic waters and mountain views, it's a peaceful Interior Alaska destination for weekend getaways.

☐ 🔖 ♡ **Liberty Falls State Recreation Site:** Near Chitina, this small day-use park centers on a dramatic waterfall cascading through a forested canyon. Picnic tables, short trails, and creekside fishing access make it a refreshing roadside stop. Popular with travelers heading toward Wrangell-St. Elias, it provides a quiet spot to stretch, relax, and enjoy Alaska's natural beauty.

☐ 🔖 ♡ **Little Nelchina State Recreation Site:** Along the Glenn Highway near the Mat-Su/Chugach region, this riverside park offers picnic areas, a boat launch, fishing, and forest trails. Anglers cast for salmon while families enjoy easy riverside walks. Its convenient access makes it a popular summer stop for travelers exploring southcentral Alaska's scenic corridors.

☐ 🔖 ♡ **Matanuska Glacier State Recreation Site:** At Mile 101 of the Glenn Highway, this 229-acre park overlooks the massive Matanuska Glacier. Visitors enjoy a small campground, picnic areas, restrooms, and the Glacier Edge Trail with interpretive signs. While it doesn't provide direct glacier access, it's a scenic stop for hiking, photography, and admiring Chugach Mountain vistas.

☐ 🔖 ♡ **Montana Creek State Recreation Site:** Near Talkeetna, this creekside park offers boat access, picnic facilities, and fishing for salmon and trout. Shaded by spruce, it's a favored local spot for paddling, riverside walks, and family outings. Its proximity to Talkeetna makes it a convenient and popular day-use destination in the Susitna Valley.

☐ 🔖 ♡ **Moon Lake State Recreation Site:** A cozy Interior lake park offering tent camping, a boat launch, swimming area, and fishing for trout. Surrounded by spruce forest, it provides a peaceful lakeside escape ideal for small boats, paddlers, and weekend campers. Its intimate size and tranquil setting make it a favorite for families and solitude seekers alike.

☐ 🔖 ♡ **Morgan's Landing State Recreation Area:** On the Kenai River near Sterling, this low-key park offers a gravel boat launch, fishing access, and picnic tables. Less crowded than other Kenai sites, it provides quiet riverside trails and a laid-back atmosphere. Anglers and paddlers use it as an alternative access point to Alaska's world-famous salmon waters.

ALASKA

☐ 🔖 ♡ **Nancy Lake State Recreation Site:** Adjacent to the larger Nancy Lake Recreation Area near Willow, this smaller site features a campground, boat launch, picnic shelters, and fishing access. Trailheads connect to a chain of canoe-friendly lakes. Surrounded by spruce woodlands, it's a gateway for paddling, birdwatching, and exploring Alaska's lake country.

☐ 🔖 ♡ **Porcupine Creek State Recreation Site:** In the Matanuska-Susitna Valley, this quiet day-use park offers picnic sites, shoreline access, forested trails, and salmon fishing. Families enjoy its easy walking paths and shaded setting, while anglers target seasonal runs. It provides a tranquil creekside environment ideal for casual recreation close to nearby communities.

☐ 🔖 ♡ **Quartz Lake State Recreation Area:** North of Glennallen, this popular lake park has campgrounds, cabins, picnic shelters, a swimming beach, boat launch, and hiking trails. Anglers target stocked rainbow trout and grayling, while families swim and paddle. Surrounded by alpine hills, it offers year-round recreation, from summer fishing trips to winter skiing and snowmachining.

☐ 🔖 ♡ **Rocky Lake State Recreation Site:** A small, secluded Interior lake park offering tent camping, boating, and trout and grayling fishing. Its quiet woodlands, berry patches, and calm waters make it ideal for off-grid weekends of paddling and solitude. With basic facilities and remote charm, it's a simple but rewarding destination for nature lovers.

☐ 🔖 ♡ **Salcha River State Recreation Site:** Southeast of Fairbanks, this 61-acre park offers campsites, a cabin, boat ramp, and king salmon and grayling fishing. In winter, cross-country skiing and snowmobiling add appeal. Families gather here for riverside picnics, camping, and angling, making it a year-round favorite along the Richardson Highway.

☐ 🔖 ♡ **Scout Lake State Recreation Site:** North of Soldotna, this spruce-fringed lake park offers a campground, boat launch, swimming beach, and picnic areas. Families enjoy paddling, fishing, and hiking short trails around the lake. With its sandy shoreline and calm waters, Scout Lake is a welcoming weekend retreat for campers, anglers, and visitors seeking a peaceful Kenai Peninsula setting.

☐ 🔖 ♡ **Squirrel Creek State Recreation Site:** A small Interior park with picnic tables, forest shade, and access to stream fishing. Short trails wind along the creek, offering quiet walks and wildlife spotting. With limited facilities, it remains a rustic stop ideal for families, anglers, and travelers seeking a tranquil outdoor pause amid Alaska's remote cabin-country landscapes.

☐ 🔖 ♡ **Stariski State Recreation Site:** Perched on the Kenai Peninsula coast, this undeveloped park provides direct access to Cook Inlet beaches. Visitors enjoy tidepooling, surf fishing, and camping amid driftwood along the shore. Sweeping views of volcanic peaks and dramatic sunsets make it a favorite for coastal exploration and quiet shoreline retreats in Southcentral Alaska.

☐ 🔖 ♡ **Summit Lake State Recreation Site:** Set along the Parks Highway, this alpine lake park offers camping, a boat launch, fishing, and picnic areas framed by mountain peaks. With clear waters and easy access, it's a popular stop for travelers heading north, as well as a destination for paddlers, anglers, and hikers seeking high-country recreation in a scenic roadside setting.

☐ 🔖 ♡ **Tok River State Recreation Site:** Near Tok on the Alaska Highway, this riverside park features a campground, boat ramp, picnic shelters, and fishing access. Travelers stop here for grayling angling, wildlife viewing, and forested trails. Its mix of quiet camping, river recreation, and highway convenience makes it a popular overnight pause in Alaska's Interior.

☐ 🔖 ♡ **Worthington Glacier State Recreation Site:** Located along the Richardson Highway near Thompson Pass, this roadside park provides direct access to Worthington Glacier. Visitors explore picnic areas, interpretive trails, and viewpoints of crevasses and icefalls. Short hikes allow close-up glacier experiences, making it a memorable and easily accessible highlight for travelers in Southcentral Alaska.

UNITED STATES EDITION

ALASKA

State & National Forests

☐ 🔖 ♡ **Chugach National Forest:** Covering over 5.4 million acres, Chugach National Forest is the second-largest in the U.S. It stretches from Prince William Sound to the Kenai Peninsula and Copper River Delta. With glaciers, fjords, rainforest, and abundant wildlife, including bears and bald eagles, it offers unmatched scenic beauty and access to wild Alaska.

☐ 🔖 ♡ **Haines State Forest:** Established in 1982, Haines State Forest spans around 286,000 acres in Southeast Alaska. Its mixed forests of spruce, hemlock, and cottonwood support logging, recreation, and subsistence uses. The forest includes part of the Chilkat River Valley, an important salmon habitat and a world-famous gathering spot for bald eagles.

☐ 🔖 ♡ **Southeast State Forest:** Created in 2010, Southeast State Forest is Alaska's newest state forest, covering roughly 48,000 acres across scattered parcels in the Panhandle region. Managed primarily for long-term timber harvest and local economic benefit, it also protects wildlife habitat and allows for recreation like hunting, fishing, and hiking.

☐ 🔖 ♡ **Tanana Valley State Forest:** Spanning over 1.8 million acres in Interior Alaska, Tanana Valley State Forest is the state's oldest and largest forest. It supports sustainable timber harvests while offering habitat for moose, bears, and migratory birds. Popular for hunting, fishing, berry picking, dog mushing, and winter sports, it's a key working forest near Fairbanks and Delta Junction.

☐ 🔖 ♡ **Tongass National Forest:** At 16.7 million acres, Tongass is the largest national forest in the U.S., encompassing much of Southeast Alaska. This vast temperate rainforest is rich with old-growth trees, glaciers, fjords, and wildlife like wolves, bears, and salmon. It supports Native cultures, subsistence lifestyles, and eco-tourism in towns like Sitka and Ketchikan.

National Scenic Byways & All-American Roads

☐ 🔖 ♡ **Alaska Marine Highway:** Designated as an All-American Road, this ferry route connects 3,500 miles of coastal Alaska through the Inside Passage, Gulf of Alaska, and Aleutian Islands. With stunning views of glaciers, islands, fjords, and wildlife, it links remote communities and offers a once-in-a-lifetime marine travel experience through some of the world's most dramatic seascapes.

☐ 🔖 ♡ **Glenn Highway Scenic Byway:** Stretching 135 miles from Anchorage to Glennallen, this National Scenic Byway traverses glaciers, braided rivers, volcanic fields, and alpine tundra. Key sights include the Matanuska Glacier and Wrangell Mountains. Originally built during WWII, the highway showcases wild beauty and geological wonder.

☐ 🔖 ♡ **Haines Highway Scenic Byway:** Connecting Haines, Alaska to Haines Junction, Yukon, this 44-mile National Scenic Byway climbs through the coastal rainforest into alpine tundra. Once a trade route for the Chilkat Tlingit people, it passes glacial valleys, the Chilkat Bald Eagle Preserve, and offers exceptional opportunities for wildlife viewing and cultural exploration.

☐ 🔖 ♡ **Parks Highway Scenic Byway (George Parks Highway):** Running from Anchorage to Fairbanks, this National Scenic Byway spans more than 320 miles, with dramatic views of Denali (North America's tallest peak). It passes through Denali State and National Parks and offers frequent wildlife sightings and panoramic access to Alaska's Interior.

☐ 🔖 ♡ **Richardson Highway Scenic Byway:** Alaska's oldest highway and a designated National Scenic Byway, this 368-mile route runs from Valdez to Fairbanks. It parallels the Trans-Alaska Pipeline and features stunning mountain scenery, glaciers, and waterfalls. Originally a gold rush trail, it's now a gateway to the Chugach and Alaska Ranges.

☐ 🔖 ♡ **Seward Highway Scenic Byway:** This National Scenic Byway and All-American Road stretches 127 miles from Anchorage to Seward, tracing Turnagain Arm and passing through fjords, boreal forest, and the Kenai Mountains. Moose, eagles, and beluga whales are common sights. It links Alaska's largest city to the Kenai Peninsula's stunning wilderness.

ALASKA

☐ 🔖 ♡ **Steese Highway Scenic Byway:** A 161-mile National Scenic Byway heading northeast from Fairbanks, the Steese Highway travels through gold rush country and vast wilderness. It provides access to the Yukon River, Circle Hot Springs, and the White Mountains. Wild, remote, and historically rich, it's a classic drive into Alaska's frontier.

☐ 🔖 ♡ **Sterling Highway Scenic Byway:** This National Scenic Byway traverses the Kenai Peninsula, connecting the towns of Soldotna, Kenai, and Homer. It follows rivers, volcanic peaks, and coastlines, offering prime fishing, bear viewing, and access to Kenai National Wildlife Refuge and Kachemak Bay. Its beauty makes it a favorite among locals and travelers alike.

☐ 🔖 ♡ **Tok Cut-Off Scenic Byway:** A remote, 125-mile National Scenic Byway linking Gakona and Tok, this route passes volcanic terrain, glacier-fed rivers, and spruce forests. Part of the greater Glenn and Alaska Highway network, it offers quiet, scenic driving through the eastern Alaska Range and connects to routes into Canada and the Lower 48.

☐ 🔖 ♡ **Valdez to Chitina Scenic Byway:** This rugged and less-traveled National Scenic Byway traverses deep valleys, waterfalls, and remote stretches along the old Copper River & Northwestern Railway. The route offers access to Wrangell-St. Elias National Park, the largest in the U.S., and traces a corridor rich in mining and indigenous history.

State Scenic Byways

☐ 🔖 ♡ **Alaska Railroad Scenic Byway:** Running 470 miles from Seward to Fairbanks, this rail byway passes glaciers, mountains, rivers, and tundra. Passengers enjoy views of Denali, crossing trestles and valleys unreachable by car. Wildlife sightings of moose, eagles, and bears are common, while the route itself is a living link to Alaska's settlement and exploration history.

☐ 🔖 ♡ **Copper River Highway Scenic Byway:** Extending from Cordova toward Childs Glacier, this partially paved route follows the Copper River Delta. Towering mountains, braided glacial rivers, and rich bird habitats define the scenery. Once part of a historic railroad corridor, it offers fishing access, wildlife viewing, and a front-row seat to Alaska's changing natural landscapes.

☐ 🔖 ♡ **Dalton Highway Scenic Byway:** Stretching 414 remote miles from Livengood to Deadhorse, this rugged byway crosses the Arctic Circle and ends at the Arctic Ocean. It passes boreal forest, the Yukon River, Brooks Range, and vast tundra. Known for solitude and extreme conditions, it's a bucket-list journey through some of the wildest landscapes in North America.

☐ 🔖 ♡ **Kachemak Bay Scenic Byway:** Starting in Homer, this route hugs the Kenai Peninsula's southern coast along Kachemak Bay. Panoramic ocean views, tide pools, and snowcapped mountains frame the corridor. Fishing villages, wildlife-rich estuaries, and dramatic sunsets showcase the blending of culture and coastal wilderness unique to Alaska's maritime frontier.

☐ 🔖 ♡ **Prince of Wales Island Scenic Byway:** Encompassing roads across the state's largest island, this byway passes temperate rainforest, salmon streams, and rugged shorelines. Small Native and fishing communities dot the corridor, offering cultural experiences. Towering spruce and cedar forests, along with abundant wildlife, make it a lush and remote coastal drive.

☐ 🔖 ♡ **Richardson Highway Scenic Byway:** Linking Valdez to Fairbanks, this historic corridor showcases glaciers, waterfalls, and the Alaska and Wrangell Mountains. Travelers encounter Thompson Pass, Worthington Glacier, and the Copper River Valley. Once a mining road, today it's a scenic route rich in natural beauty and cultural history, connecting coastal and interior Alaska.

☐ 🔖 ♡ **Taylor Highway Scenic Byway:** This 160-mile frontier road leads from Tetlin Junction near Tok to Eagle on the Yukon River. Passing through boreal forests, historic mining sites, and mountain ridges, it offers cultural history and vast wilderness views. In summer, it connects with the Top of the World Highway, opening access to Canada's Yukon.

☐ 🔖 ♡ **Top of the World Highway Scenic Byway:** Extending 79 miles from Eagle to the Canadian border, this high ridge-top road provides sweeping views of rolling tundra and distant mountains. Known for long daylight and vibrant wildflowers, it links isolated communities and offers a unique perspective of Alaska's northern frontier.

UNITED STATES EDITION

ALASKA

National Natural Landmarks

 ☐ 🔖 ♡ **Aniakchak Crater:** This vast caldera on the Alaska Peninsula became a National Natural Landmark for its exceptional preservation of volcanic activity. Formed in a massive eruption 3,500 years ago and last erupting in 1931, it contains steaming vents, lava flows, and Surprise Lake. Remote and rugged, it is one of North America's clearest examples of active volcanism.
GPS: 56.9058, -158.2089

 ☐ 🔖 ♡ **Arrigetch Peaks:** Rising like jagged towers above Arctic valleys, the Arrigetch Peaks were named a National Natural Landmark for their striking granite spires and pristine alpine setting. Located in Gates of the Arctic, they demonstrate transitions in ancient rock formations and serve as an unparalleled example of mountain geology and Arctic wilderness.
GPS: 67.4167, -154.1833

 ☐ 🔖 ♡ **Bogoslof Island:** Constantly reshaped by eruptions, this Aleutian island earned National Natural Landmark status for its outstanding record of oceanic volcanism. Its shifting landform highlights the forces of creation and erosion while providing nesting grounds for seabirds and habitat for Steller sea lions, making it both geologically and ecologically significant.
GPS: 53.9272, -168.0344

 ☐ 🔖 ♡ **Clarence Rhode National Wildlife Range:** This Yukon Delta refuge holds National Natural Landmark status for supporting some of the largest concentrations of nesting waterfowl in North America. Its expansive wetlands, lakes, and tide flats provide habitat for species such as emperor geese and black brant, demonstrating the ecological importance of tundra wetlands.
GPS: 61.2500, -148.6167

 ☐ 🔖 ♡ **Iliamna Volcano:** Standing over 10,000 feet in Lake Clark National Park, Iliamna is recognized as a National Natural Landmark for its active stratovolcano form. Fumaroles, glaciers, and ongoing seismic activity reveal the dynamic processes shaping the Chigmit Mountains, making it a natural laboratory for the interaction between volcanism and glaciation.
GPS: 60.0333, -153.0667

 ☐ 🔖 ♡ **Lake George:** Once the largest glacier-dammed lake in North America, Lake George was named a National Natural Landmark for its dramatic jökulhlaups. These sudden outburst floods reshaped the valley repeatedly, offering classic examples of glacial hydrology and demonstrating the power of ice and water in sculpting Alaska's landscapes.
GPS: 61.2500, -148.6167

 ☐ 🔖 ♡ **Malaspina Glacier:** Flowing from the St. Elias Mountains, Malaspina sprawls over 1,500 square miles, making it North America's largest piedmont glacier. Its scale and form led to its National Natural Landmark designation, as it perfectly illustrates glacial dynamics on a continental level and is visible even from space.
GPS: 59.9192, -140.5328

 ☐ 🔖 ♡ **McNeil River State Game Sanctuary:** Famed for hosting the world's largest seasonal gathering of brown bears, this sanctuary holds National Natural Landmark status for illustrating predator-prey interactions. Each summer, dozens of bears congregate to fish for salmon at McNeil River Falls, offering a dramatic demonstration of Alaska's ecological richness.
GPS: 59.0167, -154.4667

 ☐ 🔖 ♡ **Mount Veniaminof:** This massive stratovolcano is one of the only glacier-filled calderas in the world with an active vent, a rarity that earned it National Natural Landmark status. Located on the Alaska Peninsula, it blends fire and ice, with eruptions occurring alongside a vast ice field, making it a remarkable site for geologic research.
GPS: 56.1981, -159.3908

 ☐ 🔖 ♡ **Redoubt Volcano:** Dominating Cook Inlet, Redoubt is celebrated as a National Natural Landmark for being one of Alaska's most active and scientifically studied stratovolcanoes. Its 2009 eruption sent massive ash plumes skyward, underscoring its role as a powerful expression of the Pacific Ring of Fire and a prime example of volcanic hazards.
GPS: 60.4853, -152.7431

ALASKA

 **Shishaldin Volcano:** Perfectly symmetrical and rising 9,373 feet, Shishaldin on Unimak Island is a National Natural Landmark for being both the highest and one of the most active volcanoes in the Aleutians. Its frequent eruptions provide scientists with vital records of ongoing volcanic activity in this geologically restless chain.
GPS: 54.7558, -163.9675

 **Simeonof National Wildlife Refuge:** This Shumagin Islands refuge was designated a National Natural Landmark for preserving undisturbed island habitats. Rocky coasts, kelp forests, and isolation make it ideal for seabirds, sea otters, and marine mammals, providing a prime site for studying the ecological effects of isolation and oceanic environments.
GPS: 54.8948, -159.2738

 **Unga Island:** Buried volcanic ash preserved an ancient sequoia forest here, making Unga Island a National Natural Landmark for its rare fossilized trees. These remains provide paleobotanical evidence of prehistoric ecosystems in Alaska, offering critical insights into ancient climate and vegetation long before human settlement.
GPS: 55.2606, -160.6950

 **Walker Lake:** High in the Brooks Range, Walker Lake received National Natural Landmark designation for its pristine alpine waters and ecological transitions. The surrounding terrain demonstrates the shift from boreal forest to Arctic tundra, making it a living classroom for studying northern wilderness succession and cold-adapted ecosystems.
GPS: 67.1267, -154.3631

 **Walrus Islands:** These Bering Sea islands serve as a National Natural Landmark for hosting the only major bull walrus haul-out in the U.S. As the southernmost site of its kind worldwide, they are vital for walrus conservation while also supporting seabirds and marine mammals in an untouched subarctic ecosystem.
GPS: 58.6804, -160.2786

 **Worthington Glacier:** Located near Thompson Pass, Worthington Glacier is valued as a National Natural Landmark for its accessibility and textbook glacial features. Crevasses, moraines, and melt zones are easily studied here, making it one of the best outdoor laboratories for understanding valley glacier dynamics in Alaska's changing climate.
GPS: 61.1703, -145.7633

UNITED STATES EDITION

Arizona

Arizona's iconic beauty spans vibrant red rock canyons, pine-clad mountains, sweeping deserts, and ancient geological wonders. With an array of national and state parks, national forests, and remarkable landmarks, the state offers a landscape of awe-inspiring contrasts and endless opportunities for discovery and adventure.

🗓 Peak Season
March–May and October–November are the most comfortable times to visit Arizona. Spring offers desert wildflowers and pleasant hiking weather, while fall brings cooler temperatures, clear skies, and outdoor festivals.

🗓 Offseason Months
June–September can be extremely hot in the deserts, making outdoor activity challenging, though cooler mountain towns and the Grand Canyon remain popular. December–February is mild in the south but brings snow to northern regions.

🍃 Scenery & Nature Timing
Spring carpets desert valleys with cactus blooms and wildflowers. Summer heat dominates lowlands, but higher elevations offer alpine meadows. Fall colors brighten mountain canyons, while winter brings snowy vistas in the north.

✨ Special
Arizona highlights the Grand Canyon, the red rock buttes of Sedona, and giant saguaro cacti in Saguaro National Park. The Petrified Forest preserves fossilized trees, while Monument Valley, the Painted Desert, and San Francisco Peaks add striking contrasts across the landscape..

ARIZONA
State Parks

☐ 🔖 ♡ **Alamo Lake State Park:** Located in western Arizona, Alamo Lake State Park offers a remote desert lake known for excellent bass fishing. Visitors enjoy boating, camping, and stargazing in the dark skies. Wildlife viewing includes bald eagles, burros, and other desert species. The rugged, isolated setting provides peace and stunning scenery away from city crowds.

☐ 🔖 ♡ **Buckskin Mountain State Park:** Nestled along the Colorado River near Parker, this park combines desert and water recreation. Visitors boat, fish, swim, and camp along the riverbank with views of colorful mountains. Hiking trails climb into the desert hills for panoramic vistas. It's a scenic destination for water fun and camping on the Arizona–California border.

☐ 🔖 ♡ **Catalina State Park:** At the base of the Santa Catalina Mountains near Tucson, this park spans 5,500 acres of desert landscape. Over 150 bird species, rich cactus diversity, and wildlife thrive here. Hiking, biking, and horseback trails wind through rugged terrain to canyons and streams. With its dark skies and striking mountain backdrop, it's a haven for nature lovers.

☐ 🔖 ♡ **Cattail Cove State Park:** South of Lake Havasu City, this riverfront park offers a quieter alternative to busier spots on the Colorado. Its sandy beaches invite swimming and fishing, while boaters launch into calm waters. Trails lead into the desert for wildlife viewing. The combination of shoreline relaxation and scenic desert hikes makes it a family-friendly retreat.

☐ 🔖 ♡ **Colorado River State Historic Park:** Located in Yuma, this park preserves the historic Quartermaster Depot that once supplied military posts throughout the Southwest. Visitors tour restored buildings, exhibits, and artifacts that tell the story of river commerce and military history. The park offers shaded grounds and interpretive programs highlighting Yuma's role as a desert crossroads.

☐ 🔖 ♡ **Dankworth Pond State Park:** Near Safford, this small pond park offers fishing for catfish, bass, and trout, plus trails that connect to Roper Lake. Shaded picnic areas and a short interpretive trail with replica Native dwellings add cultural interest. With calm waters and a family-friendly atmosphere, it's a peaceful destination for anglers and local recreation.

☐ 🔖 ♡ **Dead Horse Ranch State Park:** Situated along the Verde River in Cottonwood, this lush riparian park features lagoons, trails, and wildlife-rich habitat. Birdwatchers flock to spot herons, eagles, and dozens of species. Visitors hike, fish, paddle, or camp in cottonwood-shaded campgrounds. Its mix of desert and river ecosystems makes it a favorite Verde Valley destination.

☐ 🔖 ♡ **Fort Verde State Historic Park:** In Camp Verde, this well-preserved 19th-century Army fort brings frontier history to life. Restored officer's quarters and exhibits tell stories of soldiers, settlers, and Native peoples. Costumed interpreters, reenactments, and artifacts immerse visitors in Territorial Arizona. The site provides a vivid window into the Indian Wars era.

☐ 🔖 ♡ **Granite Mountain Hotshots Memorial State Park:** Near Yarnell, this park honors 19 firefighters lost in the 2013 Yarnell Hill Fire. A challenging 3.5-mile trail leads to the memorial site with plaques and tributes. The hike passes through rugged desert landscapes, encouraging reflection and remembrance. The park preserves their legacy while offering visitors a solemn, moving experience.

☐ 🔖 ♡ **Homolovi State Park:** Near Winslow, this archaeological park protects ancestral Hopi pueblos with hundreds of preserved rooms and petroglyphs. Trails lead to ancient ruins, while a visitor center displays artifacts and cultural exhibits. Stargazing is excellent under its dark skies. The park provides insight into the history of the Hopi and their homeland.

☐ 🔖 ♡ **Jerome State Historic Park:** Overlooking the historic mining town of Jerome, this park centers on the Douglas Mansion built in 1916 by a copper baron. Exhibits cover geology, mining, and daily life in a boomtown. Visitors tour the mansion, enjoy panoramic views of the Verde Valley, and learn about Arizona's mining heritage in a dramatic hillside setting.

☐ 🔖 ♡ **Kartchner Caverns State Park:** Near Benson, this world-class limestone cave showcases massive stalactites, stalagmites, and other living formations. Guided tours reveal colorful chambers like the Rotunda and Throne Room. Above ground, hiking trails and a campground extend the visit. It's both a geologic wonder and a conservation success, preserving fragile subterranean beauty.

ARIZONA

☐ 🔖 ♡ **Lake Havasu State Park:** Along Lake Havasu's shoreline, this popular park features sandy beaches, swimming, fishing, and boating access. Campgrounds and cabanas line the water. Trails showcase desert flora and scenic lake views. Located near the relocated London Bridge, it's a hub for recreation and relaxation in western Arizona's desert resort region.

☐ 🔖 ♡ **Lost Dutchman State Park:** At the base of the Superstition Mountains in Apache Junction, this park offers iconic desert scenery tied to legends of a hidden gold mine. Visitors hike rugged trails into the wilderness, camp under desert skies, and enjoy cactus-filled landscapes. Its dramatic backdrop and lore make it a quintessential Arizona adventure spot.

☐ 🔖 ♡ **Lyman Lake State Park:** In eastern Arizona near St. Johns, this high-desert park features a large reservoir for boating, fishing, and swimming. Visitors explore petroglyphs on trails around the lake, while campgrounds and cabins accommodate overnight stays. Surrounded by rolling hills and wide skies, it's an ideal escape for water recreation and archaeology.

☐ 🔖 ♡ **McFarland State Historic Park:** In Florence, this park preserves the original Pinal County Courthouse, built in 1878. Exhibits highlight territorial justice and Governor Ernest McFarland's contributions to Arizona's history. The site provides a glimpse into early legal and civic life, serving as both a heritage museum and a reminder of Arizona's pioneer past.

☐ 🔖 ♡ **Oracle State Park:** Set in oak-grassland foothills near Tucson, this 4,000-acre park offers trails through desert, canyon, and mountain terrain. Wildlife sightings include deer, coyotes, and diverse birdlife. A certified International Dark Sky Park, it's excellent for stargazing. Educational programs and hiking make it a peaceful nature preserve with scientific significance.

☐ 🔖 ♡ **Patagonia Lake State Park:** In southern Arizona near Nogales, this 265-acre lake offers boating, fishing, kayaking, and swimming. Birdwatchers come to see rare species along Sonoita Creek. The park includes campgrounds, cabins, and picnic areas, making it a popular family destination. Its combination of desert scenery and riparian habitat provides year-round recreation.

☐ 🔖 ♡ **Picacho Peak State Park:** Known for its distinctive peak visible from miles away, this park offers hiking trails to its summit with panoramic desert views. It's also the site of the westernmost Civil War battle. Wildflowers blanket the park in spring, adding color to the desert landscape. Its striking landmark and history make it a favorite Arizona stop.

☐ 🔖 ♡ **Red Rock State Park:** Outside Sedona, this 286-acre park showcases brilliant red sandstone formations and lush Oak Creek riparian habitat. Trails wind through meadows, forests, and canyons. Visitors enjoy birdwatching, guided nature walks, and educational programs. The combination of geology, wildlife, and views of Cathedral Rock makes it one of Arizona's most scenic parks.

☐ 🔖 ♡ **Riordan Mansion State Historic Park:** In Flagstaff, this 1904 Arts and Crafts style mansion was home to lumber barons. Guided tours reveal original furnishings and family history. The mansion reflects early 20th-century prosperity and design. Surrounded by ponderosa pines, it offers cultural insights within a forest setting near Northern Arizona University.

☐ 🔖 ♡ **River Island State Park:** Adjacent to Buckskin Mountain along the Colorado River, this smaller park provides a sandy beach, boat launch, and shaded campsites. It's popular for boating, fishing, swimming, and wildlife watching. Hiking trails climb into surrounding desert hills. Its relaxed riverfront setting makes it ideal for family outings and camping by the water.

☐ 🔖 ♡ **Rockin' River Ranch State Park:** Near Camp Verde, this recently opened park along the Verde River protects riparian woodlands and open grasslands. Trails allow hiking and birdwatching, while picnic areas provide riverfront relaxation. Still being developed, it expands opportunities for low-impact recreation and conservation in Arizona's Verde Valley.

☐ 🔖 ♡ **Roper Lake State Park:** Near Safford, this small lake offers fishing, swimming, and boating in a scenic desert basin. Campgrounds, cabins, and hot mineral springs make it appealing for families. Trails and abundant birdlife enhance its natural charm. With nearby mountain views, it's a convenient southeastern Arizona getaway for both recreation and relaxation.

☐ 🔖 ♡ **Slide Rock State Park:** In Oak Creek Canyon near Sedona, this park is famous for its slick natural water slide over red sandstone. Visitors swim in the creek, hike canyon trails, and picnic under shady trees. The site also preserves historic orchards. Its combination of fun, scenery, and history makes it one of Arizona's most popular parks.

☐ 🔖 ♡ **Tonto Natural Bridge State Park:** Near Payson, this park features the world's largest natural travertine bridge, spanning 183 feet. Trails lead to viewpoints and beneath the bridge where waterfalls trickle into lush grottos. Visitors hike, picnic, and marvel at the geology. Its dramatic formations and surrounding pine forests make it a highlight of central Arizona.

ARIZONA

 ☐ 🔖 ♡ **Tubac Presidio State Historic Park:** Arizona's first state park preserves the site of a Spanish colonial presidio founded in 1752. Visitors explore restored adobe structures, a museum, and artifacts reflecting Native, Spanish, and Mexican heritage. The park provides cultural programs and trails linking to the historic town of Tubac along the Santa Cruz River.

☐ 🔖 ♡ **Yuma Territorial Prison State Historic Park:** In Yuma, this site preserves the infamous 19th-century prison known as the "Hellhole on the Colorado." Visitors tour original cell blocks, guard towers, and a museum with prisoner records and artifacts. The park offers vivid insights into frontier justice, Arizona's territorial past, and the harsh life of early inmates.

National Parks

 ☐ 🔖 ♡ **Canyon De Chelly National Monument:** In northeastern Arizona, this monument features towering red rock walls, ancient cliff dwellings, and cultural sites tied to the Navajo Nation. Visitors can take guided tours into the canyon, view centuries-old archaeological sites, and enjoy sweeping desert vistas while learning about Indigenous history and enduring traditions.

 ☐ 🔖 ♡ **Casa Grande Ruins National Monument:** Located in Coolidge, this monument preserves the massive four-story "Great House" built by the Hohokam people over 600 years ago. Visitors can explore the ruins, learn about the Hohokam's advanced irrigation systems, and gain insights into one of the most significant archaeological sites of the ancient Southwest.

 ☐ 🔖 ♡ **Chiricahua National Monument:** Southeastern Arizona's "Wonderland of Rocks" showcases towering rhyolite formations created by volcanic activity. Visitors hike through canyons and balanced rock spires, explore diverse "Sky Island" ecosystems, and encounter wildlife while enjoying panoramic views of surrounding valleys and mountain ranges.

 ☐ 🔖 ♡ **Coronado National Memorial:** On the U.S.-Mexico border, this site commemorates Coronado's 1540 expedition, the first major European exploration of the Southwest. Scenic trails lead to sweeping borderland views, while exhibits highlight natural and cultural history, offering perspective on the region's blend of Indigenous and European influences.

☐ 🔖 ♡ **Fort Bowie National Historic Site:** Preserving ruins of a key outpost in the Apache Wars, this site in southeastern Arizona tells the story of conflict and cultural change. Visitors hike to the fort past battlefields and springs, explore remnants of adobe buildings, and learn about the complex relationships between settlers, soldiers, and Apache people.

 ☐ 🔖 ♡ **Glen Canyon National Recreation Area:** Straddling Arizona and Utah, this vast desert landscape centers on Lake Powell, known for red rock canyons and blue waters. Visitors enjoy boating, kayaking, fishing, and hiking while experiencing stunning geological formations and the expansive beauty of the surrounding canyonlands.

 ☐ 🔖 ♡ **Grand Canyon National Park:** Arizona's most iconic landscape features immense cliffs, layered rock history, and the Colorado River. Visitors marvel at breathtaking viewpoints, hike rugged trails, raft through the canyon, and discover both Native heritage and unique ecosystems in one of the world's greatest natural wonders.

 ☐ 🔖 ♡ **Hohokam Pima National Monument:** Preserving remains of an ancient Hohokam village in Pima County, this site protects canals, ballcourts, and dwellings that highlight the culture's advanced agriculture. Although closed to the public, it remains vital for archaeological study and recognition of the Hohokam's contributions to desert life.

 ☐ 🔖 ♡ **Hubbell Trading Post National Historic Site:** Established in 1878 in Ganado, this site preserves a working Navajo trading post. Visitors tour the historic store, see traditional crafts, and learn about Navajo culture and the role of trade in connecting communities across the Southwest.

 ☐ 🔖 ♡ **Lake Mead National Recreation Area:** Stretching across Arizona and Nevada, this desert oasis features Lake Mead, America's largest reservoir. Visitors boat, fish, kayak, and camp while surrounded by stark mountain ranges, colorful rock formations, and striking desert scenery that make it a premier water-based recreation destination.

UNITED STATES EDITION

ARIZONA

Montezuma Castle National Monument: Near Camp Verde, this site preserves a dramatic five-story cliff dwelling built by the Sinagua people in the 1100s. Visitors view the well-preserved structure from below, explore interpretive trails, and learn about the ingenuity of desert communities who thrived in this harsh landscape.

Navajo National Monument: Protecting cliff dwellings of the Ancestral Puebloans, this monument in northern Arizona highlights sites such as Betatakin and Keet Seel. Visitors can take guided tours, hike scenic trails, and explore exhibits that reveal the cultural and historical significance of the region to Native peoples.

Organ Pipe Cactus National Monument: Along the Mexican border, this Sonoran Desert preserve protects rare organ pipe cactus and diverse desert ecosystems. Visitors hike desert trails, camp beneath starry skies, and encounter wildlife like javelinas and coyotes while learning about Indigenous traditions tied to this unique landscape.

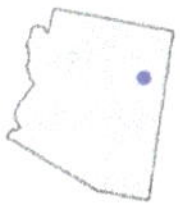

Petrified Forest National Park: Famous for its colorful fossilized trees, this park in northeastern Arizona preserves remnants of an ancient forest over 200 million years old. Visitors explore Painted Desert vistas, hike past petrified wood, and discover archaeological sites reflecting centuries of human presence in the region.

Pipe Spring National Monument: Set in the Arizona Strip, this site preserves a historic Mormon fort and the life-giving springs around it. Visitors tour the restored buildings, learn about conflicts and cooperation between Native Americans and settlers, and see how the springs sustained life in a harsh desert.

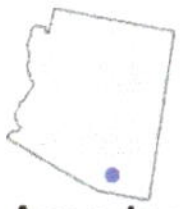

Saguaro National Park: Surrounding Tucson, this park celebrates the iconic saguaro cactus, symbol of the American West. Visitors explore Sonoran Desert landscapes through scenic drives and hiking trails, discovering diverse plant and animal life while taking in the grandeur of towering cacti and mountain backdrops.

Sunset Crater Volcano National Monument: Northern Arizona's volcanic past is revealed in this monument, where a 900-year-old eruption reshaped the landscape. Visitors hike among lava flows and cinder fields, learn about geology and Native survival in a changed environment, and enjoy striking contrasts between desert and forest.

Tonto National Monument: Protecting cliff dwellings built by the Salado people in the 13th and 14th centuries, this monument reveals stories of survival in the desert. Visitors hike to ruins perched high above the valley, explore exhibits on Salado culture, and gain perspective on ancient adaptation to arid environments.

Tumacácori National Historical Park: South of Tucson, this park preserves three Spanish colonial missions along the Santa Cruz River. Visitors tour the mission ruins, explore interpretive trails, and learn about cultural exchanges between Indigenous peoples and missionaries in the borderlands of New Spain.

Tuzigoot National Monument: Near Clarkdale, this site preserves a sprawling pueblo built by the Sinagua people atop a ridge overlooking the Verde Valley. Visitors wander through stone ruins, take in expansive views, and learn how the Sinagua developed thriving communities in the desert over 900 years ago.

Walnut Canyon National Monument: Just east of Flagstaff, this canyon shelters cliff dwellings of the Ancestral Puebloans. Visitors hike rim or island trails to view homes tucked into the canyon walls, gaining insight into the resourcefulness and daily life of ancient desert peoples.

Wupatki National Monument: North of Flagstaff, this desert landscape preserves large pueblos and ancient farming villages built by the Sinagua people. Visitors explore stone ruins, see ballcourts and dwellings, and enjoy views of the San Francisco Peaks while learning about the cultural heritage of the high desert.

ARIZONA

State & National Forests

☐ ▢ ♡ **Apache-Sitgreaves National Forests:** Encompassing over 2.6 million acres in eastern Arizona, this combined forest features cool mountain lakes, volcanic peaks, and vast ponderosa pine woodlands. The Mogollon Rim and White Mountains provide scenic backdrops for camping, fishing, hiking, and wildlife watching. Known for its high-elevation beauty, it's a summer refuge and year-round recreation haven.

☐ ▢ ♡ **Coconino National Forest:** Spanning nearly 1.9 million acres, Coconino boasts striking diversity, from Sedona's red rock canyons and the volcanic San Francisco Peaks to alpine forests and desert grasslands. Home to lava flows, cliff dwellings, and the scenic Mogollon Rim, the forest supports endless recreation, including hiking, skiing, and cultural exploration amid iconic Arizona landscapes.

☐ ▢ ♡ **Coronado National Forest:** Spread across "sky islands" in southern Arizona and extending into New Mexico, Coronado showcases dramatic mountain ranges rising from desert basins. Rich in biodiversity, it includes habitats from cactus-filled valleys to high pine forests. The Santa Catalinas, Chiricahuas, and Huachucas offer hiking, birding, and rare wildlife viewing, making it a biological treasure.

☐ ▢ ♡ **Kaibab National Forest:** Encircling both rims of the Grand Canyon, Kaibab covers 1.6 million acres of plateaus, ponderosa pine forests, and dramatic canyons. Its landscapes range from alpine meadows to desert vistas, with abundant wildlife. Offering access to remote Grand Canyon overlooks and backcountry trails, it provides solitude and unmatched views away from crowded rim areas.

☐ ▢ ♡ **Prescott National Forest:** Encompassing 1.2 million acres of central Arizona, Prescott includes the Bradshaw, Black Hills, and Mingus Mountains. Known for historic mining towns, hidden lakes, and mild climate, it offers year-round outdoor recreation: kayaking, horseback riding, hiking, and off-roading. The forest blends history, scenic mountain terrain, and diverse habitats into an inviting landscape.

☐ ▢ ♡ **Tonto National Forest:** Arizona's largest national forest at 2.9 million acres, Tonto spans rugged Sonoran Desert to alpine peaks. The Salt and Verde Rivers and six man-made lakes provide boating, fishing, and water recreation. Saguaro-studded canyons rise toward snowy summits, offering dramatic contrasts. One of the nation's most-visited forests, it blends wilderness with accessibility.

National Scenic Byways & All-American Roads

☐ ▢ ♡ **Coronado Trail Scenic Byway (US-191):** Formerly known as "The Devil's Highway" (US-666), this twisting 123-mile National Scenic Byway climbs from desert to alpine forests between Clifton and Springerville. It offers over 400 curves, pine-scented air, sweeping mountain vistas, and solitude through the Apache-Sitgreaves National Forests.

☐ ▢ ♡ **Historic Route 66 (Arizona Segment):** The Arizona stretch of this All-American Road passes through classic Americana: old diners, neon signs, and nostalgic motels. From Holbrook and Winslow to Seligman and Oatman, this scenic drive preserves roadside culture, Native history, and stunning desert and mountain landscapes along the "Mother Road."

☐ ▢ ♡ **Kaibab Plateau–North Rim Parkway (AZ-67):** This National Scenic Byway leads 44 miles through ponderosa pine and aspen forest to the Grand Canyon's North Rim. Open seasonally, it's a quiet, high-elevation route rich in wildlife and natural beauty. Visitors are rewarded with fewer crowds and breathtaking canyon overlooks.

☐ ▢ ♡ **Red Rock Scenic Byway (SR-179):** Designated an All-American Road, this 7.5-mile route south of Sedona showcases Arizona's most iconic red sandstone formations, including Cathedral Rock, Bell Rock, and Courthouse Butte. Scenic pullouts, hiking trailheads, and cultural sites like ancient petroglyphs line the drive. Renowned for its geology and views, it offers a stunning introduction to Red Rock Country.

☐ ▢ ♡ **Sky Island Scenic Byway (Catalina Highway):** Climbing over 6,000 feet in just 27 miles, this National Scenic Byway begins in Tucson's desert and ascends to alpine forests at Mount Lemmon. Often called a "biological time machine," it passes through life zones from cactus to pine. A favorite for hikers, cyclists, and stargazers.

ARIZONA

State Scenic Byways

☐ 🔖 ♡ **Apache Trail Historic Road:** Winding through the Superstition Mountains, this historic stagecoach route reveals canyons, lakes, and desert cliffs within Tonto National Forest. Travelers encounter Goldfield Ghost Town, Canyon Lake, and Roosevelt Dam along the way. Steep grades and narrow curves add to the sense of adventure on one of Arizona's most famous drives.

☐ 🔖 ♡ **Copper Corridor Scenic Road:** Linking Globe, Winkelman, and Oracle, this desert route highlights Arizona's mining heritage. It passes copper mines, rugged mountains, and the San Pedro River Valley, blending industrial history with desert beauty. Visitors encounter Biosphere 2, Aravaipa Canyon, and small towns that showcase the state's cultural and geological contrasts.

☐ 🔖 ♡ **Coronado Trail Scenic Road:** Following US 191 through eastern Arizona, this twisting mountain road offers over 400 curves in 120 miles. Towering pines, alpine meadows, and sweeping overlooks define the route. Rich in wildlife and history, it traces the path of Coronado's expedition and is celebrated as one of the nation's most scenic drives.

☐ 🔖 ♡ **Desert to Tall Pines Scenic Road:** Climbing from the desert floor near Globe to the Mogollon Rim, this drive showcases striking ecological transitions. Cacti and scrublands give way to oak, juniper, and finally ponderosa pine forests. Rugged canyons, sparkling streams, and dramatic overlooks highlight the elevation change along this spectacular mountain ascent.

☐ 🔖 ♡ **Diné Tah Scenic Road:** Meaning "Among the People," this route travels through Navajo Nation lands, connecting Window Rock, Canyon de Chelly, and tribal communities. Towering red cliffs, mesas, and cultural landmarks line the way. It offers deep insight into Navajo history, traditions, and landscapes, blending cultural heritage with breathtaking scenery.

☐ 🔖 ♡ **Dry Creek Scenic Road:** A short corridor near Sedona, this byway showcases the region's red rock formations and lush creekside scenery. Oak woodlands and riparian habitats contrast with fiery sandstone cliffs. The drive is serene yet dramatic, immersing travelers in the striking beauty that has made Sedona one of Arizona's most iconic landscapes.

☐ 🔖 ♡ **Fredonia–Vermilion Cliffs Scenic Road:** Stretching across northern Arizona, this road highlights the brilliant red Vermilion Cliffs, desert plateaus, and sweeping canyon vistas. The route includes Navajo Bridge and access to Marble Canyon. Remote and rugged, it offers awe-inspiring geology and a powerful sense of the vast Colorado Plateau.

☐ 🔖 ♡ **Gila–Pinal Scenic Road:** Running between Florence and Globe, this byway passes desert foothills, riparian corridors, and rugged mountain ridges. Travelers encounter botanical gardens, ancient cultural sites, and diverse wildlife along the way. It's a journey through changing ecosystems that reveal the rich natural and cultural heritage of central Arizona.

☐ 🔖 ♡ **Jerome–Clarkdale–Cottonwood Historic Road:** A short but colorful route through Verde Valley, this byway connects mining towns, vineyards, and historic districts. Visitors can explore Tuzigoot National Monument, museums, and riverfront parks. Red rock formations frame the landscape, blending history, culture, and scenic beauty in northern Arizona.

☐ 🔖 ♡ **Joshua Forest Scenic Road:** Located along US 93, this route passes through Arizona's largest Joshua tree forest. Quirky and iconic, the twisted trees contrast with desert basins and distant mountains. Wildlife, wildflowers, and wide-open skies create a distinctive drive, offering a rare glimpse of this unique desert ecosystem.

☐ 🔖 ♡ **Kayenta–Monument Valley Scenic Road:** Leading into the heart of Monument Valley, this byway showcases towering sandstone buttes, mesas, and desert landscapes sacred to the Navajo. The route offers iconic views seen in countless films, while cultural centers and trading posts enrich the experience. It's a journey into the soul of the American Southwest.

☐ 🔖 ♡ **Mingus Mountain Scenic Road:** This winding route climbs SR 89A through Prescott National Forest toward Jerome. Dramatic switchbacks reveal views of the Verde Valley and distant red rocks of Sedona. Dense pine forests give way to sweeping overlooks. It's a scenic ascent filled with natural beauty and historic mining heritage.

☐ 🔖 ♡ **Naat'tsis'aan–Navajo Mountain Scenic Road:** Traversing remote Navajo Nation lands, this byway highlights the massive Navajo Mountain and surrounding mesas. Stark desert landscapes, colorful cliffs, and cultural landmarks define the route. Isolated and serene, it offers a glimpse into both Navajo traditions and the raw power of the Colorado Plateau.

ARIZONA

☐ 🔖 ♡ **Organ Pipe Cactus Parkway:** Running through Organ Pipe Cactus National Monument, this drive immerses travelers in one of the most biodiverse deserts in North America. Unique cactus forests, rugged volcanic hills, and desert wildlife create a living desert museum. It's a celebration of the Sonoran Desert's beauty and resilience.

☐ 🔖 ♡ **Patagonia–Sonoita Scenic Road:** Crossing rolling grasslands and oak-dotted hills, this route links the communities of Patagonia and Sonoita. The corridor passes vineyards, birding hotspots, and ranchlands. Surrounded by sky island mountains, the drive blends pastoral charm, cultural heritage, and ecological richness in southern Arizona's wine country.

☐ 🔖 ♡ **San Francisco Peaks Scenic Road:** North of Flagstaff, this byway follows US 180 toward Arizona's highest mountains. Aspen groves, alpine meadows, and volcanic peaks dominate the scenery. Fall foliage and wildflowers add seasonal color. The route provides easy access to trails, campgrounds, and sweeping views of northern Arizona.

☐ 🔖 ♡ **Sedona–Oak Creek Canyon Scenic Road:** Carving through Oak Creek Canyon along SR 89A, this drive reveals sheer cliffs, red rock spires, and lush riparian forests. Slide Rock State Park and multiple overlooks offer scenic stops. Known for its dramatic beauty, it's one of Arizona's most beloved and photographed byways.

☐ 🔖 ♡ **Swift Trail Parkway:** Climbing SR 366 to Mount Graham, this steep and winding road passes through desert, oak, pine, and fir forests. It showcases remarkable ecological diversity within a short distance. Scenic overlooks, cool mountain air, and access to high-elevation lakes and observatories make it a unique "sky island" journey.

☐ 🔖 ♡ **Tse'nikani–Flat Mesa Rock Scenic Road:** Traveling US 191 in northeastern Arizona, this byway winds through mesas, canyons, and sandstone cliffs. Petroglyphs and cultural landmarks mark the landscape, while sweeping desert views highlight the vastness of the Colorado Plateau. It's a quiet, evocative route rich in natural and cultural history.

☐ 🔖 ♡ **White Mountain Scenic Road:** Looping through Arizona's White Mountains, this route combines SR 260, 261, and 273. Dense pine forests, cool lakes, and alpine meadows define the drive, with seasonal wildflowers and fall colors enhancing the beauty. Recreation opportunities abound, making it a popular high-country retreat.

☐ 🔖 ♡ **White River Scenic Road:** Crossing the Fort Apache Reservation, this corridor follows wooded canyons, streams, and ranchlands. Cultural sites, fish hatcheries, and scenic overlooks highlight Apache traditions and the area's natural richness. It's a peaceful drive combining heritage, ecology, and striking highland landscapes.

National Natural Landmarks

 ☐ 🔖 ♡ **Barfoot Park:** High in the Chiricahua Mountains, Barfoot Park earned National Natural Landmark status for its Madrean-influenced ponderosa pine forest. Here, elements of the Sierra Madre and Rocky Mountains meet, creating a rich mix of flora and fauna. This rare forest community is one of the best-preserved examples of its kind in the American Southwest.
GPS: 31.9151, -109.3020

 ☐ 🔖 ♡ **Barringer Meteor Crater:** Often called Meteor Crater, this site is protected as a National Natural Landmark for being the most pristine impact crater on Earth. Formed about 50,000 years ago, it measures nearly 4,000 feet across and 560 feet deep. The crater provides unmatched opportunities to study planetary impacts and even served as a training ground for astronauts.
GPS: 35.0272, -111.0225

 ☐ 🔖 ♡ **Canelo Hills Cienega Reserve:** This wetland oasis in southern Arizona holds National Natural Landmark status for preserving one of the region's last natural cienegas. Surrounded by grasslands, it sustains rare species such as the Gila chub and the Canelo Ladies Tresses Orchid. The site highlights the ecological importance of marsh habitats in otherwise arid landscapes.
GPS: 31.5622, -110.5259

 ☐ 🔖 ♡ **Comb Ridge:** Stretching 80 miles along the Arizona–Utah border, Comb Ridge was named a National Natural Landmark for its geologic and paleontological significance. It is the only North American site to yield tritylodont fossils, ancient reptile-like mammals. The ridge also preserves ancestral Puebloan dwellings and petroglyphs, combining cultural and scientific value.
GPS: 36.8188, -110.0572

ARIZONA

 ☐ 🔖 ♡ **Grapevine Mesa:** This remarkable Joshua tree forest near the Grand Canyon is a National Natural Landmark for its density and size. Ancient groves of Joshua trees flourish here, standing among sweeping desert vistas. The site exemplifies Mojave Desert resilience and preserves one of the most outstanding Joshua tree habitats in the United States.
GPS: 35.9744, -114.0816

 ☐ 🔖 ♡ **Willcox Playa:** This vast alkali flat in southeastern Arizona was named a National Natural Landmark for its importance to migratory birds. Each winter, tens of thousands of sandhill cranes stop here to feed and rest. When dry, its cracked surface illustrates desert geomorphology, while seasonal floods transform it into a vital wetland refuge.
GPS: 32.1410, -109.8480

 ☐ 🔖 ♡ **Kaibab Squirrel Area:** On the Kaibab Plateau, this site became a National Natural Landmark for being the exclusive home of the Kaibab squirrel. This tufted-eared subspecies of the Abert's squirrel lives only in the plateau's ponderosa pine forests. Its isolation highlights how geography shapes wildlife evolution and ecological specialization.
GPS: 36.4002, -112.1531

 ☐ 🔖 ♡ **Onyx Cave:** Widely regarded as Arizona's finest limestone cavern, Onyx Cave was given National Natural Landmark status for its stunning mineral formations. Delicate stalactites, soda straws, and flowstone fill its chambers, offering scientists rare insight into subterranean processes. Limited access helps ensure the preservation of its fragile features.
GPS: 31.7175, -110.7692

 ☐ 🔖 ♡ **Patagonia–Sonoita Creek:** One of southern Arizona's last perennial streams, Patagonia–Sonoita Creek was declared a National Natural Landmark for its ecological richness. Cottonwood–willow forests line its banks, providing critical habitat for native fish and migratory birds. The corridor preserves what much of the Southwest's waterways once looked like.
GPS: 31.5280, -110.7755

 ☐ 🔖 ♡ **Ramsey Canyon:** Nestled in the Huachuca Mountains, Ramsey Canyon became a National Natural Landmark for its extraordinary biodiversity. Sheer cliffs, shaded gorges, and a perennial creek support dozens of hummingbird species, rare plants, and diverse wildlife. It stands as one of Arizona's most important ecological havens in an otherwise arid region.
GPS: 31.4478, -110.3072

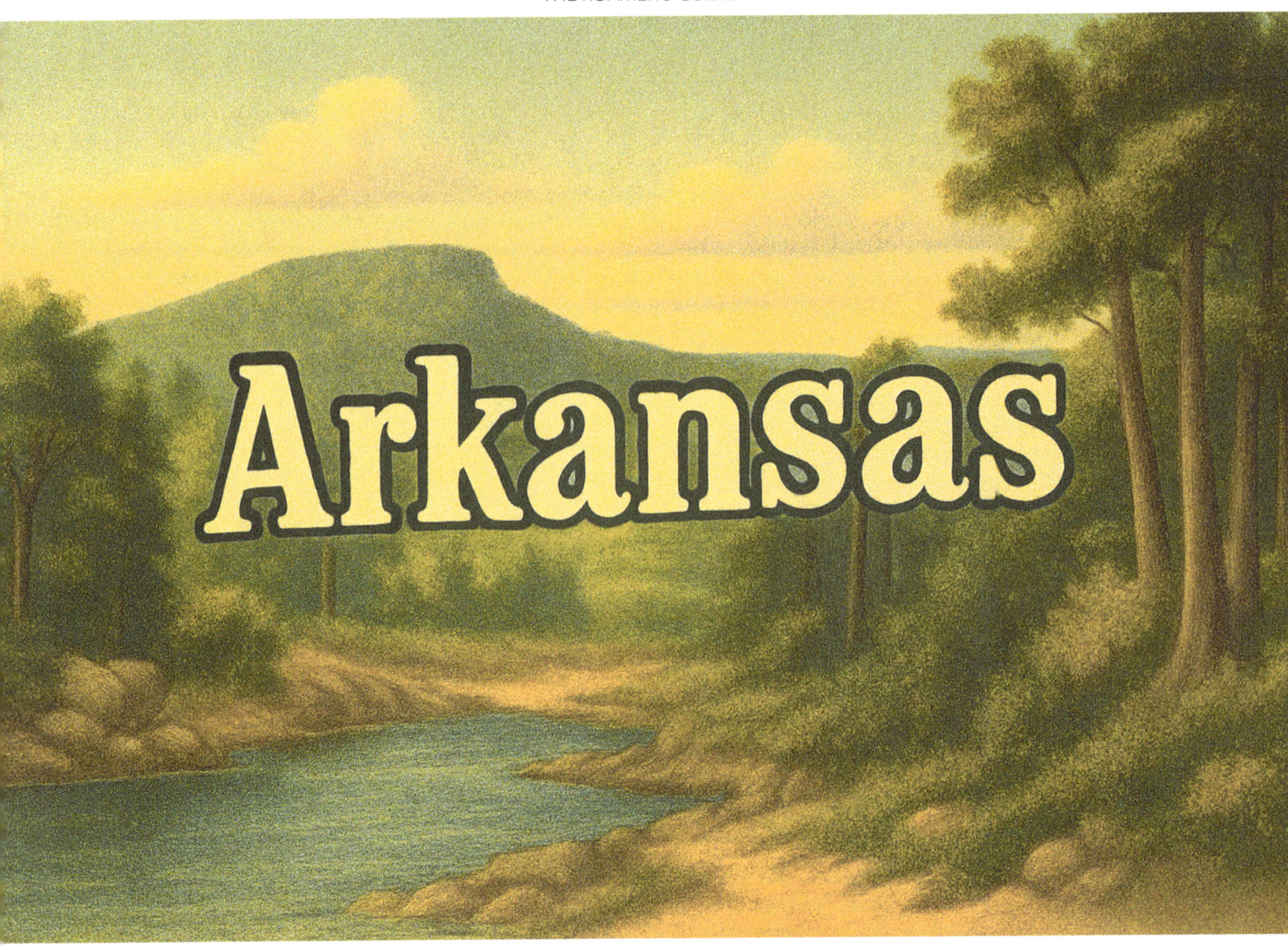

Arkansas

Arkansas is a land of natural treasures, with an abundance of state parks, national forests, a beloved national park, and unique natural landmarks. From the Ozark Mountains and sparkling lakes to rugged trails and crystal caverns, The Natural State beckons outdoor enthusiasts.

📅 Peak Season
March–May and September–November are the best times to visit Arkansas. Spring brings wildflowers, waterfalls at their fullest, and mild hiking weather, while fall offers cooler air, brilliant foliage, and lively festivals.

📅 Offseason Months
June–August is hot and humid, making midday activities less comfortable, though rivers and lakes draw summer crowds. December–February is quieter, with fewer tourists and occasional chilly conditions in the Ozarks.

🍃 Scenery & Nature Timing
Spring highlights blooming dogwoods, redbuds, and rushing waterfalls. Summer is lush and green with abundant wildlife. Fall transforms the Ozarks and Ouachitas with colorful foliage, while winter reveals clear mountain vistas.

✨ Special
Arkansas is shaped by the Ozark and Ouachita Mountains, with striking caves like Blanchard Springs Caverns and rushing waterfalls in the Ozark Highlands. Hot Springs National Park and Mammoth Spring showcase unique waters, while the Buffalo National River winds through scenic bluffs and forests.

ARKANSAS

State Parks

☐ 🔖 ♡ **Bull Shoals–White River State Park:** Below Bull Shoals Dam, this park is a premier trout-fishing destination, with cold, clear waters ideal for anglers. Campgrounds, pavilions, and hiking trails line the White River. Interpretive programs highlight ecology and dam history. With forested hills, scenic overlooks, and abundant wildlife, it's one of Arkansas's most popular recreation spots.

☐ 🔖 ♡ **Cane Creek State Park:** Nestled at the edge of the Mississippi Delta, this park offers a 1,675-acre lake surrounded by cypress sloughs and pine woods. Trails for hiking and biking connect wetlands with uplands. Fishing, paddling, and birdwatching highlight the lake, while campgrounds and cabins make it a relaxing retreat blending two Arkansas ecosystems.

☐ 🔖 ♡ **Conway Cemetery State Park:** A quiet memorial site in Bradley County, this park preserves the resting place of Arkansas's first governor, James S. Conway, and his family. Shaded by tall pines, it offers a reflective atmosphere with interpretive panels about Conway's legacy. Though small in size, it plays a meaningful role in preserving the state's early history.

☐ 🔖 ♡ **Cossatot River State Park–Natural Area:** Known as Arkansas's "Skull Crusher" for its rapids, the Cossatot River offers thrilling whitewater for kayakers and canoeists. Trails and overlooks showcase rugged Ouachita Mountain scenery, while fishing and swimming add to recreation. As both a state park and natural area, it preserves rare habitats alongside adventurous outdoor opportunities.

☐ 🔖 ♡ **Crater of Diamonds State Park:** The only public diamond mine in the world invites visitors to dig for real diamonds in a 37-acre volcanic field near Murfreesboro. Campgrounds, a museum, and a water park enhance the family-friendly experience. With hiking trails, picnic areas, and the thrill of discovery, it's one of Arkansas's most unique attractions.

☐ 🔖 ♡ **Crowley's Ridge State Park:** Perched on a rare geologic formation in northeast Arkansas, this park blends natural beauty with historic CCC craftsmanship. Cabins, trails, lakes, and picnic areas provide family recreation. Visitors explore unique terrain with hardwood forests and rolling hills, learning about Crowley's Ridge while enjoying classic state park activities.

☐ 🔖 ♡ **Daisy State Park:** Located on Lake Greeson in the Ouachitas, this park is surrounded by pine forests and scenic coves. Anglers target bass and crappie, while boaters and campers enjoy the lake's tranquil waters. Trails provide wildlife viewing and access to hidden spots. With quiet campgrounds and natural beauty, it's a beloved family getaway.

☐ 🔖 ♡ **Davidsonville Historic State Park:** Once a bustling frontier town, Davidsonville was Arkansas's first platted community and home to its first courthouse and post office. Today, ghost structures, archaeological sites, and interpretive exhibits tell its story. Visitors camp, hike, and fish along the Black River, stepping back into early 19th-century Arkansas life.

☐ 🔖 ♡ **DeGray Lake Resort State Park:** Arkansas's only resort state park combines a full-service lodge with boating, golf, hiking, and fishing on scenic DeGray Lake. Guests enjoy a marina, campgrounds, and programs on nature and astronomy. With its mix of luxury amenities and natural beauty, it's a year-round destination for recreation and relaxation.

☐ 🔖 ♡ **Delta Heritage Trail State Park:** A rail-to-trail project stretching through the Arkansas Delta, this park offers scenic biking, hiking, and birdwatching. Running along an abandoned rail line, it passes wetlands, farmland, and bottomland forests. Interpretive stops highlight regional history and wildlife, making it a blend of cultural heritage and outdoor adventure.

☐ 🔖 ♡ **Devil's Den State Park:** A CCC-built gem in the Ozark Mountains, Devil's Den is known for caves, bluffs, and clear mountain streams. Trails lead to waterfalls and unique rock formations, while rustic cabins and campgrounds welcome overnight visitors. With abundant wildlife and historic stonework, it's one of Arkansas's most iconic and scenic parks.

☐ 🔖 ♡ **Hampson Archeological Museum State Park:** Located in Wilson, this museum displays artifacts from the Nodena Site, a large Mississippian village that thrived 500 years ago. Exhibits include intricate pottery, tools, and reconstructions of daily life. Visitors learn about agriculture, trade, and cultural practices of one of Arkansas's most important prehistoric communities.

ARKANSAS

☐ 🔖 ♡ **Herman Davis State Park:** In Manila, this small park honors WWI hero Herman Davis, ranked among America's top soldiers by General Pershing. A statue and granite memorial pay tribute, while shaded grounds invite reflection. Though modest, it preserves the legacy of a native son whose mark on history is far larger than the park itself.

☐ 🔖 ♡ **Historic Washington State Park:** Once Arkansas's Confederate capital, this preserved 19th-century village features historic homes, blacksmith shops, and museums. Guided tours and demonstrations bring frontier life to life. Surrounded by ancient oaks and heritage landscapes, it offers visitors an immersive journey into Civil War-era and antebellum Arkansas.

☐ 🔖 ♡ **Hobbs State Park–Conservation Area:** The largest in Arkansas, spanning 12,000 acres in the Ozarks, Hobbs focuses on conservation and recreation. Trails for hiking, biking, and horseback riding wind through forested ridges and streams. A modern visitor center offers exhibits and programs. It's a hub for both outdoor adventure and environmental education.

☐ 🔖 ♡ **Jacksonport State Park:** At the meeting of the White and Black rivers, this park preserves a restored 1872 courthouse and celebrates Arkansas's steamboat era. Campsites, boat ramps, and exhibits immerse visitors in river history. Festivals and programs bring 19th-century culture alive, making it both scenic and historically rich.

☐ 🔖 ♡ **Jenkins' Ferry Battleground State Park:** This quiet site preserves an 1864 Civil War battle fought in swampy terrain. Trails and interpretive signs describe the hardships of the Camden Expedition and honor those who fought. Shaded by dense woods, it's a somber but important reminder of Arkansas's wartime history.

☐ 🔖 ♡ **Lake Catherine State Park:** Nestled in the Ouachita Mountains near Hot Springs, this park offers fishing, boating, and swimming on a scenic lake. Cabins, campgrounds, and trails to waterfalls invite overnight stays and exploration. Its wooded hillsides, family programs, and year-round accessibility make it one of Arkansas's most visited and beloved parks.

☐ 🔖 ♡ **Lake Charles State Park:** In northeast Arkansas, this park surrounds a 645-acre lake known for great bass, catfish, and crappie fishing. Campgrounds, trails, and picnic sites make it family-friendly. Birdwatchers enjoy abundant species, while rolling hills and quiet woodlands frame the lake. It's a relaxing retreat that blends scenic beauty, recreation, and wildlife watching.

☐ 🔖 ♡ **Lake Chicot State Park:** On Lake Chicot, Arkansas's largest natural lake, this Delta park offers boating, fishing, and birdwatching. A marina, campgrounds, and trails make it a hub for outdoor recreation. Migratory waterfowl flock here each season, creating prime viewing opportunities. With shady lakeside sites, it's a serene destination for families and anglers alike.

☐ 🔖 ♡ **Lake Dardanelle State Park:** Spanning two sites on Lake Dardanelle, this park combines world-class fishing with cultural history. Its visitor center features aquariums, exhibits, and interpretive programs, while piers and ramps provide easy lake access. Designated as part of the Trail of Tears National Historic Trail, it blends recreation with heritage significance.

☐ 🔖 ♡ **Lake Fort Smith State Park:** In the Boston Mountains, this modern park features a lodge, cabins, marina, and campgrounds along the scenic lake. Trails link to the Ozark Highlands Trail, offering rugged hiking. Visitors enjoy fishing, kayaking, and cool mountain breezes. With historic ties and modern amenities, it's a top retreat for Ozark exploration.

☐ 🔖 ♡ **Lake Frierson State Park:** Located on Crowley's Ridge, this quiet park features a 335-acre lake great for bass, catfish, and crappie fishing. Campgrounds, hiking trails, and shaded picnic areas provide a peaceful setting. Birdwatchers find diverse species among hardwoods. Its intimate scale makes it a hidden gem for outdoor enthusiasts seeking solitude.

☐ 🔖 ♡ **Lake Ouachita State Park:** On one of the cleanest lakes in the nation, this park is surrounded by forested Ouachita Mountains. Crystal-clear water invites boating, swimming, fishing, and scuba diving. Trails and campsites provide land-based fun. With its marina and interpretive programs, it's a premier destination for outdoor adventure and natural beauty.

☐ 🔖 ♡ **Lake Poinsett State Park:** In northeast Arkansas, this Delta park surrounds a 132-acre lake recently restored for anglers. Visitors fish, paddle, and camp in shaded sites. Trails wind through unique ridge terrain, offering wildlife viewing and nature exploration. With family-friendly facilities and a quiet setting, it's a popular weekend destination.

ARKANSAS

☐ 🔖 ♡ **Logoly State Park:** Arkansas's first environmental education park focuses on nature study and conservation. Mineral springs, shaded forests, and rare plants make it a hotspot for learning. Trails loop through unique habitats, while picnic areas and programs attract families and school groups. Though small, its focus on ecology makes it a vital outdoor classroom.

☐ 🔖 ♡ **Louisiana Purchase State Park:** Deep in a Delta swamp, this National Historic Landmark preserves the survey point that began mapping the Louisiana Purchase. A boardwalk takes visitors through rare headwater wetlands to a stone monument. Interpretive signs tell the story of westward expansion. It's both a historic and natural treasure tucked in a secluded setting.

☐ 🔖 ♡ **Lower White River Museum State Park:** In Des Arc, this museum explores life along the White River from 1830–1900. Exhibits highlight steamboats, commerce, and daily frontier life. Visitors discover artifacts, interpretive panels, and stories that bring river culture alive. It's a cultural stop offering insights into Arkansas's role as a river-based economy.

☐ 🔖 ♡ **Mammoth Spring State Park:** Centered on one of the largest springs in the U.S., discharging 9 million gallons per hour, this park showcases the spring, a hydroelectric plant, and a historic train depot. Trails, fishing, and picnic spots make it popular. Its mix of natural wonder and historic features creates a destination rich in both scenery and heritage.

☐ 🔖 ♡ **Marks' Mills Battleground State Park:** This wooded park preserves the site of an 1864 Civil War ambush during the Camden Expedition. Interpretive signs detail the events and significance of the battle. Quiet trails encourage reflection, while shaded forests offer a peaceful setting. It's one of three state parks commemorating this chapter of Arkansas's wartime history.

☐ 🔖 ♡ **Millwood State Park:** Along Millwood Lake in southwest Arkansas, this park is a top destination for fishing, especially largemouth bass. Birdwatchers flock to see hundreds of species in wetlands and forests. Campgrounds, boat ramps, and trails support year-round recreation. With 29,000 acres of water, it's a haven for anglers and outdoor enthusiasts.

☐ 🔖 ♡ **Mississippi River State Park:** Within the St. Francis National Forest, this park gives direct access to the Mississippi River, lakes, and Crowley's Ridge. Trails and campgrounds complement fishing and boating opportunities. Cypress swamps and hardwood forests provide rich wildlife habitats. It's a unique blend of national forest and state park recreation.

☐ 🔖 ♡ **Moro Bay State Park:** At the confluence of rivers and bayous, Moro Bay offers fishing, boating, and peaceful camping under cypress trees draped in Spanish moss. A ferry replica and interpretive exhibits recall the area's transportation history. Trails, picnic areas, and abundant wildlife make it a quiet, nature-filled retreat in southern Arkansas.

☐ 🔖 ♡ **Mount Magazine State Park:** Arkansas's highest point, Mount Magazine rises 2,753 feet and offers stunning views, hiking, biking, and even hang gliding. A lodge, cabins, and visitor center provide modern amenities. Rugged trails and overlooks highlight the mountain's dramatic landscape. Its mix of adventure and scenery makes it a premier destination.

☐ 🔖 ♡ **Mount Nebo State Park:** Overlooking the Arkansas River Valley, Mount Nebo features dramatic bluffs, historic CCC-built cabins, and sweeping vistas. Visitors hike, bike, and explore scenic trails, while hang gliders launch from its cliffs. Rustic stonework preserves its heritage. Its combination of recreation and history makes it a beloved state park.

☐ 🔖 ♡ **Ozark Folk Center State Park:** In Mountain View, this cultural park preserves Ozark heritage through live music, folk dancing, and traditional crafts. Visitors watch artisans at work, join workshops, and hear authentic mountain music. With a theater, craft village, and gardens, it's a living museum of Ozark culture and a celebration of regional traditions.

☐ 🔖 ♡ **Parkin Archeological State Park:** On the St. Francis River, this site preserves a large Mississippian village occupied over 500 years ago. Trails and a museum display artifacts such as pottery, tools, and ornaments. Archaeological research continues, revealing insights into pre-Columbian life. Visitors explore a mound site rich in Native American history.

☐ 🔖 ♡ **Petit Jean State Park:** Arkansas's first state park, Petit Jean is famed for Cedar Falls, towering bluffs, and CCC-built stone structures. Trails explore caves, canyons, and forests. The lodge and cabins provide overnight stays, while picnic areas and overlooks invite day use. Its history, scenery, and accessibility make it a crown jewel of the state park system.

☐ 🔖 ♡ **Pinnacle Mountain State Park:** Just outside Little Rock, this park is centered on the iconic Pinnacle Mountain, whose trails lead to panoramic vistas of the Arkansas River Valley. Families enjoy picnics, hiking, and educational exhibits at the visitor center. With riverside boardwalks, birdwatching, and outdoor programs, it's a premier urban natural escape.

ARKANSAS

☐ ▢ ♡ **Plum Bayou Mounds Archeological State Park:** Formerly Toltec Mounds, this park preserves 18 Native American earthworks built by the Plum Bayou culture between 600–1050 A.D. Trails and exhibits explain mound-building practices and cultural life. Interpretive panels, artifacts, and scenic views highlight the significance of this prehistoric ceremonial site.

☐ ▢ ♡ **Poison Springs Battleground State Park:** Commemorating an 1864 Civil War clash, this site interprets the Battle of Poison Springs, where African American Union troops fought bravely but suffered heavy losses. Interpretive signs explain the battle's role in the Camden Expedition. Today, shaded trails and quiet woods make it a reflective, historic landscape.

☐ ▢ ♡ **Powhatan Historic State Park:** Along the Black River, this park preserves a 19th-century river port town with its courthouse, jail, and restored buildings. Guided tours and living history events highlight commerce, law, and culture of frontier Arkansas. With views of the river and preserved heritage, it offers a step back into the 1800s.

☐ ▢ ♡ **Prairie Grove Battlefield State Park:** This park preserves the 1862 Civil War Battle of Prairie Grove, one of the most significant in Arkansas. A museum, driving tour, and interpretive trails explain troop movements and battlefield history. Living history events bring the site alive. It's a solemn and educational destination for history enthusiasts.

☐ ▢ ♡ **Queen Wilhelmina State Park:** On Rich Mountain, Arkansas's second-highest peak, this park offers sweeping Ouachita Mountain views. A historic lodge, nicknamed the "Castle in the Sky", serves visitors, while trails and overlooks showcase the scenery. With seasonal wildflowers, wildlife, and crisp air, it's a mountaintop retreat for relaxation and exploration.

☐ ▢ ♡ **Village Creek State Park:** Spanning nearly 7,000 acres along Crowley's Ridge, this large park offers diverse recreation. Two lakes provide fishing and paddling, while trails welcome hikers, bikers, and horseback riders. A golf course and campsites add to its appeal. Segments of the Trail of Tears pass through, linking outdoor fun with history.

☐ ▢ ♡ **White Oak Lake State Park:** In southwest Arkansas, this quiet park surrounds a 725-acre lake known for fishing, birding, and boating. Trails wind through pine and hardwood forests rich with wildlife. Campgrounds and picnic sites make it a family destination. With its peaceful atmosphere, it's a prime spot for anglers and nature enthusiasts alike.

☐ ▢ ♡ **Withrow Springs State Park:** In the Ozarks, this park is centered on a spring-fed stream ideal for fishing and paddling. Hiking trails explore bluff-lined hollows, caves, and hardwood forests. Shaded campgrounds and picnic areas provide comfort, while interpretive programs connect visitors with the area's natural and cultural heritage.

☐ ▢ ♡ **Woolly Hollow State Park:** North of Conway, this park surrounds 40-acre Lake Bennett, offering swimming, fishing, and paddleboats. Trails loop through forests and past historic farmsteads. With a beach, picnic areas, and campgrounds, it's family-oriented and scenic. Its combination of recreation and history makes it a charming retreat in central Arkansas.

National Parks

☐ ▢ ♡ **Arkansas Post National Memorial:** Preserving the site of Arkansas's first European settlement and the Civil War Battle of Arkansas Post, this memorial highlights centuries of layered history. Visitors can walk scenic trails, explore museum exhibits, and learn about colonial trade, frontier life, and the strategic importance of the area during conflict.

☐ ▢ ♡ **Buffalo National River:** Flowing freely for 135 miles in northern Arkansas, this river is one of the few remaining undammed in the lower 48 states. Visitors enjoy canoeing, kayaking, fishing, and hiking along towering bluffs, crystal-clear waters, and lush forests, while spotting wildlife in one of the state's most pristine natural landscapes.

ARKANSAS

☐ 🔖 ♡ **Fort Smith National Historic Site:** On the Arkansas-Oklahoma border, this site preserves two frontier forts and the story of law and order in the 19th century. Visitors explore courthouse ruins, jail cells, and exhibits that tell of Indian Removal, the Trail of Tears, and the role Fort Smith played in westward expansion and frontier justice.

☐ 🔖 ♡ **Hot Springs National Park:** Nestled in the Ouachita Mountains, this park is famed for its thermal waters and historic bathhouses. Visitors can stroll Bathhouse Row, hike scenic mountain trails, bike forested roads, and even soak in spring-fed pools, experiencing a unique blend of natural beauty, wellness traditions, and cultural history.

☐ 🔖 ♡ **Little Rock Central High School National Historic Site:** This landmark tells the story of the 1957 desegregation crisis, when nine African American students, the "Little Rock Nine," courageously integrated the school under federal protection. Visitors can tour the still-operating high school and explore exhibits on civil rights and social change.

☐ 🔖 ♡ **Pea Ridge National Military Park:** Covering 4,300 acres in northwest Arkansas, this site preserves the 1862 Civil War battlefield where Union forces secured control of the Ozarks. Visitors can follow an interpretive driving tour, walk historic trails, view monuments and artifacts, and gain perspective on the battle's pivotal role in the war's Western Theater.

☐ 🔖 ♡ **President William Jefferson Clinton Birthplace Home National Historic Site:** Located in Hope, this site preserves the childhood home of the 42nd U.S. president. Visitors can tour the modest house where Bill Clinton lived with his grandparents, explore exhibits at the visitor center, and learn about his formative years and rise to national leadership.

State & National Forests

☐ 🔖 ♡ **Ouachita National Forest:** Spanning 1.8 million acres in western Arkansas and eastern Oklahoma, Ouachita is the oldest National Forest in the South. Known for the rugged Ouachita Mountains, the forest offers crystal-clear creeks, scenic drives like Talimena, and solitude for hiking, horseback riding, camping, and wildlife observation in mixed pine-hardwood landscapes.

☐ 🔖 ♡ **Ozark-St. Francis National Forests:** Together covering over 1.2 million acres, these twin forests offer distinct ecosystems. The Ozark section is mountainous and scenic with waterfalls and trails, while the St. Francis section protects Delta lowlands. The forests support activities from rock climbing to fishing and are home to the highest point in Arkansas, Mount Magazine.

☐ 🔖 ♡ **Poison Springs State Forest:** Located in southern Arkansas, this 22,000-acre working forest blends timber production, habitat restoration, and historical preservation. It was the site of a Civil War battle and now supports pine reforestation, fire ecology research, and outdoor recreation like hunting and wildlife watching, all within a managed forest landscape.

National Scenic Byways & All-American Roads

☐ 🔖 ♡ **Crowley's Ridge Parkway:** This National Scenic Byway runs 198 miles through eastern Arkansas along a unique geologic formation rising above the Mississippi Delta. It passes rich farmland, Civil War sites, state parks, and hardwood forests. With rolling hills and cultural heritage, the route offers a surprising contrast to the surrounding flatlands.

☐ 🔖 ♡ **Great River Road (Arkansas Segment):** Part of the 10-state Great River Road All-American Road system, this scenic corridor traces the Mississippi River along Arkansas's eastern border. Travelers experience riverside towns, wildlife refuges, historic plantations, and Delta blues heritage, highlighting the cultural and natural richness of the Mississippi Valley.

ARKANSAS

☐ ▢ ♡ **Talimena Scenic Drive (Arkansas Segment):** This National Scenic Byway runs 18 miles through the Ouachita Mountains in western Arkansas before continuing into Oklahoma. It follows ridgelines with long-range views, wildflower fields, and overlooks. Especially popular in fall, it's one of the best places in the state for autumn foliage.

State Scenic Byways

☐ ▢ ♡ **Arkansas Scenic 7 Byway:** Stretching from the Louisiana border to Harrison, this route traverses pine-covered hills, river valleys, and the Ouachita and Ozark National Forests. Scenic overlooks, waterfalls, and small mountain towns highlight the journey. It's celebrated for dramatic seasonal color, rolling ridges, and winding roads that showcase the natural beauty of Arkansas.

☐ ▢ ♡ **Boston Mountains Scenic Loop:** Combining US 71 and I-49, this loop winds through the rugged Boston Mountains in the Ozark National Forest. Travelers encounter sweeping views of forested ridges, deep valleys, and historic towns. The slower US 71 emphasizes heritage and charm, while I-49 delivers quick access to overlooks, creating a scenic and cultural pairing.

☐ ▢ ♡ **Camden Expedition Scenic Byway:** Following the path of the Union campaign of 1864, this heritage-rich route connects battlefields, historic towns, and rolling farmland. Travelers explore preserved Civil War sites, interpretive centers, and small communities tied to Arkansas's wartime past. Scenic stretches of countryside provide both natural beauty and cultural reflection.

☐ ▢ ♡ **Ozark Highlands Scenic Byway (Highway 21):** Running 35 miles from Clarksville to the Buffalo National River, this byway cuts through the heart of the Ozark National Forest. Towering bluffs, hardwood forests, and winding rivers define the scenery. Overlooks, trailheads, and historic bridges provide access to outdoor adventure and breathtaking landscapes.

☐ ▢ ♡ **Interstate 530 Scenic Byway:** A short but varied 15-mile corridor south of Pine Bluff, this route highlights oak woodlands, rivers, and farm country. Wildlife thrives in the surrounding landscape, offering birdwatching and seasonal color. As a transition from city to rural countryside, it provides a scenic interlude along a major highway.

☐ ▢ ♡ **Mount Magazine Scenic Byway (Highway 309):** Ascending Arkansas's tallest peak, this drive passes through the Ozark National Forest, delivering sweeping vistas and cooler mountain air. Panoramic overlooks, hiking trails, and recreation areas near the summit highlight the route. The dramatic climb captures the grandeur of the state's highest point.

☐ ▢ ♡ **Pig Trail Scenic Byway (Highway 23):** Known for its twisting curves and forested beauty, this byway winds through the Ozark National Forest from Ozark to Eureka Springs. Dense woodlands, wildflowers, and autumn foliage create a colorful backdrop. A favorite for motorcyclists, it blends thrilling driving with rugged natural charm.

☐ ▢ ♡ **Sylamore Scenic Byway:** A 26.5-mile stretch through the Ozark National Forest, this route passes towering limestone bluffs, rolling rivers, and dense hardwood forests. Starting near Blanchard Springs Caverns, it showcases caves, streams, and recreational areas. The byway offers peaceful scenery, outdoor adventure, and a strong connection to Arkansas's natural heritage.

☐ ▢ ♡ **West–Northwest Scenic Byway:** Extending over 260 miles, this route links Mena, Ola, and Fort Smith with forested ridges, farmland, and historic small towns. Long stretches pass through quiet backcountry and natural landscapes, offering solitude and sweeping views. It captures the diversity of Arkansas scenery, from mountain slopes to pastoral valleys.

ARKANSAS

National Natural Landmarks

☐ 🔖 ♡ **Big Lake Natural Area:** Within Big Lake National Wildlife Refuge, this site is a National Natural Landmark for preserving a remnant of the vast Mississippi Alluvial Plain. Bottomland hardwood forests, oxbow lakes, and marshes create essential habitat for migratory waterfowl, making it one of the most ecologically important wetland systems in the state.
GPS: 35.9135, -90.1176

☐ 🔖 ♡ **Lake Winona Research Natural Area:** Deep in the Ouachita National Forest, Lake Winona's Research Natural Area holds National Natural Landmark status for its undisturbed shortleaf pine forest. Protecting a rare upland ecosystem, it offers scientists a chance to study natural fire regimes, forest succession, and the pre-settlement conditions of Arkansas's pine woodlands.
GPS: 34.7102, -94.4244

☐ 🔖 ♡ **Mammoth Spring:** One of the largest natural springs in the central United States, Mammoth Spring was named a National Natural Landmark for its immense discharge, over nine million gallons an hour. The spring creates the Spring River and links hydrologically to Missouri's Grand Gulf, forming a rare interstate karst system of geological significance.
GPS: 36.4978, -91.5359

☐ 🔖 ♡ **Roaring Branch Research Natural Area:** This rugged ravine in the Ouachitas is a National Natural Landmark for protecting one of the last virgin stands of mixed pine and hardwoods. Its cascading stream, steep slopes, and untouched canopy preserve a rare glimpse into Arkansas's pre-settlement forests, serving as a living record of natural heritage.
GPS: 34.3730, -93.9780

☐ 🔖 ♡ **White River Sugarberry Natural Area:** Situated within White River National Wildlife Refuge, this site holds National Natural Landmark status for showcasing a pristine bottomland hardwood floodplain. Dominated by mature sugarberry and associated species, it represents one of the richest and best-preserved examples of Lower Mississippi Valley forest ecosystems.
GPS: 34.3500, -91.1000

California

California offers unmatched outdoor diversity, with a vast network of state parks, towering national forests, legendary national parks, and a wealth of natural landmarks. From rugged coastlines and redwood forests to desert valleys and alpine peaks, the Golden State is a playground for adventure.

🗓 Peak Season
May–October is California's peak season, bringing warm, dry weather across much of the state. Summer is busiest along the beaches, national parks, and major cities, with long days and ideal conditions for outdoor activities.

🗓 Offseason Months
November–April is the offseason, marked by cooler temperatures and winter rains along the coast, plus heavy snowfall in the Sierra Nevada. While some high-elevation roads close, cities and coastal areas are quieter with lighter crowds.

🍃 Scenery & Nature Timing
Spring fills valleys with wildflowers in places like Antelope Valley and Carrizo Plain. Summer highlights beaches and alpine lakes. Fall brings grape harvests and colorful Sierra foliage, while winter showcases snowy peaks and gray whale migrations.

✨ Special
California features Yosemite's granite cliffs, giant sequoias in Sequoia and Kings Canyon, and towering coastal redwoods. Death Valley's deserts erupt in spring superblooms, while Big Sur's cliffs, Lake Tahoe's waters, and Mount Shasta's volcanic peak add to the state's dramatic landscapes.

UNITED STATES EDITION

CALIFORNIA

State Parks

☐ 🔖 ♡ **Ahjumawi Lava Springs State Park:** Accessible only by boat, this remote northeastern California park protects one of the largest systems of underwater springs in the nation. Lava flows, crystal-clear waters, and wetlands create habitats for fish, waterfowl, and wildlife. Visitors enjoy canoeing, kayaking, fishing, hiking, and primitive camping while experiencing volcanic landscapes and serene seclusion.

☐ 🔖 ♡ **Andrew Molera State Park:** Located in Big Sur, Andrew Molera retains a rustic charm with limited development. The park features meadows, beaches, redwoods, and the Big Sur River. Miles of trails allow hiking, horseback riding, and beachcombing along the rugged coastline. Wildlife abounds, including condors and sea otters. Campers can stay in walk-in sites, offering a quieter alternative to busier Big Sur parks.

☐ 🔖 ♡ **Angel Island State Park:** Situated in San Francisco Bay, Angel Island offers a mix of natural beauty and cultural history. Accessible by ferry, the island provides panoramic views of San Francisco, the Golden Gate, and Marin. It was once a military base and immigration station. Today, visitors hike, bike, or tour historic sites, while camping and picnicking opportunities create an immersive island experience.

☐ 🔖 ♡ **Anza-Borrego Desert State Park:** California's largest state park covers 585,000 acres of desert wilderness. Known for seasonal wildflower "superblooms," the park features badlands, palm oases, slot canyons, and rugged mountains. Stargazing under its dark skies is exceptional. Visitors can hike, camp, drive off-road, or join ranger programs that showcase desert wildlife, geology, and Native American history.

☐ 🔖 ♡ **Bidwell-Sacramento River State Park:** Near Chico, this park protects riparian forests along the Sacramento River. Trails wind through cottonwoods, sycamores, and oaks, creating habitat for birds and wildlife. Boating and fishing are popular, with salmon and steelhead runs drawing anglers. Picnicking, paddling, and wildlife viewing provide peaceful recreation while preserving one of the valley's most important river habitats.

☐ 🔖 ♡ **Big Basin Redwoods State Park:** Established in 1902 as California's first state park, Big Basin protects ancient coast redwoods. Though wildfires in 2020 devastated parts of the forest, recovery is underway. Visitors can still hike trails to waterfalls and groves of towering trees. Camping, backpacking, and interpretive programs highlight the park's ecological importance and its role in the state's conservation legacy.

☐ 🔖 ♡ **Border Field State Park:** At California's southwest corner near the U.S.–Mexico border, this park encompasses beaches, estuaries, and wetlands within the Tijuana River Reserve. Birdwatching is exceptional, with many migratory species. Trails and horseback riding routes cross the dunes and salt marshes. Friendship Park, at the border fence, serves as a binational gathering place where families and friends connect.

☐ 🔖 ♡ **Bothe-Napa Valley State Park:** Set in Napa Valley, this park preserves forests of redwoods, Douglas-fir, and oak woodlands. It protects the farthest inland coast redwoods in California. Visitors enjoy hiking, swimming in a spring-fed pool, and camping in cabins or yurts. The park contrasts with surrounding vineyards, offering shaded trails, creeks, and a quiet natural refuge within the famous wine country.

☐ 🔖 ♡ **Burton Creek State Park:** Located near Tahoe City, this quiet forested park covers over 2,000 acres of conifer woods, meadows, and creeks. Trails accommodate hiking, biking, and horseback riding, while winter brings cross-country skiing and snowshoeing. With no developed facilities, it's a tranquil retreat for outdoor enthusiasts seeking solitude and scenic mountain beauty away from Lake Tahoe's busy recreation hubs.

☐ 🔖 ♡ **Butano State Park:** Nestled in the Santa Cruz Mountains near Pescadero, Butano features towering redwoods, fern-lined canyons, and over 40 miles of hiking trails. The park is known for its quiet, less-crowded atmosphere compared to nearby parks. Visitors enjoy camping, birdwatching, and exploring lush forests filled with varied wildlife. Its cool, shaded trails make it a hidden gem along the central coast.

☐ 🔖 ♡ **Calaveras Big Trees State Park:** This Sierra Nevada park preserves groves of giant sequoias, some thousands of years old. Established in 1931, it protects both the North and South Groves. Visitors marvel at the immense trees, hike interpretive trails, and camp in forested sites. In winter, snow brings opportunities for cross-country skiing. The park highlights the legacy of early conservation in California.

☐ 🔖 ♡ **Castle Crags State Park:** Dominated by granite spires rising dramatically above the Sacramento River, this park offers rugged scenery and recreation. Trails climb into wilderness areas with views of Mount Shasta and the crags. Camping, hiking, and fishing draw visitors, while climbers tackle the imposing rock faces. The park blends striking geology, forest habitats, and cultural history tied to early settlers.

CALIFORNIA

☐ 🔖 ♡ **Castle Rock State Park:** Along the crest of the Santa Cruz Mountains, this park features sandstone cliffs, dense forests, and sweeping views of the Pacific. Popular with hikers and rock climbers, it's also a gateway to the 50-mile Skyline-to-the-Sea Trail. Wildlife, wildflowers, and scenic overlooks enrich the experience. Backpacking camps provide overnight opportunities in a rugged but accessible wilderness setting.

☐ 🔖 ♡ **China Camp State Park:** On San Pablo Bay near San Rafael, China Camp preserves a historic 19th-century Chinese shrimp-fishing village. Visitors explore restored buildings, a museum, and cultural exhibits that honor Chinese American history. Trails for hiking, biking, and horseback riding traverse oak woodlands and marshes. Camping, kayaking, and birdwatching round out the experiences in this cultural and natural park.

☐ 🔖 ♡ **Crystal Cove State Park:** Stretching along 3 miles of Orange County coastline, Crystal Cove combines sandy beaches, tidepools, and backcountry wilderness. Visitors hike through canyons, bike coastal bluffs, or explore the historic beach cottages of the 1930s district. With camping, surfing, snorkeling, and scenic trails, it blends natural beauty, recreation, and cultural heritage in one destination.

☐ 🔖 ♡ **Del Norte Coast Redwoods State Park:** Part of the Redwood National and State Parks, this coastal park features towering old-growth redwoods, rugged cliffs, and dramatic ocean views. Trails wind through lush forests and along secluded beaches. Visitors enjoy hiking, camping, and wildlife watching, including Roosevelt elk. The park highlights California's unique blend of coastal wilderness and ancient trees.

☐ 🔖 ♡ **Ed Z'Berg Sugar Pine Point State Park:** On Lake Tahoe's west shore, this park protects dense pine forests and two miles of shoreline. Visitors explore trails, camp, fish, and enjoy swimming or boating in summer. Winter brings cross-country skiing on historic Olympic trails. The Hellman-Ehrman Mansion offers guided tours, showcasing Tahoe's cultural heritage alongside the park's scenic natural beauty.

☐ 🔖 ♡ **Emerald Bay State Park:** One of Lake Tahoe's most photographed destinations, Emerald Bay dazzles with turquoise waters, granite peaks, and the only island in the lake. Visitors can hike to Eagle Falls, kayak the bay, or explore Vikingsholm Castle, a Scandinavian-style mansion. Underwater, a state preserve protects historic shipwrecks. Camping, boating, and sightseeing make it a jewel of the Sierra Nevada.

☐ 🔖 ♡ **Fort Ord Dunes State Park:** On Monterey Bay, this park preserves 4 miles of shoreline once used as a U.S. Army training base. Visitors explore beaches, dunes, and coastal scrub habitat along trails and a paved bike path. Interpretive signs tell the story of Fort Ord's military past. Today, the park provides wildlife habitat, peaceful recreation, and sweeping ocean vistas.

☐ 🔖 ♡ **Fort Ross State Historic Park:** Located on the Sonoma Coast, Fort Ross preserves a Russian-American Company settlement established in 1812. Restored buildings, including the chapel and stockade, showcase early Russian colonial history in California. Trails lead along coastal bluffs and forests, offering dramatic Pacific views. Visitors enjoy cultural festivals, picnicking, and exploring this unique blend of natural and historic heritage.

☐ 🔖 ♡ **Fort Tejon State Historic Park:** In the Tehachapi Mountains, Fort Tejon preserves a mid-19th-century U.S. Army post. Restored adobe buildings, reenactments, and exhibits bring frontier military history to life. The park also protects oak woodlands and wildlife habitats. Visitors can hike shaded trails, tour historic sites, and learn about the fort's role in guarding early travel routes through California.

☐ 🔖 ♡ **Fremont Peak State Park:** Overlooking the Salinas Valley and Monterey Bay, this park offers panoramic views and night skies prized by stargazers. Trails wind through pine and oak woodlands, while campgrounds provide quiet mountain retreats. The park is home to Fremont Peak Observatory, where astronomy programs highlight its dark-sky setting. It combines natural beauty, recreation, and scientific discovery.

☐ 🔖 ♡ **Garrapata State Park:** Along Highway 1 in Big Sur, Garrapata features rugged coastal cliffs, wildflower-covered hills, and redwood canyons. Trails lead to hidden beaches, bluff overlooks, and scenic coastal headlands. Wildlife viewing includes sea otters, sea lions, and migrating whales offshore. With its mix of mountains and shoreline, the park offers dramatic scenery and unspoiled coastal hiking experiences.

☐ 🔖 ♡ **Grizzly Creek Redwoods State Park:** A hidden gem in Humboldt County, this park protects small groves of ancient coast redwoods along the Van Duzen River. Visitors enjoy camping, fishing, swimming, and hiking in a tranquil setting. Its small size makes it less crowded than other redwood parks, offering a peaceful atmosphere and intimate experience among towering trees.

CALIFORNIA

☐ ◫ ♡ **Grover Hot Springs State Park:** Tucked in the Sierra Nevada near Markleeville, this park features a hot spring pool complex surrounded by pine forests and granite peaks. Visitors hike to waterfalls and meadows, camp in shaded sites, or soak in the mineral pools. Winter brings snowshoeing and skiing. It's a year-round destination blending natural thermal waters with mountain wilderness recreation.

☐ ◫ ♡ **Humboldt Lagoons State Park:** North of Eureka, this park preserves a chain of lagoons separated from the Pacific by narrow sand spits. It provides critical wetland habitat for birds and fish. Visitors kayak, fish, and hike scenic trails while observing diverse wildlife. Agate Beach offers beachcombing opportunities. The park protects fragile ecosystems while offering a peaceful coastal escape.

☐ ◫ ♡ **Humboldt Redwoods State Park:** Encompassing the largest remaining contiguous old-growth redwood forest on Earth, this park is home to the famous Avenue of the Giants. Trails and campgrounds immerse visitors in towering redwoods, rivers, and meadows. Wildlife thrives beneath the canopy. The park offers hiking, camping, and interpretive programs that celebrate the ecological significance of California's ancient forests.

☐ ◫ ♡ **Indian Grinding Rock State Historic Park:** Near Pine Grove in the Sierra foothills, this park preserves a large outcropping of limestone with over 1,100 mortar holes created by Miwok people for acorn grinding. It's the largest such site in North America. The park also features a museum, reconstructed village, and trails. Visitors learn about Native American culture and enjoy picnicking and camping.

☐ ◫ ♡ **Jack London State Historic Park:** In Glen Ellen, this park preserves the home, ranch, and gravesite of author Jack London. Trails explore forests, vineyards, and historic ruins of London's "Wolf House." Visitors tour the cottage and museum exhibits while enjoying hikes with sweeping views. The park celebrates literature, history, and nature in the heart of Sonoma's wine country.

☐ ◫ ♡ **Jedediah Smith Redwoods State Park:** Near Crescent City, this park protects some of the densest old-growth redwoods in the world. Trails and scenic drives wind through towering groves, while the Smith River offers crystal-clear waters for fishing and kayaking. Campgrounds immerse visitors in redwood forests. The park provides a serene, awe-inspiring experience among the planet's tallest trees.

☐ ◫ ♡ **Julia Pfeiffer Burns State Park:** Famous for McWay Falls, an 80-foot waterfall that drops onto the beach, this Big Sur park offers iconic coastal scenery. Trails wind through redwoods, cliffs, and wildflower meadows. Wildlife such as sea otters, seals, and migrating whales are often seen offshore. The park's dramatic views and natural features make it one of California's most photographed destinations.

☐ ◫ ♡ **Kruse Rhododendron State Natural Reserve:** Nestled next to Salt Point along the Sonoma coast, this quiet forest preserve bursts with pink rhododendron blooms each May. Trails wind through redwoods, Douglas fir, and tanoak forests, offering peaceful hikes year-round. Without campgrounds or major facilities, it remains a serene destination for day hikes, birdwatching, and spring wildflower photography.

☐ ◫ ♡ **Leo Carrillo State Park:** Stretching along the Malibu coast, this park offers sandy beaches, tidepools, and sea caves paired with backcountry canyons and ridges. Campgrounds shaded by sycamores provide a base for exploring trails, surfing, or swimming. Named after actor-conservationist Leo Carrillo, it's a blend of ocean recreation and rugged wilderness within the Santa Monica Mountains.

☐ ◫ ♡ **Limekiln State Park:** Situated along Big Sur's rugged coast, this park features historic limekilns, redwood groves, and a dramatic beach cove. Trails lead through towering forests to waterfalls and historic sites. Camping beneath redwoods offers a classic Big Sur experience. Its mix of cultural history and natural beauty makes it a distinctive stop on California's iconic coastal highway.

☐ ◫ ♡ **Malakoff Diggins State Historic Park:** Preserving California's largest hydraulic gold mine, this Sierra Nevada park showcases Gold Rush history with a ghost town, museum, and massive mining pits. Visitors explore scenic trails, campgrounds, and remnants of mining life. The park blends outdoor recreation with stark reminders of the environmental impact of 19th-century mining practices.

☐ ◫ ♡ **Manchester State Park:** On the Mendocino Coast, this park boasts long sandy beaches, windswept dunes, and diverse birdlife. Visitors hike along coastal trails, fish in nearby creeks, or camp among grassy bluffs. Offshore lies the Point Arena Lighthouse and seasonal gray whale migrations. The park offers solitude, scenic beauty, and access to a rugged stretch of Northern California shoreline.

CALIFORNIA

- ☐ 🔖 ♡ **Mendocino Headlands State Park:** Surrounding the town of Mendocino, this park features dramatic bluffs, hidden beaches, and wildflower meadows. Trails wind along the headlands with sweeping ocean views, while wildlife includes harbor seals and seabirds. The park preserves both natural beauty and cultural landscapes, complementing Mendocino's historic architecture and artistic community.

- ☐ 🔖 ♡ **Montaña de Oro State Park:** Near Morro Bay, this park spans rugged cliffs, sandy beaches, and coastal hills blanketed with wildflowers in spring. Trails like the Bluff Trail and Valencia Peak climb through diverse terrain. Visitors enjoy tidepooling, horseback riding, and camping in coastal valleys. Its name means "Mountain of Gold," reflecting the park's seasonal floral displays.

- ☐ 🔖 ♡ **Mount Diablo State Park:** Rising dramatically from the East Bay, Mount Diablo offers sweeping views across Central California. Trails climb through chaparral, oak woodlands, and rock formations to the summit. Campgrounds, rock climbing, and interpretive programs attract outdoor enthusiasts. The mountain is rich in geology and Native American history, and on clear days, views can stretch for hundreds of miles.

- ☐ 🔖 ♡ **Mount San Jacinto State Park:** Accessible by the Palm Springs Aerial Tramway or mountain trails, this high-altitude park protects alpine forests and granite peaks. Visitors hike to San Jacinto Peak at 10,834 feet or explore meadows filled with wildflowers. Camping and backcountry trails offer wilderness escapes above the desert. The park is celebrated for its stark elevation contrasts and panoramic views.

- ☐ 🔖 ♡ **Mount Tamalpais State Park:** Overlooking the Golden Gate and Bay Area, this park features redwood canyons, grassy hills, and panoramic ridges. Miles of trails, including part of the Dipsea Trail, attract hikers and mountain bikers. The East Peak summit provides sweeping vistas of the Pacific and Bay. The park is a cornerstone of Bay Area outdoor culture and scenic beauty.

- ☐ 🔖 ♡ **Navarro River Redwoods State Park:** Following the Navarro River to the Mendocino coast, this park preserves towering redwoods along a scenic drive. Campgrounds and trails provide access to the river and forest. Visitors enjoy kayaking, fishing, and wildlife viewing. The park connects inland valleys to the Pacific, blending riparian woodlands with dramatic coastal landscapes.

- ☐ 🔖 ♡ **Palomar Mountain State Park:** Nestled in San Diego County, this park offers cool forests of conifers, meadows, and a peaceful mountain setting. Trails lead to scenic viewpoints, while Doane Pond provides fishing and picnicking. The park's high elevation contrasts sharply with the surrounding desert, making it a popular retreat for hiking, camping, and stargazing under dark skies.

- ☐ 🔖 ♡ **Pfeiffer Big Sur State Park:** A jewel of Big Sur, this park lies along the Big Sur River and features redwood groves, waterfalls, and dramatic ridges. Campgrounds under redwoods attract visitors year-round, while trails climb to overlooks with sweeping coastal and canyon views. Often called a "mini Yosemite," it's a prime destination for hiking, camping, and exploring California's wild coast.

- ☐ 🔖 ♡ **Plumas-Eureka State Park:** Located in the Sierra Nevada, this park blends Gold Rush history with alpine beauty. Visitors tour a historic mining area, blacksmith shop, and museum while hiking trails lead to lakes and peaks. Campgrounds, fishing, and winter snowshoeing offer year-round recreation. The park preserves both natural landscapes and California's rich mining heritage.

- ☐ 🔖 ♡ **Point Mugu State Park:** Stretching along the Pacific in Ventura County, this park offers five miles of beaches backed by rugged canyons and peaks. Trails lead through chaparral-covered hills, while the coastline invites surfing, fishing, and tidepool exploration. Its blend of mountains and sea makes it one of Southern California's most diverse and scenic coastal parks.

- ☐ 🔖 ♡ **Portola Redwoods State Park:** Tucked deep in the Santa Cruz Mountains, this quiet forest park shelters towering coast redwoods, fern-filled gullies, and babbling creeks. Trails lead to waterfalls and secluded groves, while campgrounds offer peaceful escapes from urban life. Its shaded trails and cool streams provide a classic redwood experience in a less-visited setting.

- ☐ 🔖 ♡ **Prairie Creek Redwoods State Park:** A UNESCO World Heritage Site, this park protects ancient coast redwoods, lush prairies, and scenic coastal bluffs. Visitors encounter Roosevelt elk, hike Fern Canyon's mossy walls, and camp among giants. The park's breathtaking landscapes and wildlife diversity make it one of the crown jewels of California's redwood country.

- ☐ 🔖 ♡ **Robert Louis Stevenson State Park:** North of Calistoga, this rugged park features volcanic peaks, chaparral, and sweeping views of Napa Valley. Trails climb to Mount St. Helena, where Stevenson once stayed, inspiring his novel The Silverado Squatters. Hiking, wildflower viewing, and history combine in this wild, undeveloped park honoring the famed author.

CALIFORNIA

☐ ◻ ♡ **Russian Gulch State Park:** Near Mendocino, this park blends a dramatic coastal cove with redwood forests and waterfalls. Trails lead to a 36-foot waterfall and along bluffs overlooking sea arches. Visitors enjoy camping, tidepooling, and biking. Its combination of ocean scenery, forested canyons, and unique natural features makes it a standout on California's north coast.

☐ ◻ ♡ **Salt Point State Park:** Located on the Sonoma Coast, this park features rugged cliffs, tidepools, pygmy forests, and underwater preserves for divers. Trails traverse meadows and forested headlands, while camping and fishing are popular. The park's sandstone formations supplied blocks for San Francisco buildings, adding cultural history to its natural beauty.

☐ ◻ ♡ **Samuel P. Taylor State Park:** Nestled in Marin County, this park protects redwood groves and open grasslands along Lagunitas Creek. Popular for camping, hiking, and cycling, it offers shady trails, salmon spawning viewing, and historical remnants of an early paper mill. Its proximity to the Bay Area makes it a cherished escape into nature.

☐ ◻ ♡ **Shasta State Historic Park:** Near Shasta Lake, this park preserves the ruins of Shasta City, a Gold Rush town once bustling with activity. Visitors explore brick ruins, a restored courthouse, and museum exhibits while enjoying views of the Trinity Mountains. The park combines rich history with surrounding natural beauty, offering insight into California's boomtown era.

☐ ◻ ♡ **Sinkyone Wilderness State Park:** Part of the remote Lost Coast, this rugged park features black sand beaches, redwood groves, and dramatic coastal bluffs. Popular with backpackers, its Lost Coast Trail offers solitude, sweeping ocean views, and encounters with Roosevelt elk. Former logging lands now preserve wild beauty, making it one of California's most remote coastal treasures.

☐ ◻ ♡ **Sonoma Coast State Park:** Stretching along 17 miles of rugged shoreline, this park includes secluded coves, headlands, and sandy beaches framed by dramatic cliffs. Visitors enjoy tidepooling, hiking coastal bluffs, and exploring driftwood-strewn shores. Camping and picnicking add to the experience, with iconic sea stacks and Pacific sunsets making it a favorite coastal escape.

☐ ◻ ♡ **Sue-meg State Park:** Overlooking the rugged Humboldt coast, this park protects cliffs, coastal prairies, and spruce forests. Visitors can comb Agate Beach for colorful stones, explore tidepools, hike to Wedding Rock, and camp with Pacific views. Yurok heritage is honored through a recreated village and cultural exhibits, blending Indigenous history with stunning natural scenery.

☐ ◻ ♡ **Sugarloaf Ridge State Park:** Located in the Mayacamas Mountains near Santa Rosa, this park features volcanic ridges, oak woodlands, and riparian valleys. Trails climb to Bald Mountain for sweeping views of the Bay Area and beyond. With camping, waterfalls, and a public observatory, it offers both outdoor adventure and celestial discovery in one destination.

☐ ◻ ♡ **The Forest of Nisene Marks State Park:** Located in the Santa Cruz Mountains, this redwood forest preserves second-growth groves regenerating from historic logging. Trails wind through shaded canyons, waterfalls, and fern gullies. Popular for hiking, running, and mountain biking, the park showcases nature's resilience while offering peaceful escapes near urban centers.

☐ ◻ ♡ **Tomales Bay State Park:** Tucked into sheltered coves along Tomales Bay, this park features calm waters perfect for swimming, kayaking, and picnicking. Hiking trails lead through forests and to sandy beaches rich in marine life. With its tranquil shoreline, wildlife, and scenic coastal beauty, it offers a gentler counterpart to the nearby open Pacific.

☐ ◻ ♡ **Topanga State Park:** Part of the Santa Monica Mountains, this park lies entirely within Los Angeles city limits, making it one of the largest urban wilderness areas in the U.S. Trails traverse canyons, ridges, and oak woodlands with sweeping ocean and city views. Hiking, horseback riding, and mountain biking make it a hub for outdoor recreation.

☐ ◻ ♡ **Torrey Pines State Natural Reserve:** Famous for its rare Torrey pine trees, this coastal park near San Diego features sandstone cliffs, desert flora, and sweeping ocean views. Trails lead to overlooks and beaches, while the reserve preserves fragile ecosystems. It's one of California's most iconic natural coastal landscapes.

☐ ◻ ♡ **Trione-Annadel State Park:** Situated near Santa Rosa, this park offers oak woodlands, meadows, and volcanic rock formations. Trails for hiking, biking, and horseback riding wind past wildflower-filled hills in spring. Lake Ilsanjo provides fishing and picnicking, making the park a year-round recreational haven in the North Bay.

CALIFORNIA

☐ 🔖 ♡ **Van Damme State Park:** Located on the Mendocino coast, this park features fern canyons, redwood groves, and scenic beaches. Visitors enjoy hiking through lush forests, kayaking in the protected cove, and exploring the nearby pygmy forest with its stunted trees. Its mix of marine and forest habitats makes it a popular year-round destination.

☐ 🔖 ♡ **Washoe Meadows State Park:** Situated in South Lake Tahoe, this undeveloped park protects open meadows, forests, and river habitats important for wildlife. Popular with hikers, birdwatchers, and anglers, it provides a quiet alternative to busier Tahoe parks. Its preservation focus highlights natural landscapes and watershed protection.

☐ 🔖 ♡ **Weaverville Joss House State Historic Park:** This Taoist temple, built in 1874, is the oldest continuously used Chinese temple in California. Located in Weaverville, it preserves the cultural and spiritual traditions of early Chinese immigrants. Guided tours highlight ornate altars, artifacts, and stories of the Gold Rush–era Chinese community.

☐ 🔖 ♡ **Wildwood Canyon State Park:** Located in the foothills near Yucaipa, this park preserves chaparral, oak woodlands, and riparian areas. Visitors hike trails with views of San Bernardino peaks and San Gorgonio Mountain. The park emphasizes open space and habitat conservation while offering peaceful outdoor exploration.

State Beaches

☐ 🔖 ♡ **Asilomar State Beach:** Along the Monterey Peninsula, Asilomar mixes rocky coves, sandy pockets, and rich tidepools within a protected marine reserve. Boardwalks wind through restored dunes where shorebirds nest and wildflowers bloom. Cool water and changeable surf make it better for strolling, photography, and tidepooling than swimming. Sunsets glow over cypress silhouettes and granite outcrops.

☐ 🔖 ♡ **Bean Hollow State Beach:** South of Pescadero, Bean Hollow's rugged shoreline reveals tafoni honeycomb rocks, pebble pockets, and lively tidepools. Short bluff trails link Arroyo de los Frijoles and Pebble Beach, with spring wildflowers and harbor-seal sightings offshore. Strong currents and rip tides make it unsafe for swimming, but beachcombing, fishing, and coastal geology shine.

☐ 🔖 ♡ **Bolsa Chica State Beach:** Wide, golden sand, steady surf, and long multi-use paths define this Huntington Beach favorite. Families gather at fire rings for sunset, while cyclists and skaters cruise the oceanfront trail. Across PCH, Bolsa Chica Ecological Reserve adds wetlands and prime birding. Lifeguards, concessions, and ample parking make easy logistics for a classic SoCal beach day.

☐ 🔖 ♡ **Cardiff State Beach:** Gently sloped sand and reef breaks draw swimmers and longboarders to this Encinitas strand. Tidepools emerge at low tide, and beach walks connect to San Elijo and Seaside. Parking, restrooms, and nearby cafés keep things convenient, yet the shoreline still feels relaxed. Arrive near golden hour for glowing cliffs, dolphins offshore, and pastel sunsets.

☐ 🔖 ♡ **Carlsbad State Beach:** Also called Tamarack, this bluff-backed beach pairs easy access with seasonal lifeguards and a paved promenade above the surf. Families swim and sun while surfers chase consistent peaks. Benches and overlooks make ideal sunset perches, and showers, restrooms, and picnic spots keep it simple. It's a versatile coastal hub close to downtown Carlsbad.

☐ 🔖 ♡ **Carmel River State Beach:** A sweeping crescent at the river mouth, with a lagoon and wetlands prized by birders. Views stretch toward Point Lobos as kayakers explore calm estuary water. Powerful surf and rip currents call for caution, so most visitors come for photography, beach walks, and wildlife (pelicans, otters, and seasonal shorebirds) beneath often-misty skies.

☐ 🔖 ♡ **Carpinteria State Beach:** Known for gentle surf and wide, family-friendly sands, Carpinteria adds tidepools, seaside campgrounds, and an easy coastal trail. Winter brings a nearby harbor-seal rookery (view respectfully from a distance). Downtown shops and cafés are a short stroll away, blending low-key camping with marine life, soft-wave swimming, and mellow Central Coast charm.

☐ 🔖 ♡ **Caspar Headlands State Beach:** A sheltered cove near Mendocino with sandy shore framed by rocky headlands and kelp-rich water. Kayakers and divers favor the calm conditions, while short trails climb to overlooks where wildflowers and seabirds thrive. Limited amenities preserve a quiet feel. It's a photogenic North Coast stop for picnics, tidepooling, and paddling.

CALIFORNIA

☐ 🔖 ♡ **Cayucos State Beach:** Centered on a historic wooden pier, this town beach delivers small-town vibe with easy surf, fishing, and sandy strolls. Families spread out near the pier while surfers hunt peaks along the sandbars. With cafés, bakeries, and antique shops just steps away, it's an inviting base for sunsets over Morro Bay and relaxed Central Coast days.

☐ 🔖 ♡ **Corona del Mar State Beach:** A half-mile sandy crescent backed by cliffs in Newport Beach, Orange County. Popular with swimmers, divers, and families, it offers gentle surf, fire pits, and views of Newport Harbor's entrance. Facilities include restrooms, outdoor showers, and snack concessions. Its sheltered location and iconic scenery make it a classic SoCal beach outing.

☐ 🔖 ♡ **Cowell Ranch State Beach:** A secluded Half Moon Bay cove reached by a bluff-top trail across coastal farmland. Expect dramatic cliffs, a long stair descent, and seasonal harbor-seal viewing from designated overlooks. With no services on the sand, it stays peaceful, ideal for picnics, whale watching, and wildflower walks along windswept headlands above the surf.

☐ 🔖 ♡ **Dockweiler State Beach:** Beneath LAX's flight path, Dockweiler pairs a broad sandy shore with bonfire rings, a beachfront bike path, and RV camping. Families gather for sunsets as jets thunder overhead, part spectacle, part soundtrack. Simple amenities and lifeguards keep it friendly, while long shoreline walks and sandcastle territory stretch toward Playa del Rey.

☐ 🔖 ♡ **Doheny State Beach:** One of California's original state beaches, Doheny mixes grassy picnic lawns with a protected cove perfect for beginners and families. Lifeguards, a near-the-sand campground, tidepools, and flat bike paths make all-day visits easy. Stroll the breakwater, watch longboarders at the point, and explore exhibits highlighting Dana Point's coastal ecology.

☐ 🔖 ♡ **El Capitán State Beach:** On the Gaviota Coast, sycamore-shaded camps sit above a shoreline of cobbles, tidepools, and golden sand. Paddle calm morning water, wander bluff trails, or beachcomb after winter swells. Marine life (dolphins, pelicans, and occasional gray whales) adds drama offshore. Paired with nearby Refugio, it's a quieter Central Coast alternative with classic ocean-cliff scenery.

☐ 🔖 ♡ **Emma Wood State Beach:** Just west of Ventura, this narrow, wave-washed shore fronts a primitive ocean-side campground popular with RVs. Surfers chase sandbar peaks; anglers and walkers roam long cobble stretches. The Ventura River estuary and coastal scrub host birdlife, while trains and sunsets provide a uniquely coastal soundtrack in a raw, elemental setting.

☐ 🔖 ♡ **Gray Whale Cove State Beach:** A pocket cove south of Pacifica with steep stair access, rugged cliffs, and seasonal whale sightings. Strong surf and rip currents make swimming risky, but picnics, photography, and winter storm watching excel. Bluff trails above the beach offer sweeping San Mateo County vistas. Limited parking helps keep this dramatic spot peaceful.

☐ 🔖 ♡ **Greenwood State Beach:** In Elk, Mendocino County, Greenwood blends a quiet beach at the mouth of Greenwood Creek with windswept headlands and village history. Explore picnic spots and bluff-top views of sea arches and offshore stacks. Facilities are minimal, keeping the pace mellow. It's a scenic pause on Highway 1, perfect for tidepooling and fog-and-sun North Coast days.

☐ 🔖 ♡ **Half Moon Bay State Beach:** Four linked units (Francis, Venice, Dunes, and Roosevelt) create miles of walkable sand backed by a bluff-top segment of the Coastal Trail. Expect fishing, kites, and seasonal wildflowers, with a year-round campground at Francis. Pelicans skim wave crests at sunset, and winter storms reshape the shoreline in this beloved Bay Area escape.

☐ 🔖 ♡ **Huntington State Beach:** Two miles of broad sand, steady surf, and volleyball courts define this Orange County icon. Lifeguards patrol daily; fire rings spark golden-hour gatherings. Bike paths connect north and south, and nearby wetlands offer birding breaks. It's quintessential SoCal, active by day, glowing at dusk, where beach culture, board sports, and big skies meet.

☐ 🔖 ♡ **Las Tunas State Beach:** A narrow Malibu strand tucked below Pacific Coast Highway, favored by anglers, tidepoolers, and divers when conditions allow. Rocky sections and high-tide swallows keep swimming limited; parking is roadside and facilities are sparse. Come for coastal views, seabirds, and quieter pockets between livelier Malibu stops on a scenic drive.

☐ 🔖 ♡ **Leucadia State Beach:** Also known as Beacon's, this Encinitas favorite sits below golden bluffs reached by a steep stairway. Surfers chase mellow point and beach breaks; beachgoers spread out on the broad, sandy apron. Limited parking preserves a low-key vibe. Expect cool water, afternoon winds, and glowing sunsets, classic North County San Diego in a compact, scenic package.

CALIFORNIA

☐ 🔖 ♡ **Lighthouse Field State Beach:** A small Santa Cruz strand below West Cliff Drive, steps from the Surfing Museum at the lighthouse and legendary Steamer Lane. Strong rip currents keep most visitors on the sand or bluff path, watching surfers carve the point and whales migrate offshore. Tidepools dot the rocks at low tide; sunsets fire up the coast. Dogs on leash; facilities are limited, come for views and sea air.

☐ 🔖 ♡ **Little River State Beach:** North of McKinleyville, this broad, dune-backed beach fronts the Little River mouth and offers windswept solitude. Expect chilly water, fog, and strong currents. Better for walking, birding, and beachcombing than swimming. Sensitive dune habitat shelters wildflowers and shorebirds; amenities are minimal, preserving a wild North Coast feel between Trinidad and Clam Beach.

☐ 🔖 ♡ **Malibu Lagoon State Beach:** Where Malibu Creek meets the sea, this park blends a famed right point break (Surfrider) with restored wetlands rich in birdlife. Stroll boardwalks, visit the adjacent pier, and watch longboarders slide peeling waves. Trails and exhibits interpret lagoon ecology. Parking is limited; tides and sandbar shifts shape the surf and the lagoon's ever-changing mouth.

☐ 🔖 ♡ **Mandalay State Beach:** A protected swath of Oxnard dunes and shorebird habitat with few facilities and a wild feel. Boardwalks cross fragile foredunes to a wide, uncrowded beach where winds, waves, and fog often set the mood. Snowy plovers nest seasonally; respect closures. Come for long walks, shell hunting, and sunset color. Nature first, recreation second.

☐ 🔖 ♡ **Manresa State Beach:** South of Aptos, long, open sand invites sunrise jogs, kite flying, and classic surf sessions. Powerful shorebreak and rip currents mean cautious swimming. Above the bluffs, Manresa Uplands campground (seasonal) keeps you close to the roar of Monterey Bay. Simple amenities, cool breezes, and big skies define this mellow, uncrowded stretch.

☐ 🔖 ♡ **Marina State Beach:** Known for tall dunes and steady winds, Marina draws hang gliders, paragliders, and kite flyers. A short path crosses protected dunes to a wide, often quiet shoreline with far-reaching views of Monterey Bay. Strong currents make it better for walking, photography, and wildlife watching. Facilities are simple; sunsets can be spectacular.

☐ 🔖 ♡ **McGrath State Beach:** At the Santa Clara River estuary near Ventura, McGrath protects wetlands vital to Pacific Flyway birds. Seasonal flooding can limit access, but when open you'll find long, wave-washed sands, birding, and a rustic campground. Surf can be powerful; most come for nature walks, dune strolls, and the sound of shorebirds over the river mouth.

☐ 🔖 ♡ **Montara State Beach:** A dramatic San Mateo Coast sweep of golden sand beneath rugged cliffs, popular with photographers, anglers, and tidepoolers. Surf is powerful and cold; swimming is not advised. Trailheads link to nearby bluff routes, while spring wildflowers light up the headlands. Limited services preserve a wild, windswept character minutes from Highway 1.

☐ 🔖 ♡ **Monterey State Beach:** A family-friendly arc from Del Monte to Seaside with gentle shorebreak in spots, easy parking, and the Coastal Trail just inland. Launch a kayak, cast for surfperch, or settle in for fog-kissed mornings and glowing sunsets. Dune restorations protect habitat; lifeguards patrol in season. It's a versatile base near Cannery Row and the aquarium.

☐ 🔖 ♡ **Moonlight State Beach:** Located in Encinitas, San Diego County, Moonlight is a wide sandy beach with gentle surf, lifeguards, and family-friendly amenities. Picnic areas, volleyball courts, playground, and a snack bar keep it lively. Historically the town's social hub, it remains a centerpiece for summer gatherings, surf sessions, and sunsets along North County's coastline.

☐ 🔖 ♡ **Morro Strand State Beach:** A long ribbon of sand between Cayucos and Morro Rock, ideal for quiet walks, shorebird watching, and surf fishing. Breezes and marine haze are common; the campground sits just behind the foredunes. Powerful surf and rip currents warrant caution. On clear evenings, the Rock silhouettes against pastel skies: classic Central Coast mood.

☐ 🔖 ♡ **Moss Landing State Beach:** Straddling the harbor mouth to Elkhorn Slough, this beach pairs bird-rich wetlands with a windswept shoreline. Watch sea otters in the channel, scan for whales offshore, and photograph working boats at golden hour. Strong currents near the jetties make swimming hazardous; most visitors stroll, fish, or picnic amid coastal dunes and seabreezes.

☐ 🔖 ♡ **Natural Bridges State Beach:** Famous for its remaining sea arch, this compact park also shelters a monarch butterfly grove each winter. Explore tidepools teeming with anemones and sea stars, then wander boardwalks through coastal scrub and seasonal wetlands. Surf can be rough; come for intertidal life, seabirds, and fiery Santa Cruz sunsets over sculpted rock.

CALIFORNIA

☐ ◫ ♡ **New Brighton State Beach:** A bluff-backed Aptos strand with a popular campground steps from the sand. Families spread out on the broad beach, stroll toward Capitola, and watch pelicans skim the surf at dusk. Gentle waves often suit wading, though rip currents occur. Interpretive panels touch on local geology and Ohlone heritage amid eucalyptus and Monterey pine.

☐ ◫ ♡ **Pacifica State Beach:** Also known as Linda Mar, this mile-long San Mateo County shoreline is one of the Bay Area's most popular beginner surfing spots. Nestled in a crescent cove with scenic headlands, it features a restored wetland, paved walking trail, and beach access from Highway 1. Families, dog walkers, and surfers share this sandy, often fog-kissed strand.

☐ ◫ ♡ **Pelican State Beach:** California's northernmost ocean beach, a quiet, undeveloped stretch just south of the Oregon line. No facilities, often foggy, and swept by cold currents; perfect for solitude, beachcombing, and watching offshore seabirds. Shifting sandbars and driftwood frame big-sky views; bring layers and self-sufficiency to this far-flung Del Norte County edge.

☐ ◫ ♡ **Pescadero State Beach:** Rugged headlands, pocket coves, and tidepools define this San Mateo Coast favorite. Cross Highway 1 to explore Pescadero Marsh's herons and red-winged blackbirds, then return for wave watching and shell hunting. Strong surf discourages swimming; come for geology (tafoni sandstone, sea stacks, and layered bluffs) and windswept wildflower displays in spring.

☐ ◫ ♡ **Pismo State Beach:** Classic Central Coast sands linking Oceano, Grover Beach, and Pismo. Camp near the dunes, watch monarch butterflies overwinter nearby, and stroll wide, flat shores at sunrise. Surfing, clamming (seasonally regulated), birding, and horseback rides all feature. Adjacent Oceano Dunes SVRA offers OHV access, while this unit leans family-friendly.

☐ ◫ ♡ **Point Dume State Beach:** A Malibu crescent below sandstone cliffs with tidepools at low tide and a short bluff-top loop to whale-watching overlooks. Limited parking preserves a peaceful feel; arrive early for calm water and cobalt views. Strong rip currents can appear - heed lifeguards. Spring brings wildflowers to the headland; year-round sunsets are stellar.

☐ ◫ ♡ **Point Sal State Beach:** A remote, rugged expanse in northern Santa Barbara County, Point Sal features steep cliffs, dunes, and a 1.5-mile sandy shoreline. Accessible only by a strenuous hike or walk-in route, it remains largely undeveloped. Cold water, rip currents, and limited access keep it wild, rewarding visitors with solitude, wildlife, and panoramic coastal vistas.

☐ ◫ ♡ **Pomponio State Beach:** A scenic San Mateo County cove where Pomponio Creek meets the sea. Picnic tables on the bluff, stairs to broad sand, and sculpted cliffs invite relaxed afternoons. Surf and rip currents can be dangerous, so most visitors beachcomb, fish from shore, or explore small sea caves at low tide. Simple facilities keep the vibe unhurried.

☐ ◫ ♡ **Refugio State Beach:** Palm-lined and cove-sheltered on the Gaviota Coast, Refugio offers family-friendly swimming, kayak launches, and a popular campground under coastal bluffs. A paved path links toward El Capitán for easy bike rides. Dolphins and pelicans animate calm mornings; breezes rise by afternoon. It's a quintessential Santa Barbara retreat with mellow surf and golden sunsets.

☐ ◫ ♡ **Robert H. Meyer Memorial State Beach:** Three Malibu pocket coves (El Matador, La Piedra, and El Pescador) showcase sea stacks, arches, and tidepools beneath sculpted bluffs. Steep trails lead to narrow, photogenic sands best at low tide. Facilities are minimal; bring water and good footwear. Expect chilly water, strong surf at times, and unforgettable golden-hour light along one of California's most dramatic shorelines.

☐ ◫ ♡ **Robert W. Crown Memorial State Beach:** On Alameda's bayfront, this broad, gently sloping beach features warm, shallow water, lawns for picnics, and miles of paved Bay Trail. Windsurfers and kiteboarders skim breezy afternoons; families wade and build sandcastles at low tide. Views span the San Francisco skyline and Bay Bridge. With restrooms, concessions, and easy access, it's an inviting urban shoreline.

☐ ◫ ♡ **Salinas River State Beach:** A quiet Monterey County strand backed by dunes and farmland, popular for fishing, birding, and long walks. Cold, powerful surf and rip currents make swimming hazardous; most visitors beachcomb or watch pelicans and sea otters offshore. Sensitive snowy plover habitat prompts seasonal protections. Simple access points keep the mood low-key along this wind-scrubbed coast.

☐ ◫ ♡ **San Buenaventura State Beach:** A wide Ventura beach with volleyball courts, bike path, and easy access to the historic pier. Families spread out on soft sand while surfers hunt peaks near jetties. Rent a cruiser, picnic under palms, or watch Channel Islands sunsets flare beyond the harbor. Lifeguards in season and nearby cafés make this a relaxed, full-service coastal day.

CALIFORNIA

☐ 🔖 ♡ **San Clemente State Beach:** Steep sandstone bluffs frame a classic South OC shoreline known for consistent waves and a bluff-top campground with ocean views. Stroll the beach trail along the rails, swim or surf near the rivermouth, and explore tidepools at low tide. Trains, swallows, and golden evening light give it a nostalgic beach-town feel with modern amenities close by.

☐ 🔖 ♡ **San Elijo State Beach:** Hugging the Encinitas bluffs, this beach pairs a popular campground with stair access to surf breaks like Pipes and nearby Cardiff Reef. Tidepools emerge on low tides; sunsets glow over kelp lines. Facilities include showers, restrooms, and a store. Strong rip currents can occur. Heed lifeguards. It's a lively coastal strip blending family camping with classic North County surf culture.

☐ 🔖 ♡ **San Gregorio State Beach:** Where San Gregorio Creek meets the Pacific, this San Mateo cove offers broad sand, picnic tables, and high, stratified cliffs. Strong currents and cool water limit swimming, but low-tide rambles reveal sea caves and sculpted tafoni. Birdlife works the estuary, and spring wildflowers dot the bluffs. Simple facilities keep the focus on geology, views, and quiet walks.

☐ 🔖 ♡ **San Onofre State Beach:** A beloved surf coast spanning Surf Beach, the Bluffs, and San Mateo. World-class waves at Trestles draw shortboarders; mellow breaks and cobbles suit longboard style at Old Man's. Trails descend from blufftop parking to wide, pebbly sands. Expect limited shade, rustic amenities, and steady sea breezes. Culture and coastline meet at one of SoCal's surfing hearts.

☐ 🔖 ♡ **Santa Monica State Beach:** Stretching 3.5 miles along the Pacific, Santa Monica State Beach is a lively coastal destination famed for its wide sandy shoreline, palm-lined pathways, and iconic pier with its amusement park and aquarium. Visitors enjoy swimming, surfing, volleyball, biking the scenic path, or simply relaxing with views of the Santa Monica Mountains meeting the ocean.

☐ 🔖 ♡ **Schooner Gulch State Beach:** Near Point Arena, this Mendocino Coast gem is famed for "Bowling Ball Beach," where spherical rock concretions stud the intertidal at low tide. Access can be steep or muddy; check tides for safe viewing. Expect rugged cliffs, driftwood, and offshore stacks, plus minimal facilities. Bring layers and curiosity. Geology steals the show along this wild shoreline.

☐ 🔖 ♡ **Seacliff State Beach:** Bluff-backed sand in Aptos anchored by a pier and the historic concrete ship SS Palo Alto. Camp near the surf, stroll the long, flat shoreline, and watch pelicans skim the waves at dusk. Erosion and storms can affect access and the pier's condition, but calm mornings reward walkers and photographers. Facilities, lifeguards in season, and easy parking make visits simple.

☐ 🔖 ♡ **Silver Strand State Beach:** An isthmus park between the Pacific and San Diego Bay with RV camping, beach access on both sides, and miles of sand. Mornings suit paddling and mellow swims; afternoons bring wind for kites and sails. Bike paths connect to Coronado, and sunsets blaze over the ocean as the bay glows behind you. Facilities are ample; plan for breezes and bright sun.

☐ 🔖 ♡ **South Carlsbad State Beach:** Long bluffs, stairways to pocket coves, and a popular cliff-top campground define this stretch of North County coast. Surfers chase peaks along shifting sandbars; families stake out day-use spots below the stairs. Restrooms, showers, and camp amenities keep it easy. Expect cool water, afternoon winds, and golden sunsets from your campsite above the surf.

☐ 🔖 ♡ **Sunset State Beach:** Dune-backed sands south of Santa Cruz with camp loops tucked behind foredunes. Long beach walks, surf-perch fishing, and big, colorful sunsets set a tranquil tone. Facilities are simple; winds and cool water are common. Snowy plover protections apply seasonally. It's a peaceful alternative to busier Monterey Bay beaches, perfect for unhurried coastal days.

☐ 🔖 ♡ **Thornton State Beach:** Windswept bluffs south of San Francisco preserved as open space with limited beach access due to erosion. Trails atop the ridge offer sweeping Pacific views and native plant restorations; raptors and migrating seabirds ride the wind. It's more about vistas than swimming, with few facilities and frequent fog. An untamed edge to the urban peninsula.

☐ 🔖 ♡ **Topanga State Beach:** At the mouth of Topanga Canyon, this narrow Malibu-adjacent strand fronts a classic right point break. Tidepools gleam at low tide; anglers try the rocky point while sunbathers claim small sandy pockets. Facilities include restrooms and showers; parking is limited. Expect cobbles, cool water, and a laid-back vibe where mountains meet the sea.

CALIFORNIA

☐ 🔖 ♡ **Torrey Pines State Beach:** Below sculpted sandstone cliffs and rare Torrey pines, this San Diego favorite offers surfing, swimming, and long shoreline walks. Trails from the reserve descend to the sand, linking bluff-top vistas with tidepools and cobble pockets. Mornings are calmest; afternoons bring wind and glow. Facilities are split between North and South lots; heed rip currents.

☐ 🔖 ♡ **Trinidad State Beach:** North Coast headlands, spruce-rimmed bluffs, and offshore sea stacks frame postcard views. Wander to College Cove at low tide, scan for whales, and explore tidepools in sheltered corners. Picnic tables perch above the surf; fog and sun trade places often, so bring layers. The nearby fishing village adds historic charm to this dramatic Humboldt shoreline.

☐ 🔖 ♡ **Twin Lakes State Beach:** Adjacent to Santa Cruz Harbor, Twin Lakes blends a family-friendly swim area with paddleboarding and mellow surf. Walk the jetty to the small lighthouse, grab snacks from cafés, and linger for sunsets over the bay. Lifeguards in season, restrooms, and easy access make it a convenient choice with lively harbor energy and relaxed beachfront hangs.

☐ 🔖 ♡ **Westport-Union Landing State Beach:** A 3-mile Mendocino bluff-top corridor with rugged coves, crashing surf, and wide-open vistas. Primitive camp areas sit steps from the edge, perfect for storm watching or starry nights. Steep paths lead to pocket beaches; strong currents and cold water discourage swimming. Sparse facilities, big skies, and wind define this remote, dramatic coast.

☐ 🔖 ♡ **Will Rogers State Beach:** Between Santa Monica and Pacific Palisades, this wide strand offers year-round lifeguards, restrooms, showers, and volleyball courts beside the Marvin Braude Bike Trail. Gentle slopes suit swimming and sunbathing; small peaks tempt surfers and paddleboarders. Parking is easier than nearby beaches, and dolphin sightings are common. Expect cool water, afternoon breezes, and occasional rip currents with classic SoCal sunsets included.

☐ 🔖 ♡ **William Randolph Hearst Memorial State Beach:** Below San Simeon Point, this sheltered cove pairs a long fishing pier with a sandy launch for kayaks and SUPs, plus picnic lawns shaded by cypress. Tidepools and seabirds reward low-tide wanders; the elephant seal rookery at Piedras Blancas lies just north (view from overlooks). Services are limited and afternoons can be windy or foggy. A calm Highway 1 stop with historic ties to Hearst Castle.

☐ 🔖 ♡ **Zmudowski State Beach:** At the Pajaro River mouth in northern Monterey County, this remote, dune-backed shore offers long walks, birding over lagoon wetlands, and productive surf fishing. Cold water and powerful rip currents make swimming hazardous; there are no lifeguards and few amenities. Come for solitude, big skies, and wildlife. Respect seasonal snowy plover closures, keep to signed routes, and bring layers for wind and fog.

National Parks

☐ 🔖 ♡ **Cabrillo National Monument:** Perched on Point Loma Peninsula in San Diego, this monument honors Juan Rodríguez Cabrillo's 1542 landing, the first European expedition to the West Coast. Visitors explore tidepools, historic lighthouses, and cultural exhibits, while panoramic views showcase San Diego Bay, the Pacific, and even migrating gray whales offshore.

☐ 🔖 ♡ **Castle Mountains National Monument:** Protecting a remote stretch of the Mojave Desert, this monument features sweeping valleys, Joshua tree forests, and historic mining ruins. Visitors hike desert trails, spot wildlife like bighorn sheep, and explore remnants of boomtown life, all within a landscape that bridges cultural history and rugged wilderness solitude.

☐ 🔖 ♡ **César E. Chávez National Monument:** Located in Keene, this site preserves the home, office, and gardens of labor leader César Chávez. Visitors explore exhibits on the farm worker movement, walk peaceful grounds, and gain insight into the life and legacy of the activist whose organizing transformed labor rights and inspired social justice nationwide.

☐ 🔖 ♡ **Channel Islands National Park:** Encompassing five remote islands off California's coast, this park protects unique species, rugged cliffs, and sea caves. Visitors kayak crystal waters, snorkel with seals, hike scenic ridges, and explore cultural sites left by Indigenous peoples. Accessible only by boat or plane, it offers an unmatched wilderness escape.

CALIFORNIA

☐ 🔖 ♡ **Death Valley National Park:** Spanning California and Nevada, this park contains the hottest, driest, and lowest U.S. landscape. Visitors explore salt flats at Badwater Basin, hike golden dunes, tour ghost towns, and marvel at colorful canyons. Despite its name, the park teems with life and offers world-class stargazing in its dark desert skies.

☐ 🔖 ♡ **Devils Postpile National Monument:** Nestled in the Sierra Nevada, this monument features striking basalt columns formed by ancient lava flows. Visitors hike to the geometric cliffs, continue on to Rainbow Falls, and explore surrounding meadows and mountain trails. The site blends geological wonders with alpine scenery, offering adventure for all ages.

☐ 🔖 ♡ **Eugene O'Neill National Historic Site:** In Danville's rolling hills, this site preserves Tao House, the retreat of playwright Eugene O'Neill. Visitors tour his home and gardens, where he penned some of his greatest works, including "Long Day's Journey Into Night." Exhibits highlight his life, struggles, and creative contributions to American theater.

☐ 🔖 ♡ **Fort Point National Historic Site:** Beneath San Francisco's Golden Gate Bridge, this brick fort once guarded the bay during the Civil War. Visitors explore cannon-lined walls, arched corridors, and barracks, learning about coastal defense history. The fort's vantage offers some of the most iconic views of the Golden Gate and city skyline.

☐ 🔖 ♡ **Golden Gate National Recreation Area:** Stretching across San Francisco and Marin County, this vast recreation area offers trails, beaches, and historic sites. Visitors explore Alcatraz, Presidio ruins, and coastal bluffs, while enjoying activities like hiking, cycling, and birdwatching. Its landscapes combine natural beauty with rich cultural heritage.

☐ 🔖 ♡ **John Muir National Historic Site:** In Martinez, this site honors conservationist John Muir. Visitors tour his Victorian home, orchards, and surrounding landscapes, reflecting on his role in protecting wilderness and shaping the National Park System. Exhibits highlight his writings and Sierra Club work, inspiring ongoing efforts in environmental stewardship.

☐ 🔖 ♡ **Joshua Tree National Park:** Famed for its namesake Joshua trees, this desert park showcases otherworldly rock formations and vast starlit skies. Visitors hike trails through rugged terrain, climb granite monoliths, and explore ecosystems where the Mojave and Colorado Deserts meet, creating a striking blend of plant life, wildlife, and geologic wonders.

☐ 🔖 ♡ **Kings Canyon National Park:** Sharing a boundary with Sequoia, this park features one of the deepest canyons in North America, alongside giant sequoia groves and thundering waterfalls. Visitors hike glacial valleys, camp beneath granite cliffs, and explore wilderness backcountry, experiencing dramatic Sierra Nevada landscapes shaped by ice and time.

☐ 🔖 ♡ **Lassen Volcanic National Park:** This northern California park showcases steaming fumaroles, boiling springs, and an active volcano. Visitors hike to bubbling mud pots, climb Lassen Peak, and explore alpine lakes surrounded by wildflower meadows. Its dynamic geology offers a living laboratory of volcanic forces and natural renewal.

☐ 🔖 ♡ **Lava Beds National Monument:** Located near the Oregon border, this monument contains over 700 lava tube caves, Native rock art, and battlefield history from the Modoc War. Visitors spelunk underground passages, hike cinder cones, and discover volcanic landscapes shaped by millennia of eruptions, creating one of America's most unique park experiences.

☐ 🔖 ♡ **Manzanar National Historic Site:** In Owens Valley, this site preserves a WWII internment camp where thousands of Japanese Americans were forcibly relocated. Visitors tour barracks, exhibits, and the visitor center, reflecting on civil liberties, resilience, and the enduring stories of those who lived through this difficult chapter of U.S. history.

☐ 🔖 ♡ **Mojave National Preserve:** Covering 1.6 million acres, this desert preserve features sand dunes, cinder cones, and Joshua tree forests. Visitors hike Kelso Dunes, explore volcanic landscapes, and visit historic railroad depots. Its sweeping wilderness provides solitude, stargazing, and a chance to experience the varied ecosystems of the Mojave Desert.

CALIFORNIA

Muir Woods National Monument: Just north of San Francisco, this park protects ancient coastal redwoods, some over 1,000 years old. Visitors walk shaded trails, listen to the quiet of cathedral-like groves, and learn about redwood ecology. Easy access and timeless beauty make it one of California's most cherished natural sanctuaries.

Pinnacles National Park: Famous for towering spires and talus caves, Pinnacles offers world-class hiking and rock climbing. Visitors explore unique volcanic formations, watch for endangered California condors, and traverse landscapes ranging from oak woodlands to chaparral. The park's dramatic scenery reveals the power of geologic forces over time.

Point Reyes National Seashore: On the California coast, this preserve protects rugged cliffs, beaches, and tule elk herds. Visitors hike to Point Reyes Lighthouse, enjoy whale watching, and explore estuaries rich in birdlife. Its wild coastal landscapes highlight the meeting of land and sea, preserving both cultural heritage and natural beauty.

Port Chicago Naval Magazine National Memorial: In Concord, this memorial honors 320 sailors and civilians who died in a 1944 munitions explosion. Most victims were African American, and the tragedy led to the largest mutiny trial in U.S. naval history. Visitors learn how the disaster shaped military labor reforms and advanced civil rights.

Redwood National Park: Protecting the tallest trees on Earth, this network preserves ancient redwood groves, coastal bluffs, and wild rivers. Visitors hike fern-filled canyons, camp in primeval forests, and explore beaches teeming with wildlife. The parks showcase biodiversity and safeguard some of the planet's most awe-inspiring natural wonders.

Rosie the Riveter/WWII Home Front National Historical Park: Located in Richmond, this park commemorates civilian contributions during World War II, especially women working in defense industries. Visitors explore historic shipyards, exhibits, and interpretive centers that honor the spirit of the "Rosie" generation and their role in reshaping America's workforce.

San Francisco Maritime National Historical Park: On the city's northern waterfront, this park preserves historic ships, a visitor center, and a maritime museum. Visitors board tall ships, steam vessels, and tugboats while learning about San Francisco's seafaring past. The park blends waterfront scenery with immersive maritime history.

Santa Monica Mountains National Recreation Area: Spanning rugged terrain above Los Angeles, this area offers hiking, horseback riding, and scenic drives. Visitors explore chaparral, oak woodlands, and coastal canyons while enjoying views of the Pacific. It also preserves Native American sites, historic ranches, and diverse ecosystems close to urban life.

Sequoia National Park: Famous for groves of giant sequoias, including the General Sherman Tree, the world's largest by volume, this park offers wilderness adventures in the Sierra Nevada. Visitors hike alpine trails, explore caves, and marvel at towering forests. Together with Kings Canyon, it preserves some of California's most iconic landscapes.

Tule Lake National Monument: Near the Oregon border, this site preserves a WWII internment camp where Japanese Americans endured confinement. Visitors tour remnants of barracks and explore exhibits that reveal stories of resilience, loyalty questions, and civil rights struggles. It's a sobering reminder of wartime injustice and its lasting impacts.

Whiskeytown National Recreation Area: In northern California, this vast area features Whiskeytown Lake, Shasta-Trinity mountains, and forests. Visitors boat, swim, fish, and camp while exploring waterfalls and trails. The recreation area balances outdoor fun with natural beauty, offering both water-based activities and rugged wilderness experiences.

Yosemite National Park: A crown jewel of the Sierra Nevada, Yosemite is famed for granite icons El Capitan and Half Dome, thundering waterfalls, and giant sequoias. Visitors hike valleys, climb cliffs, and camp under starry skies. Designated a UNESCO World Heritage Site, it remains a global symbol of America's national parks.

CALIFORNIA

State & National Forests

☐ 🔖 ♡ **Angeles National Forest:** Angeles National Forest covers the San Gabriel Mountains north of Los Angeles. It offers rugged wilderness, alpine peaks, and miles of trails just minutes from the city. Popular spots include Mount Baldy, the Pacific Crest Trail, and scenic drives like the Angeles Crest Highway. It's a vital escape for outdoor recreation in Southern California.

☐ 🔖 ♡ **Boggs Mountain Demonstration State Forest:** Near Cobb in Lake County, this CAL FIRE forest serves as a research and education site for sustainable forestry and fire recovery. Pine and fir woodlands host trails for hiking, biking, and horseback riding. Once devastated by wildfire, it now demonstrates forest resilience while offering recreation in a recovering landscape.

☐ 🔖 ♡ **Cleveland National Forest:** Cleveland National Forest lies in Southern California's Peninsular Ranges near San Diego. It features chaparral-covered hills, oak woodlands, and scenic overlooks. Key areas include Palomar Mountain and Laguna Mountain. The forest offers hiking, camping, and off-roading amid a semi-arid, rugged landscape.

☐ 🔖 ♡ **Eldorado National Forest:** Stretching from the foothills to the crest of the Sierra Nevada, Eldorado National Forest features pine forests, granite peaks, and alpine lakes. It's a popular destination for hiking, camping, and snow sports, especially around Desolation Wilderness and the Crystal Basin area. The forest also supports historic gold rush sites.

☐ 🔖 ♡ **Humboldt–Toiyabe National Forest:** Spanning Nevada and eastern California, this is the largest national forest outside Alaska. In California, it protects alpine basins, desert canyons, and stretches of the Eastern Sierra. Visitors hike remote wilderness, fish in cold streams, and explore rugged ranges. Its vast, varied terrain showcases solitude and dramatic high desert–mountain contrasts.

☐ 🔖 ♡ **Inyo National Forest:** Stretching along the Eastern Sierra and White Mountains, Inyo features jagged peaks, alpine lakes, volcanic craters, and the world's oldest trees, the ancient bristlecone pines. Home to Mount Whitney and Mammoth Lakes, it offers hiking, climbing, skiing, and stargazing in vast wilderness. Its dramatic contrasts span desert basins to glaciated high country.

☐ 🔖 ♡ **Jackson Demonstration State Forest:** Located near Fort Bragg, Jackson is California's largest state forest and a hub for sustainable forestry research. With redwood groves, hiking trails, and educational signage, it balances public recreation with active timber harvesting. Visitors enjoy shaded paths, mushroom foraging, and mountain biking.

☐ 🔖 ♡ **Klamath National Forest:** Klamath National Forest spans rugged mountains, deep canyons, and wild rivers near the Oregon border. It includes part of the Klamath-Siskiyou range, known for rich biodiversity. Popular for whitewater rafting, hiking, and fishing, the forest also features portions of the Pacific Crest Trail and several wilderness areas.

☐ 🔖 ♡ **Lake Tahoe Basin Management Unit:** Though not a traditional forest, this unit of the U.S. Forest Service protects the Lake Tahoe watershed and surrounding forests. It offers breathtaking alpine scenery, crystal-clear waters, and year-round recreation including boating, hiking, and skiing. Conservation efforts focus on reducing erosion and preserving lake clarity.

☐ 🔖 ♡ **Las Padres National Forest:** Stretching along the California coast from Ventura to Big Sur, Las Padres offers dramatic cliffs, chaparral hills, and redwood groves. It includes wilderness areas like Ventana and Sespe. The forest supports hiking, backcountry camping, and scenic drives through remote mountain terrain and coastal canyons.

☐ 🔖 ♡ **Las Posadas State Forest:** Tucked in Napa County, this small research forest preserves mixed conifers and chaparral on volcanic soils. Managed for forestry studies, it also allows hiking, hunting, and wildlife observation. Its oak woodlands and scenic ridges contribute to local watershed health, making it an important though lesser-known piece of California's state forest system.

☐ 🔖 ♡ **Lassen National Forest:** Surrounding Lassen Volcanic National Park, this forest is known for its geothermal activity, lava tubes, and mountain lakes. It includes Hat Creek Rim and the scenic Bizz Johnson Trail. The forest is shaped by volcanic history and offers camping, fishing, and snow sports in a landscape of conifers and meadows.

CALIFORNIA

☐ 🔖 ♡ **LaTour Demonstration State Forest:** Located in Shasta County, LaTour serves as a research site for sustainable forestry practices. It features mixed conifer forests, volcanic soils, and cool high elevations. While not heavily developed for recreation, it provides access for hiking, hunting, and educational tours.

☐ 🔖 ♡ **Mendocino National Forest:** Mendocino National Forest is California's only national forest without a major paved road crossing it, preserving a truly remote wilderness experience. Located north of Clear Lake, it features oak woodlands, rugged peaks, and hidden lakes. Popular for off-roading, hunting, and backcountry camping, it's a haven for solitude seekers.

☐ 🔖 ♡ **Modoc National Forest:** In California's northeast corner, this forest blends volcanic plateaus, pine forests, and high desert. Lava flows, cinder cones, wetlands, and meadows create diverse habitats for pronghorn, eagles, and waterfowl. Visitors enjoy camping, horseback riding, and fishing in remote lakes. With few crowds, it's a quiet landscape of solitude and geologic wonder.

☐ 🔖 ♡ **Mountain Home Demonstration State Forest:** Nestled in the Sierra Nevada, this forest protects ancient groves of giant sequoias, some over 2,000 years old. It's a research site for forest management and fire ecology, with interpretive trails, quiet campsites, and access to the larger Sequoia National Forest. Visitors find towering trees and peaceful woodland.

☐ 🔖 ♡ **Plumas National Forest:** Located in northeastern California, Plumas National Forest features deep river canyons, high granite ridges, and over 1,000 miles of streams. With areas like Bucks Lake Wilderness and the Feather River Scenic Byway, it's ideal for camping, fishing, and scenic drives. Historic gold-mining towns also dot the region.

☐ 🔖 ♡ **San Bernardino National Forest:** San Bernardino National Forest spans the San Gabriel, San Bernardino, and San Jacinto mountains. Near Los Angeles, it offers alpine lakes, forested peaks, and snow-covered trails. Popular sites include Big Bear Lake and Mount San Jacinto. It's a year-round escape for hiking, skiing, and scenic drives.

☐ 🔖 ♡ **Sequoia National Forest:** Home to some of the largest trees in the world, Sequoia National Forest surrounds the famed Giant Sequoia National Monument. It features towering groves, rugged Sierra Nevada peaks, and deep river canyons. Highlights include the Kern River, Trail of 100 Giants, and alpine recreation areas like Hume Lake.

☐ 🔖 ♡ **Shasta-Trinity National Forest:** The largest national forest in California, it spans volcanic peaks, pristine lakes, and vast wilderness. Home to Mount Shasta, Castle Crags, and Trinity Alps, it offers endless opportunities for hiking, boating, and fishing. The forest contains both alpine and forested landscapes with rich cultural and natural history.

☐ 🔖 ♡ **Sierra National Forest:** East of Fresno in the central Sierra Nevada, this forest is the gateway to Yosemite and Kings Canyon. It features granite cliffs, wild rivers, and alpine meadows. Known for the Kaiser Wilderness and Dinkey Lakes, it's a hub for camping, backpacking, and fishing, with a mix of easy access and backcountry solitude.

☐ 🔖 ♡ **Six Rivers National Forest:** Covering 1 million acres along California's north coast, this forest stretches from redwood groves to rugged mountains and wild rivers like the Klamath, Trinity, and Smith. Renowned for salmon and steelhead fishing, it also offers rafting, camping, and hiking. Remote peaks and lush valleys make it a haven for wildlife and outdoor adventure.

☐ 🔖 ♡ **Soquel Demonstration State Forest:** Near Santa Cruz, Soquel is a coastal redwood forest managed for sustainable forestry, education, and recreation. It's especially popular with mountain bikers, offering steep, flowing trails under towering trees. The forest also plays a role in watershed protection and timber research.

☐ 🔖 ♡ **Stanislaus National Forest:** Bordering Yosemite National Park, Stanislaus features wild rivers, scenic byways, and coniferous forests. Visitors enjoy camping, hiking, and rafting along the Tuolumne and Stanislaus Rivers. The forest is also known for its volcanic geology and historic mining heritage, with elevations ranging from 1,500 to over 11,000 feet.

☐ 🔖 ♡ **Tahoe National Forest:** This northern Sierra forest includes parts of the Pacific Crest Trail, Donner Summit, and beautiful alpine lakes. Popular for hiking, skiing, and paddling, it offers a balance of accessible recreation and deep wilderness. The forest plays a key role in protecting the headwaters of the Yuba and American Rivers.

CALIFORNIA

National Grasslands

☐ 🔖 ♡ **Butte Valley National Grassland**: Located in northern California near the Oregon border, Butte Valley National Grassland lies in the shadow of Mount Shasta and features a mix of native bunchgrasses, sagebrush, and wetlands. Once farmland, the area was restored to native grassland and now supports raptors, waterfowl, and pronghorn. It's a quiet spot for wildlife viewing and stargazing.

National Scenic Byways & All-American Roads

☐ 🔖 ♡ **Arroyo Seco Historic Parkway (Route 110):** America's first freeway and a National Scenic Byway, this historic 8-mile parkway links Los Angeles and Pasadena. Built in the 1930s, it features graceful curves, landscaped medians, and stone bridges in the Arts & Crafts style. Drivers experience early parkway design while enjoying views of the San Gabriel Mountains and Arroyo Seco corridor.

☐ 🔖 ♡ **Big Sur Coast Highway (Route 1):** Designated an All-American Road, this 71-mile stretch of Highway 1 hugs cliffs between Carmel and San Simeon. Travelers pass redwood canyons, Bixby Creek Bridge, pounding surf, and endless Pacific vistas. Known worldwide as one of the most beautiful drives, it combines dramatic geology, coastal ecosystems, and iconic California scenery.

☐ 🔖 ♡ **California Historic Route 66 – Needles to Barstow:** This National Scenic Byway preserves the legendary Mother Road across the Mojave Desert. Travelers encounter vintage motels, neon signs, and trading posts recalling the golden age of road trips. Expansive desert vistas, volcanic peaks, and cultural landmarks tell the story of migration, commerce, and resilience along Route 66.

☐ 🔖 ♡ **Death Valley Scenic Byway (Highway 190):** Crossing Death Valley National Park, this National Scenic Byway traverses salt flats, badlands, dunes, and desert mountains. Stops include Zabriskie Point, Badwater Basin, the lowest point in North America, and colorful canyons. The stark desert beauty, extreme contrasts, and mining history make this one of the nation's most unique drives.

☐ 🔖 ♡ **Ebbetts Pass Scenic Byway (Highway 4):** A narrow Sierra Nevada crossing, this National Scenic Byway climbs over 8,700-ft Ebbetts Pass between Arnold and Markleeville. Winding roads reveal granite peaks, alpine lakes, volcanic outcrops, and wildflower meadows. Popular with adventurous drivers and cyclists, it offers solitude, geologic wonders, and high-country beauty off the beaten path.

☐ 🔖 ♡ **San Luis Obispo North Coast Byway (Route 1):** An All-American Road, this 57-mile drive follows the rugged coast from Cambria to Ragged Point. Visitors pass Hearst Castle, Piedras Blancas Lighthouse, and elephant seal rookeries, with cliffs plunging to the Pacific. It blends cultural landmarks with unspoiled scenery, serving as the southern gateway to Big Sur.

☐ 🔖 ♡ **Tioga Road / Big Oak Flat Road (Yosemite, Route 120):** A National Scenic Byway, this high-country route crosses Yosemite above 9,000 feet. Drivers encounter granite domes, meadows, and alpine lakes with sweeping Sierra views. Seasonal access (summer–fall) makes it special. It's the gateway to Tuolumne Meadows, linking Yosemite Valley to the eastern Sierra.

☐ 🔖 ♡ **Volcanic Legacy Scenic Byway:** An All-American Road stretching from Lassen Volcanic National Park into Oregon, this route showcases lava flows, cinder cones, and snow-capped peaks. Stops include Lassen Peak, Lava Beds caves, and wildlife-rich wetlands. It highlights volcanic geology, cultural history, and diverse ecosystems across one of America's most dramatic volcanic landscapes.

CALIFORNIA

State Scenic Byways

☐ 🔖 ♡ **Ancient Bristlecone Scenic Byway (SR 168):** High in the White Mountains, this road leads to groves of bristlecone pines, the oldest trees on Earth. Views stretch across the Sierra Nevada while alpine meadows and rugged ridges surround travelers. Remote and otherworldly, the byway highlights endurance and solitude in one of California's most extreme environments.

☐ 🔖 ♡ **Angeles Crest Scenic Byway (SR 2):** Winding through the San Gabriel Mountains above Los Angeles, this route offers a swift escape from city bustle. Pine forests, rugged cliffs, and alpine meadows line the way, with overlooks revealing both deserts and the city skyline. Popular for hiking, skiing, and scenic drives, it blends urban proximity with wilderness.

☐ 🔖 ♡ **Arroyo Seco Historic Parkway (SR 110):** America's first freeway doubles as a state scenic byway. Linking Pasadena with Los Angeles, it combines landscaped medians, historic bridges, and curving lanes with urban greenery. Though busy, it preserves early 20th-century parkway design and offers a living piece of California's transportation heritage.

☐ 🔖 ♡ **Big Bear Lake Scenic Byway (SR 18):** Circling Big Bear Lake in the San Bernardino Mountains, this route showcases alpine forests, sparkling waters, and year-round recreation. Summer brings boating and fishing, fall adds golden foliage, and winter offers snowy peaks and skiing. It's a four-season escape into Southern California's mountain playground.

☐ 🔖 ♡ **Big Sur Coast Highway (SR 1):** Hugging cliffs above the Pacific, this world-famous drive reveals rugged headlands, redwood groves, and iconic landmarks like Bixby Creek Bridge. Pullouts showcase whales, sea otters, and pounding surf. With unmatched ocean vistas and dramatic coastal terrain, it remains one of America's premier scenic highways.

☐ 🔖 ♡ **Bradshaw Trail Scenic Byway:** A historic freight route turned desert backroad, this byway crosses remote washes and rocky terrain of Southern California's desert. Vast skies, rugged mountains, and pioneer history frame the drive. Lightly traveled, it offers solitude and stark desert beauty, echoing the frontier spirit that shaped the region.

☐ 🔖 ♡ **Carmel Valley Road Scenic Byway:** Narrow and winding, this road threads through golden oak-studded hills, ranchlands, and vineyards east of Monterey. Scenic overlooks showcase Carmel Valley's wine country charm, while wildflowers brighten the roadside in spring. The byway reflects California's rural Mediterranean landscape with a rustic, pastoral character.

☐ 🔖 ♡ **Carson Pass Scenic Byway (SR 88):** Crossing the Sierra Nevada, this historic emigrant route crests at Carson Pass. Alpine lakes, granite domes, and meadows of summer wildflowers line the road. In fall, aspens glow gold; in winter, snow transforms the pass into a frozen wonderland. It captures the Sierra's rugged beauty in every season.

☐ 🔖 ♡ **Death Valley Scenic Byway (SR 190):** Entering the lowest point in North America, this drive unveils salt flats, colorful badlands, sand dunes, and stark desert mountains. Sunrises and sunsets wash the landscape in vivid hues, while spring wildflowers sometimes blanket the desert. Harsh yet beautiful, it reveals the drama of Earth's extremes.

☐ 🔖 ♡ **Dinosaur Diamond Scenic Byway (SR 139/US 40):** In far northwestern California, this route showcases fossil beds, petroglyphs, and rugged red-rock canyons. Dinosaur National Monument highlights deep time and geologic drama, while sagebrush plains and river valleys add variety. The drive blends prehistory, Native heritage, and desert beauty into a unique journey.

☐ 🔖 ♡ **Eastern Sierra Scenic Byway (US 395):** Stretching from Lone Pine to the Nevada line, this long corridor follows the dramatic eastern escarpment of the Sierra Nevada. Jagged peaks tower over desert basins, while hot springs, alpine lakes, and small towns add interest. It's one of California's most iconic road trips, offering endless mountain vistas.

☐ 🔖 ♡ **Ebbetts Pass Scenic Byway (SR 4):** Narrow and winding, this Sierra crossing passes volcanic ridges, granite peaks, and deep forests. Alpine lakes and wildflower meadows reward adventurous travelers. With few services and little traffic, it feels remote and pristine, capturing the raw spirit of California's high mountain backcountry.

☐ 🔖 ♡ **Emigrant Trail Scenic Byway (US 395 segments):** Tracing historic pioneer migration routes, this byway crosses sagebrush plains and skirts the Sierra's eastern edge. Interpretive sites recall westward journeys, while geothermal springs and volcanic ridges enrich the scenery. It blends cultural heritage with stark natural beauty in a land of transition.

CALIFORNIA

☐ 🔖 ♡ **Feather River Scenic Byway (SR 70):** Following the river through its namesake canyon, this road showcases waterfalls, granite cliffs, and pine forests. Railroad bridges and tunnels highlight historic engineering, while turnouts provide sweeping views. Wildlife, seasonal foliage, and rushing waters enrich the canyon, making it a lush Sierra passage.

☐ 🔖 ♡ **Feather River West Scenic Byway (SR 70 alternate):** This western segment emphasizes waterfalls, canyon walls, and railroad history in a slightly different stretch of the Feather River corridor. Bridges, tunnels, and deep gorges define the landscape, while forests and wildflowers soften the ruggedness. A companion route to the main Feather River drive.

☐ 🔖 ♡ **High Desert Scenic Byway (US 395):** Traversing sagebrush basins and volcanic plateaus, this byway highlights the stark beauty of California's arid east. Snowcapped Sierra peaks rise dramatically above desert plains. Hot springs, lava flows, and wide horizons create a striking landscape where geology, ecology, and pioneer history converge.

☐ 🔖 ♡ **Jacinto Reyes Scenic Byway (SR 33):** Climbing into Los Padres National Forest, this route passes chaparral hillsides, rocky outcrops, and pine forests. Scenic overlooks reveal the Ojai Valley and Channel Islands beyond. Popular with motorcyclists, it blends rugged mountain driving with forested serenity and panoramic coastal views.

☐ 🔖 ♡ **June Lake Loop Scenic Byway (SR 158):** A short but spectacular Eastern Sierra loop, this route circles alpine lakes beneath jagged peaks. Aspen groves glow golden in fall, while fishing, boating, and hiking fill summer days. Winter snows create a serene alpine setting. Its intimate scale makes it a Sierra Nevada jewel.

☐ 🔖 ♡ **Kings Canyon Scenic Byway (SR 180):** Leading deep into one of North America's deepest canyons, this road follows a glacial river valley framed by granite cliffs. Giant sequoias, waterfalls, and alpine meadows enrich the journey. The road ends in remote Cedar Grove, immersing travelers in the raw power of Kings Canyon.

☐ 🔖 ♡ **Klamath River Scenic Byway (SR 96):** Meandering through rugged northern California, this route follows the Klamath River past Native communities, fishing sites, and deep forest canyons. Salmon runs and rafting highlight the river's vitality, while interpretive stops share cultural history. It's a blend of wild scenery and living heritage.

☐ 🔖 ♡ **Lassen Scenic Byway (SR 89):** Encircling Lassen Volcanic National Park, this drive highlights geothermal features, lava fields, and alpine lakes. Snow-capped peaks rise above meadows bursting with wildflowers in summer. Visitors encounter steaming fumaroles, pristine forests, and volcanic landscapes, creating a dramatic journey through one of California's most geologically active regions.

☐ 🔖 ♡ **Lee Vining Canyon Scenic Byway (SR 120):** Ascending from Mono Lake to Yosemite's Tioga Pass, this steep canyon route reveals waterfalls, glacial-carved cliffs, and colorful aspen groves. Granite walls tower above the road, while scenic pullouts provide sweeping vistas. Linking desert basin to alpine heights, it showcases one of the Sierra Nevada's most striking vertical transitions.

☐ 🔖 ♡ **Mariposa–Sequoia Grove Scenic Byway (SR 41):** Entering Yosemite from the south, this route passes oak woodlands before climbing to giant sequoia groves. Scenic turnouts reveal rolling foothills, granite ridges, and sweeping mountain views. The Mariposa Grove offers close encounters with some of the world's largest trees, blending natural wonder with cultural heritage.

☐ 🔖 ♡ **Mendocino Coast Scenic Byway (SR 1):** Hugging Northern California's rugged shoreline, this route passes dramatic headlands, secluded coves, and charming coastal villages. Towering redwoods frame ocean vistas, while lighthouses and historic towns enrich the journey. Whale-watching, tidepools, and endless Pacific horizons make it a breathtaking coastal experience.

☐ 🔖 ♡ **Mulholland Highway Scenic Byway:** Twisting through the Santa Monica Mountains, this route offers sweeping views of the Pacific Ocean, chaparral hillsides, and canyon landscapes. Popular with drivers and cyclists, it links state parks, historic ranchlands, and overlooks. Its cultural cachet and natural beauty make it an iconic Southern California scenic drive.

☐ 🔖 ♡ **Pacific Coast Highway (SR 1, Northern):** North of San Francisco, this legendary stretch of SR 1 traverses bluffs, beaches, and fishing villages along the rugged coast. Redwoods rise inland while surf pounds rocky coves. With picturesque lighthouses, marine preserves, and sweeping ocean views, it captures the wild essence of California's northern shoreline.

☐ 🔖 ♡ **Pines to Palms Scenic Byway (SR 74):** Dropping from mountain forests into the Coachella Valley, this drive showcases dramatic ecological transitions. Towering pines give way to desert palms as the road descends. Scenic overlooks reveal deep canyons, San Jacinto's granite peaks, and vast desert basins, making it a striking showcase of California's diversity.

CALIFORNIA

☐ 🔖 ♡ **Plumas Scenic Byway (SR 89):** Traveling through Plumas National Forest, this corridor highlights alpine lakes, meadows, and evergreen ridges. Historic mining towns, campgrounds, and river valleys enrich the scenery. With opportunities for hiking, fishing, and wildlife viewing, it emphasizes the Sierra's quieter beauty, away from more heavily traveled routes.

☐ 🔖 ♡ **Redwood Highway (US 101):** Stretching through towering redwood groves in Humboldt and Del Norte Counties, this byway immerses travelers in cathedral-like forests. Rivers, misty coastline, and historic logging towns accompany the drive. It connects multiple parks preserving the world's tallest trees, blending natural grandeur with cultural heritage.

☐ 🔖 ♡ **Rim of the World Scenic Byway (SR 38):** Running along the spine of the San Bernardino Mountains, this lofty road lives up to its name with expansive views over valleys and deserts. Forests of pine and fir line the route, while overlooks showcase alpine lakes and distant peaks. Seasonal wildflowers and fall foliage enhance the high-altitude beauty.

☐ 🔖 ♡ **Route of the Ancients Scenic Byway (Modoc Plateau):** Crossing California's remote northeast, this byway highlights Lava Beds National Monument, petroglyphs, and volcanic landscapes. Sagebrush plateaus, lava flows, and caves tell stories of Native culture and geologic history. Isolated and stark, it connects travelers to timeless natural and cultural heritage.

☐ 🔖 ♡ **Route of the Silver Kings Scenic Byway (SR 4):** This corridor through Alpine County reflects the state's silver-mining era. Ghost towns, alpine passes, and forested ridges punctuate the drive, while interpretive sites share mining history. Scenic overlooks reveal rugged terrain and high-country lakes, blending cultural heritage with pristine Sierra beauty.

☐ 🔖 ♡ **San Gabriel Canyon Scenic Byway (SR 39):** Climbing from Azusa into the San Gabriel Mountains, this road follows steep canyons, streams, and forested slopes. Overlooks reveal dramatic ridges, while picnic areas and trailheads line the corridor. It's a quick gateway from urban Southern California to mountain wilderness and outdoor adventure.

☐ 🔖 ♡ **San Juan Bautista Scenic Byway (SR 156/25):** Linking fertile farmland with the historic town of San Juan Bautista, this byway highlights mission-era heritage and rolling golden hills. Scenic views encompass ranchlands, wildflower fields, and cultural landmarks. It connects California's agricultural heart with its early Spanish colonial history.

☐ 🔖 ♡ **San Luis Obispo North Coast Scenic Byway (SR 1):** Running from San Simeon past Morro Bay, this coastal route features rocky bluffs, sea stacks, and pristine beaches. Elephant seals, seabirds, and tidepools enrich the natural experience, while historic piers and lighthouses add cultural depth. It's a quintessential Central Coast journey.

☐ 🔖 ♡ **Santa Monica Mountains Scenic Byway (SR 27):** Following Topanga Canyon Road, this route winds through oak woodlands, rugged hills, and chaparral landscapes. Scenic overlooks provide views of the Pacific and hidden valleys. Linking coastal communities with mountain trails, it captures the wild side of Los Angeles's backyard.

☐ 🔖 ♡ **Shasta Volcanic Scenic Byway (SR 89/US 97):** Traversing northern California's volcanic landscapes, this corridor showcases Mount Shasta, cinder cones, lava flows, and alpine lakes. Interpretive sites reveal Native history and geologic change. With opportunities for recreation and sweeping mountain vistas, it's a dynamic and diverse byway.

☐ 🔖 ♡ **Sierra Heritage Scenic Byway (SR 168):** Climbing into Sierra National Forest, this drive offers chaparral foothills, volcanic ridges, and granite canyons. Interpretive sites highlight logging and Native heritage. Scenic overlooks and forested trails reveal the Sierra's varied ecosystems, blending cultural history with natural grandeur.

☐ 🔖 ♡ **Sierra Vista Scenic Byway:** Circling through Sierra foothills near Oakhurst, this route reveals oak-dotted meadows, granite domes, and seasonal wildflowers. Historic logging sites and interpretive pullouts enrich the journey. The byway blends cultural heritage, rural landscapes, and mountain views into a quiet escape into California's backcountry.

☐ 🔖 ♡ **Smith River Scenic Byway (US 199):** Following the emerald-green Smith River in far northern California, this road passes through towering redwoods and rugged canyons. Scenic pullouts highlight pristine waters, old-growth forests, and abundant wildlife. Its wild and scenic status underscores its ecological importance as one of the West's last undammed rivers.

☐ 🔖 ♡ **Sonoma Coast Scenic Byway (SR 1):** Running from Bodega Bay to Jenner, this stunning coastal drive reveals rugged cliffs, sandy beaches, and pounding surf. Wildflowers carpet the bluffs in spring, while seabirds and seals thrive year-round. Lighthouses, fishing villages, and state parks add cultural and recreational depth to this dramatic Pacific shoreline route.

CALIFORNIA

☐ ▢ ♡ **Sunrise Scenic Byway (SR 180):** High in Sequoia National Park, this ascent showcases towering sequoias, alpine meadows, and sweeping Sierra vistas. Named for the brilliant morning light on its ridges, the byway offers access to trailheads, overlooks, and picnic areas. It's a short but unforgettable window into California's mountain wilderness.

☐ ▢ ♡ **Tioga Road Scenic Byway (SR 120):** Crossing Yosemite's high country, this alpine highway climbs over 9,900 feet at Tioga Pass. Along the way, granite domes, pristine lakes, and Tuolumne Meadows highlight the grandeur of the Sierra Nevada. Open only in summer, the road offers spectacular scenery and connects Yosemite Valley with the eastern Sierra.

☐ ▢ ♡ **Trinity Scenic Byway (SR 299):** Cutting through the rugged Trinity Alps, this winding route follows the Trinity River. Anglers and rafters prize its waters, while granite peaks and evergreen forests frame the drive. Historic mining towns add cultural interest, and scenic overlooks reveal one of Northern California's most pristine wilderness corridors.

☐ ▢ ♡ **US 395 Scenic Byway (Owens Valley):** South of Bishop, this byway runs along the Sierra Nevada's dramatic eastern escarpment. Snowcapped peaks loom over sagebrush plains, while hot springs, small towns, and historic sites enrich the corridor. It's a striking blend of high desert and towering mountains, offering endless vistas and recreation.

☐ ▢ ♡ **Volcanic Legacy Scenic Byway (SR 89/44/36):** This multi-state route highlights volcanic landscapes shaped by Lassen Peak and Mount Shasta. Travelers encounter lava tubes, cinder cones, waterfalls, and alpine lakes. Interpretive stops reveal geologic and cultural history. The drive blends fiery volcanic heritage with tranquil mountain scenery in Northern California.

☐ ▢ ♡ **West Side Highway Scenic Byway (SR 33):** Stretching along the western edge of the Central Valley, this corridor passes rolling hills, ranchlands, and orchards. Views of the Coast Ranges frame the horizon. The route highlights California's agricultural heartland while providing a peaceful alternative to busy interstates, with sweeping rural landscapes.

☐ ▢ ♡ **Whitmore Trough Scenic Byway:** A quiet Eastern Sierra corridor near Mammoth Lakes, this road passes volcanic tablelands, hot springs, and wide sagebrush basins. Panoramic views of the Sierra crest dominate the skyline. Remote and lightly traveled, it offers solitude, geologic intrigue, and a sense of the high desert's vastness.

☐ ▢ ♡ **Whitmore Valley Scenic Byway:** Nestled east of the Sierra, this short route reveals open valleys, volcanic ridges, and seasonal wildflower displays. Ranchlands and rolling terrain frame distant mountain backdrops. It's a quiet drive that emphasizes California's wide, open spaces and pastoral landscapes away from busy tourist routes.

☐ ▢ ♡ **Wildwood Road Scenic Byway:** This Trinity County backroad winds through mixed forests and small valleys. The corridor highlights rural heritage and access to Trinity River recreation. Dense woodlands, streams, and seasonal color provide a peaceful backdrop, making it a low-key but scenic route through Northern California's countryside.

☐ ▢ ♡ **Yankee Jims Road Scenic Byway:** A rugged historic mining trail near Foresthill, this narrow route recalls California's Gold Rush heritage. Crossing wooden bridges and steep ridges, it offers dramatic canyon views and traces of early settlements. Remote and adventurous, it connects travelers to both cultural history and rugged Sierra scenery.

☐ ▢ ♡ **Yolo Causeway Scenic Byway (I-80 segment):** Spanning wetlands between Sacramento and Davis, this elevated causeway provides sweeping views of rice fields, migratory birds, and open sky. Seasonal waterfowl migrations make it a birdwatcher's delight. It highlights the importance of Central Valley wetlands while connecting urban centers across a natural landscape.

☐ ▢ ♡ **Yosemite Valley Scenic Byway (SR 140):** Entering Yosemite National Park from the west, this byway follows the Merced River into the valley. Granite cliffs, waterfalls, and meadows create iconic views, culminating at El Capitan and Half Dome. It's one of the most famous scenic drives in the world, embodying California's natural majesty.

☐ ▢ ♡ **Yuba–Donner Scenic Byway (SR 49/20/89):** Linking historic mining towns with Donner Summit, this route traverses Gold Rush country and Sierra passes. Interpretive sites reveal pioneer hardships, while alpine lakes and forests enrich the scenery. It blends cultural history with mountain beauty, offering one of Northern California's most diverse scenic experiences.

☐ ▢ ♡ **Yurok Scenic Byway (US 101/SR 169):** Highlighting the heritage of the Yurok Tribe, this byway follows the Klamath River to the Pacific. Visitors encounter redwoods, river valleys, and cultural interpretive centers. It blends Native traditions with natural beauty, offering a meaningful journey through one of California's most significant cultural landscapes.

UNITED STATES EDITION

CALIFORNIA

National Natural Landmarks

 ☐ 🔖 ♡ **Amboy Crater:** Rising starkly from the Mojave Desert, Amboy Crater illustrates recent volcanism with its 6,000-year-old cinder cone and surrounding basaltic lava flows. Named a National Natural Landmark for its textbook volcanic form, it offers hikers the chance to climb to the rim while preserving an excellent example of desert geology near historic Route 66.
GPS: 34.5199, -115.7241

 ☐ 🔖 ♡ **American River Bluffs and Phoenix Park Vernal Pools:** This Central Valley site holds National Natural Landmark status for its rare vernal pools and blue oak woodlands. Seasonal wetlands nurture endangered fairy shrimp and spring wildflowers, while intact oak bluffs shelter native grasses, offering one of California's best examples of fragile vernal pool ecosystems.
GPS: 38.6529, -121.2167

 ☐ 🔖 ♡ **Año Nuevo State Reserve:** One of the world's largest mainland elephant seal colonies makes Año Nuevo a National Natural Landmark. Its dunes, terraces, and rocky bluffs protect diverse upland and marine life. The site preserves critical breeding habitat while highlighting the interaction between coastal ecosystems and marine mammal conservation.
GPS: 37.1187, -122.3067

 ☐ 🔖 ♡ **Anza-Borrego Desert:** The largest state park in the nation, Anza-Borrego was named a National Natural Landmark for its outstanding desert geology and ecology. Rugged badlands, palm oases, and slot canyons preserve fossils and rare habitats. Spring wildflowers and vast arid landscapes make it a premier site for studying desert processes and biodiversity.
GPS: 33.2493, -116.4068

 ☐ 🔖 ♡ **Audubon Canyon:** This sanctuary in Marin County gained National Natural Landmark recognition as the Pacific Coast's largest rookery for herons and egrets. Surrounded by redwoods, wetlands, and meadows, it provides essential nesting habitat while doubling as an outdoor classroom for conservation, linking bird survival with habitat protection.
GPS: 37.9294, -122.6822

 ☐ 🔖 ♡ **Black Chasm Cave:** Black Chasm Cave is celebrated as a National Natural Landmark for its delicate helictites which are uncommon mineral formations that twist in unusual directions. Alongside flowstone, stalactites, and underground lakes, its chambers preserve fragile karst features, offering one of California's most valuable subterranean landscapes for science and education.
GPS: 38.4343, -120.6265

 ☐ 🔖 ♡ **Burney Falls:** Fed by underground springs, Burney Falls flows year-round, cascading 129 feet over volcanic basalt. Named a National Natural Landmark for its exceptional hydrology and scenic beauty, the falls were once called the "Eighth Wonder of the World." Its misty spray supports lush vegetation, showcasing the ecological richness of Northern California.
GPS: 41.0122, -121.6519

 ☐ 🔖 ♡ **Cinder Cone Natural Area:** This Mojave Desert site contains more than 20 volcanic cones and expansive lava flows, earning National Natural Landmark status for its dramatic record of volcanism. Black and red cinders and ash fields create stark terrain that illustrates how desert geology is shaped by relatively recent eruptions.
GPS: 35.2894, -115.5853

 ☐ 🔖 ♡ **Cosumnes River Riparian Woodlands:** One of the last free-flowing rivers in the Central Valley, the Cosumnes is a National Natural Landmark for preserving floodplain habitats of riparian forest, vernal pools, and wetlands. It sustains migratory birds, fish, and endangered species, providing a living remnant of California's once-vast riverine landscapes.
GPS: 38.2657, -121.4392

 ☐ 🔖 ♡ **Deep Springs Marsh:** East of the Sierra Nevada, this isolated desert wetland was designated a National Natural Landmark for its rare ecological setting. It supports native grasses, desert plants, and migratory waterfowl, functioning as a critical oasis in an arid environment and demonstrating the role of wetlands in desert survival.
GPS: 37.3333, -118.0175

CALIFORNIA

Dixon Vernal Pools: This Central Valley preserve was named a National Natural Landmark for containing some of the best vernal pool–grassland complexes in California. Endangered crustaceans such as fairy shrimp thrive in its seasonal pools, which also host vibrant wildflower blooms, making it a critical remnant of threatened wetland habitats.
GPS: 38.2754, -121.8237

Elder Creek: Within the Eel River Basin, Elder Creek is a National Natural Landmark for its pristine watershed. Flowing through steep canyons and ancient Douglas-fir forests, it allows scientists to study redwood succession and watershed processes in a virtually undisturbed state, providing one of California's finest long-term ecological research sites.
GPS: 39.7256, -123.6262

Emerald Bay: A glacier-carved inlet on Lake Tahoe's west shore, Emerald Bay was recognized as a National Natural Landmark for its scenic and geologic value. Granite cliffs frame the bay, Eagle Falls tumbles nearby, and Tahoe's only island lies within its waters. The site blends alpine beauty with a record of glacial history.
GPS: 38.9571, -120.0934

Eureka Dunes: Towering 680 feet, Eureka Dunes in Death Valley are among the tallest in North America. Named a National Natural Landmark for their rare booming sands and endemic plants, they provide both geologic intrigue and biological uniqueness. The dunes exemplify how desert winds and isolation create exceptional natural features.
GPS: 37.0960, -117.6750

Fish Slough ACEC: This desert wetland north of Bishop earned National Natural Landmark status for its unusual mix of alkali meadows, volcanic tablelands, and rare plants such as the alkali mariposa lily. Endangered Owens pupfish swim in its waters, making it a vital preserve for biodiversity in California's Eastern Sierra.
GPS: 37.4691, -118.4009

Guadalupe–Nipomo Dunes: Stretching along the Central Coast, these dunes are a National Natural Landmark for being one of California's largest and most intact dune systems. They shelter endangered birds and rare plants while balancing recreation with conservation, demonstrating the fragility and resilience of coastal ecosystems.
GPS: 34.9656, -120.6503

Imperial Sand Hills (Algodones Dunes): These vast dunes, created by winds over ancient lakebeds, were designated a National Natural Landmark for their scale and ecological importance. Covering miles of desert, they support unique species like the desert pupfish and illustrate the ongoing processes of sand movement in arid environments.
GPS: 32.9167, -115.0500

Irvine Ranch Natural Landmarks: This Orange County landscape is a National Natural Landmark for preserving a complete geologic sequence from the Cretaceous to the present. Coastal sage scrub, oak woodlands, and fossil-rich strata highlight both ecological and paleontological importance making it a premier site for conservation and study.
GPS: 33.7315, -117.6930

La Brea Tar Pits (Rancho La Brea): In the heart of Los Angeles, the La Brea Tar Pits earned National Natural Landmark status for preserving one of the richest Ice Age fossil records in the world. Natural asphalt seeps trapped animals such as mammoths and saber-toothed cats, creating a site of global importance for paleontology.
GPS: 34.0630, -118.3560

Lake Shasta Caverns: Accessible only by boat, Lake Shasta Caverns are a National Natural Landmark for their outstanding karst features. Inside, visitors find flowstone, stalactites, and calcite formations that illustrate subterranean water processes. The caves showcase the complexity of limestone geology and provide a natural classroom for hydrogeology.
GPS: 40.8045, -122.3044

Lanphere Dunes and Ma-le'l Dunes: Near Humboldt Bay, these dunes earned National Natural Landmark status for being among the largest and most intact dune systems on the Pacific Coast. Shifting sands, wetlands, and forests support rare plants and wildlife, illustrating the ecological value and fragility of California's dynamic coastal dune landscapes.
GPS: 40.8520, -124.1490

CALIFORNIA

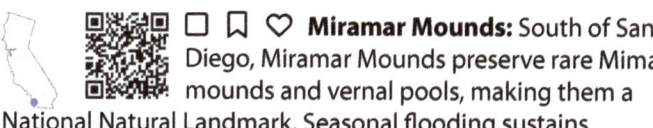 **Miramar Mounds:** South of San Diego, Miramar Mounds preserve rare Mima mounds and vernal pools, making them a National Natural Landmark. Seasonal flooding sustains endangered species and wildflowers in this unusual soil formation. Once widespread in California's coastal valleys, mound-and-pool systems now survive only in scattered remnants like this.
GPS: 32.8453, -117.1386

 **Mitchell Caverns and Winding Stair Cave:** Within the Mojave Desert, these limestone caves hold National Natural Landmark status for their delicate speleothems. Stalactites, columns, and flowstone decorate the chambers, offering a rare karst system in an arid setting. They reveal the surprising presence of subterranean beauty in California's desert geology.
GPS: 34.9408, -115.5144

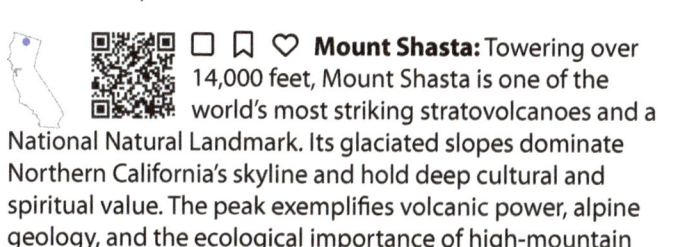 **Mount Shasta:** Towering over 14,000 feet, Mount Shasta is one of the world's most striking stratovolcanoes and a National Natural Landmark. Its glaciated slopes dominate Northern California's skyline and hold deep cultural and spiritual value. The peak exemplifies volcanic power, alpine geology, and the ecological importance of high-mountain environments.
GPS: 41.4099, -122.1949

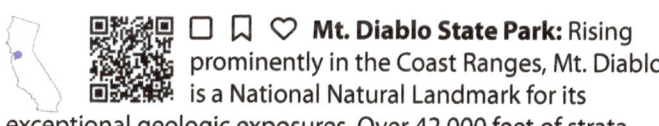 **Mt. Diablo State Park:** Rising prominently in the Coast Ranges, Mt. Diablo is a National Natural Landmark for its exceptional geologic exposures. Over 42,000 feet of strata record tectonic uplift, sedimentation, and mountain-building from the Jurassic to the Tertiary. Its summit provides sweeping views and a rare outdoor record of Earth's geologic past.
GPS: 37.8772, -121.9238

Pixley Vernal Pools: Located in the San Joaquin Valley, Pixley Vernal Pools are a National Natural Landmark for preserving one of the last intact vernal pool complexes. These seasonal wetlands support endangered fairy shrimp and rare invertebrates, while spring wildflower blooms showcase the biodiversity and beauty of ephemeral habitats.
GPS: 35.9844, -119.2125

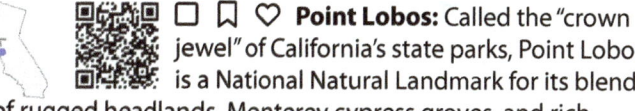 **Point Lobos:** Called the "crown jewel" of California's state parks, Point Lobos is a National Natural Landmark for its blend of rugged headlands, Monterey cypress groves, and rich marine life. Offshore kelp forests and coastal ecosystems illustrate the interaction of land and sea, making it one of the most biologically rich sites on the Pacific coast.
GPS: 36.5171, -121.9426

 **Pygmy Forest at Jug Handle State Natural Reserve:** This reserve is a National Natural Landmark for its five-level ecological staircase, which records 500,000 years of uplift and soil development. At the highest terrace lies a pygmy forest, where acidic soils stunt cypress and pine into miniature forms, creating a unique ecological community.
GPS: 39.3748, -123.7895

 **Rainbow Basin:** Near Barstow, Rainbow Basin is a National Natural Landmark for its colorful badlands and fossil-rich sedimentary layers. Miocene deposits preserve ancient mammals and document desert evolution. Its eroded terrain tells the story of prehistoric ecosystems, making it a key site for paleontology and geologic research in the Mojave Desert.
GPS: 35.0294, -117.0367

 **San Andreas Fault:** One of the most famous geologic features on Earth, the San Andreas Fault was named a National Natural Landmark for its visible surface traces and scientific importance. Marking the boundary between the Pacific and North American plates, it dramatically demonstrates crustal movement and seismic processes shaping California's landscapes.
GPS: 35.9150, -120.5310

 **San Felipe Creek Area:** In the Colorado Desert, San Felipe Creek is a National Natural Landmark for preserving California's last perennial desert stream. Its marshes support endangered fish and desert wildlife, offering a rare glimpse into natural desert hydrology. This oasis highlights the ecological value of scarce water in arid environments.
GPS: 33.1697, -115.8219

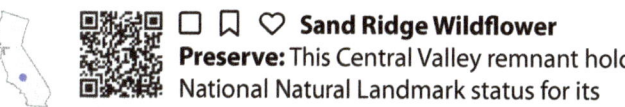 **Sand Ridge Wildflower Preserve:** This Central Valley remnant holds National Natural Landmark status for its sandy soils and unique plant life. It shelters rare wildflowers and the endangered Bakersfield cactus, species found nowhere else. The site demonstrates how microhabitats in arid valleys support biodiversity and preserve fragile desert ecosystems.
GPS: 35.3087, -118.7901

CALIFORNIA

Sharktooth Hill: Near Bakersfield, Sharktooth Hill is one of the richest Miocene fossil sites in the world and a National Natural Landmark. Fossil beds preserve sharks, whales, and rays, offering an unmatched record of prehistoric marine life. The site provides scientists with invaluable evidence of California's ancient ocean ecosystems.
GPS: 35.4418, -118.9406

Tijuana River Estuary: This coastal wetland was recognized as a National Natural Landmark for being one of the largest remaining in Southern California. Mudflats, salt marshes, and uplands support migratory birds and endangered species. Straddling the U.S.–Mexico border, it illustrates the global importance of wetland preservation.
GPS: 32.5520, -117.1193

Torrey Pines State Reserve: Home to one of the world's rarest trees, Torrey Pines State Reserve is a National Natural Landmark for protecting this unique coastal habitat. Steep cliffs and ravines frame trails overlooking the Pacific, preserving both ecological and scenic value in one of California's most remarkable coastal ecosystems.
GPS: 32.9166, -117.2496

Trona Pinnacles: Rising from an ancient dry lakebed, the Trona Pinnacles were named a National Natural Landmark for their hundreds of tufa spires. Formed underwater during the Pleistocene, these towers of calcium carbonate create an otherworldly landscape, often featured in films, while offering insight into desert paleoenvironments.
GPS: 35.6177, -117.3681

Turtle Mountain: Near the Colorado River, Turtle Mountain holds National Natural Landmark status for its diverse geology. Two distinct rock masses form its colorful, folded terrain, illustrating tectonic forces that shaped the desert. The site provides researchers with a clear window into geologic processes in California's arid regions.
GPS: 34.3182, -114.8520

COLORADO

Colorado's landscapes stretch from the soaring Rocky Mountains to sweeping high plains and deep canyons carved by rivers. National and state parks, vast forests, and striking natural landmarks provide endless opportunities to experience the state's rugged beauty and remarkable diversity.

📅 Peak Season
June–September is Colorado's peak season, with warm days, cool mountain nights, and full access to trails, parks, and alpine passes. Summer brings the largest crowds, especially in national parks and resort towns.

📅 Offseason Months
November–April is the primary offseason for general travel, with cold temperatures and snow limiting access to many high-elevation areas. Winter, however, is peak for ski resorts, while spring and late fall remain quieter with lighter visitation.

🍃 Scenery & Nature Timing
Spring brings wildflowers to the foothills and melting snow fills rivers for rafting. Summer offers alpine meadows and accessible high peaks. Fall is famous for golden aspen groves, while winter covers the Rockies in deep snow and clear skies.

✨ Special
Colorado showcases the Rocky Mountains with fourteeners like Mount Elbert, dramatic canyons such as Black Canyon of the Gunnison, and vast sand dunes at Great Sand Dunes National Park. Mesa Verde preserves ancient cliff dwellings, while alpine tundra, red rock mesas, and rushing rivers highlight its diverse landscapes.

COLORADO

State Parks

☐ 🔖 ♡ **Barr Lake State Park:** Just northeast of Denver, Barr Lake is known for birdwatching, especially bald eagles. A flat, 8.8-mile trail loops the lake, perfect for hiking and biking. The park includes wetlands, fishing piers, boat ramps (no wake), and a nature center. Its diverse habitats and peaceful views make it a haven for wildlife lovers and casual explorers alike.

☐ 🔖 ♡ **Boyd Lake State Park:** Situated near Loveland, Boyd Lake is ideal for boating, fishing, swimming, and jet skiing on its 1,700-acre reservoir. The park features paved trails, shaded picnic areas, and year-round camping. Its convenient access and wide variety of water and land activities make it one of northern Colorado's most popular family-friendly destinations.

☐ 🔖 ♡ **Castlewood Canyon State Park:** Located near Franktown, this park features a dramatic canyon carved by Cherry Creek and the ruins of the historic Castlewood Dam. Visitors enjoy scenic hiking trails, birdwatching, rock climbing, and wildflower viewing. With its diverse terrain and fascinating history, it's a unique blend of nature and heritage just southeast of Denver.

☐ 🔖 ♡ **Chatfield State Park:** Southwest of Denver, Chatfield offers a large reservoir for boating, paddleboarding, fishing, and swimming. Visitors enjoy 26 miles of trails, an off-leash dog park, and campgrounds with full hookups. Surrounded by foothills and wetlands, the park provides scenic recreation close to the city, attracting water lovers and wildlife watchers alike.

☐ 🔖 ♡ **Cherry Creek State Park:** In suburban Aurora, Cherry Creek offers a 880-acre reservoir for sailing, kayaking, swimming, and fishing. Paved and natural trails weave through grasslands and wetlands, supporting biking, horseback riding, and nature walks. Campgrounds, boat ramps, picnic shelters, and a family-friendly beach make this a year-round urban oasis.

☐ 🔖 ♡ **Cheyenne Mountain State Park:** Just outside Colorado Springs, this 2,700-acre park offers over 28 miles of trails through diverse ecosystems. Visitors enjoy hiking, mountain biking, and camping with panoramic views of Cheyenne Mountain. Wildlife is abundant, with deer, turkeys, and bears commonly seen. An archery range and nature programs add to the offerings.

☐ 🔖 ♡ **Crawford State Park:** Set in western Colorado, Crawford surrounds a peaceful reservoir ideal for boating, water skiing, and warm-water fishing. The park features lakeside campsites, picnic areas, and wildlife viewing against a backdrop of the West Elk Mountains. It offers easy access to the nearby Black Canyon of the Gunnison for further outdoor adventures.

☐ 🔖 ♡ **Eldorado Canyon State Park:** Located just south of Boulder, Eldorado Canyon is a rock climber's paradise, with towering sandstone walls and world-renowned routes. Visitors also enjoy hiking, picnicking, fishing, and spotting golden eagles. Scenic trails wind through the canyon and connect to Boulder's trail system, making it a favorite day trip for locals.

☐ 🔖 ♡ **Eleven Mile State Park:** Near Lake George, Eleven Mile Reservoir offers excellent trout and pike fishing, sailing, kayaking, and winter ice fishing. Dozens of campsites dot the shoreline, and trails like Black Bear and Lakeview provide scenic hiking and wildlife watching. Its wide-open views and quiet ambiance appeal to anglers and nature lovers alike.

☐ 🔖 ♡ **Elkhead Reservoir State Park:** Located near Craig in northwestern Colorado, this park surrounds a quiet reservoir ideal for fishing, boating, and swimming. Visitors enjoy shaded campsites, birdwatching, and hiking in a peaceful setting. Elkhead offers a relaxed atmosphere with scenic views, especially popular during summer holidays and music festival weekends.

☐ 🔖 ♡ **Fishers Peak State Park:** Colorado's newest state park, located near Trinidad, protects over 19,000 acres including the 9,633-foot Fishers Peak. Still under development, the park offers limited trails and rugged backcountry experiences. It's home to elk, black bears, and cougars, and is a future hub for hiking, climbing, and conservation in southern Colorado.

☐ 🔖 ♡ **Golden Gate Canyon State Park:** Just 30 miles west of Denver, this park offers more than 35 miles of trails through forests, meadows, and aspen groves. It features scenic overlooks, backcountry campsites, yurts, and cabins. Popular for hiking, biking, and snowshoeing, the park's high elevations provide stunning views of the Continental Divide and fall colors.

COLORADO

☐ 🔖 ♡ **Harvey Gap State Park:** Near Rifle, Harvey Gap surrounds a 190-acre lake known for its quiet beauty and excellent fishing. Only wakeless boating is allowed, preserving a peaceful atmosphere for paddleboarding and wildlife watching. The day-use park also offers a swim beach and shaded picnic areas, making it a perfect spot for relaxing with mountain views.

☐ 🔖 ♡ **Highline Lake State Park:** Located near Fruita, Highline Lake offers warm-weather fun with boating, swimming, paddleboarding, and fishing. It's also a gateway for mountain bikers heading to the nearby Kokopelli Trail. Birdwatchers enjoy sightings of herons and eagles. With campgrounds and desert views, it's a favorite for both locals and road-trippers alike.

☐ 🔖 ♡ **Jackson Lake State Park:** Set on Colorado's eastern plains, this park offers a large reservoir popular for boating, jet skiing, and fishing. Sandy beaches and shallow coves attract swimmers and waterfowl alike. Campgrounds, nature trails, and birding hotspots make it a quiet but well-equipped getaway, especially during spring and fall migration seasons.

☐ 🔖 ♡ **James M. Robb – Colorado River State Park:** This unique five-section park spans the Colorado River between Palisade and Fruita. Visitors enjoy kayaking, fishing, biking, and camping at various riverfront sites. The park highlights the Grand Valley's red rock beauty and riparian habitat, with paved trails connecting scenic overlooks and picnic spots.

☐ 🔖 ♡ **John Martin Reservoir State Park:** Known for vast skies and quiet waters, this southeastern Colorado park offers top-tier birdwatching and fishing. The reservoir is ideal for boating and watersports, while nearby trails explore the area's Santa Fe Trail history. With roomy campsites and stargazing potential, it's a peaceful spot off the beaten path.

☐ 🔖 ♡ **Lake Pueblo State Park:** With 60 miles of shoreline, Lake Pueblo is one of Colorado's top water recreation spots. Boaters, anglers, and swimmers flock to the large reservoir, which also supports two marinas and dozens of campsites. Over 30 miles of trails attract hikers and bikers. The high-desert terrain and warm climate allow year-round visits.

☐ 🔖 ♡ **Lathrop State Park:** Colorado's first state park, Lathrop is located near Walsenburg and features two lakes, Martin and Horseshoe, for boating, swimming, and fishing. Framed by the Spanish Peaks, the park offers scenic trails, golf, and diverse campsites. With both motorized and wakeless water areas, it's perfect for families and outdoor recreation in southern Colorado.

☐ 🔖 ♡ **Lory State Park:** West of Fort Collins, Lory offers trails for hiking, mountain biking, and horseback riding through ridges and forests along the foothills. The park provides access to Horsetooth Reservoir and features climbing routes, picnic areas, and wildlife viewing. It's a favorite for locals seeking nature close to the city with dramatic rock outcrops.

☐ 🔖 ♡ **Mancos State Park:** Near Mesa Verde, Mancos State Park offers a quiet forested retreat around Jackson Gulch Reservoir. Visitors enjoy canoeing, fishing, cross-country skiing, and snowshoeing. With scenic campsites, yurts, and mountain views, it's a four-season destination ideal for escaping crowds and exploring Colorado's southwest heritage landscapes.

☐ 🔖 ♡ **Mueller State Park:** This 5,000-acre park near Divide boasts more than 50 miles of trails through rolling meadows, dense forests, and scenic ridgelines. Visitors enjoy camping, horseback riding, snowshoeing, and wildlife watching, especially elk and bears. Mueller offers cabins, campsites, and quiet access to Pikes Peak country with year-round outdoor options.

☐ 🔖 ♡ **Navajo State Park:** Often called the "Lake Powell of Colorado," Navajo Reservoir spans into New Mexico and offers 15,000 acres of water for boating, sailing, and housebarating. The park has marinas, campgrounds, and rental cabins. With excellent fishing, sunny weather, and expansive views, it's a southern Colorado hub for water lovers and weekend getaways.

☐ 🔖 ♡ **North Sterling State Park:** Located in northeastern Colorado, this park surrounds a large reservoir that's popular for boating, swimming, and walleye fishing. It offers shaded campsites, a sandy swim beach, and birdwatching opportunities. The wide-open prairie setting provides spectacular sunrises, quiet trails, and a relaxing atmosphere away from city crowds.

COLORADO

☐ 🔖 ♡ **Pearl Lake State Park:** Tucked in the Routt National Forest near Steamboat Springs, this serene, no-wake lake is surrounded by aspen groves and mountains. Ideal for canoeing, fishing, and paddleboarding, the park offers walk-in campsites and yurts. Pearl Lake is a peaceful, scenic alternative to busier alpine lakes, especially during the golden fall season.

☐ 🔖 ♡ **Rifle Falls State Park:** Known for its iconic 70-foot triple waterfall, Rifle Falls offers lush greenery, trout-filled streams, and limestone caves to explore. It's one of Colorado's most photogenic parks, ideal for hiking, camping, and wildlife viewing. Shaded trails and cool spray from the falls provide a refreshing escape in summer and a magical winter retreat.

☐ 🔖 ♡ **Rifle Gap State Park:** Just north of Rifle Falls, this park centers on a clear, cold-water reservoir ideal for boating, windsurfing, and swimming. Popular with anglers, Rifle Gap is stocked with trout, perch, and northern pike. Campgrounds and day-use areas line the shore, with dramatic views of the surrounding mesas and cliffs enhancing the outdoor experience.

☐ 🔖 ♡ **Roxborough State Park:** This quiet, day-use park southwest of Denver features stunning red sandstone formations, similar to those in Garden of the Gods. Hiking trails wind through prairie and foothills habitats rich in deer, birds, and wildflowers. With no bikes or pets allowed, it maintains a peaceful, natural feel perfect for quiet reflection and photography.

☐ 🔖 ♡ **Spinney Mountain State Park:** Renowned for trophy trout and pike fishing, this high-elevation reservoir near Hartsel is a favorite for anglers and birdwatchers. Only hand-launched, wakeless boats are allowed, preserving the calm, open waters. With wide views of the Collegiate Peaks and Gold Medal waters, it's a peaceful, uncrowded spot for solitude and sport.

☐ 🔖 ♡ **St. Vrain State Park:** Near Longmont, St. Vrain offers a quiet escape with several small ponds perfect for kayaking, fishing, and birdwatching. The park features full-hookup RV campsites, easy walking paths, and wildlife like herons, pelicans, and coyotes. Close to I-25, it's ideal for travelers and families seeking nature without a long drive.

☐ 🔖 ♡ **Stagecoach State Park:** Located near Steamboat Springs, this park surrounds a 780-acre reservoir perfect for fishing, boating, and paddleboarding. It features a beach, scenic trails, and camping, with winter activities like ice fishing and snowshoeing. Wildlife including elk, moose, and eagles are frequently seen in this quiet, scenic corner of northern Colorado.

☐ 🔖 ♡ **State Forest State Park:** Colorado's largest state park, covering 71,000 acres in the Medicine Bow Mountains, offers alpine lakes, meadows, and over 70 miles of trails. It's a premier destination for moose watching and backcountry exploration. Visitors enjoy hiking, fishing, skiing, snowmobiling, and cozying up in cabins or yurts in all four seasons.

☐ 🔖 ♡ **Staunton State Park:** One of Colorado's newest parks, Staunton features granite cliffs, alpine meadows, and cascading waterfalls within an hour of Denver. It offers rock climbing, accessible trails, backcountry huts, and over 30 miles of hiking and biking routes. Its dramatic scenery and diverse terrain make it ideal for day trips and weekend adventures.

☐ 🔖 ♡ **Steamboat Lake State Park:** Located beneath Hahn's Peak, this alpine park is beloved for boating, camping, and snowmobiling. The reservoir supports cold-water fishing, and nearby trails lead through flower-filled meadows and forests. With yurts, cabins, and spectacular views, it's a year-round escape into the beauty of Colorado's northern mountains.

☐ 🔖 ♡ **Sweitzer Lake State Park:** This small, day-use park near Delta surrounds a 137-acre lake ideal for swimming, paddleboarding, and wakeless boating. Open landscapes and shaded picnic shelters make it great for relaxing or hosting gatherings. While there's no camping, the park is popular in summer with locals looking for simple, uncrowded water recreation.

☐ 🔖 ♡ **Sylvan Lake State Park:** Set in a forested valley near Eagle, this alpine lake park offers fishing, canoeing, and non-motorized boating amid lush scenery. Cabins, yurts, and campsites provide lodging year-round. Trails lead into the surrounding wilderness for hiking, wildlife viewing, snowshoeing, and quiet immersion in nature's mountain beauty.

UNITED STATES EDITION

COLORADO

☐ ⛉ ♡ **Trinidad Lake State Park:** Overlooking the historic town of Trinidad, this reservoir park offers hiking trails with mountain views, boating, and fishing. Its campground provides scenic spots for tents and RVs, and the nearby coal mining museum adds historical depth. The park is a relaxing base for exploring southern Colorado's unique culture and nature.

☐ ⛉ ♡ **Vega State Park:** Located on the Grand Mesa near Collbran, Vega offers quiet water recreation with fishing, canoeing, and ice fishing in winter. Campgrounds, cabins, and trails are nestled among aspens and spruce forests. Wildlife like moose and foxes roam nearby. It's a peaceful destination for four-season adventure in Colorado's high country.

☐ ⛉ ♡ **Yampa River State Park:** This linear park follows the Yampa River between Hayden and Dinosaur, offering rafting, fishing, and riverside camping. Multiple access points support day-use and overnight trips, with a visitor center and trails along the river corridor. It's a haven for paddlers, anglers, and birders exploring Colorado's remote northwest.

National Parks

☐ ⛉ ♡ **Bent's Old Fort National Historic Site:** In La Junta, this reconstructed 1840s adobe fort recreates a vital fur trading hub on the Santa Fe Trail. Visitors step into frontier history with costumed interpreters, artifacts, and exhibits showcasing the cultural crossroads where traders, trappers, Native Americans, and settlers once converged in the American West.

☐ ⛉ ♡ **Black Canyon of the Gunnison National Park:** Western Colorado's Black Canyon features sheer cliffs and narrow gorges carved by the Gunnison River. Visitors hike rim trails, peer into dramatic depths, and marvel at ancient rock walls among the steepest in North America. The park offers fishing, rafting, and stargazing in a rugged wilderness setting.

☐ ⛉ ♡ **Colorado National Monument:** Near Grand Junction, this monument showcases towering monoliths, red rock canyons, and desert plateaus. The scenic Rim Rock Drive offers sweeping views, while trails wind past arches, spires, and juniper forests. Wildlife like bighorn sheep thrive here, making it a favorite for hikers, cyclists, and photographers.

☐ ⛉ ♡ **Curecanti National Recreation Area:** Stretching along the Gunnison River, this recreation area features three reservoirs, including Blue Mesa, Colorado's largest. Visitors enjoy boating, swimming, fishing, and camping amid high mesas and dramatic cliffs. Trails lead to overlooks and historic sites, offering a blend of water recreation and mountain scenery.

☐ ⛉ ♡ **Dinosaur National Monument:** Straddling Colorado and Utah, this monument preserves world-class fossil beds where visitors can see dinosaur bones still embedded in rock. Beyond paleontology, the park features rugged canyons, petroglyphs, and rafting on the Yampa and Green Rivers. It's a place where geology, history, and adventure meet.

☐ ⛉ ♡ **Florissant Fossil Beds National Monument:** In central Colorado, ancient volcanic mudflows preserved massive redwood stumps and thousands of insect and plant fossils. Visitors explore trails, exhibits, and paleontology programs that reveal a 34-million-year-old ecosystem. The site highlights Earth's changing climates and Colorado's prehistoric life.

☐ ⛉ ♡ **Great Sand Dunes National Park & Preserve:** Home to the tallest dunes in North America, this park offers a surreal landscape of shifting sand against alpine peaks. Visitors hike, sled, or sandboard the dunes, splash in Medano Creek, and explore surrounding grasslands and forests. It's a dynamic mix of desert and mountain wilderness.

☐ ⛉ ♡ **Hovenweep National Monument:** On the Colorado–Utah border, Hovenweep protects six villages of stone towers built by Ancestral Puebloans. Trails wind past perched dwellings and cliffside structures set amid stark canyons. Visitors learn about the ingenuity and resilience of the ancient culture while experiencing a remote, quiet landscape.

COLORADO

Mesa Verde National Park: A UNESCO World Heritage Site, Mesa Verde preserves over 600 cliff dwellings built by Ancestral Puebloans. Visitors tour Cliff Palace, Balcony House, and other archaeological wonders while learning about centuries of native culture. Scenic overlooks and hiking trails complement the park's cultural significance.

Sand Creek Massacre National Historic Site: In eastern Colorado, this solemn site memorializes the 1864 massacre where U.S. troops killed hundreds of Cheyenne and Arapaho people. Visitors walk interpretive trails, attend ranger talks, and reflect on a tragedy that profoundly shaped Native and U.S. history. It's a place of remembrance and healing.

Rocky Mountain National Park: Encompassing alpine peaks, tundra, and valleys, this park offers 350+ miles of trails, wildlife like elk and bighorn sheep, and jaw-dropping scenery. Trail Ridge Road crosses the Continental Divide at over 12,000 feet. Hiking, camping, fishing, and mountaineering make it one of America's premier mountain parks.

Yucca House National Monument: Near Cortez, this largely unexcavated Ancestral Puebloan site preserves a massive pueblo complex left undisturbed for centuries. With no visitor facilities, it offers a rare opportunity to quietly explore ancient ruins in a natural setting, connecting modern visitors to the enduring legacy of the Pueblo people.

State & National Forests

Arapaho National Forest: Arapaho National Forest spans the central Rockies west of Denver and includes portions of the Continental Divide. Known for alpine lakes, high peaks, and access to the Front Range, it's home to Mount Evans, Berthoud Pass, and the scenic Peak to Peak Byway. Visitors enjoy hiking, skiing, and wildlife watching year-round.

Medicine Bow-Routt National Forest: Stretching into northern Colorado, this forest features rugged peaks, scenic byways, and the Mount Zirkel Wilderness. Popular activities include hiking, snowshoeing, and horseback riding. Its varied ecosystems range from sagebrush foothills to high alpine ridges rich in wildlife.

Colorado State Forest: Colorado's only designated state forest, located in Jackson County, spans over 70,000 acres in the Medicine Bow Mountains. Managed for sustainable forestry and recreation, it overlaps with State Forest State Park. Visitors enjoy hiking, camping, and wildlife viewing - especially moose. It's a rugged, scenic destination known for its alpine terrain and remote beauty.

Pike National Forest: Located southwest of Denver and Colorado Springs, Pike National Forest features iconic peaks like Pikes Peak and rugged wilderness areas such as Lost Creek. It offers scenic drives, rock climbing, hiking, and camping amid granite domes, ponderosa pines, and river canyons. It's a favorite for Front Range outdoor enthusiasts.

Grand Mesa National Forest: Perched atop the world's largest flat-top mountain, Grand Mesa National Forest features more than 300 lakes, alpine forests, and wildflower meadows. Popular for fishing, hiking, and snowmobiling, it offers sweeping views and solitude above the Colorado Plateau. The forest also connects with the Grand Mesa Scenic Byway.

Rio Grande National Forest: Encompassing the San Luis Valley and parts of the San Juan Mountains, Rio Grande National Forest is one of Colorado's most remote and scenic public lands. It includes the headwaters of the Rio Grande River, high alpine basins, and peaks like Mount Blanca. It's a haven for hiking, fishing, and solitude.

Gunnison National Forest: Surrounding the town of Gunnison, this forest features steep canyons, aspen groves, and alpine meadows. It includes parts of the Elk and West Elk Mountains, and iconic spots like the Fossil Ridge Wilderness and Taylor Reservoir. Outdoor lovers find solitude and adventure through hiking, fishing, and cross-country skiing.

Roosevelt National Forest: Bordering Rocky Mountain National Park, Roosevelt National Forest stretches along Colorado's Front Range. It features rugged canyons, scenic overlooks, and dense pine forests. Popular for hiking, camping, and off-roading, it includes parts of the Cache la Poudre River, a designated National Wild and Scenic River.

COLORADO

☐ 🔖 ♡ **Routt National Forest:** Located in northwestern Colorado, Routt National Forest includes the Flat Tops Wilderness and stretches across the Elkhead and Park Ranges. Known for its wide valleys, abundant wildlife, and peaceful lakes, it offers year-round recreation including backcountry skiing, horseback riding, and fly fishing in alpine streams.

☐ 🔖 ♡ **San Isabel National Forest:** This forest contains some of Colorado's highest peaks, including more than a dozen 14ers like Mount Elbert, the state's tallest. With vast aspen forests, alpine lakes, and popular climbing routes, it's a prime destination for hikers and campers. Scenic byways wind through historic mining towns and mountain passes.

☐ 🔖 ♡ **San Juan National Forest:** Nestled in the remote southwestern corner of the state, San Juan National Forest includes dramatic peaks, mesa tops, and deep river gorges. It surrounds Durango and includes parts of the San Juan Skyway and Weminuche Wilderness. Visitors come for hiking, skiing, mountain biking, and stunning fall colors.

☐ 🔖 ♡ **Uncompahgre National Forest:** Part of the Grand Mesa–Uncompahgre–Gunnison (GMUG) complex, this forest stretches across the San Juan Mountains and offers iconic views of dramatic peaks and colorful cliffs. Its landscape supports hiking, off-roading, and fishing, with highlights including the Alpine Loop Scenic Byway and Mount Sneffels Wilderness.

☐ 🔖 ♡ **White River National Forest:** One of the most visited national forests in the U.S., White River surrounds popular ski resorts like Aspen, Vail, and Breckenridge. It includes the Maroon Bells, Flat Tops Wilderness, and parts of the Continental Divide. From wildflower-filled valleys to snowy slopes, it offers four-season adventure in dramatic alpine landscapes.

National Grasslands

☐ 🔖 ♡ **Comanche National Grassland:** Spanning southeastern Colorado, Comanche National Grassland features vast prairies, canyons, and ancient petroglyphs. Rich in cultural and natural history, it was once home to prehistoric peoples and roaming bison. Visitors can explore dinosaur tracks, hike Picketwire Canyonlands, and experience the wide-open beauty of the High Plains ecosystem.

☐ 🔖 ♡ **Pawnee National Grassland:** Nestled in northeastern Colorado, Pawnee National Grassland showcases sweeping shortgrass prairie, dramatic buttes, and seasonal wildflower blooms. A haven for birdwatchers and naturalists, it supports prairie dogs, burrowing owls, and ferruginous hawks. The Pawnee Buttes Trail offers iconic views of this serene and ecologically vital landscape.

National Scenic Byways & All-American Roads

☐ 🔖 ♡ **Colorado River Headwaters Scenic Byway:** Beginning near Grand Lake and tracing the early course of the Colorado River, this route winds through mountain ranchlands, canyon walls and hot springs. Forested slopes and riparian corridors frame the young river as it collects its headwaters, offering fishing, rafting, and dramatic western-Colorado landscapes.

☐ 🔖 ♡ **Dinosaur Diamond Prehistoric Highway:** Looping through northwestern Colorado and into eastern Utah, this byway reveals fossil quarries, dinosaur tracks, red-rock canyons and ancient petroglyphs. Visitors explore deep geologic time, Indigenous heritage and desert walls carved across millennia: a journey where every mile is a story in prehistoric life and dramatic terrain.

☐ 🔖 ♡ **Frontier Pathways Scenic & Historic Byway:** Stretching from Pueblo toward Westcliffe, this route crosses the Wet Mountains, historic ranchlands and mining settlements. Along the way are Spanish missions, frontier-era towns and scenic mountain passes. Wildflower meadows, piñon-juniper slopes and aspen groves frame a corridor steeped in Colorado's pioneer and cultural history.

☐ 🔖 ♡ **Gold Belt Tour Scenic & Historic Byway:** Circling the central Colorado canyons around Cañon City, Victor and Cripple Creek, this byway follows the rugged corridor of Phantom Canyon, Shelf Road and old narrow-gauge rail grades. Historic mining towns, ghost-town relics and canyon walls combine with aspen glades and scenic overlooks for a drive through gold-rush heritage and canyon country.

COLORADO

☐ 🔖 ♡ **Grand Mesa Scenic & Historic Byway:** Ascending from the Grand Valley onto the vast summit of the world's largest flat-top mountain, this route climbs to around 11,000 ft with hundreds of lakes, aspen and pine forests, wildflower meadows and sweeping overlooks. It offers a high-elevation escape across western Colorado's plateau country with unique geological character.

☐ 🔖 ♡ **Lariat Loop Scenic & Historic Byway:** A roughly 40-mile drive west of Denver connecting Golden, Morrison and Evergreen, this loop skirts the foothills and offers scenic views of the plains and mountains. Stops include Red Rocks Amphitheatre, Dinosaur Ridge and historic mountain parks, blending accessible nature, cultural landmarks and Colorado's early recreation history.

☐ 🔖 ♡ **San Juan Skyway Scenic & Historic Byway:** This 236-mile loop through the San Juan Mountains links Durango, Telluride, Silverton, Ouray and back. Towering 14,000-foot peaks, ghost towns, alpine passes, narrow-gauge railroads and Native archaeological sites combine in one of Colorado's most breathtaking and varied drives — a true All-American Road.

☐ 🔖 ♡ **Santa Fe Trail Scenic & Historic Byway:** Traversing southeastern Colorado from Lamar to Trinidad, this historic corridor follows the Santa Fe Trail across rolling prairie, buttes and heritage sites. Interpretive stops highlight frontier trade and migration, buffalo-era plains and Hispanic culture, while expansive skies and open terrain frame the journey across Colorado's historic east.

☐ 🔖 ♡ **Scenic Highway of Legends:** Looping from Trinidad through Cuchara and La Veta to Walsenburg, this route encircles the Spanish Peaks region of southern Colorado. Volcanic dikes, aspen forests, ranching history and coal-mining towns knit together natural drama and cultural stories in a scenic and storied mountain corridor.

☐ 🔖 ♡ **Silver Thread Scenic & Historic Byway:** Running from South Fork through Creede to Lake City, this high-mountain route threads historic silver-mining towns, alpine valleys, waterfalls and high passes in the San Juans. The narrow ribbon of road provides solitude, scenic peaks and a powerful sense of Colorado's mining past and remote wilderness.

☐ 🔖 ♡ **Top of the Rockies Scenic Byway:** Linking Leadville, Twin Lakes and Minturn/Copper Mountain, this elevated route rides above 9,000 ft along the Continental Divide through mining relics, alpine lakes and sweeping mountain ridges. With high altitudes, ghost towns and rich terrain, it's one of Colorado's most dramatic scenic drives.

☐ 🔖 ♡ **Trail of the Ancients Scenic & Historic Byway:** In the southwest corner of Colorado, this route links Mesa Verde, Hovenweep and Canyons of the Ancients through desert mesas, rock art and cliff dwellings. Visitors explore ancient cultural landscapes, archaeological treasures and dramatic canyon scenery in a journey that spans centuries of human and natural history.

☐ 🔖 ♡ **Trail Ridge Road/Beaver Meadow Scenic Byway:** Traversing from Estes Park to Grand Lake through Rocky Mountain National Park, this high-elevation route crosses above timberline with sweeping tundra, snowfields and panoramic ridgelines. At over 12,000 feet, this is the highest continuous paved road in North America — an iconic alpine drive.

State Scenic Byways

☐ 🔖 ♡ **Alpine Loop Scenic Byway:** A rugged 65-mile 4WD route linking Ouray, Silverton, and Lake City through alpine tundra, meadows, and mining ghost towns. Crossing Engineer and Cinnamon Passes above 12,000 feet, it reveals waterfalls, wildflowers, and sweeping San Juan vistas—a true backcountry adventure for skilled drivers.

☐ 🔖 ♡ **Cache la Poudre–North Park Scenic Byway:** Following the Wild & Scenic Poudre River from Fort Collins to Walden, this drive climbs through granite canyons, forests, and alpine meadows. Wildlife is abundant, from moose to raptors, while anglers and hikers enjoy unspoiled wilderness along Colorado's only federally protected river.

☐ 🔖 ♡ **Colorado River Headwaters Scenic Byway:** Beginning near Granby, this byway follows the upper Colorado River past Hot Sulphur Springs and Gore Canyon to State Bridge. It traces the river's first miles from the Continental Divide through ranchlands and canyons, showcasing the lifeblood of Colorado's western landscapes.

☐ 🔖 ♡ **Collegiate Peaks Scenic Byway:** Framed by 14,000-foot summits named for Ivy League schools, this route runs through the Arkansas River Valley. Travelers find rafting, fishing, and trails surrounded by alpine grandeur. Historic towns, hot springs, and mountain panoramas define Colorado's rugged heartland.

COLORADO

☐ 🔖 ♡ **Dinosaur Diamond Scenic & Historic Byway:** Crossing northwest Colorado, this byway unveils red-rock canyons, ancient fossils, and Native petroglyphs. Stops at Dinosaur National Monument and old quarries reveal prehistoric life and stunning desert geology, creating a journey through deep time and dramatic landscapes.

☐ 🔖 ♡ **Flat Tops Trail Scenic Byway:** Linking Meeker and Yampa, this 82-mile high-country drive climbs through volcanic cliffs, alpine lakes, and vast plateaus. With access to the Flat Tops Wilderness, it's a peaceful escape filled with aspen forests, wildlife, and breathtaking views of Colorado's unspoiled western highlands.

☐ 🔖 ♡ **Frontier Pathways Scenic & Historic Byway:** Stretching from Pueblo to Westcliffe, this drive crosses the Wet Mountains through mining towns, missions, and ranches. The byway highlights Spanish and pioneer heritage against the backdrop of the Sangre de Cristo range—a vivid blend of history and mountain scenery.

☐ 🔖 ♡ **Gold Belt Tour Scenic & Historic Byway:** Linking Cañon City, Florence, Cripple Creek, and Victor, this byway follows old stagecoach and railroad routes from Colorado's gold rush era. Rugged canyons, ghost towns, and mining relics line a journey that connects frontier history with striking geologic beauty.

☐ 🔖 ♡ **Grand Mesa Scenic & Historic Byway:** Rising from the Grand Valley to 11,000 feet atop the world's largest flat-top mountain, this route passes lakes, aspen groves, and wildflower meadows. Panoramic overlooks and alpine forests make it a refreshing, high-elevation drive across western Colorado's natural crown.

☐ 🔖 ♡ **Guanella Pass Scenic & Historic Byway:** From Georgetown to Grant, this paved mountain route ascends to 11,669 feet through tundra, glacial basins, and wildflower fields. Views of Mount Bierstadt and Evans accompany moose and marmot sightings, making it a beloved alpine escape close to Denver.

☐ 🔖 ♡ **Highway of Legends Scenic Byway:** Encircling the Spanish Peaks from Trinidad to Walsenburg, this 82-mile loop traverses volcanic dikes, aspen groves, and mountain passes. Along the way, it reveals Native legends, coal mining history, and southern Colorado's rich cultural and geological tapestry.

☐ 🔖 ♡ **Lariat Loop Scenic & Historic Byway:** A 40-mile foothills circuit west of Denver connecting Golden, Morrison, and Evergreen. The route features Red Rocks Amphitheatre, Lookout Mountain, and Dinosaur Ridge, blending early tourism history with mountain views that capture Colorado's front range charm.

☐ 🔖 ♡ **Los Caminos Antiguos Scenic & Historic Byway:** Through the San Luis Valley, this byway highlights Hispanic and Native heritage. Stops include Fort Garland, San Luis, and Great Sand Dunes National Park. Surrounded by the Sangre de Cristos, it blends cultural legacy with stunning open-valley scenery.

☐ 🔖 ♡ **Mount Blue Sky Scenic & Historic Byway:** Formerly Mount Evans, this byway climbs from Idaho Springs to over 14,000 feet—the highest paved road in North America. Passing Echo and Summit Lakes, it reveals tundra, glaciers, and mountain goats amid breathtaking alpine panoramas above the clouds.

☐ 🔖 ♡ **Pawnee Pioneer Trails Scenic Byway:** Crossing Colorado's northeastern plains, this route traverses the Pawnee National Grassland with views of buttes, vast skies, and prairie wildlife. Interpretive stops tell stories of Native peoples and homesteaders who braved this wide-open, windswept landscape.

☐ 🔖 ♡ **Peak to Peak Scenic & Historic Byway:** Colorado's oldest scenic byway runs 55 miles from Black Hawk to Estes Park. It follows the edge of the Continental Divide through mining towns and golden aspen forests, revealing alpine lakes, meadows, and timeless Rocky Mountain beauty at every bend.

☐ 🔖 ♡ **Silver Thread Scenic & Historic Byway:** A 117-mile route connecting Lake City, Creede, and South Fork, this drive follows the Rio Grande through historic mining country. Alpine valleys, waterfalls, and ghost towns tell stories of frontier endurance amid some of Colorado's most breathtaking scenery.

☐ 🔖 ♡ **South Platte River Trail Scenic & Historic Byway:** Near Julesburg, this byway follows the path of pioneers and Pony Express riders. Interpretive signs mark Overland Trail sites along cottonwood-lined riverbanks, where quiet prairie towns preserve the legacy of early travelers heading west.

☐ 🔖 ♡ **Tracks Across Borders Scenic & Historic Byway:** Extending from Durango to New Mexico, this byway crosses Southern Ute lands through mesas and river valleys. It showcases Native, Hispanic, and railroad heritage while offering sweeping Four Corners views across rugged, red-rock terrain.

☐ 🔖 ♡ **Top of the Rockies Scenic & Historic Byway:** Connecting Leadville, Twin Lakes, and Minturn, this byway soars above 10,000 feet with spectacular views of Mount Elbert and Massive. Mining relics, alpine lakes, and glacial valleys line a route that celebrates Colorado's highest and most awe-inspiring peaks.

COLORADO

☐ 🔖 ♡ **Trail of the Ancients Scenic & Historic Byway:** Exploring the southwest corner, this byway links Mesa Verde, Hovenweep, and Canyons of the Ancients. Ancient cliff dwellings, rock art, and desert mesas reveal the enduring legacy of the Ancestral Puebloans amid striking red-rock scenery.

☐ 🔖 ♡ **Unaweep Tabeguache Scenic & Historic Byway:** A 133-mile route from Whitewater to Placerville through canyons, mesas, and forests. The unique double canyon of Unaweep and the red sandstone cliffs create a dramatic landscape blending desert solitude with mountain grandeur.

☐ 🔖 ♡ **West Elk Loop Scenic & Historic Byway:** A 205-mile circuit around the West Elk Mountains connecting Carbondale, Crested Butte, and Paonia. It crosses McClure and Kebler Passes through lush aspen forests, orchards, and ranchlands—showcasing the wild beauty of Colorado's western slope.

National Natural Landmarks

 ☐ 🔖 ♡ **Big Spring Creek:** Flowing from an unconfined aquifer, Big Spring Creek in the San Luis Valley became a National Natural Landmark for its rare spring-fed wetland. In an otherwise arid environment, it sustains lush vegetation, uncommon plants, and wildlife dependent on cool, mineral-rich water, standing out as an oasis in southern Colorado.
GPS: 37.7667, -105.6250

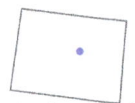 ☐ 🔖 ♡ **Garden of the Gods:** Towering red sandstone spires and tilted hogbacks make Garden of the Gods a National Natural Landmark. Formed during the Laramide orogeny, its rocks reveal millions of years of geologic history. The site also harbors diverse ecosystems and wildlife, blending dramatic natural beauty with rich scientific value.
GPS: 38.8678, -104.8911

 ☐ 🔖 ♡ **Garden Park Fossil Area:** This fossil-rich landscape near Cañon City is a National Natural Landmark for its Jurassic deposits. Dinosaurs like Stegosaurus and Allosaurus were first uncovered here in the 19th century, and new finds continue today. The exposures provide invaluable evidence of ancient ecosystems and the evolution of vertebrate life.
GPS: 38.5350, -105.2217

 ☐ 🔖 ♡ **Hanging Lake:** Perched above Glenwood Canyon, Hanging Lake is a turquoise travertine pool recognized as a National Natural Landmark. Fed by waterfalls, it sustains fragile hanging gardens and showcases delicate limestone deposition. The site offers a rare and beautiful example of a travertine system thriving in a rugged alpine setting.
GPS: 39.6014, -107.1917

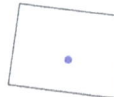 ☐ 🔖 ♡ **Indian Springs Trace Fossil Site:** Preserved within Ordovician rock, Indian Springs is a National Natural Landmark for its abundance of ancient trace fossils. Trackways and burrows capture the movements of early marine life 450 million years ago, offering scientists one of the continent's best records of animal behavior on ancient seafloors.
GPS: 38.3675, -105.4853

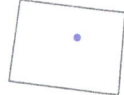 ☐ 🔖 ♡ **Lost Creek Scenic Area:** Hidden in Pike National Forest, Lost Creek Scenic Area became a National Natural Landmark for its unusual granite domes, twisting formations, and disappearing streams. These features illustrate distinctive hydrologic processes, making the landscape a striking example of Colorado's diverse and rugged backcountry geology.
GPS: 39.2686, -105.4681

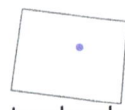 ☐ 🔖 ♡ **Morrison–Golden Fossil Areas:** Along the Front Range, these fossil sites earned National Natural Landmark status for preserving dinosaur tracks and plant remains from the Jurassic and Cretaceous. Their layers also record mountain uplift and erosion, offering a dual record of paleontological treasures and the building of the Rockies.
GPS: 39.6811, -105.1925

 ☐ 🔖 ♡ **Raton Mesa:** Marked by basalt-capped mesas, this dramatic landform was designated a National Natural Landmark for its resistance to erosion and striking geology. Its rugged cliffs and plateaus also sustain rich biodiversity, from elk and bear to mountain lions, making it both a natural refuge and a geological showcase.
GPS: 37.0978, -104.4628

UNITED STATES EDITION

COLORADO

 **Roxborough State Park:** Southwest of Denver, Roxborough is a National Natural Landmark for its spectacular Fountain Formation sandstone. Red rock hogbacks, ancient fossils, and unique plant communities create a living classroom of geology and ecology, where tilted strata meet thriving ecosystems along the Front Range.
GPS: 39.4292, -105.0683

 **Russell Lakes:** In the San Luis Valley, Russell Lakes was named a National Natural Landmark for preserving Colorado's largest bulrush marsh. This wetland supports migratory birds, amphibians, and native vegetation, serving as a critical stopover in an otherwise dry basin and demonstrating the ecological importance of valley wetlands.
GPS: 37.9447, -106.1200

 **Sand Creek:** Straddling the Colorado–Wyoming line, Sand Creek became a National Natural Landmark for its dramatic sandstone cliffs, topple blocks, and fossil-bearing strata. The formations showcase cross-bedded layers and erosion processes, while surrounding habitats support plants and wildlife adapted to this rugged environment.
GPS: 40.9958, -105.7681

 **Slumgullion Earthflow:** This massive landslide near Lake City is one of the best-studied active earthflows in the world and a National Natural Landmark. Ancient and modern flows overlap, altering drainage patterns and forming Lake San Cristobal, giving scientists a natural laboratory for observing mass wasting in real time.
GPS: 37.9986, -107.2450

 **Spanish Peaks:** Rising above southern Colorado, the Spanish Peaks are a National Natural Landmark for their more than 500 exposed radial dikes, dramatic igneous intrusions formed during volcanic activity. They are geologically unique, ecologically diverse, and hold deep cultural significance as landmarks of the American West.
GPS: 37.3756, -104.9936

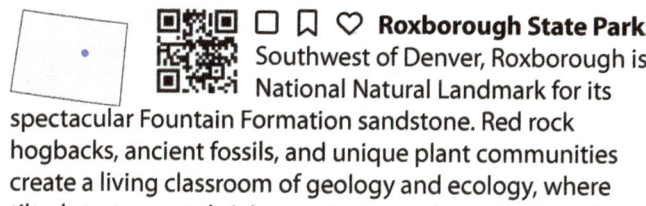 **Sulphur Cave and Spring:** Beneath Steamboat Springs, this unusual cave system holds National Natural Landmark status for its sulfuric acid speleogenesis. Biovermiculations and rare microbial formations thrive here, creating a living example of how chemistry and biology interact underground to shape cave ecosystems.
GPS: 40.4836, -106.8400

 **Summit Lake:** At nearly 13,000 feet on Mount Evans, Summit Lake is a National Natural Landmark for preserving Arctic-like tundra in the lower 48 states. Its glacial basin shelters rare cold-adapted plants and wildlife, demonstrating ecological survival in extreme alpine conditions and making it a vital high-elevation refuge.
GPS: 39.5983, -105.6444

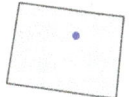 **West Bijou Site:** On Colorado's plains, West Bijou was named a National Natural Landmark for preserving the Cretaceous–Paleogene boundary. Its fossil-rich layers record Earth's last mass extinction, including the asteroid impact that ended the dinosaurs, making it a globally significant reference site for geologic and paleontological research.
GPS: 39.6811, -104.7358

Connecticut

Connecticut's natural charm lies in its wooded hills, scenic rivers, coastal marshes, and peaceful lakes. With an inviting mix of state parks, forests, national scenic trails, and distinctive landmarks, the state offers serene outdoor escapes, from quiet shoreline walks to winding woodland hikes and historic landscapes.

📅 Peak Season
May–October is Connecticut's peak season, with warm weather, lush greenery, and vibrant fall foliage. Summer brings the busiest crowds along the shoreline and lakes, while autumn draws visitors for its colorful landscapes.

📅 Offseason Months
November–April is the offseason, with colder weather, snow in the interior, and quieter coastal towns. Winter offers opportunities for skiing and cozy retreats, but overall visitation is lighter outside the holidays.

🍃 Scenery & Nature Timing
Spring brings blooming dogwoods and cherry blossoms, especially in parks and historic towns. Summer highlights sandy beaches and wooded trails. Fall is celebrated for brilliant foliage in the Litchfield Hills, while winter creates snowy countryside and frozen lakes.

✨ Special
Connecticut features rugged Appalachian ridges, the scenic Connecticut River Valley, and Long Island Sound's coastal shores. The Thimble Islands dot the southern coast, while waterfalls, rolling hills, and forested state parks add to the state's natural variety.

CONNECTICUT

State Parks

☐ 🔖 ♡ **Above All State Park:** Located in Warren, this 31-acre undeveloped park preserves the wooded summit of a Cold War–era radar site. Visitors find remnants of the former SAGE installation, including foundations and pads, but no formal trails or facilities. The quiet forest setting offers solitude, birdwatching, and a glimpse into military history amid the scenic Litchfield Hills.

☐ 🔖 ♡ **Auerfarm State Park Scenic Reserve:** A 40-acre reserve in Bloomfield, this former farm offers meadows, woodlands, and a pond used for outdoor education and community programs. Ideal for birdwatching, walking, or quiet reflection, it preserves Connecticut's agricultural past while providing an accessible green space for schools, families, and nature lovers.

☐ 🔖 ♡ **Beaver Brook State Park:** Encompassing 401 acres in Chaplin and Windham, this park surrounds Bibbins Pond and Beaver Brook. Visitors enjoy canoeing, fishing, hiking, and picnicking along peaceful wooded paths. Trails connect to the Air Line State Park Trail, offering extended exploration through Connecticut's eastern forests and wetlands.

☐ 🔖 ♡ **Becket Hill State Park Reserve:** This 260-acre undeveloped reserve in Lyme borders Nehantic State Forest and surrounds Uncas Pond. Popular for hiking, birding, and paddling, it offers solitude and rustic charm. Its quiet forest trails and pond access make it an ideal retreat for those seeking a backcountry experience in eastern Connecticut.

☐ 🔖 ♡ **Bennett's Pond State Park:** At 460 acres straddling Ridgefield and Danbury, this park surrounds scenic Bennett's Pond. Visitors can fish, boat, hike woodland trails, or enjoy a picnic. Once part of a private estate, the park blends open water, forest, and shoreline into a relaxing natural destination serving greater Fairfield County.

☐ 🔖 ♡ **Bigelow Hollow State Park:** Situated in Union, this 516-acre park features Bigelow Pond and access to the larger Mashapaug Lake. Surrounded by Nipmuck State Forest, it offers boating, fishing, picnicking, and miles of forest trails that lead to quiet ponds and wetlands. With no designated swim beach, it remains a wild, scenic retreat for hiking, paddling, and exploring northeastern Connecticut.

☐ 🔖 ♡ **Black Rock State Park:** This 444-acre park in Watertown features Black Rock Pond, rugged cliffs, and scenic overlooks. Swimming, fishing, camping, and hiking on the Mattatuck Trail draw visitors. With its mix of woodland and dramatic landscapes, the park is a top choice for those seeking both recreation and natural beauty.

☐ 🔖 ♡ **Bluff Point State Park:** A coastal preserve in Groton, this 806-acre peninsula includes hiking and bridle trails, salt marshes, beach access, and a boat launch. Birdwatchers flock to its tidal habitats, while anglers and paddlers enjoy Long Island Sound. Its combination of shoreline and forest makes it one of Connecticut's most diverse natural areas.

☐ 🔖 ♡ **Bolton Notch State Park:** This 95-acre preserve in Bolton is famed for traprock cliffs, caves, and dramatic ledges. Trails explore rugged outcrops and connect directly to the Hop River State Park Trail, part of the regional greenway. With picnic areas and wooded corridors, the park offers striking geology and an accessible escape into nature near Hartford.

☐ 🔖 ♡ **Brainard Homestead State Park:** This 25-acre undeveloped preserve in East Haddam protects meadow and forestland surrounding the historic Brainard homestead. Visitors can walk informal trails, observe wildlife, and enjoy the quiet atmosphere. With its rustic charm and ties to local history, it offers a peaceful escape in the lower Connecticut River Valley.

☐ 🔖 ♡ **Burr Pond State Park:** In Torrington, this 438-acre park centers on Burr Pond, created in the 1800s by damming local streams. It features a sandy beach for swimming, a boat launch, and wooded trails that link to Sunnybrook and Paugnut State Parks. Anglers, paddlers, and picnickers enjoy its calm waters and shady groves, making it a family-friendly hub for summer recreation in Litchfield County.

☐ 🔖 ♡ **Camp Columbia State Park:** In Morris, this 600-acre site was once Columbia University's engineering camp. Today it's an undeveloped park with hiking, hunting, and wildlife viewing, plus remnants like the stone observation tower recalling its academic past. With forested ridges, quiet trails, and historic intrigue, it's a rustic destination blending history and back-to-nature exploration.

CONNECTICUT

☐ 🔖 ♡ **Campbell Falls State Park:** On the Massachusetts border in Norfolk, this scenic park features a 50-foot waterfall surrounded by dense woods. Short hiking trails lead to the falls, making it an ideal destination for photography, picnicking, and tranquil walks. Its remote setting and natural beauty make it a hidden treasure in Connecticut's northwest hills.

☐ 🔖 ♡ **Chatfield Hollow State Park:** Located in Killingworth, this park offers rugged trails, a swimming pond, trout fishing, and wooden bridges across rocky gorges. Visitors enjoy Native American rock shelters, a covered bridge, and a small nature center. Its blend of natural features and cultural history makes it one of Connecticut's most scenic inland parks.

☐ 🔖 ♡ **Collis P. Huntington State Park:** Spanning over 1,000 acres in Redding, this park is known for its forested trails, fishing ponds, and horseback riding paths. Near the entrance, granite sculptures by artist Anna Hyatt Huntington add artistic flair. With hiking, biking, and wildlife viewing, it's a diverse year-round destination for outdoor enthusiasts.

☐ 🔖 ♡ **Connecticut Valley Railroad State Park:** In Essex, this heritage park preserves part of the historic Valley Railroad. Visitors can ride vintage trains along the Connecticut River, enjoy scenic views, or picnic by the tracks. It's a unique blend of history and recreation, offering a window into the state's 19th-century transportation era.

☐ 🔖 ♡ **Dart Island State Park:** This undeveloped island in the Connecticut River near Middletown is accessible only by boat. It provides paddlers with a peaceful retreat for fishing, picnicking, and wildlife observation. With no facilities, the park offers solitude and a chance to experience the river's ecosystems up close.

☐ 🔖 ♡ **Day Pond State Park:** A small but charming park in Colchester, Day Pond features a swimming beach, picnic areas, and trails through surrounding woodlands. Anglers enjoy fishing in the pond, while hikers connect to Salmon River State Forest trails leading to waterfalls and scenic overlooks. It's a popular family spot with four-season appeal.

☐ 🔖 ♡ **Dennis Hill State Park:** Perched at 1,620 feet in Norfolk, this 240-acre park features a stone pavilion and sweeping vistas of the Litchfield Hills. Once a private estate, it now offers hiking, picnicking, and some of the state's best fall foliage views. Its hilltop location makes it a peaceful yet dramatic retreat.

☐ 🔖 ♡ **Devil's Hopyard State Park:** Located in East Haddam, this 860-acre park is home to Chapman Falls, a striking 60-foot cascade. Trails wind through forest and over wooden bridges, while fishing and picnicking add to the appeal. Unique pothole rock formations give the park its curious name, making it a geological and scenic highlight.

☐ 🔖 ♡ **Dinosaur State Park:** In Rocky Hill, this park preserves one of the largest dinosaur track sites in North America, with more than 500 Jurassic-era footprints displayed beneath a geodesic dome. Visitors can explore educational exhibits, walk nature trails, picnic outdoors, and let children enjoy discovery activities. It's a unique destination blending science, history, and family recreation.

☐ 🔖 ♡ **Eagle Landing State Park:** Found in Haddam, this riverside park offers a boat launch, picnic spots, and sweeping views of the Connecticut River. Known as a bald eagle watching hotspot, especially in winter, it's also popular for kayaking, fishing, and photography. With its open riverfront setting and peaceful atmosphere, it's a perfect escape for wildlife and nature lovers.

☐ 🔖 ♡ **Farm River State Park:** This 62-acre coastal preserve in East Haven provides tidal wetlands, forest trails, and access to the Farm River. Visitors can paddle, fish, or hike short paths through woodlands that open to scenic overlooks. Birdwatching is excellent, and the park's peaceful mix of shoreline and quiet forest provides an accessible natural retreat near urban areas.

☐ 🔖 ♡ **Fort Griswold Battlefield State Park:** Located in Groton, this historic Revolutionary War site preserves the earthworks of a colonial fort and a monument honoring soldiers lost in the 1781 battle. Visitors can climb the granite monument tower for views of the Thames River, walk the grounds, and learn about Connecticut's role in early American history. It's both educational and reflective.

☐ 🔖 ♡ **Fort Trumbull State Park:** This restored 19th-century coastal fort in New London offers exhibits and guided tours on military history, from colonial defenses to World War II. Its grassy ramparts provide sweeping harbor views, while a scenic waterfront walkway and fishing pier attract visitors. The blend of history, architecture, and shoreline access creates a distinctive park experience.

CONNECTICUT

Gardner Lake State Park: In Salem, this 10-acre waterfront park provides public access to the 529-acre Gardner Lake. A sandy beach, picnic grove, and boat launch make it a family favorite for summer swimming, fishing, and paddling. The lake's clear waters, scenic surroundings, and laid-back atmosphere create an inviting spot for recreation and relaxation in southeastern Connecticut.

Gay City State Park: Spanning 1,500 acres in Hebron, this park features forested trails, a pond for swimming and fishing, and the stone remains of a 19th-century mill town. Visitors can hike, bike, picnic, or explore the ruins of historic foundations. Combining natural beauty with cultural intrigue, the park offers outdoor adventure with a fascinating glimpse into the past.

George Dudley Seymour State Park: Situated near Haddam, this undeveloped preserve protects forest, meadow, and riverfront along the Connecticut River. Visitors hike or birdwatch along informal trails with scenic overlooks. With no facilities, it appeals to those seeking solitude and quiet immersion in nature. The park highlights Connecticut's natural heritage while providing peaceful escape.

George Waldo State Park: This rugged, 150-acre preserve in Southbury offers forested trails and access to Lake Lillinonah. Visitors enjoy hiking, horseback riding, mountain biking, and fishing or paddling from the shoreline. With limited development, it provides quiet outdoor recreation and scenic lake views. The park's rustic character makes it a favorite for those seeking solitude.

Gillette Castle State Park: Located in East Haddam, this whimsical stone mansion built by actor William Gillette overlooks the Connecticut River. Visitors tour the medieval-inspired home, hike trails with dramatic vistas, and picnic on terraced grounds. The park blends architecture, theater history, and natural beauty, creating one of the state's most iconic and distinctive attractions.

Haddam Island State Park: Accessible only by boat, this forested island in the Connecticut River offers primitive camping, fishing, and birdwatching. With no facilities or development, it provides a back-to-basics wilderness experience. Its seclusion and wildlife habitat make it ideal for paddlers seeking a quiet destination surrounded by river scenery and natural beauty.

Haddam Meadows State Park: Located on the Connecticut River, this open, grassy park offers picnic areas, a boat launch, and riverside trails. Visitors come for kayaking, fishing, birdwatching, and relaxing by the water. The meadows provide panoramic views, making the park a popular and accessible riverside retreat with plenty of space for simple outdoor recreation.

Haley Farm State Park: In Groton, this 200-acre coastal park preserves rolling fields, stone walls, and remnants of a colonial farm. Its bike and walking trails connect to Bluff Point, creating a popular route for cyclists, walkers, and birdwatchers. With its mix of history, open meadows, and tidal estuary views, it's a peaceful place for outdoor exploration.

Hammonasset Beach State Park: Connecticut's largest shoreline park, in Madison, offers more than two miles of sandy beach along Long Island Sound. Families enjoy swimming, sunbathing, camping, hiking, and visiting the Meigs Point Nature Center. With boardwalks, ample facilities, and wide open shores, it's the state's most visited park and a centerpiece for summer recreation.

Harkness Memorial State Park: Located in Waterford, this elegant estate features the grand Eolia mansion, formal gardens, and sweeping lawns overlooking Long Island Sound. Visitors stroll through manicured grounds, picnic under shade trees, and admire waterfront views. Often used for weddings and events, the park is both scenic and historic, blending natural beauty with cultural heritage.

Haystack Mountain State Park: Found in Norfolk, this park's summit stone tower provides panoramic views of the northwest hills and Berkshires. A steep but short trail climbs through hardwood forest to the tower, popular for foliage hikes in autumn. With picnic areas and scenic landscapes, the park offers a satisfying mix of outdoor recreation and striking vistas.

Higganum Reservoir State Park: Located in Haddam, this small, undeveloped preserve protects forested shoreline around the reservoir. Anglers fish in its quiet waters, while birdwatchers and walkers enjoy a tranquil, natural setting. With no developed facilities, the park remains peaceful and rustic, offering a low-key outdoor experience close to the village of Higganum.

CONNECTICUT

☐ 🔖 ♡ **Hop River State Park Trail:** This 20-mile linear park follows a former rail line through Columbia, Coventry, Bolton, and beyond. Its multi-use path supports hiking, biking, and horseback riding, with bridges, streams, and wooded scenery along the way. As part of the East Coast Greenway, it links communities while offering a quiet, scenic outdoor corridor.

☐ 🔖 ♡ **Hopemead State Park:** A 60-acre undeveloped preserve in Bozrah, this park borders Gardner Lake and offers hiking, fishing, and birdwatching. Trails lead through woodlands and open to the shoreline. With no amenities, it's valued for its quiet, natural setting. Its combination of lake access and rustic forest trails makes it a hidden gem for peaceful outdoor activity.

☐ 🔖 ♡ **Hopeville Pond State Park:** Located in Griswold, this 544-acre park surrounds Hopeville Pond, where visitors swim, boat, and fish. A sandy beach, shaded picnic groves, and family campground draw summer crowds. Trails explore the forest and connect to the larger Pachaug State Forest. It's a versatile destination combining water recreation with classic woodland camping.

☐ 🔖 ♡ **Horse Guard State Park Reserve:** Situated in Avon, this rugged, undeveloped preserve protects a forested ridgeline along the Metacomet Trail. It honors the legacy of the Governor's Horse Guard with its name. Though it has no facilities, hikers enjoy scenic overlooks, birdwatching, and solitude. Its natural beauty and historical ties create a quiet but meaningful destination.

☐ 🔖 ♡ **Housatonic Meadows State Park:** In Sharon, this riverside park offers camping, fly-fishing, and canoeing along the Housatonic River. Forested campsites nestle near the water, while trails climb to ridgeline views. A favorite in autumn for brilliant foliage, it attracts anglers, hikers, and families seeking a peaceful outdoor retreat in the northwest hills.

☐ 🔖 ♡ **Humaston Brook State Park:** Found in Litchfield, this undeveloped park preserves woodlands and a namesake brook. With no formal trails or amenities, it caters to birdwatchers, explorers, and those seeking solitude. Its off-the-beaten-path character provides a natural sanctuary for quiet reflection and low-impact recreation amid rural Litchfield County.

☐ 🔖 ♡ **Hurd State Park:** Located in East Hampton along the Connecticut River, this park offers picnic areas, hiking trails, and a boat launch. Its wooded terrain and dramatic river views provide a peaceful backdrop for paddling, fishing, or simply relaxing outdoors. Seasonal wildflowers and abundant wildlife enhance the experience, making it a scenic riverside destination.

☐ 🔖 ♡ **Indian Well State Park:** In Shelton, this popular park is named for its striking waterfall, which plunges into a shaded pool. Set along the Housatonic River, it also offers swimming at a sandy beach, picnicking, and hiking forested trails. Its mix of dramatic natural features and family-friendly amenities makes it a favorite summer gathering spot.

☐ 🔖 ♡ **John A. Minetto State Park:** Spanning Torrington and Goshen, this quiet park surrounds a small reservoir. Visitors enjoy fishing, picnicking, hiking open fields, and relaxing in shaded groves. Formerly known as Hall Meadow, the park provides a low-key natural escape with scenic views of the Litchfield Hills and abundant wildlife.

☐ 🔖 ♡ **Kent Falls State Park:** A jewel of northwestern Connecticut, this park features a spectacular series of cascading waterfalls dropping nearly 250 feet. A stair trail climbs beside the falls, with viewing platforms offering dramatic perspectives. Picnic areas at the base and easy accessibility make it a favorite for families, photographers, and nature lovers year-round.

☐ 🔖 ♡ **Kettletown State Park:** Located in Southbury along Lake Zoar, this 605-acre park offers camping, hiking, swimming, and boating. Trails wind through wooded hillsides with scenic overlooks, while the campground provides a peaceful retreat near the water. Its combination of shoreline and forested terrain creates a balanced destination for both day-trippers and campers.

☐ 🔖 ♡ **Killingly Pond State Park:** Straddling the Connecticut–Rhode Island border, this 162-acre park provides access to a 122-acre pond. Visitors enjoy boating, fishing, and swimming in the clear waters, with a boat launch and picnic spots available. Surrounded by woodlands and quiet shoreline, it's a laid-back park for water-based recreation and peaceful outdoor escapes.

UNITED STATES EDITION

CONNECTICUT

☐ ◫ ♡ **Lake Waramaug State Park:** In Kent, this scenic park borders part of Lake Waramaug, considered one of Connecticut's most beautiful natural lakes. It offers swimming, camping, fishing, and canoeing, with shaded picnic areas nearby. Surrounded by hills and vineyards, the lake's picturesque charm makes it a sought-after destination for summer vacations and autumn foliage trips.

☐ ◫ ♡ **Lamentation Mountain State Park:** An undeveloped preserve in Berlin and Meriden, this rocky ridgeline offers sweeping views of the Quinnipiac Valley. The Mattabesett Trail crosses its slopes, making it a destination for hikers seeking challenging terrain and panoramic vistas. Its rugged setting and seasonal wildflowers attract those who prefer solitude in nature.

☐ ◫ ♡ **Lover's Leap State Park:** Located in New Milford, this park features dramatic cliffs above the Housatonic River and a historic 19th-century iron bridge. Trails pass Native American cultural sites and forested slopes with scenic overlooks. Steeped in legend and natural beauty, the park offers both romantic lore and striking views, making it a popular hiking spot.

☐ ◫ ♡ **Macedonia Brook State Park:** Nestled in Kent's rugged hills, this 2,300-acre park offers steep Blue-Blazed trails with sweeping views of the Catskills and Taconic ranges. A clear brook winds through forests and rocky ridges, ideal for fishing and quiet picnics. With a seasonal campground and challenging hikes, it's a top choice for outdoor adventurers in northwestern Connecticut.

☐ ◫ ♡ **Machimoodus State Park:** In East Haddam, this 300-acre park overlooks the Salmon and Moodus Rivers. Trails pass through open fields, woodlands, and ridgelines with sweeping river views. Once the site of a summer resort, it's now a quiet preserve for birdwatching, hiking, and fishing. Seasonal wildflowers and abundant wildlife make it a peaceful natural retreat year-round.

☐ ◫ ♡ **Mansfield Hollow State Park:** Surrounding Mansfield Hollow Lake, this 2,300-acre park offers boating, kayaking, and fishing along scenic shorelines. Trails wind through wetlands and forests, making it ideal for hiking, biking, and wildlife watching. With open fields, shaded picnic areas, and broad lake views, it's a family-friendly spot with plenty of outdoor variety.

☐ ◫ ♡ **Mashamoquet Brook State Park:** Located in Pomfret, this historic park features the Wolf Den, where Israel Putnam is said to have slain Connecticut's last wolf. Trails explore woodlands, streams, and cultural landmarks like Indian Chair. With camping, fishing, and picnicking, it's a blend of history and natural beauty, offering both educational and recreational opportunities.

☐ ◫ ♡ **Millers Pond State Park:** Straddling Durham and Haddam, this 30-acre pond is surrounded by forested land, creating a quiet setting for fishing, kayaking, and hiking. The clear waters and undeveloped shoreline attract those seeking peace away from busier parks. Trails link to Cockaponset State Forest, extending opportunities for exploration in a rustic landscape.

☐ ◫ ♡ **Minnie Island State Park:** Connecticut's smallest state park, this tiny island sits in Gardner Lake between Salem and Montville. Accessible only by boat, it offers rustic picnicking, paddling, and swimming. The wooded island provides a quirky, memorable day-trip destination. With its novelty status and scenic location, it's a favorite stop for adventurous visitors.

☐ ◫ ♡ **Mohawk Mountain State Park:** Located in Cornwall, this rugged park features ridgeline trails, Lookout Point, and links to the Appalachian Trail. Visitors hike, picnic, or explore old forest roads through hardwood stands. In winter, its proximity to Mohawk Mountain Ski Area makes it popular year-round. Panoramic views reward hikers across the northwest highlands.

☐ ◫ ♡ **Moosup Valley State Park Trail:** Running through Plainfield and Sterling to the Rhode Island border, this linear trail follows a historic rail corridor. Ideal for hiking, biking, and horseback riding, it connects to the East Coast Greenway. Shaded woods, streams, and quiet rural scenery line the route, making it a peaceful place for recreation and exploration.

☐ ◫ ♡ **Mooween State Park:** In Lebanon, this park surrounds Red Cedar Lake, offering fishing, paddling, and hiking. Once a boys' summer camp, remnants of rustic structures remain. The lake's clear waters and forested trails provide tranquility, while its quiet setting appeals to families and birdwatchers. It's a peaceful destination for those seeking a low-key outdoor escape.

CONNECTICUT

☐ ▯ ♡ **Mount Bushnell State Park:** This 214-acre undeveloped park in Washington is mostly forested ridgeline above Lake Waramaug. With no facilities, it offers hiking, birdwatching, and solitude for those who enjoy backcountry experiences. Its rugged terrain and high vantage points provide sweeping views of the lake and surrounding hills, rewarding those who make the climb.

☐ ▯ ♡ **Mount Riga State Park:** Located in Salisbury, this 276-acre park offers a gateway to some of Connecticut's most rugged hiking, including access to the Appalachian Trail and nearby Bear Mountain. Known for its scenic wilderness, it's popular with backpackers, birdwatchers, and serious hikers. Its forested slopes and sweeping vistas highlight the northwest corner's wild beauty.

☐ ▯ ♡ **Mount Tom State Park:** Near Litchfield, this 231-acre park features Mount Tom Pond for swimming, fishing, and paddling. A short but steep hike leads to a historic stone observation tower with panoramic views of surrounding countryside. Picnic areas and a sandy beach make it a family favorite, especially during summer and fall foliage seasons.

☐ ▯ ♡ **Old Furnace State Park:** In Killingly, this rugged park features forest trails, rocky cliffs, and the remains of an old iron furnace. A steep hike rewards visitors with sweeping views from Ross Cliffs, particularly striking in fall. Fishing, hiking, and exploring make it a favorite for outdoor enthusiasts seeking a mix of history and nature.

☐ ▯ ♡ **Osbornedale State Park:** Situated in Derby, this 417-acre park offers wooded trails, meadows, and fishing at Pickett's Pond. Visitors enjoy picnicking, wildlife observation, and exploring the historic Osborne Homestead Museum nearby. With its blend of natural beauty and cultural heritage, it provides a relaxing green space in the Naugatuck Valley.

☐ ▯ ♡ **Penwood State Park:** In Bloomfield, this 787-acre park lies along Talcott Mountain Ridge. Donated by Curtis Veeder, it features forested trails, a section of the Metacomet Trail, and scenic overlooks of the Farmington Valley. Ideal for hiking, biking, and birding, its ridgeline paths and connections to Talcott Mountain State Park provide dramatic vistas.

☐ ▯ ♡ **Platt Hill State Park:** Located in Winchester, this small, undeveloped park features grassy meadows and wooded ridgelines with scenic views. Visitors enjoy hiking, birdwatching, and quiet picnics in its open spaces. With no formal facilities, it appeals to those seeking solitude, stargazing, or simply a peaceful connection with Connecticut's backcountry landscapes.

☐ ▯ ♡ **Pomeroy State Park:** This undeveloped preserve in Lebanon is a peaceful retreat for hiking, birdwatching, and quiet exploration. With no facilities or marked trails, it maintains a rustic, natural atmosphere. Visitors seeking solitude will appreciate its forested landscape and simple charm, making it a reminder of Connecticut's preserved wild spaces.

☐ ▯ ♡ **Putnam Memorial State Park:** Connecticut's oldest state park, located in Redding, commemorates General Israel Putnam's 1778–79 winter encampment. Visitors explore preserved foundations, reconstructed log huts, a museum, and interpretive trails. The wooded battlefield landscape offers history alongside outdoor recreation, creating a rich blend of cultural heritage and natural beauty.

☐ ▯ ♡ **Quaddick State Park:** In Thompson, this 116-acre park lies along the 407-acre Quaddick Reservoir. It offers a sandy swimming beach, picnic groves, and a boat launch for fishing and boating. Surrounded by pine and hardwood forests, it's a popular family spot for water recreation and nature observation. Its balance of facilities and forest makes it versatile and inviting.

☐ ▯ ♡ **Quinebaug Lake State Park:** In Killingly, this 181-acre park centers on an 88-acre spring-fed lake with exceptionally clear waters. Popular for fishing, kayaking, and canoeing, it provides a peaceful setting with a boat launch and limited shoreline facilities. Surrounded by quiet forest, it's ideal for paddlers and anglers seeking a serene, undeveloped retreat.

☐ ▯ ♡ **Quinnipiac River State Park:** Located in North Haven, this 323-acre preserve protects valuable floodplain forests and wetlands along the Quinnipiac River. Birdwatchers and kayakers enjoy exploring the diverse habitats, while trails provide opportunities for hiking and wildlife observation. With minimal development, it serves as an important natural buffer and quiet riverside escape.

CONNECTICUT

☐ 🔖 ♡ **River Highlands State Park:** In Cromwell, this 177-acre bluff-top park features forested trails, scenic overlooks, and picnic areas high above the Connecticut River. Known for its dramatic "bluff point" views, it offers a mix of hiking, birdwatching, and peaceful riverside scenery. Its elevated vantage points make it a rewarding destination for nature enthusiasts.

☐ 🔖 ♡ **Rocky Glen State Park:** A small, undeveloped preserve in Newtown, this park protects forested land along the Pootatuck River. With no amenities, it offers a rustic experience for hiking, birding, and quiet reflection. Its river corridor provides important habitat, making it a hidden natural gem for those seeking solitude in western Connecticut.

☐ 🔖 ♡ **Rocky Neck State Park:** Found in East Lyme, this 710-acre coastal park combines sandy beaches, tidal marshes, and wooded trails. Visitors enjoy swimming, camping, and picnicking, while boardwalks provide access to diverse habitats. Its stone beach pavilion and abundant wildlife make it one of the most popular and family-friendly shoreline destinations in the state.

☐ 🔖 ♡ **Ross Pond State Park:** Located in Killingly, this quiet park offers a boat launch, fishing on Ross Pond, and wooded trails that connect to Old Furnace State Park. Visitors can hike, paddle, or enjoy a picnic in a peaceful forest setting. With its low-key atmosphere and natural character, it's a great destination for solitude and outdoor relaxation.

☐ 🔖 ♡ **Scantic River State Park:** Spread across Enfield, East Windsor, and Somers, this park preserves sections of the Scantic River corridor. It offers fishing, paddling, and hiking trails through meadows and forested floodplains. With multiple access points, it provides a variety of quiet outdoor activities. Its mix of water and woodland habitats makes it a diverse, under-the-radar destination.

☐ 🔖 ♡ **Selden Neck State Park:** Accessible only by boat, this 607-acre island in the Connecticut River offers a wilderness setting with hiking trails, primitive campsites, and abundant wildlife. The park also contains remnants of a historic granite quarry. With its remote charm and scenic views, it's a favorite for paddlers, campers, and adventurers seeking backcountry solitude.

☐ 🔖 ♡ **Seth Low Pierrepont State Park Reserve:** In Ridgefield, this 305-acre reserve surrounds Pierrepont Lake and features hiking trails, fishing, and kayaking opportunities. Trails loop around the lake and climb forested ridges to overlooks. With its diverse habitats and quiet atmosphere, it's a versatile destination for year-round recreation, nature study, and scenic relaxation.

☐ 🔖 ♡ **Sherwood Island State Park:** Connecticut's first state park, located in Westport, features sandy beaches, salt marshes, and grassy picnic areas along Long Island Sound. Visitors swim, fish, and explore trails with coastal views. The 9/11 Living Memorial offers a tranquil overlook. With ample facilities and broad appeal, it's both recreational and reflective.

☐ 🔖 ♡ **Silver Sands State Park:** In Milford, this shoreline park offers a long sandy beach, dunes, tidal marshes, and a boardwalk to Walnut Beach. Charles Island, accessible by a sandbar at low tide, adds adventure and history. Swimming, birdwatching, and walking make it a favorite for families and nature enthusiasts. Its varied habitats support abundant wildlife.

☐ 🔖 ♡ **Sleeping Giant State Park:** In Hamden, this iconic 1,465-acre park is named for the traprock ridge resembling a giant at rest. Popular trails climb to a stone observation tower, offering sweeping views of the Quinnipiac Valley. With cliffs, woodlands, and panoramic vistas, it's one of Connecticut's most beloved hiking destinations and a symbol of local outdoor culture.

☐ 🔖 ♡ **Southford Falls State Park:** In Southbury, this scenic park is known for its waterfalls, covered bridge, and trout stream. Hiking trails loop through woodlands and past cascading falls, while picnic areas provide relaxing spots near the water. Anglers enjoy stocked fishing areas, and seasonal wildflowers and foliage add color to its natural charm.

☐ 🔖 ♡ **Squantz Pond State Park:** Located in New Fairfield, this park borders Candlewood Lake and features a sandy beach, boat launch, and picnic areas. Hiking trails climb steep terrain, offering dramatic views of wooded hills. It's especially popular for swimming, boating, and fall foliage hikes. Its scenic waters and rugged terrain make it a year-round favorite.

CONNECTICUT

☐ ▢ ♡ **Stillwater Pond State Park:** Located in Torrington, this small but scenic park surrounds Stillwater Pond, offering boating, fishing, and quiet picnicking. A boat launch provides easy access, while the tranquil waters attract paddlers and anglers. Surrounded by forested hillsides, the park's peaceful atmosphere and lack of development make it a relaxing natural retreat.

☐ ▢ ♡ **Stoddard Hill State Park:** A riverside park in Ledyard, it includes tidal access to the Thames River, a boat launch, and a trail to a hilltop overlook. Visitors enjoy fishing, paddling, and hiking through wooded uplands. With its blend of shoreline and forest, it offers quiet recreation and panoramic river views away from busy coastal areas.

☐ ▢ ♡ **Stratton Brook State Park:** Located in Simsbury, this park offers a pond with a sandy swimming area, fishing, picnic facilities, and shaded trails. A covered bridge and scenic boardwalk add charm. Wheelchair-accessible amenities make it welcoming to all visitors. In winter, the flat terrain is popular for cross-country skiing, adding four-season appeal.

☐ ▢ ♡ **Sunnybrook State Park:** Found in Torrington, this tranquil park offers hiking along the East Branch of the Naugatuck River, fishing access, and picnic groves. Trails connect to Paugnut State Forest and the John Muir Trail. Its undeveloped feel, wooded riverbanks, and quiet scenery provide a relaxing retreat for nature lovers seeking low-key recreation.

☐ ▢ ♡ **Sunrise State Park:** In East Haddam, this 143-acre property was once a resort, now returned to nature. Visitors can explore open fields, wooded trails, and river access along the Moodus. It's a quiet destination for birdwatching, fishing, and walking. With its mix of history and natural character, it provides a peaceful outdoor setting with rustic charm.

☐ ▢ ♡ **Talcott Mountain State Park:** In Simsbury, this ridgeline park is crowned by the historic Heublein Tower, accessible via a steep but rewarding hike. From the summit, visitors enjoy sweeping views of the Farmington Valley and beyond. Trails connect to the Metacomet Trail, making it part of a regional hiking network. It's a premier destination for dramatic scenery.

☐ ▢ ♡ **Tri-Mountain State Park:** Spanning Wallingford, Durham, and Middletown, this undeveloped park protects rugged traprock ridges along the Mattabesett Trail. With no facilities, it appeals to experienced hikers seeking solitude, challenging climbs, and sweeping vistas. Its forested slopes and rocky outcrops highlight Connecticut's dramatic geology in a remote, natural setting.

☐ ▢ ♡ **Trout Brook Valley State Park Reserve:** In Easton and Weston, this 300-acre preserve is part of a larger land trust. Trails lead through meadows, wetlands, and forests with views of surrounding countryside. Visitors enjoy birdwatching, hiking, and seasonal foliage walks. Its peaceful character and diverse habitats make it a favorite for quiet, scenic outdoor recreation.

☐ ▢ ♡ **Wadsworth Falls State Park:** Located in Middletown and Middlefield, this popular park features two waterfalls, forest trails, and a sandy swimming area. Visitors hike along the Coginchaug River, picnic in shady groves, and admire scenic cascades. Its combination of natural beauty and family-friendly amenities makes it one of Connecticut's most treasured inland parks.

☐ ▢ ♡ **West Rock Ridge State Park:** Overlooking New Haven, this 1,700-acre park offers dramatic cliffside views and rugged trails, including the historic Regicides Trail. Lake Wintergreen provides opportunities for fishing and boating. Its mix of geology, history, and outdoor recreation makes it a top urban escape, combining wild ridgelines with city proximity.

☐ ▢ ♡ **Wharton Brook State Park:** In Wallingford, this compact park features a pond for fishing and seasonal swimming, along with picnic areas and easy walking paths. Families appreciate its accessibility and shady groves. Close to I-91, it's a convenient quick getaway, offering nature, relaxation, and birdwatching in a small but welcoming setting.

☐ ▢ ♡ **Whittemore Glen State Park:** Bordering Naugatuck and Middlebury, this undeveloped tract connects to the Mattatuck Trail. It offers rugged woodland hiking and wildlife observation in a quiet natural setting. With no facilities, it's ideal for back-to-nature exploration. Its trails provide access to a larger regional system, rewarding those who enjoy solitude.

☐ ▢ ♡ **Windsor Meadows State Park:** This linear riverside park in Windsor provides access to the Connecticut River for fishing, paddling, and walking. Flat trails follow the water, making it popular for cycling and jogging. Serving as a greenway link, it's both recreational and scenic, offering peaceful river views near urban areas.

☐ ▢ ♡ **Wooster Mountain State Park:** Found in Danbury, this rugged, forested park provides hiking, hunting, and access to the Wooster Mountain Shooting Range. Its trails pass through quiet woodlands with opportunities for wildlife viewing. With limited development, it's a lesser-known park that appeals to outdoor enthusiasts seeking solitude and rustic recreation.

UNITED STATES EDITION

CONNECTICUT

National Parks

☐ 🔖 ♡ **Appalachian National Scenic Trail:** Spanning more than 2,100 miles from Georgia to Maine, the Appalachian Trail is one of the world's most iconic long-distance hiking routes. Winding through forests, mountains, and small towns, it offers a blend of breathtaking vistas, diverse ecosystems, and cultural heritage. Both day hikers and seasoned backpackers find unforgettable adventures along its path.

☐ 🔖 ♡ **Weir Farm National Historic Park:** Nestled in Ridgefield, Connecticut, Weir Farm preserves the home and studios of Impressionist painter J. Alden Weir. The site celebrates American art, with gardens, meadows, and landscapes that inspired generations of artists. Visitors explore historic buildings, trails, and cultural exhibits, experiencing the intersection of creativity and natural beauty.

State & National Forests

☐ 🔖 ♡ **Algonquin State Forest:** Nestled in Connecticut's northwest hills, Algonquin protects rugged terrain along Sandy Brook and includes the Kitchel Wilderness Natural Area. With trails for hiking and birdwatching, it serves as both a recreation area and conservation zone. Its quiet, forested landscape preserves classic New England hardwood habitats and offers peaceful solitude.

☐ 🔖 ♡ **American Legion State Forest:** Located along the Farmington River in Barkhamsted, this forest offers scenic trails like the Henry Buck and Turkey Vultures Ledges. It's adjacent to Peoples State Forest, providing river access, camping, and hardwood and hemlock forest exploration. It's a favorite for fishing, leaf-peeping, and hiking in Connecticut's northwest corner.

☐ 🔖 ♡ **Camp Columbia State Forest:** A small state forest near Morris, this area was once home to Columbia University's engineering camp. Today it's managed for wildlife and low-impact recreation. It features short trails, quiet woods, and historical remains like the Camp Columbia tower offering sweeping views of the Litchfield Hills.

☐ 🔖 ♡ **Centennial Watershed State Forest:** One of the largest forests in southwestern Connecticut, this forest protects public drinking water and native habitats. Access is by permit only, preserving sensitive ecosystems. Managed jointly by the state and private landowners, it serves as a model of cooperative conservation across watersheds and woodlands.

☐ 🔖 ♡ **Cockaponset State Forest:** Spanning over 17,000 acres in southern Connecticut, Cockaponset features forested ridges, wetlands, and diverse trails including the Pattaconk area and Cedar Swamp Trail. It supports hiking, mountain biking, fishing, and seasonal hunting, and is named for a Native American chief who once lived in the area.

☐ 🔖 ♡ **Enders State Forest:** Enders offers a peaceful escape with a series of waterfalls, hardwood groves, and hemlock stands near Granby. It's ideal for hiking, photography, and quiet nature exploration. The falls are beautiful but slippery, so caution is encouraged. This forest is known for its scenic beauty and natural cascades in all seasons.

☐ 🔖 ♡ **Housatonic State Forest:** Scattered across northwestern Connecticut, this forest protects parts of the Housatonic River watershed. With access to the Appalachian Trail and remote ridgelines, it's a quiet forest ideal for backpacking, birding, and fishing. It plays a key role in maintaining the region's wild and scenic character.

☐ 🔖 ♡ **James L. Goodwin State Forest:** Located in Hampton, this forest includes Pine Acres Lake and a conservation center offering programs and exhibits. With interpretive trails, boardwalks, and wildlife viewing, it balances recreation with forestry education. It's a model site for sustainable land management and is especially family- and birdwatcher-friendly.

☐ 🔖 ♡ **Massacoe State Forest:** A small forest in Simsbury, Massacoe protects wetlands, hardwood groves, and the Stratton Brook watershed. It supports passive recreation like walking and birdwatching. Although modest in size, it contributes to local conservation and provides green space in a developed area near the Farmington Valley.

☐ 🔖 ♡ **Mattatuck State Forest:** A patchwork forest in western Connecticut known for waterfalls, rock ledges, and Leatherman's Cave. Its trails link to the Blue-Blazed Mattatuck Trail, and popular spots include Black Rock and Buttermilk Falls. It offers hiking, biking, and scenic views across its rugged, varied terrain.

CONNECTICUT

☐ 🔖 ♡ **Meshomasic State Forest:** Connecticut's first state forest, established in 1903, Meshomasic lies east of the Connecticut River. It features oak ridges, the Shenipsit Trail, and scenic overlooks. With forestry research plots and historic fire towers, it's a blend of conservation and recreation steeped in early 20th-century land stewardship.

☐ 🔖 ♡ **Mohawk State Forest:** In the Litchfield Hills, Mohawk offers highland forests, historic CCC-built roads and campgrounds, and sweeping vistas from Mohawk Mountain. It's a top fall foliage destination with the Mattatuck and Mohawk Trails traversing its ridges. Snowshoeing, hiking, and nature study are popular activities year-round.

☐ 🔖 ♡ **Mohegan State Forest:** A quiet forest in Scotland and Sprague, Mohegan supports sustainable forestry and wildlife habitat. It includes mixed hardwood stands and wetlands, and allows limited hiking, hunting, and seasonal use. While less visited than other forests, it provides an important ecological buffer in eastern Connecticut.

☐ 🔖 ♡ **Nassahegon State Forest:** Located in Burlington, Nassahegon features the Nassahegon Trail, trout-stocked streams, and proximity to Sessions Woods Wildlife Management Area. It's popular with mountain bikers, hikers, and birders, and includes hardwood and pine forests that support a wide range of wildlife species.

☐ 🔖 ♡ **Natchaug State Forest:** Located in Eastford and Chaplin, Natchaug protects scenic rivers, old growth forests, and the CCC-built CCC Forest Camp. It includes part of the Natchaug Trail and is ideal for fishing, hiking, and horseback riding. This forest blends recreation with heritage, forestry education, and historical charm.

☐ 🔖 ♡ **Nathan Hale State Forest:** This forest, gifted by descendants of Revolutionary War hero Nathan Hale, includes over 1,400 acres of forestland in Coventry and Andover. It supports timber research, hunting, and walking trails, and borders the Nathan Hale Homestead, preserving both historical and ecological legacy.

☐ 🔖 ♡ **Naugatuck State Forest:** Composed of five non-contiguous blocks, Naugatuck covers ridges, reservoirs, and Blue-Blazed Trails like the Quinnipiac and Naugatuck Trails. Popular for hunting, hiking, rock climbing, and fishing, it blends rugged terrain with easy access from urban areas like Waterbury and Beacon Falls.

☐ 🔖 ♡ **Nehantic State Forest:** This coastal forest in Lyme and East Lyme includes a dense mix of pine, oak, and swamp habitat. Trails wind through varied landscapes with options for hiking, seasonal hunting, and nature observation. It connects to other local preserves, offering continuity for wildlife and quiet woodland walks.

☐ 🔖 ♡ **Nepaug State Forest:** West of New Hartford, Nepaug includes scenic trails, forest roads, and sections of the Farmington River. It's a great place for hiking, mountain biking, and cross-country skiing, with the Tunxis Trail winding through shaded glades, stone walls, and glacial outcroppings typical of Connecticut's uplands.

☐ 🔖 ♡ **Nipmuck State Forest:** Spanning Union and surrounding towns, Nipmuck includes the northernmost section of the Blue-Blazed Nipmuck Trail. Its pine-oak woods and kettle ponds provide quiet hiking and snowshoeing opportunities. This forest also contains Bigelow Hollow State Park, making it a gateway to some of the state's most remote areas.

☐ 🔖 ♡ **Nye-Holman State Forest:** Located in Tolland, Nye-Holman is a lesser-known forest with woodland trails and access to Willimantic River fishing. It's quiet, undeveloped, and used primarily for forest management, birdwatching, and seasonal hunting. Its modest size contributes to habitat protection in the region.

☐ 🔖 ♡ **Pachaug State Forest:** Connecticut's largest state forest spans over 26,000 acres in the state's southeastern corner. It includes campgrounds, multiple hiking trails like the Narragansett Trail, and features like Mount Misery and the Rhododendron Sanctuary. The forest offers opportunities for ORV use, fishing, horseback riding, and backpacking.

☐ 🔖 ♡ **Paugnut State Forest:** Located in Torrington, Paugnut is a small forest with trail connections to Burr Pond and Sunnybrook State Parks. It provides quiet, wooded trails for hiking and wildlife observation and is part of the Tunxis Heritage Corridor, preserving cultural and natural landscapes in northwest Connecticut.

☐ 🔖 ♡ **Paugussett State Forest:** Situated in Newtown, Paugussett protects rolling woodlands and riparian corridors. It supports hunting and passive recreation, with trails linking to the Upper Paugussett State Forest and Lake Lillinonah. Its preserved lands help maintain watershed quality and provide forested green space near growing communities.

CONNECTICUT

☐ ▢ ♡ **Peoples State Forest:** Adjacent to American Legion State Forest, Peoples includes the Jessie Gerard Trail and view-packed ledges over the Farmington Valley. It contains a small museum, seasonal interpretive programs, and miles of trails for hiking, cross-country skiing, and exploring old-growth woodlands and historic CCC sites.

☐ ▢ ♡ **Pootatuck State Forest:** A quiet preserve near New Fairfield, Pootatuck protects steep hills, hardwood forests, and parts of the Still River watershed. It's used for hunting, hiking, and habitat protection. The forest sees little traffic and offers solitude close to the New York state line and Candlewood Lake region.

☐ ▢ ♡ **Quaddick State Forest:** Located near Thompson and adjacent to Quaddick State Park, this forest protects woodland and wetland habitats in the state's northeast corner. It offers hunting and informal hiking access and helps maintain water quality in the Quinebaug River Basin. It's a peaceful retreat in Connecticut's Quiet Corner.

☐ ▢ ♡ **Salmon River State Forest:** This forest preserves a scenic section of the Salmon River watershed near Marlborough and Colchester. It's known for the Comstock Covered Bridge, wild trout fishing, and miles of trails including the Airline State Park Trail. The area supports biking, equestrian use, and year-round exploration.

☐ ▢ ♡ **Shenipsit State Forest:** Spanning several parcels, this north-central forest includes Soapstone Mountain, topped with a fire tower offering panoramic views. It contains trails, old stone walls, and the Shenipsit Trail, making it a favorite for fall hikes, nature walks, and wildlife observation amid central Connecticut woodlands.

☐ ▢ ♡ **The Preserve State Forest:** Acquired in 2015, The Preserve protects 1,000 acres of forest and wetland in Old Saybrook, Essex, and Westbrook. It's home to vernal pools, migratory birds, and amphibians, with hiking trails winding through one of the largest unfragmented coastal forests remaining in southern New England.

☐ ▢ ♡ **Topsmead State Forest:** Once a private estate, this forest includes the historic Topsmead mansion, meadows, and hardwood groves. Located in Litchfield, it offers manicured trails, educational programs, and one of the most picturesque picnic and walking destinations in the state. It blends nature, history, and landscape design.

☐ ▢ ♡ **Tunxis State Forest:** Near the Massachusetts border in Hartland, Tunxis features remote trails, waterfalls, and backcountry experiences. It includes sections of the Tunxis Trail and offers hunting, hiking, snowmobiling, and quiet exploration. The rugged terrain and conservation focus make it a favorite for experienced hikers.

☐ ▢ ♡ **Wyantenock State Forest:** Scattered across western Connecticut, Wyantenock preserves a patchwork of ridges, wetlands, and river corridors near Washington and Warren. It supports seasonal hunting, birdwatching, and passive recreation, and helps preserve the headwaters of the Shepaug River in a region of rich ecological value.

National Scenic Byways & All-American Roads

☐ ▢ ♡ **Connecticut State Route 169 Scenic Byway:** A National Scenic Byway traversing 32 miles from Lisbon to the Massachusetts border in northeast CT. Winding through "Quiet Corner" landscapes, it passes colonial homesteads, churches, stone walls, meetinghouses, pine and maple forests, and glacial boulders—showcasing rich New England heritage and vibrant fall foliage.

☐ ▢ ♡ **Merritt Parkway (Route 15):** A National Scenic Byway and historic parkway from Greenwich to Milford, famed for Art Deco and Moderne-style overpasses amid woodland scenery. Completed in the 1930s, it offers a commuter experience uniquely preserved from commercial vehicles—renowned for its elegant design and spectacular seasonal foliage.

CONNECTICUT

State Scenic Byways

☐ 🔖 ♡ **Route 1 (Madison):** This short coastal stretch winds through Madison's shoreline, where tidal marshes, colonial homes, and tree-lined streets showcase New England charm. Views of Long Island Sound and quiet village roads create a peaceful corridor blending maritime heritage with small-town character, offering travelers a glimpse of Connecticut's historic coast.

☐ 🔖 ♡ **Route 1 (Old Lyme):** Less than a mile in length, this byway preserves Old Lyme's maritime and artistic heritage. Passing tidal coves, historic homes, and shady roadside landscapes, it reflects the town's roots as an artist colony while highlighting the ecological richness of the shoreline. It offers a brief yet meaningful scenic snapshot of coastal Connecticut.

☐ 🔖 ♡ **Route 4 (Farmington/Burlington):** This byway features rolling farmland, river crossings, and stone walls emblematic of Connecticut's rural identity. Historic homes and forested hillsides add depth to the landscape, while seasonal foliage paints it with vibrant color. The corridor captures the blend of cultural heritage and natural scenery central to New England's appeal.

☐ 🔖 ♡ **Route 4 (Sharon – Segment 1):** A 3.17-mile corridor in Sharon highlights meadows, ridges, and stone fences that frame traditional farmhouses. The road winds gently through quiet countryside, reflecting Litchfield County's timeless agricultural heritage. Seasonal beauty enhances the experience, making it a quintessential New England scenic drive.

☐ 🔖 ♡ **Route 4 (Sharon – Segment 2):** At just over a mile, this segment continues Sharon's pastoral charm with wooded edges and historic farmsteads. Stone walls trace the roadway, and the gentle landscape preserves the area's rural essence. Though short, it offers a rich impression of northwestern Connecticut's traditional countryside.

☐ 🔖 ♡ **Route 4 (Harwinton):** This 1.5-mile stretch blends shaded forest, fields, and historic homes into a serene drive. The corridor emphasizes Connecticut's quiet rural landscapes, where farmland meets woodlands. It highlights the enduring connection between natural scenery and small-town heritage in the state's interior hills.

☐ 🔖 ♡ **Route 7 (Sharon):** Passing through the Housatonic River Valley, this 4.3-mile segment features farm fields, river views, and colonial architecture. Historic mills and barns sit alongside stone fences, blending culture and landscape. Its pastoral scenery and heritage make it a highlight of northwestern Connecticut's scenic network.

☐ 🔖 ♡ **Route 7 (Kent):** Ten miles of Route 7 reveal covered bridges, river valleys, and vibrant village centers. Farms and forests frame the corridor, while autumn foliage creates some of the state's most iconic views. This drive combines cultural richness with natural splendor, making it one of Connecticut's most celebrated byways.

☐ 🔖 ♡ **Route 7 (Cornwall):** This 3.6-mile corridor captures the essence of small-town New England with riverside vistas, historic bridges, and shaded woodlands. It emphasizes the balance between preserved heritage and natural beauty, inviting travelers to slow down and enjoy Connecticut's quiet countryside.

☐ 🔖 ♡ **Route 7 (Salisbury–Sharon–Canaan):** Stretching more than 10 miles, this section passes rolling hills, open farmland, and historic town centers. Stone churches, barns, and village greens punctuate the landscape, while seasonal colors make it a favorite drive. It offers a rich blend of rural heritage and scenic charm.

☐ 🔖 ♡ **Route 10 (Farmington):** Just over a mile long, this corridor features colonial architecture, meadows, and stone walls. Shady tree canopies frame the road, highlighting the historic core of Farmington. The route emphasizes the harmony of natural beauty and small-town heritage in Connecticut's central valley.

☐ 🔖 ♡ **Route 14 (Windham/Scotland):** Nearly 4.5 miles long, this route highlights open farmland, streams, and preserved colonial homes. Historic churches and stone walls frame the corridor, which winds through quiet villages. It represents eastern Connecticut's enduring agricultural traditions and cultural roots.

☐ 🔖 ♡ **Route 14A (Sterling):** Less than a mile in length, this segment offers a concentrated view of Sterling's pastoral character. Farmhouses, fields, and wooded edges define the landscape, while the road's quiet, rural charm provides a timeless New England snapshot. It remains a preserved link to Connecticut's countryside past.

☐ 🔖 ♡ **Route 17 (Durham):** This 1.5-mile scenic stretch emphasizes wooded ridges, open farmland, and historic homes. Its landscape reflects central Connecticut's agricultural and cultural heritage. With shaded lanes and small-town charm, it provides a tranquil and authentic drive through the region's countryside.

CONNECTICUT

☐ 🔖 ♡ **Route 27 (Stonington/Groton):** Following the Mystic River, this corridor features tidal marshes, historic shipyards, and colonial architecture. It preserves maritime history while offering expansive water views. The route connects the vibrant village of Mystic with surrounding cultural and natural landmarks in southeastern Connecticut.

☐ 🔖 ♡ **Route 30 (Tolland):** A short but meaningful corridor, this stretch features meadows, woodlands, and historic homes. Its quiet rural landscape reflects Tolland's agricultural heritage, offering a snapshot of countryside beauty. The byway highlights the value of preserving traditional New England scenery.

☐ 🔖 ♡ **Route 33 (Wilton):** Extending nearly five miles, this route showcases stone walls, forested ridges, and historic farmhouses. Its shady canopies and rural character emphasize timeless New England charm. The corridor blends heritage with natural beauty, creating a peaceful and evocative drive through Wilton.

☐ 🔖 ♡ **Route 41 (Multiple Towns):** Spanning over 15 miles through Salisbury, Sharon, and beyond, this corridor highlights valleys, ridges, and historic villages. Travelers experience old mills, farmland, and seasonal beauty at every turn. Its length and diversity make it one of Connecticut's most scenic rural routes.

☐ 🔖 ♡ **Route 44 (Norfolk):** This corridor winds through Norfolk's quiet countryside, with woodlands, historic homes, and stone churches. It highlights the area's cultural and natural heritage in a compact scenic stretch. Colonial architecture and pastoral charm define this peaceful New England drive.

☐ 🔖 ♡ **Route 45 (Washington/Warren):** Hugging the shoreline of Lake Waramaug for just over two miles, this byway provides dramatic water views framed by vineyards and wooded hills. Historic villages and farmland enhance its appeal. It is a popular drive for recreation, foliage, and tranquil New England scenery.

☐ 🔖 ♡ **Route 49 (Voluntown–Sterling):** Extending 18 miles, this byway runs through Pachaug State Forest and rural farmland. Dense woodlands, streams, and stone fences create an immersive natural experience. The corridor reflects eastern Connecticut's rustic charm and offers one of the state's most tranquil scenic drives.

☐ 🔖 ♡ **Route 53 (Redding/Weston):** This corridor winds through wooded hills, open meadows, and small rural villages. Stone walls, colonial homes, and historic churches highlight the area's heritage. The drive offers a peaceful retreat into southwestern Connecticut's preserved countryside, showcasing a blend of natural beauty and traditional New England charm.

☐ 🔖 ♡ **Route 63 (Litchfield):** Passing through Litchfield's scenic countryside, this 3.4-mile segment features rolling farmland, shaded forests, and historic town greens. Colonial houses, stone walls, and small churches frame the route. The byway captures a timeless New England atmosphere, especially beautiful during autumn foliage.

☐ 🔖 ♡ **Route 67 (Roxbury):** This short byway highlights wooded hillsides, stream crossings, and pastoral farmland. Historic homes and quiet stone fences line the corridor, while shaded canopies add to its appeal. It reflects the peaceful character of rural Connecticut and preserves the state's agrarian traditions within a compact scenic drive.

☐ 🔖 ♡ **Route 74 (Tolland/Vernon):** Winding through northeastern Connecticut, this scenic corridor features fields, woodlands, and historic village centers. Stone walls, churches, and colonial homes create a cultural backdrop. The route preserves the region's rural beauty while connecting travelers to the area's small-town heritage.

☐ 🔖 ♡ **Route 75 (Windsor Locks/East Granby):** Near Bradley International Airport, this corridor highlights colonial-era homes, old tobacco barns, and shaded village greens. Rolling farmland and historic architecture create a setting steeped in tradition. It blends agricultural and cultural heritage along a peaceful stretch of rural roadway.

☐ 🔖 ♡ **Route 77 (Guilford/Durham):** This corridor travels from the Guilford Green north through farms, forests, and small lakes. Stone walls and tree-lined roads highlight its rustic charm. The byway captures classic inland Connecticut scenery, connecting coastal heritage with central farmland in a peaceful and scenic drive.

☐ 🔖 ♡ **Route 80 (Multiple Towns):** Stretching across southern Connecticut, this byway features shaded forests, small villages, and farmlands. Colonial homes and churches line the corridor, adding cultural depth. Scenic ridges, stone bridges, and seasonal beauty make it a route where history and natural splendor intertwine.

☐ 🔖 ♡ **Route 82 (Salem/East Haddam):** A short corridor crossing the Connecticut River near East Haddam, this byway highlights sweeping river views and the historic Goodspeed Opera House. Forested ridges and open meadows frame the road, creating a memorable drive that balances cultural heritage with natural beauty.

☐ 🔖 ♡ **Route 85 (Hebron/Colchester):** This corridor passes through open farmland, forested ridges, and historic crossroads towns. Colonial homes and traditional stone walls frame the route, while meadows and streams add natural charm. It showcases eastern Connecticut's quiet countryside character and rural heritage.

CONNECTICUT

☐ 🔖 ♡ **Route 87 (Lebanon/Columbia):** Passing through Lebanon's historic green and surrounding farmland, this corridor highlights stone fences, farmhouses, and village churches. Wooded edges and meadows create a peaceful atmosphere. It reflects Connecticut's colonial heritage and enduring agricultural landscapes in a tranquil drive.

☐ 🔖 ♡ **Route 94 (Glastonbury/Hebron):** This corridor winds past forested hills, brooks, and historic homes. Agricultural lands mix with wooded ridges to create varied scenery. With its quiet villages and stone bridges, the byway preserves the balance of natural beauty and cultural history typical of central Connecticut.

☐ 🔖 ♡ **Route 97 (Hampton/Scotland/Sprague):** This byway follows the Shetucket River, passing through historic mill towns, forests, and open farmland. Old textile mills, churches, and bridges add cultural interest, while the river's scenery provides a natural backdrop. It highlights eastern Connecticut's industrial and agricultural heritage.

☐ 🔖 ♡ **Route 136 (Westport/Norwalk):** This coastal corridor passes through shoreline neighborhoods, salt marshes, and historic harbor districts. It highlights maritime heritage and scenic estuaries while connecting small coastal towns. The byway preserves Connecticut's shoreline charm and cultural character within a compact but diverse drive.

☐ 🔖 ♡ **Route 139 (Branford/North Branford):** This short byway features historic farmsteads, shaded forests, and rolling fields. Its stone walls and colonial homes preserve traditional New England character. The corridor showcases Connecticut's agricultural heritage while offering a quiet alternative to larger highways.

☐ 🔖 ♡ **Route 148 (Chester/Haddam):** Crossing the Connecticut River on the historic Chester–Hadlyme Ferry, this corridor highlights river views, small villages, and wooded hillsides. The ferry crossing itself is a cultural landmark, making this byway a unique blend of transportation history and scenic beauty.

☐ 🔖 ♡ **Route 154 (Old Saybrook/Essex):** This coastal byway winds along the lower Connecticut River, passing historic shipyards, colonial homes, and tidal marshes. It highlights maritime heritage and natural estuaries, connecting picturesque towns with preserved waterfront landscapes. Seasonal foliage enhances the scenic experience.

☐ 🔖 ♡ **Route 160 (Rocky Hill/Glastonbury):** A short but historic corridor that includes the Rocky Hill–Glastonbury Ferry, the oldest continuously operating ferry in the U.S. The route offers river views, farmland, and small-town charm. It blends cultural heritage with scenic beauty in central Connecticut.

☐ 🔖 ♡ **Route 169 (Lisbon/Canterbury/Chaplin):** Though nationally recognized, state designation also applies. This corridor features 32 miles of rolling farmland, colonial homes, and historic churches. Passing through quiet towns, it reflects New England's rural heritage and remains one of Connecticut's most iconic scenic drives.

☐ 🔖 ♡ **Route 171 (Woodstock/Putnam):** Passing through Connecticut's northeast corner, this byway highlights rolling farmland, historic mills, and stone bridges. Village greens and colonial homes define the corridor, while open meadows and forests showcase natural beauty. It is a peaceful drive steeped in heritage.

☐ 🔖 ♡ **Route 177 (Farmington/Plainville):** This corridor features wooded ridges, brooks, and historic homes. Stone walls and village centers highlight Connecticut's colonial heritage. Seasonal scenery adds to the charm, making it a quiet and picturesque roadway linking small towns with natural landscapes.

☐ 🔖 ♡ **Route 179 (Barkhamsted/Canton):** This byway winds along the Farmington River, offering wooded banks, stone bridges, and village scenery. It highlights Barkhamsted Reservoir and colonial-era architecture. The corridor combines natural river beauty with historic features, making it a serene and culturally rich drive through northwestern Connecticut.

☐ 🔖 ♡ **Route 181 (Barkhamsted):** Passing through the People's State Forest area, this route features rugged woodland, river overlooks, and scenic ridgelines. Stone walls and early 20th-century conservation efforts are visible along the way. The byway emphasizes Connecticut's natural preservation heritage and forested landscapes.

☐ 🔖 ♡ **Route 182/182A (Colebrook/Norfolk):** These parallel byways traverse rolling farmland, small villages, and shaded woodlands. Historic churches, open meadows, and stone walls highlight Litchfield County's timeless charm. Seasonal color brings dramatic beauty to these quiet roads, reflecting Connecticut's enduring rural character.

☐ 🔖 ♡ **Route 185 (Simsbury/Bloomfield):** Crossing the Talcott Mountain area, this corridor offers sweeping ridgeline views, woodlands, and access to Heublein Tower. The road showcases dramatic elevation changes and natural scenery. With cultural landmarks and natural splendor, it represents one of Connecticut's most striking short byways.

☐ 🔖 ♡ **Route 186 (East Longmeadow Border):** Near the Massachusetts line, this byway features shaded corridors, farmland, and historic homes. Its quiet lanes preserve the small-town charm of northern Connecticut, offering a peaceful drive through rolling countryside that reflects the state's rural heritage.

CONNECTICUT

☐ ▢ ♡ **Route 187 (Bloomfield/Windsor):** Passing farmland, brooks, and historic churches, this byway highlights Connecticut's agricultural past. Shady stretches and stone fences provide natural charm, while village greens and colonial homes add cultural depth. It blends preserved rural landscapes with heritage landmarks.

☐ ▢ ♡ **Route 191 (Enfield):** This corridor features tobacco barns, open farmland, and historic neighborhoods. It reflects north-central Connecticut's agricultural identity while offering scenic pastoral views. Seasonal changes highlight its character, making it a drive that blends cultural history with rustic charm.

☐ ▢ ♡ **Route 193 (Union):** A quiet corridor through Connecticut's northeast corner, this route highlights forests, stone walls, and historic farms. Its remote atmosphere and pastoral character provide a tranquil escape, showcasing a preserved landscape that connects travelers to the state's rural traditions.

☐ ▢ ♡ **Route 254 (Thomaston/Litchfield):** This byway follows the Naugatuck River Valley, offering wooded ridges, mills, and farmland. Historic bridges and colonial architecture mark the corridor, while open fields and forests provide natural charm. It's a diverse scenic drive balancing cultural heritage with rural beauty.

☐ ▢ ♡ **Route 272 (Torrington/Norfolk):** Extending through the northwest hills, this corridor highlights forested ridges, streams, and historic town centers. Its stone walls, old farms, and shaded lanes emphasize classic New England scenery. Seasonal foliage and quiet charm make it a favorite in Litchfield County.

☐ ▢ ♡ **Route 341 (Kent/Warren):** This byway crosses the Housatonic River and winds through farmland, meadows, and forested slopes. Covered bridges, colonial homes, and stone walls define the corridor. It highlights both cultural heritage and natural beauty, providing a peaceful and authentic Connecticut drive.

National Natural Landmarks

 ☐ ▢ ♡ **Bartholomew's Cobble:** Straddling the Connecticut–Massachusetts border, Bartholomew's Cobble is a National Natural Landmark for its remarkable biodiversity. It contains the richest fern community in North America, with over 800 plant species thriving on limestone soils. Trails, scenic river views, and a visitor center make it both a research site and a natural retreat.
GPS: 42.0572, -73.3508

 ☐ ▢ ♡ **Beckley Bog:** Tucked in northwestern Connecticut, Beckley Bog became a National Natural Landmark as the southernmost sphagnum-heath-black spruce bog in New England. Its acidic soils, peat moss, and stunted conifers support rare plants and wildlife. The bog offers a fragile and irreplaceable glimpse into boreal wetland ecosystems at the edge of their natural range.
GPS: 41.9689, -73.1622

 ☐ ▢ ♡ **Bingham Pond Bog:** This secluded wetland is a National Natural Landmark for its unusual dominance of black spruce without the typical sphagnum moss cover. Its largely undisturbed state makes it invaluable for studying rare northern bog ecosystems in southern New England, where such habitats are scarce. It preserves distinctive conditions for plants and wildlife.
GPS: 42.0203, -73.4664

 ☐ ▢ ♡ **Cathedral Pines:** Once among the finest old-growth white pine–hemlock forests in New England, Cathedral Pines is a National Natural Landmark that now tells a story of resilience. Though a tornado in 1989 leveled much of it, the site remains a living case study in forest disturbance, natural regeneration, and the enduring ecology of northeastern woodlands.
GPS: 41.8360, -73.3252

 ☐ ▢ ♡ **Chester Cedar Swamp:** Within Cockaponset State Forest, Chester Cedar Swamp is recognized as a National Natural Landmark for its rare Atlantic white cedar wetland. Cool, acidic conditions nurture specialized plants, while the swamp's intact hydrology helps filter water, store carbon, and provide sanctuary for biodiversity in Connecticut's shrinking cedar habitats.
GPS: 41.3875, -72.4890

 ☐ ▢ ♡ **Dinosaur Trackway:** Preserved in Jurassic sandstone, this site holds National Natural Landmark status for containing one of North America's largest collections of fossilized dinosaur tracks. Over 200 million years old, the prints reveal the movement and behavior of ancient reptiles, making it a globally significant site for paleontology and Earth history.
GPS: 41.6519, -72.6569

CONNECTICUT

 ☐ 🔖 ♡ **McLean Game Refuge Natural Areas:** Spread across 4,400 acres, McLean Game Refuge is a National Natural Landmark for its glacial landforms and ecological diversity. Ridges, wetlands, and forests provide habitats for wildlife while demonstrating Connecticut's natural history. Established by Senator George P. McLean, it remains a model of long-term conservation.
GPS: 41.9205, -72.7885

 ☐ 🔖 ♡ **Pachaug–Great Meadow Swamp:** In the heart of Pachaug State Forest, this swamp is a National Natural Landmark for preserving one of southern New England's largest intact Atlantic white cedar wetlands. Fed by the Pachaug River and Great Meadow Brook, it sustains diverse flora and fauna while showcasing the importance of intact hydrologic systems.
GPS: 41.5992, -71.8781

Delaware

Delaware's landscapes blend sandy beaches, quiet forests, and historic trails. With inviting state parks, a national park unit, and notable natural landmarks, the state provides a peaceful coastal gateway to nature, offering bird-rich marshes, riverfront scenery, and miles of shoreline to explore.

🗓 Peak Season
June–August is Delaware's peak season, when warm weather draws visitors to its Atlantic beaches and coastal towns. Summer festivals and long days bring the highest crowds and busiest travel period.

🗓 Offseason Months
November–April is the offseason, with colder weather, quieter beaches, and fewer visitors. Winter is calm and peaceful along the coast, while spring and late fall see lighter crowds before and after the busy summer.

🍃 Scenery & Nature Timing
Spring highlights coastal marshes and bird migrations, especially at Bombay Hook and Prime Hook refuges. Summer offers lively beaches and boating. Fall colors brighten inland forests, while winter brings quiet wildlife viewing in marshes and along the bays.

✨ Special
Delaware features the sandy shores of Rehoboth and Bethany Beaches, tidal marshes at Bombay Hook and Prime Hook, and the rolling Brandywine Valley. Cape Henlopen's dunes and the Delaware Bay estuary highlight the state's coastal beauty.

DELAWARE

State Parks

☐ ◫ ♡ **Alapocas Run State Park:** Located in New Castle County, this 359-acre urban park blends natural beauty with recreation. It features rock climbing walls, scenic wooded trails, and the historic Blue Ball Barn, home to the Delaware Folk Art Collection. Visitors enjoy walking, biking, and exploring Brandywine Creek in a peaceful forested setting close to Wilmington.

☐ ◫ ♡ **Auburn Valley State Park:** Nestled in Yorklyn, this park preserves the estate of the Marshall family, including Auburn Heights Mansion and the Marshall Steam Museum, showcasing antique steam cars. The park offers hiking trails, scenic views, and a deep dive into Delaware's industrial and transportation history amid rolling hills and tranquil woodlands.

☐ ◫ ♡ **Bellevue State Park:** Situated on a former du Pont estate in Wilmington, this 331-acre park features Bellevue Hall, formal gardens, and horse stables. Visitors enjoy tennis courts, picnic areas, and walking trails through meadows and woodlands. The park merges recreation with historical charm, offering year-round events and cultural activities.

☐ ◫ ♡ **Brandywine Creek State Park:** Spanning 951 acres near Wilmington, this park offers beautiful trails through meadows and woodlands along the Brandywine Creek. Popular for hiking, fishing, and birdwatching, it also houses the Brandywine Creek Nature Center. The park preserves land once owned by the du Pont family and supports environmental education.

☐ ◫ ♡ **Cape Henlopen State Park:** Located at the mouth of the Delaware Bay, this 5,193-acre park offers beaches, dunes, salt marshes, and maritime forests. Visitors enjoy swimming, cycling, fishing, camping, and exploring WWII-era observation towers. The Seaside Nature Center provides exhibits and aquariums, enriching the experience with coastal education.

☐ ◫ ♡ **Delaware Seashore State Park:** This 2,825-acre park lies between the Atlantic Ocean and Indian River Bay, offering ocean beaches, a marina, and opportunities for swimming, surfing, and boating. The historic Indian River Life-Saving Station Museum highlights maritime heritage. It's a popular destination for anglers, campers, and beach lovers.

☐ ◫ ♡ **Fenwick Island State Park:** This 344-acre park sits on a narrow strip between the Atlantic Ocean and Little Assawoman Bay. Known for its quiet beaches, it offers surf fishing, swimming, kayaking, and windsurfing. With fewer crowds than nearby resorts, Fenwick Island is ideal for relaxing beach days and scenic coastal views.

☐ ◫ ♡ **First State Heritage Park:** Located in the heart of Dover, this urban park links historic and cultural sites, including Legislative Hall, the Old State House, and the John Bell House. It offers guided tours, living history programs, and seasonal events, serving as Delaware's "park without boundaries" to celebrate its colonial and civic heritage.

☐ ◫ ♡ **Fort Delaware State Park:** Situated on Pea Patch Island in the Delaware River, this park features a Civil War-era fort that once held Confederate prisoners. Visitors take a ferry from Delaware City to explore the fort's history through reenactments and tours. The island is also a bird sanctuary, especially for nesting herons and egrets.

☐ ◫ ♡ **Fort DuPont State Park:** Located near Delaware City, this park preserves a former military installation that was active from the Civil War through WWII. Today, it offers walking trails, historic structures, and open spaces along the Delaware River. It's a peaceful spot to enjoy nature while exploring the state's military past.

☐ ◫ ♡ **Fox Point State Park:** Overlooking the Delaware River in New Castle, this small but scenic park features walking and biking paths with panoramic views of river traffic and the industrial skyline. It's a favorite for picnics, casual strolls, and enjoying ships passing by, while learning about local environmental restoration efforts.

☐ ◫ ♡ **Holts Landing State Park:** Located on Indian River Bay near Millville, this 203-acre park includes forests, salt marshes, and bay shorelines. Visitors enjoy crabbing, fishing, hiking, and kayaking. The park's boat launch and bayfront picnic area make it a serene spot for outdoor recreation and wildlife viewing in a coastal habitat.

☐ ◫ ♡ **Killens Pond State Park:** Centered around a 66-acre pond in Felton, this 1,443-acre park offers boating, fishing, and a water park for summer fun. It features campgrounds, hiking and biking trails, and a nature center. Popular with families, Killens Pond provides year-round activities in a tranquil wooded environment.

DELAWARE

☐ 🔖 ♡ **Lums Pond State Park:** Located near Bear, this 1,790-acre park surrounds Delaware's largest freshwater pond. It offers kayaking, fishing, zip lining, hiking, horseback riding, and camping. The park features varied habitats and wildlife, including bald eagles. It's a favorite for outdoor enthusiasts seeking diverse recreation.

☐ 🔖 ♡ **Trap Pond State Park:** Located in Laurel, this park protects one of the northernmost natural stands of bald cypress trees in the U.S. The pond is ideal for kayaking, fishing, and birdwatching. With trails, campgrounds, and a nature center, it offers a rich blend of recreation and natural beauty in Delaware's wetlands.

☐ 🔖 ♡ **White Clay Creek State Park:** Spanning over 3,600 acres near Newark, this park features forested hills, rolling meadows, and the scenic White Clay Creek. It's popular for hiking, mountain biking, and trout fishing. The park supports diverse plant and animal species and connects to trails extending into neighboring Pennsylvania.

National Parks

☐ 🔖 ♡ **First State National Historical Park:** Located in Delaware, this park preserves significant sites related to the founding of the United States, including the historic New Castle district and the Old New Castle Courthouse. Visitors can explore the early history of the nation and the events leading to the creation of Delaware, the first state to ratify the U.S. Constitution.

State & National Forests

☐ 🔖 ♡ **Blackbird State Forest:** Nestled in northern Delaware along the Blackbird Creek, this forest preserves mature hardwood swamps and tidal marshes. It's managed for timber, wildlife habitat, and water quality. Visitors can enjoy tranquil walking trails, seasonal birdwatching—especially during migrations—and educational signage that interprets the forest's ecological role.

☐ 🔖 ♡ **Redden State Forest:** Located in Sussex County near Georgetown, Redden State Forest spans rolling uplands and pine-oak woodlands. Named after the historic Redden Lodge, it offers a mix of recreation and education. Hiking, mountain biking, and horseback riding trails wind through pine plantation areas, along with wildlife viewing opportunities and controlled timber management.

☐ 🔖 ♡ **Taber State Forest:** Situated in Kent and Sussex counties near Felton, Taber State Forest protects mixed pine and hardwood stands with a sandy coastal plain setting. Managed for sustainable timber harvest and habitat conservation, it offers forest roads for walking and cycling. Birders may spot migrating shorebirds, and the forest contributes to groundwater recharge and native species preservation.

National Scenic Byways & All-American Roads

☐ 🔖 ♡ **Brandywine Valley National Scenic Byway:** This 12-mile route runs from Wilmington to the Pennsylvania border, winding along Brandywine Creek. Lined with grand du Pont estates, manicured gardens, historic mills, and art museums, the byway blends scenic pastoral beauty with early American industrial and cultural heritage, making it a refined escape into Delaware's "Château Country."

☐ 🔖 ♡ **Delaware Bayshore National Scenic Byway:** Stretching along Routes 1 and 9 from Lewes to New Castle, this stunning route traces Delaware Bay and the Delaware River shoreline. Pass through tidal marshes, coastal farmland, fishing villages, and wildlife refuges like Bombay Hook. Rich in birding, heritage lighthouses, and coastal ecology, it's a peaceful shore-to-river journey.

DELEWARE

☐ ▢ ♡ **Red Clay Scenic Byway:** A state-designated route along DE 82 from Greenville to the Pennsylvania line, following Red Clay Creek. It winds through lush woodlands, historic mills, covered bridges, and rolling farmland. The scenic valley is steeped in early industry, Quaker history, and natural beauty—aglow with fall foliage in autumn and perfect for quiet country drives.

State Scenic Byways

☐ ▢ ♡ **Harriet Tubman Underground Railroad Byway:** This route traces the secret paths enslaved people once took through Delaware to freedom. Interpretive sites, churches, and historic markers highlight the state's critical role in the Underground Railroad. Travelers experience both cultural heritage and quiet rural landscapes that preserve a moving story of courage and resilience.

☐ ▢ ♡ **Historic Lewes Byway, Gateway to the Bayshore:** Centered in Lewes, Delaware's first town, this byway showcases maritime heritage, lighthouses, and coastal habitats. It highlights Cape Henlopen State Park, preserved historic districts, and scenic bayshore drives, offering travelers a mix of seafaring history, natural beauty, and the charm of a storied coastal community.

☐ ▢ ♡ **Nanticoke Heritage Byway:** Stretching through western Sussex County, this byway follows the Nanticoke River corridor and surrounding countryside. It passes through towns like Seaford, blending Native American heritage, maritime history, and agricultural landscapes. The route offers access to parks, river overlooks, and cultural sites that define Delaware's rural identity.

☐ ▢ ♡ **Red Clay Scenic Byway:** Winding through rolling hills and valleys in northern Delaware, this byway highlights the Brandywine Valley's lesser-known landscapes. It features stone walls, historic mills, and preserved villages amid lush woodlands and farmland. The route offers a peaceful drive rich with scenery, history, and conservation areas tied to the Red Clay watershed.

National Natural Landmarks

☐ ▢ ♡ **Great Cypress Swamp:** Stretching across the Delaware–Maryland border, the Great Cypress Swamp is a National Natural Landmark for being one of North America's northernmost bald cypress wetlands. As the largest forested swamp on the Delmarva Peninsula, it shelters rare plants, migratory birds, and diverse wildlife, preserving a vital remnant of ancient wetland ecosystems.
GPS: 38.5183, -75.3544

UNITED STATES EDITION

Florida

Florida's outdoor wonders include tropical wetlands, crystal-clear springs, coastal dunes, and vast mangrove forests. Through a vibrant network of state parks, national forests, iconic national parks, and remarkable natural landmarks, the Sunshine State invites endless exploration year-round.

📅 Peak Season
December–April is Florida's peak season, with warm, dry weather and an influx of visitors escaping colder climates. Beaches, theme parks, and natural areas are busiest during winter and spring break periods.

📅 Offseason Months
June–September is the offseason, bringing hot, humid weather, heavy afternoon storms, and hurricane risk. Travel is quieter outside of holidays, though summer remains popular along beaches and springs.

🍃 Scenery & Nature Timing
Spring brings wildflowers and pleasant outdoor weather before the heat sets in. Summer showcases sea turtle nesting on Atlantic beaches. Fall highlights bird migrations across wetlands, while winter is peak for manatee viewing in warm springs and clear, dry skies for exploration.

✨ Special
Florida features the Everglades' vast wetlands, coral reefs in Biscayne and the Florida Keys, and the freshwater springs of central Florida. The Gulf Coast showcases white-sand beaches, while the Panhandle and Big Cypress Swamp highlight the state's rich natural diversity.

FLORIDA

State Parks

☐ 🔖 ♡ **Addison Blockhouse Historic State Park:** A protected ruin in the Tomoka River floodplain near Ormond Beach. The coquina blockhouse is not open for general visitation and has no facilities; it's typically viewed by boat from the river or during special programs. Treat it as a sensitive cultural resource and check advisories—this unit prioritizes preservation over on-site recreation like hiking or picnicking.

☐ 🔖 ♡ **Alafia River State Park:** Reclaimed phosphate country near Tampa transformed into a premier mountain-biking playground, with miles of flowy to expert singletrack over dramatic mine spoils. Off the bike, hike shady loops, ride equestrian trails, or paddle and fish the lakes and river. Camp beneath longleaf pines and wake to birdsong—an action-packed hub for trail lovers in a surprisingly wild landscape.

☐ 🔖 ♡ **Alfred B. Maclay Gardens State Park:** Located in Leon County, this former governor's estate surrounds Cypress Lake with meticulously landscaped gardens bursting with azaleas, camellias, and tall pines. Visitors stroll formal pathways, fish or paddle on the lake, admire the Mediterranean-Revival mansion, and enjoy seasonal blooms in a tranquil horticultural retreat.

☐ 🔖 ♡ **Amelia Island State Park:** Set on Nassau County's barrier island, this 2-mile stretch of beach is framed by dunes and maritime forests. It's one of the few Florida parks permitting horseback riding on the beach. Visitors also enjoy swimming, shelling, wildlife spotting, hiking sandy trails, and savoring a serene beach experience just north of Fernandina Beach.

☐ 🔖 ♡ **Anastasia State Park:** A 1,600-acre coastal gem near St. Augustine that combines wide sandy beaches, salt marshes, dunes, tidal creeks, and pine woods. Ideal for swimming, fishing, birdwatching, hiking, biking, and wildlife viewing. Osprey, turtles, and shorebirds abound, and visitors can stroll shaded paths amid scenic dunes and maritime habitats.

☐ 🔖 ♡ **Anclote Key Preserve State Park:** Accessible only by boat, this barrier island park off Tarpon Springs features remote white-sand beaches, a historic 19th-century lighthouse, and pine flatwoods. Visitors enjoy swimming, shelling, birdwatching, and primitive camping. The park's seclusion makes it a peaceful haven for wildlife and solitude seekers.

☐ 🔖 ♡ **Avalon State Park:** This St. Lucie County park boasts nearly a mile of undeveloped beachfront along the Atlantic. Popular for surf fishing, beachcombing, and wildlife observation, it's also known for nesting sea turtles. The shoreline's natural beauty and quiet atmosphere provide a peaceful alternative to Florida's more crowded beaches.

☐ 🔖 ♡ **Bahia Honda State Park:** Located in the Lower Florida Keys, this park offers turquoise waters, sandy beaches, and iconic views of the Old Bahia Honda Bridge. Popular activities include swimming, snorkeling, kayaking, and camping. The park's tropical setting and marine life make it one of Florida's top destinations for beachgoers and nature lovers.

☐ 🔖 ♡ **Bald Point State Park:** Situated on Florida's Panhandle, this park features coastal marshes, pine flatwoods, and pristine Gulf shoreline. It's a hotspot for migratory birdwatching, fishing, and kayaking. The park's trails and boardwalks offer access to scenic viewpoints, and its quiet beaches are ideal for nature photography and peaceful recreation.

☐ 🔖 ♡ **Big Lagoon State Park:** Located near Pensacola, this park encompasses tidal marshes, pine forests, and coastal bays. Visitors enjoy paddling, hiking, fishing, and birdwatching along the Great Florida Birding Trail. Boardwalks and observation towers provide views of wildlife-rich habitats and stunning sunsets over the water.

☐ 🔖 ♡ **Big Shoals State Park:** Home to Florida's largest whitewater rapids, this north-central park features limestone bluffs and over 28 miles of trails for hiking, biking, and horseback riding. Visitors can kayak the Suwannee River during high water or enjoy scenic vistas from the bluffs. The park also offers excellent wildlife viewing and picnicking areas.

☐ 🔖 ♡ **Bill Baggs Cape Florida State Park:** Key Biscayne's quiet escape with wide beaches, shady picnic groves, bike paths, and calm paddling on Biscayne Bay. Add history at the 1825 Cape Florida Lighthouse—tours run on select days with limited capacity, so check the schedule or arrive early. Migratory birds, manatees offshore, and sunset views make it a Miami standout.

FLORIDA

☐ 🔖 ♡ **Blackwater River State Park:** This Panhandle park is known for its white sandy beaches and one of the purest sand-bottom rivers in the country. It's a prime location for canoeing, tubing, and fishing. Visitors also enjoy hiking trails through longleaf pine forests and camping under the stars in a peaceful, wooded environment.

☐ 🔖 ♡ **Blue Spring State Park:** A crystal spring run and boardwalks along the St. Johns that turn into a manatee refuge each winter. From roughly mid-November to March, swimming, snorkeling, and paddling close in the spring to protect manatees using the 72°F water. Outside refuge season, enjoy tubing, kayaking, river cruises, and prolific wildlife in a lush, easy-to-love setting.

☐ 🔖 ♡ **Bulow Creek State Park:** Located near Ormond Beach, this park preserves one of the largest stands of southern live oak in Florida, including the massive Fairchild Oak. Visitors enjoy hiking trails, birdwatching, and picnicking beneath the ancient canopy. The park offers access to nearby ruins of sugar plantations and historical landmarks.

☐ 🔖 ♡ **Bulow Plantation Ruins Historic State Park:** This site features the remnants of a sugar plantation destroyed during the Second Seminole War. The park offers trails through lush hammocks and access to Bulow Creek for paddling. Visitors can explore coquina foundations, a scenic boat launch, and a glimpse into 19th-century Florida history.

☐ 🔖 ♡ **Caladesi Island State Park:** Accessible only by boat or ferry, this barrier island near Clearwater features unspoiled beaches, kayak trails through mangrove tunnels, and coastal hammocks. Visitors enjoy swimming, hiking, birdwatching, and shelling. The park's natural beauty and tranquil setting make it one of Florida's top coastal escapes.

☐ 🔖 ♡ **Camp Helen State Park:** Nestled between the Gulf of Mexico and Lake Powell near Panama City Beach, this park features rare coastal dune lakes, salt marshes, and historic resort buildings. Visitors can hike scenic trails, fish, or enjoy birdwatching. The blend of natural and cultural resources makes it a hidden gem along the Panhandle.

☐ 🔖 ♡ **Cayo Costa State Park:** Remote, boat-access barrier island with nine miles of undeveloped Gulf shoreline, sweeping dunes, and coastal hammock. Come for shelling, snorkeling, paddling, and miles of quiet beach; watch for sea turtles and shorebirds, then linger under star-bright skies. Sand roads, tropical pines, and turquoise water make this a rare slice of wild Florida.

☐ 🔖 ♡ **Cedar Key Museum State Park:** Located in the historic fishing village of Cedar Key, this small park features exhibits on local history, Native American artifacts, and the restored 1920s St. Clair Whitman house. Visitors enjoy nature trails and birdwatching while learning about the town's 19th-century prominence as a shipping port.

☐ 🔖 ♡ **Charlotte Harbor Preserve State Park:** One of Florida's largest preserves, this park protects 45,000 acres of coastal habitat along Charlotte Harbor. Visitors can paddle through mangrove tunnels, hike scenic trails, and observe wading birds, dolphins, and manatees. The park's vast wilderness offers a peaceful escape for outdoor exploration.

☐ 🔖 ♡ **Collier-Seminole State Park:** Located near Naples, this park showcases diverse ecosystems from mangroves to cypress swamps. Visitors can hike the nature trails, paddle the Blackwater River, or view rare plants and wildlife. The park is also home to a 1920s Bay City Walking Dredge, a National Historic Mechanical Engineering Landmark.

☐ 🔖 ♡ **Colt Creek State Park:** Located in Lakeland, this park spans more than 5,000 acres of pine flatwoods, cypress domes, and freshwater lakes. Visitors can hike, bike, or ride horses on over 15 miles of trails, or enjoy fishing and kayaking. The park is also home to diverse wildlife like deer, otters, and wading birds, offering a peaceful retreat in Central Florida.

☐ 🔖 ♡ **Constitution Convention Museum State Park:** Situated in Port St. Joe, this park commemorates the site of Florida's first constitutional convention in 1838. The museum features exhibits and life-sized figures representing key delegates. Visitors can explore the surrounding grounds, picnic under trees, and reflect on Florida's early path to statehood.

☐ 🔖 ♡ **Crystal River Archaeological State Park:** This coastal site preserves six Native American temple mounds and middens used between 200 BC and AD 1000. Visitors walk interpretive trails among the earthworks and enjoy views of the Crystal River. The park offers insights into pre-Columbian life and access to a scenic coastal environment.

FLORIDA

☐ 🔖 ♡ **Curry Hammock State Park:** Located in the Middle Keys, this park protects large areas of mangrove swamp, seagrass beds, and coastal hammock. Visitors enjoy kayaking, kiteboarding, and beachcombing along the Atlantic shoreline. Campsites provide oceanfront views, and the park's shallow waters attract shorebirds and marine wildlife.

☐ 🔖 ♡ **Dagny Johnson Key Largo Hammock Botanical State Park:** This park preserves one of the largest tracts of subtropical hardwood hammock in the Keys. Located in Key Largo, it offers paved trails for walking, wildlife viewing, and guided tours. The park is home to endangered species like the Key Largo woodrat and the American crocodile.

☐ 🔖 ♡ **De Leon Springs State Park:** Near DeLand, a 72°F spring invites swimming, snorkeling, and paddling the spring run beneath shady live oaks. Inside the historic mill, the Sugar Mill Restaurant now operates the beloved cook-your-own pancake griddles. Boardwalks, boat tours, and exhibits interpret Indigenous history, Spanish settlement, and milling heritage in a leafy, family-friendly setting.

☐ 🔖 ♡ **DeSoto Site Historic State Park:** Located in Tallahassee, this park marks the winter encampment of Spanish explorer Hernando de Soto in 1539–1540. A museum and interpretive exhibits tell the story of early European contact. Trails wind through hardwood forests and archaeological sites rich in Florida's colonial-era history.

☐ 🔖 ♡ **Don Pedro Island State Park:** Accessible only by boat, this barrier island near Cape Haze features a long stretch of secluded beach, mangrove forests, and coastal dunes. Visitors enjoy swimming, shelling, fishing, and picnicking in a tranquil environment. The island's remote feel makes it ideal for quiet beach days and wildlife observation.

☐ 🔖 ♡ **Dudley Farm Historic State Park:** Located in Newberry, this working farm depicts Florida rural life from the late 1800s to early 1900s. Costumed interpreters demonstrate traditional skills like blacksmithing, gardening, and animal care. Visitors can tour the original homestead, barns, and outbuildings set amid rolling pastureland.

☐ 🔖 ♡ **Dunns Creek State Park:** Near Palatka, this 6,200-acre park protects a mosaic of sandhills, floodplains, and wetlands along the St. Johns River basin. Visitors hike or ride horses on miles of trails through pine forests and along Dunns Creek. The park offers quiet wildlife viewing, paddling access, and glimpses of Florida's natural beauty.

☐ 🔖 ♡ **Econfina River State Park:** Located along the Gulf Coast in Taylor County, this remote park features pine flatwoods, salt marshes, and the winding Econfina River. Visitors enjoy paddling, fishing, hiking, and horseback riding. The park offers elevated boardwalks and river overlooks, ideal for birdwatching and spotting coastal wildlife.

☐ 🔖 ♡ **Eden Gardens State Park:** Centered on the 1897 Wesley House, this Bay-side retreat near Point Washington pairs formal gardens, reflecting pools, and massive live oaks with quiet nature trails. Tour the period-furnished mansion, picnic under shady lawns, and watch herons hunt on Tucker Bayou. A serene counterpoint to nearby beaches, it blends Panhandle history, horticulture, and easy strolling in a postcard setting.

☐ 🔖 ♡ **Edward Ball Wakulla Springs State Park:** Home to one of the world's largest and deepest freshwater springs, this park near Tallahassee offers swimming, glass-bottom boat tours, and river cruises. Visitors can explore the historic Wakulla Springs Lodge and view manatees, alligators, and wading birds in the spring's clear waters.

☐ 🔖 ♡ **Egmont Key State Park:** Located at the mouth of Tampa Bay, this island park is accessible only by boat and features historic ruins from Fort Dade, a still-operating lighthouse, and pristine beaches. Visitors can snorkel, fish, or hike sandy trails. The island's isolation makes it ideal for quiet exploration and wildlife watching.

☐ 🔖 ♡ **Ellie Schiller Homosassa Springs Wildlife State Park:** A showcase for native Florida wildlife anchored by a first-magnitude spring. View manatees from the underwater "Fish Bowl," then meet ambassadors like black bear, panther, bobcat, and birds of prey. Tram and boat rides link the visitor center to shady boardwalks and exhibits, offering an up-close, educational experience in Citrus County's crystal waters and hammocks.

☐ 🔖 ♡ **Fakahatchee Strand Preserve State Park:** Florida's largest state park spans part of the Everglades ecosystem in Collier County. It's known for rare orchids, ghost trees, and elusive wildlife like panthers and black bears. Visitors hike through swampy terrain, explore boardwalks, or take guided swamp walks through the "Amazon of North America."

☐ 🔖 ♡ **Falling Waters State Park:** Located near Chipley, this park features Florida's highest waterfall, where water tumbles 73 feet into a sinkhole. Visitors enjoy boardwalk trails, swimming in a lake, and camping beneath tall pines. The park's unique geology includes sinkholes, caverns, and towering longleaf pines.

FLORIDA

☐ 🔖 ♡ **Fanning Springs State Park:** Situated along the Suwannee River, this park features a second-magnitude spring with crystal-clear waters perfect for swimming and snorkeling. Visitors enjoy picnicking, hiking, and spotting manatees in cooler months. The spring's steady 72-degree water and scenic surroundings offer a refreshing natural retreat.

☐ 🔖 ♡ **Florida Caverns State Park:** This park in Marianna is the only Florida state park offering guided tours of dry (air-filled) caves. Visitors explore limestone caverns with stalactites and flowstones. Above ground, the park features hiking, biking, camping, and paddling opportunities, with scenic bluffs and floodplain forests along the Chipola River.

☐ 🔖 ♡ **Fort Clinch State Park:** On Amelia Island's northern tip, this brick guardian of Cumberland Sound pairs Civil War history with wild coast. Explore vaulted casemates, earthworks, and living-history weekends, then roam dunes, maritime hammock, and shell-strewn beaches. Bike the park road or shaded trails, fish the inlet, and camp beneath twisting oaks where seabreezes and cannon echoes meet.

☐ 🔖 ♡ **Fort Cooper State Park:** Located in Inverness, this 700-acre park surrounds a spring-fed lake and commemorates an 1836 Seminole War fort site. Visitors can hike wooded trails, paddle on the lake, picnic, and observe wildlife. The park also hosts annual reenactments and offers peaceful natural settings for learning about Florida's frontier history.

☐ 🔖 ♡ **Fort Foster Historic Site:** Located within Hillsborough River State Park, this reconstructed 1830s fort represents Florida's role in the Second Seminole War. Accessible by ranger-led tours only, the site includes wooden palisades, blockhouses, and exhibits. It offers a glimpse into military history and life on the Florida frontier.

☐ 🔖 ♡ **Fort George Island Cultural State Park:** Centered on the restored Ribault Club, this coastal retreat offers scenic drives through maritime hammock, multi-use trails, a boat launch on the St. Johns, and tabby ruins tracing centuries of human history. Pair your visit with nearby Kingsley Plantation in the Timucuan Preserve, then linger for river views and quiet, moss-draped roads.

☐ 🔖 ♡ **Fort Mose Historic State Park:** Just north of St. Augustine, Fort Mose was the first free Black settlement legally sanctioned in what is now the U.S. The park includes a visitor center, boardwalks through salt marsh, and interpretive exhibits. It honors the legacy of escaped slaves who found freedom in Spanish Florida in the 1700s.

☐ 🔖 ♡ **Fort Zachary Taylor Historic State Park:** Located at the southern tip of Key West, this park offers guided tours of a Civil War-era fort and some of the island's best beaches. Visitors enjoy swimming, snorkeling, biking, and sunset views. The park combines military history with tropical coastal recreation in a unique setting.

☐ 🔖 ♡ **George Crady Bridge Fishing Pier State Park:** Located on the Nassau-Sound bridge, this park is a mile-long pedestrian fishing pier extending into the Atlantic. It offers year-round saltwater fishing for species like red drum, flounder, and whiting. The pier provides a relaxing coastal fishing spot with panoramic water views.

☐ 🔖 ♡ **Grayton Beach State Park:** Sugar-white quartz sands and turquoise Gulf waters meet pine flatwoods and the scenic shores of Western Lake, a coastal dune lake. Swim, paddle, and beachcomb, then hike or bike shady trails through scrub and longleaf. Book rustic-chic cabins or a pine-scented campsite and savor blazing sunsets, starry nights, and quiet mornings along 30A's wild heart.

☐ 🔖 ♡ **Henderson Beach State Park:** Near Destin, this park features sugar-white sand dunes and emerald Gulf waters. Visitors enjoy swimming, sunbathing, picnicking, and hiking a nature trail through coastal scrub. The park includes a popular campground just steps from the beach, offering easy access to one of Florida's most scenic shorelines.

☐ 🔖 ♡ **Highlands Hammock State Park:** One of Florida's oldest state parks, this Sebring-area preserve offers ancient oak trees, a scenic boardwalk through cypress swamp, and nine miles of hiking and biking trails. Visitors enjoy tram tours, wildlife viewing, and learning about CCC-era park history. It's a lush and shady escape into old-growth Florida.

☐ 🔖 ♡ **Hillsborough River State Park:** Located near Tampa, this park features class II river rapids, a rare sight in Florida. Visitors can paddle, camp, hike seven miles of trails, or swim in the pool. The park also contains Fort Foster Historic Site and offers a scenic blend of natural and historical attractions along the wooded riverbanks.

FLORIDA

☐ ☐ ♡ **Honeymoon Island State Park:** Miles of natural beach, shell-studded shoreline, and wind-twisted sand pines define Dunedin's beloved barrier island. Walk the Osprey Trail through rare slash pine forest, watch shorebirds feed on tidal flats, or cast for mackerel from the surf. Swim, paddle calm coves, and look for dolphins—then ferry to neighboring Caladesi for a two-island day.

☐ ☐ ♡ **Hontoon Island State Park:** Accessible only by boat or ferry on the St. Johns River near DeLand, this island park features lush hammocks, pine forests, and shell mounds left by Native Americans. Visitors enjoy kayaking, hiking, biking, camping, and wildlife watching in a peaceful, car-free environment.

☐ ☐ ♡ **Hugh Taylor Birch State Park:** Located in Fort Lauderdale, this coastal urban oasis offers walking and biking trails, kayak rentals along a freshwater lagoon, and shaded picnic areas. Once a private estate, the park preserves a slice of native coastal habitat and provides green space steps from bustling beachside development.

☐ ☐ ♡ **Ichetucknee Springs State Park:** Famous for tubing in its clear, spring-fed river, this park near Fort White is also great for snorkeling, swimming, and paddling. The 6-mile Ichetucknee River winds through shaded hammocks and offers abundant wildlife viewing. It's a popular summer escape into pristine, refreshing waters.

☐ ☐ ♡ **Indian Key Historic State Park:** Accessible only by boat from Islamorada, this small island contains the ruins of a 19th-century shipwreck salvage settlement. Visitors can snorkel, paddle, and walk interpretive trails through tropical vegetation. The park blends history and nature with scenic views of the surrounding turquoise waters.

☐ ☐ ♡ **John D. MacArthur Beach State Park:** Located on Singer Island, this barrier island park protects rare coastal habitats including dunes, maritime hammocks, and estuaries. Visitors enjoy kayaking, snorkeling, hiking, and visiting the nature center. A boardwalk and beach access provide opportunities to explore both land and sea.

☐ ☐ ♡ **John Gorrie Museum State Park:** In Apalachicola, this museum honors Dr. John Gorrie, a pioneer of air conditioning and refrigeration. Visitors learn about his 19th-century inventions and contributions to medical science. The small park also highlights local history and provides access to downtown Apalachicola's scenic riverfront.

☐ ☐ ♡ **John Pennekamp Coral Reef State Park:** Located in Key Largo, this was the first underwater park in the U.S. Visitors can snorkel or dive among vibrant coral reefs and marine life, take glass-bottom boat tours, or kayak through mangrove channels. The park also offers sandy beaches, a visitor center with aquariums, and opportunities for camping in a tropical setting.

☐ ☐ ♡ **Jonathan Dickinson State Park:** Situated in Hobe Sound, this is one of Florida's largest parks, featuring rivers, pine flatwoods, and sand pine scrub. Visitors can hike, bike, ride horses, kayak the Loxahatchee River, or tour historic Trapper Nelson's homestead. It's a haven for outdoor enthusiasts with abundant wildlife and varied landscapes.

☐ ☐ ♡ **Kissimmee Prairie Preserve State Park:** A 54,000-acre ocean of grass where crested caracara and the endangered Florida grasshopper sparrow ride the wind. Hike, bike, or ride horseback on sand tracks beneath endless sky, scanning for deer, burrowing owls, and wildflowers. At night, some of Florida's darkest skies reveal the Milky Way; astronomy pads and remote camps reward stargazers.

☐ ☐ ♡ **Koreshan State Park:** Located near Estero, this park preserves the remains of a 19th-century utopian settlement. Visitors can tour historic buildings, stroll riverside trails, and camp under towering oaks. The park offers kayaking on the Estero River and interpretive programs that highlight the fascinating history of the Koreshan Unity community.

☐ ☐ ♡ **Lake Griffin State Park:** Near Leesburg, this park offers a quiet retreat with access to Lake Griffin, part of the Harris Chain of Lakes. Visitors enjoy boating, fishing, and camping among towering oak trees. A highlight is Florida's second-largest live oak tree, which draws nature lovers and photographers to this peaceful setting.

☐ ☐ ♡ **Lake Jackson Mounds Archaeological State Park:** Near Tallahassee, this park protects several earthen mounds built by the Fort Walton culture over 800 years ago. Visitors can hike nature trails through pine woods and oak hammocks while learning about Native American ceremonial and political life in prehistoric Florida.

FLORIDA

☐ 🔖 ♡ **Lake June-in-Winter Scrub State Park:** On the Lake Wales Ridge near Lake Placid, this quiet preserve protects ancient scrub and rare plants amid rolling white sands. Look for Florida scrub-jays and gopher tortoises along sunlit loops, then cool off at the lake's shoreline for fishing or hand-launched paddling. Minimal facilities, maximum solitude—an intimate window into old Florida uplands.

☐ 🔖 ♡ **Lake Kissimmee State Park:** This 5,930-acre park near Lake Wales offers vast prairies, pine flatwoods, and marshes. Visitors enjoy boating, fishing, horseback riding, and hiking over 13 miles of trails. The park features a living history exhibit of a 19th-century cow camp, providing insight into Florida's cattle ranching heritage.

☐ 🔖 ♡ **Lake Louisa State Park:** Nestled in Clermont, this park features rolling hills, clear lakes, and diverse ecosystems. Visitors enjoy kayaking, fishing, swimming, and hiking over 20 miles of trails. The park offers cabins and campgrounds, making it ideal for an overnight escape into nature with scenic lakefront views.

☐ 🔖 ♡ **Lake Manatee State Park:** Located east of Bradenton, this park offers boating, fishing, and swimming in a reservoir along the Manatee River. Visitors hike through pine flatwoods and scrub habitats while spotting wildlife like deer and wading birds. The park includes a family-friendly campground and picnic areas for a full day of fun.

☐ 🔖 ♡ **Lake Talquin State Park:** Situated near Tallahassee, this small park overlooks scenic Lake Talquin, a reservoir on the Ochlockonee River. Visitors can hike wooded trails, fish from the pier, and enjoy birdwatching in a peaceful setting. The park's rolling hills and picnic facilities make it a quiet retreat for nature lovers.

☐ 🔖 ♡ **Letchworth-Love Mounds Archaeological State Park:** Located near Monticello, this park protects Florida's tallest Native American ceremonial earthwork, dating back over 1,000 years. Visitors can hike interpretive trails, view the mounds, and learn about the prehistoric Weedon Island culture. The serene woodland setting offers a glimpse into ancient Florida.

☐ 🔖 ♡ **Lignumvitae Key Botanical State Park:** Accessible only by boat, this small island park in the Keys preserves tropical hardwood hammock and a historic caretaker's house. Visitors can take guided tours, explore native vegetation, and enjoy a glimpse of the Keys' ecological and cultural history in a quiet, remote environment.

☐ 🔖 ♡ **Little Manatee River State Park:** Near Wimauma, this park features 2,400 acres of sandhills, river swamps, and pine flatwoods. Visitors can kayak the winding river, hike 15 miles of trails, or camp under shady oaks. The park is popular for its scenic beauty and abundant wildlife, including deer, otters, and wading birds.

☐ 🔖 ♡ **Little Talbot Island State Park:** This barrier island near Jacksonville boasts five miles of undeveloped beaches and maritime forests. Visitors can swim, surf, fish, hike along dunes, and explore salt marshes. The park offers camping facilities and is home to rare coastal habitats, making it a top destination for beach lovers seeking solitude.

☐ 🔖 ♡ **Long Key State Park:** Located in the Middle Keys, this park offers oceanfront campsites, nature trails, and opportunities for snorkeling, fishing, and kayaking. Visitors can enjoy sweeping views of turquoise waters and mangroves, making it an ideal destination for those seeking a peaceful, tropical escape.

☐ 🔖 ♡ **Lovers Key State Park:** Found near Fort Myers Beach, this park includes barrier islands and tidal lagoons perfect for kayaking, fishing, and birdwatching. It's renowned for its quiet beaches and wildlife, including manatees and dolphins. The park offers hiking trails and is a favorite spot for weddings and sunsets.

☐ 🔖 ♡ **Madison Blue Spring State Park:** Near the town of Madison, this park boasts a first-magnitude spring that bubbles up in a limestone basin along the Withlacoochee River. Visitors can swim in the vibrant blue waters, explore underwater caves (for certified divers), and hike riverside trails. It's one of Florida's most photogenic springs.

☐ 🔖 ♡ **Manatee Springs State Park:** Near Chiefland, this park features a first-magnitude spring that flows into the Suwannee River. Visitors swim, snorkel, and dive in the crystal-clear waters or walk boardwalks through cypress swamps. The park offers camping and is a winter refuge for manatees, making it a favorite for wildlife lovers.

FLORIDA

☐ ◻ ♡ **Marjorie Kinnan Rawlings Historic State Park:** Located in Cross Creek, this park preserves the home and grove of the Pulitzer Prize-winning author of The Yearling. Visitors can tour her 1930s farmhouse, walk scenic trails, and explore the landscape that inspired her writings. It's a literary and historical gem in rural Florida.

☐ ◻ ♡ **Mike Roess Gold Head Branch State Park:** Situated on rolling sandhills near Keystone Heights, this park features ravines, lakes, and pine forests. Visitors enjoy hiking, swimming, fishing, and camping in historic CCC-built cabins. The park's scenic beauty and elevation changes make it one of Florida's most picturesque inland parks.

☐ ◻ ♡ **Mound Key Archaeological State Park:** Only accessible by boat in Estero Bay, this park preserves a shell mound island once home to the Calusa, a powerful Native American civilization. Visitors can kayak to the island and explore short trails through mangrove forests and learn about the Calusa's impressive shell architecture.

☐ ◻ ♡ **Myakka River State Park:** One of Florida's oldest and largest parks, located near Sarasota. It features vast wetlands, prairies, and a scenic river perfect for kayaking and airboat tours. Visitors enjoy hiking, wildlife viewing, camping, and the famous canopy walkway for treetop views of the park's lush ecosystem.

☐ ◻ ♡ **Natural Bridge Battlefield Historic State Park:** This park near Tallahassee commemorates the 1865 Civil War battle where Confederate troops repelled Union forces, preserving Tallahassee from capture. Visitors walk trails past earthworks and interpretive signs, and each March, a battle reenactment honors this important Southern victory.

☐ ◻ ♡ **O'Leno State Park:** Located along the Santa Fe River near High Springs, this park is known for its disappearing river, where the water flows underground through limestone caverns. Visitors enjoy hiking, biking, camping, and exploring historic CCC structures. The park offers natural beauty, deep forests, and unique geology.

☐ ◻ ♡ **Ochlockonee River State Park:** Located in Florida's Panhandle, this peaceful riverside park is a haven for wildlife such as white squirrels, black bears, and bald eagles. Visitors enjoy paddling, hiking, and fishing along the river's scenic banks. The park's quiet atmosphere makes it ideal for relaxing and connecting with nature.

☐ ◻ ♡ **Oleta River State Park:** Miami's wild side: mangrove-lined waterways, a sandy bayfront beach, and miles of off-road bike trails inside Florida's largest urban park. Kayak the tidal river, spot manatees and herons, or rent a board and glide Biscayne Bay. Shaded picnic areas, simple cabins, and golden-hour skyline views deliver a nature escape minutes from the city.

☐ ◻ ♡ **Olustee Battlefield Historic State Park:** Located in Baker County, this site preserves the location of Florida's largest Civil War battle. Visitors can walk shaded trails past historical markers, tour the small interpretive center, and attend annual reenactments. The park honors those who fought and died in the 1864 conflict.

☐ ◻ ♡ **Orman House Historic State Park:** In Apalachicola, this park showcases a beautifully restored antebellum home built in 1838 by merchant Thomas Orman. Visitors tour period-furnished rooms and stroll adjacent gardens. The park offers insight into 19th-century Gulf Coast life and highlights the region's shipping and trade heritage.

☐ ◻ ♡ **Oscar Scherer State Park:** Located in Osprey, this park preserves rare scrubby flatwoods and is one of the best places to see the endangered Florida scrub-jay. Visitors enjoy biking, hiking, kayaking, and swimming in Lake Osprey. The park's trails and habitats offer year-round opportunities for wildlife viewing.

☐ ◻ ♡ **Paynes Creek Historic State Park:** Located near Bowling Green, this park commemorates the site of an 1849 attack that led to the Seminole Wars. Visitors can hike trails through pine woods, visit a small museum, and view the reconstructed trading post area. The park combines history with a peaceful natural setting.

☐ ◻ ♡ **Paynes Prairie Preserve State Park:** South of Gainesville, this 22,000-acre park features sweeping grasslands, bison, wild horses, and over 270 bird species. Visitors enjoy panoramic views from an observation tower, hike trails through varied habitats, and paddle freshwater creeks. It's one of the most unique ecosystems in Florida.

☐ ◻ ♡ **Peacock Springs State Park:** Near Live Oak, this park protects two major springs and one of the longest underwater cave systems in the U.S. It's a favorite for cave diving, swimming, and picnicking. Visitors can also explore nature trails through hardwood hammocks. Clear spring water and unique geology define this peaceful park.

FLORIDA

☐ 🔖 ♡ **Perdido Key State Park:** Located on a narrow barrier island near Pensacola, this Gulf-front park offers white sand beaches and dunes that are ideal for swimming, sunbathing, and surf fishing. It's also a nesting site for sea turtles and shorebirds. The park provides a quiet alternative to more developed beaches nearby.

☐ 🔖 ♡ **Pumpkin Hill Creek Preserve State Park:** Located in northeast Jacksonville, this park protects hardwood forests, tidal creeks, and salt marshes along the Nassau and St. Johns Rivers. Visitors enjoy hiking, kayaking, and horseback riding. The park offers excellent birdwatching and connects to larger conservation lands and paddling trails.

☐ 🔖 ♡ **Rainbow Springs State Park:** Near Dunnellon, this park features Florida's fourth-largest spring, surrounded by lush gardens and waterfalls. Visitors can swim, kayak, and hike trails through hardwood forest and rolling hills. Formerly a 1930s tourist attraction, the park now offers a scenic, natural getaway with crystal-clear waters.

☐ 🔖 ♡ **Ravine Gardens State Park:** Near Palatka, this park features steep ravines and formal gardens filled with azaleas, especially vibrant in spring. Visitors hike suspension bridges and scenic trails that wind through the lush terrain. Built by the CCC in the 1930s, the park offers both natural beauty and historical architecture.

☐ 🔖 ♡ **River Rise Preserve State Park:** Located just north of High Springs, this park is where the Santa Fe River reemerges from underground after disappearing in O'Leno State Park. It features equestrian trails, hardwood hammocks, and tranquil woods. A great destination for horseback riding, hiking, and quiet nature experiences.

☐ 🔖 ♡ **Rock Springs Run State Reserve:** Located in Sorrento, this 14,000-acre park features pine flatwoods, swamps, and the clear waters of Rock Springs Run. Visitors can hike, horseback ride, or paddle through scenic wilderness. The park is also a habitat for black bears and Florida scrub-jays and offers backcountry camping opportunities.

☐ 🔖 ♡ **San Felasco Hammock Preserve State Park:** Near Gainesville, this park protects one of Florida's largest remaining hardwood forests. Visitors hike or bike miles of trails through rolling terrain and shady hammocks. The park also offers horseback riding and is known for its biodiversity and peaceful natural setting.

☐ 🔖 ♡ **San Marcos de Apalache Historic State Park:** Located in St. Marks, this park preserves the ruins of a Spanish fort built in the 1600s. Visitors can explore the museum, walk scenic riverfront trails, and view historic earthworks. The park's setting at the confluence of two rivers offers great birdwatching and rich cultural history.

☐ 🔖 ♡ **San Pedro Underwater Archaeological Preserve State Park:** Located off Islamorada in the Florida Keys, this underwater park protects the remains of the 18th-century Spanish ship San Pedro. Divers and snorkelers explore coral-encrusted ballast stones, cannons, and marine life in crystal-clear waters. It's a unique mix of history and reef ecology.

☐ 🔖 ♡ **Savannas Preserve State Park:** Stretching along Florida's southeast coast, this park protects a rare freshwater marsh ecosystem. Visitors can paddle quiet waterways, hike sandy trails, and spot wildlife such as sandhill cranes and alligators. The park offers solitude and scenic beauty amid urban surroundings.

☐ 🔖 ♡ **Seabranch Preserve State Park:** Situated in Martin County, this quiet preserve protects pine flatwoods and scrub habitats. Visitors enjoy hiking and birdwatching on low-impact trails. The park's undeveloped nature makes it ideal for peaceful exploration of native plant communities and Florida's seasonal wildlife.

☐ 🔖 ♡ **Sebastian Inlet State Park:** Located where the Indian River Lagoon meets the Atlantic, this park is famous for surfing, fishing, and beachcombing. Visitors also explore nature trails, a fishing museum, and historical exhibits. It's a hotspot for manatee viewing, wading birds, and coastal recreation on Florida's east coast.

☐ 🔖 ♡ **Silver Springs State Park:** Near Ocala, this park is famous for its glass-bottom boat tours over crystal-clear springs. The park also offers kayaking, hiking trails, and a museum on Florida's natural and cultural history. It's one of the oldest tourist attractions in the state and a showcase of spring-fed ecosystems.

☐ 🔖 ♡ **Skyway Fishing Pier State Park:** Spanning Tampa Bay, this park is the world's longest fishing pier, built on the remains of the old Sunshine Skyway Bridge. It's open 24/7 and offers fishing for snook, tarpon, and grouper. With panoramic views and easy access, it's a favorite for both serious anglers and casual visitors.

FLORIDA

☐ 🔖 ♡ **St. Andrews State Park:** Located in Panama City Beach, this popular park offers sugar-white sands, emerald waters, and excellent opportunities for swimming, snorkeling, kayaking, and fishing. Visitors can explore nature trails, birdwatch, or take a shuttle to Shell Island. The park also features a large campground and scenic picnic areas.

☐ 🔖 ♡ **St. George Island State Park:** Situated on a barrier island along the Gulf Coast, this park features nine miles of pristine beach ideal for shelling, sunbathing, and stargazing. Visitors can camp in dunes, paddle in Apalachicola Bay, and enjoy hiking and birdwatching. It's a peaceful destination known for natural beauty and wildlife.

☐ 🔖 ♡ **St. Lucie Inlet Preserve State Park:** Accessible only by boat, this park on Florida's east coast offers a quiet retreat with coastal hammocks, mangroves, and unspoiled Atlantic beaches. Visitors can hike scenic trails, snorkel near the reef, or paddle the calm estuary. It's a sanctuary for sea turtles and migratory birds.

☐ 🔖 ♡ **St. Marks River Preserve State Park:** This quiet preserve near Tallahassee protects swamps, flatwoods, and sandhills along the St. Marks River corridor. Visitors enjoy primitive hiking, biking, and horseback riding on forested trails. The park supports water quality and habitat conservation in one of Florida's oldest river systems.

☐ 🔖 ♡ **St. Sebastian River Preserve State Park:** Spanning over 22,000 acres in Brevard and Indian River counties, this park protects longleaf pine and scrub habitats along the St. Sebastian River. Visitors enjoy birding, horseback riding, and hiking through undeveloped wilderness. The preserve is home to rare species and offers peaceful solitude.

☐ 🔖 ♡ **Stephen Foster Folk Culture Center State Park:** Located in White Springs along the Suwannee River, this park celebrates the music of composer Stephen Foster. Visitors can explore exhibits, a carillon tower, craft demonstrations, and nature trails. The park hosts festivals and provides a cultural experience in a natural riverfront setting.

☐ 🔖 ♡ **Stump Pass Beach State Park:** Found at the southern tip of Manasota Key, this park features quiet Gulf beaches, tidal mangroves, and nature trails. Visitors enjoy beachcombing, fishing, kayaking, and spotting dolphins and seabirds. It's a peaceful alternative to more developed beaches with scenic views and shallow waters.

☐ 🔖 ♡ **Suwannee River State Park:** Located where the Suwannee and Withlacoochee Rivers meet, this park features river bluffs, hardwood forests, and historic Civil War-era earthworks. Visitors can hike scenic trails, camp, paddle the rivers, and fish in shaded waters. The park's peaceful ambiance and rich history make it a hidden gem.

☐ 🔖 ♡ **T.H. Stone Memorial St. Joseph Peninsula State Park:** Situated on a narrow peninsula near Port St. Joe, this park offers tall dunes, white sand beaches, and rich coastal habitats. Visitors enjoy camping, fishing, swimming, hiking, and birdwatching. Its natural beauty and quiet setting make it one of the Panhandle's top coastal parks.

☐ 🔖 ♡ **Tarkiln Bayou Preserve State Park:** Located in Escambia County, this park protects a rare wet prairie ecosystem and is home to the endangered white-top pitcher plant. Visitors can explore boardwalks and trails through pine flatwoods and wetland habitats. It's a peaceful spot for nature walks and observing rare native flora.

☐ 🔖 ♡ **Terra Ceia Preserve State Park:** A lesser-known preserve near Tampa Bay, this park offers tidal marshes, mangroves, and hiking trails ideal for birdwatching and quiet exploration. It provides important estuarine habitat and access to kayak routes through Terra Ceia Bay. The park is undeveloped and perfect for nature immersion.

☐ 🔖 ♡ **Three Rivers State Park:** Near Sneads in the Panhandle, this park sits at the confluence of the Chattahoochee, Flint, and Apalachicola Rivers. Visitors enjoy boating, fishing, hiking, and camping among rolling hills and scenic lakefronts. The park's peaceful vibe and high bluffs offer sweeping water views and excellent wildlife viewing.

☐ 🔖 ♡ **Tomoka State Park:** Located near Ormond Beach, this park surrounds the Tomoka River and is rich in history and wildlife. Visitors can paddle winding waterways, camp under oak canopies, and visit the ancient site of the Timucuan village of Nocoroco. It's a peaceful retreat with excellent fishing and birding opportunities.

☐ 🔖 ♡ **Topsail Hill Preserve State Park:** Towering "topsail" dunes, three rare coastal dune lakes, and over three miles of uncrowded sugar-sand beach anchor this 30A favorite. Ride the tram or hike to turquoise Gulf water, then explore longleaf pine trails alive with deer and songbirds. Camp or stay in cabins, bike paved paths, and watch pastel sunsets melt into starry Panhandle nights.

FLORIDA

☐ ▯ ♡ **Torreya State Park:** Known for its high bluffs and rare Torreya trees, this park near Bristol offers dramatic views of the Apalachicola River. Visitors hike challenging trails, explore a historic plantation house, and camp in shaded sites. The park is prized for its steep terrain, unique geology, and rich biodiversity.

☐ ▯ ♡ **Troy Spring State Park:** Located near Branford, this park features a clear spring with depths up to 70 feet, ideal for swimming and diving. Visitors can also see the submerged remains of a Confederate steamboat, the Madison, scuttled during the Civil War. Shady trails and peaceful picnic areas enhance this riverfront gem.

☐ ▯ ♡ **Waccasassa Bay Preserve State Park:** Located on Florida's Gulf Coast, this remote and undeveloped park is accessible only by boat. It protects salt marshes, tidal creeks, and hammocks that serve as critical habitat for manatees, birds, and fish. It's a quiet destination for paddling and solitude in a wild coastal environment.

☐ ▯ ♡ **Washington Oaks Gardens State Park:** Located in Palm Coast, this park is renowned for its formal gardens, majestic live oaks, and coquina rock formations along the Atlantic shoreline. Visitors stroll garden paths, picnic beneath the trees, and explore nature trails through coastal hammock. It's a peaceful blend of cultivated beauty and wild scenery.

☐ ▯ ♡ **Weeki Wachee Springs State Park:** Where mermaids meet a spring of dazzling blue. The classic underwater theater hosts live shows, while Buccaneer Bay adds slides and a sandy swim area. Paddle the clear Weeki Wachee River past turtles and manatees, stroll shady gardens, and soak in mid-century roadside charm wrapped around a first-magnitude spring that never stops flowing.

☐ ▯ ♡ **Wekiwa Springs State Park:** Situated near Orlando, this park features a crystal-clear spring perfect for swimming, snorkeling, and kayaking. Visitors can hike through pine flatwoods, bike shaded trails, and camp under the stars. The springhead offers year-round cool water and is a popular escape into nature just minutes from the city.

☐ ▯ ♡ **Werner-Boyce Salt Springs State Park:** Near Port Richey, this park protects coastal marshes, mangrove islands, and a spring that flows into the Gulf. Visitors can kayak winding waterways, hike nature trails, and fish from the shore. The park's rich estuarine environment supports dolphins, wading birds, and other coastal wildlife.

☐ ▯ ♡ **Windley Key Fossil Reef Geological State Park:** Located in Islamorada, this park showcases a fossilized coral reef exposed in an old quarry once used by Henry Flagler's railroad. Visitors explore trails with educational exhibits on the reef's formation and see ancient coral beds embedded with fossils. It's a unique geological site in the Keys.

☐ ▯ ♡ **Yellow Bluff Fort Historic State Park:** Located near Jacksonville, this park preserves the remains of a Civil War-era encampment used to guard the St. Johns River. Visitors explore interpretive signs, shaded trails, and earthwork remnants. Though small, it offers a glimpse into Florida's military history in a serene riverside setting.

☐ ▯ ♡ **Yulee Sugar Mill Ruins Historic State Park:** Near Homosassa, this small park features the stone ruins of a 19th-century sugar mill used during the Civil War. Visitors can view the preserved machinery and learn about Florida's sugar plantation history. The site is shaded by live oaks and includes picnic areas for a quiet historical stop.

National Parks

 ☐ ▯ ♡ **Big Cypress National Preserve:** Protecting one of the largest wetlands in the U.S., Big Cypress is a vast mosaic of cypress swamps, prairies, and tropical forests. Visitors can hike, paddle, birdwatch, or drive scenic routes while spotting wildlife like alligators, wading birds, and the elusive Florida panther. The preserve serves as a vital buffer for the Everglades ecosystem.

 ☐ ▯ ♡ **Biscayne National Park:** Just south of Miami, Biscayne protects coral reefs, mangrove forests, and the clear waters of Biscayne Bay. Over 90% of the park is underwater, making it a paradise for snorkeling, diving, and boating. Visitors can explore shipwrecks, kayak around islands, and discover the area's cultural history alongside its vibrant marine life.

FLORIDA

 **Canaveral National Seashore:** This undeveloped stretch of Florida's east coast preserves barrier islands, dunes, lagoons, and tidal marshes. It offers quiet beaches, excellent birdwatching, and seasonal sea turtle nesting. Visitors enjoy swimming, hiking trails, and the rare chance to experience Florida's shoreline in its natural, largely untouched state.

 **Castillo de San Marcos National Monument:** Standing in St. Augustine, this 17th-century Spanish fortress is the oldest masonry fort in the continental U.S. Built of coquina stone, it protected Spain's colonial interests for centuries. Today, visitors tour its bastions, explore exhibits, and enjoy sweeping views of Matanzas Bay from the ramparts.

 **De Soto National Memorial:** Located in Bradenton, this site commemorates Hernando de Soto's 1539 expedition and its impact on Native peoples. Visitors can walk shaded trails, view living history demonstrations, and explore exhibits that highlight the clash of cultures during early European colonization of the Southeast.

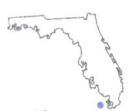 **Dry Tortugas National Park:** Seventy miles west of Key West, this remote park features Fort Jefferson, coral reefs, and seven small islands. Accessible only by boat or seaplane, it offers snorkeling, birdwatching, camping, and a sense of solitude. Its mix of history and marine wilderness makes it one of the most unique national parks.

 **Everglades National Park:** Covering 1.5 million acres, Everglades protects vast wetlands of sawgrass, mangroves, and cypress. It's home to alligators, manatees, panthers, and countless bird species. Visitors explore by foot, bike, kayak, or airboat, experiencing a rare subtropical wilderness that plays a vital role in global biodiversity.

 **Fort Caroline National Memorial:** In Jacksonville, this memorial honors the short-lived French Huguenot colony of 1564. Visitors explore reconstructed fort structures, nature trails, and exhibits telling the story of European colonization and its consequences, all within a landscape of coastal forests and marshlands.

 **Fort Matanzas National Monument:** Built in 1742 to guard St. Augustine, this small Spanish fort sits on Rattlesnake Island. Accessible by ferry, the site preserves colonial military history and offers nature trails, fishing areas, and wildlife viewing. Visitors enjoy both the historical significance and the scenic coastal setting.

 **Gulf Islands National Seashore:** Spanning Florida and Mississippi, this park protects sugar-white beaches, dunes, and barrier islands along the Gulf Coast. Historic forts, such as Fort Pickens, highlight military history, while visitors enjoy camping, hiking, swimming, and birdwatching in a serene, unspoiled coastal environment.

 **Timucuan Ecological and Historic Preserve:** This Jacksonville preserve protects over 46,000 acres of salt marshes, forests, and historic sites like Kingsley Plantation. It highlights 6,000 years of human history, from Indigenous cultures to European settlers. Visitors enjoy hiking, paddling, and exploring one of Florida's last unspoiled coastal wetlands.

State & National Forests

Apalachicola National Forest: Florida's largest national forest spans the Panhandle with longleaf pine flatwoods, cypress swamps, and bogs. It includes two wilderness areas, Bradwell Bay and Mud Swamp, and offers abundant recreation including hiking, hunting, off-roading, and paddling. It's a haven for rare plants and species like the red-cockaded woodpecker.

Belmore State Forest: Located near Green Cove Springs, Belmore offers pine flatwoods, scrubby sandhills, and access to the Satsuma Trail. The forest supports sustainable timber, water recharge, and wildlife habitat. Visitors enjoy hiking, horseback riding, and seasonal hunting in this quiet and ecologically diverse corner of northeast Florida.

FLORIDA

☐ 🔖 ♡ **Big Shoals State Forest:** Adjacent to Big Shoals State Park near White Springs, this forest features the only Class III whitewater rapids in Florida. Visitors enjoy hiking trails, birdwatching, and views of limestone bluffs along the Suwannee River. It's a protected floodplain forest that supports rare aquatic and hardwood species.

☐ 🔖 ♡ **Blackwater River State Forest:** Florida's largest state forest, near Milton, features longleaf pine ecosystems, pitcher plant bogs, and the clear Blackwater River. Known for scenic paddling, hiking, and equestrian trails, it's part of a regional corridor protecting the Florida Panhandle's biodiversity and historic landscapes.

☐ 🔖 ♡ **Carl Duval Moore State Forest:** A small forest in Putnam County, this preserve features bottomland hardwood swamps and mixed pine stands. Managed primarily for water resource protection and floodplain conservation, it offers limited recreation including nature viewing and environmental education.

☐ 🔖 ♡ **Cary State Forest:** Located northwest of Jacksonville, Cary includes over 35,000 acres of pine flatwoods, wetlands, and upland hammocks. Visitors enjoy horseback riding, hiking, hunting, and off-road biking. It serves as an important wildlife corridor and protects the headwaters of the St. Marys River.

☐ 🔖 ♡ **Charles H. Bronson State Forest:** Adjacent to the Little Big Econ State Forest, this forest near Christmas offers 11,000 acres of pine flatwoods and hydric hammocks. Trails support hiking, biking, and horseback riding. The forest also protects vital water recharge zones and wildlife corridors in fast-growing central Florida.

☐ 🔖 ♡ **Cottage Hill State Forest:** A small Florida Forest Service tract in Escambia County, this pocket forest protects pine flatwoods and hardwood swales on the western Panhandle's uplands. With no developed facilities, it's a low-key spot for quiet walks, birding, and forest management research. Access and activities are limited—expect an undeveloped setting focused on habitat conservation and stewardship.

☐ 🔖 ♡ **Deep Creek State Forest:** A small, quiet forest near Hastings in St. Johns County, Deep Creek protects sensitive creekside habitats and mixed pine hardwood uplands. While undeveloped for recreation, it plays an important role in water protection and wildlife habitat in Florida's northeastern coastal plain.

☐ 🔖 ♡ **Etoniah Creek State Forest:** Located near Palatka, this forest protects sandhills, pine flatwoods, and seepage streams. Home to the endangered Etonia rosemary, it offers hiking trails and backcountry camping in a scrubby, scenic landscape. It also supports habitat corridors for wide-ranging wildlife like black bears.

☐ 🔖 ♡ **Four Creeks State Forest:** This forest near Callahan protects the headwaters of four creeks and includes upland pine, cypress swamps, and blackwater streams. It provides habitat for migratory birds and is used for horseback riding, hunting, and nature study, while also serving as a regional conservation buffer.

☐ 🔖 ♡ **Goethe State Forest:** Located in Levy County, Goethe spans more than 50,000 acres of pine plantations, wet prairies, and dome swamps. It's home to one of the largest remaining longleaf pine ecosystems and offers trails for horseback riding, hiking, and hunting. The forest is also vital for aquifer recharge and wildlife habitat.

☐ 🔖 ♡ **Holopaw State Forest:** One of Florida's smallest forests, Holopaw near Osceola County covers less than 60 acres. It preserves pine flatwoods and provides habitat for gopher tortoises and scrub species. It has no recreational facilities and is managed primarily for conservation and restoration of native vegetation.

☐ 🔖 ♡ **Indian Lake State Forest:** Near Ocala, this forest is known for sinkhole lakes, scrub habitat, and longleaf pine restoration. Hiking and wildlife observation are available along its trails, and the forest is part of a wider effort to protect Florida's karst topography and recharge zones in Marion County.

☐ 🔖 ♡ **Jennings State Forest:** West of Jacksonville, Jennings includes hardwood swamps, longleaf pine, and rare plant bogs like the pitcher plant prairie. It offers trails for hiking, horseback riding, and nature study, with access to Black Creek and diverse flora and fauna across nearly 25,000 acres.

☐ 🔖 ♡ **John M. Bethea State Forest:** Spreading across Baker County between Osceola National Forest and Okefenokee, this ~37,700-acre corridor protects longleaf pine flatwoods, sandhills, and St. Marys River headwaters. Expect remote roads and trails for wildlife viewing, hiking, and seasonal hunting within the WMA—an expansive, fire-managed landscape anchoring one of North Florida's wildest regions.

FLORIDA

☐ 🔖 ♡ **Kissimmee Bend State Forest:** Along the Kissimmee River north of Lake Okeechobee, this ~1,990-acre forest is managed with FWC as part of the Everglades Headwaters WMA. Levee paths and sand roads invite hiking, biking, or horseback riding; anglers and paddlers use river access; broad restored floodplain prairies draw wading birds and raptors—big-sky sunsets are a bonus.

☐ 🔖 ♡ **Lake George State Forest:** Located west of Daytona Beach, Lake George protects hardwood floodplains, pine flatwoods, and blackwater creeks. It helps buffer the St. Johns River and includes trails for hiking, wildlife observation, and seasonal hunting. The forest also supports aquifer recharge and biodiversity conservation.

☐ 🔖 ♡ **Lake Talquin State Forest:** A mosaic of tracts west of Tallahassee—Fort Braden, Bear Creek, and more—protecting steephead ravines, longleaf pine, and oak bluffs above Lake Talquin. Ride equestrian/hiking loops at Fort Braden, explore family-friendly trails and programs at Bear Creek Educational Forest, and enjoy lake overlooks and rich birdlife across shady sandhills and floodplain woods.

☐ 🔖 ♡ **Lake Wales Ridge State Forest:** This forest preserves one of Florida's oldest geological features—a sandy ridge rich in endemic plants. Located near Frostproof, it supports rare scrub species, sandhill habitats, and the endangered Florida scrub-jay. Trails allow hiking and equestrian use across fragile upland ecosystems.

☐ 🔖 ♡ **Little Big Econ State Forest:** Spanning more than 10,000 acres along the Econlockhatchee River near Orlando, this forest offers scenic paddling, hiking, and primitive camping. Known for its steep bluffs and floodplain trails, it provides a close-to-home wild area with boardwalks and rich birdlife along central Florida's blackwater rivers.

☐ 🔖 ♡ **Matanzas State Forest:** Situated near the Atlantic coast south of St. Augustine, Matanzas protects maritime forests, flatwoods, and estuarine marshes. It offers primitive trails, wildlife viewing, and educational opportunities while buffering the Matanzas River and preserving coastal biodiversity in a rapidly developing region.

☐ 🔖 ♡ **Myakka State Forest:** Near Sarasota, Myakka preserves pine flatwoods, wetlands, and prairies in the Myakka River basin. Trails for hiking and horseback riding loop through varied terrain, while canoe access and birdwatching are popular. The forest supports vital wildlife corridors between coastal and inland ecosystems.

☐ 🔖 ♡ **Newnans Lake State Forest:** Adjacent to Gainesville, this forest helps protect wetlands and hardwood swamps around Newnans Lake. It supports biodiversity, water quality, and passive recreation including birdwatching and walking trails. It's an important green space close to urban areas.

☐ 🔖 ♡ **Ocala National Forest:** Covering over 430,000 acres in central Florida, Ocala is known for clear springs, sand pine scrub, and extensive ATV and hiking trail systems. Visitors flock to Juniper, Alexander, and Salt Springs for swimming and paddling. It's the oldest National Forest east of the Mississippi and a hotspot for biodiversity and recreation.

☐ 🔖 ♡ **Okaloacoochee Slough State Forest:** Located in southwest Florida, this forest preserves vast wetlands, sloughs, and pine uplands. It supports endangered species like the Florida panther and offers limited trails and primitive camping. The landscape is remote and wild, offering unique insight into Florida's natural hydrology.

☐ 🔖 ♡ **Osceola National Forest:** North of Lake City, Osceola protects pine flatwoods, cypress swamps, and the Big Gum Swamp Wilderness. It includes part of the Florida Trail and offers hunting, hiking, fishing, and equestrian use. This compact yet diverse national forest plays a critical role in conserving the state's northern wetland ecosystems.

☐ 🔖 ♡ **Peace River State Forest:** A small forest near Wauchula, Peace River protects hardwood hammocks and floodplain ecosystems along its namesake river. The area provides access to paddling routes, birdwatching, and seasonal wildlife. Its strategic location contributes to regional conservation goals in central Florida.

☐ 🔖 ♡ **Picayune Strand State Forest:** Located near Naples, this 80,000-acre forest is part of a massive Everglades restoration project converting old subdivisions into wetlands. Visitors enjoy hiking, wildlife viewing, and backcountry trails through slash pine, cypress domes, and wet prairie ecosystems vital to regional water flow.

FLORIDA

☐ 🔖 ♡ **Pine Log State Forest:** Florida's oldest state forest, Pine Log lies near Panama City and offers sandhill pine forests, fishing lakes, and campgrounds. Trails support hiking, horseback riding, and wildlife watching in a rolling landscape of upland pine and wiregrass. It's a great destination for outdoor recreation in the Panhandle.

☐ 🔖 ♡ **Plank Road State Forest:** This forest protects a mix of sand pine scrub and pine flatwoods near Lake Placid. It's used for habitat protection, timber research, and passive recreation. Trails allow access to dry upland communities, and the area supports gopher tortoises, fox squirrels, and other threatened species.

☐ 🔖 ♡ **Point Washington State Forest:** Situated near the Emerald Coast, this forest features coastal dune lakes, wet prairies, and pine uplands. Visitors enjoy hiking, birdwatching, and camping along the Longleaf Greenway Trail. It provides critical habitat in a high-growth tourism zone while linking larger Gulf Coast conservation areas.

☐ 🔖 ♡ **Ralph E. Simmons Memorial State Forest:** Bordering the St. Marys River, this northeastern forest features hardwood hammocks, pine forests, and sandy bluffs. Trails follow the river and offer fishing, hiking, and hunting opportunities in a quiet, biologically rich corridor at the Florida–Georgia line.

☐ 🔖 ♡ **Ross Prairie State Forest:** Located in Marion County, this forest includes scrub and flatwoods near the Cross Florida Greenway. It provides hiking trails, equestrian facilities, and primitive camping close to Ocala. Its strategic location links habitat corridors and recreation areas in central Florida.

☐ 🔖 ♡ **Seminole State Forest:** Covering over 25,000 acres near Mount Dora, Seminole includes sandhill ridges, flatwoods, and parts of the Florida National Scenic Trail. It offers backcountry hiking, wildlife watching, and remote campsites. This forest is one of the best places in Florida to experience pine uplands and rare plants.

☐ 🔖 ♡ **Tate's Hell State Forest:** Located near Carrabelle in the Panhandle, Tate's Hell spans over 200,000 acres of swamp, pine flatwoods, and wet prairie. The forest includes part of the Florida Trail and is known for wild hogs, carnivorous plants, and the tale of Cebe Tate. It offers camping, paddling, and rugged backcountry exploration.

☐ 🔖 ♡ **Tiger Bay State Forest:** Just west of Daytona Beach, Tiger Bay protects wetlands, cypress domes, and pine ridges. It helps recharge the Floridan Aquifer and supports hiking, horseback riding, and wildlife viewing. The forest also buffers natural communities in a rapidly developing region of east-central Florida.

☐ 🔖 ♡ **Twin Rivers State Forest:** Located along the Suwannee and Withlacoochee Rivers near Live Oak, Twin Rivers features floodplain hardwoods, sandhills, and blackwater creeks. It includes riverfront trails and paddling access and supports species like alligators, otters, and prothonotary warblers. It's ideal for water-based recreation and scenic views.

☐ 🔖 ♡ **Wakulla State Forest:** Situated south of Tallahassee, Wakulla protects bottomland hardwood forests, ephemeral wetlands, and mesic flatwoods. It helps protect the Wakulla Springs watershed and provides quiet hiking and hunting opportunities. It plays a vital role in protecting one of the largest freshwater springs in the world.

☐ 🔖 ♡ **Watson Island State Forest:** A small forest in Columbia County, Watson Island includes pine flatwoods and bottomland hardwoods. It's managed for timber, wildlife habitat, and conservation. While it has no developed recreation, it contributes to broader habitat preservation in north-central Florida.

☐ 🔖 ♡ **Welaka State Forest:** Located along the St. Johns River in Putnam County, Welaka features hardwood hammocks, equestrian trails, and a fish hatchery. It offers hiking, wildlife viewing, and camping under shady oak canopies. Its trails wind through uplands and wet lowlands, supporting both recreation and conservation in a scenic riverside setting.

☐ 🔖 ♡ **Withlacoochee State Forest:** One of Florida's largest, Withlacoochee includes six separate tracts across central Florida. It features longleaf pine, wetlands, caves, and extensive recreation like hiking, biking, camping, and horseback riding. The forest also protects karst landscapes and aquifer recharge zones across a broad ecological corridor.

FLORIDA

National Scenic Byways & All-American Roads

☐ 🔖 ♡ **A1A Scenic & Historic Coastal Byway:** Stretching 72 miles along Florida's northeast coast, this All-American Road passes beaches, estuaries, and barrier islands while connecting towns like St. Augustine and Fernandina. Visitors explore lighthouses, historic districts, state parks, and coastal habitats that highlight beach culture, maritime heritage, and Florida's natural beauty.

☐ 🔖 ♡ **Big Bend Scenic Byway:** Covering 220 miles of Florida's Big Bend, this National Scenic Byway traces marshes, flatwoods, and undeveloped Gulf beaches. Linking Apalachicola to St. Marks, it provides solitude, birdwatching, fishing, and rustic beauty. It's a journey through Florida's least-developed coast, showcasing rich biodiversity and unspoiled natural landscapes.

☐ 🔖 ♡ **Florida Black Bear Scenic Byway:** Winding 123 miles through Ocala National Forest, this National Scenic Byway showcases springs, pine flatwoods, and shady hammocks. Visitors may spot Florida black bears and other wildlife while hiking, camping, paddling, or riding forest trails. It's an immersive drive through one of Florida's wildest landscapes.

☐ 🔖 ♡ **Florida Keys Scenic Highway:** Following US 1 for 110 miles from Key Largo to Key West, this All-American Road crosses turquoise waters and coral reefs via the famous Overseas Highway bridges. Visitors encounter tropical islands, historic towns, diving sites, and ocean vistas—making it one of America's most iconic road trips.

☐ 🔖 ♡ **Indian River Lagoon National Scenic Byway:** Covering 150 miles from Oak Hill to Wabasso, this byway traces the biodiverse Indian River Lagoon. Visitors encounter estuary views, barrier islands, Kennedy Space Center, and fishing towns. Birdwatching, paddling, and cultural stops highlight the lagoon's role as one of North America's most vibrant ecosystems.

☐ 🔖 ♡ **Ormond Scenic Loop & Trail:** A 34-mile National Scenic Byway circling Tomoka Peninsula near Ormond Beach, this loop winds through oak-shaded roads, tidal creeks, and beachside parks. Visitors enjoy wildlife habitats, historic markers, and cultural sites along the coast, creating a memorable drive through woodlands and shoreline landscapes.

☐ 🔖 ♡ **River of Lakes Heritage Corridor:** A 156-mile National Scenic Byway tracing the St. Johns River and its chain of lakes through West Volusia and Seminole. Cruise oak-canopy roads linking DeLand, DeBary, Sanford and riverside fish camps; stop for manatees at Blue Spring and history at DeLeon Springs. Boardwalks, birding, and easy paddles showcase marshes, backwaters, and classic "Old Florida" vistas.

☐ 🔖 ♡ **Scenic Highway 30A:** A 33-mile National Scenic Byway along the Emerald Coast, this route travels through coastal dune lakes, beach towns like Seaside and Grayton, and state parks. Visitors enjoy white-sand beaches, rolling woodlands, and pastel coastal communities, making it a scenic and cultural gem on Florida's Gulf shoreline.

State Scenic Byways

☐ 🔖 ♡ **Big Bend Scenic Byway – Coastal Trail:** This route follows the Gulf coast through Franklin and Wakulla counties, showcasing tidal flats, salt marshes, fishing villages, and pine forests. It highlights the ecological richness of the Big Bend, with birding, seafood culture, and Gulf views, offering a glimpse of Florida's undeveloped and wild shoreline landscapes.

☐ 🔖 ♡ **Big Bend Scenic Byway – Forest Trail:** Traversing Apalachicola National Forest and St. Marks National Wildlife Refuge, this trail winds through longleaf pine forests, wetlands, and sinkholes. It highlights unique ecosystems and recreational stops for hiking, paddling, and wildlife watching, immersing travelers in Florida's largest and most biodiverse national forest.

☐ 🔖 ♡ **Biscayne–Everglades Greenway Scenic Highway:** Linking Biscayne and Everglades National Parks in southern Miami-Dade County, this corridor travels through farmland, hammocks, and wetlands. It provides a unique connection between two UNESCO sites, highlighting the cultural and ecological significance of the region's coastal and inland environments.

☐ 🔖 ♡ **Black Bear Scenic Byway – Ocala National Forest Spur:** A state-level spur of the Black Bear Scenic Byway, this route explores the Ocala National Forest with longleaf pine flatwoods, springs, and lakes. It highlights habitats supporting Florida black bears and bald eagles, offering travelers a deeper look into north-central Florida's wild interior.

FLORIDA

☐ ▢ ♡ **Courtney Campbell Scenic Highway:** Stretching across Old Tampa Bay, this byway links Clearwater and Tampa via a sweeping causeway. The route features panoramic water views, fishing piers, recreational trails, and birding spots, making it both a vital transportation corridor and a celebrated landmark for recreation and coastal scenery.

☐ ▢ ♡ **Cultural Coast Scenic Highway:** Located in Sarasota and Manatee counties, this route emphasizes the area's artistic and cultural heritage. It highlights theaters, museums, historic neighborhoods, and Gulf Coast beaches, offering travelers a mix of leisure and heritage in one of Florida's most vibrant cultural destinations.

☐ ▢ ♡ **Gainesville–Hawthorne State Trail Scenic Byway:** Following a 16-mile paved rail-trail between Gainesville and Hawthorne, this byway showcases shady hammocks, wetlands, and prairie ecosystems. A favorite for cyclists, hikers, and equestrians, it offers a quiet retreat through the inland landscapes of north Florida with abundant wildlife viewing opportunities.

☐ ▢ ♡ **Green Mountain Scenic Byway:** Stretching along Lake Apopka's western ridge, this byway winds through rolling hills, citrus groves, and preserves. Known for birdwatching and cycling, it highlights rare elevation in central Florida, offering sweeping views, historic communities, and access to trails that celebrate natural beauty and conservation.

☐ ▢ ♡ **Heritage Crossroads: Miles of History Scenic Highway:** Situated in Flagler County, this route links the Atlantic coast with inland farmland. It preserves traces of Florida's colonial and pioneer history with plantations, homesteads, and historic roadbeds. The byway offers a journey through centuries of heritage across diverse cultural landscapes.

☐ ▢ ♡ **Indian River Lagoon Scenic Highway – State Spur:** While the federally designated corridor highlights the main lagoon route, this state spur explores adjoining segments. It connects small towns, fishing docks, and conservation lands along the lagoon, one of North America's most biodiverse estuaries, offering travelers authentic cultural and ecological experiences.

☐ ▢ ♡ **J.C. Penney Memorial Scenic Highway:** Located near Penney Farms in Clay County, this short byway commemorates retailer J.C. Penney's utopian settlement project. It passes through a historic rural community with tree-lined roads, churches, and farms, reflecting a blend of cultural heritage, philanthropy, and small-town charm in northeast Florida.

☐ ▢ ♡ **Lemon Bay/Myakka Trail Scenic Highway:** Winding through Charlotte and Sarasota counties, this route highlights estuaries, state parks, and barrier islands. It blends Gulf Coast scenery with inland wetlands, offering birdwatching, paddling, and fishing, while connecting beach towns and nature preserves that reflect Florida's natural and recreational treasures.

☐ ▢ ♡ **Old Florida Heritage Highway:** Near Gainesville, this corridor preserves the charm of north Florida's small towns, farms, and natural landscapes. Lined with moss-draped oaks, it links historic communities, springs, and Paynes Prairie Preserve State Park. Travelers experience traditional "Old Florida" culture, history, and natural beauty along the route.

☐ ▢ ♡ **Ormond Scenic Loop and Trail:** This coastal and inland circuit near Ormond Beach passes through live oak canopies, salt marshes, state parks, and scenic waterways. Known for its cycling and birding opportunities, the route combines natural beauty with history, including plantations, Native heritage, and a vibrant seaside community.

☐ ▢ ♡ **Pensacola Scenic Bluffs Highway:** Stretching along U.S. 90 northeast of Pensacola, this byway follows Florida's highest coastal bluffs overlooking Escambia Bay. It highlights unique geology, historic settlements, and longleaf pine forests, offering travelers striking bay vistas, cultural heritage sites, and access to recreation along a dramatic coastal landscape.

☐ ▢ ♡ **River of Lakes Heritage Corridor Scenic Highway:** Located in Volusia County, this inland byway follows the St. Johns River and interconnected lakes. It highlights historic river towns, Native heritage, citrus groves, and eco-tourism opportunities. Visitors discover a landscape where culture, recreation, and waterways intertwine in central Florida's heartland.

☐ ▢ ♡ **Scenic Highway 30A:** This byway runs along the Gulf in Walton County, linking beachside communities and coastal dune lakes. It highlights sugar-white beaches, rare coastal ecosystems, state parks, and vibrant arts districts. Scenic 30A blends leisure, ecology, and culture in one of Florida's most celebrated coastal destinations.

☐ ▢ ♡ **Scenic Sumter Heritage Byway:** Encircling Sumter County, this byway highlights historic courthouses, cattle ranches, oak canopies, and rural charm. It showcases Florida's agricultural and pioneer traditions while linking small towns, heritage landmarks, and countryside landscapes that preserve the essence of inland "Old Florida."

FLORIDA

☐ ▢ ♡ **William Bartram Scenic Highway:** Following State Road 13 along the St. Johns River in St. Johns County, this byway honors naturalist William Bartram's 18th-century explorations. It passes historic plantations, oak hammocks, and river views. Interpretive sites highlight Bartram's writings and Florida's early cultural and ecological history.

National Natural Landmarks

 ☐ ▢ ♡ **Archbold Biological Station:** On the Lake Wales Ridge, Archbold is a National Natural Landmark for preserving the largest undisturbed tract of ancient sandhill. Its unique soils and isolation foster species found nowhere else. As one of the world's premier ecological field stations, it supports decades of research and protects globally rare biodiversity.
GPS: 27.1806, -81.3500

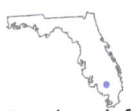 ☐ ▢ ♡ **Big Cypress Bend:** Within Fakahatchee Strand Preserve, Big Cypress Bend is a National Natural Landmark for protecting the largest royal palm grove in the U.S. alongside old-growth cypress. Panthers, orchids, and alligators inhabit its lush swamp, making it one of the finest surviving examples of Florida's original subtropical forested wetlands.
GPS: 25.8589, -81.0339

 ☐ ▢ ♡ **Corkscrew Swamp Sanctuary:** This Audubon preserve holds National Natural Landmark status for containing North America's largest virgin bald cypress stand. Towering centuries-old trees rise from wetlands that shelter wood storks, otters, and alligators. A boardwalk through the swamp allows visitors to experience Florida's most iconic wetland ecosystem.
GPS: 26.4179, -81.5384

 ☐ ▢ ♡ **Devil's Millhopper:** A 120-foot sinkhole near Gainesville, Devil's Millhopper is a National Natural Landmark for its geology and hydrology. Exposed limestone walls contain fossils, while the cool, moist slopes support ferns and mosses that create a miniature rainforest. The site highlights Florida's karst processes and groundwater systems.
GPS: 29.7069, -82.3950

 ☐ ▢ ♡ **Emeralda Marsh:** Emeralda Marsh is a National Natural Landmark for being one of Florida's most intact freshwater wetlands. Its sawgrass marshes support herons, ibises, and alligators while also filtering water and reducing floods. As part of the Great Florida Birding Trail, it illustrates the ecological importance of inland wetlands.
GPS: 28.9671, -81.8039

 ☐ ▢ ♡ **Florida Caverns Natural Area:** Within Florida Caverns State Park, this site is a National Natural Landmark for protecting the state's only air-filled limestone caves. Stalactites, stalagmites, and flowstone decorate chambers that also shelter Indiana bats. Public tours highlight the region's rare karst geology and subterranean biodiversity.
GPS: 30.8139, -85.2331

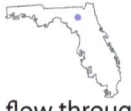 ☐ ▢ ♡ **Ichetucknee Springs:** This artesian spring system is a National Natural Landmark for its crystal-clear flow through forested surroundings. Its spring run sustains manatees, fish, aquatic vegetation, and birdlife. As one of Florida's most intact groundwater-fed rivers, Ichetucknee showcases the ecological value of healthy spring ecosystems.
GPS: 29.9674, -82.7761

 ☐ ▢ ♡ **Lignumvitae Key:** Accessible only by boat, Lignumvitae Key is a National Natural Landmark for containing the Florida Keys' best-preserved tropical hardwood hammock. Rare trees such as lignum vitae grow here, alongside subtropical birds. The island preserves a vital remnant of the dense forests that once covered the Keys.
GPS: 24.9020, -80.6993

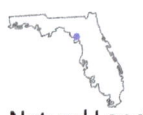 ☐ ▢ ♡ **Manatee Springs:** This artesian spring, discharging over 100 million gallons daily, is a National Natural Landmark for exemplifying Florida's spring ecosystems. Its clear waters feed the Suwannee River, while adjacent cypress swamps provide critical winter refuge for manatees and habitat for freshwater fish and wildlife.
GPS: 29.4904, -82.9771

UNITED STATES EDITION

FLORIDA

 ☐ 🔖 ♡ **Osceola Research Natural Area:** In Osceola National Forest, this tract is a National Natural Landmark for its old-growth bald cypress and diverse hardwood forest. Undisturbed and pristine, it provides a reference site for scientists studying southeastern swamps, serving as a benchmark for long-term ecological change and forest dynamics.
GPS: 30.2906, -82.3217

 ☐ 🔖 ♡ **Paynes Prairie:** This massive wetland south of Gainesville is a National Natural Landmark for its formation in a sinkhole basin. It is one of Florida's most diverse ecosystems, where bison, wild horses, alligators, and migratory birds coexist. The prairie highlights the richness and ecological value of inland wetlands.
GPS: 29.5669, -82.3811

 ☐ 🔖 ♡ **Rainbow Springs:** Florida's second-largest artesian spring, Rainbow Springs is a National Natural Landmark for its clear waters and rich aquatic habitats. Once a private attraction, it now flourishes as a state park with trails, gardens, and waterfalls, representing the ecological and scenic value of spring ecosystems in the state.
GPS: 29.1027, -82.4371

 ☐ 🔖 ♡ **Reed Wilderness Seashore Sanctuary:** Along the Atlantic coast, Reed Wilderness is a National Natural Landmark for preserving Florida's longest undeveloped shoreline. Its beaches, dunes, and maritime forests provide essential nesting habitat for loggerhead turtles and migratory birds, offering a rare glimpse of intact coastal ecosystems.
GPS: 27.0405, -80.1137

 ☐ 🔖 ♡ **San Felasco Hammock:** San Felasco Hammock near Gainesville is a National Natural Landmark for its biological diversity. This preserve protects upland hardwood forests, sinkholes, and karst features. Its ecosystems support abundant plant and animal life, offering both ecological research opportunities and recreational access to rare hammocks.
GPS: 29.7289, -82.4419

☐ 🔖 ♡ **Silver Springs:** Known for its glass-bottom boat tours, Silver Springs is a National Natural Landmark for being Florida's largest artesian spring. Its waters sustain manatees, fish, and submerged vegetation. The site blends ecological importance with cultural heritage, standing as one of Florida's most famous natural attractions.
GPS: 29.2164, -82.0578

 ☐ 🔖 ♡ **Torreya State Park:** Overlooking the Apalachicola River, Torreya State Park is a National Natural Landmark for protecting steep ravines and bluffs that shelter the endangered Torreya tree. This rare habitat mixes Appalachian-like conditions with Florida ecology, creating a unique refuge for threatened species and biodiversity.
GPS: 30.5689, -84.9481

 ☐ 🔖 ♡ **Waccasassa Bay Preserve State Park:** On Florida's Gulf Coast, Waccasassa Bay is a National Natural Landmark for its tidal creeks, marshes, and mangroves. Brackish estuaries here shelter fish, birds, and other wildlife while buffering inland areas from storms, showing the importance of coastal wetlands for ecological resilience.
GPS: 29.1790, -82.9306

 ☐ 🔖 ♡ **Wakulla Springs:** South of Tallahassee, Wakulla Springs is a National Natural Landmark for being the deepest artesian spring in the Southeast. Its clear waters harbor manatees, fossils, and diverse aquatic life. Surrounded by cypress and moss-draped oaks, it supports tours and research into Florida's spring geology and ecology.
GPS: 30.2328, -84.2922

GEORGIA

Georgia's rich natural beauty extends from the Blue Ridge Mountains to coastal marshes and barrier islands. Its mix of state parks, national forests, a celebrated national park, and diverse natural landmarks provides endless opportunities for outdoor adventure, from mountain summits to quiet tidal shores.

📅 Peak Season
March–May and September–November are Georgia's peak seasons, with mild weather, spring blooms, and colorful fall foliage. These months are most comfortable for hiking, sightseeing, and exploring both mountains and coast.

📅 Offseason Months
June–August is hot and humid, especially inland, though beaches and mountain retreats remain popular. December–February is generally quieter, with cooler temperatures and lighter tourist traffic outside of holiday periods.

🍃 Scenery & Nature Timing
Spring brings azaleas, dogwoods, and wildflowers to parks and gardens. Summer offers lush greenery and river activities. Fall transforms the Blue Ridge Mountains with vivid foliage, while winter highlights crisp skies and occasional snowfall in the north.

✨ Special
Georgia features the Blue Ridge Mountains, the Okefenokee Swamp, and scenic coastal barrier islands like Cumberland and Jekyll. Tallulah Gorge and Amicalola Falls showcase dramatic landscapes, while the Chattahoochee River winds from the mountains to the coastal plain.

GEORGIA

State Parks

☐ 🔖 ♡ **A.H. Stephens State Park:** Located in Crawfordville, this tranquil park honors Confederate Vice President Alexander Stephens with a museum and his restored home. The park features a fishing lake, wooded trails, and shady campgrounds, blending Civil War heritage with outdoor recreation. Visitors enjoy a peaceful mix of history, nature, and Southern charm in a quiet rural setting.

☐ 🔖 ♡ **Amicalola Falls State Park & Lodge:** Home to Georgia's tallest waterfall at 729 feet, this Dawsonville park is a gateway to adventure. The Appalachian Trail approach begins here, leading hikers through steep, scenic terrain. Visitors enjoy a mountaintop lodge, camping, and sweeping North Georgia views, making it one of the state's premier destinations for hiking, photography, and natural beauty.

☐ 🔖 ♡ **Black Rock Mountain State Park:** Georgia's highest state park, at 3,640 feet, offers cool breezes and breathtaking views of four states. Located near Clayton, it features scenic overlooks, wooded trails, a peaceful lake, and rustic campsites. Known for its vibrant fall color and rugged mountain setting, the park is a year-round destination for hikers, campers, and those seeking panoramic vistas.

☐ 🔖 ♡ **Chattahoochee Bend State Park:** Stretching along five miles of river near Newnan, this 2,910-acre park is a haven for paddlers, anglers, and campers. Visitors explore trails through forests and fields, stay in rustic cabins, or launch boats from ramps. Rich in birdlife and wildlife, it's one of Georgia's largest state parks, offering a mix of outdoor recreation and scenic river views.

☐ 🔖 ♡ **Cloudland Canyon State Park:** Perched on Lookout Mountain, this park showcases dramatic canyons, sandstone cliffs, waterfalls, and miles of trails. The Overlook Trail offers breathtaking vistas, while challenging hikes descend into the canyon floor. With cottages, yurts, and campgrounds, it's popular for adventure seekers, photographers, and families exploring one of Georgia's most striking landscapes.

☐ 🔖 ♡ **Crooked River State Park:** Near St. Marys on Georgia's southern coast, this scenic park offers views of salt marshes and maritime forests. Visitors enjoy kayaking, fishing, and birdwatching, with easy access to nearby Cumberland Island. Cabins, campsites, and trails provide a peaceful retreat, while tidal waterways and abundant wildlife make it a favorite for coastal exploration.

☐ 🔖 ♡ **Don Carter State Park:** Set on the north end of Lake Lanier near Gainesville, this is Georgia's only state park on the lake. It features a sandy swimming beach, boat ramps, cabins, and multi-use trails. Families enjoy fishing, paddling, and camping, while the lakefront setting provides a quiet getaway within reach of metro Atlanta. It's a top spot for recreation and relaxation.

☐ 🔖 ♡ **Elijah Clark State Park:** Located on Clarks Hill Lake near Lincolnton, this wooded park honors Revolutionary War hero Elijah Clark with a reconstructed log cabin. Visitors enjoy lakeside camping, boat ramps, a sandy beach, and cottages. Shady trails wind through the forest, while the lake offers boating, fishing, and peaceful retreats along the expansive shoreline.

☐ 🔖 ♡ **F.D. Roosevelt State Park:** Georgia's largest state park covers 9,049 acres in Pine Mountain. Built by the Civilian Conservation Corps, it preserves CCC structures and Roosevelt history. More than 40 miles of trails lead to scenic overlooks, waterfalls, and quiet lakes. Popular for hiking, horseback riding, and nature study, the park blends history, recreation, and sweeping mountain views.

☐ 🔖 ♡ **Florence Marina State Park:** On Lake Walter F. George in southwest Georgia, this park is a boating and fishing hub. It offers a marina, cottages, campsites, trails, and birding opportunities along the Chattahoochee River corridor. Nearby Kolomoki Mounds add cultural interest. Visitors enjoy both water-based recreation and peaceful nature retreats in a relaxed setting.

☐ 🔖 ♡ **Fort McAllister State Park:** Near Richmond Hill, this coastal park preserves some of the best-preserved Confederate earthworks from the Civil War. A museum interprets its history, while shaded trails lead through salt marshes and live oak forests. Visitors enjoy camping, fishing, boating, and hiking, combining Southern history with natural coastal beauty.

☐ 🔖 ♡ **Fort Mountain State Park:** In the Cohutta Mountains near Chatsworth, this park is known for its mysterious ancient stone wall. It offers 25 miles of hiking, biking, and horseback trails, scenic overlooks, and a lake for swimming and fishing. Campers, history enthusiasts, and adventurers alike enjoy exploring the Appalachian forests, mountain ridges, and legends of this unique park.

GEORGIA

☐ 🔖 ♡ **Fort Yargo State Park:** Located in Winder, this park features a 260-acre lake with a beach, paddling, and fishing. Visitors explore wooded trails, disc golf, and a reconstructed 1790s log fort. With campsites, cabins, and yurts, it's a family favorite close to Atlanta, offering both history and outdoor recreation in a peaceful, accessible setting.

☐ 🔖 ♡ **General Coffee State Park:** Near Douglas, this park highlights South Georgia's agricultural heritage with a heritage farm, historic buildings, and barnyard animals. Visitors explore cypress swamps on boardwalks, hike through sandhills, or camp beneath pine forests. With cabins, trails, and abundant wildlife, it's a quiet retreat blending history, education, and natural beauty.

☐ 🔖 ♡ **George L. Smith State Park:** Near Twin City, this peaceful park features a mill pond surrounded by cypress and tupelo trees, perfect for paddling and photography. Visitors can kayak under moss-draped branches, hike quiet woodland trails, and explore a historic covered bridge and gristmill. Cabins and campsites make it a favorite for families, birders, and nature enthusiasts seeking relaxation.

☐ 🔖 ♡ **George T. Bagby State Park:** Nestled along the shores of Lake Walter F. George in southwest Georgia, this park offers a peaceful retreat with fishing, boating, and scenic hiking trails. Once home to a lodge and golf course, it now highlights natural beauty with lakeside picnic areas, camping, and abundant birdlife. The park provides a quiet, family-friendly getaway in a serene lakeside setting.

☐ 🔖 ♡ **Georgia Veterans State Park:** Situated on Lake Blackshear near Cordele, this expansive park honors U.S. military veterans with a museum displaying aircraft, vehicles, and artifacts. Guests enjoy golf, boating, fishing, camping, and access to the resort and conference center. A scenic railroad adds to its family appeal, making it a unique blend of recreation, lakeside relaxation, and military history.

☐ 🔖 ♡ **Hamburg State Park:** Tucked in Washington County, this rustic park preserves Georgia's rural history with a 1920s gristmill still in operation. Visitors camp under shady pines, fish in the pond, or picnic by the water. It's ideal for history lovers and those seeking a slower pace, where outdoor recreation is paired with a glimpse into the state's early 20th-century agricultural life.

☐ 🔖 ♡ **Hard Labor Creek State Park:** Near Rutledge, this scenic park features a 275-acre lake for fishing and paddling, miles of hiking and horseback trails, and one of Georgia's top public golf courses. Campers enjoy shaded sites and cottages surrounded by pine forest. Wildlife, quiet waters, and wide-open spaces make it a relaxing escape that balances outdoor adventure with tranquility.

☐ 🔖 ♡ **High Falls State Park:** Just north of Macon near Jackson, this popular park is famed for its cascading waterfalls on the Towaliga River. Visitors hike scenic trails past rapids and mill ruins, fish or boat on the lake, and enjoy family-friendly camping. With its mix of natural beauty, history, and recreation, it's a favorite for day-trippers, photographers, and weekend getaways.

☐ 🔖 ♡ **Indian Springs State Park:** One of the nation's oldest state parks, located near Flovilla, it's famed for natural spring water once thought to have healing powers. Guests enjoy wading in the spring, swimming at the lake, or hiking wooded trails. A museum, historic stone pavilion, and Creek Indian history add cultural depth. It's a blend of recreation, history, and therapeutic tradition.

☐ 🔖 ♡ **Jack Hill State Park:** Situated in Reidsville, this family-friendly park surrounds a tranquil fishing lake with a sandy swimming beach and shaded campsites. It offers disc golf, hiking, and cozy cottages for overnight stays. Once called Gordonia-Alatamaha, it was renamed to honor Senator Jack Hill. With small-town charm and a relaxed atmosphere, it's a quiet southeastern Georgia getaway.

☐ 🔖 ♡ **James H. (Sloppy) Floyd State Park:** Nestled in the foothills near Summerville, this park features two peaceful lakes, wooded trails, and picnic areas. Visitors enjoy birdwatching, fishing, and camping in a serene setting. Trails connect to nearby Chattahoochee National Forest, offering extended hikes. Its calm atmosphere and natural beauty make it a hidden gem for outdoor lovers seeking solitude.

☐ 🔖 ♡ **Kolomoki Mounds State Park:** Near Blakely, this park preserves one of the most significant Woodland-era Native American mound complexes in the Southeast. Visitors explore ancient ceremonial mounds, a museum, and a scenic lake surrounded by forest. With hiking, boating, and picnicking, it offers a unique combination of cultural history and outdoor recreation in Georgia's rural southwest region.

GEORGIA

☐ 🔖 ♡ **Laura S. Walker State Park:** Adjacent to the Okefenokee Swamp near Waycross, this park highlights southeastern Georgia's natural diversity. It features a 120-acre lake, nature trails, golf course, and shaded campgrounds. Visitors kayak among cypress trees, hike through pine flatwoods, or relax in peaceful surroundings. Named for a Georgia conservationist, it serves as a gateway to swamp ecosystems.

☐ 🔖 ♡ **Little Ocmulgee State Park & Lodge:** Set near McRae-Helena, this park centers on a 265-acre lake with a swimming beach, boat rentals, and fishing piers. It includes a lodge, cottages, and a golf course, making it ideal for family vacations and group gatherings. Tall pines, sandhills, and wetland boardwalks create a relaxing environment where recreation meets Georgia's natural beauty.

☐ 🔖 ♡ **Magnolia Springs State Park:** Near Millen, this scenic park is renowned for crystal-clear springs that flow at seven million gallons a day. A boardwalk winds through wetlands where alligators, turtles, and wading birds thrive. The park also preserves remnants of a Civil War prison camp. With camping, fishing, and lush scenery, it's both a natural and historical treasure in southeast Georgia.

☐ 🔖 ♡ **Mistletoe State Park:** Located on the shores of Clarks Hill Lake near Augusta, this park is a favorite for anglers, boaters, and hikers. It offers cottages, shaded campsites, and trails through hardwood forests rich in birdlife. Known for quiet coves and wide lake views, it provides a peaceful retreat. Its large, scenic lake makes it one of Georgia's premier spots for water recreation.

☐ 🔖 ♡ **Moccasin Creek State Park:** Nestled on Lake Burton in the North Georgia mountains, this small but popular park offers lakeside camping, trout fishing, and easy access to mountain hiking. Especially welcoming to senior anglers, it provides a calm, family-friendly setting. Surrounded by forested peaks, it's a peaceful basecamp for exploring waterfalls, boating, or simply enjoying lakefront relaxation.

☐ 🔖 ♡ **Panola Mountain State Park:** Just outside Atlanta, this protected monadnock preserves rare ecosystems similar to nearby Stone Mountain but without heavy development. Guided hikes help protect fragile habitats. The park offers trails for hiking and biking, a treetop rope course, archery, fishing, and scenic views. Its unique mix of recreation and conservation makes it a natural escape close to the city.

☐ 🔖 ♡ **Providence Canyon State Park:** Nicknamed "Georgia's Little Grand Canyon," this striking park near Lumpkin features dramatic gullies up to 150 feet deep formed by erosion. Visitors hike rim trails or explore the colorful canyon floor, photographing vivid red, orange, and purple soils. With camping, astronomy programs, and educational exhibits, it's a geological and recreational highlight of southwest Georgia.

☐ 🔖 ♡ **Red Top Mountain State Park:** Situated on Lake Allatoona near Cartersville, this popular park offers swimming, boating, fishing, and over 15 miles of hiking trails. Its history as an iron mining site is preserved in a reconstructed homestead. With cottages, campgrounds, and a sandy beach, it's a top spot for summer recreation, family vacations, and exploring northwest Georgia's scenic woodlands.

☐ 🔖 ♡ **Reed Bingham State Park:** Near Adel in South Georgia, this park is known for its 375-acre lake ideal for boating, fishing, and paddling. Trails wind through sandhills, swamps, and pine flatwoods, offering habitats for gopher tortoises, bald eagles, and migratory birds. With camping, picnicking, and family-friendly amenities, it's a natural oasis bridging Georgia's coastal plain and upland ecosystems.

☐ 🔖 ♡ **Richard B. Russell State Park:** Nestled on Lake Richard B. Russell near Elberton, this park features excellent fishing, swimming, and boating opportunities along with a championship golf course. Visitors can enjoy quiet coves, wooded trails, and lakeside cottages. Its blend of recreation, natural scenery, and comfortable lodging makes it a popular spot for both families and weekend getaways.

☐ 🔖 ♡ **Seminole State Park:** Located on Lake Seminole in southwest Georgia, this park is a hub for anglers and birdwatchers, with abundant bass fishing and migratory waterfowl. Shady campgrounds and lakeside cottages provide peaceful lodging, while trails, picnic areas, and boat ramps make it ideal for water recreation. Its cypress-studded shoreline captures the charm of Georgia's southern wetlands.

☐ 🔖 ♡ **Skidaway Island State Park:** Near Savannah, this coastal park offers trails through maritime forest, salt marsh, and tidal creeks. Elevated boardwalks showcase habitats where fiddler crabs, egrets, and ospreys thrive. Campgrounds and cabins allow extended stays, making it a favorite base for exploring Savannah's history while enjoying natural quiet. It's a coastal gem blending wildlife and recreation.

GEORGIA

☐ 🔖 ♡ **Smithgall Woods State Park:** Near Helen in North Georgia, this park preserves a vast tract of hardwood forest and trout streams. Known for its catch-and-release fly fishing, it also offers secluded cottages, hiking, and biking. Wildlife like deer and black bear roam the hills, while Dukes Creek waterfalls provide a scenic highlight. Its blend of wilderness and luxury makes it unique.

☐ 🔖 ♡ **Stephen C. Foster State Park:** A gateway to the Okefenokee Swamp, this park near Fargo provides access to blackwater channels, cypress forests, and abundant wildlife including alligators, herons, and otters. Visitors enjoy boat tours, stargazing in designated dark skies, and rustic camping. As one of Georgia's wildest landscapes, it immerses travelers in swamp ecology and quiet natural wonder.

☐ 🔖 ♡ **Sweetwater Creek State Park:** Just west of Atlanta, this park features wooded trails leading to the ruins of a Civil War-era textile mill along a rushing creek. It's popular for hiking, fishing, kayaking, and picnicking. Visitors enjoy waterfalls, rugged bluffs, and wildlife in a natural setting close to the city. With history and scenery, it's one of Georgia's most-visited urban escapes.

☐ 🔖 ♡ **Tallulah Gorge State Park:** Near Clayton, this park protects a two-mile-long gorge nearly 1,000 feet deep carved by the Tallulah River. Visitors hike rim trails, cross a suspension bridge, or get permits to descend into the gorge floor. Waterfalls, overlooks, and seasonal whitewater releases attract adventurers. With rugged terrain and breathtaking vistas, it's a crown jewel of Georgia's natural wonders.

☐ 🔖 ♡ **Tugaloo State Park:** On Lake Hartwell near Lavonia, this park offers sandy beaches, fishing docks, and boat ramps perfect for water recreation. Its cabins, campgrounds, and yurts provide varied lodging. Trails wind through forested hillsides, while wildlife abounds along the lake's quiet coves. A family-friendly destination, it's a popular place to enjoy Georgia's northeastern lake country.

☐ 🔖 ♡ **Unicoi State Park:** Located near Helen in the North Georgia mountains, this park centers on Unicoi Lake and offers boating, fishing, swimming, and zip-lining. Trails connect to nearby Anna Ruby Falls, while cottages and a lodge host visitors year-round. Surrounded by forested peaks, it blends outdoor adventure with modern amenities, making it a popular mountain retreat.

☐ 🔖 ♡ **Victoria Bryant State Park**: A quiet Piedmont retreat centered around a CCC-built, spring-fed lake from the 1930s. Gentle trails, uncrowded fishing spots, and excellent birdwatching make this a favorite for those seeking solitude. Its small size and low visitation offer a peaceful alternative to Georgia's busier parks.

☐ 🔖 ♡ **Vogel State Park:** One of Georgia's oldest and most beloved state parks, Vogel lies at the base of Blood Mountain in the Chattahoochee National Forest. It features a 22-acre lake, waterfalls, cabins, and scenic trails including part of the Appalachian Trail. With mountain views, vibrant fall foliage, and rich history, it's a classic North Georgia destination for campers and hikers.

☐ 🔖 ♡ **Watson Mill Bridge State Park:** Near Comer, this park is home to Georgia's longest covered bridge, a 229-foot structure spanning the South Fork River. Visitors enjoy picnicking by shoals, camping, fishing, and horseback riding. Trails wind through hardwood forest, offering peaceful scenery. Combining history with natural beauty, it's a picturesque retreat where rural charm and outdoor fun meet.

National Parks

☐ 🔖 ♡ **Andersonville National Historic Site:** Located in Georgia, this site preserves the infamous Civil War prison where thousands of Union soldiers perished. Visitors explore the National Prisoner of War Museum, walk through the cemetery, and reflect on the sacrifices of those held captive. The grounds offer a solemn reminder of wartime hardship and honor the memory of all American POWs.

☐ 🔖 ♡ **Appalachian National Scenic Trail:** Stretching over 2,100 miles from Georgia to Maine, this iconic footpath follows the Appalachian Mountains. Hikers experience diverse forests, ridges, and valleys while tackling a journey that is both scenic and challenging. The trail showcases the beauty of the eastern U.S. and remains a symbol of endurance, conservation, and outdoor adventure.

GEORGIA

 ☐ 🔖 ♡ **Chattahoochee River National Recreation Area:** Near Atlanta, this park preserves 48 miles of the Chattahoochee River and its natural landscapes. Visitors kayak, fish, and hike along wooded trails while spotting wildlife. The area highlights the river's cultural history and ecological importance, providing a peaceful retreat with easy access to both nature and urban surroundings.

 ☐ 🔖 ♡ **Chickamauga and Chattanooga National Military Park:** Spanning Georgia and Tennessee, this park preserves the sites of two pivotal Civil War battles. Visitors explore battlefields, monuments, and historic markers while learning about the Union's push toward Atlanta. Scenic drives, trails, and guided tours reveal the strategic significance of these campaigns and honor the soldiers who fought there.

 ☐ 🔖 ♡ **Cumberland Island National Seashore:** Off Georgia's coast, this barrier island features windswept beaches, wild horses, and moss-draped forests. Trails lead to historic ruins of Carnegie family estates and through diverse habitats. Visitors can camp, hike, and enjoy birding in one of the most unspoiled natural landscapes on the Atlantic coast, blending wilderness and history.

 ☐ 🔖 ♡ **Fort Frederica National Monument:** On St. Simons Island, this site preserves the remains of an 18th-century British fort and town built to defend the Georgia colony. Visitors explore ruins, archaeological sites, and scenic marshland while learning about early colonial struggles between Britain and Spain. The park blends coastal beauty with centuries-old military history.

 ☐ 🔖 ♡ **Fort Pulaski National Monument:** Situated on Cockspur Island, this preserved Civil War-era fort once protected Savannah. Famous for its masonry walls breached by Union rifled cannon, it marks a turning point in military history. Visitors can tour the fort, walk scenic dikes and marsh trails, and learn about its defenses, siege, and role in the broader conflict.

 ☐ 🔖 ♡ **Jimmy Carter National Historic Site:** In Plains, Georgia, this site honors the 39th President of the United States. Visitors tour his boyhood farm, campaign headquarters, and local school, gaining insight into his humble beginnings. Exhibits highlight Carter's presidency, human rights efforts, and legacy of peace, celebrating his lasting impact at both local and global levels.

  ☐ 🔖 ♡ **Kennesaw Mountain National Battlefield Park:** Located northwest of Atlanta, this battlefield preserves the site of a major clash during the Civil War's Atlanta Campaign. Visitors hike wooded trails to mountain overlooks, tour historic earthworks, and learn about the battle's impact. The park blends history, natural scenery, and reflection on a defining moment of the war.

 ☐ 🔖 ♡ **Martin Luther King, Jr. National Historical Park:** In Atlanta, this site preserves landmarks tied to Dr. King's life and the Civil Rights Movement. Visitors can tour his childhood home, Ebenezer Baptist Church, and The King Center, where his legacy is honored. The park tells the story of his fight for equality, justice, and peace, inspiring generations worldwide.

  ☐ 🔖 ♡ **Ocmulgee Mounds National Historical Park:** Located in Macon, this park protects ancient earthworks built by the Muscogee people. Trails lead past temple and burial mounds, ceremonial sites, and archaeological exhibits. Visitors learn about 17,000 years of human history, from early hunter-gatherers to thriving Indigenous cultures, in a landscape that blends heritage and natural beauty.

GEORGIA

State & National Forests

☐ 🔖 ♡ **Bartram Forest:** A 2,113-acre stewardship forest spanning Baldwin & Wilkinson counties. Managed by Georgia Forestry Commission, it features pine stands, wetlands, and beaver ponds. Ideal for hiking, mountain biking, and archery hunting, it balances timber production with wildlife habitat, water quality, and public recreation along rolling central Georgia terrain.

☐ 🔖 ♡ **Broxton Rocks Forest:** A 350-acre tract in Coffee County, named for its scenic rocky outcrops. Managed for timber, water conservation, and native longleaf pine restoration, it features trails through loblolly and longleaf pine and rare bottomland hardwoods. Public access is foot-travel-only to protect habitat integrity.

☐ 🔖 ♡ **Chattahoochee-Oconee National Forests:** Encompassing ~867,000 acres across northern and central Georgia, these combined forests protect Appalachian Mountains terrain, trout-rich streams, waterfalls, and over 850 miles of trails. Includes Brasstown Bald, Springer Mountain, and the southern approach to the Appalachian Trail. Offers hiking, camping, fishing, hunting, OHV use.

☐ 🔖 ♡ **Dawson Forest:** A 10,130-acre City of Atlanta tract in Dawson County, managed for conservation and forestry. Includes mixed pine stands, habitat restoration, and trail networks for hiking, horseback riding, and mountain biking. Also part of a wildlife management area with primitive camping near Atlanta backcountry.

☐ 🔖 ♡ **Dixon Memorial State Forest:** Georgia's largest state forest (~35,000 acres) on the Okefenokee's northern edge in Ware & Brantley counties. Historically a federal land program, now managed for longleaf, slash, and loblolly pine, with pond cypress wetlands. Supports timber, research, wildlife habitat, hunting, and education.

☐ 🔖 ♡ **Hightower Forest:** A 142-acre education forest in Dawson County along the Etowah River. Managed by GFC, it provides environmental learning opportunities for students and the public. Consists of pine-hardwood stands and supports fire-control efforts and ecology studies.

☐ 🔖 ♡ **Paulding Forest:** A 10,000-acre City of Atlanta tract scattered across Paulding County. Managed for timber, wildlife, and watershed health under GFC stewardship. Offers hiking, primitive camping, wildlife viewing, and canoeing opportunities on small lakes, with regulated hunting and forest management for health and fire control.

☐ 🔖 ♡ **Spirit Creek Forest:** A 725-acre working forest near Augusta in Richmond County. A mix of planted loblolly pine and bottomland hardwoods around wetlands. Managed for timber, wildlife, soil and water conservation, aesthetics, and education. Offers passive recreation and learning opportunities.

National Scenic Byways & All-American Roads

☐ 🔖 ♡ **Russell–Brasstown Scenic Byway:** Georgia's only National Scenic Byway, this 41-mile loop through the Chattahoochee-Oconee National Forest crosses SR 348, SR 180, SR 17/75. It ascends to Brasstown Bald (the state's high point), passes waterfall overlooks, Appalachian Trail junctions, dense forest, and mountain vistas—Georgia's top scenic mountain drive.

State Scenic Byways

☐ 🔖 ♡ **Altamaha Historic Scenic Byway:** A ~17-mile coastal drive between Meridian and Darien that skirts shimmering tidal marsh, live-oak corridors, and tabby ruins. Roll past rice-canal remnants and Gullah-Geechee heritage sites, pause at Fort King George, and continue toward the Sapelo Island ferry. A serene ribbon of estuarine vistas, working waterfronts, and Lowcountry history in Georgia's coastal plain.

☐ 🔖 ♡ **Cohutta–Chattahoochee Scenic Byway:** Trace the edge of the Cohutta Wilderness on quiet mountain highways and backroads, with pullouts for trout streams, orchard valleys, and waterfall hikes. Fort Mountain vistas, hardwood ridges, and small hamlets give this loop a classic North Georgia feel. Expect switchbacks, overlooks, and crisp forest air as ridge and river trade the lead.

GEORGIA

☐ 🔖 ♡ **Enduring Farmlands Scenic Byway:** A mellow circuit around Hawkinsville through quilt-work fields, pecan groves, and piney uplands. Pass country churches, tin-roof barns, syrup sheds, and courthouse squares where agriculture still sets the pace. Farmstands, heritage markers, and slow, open horizons deliver a living portrait of working landscapes and small-town hospitality.

☐ 🔖 ♡ **Historic Dixie Highway:** Follow the early auto-era route on US 19/US 41 through west-central Georgia. Roll by brick-front squares, vintage motor courts, murals, and roadside diners, tracing the path snowbirds once drove to Florida. Wayside museums and courthouse lawns add context as gentle hills, pines, and pastures frame this nostalgic corridor.

☐ 🔖 ♡ **Historic Effingham–Ebenezer Scenic Byway:** A quiet Lowcountry drive linking the colonial townsite of Ebenezer, 18th-century churches, and Savannah River marsh. Cypress shadows, tidal breezes, and Salzburger heritage shape the story along shaded lanes and river overlooks. Expect birdlife, history, and reflective stops in a peaceful coastal landscape.

☐ 🔖 ♡ **Historic Piedmont Scenic Byway:** Meander country lanes over red-clay hills past antebellum homes, dairy farms, and hardwood bottoms. Courthouse squares, mill villages, and oak-lined avenues reveal the Piedmont's agrarian roots. Rolling vistas, fence-rows, and heritage markers sketch a timeless portrait of central Georgia's working countryside.

☐ 🔖 ♡ **Interstate 185 Scenic Byway:** An 18-mile, green-framed corridor from Columbus toward LaGrange where pine uplands, river crossings, and glimpses of recreation lands soften the ride. Trailheads, overlooks, and nearby Chattahoochee sites make easy detours. A surprisingly scenic slice of interstate travel in west-central Georgia.

☐ 🔖 ♡ **Meriwether–Pike Scenic Byway:** A 40-mile wander through rolling pasture, pine forest, and creek bottoms between country towns. Look for white-steepled churches, historic mills, and covered-bridge charm amid hayfields and fencerows. Unhurried and pastoral, it's a quiet sampler of rural west Georgia.

☐ 🔖 ♡ **Millen–Jenkins County Scenic Byway:** Drift along two-lane roads where farmland mosaics, longleaf stands, and family cemeteries share the view. Pause in Millen's square or detour to nearby Magnolia Springs for boardwalks and wildlife. A low-traffic corridor that captures the rhythms of southeastern Georgia backroads.

☐ 🔖 ♡ **Monticello Crossroads Scenic Byway:** A ~29-mile loop on SR 11/SR 83 circling courthouse-centric Monticello. Roll past oak-canopy lanes, pastureland, and National Register districts; echoes of Native trade paths and early Methodist circuits linger at roadside markers. A graceful blend of small-town heritage and Piedmont scenery.

☐ 🔖 ♡ **Ocmulgee–Piedmont Scenic Byway:** Follow gentle ridges and river tributaries through the heart of the Piedmont. Farm fields, clapboard chapels, and mill-town streets line the way, with cemetery hills and hardwood hollows recalling 19th-century rural Georgia. A contemplative drive of rolling hills and watershed views.

☐ 🔖 ♡ **Ridge & Valley Scenic Byway:** A northwest Georgia ramble across folded ridgelines and broad limestone valleys. Pastoral views, rail-town history, and scenic pullouts reveal classic ridge-and-valley physiography at the Appalachian's doorstep. Expect long sightlines, patchwork farms, and forested spines rising above the fields.

☐ 🔖 ♡ **South Fulton Scenic Byway:** A 29-mile loop through Chattahoochee Hill Country on Cochran Mill, Hutcheson Ferry, and Campbellton-Redwine roads. Creek gorges, farmsteads, and historic structures anchor a rare greenbelt just beyond metro Atlanta. Trailheads, waterfalls, and wide rural views define this close-to-town escape.

☐ 🔖 ♡ **Warren County–Piedmont Scenic Byway:** Thread quiet backroads across Warren, Glascock, and Jefferson counties, where churchyards, piney ridges, and fencerows define the horizon. Heritage markers, small crossroads, and long, open views deliver a serene, lesser-traveled portrait of east-central Georgia's pastoral character.

GEORGIA

National Natural Landmarks

 **Big Hammock Natural Area:** In Georgia's Coastal Plain, Big Hammock became a National Natural Landmark for protecting one of the last broadleaf evergreen hammock forests. Its dense canopy and rich understory sustain exceptional biodiversity, offering a rare glimpse into an ecosystem once widespread but now fragmented across the Southeast.
GPS: 31.8613, -82.0582

 **Camp E.F. Boyd Natural Area:** This site is nationally recognized for conserving one of the best upland sand ridge ecosystems in the Southeast. Longleaf pine forests thrive in dry, sandy soils, a habitat type once common across the Coastal Plain but now scarce. Its designation as a National Natural Landmark highlights its ecological and research value.
GPS: 32.3958, -82.4452

 Cason J. Calloway Memorial Forest: Transition zones between hardwoods and southern conifers earned this forest National Natural Landmark status. The mosaic of species reflects long-term ecological responses to fire, soils, and climate. Today, it provides scientists with a living classroom to study forest dynamics across the southeastern United States.
GPS: 32.7527, -84.9478

 **Ebenezer Creek Swamp:** Recognized as a National Natural Landmark, Ebenezer Creek is the finest cypress–gum swamp in the Savannah River basin. Towering trees rise above seasonally flooded wetlands that shelter aquatic life and migratory birds. Its intact ecosystem represents one of the Southeast's most pristine swamp forests.
GPS: 32.3658, -81.2971

 **Heggie's Rock:** Designated a National Natural Landmark for being the best granite outcrop ecosystem in eastern North America, Heggie's Rock supports rare and endemic plants found only on isolated rock islands. This exposed dome illustrates how geology shapes unique biological communities and preserves specialized habitats.
GPS: 33.5416, -82.2536

 **Lewis Island Tract:** One of Georgia's most extensive bottomland hardwood swamps, Lewis Island Tract is a National Natural Landmark for its largely undisturbed floodplain forest. Seasonal flooding nurtures diverse plant and animal life, preserving critical wetland functions and demonstrating the importance of intact riverine ecosystems.
GPS: 31.3852, -81.5209

 **Marshall Forest:** National Natural Landmark status was awarded to Marshall Forest for its rare old-growth loblolly–shortleaf pine community. Believed to have regenerated after fires during Cherokee removal, it now stands as an ecological and cultural resource, providing insights into fire history, succession, and forest resilience.
GPS: 34.2509, -85.1954

 **Okefenokee Swamp:** Covering vast portions of southern Georgia, the Okefenokee is a National Natural Landmark for being one of North America's largest and most pristine swamps. Its peat bogs, blackwater rivers, and wetlands harbor rare species and ancient landscapes, offering an example of a southern wetland ecosystem.
GPS: 30.6167, -82.3167

 **Panola Mountain:** Unlike other quarried granite domes, Panola Mountain retains its natural integrity, making it a National Natural Landmark. Rare lichens, mosses, and glade species cling to its rocky surface. As the least disturbed of Georgia's granite outcrops, it illustrates the fragility and uniqueness of this ecosystem type.
GPS: 33.6353, -84.1703

 **Wade Tract Preserve:** One of the finest old-growth longleaf pine savannas left in North America, the Wade Tract is a National Natural Landmark for demonstrating the ecological importance of fire-dependent landscapes. Endangered species like the red-cockaded woodpecker thrive among its ancient pines and fire-adapted grasses.
GPS: 30.7500, -84.0000

 **Wassaw Island:** National recognition came to Wassaw Island for being Georgia's only barrier island with its original maritime forest intact. The island also preserves salt marshes, dunes, and beaches that support nesting sea turtles and migratory birds, making it an irreplaceable refuge along the Atlantic coast.
GPS: 31.9003, -80.9822

UNITED STATES EDITION

HAWAII

Hawaii's island landscapes are uniquely captivating, with volcanic craters, black sand beaches, lush rainforests, and dramatic sea cliffs. With state and national parks, historic sites, and natural landmarks, Hawaii offers unforgettable nature experiences found nowhere else in the world.

📅 Peak Season
December–April and June–August are peak seasons in Hawaii. Winter draws visitors escaping colder climates, while summer is busy with families on vacation. Both periods bring higher prices and larger crowds at beaches and resorts.

📅 Offseason Months
May and September–November are the quieter months, with fewer tourists, more affordable lodging, and generally pleasant weather. These shoulder seasons are among the best times for less-crowded exploration.

🍃 Scenery & Nature Timing
Spring highlights lush valleys and waterfalls fed by winter rains. Summer offers calm seas and excellent snorkeling. Fall provides warm water and fewer crowds, while winter brings big waves to the North Shore and humpback whale migrations.

✨ Special
Hawaii showcases volcanic wonders like Kīlauea and Mauna Loa on the Big Island, the dramatic Nā Pali Coast on Kauaʻi, and Haleakalā's massive crater on Maui. Black and green sand beaches, towering sea cliffs, and lush rainforests add to the islands' extraordinary landscapes.

HAWAII

State Parks

☐ ♡ **Ahupua'a 'O Kahana State Park:** Located on O'ahu's windward coast, this park preserves one of the few remaining intact ahupua'a (traditional Hawaiian land divisions). It features lush forests, two hiking trails, cultural demonstrations, and access to a serene bay. Visitors ca'n explore native flora, traditional Hawaiian practices, and archaeological sites in a living cultural landscape.

☐ ♡ **'Akaka Falls State Park:** On the Big Island near Hilo, this park is home to the breathtaking 442-foot 'Akaka Falls and the smaller Kahuna Falls. A paved loop trail winds through lush rainforest filled with bamboo, wild orchids, and giant ferns. It's a top destination for nature photography and sightseeing, offering a short, family-friendly walk with stunning views.

☐ ♡ **Hā'ena State Park:** Located at the end of Kaua'i's North Shore, this park offers access to the world-famous Kalalau Trail along the Nāpali Coast. Visitors can explore pristine beaches, ancient Hawaiian sites, and the Limahuli Stream. Advance reservations are required due to limited entry, ensuring preservation of this ecologically and culturally significant landscape.

☐ ♡ **He'eia State Park:** On O'ahu's windward coast, this 18-acre park overlooks Kāne'ohe Bay and offers oceanfront lawns, a cultural learning center, and kayak rentals. Managed by a nonprofit, it focuses on environmental education and Hawaiian cultural programs. The park is a great launch point for kayaking to Coconut Island and exploring the bay's marine life.

☐ ♡ **Ka'ena Point State Park:** Located at the northwestern tip of O'ahu, this rugged coastal park is home to native seabirds, tide pools, and cultural sites. Hikers can access the remote Ka'ena Point Natural Area Reserve via trails from Wai'anae or Mokulē'ia. The park protects endangered species like the Hawaiian monk seal and preserves a wild, untouched landscape.

☐ ♡ **Kaiwi State Scenic Shoreline:** Skirting O'ahu's wild southeast coast between Koko Head and Makapu'u, this preserve protects sheer sea cliffs, lava headlands, and panoramic ocean vistas. Walk the paved 2-mile Makapu'u Point Lighthouse Trail for sunrise views and winter humpback whale-watching, or pause at lookouts toward Mānana (Rabbit) and Kāohikaipu islets. Little shade or water—surf, cliffs, and tidepools are hazardous.

☐ ♡ **Kealakekua Bay State Historical Park:** On the Big Island, this bay marks the site of Captain James Cook's arrival and death in 1779. The area is now a marine life conservation district, ideal for kayaking and snorkeling. A monument to Cook stands across the bay, accessible by hike or boat. The park preserves both Hawaiian and global historical significance.

☐ ♡ **Kekaha Kai (Kona Coast) State Park:** Located north of Kailua-Kona on the Big Island, this sprawling coastal park includes Mahai'ula Beach, Makalawena Beach, and Manini'ōwali Bay. It offers white sand beaches, lava fields, hiking trails, and swimming spots. Visitors can enjoy birdwatching and sunbathing in one of the island's most scenic coastal areas.

☐ ♡ **Kīholo State Park Reserve:** Situated on the Big Island's west coast, this coastal reserve features black sand beaches, turquoise lagoons, and ancient fishponds. Ideal for hiking, camping (by permit), and snorkeling, the park supports native species and cultural preservation. It's a peaceful, off-the-beaten-path destination with unique volcanic scenery.

☐ ♡ **Kōke'e State Park:** High above Waimea Canyon on Kaua'i, this mountain park features native forests, cool air, and trails leading to breathtaking overlooks of the Nāpali Coast. It offers cabins, a natural history museum, and diverse hiking opportunities. The park supports native bird habitat and is ideal for exploring the upland wilderness of Kaua'i.

☐ ♡ **Lapakahi State Historical Park:** Located on the Big Island's Kohala Coast, this coastal park preserves the partially restored remains of an ancient Hawaiian fishing village. Self-guided walking trails lead through archaeological sites that reveal daily life, agriculture, and craftsmanship of early Hawaiians. It offers both scenic views and cultural education.

☐ ♡ **Lydgate State Park:** Located near Wailua on Kaua'i, this family-friendly beach park features protected swimming areas, picnic pavilions, a playground, and paved walking paths. A rock-walled lagoon offers safe snorkeling and wading, especially for kids. The park is popular for family outings, and nearby cultural sites enhance its appeal.

HAWAII

☐ 🔖 ♡ **Mākena State Park:** On Maui's south shore, this rugged coastal park wraps the Puʻu Ōlaʻi cinder cone with three distinct beaches: broad golden Big Beach (ʻOneloa) with lifeguards, tucked-away Little Beach over the lava bluff, and Oneʻuli black sand. Powerful shorebreak is common—swim only in calm conditions. Wander lava-fringed trails under kiawe, spot Molokini and Kahoʻolawe offshore, and expect limited shade and facilities.

☐ 🔖 ♡ **Nā Pali Coast State Wilderness Park:** Located on Kauaʻi's rugged north shore, this park is known for its towering sea cliffs, lush valleys, and remote beaches. The famed Kalalau Trail traverses 11 miles through dramatic terrain, accessible only by foot or boat. Rich in natural beauty and cultural sites, the park offers an unforgettable wilderness experience for hikers and adventurers.

☐ 🔖 ♡ **Pāʻulaʻula State Historic Site:** Situated near Waimea on Kauaʻi, this park preserves the remains of a fort built by Russians in 1817 during an alliance with a Hawaiian chief. Stone walls, interpretive signs, and ocean views tell the story of this brief colonial presence. It's a unique blend of Hawaiian and international history.

☐ 🔖 ♡ **Pālāʻau State Park:** The only state park on Molokaʻi, Pālāʻau offers panoramic views of the Kalaupapa Peninsula and sea cliffs. It features short hiking trails, picnic areas, and a serene forest setting. The park is also home to a sacred phallic fertility stone (Kauleonanahoa), linking it to ancient Hawaiian spiritual practices and cultural traditions.

☐ 🔖 ♡ **Polihale State Park:** Located at the western end of Kauaʻi, this remote beach park offers miles of white sand backed by towering dunes. Accessible via a rough, unpaved road, it's perfect for stargazing, sunset viewing, and solitude. Though camping is allowed, strong currents often make ocean activities hazardous. It borders the dramatic cliffs of the Nā Pali Coast.

☐ 🔖 ♡ **Puʻu o Mahuka Heiau State Historic Site:** Overlooking Waimea Bay on Oʻahu's North Shore, this site preserves the largest heiau (temple) on the island. Believed to have served religious and possibly sacrificial functions, it offers insight into ancient Hawaiian spiritual practices. Visitors enjoy expansive coastal views alongside cultural interpretation.

☐ 🔖 ♡ **Puʻu ʻUalakaʻa State Wayside:** Perched above Honolulu in Tantalus, this scenic wayside offers panoramic views of Diamond Head, Waikīkī, and the southern coastline of Oʻahu. A short loop trail winds through native and introduced forest. It's a popular spot for picnicking, photography, and watching sunsets over the city.

☐ 🔖 ♡ **Waiʻānapanapa State Park:** Near Hāna on Maui, this park is famed for its black sand beach, sea caves, coastal lava tubes, and freshwater pools. It offers cabins, camping, and the start of the Piʻilani Trail. Visitors explore dramatic volcanic scenery and culturally significant sites, including ancient burial grounds and Hawaiian legends tied to the land.

☐ 🔖 ♡ **Wailua River State Park:** Located on Kauaʻi, this scenic park centers around Hawaii's only navigable river. Visitors can kayak or take boat tours to sites like Fern Grotto and Secret Falls. The park also includes sacred Hawaiian temples (heiau), ancient rock carvings, and Wailua Falls. It blends cultural significance with stunning river valley views.

☐ 🔖 ♡ **Waimea Canyon State Park:** Often called the "Grand Canyon of the Pacific," this park on Kauaʻi showcases a vast canyon with red cliffs, waterfalls, and forested ridges. Multiple lookouts and hiking trails offer sweeping views of the canyon and beyond. It's a must-see destination for its geological wonder and accessibility by car and trail.

State Monuments

☐ 🔖 ♡ **Diamond Head State Monument:** One of Hawaii's most iconic landmarks, Diamond Head (Lēʻahi) on Oʻahu features a popular hiking trail up the crater's interior to panoramic views of Honolulu. The 0.8-mile hike includes tunnels, stairs, and historic military bunkers. It's a must-see for visitors seeking a mix of geology, history, and breathtaking scenery.

☐ 🔖 ♡ **Halekiʻi-Pihana Heiau State Monument:** Located in central Maui, this monument preserves two significant ancient Hawaiian temple sites once used for political and religious ceremonies. Set on a hill overlooking Wailuku and ʻĪao Valley, it offers educational panels and sweeping views. Visitors gain insight into Maui's pre-contact history and the island's ancient power centers.

HAWAII

☐ 🔖 ♡ **Kohala Historical Sites State Monument:** On Hawai'i Island's windswept Upolu Point, this monument protects Mo'okini Heiau—one of Hawai'i's oldest and most sacred temples—and the nearby birthplace of Kamehameha I. A rough road leads across pasture to lava-walled ruins and coastal vistas to Maui. No facilities; stay on paths, don't climb stones, and visit with respect for cultural traditions.

☐ 🔖 ♡ **'Īao Valley State Monument:** Located in central Maui, this park is famous for the 'Īao Needle, a 1,200-foot green-mantled peak. The site holds deep historical significance as the 1790 Battle of Kepaniwai occurred here. Short paved trails and scenic viewpoints make it accessible for all visitors. The lush valley is rich in native plants and offers insight into Maui's cultural past.

☐ 🔖 ♡ **Lava Tree State Monument:** Near Pāhoa on the Big Island, this unique park showcases lava molds of tree trunks created by a 1790 lava flow. A loop trail winds through eerie lava formations and regenerating forest. It's a quick and fascinating stop that highlights the dynamic volcanic forces that have shaped Hawaii's landscapes.

State Recreational Areas

☐ 🔖 ♡ **Hāpuna Beach State Recreation Area:** Located on the Kohala Coast of the Big Island, Hāpuna Beach is one of Hawaii's largest white sand beaches. Known for excellent swimming and bodyboarding in calm conditions, it also features pavilions, restrooms, and picnic areas. The park is a family favorite and a prime destination for sunbathing and ocean recreation.

☐ 🔖 ♡ **Kalōpā State Recreation Area:** Nestled in the Hāmākua region of the Big Island, this cool, forested park offers cabin and tent camping, a nature trail, and a native forest arboretum. At 2,000 feet elevation, it provides a peaceful escape into 'ōhi'a and koa woodland. The park is ideal for birdwatching and short, shaded hikes in a misty upland setting.

☐ 🔖 ♡ **Keaīwa Heiau State Recreation Area:** Situated in 'Aiea Heights on O'ahu, this park features a forested campground, scenic trails, and the ancient Keaīwa Heiau—a medicinal healing temple. The 'Aiea Loop Trail offers panoramic views of Pearl Harbor. The park blends natural and cultural elements and provides a peaceful retreat from urban Honolulu.

☐ 🔖 ♡ **Sand Island State Recreation Area:** Adjacent to Honolulu Harbor, this coastal park offers open fields, picnic areas, and a beach with views of downtown and the ocean. Once used as an internment camp during WWII, the area has been reclaimed for public recreation. It's popular for gatherings, walking, and watching planes and ships pass by.

☐ 🔖 ♡ **Wailoa River State Recreation Area:** In the heart of Hilo, this waterfront park rings brackish lagoons where the Wailoa River meets Hilo Bay. Stroll lawns and bridges, fish from piers, or launch a kayak on calm water. The Wailoa Center hosts art and cultural exhibits, while the park's King Kamehameha I statue honors island history. Created as a post-tsunami buffer, it's a quiet urban refuge for birds and people.

National Parks

 ☐ 🔖 ♡ **Ala Kahakai National Historic Trail:** Stretching 175 miles along Hawai'i Island's western and southern coasts, this trail links ancient footpaths once used by Native Hawaiians. It passes sacred temples, fishing villages, lava fields, and beaches, connecting cultural landmarks with natural beauty. Visitors can hike portions of the route to explore Hawai'i's living history.

 ☐ 🔖 ♡ **Haleakalā National Park:** On Maui, this park features the massive Haleakalā Crater, a dormant volcano surrounded by alpine deserts, cloud forests, and lush valleys. Visitors hike among rare plants, witness breathtaking sunrises and sunsets above the clouds, and stargaze under pristine skies. The park also preserves cultural sites tied to Native Hawaiian traditions.

HAWAII

 **Hawai'i Volcanoes National Park:** Located on the Big Island, this park protects Kīlauea and Mauna Loa, two of the world's most active volcanoes. Visitors explore lava fields, steam vents, lush forests, and dramatic craters while learning about geology and Hawaiian culture. Trails, scenic drives, and volcanic activity offer a living view of Earth's creation in motion.

 **Honouliuli National Historic Site:** On O'ahu, this site preserves the Honouliuli Internment Camp, where Japanese Americans and others were forcibly confined during World War II. Exhibits highlight the injustices faced, the resilience of internees, and the camp's role in Hawaii's wartime history. It serves as a reminder of civil liberties lost and lessons learned.

 **Kalaupapa National Historical Park:** On Moloka'i, this park preserves the Kalaupapa settlement, where those with Hansen's disease were isolated for decades. It honors their resilience, the care provided by Saint Damien and Mother Marianne, and the deep history of the Hawaiian community. Remote and deeply moving, it offers powerful stories of courage and faith.

 **Kaloko-Honokōhau National Historical Park:** On the Big Island, this coastal park protects ancient Hawaiian fishponds, sacred sites, and petroglyphs. Visitors walk through lava fields, sandy beaches, and wetlands, learning how traditional aquaculture sustained Hawaiian communities. It's a living connection to the culture, ingenuity, and spirit of early Hawaiians.

 **Pearl Harbor National Memorial:** On O'ahu, this memorial honors those lost in the December 7, 1941 attack. Sites include the USS Arizona Memorial, USS Missouri, and interpretive exhibits. Visitors reflect on the day that brought the U.S. into World War II, exploring both tragedy and resilience while standing at one of America's most significant historic landmarks.

 **Pu'uhonua o Hōnaunau National Historical Park:** On the Big Island, this sacred site served as a refuge for those who broke ancient Hawaiian laws. Restored temples, royal grounds, and coastal fishponds tell stories of forgiveness and renewal. Visitors experience Hawaiian traditions, spiritual practices, and the power of a place central to island life and belief.

 **Pu'ukoholā Heiau National Historic Site:** On the Big Island, this site preserves the massive temple built by King Kamehameha I to fulfill prophecy and unify the Hawaiian Islands. Visitors walk along the heiau's stone terraces, learn about the political and cultural forces shaping Hawaii, and reflect on its role as both a sacred space and a symbol of unification.

State & National Forests

'Ewa Forest Reserve: Established in 1916 on O'ahu's Wai'anae foothills, this dry forest reserve was among the earliest created to combat deforestation and watershed loss. Today it protects rare native shrublands, reforested slopes, and aquifer recharge zones. Access is restricted, with management focused on erosion control, fire protection, and restoration of native vegetation.

Halele'a Forest Reserve: Located on Kaua'i's north shore uplands, this reserve protects misty ridges that feed Hanalei River and other watersheds. Dense forests of 'ōhi'a and koa harbor rare plants and birds while buffering erosion on steep slopes. Limited roads provide hunting access; DOFAW's efforts focus on maintaining watershed health and forest restoration.

Hāna Forest Reserve: Spanning East Maui's wet windward slopes, this reserve encompasses gulches, streams, and lush 'ōhi'a-koa forests nourished by steady rainfall. It safeguards critical headwaters for local communities while supporting native biodiversity. Management emphasizes watershed protection, invasive species removal, and compatible public access via select roads and trails.

Hanawi Natural Area & Forest Reserve: Part of East Maui's rain-soaked slopes, Hanawi supports some of the wettest ecosystems on earth, sustaining pristine montane forests and streams. It provides habitat for endangered native birds like the Maui parrotbill. Management highlights include watershed conservation, native plant protection, and carefully managed access for research.

HAWAII

Hilo Forest Reserve: Stretching across windward Hawai'i Island, this vast reserve covers rainforests, lava flows, and stream-fed valleys that recharge groundwater. Established in 1906, it was one of Hawai'i's earliest forest reserves. Today it remains vital for biodiversity, cultural resources, and public recreation, offering hunting, hiking, and birdwatching opportunities.

Honolulu Watershed Forest Reserve: High above Honolulu on O'ahu's Ko'olau Range, this steep reserve preserves critical watersheds supplying urban areas. Its native rainforests, cloud forests, and stream valleys store rainfall that sustains aquifers. Access is limited to protect fragile ecosystems, but it remains central to water security and biodiversity on the island.

Ka'ū Forest Reserve: On the southeastern slopes of Mauna Loa, this vast Hawai'i Island reserve shelters one of the largest remaining native forests. It provides refuge for endangered birds such as the 'akiapōlā'au and 'io (Hawaiian hawk). Management emphasizes habitat conservation, watershed protection, and cultural uses, with limited hunting opportunities.

Ka'ūpūlehu Forest Reserve: Situated on the Kona side of Hawai'i Island, Ka'ūpūlehu conserves rare dryland forests once widespread across West Hawai'i. Ancient wiliwili and sandalwood once dominated here. Management seeks to recover this endangered ecosystem while preventing wildfire and invasive species impacts. Limited access supports research and cultural practices.

Kahaualeʻa Forest Reserve: Bordering Hawai'i Volcanoes National Park, this reserve preserves young forests growing over recent lava flows. Lush 'ōhi'a woodlands host rare plants and native honeycreepers. Its landscape illustrates natural succession after eruptions, while management protects biodiversity and provides scientific and cultural study opportunities.

Kahikinui Forest Reserve: On Maui's leeward southern slopes, Kahikinui encompasses rugged, dry forests once heavily grazed. Restoration is ongoing to stabilize soils, restore native plants, and reestablish forest cover. While remote and difficult to access, the area plays a vital role in watershed recharge and offers traditional cultural uses for local communities.

Kahuku Forest Reserve: Located on Hawai'i Island's Ka'ū District, this reserve features native dry and mesic forests transitioning up Mauna Loa's southern flanks. It sustains habitat for endemic species and stabilizes fragile volcanic soils. Access is challenging, but management aims to restore native cover and safeguard long-term watershed health.

Kapāpala Forest Reserve: One of Hawai'i Island's largest reserves, Kapāpala covers vast slopes of Mauna Loa and diverse ecosystems from wet forests to dry shrublands. It supports endangered birds and rare plants while serving as a key hunting area. Management balances recreation, cultural uses, and conservation of critical watersheds and habitats.

Kīpahulu Forest Reserve: High above Hāna, Maui, this reserve protects lush rainforests and gulches feeding waterfalls like those in Kīpahulu Valley. It harbors endangered birds and rare plants found only in East Maui. Access is restricted to safeguard sensitive ecosystems, with management focusing on watershed protection and native species recovery.

Kohala Forest Reserve: Encompassing the windward and leeward slopes of Kohala Mountain, this Hawai'i Island reserve shelters some of the island's oldest forests. Mist-fed rainforests, valleys, and waterfalls supply water to North Kohala. Cultural sites, bird habitat, and hunting opportunities make it both ecologically and historically important for the region.

Koloa Forest Reserve: Found in Kaua'i's uplands, Koloa FR protects steep ridges and valleys clothed in native koa and 'ōhi'a. Its ecosystems buffer erosion and contribute to aquifer recharge. Hunting and cultural practices are supported, while management combats invasive plants and prioritizes watershed health for downstream agriculture and communities.

Koolau Forest Reserve: Spanning much of O'ahu's Ko'olau Range, this large reserve protects lush valleys, waterfalls, and rainforests that recharge aquifers for Honolulu. Trails like those near Mānoa Valley touch its edge, though interior access is rugged. Management emphasizes watershed stability, erosion control, and protecting native ecosystems critical for biodiversity and water supply.

HAWAII

☐ 🔖 ♡ **Laupāhoehoe Forest Reserve:** On Hawaiʻi Island's windward Hamakua Coast, this reserve preserves old-growth ʻōhiʻa and koa forests with intact understory. It is a refuge for rare birds including the Hawaiʻi creeper and ʻakiapōlāʻau. Trails like the Laupāhoehoe Trail provide access for hiking and hunting. State management stresses biodiversity protection and watershed health.

☐ 🔖 ♡ **Līhuʻe-Koloa Forest Reserve:** Covering central Kauaʻi, this reserve includes upland forests, valleys, and ridges draining into the Wailua River. It shelters koa-ʻōhiʻa forests, supports hunting, and preserves cultural resources. Its mist-fed slopes stabilize soils and aquifers vital for communities. DOFAW manages invasive species while balancing recreation and watershed protection.

☐ 🔖 ♡ **Makawao Forest Reserve:** Located on Maui's northwest slopes of Haleakalā, Makawao is a popular recreation forest known for trails like Kahakapao Loop, popular with hikers and bikers. It protects koa-ʻōhiʻa forests, provides habitat for native species, and supplies water resources. Management balances recreation with invasive species control and watershed restoration.

☐ 🔖 ♡ **Manuka Forest Reserve:** Covering a vast area of South Kona, Hawaiʻi Island, Manuka encompasses old lava flows, dry forests, and native shrublands. It is habitat for rare plants and birds adapted to arid ecosystems. Hunting and research are permitted, while management focuses on protecting sensitive dryland forests and preventing wildfires and invasives.

☐ 🔖 ♡ **Molokaʻi Forest Reserve:** Dominating the island's mountainous spine, this reserve protects rainforests, cloud forests, and stream valleys that provide all of Molokaʻi's drinking water. It harbors rare birds and plants unique to the island. Management emphasizes watershed protection and invasive species control, with limited public access to safeguard fragile habitats.

☐ 🔖 ♡ **Na Pali-Kona Forest Reserve:** One of Hawaiʻi's largest, spanning central Kauaʻi's rugged mountains, cliffs, and valleys. It includes iconic Nā Pali ridges and vast uplands crucial for watershed health. It shelters rare ecosystems and supports hunting access. Management focuses on preventing erosion, safeguarding biodiversity, and sustaining native forests that define Kauaʻi's landscape.

☐ 🔖 ♡ **Nānāwale Forest Reserve:** On Hawaiʻi Island's Puna District, this reserve preserves lush native forests growing on young lava flows. ʻŌhiʻa woodlands support native birds and plants, while roads provide access for hunting. It helps protect watersheds in an area prone to volcanic change. State efforts emphasize invasive species control and habitat stability.

☐ 🔖 ♡ **Pepeʻekeo Forest Reserve:** Along Hawaiʻi Island's Hamakua Coast, this small reserve protects stream valleys and native rainforests. It contributes to groundwater recharge and provides habitat for native birds. Its steep terrain is difficult to access, so management prioritizes invasive species removal and watershed health over recreation. Hunting opportunities exist on its margins.

☐ 🔖 ♡ **Puʻu Ka Pele Forest Reserve:** On Kauaʻi's west side, near Waimea Canyon, this reserve encompasses dry upland forests and striking cliffs. It stabilizes watersheds feeding the canyon and provides public hunting access. Its unique mix of dryland species contrasts with wetter forests elsewhere on the island. Management focuses on habitat stability and fire prevention.

☐ 🔖 ♡ **Puʻu Waʻawaʻa Forest Reserve:** On Hawaiʻi Island's North Kona District, this large reserve includes dryland forests, cinder cones, and unique volcanic landscapes. It supports rare ecosystems and extensive hunting areas. Popular for hiking and cultural activities, it is co-managed with community partners. Restoration focuses on native species recovery and wildfire control.

☐ 🔖 ♡ **Tantalus Forest Reserve:** Overlooking Honolulu, Tantalus FR preserves rainforest slopes in the Koʻolau Range. It is known for winding roads, hiking trails, and panoramic city views. Established early in the forest reserve system, it plays a key role in aquifer recharge and recreation. Management balances heavy visitor use with conservation and invasive control.

☐ 🔖 ♡ **Upper Waiākea Forest Reserve:** On Hawaiʻi Island's windward slopes of Mauna Loa, this expansive reserve includes old-growth rainforest and younger successional forests. It provides habitat for native birds and critical groundwater recharge. Hunting and recreation are allowed in designated zones. Management stresses watershed protection and restoration of native ecosystems.

HAWAII

☐ 🔖 ♡ **Wai'anae Kai Forest Reserve:** On O'ahu's rugged Wai'anae Range, this reserve protects steep ridges, gulches, and native dry forests critical for aquifer recharge on the leeward side. Popular for hiking via trails like Mā'ili and Wai'anae Kai, it supports hunting and cultural use. Management balances public access with fire prevention, erosion control, and habitat restoration.

☐ 🔖 ♡ **Waiawa Forest Reserve:** Located above Pearl City on O'ahu, this reserve conserves Ko'olau foothill forests and aquifer recharge zones for urban Honolulu. Steep terrain makes access limited, but its forests are crucial for water resources. Management focuses on invasive species removal, watershed health, and protecting remaining native ecosystems in central O'ahu.

☐ 🔖 ♡ **Waihou Spring Forest Reserve:** Nestled above Kula on Maui, this small reserve is known for the popular Waihou Spring Trail, leading to a picturesque forest and spring-fed gorge. It provides local groundwater recharge and offers family-friendly recreation. Management balances public use with forest protection, ensuring long-term stability of upland ecosystems.

☐ 🔖 ♡ **Waikamoi Forest Reserve:** On the northeast slopes of Haleakalā, Maui, Waikamoi is one of the most important conservation areas, harboring rare plants and endangered birds like the 'ākohekohe. Its rainforests provide major watershed protection. Public access is restricted to guided trips to safeguard sensitive ecosystems. Management emphasizes biodiversity and watershed resilience.

☐ 🔖 ♡ **Wailuku Forest Reserve:** Just above Hilo on Hawai'i Island, Wailuku protects the headwaters of the Wailuku River, famed for Rainbow Falls. Dense rainforests, gulches, and waterfalls provide aquifer recharge and cultural significance. Popular trails like Kaumana Caves lie nearby, though core areas remain closed. Management stresses watershed security and forest restoration.

☐ 🔖 ♡ **Waimea Canyon Forest Reserve:** On Kaua'i's west side, this reserve frames the "Grand Canyon of the Pacific." It encompasses steep cliffs, valleys, and dry forests feeding Waimea River. Scenic lookouts and hunting access attract visitors, while management priorities include fire prevention, watershed health, and restoration of native dryland species unique to the region.

☐ 🔖 ♡ **West Maui Forest Reserve:** Encompassing the misty ridges and valleys of Maui's West Mountains, this reserve safeguards rainforests, cloud forests, and streams that feed Lahaina and Wailuku. It harbors endangered plants and rare birds like the Maui parrotbill. Public access is limited, with management focusing on watershed recharge, erosion control, and invasive species removal.

State Scenic Byways

☐ 🔖 ♡ **Holoholo Kōloa Scenic Byway:** A State scenic route on Kauai's south shore, weaving through sugarcane-era Kōloa, coastal farmlands, salt ponds, and beach vistas. Passing by historic plantation town landscapes, seaside parks, and cultural sites, the drive offers gentle coastal charm amid Kona winds and ancient Hawaiian shoreline life.

☐ 🔖 ♡ **Ka'ū Scenic Byway – Slopes of Maunaloa (Hwy 11):** A 54-mile State scenic byway along Hawai'i Island's southern belt road. It crosses rolling lava fields, black-sand Punalu'u Beach, native dryland forests, ancient cave systems, and panoramic ocean and volcano views—offering a quiet, evocative journey around Mauna Loa's slopes to the gates of Volcanoes National Park.

☐ 🔖 ♡ **Māmalahoa Kona Heritage Corridor (Hawaii Belt Road / Hwy 11/180):** A 10-mile State scenic segment on the Kona coast honoring Kamehameha's "Law of the Splintered Paddle." Past Hōlualoa's art galleries, Kona coffee farms, historic shrines, and Kona village architecture, the route follows ancient footpaths and cultural landmarks overlooking Kailua-Kona and blue ocean vistas.

☐ 🔖 ♡ **Maunalua–Makapu'u Scenic Byway:** Stretching along O'ahu's southeastern shore, this coastal byway traces the dramatic Ka Iwi coastline from Hawai'i Kai through Koko Head, Sandy Beach, and Makapu'u Point. Panoramic ocean vistas, rugged sea cliffs, tidepools, and whale-watching lookouts define the route. It highlights ancient fishing shrines, volcanic landmarks, and sweeping views toward Moloka'i and Lana'i.

HAWAII

☐ 🔖 ♡ **Royal Footsteps Along the Kona Coast (Ali'i Drive):** This 7-mile State scenic stretch in Kailua-Kona traces ancient royal pathways along Ali'i Drive. It connects four historical royal centers—Hulihe'e Palace, kahua heiau, royal surfing grounds, and early Christian church sites—while offering oceanfront greenery and a living corridor of Hawaiian chiefs and culture.

National Natural Landmarks

 ☐ 🔖 ♡ **Diamond Head (Lē'ahi):** Towering above Honolulu, Diamond Head is celebrated as a National Natural Landmark for its textbook example of tuff cone volcanism. Formed about 300,000 years ago during the Honolulu Volcanic Series, it preserves clear evidence of O'ahu's fiery past. The crater and rim offer sweeping island views while serving as a natural geologic classroom.
GPS: 21.2615, -157.8081

 ☐ 🔖 ♡ **I'ao Valley:** Lush and steep-sided, I'ao Valley on Maui earned National Natural Landmark status for showcasing dramatic volcanic erosion. The valley's centerpiece, the I'ao Needle, stands as a remnant of basalt carved by centuries of weathering. Its rainforest and cloud forest ecosystems nurture diverse species while preserving an important cultural landscape.
GPS: 20.8886, -156.5222

 ☐ 🔖 ♡ **Kanahā Pond State Wildlife Sanctuary:** Kanahā Pond became a National Natural Landmark because it preserves one of Hawai'i's last intact coastal wetlands. Once a royal fishpond, it is now a refuge for endangered native birds like the Hawaiian stilt and coot. Its brackish waters and mudflats demonstrate the ecological importance of wetland protection in the islands.
GPS: 20.8972, -156.4575

 ☐ 🔖 ♡ **Ko'olau Range Pali:** The dramatic cliffs of the Ko'olau Pali highlight the exposed eastern flank of O'ahu's shield volcano and are protected as a National Natural Landmark. Massive landslides and relentless erosion sculpted these vertical walls, which today support tropical vegetation and cloud forests while preserving evidence of catastrophic volcanic collapse.
GPS: 21.3842, -157.8033

 ☐ 🔖 ♡ **Makalawena Marsh:** This rare coastal marsh on Hawai'i Island holds National Natural Landmark distinction for its role as critical habitat for endangered species such as the Hawaiian stilt. Volcanic flows and oceanic forces shaped the wetland, which endures as one of the most ecologically significant marshes in the islands' dry coastal zones.
GPS: 19.7915, -156.0269

 ☐ 🔖 ♡ **Mauna Kea:** Rising 13,800 feet above sea level, Mauna Kea is a National Natural Landmark both for its geology and its ecology. It is Earth's tallest mountain from base to summit and hosts unique alpine environments rarely seen in the tropics. The volcano also supports world-class observatories, blending natural significance with scientific achievement.
GPS: 19.8206, -155.4681

 ☐ 🔖 ♡ **North Shore Cliffs:** On Moloka'i, the North Shore Cliffs plunge more than 3,000 feet into the sea, earning their place as a National Natural Landmark. These are among the tallest sea cliffs on Earth, formed by volcanic collapse and erosion. Beyond their breathtaking scale, the cliffs provide nesting habitat for seabirds and refuge for rare native plants.
GPS: 21.1458, -156.8625

IDAHO

Idaho's rugged beauty spans jagged peaks, alpine lakes, deep canyons, and scenic rivers. With a tapestry of state parks, vast national forests, a national park, and awe-inspiring natural landmarks, Idaho is a haven for those seeking wild solitude, outdoor adventure, and pristine wilderness escapes.

📅 Peak Season
June–September is Idaho's peak season, with warm weather, clear skies, and full access to mountain trails, lakes, and rivers. These months are busiest for hiking, camping, and water recreation across the state.

📅 Offseason Months
November–April is the offseason for most areas, with cold weather and snow limiting access to high elevations. Winter, however, is peak season for skiing and snow sports in Sun Valley and other mountain resorts.

🍃 Scenery & Nature Timing
Spring brings wildflowers and swelling rivers from snowmelt. Summer highlights alpine lakes, river rafting, and mountain meadows. Fall offers golden larch and aspen foliage, while winter covers the Sawtooths and other ranges in deep snow.

✨ Special
Idaho features the jagged Sawtooth Mountains, Hells Canyon—the deepest gorge in North America—and Shoshone Falls, known as the "Niagara of the West." Craters of the Moon's lava fields, alpine lakes, and vast wilderness areas showcase the state's rugged beauty.

IDAHO

State Parks

☐ 🔖 ♡ **Ashton–Tetonia Trail State Park**: Situated in the picturesque Teton Valley, this 28-mile rail-trail runs from Ashton to Tetonia, offering stunning views of the Teton Mountains. The trail is perfect for biking, hiking, and wildlife watching, providing an ideal spot for outdoor enthusiasts. Visitors can enjoy the scenic beauty of Idaho's farmland and mountain vistas, making it a great place for nature lovers and photographers.

☐ 🔖 ♡ **Bear Lake State Park**: Located on the shores of Bear Lake, this park is known for its striking turquoise waters and sandy beaches. Popular for boating, fishing, and camping, Bear Lake is a serene destination that offers swimming, hiking, and picnicking. The park also features excellent birdwatching opportunities, with numerous migratory bird species frequenting the area.

☐ 🔖 ♡ **Bruneau Dunes State Park**: Home to North America's tallest single-structured sand dune, Bruneau Dunes offers a unique landscape for outdoor recreation. Visitors can hike or sandboard down the dunes, stargaze at the observatory, or explore the park's diverse ecosystems. The park's tranquil surroundings and the nearby Bruneau River make it a peaceful retreat for nature lovers.

☐ 🔖 ♡ **Castle Rocks State Park**: Located near the City of Rocks National Reserve, Castle Rocks offers visitors a chance to experience rock climbing, hiking, and camping amidst stunning granite formations. The park is rich in history, featuring ancient emigrant inscriptions along the California Trail. With its towering spires and picturesque landscapes, it's a haven for outdoor adventurers and photographers.

☐ 🔖 ♡ **Coeur d'Alene Parkway State Park**: Situated along the scenic shores of Lake Coeur d'Alene, this urban trail system is perfect for walking, cycling, and enjoying lakeside views. The park connects various waterfront locations, offering easy access to parks, beaches, and picnic areas. It's a relaxing destination for families and outdoor enthusiasts looking to enjoy the beauty of Coeur d'Alene's lakefront.

☐ 🔖 ♡ **Dworshak State Park**: Nestled along the shores of Dworshak Reservoir, this park offers ample opportunities for boating, fishing, and camping. Surrounded by dense forests and towering mountains, it's a great spot for hiking, wildlife watching, and enjoying Idaho's natural beauty. The park is a peaceful retreat for those looking to escape into nature.

☐ 🔖 ♡ **Eagle Island State Park**: Located near Boise, Eagle Island is a family-friendly park featuring a swimming beach, picnic areas, and equestrian trails. The park is ideal for hiking, birdwatching, and enjoying water activities like kayaking and paddleboarding. It's a relaxing spot for picnics or a day spent swimming in the freshwater lake.

☐ 🔖 ♡ **Farragut State Park**: Situated on Lake Pend Oreille, Farragut State Park offers hiking, biking, and water activities, along with fascinating historical sites from its past as a naval training base. Visitors can enjoy hiking trails that meander through dense forests, or simply relax by the lake. The park also has ample camping facilities and picnic areas.

☐ 🔖 ♡ **Harriman State Park**: Located in the Greater Yellowstone Ecosystem, Harriman State Park is a nature lover's paradise, providing excellent opportunities for fly fishing, hiking, and wildlife viewing. The park is home to numerous bird species and offers spectacular views of the surrounding mountains. It's a peaceful, serene destination for those seeking solitude and outdoor recreation.

☐ 🔖 ♡ **Hells Gate State Park**: Situated at the confluence of the Snake and Clearwater Rivers, Hells Gate is a popular park for jet boating, fishing, and camping. The park offers scenic views of the Hells Canyon, the deepest river gorge in North America, and is a great place to explore the surrounding landscapes by boat or foot. Visitors can also hike, picnic, and enjoy wildlife viewing in this beautiful river setting.

☐ 🔖 ♡ **Henrys Lake State Park**: A premier destination for anglers, this park is known for its excellent fishing opportunities on Henrys Lake, where anglers can catch a variety of species including trout. The park offers camping, boating, and birdwatching, making it a peaceful retreat for outdoor enthusiasts looking to enjoy the serene beauty of Idaho's natural landscapes.

☐ 🔖 ♡ **Heyburn State Park**: Idaho's oldest state park, Heyburn offers a mix of lakes, forests, and trails, perfect for hiking, biking, and wildlife watching. It's an excellent spot for camping and enjoying a variety of water activities on Chatcolet and Benewah Lakes. Visitors can also explore the park's rich history, with interpretive exhibits and educational programs on the region's natural and cultural heritage.

IDAHO

☐ 🔖 ♡ **Lake Cascade State Park**: Located on Lake Cascade, this park is a favorite for boating, fishing, and camping. With its beautiful sandy beaches and scenic views, it's also a great spot for picnics and hiking. The park offers various facilities for RV camping, making it ideal for a weekend getaway or family retreat by the lake.

☐ 🔖 ♡ **Lake Walcott State Park**: Situated on the Snake River, this park offers boating, fishing, and birdwatching opportunities. It's particularly known for its waterfowl habitats, making it a haven for bird watchers. The park has a relaxed atmosphere, with plenty of picnic spots and camping areas, perfect for families and nature lovers seeking a quiet place to unwind.

☐ 🔖 ♡ **Land of the Yankee Fork State Park**: Rich in mining history, this park offers visitors a chance to explore Idaho's gold rush past, with interpretive sites, hiking trails, and opportunities to learn about the area's historical significance. It also provides camping and picnicking opportunities, making it a great spot for both history buffs and nature enthusiasts.

☐ 🔖 ♡ **Lucky Peak State Park**: Near Boise, Lucky Peak offers boating, fishing, and picnicking, with scenic views of the Boise River. The park is a popular spot for locals to enjoy outdoor activities such as swimming, paddleboarding, and relaxing by the water. It's a great place for a quick escape to nature, with easy access from Boise.

☐ 🔖 ♡ **Mary Minerva McCroskey State Park**: Located in the Palouse region, McCroskey offers panoramic views, hiking trails, and a tranquil forest setting. The park is known for its peace and quiet, making it a perfect spot for nature walks, birdwatching, and photography. The park's accessible location and scenic beauty make it a great retreat for those looking to escape into nature.

☐ 🔖 ♡ **Massacre Rocks State Park**: A historical site along the Oregon Trail, Massacre Rocks features interpretive exhibits, hiking trails, and a disc golf course. The park commemorates an infamous battle and offers visitors a chance to learn about the hardships faced by emigrants traveling west. It also provides ample opportunities for hiking and enjoying Idaho's wide-open spaces.

☐ 🔖 ♡ **Old Mission State Park**: Home to the historic Cataldo Mission, this park offers cultural insights, hiking, and picnicking opportunities. It's the site of Idaho's oldest building and is an important landmark in the region's history. Visitors can learn about the mission's history, hike the surrounding trails, and enjoy a picnic in a picturesque setting.

☐ 🔖 ♡ **Ponderosa State Park**: Situated on Payette Lake, Ponderosa offers hiking, biking, and water activities, along with winter recreation options. The park features forested areas and scenic views of the lake, making it an ideal spot for outdoor activities year-round. During winter, visitors can enjoy cross-country skiing, snowshoeing, and ice fishing.

☐ 🔖 ♡ **Priest Lake State Park**: Nestled in the Selkirk Mountains, Priest Lake offers boating, fishing, and camping amidst pristine forested landscapes. The park's remote location makes it a peaceful destination, perfect for outdoor enthusiasts seeking solitude. Hiking, wildlife watching, and exploring the beautiful forest are also popular activities.

☐ 🔖 ♡ **Round Lake State Park**: A small, serene park offering fishing, hiking, and wildlife viewing in a peaceful setting. Located in the northern part of Idaho, it provides a quiet retreat for visitors looking to enjoy a relaxing day surrounded by nature. The park is ideal for birdwatching and offers great opportunities for photography.

☐ 🔖 ♡ **Thousand Springs State Park**: Known for its dramatic springs and waterfalls, this park offers hiking, photography, and exploration opportunities. The park is located in the Magic Valley and features stunning natural beauty with crystal-clear springs cascading into the Snake River. It's a great spot for nature walks, photography, and enjoying the scenic views.

☐ 🔖 ♡ **Three Island Crossing State Park**: A historical site along the Oregon Trail, featuring interpretive exhibits, hiking trails, and a campground. The park is an important landmark in Idaho's history, where emigrants crossed the Snake River on their way to the western United States. It also offers opportunities for picnicking, wildlife viewing, and outdoor exploration.

☐ 🔖 ♡ **Winchester Lake State Park**: Located in the Clearwater Mountains, it offers fishing, hiking, and camping amidst lush forests. The park provides a peaceful setting for fishing and wildlife viewing, with ample opportunities for hiking and picnicking. The surrounding forest offers plenty of trails and scenic views, making it a perfect spot for nature enthusiasts.

UNITED STATES EDITION

IDAHO

National Parks

☐ 🔖 ♡ **City of Rocks National Reserve:** Located in southern Idaho, this reserve is famed for its dramatic granite spires, historic emigrant trails, and world-class climbing. Visitors can hike through striking landscapes, camp under clear skies, and follow the route of pioneers on the California Trail. The reserve blends natural beauty, recreation, and cultural history in one unforgettable setting.

☐ 🔖 ♡ **Craters of the Moon National Monument & Preserve:** This vast volcanic landscape showcases craters, lava flows, and unique formations created by ancient eruptions. Visitors can explore rugged trails, learn about the area's geologic history, and experience an otherworldly wilderness of black rock, cinder cones, and lava tubes. It's one of Idaho's most dramatic and unusual natural wonders.

☐ 🔖 ♡ **Hagerman Fossil Beds National Monument:** Known for one of the richest fossil deposits in North America, this site preserves remains of prehistoric horses, mammoths, and other Ice Age species. Visitors can explore trails, view fossil replicas at the visitor center, and learn about the ancient ecosystems that once thrived here. The monument offers a fascinating window into Idaho's deep past.

☐ 🔖 ♡ **Minidoka National Historic Site:** This site preserves the history of the Minidoka Internment Camp, where Japanese Americans were unjustly incarcerated during World War II. Visitors can walk among historic structures, learn about the hardships endured by internees, and reflect on the lessons of this difficult chapter in U.S. history. The park honors resilience and the pursuit of justice.

☐ 🔖 ♡ **Nez Perce National Historical Park:** Spanning sites in Idaho, Montana, and Washington, this park honors the Nez Perce people and their struggle against forced removal in the 19th century. Visitors can explore cultural centers, historic battlefields, and sacred landscapes while learning about the tribe's traditions, resilience, and the legacy of the Nez Perce War.

☐ 🔖 ♡ **Yellowstone National Park:** America's first national park extends into Idaho, Wyoming, and Montana, showcasing geothermal wonders like Old Faithful, colorful hot springs, and steaming geysers. Visitors can hike, camp, and explore landscapes teeming with bison, elk, wolves, and grizzly bears. Its mix of volcanic features and thriving ecosystems makes Yellowstone world-renowned.

State & National Forests

☐ 🔖 ♡ **Boise National Forest:** Spanning 2.2 million acres from sagebrush steppe to alpine forests, this forest features over 70 campgrounds, 1,300 miles of trails, hot springs, and wild rivers. Whitewater rafting, fishing, and wildlife like wolves, mountain goats, and bald eagles thrive here. Seasonal wildflowers, including rare Sacajawea's bitterroot, add to its natural diversity.

☐ 🔖 ♡ **Caribou-Targhee National Forest:** Covering 2.6 million acres across southeast Idaho into Wyoming, this forest is part of the Greater Yellowstone Ecosystem. Rugged peaks, pristine rivers, and abundant wildlife including moose, elk, and grizzlies define its terrain. It connects seamlessly to Yellowstone and Grand Teton National Parks, offering hiking, skiing, and backcountry solitude.

☐ 🔖 ♡ **Clearwater National Forest:** Situated in north-central Idaho, this forest features deep canyons, towering old-growth stands, and access to the Selway–Bitterroot Wilderness. Visitors enjoy whitewater trips, fishing, and backpacking through remote terrain supporting salmon, steelhead, and diverse wildlife. Its vast wild areas offer a chance to experience Idaho's rugged backcountry.

☐ 🔖 ♡ **Idaho Panhandle National Forests:** Encompassing 3.2 million acres across northern Idaho, this unit combines the Coeur d'Alene, St. Joe, and Kaniksu forests. The region is rich with mountain lakes, rivers, and dense forests home to elk, wolves, and eagles. Hiking, camping, and fishing abound, with scenic drives and remote trails offering both relaxation and adventure.

☐ 🔖 ♡ **Nez Perce-Clearwater National Forests:** Spanning nearly 4 million acres, these combined forests protect vast wilderness including the Selway–Bitterroot and Frank Church–River of No Return. Renowned for its wild rivers, rugged terrain, and critical fish habitat, it offers rafting, hunting, hiking, and backcountry experiences in some of Idaho's most remote landscapes.

☐ 🔖 ♡ **Payette National Forest:** Stretching across central Idaho, this forest includes alpine lakes, hot springs, and sections of the Frank Church Wilderness. Its Salmon and Payette Rivers are prized for whitewater kayaking and rafting. With scenic trails, winter snowmobiling, and wildlife viewing, the Payette is a year-round destination for recreation and nature immersion.

IDAHO

☐ ⌘ ♡ **Salmon–Challis National Forest:** Covering 4.2 million acres, this forest contains Mount Borah, Idaho's highest peak, and much of the Frank Church Wilderness. Visitors find rugged mountains, canyons, wild rivers, and 80 campgrounds. Known for its epic backpacking terrain and remote solitude, it offers a true wilderness experience in the heart of Idaho.

☐ ⌘ ♡ **Sawtooth National Forest:** Encompassing over 2.1 million acres, this iconic forest includes the jagged Sawtooth Mountains and Sawtooth National Recreation Area. With alpine lakes, granite peaks, and 1,000 miles of trails, it's a premier destination for hiking, camping, skiing, and hot springs. Its diverse wildlife and dramatic scenery make it one of Idaho's crown jewels.

National Grasslands

☐ ⌘ ♡ **Curlew National Grassland**: Tucked in southeastern Idaho near the Utah border, Curlew National Grassland spans valleys and low hills once traveled by Native peoples and early settlers. It's home to sagebrush steppe, native grasses, and diverse wildlife including elk, hawks, and sage-grouse. Popular for hunting, hiking, and birdwatching, it offers peaceful views of wide-open rangeland and sky.

National Scenic Byways & All-American Roads

☐ ⌘ ♡ **City of Rocks Back Country Byway:** Winding 49 miles between Albion and Almo, this byway showcases southern Idaho's dramatic granite spires, open ranchlands, and historic emigrant routes. Travelers pass the City of Rocks National Reserve, famed for pioneer inscriptions and world-class climbing. With sweeping vistas and unique geology, it blends frontier history with rugged beauty.

☐ ⌘ ♡ **Elk River Back Country Byway:** This rugged loop winds through the upper Elk River drainage near North Fork, crossing forested slopes, streams, and steep mountain terrain. Popular with off-road vehicles, anglers, and hikers, it offers remote trails, river crossings, and solitude in a wild setting where backcountry adventure and pristine nature meet.

☐ ⌘ ♡ **International Selkirk Loop:** Idaho's only All-American Road, this 144-mile loop meanders through the Selkirk Mountains, connecting forests, lakes, waterfalls, and alpine meadows. Crossing into Canada, it highlights Sandpoint and other charming towns. Visitors enjoy mountain drives, scenic overlooks, wildlife viewing, and cross-border adventure in a pristine northern landscape.

☐ ⌘ ♡ **Lewis & Clark Back Country Byway:** A 36-mile loop near Lemhi Pass in eastern Idaho, this byway follows the Continental Divide and the Lewis & Clark Trail. Ascending more than 4,000 feet, it passes valleys, wildflower meadows, and evergreen forests. Hikers, anglers, and history enthusiasts enjoy its blend of wilderness and exploration heritage.

☐ ⌘ ♡ **Main Oregon Trail Back Country Byway:** Stretching 102 miles through the high desert between I-84 near Mountain Home and I-86 near Burley, this route follows emigrant wagon ruts and stagecoach roads across wide sagebrush plains. Visitors see historic sites like Rock Creek Station, Kelton Road, and authentic trail remnants, while enjoying vast open skies and glimpses of Idaho's Oregon Trail past.

☐ ⌘ ♡ **Northwest Passage Scenic Byway:** Designated an All-American Road, this 202-mile route traces the Lewis & Clark Expedition from Lewiston to Lolo Pass. It follows the Clearwater and Lochsa Rivers through pine forests and mountain landscapes. Blending recreation with history, it offers rafting, fishing, scenic drives, and connections across Idaho into Montana.

☐ ⌘ ♡ **Owyhee Uplands Back Country Byway:** This 103-mile gravel loop through the remote Owyhee Canyonlands offers solitude and striking desert scenery. Travelers encounter volcanic mesas, juniper-clad ridges, wildflower meadows, and deep river canyons. Wildlife such as pronghorn, raptors, and sage-grouse thrive here. It's a rugged adventure route where Idaho's wildest landscapes and frontier spirit endure.

☐ ⌘ ♡ **Payette River Scenic Byway (SH 55):** Following the North Fork Payette River from Eagle to New Meadows, this byway offers canyon views, rushing whitewater, and pine-clad ridges. Travelers pass through alpine valleys, mountain towns, and lake vistas. Popular for rafting, fishing, and fall colors, it is one of Idaho's premier scenic corridors.

IDAHO

☐ 🔖 ♡ **Pend Oreille Scenic Byway (SH 200):** This 33-mile lakeside route traces the northern edge of Lake Pend Oreille. With rolling hills, pine forests, campgrounds, and marinas, it highlights Idaho's largest lake. Visitors enjoy boating, birdwatching, fishing, and peaceful drives through charming lakeside communities framed by water and mountain scenery.

☐ 🔖 ♡ **Pioneer Historic Byway (US 91/SH 34):** Covering 128 miles from Preston to the Wyoming border, this byway follows Mormon pioneer and Oregon Trail routes. It passes rural towns, cemeteries, and agricultural landscapes alongside rivers and foothills. Visitors explore a blend of history, open vistas, and quiet roads steeped in pioneer heritage.

☐ 🔖 ♡ **Western Heritage Historic Byway:** From Swan Falls Dam near Kuna to Meridian, this route traces SH 69 through Snake River Canyon country. Visitors see basalt cliffs, sweeping river views, and historic sites tied to Idaho's early settlement. The byway highlights the region's cultural legacy and natural beauty with trails and recreation along the way.

State Scenic Byways

☐ 🔖 ♡ **Fort Henry Historic Byway:** Stretching from Rexburg toward Island Park, this byway follows Henry's Fork of the Snake River through rich farmland, volcanic terrain, and sand dunes. Visitors pass the Fort Henry Monument, one of Idaho's earliest settlements, while enjoying views of the Tetons and abundant wildlife. It blends pioneer history, wide-open landscapes, and quiet rural charm.

☐ 🔖 ♡ **Gold Rush Historic Byway:** Running through north-central Idaho, this byway follows the Clearwater River into historic mining country. Travelers encounter remnants of 19th-century gold camps, rustic homesteads, and small communities shaped by boom-and-bust fortunes. Scenic river valleys and wooded hills frame a journey that highlights both Idaho's natural beauty and frontier past.

☐ 🔖 ♡ **Hells Canyon Scenic Byway:** This drive skirts the Snake River and into Hells Canyon, the deepest gorge in North America. Towering canyon walls, rugged plateaus, and sweeping river views define the route. Wildlife, fishing, and hiking opportunities abound, with overlooks showcasing dramatic vistas. The byway offers a powerful look into Idaho's untamed canyon country.

☐ 🔖 ♡ **Lake Coeur d'Alene Scenic Byway (SH 97):** Following the lake's eastern shoreline, this byway reveals sparkling blue waters framed by pine-clad hills. Travelers encounter small lakeside towns, marinas, and campgrounds, with easy access to boating, fishing, and birdwatching. Scenic pullouts provide postcard views, making this one of northern Idaho's most tranquil and beautiful drives.

☐ 🔖 ♡ **Lost Gold Trails Loop:** Winding through eastern Idaho, this loop traces the paths of early miners and settlers. The drive passes ghost towns, forested valleys, and open rangelands rich with history. Interpretive sites recount the struggles and triumphs of the mining era, while today's visitors enjoy peaceful scenery, wildlife, and glimpses into Idaho's frontier heritage.

☐ 🔖 ♡ **Lower Payette River Heritage Byway:** This byway follows the Lower Payette River through fertile valleys, rugged canyons, and farmland that has long sustained Idaho communities. Rapids and calm waters alternate along the route, offering opportunities for boating, fishing, and wildlife viewing. Historic farmsteads and wide river vistas provide a blend of culture and nature.

☐ 🔖 ♡ **Mesa Falls Scenic Byway:** Leading to the spectacular Upper and Lower Mesa Falls, this route winds through forests, meadows, and volcanic landscapes along the Henry's Fork. Thundering waterfalls drop dramatically into deep gorges, creating breathtaking views. Along the way, visitors find hiking trails, wildlife, and interpretive sites that showcase the region's geologic and cultural history.

☐ 🔖 ♡ **Oregon Trail–Bear Lake Scenic Byway:** This historic route traces Oregon Trail paths through the Bear Lake Valley, where emigrants once crossed rivers and camped in sagebrush flats. Today, travelers find turquoise Bear Lake, rolling ranchlands, and sites tied to Mormon pioneer settlements. The byway highlights both dramatic scenery and the endurance of westward migration.

IDAHO

☐ ▢ ♡ **Panhandle Historic Rivers Passage Scenic Byway:** Following the Kootenai and Moyie Rivers near the Canadian border, this route showcases forested valleys, rushing waters, and historic bridges. Towns like Bonners Ferry offer cultural stops, while overlooks reveal panoramic views of river canyons and surrounding mountains. It's a scenic blend of frontier history and natural grandeur.

☐ ▢ ♡ **Peaks to Craters Scenic Byway:** Crossing south-central Idaho, this byway connects the towering Lost River Range—including Mount Borah—with the volcanic flows of Craters of the Moon. The drive spans high peaks, wide valleys, and ancient lava fields. Visitors experience stark contrasts of alpine beauty and surreal volcanic terrain, making it one of Idaho's most dramatic routes.

☐ ▢ ♡ **Ponderosa Pine Scenic Byway (SH 21):** Running from Boise to Stanley, this mountain route climbs through pine forests, river canyons, and gold-rush towns like Idaho City. Scenic pullouts showcase sweeping vistas of the Boise Mountains, while recreation abounds with hiking, camping, and fishing. Named for its towering pines, the byway highlights Idaho's wild heart.

☐ ▢ ♡ **Sacajawea Historic Byway:** Following SH-28 in eastern Idaho, this route honors Sacajawea and the Lewis & Clark Expedition. It passes through valleys, sagebrush plains, and landmarks tied to the Shoshone people and early explorers. Interpretive sites tell stories of cultural resilience, while sweeping landscapes and abundant wildlife provide a striking backdrop to history.

☐ ▢ ♡ **Salmon River Scenic Byway:** This drive parallels the "River of No Return" from Stanley to North Fork, showcasing deep canyons, rugged mountains, and historic sites. Hot springs, wildlife, and river access invite recreation, while the Salmon River's dramatic rapids roar alongside. The route blends adventure, scenery, and a sense of Idaho's remote wilderness.

☐ ▢ ♡ **Sawtooth Scenic Byway:** Beginning in Shoshone and stretching north past Sun Valley into Stanley, this byway highlights jagged peaks, alpine lakes, and wide ranching valleys. Seasonal wildflowers paint meadows, while winter brings snow-covered grandeur. Scenic turnouts and trailheads provide access to recreation, making it one of Idaho's most iconic mountain corridors.

☐ ▢ ♡ **Snake River Canyon Scenic Byway:** Traversing southwestern Idaho's wine country and farmlands, this route offers sweeping views of the Snake River Canyon and Owyhee Mountains. Orchards, vineyards, and historic towns line the way, blending agriculture with natural beauty. The byway highlights fertile valleys, rugged cliffs, and opportunities for tasting local wines and produce.

☐ ▢ ♡ **St. Joe River Scenic Byway:** This northern Idaho route follows the wild St. Joe River through dense forests, mountain valleys, and remote backcountry. Anglers and rafters flock to its pristine waters, while hikers and campers explore surrounding wilderness. Scenic overlooks reveal sweeping views, making it a premier destination for solitude and outdoor adventure.

☐ ▢ ♡ **Teton Scenic Byway:** On Idaho's eastern edge, this drive offers unmatched views of the western slope of the Teton Range. The byway passes farmland, historic towns, and wildlife-rich meadows framed by jagged peaks. Seasonal wildflowers, autumn colors, and crisp mountain air make it a year-round showcase of natural beauty and rural heritage.

☐ ▢ ♡ **Thousand Springs Scenic Byway:** Following the Snake River in south-central Idaho, this byway features dramatic waterfalls and crystal springs spilling from canyon walls. The route passes through the Hagerman Valley, known for its fossil beds, wildlife refuges, and rich farmland. Scenic pullouts and parks highlight one of Idaho's most unique and beautiful landscapes.

☐ ▢ ♡ **White Pine Scenic Byway:** Stretching from Potlatch through the St. Joe National Forest, this route takes its name from towering white pines that once dominated the region. Visitors encounter small towns, forested ridges, and river valleys rich in logging history. Scenic and quiet, the drive offers both cultural heritage and natural beauty.

☐ ▢ ♡ **Wild Horse Trail Scenic Byway:** Near the Canadian border, this byway follows US-95 through the rugged Selkirk Mountains. Named for wild herds that once roamed the valleys, it offers panoramic views of Kootenai Valley and Lake Pend Oreille. Wildlife sightings are common, and the route provides a peaceful, scenic link to northern Idaho's wild landscapes.

☐ ▢ ♡ **Wildlife Canyon Scenic Byway:** Following the Payette River south of Banks, this byway winds through a narrow canyon renowned for whitewater rafting and abundant wildlife. Deer, elk, and raptors are often seen along the route. Towering cliffs and rushing rapids provide dramatic scenery, while pullouts and trails invite exploration of this rugged corridor.

National Natural Landmarks

 **Big Southern Butte:** Rising 2,500 feet above the Snake River Plain, Big Southern Butte is an NNL for being one of the world's largest rhyolitic domes. Its immense size and lava composition provide insight into Quaternary volcanism and dome formation in the western U.S., making it a premier site for understanding volcanic processes and Idaho's geologic history.
GPS: 43.4014, -113.0239

 **Big Springs:** Big Springs is a National Natural Landmark for being the only first-magnitude spring in the U.S. that emerges from rhyolitic lava. Its crystal-clear, cold waters flow into Henrys Fork River, supporting robust trout populations. The spring is both hydrologically significant and scenically stunning, highlighting the link between volcanic geology and groundwater systems.
GPS: 44.5003, -111.2553

 **Cassia Silent City of Rocks:** Granite monoliths and spires define the Cassia Silent City of Rocks, a National Natural Landmark for its textbook display of granitic weathering. Towering plutons shaped by exfoliation create a dramatic landscape studied by geologists and cherished by climbers. The site offers one of Idaho's best examples of exposed granite formations and natural sculpting.
GPS: 42.0760, -113.7017

 **Crater Rings:** Near Mountain Home, the Crater Rings are a National Natural Landmark for being rare pit craters in the continental U.S. These nearly symmetrical depressions formed through volcanic explosions or collapse, preserving a striking geologic feature of the Snake River Plain. Their rarity and clarity make them exceptional for studying volcanic landforms.
GPS: 43.1907, -115.8597

 Great Rift of Idaho: Stretching more than 50 miles, the Great Rift is a National Natural Landmark for showcasing rift volcanism. Its fissures, cracks, and lava flows reveal Earth's crust under tension and illustrate how massive eruptions shaped Idaho's landscape. The site provides a dramatic natural laboratory for studying tectonic and volcanic processes.
GPS: 43.4617, -113.5628

 **Hagerman Fauna Sites:** These fossil beds are a National Natural Landmark for preserving one of the world's richest Upper Pliocene terrestrial deposits. Known especially for the Hagerman horse, the site also contains mastodons and other extinct animals. It offers an unparalleled view into ancient ecosystems, making it a cornerstone of North American paleontology.
GPS: 42.7906, -114.9448

 **Hell's Half Acre Lava Field:** Hell's Half Acre is an NNL for its extensive pahoehoe basalt flows, formed by eruptions only a few thousand years ago. Covering more than 150 square miles, the lava field demonstrates ropy textures and surface features characteristic of basaltic volcanism. Easily accessed from Interstate 15, it provides an outstanding example of recent volcanic activity.
GPS: 43.5000, -112.4500

 **Hobo Cedar Grove Botanical Area:** In Idaho's Panhandle, this grove is a National Natural Landmark for preserving a pristine western red cedar forest. Some trees exceed 500 years in age, creating a living museum of old-growth ecology. The cool, moist forest contrasts sharply with surrounding landscapes, offering a rare glimpse into ancient Northern Rocky ecosystems.
GPS: 47.0911, -116.1270

 **Menan Buttes:** The Menan Buttes, near Rexburg, are National Natural Landmarks for being rare examples of volcanic cones formed in freshwater. Created by explosive hydrovolcanic eruptions, their glass tuff deposits illustrate phreatomagmatic processes. The buttes are scientifically significant as some of the only known rhyolitic tuff cones in the U.S., and they remain striking natural features.
GPS: 43.6000, -111.5000

 **Niagara Springs:** Emerging dramatically from Snake River Canyon's walls, Niagara Springs is a National Natural Landmark for illustrating aquifer-fed spring systems. Its cold waters gush into the Snake River, sustaining unique ecosystems. Less developed than other large springs, the site highlights the geologic and hydrologic forces that shape Idaho's landscape.
GPS: 42.8578, -114.8764

IDAHO

 ▫ 🔖 ♡ **Sheep Rock:** Sheep Rock in Hells Canyon is a National Natural Landmark for its layered Columbia River basalt flows. The stacked lava sequences provide a clear geologic record of massive eruptions that once inundated the region. Its dramatic cliffs showcase volcanic processes while offering sweeping scenery in one of Idaho's most rugged landscapes. *GPS: 45.1917, -116.6713*

ILLINOIS

Illinois reveals natural beauty in its sandstone canyons, rolling prairies, quiet forests, and river bluffs. With an array of state parks, national forests, a treasured national historic site, and unique natural landmarks, the state offers outdoor escapes for all seasons, from hiking and wildlife watching to riverside trails and scenic drives.

📅 Peak Season
May–October is Illinois's peak season, with warm weather, long days, and comfortable conditions for exploring cities, parks, and farmland. Summer is busiest in Chicago and at lakes, while fall draws visitors for colorful foliage.

📅 Offseason Months
November–April is the offseason, with cold winters and snow in the north. Tourism slows outside of holiday periods, though spring flowers and early festivals begin drawing visitors before the peak season.

🍃 Scenery & Nature Timing
Spring highlights blooming prairies and flowering trees. Summer is prime for lakefront activities and river recreation. Fall transforms forests with vivid colors, especially in the Shawnee Hills. Winter brings snow to northern regions and quiet landscapes statewide.

✨ Special
Illinois features the sandstone canyons and waterfalls of Starved Rock State Park, the rolling Shawnee National Forest, and the Illinois River Valley. Lake Michigan's shoreline shapes Chicago, while prairies, wetlands, and bluffs add to the state's natural diversity.

ILLINOIS

State Parks

☐ 🔖 ♡ **Adeline Jay Geo-Karis Illinois Beach State Park:** Located along Lake Michigan in Zion, this 4,160-acre park features beaches, dunes, marshes, and forests. Visitors can enjoy swimming, hiking, camping, and birdwatching. The park preserves one of the last remaining lakefront ecosystems in Illinois, making it a popular destination for nature lovers and outdoor recreation.

☐ 🔖 ♡ **Apple River Canyon State Park:** Tucked in the northwest corner of Illinois, this scenic park features rugged limestone bluffs, deep ravines, and the winding Apple River. Visitors enjoy hiking, fishing, and observing wildlife in a peaceful natural setting. The park is also known for its unique geology and serves as a quiet retreat for outdoor enthusiasts and photographers.

☐ 🔖 ♡ **Argyle Lake State Park:** Near Colchester, this 1,700-acre park surrounds a 93-acre lake ideal for fishing, boating, and swimming. Visitors can explore wooded trails, enjoy camping, and relax in scenic picnic areas. Wildlife is abundant, and the park is especially popular in fall for its brilliant foliage and peaceful, forested hills that make for a tranquil getaway.

☐ 🔖 ♡ **Beall Woods State Park:** Located along the Wabash River, this park protects a rare old-growth forest with towering oaks, hickories, and maples. Trails wind through the woods, offering a glimpse of Illinois' pre-settlement ecology. The visitor center features educational exhibits, and the park is a haven for birdwatchers, hikers, and those seeking natural solitude.

☐ 🔖 ♡ **Beaver Dam State Park:** Situated in Macoupin County near Carlinville, this 750-acre park centers around a scenic 59-acre lake known for fishing and boating. Visitors enjoy shaded hiking trails, wooded picnic areas, and peaceful camping spots. Wildlife abounds in the forested surroundings, making it a quiet and relaxing destination for families and nature lovers.

☐ 🔖 ♡ **Buffalo Rock State Park:** Overlooking the Illinois River near Ottawa, this 298-acre park offers bluff-top trails, prairie landscapes, and panoramic views. It features a small bison herd, large-scale earth sculptures, and peaceful picnic areas. The park's rich natural and cultural history makes it a favorite for hikers, wildlife watchers, and fans of Illinois river scenery.

☐ 🔖 ♡ **Castle Rock State Park:** Located along the Rock River in Ogle County, this park features dramatic sandstone formations, forested trails, and scenic river overlooks. Hikers can explore bluffs and wooded ridges, while anglers enjoy shoreline fishing. The park's geological features and tranquil setting attract outdoor adventurers and nature photographers year-round.

☐ 🔖 ♡ **Cave-In-Rock State Park:** Set along the Ohio River in Hardin County, this park is named for its massive limestone cave, once a legendary hideout for river pirates. Visitors can explore the cave, hike forested trails, and enjoy scenic river views. The park also offers cabins, picnic areas, and a lodge, making it a historic and picturesque spot for exploration.

☐ 🔖 ♡ **Chain O'Lakes State Park:** Located in northeastern Illinois, this 6,000-acre park is surrounded by the Fox River and ten interconnecting lakes. It's a top destination for boating, fishing, hiking, and camping. The park also offers equestrian trails, wetlands for birdwatching, and winter sports, providing year-round recreation just a short drive from Chicago suburbs.

☐ 🔖 ♡ **Channahon State Park:** Situated at the confluence of the DuPage, Des Plaines, and Kankakee Rivers, this small park preserves a portion of the historic I&M Canal. Visitors enjoy hiking, fishing, and canoeing while exploring canal-era towpaths and restored locks. The peaceful setting offers a blend of natural beauty and early transportation history.

☐ 🔖 ♡ **Delabar State Park:** Nestled along the Mississippi River in Henderson County, this peaceful park features hardwood forests and scenic river views. Visitors enjoy fishing, hiking, and birdwatching in a tranquil setting. With shaded picnic areas and opportunities for spotting eagles and songbirds, it's an ideal spot for a relaxing nature retreat near the river.

☐ 🔖 ♡ **Dickson Mounds State Park:** Located near Lewistown, this park combines archaeology and nature with preserved Native American burial sites and an on-site museum. Trails lead through prairies and woodlands, offering views of the Illinois River Valley. It's a unique blend of cultural history and natural beauty, perfect for quiet hikes, learning, and reflection.

ILLINOIS

☐ 🔖 ♡ **Dixon Springs State Park:** Found in the Shawnee Hills region, this park is known for its scenic bluffs, bubbling springs, and deep ravines. Visitors enjoy hiking wooded trails, fishing in a small creek, and relaxing in shaded picnic areas. A seasonal swimming pool and unique rock formations make it a family-friendly destination for Southern Illinois explorers.

☐ 🔖 ♡ **Ferne Clyffe State Park:** Located near Goreville, this park features stunning rock formations, seasonal waterfalls, and lush forests. Its scenic trails wind through canyons, cliffs, and wildflower-covered slopes. A favorite among photographers and hikers, it also offers camping and horseback riding, providing a secluded and dramatic natural landscape.

☐ 🔖 ♡ **Fort Massac State Park:** Situated on the Ohio River in Metropolis, this historic park preserves the site of an 18th-century fort. A full-scale replica, interpretive programs, and reenactments showcase its military past. Trails, picnic areas, and river views make it a great spot for both history buffs and outdoor enthusiasts looking for a scenic place to explore.

☐ 🔖 ♡ **Fox Ridge State Park:** Located in Coles County near Charleston, this wooded park is known for steep ridges, deep ravines, and quiet hiking trails. The park overlooks the Embarras River and features scenic picnic areas, rustic shelters, and abundant wildlife. Its peaceful setting and varied terrain make it perfect for relaxing day hikes and birdwatching.

☐ 🔖 ♡ **Franklin Creek State Park:** Found in Lee County near Franklin Grove, this 1,000-acre park features a crystal-clear creek, restored prairie, and a functioning grist mill. Trails meander through woods and grasslands, offering fishing, hiking, and educational opportunities. It's a serene place to experience Illinois' natural and cultural heritage.

☐ 🔖 ♡ **Gebhard Woods State Park:** Located in Morris, this small yet charming park lies along the I&M Canal and features shady trails, picnic areas, and fishing access. It's ideal for peaceful walks and connecting with nature, especially for visitors traveling the adjacent I&M Canal State Trail. The park is known for its tranquility and historic canal-side scenery.

☐ 🔖 ♡ **Giant City State Park:** Situated in the Shawnee National Forest near Makanda, this 4,000-acre park is famous for its massive sandstone bluffs and "Giant City Streets" rock formations. It offers excellent hiking, horseback riding, rock climbing, and wildlife viewing. With a historic lodge, cabins, and campsites, it's a top destination for Southern Illinois adventures.

☐ 🔖 ♡ **Goose Lake Prairie State Park:** Located in Grundy County, this park protects one of the largest remnants of prairie in Illinois. Visitors can hike through tallgrass ecosystems, view native wildlife, and explore historic farm equipment displays. Birdwatchers flock here to observe rare grassland species, making it a peaceful place to experience Illinois' natural roots.

☐ 🔖 ♡ **Hazlet State Park:** Located on the western shore of Carlyle Lake in Clinton County, this park offers 3,000 acres of outdoor recreation. Boating, fishing, hiking, and camping are popular, with scenic lake views and abundant wildlife. Trails wind through forests and wetlands, and the park is a favorite among birdwatchers and families seeking lakeside relaxation.

☐ 🔖 ♡ **Hennepin Canal Parkway State Park:** This linear park stretches over 100 miles through north-central Illinois, following a historic canal. It offers multi-use trails for hiking, biking, horseback riding, and snowmobiling. The canal itself provides fishing and paddling opportunities. Visitors enjoy the peaceful rural scenery and remnants of 19th-century engineering.

☐ 🔖 ♡ **Illini State Park:** Nestled along the Illinois River in Marseilles, this park features shaded picnic areas, wooded trails, and river access. Boating, fishing, and birdwatching are popular, and the park's mature trees offer a tranquil setting. It's an inviting spot for family outings or quiet walks along the river's edge with views of passing barges and wildlife.

☐ 🔖 ♡ **James "Pate" Philip State Park:** Located in northeastern Illinois near Bartlett, this restored natural area features prairie, wetlands, and savanna habitats. It offers trails for hiking and wildlife viewing, plus a visitor center with exhibits on ecological restoration. This peaceful suburban retreat supports native species and showcases Illinois' natural diversity.

☐ 🔖 ♡ **Johnson-Sauk Trail State Park:** Near Kewanee, this park features a 58-acre lake surrounded by wooded hills and meadows. Boating, fishing, camping, and hiking are popular activities. A restored round barn adds historic interest, and the varied habitats make it a great place to observe birds and wildlife. The setting is scenic and perfect for weekend getaways.

☐ 🔖 ♡ **Jubilee College State Park:** Located west of Peoria, this 3,200-acre park surrounds the historic site of Jubilee College, a 19th-century frontier school. Visitors enjoy hiking through oak-hickory forests, camping, horseback riding, and exploring ravines. Interpretive signs highlight the area's pioneer history alongside its peaceful natural beauty.

ILLINOIS

☐ 🔖 ♡ **Kankakee River State Park:** Spanning 4,000 acres along both sides of the Kankakee River, this park offers excellent canoeing, fishing, and hiking. Visitors enjoy wooded trails, scenic bluffs, and abundant wildlife. The park also features equestrian and biking paths, campgrounds, and picnic areas, making it a favorite year-round spot for outdoor recreation.

☐ 🔖 ♡ **Lake Le-Aqua-Na State Park:** Situated in Stephenson County, this park features a 40-acre lake perfect for fishing, swimming, and boating. Surrounding trails wind through forests and restored prairie, providing great opportunities for hiking and wildlife observation. Campgrounds and picnic areas make it a cozy and scenic destination for outdoor families.

☐ 🔖 ♡ **Lake Murphysboro State Park:** Located in Jackson County, this 1,000-acre park is centered on a 145-acre lake surrounded by woodlands and bluffs. Anglers enjoy catching bass and catfish, while trails offer scenic walks through hilly terrain. With campsites, picnic areas, and peaceful views, it's a popular spot for both relaxation and outdoor exploration.

☐ 🔖 ♡ **Lincoln Trail State Park:** Located near Marshall in Clark County, this 1,023-acre park features a 146-acre lake ideal for fishing, boating, and paddling. Trails meander through rolling woodlands and past quiet coves. Campgrounds, scenic picnic spots, and abundant wildlife make it a relaxing destination for families and outdoor lovers in east-central Illinois.

☐ 🔖 ♡ **Lowden State Park:** Perched on the Rock River near Oregon, this park is known for its scenic bluffs and the 48-foot-tall Black Hawk Statue. Visitors enjoy hiking wooded trails with panoramic river views, fishing, and camping. The park's natural beauty and cultural significance make it a popular site for both quiet reflection and active exploration.

☐ 🔖 ♡ **Matthiessen State Park:** Situated near Starved Rock in LaSalle County, this park features dramatic canyons, waterfalls, and unique rock formations. Trails lead through dense woods and past streams, staircases, and bridges. It's a favorite for photographers, hikers, and nature enthusiasts seeking rugged beauty and geological wonder in north-central Illinois.

☐ 🔖 ♡ **Mississippi Palisades State Park:** Located in Carroll County, this park boasts towering limestone bluffs with spectacular views of the Mississippi River. Its 15 miles of trails wind through wooded ravines and scenic overlooks. Popular for hiking, rock climbing, and birdwatching, it's a dramatic and peaceful destination for nature lovers and photographers.

☐ 🔖 ♡ **Moraine Hills State Park:** Found in McHenry County, this 2,200-acre park preserves glacial lakes, wetlands, and wooded hills. It features over 10 miles of paved and crushed-gravel trails for hiking and biking. The park offers great fishing, birdwatching, and scenic beauty just an hour northwest of Chicago, with tranquil views and rich wildlife habitats.

☐ 🔖 ♡ **Morrison-Rockwood State Park:** Near Morrison in Whiteside County, this 1,150-acre park is centered around Lake Carlton, a 77-acre reservoir popular for fishing and boating. Visitors enjoy hiking through prairies and forests, camping in peaceful surroundings, and spotting local wildlife. The park offers a quiet, natural setting ideal for family recreation.

☐ 🔖 ♡ **Nauvoo State Park:** Located in Hancock County near the historic town of Nauvoo, this park features a small lake, wooded picnic areas, and scenic trails. It's a peaceful setting near one of Illinois' most significant historical areas. Visitors can fish, hike, or explore nearby Mormon heritage sites while enjoying the park's calm and relaxing environment.

☐ 🔖 ♡ **Pere Marquette State Park:** Illinois' largest state park, located near Grafton, spans 8,000 acres along the Illinois River. It's famous for scenic bluff-top drives, bald eagle watching, and extensive trails through hardwood forests. The park offers a lodge, campgrounds, and interpretive programs, making it a top destination for outdoor exploration and river views.

☐ 🔖 ♡ **Rock Cut State Park:** Located in Winnebago County near Rockford, this 3,000-acre park includes two lakes—Pierce and Olson—ideal for boating, fishing, and kayaking. Miles of trails wind through forests and fields, offering hiking, biking, and winter sports. It's one of the state's most popular parks for recreation, camping, and year-round outdoor fun.

☐ 🔖 ♡ **Sangchris Lake State Park:** Spanning Christian and Sangamon Counties, this park features a 2,325-acre lake surrounded by oak-hickory forests and meadows. It's ideal for boating, fishing, and wildlife watching. Trails loop through quiet woods, and campgrounds accommodate both RVs and tents. Its tranquil setting and scenic shoreline make it a favorite for nature getaways.

☐ 🔖 ♡ **Starved Rock State Park:** One of Illinois' most iconic parks, Starved Rock in LaSalle County features 18 sandstone canyons, seasonal waterfalls, and sweeping views of the Illinois River. Hiking trails lead through forested bluffs and rock formations. A lodge, visitor center, and year-round activities make it a must-see destination for adventure and history lovers.

ILLINOIS

☐ 🔖 ♡ **Walnut Point State Park:** Tucked in Douglas County, this quiet park offers a small lake for fishing and non-motorized boating, as well as wooded trails and picnic areas. It's a serene setting with abundant wildlife and peaceful campsites. Ideal for families, birdwatchers, and anyone seeking a relaxing retreat in a lesser-known part of east-central Illinois.

☐ 🔖 ♡ **White Pines Forest State Park:** Located in Ogle County, this park preserves one of Illinois' few native white pine groves. Picturesque creeks, stone bridges, and shaded trails make it a charming escape. Visitors enjoy hiking, picnicking, and staying in historic log cabins. Its peaceful forest scenery and rustic character draw visitors year-round.

☐ 🔖 ♡ **William G. Stratton State Park:** Situated along the Illinois River in Grundy County, this park serves as a major boating access point with a large marina, ramps, and picnic areas. While smaller in natural space than other parks, it's a favorite among anglers and boaters. Its proximity to the water makes it a convenient launch site and riverside recreation area.

☐ 🔖 ♡ **Wolf Creek State Park:** Found on the east side of Lake Shelbyville in Shelby County, this park offers excellent boating, swimming, hiking, and fishing. Its spacious campgrounds, wooded trails, and scenic lake views make it ideal for weekend getaways. Popular among both water sports enthusiasts and nature lovers, it's one of central Illinois' top destinations.

National Parks

☐ 🔖 ♡ **Lincoln Home National Historic Site:** Located in Springfield, Illinois, this site preserves the only home Abraham Lincoln ever owned. Visitors can tour the restored house and surrounding neighborhood, exploring Lincoln's family life, early political career, and the pivotal years leading up to his presidency. The site offers a glimpse into the personal world of one of America's greatest leaders.

☐ 🔖 ♡ **Pullman National Historical Park:** Situated in Chicago, Illinois, this monument honors the Pullman Company and the model industrial town created for its workers. Visitors can explore historic buildings, learn about the role of George Pullman in railroad car innovation, and discover the labor struggles that shaped the American labor movement and workers' rights.

State & National Forests

☐ 🔖 ♡ **Big River State Forest:** Situated in Henderson County along the Mississippi River bluffs, Big River State Forest preserves oak-hickory woodlands and floodplain habitats. Managed for sustainable timber, wildlife, and recreation, it offers scenic trails, hunting, and birdwatching amid a tranquil forest setting in western Illinois.

☐ 🔖 ♡ **Hidden Springs State Forest:** Located in Shelby County, Hidden Springs protects upland hardwood forests and springs. Though relatively small and undeveloped, it supports wildlife habitat, watershed health, and low-impact recreation like hiking and birding. Its rolling terrain and spring-fed streams form a quiet natural oasis.

☐ 🔖 ♡ **Lowden-Miller State Forest:** Found in Ogle County near Oregon, the forest features hardwood and pine woodlands across rolling glacial terrain. Managed by the Illinois Department of Natural Resources, it supports timber research, wildlife habitat, and passive recreation through trails and nature study opportunities.

☐ 🔖 ♡ **Sand Ridge State Forest:** Illinois's largest state forest (≈7,200 acres) in Mason County, it protects rare sand prairie and oak-hickory woods on ancient dunes beside the Illinois River. With 44 miles of hiking trails, campgrounds, equestrian areas, and fire-lane access, it's a hotspot for birding, hunting, and conservation research.

☐ 🔖 ♡ **Shawnee National Forest:** The only U.S. National Forest in Illinois, Shawnee spans ~498,600 acres in southern Illinois along the Ohio River. Features include rock bluffs, canyons, wetlands, and trails like Garden of the Gods. Popular for hiking, camping, horseback riding, and wildlife viewing, it's a biodiversity-rich, scenic forest.

☐ 🔖 ♡ **Trail of Tears State Forest:** Located in Union County near southeast Illinois, this forest commemorates the Cherokee removal route. It protects bottomland hardwood forests and offers trails, hunting, and watershed protection. Its forests support wildlife and stand as a historic, conservation-minded site.

ILLINOIS

National Scenic Byways & All-American Roads

☐ 🔖 ♡ **Great River Road:** An All-American Road and National Scenic Byway tracing the Mississippi River across Illinois for over 550 miles. It passes limestone bluffs, historic river towns, scenic overlooks, wildlife refuges, and heritage sites. Highlights include Galena's quaint downtown, the Quad Cities, Heartland farmland, and the journey toward southern river swamplands.

☐ 🔖 ♡ **Historic Route 66 (Illinois Route 66 Scenic Byway):** This National Scenic Byway covers all 436 miles of Route 66 through Illinois from Chicago to the Mississippi River. It showcases classic diners, neon signs, retro motels, museums, and small towns like Joliet, Pontiac, and Springfield—celebrating Americana, roadside culture, and Illinois's role in the "Mother Road" legacy.

☐ 🔖 ♡ **Illinois River Road:** A National Scenic Byway following the Illinois River between Ottawa and Havana for about 291 miles. It meanders through forested bluffs, wetlands, and prairie views, linking state parks like Starved Rock and Buffalo Rock. The route offers hiking, fishing, canoeing, birding, and scenic drives along rivers carved by glacial melt.

☐ 🔖 ♡ **Lincoln Highway:** Illinois's segment of the nation's first transcontinental highway, this 179-mile National Scenic Byway runs from Lynwood to Fulton. It passes rolling farmland, early roadside attractions, historic towns, Lincoln's Springfield, and remnants of early automobile-era culture—preserving Midwest heritage and the dawn of cross-country travel.

☐ 🔖 ♡ **Meeting of the Great Rivers Scenic Route:** A 33-mile National Scenic Byway near Alton tracing the confluence of the Mississippi, Illinois, and Missouri Rivers. Framed by towering limestone bluffs, it links Pere Marquette State Park to Lewis & Clark Historic Site. Features include riverfront parks, birdwatching, historic towns, and scenic overlooks of Midwest waterways.

☐ 🔖 ♡ **Ohio River Scenic Byway:** This 188-mile National Scenic Byway follows the Ohio River's Illinois corridor through Shawnee National Forest. It travels woodland bluffs, riverfront towns, and rural landscapes. The route offers a blend of cultural heritage—Native American, early settler, and Civil War—paired with hiking, camping, and waterway access.

National Natural Landmarks

☐ 🔖 ♡ **Allerton Natural Area:** Recognized as a National Natural Landmark for preserving Illinois stream valley ecosystems, Allerton Natural Area contains both bottomland and upland forests that remain minimally disturbed. The diverse flora and fauna, supported by fertile soils and riparian habitats, provide a living example of pre-settlement conditions in central Illinois.
GPS: 39.9981, -88.6500

☐ 🔖 ♡ **Bell Smith Springs:** Bell Smith Springs was designated a National Natural Landmark for its sandstone cliffs, sculpted passageways, and pristine streams within Shawnee National Forest. The area's dramatic geology and rich biodiversity showcase natural processes of erosion and forest growth, making it one of southern Illinois' finest natural areas for conservation and study.
GPS: 37.5186, -88.6561

☐ 🔖 ♡ **Busse Forest Nature Preserve:** This site is a National Natural Landmark for representing one of the best remaining oak and hickory woodlands in Illinois' Central Lowlands. Its mesic and dry-mesic upland forests offer critical habitat for native species while providing an invaluable natural refuge and research site within the heavily developed Chicago metropolitan region.
GPS: 42.0422, -88.0033

☐ 🔖 ♡ **Forest of the Wabash:** Designated a National Natural Landmark for its rare tract of virgin oak-hickory forest, Forest of the Wabash lies within Beall Woods State Park. These undisturbed upland and bottomland woods support diverse songbirds, mammals, and understory plants, making the site an irreplaceable remnant of Illinois' original forest ecosystems.
GPS: 38.3586, -87.8250

ILLINOIS

Fults Hill Prairie Nature Preserve: This preserve is a National Natural Landmark for its pristine loess hill prairie perched on Mississippi River bluffs. Native grasses, wildflowers, and rare prairie wildlife flourish here, representing one of the finest and least disturbed examples of this fragile ecosystem type in Illinois and highlighting the importance of prairie conservation.
GPS: 37.9775, -89.8006

Funks Grove Nature Preserve: Funks Grove is recognized as a National Natural Landmark for its remnant of virgin forest near the western edge of the Eastern Mesophytic Forest region. Towering hardwoods, vibrant spring wildflowers, and rare species thrive in this transitional community, where oak-hickory and maple-beech ecosystems overlap in an intact woodland setting.
GPS: 40.3636, -89.1144

Giant City Geological Area: Named a National Natural Landmark for its dramatic sandstone formations, Giant City Geological Area in Shawnee National Forest features towering cliffs, narrow passageways, and massive block structures formed by gravity sliding. The surrounding forests include maple, oak-hickory, and upland species, offering a landscape rich in geologic and ecological diversity.
GPS: 37.6050, -89.1883

Heron Pond – Little Black Slough: This southern Illinois wetland is a National Natural Landmark for preserving the state's largest remnant of cypress-tupelo swamp. The site supports a thriving heron rookery, rare aquatic species, and layered wetland soils shaped by alluvial and lacustrine processes, making it one of the most significant wetland ecosystems in Illinois.
GPS: 37.3669, -88.9500

Horseshoe Lake: Horseshoe Lake earned National Natural Landmark designation for its large oxbow lake, bald cypress stands, and surrounding bottomland hardwood forests. As a floodplain ecosystem, it provides vital habitat for migratory waterfowl and overwintering geese while illustrating the natural river dynamics that once shaped much of the Mississippi Valley landscape.
GPS: 37.1489, -89.3550

Illinois Beach Nature Preserve: Illinois Beach was designated a National Natural Landmark for its rare mix of sand dunes, prairies, marshes, and forests along Lake Michigan. Supporting endangered species and one of the most diverse plant communities in the state, the preserve represents one of the richest and most ecologically significant stretches of shoreline in Illinois.
GPS: 42.4172, -87.8117

LaRue–Pine Hills Ecological Area: Designated a National Natural Landmark for its extraordinary diversity, LaRue–Pine Hills hosts over 40 rare plant species within Shawnee National Forest. Its steep limestone bluffs, swampy bottomlands, and upland forests create distinct habitats where northern and southern species overlap, making it one of Illinois' richest ecological sites.
GPS: 37.5833, -89.4167

Little Grand Canyon: Little Grand Canyon is recognized as a National Natural Landmark for its dramatic sandstone cliffs, waterfalls, and deep canyon carved by erosion. This Shawnee National Forest site contains oak-hickory forests, prairie remnants, and sheltered niches that provide habitat for reptiles, including hibernating snakes, in a rugged and biologically diverse landscape.
GPS: 37.6864, -89.3983

Lower Cache River Swamp: This swamp was designated a National Natural Landmark for preserving ancient bald cypress trees, some of the largest in Illinois. As a remnant of an extensive wetland system, it shelters amphibians, migratory birds, and record-sized trees, offering a rare and irreplaceable glimpse into the state's prehistoric wetland ecosystems.
GPS: 37.0669, -89.1728

Lusk Creek Canyon: Recognized as a National Natural Landmark for its scenic Pennsylvanian sandstone gorge, Lusk Creek Canyon features rugged cliffs, rich forests, and habitats for endangered plants. The area contains both upland and bottomland ecosystems, offering solitude and a living record of the natural diversity found in southern Illinois' Shawnee National Forest.
GPS: 37.5189, -88.5400

ILLINOIS

Markham Prairie: Markham Prairie is a National Natural Landmark for protecting one of Illinois' largest and highest quality prairie remnants. This site preserves tallgrass, sand prairie, beach ridges, and a natural lakebed, reflecting ecosystems that once dominated the state. Its plant diversity and rarity make it invaluable for conservation and ecological study.
GPS: 41.6069, -87.6878

Mississippi Palisades: Designated a National Natural Landmark for its imposing limestone bluffs and caves, Mississippi Palisades State Park showcases geologic history shaped by erosion along the Mississippi River. The site's diverse ravines and forests provide habitat for rare birds and wildflowers, while offering sweeping river views and outstanding natural beauty.
GPS: 42.1383, -90.1589

Volo Bog Nature Preserve: This site is a National Natural Landmark for being a textbook example of a quaking bog. Volo Bog features a sphagnum moss mat floating over a deep peat-filled basin, supporting tamarack, pitcher plants, and orchids. As the only open-water bog in Illinois, it illustrates post-glacial wetland succession and hosts unique wildlife communities.
GPS: 42.3517, -88.1861

Wauconda Bog Nature Preserve: Wauconda Bog was designated a National Natural Landmark for its relict glacial bog community, the southernmost of its kind in the state. Sphagnum moss, tamarack, and acid-loving shrubs thrive in its peat soils, making it an invaluable site for studying post-glacial ecology and protecting rare plant and animal species in Illinois.
GPS: 42.2539, -88.1303

INDIANA

Indiana's landscapes invite discovery, from the sandy dunes of Lake Michigan to wooded trails and limestone caves. Through a network of state parks, a national forest, a treasured national park, and distinctive natural landmarks, Indiana provides outdoor adventures close to home.

📅 Peak Season
May–October is Indiana's peak season, with warm weather, blooming landscapes, and fall foliage drawing visitors. Summer is busiest at lakes and parks, while autumn highlights colorful forests and comfortable hiking conditions.

📅 Offseason Months
November–April is the offseason, with cold winters, occasional snow, and lighter tourist traffic. Winter is quieter outdoors, though some areas see activity for skiing and seasonal festivals.

🍃 Scenery & Nature Timing
Spring brings wildflowers and greening farmland. Summer is prime for boating, hiking, and camping. Fall transforms forests in Brown County and the Hoosier National Forest with vibrant color, while winter offers snowy woods and frozen lakes.

✨ Special
Indiana features the Indiana Dunes along Lake Michigan, the sandstone gorges of Turkey Run State Park, and rolling hills of Brown County. The Wabash and Ohio Rivers carve scenic valleys, while karst caves and hardwood forests add to its natural character.

INDIANA

State Parks

☐ 🔖 ♡ **Brown County State Park:** Indiana's largest state park, spanning over 15,000 acres of forested hills, ridges, and valleys. Known as the "Little Smokies," it draws visitors for brilliant fall foliage, scenic drives, mountain biking, and horseback riding. With two lakes, campgrounds, and the historic Abe Martin Lodge, it's a premier outdoor destination.

☐ 🔖 ♡ **Chain O'Lakes State Park:** Centered around nine interconnected kettle lakes, this park in northeast Indiana is a paradise for paddlers and anglers. Visitors can canoe from lake to lake, fish, swim, or hike the many wooded trails. Its campgrounds and nature-rich setting make it a top choice for birdwatching and peaceful getaways on the water.

☐ 🔖 ♡ **Charlestown State Park:** Set on former ammunition plant lands along the Ohio River, this park features rugged hills, deep ravines, and riverside overlooks. It's popular for hiking, birdwatching, and exploring historic remnants. Visitors can access the Knobstone Trail and enjoy spacious campgrounds while experiencing southern Indiana's wild beauty.

☐ 🔖 ♡ **Clifty Falls State Park:** Famous for its dramatic waterfalls plunging through rocky gorges, this park in Madison showcases nature's power in every season. Trails wind past deep canyons, fossil-rich rocks, and scenic overlooks of the Ohio River. With camping, picnicking, and a nature center, it's a photographer's and hiker's haven.

☐ 🔖 ♡ **Falls of the Ohio State Park:** Located along the Ohio River in Clarksville, this site preserves world-renowned Devonian fossil beds, offering a rare look into 390-million-year-old life. Visitors explore interpretive exhibits, riverside trails, and panoramic views of Louisville. The park blends natural history with cultural heritage in a unique setting.

☐ 🔖 ♡ **Fort Harrison State Park:** A former military base near Indianapolis, this park now provides an oasis of woodlands, meadows, and waterways. Hiking trails, fishing ponds, and picnic areas make it a local favorite. Visitors also find a golf course, historic buildings, and an inn, blending recreation with military heritage.

☐ 🔖 ♡ **Harmonie State Park:** Nestled near the historic town of New Harmony, this park features rolling hills, lush forests, and the Wabash River. Visitors enjoy hiking, fishing, swimming, and picnicking in a peaceful setting. With campgrounds, a nature center, and opportunities for birdwatching, it's a perfect blend of history and natural beauty.

☐ 🔖 ♡ **Indiana Dunes State Park:** Covering over 2,000 acres on Lake Michigan's southern shore, this park boasts towering sand dunes, wetlands, prairies, and woodlands. Popular for hiking, swimming, and birding, it offers some of the Midwest's best beaches. Campgrounds, trails, and a nature center make it a destination for year-round exploration.

☐ 🔖 ♡ **Lincoln State Park:** Across from the Lincoln Boyhood National Memorial in Lincoln City, this park blends history with recreation. Forested trails, rolling hills, and Lake Lincoln offer boating, swimming, and fishing. Visitors can hike, camp, picnic, or attend seasonal events in the park's amphitheater, connecting Abraham Lincoln's early life with Indiana's natural beauty.

☐ 🔖 ♡ **McCormick's Creek State Park:** Indiana's first state park, established in 1916, near Spencer. It showcases a dramatic limestone canyon, waterfalls, and rugged hiking trails through hardwood forests. Visitors can explore Wolf Cave, stay at the historic Canyon Inn, or camp under the stars. A nature center, picnic areas, and scenic overlooks make it a year-round favorite for families and adventurers.

☐ 🔖 ♡ **Mounds State Park:** Located in Anderson, this park preserves ten prehistoric earthworks built by the Adena and Hopewell cultures. Interpretive trails wind past ceremonial mounds and along the White River, blending archaeology with nature. Visitors enjoy hiking, birdwatching, and picnicking while learning about ancient Native heritage. A modern campground and nature center add to the experience.

☐ 🔖 ♡ **O'Bannon Woods State Park:** Near Corydon, this rugged park anchors Indiana's Ohio River hill country. It features hiking and horse trails, the Blue River for fishing and paddling, and a working pioneer farmstead. Once part of Wyandotte Woods, it provides access to Wyandotte Caves. With camping, picnicking, and a nature center, it combines cultural history with outdoor adventure.

☐ 🔖 ♡ **Ouabache State Park:** Situated near Bluffton, this park highlights prairie restoration and a small bison herd grazing in the grasslands. Kunkel Lake offers boating, swimming, and fishing, while wooded trails and bike paths invite exploration. Visitors can camp, picnic, or attend educational programs at the nature center, experiencing both Indiana's natural and cultural heritage.

INDIANA

☐ 🔖 ♡ **Pokagon State Park:** Located in Angola, Pokagon is famed for its refrigerated toboggan run, drawing visitors in winter, while summer brings boating, swimming, and fishing on Lake James and Snow Lake. The park offers hiking, horseback riding, camping, and the Potawatomi Inn. With a nature center and year-round recreation, it's one of Indiana's most popular state parks.

☐ 🔖 ♡ **Potato Creek State Park:** In North Liberty, this 3,800-acre park surrounds a 327-acre lake and showcases wetlands, woodlands, and prairies. Visitors enjoy fishing, boating, hiking, biking, and birdwatching. With modern campgrounds, family cabins, and a nature center, it's a versatile destination for outdoor activities in northern Indiana, appealing to both casual visitors and nature lovers.

☐ 🔖 ♡ **Prophetstown State Park:** Near West Lafayette, this park features restored tallgrass prairies, wetlands, and woodlands that recreate Indiana's early landscapes. Visitors can bike or hike trails, view bison herds, and learn about Native history at the Farm at Prophetstown. With modern camping facilities and access to Tippecanoe Battlefield nearby, it blends ecology, history, and recreation.

☐ 🔖 ♡ **Shades State Park:** Situated in Waveland, this park is known for its deep sandstone ravines, shaded gorges, and quiet natural beauty. Trails follow streams, cliffs, and hardwood forests, offering scenic overlooks and access to Sugar Creek. Popular for hiking, birdwatching, and photography, it also has a nature preserve, primitive camping, and picnic areas for peaceful escapes.

☐ 🔖 ♡ **Shakamak State Park:** Located near Jasonville, this former strip-mined land is now a 1,766-acre park with three man-made lakes. Fishing and boating are central activities, alongside hiking trails and camping areas. Shakamak's shaded woodlands and waters make it ideal for family outings, while the nature center, picnic areas, and group camps offer educational and recreational opportunities.

☐ 🔖 ♡ **Spring Mill State Park:** Nestled in Mitchell, this park blends history and nature with a restored pioneer village, historic gristmill, and memorial to astronaut Gus Grissom. Caves and rugged karst landscapes add adventure, while trails, camping, and a nature center offer outdoor exploration. It's a place where Indiana's pioneer past meets geology and space-age heritage.

☐ 🔖 ♡ **Summit Lake State Park:** Located in New Castle, this 2,680-acre park centers on an 800-acre lake popular for fishing, boating, and birdwatching. Surrounded by rolling woodlands and wetlands, it provides camping, trails, and picnic areas for a peaceful retreat. The lake attracts waterfowl and anglers alike, making Summit Lake a favorite for both recreation and wildlife viewing.

☐ 🔖 ♡ **Tippecanoe River State Park:** Stretching along the Tippecanoe River in Winamac, this 2,761-acre park offers canoeing, kayaking, fishing, and trails through old-growth white pine and oak forests. A fire tower provides sweeping views, while campgrounds and picnic areas support extended visits. The park blends natural beauty with opportunities to experience Indiana's scenic waterways.

☐ 🔖 ♡ **Turkey Run State Park:** Near Marshall, this iconic park is famed for sandstone gorges, cliffs, and Sugar Creek's winding course. Hiking trails with ladders, bridges, and ravines create rugged adventures, while horseback riding and canoeing add variety. With camping, an inn, and nature programs, Turkey Run remains one of Indiana's most beloved outdoor destinations.

☐ 🔖 ♡ **Versailles State Park:** Southeast Indiana's largest state park spans nearly 6,000 acres of forested hills, meadows, and a scenic 230-acre lake. Boating, swimming, and fishing are popular, along with hiking and biking trails. Camping facilities and equestrian trails add to its appeal, making Versailles a diverse destination for relaxation and recreation in a natural setting.

☐ 🔖 ♡ **White River State Park:** Located in downtown Indianapolis, this urban state park combines green space with cultural attractions. Visitors can stroll along the canal, explore gardens, or visit museums, the Indianapolis Zoo, and Victory Field. Amphitheater concerts, trails, and public art enhance the city experience, making it a hub of recreation, history, and entertainment.

☐ 🔖 ♡ **Whitewater Memorial State Park:** Created as a memorial to WWII veterans, this Liberty-based park offers 1,710 acres anchored by a 200-acre lake. Fishing, boating, and swimming draw visitors, while wooded trails, horseback riding, and picnicking provide variety. Its campgrounds and nature center make it a favorite family destination blending recreation and remembrance.

INDIANA

National Parks

George Rogers Clark National Historical Park: Situated in Vincennes, this park honors George Rogers Clark's 1779 capture of Fort Sackville, a key Revolutionary War victory that secured the western frontier. The grand memorial tells the story of Clark and his men's arduous winter march, offering exhibits, films, and ranger programs that highlight early frontier struggles and triumphs.

Indiana Dunes National Park: Stretching for 15 miles along Lake Michigan, this park protects sweeping sand dunes, oak savannas, wetlands, and prairies. Visitors can hike 50 miles of trails, birdwatch along migration flyways, or enjoy sandy beaches and swimming. With remarkable biodiversity near Chicago, the park blends outdoor recreation with rich ecological exploration.

Lincoln Boyhood National Memorial: In Lincoln City, this site preserves the farm where young Abraham Lincoln lived from age 7 to 21. The memorial building and visitor center showcase exhibits on his frontier childhood, while the Living Historical Farm recreates pioneer life. Trails, gardens, and a quiet setting highlight the environment that shaped America's 16th president.

State & National Forests

Clark State Forest: Established in 1903, Clark is Indiana's oldest state forest, located near Henryville. It spans over 24,000 acres of oak and hickory forests, with scenic ridges and ravines. It offers hiking, hunting, camping, horseback riding, and access to the Knobstone Trail, making it a cornerstone of Indiana's early forestry and recreation programs.

Ferdinand State Forest: Located in Dubois County, this 7,800-acre forest features rugged hills, hardwood stands, and quiet fishing lakes. It's ideal for hiking, camping, and wildlife viewing, with trails like the Twin Lakes Loop. Originally established for erosion control, it now serves multiple uses including timber management and recreation.

Frances Slocum State Forest: A small 516-acre forest near Peru, it preserves bottomland hardwoods and wetlands. Named for a woman captured and raised by Native Americans, the forest offers quiet, undeveloped nature with hiking, seasonal hunting, and wildlife viewing amid a peaceful historic setting.

Greene–Sullivan State Forest: Once a coal-mining area, this 9,000-acre forest near Dugger features over 100 lakes, reclaimed land, and rolling forests. It's popular for camping, fishing, horseback riding, and trail hiking. The forest is a successful model of land restoration and recreational transformation in southern Indiana.

Harrison–Crawford State Forest: Spanning over 24,000 acres near Corydon, this forest features steep ridges, deep ravines, and the Blue River. It supports hunting, horseback riding, camping, and hiking. Part of the forest borders O'Bannon Woods State Park, creating a vast area for outdoor adventure and habitat preservation.

Hoosier National Forest: Indiana's only national forest, covering over 200,000 acres of rolling hills, karst formations, and dense hardwoods. Located in south-central Indiana, it includes the Charles C. Deam Wilderness, over 260 miles of trails, and campgrounds. Popular for backpacking, horseback riding, and historic site exploration.

Jackson–Washington State Forest: Located in the hills of Jackson and Washington counties, this 18,000-acre forest offers camping, fishing, horseback riding, hiking, and hunting. Its Knobstone Trail section is a highlight, and CCC-built structures provide historic charm alongside dense oak-hickory woods and limestone outcrops.

Martin State Forest: This 8,500-acre forest in Martin County offers a mix of hardwood ridges and pine plantings. Used for sustainable forestry, it also supports hunting, primitive camping, and trails for hiking and horseback riding. The forest is a low-traffic destination known for peaceful woodland settings and wildlife.

INDIANA

☐ 🔖 ♡ **Morgan–Monroe State Forest:** One of Indiana's largest state forests at 24,000+ acres, located between Bloomington and Martinsville. It offers scenic trails, including the popular Low Gap and Mason Ridge loops. With deep ravines, hardwood forests, and a historic fire tower, it blends recreation, research, and forest conservation.

☐ 🔖 ♡ **Mountain Tea State Forest:** A quiet 1,200-acre preserve near Nashville, this forest is named for a native plant once brewed for tea. It features rolling ridges, oak-hickory woods, and a secluded atmosphere. Though lightly developed, it supports hunting, hiking, and wildlife habitat in Indiana's upland forest region.

☐ 🔖 ♡ **Owen–Putnam State Forest:** Covering 6,600 acres across Owen and Putnam counties, this forest protects hardwood hills and ravines. It's known for scenic trails, primitive camping, and the Rattlesnake Camp area. Managed for multiple uses, including timber and watershed conservation, it's a great destination for low-impact forest exploration.

☐ 🔖 ♡ **Pike State Forest:** A 5,000-acre forest in southwestern Indiana with a mix of oak-hickory and pine plantations. Offers seasonal hunting, hiking, and off-road trails. Originally purchased for reforestation, it now provides habitat, recreation, and an educational glimpse into Indiana's forest management efforts.

☐ 🔖 ♡ **Ravinia State Forest:** Located in Morgan County, Ravinia spans 1,400+ acres of rolling woodland. It is managed for forest health, wildlife habitat, and watershed protection. While lacking developed facilities, it offers a natural setting for hunting, birdwatching, and passive recreation in central Indiana's rural heartland.

☐ 🔖 ♡ **Salamonie River State Forest:** Situated in Wabash County, this 950-acre forest includes the Salamonie River and wooded bluffs. It offers hiking trails, fishing access, and birdwatching. Combined with nearby recreation areas, it supports conservation, watershed protection, and outdoor education in northeast Indiana.

☐ 🔖 ♡ **Selmier State Forest:** Indiana's smallest state forest at just over 350 acres, located near North Vernon. Donated by Frank Selmier in 1927, it's managed for timber and wildlife. With trails through young hardwoods and former agricultural fields, it offers a peaceful walk through regenerating Indiana forestland.

National Scenic Byways & All-American Roads

☐ 🔖 ♡ **Historic National Road:** This All-American Road crosses Indiana along the original route of the National Road, the nation's first federally funded highway. It passes through early western-expansion towns like Terre Haute, Plainfield, and Richmond, featuring historic architecture, roadside heritage, and timeless American cross-country travel charm.

☐ 🔖 ♡ **Indiana's Historic Pathways Scenic Byway:** A National Scenic Byway stretching roughly 250 miles across southern Indiana, following Native American trails and buffalo traces later used by settlers. Traveling from the Ohio River to the Wabash Valley, the route passes through forests, farmland, historic small towns, and pioneer-era sites—blending natural corridors and deep history.

☐ 🔖 ♡ **Ohio River Scenic Byway:** A National Scenic Byway tracing Indiana's southern border along the Ohio River. It follows US 50 and parallel roads through river towns, forested bluffs, riverfront parks, historic architecture, and scenic bridges—a scenic corridor with waterway heritage and Appalachian foothill scenery.

☐ 🔖 ♡ **Whitewater Canal Scenic Byway:** A National Scenic Byway following the historic Whitewater Canal corridor from Lawrenceburg toward Columbus. It tracks the towpath and canal locks, passing historic mills, river valleys, waterfalls, and canal-era structures. The byway celebrates 19th-century industrial heritage set in scenic rural landscapes.

State Scenic Byways

☐ 🔖 ♡ **Dearborn–Ripley Loop Scenic Byway:** A State byway looping through rolling farmland and small towns in southeastern Indiana's Dearborn and Ripley counties. It weaves past historic barns, old railroad depots, forested ridges, and river valleys—ideal for leisurely country drives, birding, and exploring rural heritage landscapes.

☐ 🔖 ♡ **East Fork Loop Scenic Byway:** A State byway circling the scenic Lake Monroe arm via county roads near Bloomington. It passes wooded hillsides, rippling lakeshores, recreational areas, and rural homesteads. The route showcases Central Indiana's natural beauty and recreation spots while staying off the main highways.

INDIANA

☐ 🔖 ♡ **Historic Michigan Road Byway:** A State-designated byway tracing part of the 19th-century Michigan Road from Indianapolis to the Michigan border. It runs along tree-lined roads passing historic courthouse towns, early settlement landscapes, churches, and agricultural vistas—highlighting a corridor that helped connect early Indiana communities.

☐ 🔖 ♡ **Hoosier Hills Scenic Byway:** A State byway winding through southeastern Indiana's forested hills, limestone bluffs, and fertile valleys. It connects small historic towns, covered bridges, and cultural landmarks while showcasing rolling farmland and hardwood forests. Travelers encounter scenic overlooks, wildlife areas, and reminders of Indiana's pioneer past, making it a route rich in natural beauty and heritage charm.

☐ 🔖 ♡ **Indiana Lincoln Highway Historic Byway:** A State byway on sections of the original Lincoln Highway—the first transcontinental US highway—running through northern Indiana farmland, small towns, vintage service stations, and historic bridges. It recalls early automobile travel with timeless roadside Americana character.

☐ 🔖 ♡ **Ohio River Scenic Byway Extension:** A State byway extending the National Ohio River Scenic Byway deeper inland. It continues the river-edge journey across forested ridges, woodlands, and backcountry roads—adding rural charm and natural green corridors away from the main highway.

☐ 🔖 ♡ **Oldenburg–Batesville Loop Scenic Byway:** A State byway connecting the German-influenced towns of Oldenburg and Batesville via rural roads. It winds through farmland, woodlots, historic churches, and small breweries. The route highlights cultural heritage, agritourism, and small-town charm nestled in southeastern Indiana.

☐ 🔖 ♡ **Wabash River Scenic Byway:** A State byway paralleling the winding Wabash River through north-central Indiana. The route links river towns, wetlands, forested floodplains, and parklands—offering canoe launches, wildlife-viewing spots, historic bridges, and peaceful countryside ambiance along the longtime waterway of early Indiana.

National Natural Landmarks

☐ 🔖 ♡ **Big Walnut Creek:** Big Walnut Creek is a National Natural Landmark because it preserves a rare Genesee soil forest ecosystem. Here, beech, sugar maple, and tulip poplar grow together in a floodplain shaped by alluvial processes. The mix of nutrient-rich soils and diverse trees creates an uncommon habitat that reflects pre-settlement conditions once widespread in Indiana.
GPS: 39.7967, -86.7775

☐ 🔖 ♡ **Cabin Creek Raised Bog:** Cabin Creek Raised Bog holds landmark status as one of the few inland raised bogs in the United States. Its acidic peat layers and cool waters nurture orchids, sedges, and plants at the edge of their range. This remnant of glacial ecosystems offers scientists a living archive of postglacial ecology and demonstrates how unique wetlands evolve over millennia.
GPS: 40.1368, -85.1257

☐ 🔖 ♡ **Calvert and Porter Woods:** These woods are a National Natural Landmark for preserving one of the last near-virgin forests on Indiana's Tipton Till Plain. Dominated by towering beech, maple, and oak, the site shows what central Indiana's forests looked like before widespread settlement. Minimal human disturbance makes this an invaluable reference point for studying old-growth ecology.
GPS: 40.0228, -86.7218

☐ 🔖 ♡ **Cowles Bog:** Cowles Bog became a National Natural Landmark because of its historic role in ecology and its diverse plant succession. Once studied by Henry Cowles, it demonstrates the natural progression from wetland to forest in a dynamic dune landscape. Its mix of marshes, dunes, and forests shelters rare species, making it one of the Midwest's most biologically rich sites.
GPS: 41.6375, -87.0922

☐ 🔖 ♡ **Davis–Purdue Agriculture Center Forest:** This forest is a National Natural Landmark for representing the best example of old-growth oak–hickory woodland on the Tipton Till Plain. Mature hardwoods rise above a diverse understory, offering a benchmark for restoration projects. Its ecological integrity allows researchers to examine natural forest succession in Indiana's historic landscape.
GPS: 40.2533, -85.1480

☐ 🔖 ♡ **Donaldson Cave System and Woods:** Donaldson Cave was designated a National Natural Landmark for its combination of karst geology and ecological diversity. A spring-fed stream emerges from a limestone cave and flows through a deep gorge, while forested cliffs above create rich habitats. The site illustrates how underground hydrology and surface ecosystems interact in dramatic fashion.
GPS: 38.7302, -86.4153

UNITED STATES EDITION

INDIANA

Dunes Nature Preserve: Indiana's Dunes Nature Preserve is a National Natural Landmark because of its exceptional dune and wetland systems along Lake Michigan. Inter-dunal ponds, blowouts, and shifting sands reveal how wind and water continuously reshape the landscape. This living laboratory of coastal change provides habitat for rare species and showcases ongoing ecological succession.
GPS: 41.6600, -87.0400

Fern Cliff Nature Preserve: Fern Cliff gained National Natural Landmark recognition for its remarkable bryophyte diversity. Shady sandstone cliffs and moist ravines support an abundance of mosses and liverworts rarely found elsewhere in the state. The preserve illustrates how geology and microclimate foster specialized plant communities, making it a treasure for conservation and science.
GPS: 39.6110, -86.9637

Hanging Rock and Wabash Reef: Hanging Rock is a National Natural Landmark for preserving a 75-foot Silurian fossil reef above the Wabash River. The undercut bluff reveals coral and marine fossils nearly 400 million years old, offering one of the clearest reef exposures in the Midwest. It is a striking geologic feature that helps scientists study ancient marine ecosystems.
GPS: 40.8300, -85.7072

Harrison Spring: Harrison Spring holds National Natural Landmark designation as Indiana's largest spring. Fed by underground karst channels, it discharges millions of gallons daily into nearby waterways. The constant flow sustains aquatic habitats and provides a clear example of subterranean hydrology, making it vital for understanding regional groundwater and spring systems.
GPS: 38.2448, -86.2251

Hemmer Woods: Hemmer Woods is recognized as a National Natural Landmark for preserving a rare remnant of southwestern Indiana's oak–hickory forests. The site remains largely undisturbed, allowing mature hardwoods and diverse understory plants to thrive. Its ecological integrity provides an invaluable window into pre-settlement forest conditions and long-term natural succession.
GPS: 38.2308, -87.3709

Hoosier Prairie: Hoosier Prairie was designated a National Natural Landmark because it protects one of the last wetland prairies in the Midwest. Containing sand flats, sedge meadows, and marshes, the preserve reflects landscapes once widespread across Indiana. Its varied habitats support rare species, making it an essential refuge for biodiversity within Indiana Dunes National Park.
GPS: 41.5227, -87.4576

Hoot Woods: Hoot Woods stands as a National Natural Landmark for being one of Indiana's few intact climax beech–maple forests. Isolated and minimally disturbed, it shelters mature trees and sensitive species that reflect the forest structure common before settlement. Its preservation allows scientists to study old-growth dynamics in a rare and undisturbed environment.
GPS: 39.2499, -86.8895

Kramer Woods: Kramer Woods earned National Natural Landmark status as the only sizeable Indiana forest dominated by Shumard's red oak, pin oak, and hickory. This lowland woodland represents a distinctive ecological community type seldom preserved in the state. The site highlights the diversity of Indiana's bottomland forests and offers a living record for ecological study.
GPS: 37.8439, -87.1380

Marengo Cave: Marengo Cave is a National Natural Landmark for its spectacular karst features and accessible passages. Formed over millions of years, its limestone chambers display stalactites, stalagmites, and intricate formations. The cave system illustrates the geologic processes shaping Indiana's underground landscapes, while also serving as a destination for education and exploration.
GPS: 38.3756, -86.3399

Meltzer Woods: Meltzer Woods was recognized as a National Natural Landmark for its outstanding old-growth character. It protects tulip poplar, white oak, and beech trees of exceptional size, along with rich understory vegetation. As one of Indiana's oldest undisturbed woodlands, it serves as a vital example of pre-settlement forest ecology and long-term conservation.
GPS: 39.5028, -85.6678

INDIANA

 ☐ 🔖 ♡ **Officer's Woods:** Officer's Woods holds National Natural Landmark status as a premier remnant of southern Indiana's beech–maple forest. Its two distinct stands are remarkable for their concentration of black gum trees, a rarity in the region. This woodland highlights the ecological variety possible within a single site and offers an important refuge for native biodiversity.
GPS: 38.8000, -85.5000

 ☐ 🔖 ♡ **Ohio Coral Reef:** Ohio Coral Reef was designated a National Natural Landmark because it preserves one of the nation's most extensive Silurian and Devonian fossil beds. Located at Falls of the Ohio, this ancient reef records coral and marine life that flourished more than 350 million years ago. Its exposures provide a world-class site for geology and paleontology.
GPS: 38.2767, -85.7654

 ☐ 🔖 ♡ **Pine Hills Natural Area:** Pine Hills is recognized as a National Natural Landmark for its deep gorges and towering ridges carved by glacial meltwaters. Part of Shades State Park, the area's rugged terrain supports unique plant communities and rare habitats. It demonstrates the interplay of glacial history and natural processes that shaped Indiana's diverse landscapes.
GPS: 39.9428, -87.0493

 ☐ 🔖 ♡ **Pinhook Bog:** Pinhook Bog became a National Natural Landmark for its rare acidic bog environment, formed in a glacial kettle over 14,000 years ago. Pitcher plants, sphagnum moss, and other boreal species thrive in this fragile ecosystem, making it an exceptional example of postglacial wetland succession. It remains one of Indiana's most unique and scientifically valuable bogs.
GPS: 41.6150, -86.8483

 ☐ 🔖 ♡ **Pioneer Mothers Memorial Forest:** Pioneer Mothers Memorial Forest is a National Natural Landmark because it preserves one of the last untouched old-growth forests in Indiana. Towering hardwoods, including tulip poplar and oak, rise above a rich understory, offering a rare glimpse into pre-settlement woodlands. Its pristine condition makes it a vital site for conservation and ecological study.
GPS: 38.5360, -86.4590

 ☐ 🔖 ♡ **Portland Arch Nature Preserve:** Portland Arch Nature Preserve was designated a National Natural Landmark for its striking sandstone arch, formed by Bear Creek cutting through bedrock. Deep ravines and rugged cliffs frame diverse habitats supporting rare plants and animals. The site highlights both Indiana's geologic variety and the ecological richness of its preserved landscapes.
GPS: 40.2186, -87.3358

 ☐ 🔖 ♡ **Rise at Orangeville:** The Rise at Orangeville earned National Natural Landmark recognition for being Indiana's second-largest spring and a key feature of the Lost River karst system. Water emerges dramatically from underground channels, creating an ecologically important aquatic habitat. Its connection to regional hydrology makes it an invaluable site for geology and water studies.
GPS: 38.6312, -86.5571

 ☐ 🔖 ♡ **Rocky Hollow–Falls Canyon Nature Preserve:** Rocky Hollow–Falls Canyon is a National Natural Landmark for its dramatic sandstone gorges and seasonal waterfalls. Located in Turkey Run State Park, the preserve protects unique microclimates and diverse plant communities. Its striking terrain, sculpted by erosion, offers a living classroom for understanding Indiana's geology and ecological diversity.
GPS: 39.8937, -87.2046

 ☐ 🔖 ♡ **Shrader–Weaver Woods:** Shrader–Weaver Woods holds National Natural Landmark status as an excellent example of Indiana's remaining old-growth beech–maple forest. Massive tulip poplar, walnut, and cherry trees dominate the canopy, while a pioneer homestead provides historical context. This blend of natural and cultural heritage underscores the forest's ecological and historical importance.
GPS: 39.7203, -85.2223

 ☐ 🔖 ♡ **Tamarack Bog:** Tamarack Bog was recognized as a National Natural Landmark for preserving a rare boreal wetland ecosystem within Indiana. Located in the Pigeon River Fish and Wildlife Area, it harbors tamarack trees, sphagnum moss, and plant species uncommon this far south. The bog provides a critical refuge for biodiversity and illustrates glacial-era ecological processes.
GPS: 41.6764, -85.2623

UNITED STATES EDITION

INDIANA

Tolliver Swallowhole: Tolliver Swallowhole is a National Natural Landmark because it exemplifies karst hydrology in action. Here, surface waters vanish into underground limestone channels, demonstrating the dynamic connection between geology and water flow. This feature illustrates the processes shaping Indiana's karst landscapes and serves as a valuable site for geological education.
GPS: 38.6162, -86.4946

Wesley Chapel Gulf (Elrod Gulf): Wesley Chapel Gulf, also known as Elrod Gulf, achieved National Natural Landmark designation as Indiana's largest sinkhole. Formed by limestone dissolution, the dramatic depression is encircled by rich forest habitat. It demonstrates karst processes at a grand scale, offering insight into both geology and the unique ecology of sinkhole environments.
GPS: 38.6225, -86.5219

Wesselman Woods Nature Preserve: Wesselman Woods Nature Preserve is a National Natural Landmark for being one of the largest old-growth forests inside any U.S. city. Located in Evansville, it protects towering hardwoods and diverse wildlife within an urban setting. The preserve showcases the ecological importance of conserving remnants of pre-settlement forest amidst modern development.
GPS: 37.9847, -87.5061

Wyandotte Caves: Wyandotte Caves earned National Natural Landmark recognition for their extensive limestone passages formed over two million years ago. With vast chambers, speleothems, and underground streams, they highlight Southern Indiana's karst geology. The caves also hold cultural significance as early exploration sites, blending natural wonder with human history.
GPS: 38.2281, -86.2961

Iowa

Iowa's scenic heartland features rolling prairies, river bluffs, mysterious caves, and glacial formations. Its blend of state parks, recreation areas, a national monument, and notable natural landmarks offers peaceful beauty, hidden wonders, and countless opportunities to explore the state's quiet natural charm.

📅 Peak Season
May–October is Iowa's peak season, offering mild to warm weather, green landscapes, and busy state parks. Summer brings the largest crowds for festivals, lake recreation, and scenic drives through rolling farmland and river valleys.

📅 Offseason Months
November–April is the offseason, with cold winters and snow across much of the state. Outdoor activities slow, though winter birding, cross-country skiing, and quiet park exploration remain available.

🍃 Scenery & Nature Timing
Spring brings wildflowers and migrating birds along river corridors. Summer showcases lush prairies and boating on lakes. Fall features colorful foliage and harvest landscapes, while winter reveals peaceful countryside and frosted woodlands.

✨ Special
Iowa highlights include the limestone bluffs of the Driftless Area, the Loess Hills' rare wind-formed ridges, and caves at Maquoketa Caves State Park. The Mississippi and Des Moines Rivers shape scenic valleys, while prairies and glacial lakes define its heartland beauty.

UNITED STATES EDITION

IOWA

State Parks

☐ 🔖 ♡ **Ambrose A. Call State Park:** In Algona, this park honors pioneer Ambrose A. Call with a reconstructed log cabin amid wooded hills. Visitors enjoy quiet hiking trails and shaded picnic spots, while a small lake offers fishing and relaxation. Its mix of historic charm and natural beauty makes it a favorite for both history lovers and outdoor enthusiasts seeking tranquility.

☐ 🔖 ♡ **Backbone State Park:** Established in 1920 near Strawberry Point, it's Iowa's first state park and remains a crown jewel. Famous for rugged dolomite formations, including the "Devil's Backbone" ridge, it offers scenic hiking, climbing, and trout fishing. The lake invites boating and swimming, while campgrounds and CCC-built lodges showcase history within stunning natural surroundings.

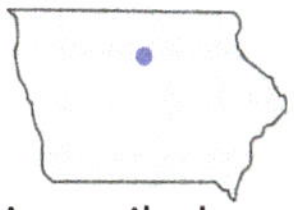

☐ 🔖 ♡ **Beed's Lake State Park:** At Hampton, this 319-acre park surrounds a picturesque 99-acre lake. Its signature feature is a mile-long stone causeway built by the CCC, offering unique lake views. Visitors enjoy fishing, boating, and swimming, along with shady trails and picnic spots. With historic charm and natural beauty, it's a peaceful destination for families and nature seekers alike.

☐ 🔖 ♡ **Bellevue State Park:** High above the Mississippi River at Bellevue, this park offers dramatic blufftop views and rich wildlife. Visitors stroll trails through woodland and prairie, explore a butterfly garden, and learn at the nature center. Spring wildflowers, migrating birds, and the changing river landscape make it a year-round favorite for photography, hiking, and quiet reflection.

☐ 🔖 ♡ **Big Creek State Park:** Just north of Des Moines in Polk City, this park features an 866-acre lake built for flood control but beloved for recreation. Visitors swim at Iowa's largest sandy beach, fish for walleye and bass, or launch boats from modern ramps. Trails, picnic shelters, and nearby bike paths make it a popular destination for families and weekend outings.

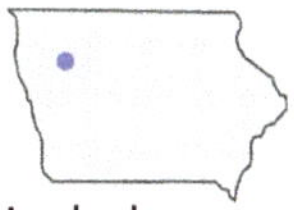

☐ 🔖 ♡ **Black Hawk State Park:** On Black Hawk Lake at Lake View, this park honors the Sauk leader Black Hawk. The 957-acre area includes camping, fishing, boating, and a lakeside trail with excellent wildlife viewing. Picnic shelters and CCC-built structures highlight its history. Its scenic setting on Iowa's southernmost natural glacial lake makes it a treasured gathering place.

☐ 🔖 ♡ **Blackburn State Park:** In Thurman, this quiet Loess Hills park offers rolling terrain, prairie vistas, and woodland trails. Visitors find opportunities for hiking, birdwatching, and peaceful picnics in a secluded natural setting. With its gentle ridges and unique geography, Blackburn provides a tranquil escape for those seeking solitude and scenic beauty within Iowa's western hill country.

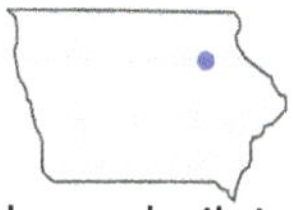

☐ 🔖 ♡ **Cedar Rock State Park:** In Quasqueton, this 423-acre park preserves "Cedar Rock," a Frank Lloyd Wright Usonian home built in 1950. Visitors tour the architecturally significant house and stroll along the Wapsipinicon River. The surrounding natural landscape of woods and fields provides quiet trails and picnic spots, blending mid-century design heritage with scenic Iowa beauty.

☐ 🔖 ♡ **Clear Lake State Park:** On the shores of Clear Lake, this park is a boating, fishing, and swimming hotspot. Its sandy beach, shaded campground, and picnic areas make it a family favorite. Trails wind through oak forests and prairie remnants, offering wildlife viewing and birding. Its location near downtown Clear Lake ensures both natural serenity and easy access to amenities.

☐ 🔖 ♡ **Coralville Lake State Park:** Adjacent to Coralville Reservoir, this 5,000-acre recreation hub offers boating, fishing, hiking, and camping. Trails explore wooded bluffs and wetlands, while campgrounds host visitors year-round. The nature center provides educational programs on wildlife and water resources. Its proximity to Iowa City makes it an accessible escape with rich outdoor opportunities.

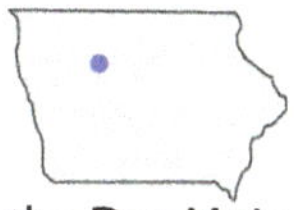

☐ 🔖 ♡ **Dolliver Memorial State Park:** In Webster County, this 594-acre park showcases dramatic sandstone bluffs, steep ravines, and the Des Moines River valley. Trails wind through unique geological formations, including Boneyard Hollow. Picnic areas and campsites rest beneath towering trees. With its mix of scenic beauty and natural history, Dolliver offers a peaceful retreat for exploration.

☐ 🔖 ♡ **Elinor Bedell State Park:** On East Okoboji Lake near Spirit Lake, this small 80-acre park provides boat access, fishing piers, and open space for picnics. Trails explore restored prairie and wetlands rich with birds and wildlife. Donated by former Congressman Berkley Bedell and his wife, the park honors their conservation legacy while offering a serene natural getaway.

IOWA

☐ 🔖 ♡ **Elk Rock State Park:** On Lake Red Rock near Knoxville, this 850-acre park provides expansive water recreation opportunities. Boaters and anglers enjoy the reservoir, while trails pass through hardwood forests and prairies. Scenic overlooks reveal lake vistas and wildlife. Modern campgrounds and equestrian facilities make Elk Rock a versatile destination for outdoor adventurers.

☐ 🔖 ♡ **Fort Defiance State Park:** Near Estherville, this 191-acre park blends wooded hills and prairie ridges with sweeping views of the Des Moines River valley. Trails lead to overlooks, while meadows attract deer and songbirds. Its historic name honors a frontier fort, though none remains. Today it's valued for its peaceful atmosphere, picnicking, and family-friendly hiking experiences.

☐ 🔖 ♡ **Geode State Park:** Near Danville, this 1,640-acre park is named for Iowa's state rock, often found in the region. Its 187-acre lake offers boating, fishing, and swimming. Trails weave through forests and prairie, providing excellent birdwatching and wildlife viewing. Shaded picnic areas, campsites, and a visitor-friendly landscape make it one of southeast Iowa's most popular destinations.

☐ 🔖 ♡ **George Wyth Memorial State Park:** In Waterloo, this 1,200-acre park preserves natural areas along the Cedar River and several lakes. Anglers and paddlers enjoy abundant water access, while trails connect to regional bike paths. The park is a haven for birdwatchers, with over 200 recorded species. Its location within a metro area makes it a unique urban-nature blend.

☐ 🔖 ♡ **Green Valley State Park:** Near Creston, this 1,060-acre park features a 390-acre reservoir surrounded by woodland and prairie. Fishing and boating are popular, while trails and a lakeside multi-use path provide recreation for hikers and cyclists. Campgrounds, playgrounds, and picnic shelters make it a family-friendly destination, offering both natural beauty and modern conveniences.

☐ 🔖 ♡ **Gull Point State Park:** On West Okoboji Lake, this park is a centerpiece of the Iowa Great Lakes. Its sandy beach, boat ramps, and fishing piers make it a summer favorite, while trails wind through woodland and prairie rich in wildlife. Campgrounds and picnic areas provide comfort, and its central location makes Gull Point a hub for exploring nearby lake attractions year-round.

☐ 🔖 ♡ **Honey Creek State Park:** Near Moravia, this 828-acre park lies on Rathbun Lake, Iowa's second-largest reservoir. It offers boating, fishing, and swimming, plus hiking trails through rolling woodland and prairie. Wildlife is abundant, from deer to waterfowl. Campgrounds and picnic shelters make it a family destination, while its lake views and quiet setting draw outdoor enthusiasts.

☐ 🔖 ♡ **Lacey-Keosauqua State Park:** Along the Des Moines River in southeast Iowa, this 1,653-acre park is Iowa's second-oldest. It features CCC-built stone lodges, a 30-acre lake, and trails through oak-hickory forest. Wildlife is plentiful, including bald eagles. Archaeological sites highlight ancient cultures. Campgrounds, picnics, and hiking combine natural beauty with deep cultural history.

☐ 🔖 ♡ **Lake Ahquabi State Park:** Near Indianola, this 770-acre park centers on a 115-acre lake ideal for fishing, swimming, and paddling. Trails circle through forest and prairie, offering wildlife encounters and scenic views. With modern campgrounds and picnic spots, it provides a tranquil retreat within an easy drive of Des Moines, perfect for family outings and weekend getaways.

☐ 🔖 ♡ **Lake Anita State Park:** In southwest Iowa, this 1,062-acre park is anchored by a 171-acre reservoir stocked with bass, crappie, and catfish. Its sandy swimming beach, boat ramps, and trails attract families and anglers alike. Shady campgrounds and picnic areas offer comfort, while the lake's peaceful setting makes it a favored destination for relaxation and outdoor recreation.

☐ 🔖 ♡ **Lake Darling State Park:** Near Brighton, this 1,387-acre park surrounds a 302-acre lake named for conservationist J.N. "Ding" Darling. Visitors fish, boat, and swim, while trails explore oak woods and prairie. Campgrounds with modern amenities, playgrounds, and picnic shelters welcome families. The park's wildlife, natural scenery, and restored habitats highlight Darling's conservation legacy.

☐ 🔖 ♡ **Lake Keomah State Park:** Just east of Oskaloosa, this 366-acre park features an 83-acre lake for boating, swimming, and fishing. Trails loop through woodlands and restored prairie, offering wildlife viewing and quiet escapes. A modern campground, picnic shelters, and open fields make it family-friendly, while its small size and tranquil setting create a peaceful retreat.

IOWA

☐ 🔖 ♡ **Lake Macbride State Park:** Near Solon, this 2,180-acre park is Iowa's largest. Its 812-acre lake offers two swimming beaches, excellent fishing, and ample boating. Trails pass through woodland, prairie, and shoreline. Picnic shelters, campgrounds, and a spillway popular for wading enhance its appeal. Close to Iowa City, it's one of the state's most visited recreation destinations.

☐ 🔖 ♡ **Lake Manawa State Park:** At Council Bluffs, this 1,529-acre park centers on a 772-acre oxbow lake formed by the Missouri River. Boaters, anglers, and swimmers flock to its waters, while trails and picnic areas offer land-based fun. Campgrounds and wildlife-rich habitats make it versatile, and its location near Omaha-Council Bluffs ensures steady popularity for family recreation.

☐ 🔖 ♡ **Lake of Three Fires State Park:** In Bedford, this 1,155-acre park features an 85-acre lake stocked with fish and ideal for boating and paddling. Trails wind through oak-hickory forest and prairie, with campgrounds and cabins available. Wildlife is abundant, and the park's quiet setting makes it perfect for family gatherings, fishing trips, and scenic exploration year-round.

☐ 🔖 ♡ **Lake Wapello State Park:** Near Drakesville, this 1,150-acre park surrounds a 289-acre natural lake. It offers a sandy swimming beach, fishing piers, and boat rentals. A 6.6-mile trail encircles the lake, providing scenic hiking and biking. Cabins, campgrounds, and picnic shelters make it family-friendly, while its clear waters and wooded hills create a classic Iowa retreat.

☐ 🔖 ♡ **Ledges State Park:** Near Boone, this 1,200-acre park is famed for sandstone canyons carved by Pea's Creek. Trails pass through cliffs and wooded ridges, offering spectacular views of the Des Moines River valley. CCC-built bridges and shelters add history. A mix of geology, hiking, camping, and picnic areas make it one of Iowa's most dramatic natural parks.

☐ 🔖 ♡ **Lewis and Clark State Park:** In Onawa, this 176-acre park sits on Blue Lake, a Missouri River oxbow. It commemorates the 1804 Lewis and Clark expedition campsite with interpretive displays and a replica keelboat. Fishing, boating, and birdwatching are popular, while shaded picnic grounds and a modern campground make it a blend of history and outdoor recreation.

☐ 🔖 ♡ **Maquoketa Caves State Park:** Near Maquoketa, this 370-acre park is home to Iowa's largest collection of caves. Visitors explore Dancehall Cave and other formations via rugged trails, while limestone bluffs, sinkholes, and scenic woodlands add variety. A visitor center interprets geology and history. Camping, picnicking, and year-round exploration make it one of Iowa's most unique parks.

☐ 🔖 ♡ **McIntosh Woods State Park:** Near Ventura on Clear Lake, this 62-acre park features a boat ramp, fishing jetty, and sandy beach. Trails pass through old-growth forest rich with songbirds, while a modern campground and four yurts offer unique stays. Its lakeshore location combines boating and swimming with woodland exploration, making it a versatile year-round destination.

☐ 🔖 ♡ **Mineral Springs Park:** In Keokuk, this historic park overlooks the Mississippi River and features spring-fed ponds, wooded trails, and picnic areas. Visitors enjoy fishing, wildlife watching, and exploring the city's riverfront heritage. Its scenic setting and historic charm make it both a local gathering spot and a peaceful retreat for nature and history lovers alike.

☐ 🔖 ♡ **Mini-Wakan State Park:** On the north shore of Spirit Lake, this 20-acre park provides a scenic lakeside escape. Anglers and boaters enjoy access to Iowa's largest natural lake, while picnic areas and open lawns provide space for family gatherings. Its quiet shoreline, birdlife, and connection to the surrounding Great Lakes region make it a serene yet active destination.

☐ 🔖 ♡ **Nine Eagles State Park:** Near Davis City, this 1,119-acre park is known for its wooded ridges, valleys, and scenic 64-acre lake. Trails wind through forest and prairie, with opportunities for hiking, horseback riding, and wildlife viewing. Fishing, boating, and camping facilities attract families, while the park's rugged beauty makes it a favorite for outdoor adventure.

☐ 🔖 ♡ **Okamanpedan State Park:** On the Iowa-Minnesota border near Dolliver, this 19-acre park offers public access to Tuttle Lake (Okamanpeedan). Anglers and boaters use its ramps and shoreline, while shaded picnic areas provide relaxation. Its modest size and peaceful lakeside setting make it ideal for quiet recreation and enjoying the natural scenery of Iowa's northern tier.

IOWA

☐ 🔖 ♡ **Palisades-Kepler State Park:** East of Cedar Rapids, this 840-acre park highlights rugged limestone bluffs, ravines, and rich forests along the Cedar River. Trails lead to dramatic overlooks, while fishing and canoeing are popular on the river. CCC-era stone shelters add history. With camping, picnicking, and abundant wildlife, it blends natural drama and cultural heritage.

☐ 🔖 ♡ **Pikes Peak State Park:** Near McGregor, this 960-acre park features one of Iowa's most iconic Mississippi River overlooks. Trails wind through wooded bluffs, waterfalls, and effigy mounds, offering cultural as well as scenic interest. Visitors picnic under shade trees or camp nearby. With breathtaking views and natural beauty, it's a must-see destination in northeast Iowa.

☐ 🔖 ♡ **Pikes Point State Park:** On Spirit Lake, this 15-acre park offers one of the Great Lakes region's most popular sandy swimming beaches. Families enjoy picnicking and open space for play, while anglers cast from shore. Though small, its prime location and recreational amenities make it a lively summertime gathering spot with beautiful lake views and easy access.

☐ 🔖 ♡ **Pilot Knob State Park:** Near Forest City, this 700-acre park is known for its observation tower atop Iowa's second-highest point. Trails lead through forest, prairie, and wetlands, offering scenic overlooks and wildlife encounters. A small glacial pond, picnic shelters, and campgrounds enhance its appeal. Its mix of landscapes and historic CCC structures make it a unique destination.

☐ 🔖 ♡ **Pine Lake State Park:** At Eldora, this 668-acre park preserves rare stands of old-growth white pine along the Iowa River. Two lakes provide boating, fishing, and swimming, while wooded trails offer scenic exploration. Campgrounds, picnic areas, and CCC-built shelters highlight its heritage. Combining natural beauty, water recreation, and history, Pine Lake is a beloved Iowa treasure.

☐ 🔖 ♡ **Pottawattamie State Park:** Nestled in Iowa's western hills, this small park offers hiking, fishing, and picnicking in a quiet natural setting. Known for its CCC-era stone structures, it preserves both natural beauty and Depression-era history. With shaded picnic grounds, a small lake, and wildlife habitat, it provides a peaceful stop for families and outdoor enthusiasts.

☐ 🔖 ♡ **Prairie Rose State Park:** Near Harlan, this 707-acre park surrounds a 218-acre lake known for fishing, boating, and swimming. Trails circle the water, offering scenic hikes and birdwatching. Campgrounds and cabins accommodate visitors year-round. With playgrounds, picnic shelters, and open fields, it's a popular destination for families seeking outdoor recreation in western Iowa.

☐ 🔖 ♡ **Preparation Canyon State Park:** In the Loess Hills near Moorhead, this 344-acre park preserves rugged bluffs and quiet prairies. Trails wind through hills with scenic overlooks, while shaded picnic areas provide peaceful rest. The park's history includes the site of a Mormon settlement. Today it offers seclusion and striking landscapes for hikers, photographers, and nature lovers.

☐ 🔖 ♡ **Red Haw State Park:** Near Chariton, this 649-acre park is especially famous in spring when redbud trees bloom around its 72-acre lake. Visitors enjoy fishing, boating, and trails that loop through woodland and meadows. Campgrounds, picnic areas, and scenic views make it family-friendly, while its seasonal beauty and quiet atmosphere draw nature lovers year-round.

☐ 🔖 ♡ **Rice Lake State Park:** Near Lake Mills, this 15-acre park sits on a 1,200-acre glacial lake. Anglers fish for northern pike, walleye, and panfish, while birdwatchers spot migrating waterfowl. A boat ramp and picnic areas enhance its simple charm. Though small, Rice Lake's natural setting and fishing opportunities make it a valued stop in northern Iowa.

☐ 🔖 ♡ **Rock Creek State Park:** Near Kellogg, this 1,697-acre park features a 602-acre lake ideal for boating, fishing, and swimming. Trails encircle the water for hiking, biking, and wildlife watching. Campgrounds, picnic shelters, and playgrounds make it family-friendly. Known for its excellent angling and scenic shoreline, Rock Creek is a central Iowa favorite for recreation.

☐ 🔖 ♡ **Springbrook State Park:** In Guthrie County, this 930-acre park surrounds a scenic 17-acre lake. Anglers and paddlers enjoy the water, while trails offer hiking, biking, and horseback riding through woodlands and prairies. A modern campground, picnic shelters, and environmental education center make it versatile. Its blend of natural beauty and recreation draws families year-round.

IOWA

☐ 🔖 ♡ **Stone State Park:** In Sioux City, this 1,069-acre park protects dramatic Loess Hills landscapes. Trails for hiking and horseback riding lead to overlooks with sweeping views. Picnic shelters and campgrounds welcome visitors, while abundant wildlife and rare plants thrive in its rugged terrain. Its proximity to the city makes it an urban escape with wild character.

☐ 🔖 ♡ **Summerset State Park:** Between Des Moines and Indianola, this park transforms former strip mine pits into scenic lakes. Anglers enjoy stocked waters, while trails invite hikers and mountain bikers through reclaimed prairie and woodland. Wildlife is abundant, from deer to songbirds. With picnic areas and lake overlooks, it blends recreation with habitat restoration.

☐ 🔖 ♡ **Trapper's Bay State Park:** On Silver Lake near Lake Park, this 111-acre site provides shoreline access for boating, fishing, and birdwatching. Picnic areas and shaded groves make it inviting for families, while migrating waterfowl attract birders. Modest in size but rich in charm, it offers peaceful recreation within the Iowa Great Lakes region's natural landscapes.

☐ 🔖 ♡ **Twin Lakes State Park:** Near Rockwell City, this 15-acre park lies on North Twin Lake, offering a sandy swimming beach, boat ramp, and shaded picnic grounds. Anglers cast for bass and crappie, while families enjoy playgrounds and open lawns. Though small, its lakefront setting and recreational amenities make it a popular summer destination for locals and visitors alike.

☐ 🔖 ♡ **Union Grove State Park:** Near Gladbrook, this 282-acre park surrounds a 110-acre lake stocked with fish and open to boating and swimming. Trails wind through woodland and prairie, while campgrounds and picnic shelters host family gatherings. Abundant wildlife and seasonal beauty make it a tranquil, versatile destination for outdoor fun in central Iowa year-round.

☐ 🔖 ♡ **Viking Lake State Park:** In southwest Iowa, this 1,000-acre park features a 136-acre lake popular for fishing, boating, and swimming. Trails weave through wooded hills and prairie, offering wildlife encounters and scenic views. Campgrounds and picnic areas make it family-friendly, while the lake's quiet beauty provides a relaxing retreat for nature lovers and outdoor adventurers.

☐ 🔖 ♡ **Walnut Woods State Park:** On the Raccoon River near West Des Moines, this 260-acre park preserves Iowa's largest stand of native black walnut trees. Trails explore woodland rich with songbirds, while fishing and picnicking are popular along the river. A modern campground and open spaces provide easy access, making it a natural escape close to the metro area.

☐ 🔖 ♡ **Wapsipinicon State Park:** At Anamosa, this 400-acre park features striking limestone bluffs, caves, and the Wapsipinicon River. Visitors explore Horse Thief Cave, hike wooded trails, and fish or paddle the river. CCC-built picnic shelters and bridges add history. With scenic beauty, geology, and abundant wildlife, it remains a classic Iowa state park experience.

☐ 🔖 ♡ **Waubonsie State Park:** In the Loess Hills of southwest Iowa, this 2,000-acre park offers dramatic overlooks of the Missouri River valley. Trails explore prairie and woodland, attracting hikers and birdwatchers. Campgrounds and picnic areas provide comfort, while fall foliage and seasonal wildlife add beauty. Its unique terrain makes it a premier destination for outdoor recreation.

☐ 🔖 ♡ **Wildcat Den State Park:** Near Muscatine, this 600-acre park is famed for sandstone bluffs, Pine Creek Grist Mill, and CCC-era buildings. Trails lead through rugged canyons and streams, while historic sites tell Iowa's pioneer story. With picnic areas, camping nearby, and abundant natural scenery, Wildcat Den combines outdoor adventure with heritage exploration in a scenic setting.

National Parks

 ☐ 🔖 ♡ **Effigy Mounds National Monument:** Nestled along the Mississippi River in northeast Iowa, this monument protects over 200 prehistoric burial mounds built by Native American cultures, many shaped like animals such as bears and birds. Visitors can hike forested trails with scenic overlooks, explore the mounds' spiritual and cultural significance, and learn about ancient traditions that shaped the region.

 ☐ 🔖 ♡ **Herbert Hoover National Historic Site:** In West Branch, this site honors the life of America's 31st president. Visitors can tour Hoover's humble birthplace cottage, his boyhood neighborhood, and the Presidential Library and Museum. The grounds highlight his humanitarian legacy, Quaker roots, and leadership during the Great Depression, offering an inspiring look at his enduring impact.

IOWA

State & National Forests

☐ 🔖 ♡ **Backbone State Forest:** Tucked in Delaware County, this 186-acre oak-hickory woodland sits atop limestone bluffs near the Maquoketa River valley. Managed by Iowa DNR, it provides rugged hiking terrain, rich wildlife habitat, and overlooks of the driftless landscape. The forest complements nearby Backbone State Park, offering a quieter, more secluded escape for nature enthusiasts.

☐ 🔖 ♡ **Gifford State Forest:** Located in Pottawattamie County, this small forest along the Missouri River corridor preserves unmanaged riparian woodlands. Though lacking facilities or trails, it serves as an important habitat for birds and other wildlife while enhancing Iowa's limited western forest cover. Its conservation focus makes it a quiet link in the state's ecological network.

☐ 🔖 ♡ **Loess Hills State Forest:** Stretching 10,600 acres across Harrison and Monona counties, this forest showcases dramatic loess ridges, oak-hickory woodlands, and rare prairie remnants. With over 50 miles of multi-use trails, it offers hiking, biking, and horseback riding amid sweeping vistas. The forest protects one of the Midwest's most unique geologic landscapes, carved by ancient winds.

☐ 🔖 ♡ **Pilot Mound State Forest:** Encompassing 34 acres in Boone County, Pilot Mound preserves rolling upland hardwoods atop a glacially formed hill. Though small and minimally developed, it provides habitat for native species and serves as a forestry demonstration area. Visitors seeking solitude and ecological insight will find a quiet pocket of Iowa's woodland heritage here.

☐ 🔖 ♡ **Shimek State Forest:** Covering 9,148 acres in Lee and Van Buren counties, Shimek is southeast Iowa's largest public forest. It features oak-hickory stands, pine plantations, lakes, and campgrounds. Visitors enjoy hiking, horseback riding, fishing, and wildlife watching across multiple units. Named for naturalist Bohumil Shimek, it preserves one of the state's richest woodland landscapes.

☐ 🔖 ♡ **Stephens State Forest:** Iowa's largest state forest, Stephens spans about 15,500 acres across seven southern counties. Planted by the CCC in the 1930s, it has grown into diverse woodlands, lakes, and grasslands. Today it's a hub for camping, hiking, hunting, and bird conservation. Its patchwork of units demonstrates long-term land stewardship and reclaimed forest success.

☐ 🔖 ♡ **White Pine Hollow State Forest:** This 712-acre preserve in Dubuque County protects rare stands of native white pine growing on steep limestone slopes. Its oak-hickory woodlands and thin-soiled ridges harbor unique plant and animal life. Managed for conservation, it links with surrounding public lands, creating a haven for biodiversity in Iowa's rugged northeast corner.

☐ 🔖 ♡ **Yellow River State Forest:** Encompassing 8,500 acres in Allamakee County, this forest is known for its trout streams, hardwood valleys, and driftless-area bluffs. It offers campgrounds, equestrian trails, biking, and Iowa's only fire tower with sweeping views. Established in the 1930s by the CCC, it remains a rugged outdoor destination blending history, scenery, and recreation.

National Scenic Byways & All-American Roads

☐ 🔖 ♡ **Great River Road:** Following 328 miles of the Mississippi River along Iowa's eastern edge, this federally designated byway showcases limestone bluffs, wildlife refuges, and historic towns such as Dubuque and Lansing. Travelers encounter scenic overlooks, Effigy Mounds, and river culture, connecting nature, heritage, and one of America's iconic waterways.

☐ 🔖 ♡ **Lincoln Highway Heritage Byway:** Stretching 372 miles across Iowa, this historic route honors America's first transcontinental highway. Visitors encounter restored gas stations, vintage roadside diners, and classic main streets reflecting early automobile tourism. Blending cultural history with rolling farmland scenery, it preserves the nostalgia and innovation of cross-country travel.

☐ 🔖 ♡ **Loess Hills Scenic Byway:** Running 220 miles along Iowa's western border, this byway winds through rare loess soil formations, oak savannas, and dramatic bluffs overlooking the Missouri River valley. Scenic overlooks, prairies, and winding roads reveal one of the Midwest's most unique landscapes, with trails and preserves offering abundant opportunities for exploration.

IOWA

State Scenic Byways

☐ 🔖 ♡ **Covered Bridges Scenic Byway:** Stretching 82 miles through Madison County, this route highlights Iowa's famous 19th-century covered bridges and pastoral countryside. Stops include Winterset, the birthplace of John Wayne, plus quilt shops, historic architecture, and rolling farmland. Restored bridges and backroads make it a nostalgic journey into Iowa's rural heritage.

☐ 🔖 ♡ **Delaware Crossing Scenic Byway:** Following 44 miles of the Maquoketa River valley, this drive winds past limestone bluffs, wooded hills, and quilt-marked barns. Small towns like Manchester feature a whitewater park and cultural stops. Scenic overlooks, recreation areas, and rural charm combine for a route that blends beauty and community character.

☐ 🔖 ♡ **Driftless Area Scenic Byway:** Covering about 100 miles in northeast Iowa, this byway traverses a rare unglaciated region of rugged bluffs, winding valleys, and limestone ridges. The corridor features trout streams, birding hotspots, and panoramic overlooks, offering travelers a striking glimpse of Iowa's pre-glacial natural heritage.

☐ 🔖 ♡ **Glacial Trail Scenic Byway:** Spanning 36 miles in northwest Iowa, this short but scenic route highlights moraines, kettle lakes, and glacier-shaped terrain. Interpretive signs share geological history, while nearby lakes and small towns provide fishing, boating, and relaxed exploration amid rolling farmland and wooded pockets.

☐ 🔖 ♡ **Grant Wood Scenic Byway:** Extending 68 miles in eastern Iowa, this drive celebrates the landscapes that inspired artist Grant Wood. Rolling fields, stone churches, and farmsteads echo his iconic paintings. Travelers can stop at art galleries, cultural landmarks, and historic towns that showcase the authentic Midwest captured in his work.

☐ 🔖 ♡ **Historic Hills Scenic Byway:** A 110-mile route in southeast Iowa's wooded "hill country," this byway meanders past Amish communities, state forests, and limestone bluffs. Visitors enjoy parks, trails, and cultural detours into hidden valleys. Its less-traveled backroads offer rustic charm, scenic views, and abundant wildlife.

☐ 🔖 ♡ **Iowa Valley Scenic Byway:** Stretching 77 miles across east-central Iowa, this route follows river valleys, oak woodlands, and rural communities. Highlights include historic barns, Meskwaki Nation heritage sites, and local art. Scenic overlooks and vibrant fall colors provide a tranquil glimpse of Iowa's cultural and natural traditions.

☐ 🔖 ♡ **Jefferson Highway Heritage Byway:** Running about 220 miles, this route retraces the historic Jefferson Highway, once called the "Pine to Palm" road. Vintage roadside architecture, rolling farmland, and small-town main streets reflect the dawn of automobile tourism, preserving a piece of early 20th-century road history.

☐ 🔖 ♡ **River Bluffs Scenic Byway:** Covering 109 miles in northeast Iowa, this byway features limestone cliffs, forested hollows, and winding valleys near the Mississippi watershed. Travelers pass through small Scandinavian-influenced towns, hike woodland trails, and enjoy dramatic overlooks of one of the state's most rugged landscapes.

☐ 🔖 ♡ **Western Skies Scenic Byway:** Spanning 142 miles across western Iowa, this route crosses open prairies, historic homesteads, and wind-turbine landscapes. Danish-heritage towns like Elk Horn and Kimballton add cultural richness. Open horizons and vibrant communities define this drive through Iowa's western edge.

☐ 🔖 ♡ **White Pole Road Scenic Byway:** This 26-mile corridor near Redfield follows a historic auto route once marked by painted white poles. Visitors encounter farmland, roadside attractions, and nostalgic Americana tied to early road travel. Its short length makes it a perfect half-day journey through Iowa's small-town charm.

National Natural Landmarks

 ☐ 🔖 ♡ **Anderson Goose Lake:** Anderson Goose Lake was designated a National Natural Landmark for being one of the last natural glacial pothole lakes in Iowa. Its shallow basin and surrounding marshland, shaped by retreating glaciers, support native prairie vegetation and diverse waterfowl. The site preserves a vanishing habitat type once common across the northern plains.
GPS: 42.3156, -93.6239

 ☐ 🔖 ♡ **Cayler Prairie:** Cayler Prairie is recognized as a National Natural Landmark for preserving a pristine remnant of tallgrass prairie, a landscape that once blanketed much of Iowa. Native grasses such as big bluestem and Indian grass thrive here alongside spring wildflowers and rare species, offering a vivid glimpse into the region's ecological heritage.
GPS: 43.3972, -95.2439

THE ROAMER'S GUIDE

IOWA

 **Cold Water Cave:** Cold Water Cave achieved National Natural Landmark status as Iowa's longest cave system, extending more than 16 miles beneath the Driftless Area. Its limestone passages contain delicate speleothems, clear underground streams, and rare cave-dwelling fauna, providing an exceptional example of Midwestern karst geology and subterranean biodiversity.
GPS: 43.4411, -91.9603

 **Dewey's Pasture and Smith's Slough:** This wetland complex is a National Natural Landmark for its outstanding glacial pothole and northern tallgrass prairie ecosystems. Sedge meadows, shallow wetlands, and prairie vegetation create critical habitat for migratory birds and waterfowl. The landscape reflects the ecological richness shaped by glacial retreat.
GPS: 43.1965, -94.9217 (Dewey's Pasture)
GPS: 43.1875, -94.9323 (Smith's Slough)

 **Hayden Prairie State Preserve:** Hayden Prairie was named a National Natural Landmark for being one of Iowa's largest remaining tracts of undisturbed tallgrass prairie. With more than 200 native plant species—including blazing star and gentian—it shelters butterflies and prairie chickens, preserving the ecological diversity once widespread across the Midwest.
GPS: 43.4395, -92.3831

 **Loess Hills:** The Loess Hills were designated a National Natural Landmark because they form one of the world's most extensive loess deposits, with silt layers rising up to 200 feet. Their steep ridges and valleys host rare prairie and forest communities, making the Missouri River bluffs both a geological wonder and an ecological treasure.
GPS: 41.8013, -95.9950

White Pine Hollow State Forest: White Pine Hollow is a National Natural Landmark for containing Iowa's only native stand of white pine, sheltered in a cool ravine of the Driftless Area. Its moist microclimate sustains ferns, mosses, and northern plant species found far from their usual range, creating an island of biodiversity in the state.
GPS: 42.6297, -91.1121

Kansas

Kansas offers wide-open wonders, with tallgrass prairies, striking rock formations, quiet lakes, and expansive skies. Through its collection of state parks, national historic sites and trails, and notable natural landmarks, Kansas reveals its understated outdoor charm, where endless horizons meet peaceful trails and timeless prairie beauty.

📅 Peak Season
May–October is Kansas's peak season, with warm days, clear skies, and blooming prairies. Spring and fall bring the most comfortable weather for hiking, scenic drives, and exploring parks and historic sites.

📅 Offseason Months
November–April is the offseason, with colder temperatures, occasional snow, and quieter travel across the plains. Winter offers peaceful open landscapes and clear views, though outdoor activity is limited.

🍃 Scenery & Nature Timing
Spring fills the prairies with wildflowers and active wildlife. Summer brings green grasslands and vivid sunsets. Fall offers cooler air and golden fields, while winter highlights stark prairie beauty and migratory birds.

✨ Special
Kansas features the tallgrass prairies of the Flint Hills, the striking chalk formations of Monument Rocks, and the gypsum dunes of Little Sahara near Medicine Lodge. Rolling plains, meandering rivers, and expansive skies define its natural landscape.

KANSAS

State Parks

☐ 🔖 ♡ **Cedar Bluff State Park:** Encompassing ~850+ acres in north-central Kansas, this park surrounds a 3,500-acre reservoir framed by striking chalk bluffs. Known for boating, fishing, and camping, it also offers hiking trails, picnic sites, and fossil-rich rock formations over 85 million years old. Visitors enjoy panoramic views, rich geology, and water recreation in a dramatic High Plains setting.

☐ 🔖 ♡ **Cheney State Park:** Spread across 1,500 acres in south-central Kansas, Cheney State Park surrounds Cheney Reservoir, a hub for fishing, sailing, and swimming. Its campgrounds, hiking trails, and picnic spots draw families and outdoor enthusiasts year-round. Known for its wind and open water, it's a favorite among sailors and birdwatchers, with scenic prairie and lake views enhancing the experience.

☐ 🔖 ♡ **Clinton State Park:** Near Lawrence, this 1,500-acre park borders Clinton Lake and offers abundant outdoor recreation. Boaters, anglers, and swimmers flock to its waters, while hikers and bikers enjoy miles of wooded trails. Campgrounds, picnic areas, and wildlife observation points make it a popular family getaway, blending natural beauty with easy access to nearby cultural and historic sites.

☐ 🔖 ♡ **Crawford State Park:** Nestled in southeast Kansas, this 500-acre park surrounds Crawford State Lake, offering serene fishing, boating, and camping opportunities. Shaded trails wind through hardwood forests, while picnic areas provide lakeside views. The park's quiet setting, diverse wildlife, and peaceful waters make it a retreat for nature lovers seeking relaxation and outdoor recreation in a smaller, scenic park.

☐ 🔖 ♡ **Cross Timbers State Park:** Spanning 1,000 acres near Toronto Reservoir in east-central Kansas, this park preserves ancient oak woodlands and tallgrass prairies. Visitors enjoy boating, fishing, hiking, and camping amid rugged natural beauty. It's a top spot for birdwatching and wildlife observation, with trails showcasing unique geology and rich ecosystems that define the Cross Timbers region.

☐ 🔖 ♡ **Eisenhower State Park:** Covering 1,785 acres on Melvern Reservoir, this park honors President Dwight D. Eisenhower. It offers excellent fishing, boating, and camping, plus hiking and equestrian trails through prairie and woodland. Scenic overlooks and picnic spots make it ideal for family outings, while its mix of recreation and history reflects Kansas' natural and cultural heritage.

☐ 🔖 ♡ **El Dorado State Park:** The largest state park in Kansas, spanning 4,000+ acres around El Dorado Reservoir. Known for extensive boating, fishing, hiking, and camping, it also features nature trails, equestrian paths, and rich wildlife. With multiple campgrounds and marinas, the park serves as a recreation hub, offering year-round opportunities in a diverse prairie and woodland landscape.

☐ 🔖 ♡ **Elk City State Park:** Nestled around Elk City Lake in southeast Kansas, this 1,000-acre park offers boating, fishing, and scenic hiking. Trails like the Elk River Hiking Trail reveal limestone bluffs, dense forests, and panoramic lake views. Campgrounds and picnic areas provide a peaceful retreat, while diverse birdlife and wildlife make it a destination for nature photography and outdoor relaxation.

☐ 🔖 ♡ **Fall River State Park:** Located in southeastern Kansas, this 1,000-acre park surrounds Fall River Lake, offering boating, fishing, and swimming. Six hiking trails wind through prairie, woodland, and river valleys, providing excellent wildlife viewing. With shaded campgrounds and diverse ecosystems, it's a haven for outdoor recreation and a gateway to the Flint Hills' scenic and ecological beauty.

☐ 🔖 ♡ **Flint Hills Trail State Park:** Stretching 117 miles through eastern Kansas, this linear park is a premier hiking, biking, and horseback riding trail. Traversing the tallgrass prairie of the Flint Hills, it reveals sweeping views of rolling hills, rivers, and wildflowers. Rich in natural beauty and heritage, it links rural communities, offering multi-day adventure through Kansas' most iconic landscapes.

☐ 🔖 ♡ **Glen Elder State Park:** Encompassing 1,300 acres around Waconda Lake in north-central Kansas, this park is popular for fishing, boating, and camping. Known for its scenic lake views and abundant wildlife, it also features trails, picnic spots, and a waterfowl refuge. With family-friendly facilities and year-round recreation, it's a favored destination for anglers, birdwatchers, and lake enthusiasts.

☐ 🔖 ♡ **Hillsdale State Park:** Situated on Hillsdale Lake in northeastern Kansas, this park provides boating, fishing, swimming, and wildlife viewing across 12,000 acres of water and prairie. Its campgrounds, hiking and equestrian trails, and picnic areas make it ideal for families. Easily accessible from Kansas City, it blends natural beauty with convenient recreation for city visitors and locals alike.

KANSAS

Kanopolis State Park: Spanning 3,500 acres near Kanopolis Reservoir, this park features sandstone canyons, caves, and prairie bluffs unique to central Kansas. Popular for fishing, boating, hiking, and camping, it also borders Mushroom Rock State Park, known for odd rock formations. Trails like Horsethief Canyon highlight rugged scenery, making it a top destination for outdoor adventure and photography.

Kaw River State Park: The only urban state park in Kansas, located in Topeka along the Kansas River. It offers trails for hiking, biking, and running, plus river access for paddling and wildlife observation. Though small, it's a valuable green space blending natural beauty with city access, serving as a hub for outdoor recreation within the state capital's urban landscape.

Lake Scott State Park: Nestled in western Kansas' canyons, this park centers on Lake Scott and preserves El Cuartelejo, the state's only known Native American pueblo ruins. Visitors enjoy fishing, boating, hiking, and camping amid striking cliffs and lush valleys. Its blend of recreation, archaeology, and natural beauty makes it a National Historic Landmark and one of Kansas' most unique parks.

Lehigh Portland State Park: Centered on reclaimed quarry lands near Iola, this park features rugged trails winding through limestone bluffs, woodlands, and wetlands. Visitors can hike, bike, or run along more than 10 miles of singletrack and rail-trail connections, with access to the South Fork of the Neosho River. Its diverse terrain makes it a rising destination for outdoor adventure in southeast Kansas.

Little Jerusalem Badlands State Park: In the Smoky Hills of western Kansas, this park protects the state's largest Niobrara chalk formation. Towering white cliffs, spires, and buttes carved by erosion create a surreal landscape. Designated trails lead to dramatic overlooks, offering sweeping views of the High Plains. It's a geologic wonder and premier site for hiking, photography, and wildlife observation.

Lovewell State Park: Covering 1,160 acres around Lovewell Reservoir in north-central Kansas, this park is popular for fishing, boating, and camping. It features scenic lake views, wildlife-rich habitats, and family-friendly facilities like picnic shelters and playgrounds. Known for walleye fishing, Lovewell blends recreation and relaxation, attracting anglers and outdoor enthusiasts year-round.

Meade State Park: A tranquil 440-acre park in southwest Kansas' High Plains, centered on an 80-acre lake. Visitors enjoy boating, fishing, and camping in a prairie landscape, with trails for hiking and wildlife viewing. Shaded picnic areas and open skies make it a peaceful destination, ideal for stargazing, birdwatching, and quiet getaways in a remote but welcoming setting.

Milford State Park: Located on Milford Reservoir in northeast Kansas, this park is among the largest in the state. It offers fishing, boating, swimming, hiking, and camping across diverse habitats. Trails highlight tallgrass prairie, wetlands, and abundant wildlife, including eagles. With full-service campgrounds and year-round recreation, it's a prime destination for anglers, birders, and outdoor families.

Mushroom Rock State Park: One of Kansas' smallest parks, located in central Kansas, but home to some of its most unusual geology. The park features giant sandstone concretions eroded into mushroom-like shapes, formed millions of years ago. Though compact, it's a favorite for short hikes, photography, and picnics, offering a fascinating look at Kansas' natural history in a unique setting.

Perry State Park: Encompassing 1,200 acres on Perry Reservoir in northeast Kansas, this park offers boating, fishing, hiking, and camping. It includes equestrian and biking trails, scenic woodlands, and abundant wildlife. With multiple campgrounds, day-use areas, and lake access, it's a favorite for families, anglers, and outdoor enthusiasts seeking recreation near Lawrence and Topeka.

Pomona State Park: Located on Pomona Reservoir in east-central Kansas, this park covers 490 acres and provides year-round recreation. Visitors enjoy boating, fishing, swimming, and hiking through prairie and woodland. With scenic campgrounds, picnic shelters, and wildlife-rich landscapes, Pomona offers both relaxation and adventure, making it a popular destination for families and weekend getaways.

Prairie Dog State Park: Situated in northwest Kansas around Keith Sebelius Reservoir, this park is named for its prairie dog colony and also features restored sod and stone houses from the 19th century. It offers boating, fishing, camping, and wildlife viewing. The blend of cultural history, prairie scenery, and outdoor recreation makes it one of Kansas' most distinctive state parks.

KANSAS

☐ 🔖 ♡ **Prairie Spirit Trail State Park:** A 51-mile rail-trail stretching through eastern Kansas, ideal for hiking, biking, and horseback riding. Passing through prairie landscapes, woodlands, and small towns, it provides a unique way to explore the state's natural and cultural heritage. With multiple trailheads and gentle grades, it's perfect for both short outings and multi-day adventures.

☐ 🔖 ♡ **Sand Hills State Park:** Adjacent to Hutchinson, this 1,123-acre park preserves sand dunes, grasslands, and woodlands. It offers equestrian, hiking, and biking trails through rolling dunes and shaded groves, making it a diverse ecological landscape. Wildlife viewing and birdwatching are popular, and its unique terrain provides a rare natural setting in central Kansas.

☐ 🔖 ♡ **Tuttle Creek State Park:** Located on the 12,500-acre Tuttle Creek Reservoir near Manhattan, this park spans over 1,200 acres in four units. It offers boating, fishing, hiking, camping, and swimming, with trails highlighting prairie and woodland habitats. With picnic areas, marinas, and family-friendly facilities, it's one of Kansas' most visited and versatile recreation destinations.

☐ 🔖 ♡ **Webster State Park:** Nestled in northwestern Kansas near the Solomon River Valley, this park surrounds Webster Reservoir. Known for boating, fishing, camping, and hiking, it's especially popular during bird migrations, with excellent waterfowl viewing. Surrounded by rolling prairies and scenic hills, Webster provides a peaceful retreat and a rich habitat for wildlife lovers.

☐ 🔖 ♡ **Wilson State Park:** Set on Wilson Reservoir in central Kansas, this park spans over 900 acres and is renowned for its rugged beauty. Its hiking and biking trails wind through rocky outcrops and tallgrass prairie, offering some of the state's best scenery. Popular for boating, fishing, and camping, Wilson is considered Kansas' most picturesque park, drawing outdoor enthusiasts statewide.

National Parks

☐ 🔖 ♡ **Brown v. Board of Education National Historic Site:** Located in Topeka, this site commemorates the 1954 Supreme Court case that ended racial segregation in public schools. Centered at Monroe Elementary School, it features exhibits, films, and programs that explore the Civil Rights Movement and the ongoing struggle for equality in education and American life.

☐ 🔖 ♡ **Fort Larned National Historic Site:** Preserving one of the best-kept frontier Army posts from the Indian Wars era, Fort Larned offers a look into 19th-century military life on the plains. Original sandstone buildings, costumed interpreters, and exhibits bring to life the fort's role in protecting trade routes and managing relations with Native Americans.

☐ 🔖 ♡ **Fort Scott National Historic Site:** Situated in Fort Scott, this 19th-century fort reveals the region's turbulent history during Indian Removal, Bleeding Kansas, and the Civil War. Visitors can explore preserved buildings, parade grounds, and exhibits that highlight the U.S. Army's role in expansion, conflict, and compromise on the western frontier.

☐ 🔖 ♡ **Nicodemus National Historic Site:** In Graham County, this site preserves the history of Nicodemus, a settlement founded by formerly enslaved African Americans after the Civil War. Visitors can tour historic structures and learn how this unique community thrived despite hardships, symbolizing resilience, freedom, and opportunity in the Great Plains.

☐ 🔖 ♡ **Tallgrass Prairie National Preserve:** Located in the Flint Hills, this preserve protects one of the last remaining sections of North America's tallgrass prairie. Visitors can hike rolling grasslands, spot bison and prairie wildlife, and tour historic ranch buildings, discovering the ecological and cultural heritage of a landscape that once covered millions of acres.

KANSAS

National Grasslands

☐ ◫ ♡ **Cimarron National Grassland:** A current National Grassland administered by the U.S. Forest Service, covering 108,175 acres in Morton and Stevens Counties. Characterized by semi-arid shortgrass prairie, sand sagebrush flats, and the Cimarron River corridor. Offers scenic drives, wildlife watching (elk, prairie chickens), hiking, camping, and historic Santa Fe Trail landmarks.

National Scenic Byways & All-American Roads

☐ ◫ ♡ **Flint Hills Scenic Byway (K-177):** This 47-mile National Scenic Byway winds through Kansas's Flint Hills, one of the last tallgrass prairies in North America. Travelers see sweeping vistas, wildflowers, bison herds, and historic ranches. With interpretive stops and hiking access, it's an immersive way to explore the region's natural beauty and cultural heritage.

☐ ◫ ♡ **Wetlands & Wildlife Scenic Byway:** This 72-mile National Scenic Byway loops through central Kansas wetlands, including Cheyenne Bottoms and Quivira National Wildlife Refuge. Seasonal migrations bring hundreds of bird species, including cranes and shorebirds. Interpretive sites, observation points, and marsh vistas highlight the area's ecological significance.

State Scenic Byways

☐ ◫ ♡ **Glacial Hills Scenic Byway:** Running through northeast Kansas along K-7, this byway winds across glacier-carved hills, wooded ridges, and fertile valleys. Travelers encounter scenic farmland, river overlooks, and historic towns like Leavenworth and Atchison. Interpretive stops highlight Ice Age geology, Native American history, and early settlement, making it a varied and picturesque route.

☐ ◫ ♡ **Gypsum Hills Scenic Byway:** This 42-mile drive west of Medicine Lodge showcases red mesas, buttes, and gypsum-rich outcrops unique to the High Plains. Contrasting green grasslands and blue skies create striking scenery, while ranching heritage, wildlife, and recreational opportunities enrich the route. Scenic pullouts and trails make it a popular destination for photographers and explorers.

☐ ◫ ♡ **Land and Sky Scenic Byway:** Kansas's first multi-county byway highlights the state's agricultural heartland. Running 88 miles through Cheyenne, Sherman, and Wallace Counties, it offers endless horizons of wheat, corn, and sunflowers framed by the High Plains. Interpretive sites reveal farming traditions, wildlife, and natural grasslands, celebrating both the land's productivity and its wide-open beauty.

☐ ◫ ♡ **Native Stone Scenic Byway:** Located along K-99 in the Flint Hills, this byway highlights the region's native limestone heritage. Dry-laid stone fences, barns, and historic bridges line rolling prairies and oak-filled valleys. Travelers see how geology shaped both landscape and architecture, blending natural beauty with pioneer craftsmanship in one of Kansas's most culturally rich drives.

☐ ◫ ♡ **Post Rock Scenic Byway:** This 18-mile route along K-232 between Wilson and Lucas is framed by Smoky Hills scenery and the shores of Wilson Lake. The byway celebrates the region's hand-quarried limestone "post rocks," once used for fencing and building. Scenic pullouts, cultural attractions, and lake views highlight the area's blend of history, geology, and striking prairie landscapes.

☐ ◫ ♡ **Prairie Trail Scenic Byway:** Stretching 56 miles through central Kansas, this byway links Canton, Lindsborg, and Marquette with farmland, Smoky Hill River overlooks, and wildlife refuges. Highlights include Maxwell Wildlife Refuge, where bison and elk roam, and Lindsborg's Swedish heritage. The route blends prairie scenery with cultural experiences, offering both natural and historic richness.

☐ ◫ ♡ **Smoky Valley Scenic Byway:** This 60-mile drive loops through Trego and Ness Counties, showcasing rolling Smoky Hill River valleys, prairie bluffs, and wildlife habitats. Points of interest include Cedar Bluff Reservoir, state fishing lakes, and historic trails once used by pioneers. Quiet roads, scenic overlooks, and birdwatching opportunities make it a peaceful Great Plains journey.

KANSAS
National Natural Landmarks

Baldwin Woods: Recognized as a National Natural Landmark, Baldwin Woods represents a rare remnant of the oak–hickory forests that once blanketed eastern Kansas. Its mature canopy and rich understory provide habitat for native mammals, birds, and wildflowers. The forest's isolation has preserved its biodiversity, making it a valuable link to the region's natural past.
GPS: 38.7539, -95.2186

Big Basin Prairie Preserve: Big Basin Prairie Preserve holds National Natural Landmark status for its remarkable sinkholes and collapse features formed by groundwater action. Encompassing mixed-grass prairie with buffalo grass and seasonal wildflowers, it also shelters wildlife around a spring-fed pond. This site highlights both ecological diversity and the geology of the High Plains.
GPS: 37.2403, -99.9975

Haskell-Baker Wetlands: Haskell-Baker Wetlands is a National Natural Landmark for preserving one of Kansas's finest wetland prairies. Its seasonally flooded habitat sustains migratory birds, amphibians, and diverse plant life. Beyond its ecological richness, the site serves as a living classroom for researchers and students, illustrating the value of prairie wetland ecosystems.
GPS: 38.9167, -95.2333

Monument Rocks: Monument Rocks was designated a National Natural Landmark for its towering chalk formations carved from the Niobrara Formation. Rising from western Kansas plains, these spires and arches contain 80-million-year-old fossils, evidence of the inland sea that once covered the region. Their dramatic form makes them both a geologic and scenic wonder.
GPS: 38.7906, -100.7625

Rock City: Rock City is a National Natural Landmark for its cluster of about 200 massive sandstone concretions, some nearly 20 feet across. Scattered across a prairie hillside, these spherical boulders reveal rare geologic concretion processes. Their size and abundance make Rock City one of the most striking examples of its kind in North America.
GPS: 39.0909, -97.7356

KENTUCKY

Kentucky's landscapes span from the world's longest cave system to forested mountains, rolling hills, and scenic lakes. With an inviting mix of state parks, national forests, a celebrated national park, and fascinating natural landmarks, the Bluegrass State promises rich adventures amid timeless natural beauty and outdoor discovery.

📅 Peak Season
April–June and September–October are Kentucky's peak seasons, offering mild temperatures, blooming landscapes, and colorful fall foliage. These months are ideal for hiking, horseback riding, and exploring caves and parks.

📅 Offseason Months
November–March is the offseason, with colder weather and occasional snow, especially in higher elevations. Winter is quieter, though many scenic areas remain open for hiking and wildlife viewing.

🍃 Scenery & Nature Timing
Spring brings dogwoods, redbuds, and wildflowers across hills and valleys. Summer offers lush forests and lake recreation. Fall transforms the Appalachians and rolling Bluegrass hills with brilliant color, while winter provides peaceful wooded scenery.

✨ Special
Kentucky showcases Mammoth Cave, the world's longest known cave system, and the sandstone arches of Red River Gorge. The Cumberland Falls "moonbow," the rugged Cumberland Plateau, and the rolling Bluegrass region highlight the state's diverse natural beauty.

KENTUCKY

State Parks

☐ 🔖 ♡ **Barren River Lake State Resort Park**: Situated in southern Kentucky, Barren River Lake State Resort Park spans over 1,000 acres and is centered around Barren River Lake. The park offers excellent boating, fishing, and swimming opportunities. Visitors can enjoy the scenic beauty while hiking along the trails or picnicking in the park's designated areas. It also features a lodge, restaurant, and campground, making it a popular destination for a weekend getaway.

☐ 🔖 ♡ **Big Bone Lick State Park**: Located in northern Kentucky, Big Bone Lick State Park is a unique historical and natural park known as the "Birthplace of American Vertebrate Paleontology." The park features salt springs and a museum showcasing prehistoric fossils of mammoths and mastodons. The park offers hiking trails, picnic areas, and a visitor center, making it both an educational and recreational destination for families.

☐ 🔖 ♡ **Blue Licks Battlefield State Resort Park**: Found in central Kentucky, Blue Licks Battlefield State Resort Park commemorates the site of the last battle of the American Revolution fought in Kentucky. The park offers a museum, hiking trails, and a picturesque picnic area with a view of the Licking River. Visitors can learn about the historic battle and enjoy outdoor activities like fishing, hiking, and camping.

☐ 🔖 ♡ **Breaks Interstate Park**: Located on the Kentucky-Virginia border, Breaks Interstate Park is often referred to as the "Grand Canyon of the South" due to its deep gorge and stunning views. The park offers hiking trails, fishing, and camping, along with a lodge that provides panoramic views of the gorge. The park's rich biodiversity and dramatic landscapes make it a perfect destination for nature lovers.

☐ 🔖 ♡ **Buckhorn Lake State Resort Park**: Situated in the Daniel Boone National Forest, Buckhorn Lake State Resort Park offers over 1,000 acres of outdoor recreational activities, including boating, fishing, and hiking. The park is set around Buckhorn Lake and provides opportunities for camping, hiking trails, and picnicking, making it a favorite among families and outdoor enthusiasts.

☐ 🔖 ♡ **Carr Creek State Park**: Located in eastern Kentucky, Carr Creek State Park is a beautiful park set around Carr Creek Lake. Visitors can enjoy fishing, boating, and swimming, with the surrounding forests providing excellent hiking opportunities. The park features picnic areas and camping facilities, making it an ideal location for a peaceful retreat in the Appalachian foothills.

☐ 🔖 ♡ **Carter Caves State Resort Park**: Found in northeastern Kentucky, Carter Caves State Resort Park is known for its limestone caves and unique geological features. Visitors can explore the park's caves, including the popular X-Cave and Cascade Cave, or hike the numerous trails that wind through lush woodlands. The park also offers a lodge, camping facilities, and opportunities for fishing and picnicking.

☐ 🔖 ♡ **Columbus-Belmont State Park**: Located in western Kentucky, this park is known for its historical significance during the Civil War. The park features a museum and interpretive exhibits about the Battle of Belmont, along with picnic areas and hiking trails. The park offers beautiful views of the Mississippi River, making it a great spot for history buffs and nature lovers alike.

☐ 🔖 ♡ **Cumberland Falls State Resort Park**: Often referred to as the "Niagara of the South," Cumberland Falls is one of the most famous state parks in Kentucky. The park is known for its 68-foot waterfall and the rare moonbow phenomenon, which occurs on clear nights during a full moon. Visitors can hike the surrounding trails, fish, and camp, or simply enjoy the breathtaking views of the falls and the Cumberland River.

☐ 🔖 ♡ **Dale Hollow Lake State Resort Park**: Located in southern Kentucky, Dale Hollow Lake State Resort Park is centered around a 27,000-acre lake known for its crystal-clear waters. The park offers a wide range of activities including boating, fishing, hiking, and camping. It also features a golf course and a lodge, making it a popular destination for water sports and outdoor relaxation.

KENTUCKY

☐ 🔖 ♡ **E. P. "Tom" Sawyer State Park**: Located in Louisville, E. P. "Tom" Sawyer State Park is an urban park offering a variety of recreational activities. It features hiking and biking trails, sports fields, a swimming pool, and a pond for fishing. The park is popular among locals for its wide range of amenities and accessible location, providing a perfect escape for outdoor enthusiasts within the city.

☐ 🔖 ♡ **Fishtrap Lake State Park**: Tucked into the Appalachian hills of Pike County, Fishtrap Lake State Park is centered on a 1,100-acre lake built by the U.S. Army Corps of Engineers. Known for its peaceful, undeveloped shoreline, the park offers boating, kayaking, and some of the region's best bass and crappie fishing. Hiking trails, camping areas, and quiet picnic spots make it a serene retreat for outdoor enthusiasts.

☐ 🔖 ♡ **Fort Boonesborough State Park**: Situated in central Kentucky, Fort Boonesborough State Park commemorates the historic fort established by Daniel Boone and his settlers in 1775. The park features a reconstructed fort, a museum, and educational exhibits on pioneer life. Visitors can also enjoy hiking trails, fishing, and camping within the park's scenic landscapes.

☐ 🔖 ♡ **General Burnside Island State Park**: Located in southern Kentucky, General Burnside Island State Park is situated on an island in Lake Cumberland. The park features a golf course, hiking trails, and several boating and fishing opportunities. It's an ideal spot for outdoor activities and offers a lodge with spectacular views of the lake.

☐ 🔖 ♡ **General Butler State Resort Park**: Found in northern Kentucky, General Butler State Resort Park offers a variety of outdoor activities such as hiking, fishing, and picnicking. The park also features a golf course and lodge, making it a popular destination for both relaxation and recreation. Visitors can enjoy scenic views of the Ohio River from the park's many vantage points.

☐ 🔖 ♡ **Grayson Lake State Park**: Situated in northeastern Kentucky, Grayson Lake State Park is centered around Grayson Lake and offers boating, fishing, hiking, and camping opportunities. The park is known for its beautiful landscapes, including rolling hills and forested areas that provide a perfect setting for outdoor activities.

☐ 🔖 ♡ **Green River Lake State Park**: Located in central Kentucky, Green River Lake State Park offers a 1,000-acre lake that is perfect for boating, fishing, and swimming. The park also features hiking trails, picnicking areas, and camping facilities, making it a great place for family outings and outdoor adventures.

☐ 🔖 ♡ **Greenbo Lake State Resort Park**: Found in northeastern Kentucky, Greenbo Lake State Resort Park offers a beautiful 10-acre lake, ideal for fishing and boating. The park also features hiking trails, a marina, and several picnic areas, providing a peaceful environment for outdoor activities. It's also known for its natural beauty and rich history.

☐ 🔖 ♡ **Jenny Wiley State Resort Park**: Located in eastern Kentucky, Jenny Wiley State Resort Park offers hiking, fishing, boating, and camping opportunities. The park is named after Jenny Wiley, a pioneer woman who survived captivity by Native Americans, and the area offers both historical significance and outdoor recreation.

☐ 🔖 ♡ **John James Audubon State Park**: Situated in western Kentucky, this park is dedicated to the life and work of the famous naturalist, John James Audubon. Visitors can explore the park's museum, hike nature trails, and observe a variety of bird species in their natural habitat. The park is known for its diverse wildlife and beautiful landscapes.

☐ 🔖 ♡ **Kenlake State Resort Park**: Nestled on the western shore of Kentucky Lake, Kenlake State Resort Park is known for its panoramic waterfront views and access to the massive Land Between the Lakes region. The park features a lodge, cottages, marina, and tennis center, along with hiking trails and picnic areas. Its combination of outdoor adventure and comfortable amenities makes it a premier lakeside getaway.

☐ 🔖 ♡ **Kentucky Dam Village State Resort Park**: Situated on the northern tip of Kentucky Lake, Kentucky Dam Village State Resort Park is one of the state's largest and most popular parks. It offers a marina, beach, golf course, lodge, cottages, and campgrounds. With boating, fishing, hiking, and birdwatching opportunities, it serves as a hub for water recreation and a gateway to the Land Between the Lakes region.

KENTUCKY

☐ 🔖 ♡ **Kincaid Lake State Park:** Located in northern Kentucky near Falmouth, Kincaid Lake State Park surrounds a 183-acre lake popular for boating, swimming, and fishing for bass, catfish, and crappie. The park offers a campground, mini-golf, hiking trails, and a sandy beach for summer fun. With picnic shelters and a family-friendly atmosphere, it's a favorite spot for both relaxation and recreation.

☐ 🔖 ♡ **Kingdom Come State Park:** Perched atop Pine Mountain in southeastern Kentucky, Kingdom Come State Park offers dramatic vistas from 2,700 feet, with overlooks like Raven Rock and Log Rock. The park features eight miles of hiking trails, a serene mountain lake for paddling and fishing, and abundant wildlife viewing. Its rugged cliffs, cool forests, and sweeping mountain scenery make it a true Appalachian treasure.

☐ 🔖 ♡ **Lake Barkley State Resort Park:** Stretching along the eastern shore of Lake Barkley, this expansive resort park offers a marina, lodge, cottages, golf course, campground, and swimming beach. Surrounded by rolling woodlands, it's perfect for fishing, boating, hiking, and wildlife viewing. Its location near Land Between the Lakes makes it a hub for exploring one of Kentucky's most scenic regions.

☐ 🔖 ♡ **Lake Cumberland State Resort Park:** Perched above the shores of one of the nation's largest man-made lakes, this resort park spans 1,400 acres and is a hub for boating, fishing, and water sports. Visitors enjoy a full-service marina, lodge, cottages, and a lakeside restaurant, along with hiking trails and campgrounds. Its sweeping vistas make it a premier Kentucky destination for outdoor adventure.

☐ 🔖 ♡ **Lake Malone State Park:** Nestled among sandstone bluffs and dense hardwood forest in western Kentucky, Lake Malone State Park surrounds a 788-acre lake ideal for swimming, boating, and fishing. The park features a campground, sandy beach, and scenic hiking trails like the Laurel Trail, which winds through wildflowers and cliff formations. It's a tranquil spot for families and nature lovers alike.

☐ 🔖 ♡ **Lincoln Homestead State Park:** Found in central Kentucky, Lincoln Homestead State Park is the birthplace of Abraham Lincoln's parents. Visitors can tour the historic cabin, explore the museum, and enjoy picnicking areas in this peaceful and historically significant park.

☐ 🔖 ♡ **Mineral Mound State Park:** Located in western Kentucky, Mineral Mound State Park offers scenic views of Lake Barkley and provides opportunities for hiking, fishing, and picnicking. The park also features a golf course, making it an ideal destination for both outdoor activities and relaxation in a peaceful environment.

☐ 🔖 ♡ **My Old Kentucky Home State Park:** Situated in Bardstown, this state park is dedicated to the memory of the home of U.S. Congressman and famous composer Stephen Foster. The park offers tours of the historic mansion, which inspired Foster's song "My Old Kentucky Home." The park also features gardens, hiking trails, and picnic areas, making it a perfect blend of history and outdoor beauty.

☐ 🔖 ♡ **Natural Bridge State Resort Park:** Located in the Red River Gorge area, Natural Bridge State Resort Park is famous for its 78-foot natural sandstone arch spanning 65 feet. The park offers over 20 miles of hiking trails, a sky lift to the arch, and access to world-renowned climbing and natural scenery. Visitors can enjoy a lodge, cabins, and picnicking, making it a destination for both outdoor adventure and relaxation.

☐ 🔖 ♡ **Nolin Lake State Park:** Found in central Kentucky, Nolin Lake State Park is set around Nolin Lake, which offers opportunities for boating, fishing, and swimming. The park features hiking trails and picnicking areas, providing a relaxing environment for families and outdoor enthusiasts. The scenic views of the lake and surrounding forest make it a great spot for a day out in nature.

☐ 🔖 ♡ **Old Fort Harrod State Park:** Located in Harrodsburg, this park preserves the site of the first permanent settlement in Kentucky. The park features a reconstructed fort, a museum, and exhibits detailing the early history of Kentucky's settlement. Visitors can explore the fort, hike nearby trails, and learn about the state's pioneer history.

☐ 🔖 ♡ **Paintsville Lake State Park:** Situated in eastern Kentucky, Paintsville Lake State Park offers a scenic 72-acre lake, making it ideal for boating, fishing, and swimming. The park also features hiking trails, picnicking areas, and camping facilities. The park's natural beauty and outdoor opportunities make it a favorite among those seeking a peaceful retreat.

UNITED STATES EDITION

KENTUCKY

☐ 🔖 ♡ **Pennyrile Forest State Resort Park**: Located in western Kentucky, this park is known for its dense forests and serene atmosphere. It offers hiking trails, fishing opportunities, and picnicking areas. The park's lodge and cottages provide accommodations for visitors looking to explore the beauty of the Pennyrile Forest and enjoy outdoor activities like wildlife viewing and horseback riding.

☐ 🔖 ♡ **Pine Mountain State Resort Park**: Situated in southeastern Kentucky, Pine Mountain State Resort Park is the state's first state park and offers over 1,400 acres of outdoor recreation. The park features hiking trails, including the challenging Pinnacle Trail, which offers panoramic views of the Appalachian Mountains. The park also offers cabins, a lodge, and picnic areas for a perfect outdoor getaway.

☐ 🔖 ♡ **Rough River Dam State Resort Park**: Located in western Kentucky, Rough River Dam State Resort Park is centered around Rough River Lake. The park offers boating, fishing, hiking, and picnicking opportunities, along with a lodge and restaurant for visitors. The park is a popular destination for water sports and family activities in a tranquil setting.

☐ 🔖 ♡ **Taylorsville Lake State Park**: Located in central Kentucky, this park is centered around Taylorsville Lake and provides excellent opportunities for fishing, boating, and swimming. The park also offers hiking trails and camping facilities, making it a great place for families and outdoor adventurers to enjoy a day on the water or explore the surrounding nature.

☐ 🔖 ♡ **Whitley State Park**: Located in southeastern Kentucky, Whitley State Park is a peaceful park offering fishing, boating, and hiking opportunities. The park is centered around a 60-acre lake and features several miles of hiking trails, making it a perfect destination for those seeking a relaxing day surrounded by nature.

☐ 🔖 ♡ **Yatesville Lake State Park**: Located in eastern Kentucky near Louisa, Yatesville Lake State Park features a 2,300-acre lake with three boat ramps, a full-service marina, and some of the best bass fishing in the region. The park also offers an 18-hole golf course, hiking trails, camping, and scenic picnic spots, making it a favorite for boating, fishing, and family recreation in a peaceful Appalachian setting.

National Parks

☐ 🔖 ♡ **Abraham Lincoln Birthplace National Historical Park**: Located in Hodgenville, Kentucky, this park preserves the birthplace and boyhood home of Abraham Lincoln. Visitors can see the Birth Cabin Memorial, walk the historic farm, and explore exhibits about Lincoln's early life. The site reflects how his rural upbringing shaped his values and leadership during the nation's most turbulent era.

☐ 🔖 ♡ **Big South Fork National River and Recreation Area**: Straddling the Tennessee–Kentucky border, this recreation area protects a scenic stretch of the Big South Fork River. Surrounded by sandstone bluffs, natural arches, and forested gorges, it offers hiking, horseback riding, camping, and paddling. The park showcases rugged Appalachian beauty, abundant wildlife, and opportunities for outdoor adventure.

☐ 🔖 ♡ **Camp Nelson Heritage National Monument**: Situated in Jessamine County, Kentucky, this historic site preserves one of the Union's largest Civil War supply depots and recruitment centers. It became a vital refuge for formerly enslaved people and a key training ground for African American soldiers. Visitors explore preserved buildings, exhibits, and monuments honoring freedom and military service.

☐ 🔖 ♡ **Cumberland Gap National Historical Park**: At the crossroads of Kentucky, Tennessee, and Virginia, this park safeguards the historic Cumberland Gap, once a gateway for westward settlers. Trails lead through forests, caves, and overlooks with sweeping mountain views. The site highlights the natural passageway's role in American migration and its enduring cultural significance.

KENTUCKY

Mammoth Cave National Park: Home to the world's longest known cave system, this Kentucky park offers guided tours into vast underground chambers and labyrinthine passages. Above ground, visitors find hiking trails, rivers, and forest habitats supporting diverse wildlife. The park blends geology, ecology, and history, making it a globally significant natural wonder.

Mill Springs Battlefield National Monument: Located in Pulaski County, Kentucky, this site preserves the battlefield of a pivotal 1862 Union victory. The engagement marked a turning point in securing Kentucky for the North during the Civil War. Visitors can tour interpretive trails, monuments, and exhibits that reveal the battle's importance in the western theater.

State & National Forests

Big Rivers State Forest & Wildlife Management Area: Located in Union and Crittenden counties along the Ohio and Mississippi Rivers, this forest preserves bottomland hardwood ecosystems and provides critical habitat for migratory birds. It supports controlled timber management, wildlife conservation, and seasonal recreation such as hunting, fishing, and birdwatching across a varied riverine landscape.

Daniel Boone National Forest: Covering approximately 708,000 acres of federal land within a 2.1 million-acre boundary across 21 eastern Kentucky counties, this rugged forest lies along the Appalachian Plateau. Established in 1937 (renamed in 1966), it features over 600 miles of trails, two wilderness areas, sandstone cliffs, waterfalls, and diverse recreation including hiking, camping, rock climbing, boating, and hunting.

Dewey Lake State Forest: A ~7,350-acre forest in Floyd County, leased from the Army Corps and established near Dewey Lake. It features mixed hardwood and pine stands along rolling hills and shorelines. The forest supports timber research, watershed protection, and passive recreation including hiking, wildlife observation, and hunting.

Green River State Forest: Located just east of Henderson, this 1,092-acre forest centers on bottomland hardwood and cedar swamp along the Green and Ohio rivers. Established in 1998, it is Kentucky's first carbon-sequestration project with hardwood regeneration and wetland restoration. Offers hiking, birdwatching, hunting, and educational recreation along floodplain forests.

Kentenia State Forest: The first state forest in Kentucky, established in 1919 across seven tracts totaling about 4,277 acres on Pine Mountain near Harlan. Donated by a coal company, it supports oak-hickory woodland conservation and sustainable timber management. Includes scenic Little Shepherd Trail along the ridge—popular for hiking and forestry research.

Kentucky Ridge State Forest: Located in Bell County, this ~15,250-acre forest was created in 1930 from federal lands and transferred to state management in 1954. It occupies Pine Mountain's forested ridge, offering mixed hardwood and pine ecosystems. The property includes Pine Mountain State Resort Park and supports recreation, conservation, and watershed stewardship.

Knobs State Forest and Wildlife Management Area: Established in 2006 near Shepherdsville, this 2,035-acre forest protects upland hardwoods on the Knobs. Managed for sustainable timber production and wildlife habitat, it offers about six miles of hiking trails and controlled hunting opportunities within rolling, forested terrain. A former tree farm conserved for public use.

Marion County State Forest & Wildlife Management Area: Located in Marion County, this state forest supports mixed pine-hardwood stands and wildlife conservation efforts. It functions as a wildlife management area with controlled hunting, forestry research, and habitat restoration, although public trails and facilities are limited.

Marrowbone State Forest & Wildlife Management Area: Spanning Metcalfe and Cumberland counties, this forest supports mixed hardwood conservation and wildlife habitat. Managed under a cooperative model as a wildlife management area, it allows seasonal hunting, limited recreation, and supports sustainable forestry practices.

KENTUCKY

☐ 🔖 ♡ **Olympia State Forest:** A 780-acre forest in Bath County near Morehead, Olympia consists of upland hardwood and pine stands. Established for demonstration forestry and conservation education, it provides a natural woodland backdrop for passive recreation, tree research, and limited wildlife observation.

☐ 🔖 ♡ **Pennyrile State Forest:** Adjacent to Pennyrile Forest State Resort Park in Christian County, this forest supports pine-hardwood ecosystems. It manages sustainable timber harvesting and watershed protection while offering trails, wildlife habitat, and habitat corridors that enhance the surrounding state park experience.

☐ 🔖 ♡ **Tygarts State Forest:** Located near Carter Caves State Resort Park in Carter County, this 874-acre forest was established in 1957. Characterized by mixed woodlands of hardwoods and pines on plateau terrain, it supports forest research, habitat conservation, and low-impact recreation such as wildlife viewing and nature study.

National Scenic Byways & All-American Roads

☐ 🔖 ♡ **Country Music Highway:** Following US 23 in eastern Kentucky, this 144-mile National Scenic Byway honors the region's legendary country musicians, including Loretta Lynn, Ricky Skaggs, and Dwight Yoakam. Museums, markers, and coalfield towns celebrate Appalachian culture. Panoramic vistas of forested hills, historic communities, and rich musical heritage define the drive.

☐ 🔖 ♡ **Great River Road:** Kentucky's stretch of this All-American Road traces the Mississippi River through western counties. Scenic overlooks, bluffs, ferry crossings, and wildlife refuges highlight river life. Linking small towns with historic trade routes, the drive connects travelers to both regional culture and the sweeping landscapes of America's iconic waterway.

☐ 🔖 ♡ **Lincoln Heritage Scenic Highway:** This 71-mile National Scenic Byway runs from Hodgenville to Danville, connecting sites tied to Abraham Lincoln's early life. Stops include his birthplace, Civil War landmarks, bourbon distilleries, and historic farm country. Rolling Bluegrass hills and cultural attractions blend presidential heritage with Kentucky tradition.

☐ 🔖 ♡ **Old Frankfort Pike Historic and Scenic Byway:** A short but iconic National Scenic Byway between Lexington and Frankfort, this road showcases Kentucky's horse country. Stone fences, elegant horse farms, and historic estates line the corridor. Recognized for its preserved landscape and equestrian culture, it's one of the most picturesque drives in the Bluegrass region.

☐ 🔖 ♡ **Red River Gorge Scenic Byway:** Winding through Daniel Boone National Forest, this National Scenic Byway passes towering sandstone cliffs, natural arches, and deep ravines. Trailheads, picnic areas, and overlooks immerse travelers in one of Kentucky's most beloved natural areas. The byway is a gateway to world-class climbing, hiking, and wilderness scenery.

☐ 🔖 ♡ **Wilderness Road Heritage Highway:** Stretching 94 miles from Cumberland Gap to Berea, this National Scenic Byway follows Daniel Boone's frontier route. Historic settlements, Civil War sites, Appalachian ridges, and mountain valleys line the way. The route honors Kentucky's pioneer heritage while revealing rugged landscapes and cultural landmarks of the Cumberland Plateau.

☐ 🔖 ♡ **Woodlands Trace National Scenic Byway (The Trace):** Running 43 miles through Land Between the Lakes National Recreation Area, this ridge-top byway connects lakes, forests, and wildlife areas. Overlooks, visitor centers, and trails reveal one of the Southeast's largest recreation corridors. It's a tranquil journey through rich natural habitats and outdoor adventure areas.

KENTUCKY

State Scenic Byways

☐ 🔖 ♡ **Big Bone Lick/Middle Creek Parkway:** This byway links Big Bone Lick State Park with surrounding marshes, farmland, and river views. Fossil beds, historic salt licks, and pastoral scenery highlight the region's paleontological and cultural heritage while offering a peaceful countryside drive in Boone County.

☐ 🔖 ♡ **Bill Monroe Bluegrass Trail:** Spanning central Kentucky, this byway celebrates the Father of Bluegrass through markers, towns, and landscapes tied to Monroe's legacy. Rolling farmland, limestone fences, and cultural sites provide a journey that blends rural charm with the birthplace of one of America's most enduring musical genres.

☐ 🔖 ♡ **Everly Brothers Rock-N-Roll Route:** Nearly 100 miles through western Kentucky, this route honors the Everly Brothers. Murals, music markers, and historic venues spotlight early rock and roll while farm country and small towns add authentic rural scenery. The drive mixes cultural history with a landscape that inspired a musical revolution.

☐ 🔖 ♡ **W.C. Handy Blues Route:** This route traces the life of W.C. Handy, the "Father of the Blues," through western Kentucky's river towns. Travelers encounter blues heritage museums, historic markers, and pastoral farmland. The byway highlights the cultural roots of a genre that shaped American music while offering scenic and historic variety.

☐ 🔖 ♡ **Boone Creek Scenic Byway:** Southeast of Lexington, this loop meanders past limestone ravines, wooded ridges, and pastoral horse farms. Historic stone fences line the route, adding to its timeless Bluegrass character. Visitors discover quiet creek valleys and rolling farmland within easy reach of the city, blending scenic beauty with rural tranquility.

☐ 🔖 ♡ **Cordell Hull Highway:** Named for the U.S. statesman, this byway links Cumberland Gap to Mammoth Cave. Winding through forested hills and rural valleys, it highlights historic churches, timber country, and Appalachian scenery. The drive preserves pioneer heritage while offering travelers sweeping mountain landscapes and rustic cultural landmarks.

☐ 🔖 ♡ **Cumberland Cultural Heritage Highway:** Nearly 200 miles of southeastern Kentucky roadway, this byway showcases Appalachian culture through Civil War sites, coal towns, small museums, and forested valleys. Scenic lakes, rivers, and mountain ridges accompany the journey, preserving local traditions while immersing travelers in rugged natural beauty.

☐ 🔖 ♡ **Duncan Hines Scenic Road:** Near Bowling Green, this route honors America's famous food critic. Travelers encounter rolling farmland, small towns, and roadside Americana tied to mid-20th-century heritage. Historic homes, barns, and community markers capture an era of dining and travel, blending cultural stories with pastoral Kentucky scenery.

☐ 🔖 ♡ **Highway 524 Loop:** A rural loop in Oldham County, this short byway travels through rolling farmland, wooded hollows, and historic farmsteads. Quiet and lightly traveled, it provides a glimpse into Kentucky's traditional agrarian landscape. The corridor reflects the enduring agricultural heritage of the state's northern region.

☐ 🔖 ♡ **Hughes Lane:** Nestled in Fayette County, this short byway preserves the quiet beauty of Bluegrass farmland. Stone fences, open pastures, and historic farms create a quintessential Kentucky scene. It offers a brief but charming drive highlighting equestrian heritage and the timeless agricultural landscapes of central Kentucky.

☐ 🔖 ♡ **Ironworks Pike:** Running through Fayette County, this route passes horse farms, pastures, and historic estates. The byway highlights Kentucky's equestrian culture while showcasing preserved rural scenery at the edge of suburban growth. It's a scenic corridor that reflects both heritage and the ongoing identity of Bluegrass country.

☐ 🔖 ♡ **Ridgetop Scenic Byway (KY 89):** A 35-mile route along upland ridges, this byway winds through small rural communities and overlooks rolling valleys. The drive highlights traditional homesteads, forested hills, and broad ridgeline perspectives. It's a quiet escape that blends cultural heritage with Kentucky's scenic mountain character.

☐ 🔖 ♡ **Black Mountain Scenic Byway (KY 160):** Climbing into Harlan County's mountains, this route offers panoramic views near Kentucky's highest point. The road reveals coal-mining history, Appalachian culture, and rugged forested terrain. Its sharp curves and ridgeline scenery showcase the dramatic landscapes of southeastern Kentucky.

☐ 🔖 ♡ **Mary Ingles Highway:** Following the Ohio River, this byway recalls the pioneer journey of Mary Ingles. Historic river towns, scenic bluffs, and fertile floodplains line the route, preserving both natural and cultural heritage. The drive offers peaceful river views alongside stories of early frontier survival and settlement.

KENTUCKY

☐ ◻ ♡ **North Cleveland Road:** A short rural corridor in central Kentucky, this byway travels through farmland, stone-lined fields, and wooded hollows. It preserves the pastoral landscapes of the Bluegrass while connecting communities with a traditional scenic route. Its charm lies in the quiet continuity of Kentucky's agrarian heritage.

☐ ◻ ♡ **Old Kentucky Turnpike:** Once a key travel corridor, this historic route preserves the look and feel of early Kentucky roadways. Stone fences, farmsteads, and small towns recall 19th-century travel. Today, it provides a quiet drive blending history with the enduring beauty of Bluegrass fields and rural cultural landscapes.

☐ ◻ ♡ **Pisgah Pike Scenic Byway:** This road runs through one of Kentucky's most celebrated equine regions. Horse farms, historic barns, and elegant stone fences define the route. Rolling fields and pastures offer iconic Bluegrass scenery, while the area's preserved architecture highlights the deep cultural connection between Kentucky and horse breeding.

☐ ◻ ♡ **Midway–Versailles Road (US 62):** Between two charming small towns, this byway winds through Kentucky's horse country. Limestone walls, historic farms, and lush fields reflect equestrian heritage. The route captures the timeless character of the Bluegrass region while connecting vibrant communities rooted in agricultural and cultural traditions.

☐ ◻ ♡ **Riverboat Row Scenic Byway:** A short stretch in Newport along the Ohio River, this byway highlights river heritage with views of historic boats, parks, and the urban waterfront. Blending old and new, it celebrates Northern Kentucky's connection to the river and its evolving cultural identity as a city on the water.

☐ ◻ ♡ **Shakertown Road Scenic Byway:** Leading to Shaker Village of Pleasant Hill, this byway travels past farmland, stone fences, and equine estates. The journey culminates in one of Kentucky's best-preserved historic sites, where Shaker architecture and cultural heritage blend with scenic Bluegrass landscapes for a drive steeped in history.

☐ ◻ ♡ **US 42 Scenic Byway:** Running between Goshen and Louisville's outskirts, this route features farmland, historic estates, and limestone cuttings. It transitions from quiet countryside to suburban communities while preserving glimpses of Kentucky's agricultural past. Scenic views and cultural heritage combine along this northern corridor.

☐ ◻ ♡ **US 68 Scenic Byway:** Spanning much of the state, this byway links bourbon distilleries, historic towns, and rolling Bluegrass landscapes. From small communities to major landmarks, the route highlights Kentucky's pioneer heritage, equestrian tradition, and agricultural richness while offering a scenic journey across varied regions.

☐ ◻ ♡ **Zilpo Road Scenic Byway:** Winding nine miles through Daniel Boone National Forest, this byway connects forested ridges with Cave Run Lake. Hardwood stands, lakeshore overlooks, and campgrounds make it a serene drive for nature lovers. It highlights the forest's recreational treasures while preserving its wild Appalachian character.

National Natural Landmarks

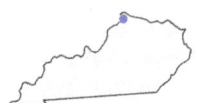 ☐ ◻ ♡ **Big Bone Lick:** Big Bone Lick holds National Natural Landmark status as the "birthplace of American vertebrate paleontology." Salt springs here drew mammoths, mastodons, and other Ice Age animals, leaving behind fossil-rich deposits. The site preserves an irreplaceable record of Pleistocene megafauna and the natural history of North America.
GPS: 38.8869, -84.7478

 ☐ ◻ ♡ **Creelsboro Natural Bridge:** Creelsboro Natural Bridge was designated a National Natural Landmark for being one of Kentucky's largest natural arches. Spanning 104 feet, it was carved by the Cumberland River through subterranean erosion of limestone. The arch showcases the power of water in shaping karst terrain and offers a dramatic example of stream diversion in action.
GPS: 36.8850, -85.2364

KENTUCKY

Henderson Sloughs: Henderson Sloughs earned National Natural Landmark status as one of Kentucky's most important wetland complexes. Its bottomland hardwoods, swamps, and backwater lakes provide critical habitat for migratory birds, amphibians, and fish. Beyond its biodiversity, the sloughs play a vital role in water purification and flood control in the Ohio River Valley.
GPS: 37.8604, -87.7801

Lilley Cornett Woods: Recognized as a National Natural Landmark, Lilley Cornett Woods preserves one of Kentucky's last tracts of virgin mixed mesophytic forest. With towering beech, maple, and tulip poplar trees over 300 years old, it supports extraordinary plant and animal diversity. The site offers rare insight into the untouched ecosystems of the Appalachian Plateau.
GPS: 37.0879, -82.9925

Ohio Coral Reef: At the Falls of the Ohio, this fossil-rich site is recognized as a National Natural Landmark for preserving Silurian and Devonian coral reef communities. Once part of a shallow tropical sea, the exposed limestone beds provide rare access to over 400-million-year-old marine fossils, offering unmatched opportunities for research and education.
GPS: 38.2767, -85.7654

Red River Gorge: Red River Gorge was designated a National Natural Landmark for its remarkable sandstone cliffs, rock shelters, and more than 100 natural arches. This rugged canyon system combines outstanding geologic features with rich biodiversity. It is both a scientific treasure and a world-class recreation area for hiking, climbing, and exploring Kentucky's wild landscapes.
GPS: 37.8339, -83.6078

Rock Creek Research Natural Area: This secluded gorge in Kentucky is a National Natural Landmark for protecting one of the last virgin hemlock–hardwood forests in the state. Its centuries-old trees thrive in an undisturbed setting, offering scientists an invaluable site to study old-growth ecosystems, Appalachian forest succession, and long-term ecological processes.
GPS: 37.2881, -83.8753

LOUISIANA

Louisiana's wild beauty shines in its cypress swamps, bayous, barrier islands, and bird-filled wetlands. Through its array of state parks, national forests, national park sites, and natural landmarks, Louisiana offers soulful and diverse outdoor experiences, where water, wildlife, and culture blend in a landscape unlike any other.

📅 Peak Season
March–May and October–November are Louisiana's peak seasons, with warm, pleasant weather and lower humidity. These months are ideal for outdoor festivals, swamp tours, and exploring parks and bayous before or after the summer heat.

📅 Offseason Months
June–September is the offseason, bringing high heat, humidity, and frequent thunderstorms. Winter (December–February) is generally mild and quieter, though it can still draw visitors to southern coastal regions.

🍃 Scenery & Nature Timing
Spring highlights blooming cypress swamps, bird migrations, and mild conditions. Summer brings lush wetlands and wildlife activity. Fall offers cooler air and golden marsh grasses, while winter attracts migratory birds to coastal refuges.

✨ Special
Louisiana features the vast Atchafalaya Basin, cypress swamps draped in Spanish moss, and the bayous of the Mississippi Delta. The Kisatchie National Forest, coastal wetlands, and barrier islands showcase the state's rich and fragile ecosystems.

LOUISIANA

State Parks

☐ 🔖 ♡ **Bogue Chitto State Park:** This 1,786-acre park in Washington Parish blends cypress-tupelo swamps, hardwood forests, and the spring-fed Bogue Chitto River. Visitors float the clear waters by tube, canoe, or kayak, and explore miles of hiking, biking, and equestrian trails. Cabins, campgrounds, and a bluff-top visitor center make it a family-friendly hub for outdoor adventure.

☐ 🔖 ♡ **Chemin-A-Haut State Park:** On a high bluff above Bayou Bartholomew, this 500-acre northern Louisiana park features scenic overlooks and hardwood forests ideal for hiking and birding. Anglers fish from bayou banks, while families picnic under shady groves. Cabins and campgrounds allow overnight guests to enjoy the peaceful setting steeped in natural and cultural history.

☐ 🔖 ♡ **Chicot State Park:** Louisiana's largest state park surrounds 1,600-acre Lake Chicot with 6,400 acres of rolling forests and wetlands. It's also home to the Louisiana State Arboretum, a living museum showcasing native plants. Hiking, boating, and wildlife viewing abound, while cabins, campgrounds, and picnic areas invite extended stays in this diverse natural retreat.

☐ 🔖 ♡ **Cypremort Point State Park:** On Vermilion Bay near the Gulf, this coastal park offers a rare sandy beach for swimming, picnicking, and relaxing. Anglers prize its waters for redfish and speckled trout, while a boat launch caters to boating and water sports. Trails wind through marshes and coastal habitats, making it a prime spot for wildlife and sunsets.

☐ 🔖 ♡ **Fairview-Riverside State Park:** Nestled along the Tchefuncte River, this small but scenic park blends natural beauty with history. The 19th-century Otis House Museum provides cultural insight, while riverbanks invite fishing and picnicking. Shaded trails and a peaceful campground make it a restful destination, combining Louisiana heritage with tranquil riverside recreation.

☐ 🔖 ♡ **Fontainebleau State Park:** On Lake Pontchartrain's north shore, this 2,800-acre park offers sandy beaches, forested trails, and abundant birdwatching. Once the site of a 19th-century sugar plantation, it now features campgrounds, cabins, and picnic areas. Visitors enjoy swimming, hiking through live oaks and pines, and spotting herons, egrets, and migratory waterfowl.

☐ 🔖 ♡ **Grand Isle State Park:** Louisiana's only inhabited barrier island, Grand Isle offers sandy beaches along the Gulf perfect for swimming, shelling, and picnicking. Renowned for birdwatching and sportfishing, it attracts anglers chasing redfish and speckled trout. A campground provides overnight stays, with the island's unique coastal culture nearby for exploration.

☐ 🔖 ♡ **Jimmie Davis State Park:** On scenic Caney Lake, this north-central park honors the country singer and former governor. Fishing, boating, and water recreation dominate, while hiking trails explore the wooded landscape. Cabins, a lodge, and campgrounds accommodate visitors, who also enjoy picnic pavilions and lakefront views in a setting rich with music heritage.

☐ 🔖 ♡ **Lake Bistineau State Park:** In northwestern Louisiana, this park spans cypress-lined shores of Lake Bistineau. Visitors enjoy boating, fishing, and paddling across moss-draped waters. Trails wind through hardwood forests, and a nature center highlights local ecosystems. With camping, picnicking, and abundant wildlife, it's a haven for outdoor exploration and relaxation.

☐ 🔖 ♡ **Lake Bruin State Park:** Centered on an oxbow lake of the Mississippi, this 1,100-acre lake is famed for its fishing. The park offers boat rentals, piers, and sandy swimming areas, plus hiking and picnicking. Campsites and cabins let guests linger along tranquil waters, making it a relaxing destination for anglers and families alike.

☐ 🔖 ♡ **Lake Claiborne State Park:** Set in pine forests around the 6,400-acre Lake Claiborne, this park offers sandy beaches, fishing, boating, and water sports. Trails explore rolling woodlands and wetlands, while campsites and cabins provide a range of accommodations. Its lodge and picnic facilities make it a versatile spot for group gatherings or quiet escapes.

☐ 🔖 ♡ **Lake D'Arbonne State Park:** Spread along the 15,000-acre Lake D'Arbonne in Union Parish, this park offers endless opportunities for boating, crappie fishing, and wildlife viewing. Trails meander through pine forests and gentle hills, while picnic pavilions, cabins, and campgrounds welcome visitors. Sunsets over the reservoir highlight its peaceful and scenic charm.

LOUISIANA

☐ 🔖 ♡ **Lake Fausse Pointe State Park:** Immersed in the Atchafalaya Basin, this park highlights Louisiana's wetlands and bayous. Canoeing, boating, and fishing offer close encounters with wildlife including alligators, herons, and egrets. Trails and boardwalks lead through cypress swamps, while cabins and campgrounds extend stays in one of the state's most iconic ecosystems.

☐ 🔖 ♡ **North Toledo Bend State Park:** Along the reservoir's western shore, this park is popular with anglers seeking bass and catfish. It also offers boating, hiking trails, and lakefront picnicking. Campgrounds and cabins accommodate families, while abundant wildlife and broad water views create a peaceful retreat in Louisiana's western uplands.

☐ 🔖 ♡ **Palmetto Island State Park:** Set on the Vermilion River, this park highlights Louisiana's lush wetlands. Canoeing, fishing, and hiking immerse visitors in habitats filled with wading birds, turtles, and native plants. Cabins and campgrounds offer overnight stays, while picnic areas provide riverside relaxation. It's a peaceful retreat blending bayous, wildlife, and Cajun country scenery.

☐ 🔖 ♡ **Poverty Point Reservoir State Park:** Anchored by a 2,700-acre lake, this northeastern Louisiana park is known for fishing, boating, and birding. It also connects to the Poverty Point UNESCO World Heritage Site, an ancient Native American earthworks complex. With trails, campgrounds, and cabins, the park combines outdoor recreation with cultural and archaeological significance.

☐ 🔖 ♡ **Sam Houston Jones State Park:** In southwest Louisiana, this park features pine forests, hardwoods, and cypress wetlands surrounding Calcasieu River tributaries. Fishing, hiking, and boating are popular, with trails offering wildlife sightings of deer, birds, and small mammals. With campgrounds, cabins, and picnic pavilions, it balances nature with visitor comfort.

☐ 🔖 ♡ **South Toledo Bend State Park:** Located on the reservoir's eastern shore, this park draws anglers for world-class freshwater fishing. Hiking trails and overlooks showcase lake vistas, while birdwatchers spot migratory species. Campgrounds, cabins, and picnic areas extend stays, making it a versatile destination for recreation on Louisiana's largest man-made lake.

☐ 🔖 ♡ **St. Bernard State Park:** Near New Orleans, this small but charming park offers picnic areas, trails, and playgrounds under shady groves. Wetlands and marshes surround the area, inviting birdwatching and quiet exploration. It provides a refreshing natural escape from the nearby city, with a family-friendly atmosphere and glimpses of Louisiana's coastal ecosystems.

☐ 🔖 ♡ **Tickfaw State Park:** Immersing visitors in four ecosystems—swamps, bottomland hardwoods, pine forests, and river habitats—this park offers canoeing, hiking, and elevated boardwalks. A nature center interprets local wildlife, while picnic pavilions and campgrounds invite family outings. Rich in biodiversity, it blends education, adventure, and serene Louisiana landscapes.

National Parks

 ☐ 🔖 ♡ **Cane River Creole National Historical Park:** In Natchitoches Parish, this park preserves two historic plantations along the Cane River—Oakland and Magnolia. It tells the story of Creole families, plantation agriculture, and the lives of enslaved people who shaped the region. Visitors explore preserved homes, landscapes, and outbuildings tied to Louisiana's Creole heritage.

☐ 🔖 ♡ **Jean Lafitte National Historical Park and Preserve:** Spanning Louisiana's wetlands and cultural sites, this park protects swamps, marshes, and bayous while interpreting the state's colonial past. It highlights the legacy of Jean Lafitte, a 19th-century pirate and privateer, and offers trails, visitor centers, and programs that explore both natural ecosystems and cultural traditions.

 ☐ 🔖 ♡ **New Orleans Jazz National Historical Park:** In the heart of New Orleans, this site honors the birthplace of jazz. Exhibits, performances, and ranger-led programs showcase the music's history and evolution. Visitors can join walking tours through the French Quarter, listen to live jazz, and learn how the city's unique blend of cultures created a sound that shaped America's music.

 ☐ 🔖 ♡ **Poverty Point National Monument:** In northeast Louisiana, this ancient site preserves massive earthworks created more than 3,000 years ago by the Poverty Point culture. Visitors walk among mounds and ridges that reveal the ingenuity of early Native Americans. The site also interprets their role in long-distance trade, community life, and early North American cultural development.

LOUISIANA

☐ 🔖 ♡ **Vicksburg National Military Park:** Across the Mississippi River from Louisiana, this battlefield commemorates the decisive Civil War siege of Vicksburg. The Union victory here gave control of the river and split the Confederacy. Visitors explore preserved trenches, historic monuments, memorials, and interpretive exhibits that bring to life the strategies and struggles of 1863.

State & National Forests

☐ 🔖 ♡ **Alexander State Forest:** Established in 1923 near Woodworth, Alexander is Louisiana's oldest state forest and serves as a model for sustainable forestry. It supports timber production, research, and recreation, including fishing and boating on Indian Creek Lake. The forest also hosts demonstration areas that highlight reforestation, wildlife habitat, and long-term land stewardship.

☐ 🔖 ♡ **Kisatchie National Forest:** Louisiana's only national forest spans 604,000 acres across eight parishes. It protects longleaf pine forests, red clay hills, and unique wilderness areas like Kisatchie Hills. Popular for hiking, hunting, camping, and mountain biking, it also offers scenic byways such as the Longleaf Trail. Kisatchie blends recreation, history, and critical conservation work.

National Scenic Byways & All-American Roads

☐ 🔖 ♡ **Bayou Teche Scenic Byway:** This 184-mile National Scenic Byway traces Bayou Teche from Morgan City to Arnaudville, passing plantation homes, sugarcane fields, and oak-lined levees. It highlights Cajun and Creole towns alive with food, music, and festivals. The route blends natural beauty with living culture, offering a rich journey through Acadiana's historic heartland.

☐ 🔖 ♡ **Boom or Bust Byway:** A National Scenic Byway along 136 miles of LA 2 in northern Louisiana, this route tells the story of oil, gas, and timber booms that shaped the region. Pumpjacks, sawmill relics, and historic towns reveal cycles of growth and decline. Travelers encounter rural charm, roadside stories, and pine forests along one of Louisiana's most storied corridors.

☐ 🔖 ♡ **Creole Nature Trail (All-American Road):** Designated an All-American Road, this 207-mile "Louisiana Outback" drive explores prairies, marshes, beaches, and barrier islands. Wildlife refuges teem with alligators and wading birds, while fishing and Gulf vistas draw outdoor enthusiasts. It offers an authentic, immersive look at Louisiana's wild coastal ecosystems and fragile beauty.

☐ 🔖 ♡ **Great River Road (All-American Road):** Louisiana's section of this iconic national route follows the Mississippi River, linking plantations, levees, and historic river towns. Scenic overlooks, antebellum homes, and cultural landmarks highlight the river's role in shaping trade, culture, and identity. As an All-American Road, it captures the timeless power of the Mississippi.

State Scenic Byways

☐ 🔖 ♡ **Cajun Corridor Byway:** This 34-mile drive along LA 14 links Gueydan, Abbeville, and Delcambre, showcasing Cajun food, crawfish farms, and seafood docks. Historic downtowns brim with culture, while festivals and music halls celebrate Cajun traditions. It's a compact byway offering a flavorful slice of southern Louisiana's prairie life.

☐ 🔖 ♡ **Cane River National Heritage Trail:** Spanning 71 miles along LA 1, 119, and 494, this byway highlights Creole heritage through plantations, French architecture, and historic Natchitoches. Oxbow lakes and riverside views frame antebellum homes and rural villages. It's a cultural corridor linking scenic landscapes with Louisiana's Creole identity.

☐ 🔖 ♡ **Flyway Byway:** A 55-mile loop through Jefferson Davis Parish, this byway crosses rice fields, marshes, and prairies alive with migratory birds. Jennings, Lake Arthur, and small Cajun towns add cultural depth with music halls, hunting traditions, and local festivals. It's an ecotourism route mixing wildlife and community heritage.

☐ 🔖 ♡ **Historic US 80 / Dixie Overland Byway:** Covering 113 miles from Ruston to the Mississippi River, this route recalls America's highway heyday. Travelers find pine forests, Civil War sites, and WWII relics alongside classic diners, motels, and roadside stops. It preserves the nostalgic spirit of the Dixie Overland road across the South.

LOUISIANA

☐ ◫ ♡ **Longleaf Trail Scenic Byway:** A 17-mile drive through Kisatchie National Forest, this route showcases restored longleaf pine ecosystems. Streams, ridges, and wildflowers line the road, with trailheads and campsites nearby. Compact but scenic, it offers solitude, upland views, and a glimpse of Louisiana's once-vast longleaf landscapes.

☐ ◫ ♡ **Louisiana Colonial Trails:** This 484-mile network winds through central Louisiana along historic colonial routes. Travelers encounter mission sites, plantations, small towns, and oxbow lakes. The byway highlights French, Spanish, and Native American legacies, offering a diverse journey where cultures blended to shape Louisiana's early identity.

☐ ◫ ♡ **Myths & Legends Byway:** Stretching 181 miles through Beauregard and Allen parishes, this route is steeped in folklore and timber history. It passes tribal lands, logging ghost towns, and pine forests tied to old legends. Interpretive stops share ghost stories and cultural lore, creating a drive that blends mystery with rural landscapes.

☐ ◫ ♡ **Northup Trail:** This 123-mile byway along US 71 traces the path of Solomon Northup, author of Twelve Years a Slave. Antebellum homes, plantations, and museums highlight his story and the legacy of slavery. Oak-lined roads and historic markers connect cultural memory with Louisiana's plantation-era heritage.

☐ ◫ ♡ **San Bernardo Byway:** Running 35 miles along LA 46 east of New Orleans, this byway explores St. Bernard Parish's fishing villages, levees, and colonial churches. Shrimp docks, historic shrines, and Creole traditions enrich the route, reflecting coastal Louisiana's multicultural communities and enduring ties to water and heritage.

☐ ◫ ♡ **Southern Swamps Byway:** A 69-mile corridor between Sorrento and Ponchatoula, this byway immerses travelers in cypress swamps, bayous, and mossy forests. Canoe launches, fishing camps, and wildlife sightings bring wetland culture alive. It captures a landscape where daily life is shaped by water and wilderness.

☐ ◫ ♡ **Toledo Bend Forest Scenic Byway:** Spanning 78 miles along LA 191, this route hugs the Toledo Bend Reservoir. Rolling hills, pine uplands, and lake overlooks offer recreation and wildlife viewing. Boat ramps and campgrounds dot the drive, creating a peaceful experience along one of the South's largest reservoirs.

☐ ◫ ♡ **Tunica Trace Byway:** Covering 20 miles along LA 66, this route winds from US 61 to Angola through hardwood ridges, plantations, and historic sites. Scenic overlooks and markers tell stories of rural life, prisons, and cultural change. Compact yet layered, it blends striking scenery with Louisiana's complex history.

☐ ◫ ♡ **Wetlands Cultural Byway:** At 282 miles through Bayous Lafourche and Terrebonne, this route reveals Cajun and Creole life along docks, shrimp boats, and working wetlands. Salt marshes and barrier islands form a backdrop to seafood culture and festivals. It's a story of resilience in communities tied to fragile coasts.

☐ ◫ ♡ **Zydeco Cajun Prairie Byway:** This 283-mile byway crosses Acadiana, linking towns like Opelousas and Crowley. Zydeco music halls, crawfish farms, and prairie remnants define the journey. Festivals, food, and dance highlight Creole and Cajun heritage, making the route a joyful immersion into Louisiana's living prairie culture.

MAINE

Maine's untamed beauty stretches from rugged coastlines and granite peaks to dense forests and pristine lakes. With an inspiring blend of state parks, a vast national forest, a cherished national park, and striking natural landmarks, Maine captivates outdoor enthusiasts with its wild scenery, maritime charm, and timeless natural spirit.

📅 Peak Season
June–October is Maine's peak season, offering mild weather, clear skies, and scenic beauty from coast to mountains. Summer is busiest along the beaches and Acadia National Park, while fall draws travelers for brilliant foliage.

📅 Offseason Months
November–April is the offseason, bringing cold temperatures and heavy snow inland. Winter is quiet except in ski areas, though coastal towns and forests remain open for serene exploration and winter recreation.

🍃 Scenery & Nature Timing
Spring brings wildflowers and thawed rivers, though conditions can be cool and damp. Summer highlights rugged coasts, lighthouses, and lush forests. Fall peaks with vibrant foliage in September–October, while winter blankets mountains and lakes in snow.

✨ Special
Maine sees the nation's first sunrise atop Cadillac Mountain and dramatic tides along the Bay of Fundy. Summer bioluminescence glows in Frenchman Bay near Bar Harbor and Castine Harbor, while sea caves, fog banks, and vivid fall colors define its seasonal beauty.

UNITED STATES EDITION

MAINE

State Parks

☐ 🔖 ♡ **Androscoggin Riverlands State Park:** Stretching across 2,600 acres in Turner, this park offers 12 miles of river frontage along the Androscoggin. Ideal for paddling, fishing, and birdwatching, it also has 10 miles of multi-use trails for hiking, biking, and snowmobiling. Wildlife abounds in its forests and wetlands, while scenic overlooks provide peaceful views of the broad, winding river.

☐ 🔖 ♡ **Aroostook State Park:** Established in 1939, this is Maine's first state park, located near Presque Isle. Nestled at the base of Quaggy Jo Mountain, it offers hiking trails to rocky overlooks, a small lake for fishing and swimming, and abundant northern forest wildlife. Its serene setting and historic significance make it a popular spot for year-round outdoor recreation in Aroostook County.

☐ 🔖 ♡ **Baxter State Park:** Encompassing more than 200,000 acres, this rugged wilderness in northern Maine is home to Mount Katahdin, the state's highest peak and the northern terminus of the Appalachian Trail. The park offers over 200 miles of hiking trails, pristine lakes for fishing, and backcountry camping. Famous for the Knife Edge Trail, it's a premier destination for experienced adventurers.

☐ 🔖 ♡ **Birch Point State Park:** Tucked into Owls Head, this small coastal park features a quiet, crescent-shaped beach on Penobscot Bay. Visitors enjoy swimming, picnicking, and beachcombing in a peaceful setting with gentle waves and ocean breezes. Its relatively low visitation offers a tranquil seaside retreat, perfect for families and those seeking solitude by the shore.

☐ 🔖 ♡ **Bradbury Mountain State Park:** Located in Pownal, this 800-acre park is centered on Bradbury Mountain, a modest peak with big views of Casco Bay and the western mountains. Popular for hiking, picnicking, and birdwatching, especially during hawk migration, it also has trails for mountain biking and horseback riding. Its accessibility makes it a year-round favorite for outdoor enthusiasts.

☐ 🔖 ♡ **Camden Hills State Park:** Overlooking Penobscot Bay, this 5,700-acre park near Camden offers sweeping coastal views from Mount Battie and Mount Megunticook. Trails range from short walks to rugged hikes, and the park includes camping, picnicking, and birdwatching opportunities. With ocean vistas, forested ridges, and mountain peaks, it's a favorite for outdoor enthusiasts year-round.

☐ 🔖 ♡ **Cobscook Bay State Park:** Located near Dennysville, this coastal gem is known for its 24-foot tides that transform the shoreline twice daily. Visitors enjoy camping, hiking through forests and salt marshes, and birdwatching for bald eagles, ospreys, and migrating shorebirds. Its remote setting and unique ecosystem make it a peaceful destination for nature lovers and coastal explorers.

☐ 🔖 ♡ **Crescent Beach State Park:** In Cape Elizabeth, this mile-long crescent of sand is ideal for swimming, sunbathing, and beachcombing along Casco Bay. The park also offers trails for hiking, cross-country skiing, and access to fishing and sea kayaking. Backed by dunes and woodlands, Crescent Beach combines scenic beauty with diverse recreation, making it a popular year-round coastal escape.

☐ 🔖 ♡ **Damariscotta Lake State Park:** Situated in Jefferson, this family-friendly park offers a sandy swimming beach on the clear waters of Damariscotta Lake. Visitors enjoy fishing, picnicking, and paddling, while surrounding forests provide shade and wildlife habitat. Its easy access and tranquil setting make it a popular day-use destination for outdoor recreation in mid-coast Maine.

☐ 🔖 ♡ **Ferry Beach State Park:** Located in Saco, this park features a sandy beach on Saco Bay and a network of trails winding through woodlands and rare tupelo swamps. Visitors enjoy swimming, picnicking, and birdwatching, with opportunities to spot warblers and shorebirds. Combining beach and forest, it offers a unique mix of coastal recreation and ecological diversity.

☐ 🔖 ♡ **Fort Point State Park:** Perched on Penobscot Bay in Stockton Springs, this park combines history and scenery with its preserved 19th-century Fort Pownall and lighthouse. Visitors can explore the historic site, picnic by the shore, or relax on the small beach. With panoramic coastal views and cultural heritage, it provides both outdoor recreation and a glimpse into Maine's past.

☐ 🔖 ♡ **Grafton Notch State Park:** Located in Newry, this rugged 3,000-acre park features dramatic mountains, deep gorges, and waterfalls. Hikers can explore trails leading to Screw Auger Falls, Moose Cave, and panoramic summits, including stretches of the Appalachian Trail. Popular for its challenging terrain, scenic vistas, and striking geology, it's a premier destination for outdoor adventure.

MAINE

☐ 🔖 ♡ **Lake St. George State Park:** Nestled in Liberty, this lakeside park provides sandy beaches, picnic areas, and wooded trails around the clear waters of Lake St. George. Visitors enjoy swimming, boating, and fishing for landlocked salmon and brook trout. With a family-friendly campground and peaceful setting, it's a popular summer retreat for relaxation and recreation in central Maine.

☐ 🔖 ♡ **Lamoine State Park:** On Frenchman Bay near Ellsworth, this coastal park offers sweeping views of Mount Desert Island and easy access to Acadia National Park. Campgrounds and picnic areas sit among fields and shoreline, with opportunities for swimming, kayaking, and wildlife watching. Its quiet, affordable setting makes it a convenient base for exploring Maine's scenic Downeast coast.

☐ 🔖 ♡ **Lily Bay State Park:** Located in Greenville on Moosehead Lake's eastern shore, this 925-acre park offers boating, fishing, hiking, and a family-friendly swimming beach. Two campgrounds provide lakeside camping with mountain views, and trails wind through forests rich in wildlife. Its tranquil setting on Maine's largest lake makes it ideal for both quiet retreats and active adventures.

☐ 🔖 ♡ **Mackworth Island State Park:** A 100-acre island connected to Falmouth by causeway, Mackworth features a 1.25-mile shoreline trail with sweeping views of Casco Bay. The island hosts the Baxter Memorial, birdwatching opportunities, and the whimsical "Fairy Village" built by children. With its mix of nature, history, and creativity, it's a unique coastal destination near Portland.

☐ 🔖 ♡ **Moose Point State Park:** Situated in Searsport, this coastal park overlooks Penobscot Bay with picnic areas shaded by spruce and fir. Short nature trails provide opportunities for birdwatching and peaceful walks along rocky shores. Known for its scenic views and serene atmosphere, it's a popular spot for family outings, small gatherings, or simply relaxing with ocean breezes.

☐ 🔖 ♡ **Mount Blue State Park:** Encompassing nearly 8,000 acres in Weld, this park surrounds Webb Lake and offers a wide range of recreation including hiking Mount Blue, fishing, boating, and swimming. Campgrounds and picnic areas provide extended stays amid mountain scenery. With year-round activities, from winter sports to summer camping, it's one of Maine's premier outdoor destinations.

☐ 🔖 ♡ **Owl's Head State Park:** Overlooking Penobscot Bay near Rockland, this small coastal park is home to the historic 1852 Owl's Head Light. Visitors can stroll wooded paths, picnic by the shoreline, and enjoy sweeping ocean views dotted with islands and passing schooners. The lighthouse and beach access make it a popular stop for sightseeing, photography, and a taste of Maine's maritime charm.

☐ 🔖 ♡ **Peaks-Kenny State Park:** Nestled on Sebec Lake near Dover-Foxcroft, this 839-acre park combines a sandy beach, boating access, and miles of hiking trails. The campground offers wooded sites for tents and RVs, making it popular with families. Swimming, fishing, and picnicking round out the activities. Its peaceful forest-and-lake setting creates an ideal balance of recreation and relaxation.

☐ 🔖 ♡ **Popham Beach State Park:** One of Maine's most popular beaches, this Phippsburg park offers a sweeping sandy shoreline along the Atlantic. Visitors enjoy swimming, picnicking, and exploring tidal pools and shifting sandbars that reveal trails to nearby islands at low tide. With dramatic coastal scenery and ample space, it's a favorite destination for both day trips and ocean lovers.

☐ 🔖 ♡ **Quoddy Head State Park:** At Lubec's rugged coast, this park is home to the iconic red-striped West Quoddy Head Lighthouse, marking the easternmost point in the continental U.S. Trails traverse bogs, forests, and cliffs overlooking the Bay of Fundy, where whale and seabird sightings are common. Combining dramatic scenery with historic significance, it offers a uniquely Maine coastal experience.

☐ 🔖 ♡ **Range Pond State Park:** Located in Poland, this park features a wide sandy beach with lifeguards, picnic areas, and wooded trails. Its calm waters are ideal for swimming, kayaking, and fishing, while open lawns invite family activities. Easily accessible and popular with locals, Range Pond offers a relaxed, welcoming setting for outdoor recreation in southern Maine.

☐ 🔖 ♡ **Rangeley Lake State Park:** On the shores of Rangeley Lake, this 869-acre park is surrounded by the mountains of western Maine. Visitors can swim, fish for trout and salmon, hike nearby trails, or watch for moose and loons. Campgrounds and picnic areas provide extended stays in a scenic wilderness setting. Its mix of recreation and natural beauty makes it a classic North Woods destination.

MAINE

☐ ▯ ♡ **Reid State Park:** Located on Georgetown Island, this 770-acre park features long sandy beaches, rare dunes, rocky tidepools, and a tidal lagoon with warmer water than the open ocean. Popular for swimming, surfing, picnicking, and hiking, its trails wind through forests and along salt marshes. Scenic lookouts at Griffith Head offer sweeping views of lighthouses, islands, and seabird habitat.

☐ ▯ ♡ **Roque Bluffs State Park:** Nestled in Washington County, this coastal park combines a freshwater pond with a half-mile saltwater beach on Englishman Bay. Visitors enjoy swimming, picnicking, and exploring tidal pools, along with trails through forests and meadows rich in birdlife. Its unique mix of inland and coastal ecosystems makes it a favorite for both relaxation and exploration.

☐ ▯ ♡ **Scarborough Beach State Park:** Stretching along Prouts Neck, this coastal park is known for some of Maine's warmest ocean waters and prime surf. A long sandy shoreline with dunes makes it a favorite for sunbathing, shelling, and swimming, with lifeguards posted in summer. Facilities include restrooms, concessions, and rentals, though parking fills quickly on busy days.

☐ ▯ ♡ **Sebago Lake State Park:** One of Maine's first state parks, this 1,400-acre gem on the shores of Sebago Lake offers sandy beaches, extensive hiking and biking trails, and prime boating and fishing. Located in Casco and Naples, it's a hub for year-round recreation. The park's woodlands and waterfront make it a destination for camping, swimming, and enjoying Maine's largest lake.

☐ ▯ ♡ **Shackford Head State Park:** Overlooking Cobscook Bay in Eastport, this rugged park features 2.5 miles of trails winding through forests, fields, and rocky shorelines. Scenic overlooks provide panoramic views of nearby islands and wildlife-rich waters. Known for birdwatching, peaceful hikes, and its quiet coastal charm, the park offers a natural retreat on Maine's eastern edge.

☐ ▯ ♡ **Swan Lake State Park:** Set on the shores of 1,400-acre Swan Lake in Swanville, this park is a family-friendly spot for swimming, fishing, and boating. A sandy beach with picnic areas provides summer relaxation, while surrounding forests offer shaded trails and wildlife habitat. The calm waters and scenic views make it an ideal destination for both day trips and outdoor getaways.

☐ ▯ ♡ **Two Lights State Park:** Perched along Maine's rocky southern coast in Cape Elizabeth, this 41-acre park features sweeping ocean vistas and picnic areas overlooking Casco Bay. Named after two historic lighthouses nearby, it offers trails, tidal pool exploration, and dramatic shoreline scenery. A favorite for photographers and families, it provides a classic Maine coastal experience.

☐ ▯ ♡ **Vaughan Woods Memorial State Park:** Known locally as "the Hamilton House Woods," this South Berwick park blends history and nature. Visitors can explore wooded trails along the Salmon Falls River, admire historic stone bridges, and enjoy the grounds of the 1785 Hamilton House. With its scenic landscapes and ties to Maine's past, it's a peaceful spot for hiking and reflection.

☐ ▯ ♡ **Warren Island State Park:** Accessible only by boat, this 70-acre island in Penobscot Bay offers a secluded escape with primitive campsites, hiking trails, and sheltered coves for kayaking. Its rugged beauty and quiet atmosphere attract campers, paddlers, and birdwatchers seeking solitude. With its mix of forest and shoreline, the island provides a true back-to-nature adventure.

☐ ▯ ♡ **Wolfe's Neck Woods State Park:** Located near Freeport, this coastal park features trails winding through forests, salt marshes, and rocky shoreline with views of Casco Bay and the Ovens Mouth islands. Known for osprey nesting areas, it's a top spot for birdwatching, picnicking, and family hikes. Its convenient location and diverse habitats make it both accessible and scenic.

National Parks

☐ ▯ ♡ **Acadia National Park:** Nestled on Maine's rugged coast, Acadia blends rocky shorelines, dense forests, and granite peaks. Visitors can hike Cadillac Mountain, the first spot to see sunrise in the U.S., or drive the scenic Park Loop Road. With biking, kayaking, wildlife viewing, and iconic coastal scenery, Acadia remains one of the Northeast's most beloved and visited national parks.

☐ ▯ ♡ **Appalachian National Scenic Trail:** Stretching over 2,100 miles from Georgia to Maine, the Appalachian Trail is among the world's longest continuous footpaths. Hikers traverse forests, ridgelines, and mountain peaks, experiencing diverse ecosystems and sweeping vistas. Whether on a day hike or a thru-hike, visitors immerse themselves in nature along this iconic corridor of the eastern U.S.

MAINE

☐ 🔖 ♡ **Katahdin Woods and Waters National Monument:** In northern Maine, this remote monument preserves pristine wilderness surrounding Mount Katahdin, the northern end of the Appalachian Trail. The area offers hiking, canoeing, camping, and wildlife viewing amid forested rivers and rugged landscapes. Rich in history and natural beauty, it's a sanctuary for exploration and solitude.

☐ 🔖 ♡ **Saint Croix Island International Historic Site:** Located in Maine's Passamaquoddy Bay, this site honors Saint Croix Island, where French settlers established one of North America's earliest colonies in 1604. Visitors discover the hardships faced by the colonists through exhibits and trails with scenic views. The site blends natural beauty with deep cultural and historical significance.

State & National Forests

☐ 🔖 ♡ **Durham State Forest:** This small single-unit forest in Waldo County preserves mixed hardwood stands while offering limited but meaningful public access. Managed as a demonstration and community forest, it provides shaded trails for low-impact recreation and supports diverse wildlife habitats. Its compact footprint highlights Maine's ongoing commitment to sustainable forest stewardship.

☐ 🔖 ♡ **Sebago Lake State Forest (Public Reserved Land Unit):** West of Portland, this important unit balances recreation, commercial forestry, and watershed protection for Sebago Lake. Visitors enjoy trails, boat launches, camping areas, and ATV routes, while timber harvesting supports local economies. The forest also safeguards the lake's water quality, vital for southern Maine's communities and ecosystems.

☐ 🔖 ♡ **Togue Pond Unit (Public Reserved Land):** Spanning 15,000 acres in Maine's north woods, this unit features lakes, wetlands, and mixed forest managed for timber, habitat, and recreation. Backcountry camping, hunting, fishing, and canoeing opportunities abound, while forest roads provide access. Its remote setting offers visitors a rugged wilderness escape surrounded by scenic and ecologically rich landscapes.

☐ 🔖 ♡ **White Mountain National Forest:** Stretching across rugged peaks and deep valleys, the White Mountain National Forest lies mostly in New Hampshire but extends into Maine's western highlands. It features alpine forests, pristine lakes, and hundreds of miles of trails, including the Appalachian Trail. Renowned for its four-season beauty, it draws hikers, campers, and outdoor adventurers year-round.

National Scenic Byways & All-American Roads

☐ 🔖 ♡ **Acadia All-American Road:** A 40-mile loop across Mount Desert Island, this All-American Road combines rocky shores, granite peaks, spruce forests, and Bar Harbor charm. It follows the Park Loop Road with stops at Cadillac Mountain, Jordan Pond, and Thunder Hole, plus access to historic carriage roads. The drive showcases Acadia's most iconic coastal and mountain scenery.

☐ 🔖 ♡ **Bold Coast Scenic Byway:** Stretching 125 miles from Milbridge to Lubec and Eastport, this byway highlights Downeast Maine's rugged shoreline, fishing villages, blueberry barrens, and dramatic headlands. Visitors encounter lighthouses, tidal marshes, and cliffside trails with sweeping Atlantic vistas. It captures both the wild beauty and maritime culture of Maine's eastern edge.

☐ 🔖 ♡ **Katahdin Woods & Waters Scenic Byway:** Encircling Baxter State Park's southern edge, this 100-mile route passes through Millinocket and Patten, with views of Katahdin, forested ridges, and the East Branch of the Penobscot River. It offers abundant wildlife, scenic overlooks, and trailheads, serving as a gateway to Katahdin Woods and Waters National Monument and Maine's remote north woods.

☐ 🔖 ♡ **Old Canada Road National Scenic Byway:** Following U.S. Route 201 for 78 miles from Solon to Jackman, this corridor traces the Kennebec and Dead Rivers through forests, mountains, and historic villages. Pull-offs reveal sweeping river views and moose habitat, while fall foliage draws visitors each autumn. It preserves the classic character of the North Woods and Maine's route into Quebec.

☐ 🔖 ♡ **Rangeley Lakes National Scenic Byway:** A 36-mile loop through western Maine's mountains, this byway links Rangeley and Oquossoc along Routes 4 and 17. Highlights include the famed Height of Land overlook, Rangeley Lake, and nearby waterfalls. Scenic ridges, trout waters, and moose habitat make it a four-season destination for fishing, hiking, and admiring vast alpine views.

☐ 🔖 ♡ **Schoodic National Scenic Byway:** A 29-mile loop around Acadia's quieter Schoodic Peninsula, this route explores rocky headlands, spruce forests, fishing harbors, and small villages. Less crowded than Mount Desert Island, it provides coastal trails, lighthouses, and authentic Downeast character. With its working waterfronts and dramatic Atlantic outlooks, it offers a peaceful Acadia alternative.

MAINE

☐ 🔖 ♡ **St. John Valley Cultural Byway / Fish River Scenic Byway:** Together forming 134 miles across Aroostook County, these twin byways highlight Acadian heritage, farmland, and river valleys. The route includes French-speaking villages, forested ridges, and panoramic views toward Canada. Churches, museums, and festivals celebrate Franco-American culture amid northern Maine's pastoral and wild beauty.

State Scenic Byways

☐ 🔖 ♡ **Blackwoods Scenic Byway:** Following Route 182 for 12 miles between Franklin and Cherryfield, this corridor links forests, lakes, and ridges in Downeast Maine. It provides quiet access to Schoodic and Acadia's less-traveled areas. Scenic ponds, blueberry barrens, and wildlife habitat line the drive, offering a tranquil alternative to busier coastal routes.

☐ 🔖 ♡ **Grafton Notch Scenic Byway:** Running 21 miles along Route 26 between Newry and Upton, this mountain corridor passes waterfalls like Screw Auger and Mother Walker Falls, dramatic gorges, and access to Appalachian Trail segments. Autumn foliage draws many visitors, while summer brings hikers, paddlers, and campers into the rugged western Maine highlands.

☐ 🔖 ♡ **Million Dollar View Scenic Byway:** A short 8-mile stretch of U.S. Route 1 near Danforth showcases expansive views of East Grand, Deering, and Brackett Lakes with Mount Katahdin on the horizon. Pull-offs provide panoramic overlooks, especially vibrant in fall. This compact route highlights the pristine lake country and the vastness of northern Maine's forests.

☐ 🔖 ♡ **Moosehead Lake Scenic Byway:** A 59-mile loop around Maine's largest lake, this byway follows Routes 15 and 6 through Greenville, Rockwood, and Kokadjo. Visitors enjoy lakefront vistas, the cliffs of Mount Kineo, and wildlife like moose and loons. Year-round recreation includes boating, fishing, snowmobiling, and hiking in Maine's famed north woods setting.

☐ 🔖 ♡ **Pequawket Trail Scenic Byway:** Stretching 60 miles along Route 113 from Standish to Gilead, this corridor traces the Saco River past pine forests, covered bridges, and granite ridges. Small towns, farm stands, and scenic riverside pull-offs highlight its charm. It serves as a transition from Maine's coastal plain to the White Mountains of New Hampshire.

☐ 🔖 ♡ **State Route 27 High Peaks Scenic Byway:** Covering 47 miles from Kingfield to Coburn Gore, this byway climbs through western Maine's High Peaks region, with trailheads to the Bigelow Range and Sugarloaf Mountain. Panoramic overlooks, river cascades, and seasonal foliage make it a striking mountain drive, offering access to recreation hubs and wilderness landscapes.

National Natural Landmarks

  ☐ 🔖 ♡ **Appleton Bog Atlantic White Cedar Stand:** Appleton Bog is a National Natural Landmark for preserving a rare Atlantic white cedar stand within an extensive peatland. Its hummock-and-hollow topography, intact hydrology, and continuous forest cover sustain mosses, ferns, amphibians, and wetland birds, making it a vital refuge for peatland biodiversity.
GPS: 43.5500, -70.4667

 ☐ 🔖 ♡ **Carrying Place Cove Bog:** Carrying Place Cove Bog earned National Natural Landmark status as a rare eroded tombolo bog shaped by coastal processes. Wave action sculpted its sand spit, creating a unique wetland within a lake system. The bog supports sphagnum mosses, cranberries, and salt-tolerant wetland plants, illustrating the blend of marine and freshwater ecology.
GPS: 44.5451, -67.7844

MAINE

 **Colby–Marston Preserve:** This kettle-hole bog was designated a National Natural Landmark for its 40-foot-thick peat mat, one of the deepest in Maine. Acidic, nutrient-poor conditions sustain carnivorous plants, bryophytes, and cranberries. Its undisturbed layers preserve a long record of peatland development, offering rare insight into carbon storage and glacial history.
GPS: 44.4761, -69.8378

 Crystal Bog: Crystal Bog is recognized as a National Natural Landmark for being one of Maine's largest and most pristine sphagnum bogs. Its raised peat dome, surrounded by forest, supports carnivorous plants such as pitcher plants and sundews, alongside diverse sphagnum species. The bog exemplifies intact peatland processes and wetland biodiversity.
GPS: 46.0345, -68.3304

 Gulf Hagas: Known as the "Grand Canyon of the East," Gulf Hagas is a National Natural Landmark for its dramatic gorge carved into sandstone. Waterfalls up to 40 feet plunge into the canyon, while spruce-fir and hardwood forests cloak the cliffs. Shaded microclimates shelter rare plants, showcasing the interplay of geology and ecology.
GPS: 45.4841, -69.3230

 Monhegan Island: Monhegan Island became a National Natural Landmark for its intact coastal spruce forest and exceptional plant diversity, with over 400 flowering species. Bedrock outcrops, cliffs, and salt spray create unique habitats, while seabird nesting colonies thrive along the rugged shoreline. Its seclusion preserves botanical and ecological richness.
GPS: 43.7622, -69.3203

 **Mount Bigelow:** This glaciated mountain earned National Natural Landmark status for its alpine meadows, cirques, and rugged summits. Rising above spruce-fir forests, Mount Bigelow hosts rare alpine vegetation found only in the highest eastern peaks. Its scenery, glacial landforms, and biodiversity make it a natural treasure of Maine's mountains.
GPS: 45.1473, -70.2892

 Mount Katahdin: Designated a National Natural Landmark, Katahdin is Maine's highest peak and a premier record of Pleistocene glaciation. Its summit and slopes display eskers, drumlins, kames, and erratics, preserving textbook glacial features. Alpine and subalpine plant communities thrive here, linking geology with northern ecological systems.
GPS: 45.9044, -68.9213

 New Gloucester Black Gum Stand: The New Gloucester Black Gum Stand is a National Natural Landmark for conserving an ancient swamp forest of virgin black gum trees. This rare ecosystem supports wetland-adapted plants and wildlife, representing a remnant of Maine's pre-settlement coastal plain forests with exceptional ecological and historical value.
GPS: 43.9620, -70.2760

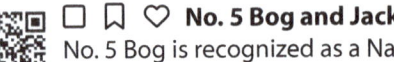 **No. 5 Bog and Jack Pine Stand:** No. 5 Bog is recognized as a National Natural Landmark for being Maine's only large intermontane peatland. Its sphagnum mats and jack pine groves support rare bog flora and fauna. The undeveloped, pristine character of this site illustrates the enduring resilience of northeastern peatland ecosystems.
GPS: 45.1300, -69.5000

 **Orono Bog:** Orono Bog was designated a National Natural Landmark for exemplifying a classic kettle-hole sphagnum bog. Its peat layers, mats, and fen communities support rare plants like bog laurel and sundews. Researchers value the site as a living laboratory for studying hydrology, peat accumulation, and bog ecology.
GPS: 44.8691, -68.7257

 **Passadumkeag Marsh and Bogland:** This vast wetland complex holds National Natural Landmark status for its unspoiled marshes, bogs, and swamps. It provides critical habitat for carnivorous plants, amphibians, and migratory birds. Its nutrient cycling, flood control, and intact ecology illustrate the importance of large wetlands to Maine's environment.
GPS: 45.1000, -68.4000

MAINE

Penny Pond–Joe Pond Complex: Recognized as a National Natural Landmark, this paired kettle-hole pond and bog system retains undisturbed sphagnum carpets, peatlands, and specialized flora. Its hydrology supports migratory birds and rare wetland plants, making it a pristine example of glacial wetland formation in Maine's forested landscapes.
GPS: 44.3550, -69.8000

The Hermitage: The Hermitage holds National Natural Landmark designation as one of New England's last old-growth white pine stands. Towering pines dating back centuries mix with hardwoods and a diverse understory. This uncut forest preserves northern woodland conditions that predate colonial logging, offering rare continuity of structure and habitat.
GPS: 45.4860, -68.0840

MARYLAND

Maryland's natural wonders unfold from forested Appalachian foothills to Chesapeake Bay tidal marshes and coastal dunes. With a rich collection of state parks, a national forest, national park sites, and natural landmarks, Maryland invites year-round exploration and discovery across its remarkably varied landscapes.

📅 Peak Season
May–October is Maryland's peak season, with warm weather, long days, and full access to beaches, trails, and parks. Summer is busiest along the Chesapeake Bay and Atlantic Coast, while fall brings colorful forests and comfortable temperatures.

📅 Offseason Months
November–April is the offseason, bringing cooler weather and lighter crowds. Winter is mild near the coast but colder in the mountains, offering quiet outdoor exploration and occasional snow in western regions.

🍃 Scenery & Nature Timing
Spring showcases blooming dogwoods and migrating waterfowl along the bay. Summer highlights boating, beaches, and green forests. Fall peaks with vibrant color in the Appalachians, while winter offers crisp coastal views and quiet hiking trails.

✨ Special
Maryland showcases the tidal rhythms of the Chesapeake Bay, glowing plankton in summer waters near Solomons Island, and wild horses roaming Assateague Island's beaches. The Appalachian ridges of western Maryland blaze with fall color, while dense coastal fog drifts over the bay in spring.

UNITED STATES EDITION

MARYLAND

State Parks

☐ 🔖 ♡ **Assateague State Park:** Maryland's only oceanfront state park, located on Assateague Island, features sandy beaches, dunes, and salt marshes. Visitors enjoy swimming, surfing, fishing, and camping beside the Atlantic, with opportunities to see the island's famous wild horses. The park also provides boat launches, nature trails, and abundant birdwatching along the coastal ecosystem.

☐ 🔖 ♡ **Big Run State Park:** Nestled in Garrett County along the Savage River Reservoir, this small, rustic park is surrounded by steep forested ridges and offers opportunities for camping, picnicking, and hiking. It provides water access for boating and fishing while serving as a gateway to the larger Savage River State Forest. Its remote setting makes it a peaceful retreat for nature lovers.

☐ 🔖 ♡ **Bill Burton Fishing Pier State Park:** Spanning the Choptank River between Dorchester and Talbot counties, this park features a repurposed section of the historic U.S. Route 50 bridge. Anglers flock here for striped bass, perch, and catfish, while visitors enjoy scenic views and picnicking. The park honors outdoor writer Bill Burton and serves as a community gathering spot on the Eastern Shore.

☐ 🔖 ♡ **Bohemia River State Park:** Nestled in Cecil County, this park protects tidal wetlands, upland forests, and quiet riverfront along the Bohemia River. Visitors enjoy canoeing, kayaking, and birdwatching in a peaceful setting rich with waterfowl and forest wildlife. With its mix of habitats and scenic shoreline, the park provides both recreation and ecological conservation in eastern Maryland.

☐ 🔖 ♡ **Calvert Cliffs State Park:** Famous for its dramatic cliffs rising above the Chesapeake Bay, this park is renowned as a fossil hunter's destination. Trails lead through forest and marsh to a sandy beach where visitors may find ancient shark teeth and other marine fossils. The park also features family-friendly picnic areas and scenic views, blending natural history with outdoor exploration.

☐ 🔖 ♡ **Casselman River Bridge State Park:** Centered on the historic 1813 stone bridge, once the longest single-span arch in the U.S., this park highlights Maryland's transportation heritage. Visitors enjoy riverside picnics, photography, and seasonal foliage displays, especially in autumn. The bridge and its surrounding landscape offer a unique blend of history, engineering, and natural beauty in a compact park setting.

☐ 🔖 ♡ **Chapel Point State Park:** Located on the Port Tobacco River, this largely undeveloped park preserves quiet riverfront habitat. Anglers and hunters frequent the site, while its natural wetlands provide refuge for waterfowl and fish. With minimal infrastructure, the park offers visitors solitude, scenic views, and an authentic sense of Maryland's tidal ecosystems in their natural state.

☐ 🔖 ♡ **Chapman State Park:** Along the Potomac River in Charles County, this park encompasses historic Mount Aventine, once home to the Chapman family. Visitors can walk mansion grounds, explore trails through forests and fields, and picnic with views of the river. The park also supports fishing, birdwatching, and wildlife viewing, blending history and natural scenery in a serene riverside landscape.

☐ 🔖 ♡ **Cunningham Falls State Park:** Set in the Catoctin Mountains, this park is renowned for Maryland's tallest cascading waterfall at 78 feet. It offers extensive hiking trails, a lake for swimming and boating, campgrounds, and fishing areas. The mix of mountain terrain, forest, and water makes it a favorite for families and nature lovers seeking scenic views and outdoor adventure year-round.

☐ 🔖 ♡ **Cypress Branch State Park:** A small gem in Kent County, this park centers around a three-acre pond ideal for fishing and picnicking. Surrounded by open meadows and woodlands, it provides a quiet retreat for birdwatchers and families looking for low-key recreation. Its simplicity and natural charm offer a peaceful escape within Maryland's Eastern Shore countryside.

MARYLAND

☐ 🔖 ♡ **Dans Mountain State Park:** Overlooking the Cumberland Valley, this Allegany County park features an Olympic-sized swimming pool with a waterslide, scenic overlooks, and shaded picnic areas. Trails explore the surrounding ridges and forested slopes, making it a popular summer destination for families. The combination of mountain scenery and recreational amenities creates a versatile park experience.

☐ 🔖 ♡ **Deep Creek Lake State Park:** Nestled in western Maryland, this park surrounds the state's largest freshwater lake. Visitors enjoy boating, fishing, swimming, and hiking against a backdrop of Appalachian ridges. The park offers campgrounds, cabin rentals, and interpretive programs, making it a year-round hub for outdoor recreation while also protecting one of the region's most scenic mountain lakes.

☐ 🔖 ♡ **Elk Neck State Park:** Stretching across upland forests, marshes, and beaches at the head of the Chesapeake Bay, this park is best known for the Turkey Point Lighthouse. Visitors hike to the bluff for panoramic views, enjoy swimming and boating, or explore diverse ecosystems. Wildlife observation and family picnics round out the activities in this ecologically rich destination.

☐ 🔖 ♡ **Fort Frederick State Park:** Anchored by a massive 1750s stone fort built for frontier defense, this park preserves a vivid piece of colonial history. Visitors tour the fort, attend reenactments, and explore hiking and picnicking areas along the C&O Canal. Its blend of military heritage and riverside landscapes makes it one of Maryland's most unique historical parks.

☐ 🔖 ♡ **Fort Tonoloway State Park:** A quiet, undeveloped retreat in Washington County, this park preserves woodlands and wildlife habitat on the site of a short-lived 18th-century frontier fort. Today, it offers solitude for hikers, birdwatchers, and history enthusiasts seeking a natural escape. With minimal development, it provides a back-to-nature experience steeped in historic significance.

☐ 🔖 ♡ **Franklin Point State Park:** On Anne Arundel County's Chesapeake shoreline, this undeveloped park protects tidal marshes, dunes, and forest habitat. Visitors hike sandy trails, watch for bald eagles and herons, and enjoy quiet beaches ideal for photography and reflection. Its wild character preserves a rare slice of natural coastline amid the developed Chesapeake Bay region.

☐ 🔖 ♡ **Gambrill State Park:** Perched on the Catoctin Mountains near Frederick, this park is famed for its sweeping overlooks of the valleys below. Trails invite hiking, biking, and horseback riding through hardwood forests. Stone overlooks and picnic shelters built by the CCC add historic charm. Its combination of mountain views, recreation, and history makes it a regional favorite.

☐ 🔖 ♡ **Gathland State Park:** Once the estate of Civil War correspondent George Alfred Townsend, this South Mountain park features the War Correspondents Memorial Arch. It offers picnic areas, museum exhibits, and access to the Appalachian Trail. Visitors discover a unique mix of history, architecture, and outdoor recreation while exploring Maryland's Civil War-era landscapes.

☐ 🔖 ♡ **Greenbrier State Park:** Nestled along South Mountain, this park centers on a 42-acre man-made lake for swimming, boating, and fishing. Hiking trails wind through forested slopes, connecting to the Appalachian Trail. With sandy beaches, shaded picnic areas, and family-friendly facilities, it offers a welcoming setting for recreation in the rolling Maryland highlands.

☐ 🔖 ♡ **Greenwell State Park:** In St. Mary's County, this park features a historic manor house, scenic trails, and access to the Patuxent River. Visitors enjoy hiking, horseback riding, fishing, and non-motorized boating in a peaceful setting. With a blend of history, shoreline, and recreation, it offers a quiet retreat while preserving the character of southern Maryland's rural landscape.

☐ 🔖 ♡ **Gunpowder Falls State Park:** Spanning 18,000 acres across six distinct areas, this is one of Maryland's largest state parks. It offers extensive hiking, biking, and horseback riding trails, along with fishing, canoeing, and picnicking. Landscapes include rugged river valleys, tidal wetlands, and wooded hills, providing year-round recreation and diverse habitats just a short drive from Baltimore.

☐ 🔖 ♡ **Harriet Tubman Underground Railroad State Park:** This park honors the life and legacy of Harriet Tubman, leader of the Underground Railroad. Located in Dorchester County, it features a visitor center with exhibits, films, and interpretive programs. Surrounded by landscapes Tubman once knew, visitors gain insight into her story while exploring trails and nearby marshes of the Blackwater refuge.

MARYLAND

☐ 🔖 ♡ **Hart-Miller Island State Park:** Accessible only by boat, this unique Chesapeake Bay park features sandy beaches, hiking trails, fishing areas, and camping sites. Once a dredged material containment site, it is now a wildlife haven and recreational escape. Its seclusion offers boaters and campers rare solitude, with panoramic bay views and opportunities for birdwatching and beachcombing.

☐ 🔖 ♡ **Herrington Manor State Park:** Nestled in Garrett County, this mountain park features a 53-acre lake for swimming, fishing, and boating. Trails wind through hemlock and pine forests, with winter cross-country skiing available. Picnic areas, cabins, and campgrounds provide family-friendly amenities, making it a year-round retreat amid western Maryland's Appalachian highlands.

☐ 🔖 ♡ **Janes Island State Park:** Situated near Crisfield in Somerset County, this park offers over 30 miles of water trails through saltmarsh, islands, and tidal creeks. Popular with kayakers and canoeists, it also provides camping, cabins, hiking trails, and a sandy beach. Known for its sunsets and wildlife-rich waterways, it's a haven for paddlers and nature enthusiasts.

☐ 🔖 ♡ **Jonas Green State Park:** Overlooking the Severn River in Anne Arundel County, this historic park features fishing piers, trails, and picnic areas near the Naval Academy Bridge. Named after Maryland's colonial printer, it blends history with scenic waterfront views. Its compact size and tranquil setting make it a popular spot for anglers, walkers, and those seeking a quiet riverside escape.

☐ 🔖 ♡ **Martinak State Park:** Located along the Choptank River and Watts Creek, this Caroline County park features trails, campsites, and boat ramps. Visitors enjoy fishing, paddling, and exploring wooded nature paths rich in birdlife. Family-friendly facilities include playgrounds and picnic shelters, while its riverside setting offers both recreation and relaxation on Maryland's Eastern Shore.

☐ 🔖 ♡ **Matthew Henson State Park:** Stretching through Montgomery County suburbs, this linear greenway follows a forested stream valley. A paved trail offers space for biking, jogging, and walking while preserving habitat for wildlife. Visitors enjoy a natural escape with woodlands, creeks, and boardwalks, creating a vital corridor that blends recreation with conservation in an urbanizing region.

☐ 🔖 ♡ **New Germany State Park:** Tucked in Garrett County's Savage River State Forest, this park features a 13-acre lake surrounded by hemlock and spruce. Popular for swimming, fishing, and boating in summer, it transforms into a cross-country skiing hub in winter. With campgrounds, cabins, and wooded trails, it offers a year-round mountain retreat rich in quiet charm and natural beauty.

☐ 🔖 ♡ **Newtowne Neck State Park:** In St. Mary's County, this 776-acre peninsula offers forest, farmland, and shoreline along the Potomac. Visitors enjoy hiking, biking, and paddling in a tranquil natural setting rich in history dating back to early colonial settlements. Its quiet trails and water access make it an ideal retreat for birdwatching and low-impact recreation.

☐ 🔖 ♡ **North Point State Park:** Located in Edgemere on the Chesapeake Bay, this park features tidal wetlands, woodlands, and scenic views. Once home to Bay Shore Amusement Park, it now offers trails, fishing, and birdwatching. With picnic areas and historic remnants, it provides both recreation and a glimpse of the bayfront's cultural past in a peaceful waterfront setting.

☐ 🔖 ♡ **Palmer State Park:** Nestled in Harford County near the Deer Creek, this undeveloped park preserves forests, meadows, and riparian habitat. It offers fishing, canoeing, and hiking opportunities with minimal infrastructure, making it a serene place for solitude and nature study. Its unspoiled character attracts birdwatchers, anglers, and those seeking a quiet, back-to-nature escape.

☐ 🔖 ♡ **Patapsco Valley State Park:** Stretching 32 miles along the Patapsco River, this 16,000-acre park is one of Maryland's oldest. With over 200 miles of trails, it offers hiking, biking, horseback riding, and fishing. Visitors can explore ruins, bridges, and waterfalls in diverse ecosystems from dense forests to open meadows, making it a popular year-round recreation hub.

☐ 🔖 ♡ **Patuxent River State Park:** Spanning Montgomery and Howard counties, this largely undeveloped park preserves forests, fields, and river corridors. Known for hiking, horseback riding, and trout fishing, it offers rustic trails and a peaceful natural setting. Wildlife enthusiasts enjoy birding and exploring its habitats, making it a quiet retreat from nearby urban areas.

MARYLAND

☐ ◫ ♡ **Pocomoke River State Park:** Located in Snow Hill, this park showcases Maryland's cypress swamps and hardwood forests. Popular for canoeing, kayaking, and fishing, it also offers camping, trails, and nature programs. The river's dark, tannin-stained waters host abundant wildlife, making it one of the Eastern Shore's most distinctive natural destinations for outdoor recreation.

☐ ◫ ♡ **Point Lookout State Park:** Situated at Maryland's southern tip, this park combines history and coastal beauty. The site of a Civil War prison camp, it offers a museum, historic lighthouse, and interpretive programs. Visitors also enjoy sandy beaches, fishing piers, camping, and hiking trails. Its unique blend of heritage and Chesapeake Bay scenery draws families and history buffs alike.

☐ ◫ ♡ **Rocks State Park:** Located in Harford County, this scenic park is famed for the King and Queen Seat, a dramatic rock outcrop with sweeping valley views. Trails wind through forests and along Deer Creek, offering hiking, fishing, and picnicking. The rugged cliffs, clear streams, and wooded hillsides make it a favorite spot for outdoor adventure and photography.

☐ ◫ ♡ **Rocky Gap State Park:** Nestled in Allegany County's mountains, this park surrounds Lake Habeeb, known for its clear, spring-fed waters. Popular for boating, swimming, and fishing, it also offers trails, camping, and a resort lodge. With rocky ridges, forested slopes, and abundant wildlife, Rocky Gap blends outdoor recreation with scenic mountain landscapes year-round.

☐ ◫ ♡ **Rosaryville State Park:** Near Upper Marlboro, this 1,000-acre park offers miles of multi-use trails through forests and fields. Horseback riders, hikers, and cyclists frequent its scenic routes. At its heart stands the historic Mount Airy Mansion, once visited by George Washington, adding heritage to the natural beauty. It's a versatile destination for recreation and events.

☐ ◫ ♡ **Sandy Point State Park:** A popular Chesapeake Bay beach in Annapolis, this park draws swimmers, picnickers, and anglers with its sandy shoreline and views of the Bay Bridge. Visitors can launch boats, enjoy fishing piers, and explore historic sites like the Sandy Point Shoal Lighthouse. Its mix of recreation and iconic scenery makes it a regional favorite.

☐ ◫ ♡ **Sang Run State Park:** Near Deep Creek Lake, this small park preserves a historic 19th-century homestead, farm, and general store. It offers trails, river fishing, and interpretive programs highlighting Appalachian life. Its peaceful setting along the Youghiogheny River provides both cultural insights and outdoor recreation, making it a unique heritage-rich destination in Garrett County.

☐ ◫ ♡ **Seneca Creek State Park:** Located in Gaithersburg, this 6,300-acre park offers 50 miles of trails and the scenic 90-acre Clopper Lake. Visitors enjoy hiking, biking, fishing, boating, and picnicking amid forests and meadows. With playgrounds, seasonal events, and diverse habitats, it is a family-friendly park that blends recreation with rich wildlife and natural scenery.

☐ ◫ ♡ **Sideling Hill Creek State Park:** A rugged and undeveloped area in Allegany and Washington counties, this park protects a stretch of Sideling Hill Creek as it winds through forested ridges and valleys. It offers primitive hiking and wildlife viewing, with habitats supporting black bears, eagles, and brook trout. Its remote backcountry feel makes it ideal for solitude and exploration.

☐ ◫ ♡ **Smallwood State Park:** On Mattawoman Creek in Charles County, this park honors General William Smallwood with a restored 18th-century home. Visitors can explore the historic site, fish, boat, and hike trails. The park also features a marina and picnic areas, making it a unique combination of history, Chesapeake waterways, and family recreation opportunities.

☐ ◫ ♡ **South Mountain State Park:** Following 40 miles of the Appalachian Trail, this linear park stretches across Frederick and Washington counties. Visitors explore scenic overlooks, Civil War battlefields, and historic sites along the mountain ridge. With rugged trails, forested landscapes, and sweeping valley views, it offers a blend of outdoor adventure and American history.

☐ ◫ ♡ **St. Clement's Island State Park:** Accessible only by boat, this Potomac River island marks the 1634 landing of Maryland's first colonists. Visitors explore a reconstructed lighthouse, historic markers, and scenic trails. With picnic areas and sweeping river views, it combines heritage tourism with outdoor relaxation, preserving one of Maryland's most significant colonial sites.

MARYLAND

UNITED STATES EDITION

☐ 🔖 ♡ **St. Mary's River State Park:** In Leonardtown, this park features a 250-acre lake surrounded by forests and wetlands. Trails for hiking, biking, and equestrian use circle the lake, offering wildlife viewing and quiet nature escapes. Popular for fishing and paddling, the park combines recreation with diverse habitats that support rich bird and animal populations.

☐ 🔖 ♡ **Susquehanna State Park:** Near Havre de Grace, this park features scenic river views, wooded trails, and historic sites. Visitors explore the Rock Run Grist Mill, Carter-Archer Mansion, and a working blacksmith shop, alongside fishing and hiking opportunities. Its mix of cultural history and natural landscapes makes it a unique destination along Maryland's largest river.

☐ 🔖 ♡ **Swallow Falls State Park:** In Garrett County, this park is renowned for Muddy Creek Falls, Maryland's highest waterfall at 53 feet. Trails lead to additional cascades like Swallow Falls and Tolliver Falls, all surrounded by old-growth hemlock. Visitors enjoy hiking, camping, and picnicking, with the park's stunning waterfalls and forest scenery as its centerpiece.

☐ 🔖 ♡ **Tuckahoe State Park:** Stretching across Caroline and Queen Anne's counties, this park features Tuckahoe Creek with 20 miles of trails for hiking, biking, and horseback riding. Visitors enjoy paddling, fishing, camping, and picnicking in a forested setting. Its nature center, playgrounds, and wildlife-rich habitats make it a popular, family-oriented recreation spot.

☐ 🔖 ♡ **Washington Monument State Park:** On South Mountain near Middletown, this park preserves the nation's first completed monument to George Washington, built in 1827. A portion of the Appalachian Trail runs through the park, with scenic overlooks and interpretive displays. It offers hiking, history, and picnicking in a site of national and cultural significance.

☐ 🔖 ♡ **Wills Mountain State Park:** Perched on the Allegheny Highlands above Cumberland, this largely undeveloped park features forested ridges, limestone outcrops, and sweeping views over the Potomac River Valley. It preserves critical wildlife habitat and rugged Appalachian terrain. With no developed facilities, it appeals to adventurous hikers and naturalists seeking remote wilderness.

☐ 🔖 ♡ **Wolf Den Run State Park:** Maryland's newest state park, located in Garrett County, offers trails through forests, wetlands, and streams. Known for its rugged terrain, it accommodates hiking, hunting, and off-highway vehicle use. The park's remote setting provides opportunities for wildlife viewing and outdoor adventure in a wild, largely undeveloped Appalachian landscape.

☐ 🔖 ♡ **Wye Oak State Park:** In Talbot County, this small park honors the famed Wye Oak, once the largest white oak in the U.S., which stood for over 450 years before falling in 2002. The site features a preserved section of the tree, interpretive displays, and a peaceful setting for picnicking and reflection on Maryland's natural heritage.

National Parks

☐ 🔖 ♡ **Antietam National Battlefield:** Located in Sharpsburg, this historic site preserves the battlefield of Antietam, where the bloodiest single-day battle in American history occurred. Visitors can tour monuments, explore trails, and learn about the pivotal 1862 clash that shaped the Civil War and influenced the Emancipation Proclamation, forever altering the course of the nation.

☐ 🔖 ♡ **Appalachian National Scenic Trail:** Stretching over 2,100 miles from Georgia to Maine, the Appalachian Trail winds through Maryland's Appalachian Mountains and beyond. Hikers experience rugged terrain, sweeping vistas, and diverse ecosystems along this legendary footpath. It provides opportunities for both short hikes and extended treks while connecting cultural landmarks with natural beauty across the eastern U.S.

MARYLAND

 **Assateague Island National Seashore:** Along the Maryland–Virginia coast, this seashore is famed for its wild ponies, sandy beaches, dunes, and salt marshes. Visitors can swim, kayak, bike, or camp while exploring the island's coastal habitats. The undeveloped shoreline offers a rare opportunity to enjoy a pristine barrier island environment, blending wildlife observation with seaside recreation.

 **Catoctin Mountain Park:** Located in the Blue Ridge foothills of Maryland, this park offers hiking, camping, and picnicking among rocky ridges and dense forests. Trails lead to scenic overlooks, waterfalls, and wildlife-rich areas, giving visitors a peaceful escape into nature. Known for its rugged terrain and mountain vistas, it is a beloved year-round retreat for outdoor recreation.

 **Chesapeake & Ohio Canal National Historical Park:** Following the Potomac River, this park preserves the historic C&O Canal, once a vital 19th-century transportation route. Today, visitors walk or cycle the towpath, explore canal locks and aqueducts, and discover the cultural and industrial history that shaped the region. The park provides scenic beauty alongside rich heritage.

 **Clara Barton National Historic Site:** Situated in Glen Echo, this site preserves the home of Clara Barton, founder of the American Red Cross. Visitors can tour the residence, view exhibits, and learn about her humanitarian achievements, including medical care during the Civil War. The home reflects Barton's lifelong dedication to service, offering insight into her extraordinary legacy.

 **Fort McHenry National Monument and Historic Shrine:** Located in Baltimore, this fort became famous during the War of 1812, when its defense inspired Francis Scott Key to write "The Star-Spangled Banner." Visitors explore the star-shaped fort, view exhibits, and enjoy harbor views. The site preserves military history while celebrating the national anthem's enduring significance.

 **George Washington Memorial Parkway:** This scenic highway follows the Potomac River from Mount Vernon to Great Falls, linking historic sites and natural areas. Visitors can picnic, hike, and explore trails while enjoying views of the river. The parkway preserves cultural landmarks and landscapes, offering both recreation and a driving experience that honors America's first president.

 **Greenbelt Park:** Located near Washington, D.C., this wooded oasis provides a natural escape from urban life. With 174 campsites, hiking trails, and picnic areas, it offers opportunities for birdwatching, quiet reflection, and family outings. Its proximity to the capital makes it an easily accessible retreat where visitors can enjoy the tranquility of Maryland's forests and streams.

 **Hampton National Historic Site:** Situated in Towson, this estate preserves Hampton Mansion, one of America's grandest 19th-century homes. Visitors tour the mansion, gardens, and outbuildings while learning about the estate's wealthy owners and the enslaved people who lived there. The site reveals contrasts of privilege and hardship, offering insights into Maryland's complex social history.

 **Harriet Tubman Underground Railroad National Historical Park:** Located in Dorchester County, this park honors Harriet Tubman, who led enslaved people to freedom. Visitors explore her birthplace, interpretive trails, and exhibits that highlight her life and heroic work. The landscapes reflect her journey, preserving both natural beauty and the history of one of America's most inspiring figures.

 **Monocacy National Battlefield:** In Frederick, this park preserves the site of the 1864 Battle of Monocacy, where Union troops delayed Confederate forces advancing on Washington, D.C. Visitors walk trails, tour historic farmhouses, and learn how the "Battle That Saved Washington" influenced the Civil War. The park blends scenic farmland with compelling stories of sacrifice.

UNITED STATES EDITION

MARYLAND

☐ 🔖 ♡ **Piscataway Park:** Along the Potomac River, this park protects scenic views of Mount Vernon and preserves cultural heritage, including ties to the Piscataway people. Visitors explore hiking trails, wetlands, and wildlife habitats while learning about indigenous history. With fishing, birdwatching, and riverside picnicking, it offers a peaceful balance of nature and heritage.

☐ 🔖 ♡ **Thomas Stone National Historic Site:** In Port Tobacco, this site preserves the home of Thomas Stone, a signer of the Declaration of Independence. Visitors tour the mansion and grounds, exploring his contributions to America's founding. The site highlights Revolutionary-era history while reflecting the lives of both Stone's family and those enslaved on the estate.

☐ 🔖 ♡ **Potomac Heritage National Scenic Trail:** This network of trails follows the Potomac River, linking historical sites, natural areas, and cultural landmarks from the Appalachian Mountains to the Chesapeake Bay. Visitors hike, bike, or paddle along segments of the route, experiencing landscapes rich with wildlife and history. It provides a unifying journey through diverse regions.

State & National Forests

☐ 🔖 ♡ **Cedarville State Forest:** Near Brandywine in southern Maryland, Cedarville protects pine-oak woodlands, wetlands, and diverse understory plants. Managed for timber, wildlife, and public access, it offers multi-use trails for hiking, horseback riding, and biking. Visitors can also hunt seasonally. The forest highlights sustainable forestry while providing habitat and recreation close to Washington, D.C.

☐ 🔖 ♡ **Doncaster Demonstration Forest:** Located in Charles County, this 1,447-acre forest serves as a living laboratory for sustainable forestry. Hardwood and pine stands showcase restoration techniques, wildlife habitat projects, and active timber harvest. Visitors can explore wood roads and trails, gaining firsthand insight into Maryland's forest management and conservation practices in a natural setting.

☐ 🔖 ♡ **Elk Neck State Forest:** Covering about 3,300 acres in Cecil County, Elk Neck blends hardwood forests, wetlands, and cedar swamps. It includes a shooting range, hunting areas, and portions of the Mason-Dixon Trail. Hikers, birders, and hunters frequent the area, which also supports forestry education. The forest provides diverse ecosystems while highlighting Chesapeake Bay watershed conservation.

☐ 🔖 ♡ **Green Ridge State Forest:** Maryland's largest contiguous state forest, Green Ridge spans 46,000 acres in Allegany County along the Potomac River. It features rugged ridges, deep valleys, and pine-hardwood forests. Visitors enjoy camping, hunting, boating, and 50 miles of trails. Historic rail tunnels and overlooks add cultural interest, while management protects watersheds and Appalachian mountain ecosystems.

☐ 🔖 ♡ **Pocomoke State Forest:** On Maryland's Lower Eastern Shore near Snow Hill, Pocomoke contains cypress swamps, freshwater marshes, and pine uplands. Its Bald Cypress stands are the northernmost in the U.S. Trails and waterways allow canoeing, horseback riding, hiking, and birding. Forest programs emphasize pine restoration and watershed protection while offering visitors a rare glimpse of coastal ecosystems.

☐ 🔖 ♡ **Potomac-Garrett State Forest:** Spanning western Garrett County along the Potomac River headwaters, this forest protects highland watersheds and mixed hardwood-pine woodlands. It offers hunting, hiking, and forestry education programs, with trails leading into rugged terrain. Management balances conservation with timber use, ensuring long-term forest health while providing habitat and outdoor recreation opportunities.

MARYLAND

☐ 🔖 ♡ **Salem State Forest:** Located in St. Mary's County, Salem encompasses about 3,000 acres of pine and hardwood. Managed for timber production, habitat, and education, it offers hunting, birdwatching, and primitive hiking. The forest demonstrates sustainable forestry on Maryland's southern peninsula while protecting wildlife and maintaining a rural natural landscape near the Chesapeake Bay.

☐ 🔖 ♡ **Savage River State Forest:** Maryland's largest state forest, Savage River spans 54,000 acres in Garrett County. It protects rugged ridges, river corridors, and mountain reservoirs. Popular for hunting, fishing, snowmobiling, camping, and ORV use, it also contains CCC-built trails and facilities. The forest preserves Appalachian headwaters and highlights Maryland's forestry heritage in a wild, scenic landscape.

☐ 🔖 ♡ **Seth Demonstration Forest:** Near Easton in Talbot County, Seth serves as a demonstration site for pine-hardwood management, wildlife habitat enhancement, and sustainable timber harvest. With limited public access, it supports educational programs and research. Trails allow low-impact hiking, giving visitors insight into forestry practices on Maryland's Eastern Shore in a working woodland setting.

☐ 🔖 ♡ **St. Inigoes State Forest:** Found in St. Mary's County, this small state forest preserves pine and hardwood stands in a rural coastal setting. Managed for timber, habitat, and public enjoyment, it offers hiking, birdwatching, and passive recreation. The forest contributes to wildlife conservation while providing a quiet green space for residents on Maryland's southern peninsula.

☐ 🔖 ♡ **Stoney Demonstration Forest:** Located in Talbot County, Stoney serves as an outdoor classroom for forestry practices. Managed oak-pine stands showcase silviculture, wildlife diversity, and habitat projects. Visitors can walk trails and participate in seasonal educational programs. The forest demonstrates how working lands can balance timber production with conservation on Maryland's Eastern Shore.

☐ 🔖 ♡ **Wicomico Demonstration Forest:** In Wicomico County on the Eastern Shore, Wicomico provides a living demonstration of sustainable forestry. Managed plots highlight timber practices and wildlife management. Trails allow limited public access for hiking and birdwatching. The forest serves as an educational tool while conserving natural resources in the coastal plain landscape.

National Scenic Byways & All-American Roads

☐ 🔖 ♡ **Baltimore's Historic Charles Street Scenic Byway:** Designated a National Scenic Byway, this historic corridor runs through Baltimore City, showcasing centuries of architecture, cultural landmarks, and urban parks. It links Mount Vernon Place, Johns Hopkins University, and the Inner Harbor, blending museums, monuments, and vibrant neighborhoods into Maryland's oldest planned thoroughfare.

☐ 🔖 ♡ **Chesapeake Country Scenic Byway:** An All-American Road tracing the Eastern Shore from Chesapeake City to Crisfield. It passes Colonial towns, seafood docks, wildlife refuges, and tidal rivers, preserving maritime traditions and bayfront scenery. Visitors encounter charming villages, historic churches, and sweeping vistas, offering an immersive journey into Maryland's Chesapeake heritage.

☐ 🔖 ♡ **Harriet Tubman Underground Railroad Scenic Byway:** An All-American Road across Dorchester and Caroline counties that follows the landscapes of Harriet Tubman's life and freedom missions. Blackwater swamps, rural churches, safe houses, and interpretive centers bring her legacy alive. This route connects natural beauty with powerful stories of courage, resilience, and the struggle for liberty.

☐ 🔖 ♡ **Historic National Road Scenic Byway:** Maryland's portion of the first federally funded highway, now an All-American Road, stretches from Cumberland to Baltimore. It threads through Appalachian ridges, stone bridges, canal towns, and historic inns. The byway preserves the story of westward expansion, offering a blend of scenic landscapes, heritage towns, and transportation history.

☐ 🔖 ♡ **Journey Through Hallowed Ground Byway:** A National Scenic Byway entering Maryland near Emmitsburg, continuing into Virginia and Pennsylvania. This corridor preserves Civil War battlefields, historic farms, and small towns. It highlights America's struggles for freedom, linking sacred landscapes of conflict and remembrance with pastoral scenery and enduring cultural heritage.

☐ 🔖 ♡ **Religious Freedom Byway:** A National Scenic Byway in Southern Maryland that traces early colonial churches, Jesuit missions, and settlements from Port Tobacco to St. Mary's City. It highlights the roots of American religious tolerance, blending 17th-century architecture, riverside towns, and pastoral landscapes into a corridor of cultural history and coastal beauty.

MARYLAND

State Scenic Byways

☐ ▢ ♡ **Antietam Campaign Scenic Byway:** This route traces Civil War history across western Maryland, following troop movements through Sharpsburg, South Mountain, and nearby farmland. It links battlefields, historic towns, and spring-lined ridges, offering a moving journey through rural landscapes where pivotal clashes shaped the nation's destiny.

☐ ▢ ♡ **Booth's Escape Scenic Byway:** Retracing John Wilkes Booth's flight after Lincoln's assassination, this byway winds through Southern Maryland. It passes taverns, churches, ferry crossings, and the Dr. Mudd House, evoking the tense days of 1865. Today it provides a contemplative drive through quiet countryside steeped in one of America's most dramatic historical episodes.

☐ ▢ ♡ **Cape to Cape Scenic Byway:** Stretching from Ocean City to Snow Hill near the Virginia line, this coastal route features beaches, marshes, and seaside towns. Travelers encounter fishing villages, maritime history, and wildlife refuges. Its mix of Atlantic views, cultural sites, and small-town charm highlights Maryland's Eastern Shore heritage and coastal beauty.

☐ ▢ ♡ **Falls Road Scenic Byway:** Running from Baltimore north to Alesia, this scenic drive follows the Jones Falls Valley through historic mill villages, wooded ravines, and rolling farmland. Once an industrial corridor, it now showcases rural charm, urban history, and natural landscapes, connecting city neighborhoods to Maryland's pastoral countryside.

☐ ▢ ♡ **Horses & Hounds Scenic Byway:** Winding through northern Baltimore and Harford Counties, this byway highlights Maryland's equestrian traditions. It passes hunt clubs, rolling estates, valley farms, and steeplechase country. The route blends wooded lanes, historic homes, and pastoral fields, creating a graceful landscape rooted in rural culture and sporting heritage.

☐ ▢ ♡ **Lower Susquehanna Scenic Byway:** This route follows the Susquehanna River between Havre de Grace and Perryville. Visitors experience riverside towns, historic bridges, canal locks, and bluffs with sweeping views. Wildlife areas, colonial port heritage, and parks enrich the journey, making the corridor a blend of natural beauty and cultural history.

☐ ▢ ♡ **Mason & Dixon Scenic Byway:** Tracing Maryland's northern boundary, this route explores pastoral farmland, rugged ridges, and colonial homesteads. Interpretive markers highlight the famed boundary line's history, while scenic roads connect reservoirs, villages, and historic sites. The byway celebrates both cultural identity and the landscapes that shaped it.

☐ ▢ ♡ **Mountain Maryland Scenic Byway:** This loop across Allegany and Garrett Counties showcases western Maryland's natural splendor. Travelers discover waterfalls, deep forests, mining towns, lakes, and mountain resorts. The route captures Appalachian culture and scenic beauty across four seasons, from autumn foliage to winter snows, in a rugged highland landscape.

☐ ▢ ♡ **Old Main Streets Scenic Byway:** Centered in Frederick and Carroll Counties, this route highlights Victorian villages, covered bridges, farmsteads, and college towns. Travelers enjoy rolling farmland, historic architecture, and quiet crossroads. The byway preserves Maryland's small-town character, offering an inviting glimpse into rural life and community heritage.

☐ ▢ ♡ **Roots & Tides Scenic Byway:** Following the western Chesapeake shoreline, this byway connects fishing harbors, small towns, and maritime landscapes. It winds past salt marshes, seafood docks, research fields, and Annapolis architecture. The route blends working waterfronts with historic and natural sites, showcasing the traditions and beauty of Maryland's Bay region.

☐ ▢ ♡ **Star-Spangled Banner Scenic Byway:** Linking Solomons, Benedict, Bladensburg, and Baltimore's Fort McHenry, this byway traces the War of 1812. It passes shoreline battle sites, historic churches, museums, and forts, recreating the story behind the national anthem. The corridor offers both scenic coastal drives and immersive heritage experiences.

MARYLAND

National Natural Landmarks

 **Battle Creek Cypress Swamp:** Battle Creek Cypress Swamp is a National Natural Landmark for preserving one of the northernmost stands of bald cypress in North America. This remnant of a prehistoric wetland supports amphibians, reptiles, and migratory birds. Its cypress groves and marshy ecosystem highlight the persistence of southern species far beyond their usual range.
GPS: 38.4903, -76.5908

 **Belt Woods:** Belt Woods gained National Natural Landmark status as a rare old-growth upland forest on the Atlantic Coastal Plain. Towering tulip poplars, white oaks, and a closed canopy create prime habitat for neotropical songbirds. The forest's maturity and isolation preserve a woodland structure nearly lost to development in the Mid-Atlantic.
GPS: 38.9051, -76.7630

 **Cranesville Swamp Nature Sanctuary:** Cranesville Swamp is recognized as a National Natural Landmark for harboring boreal bog and conifer swamp habitats uncommon this far south. Its frost-pocket valley shelters spruce, tamarack, and sphagnum bogs more typical of Canada. The site provides a living record of glacial-era ecosystems and unusual plant and wildlife communities.
GPS: 39.5314, -79.4819

 **Gilpin's Falls:** Gilpin's Falls holds National Natural Landmark designation for exposing early Paleozoic pillow basalts, rare evidence of volcanic eruptions that occurred underwater. These formations reveal ancient oceanic crust and offer a glimpse into tectonic activity that helped shape the Appalachian Mountains, making the site geologically significant.
GPS: 39.6897, -75.8553

 **Long Green Creek and Sweathouse Branch:** Long Green Creek and Sweathouse Branch are National Natural Landmarks for their maturing upland forest and intact Piedmont stream valleys. With tulip poplar, beech, and oak forests shading steep ravines, the site preserves regional biodiversity and water quality, showing how healthy woodlands protect urban watersheds.
GPS: 39.4809, -76.5413

 **Sugarloaf Mountain:** Sugarloaf Mountain earned National Natural Landmark status for being a striking quartzite monadnock rising above the Maryland Piedmont. Its resistant rock core preserves a remnant of ancient Appalachia, while oak-hickory forests and rocky outcrops support diverse species. The peak offers sweeping vistas and a geologic window into deep time.
GPS: 39.2692, -77.3952

MASSACHUSETTS

Massachusetts blends historic coastlines, rolling hills, scenic rivers, and vibrant forests. Its diverse outdoor offerings include state parks, a national forest, national parks and trails, and treasured natural landmarks, creating a rich tapestry of natural beauty, outdoor adventure, and timeless New England charm.

📅 Peak Season
May–October is Massachusetts's peak season, bringing warm weather, lush landscapes, and bustling coastal towns. Summer draws the most visitors to Cape Cod and the islands, while fall foliage attracts travelers across western Massachusetts.

📅 Offseason Months
November–April is the offseason, with cold winters, snow inland, and quiet coastal towns. Winter offers skiing in the Berkshires and peaceful beach walks, though some seasonal attractions close.

🍃 Scenery & Nature Timing
Spring brings blooming orchards and greening hillsides. Summer highlights beaches, whale watching, and forested trails. Fall peaks with vibrant foliage in October, while winter features snow-covered hills and frozen lakes.

✨ Special
Massachusetts features Cape Cod's shifting dunes, the tidal flats of the Cape Cod National Seashore, and whale migrations off Stellwagen Bank. Autumn transforms the Berkshires with color, while sea fog and bioluminescent plankton occasionally glow along the coast.

MASSACHUSETTS

State Parks

Ames Nowell State Park: Located in Abington, this 600-acre park is centered around Cleveland Pond, offering boating, fishing, and picnicking. Trails wind through forests and wetlands, making it popular for hiking, birdwatching, and exploring diverse habitats. With its accessible location and family-friendly setting, it provides a peaceful outdoor retreat close to the South Shore.

Ashland State Park: Ashland State Park spans 472 acres and features the scenic Ashland Reservoir, perfect for swimming, fishing, and non-motorized boating. Visitors can enjoy wooded hiking trails, picnicking, and tranquil nature walks. Its peaceful lakeside setting makes it a favorite spot for family outings, outdoor relaxation, and enjoying New England's natural beauty close to town.

Bash Bish Falls State Park: Nestled in Mount Washington, this 424-acre park is home to Bash Bish Falls, Massachusetts' tallest waterfall. Hiking trails lead through rugged terrain to the spectacular cascades and scenic overlooks. A popular destination for photographers and nature lovers, the park offers a dramatic wilderness experience with the soothing backdrop of rushing water.

Borderland State Park: Spanning over 1,800 acres in Easton and Sharon, Borderland is known for its historic Ames Mansion, scenic ponds, and wooded trails. Visitors can hike, bike, horseback ride, or fish, while enjoying its rolling landscapes. Popular year-round, the park blends cultural history with natural beauty, offering one of Massachusetts' premier outdoor recreation areas.

Bradley Palmer State Park: Once part of an early 20th-century estate, this 721-acre park in Topsfield features woodlands, open fields, and the Ipswich River. Trails are popular for hiking, biking, and horseback riding, while picnicking areas provide scenic rest stops. With ties to the adjacent Willowdale State Forest, the park offers both natural beauty and historic charm.

C. M. Gardner State Park: Located in Huntington along the Westfield River, this 15-acre park offers shaded picnic areas, fishing, and waterfront access. Popular for its quiet, family-friendly atmosphere, it provides a convenient stop for travelers exploring western Massachusetts. Though small, it blends scenic river views with opportunities for relaxation and outdoor play.

Callahan State Park: Spanning 820 acres across Framingham, Marlborough, and Southborough, Callahan features forests, fields, and ponds with more than 7 miles of trails. Visitors enjoy hiking, horseback riding, mountain biking, and cross-country skiing. With open meadows for dog walking and quiet woodlands, it's a versatile recreation spot within reach of Boston's western suburbs.

Chicopee Memorial State Park: Covering 575 acres in Chicopee, this park is anchored by a large pond offering swimming, boating, and fishing. Surrounding trails provide opportunities for hiking, biking, and wildlife observation. With open spaces, picnic areas, and easy access from the city, it's a popular destination for outdoor recreation in western Massachusetts.

Clarksburg State Park: This 368-acre park in Clarksburg is centered on Mauserts Pond, ideal for kayaking, fishing, and swimming. The Pond Loop Trail provides scenic hikes through woodlands and waterfront areas. Known for its quiet charm and natural beauty, Clarksburg offers a peaceful retreat for families, day hikers, and anyone seeking relaxation in the northern Berkshires.

Cochituate State Park: Spanning 872 acres in Natick, Cochituate State Park features three linked ponds offering boating, fishing, and swimming. With picnic areas and wooded trails, the park is a popular spot for family recreation and water sports. Its combination of accessible amenities and serene waterside scenery makes it a year-round destination for outdoor fun.

Demarest Lloyd State Park: A 200-acre coastal park in Dartmouth, Demarest Lloyd features a sandy beach on Buzzards Bay with warm, calm waters ideal for swimming and wading. Visitors can also fish, picnic, or explore the adjacent salt marshes that attract diverse birdlife. With its shallow tidepools and scenic shoreline, it's a popular family destination in summer.

MASSACHUSETTS

☐ 🔖 ♡ **Dighton Rock State Park:** Located in Berkley along the Taunton River, this 85-acre park is home to Dighton Rock, a 40-ton boulder covered in ancient petroglyphs. Visitors can explore the museum, enjoy riverside picnicking, and hike shaded trails. The site's mysterious carvings make it both a cultural landmark and a scenic place to connect with Massachusetts history.

☐ 🔖 ♡ **Dunn State Park:** Located in Gardner, Dunn State Park's 132 acres are centered around Dunn Pond, where visitors can swim, boat, and fish. Trails wind through shaded forests, perfect for hiking and wildlife viewing. With picnic areas and a family-friendly atmosphere, the park provides a peaceful setting for relaxation, outdoor play, and exploring Massachusetts' woodland beauty.

☐ 🔖 ♡ **Ellisville Harbor State Park:** Located in Plymouth, this 97-acre coastal gem protects one of the state's few natural barrier beaches. Visitors can hike trails through meadows and woodlands to reach the sandy shore, where seals are often spotted in winter. Its unique blend of salt marsh, forest, and beach habitat makes it ideal for wildlife viewing and coastal exploration.

☐ 🔖 ♡ **Great Brook Farm State Park:** Encompassing 909 acres in Carlisle, this park combines recreation with a working dairy farm. Visitors can explore over 20 miles of trails for hiking, biking, and cross-country skiing, tour the farm, or relax by a scenic pond. With educational programs, picnicking areas, and family-friendly activities, it offers a unique blend of agriculture and outdoor fun.

☐ 🔖 ♡ **Halibut Point State Park:** This 55-acre coastal park in Rockport offers breathtaking views of the Atlantic and a dramatic granite quarry. Trails lead through rocky headlands and to a scenic overlook where waves crash against the shore. Ideal for birdwatching, photography, or a peaceful seaside picnic, it's a top destination for exploring Massachusetts' rugged coastal beauty.

☐ 🔖 ♡ **Hampton Ponds State Park:** A 47-acre gem in Westfield, Hampton Ponds offers swimming, fishing, and boating in a family-friendly setting. Visitors can enjoy shaded picnicking, walking trails, and wildlife watching along the water. Popular in summer for recreation and relaxation, the park provides a convenient escape into nature while still close to town amenities.

☐ 🔖 ♡ **Holyoke Heritage State Park:** A 7-acre urban park in downtown Holyoke, it celebrates the city's role in America's industrial past. Exhibits highlight textile and paper mill history, while walking paths, picnicking spots, and views of the Connecticut River connect heritage with recreation. It's a cultural and scenic stop for visitors exploring the Pioneer Valley.

☐ 🔖 ♡ **Hopkinton State Park:** This 1,245-acre park in Hopkinton is centered on the reservoir, ideal for swimming, boating, fishing, and kayaking. With wooded hiking trails, picnic facilities, and scenic overlooks, it's a popular spot for families and outdoor enthusiasts. Its spacious grounds provide both active recreation and tranquil settings for relaxation in nature.

☐ 🔖 ♡ **Lake Wyola State Park:** A quiet 42-acre park in Shutesbury, Lake Wyola offers a sandy beach, swimming, and boating. Visitors can also fish, hike nearby trails, and picnic along the waterfront. Its clear waters and scenic forest surroundings make it a peaceful, accessible destination for outdoor recreation and summer relaxation in western Massachusetts.

☐ 🔖 ♡ **Lawrence Heritage State Park:** This 50-acre urban park preserves Lawrence's industrial history along the Merrimack River. Visitors can explore exhibits about the textile mills, labor history, and immigrant communities that shaped the city. With riverfront trails, green spaces, and cultural programs, the park combines education with outdoor beauty and heritage tourism.

☐ 🔖 ♡ **Lowell Heritage State Park:** This 60-acre urban park celebrates Lowell's pivotal role in the American Industrial Revolution. Visitors can explore mill-era exhibits, enjoy walking trails along the Merrimack River, and take part in cultural programs. By blending history, green space, and riverfront scenery, the park offers a unique experience that highlights the city's heritage.

☐ 🔖 ♡ **Mary O'Malley State Park:** This 15-acre waterfront park in Chelsea sits along the Mystic River, offering stunning views of Boston Harbor. Visitors enjoy walking trails, picnicking, and relaxing by the shoreline. Once part of the U.S. Naval Hospital grounds, it blends open green space with history, providing a peaceful community park with a maritime setting.

MASSACHUSETTS

☐ ☐ ♡ **Massasoit State Park:** Located in Taunton, this 1,200-acre park features freshwater lakes surrounded by pine and oak woodlands. With opportunities for camping, swimming, boating, and fishing, it's a popular family destination. Trails wind through forests and around ponds, offering scenic spots for hiking, biking, and wildlife watching in a peaceful natural setting.

☐ ☐ ♡ **Maudslay State Park:** Spanning 480 acres along the Merrimack River in Newburyport, Maudslay preserves the grounds of a former estate. Known for its formal gardens, towering pines, and spring rhododendrons, the park offers hiking, picnicking, and birdwatching. With scenic river views and cultural programs, it blends historic charm with outdoor recreation.

☐ ☐ ♡ **Moore State Park:** Situated in Paxton, this 400-acre park blends history and nature, featuring old mill foundations, stone walls, and waterfalls. Trails wind through woodlands and fields, with spring bringing colorful wildflowers and rhododendrons. Visitors enjoy hiking, fishing, and photography in a setting that highlights both New England's past and its natural beauty.

☐ ☐ ♡ **Mount Holyoke Range State Park:** This park in Amherst and Granby preserves a rugged traprock ridge with sweeping views of the Connecticut River Valley. Part of the Metacomet-Monadnock Trail, it offers challenging hikes, birdwatching, and opportunities for picnicking. Rich in wildlife and natural beauty, it's a favorite for hikers seeking striking vistas and varied terrain.

☐ ☐ ♡ **Natural Bridge State Park:** Located in North Adams, this 48-acre park features the only natural white marble arch in North America. Visitors can explore the marble bridge and former quarry, hike short trails, and enjoy interpretive exhibits. Combining geology, industry, and scenery, the park offers a fascinating glimpse into the Berkshires' unique natural history.

☐ ☐ ♡ **Nickerson State Park:** A 1,900-acre retreat in Brewster on Cape Cod, Nickerson offers crystal-clear kettle ponds for swimming, boating, and fishing. With over 400 campsites, biking trails connecting to the Cape Cod Rail Trail, and abundant hiking paths, it's one of the state's most popular camping destinations. Its pine forests and freshwater lakes create a unique Cape setting.

☐ ☐ ♡ **Pearl Hill State Park:** Located in Townsend, this 1,000-acre park offers wooded trails, a scenic pond, and a 50-site campground. Visitors enjoy hiking, mountain biking, fishing, and picnicking in its peaceful surroundings. Known for its quiet charm and family-friendly atmosphere, Pearl Hill provides an accessible outdoor escape in northern Massachusetts' rolling landscapes.

☐ ☐ ♡ **Pilgrim Memorial State Park:** Situated in Plymouth, this waterfront park preserves one of the nation's most iconic landmarks: Plymouth Rock. Visitors can explore historic monuments, enjoy harbor views, and learn about the Pilgrims' 1620 landing. Blending history with scenic beauty, it's one of the most visited state parks in Massachusetts and a symbol of early American heritage.

☐ ☐ ♡ **Quinsigamond State Park:** This Worcester park sits along the shores of Lake Quinsigamond, a hub for rowing competitions and water recreation. Visitors enjoy swimming, sailing, fishing, and picnicking, with Regatta Point and Lake Park offering green spaces and facilities. Its lakeside setting combines active water sports with family-friendly relaxation near the city.

☐ ☐ ♡ **Robinson State Park:** Covering 800 acres in Agawam, Robinson State Park stretches along the Westfield River. It offers trails for hiking, biking, and horseback riding, as well as opportunities for swimming, fishing, and picnicking. Its mix of forests, wetlands, and riverfront scenery provides diverse habitats and makes it a vibrant destination for outdoor recreation.

☐ ☐ ♡ **Skinner State Park:** Located in Hadley, this park is home to Mount Holyoke's summit, made famous by the historic Prospect House hotel. Visitors can hike or drive to the top for sweeping views of the Connecticut River Valley. With its blend of history, scenery, and trails, the park remains a favorite destination for picnicking and exploring western Massachusetts landscapes.

☐ ☐ ♡ **South Cape Beach State Park:** A coastal treasure in Mashpee on Cape Cod, this 460-acre park features a mile of sandy beach, salt marshes, and coastal dunes. Visitors can swim, fish, birdwatch, or hike along trails connecting to Waquoit Bay. With stunning views of Vineyard Sound, it offers a perfect blend of relaxation and natural exploration by the sea.

UNITED STATES EDITION

MASSACHUSETTS

☐ 🔖 ♡ **Wahconah Falls State Park:** Located in Dalton, this small but scenic park showcases Wahconah Falls, where Cascade Brook tumbles over granite ledges in a dramatic display. Short trails lead to overlooks of the falls, and visitors enjoy picnicking in the wooded surroundings. Its intimate size and natural beauty make it a beloved spot for photography and quiet escapes.

☐ 🔖 ♡ **Wells State Park:** Covering 1,400 acres in Sturbridge, Wells State Park offers extensive hiking trails and a 60-site campground. Walker Pond is a hub for swimming, boating, and fishing, while the park's woodlands provide opportunities for wildlife viewing. With a blend of recreation and relaxation, it's a popular destination for families and nature lovers year-round.

☐ 🔖 ♡ **Western Gateway Heritage State Park:** Located in North Adams, this heritage park celebrates the Hoosac Tunnel and the region's industrial history. Visitors can explore interpretive exhibits, take guided tours, and walk scenic trails in the northern Berkshires. By blending history with natural beauty, it offers both education and recreation in one setting.

☐ 🔖 ♡ **Whitehall State Park:** Located in Hopkinton, this park surrounds the scenic 840-acre Whitehall Reservoir. It's a favorite spot for boating, canoeing, and fishing, with trails for hiking and horseback riding along the shoreline. The quiet, wooded setting and expansive waters make it an inviting retreat for outdoor recreation close to the greater Boston area.

☐ 🔖 ♡ **Wompatuck State Park:** Spanning 3,500 acres in Hingham, this park boasts over 40 miles of trails for hiking, biking, and horseback riding. Scenic ponds provide fishing and picnicking opportunities, while its campgrounds welcome overnight visitors. Rich in history and natural beauty, Wompatuck offers outdoor exploration just a short drive from Boston.

National Parks

 ☐ 🔖 ♡ **Adams National Historical Park:** Located in Quincy, this park preserves the homes and legacies of Presidents John Adams and John Quincy Adams. Visitors can tour the Adams Mansion and Stone Library while learning about the Adams family's influence on early America. The site offers a unique window into the Revolutionary period and the nation's political beginnings.

 ☐ 🔖 ♡ **Appalachian National Scenic Trail:** Stretching over 2,100 miles from Georgia to Maine, the Appalachian Trail winds through Massachusetts' Berkshires, offering hikers scenic ridgelines, forested paths, and diverse ecosystems. It provides a mix of peaceful walks and challenging climbs, making it a bucket-list destination for outdoor adventurers exploring the Eastern U.S.

 ☐ 🔖 ♡ **Blackstone River Valley National Historical Park:** Spanning Rhode Island and Massachusetts, this park highlights the birthplace of America's Industrial Revolution. Visitors can explore historic mill villages, tour the Slater Mill, and walk riverfront paths. The park preserves stories of innovation, labor, and cultural change that reshaped the nation in the 18th and 19th centuries.

 ☐ 🔖 ♡ **Boston African American National Historic Site:** This Boston site preserves 15 historic structures along the Black Heritage Trail. Visitors can learn about the city's vibrant 19th-century African American community, abolitionist leaders, and the fight for freedom. Guided tours and interpretive programs connect the nation's broader civil rights story to Boston's history.

 ☐ 🔖 ♡ **Boston Harbor Islands National Recreation Area:** Encompassing 34 islands in Boston Harbor, this park offers beaches, trails, and historic sites. Visitors can explore Fort Warren on Georges Island, visit the nation's oldest lighthouse, or hike through island ecosystems. With ferry access, it's a mix of natural beauty, maritime heritage, and family-friendly recreation.

MASSACHUSETTS

 **Boston National Historical Park:** This park connects iconic Revolutionary War sites across Boston, including the Freedom Trail, Bunker Hill Monument, and Old North Church. Visitors can walk historic streets, explore museums, and discover the events that sparked America's independence. It's a living classroom that brings Boston's colonial history to life.

 **Cape Cod National Seashore:** Protecting 40 miles of shoreline, this national seashore offers sandy beaches, dunes, salt marshes, and historic lighthouses. Visitors can hike scenic trails, bike along the Cape Cod Rail Trail, and swim in the Atlantic. The seashore blends recreation with cultural preservation, celebrating Cape Cod's unique natural and maritime heritage.

 **Frederick Law Olmsted National Historic Site:** In Brookline, this park preserves the home and office of America's foremost landscape architect. Visitors can explore the "Fairsted" estate, view original plans, and learn about Olmsted's role in designing Central Park, Boston's Emerald Necklace, and countless public spaces that shaped urban America.

 **John F. Kennedy National Historic Site:** This Brookline home preserves the birthplace and boyhood environment of John F. Kennedy, the 35th U.S. president. Visitors can explore rooms restored to their 1917 appearance, learn about Kennedy's upbringing, and gain insight into the early life of one of the nation's most influential modern leaders.

 **Longfellow House–Washington's Headquarters National Historic Site:** Located in Cambridge, this historic mansion served both as poet Henry Wadsworth Longfellow's home and George Washington's headquarters during the Revolutionary War. Visitors can tour the elegant house, stroll its gardens, and learn about its significance in both American literature and military history.

 **Lowell National Historical Park:** This park preserves the story of New England's textile mills and the rise of industry in Lowell. Visitors can explore restored mills, walk canals, and tour the Boott Cotton Mills Museum. The site highlights the workers, innovations, and cultural shifts that fueled America's transformation into an industrial power.

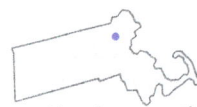 **Minute Man National Historical Park:** Located in Concord, Lincoln, and Lexington, this park preserves the landscapes where the Revolutionary War began. Visitors can walk the Battle Road Trail, stand at the North Bridge, and watch reenactments that bring April 19, 1775, to life. The park connects past struggles for liberty with modern reflections on freedom.

 **New Bedford Whaling National Historical Park:** Centered in downtown New Bedford, this park tells the story of the whaling industry that made the city the "Whaling Capital of the World." Visitors can explore cobblestone streets, visit the Whaling Museum, and learn about the diverse communities and maritime heritage that defined America's whaling era.

 **Salem Maritime National Historic Site:** Established as the first National Historic Site in the U.S., this 9-acre waterfront park preserves Salem's role in early American trade. Visitors can explore historic wharves, warehouses, the Custom House, and replica tall ships. The site highlights maritime commerce, shipbuilding, and Salem's global connections during the 18th and 19th centuries.

 **Saugus Iron Works National Historic Site:** Located on the banks of the Saugus River, this site preserves the first integrated ironworks in North America, dating to the 1640s. Visitors can tour a reconstructed blast furnace, forge, and waterwheel-powered mill. The site offers a glimpse into colonial industry and the beginnings of American iron production.

 **Springfield Armory National Historic Site:** In Springfield, this site preserves the nation's first armory, active from 1777 to 1968. For nearly two centuries it produced U.S. military firearms and pioneered manufacturing advances. Visitors can explore the museum's extensive firearms collection, learn about industrial innovations, and understand the armory's role in American defense.

UNITED STATES EDITION

MASSACHUSETTS

State & National Forests

☐ 🔖 ♡ **Beartown State Forest:** Located in the Berkshires near Great Barrington, this 12,000-acre forest features oak-chestnut ridges, rocky outcrops, and hidden waterfalls. Trails connect to Benedict Pond, caves, and scenic overlooks. Popular for hiking, camping, cross-country skiing, and foliage viewing, it balances conservation with outdoor adventure in western Massachusetts.

☐ 🔖 ♡ **Brimfield State Forest:** Covering more than 3,000 acres in south-central Massachusetts, Brimfield State Forest offers quiet woodland trails, ponds, and access to the East Brimfield Lake flood-control area. Visitors enjoy hiking, horseback riding, mountain biking, and snowmobiling in season. With its mix of pine and hardwood forests, it provides a peaceful, uncrowded outdoor escape.

☐ 🔖 ♡ **Douglas State Forest:** Situated on the Massachusetts-Rhode Island border, this 5,500-acre forest includes Wallum Lake, cedar swamps, and glacial features. It supports boating, fishing, hiking, horseback riding, and OHV use. The Midstate Trail crosses the area, which also protects rare Atlantic white cedar habitats and offers camping and interpretive programs.

☐ 🔖 ♡ **Erving State Forest:** This 2,500-acre forest in the northern Pioneer Valley centers on Laurel Lake, popular for swimming, fishing, and boating. Miles of wooded trails climb to ledges with scenic views of the Millers River Valley. Campgrounds, picnic areas, and winter recreation make it a year-round destination, blending water-based fun with upland forest adventure.

☐ 🔖 ♡ **Harold Parker State Forest:** A 3,300-acre forest in northeastern Massachusetts with mixed pine and hardwood stands, over 35 miles of trails, and several ponds. Located just north of Boston, it's popular for hiking, biking, fishing, horseback riding, and camping. The forest is also managed for sustainable timber and serves as a green buffer for nearby communities.

☐ 🔖 ♡ **Kenneth Dubuque Memorial State Forest:** Spanning over 7,400 acres in Hawley and Plainfield, this forest contains a diverse mix of hardwoods, conifers, wetlands, and streams. Known for its rustic trails, snowmobiling, and wildlife, it also contains historic cellar holes and CCC-era remains. It serves both recreation and sustainable forestry purposes.

☐ 🔖 ♡ **Leominster State Forest:** Covering over 4,200 acres in central Massachusetts, this forest features hilly terrain, pine-hardwood woods, and Crow Hill, a popular rock-climbing area. It includes trails for mountain biking, hiking, and snowmobiling, plus a beach at Crow Hill Pond. The forest is managed for recreation, timber, and wildlife conservation.

☐ 🔖 ♡ **Mohawk Trail State Forest:** Encompassing 6,000+ acres along the Deerfield River in the northern Berkshires, this forest includes some of the oldest and tallest trees in New England. With historic CCC-built cabins, scenic roads, and remote trails, it provides access to old-growth forest, mountain ridges, and riverfront camping and paddling.

☐ 🔖 ♡ **Monroe State Forest:** Located in the highlands of Franklin County, this 3,750-acre forest features steep wooded hills, streams, and quiet hiking trails. Known for Dunbar Brook and its cascades, the forest is minimally developed and managed for conservation, wildlife, and hiking. It's ideal for nature immersion away from crowds.

☐ 🔖 ♡ **Mount Grace State Forest:** Centered around Mount Grace (1,621 ft), this forest in Warwick and Northfield offers scenic trails, a fire tower, and expansive views. It includes upland hardwood forests, rocky outcrops, and wildlife habitat. The Midstate Trail passes through, making it a popular destination for hikers and outdoor enthusiasts seeking solitude and elevation.

☐ 🔖 ♡ **Myles Standish State Forest:** Encompassing more than 12,000 acres in southeastern Massachusetts, this forest includes pine barrens, kettle ponds, and cranberry bogs. It features campgrounds, equestrian trails, bike paths, and rare wildlife habitats. Located in Plymouth County, it's one of the most visited forests, offering varied year-round outdoor recreation.

☐ 🔖 ♡ **October Mountain State Forest:** The largest state forest in Massachusetts, spanning over 16,000 acres in the Berkshires. It features hardwood ridges, wetlands, and streams, with access to the Appalachian Trail. Visitors enjoy camping, hiking, fishing, snowmobiling, and wildlife watching amid the diverse terrain and scenic mountain backdrops.

MASSACHUSETTS

☐ 🔖 ♡ **Otter River State Forest:** One of Massachusetts' earliest state forests, Otter River lies in Winchendon and Templeton, offering a campground, picnic areas, and forest roads. Located along Otter and Millers Rivers, it provides hiking, mountain biking, and water access. It's part of the larger Birch Hill flood control area and supports year-round recreation.

☐ 🔖 ♡ **Pittsfield State Forest:** Covering over 10,600 acres in western Massachusetts, this forest includes Berry Pond—the highest natural body of water in the state—and mountain trails with scenic views. Offers camping, hiking, skiing, and snowmobiling. It's a key part of the Taconic Range ecosystem and includes access to Taconic Crest Trail.

☐ 🔖 ♡ **Savoy Mountain State Forest:** Located in the northwestern Berkshires, this 10,000-acre forest features mixed hardwoods and spruce-fir stands. With over 35 miles of trails, waterfalls like Tannery Falls, camping areas, and panoramic ridgeline views, it's a haven for hikers, birders, and cross-country skiers in a remote, tranquil mountain setting.

☐ 🔖 ♡ **Upton State Forest:** This 2,600-acre forest in Worcester County includes CCC-built roads and structures, a rich variety of hardwoods and pines, and part of the Midstate Trail. It's a popular site for hiking, snowshoeing, dog walking, and educational outings. The forest also protects a large vernal pool complex and historic landscape features.

☐ 🔖 ♡ **Wendell State Forest:** Located in the northern Pioneer Valley, this 7,500-acre forest includes Ruggles Pond, extensive hardwood stands, and hiking, biking, and snowmobiling trails. It offers swimming, picnicking, and backcountry camping. Managed for multiple uses, it supports biodiversity, timber harvest, and year-round outdoor activity.

National Scenic Byways & All-American Roads

☐ 🔖 ♡ **Battle Road Scenic Byway:** Designated as a National Scenic Byway, this 14-mile route runs from Arlington through Lexington and Concord, following the path of the opening battles of the American Revolution. Travelers encounter preserved colonial homes, historic farmsteads, interpretive sites, and rolling woodlands, offering a vivid journey through landscapes where the nation's fight for liberty began.

☐ 🔖 ♡ **Connecticut River Byway:** This National Scenic Byway traces the Connecticut River Valley from South Hadley north into Vermont and New Hampshire. It highlights fertile farmland, forested riverbanks, and historic mill towns, with opportunities for boating, biking, and wildlife watching. The corridor blends cultural heritage with New England scenery, offering a dynamic look at the region's natural and human history.

☐ 🔖 ♡ **Mohawk Trail Scenic Byway:** One of the nation's first scenic routes, this 65-mile National Scenic Byway follows historic Route 2 across the Berkshires. It traces an ancient Native American trade path, climbing through forested ridges and river gorges. Visitors encounter waterfalls, dramatic overlooks, and cultural landmarks like the Bridge of Flowers, making it a seasonal favorite for foliage and history alike.

☐ 🔖 ♡ **Old King's Highway (Route 6A):** This 34-mile National Scenic Byway runs along Cape Cod's northern shore from Sandwich to Orleans. Passing sea captain's homes, historic churches, cranberry bogs, and salt marshes, it showcases America's largest contiguous historic district. The route blends coastal scenery with centuries of cultural memory, offering a quintessential Cape Cod experience steeped in history.

State Scenic Byways

☐ 🔖 ♡ **Essex Coastal Scenic Byway:** Running 90 miles from Lynn to Salisbury, this State Scenic Byway highlights the North Shore's maritime heritage and coastal beauty. Passing through historic seaport towns, salt marshes, beaches, and colonial landmarks, it features lighthouses, museums, and fishing villages. The route blends New England charm with centuries of cultural and natural history.

☐ 🔖 ♡ **Jacob's Ladder Trail Scenic Byway (Route 20):** Spanning 33 miles through the Berkshire foothills, this route connects Russell to Lee along wooded valleys and mountain ridges. Once a vital 19th-century turnpike, it now showcases forested landscapes, farmlands, and rocky riversides. Cultural sites like Jacob's Pillow Dance Festival and Tanglewood enrich the journey with music and history.

UNITED STATES EDITION

MASSACHUSETTS

☐ 🔖 ♡ **Mount Greylock Scenic Byway:** A 16-mile drive ascending to Massachusetts' highest summit, this State Scenic Byway offers sweeping views across five states. The road winds through mixed forests, past trailheads and overlooks, before reaching Bascom Lodge at the summit. With its dramatic mountain scenery and rich cultural legacy, it's one of the state's most iconic highland routes.

☐ 🔖 ♡ **Route 122 Scenic Byway:** Following the Blackstone River Valley through central Massachusetts, this State Scenic Byway links mill villages, farms, and forests that tell the story of early American industry. From Worcester south to the Rhode Island border, it passes waterfalls, canals, and stone-arch bridges, blending rural beauty with the region's industrial and cultural heritage.

National Natural Landmarks

 ☐ 🔖 ♡ **Acushnet Cedar Swamp:** Recognized as a National Natural Landmark for being one of Massachusetts' largest and most pristine wetlands, Acushnet Cedar Swamp protects a classic oak–chestnut forest remnant in glaciated terrain. Its waterlogged soils sustain Atlantic white cedar, red maple, and sphagnum, offering a rare refuge for swamp biodiversity in southern New England.
GPS: 41.6922, -70.9597

 ☐ 🔖 ♡ **Bartholomew's Cobble:** This National Natural Landmark in the Housatonic Valley supports extraordinary plant richness, including North America's highest diversity of ferns. Its limestone and marble ledges mix with floodplains and upland forest to form a mosaic of habitats. With more than 800 species, the site highlights how geology shapes ecological diversity.
GPS: 42.0572, -73.3508

 ☐ 🔖 ♡ **Cold River Virgin Forest:** Designated a National Natural Landmark for preserving the last known virgin hemlock–northern hardwood forest in New England, Cold River shelters towering hemlocks and sugar maples over four centuries old. Its steep ravine setting, untouched by logging, provides scientists a living glimpse into the region's pre-settlement ecosystems.
GPS: 42.6467, -72.9464

 ☐ 🔖 ♡ **Fannie Stebbins Refuge:** A National Natural Landmark along the Connecticut River, this floodplain refuge conserves meadows, marshes, ponds, and forests that exemplify natural riverine succession. Its wetlands host migratory birds and diverse aquatic life, making it one of the best-preserved examples of river valley habitat in the Northeast.
GPS: 42.0395, -72.6026

 ☐ 🔖 ♡ **Gay Head Cliffs:** Honored as a National Natural Landmark for their vivid layers of Cretaceous through Pleistocene strata, these 150-foot cliffs on Martha's Vineyard reveal a rare geologic record. A sacred site for the Wampanoag people, the colorful clays also preserve fossil evidence and offer panoramic views of the Atlantic.
GPS: 41.3344, -70.7958

 ☐ 🔖 ♡ **Hawley Bog:** This glacial kettle-hole bog was named a National Natural Landmark for its textbook progression from open water to forested wetland. Floating mats of sphagnum, boreal plants, and spruce–fir forest illustrate classic bog succession. Its intact peatland habitats provide exceptional opportunities for research and conservation.
GPS: 42.5758, -72.8906

 ☐ 🔖 ♡ **Mt. Greylock Old Growth Spruce:** On the slopes of Massachusetts' tallest peak lies a National Natural Landmark recognized for its red spruce stands more than 150 years old. Possibly virgin, these trees are the southernmost example of such age and type in New England, offering a rare window into high-elevation forest history.
GPS: 42.6375, -73.1662

 ☐ 🔖 ♡ **Muskeget Island:** This remote, windswept island is a National Natural Landmark for its unique wildlife significance. It is the sole habitat of the Muskeget beach vole and the southernmost U.S. breeding ground for gray seals. Its dunes and nesting colonies of gulls showcase resilient coastal ecosystems shaped by ocean winds and tides.
GPS: 41.3353, -70.3042

MASSACHUSETTS

 ☐ 🔖 ♡ **North and South Rivers:** Designated a National Natural Landmark for their tidal estuarine systems, these rivers support salt, brackish, and freshwater marshes in a constantly shifting landscape. More than 45 fish species and diverse birdlife depend on their habitats, which demonstrate the ecological value of drowned river-mouth estuaries.
GPS: 42.1604, -70.7141

 ☐ 🔖 ♡ **Poutwater Pond:** This kettle-hole bog is a National Natural Landmark for exemplifying sphagnum–heath bog succession in a glacial depression. Its open pond, encircled by floating peat mats and forest, nurtures rare mosses, shrubs, and wetland bird species. The site provides one of the best illustrations of bog evolution in Massachusetts.
GPS: 42.4247, -71.8383

 ☐ 🔖 ♡ **Reedy Meadow:** Recognized as a National Natural Landmark for being the largest freshwater cattail marsh in Massachusetts, Reedy Meadow supports an impressive array of birdlife, including rare breeders like the king rail. Seasonal floods enrich its soils, sustaining a dynamic wetland ecosystem with exceptional ecological importance.
GPS: 42.5813, -71.0429

UNITED STATES EDITION

Michigan

Michigan's outdoor splendor is framed by the Great Lakes, with towering dunes, dense forests, sparkling inland waters, and island landscapes. Through its extensive state parks, national forests, a beloved national park, and exceptional natural landmarks, Michigan offers endless exploration across shorelines, wilderness trails, and serene natural retreats.

📅 Peak Season
June–September is Michigan's peak season, with warm weather, sunny days, and full access to lakes, beaches, and trails. Summer is ideal for boating and camping, while fall draws visitors for its spectacular foliage.

📅 Offseason Months
November–April is the offseason, bringing cold weather and heavy snow across much of the state. Winter is popular for skiing and snowmobiling in the north, while southern regions stay quieter.

🍃 Scenery & Nature Timing
Spring brings wildflowers and blooming orchards, especially around Traverse City. Summer highlights Great Lakes recreation and island adventures. Fall colors peak in October, while winter showcases frozen waterfalls and icy shorelines.

✨ Special
Michigan features the Sleeping Bear Dunes' massive sand cliffs, the glowing Pictured Rocks of Lake Superior, and the aurora borealis visible in the Upper Peninsula. Ice formations along the Great Lakes, thundering waterfalls, and fall color tunnels define its natural wonder.

MICHIGAN

State Parks

☐ 🔖 ♡ **Algonac State Park:** Along the St. Clair River, this 1,550-acre park is known for freighter watching and riverfront recreation. It offers camping, hiking, fishing, and picnicking, plus rare prairie habitat. The scenic shoreline makes it a favorite for birdwatchers and those seeking both water-based fun and quiet nature escapes.

☐ 🔖 ♡ **Aloha State Park:** Nestled on Mullett Lake, this 172-acre park offers sandy beaches, swimming, boating, and fishing. With its large campground and direct access to Michigan's Inland Waterway, it's a hub for water recreation. The park's peaceful setting makes it ideal for family outings, paddling adventures, or relaxing lakeside retreats.

☐ 🔖 ♡ **Baraga State Park:** Located on Lake Superior's Keweenaw Bay, this 56-acre park is a small but scenic Upper Peninsula destination. It features lakeshore camping, fishing, and easy access to hiking trails in the surrounding region. Visitors enjoy sunsets over the bay, water recreation, and a gateway location for exploring Michigan's north woods.

☐ 🔖 ♡ **Bay City State Park:** Spanning 2,389 acres on Saginaw Bay, this park includes Tobico Marsh, one of the Great Lakes' largest coastal wetlands. It offers sandy beaches, birdwatching, fishing, hiking, and family-friendly facilities. The combination of marsh, bayfront, and forest habitat makes it a top destination for both outdoor adventure and wildlife observation.

☐ 🔖 ♡ **Belle Isle Park:** A 982-acre island park in the Detroit River, Belle Isle blends city energy with natural beauty. It offers a zoo, aquarium, conservatory, beach, lighthouse, trails, and cultural landmarks. Visitors can enjoy picnics, bike rides, or shoreline walks while taking in sweeping views of Detroit and Windsor. It's Michigan's most urban state park.

☐ 🔖 ♡ **Bewabic State Park:** On Fortune Lake in the western U.P., this 315-acre park showcases wooded ridges and historic Civilian Conservation Corps stonework. It offers swimming, boating, fishing, and hiking in a peaceful setting. With lakeside campsites and scenic picnic spots, the park blends rustic charm with outdoor recreation in Iron County.

☐ 🔖 ♡ **Brimley State Park:** Located on Whitefish Bay near Sault Ste. Marie, this 151-acre park provides sandy beaches, fishing, and boating access to Lake Superior. One of the oldest state parks in the U.P., it combines family-friendly camping with big-water scenery. Its shoreline is popular for swimming, picnicking, and enjoying Upper Peninsula sunrises.

☐ 🔖 ♡ **Burt Lake State Park:** A 406-acre park on Burt Lake's sandy shoreline, this destination offers camping, swimming, boating, and fishing. Its location along the Inland Waterway makes it ideal for paddling or cruising through connected lakes and rivers. The beach and picnic areas make it especially popular with families during summer months.

☐ 🔖 ♡ **Cambridge Junction Historic State Park:** This 80-acre park centers on the restored Walker Tavern, an important 19th-century stagecoach stop. Visitors can explore the historic inn, enjoy costumed interpreters, and learn about Michigan's travel and settlement history. Scenic grounds and walking trails connect the past with outdoor relaxation.

☐ 🔖 ♡ **Cheboygan State Park:** Covering 1,250 acres along Lake Huron, this park features sandy beaches, scenic trails, and views of lighthouse ruins on nearby islands. It offers camping, fishing, and wildlife watching. The mix of shoreline, forest, and marsh makes it an attractive destination for both nature enthusiasts and history lovers.

☐ 🔖 ♡ **Clear Lake State Park:** A 290-acre retreat in northern Michigan, Clear Lake State Park offers sandy swimming beaches, wooded hiking trails, and a quiet campground. Anglers enjoy fishing for walleye and bass, while paddlers and swimmers take advantage of the pristine waters. Its forested setting provides a peaceful northern getaway.

☐ 🔖 ♡ **Craig Lake State Park:** At 8,400 acres, this remote Upper Peninsula wilderness park is Michigan's most rugged. It offers backcountry camping, fishing, paddling, and hiking among six lakes and dense forests. Wildlife such as moose and loons thrive here. Accessible mainly by rough roads, it's ideal for solitude and true wilderness experiences.

MICHIGAN

☐ ▢ ♡ **Dodge #4 State Park:** On Cass Lake in Oakland County, this 139-acre park provides a sandy swimming beach, fishing piers, and boating access. It's a favorite summer getaway for metro Detroit residents, with shaded picnic areas and family-friendly facilities. The park blends lakeside fun with convenience and accessibility.

☐ ▢ ♡ **Duck Lake State Park:** Located on Lake Michigan near Muskegon, this 728-acre park features a channel between Duck Lake and the big lake. Visitors enjoy sandy beaches, swimming, fishing, and hiking through dune and forest landscapes. The park's natural beauty and water access make it a versatile outdoor destination.

☐ ▢ ♡ **Fayette Historic State Park:** On the Garden Peninsula, this 711-acre park preserves the 19th-century townsite of Fayette, once an iron-smelting community. Restored buildings and interpretive programs tell its industrial story. Visitors also enjoy scenic cliffs, Lake Michigan shoreline, hiking, and camping, making it both a historic and recreational gem.

☐ ▢ ♡ **Fisherman's Island State Park:** Stretching along five miles of Lake Michigan shoreline near Charlevoix, this 2,678-acre park offers rustic camping, sandy beaches, and wooded dunes. Its semi-primitive setting makes it popular with those seeking solitude. Visitors can hike, fish, swim, and enjoy wildlife, with campsites located close to the shoreline for a true back-to-nature feel.

☐ ▢ ♡ **Fort Wilkins Historic State Park:** Situated at the tip of the Keweenaw Peninsula, this 700+ acre park preserves a restored 1844 military outpost. Visitors can tour the fort, see costumed interpreters, and explore exhibits on frontier life. Surrounded by Lake Fanny Hooe and Lake Superior, it also offers camping, fishing, hiking, and stunning northern scenery.

☐ ▢ ♡ **Grand Haven State Park:** This 48-acre park sits on the shores of Lake Michigan at the mouth of the Grand River. It's known for its sandy swimming beach, boardwalk, and views of the pier and lighthouse. Popular for camping, picnicking, sunbathing, and festivals, the park offers a quintessential Lake Michigan beach-town experience in the heart of Grand Haven.

☐ ▢ ♡ **Grand Mere State Park:** A 985-acre natural area along Lake Michigan, Grand Mere features three ancient inland lakes, towering dunes, wetlands, and forest trails. The park is less developed, emphasizing hiking, birdwatching, and quiet exploration. Its diverse habitats support rare plants and wildlife, making it a favorite among naturalists and solitude-seekers.

☐ ▢ ♡ **Harrisville State Park:** Nestled on Lake Huron in Alcona County, this 107-acre park combines sandy beaches, shady picnic areas, and a modern campground. It offers swimming, fishing, and nature programs. Close to town yet scenic and peaceful, it serves as a convenient family destination and a base for exploring Michigan's sunrise coast.

☐ ▢ ♡ **Hartwick Pines State Park:** At 9,672 acres, Hartwick Pines is among the largest state parks in the Lower Peninsula. It protects a rare stand of old-growth white pine, offering a glimpse into Michigan's forested past. Visitors enjoy the Michigan Forest Visitor Center, miles of trails, fishing, and camping. The towering pines provide a serene cathedral-like atmosphere.

☐ ▢ ♡ **Hoeft State Park:** Established in 1920, this 301-acre park near Rogers City offers sandy Lake Huron beaches, wooded trails, and a family-friendly campground. A paved trail connects it to Rogers City along the shoreline. With swimming, picnicking, and year-round programs, it blends natural beauty with easy access to local attractions and historic lighthouses.

☐ ▢ ♡ **Holland State Park:** A popular Lake Michigan destination, this 142-acre park features a broad sandy beach and iconic views of the "Big Red" lighthouse. Swimming, sunbathing, boating, and camping draw thousands of visitors each summer. The park's west and north units provide shoreline access, fishing piers, and a quintessential West Michigan beach-town experience.

☐ ▢ ♡ **Indian Lake State Park:** In Schoolcraft County, this 567-acre park offers sandy beaches, two campgrounds, and boating access to the state's fourth-largest inland lake. Known for fishing and swimming, the park also provides hiking and wildlife observation. Its peaceful Upper Peninsula setting makes it ideal for family camping and water recreation.

☐ ▢ ♡ **Interlochen State Park:** Established in 1917, Interlochen is Michigan's first state park. The 187-acre site lies between Duck and Green Lakes, offering swimming, boating, and fishing. Campers enjoy shaded sites close to the water. Adjacent to the Interlochen Center for the Arts, it uniquely blends outdoor recreation with cultural experiences.

☐ ▢ ♡ **J.W. Wells State Park:** On Green Bay in Menominee County, this 678-acre park offers sandy beaches, wooded trails, and a modern campground. Visitors enjoy swimming, boating, fishing, and picnicking in a quiet Upper Peninsula setting. With its shoreline and rustic charm, it provides a relaxing atmosphere for both day-trippers and campers.

MICHIGAN

☐ 🔖 ♡ **Keith J. Charters Traverse City State Park:** Just two miles from downtown Traverse City, this 75-acre park offers ¼ mile of sandy beach along Grand Traverse Bay. It features a modern campground, swimming, and access to nearby bike trails. Popular for its location, it provides a balance of city convenience and lakeshore recreation.

☐ 🔖 ♡ **Lake Gogebic State Park:** Nestled on the western shore of Lake Gogebic, the U.P.'s largest inland lake, this 360-acre park is popular for fishing, boating, and camping. With spacious wooded campsites and a sandy swimming beach, it's a peaceful base for exploring the western U.P. The park also provides access to snowmobiling and winter sports.

☐ 🔖 ♡ **Lakeport State Park:** Located along Lake Huron north of Port Huron, this 565-acre park includes two distinct campgrounds, sandy beaches, and picnic areas. It's a favorite summer spot for swimming, boating, and fishing. With wooded trails and shoreline access, the park serves as both a local getaway and a convenient stop for travelers along I-94.

☐ 🔖 ♡ **Laughing Whitefish Falls State Park:** This 960-acre park in Alger County protects one of Michigan's most stunning waterfalls, cascading nearly 100 feet through a scenic gorge. A short trail leads to viewing platforms overlooking the falls, while surrounding hardwood forest offers wildlife habitat. The park emphasizes hiking, photography, and quiet nature appreciation.

☐ 🔖 ♡ **Leelanau State Park:** At the tip of the Leelanau Peninsula, this 1,550-acre park offers hiking, camping, and scenic shoreline views of Lake Michigan. Visitors can explore the historic Grand Traverse Lighthouse, picnic by the water, and walk trails through forest, dunes, and wetlands. Its location provides sweeping vistas and a sense of seclusion on Michigan's northwest coast.

☐ 🔖 ♡ **Ludington State Park:** Spanning 5,300 acres, Ludington is one of Michigan's premier state parks, known for its sand dunes, forests, lakes, and beaches. It features the Big Sable Point Lighthouse, miles of trails, and two campgrounds. Swimming, fishing, canoeing, and wildlife viewing make it a year-round favorite for outdoor recreation along Lake Michigan.

☐ 🔖 ♡ **Mackinac Island State Park:** Established in 1895, this was Michigan's first state park and today covers over 80% of Mackinac Island. Accessible only by ferry, it offers historic sites, limestone bluffs, natural arches, and trails for hiking, biking, and horseback riding. Visitors enjoy exploring car-free roads, scenic overlooks, and the island's unique cultural heritage.

☐ 🔖 ♡ **McLain State Park:** Located on Lake Superior's Keweenaw Peninsula, this 443-acre park features sandy beaches, scenic trails, and panoramic views. Visitors enjoy swimming, fishing, picnicking, and camping with spectacular sunsets over the lake. Its location between Houghton and Calumet makes it a convenient yet scenic Upper Peninsula destination.

☐ 🔖 ♡ **Muskegon State Park:** Covering 1,233 acres along Lake Michigan and Muskegon Lake, this park offers diverse terrain including dunes, forests, and wetlands. Visitors enjoy sandy beaches, camping, hiking, and fishing. Winter brings cross-country skiing, ice skating, and luge runs. Its year-round recreation makes it one of Michigan's most versatile state parks.

☐ 🔖 ♡ **Mitchell State Park:** Located in Cadillac, this 334-acre park sits between Lake Mitchell and Lake Cadillac, connected by a historic canal. Visitors enjoy boating, fishing, swimming, and camping with easy access to both lakes. Trails and interpretive programs highlight the area's history and ecology, making it a family-friendly Lower Peninsula destination.

☐ 🔖 ♡ **Negwegon State Park:** A 4,118-acre undeveloped wilderness along Lake Huron in Alcona County, Negwegon is prized for solitude and natural beauty. Visitors hike forest trails, camp in rustic sites, or enjoy birdwatching and stargazing on its dark-sky shoreline. Its mix of rugged coast and backcountry makes it a hidden gem for quiet adventurers.

☐ 🔖 ♡ **Orchard Beach State Park:** Perched on a bluff overlooking Lake Michigan near Manistee, this 201-acre park offers sweeping shoreline views, a sandy beach, and wooded campgrounds. Established in 1921, it features historic stone structures built by the Civilian Conservation Corps. Visitors enjoy swimming, picnicking, hiking, and spectacular sunsets over the big lake from its elevated vantage.

☐ 🔖 ♡ **Otsego Lake State Park:** This 62-acre park south of Gaylord is a compact but popular destination on Otsego Lake. It offers sandy swimming beaches, shaded campsites, and boating access. Visitors enjoy fishing, picnicking, and water recreation. Its location near I-75 makes it a convenient stop for travelers heading north into Michigan's Upper Peninsula.

MICHIGAN

☐ 🔖 ♡ **Petoskey State Park:** Located on Little Traverse Bay near Petoskey, this 303-acre park is renowned for its sandy beaches and opportunities to find Michigan's state stone, the Petoskey stone. It offers swimming, hiking, picnicking, and a modern campground. Dune and forest trails provide scenic overlooks, while the bay's sunsets make it a favorite family-friendly Lake Michigan destination.

☐ 🔖 ♡ **P.J. Hoffmaster State Park:** Situated south of Muskegon, this 1,200-acre park is known for its forested dunes, three miles of sandy beach, and sweeping lake views. Trails wind through wooded terrain, and the Dune Climb offers panoramic vistas. With camping, swimming, and a nature center, it's ideal for families and dune exploration.

☐ 🔖 ♡ **Porcupine Mountains Wilderness State Park:** Michigan's largest state park at nearly 60,000 acres, the "Porkies" are famed for their rugged terrain, old-growth forests, waterfalls, and Lake of the Clouds. Visitors explore 90 miles of trails, camp in modern or backcountry sites, and enjoy fishing, skiing, and wildlife. It's the crown jewel of Michigan wilderness parks.

☐ 🔖 ♡ **Port Crescent State Park:** Located at the tip of Michigan's "Thumb," this 640-acre park offers sandy beaches on Saginaw Bay, fishing, hiking, and camping. It is also a designated dark-sky preserve, making it ideal for stargazing. Visitors enjoy shoreline walks, birdwatching, and relaxing by the water in a peaceful Lake Huron setting.

☐ 🔖 ♡ **Seven Lakes State Park:** Located in Oakland County, this 1,434-acre park is named for its chain of lakes created by a dam project. It offers fishing, swimming, camping, and hiking trails through rolling woodlands. The mix of water recreation and forested terrain makes it a convenient nature escape near the Detroit metro area.

☐ 🔖 ♡ **Silver Lake State Park:** Famous for its 2,000 acres of open sand dunes, Silver Lake offers a rare combination of off-road vehicle terrain, hiking, and beach access. Visitors can swim, boat, fish, or camp while exploring both dunes and Lake Michigan shoreline. It's a popular park for thrill-seekers and families alike, with unique dune-riding experiences.

☐ 🔖 ♡ **Sleepy Hollow State Park:** Spanning 2,678 acres in Clinton County, Sleepy Hollow centers on Lake Ovid, a reservoir created for recreation and wildlife. Visitors enjoy fishing, swimming, boating, and trails for hiking, biking, and horseback riding. With its modern campground and birdwatching opportunities, it provides a peaceful getaway in mid-Michigan.

☐ 🔖 ♡ **Tawas Point State Park:** Known as the "Cape Cod of the Midwest," this 183-acre park on Lake Huron features sandy beaches, a campground, and the historic Tawas Point Lighthouse. Its location along a major migratory flyway makes it a birdwatching hotspot. Families enjoy swimming, fishing, and picnicking while taking in stunning bay views and sunsets.

☐ 🔖 ♡ **Van Buren State Park:** Located near South Haven, this 400-acre park features high dunes, a mile-long sandy Lake Michigan beach, and wooded trails. The modern campground makes it popular for family vacations, while hiking and swimming offer day-use recreation. Its easy access and shoreline beauty draw visitors from across southwest Michigan.

☐ 🔖 ♡ **W.J. Hayes State Park:** Situated in the Irish Hills region, this 654-acre park centers on Wamplers Lake and Round Lake. It's popular for boating, swimming, and fishing, with a family-friendly modern campground and shaded picnic areas. Trails wind through rolling forests and fields, making it a convenient outdoor getaway for visitors from Ann Arbor, Detroit, and surrounding southeastern Michigan.

☐ 🔖 ♡ **Warren Dunes State Park:** One of Michigan's most visited parks, this 1,952-acre site boasts towering dunes rising 260 feet above Lake Michigan. Visitors enjoy three miles of sandy beach, hiking trails through forested dunes, camping, and hang gliding. Its sweeping vistas, diverse habitats, and family-friendly facilities make it a classic Lake Michigan destination.

☐ 🔖 ♡ **Wilderness State Park:** Spanning 10,512 acres west of Mackinaw City, this park preserves remote Lake Michigan shoreline, forest, and wetland. It offers hiking, camping, fishing, and birding, plus access to designated dark-sky viewing areas. Its vast undeveloped terrain makes it ideal for solitude, wildlife encounters, and stargazing under pristine skies.

MICHIGAN

☐ 🔖 ♡ **William C. Sterling State Park:** Michigan's only state park on Lake Erie, this 1,300-acre destination features sandy beaches, lagoons, and coastal marshes. It offers swimming, fishing, boating, and a large modern campground. Anglers prize its walleye fishing, while birdwatchers enjoy its wetlands. Located near Monroe, it provides both natural beauty and convenient access to southeastern Michigan.

☐ 🔖 ♡ **Wilson State Park:** Located on Budd Lake in Harrison, this 36-acre park offers a beach, campground, and picnic areas. It's popular for boating, fishing, and swimming, with nearby trails providing hiking opportunities. Despite its small size, the park's central Michigan location and lakefront setting make it a convenient family getaway.

☐ 🔖 ♡ **Young State Park:** On Lake Charlevoix near Boyne City, this 563-acre park offers sandy beaches, campgrounds, and a variety of recreational opportunities. Swimming, boating, hiking, and winter sports draw visitors year-round. With large family-friendly facilities and beautiful northern Michigan scenery, it's a favorite for group outings and vacations.

National Parks

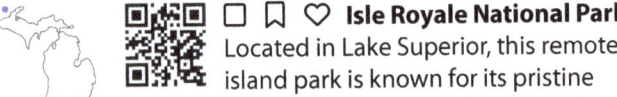 ☐ 🔖 ♡ **Isle Royale National Park:** Located in Lake Superior, this remote island park is known for its pristine wilderness, rugged trails, and abundant wildlife, including wolves and moose. Accessible only by boat or seaplane, it offers solitude and adventure with backpacking, kayaking, and camping. As one of the least-visited parks, it provides a rare untouched wilderness experience.

☐ 🔖 ♡ **Keweenaw National Historical Park:** In Michigan's Upper Peninsula, this park preserves the rich history of Copper Country and its role in America's mining heritage. Visitors can explore historic mines, preserved towns, and cultural landscapes that tell the story of the copper boom. The park highlights both industrial innovation and the lives of immigrant mining communities.

 ☐ 🔖 ♡ **Pictured Rocks National Lakeshore:** Along Lake Superior, this lakeshore is famed for its colorful sandstone cliffs, waterfalls, and pristine beaches. Visitors can hike forested trails, kayak beneath dramatic rock formations, or view landmarks like Chapel Rock and Grand Portal Point. Its blend of geology, wilderness, and shoreline beauty makes it a signature Michigan treasure.

 ☐ 🔖 ♡ **River Raisin National Battlefield Park:** Located in Monroe, this site commemorates the 1813 Battle of Frenchtown during the War of 1812. Visitors can walk the battlefield, tour exhibits at the visitor center, and learn about the soldiers, Native American alliances, and civilian impact. It preserves an important chapter of U.S. and Michigan military history.

 ☐ 🔖 ♡ **Sleeping Bear Dunes National Lakeshore:** Stretching along Lake Michigan, this park is renowned for its massive dunes, forests, and inland lakes. Visitors can hike challenging dune climbs, explore the Pierce Stocking Scenic Drive, or relax on sandy beaches. With its sweeping views, diverse habitats, and cultural sites, it offers something for every outdoor enthusiast.

MICHIGAN

State & National Forests

☐ 🔖 ♡ **Au Sable State Forest:** Spanning much of Michigan's northern Lower Peninsula, this forest protects second-growth hardwoods, pines, and unique habitats like the Roscommon Virgin Pine Stand. It safeguards watersheds around Houghton and Higgins Lakes and offers hiking, skiing, and wildlife viewing. Managed for timber and recreation, it blends conservation with outdoor adventure.

☐ 🔖 ♡ **Copper Country State Forest:** In the western Upper Peninsula, this forest grows on lands reclaimed after historic logging. Today, it's managed for reforestation, wildlife habitat, and sustainable timber. Visitors explore rustic campgrounds, forest roads, and opportunities for hunting, fishing, and hiking, making it both a working landscape and a recreation haven.

☐ 🔖 ♡ **Escanaba River State Forest:** Stretching across four U.P. counties, this forest features second-growth hardwoods and wetlands along the Escanaba River. Managed for pulpwood, wildlife, and watershed health, it also supports canoeing, hunting, fishing, and camping. Its riparian corridors connect forested habitats with outdoor opportunities.

☐ 🔖 ♡ **Hiawatha National Forest:** Covering nearly 900,000 acres across the U.P., Hiawatha embraces pine-hardwood forests, remote lakes, rivers, and six wilderness areas. It protects critical habitats while offering year-round recreation, from paddling and hiking to skiing and camping. Bordering Lakes Superior, Michigan, and Huron, it's known as "the Great Lakes National Forest."

☐ 🔖 ♡ **Huron–Manistee National Forests:** Together spanning nearly one million acres in the Lower Peninsula, these forests protect jack pine barrens vital to the endangered Kirtland's warbler, as well as dunes, rivers, and wetlands. Visitors enjoy camping, hiking, fishing, hunting, and OHV trails. They remain essential for biodiversity, timber, and outdoor recreation.

☐ 🔖 ♡ **Lake Superior State Forest:** Extending across several U.P. counties, this forest preserves hardwood and pine stands, wetlands, and wild shorelines. Managed for timber, water quality, and recreation, it offers rustic roads for access to hunting, fishing, camping, and quiet exploration in remote northern Michigan.

☐ 🔖 ♡ **Mackinaw State Forest:** Spanning over 717,000 acres in northern Lower and eastern Upper Michigan, this forest features hardwood ridges, pine stands, and cedar swamps. It's a hub for elk viewing, hunting, and ORV use, while also conserving critical habitats. Its vast size makes it a cornerstone of Michigan's forest and wildlife management.

☐ 🔖 ♡ **Ottawa National Forest:** Nearly one million acres in western Upper Michigan, Ottawa protects waterfalls, river canyons, and old-growth forest. It includes the Sylvania Wilderness, a canoeist's paradise of pristine lakes. Year-round, visitors enjoy camping, hiking, skiing, and fishing. The forest highlights both ecological richness and rugged natural beauty.

☐ 🔖 ♡ **Pere Marquette State Forest:** Stretching through Michigan's northern Lower Peninsula, this forest protects river corridors, dunes, and mixed hardwoods. Managed for pulpwood, recreation, and wildlife, it offers trails for hiking, hunting, fishing, and ORV use. Its varied terrain balances resource use with habitat conservation.

☐ 🔖 ♡ **Pigeon River Country State Forest:** Covering 109,000 acres, this forest is famed as the home of Michigan's only free-ranging elk herd. It offers backcountry camping, hiking, horseback riding, and wildlife watching across rolling hills and cedar swamps. Known as "the Big Wild," it preserves northern Michigan's most remote landscapes and rich ecology.

National Scenic Byways & All-American Roads

☐ 🔖 ♡ **Copper Country Trail:** Winding through Michigan's Keweenaw Peninsula, this route highlights the legacy of the 19th-century copper boom. Travelers encounter historic mine shafts, company towns, and striking Lake Superior views. The byway blends cultural heritage with scenic beauty, offering a drive through the industrial heart of America's Copper Country.

☐ 🔖 ♡ **River Road Scenic Byway:** Following M-65 and River Road along the Au Sable River in the Huron National Forest, this byway features overlooks, trails, and access to canoeing, fishing, and wildlife. Landmarks like Lumberman's Monument recall Michigan's logging past. Year-round, the corridor showcases both recreation and history amid the forested river valley.

MICHIGAN

☐ ▢ ♡ **Woodward Avenue (M-1) – Automotive Heritage Trail:** Known as the birthplace of the American automobile industry, this Detroit corridor showcases factories, grand theaters, neighborhoods, and museums tied to the Motor City's legacy. From cruising culture to landmarks like the Detroit Institute of Arts, it tells the story of how "Woodward put the world on wheels."

State Scenic Byways

☐ ▢ ♡ **Center Avenue Heritage Route / Bay City Historic Route:** A short 1.5-mile corridor through Bay City's Center Avenue district, this byway showcases 19th-century mansions and architecture listed on the National Register. Travelers enjoy a living museum of historic homes, leafy streets, and the cultural legacy of one of Michigan's grandest urban neighborhoods.

☐ ▢ ♡ **Chief Noonday Trail Recreational Heritage Route:** Following M-179 through the Yankee Springs region, this byway connects Gun Lake and rolling forests with access to hiking, boating, and camping. Named for a Potawatomi leader, it blends Native heritage with recreation, guiding visitors through lakes, parks, and one of southwest Michigan's most popular outdoor areas.

☐ ▢ ♡ **Copper Country Trail Heritage Route:** Traversing the Keweenaw Peninsula, this route highlights the state's copper-mining heritage with historic mine sites, boomtowns, and museums. Lake Superior views, scenic forests, and cultural landmarks make the drive a journey through both industrial history and rugged Upper Peninsula beauty.

☐ ▢ ♡ **Hidden Coast Byway (M-35):** Stretching along Lake Michigan in the Upper Peninsula, this quiet shoreline route reveals small towns, forested stretches, and long views of Green Bay's waters. Known as the "Hidden Coast," it offers an off-the-beaten-path drive where travelers discover fishing villages, scenic overlooks, and the slower rhythms of U.P. life.

☐ ▢ ♡ **I-69 Recreational Heritage Route:** This corridor through southeast Michigan highlights both natural and cultural destinations along the interstate. Travelers can access small towns, historic landmarks, and outdoor recreation areas while moving through rolling farmland and forest. The byway emphasizes the recreational and heritage richness surrounding this major travel route.

☐ ▢ ♡ **Iron County Heritage Trail:** Running along US-2 in Michigan's western Upper Peninsula, this heritage route honors the region's iron-mining history. Visitors encounter historic sites, museums, and remnants of the mining era while surrounded by forested hills, rivers, and lakes. The byway blends industrial heritage with the rugged natural beauty of the U.P.

☐ ▢ ♡ **Leelanau Scenic Byway (M-22 / Leelanau Scenic Heritage Route):** Encircling the Leelanau Peninsula, this 116-mile route offers spectacular Lake Michigan views, quaint towns like Leland and Suttons Bay, and access to Sleeping Bear Dunes. It's celebrated for wineries, fishing villages, and autumn color, making it one of Michigan's most iconic scenic drives.

☐ ▢ ♡ **Marshall's Territorial Road Historic Heritage Route:** Preserving a segment of Michigan's first land route into the interior, this byway follows the old Territorial Road. Travelers see historic inns, markers, and landscapes once used by settlers moving west. Its rural charm connects the story of early transportation with today's quiet countryside.

☐ ▢ ♡ **M-119 Tunnel of Trees Heritage Route:** One of Michigan's most famous drives, this 20-mile route hugs the Lake Michigan shoreline between Harbor Springs and Cross Village. Trees arch over the narrow road to form a tunnel of green. Scenic overlooks, fall color, and stops like Good Hart General Store make it a beloved destination year-round.

☐ ▢ ♡ **Old Mission Peninsula Heritage Route:** A short but scenic drive north from Traverse City, this route runs the length of Old Mission Peninsula, offering vineyard-dotted hills, orchards, historic farmsteads, and sweeping Grand Traverse Bay views. At its tip, the Old Mission Lighthouse and park provide a fitting landmark for this charming byway.

☐ ▢ ♡ **Tahquamenon Scenic Byway (M-123):** Stretching through Michigan's eastern Upper Peninsula, this byway leads to Tahquamenon Falls State Park, home to one of the Midwest's largest waterfalls. Forested stretches, wildlife, and rustic towns line the route, offering a classic U.P. experience with year-round opportunities for hiking, paddling, and sightseeing.

☐ ▢ ♡ **US-23 Huron Shores Heritage Route:** Following Lake Huron's shoreline from Standish to Mackinaw City, this 200-mile route links small towns, lighthouses, and beaches with sweeping Great Lakes views. It's popular for birding, beachcombing, and lakefront drives, offering travelers both historic maritime culture and unspoiled "sunrise side" scenery.

UNITED STATES EDITION

MICHIGAN

National Natural Landmarks

 **Black Spruce Bog Natural Area:** Designated a National Natural Landmark for illustrating late successional peatland stages, this boreal bog supports black spruce, tamarack, and sphagnum in Waterloo State Recreation Area. With no developed trails, it remains undisturbed, offering rare insight into the natural processes of bog forest development.
GPS: 42.3161, -84.1962

 **Dead Stream Swamp:** Recognized as a National Natural Landmark for being one of Michigan's largest, most intact cedar swamps, this Au Sable State Forest site preserves late-stage bog forest ecology. Towering northern white cedar and diverse wetland species thrive here, providing an exceptional living example of boreal swamp ecosystems.
GPS: 44.1000, -84.1700

 **Dukes Research Natural Area:** This Hiawatha National Forest tract was named a National Natural Landmark for its undisturbed old-growth swamp of cedar, hardwoods, and conifers. Rich soils nurture rare understory plants and wildlife, making it a valuable reference site for studying long-term ecological dynamics in northern wetland forests.
GPS: 46.3500, -87.1667

 **Grand Mere Lakes:** Formed in ancient glacial basins, Grand Mere's three lakes earned National Natural Landmark status for their textbook record of succession, from open water to forest. Rare plants, migratory birds, and dune systems thrive within Grand Mere State Park, illustrating the ongoing interplay of glacial, aquatic, and terrestrial processes.
GPS: 41.9931, -86.5497

 **Haven Hill State Natural Area:** This Highland Recreation Area preserve is a National Natural Landmark for containing every major southern Michigan forest type in one location. Oak-hickory, maple-beech, and conifer stands coexist, supporting more than 100 bird species. The site exemplifies biodiversity within a compact, ecologically intact landscape.
GPS: 42.6364, -83.5731

 **Newton Woods:** Newton Woods holds National Natural Landmark status as one of Michigan's last old-growth oak forests in the Lower Peninsula. Towering white, red, and black oaks dominate alongside maple and hickory. Protected by Michigan State University, the site preserves a rare remnant of pre-settlement woodland communities.
GPS: 42.0091, -85.9712

 **Porcupine Mountains:** This vast wilderness was designated a National Natural Landmark for its ancient forests of white pine and hemlock, dramatic waterfalls, and preserved glacial beach ridges. Located in the Upper Peninsula, it exemplifies Michigan's natural heritage, blending scenic beauty with intact old-growth ecosystems in a rugged setting.
GPS: 46.7667, -89.7500

 **Roscommon Virgin Pine Stand:** Within Au Sable State Forest, this site was recognized as a National Natural Landmark for its red pine stand shaped by recurring wildfires since 1798. The forest provides a living record of fire ecology and long-term pine succession, making it an invaluable research and conservation area.
GPS: 44.1000, -84.1700

 **Strangmoor Bog:** One of the southernmost patterned bogs in North America, Strangmoor is a National Natural Landmark for its string bog formation of alternating ridges and pools. Located in Seney National Wildlife Refuge, it supports boreal flora rarely found at this latitude, offering a critical record of peatland diversity.
GPS: 46.2500, -86.1000

 **Tobico Marsh:** This Bay City State Park wetland is a National Natural Landmark for its exceptional marsh, forested swamp, and open water mosaic. A vital migratory stop for waterfowl, Tobico sustains native vegetation and diverse wildlife, illustrating the ecological importance of coastal wetlands along Saginaw Bay.
GPS: 43.6975, -83.9364

MICHIGAN

 **Toumey Woodlot:** Preserved on Michigan State University's campus, Toumey Woodlot is a National Natural Landmark for being one of southern Michigan's only virgin beech-maple forests. Used for teaching and ecological research, the stand reflects the state's original woodland structure and supports species now rare in surrounding landscapes.
GPS: 42.7037, -84.4651

 **Warren Woods Natural Area:** This park protects Michigan's last sizable virgin beech-maple forest and is a National Natural Landmark for its centuries-old trees, some over 100 feet tall. Located near Lake Michigan, Warren Woods preserves the original forest character of the region, offering both scientific value and scenic beauty.
GPS: 41.8333, -86.6222

UNITED STATES EDITION

Minnesota

Minnesota's great outdoors features pristine lakes, towering pines, rolling prairies, and rugged North Shore cliffs. With a vibrant collection of state parks, national forests, a cherished national park, and remarkable natural landmarks, the state is a year-round haven for nature lovers, offering endless adventures from canoe country to frozen winter wonderlands.

📅 Peak Season
June–September is Minnesota's peak season, offering warm weather, long daylight hours, and ideal conditions for lake recreation, camping, and hiking. Summer festivals and state parks see the most visitors during this time.

📅 Offseason Months
November–April is the offseason, marked by cold temperatures and heavy snow. Winter attracts visitors for skiing, ice fishing, and snowmobiling, while early spring remains quiet before the thaw.

🍃 Scenery & Nature Timing
Spring brings wildflowers and waterfalls fueled by snowmelt. Summer offers lush forests and clear lakes for paddling and swimming. Fall showcases brilliant foliage along the North Shore, while winter covers the state in snow and ice.

✨ Special
Minnesota highlights Lake Superior's rugged North Shore, the Boundary Waters Canoe Area's labyrinth of lakes, and the headwaters of the Mississippi River. Frozen waterfalls, northern lights, and dramatic fall colors reveal its year-round natural beauty.

MINNESOTA

State Parks

☐ 🔖 ♡ **Afton State Park:** Situated along the St. Croix River, Afton State Park is a 1,600-acre retreat of prairies, woodlands, and wetlands. Trails climb to blufftop overlooks, while the river offers fishing and canoeing. In winter, cross-country skiing and snowshoeing are popular. Its proximity to the Twin Cities makes it a year-round destination blending natural beauty and outdoor recreation.

☐ 🔖 ♡ **Banning State Park:** Located near Sandstone, this 6,200-acre park highlights the Kettle River's wild rapids, sandstone cliffs, and historic quarry ruins. Trails wind through deep forests to dramatic overlooks and waterfalls, including Hell's Gate. Popular for kayaking, hiking, and rock climbing, the park blends natural beauty with industrial history.

☐ 🔖 ♡ **Bear Head Lake State Park:** In northeastern Minnesota near Ely, this 2,000-acre park centers on a pristine lake known for fishing, boating, and swimming. Trails weave through dense pine and hardwood forests, offering wildlife sightings and fall colors. Rustic campsites add to the wilderness feel, making it an ideal destination for those seeking solitude in the North Woods.

☐ 🔖 ♡ **Beaver Creek Valley State Park:** Tucked in Minnesota's southeast bluff country, this 1,000-acre park showcases limestone ridges, deep valleys, and spring-fed trout streams. Its cool, shaded woodlands make for excellent hiking, birdwatching, and photography. The park's scenic beauty and peaceful atmosphere provide a quiet escape into one of Minnesota's most picturesque landscapes.

☐ 🔖 ♡ **Big Stone Lake State Park:** Nestled along Minnesota's western border with South Dakota, this 1,000-acre park sits on a 26-mile-long glacial lake. Known for walleye and other game fish, it's a prime fishing and boating spot. Trails and picnic areas line the shore, and birdwatchers can spot migratory species along this section of the Prairie Pothole Region.

☐ 🔖 ♡ **Blue Mounds State Park:** This southwestern park spans 1,500 acres of tallgrass prairie and quartzite cliffs. Home to a managed bison herd, it offers visitors a glimpse of Minnesota's prairie past. Trails wind through wildflower-rich grasslands, up limestone bluffs, and past historical quarries. The park combines cultural history, dramatic geology, and thriving wildlife.

☐ 🔖 ♡ **Buffalo River State Park:** Covering 2,100 acres in the Red River Valley, this park highlights tallgrass prairie and riverine habitats. It features a popular swimming pond, shaded campgrounds, and fishing on the Buffalo River. Trails pass through restored prairie rich in birdlife, making it a haven for naturalists and outdoor enthusiasts.

☐ 🔖 ♡ **Camden State Park:** Set along the Redwood River in southwest Minnesota, Camden spans wooded valleys, rolling prairies, and dramatic bluffs. Fishing is popular in the river and spring-fed trout pond, while trails explore diverse terrain. The park's mix of landscapes offers scenic views and peaceful recreation close to prairie country.

☐ 🔖 ♡ **Carley State Park:** This quiet southeastern park preserves 200 acres of hardwood forest along the Whitewater River. Known for spring wildflowers and bluebells, it features picnic areas and easy hiking trails. The river offers trout fishing, while oak and maple groves provide fall color. Its small size creates a tranquil, intimate outdoor experience.

☐ 🔖 ♡ **Cascade River State Park:** Along Lake Superior's North Shore, this park showcases a series of waterfalls rushing through a rocky gorge. Trails climb to overlooks with sweeping views of Superior and the Sawtooth Mountains. Anglers enjoy trout fishing in the river, while photographers capture its dramatic cascades, rugged cliffs, and scenic shoreline.

☐ 🔖 ♡ **Charles A. Lindbergh State Park:** Located near Little Falls, this park honors the aviator with trails through hardwood forests, river overlooks, and historic sites. Visitors can tour Lindbergh's boyhood home and a WPA-era picnic shelter. The Mississippi River provides fishing and paddling, while interpretive programs highlight the family's history and conservation legacy.

☐ 🔖 ♡ **Crow Wing State Park:** At the confluence of the Mississippi and Crow Wing Rivers, this 3,000-acre park blends natural and cultural history. Trails lead to views of the rivers, pine forests, and historic fur-trade sites. Interpretive exhibits tell of Ojibwe and early settlers. The park offers camping, fishing, hiking, and a glimpse of Minnesota's frontier past.

MINNESOTA

☐ 🔖 ♡ **Father Hennepin State Park:** On Mille Lacs Lake, this 320-acre park is a summer favorite for swimming, fishing, and boating. Trails meander through hardwood forest and sandy shoreline, while picnic areas provide lakefront views. The park honors Father Louis Hennepin, an early European explorer who documented Minnesota's natural wonders in the 1600s.

☐ 🔖 ♡ **Flandrau State Park:** Near New Ulm, this 1,000-acre park offers recreation along the Big Cottonwood River. It's known for its sandy swimming beach, wooded trails, and family-friendly campsites. Wildlife thrives in its forest and prairie mix, making it ideal for birdwatching. Its combination of river access, trails, and history attracts diverse visitors.

☐ 🔖 ♡ **Forestville/Mystery Cave State Park:** This southeastern park combines rolling hills, hardwood forest, and the famous Mystery Cave—the longest cave in Minnesota. Visitors explore underground passages with stalactites and pools, or hike trails leading to historic Forestville, a restored 19th-century village. It's a unique blend of geology, history, and recreation.

☐ 🔖 ♡ **Fort Ridgely State Park:** In southern Minnesota, this 1,100-acre park preserves the site of Fort Ridgely, central to the U.S.-Dakota War of 1862. Trails wind through river valleys and prairie, while interpretive programs highlight the area's military history. The park also offers picnicking, camping, and access to fishing in the Minnesota River.

☐ 🔖 ♡ **Fort Snelling State Park:** At the confluence of the Minnesota and Mississippi Rivers, this 2,000-acre park combines rich history with outdoor recreation. Adjacent to the historic fort, the park offers hiking, biking, and fishing opportunities along floodplain forests and riverbanks. Its trails connect to regional systems, making it a green haven in the heart of the Twin Cities.

☐ 🔖 ♡ **Franz Jevne State Park:** Minnesota's smallest state park at just 118 acres, Franz Jevne sits on the Rainy River along the Canadian border. Its quiet trails lead through aspen and spruce forests with river overlooks. The park is ideal for fishing, birdwatching, and enjoying solitude in a remote setting, offering an intimate experience of northern wilderness.

☐ 🔖 ♡ **Frontenac State Park:** Overlooking the Mississippi River, this 2,300-acre blufftop park offers panoramic vistas, especially breathtaking during fall color. Trails wind through forests, prairies, and wetlands, making it a birdwatcher's paradise with over 260 species recorded. The park also provides camping, picnicking, and opportunities to explore the river valley's natural beauty.

☐ 🔖 ♡ **Glacial Lakes State Park:** In west-central Minnesota, this 2,400-acre park preserves rolling prairie hills shaped by ancient glaciers. Signalness Lake offers swimming, fishing, and canoeing, while trails cross restored tallgrass prairie alive with wildflowers and wildlife. Known for its scenic overlooks and autumn colors, the park provides a quiet retreat in prairie country.

☐ 🔖 ♡ **Gooseberry Falls State Park:** One of Minnesota's most iconic destinations, Gooseberry features dramatic waterfalls cascading through a rocky gorge into Lake Superior. The park's trails showcase basalt cliffs, wildflowers, and shoreline views. With camping, interpretive programs, and year-round recreation, it's a favorite stop along the scenic North Shore.

☐ 🔖 ♡ **Grand Portage State Park:** Located at Minnesota's northeastern tip, this 278-acre park is co-managed with the Grand Portage Band of Ojibwe. Its highlight is High Falls, the state's tallest waterfall at 120 feet. Boardwalks and trails lead to dramatic overlooks, while the park's cultural interpretation honors the Ojibwe heritage and fur trade history.

☐ 🔖 ♡ **Great River Bluffs State Park:** Set on steep Mississippi River bluffs in southeastern Minnesota, this 2,800-acre park offers stunning overlooks and quiet wooded valleys. Trails pass through prairies, forests, and goat prairies—sunny cliffside habitats. The park is a prime spot for birdwatching, hiking, and photography, with peaceful campsites among the ridges.

☐ 🔖 ♡ **Interstate State Park:** Along the St. Croix River, this park showcases world-renowned glacial potholes carved in basalt rock. With unique geology, dramatic cliffs, and scenic river views, it's a haven for hikers, canoeists, and rock climbers. Its 1,400 acres provide both natural wonder and recreational opportunities at one of the nation's oldest interstate parks.

☐ 🔖 ♡ **Itasca State Park:** Minnesota's oldest and most famous state park, Itasca preserves over 32,000 acres of forests and lakes, including the headwaters of the Mississippi River. Visitors can wade across the river's source, hike through old-growth pines, bike scenic routes, or take boat tours. Rich in history and natural beauty, it's a must-see destination.

☐ 🔖 ♡ **Jay Cooke State Park:** Spanning 8,000 rugged acres along the St. Louis River, Jay Cooke is famed for its swinging suspension bridge and rocky gorge. Trails traverse forested hills, waterfalls, and rushing rapids. Year-round activities include hiking, skiing, and snowshoeing. Its dramatic landscape and accessibility make it a favorite for adventure seekers.

MINNESOTA

☐ 🔖 ♡ **John A. Latsch State Park:** A small but challenging park in southeastern Minnesota, John A. Latsch offers steep trails climbing 500 feet to blufftop views over the Mississippi River. The 450-acre park is undeveloped, focusing on hiking and natural scenery. Its solitude and vistas make it a hidden gem along the river valley.

☐ 🔖 ♡ **Judge C.R. Magney State Park:** On Lake Superior's North Shore, this 4,600-acre park is best known for Devil's Kettle Falls, where half the river vanishes into rock. Trails lead to the falls and through rugged forested terrain. Anglers fish the Brule River, while campers and hikers enjoy a remote yet dramatic North Shore experience.

☐ 🔖 ♡ **Kilen Woods State Park:** This 222-acre park in southwestern Minnesota preserves oak savanna, prairie, and river valley landscapes. Trails explore wooded ridges and open meadows, while the Des Moines River offers fishing and paddling. Quiet campsites and wildlife observation make it a peaceful, lesser-known destination for exploring prairie country.

☐ 🔖 ♡ **Lac qui Parle State Park:** At the confluence of the Lac qui Parle River and the Minnesota River, this 530-acre park is a major stopover for migratory birds. Its wetlands and floodplain forests attract thousands of Canada geese each fall. Trails, camping, fishing, and boating offer recreation amid this vital wildlife habitat.

☐ 🔖 ♡ **Lake Bemidji State Park:** On the shore of Lake Bemidji, this 1,600-acre park features sandy beaches, swimming, and excellent fishing. Trails explore forests and bogs rich in orchids and carnivorous plants. The park offers camping, interpretive programs, and access to the Paul Bunyan State Trail, blending family recreation with northern wilderness charm.

☐ 🔖 ♡ **Lake Louise State Park:** In southeastern Minnesota, this 1,600-acre park features a peaceful lake surrounded by hardwood forest and rolling prairie. Its trails are popular for hiking, horseback riding, and snowmobiling. Visitors enjoy fishing, boating, and birdwatching in a quiet, uncrowded atmosphere. A mix of habitats creates colorful scenery year-round.

☐ 🔖 ♡ **Lake Maria State Park:** This 1,600-acre park in central Minnesota is known for its old-growth maple-basswood forest, a rarity in the region. Trails lead through hardwoods, wetlands, and lakes, offering opportunities for hiking, birdwatching, and horseback riding. Backpack campsites add a rustic feel, making it popular with those seeking quiet, wilderness-like experiences.

☐ 🔖 ♡ **Maplewood State Park:** Located in west-central Minnesota, this 9,250-acre park features rolling hills, hardwood forests, and over 20 lakes. It's especially famous for vibrant fall foliage. Trails accommodate hikers, horseback riders, and skiers, while lakes provide fishing, swimming, and paddling. Its diverse habitats support rich wildlife, offering year-round recreation and scenery.

☐ 🔖 ♡ **McCarthy Beach State Park:** North of Hibbing, this 2,471-acre park is famous for its half-mile-long sandy beach, once rated among the nation's best. Trails explore pine forests and connect to the Taconite State Trail, inviting hiking, horseback riding, and snowmobiling. With clear lakes for boating and fishing, it's a summer favorite in northern Minnesota.

☐ 🔖 ♡ **Mille Lacs Kathio State Park:** This 10,000-acre park along Mille Lacs Lake is rich in history, with archaeological sites highlighting 9,000 years of human use. Visitors enjoy climbing the fire tower, hiking forested trails, and exploring exhibits on Dakota heritage. The park also offers camping, fishing, and boating, blending culture and outdoor recreation.

☐ 🔖 ♡ **Minneopa State Park:** Famous for its double waterfalls and roaming bison herd, this 4,600-acre park near Mankato blends prairie, woodland, and river valley landscapes. Visitors hike scenic trails, picnic by the falls, or observe bison from the drive-through range. With historic sites and varied habitats, it's a southern Minnesota highlight.

☐ 🔖 ♡ **Myre-Big Island State Park:** Near Albert Lea, this 1,578-acre park features wetlands, prairies, and hardwood forest. Big Island, connected by causeway, offers trails and camping amid lake views. Birdwatchers flock here, with over 200 species recorded. Hiking, fishing, and winter skiing add to its appeal as a diverse year-round destination.

☐ 🔖 ♡ **Nerstrand Big Woods State Park:** Preserving a remnant of Minnesota's "Big Woods," this 2,882-acre park is prized for spring wildflowers and fall color. Trails lead through maple-basswood forest to Hidden Falls, a small but scenic waterfall. Birdwatching, picnicking, and peaceful camping draw visitors seeking a lush woodland experience in southern Minnesota.

☐ 🔖 ♡ **Rice Lake State Park:** A 1,029-acre park in southern Minnesota, Rice Lake is a haven for waterfowl and birdwatchers. Shallow, marshy waters attract migratory flocks, especially Canada geese. Trails explore wetlands and hardwoods, while visitors also enjoy fishing, picnicking, and camping. It's a quiet spot focused on wildlife and seasonal migrations.

MINNESOTA

☐ 🔖 ♡ **Savanna Portage State Park:** Covering 15,800 acres, this park near McGregor preserves a centuries-old Ojibwe and fur-trader canoe route across the Laurentian Divide. Visitors hike historic portage trails, fish and paddle Big Sandy Lake, or camp in wooded solitude. Its mix of cultural heritage and remote wilderness makes it one of Minnesota's most historic parks.

☐ 🔖 ♡ **Scenic State Park:** In northern Minnesota, this 3,936-acre park features pristine Sandwick Lake, towering pines, and crystal-clear waters. Known for its unspoiled wilderness character, it offers canoeing, fishing, hiking, and camping in a tranquil setting. Old-growth forest and reflective lakes make it ideal for those seeking solitude and natural beauty.

☐ 🔖 ♡ **Schoolcraft State Park:** At just 225 acres, this park sits where the Mississippi and Vermilion Rivers meet. Named for explorer Henry Schoolcraft, it offers quiet camping, fishing, and paddling in a secluded setting. Towering pines, oak forests, and river views provide a serene backdrop for hiking and picnicking, making it a small but peaceful northern retreat.

☐ 🔖 ♡ **Sibley State Park:** Near New London, this 3,419-acre park offers rolling glacial hills, prairies, and hardwood forests. Trails climb Mount Tom, providing sweeping views of central Minnesota. Visitors also enjoy swimming, fishing, and wildlife watching. With extensive campgrounds and diverse scenery, it's one of the state's most popular parks for families.

☐ 🔖 ♡ **Split Rock Lighthouse State Park:** Along Lake Superior's North Shore, this 2,200-acre park is famed for its historic lighthouse perched atop cliffs. Visitors hike scenic shoreline trails, tour the restored lighthouse, and camp along the rugged coast. It's a destination where maritime history meets the dramatic natural beauty of Minnesota's North Shore.

☐ 🔖 ♡ **St. Croix State Park:** The largest state park in Minnesota at 34,000 acres, St. Croix offers vast forests, rivers, and wetlands. Visitors canoe or fish the St. Croix and Kettle Rivers, hike 127 miles of trails, or camp year-round. A National Natural Landmark, it preserves rich ecosystems while offering extensive recreation opportunities.

☐ 🔖 ♡ **Temperance River State Park:** Along Lake Superior's North Shore, this 5,000-acre park is renowned for its dramatic river gorge, waterfalls, and cascades. Trails trace the rushing Temperance River as it drops toward Superior, offering stunning geology and wildflower-filled cliffs. Lakeshore camping and hiking provide a classic North Shore wilderness experience.

☐ 🔖 ♡ **Tettegouche State Park:** A 9,300-acre gem on Lake Superior's shore, Tettegouche is known for Shovel Point cliffs, inland lakes, and High Falls on the Baptism River. Trails suit hikers and climbers alike, while birders seek peregrine falcons. Camping and cabins make it a hub for exploration of the rugged North Shore's natural wonders.

☐ 🔖 ♡ **Whitewater State Park:** In southeastern Minnesota's bluff country, this 2,700-acre park features limestone cliffs, trout streams, and hardwood forests. Known for its dramatic scenery and lack of mosquitoes, it offers hiking, camping, and excellent trout fishing in the Whitewater River. Scenic overlooks and abundant wildlife make it a premier destination year-round.

☐ 🔖 ♡ **Wild River State Park:** Stretching along 18 miles of the St. Croix River, this 7,000-acre park highlights riparian forests, prairies, and marshes. Trails and river access provide fishing, paddling, and wildlife watching. With camping, interpretive programs, and peaceful scenery, it's an accessible yet wild-feeling park within easy reach of the Twin Cities.

☐ 🔖 ♡ **William O'Brien State Park:** Just north of Stillwater on the St. Croix River, this 1,520-acre park offers rolling hills, floodplain forest, and scenic river views. Popular activities include hiking, skiing, fishing, and birdwatching. Campgrounds and interpretive programs make it a family-friendly retreat combining natural beauty with accessibility.

☐ 🔖 ♡ **Zippel Bay State Park:** On Lake of the Woods, this 2,906-acre park features long sandy beaches and windswept pine forests. Known for excellent walleye fishing, it offers boating, birdwatching, and trails through aspen and spruce. The park's remote location and vast lake views provide a sense of wilderness adventure at Minnesota's northern edge.

MINNESOTA

National Parks

☐ 🔖 ♡ **Grand Portage National Monument:** Preserving one of the nation's most important fur trade sites, this monument in northeastern Minnesota tells the story of the Anishinaabe people and voyageurs who carried goods along the nine-mile "grand portage." Visitors explore reconstructed trading posts, historic trails, and sweeping Lake Superior overlooks, connecting culture and wilderness.

☐ 🔖 ♡ **Mississippi National River and Recreation Area:** Stretching 72 miles through the Twin Cities, this urban national park unit protects the Mississippi River's diverse habitats and history. Visitors hike, bike, and paddle along scenic corridors that blend bald eagles, floodplain forests, and historic mills. It showcases the river's role as both a natural wonder and cultural lifeline.

☐ 🔖 ♡ **Pipestone National Monument:** In southwestern Minnesota, this sacred site preserves quarries where Native peoples have harvested red pipestone for generations. Visitors walk trails past tallgrass prairie, waterfalls, and quarry pits while learning about the cultural significance of the stone. Traditional carvers continue the practice today, keeping a deeply spiritual heritage alive.

☐ 🔖 ♡ **Saint Croix National Scenic Riverway:** Flowing along the Minnesota–Wisconsin border, this protected corridor preserves 200 miles of the St. Croix and Namekagon Rivers. Paddlers, anglers, and campers experience scenic bluffs, sandy beaches, and abundant wildlife. As one of the nation's first Wild and Scenic Rivers, it offers pristine waters and quiet wilderness.

☐ 🔖 ♡ **Voyageurs National Park:** At Minnesota's northern border, Voyageurs is a watery wilderness of interconnected lakes, islands, and boreal forest. Accessible mainly by boat, it offers world-class fishing, paddling routes, and houseboat camping. Named for the French-Canadian traders who once traveled here, it blends rugged beauty, rich history, and unforgettable night skies.

State & National Forests

☐ 🔖 ♡ **Bear Island State Forest:** Centered near Ely in northeastern Minnesota, this 157,000-acre forest protects boreal landscapes of pine, spruce, aspen, and wetlands. Visitors find rugged trails for hiking, snowmobiling, and berry picking, along with abundant wildlife including loons, wolves, and black bears. Managed for timber and recreation, it offers a gateway to the northern wilderness.

☐ 🔖 ♡ **Bowstring State Forest:** Spanning 526,000 acres in north-central Minnesota, Bowstring features pine, aspen, and mixed hardwoods interlaced with lakes and bogs. It's popular for fishing, hunting, ATV riding, and snowmobiling. Quiet campgrounds and vast water access make it a haven for outdoor enthusiasts seeking remote adventures in the Chippewa National Forest region.

☐ 🔖 ♡ **Burntside State Forest:** This 74,000-acre forest near Ely is a rugged landscape of granite outcrops, boreal pines, and clear lakes. It provides a transition to the Boundary Waters region, offering rustic camping, canoeing, and fishing. Wildlife such as moose, wolves, and loons thrive here, making it a remote destination for backcountry solitude.

☐ 🔖 ♡ **Chengwatana State Forest:** Covering 29,000 acres east of Pine City, this forest of aspen, birch, and pine borders the St. Croix River. It offers ATV and snowmobile trails, dispersed camping, and hunting. Its riverside setting and mixed woods create a blend of recreation and solitude within easy reach of the Twin Cities.

☐ 🔖 ♡ **Chippewa National Forest:** Spanning 667,000 acres in north-central Minnesota, Chippewa is rich in lakes, wetlands, and towering pines. The "Lost 40" preserves virgin old-growth forest, while over 1,300 lakes invite paddling, fishing, and boating. With trails crossing the Laurentian Divide, it's a stronghold for bald eagles and a premier wilderness destination.

MINNESOTA

☐ 🔖 ♡ **Dorer Memorial Hardwood State Forest:** Nestled in southeastern Minnesota, this 1.1 million-acre forest is a patchwork of scattered tracts, farms, and river valleys. It protects rare hardwood stands and bluffland habitats. Managed for conservation and education, it offers trout streams, hiking, and wildlife viewing across a diverse and culturally rich landscape.

☐ 🔖 ♡ **Finland State Forest:** Encompassing 222,000 acres near the North Shore, Finland is defined by rugged terrain, cold trout streams, and boreal forest. Outdoor enthusiasts explore dispersed campsites, ATV and snowmobile trails, and remote trout lakes. Its wild character makes it a gateway between Lake Superior's shore and Superior National Forest's backcountry.

☐ 🔖 ♡ **George Washington State Forest:** North of Grand Rapids, this 288,000-acre forest features rolling hills, hardwoods, and over 100 lakes. It's popular for boating, swimming, and fishing, with rustic campgrounds along scenic lakeshores. Trails welcome hikers, ATV riders, and skiers, while wildlife abounds in this classic north woods landscape.

☐ 🔖 ♡ **Koochiching State Forest:** Minnesota's largest state forest at 882,000 acres, Koochiching stretches across the northern border with Canada. Vast bogs, wetlands, and spruce stands dominate, providing critical habitat for moose, wolves, and waterfowl. Visitors enjoy hunting, berry picking, snowmobiling, and paddling in this remote northern wilderness.

☐ 🔖 ♡ **Lake Jeanette State Forest:** At just 11,500 acres, this small forest north of Orr offers a quiet refuge of spruce, aspen, and mixed conifers. Centered around scenic Lake Jeanette, it's a gateway to the Boundary Waters region. Campgrounds, boating, and hiking trails provide a peaceful base for exploring the North Woods.

☐ 🔖 ♡ **Land O'Lakes State Forest:** This 52,000-acre forest in central Minnesota features rolling glacial terrain, hardwoods, and scattered lakes. Popular for fishing, camping, and ATV riding, it offers a mix of recreation and wildlife viewing. Managed forests and natural wetlands create a diverse landscape for year-round exploration.

☐ 🔖 ♡ **Pat Bayle State Forest:** Located along Minnesota's northeastern edge, this 180,000-acre forest borders the Boundary Waters and Superior National Forest. Rugged terrain, waterfalls, and boreal woodland define it. It's a haven for backpacking, fishing, and dispersed camping, offering some of the wildest country outside the BWCAW.

☐ 🔖 ♡ **Pillsbury State Forest:** Established in 1900 as Minnesota's first state forest, Pillsbury spans 25,000 acres near Brainerd. It showcases pine plantations, hardwood ridges, and remnants of old-growth red and white pine. Trails support horseback riding, hiking, skiing, and biking, while lakes offer paddling and fishing opportunities.

☐ 🔖 ♡ **Pine Island State Forest:** Covering nearly 878,000 acres in northern Minnesota, Pine Island is a vast wetland and pine mosaic. Known for solitude, it supports hunting, berry picking, and dispersed camping. Moose, wolves, and waterfowl thrive here, making it one of the state's most remote wilderness areas.

☐ 🔖 ♡ **Rum River State Forest:** Located north of the Twin Cities, this 40,000-acre forest is named for the Rum River winding through its hardwoods and wetlands. It offers ATV and snowmobile trails, rustic campgrounds, and wildlife viewing. Its mix of prairie openings and forests creates a varied habitat close to metro areas.

☐ 🔖 ♡ **Sand Dunes State Forest:** Just 6,000 acres in Sherburne County, this unique forest combines oak savanna, prairie, and shifting sand habitats. It's known for rare plants, birdlife, and horseback riding trails. Visitors also enjoy hiking, camping, and exploring its distinctive landscape shaped by windblown sands.

☐ 🔖 ♡ **Savanna State Forest:** Spanning 659,000 acres in east-central Minnesota, Savanna is a landscape of bogs, hardwood ridges, and pine plantations. It's rich in history, once crossed by fur-trade routes. Today, visitors hike, hunt, snowmobile, and camp in one of the state's largest and wildest state forests.

☐ 🔖 ♡ **Smoky Hills State Forest:** West of Detroit Lakes, this 24,000-acre forest features rolling hills cloaked in hardwoods and conifers. Scenic drives, trails, and hunting grounds attract visitors year-round. Rustic campgrounds and berry picking add to its quiet, natural charm in Minnesota's lake country.

☐ 🔖 ♡ **Snake River State Forest:** A small 4,900-acre forest near Mora, Snake River preserves lowland hardwoods and river habitats. It's valued for hunting, dispersed camping, and snowmobiling. The river winds through forested corridors, offering peaceful settings for wildlife viewing and quiet outdoor recreation.

MINNESOTA

☐ 🔖 ♡ **Solana State Forest:** Covering 59,000 acres in central Minnesota, Solana features pine plantations, hardwoods, and wetlands. Its trails and forest roads support hunting, ATV riding, and snowmobiling. Remote campsites and abundant wildlife provide a rustic north woods experience away from crowds.

☐ 🔖 ♡ **St. Croix State Forest:** Adjacent to St. Croix State Park, this 42,000-acre forest lies in east-central Minnesota. It's known for extensive ATV and snowmobile trails, camping, and hunting opportunities. Rugged terrain, river corridors, and pine forests make it a recreation hub with a true wilderness feel.

☐ 🔖 ♡ **Superior National Forest:** Stretching across 3.9 million acres of the Arrowhead, Superior is home to the Boundary Waters Canoe Area Wilderness. With over 2,000 lakes, vast boreal forests, and unmatched wildlife, it offers canoeing, fishing, hiking, and camping in one of America's premier backcountry landscapes.

☐ 🔖 ♡ **White Earth State Forest:** This 160,000-acre forest in northwestern Minnesota protects pine, hardwoods, and wetlands within the White Earth Reservation. Visitors enjoy hunting, fishing, camping, and snowmobiling. Its mix of cultural heritage and natural resources makes it a landscape rich in both tradition and outdoor opportunities.

National Scenic Byways & All-American Roads

☐ 🔖 ♡ **Edge of the Wilderness Scenic Byway:** Running 46 miles along MN-38 from Grand Rapids to Effie, this route passes through Chippewa National Forest's lakes, bogs, and pine stands. Scenic overlooks, historic sites, and wildlife abound. Known as the "Lake Country Scenic Highway," it blends peaceful wilderness with small-town character and abundant recreation opportunities.

☐ 🔖 ♡ **Grand Rounds National Scenic Byway:** Encircling Minneapolis with 50 miles of parkways, trails, and linked green spaces, the Grand Rounds is one of the nation's only urban National Scenic Byways. It connects lakes, riverfronts, gardens, and historic landmarks, offering scenic drives, biking, and walking paths. Blending natural beauty with city heritage, it's a unique urban treasure.

☐ 🔖 ♡ **Great River Road (All-American Road):** Stretching 565 miles in Minnesota, this All-American Road traces the Mississippi from its headwaters at Lake Itasca through river towns and bluffs to Iowa. Scenic overlooks, state parks, and cultural sites line the route. A national corridor of history and nature, it offers fishing, birding, and heritage tied to America's greatest river.

☐ 🔖 ♡ **Gunflint Trail Scenic Byway:** A 57-mile drive from Grand Marais into Superior National Forest, this byway leads deep into lake country and toward the Boundary Waters. Winding through boreal forest and rugged terrain, it provides access to canoe routes, hiking trails, and remote resorts. Moose, loons, and northern lights highlight the journey through pristine wilderness.

☐ 🔖 ♡ **Historic Bluff Country Scenic Byway:** Following MN-16 for 88 miles across the Driftless Area, this byway reveals limestone bluffs, trout streams, and fertile valleys. Root River towns like Lanesboro and Houston offer history, culture, and river recreation. Its unique geology, caves, and scenic overlooks make it a journey rich in natural beauty and heritage.

☐ 🔖 ♡ **Minnesota River Valley Scenic Byway:** Extending 287 miles from Big Stone Lake to Belle Plaine, this byway traces the winding Minnesota River through prairies, wetlands, and historic towns. Interpretive centers highlight Dakota heritage and frontier history. Wildlife refuges, state parks, and cultural landmarks line the route, blending river scenery with deep cultural roots.

☐ 🔖 ♡ **North Shore Scenic Drive (All-American Road):** Running 154 miles from Duluth to Grand Portage, this iconic route hugs Lake Superior's shore. It passes waterfalls, rocky cliffs, and eight state parks, with views of the Sawtooth Mountains and Superior's vast horizon. Rich in history, recreation, and natural wonder, it's one of America's most celebrated drives.

☐ 🔖 ♡ **Paul Bunyan Scenic Byway:** A 54-mile loop through lakes country in central Minnesota, this byway connects Crosslake, Pequot Lakes, and Pine River. It highlights boating, fishing, birding, and biking along quiet forested roads. Interpretive stops celebrate lumberjack folklore, while trails and resorts make it a blend of recreation, local culture, and classic north woods charm.

MINNESOTA

State Scenic Byways

☐ ▯ ♡ **Apple Blossom Drive Scenic Byway:** This 19-mile drive near La Crescent meanders through apple orchards and rolling farmland, bursting with blossoms each spring. Scenic overlooks along the Mississippi River Valley provide sweeping views of wooded bluffs and river bends. The route also offers easy access to Great River Bluffs State Park, making it a colorful and peaceful seasonal drive.

☐ ▯ ♡ **Avenue of Pines Scenic Byway:** Extending 46 miles along MN-46 from Deer River to Northome, this forested route lives up to its name with towering pines, sparkling lakes, and peat bogs. Part of Chippewa National Forest, it showcases classic North Woods scenery with abundant wildlife. The byway is popular for birding, fishing, and scenic drives, offering travelers a tranquil northern escape.

☐ ▯ ♡ **Glacial Ridge Trail Scenic Byway:** A 220-mile network of loops in central Minnesota, this route highlights rolling hills, kettle lakes, and prairies shaped by Ice Age glaciers. It links Sibley, Monson Lake, and Glacial Lakes State Parks, weaving through small towns and farmland. Visitors enjoy hiking, birding, and fishing, while autumn colors bring dramatic views to this scenic corridor.

☐ ▯ ♡ **Highway 75 "King of Trails" Scenic Byway:** Running the full 414 miles of U.S. 75 across western Minnesota, this historic corridor follows a trade and migration route once used by Native peoples and settlers. It showcases prairie landscapes, historic towns, and cultural landmarks such as Pipestone. The byway's expansive views and heritage sites connect travelers to the state's prairie frontier past.

☐ ▯ ♡ **Lady Slipper Scenic Byway:** This 28-mile route through the Chippewa National Forest is named for Minnesota's state flower, the showy lady's slipper. In late June, the roadside blooms with orchids and wildflowers, creating a colorful summer spectacle. Forested scenery, lakes, and wildlife sightings add to the experience, while interpretive stops share the region's rich natural heritage.

☐ ▯ ♡ **Lake Country Scenic Byway:** An 88-mile triangle-shaped route in north-central Minnesota, this byway links Park Rapids, Walker, and Detroit Lakes. It winds through lake country with connections to Itasca State Park and the Mississippi River headwaters. Scenic overlooks, trails, and cultural stops highlight the region's outdoor recreation, birding, and vibrant small-town character year-round.

☐ ▯ ♡ **Lake Mille Lacs Scenic Byway:** A 68-mile loop encircling Minnesota's second-largest lake, this route blends natural beauty with cultural heritage. Travelers encounter Mille Lacs Kathio and Father Hennepin State Parks, Ojibwe history, and excellent fishing waters. Scenic shoreline views, sandy beaches, and resort towns make it a favorite drive for recreation and exploration of lake country.

☐ ▯ ♡ **Otter Trail Scenic Byway:** Circling 150 miles through Otter Tail County, this byway highlights glacial hills, hardwood forests, and over 1,000 lakes. It passes through Fergus Falls and Perham, linking historic sites, fishing lakes, and quiet parks. With rolling countryside and abundant water access, the route offers a quintessential Minnesota lake-country experience across all seasons.

☐ ▯ ♡ **Saint Croix Scenic Byway:** Stretching 124 miles along the lower St. Croix River, this byway travels through rolling bluffs, forests, and historic towns. The route reveals scenic river overlooks, cultural sites, and recreational access for paddling and fishing. Visitors experience a blend of river valley landscapes, small-town charm, and the unique heritage of eastern Minnesota.

☐ ▯ ♡ **Shooting Star Scenic Byway:** Covering 32 miles along Highway 56 in southeastern Minnesota, this route passes through prairie landscapes, wildflower-rich roadsides, and small towns like LeRoy and Adams. In summer, native blossoms carpet the roadside. With its agricultural heritage, local history, and scenic views, it offers a colorful and quiet drive through Minnesota's prairie country.

☐ ▯ ♡ **Skyline Parkway Scenic Byway:** Overlooking Duluth and Lake Superior, this 28-mile urban ridge-top route offers sweeping views of the city, harbor, and vast lake horizon. Scenic overlooks highlight fall color and passing ships. Parks, gardens, and trails line the way, blending urban amenities with natural beauty. It's a unique byway that merges city life with dramatic North Shore scenery.

☐ ▯ ♡ **Superior National Forest Scenic Byway:** Spanning 78 miles from the Iron Range to Lake Superior, this route follows rugged terrain across the Laurentian Divide. It connects Iron Range mining towns with the Superior shoreline at Silver Bay. Scenic forests, waterfalls, and interpretive stops highlight the transition from industry to wilderness, offering an immersive northern Minnesota journey.

MINNESOTA

☐ ▯ ♡ **Veterans Evergreen Memorial Drive:** This short but meaningful byway near Floodwood honors veterans with a scenic drive through pine and hardwood forests. Evergreen trees line the route, providing year-round greenery and a reflective atmosphere. Picnic spots and quiet pullouts encourage visitors to pause, making the drive both a natural retreat and a living memorial to service.

☐ ▯ ♡ **Waters of the Dancing Sky Scenic Byway:** Stretching 229 miles along Minnesota's northern border, this byway follows the Rainy River, Lake of the Woods, and the Canadian boundary. Its name honors the Northern Lights, often visible in the region's dark skies. Wildlife refuges, remote towns, and Ojibwe heritage sites line the route, offering travelers a wild and culturally rich northern journey.

National Natural Landmarks

 ☐ ▯ ♡ **Ancient River Warren Channel:** Recognized as a National Natural Landmark for its massive Ice Age meltwater features, this valley was carved when glacial Lake Agassiz drained through what is now the Minnesota River. Its immense trough stretches into South Dakota, preserving one of North America's most impressive examples of catastrophic glacial outflow.
GPS: 45.5850, -96.8300

 ☐ ▯ ♡ **Cedar Creek Natural History Area:** Designated a National Natural Landmark for its convergence of prairie, deciduous forest, and boreal forest, Cedar Creek is among the most ecologically diverse sites in North America. Used for long-term ecological research, it preserves rare habitat mosaics and provides a living laboratory for understanding natural ecosystems.
GPS: 45.4020, -93.1994

 ☐ ▯ ♡ **Itasca Natural Area:** This forest near the Mississippi River's headwaters was named a National Natural Landmark for preserving red pine, spruce-fir, and mixed hardwoods in a near-virgin state. Shielded from development and logging, it provides a rare glimpse into Minnesota's pre-settlement forest ecosystems and their natural resilience.
GPS: 47.1945, -95.1653

 ☐ ▯ ♡ **Keeley Creek Natural Area:** Honored as a National Natural Landmark for its largely untouched boreal forests, Keeley Creek in Superior National Forest shelters black spruce, white pine, and northern hardwoods. It serves as a benchmark for studying forest succession, climate change impacts, and the persistence of northern ecosystems.
GPS: 47.7899, -91.7063

 ☐ ▯ ♡ **Lac la Croix Research Natural Area:** Recognized as a National Natural Landmark for containing some of the Great Lakes' finest old-growth red and white pine, this roadless forest preserves pre-settlement conditions along Minnesota's northern border. Its remoteness ensures protection of ancient trees and their associated ecosystems.
GPS: 48.3333, -92.1167

 ☐ ▯ ♡ **Lake Agassiz Peatlands Natural Area:** This vast wetland earned National Natural Landmark designation for its patterned bogs, fens, and forested peatlands formed in the basin of glacial Lake Agassiz. One of the lower 48's finest peatland complexes, it supports rare plants, boreal wildlife, and plays a key role in carbon storage.
GPS: 48.0370, -93.4750

 ☐ ▯ ♡ **Pine Point Research Natural Area:** A National Natural Landmark within Chippewa National Forest, Pine Point protects old red pine and mixed pine stands that have seen little human disturbance. The site is essential for research into forest fire history and natural succession in Minnesota's north-central woodlands.
GPS: 47.1313, -94.5553

 ☐ ▯ ♡ **Upper Red Lake Peatland:** Designated a National Natural Landmark for being one of the largest undisturbed peatlands in the contiguous U.S., this site preserves raised bogs, string bogs, and poor fens. Its intact boreal habitat supports rare flora and fauna while playing a critical role in long-term carbon sequestration.
GPS: 48.1928, -94.5119

MISSISSIPPI

Mississippi's natural beauty flows through ancient petrified forests, serene cypress swamps, winding rivers, and scenic coastal trails. With inviting state parks, vast national forests, national park sites, and notable natural landmarks, the Magnolia State offers soulful outdoor experiences rooted in nature, history, and southern charm.

🗓 Peak Season
March–May and September–November are Mississippi's peak seasons, bringing mild temperatures, blooming landscapes, and colorful foliage. These months are best for hiking, paddling, and exploring coastal and river regions.

🗓 Offseason Months
June–August is the offseason due to high heat and humidity, though beaches and lakes remain popular. December–February is cooler and quieter, with occasional cold snaps but generally mild conditions.

🍃 Scenery & Nature Timing
Spring features wildflowers and bird migrations across wetlands and forests. Summer offers lush greenery and water recreation. Fall brings golden hardwoods and comfortable air, while winter provides peaceful hiking and coastal sunsets.

✨ Special
Mississippi features the meandering Mississippi River and its fertile Delta, the cypress swamps of the Pascagoula River Basin, and the white-sand barrier islands of the Gulf Islands National Seashore. Seasonal flooding, migratory birds, and coastal marshes define its natural rhythm.

MISSISSIPPI

State Parks

Bob M. Dearing Natchez State Park: Just minutes from historic Natchez, this 230-acre park is known for its 200-acre lake that produces record-breaking largemouth bass. Visitors can enjoy fishing, boating, and quiet picnics along wooded shores, or stay overnight at campsites and cabins. Scenic trails wind through rolling hills, while the park's proximity to Natchez's cultural treasures blends outdoor adventure with history.

Buccaneer State Park: Nestled on the Gulf Coast in Waveland, Buccaneer combines beach access, oak-shaded campgrounds, and family attractions. The park features Buccaneer Bay Waterpark with slides and a wave pool, plus fishing piers and Gulf views. Birdwatchers enjoy spotting coastal species, while families relax along the sandy shoreline. Its mix of recreation, history, and natural beauty makes it a premier Mississippi destination.

Clarkco State Park: Located near Quitman, this 815-acre park centers on a sparkling lake surrounded by pine forest. Anglers fish for bass and bream, while swimmers and boaters enjoy clear waters. The park offers 58 campsites, cabins, and shaded picnic spots, plus a five-mile nature trail perfect for hiking and birdwatching. With a peaceful, family-friendly setting, it's a favorite retreat for outdoor recreation in southeast Mississippi.

George P. Cossar State Park: Perched on the shores of Enid Lake, this park is a crappie-fishing hotspot and a peaceful getaway. Visitors can explore wooded trails, enjoy picnics with lake views, or stay at campsites and cabins. A playground and ball fields add family appeal, while Enid Lake's calm waters are perfect for boating and swimming. Its mix of outdoor fun and Delta charm makes it a well-rounded destination.

Golden Memorial State Park: A tranquil 220-acre park near Walnut Grove, Golden Memorial is built around a clear, spring-fed lake. Families fish for bass and catfish, paddle along shaded banks, or hike wooded trails that showcase seasonal wildflowers and birdlife. Picnic areas under tall pines provide peaceful escapes, while its relaxed atmosphere makes it a beloved site for quiet recreation and enjoying Mississippi's natural beauty.

Great River Road State Park: Located at Rosedale, this park offers one of the most dramatic Mississippi River overlooks in the state, with a 75-foot observation tower providing sweeping views. Birdwatchers spot waterfowl and eagles, while picnic areas give visitors a peaceful place to enjoy the Delta scenery. Though less developed, its connection to the historic Great River Road makes it a memorable stop for travelers and locals alike.

Holmes County State Park: Set in Durant, this 430-acre park features two scenic lakes—English and Odum—where anglers cast for bass, crappie, and catfish. Trails weave through hardwood forests and quiet coves, offering birdwatching and photography opportunities. Campsites, cabins, and picnic shelters make it family-friendly, while the tranquil, wooded setting provides a restful atmosphere for both day trips and overnight getaways.

Hugh White State Park: Situated along Grenada Lake, this 1,200-acre park draws visitors for excellent bass fishing, boating, and swimming. It offers cabins, shaded campsites, and an 18-hole golf course for recreation. Trails meander through rolling hills, providing hiking and birding opportunities. With a blend of outdoor adventure and lakeside relaxation, it remains one of north Mississippi's most versatile destinations for family fun.

J.P. Coleman State Park: Overlooking Pickwick Lake at Iuka, this 500-acre park is a hub for water recreation. Boaters and anglers take advantage of the Tennessee River, while swimmers enjoy the pool or sandy shoreline. Cabins perched above the lake offer stunning views, and campsites accommodate overnight stays. With rugged bluffs, fishing piers, and family activities, it's a scenic destination showcasing Mississippi's northeastern beauty.

John W. Kyle State Park: Located on Sardis Reservoir, this 255-acre park blends natural beauty with recreation. Anglers and boaters flock to the reservoir, while campers and cabin guests enjoy quiet wooded surroundings. An 18-hole golf course and picnic shelters provide additional activities. With easy access to vast waters, wildlife, and forested trails, the park offers year-round outdoor fun close to the historic town of Sardis.

MISSISSIPPI

☐ 🔖 ♡ **Lake Lincoln State Park:** Nestled near Wesson, this 700-acre park centers on Lake Lincoln, a sparkling lake perfect for fishing, boating, and swimming. Shaded campsites, cabins, and day-use areas make it family-friendly, while wooded trails provide opportunities for hiking and birdwatching. With peaceful scenery, sandy swimming areas, and abundant wildlife, it's an inviting retreat for year-round recreation.

☐ 🔖 ♡ **Lake Lowndes State Park:** Near Columbus, this 150-acre lake anchors a park offering fishing, swimming, and boating opportunities. Hiking and biking trails wind through hardwood forest, while sports fields and playgrounds add to its appeal. Campgrounds and cabins allow overnight stays, making it a versatile destination where visitors can enjoy both outdoor adventure and quiet relaxation in northeast Mississippi.

☐ 🔖 ♡ **LeFleur's Bluff State Park:** A green oasis in Jackson, this 305-acre park offers urban residents a natural escape. Visitors fish or paddle on Mayes Lake, hike scenic trails, or picnic under towering hardwoods. It also houses the Mississippi Museum of Natural Science and a golf course, blending recreation with learning. Its central location makes it a unique mix of outdoor fun and cultural exploration.

☐ 🔖 ♡ **Legion State Park:** Located near Louisville, this historic park features two spring-fed lakes, quiet trails, and picnic areas. Built in the 1930s, it still showcases original Civilian Conservation Corps craftsmanship, including the rustic stone Legion Lodge. Families enjoy fishing, hiking, and camping, while its wooded setting and historical charm create a tranquil atmosphere steeped in Mississippi heritage.

☐ 🔖 ♡ **Leroy Percy State Park:** Set in the Delta near Hollandale, this 2,000-acre park preserves cypress swamps, artesian springs, and rich wetlands. Anglers fish in quiet bayous, while trails and boardwalks offer chances to spot alligators, waterfowl, and migratory birds. With its unique landscapes and abundant wildlife, it provides an intimate glimpse into Mississippi's natural diversity and Delta ecology.

☐ 🔖 ♡ **Natchez State Park:** Just north of Natchez, this 3,000-acre park offers a 230-acre lake famous for record largemouth bass. Trails wind through hardwood forest, while picnic areas and campgrounds overlook peaceful waters. Visitors enjoy boating, fishing, and hiking, with historic Natchez nearby providing cultural exploration. Its combination of outdoor recreation and southern history makes it a standout destination.

☐ 🔖 ♡ **Paul B. Johnson State Park:** Located south of Hattiesburg near McLaurin, this 805-acre park is centered on scenic Geiger Lake. Visitors swim, boat, and fish for bass and catfish, or hike wooded trails rich in pines and hardwoods. Campgrounds, cabins, and a splash pad make it family-friendly. Its combination of recreation, natural beauty, and amenities make it a popular south Mississippi getaway.

☐ 🔖 ♡ **Percy Quin State Park:** Near McComb, this 1,700-acre park blends outdoor recreation with resort-style amenities. Lake Tangipahoa provides boating, fishing, and water sports, while campgrounds and cabins offer extended stays. Visitors also enjoy hiking trails, tennis courts, and an 18-hole golf course. Its spacious grounds and variety of activities make it one of the state's most versatile parks.

☐ 🔖 ♡ **Roosevelt State Park:** Just off I-20 in Morton, this 550-acre park is centered on Shadow Lake, offering fishing, boating, and swimming. Scenic trails climb forested hills, including a Civil War historic site, while campgrounds and cabins provide overnight stays. With sports facilities, picnicking areas, and panoramic lake views, it's a convenient yet scenic spot for both relaxation and exploration.

☐ 🔖 ♡ **Shepard State Park:** Nestled in Gautier along the Singing River, this coastal park offers unique access to the Mississippi Sound. Small-craft boating, kayaking, and hiking through wooded landscapes highlight the experience. Birdwatchers enjoy spotting coastal species, while campers and picnickers relax in shaded groves. With its natural diversity and Gulf Coast location, it's a quiet escape for outdoor enthusiasts.

☐ 🔖 ♡ **Tishomingo State Park:** Set in the Appalachian foothills near Tishomingo, this 1,530-acre park features rugged Bear Creek Canyon, dramatic sandstone outcrops, and hardwood forests. Visitors hike scenic trails, canoe the creek, and climb rock formations, while campgrounds and cabins welcome overnight guests. With rich history and striking landscapes, it's one of Mississippi's most unique and adventurous parks.

☐ 🔖 ♡ **Tombigbee State Park:** Located near Tupelo, this 480-acre park features a 90-acre lake ideal for fishing and boating. Shaded campgrounds, cabins, and picnic areas provide family amenities, while trails explore rolling hills and wooded areas. A playground and sports facilities make it especially family-friendly, offering both relaxation and recreation in a scenic northeast Mississippi setting.

MISSISSIPPI

☐ 🔖 ♡ **Trace State Park:** Near Pontotoc, this 565-acre park is known for Trace Lake, offering fishing, boating, and water skiing. It's also one of the state's few parks with designated off-road vehicle trails, appealing to adventure seekers. Golfers enjoy the on-site course, while campsites and cabins provide overnight comfort. Its diverse recreation options make it a hub for outdoor fun.

☐ 🔖 ♡ **Wall Doxey State Park:** Situated near Holly Springs, this 630-acre park features Spring Lake as its centerpiece, popular for fishing, swimming, and boating. Trails circle the lake through shady hardwood forest, while campsites and cabins provide peaceful getaways. With picnicking areas and wildlife viewing, it's a quiet, scenic retreat perfect for families seeking outdoor relaxation.

National Parks

 ☐ 🔖 ♡ **Brices Cross Roads National Battlefield Site:** Near Baldwyn, this site honors the 1864 Civil War battle where Confederate forces under Nathan Bedford Forrest defeated Union troops. Visitors can walk the battlefield, view interpretive signs, and stop at the visitor center to learn about the strategy and impact of the fight, which highlighted the importance of mobility and tactics in the Western Theater.

 ☐ 🔖 ♡ **Gulf Islands National Seashore:** Stretching along the coasts of Mississippi and Florida, this seashore preserves barrier islands, white-sand beaches, and diverse ecosystems. Visitors enjoy swimming, hiking, and camping, while historic forts such as Fort Pickens showcase centuries of coastal defense. Home to sea turtles, shorebirds, and scenic Gulf waters, it blends natural beauty with cultural history.

 ☐ 🔖 ♡ **Medgar and Myrlie Evers Home National Monument:** In Jackson, this site preserves the home of civil rights leader Medgar Evers, who was assassinated here in 1963. Visitors can tour the modest house, learn about Evers' fight for equality, and reflect on the legacy continued by his wife Myrlie. The monument offers a powerful reminder of courage, sacrifice, and the struggle for justice in Mississippi.

 ☐ 🔖 ♡ **Natchez National Historical Park:** In Natchez, this park interprets the city's rich cultural heritage through historic sites including Melrose, a grand antebellum estate, and Fort Rosalie, a French colonial stronghold. Visitors explore life in the 18th and 19th centuries, walk historic grounds, and gain insight into Natchez's role as a crossroads of commerce, culture, and conflict in early America.

 ☐ 🔖 ♡ **Natchez Trace National Scenic Trail:** Winding through Mississippi, Alabama, and Tennessee, this trail follows sections of the historic Natchez Trace, once traveled by Native Americans, settlers, and traders. Modern visitors hike forested paths, view historic landmarks, and enjoy wildlife watching. The trail preserves both scenic beauty and centuries of history along one of the South's most storied routes.

 ☐ 🔖 ♡ **Natchez Trace Parkway:** Stretching 444 miles from Natchez, Mississippi, to Nashville, Tennessee, this scenic route traces the path of the historic Natchez Trace. Drivers, cyclists, and hikers explore cultural sites, ancient mounds, and peaceful forests. With picnic areas, overlooks, and interpretive stops, the parkway blends natural beauty and history, offering a leisurely journey through three states.

 ☐ 🔖 ♡ **Shiloh National Military Park:** Located in Tennessee near the Mississippi border, this park preserves the site of the 1862 Battle of Shiloh, one of the Civil War's largest and bloodiest conflicts. Visitors explore battlefields, walk trails lined with monuments, and reflect at Shiloh National Cemetery. Exhibits explain the strategies and staggering toll, marking Shiloh as a turning point in the war's western campaign.

 ☐ 🔖 ♡ **Tupelo National Battlefield:** In downtown Tupelo, this small site commemorates the July 1864 battle where Union forces clashed with Confederate troops under Forrest. Interpretive markers and monuments tell the story of the engagement, fought to protect Union supply lines. Though compact, the site provides meaningful insight into the conflict and honors those who fought in this pivotal Mississippi battle.

MISSISSIPPI

☐ 🔖 ♡ **Vicksburg National Military Park:** Overlooking the Mississippi River, this park preserves the site of the 1863 Siege of Vicksburg, a decisive Union victory that split the Confederacy. Visitors explore miles of battlefield, see reconstructed trenches, and view more than 1,300 monuments and memorials. With a national cemetery and historic gunboats, it powerfully illustrates Vicksburg's role in the Civil War.

State & National Forests

☐ 🔖 ♡ **Bienville National Forest:** Spanning 178,000 acres in central Mississippi, Bienville NF features rolling pine and oak woodlands, spring-fed creeks, and rich biodiversity. Popular spots like Marathon and Shongelo lakes provide fishing and boating, while Harrell Prairie Botanical Area protects rare tallgrass prairie. Visitors enjoy camping, hunting, and hiking in a landscape shaped by conservation and forestry.

☐ 🔖 ♡ **De Soto National Forest:** Mississippi's largest national forest at over 518,000 acres, De Soto protects longleaf pine savannas, wet flatwoods, and pitcher plant bogs. It features two wilderness areas—Black Creek and Leaf River—and is home to the Black Creek National Scenic River. Visitors hike, canoe, birdwatch, and camp while exploring one of the Southeast's most biologically rich landscapes.

☐ 🔖 ♡ **Delta National Forest:** The only bottomland hardwood national forest in the U.S., this 60,000-acre expanse in Sharkey County preserves a rare Mississippi River floodplain ecosystem. It serves as the Sunflower Wildlife Management Area, offering opportunities for hunting, canoeing, and birdwatching. Bald eagles, black bears, and rich wetland flora make it a vital sanctuary for biodiversity.

☐ 🔖 ♡ **Holly Springs National Forest:** Encompassing about 155,000 acres in northern Mississippi, this forest protects pine and hardwood hills dotted with lakes and wetlands. Visitors enjoy camping, hiking, hunting, and fishing, with recreational sites like Chewalla Lake. Created by the Civilian Conservation Corps in the 1930s, the forest combines outdoor adventure with conservation and historic landscapes.

☐ 🔖 ♡ **Homochitto National Forest:** Located in southwest Mississippi, this 191,000-acre forest is known for its pine-hardwood ridges, deep hollows, and winding streams. Rich in plant diversity, it was one of the first national forests east of the Mississippi River. Visitors fish, camp, and hike among rolling hills, while CCC-era structures remind visitors of its Depression-era origins and conservation legacy.

☐ 🔖 ♡ **Kurtz State Forest:** A small but important state forest in Jackson County, Kurtz is primarily used for forestry research, wildlife management, and demonstration of conservation practices. It helps showcase sustainable land management while preserving habitats for native plants and animals. Its limited access makes it less of a recreation site but valuable for science and stewardship.

☐ 🔖 ♡ **Tombigbee National Forest:** Covering roughly 67,000 acres in northeastern Mississippi, Tombigbee NF includes pine and oak ridges, hardwood bottoms, and scenic lakes. Managed together with Holly Springs NF, it offers hunting, horseback riding, hiking, and camping. Wildlife and forest restoration projects highlight its importance as both a recreation area and a conservation landscape.

MISSISSIPPI

National Scenic Byways & All-American Roads

☐ 🔖 ♡ **Great River Road:** Following the Mississippi River through 10 states, the Mississippi portion winds along Delta farmlands, levees, and river towns rich with blues, Civil Rights, and agricultural history. Scenic overlooks, interpretive centers, and cultural stops connect travelers to the river's heritage, offering one of America's most iconic drives.

☐ 🔖 ♡ **Natchez Trace Parkway:** Stretching 444 miles from Natchez, Mississippi, to Nashville, Tennessee, this historic route traces a centuries-old trail used by Native Americans, traders, and settlers. The parkway showcases prehistoric mounds, Civil War sites, hardwood forests, and rolling hills. With pullouts, trails, and cultural landmarks, it blends history, nature, and recreation in a seamless journey.

☐ 🔖 ♡ **Wooden Churches of the Black Belt:** Extending into Mississippi's eastern counties, this byway highlights historic African American churches that tell the story of resilience, faith, and community in the Black Belt. Simple wooden sanctuaries stand as cultural landmarks, surrounded by rural landscapes, inviting travelers to reflect on heritage, tradition, and the power of shared history.

State Scenic Byways

☐ 🔖 ♡ **Beach Boulevard Scenic Byway:** Stretching along Biloxi's Gulf Coast, this byway offers sweeping water views, the historic Biloxi Lighthouse, and access to beaches, casinos, and fresh seafood. Coastal neighborhoods and piers highlight the region's mix of natural beauty and cultural vibrancy, making it a favorite drive for both visitors and locals.

☐ 🔖 ♡ **Biloxi-D'Iberville Scenic Byway:** Connecting Biloxi to D'Iberville, this short route features views of marshlands, bridges, and coastal development along the Back Bay. It provides an easy way to experience the transition from busy waterfronts to quieter residential areas, blending natural scenery with the cultural flavor of Mississippi's Gulf Coast.

☐ 🔖 ♡ **Brice's Crossroads–Chief Tishomingo Scenic Byway:** This byway links the Brice's Crossroads National Battlefield site with areas tied to Chief Tishomingo, honoring both Civil War and Native American history. Travelers pass wooded landscapes, rolling fields, and historic markers, offering a reflective journey that showcases the cultural layers of northeast Mississippi.

☐ 🔖 ♡ **Delta Bluffs Scenic Byway:** Following the loess bluffs of the Mississippi Delta, this route offers striking views over riverside cliffs, farmlands, and small Delta towns. The byway highlights the region's agricultural heritage and scenic beauty, connecting travelers with a distinctive landscape shaped by both nature and human history.

☐ 🔖 ♡ **Gateway to History Scenic Byway:** Centered on Vicksburg, this byway connects Civil War battlefields, cemeteries, and historic structures that define the city's legacy. Scenic routes wind past preserved landscapes and interpretive sites, allowing visitors to immerse themselves in the pivotal history of the Siege of Vicksburg and its surrounding area.

☐ 🔖 ♡ **Grand Gulf–Raymond Scenic Byway:** Linking the historic river town of Grand Gulf to Raymond, this byway passes Civil War landmarks, scenic woodlands, and quiet backroads. Travelers encounter antebellum architecture, battlefield sites, and Mississippi River overlooks, blending cultural heritage with natural charm in the state's southwest corner.

☐ 🔖 ♡ **Gulf Coast Scenic Byway:** Running between Gulfport and Ocean Springs, this coastal route offers salt marshes, waterfront neighborhoods, and barrier island views. Visitors enjoy seafood stops, historic sites, and access to Ocean Springs' arts district. The blend of coastal scenery and cultural attractions makes it a highlight of Mississippi's shoreline.

☐ 🔖 ♡ **Highway 605 Scenic Byway:** Following MS 605 through Harrison County, this corridor runs between Gulfport and Long Beach, showcasing pine forests, residential communities, and nearby coastal access. Though modest in length, it offers a peaceful contrast to busier highways, providing a scenic route through southern Mississippi's landscapes.

MISSISSIPPI

☐ 🔖 ♡ **Highway 67 Scenic Byway:** Passing through Harrison County and the edge of De Soto National Forest, this byway combines pine uplands, open farmland, and small-town scenery. It highlights Mississippi's natural diversity while offering a quieter alternative to coastal routes, making it an inviting drive for travelers seeking forested beauty.

☐ 🔖 ♡ **Mississippi Delta Great River Road Scenic Byway:** This state-level designation follows the Mississippi River through Delta counties, showcasing juke joints, blues markers, plantations, and fertile farmlands. While separate from the federal Great River Road, it still highlights the Delta's unique blend of music, culture, and rich riverine heritage.

☐ 🔖 ♡ **NASA Scenic Byway to Space:** Leading toward Stennis Space Center and the Infinity Science Center, this byway blends quiet pine corridors with the high-tech legacy of space exploration. Visitors enjoy educational exhibits and interpretive stops that link Mississippi's Gulf Coast scenery to America's journey into space.

☐ 🔖 ♡ **Noxubee Hills Scenic Byway:** Winding through Oktibbeha and Winston counties, this byway features rolling hills, hardwood forests, and rural charm. Scenic views, wildlife, and quiet roads make it ideal for peaceful exploration, while nearby Noxubee National Wildlife Refuge adds opportunities for birdwatching and outdoor recreation.

☐ 🔖 ♡ **William Faulkner Scenic Byway:** Centered in Oxford and Lafayette County, this route highlights sites tied to the famed author, from Rowan Oak to the historic Square. Along the way, visitors encounter antebellum homes, university landmarks, and southern landscapes, connecting literature, culture, and Mississippi's small-town heritage.

National Natural Landmarks

☐ 🔖 ♡ **Bienville Pines Scenic Area:** Designated a National Natural Landmark for its old-growth loblolly pine, Bienville Pines within Bienville National Forest protects one of the largest remaining stands in the Southeast. Towering trees and a diverse understory preserve what Southern pine ecosystems looked like before widespread logging, offering critical habitat and scientific value.
GPS: 32.3491, -89.4711

☐ 🔖 ♡ **Chestnut Oak Disjunct:** Recognized as a National Natural Landmark for its unusual chestnut oak population, this stand lies far outside the species' normal range. Growing on dry, upland soils uncommon in Mississippi, it provides key insight into postglacial plant migration and represents a unique mix of Appalachian and Gulf Coastal Plain flora.
GPS: unlisted

☐ 🔖 ♡ **Green Ash–Overcup Oak–Sweetgum Research Natural Areas:** These tracts in Delta National Forest were named National Natural Landmarks for preserving some of the last undisturbed bottomland hardwood forests in the state. Their seasonally flooded ecosystems, rich canopy, and intact soils sustain diverse wildlife and serve as invaluable sites for ecological research.
GPS: 32.7667, -90.7833

☐ 🔖 ♡ **Harrell Prairie Hill:** This open grassland within Bienville National Forest is a National Natural Landmark for preserving a rare remnant of Jackson Prairie. Its calcareous soils support native grasses, wildflowers, and spring blooms. Once widespread, this prairie ecosystem now survives in fragments, making Harrell Hill vital for conservation and education.
GPS: 32.3358, -89.4397

☐ 🔖 ♡ **Mississippi Petrified Forest:** Honored as a National Natural Landmark for its fossilized Tertiary-era firs and maples, this site displays logs preserved by sand burial and mineralization. Visitors can follow trails through petrified trunks and explore one of the few petrified forests east of the Mississippi River, showcasing millions of years of geologic history.
GPS: 32.5207, -90.3230

Missouri

Missouri's diverse landscapes include Ozark caves, clear rivers, ancient prairies, and scenic trails. Through its inviting network of state parks, a vast national forest, national park sites, and distinctive natural landmarks, Missouri welcomes explorers of all kinds to discover its wild beauty, hidden springs, and timeless natural heritage.

📅 Peak Season
April–June and September–October are Missouri's peak seasons, offering mild temperatures, spring blooms, and colorful fall foliage. These months are ideal for hiking, floating rivers, and exploring parks and caves.

📅 Offseason Months
November–March is the offseason, with cooler weather and lighter crowds. Winter brings occasional snow, but many hiking trails and scenic areas remain open and quiet.

🍃 Scenery & Nature Timing
Spring brings wildflowers and full rivers for canoeing. Summer offers dense greenery and warm lakes. Fall transforms forests with bright color, while winter reveals open vistas and clear skies across the Ozarks.

✨ Special
Missouri showcases the Ozark Mountains, the karst caves of the Ozark National Scenic Riverways, and towering bluffs along the Mississippi River. Natural springs, waterfalls, and vast underground rivers create some of the Midwest's most unique geology.

UNITED STATES EDITION

MISSOURI

State Parks

☐ 🔖 ♡ **Babler State Park:** Located in Wildwood, this 2,400-acre park features over 15 miles of trails winding through forests, prairies, and wetlands. Visitors enjoy hiking, biking, horseback riding, and picnicking while spotting local wildlife. Close to St. Louis, it provides a peaceful natural escape with family-friendly amenities in a diverse landscape.

☐ 🔖 ♡ **Bennett Spring State Park:** Near Lebanon, this 3,300-acre park is one of Missouri's top trout-fishing destinations. Spring-fed waters and clear streams draw anglers year-round. Visitors also enjoy hiking scenic trails, exploring a historic mill, camping, and staying in rustic cabins. The park blends rich natural beauty with cultural heritage in a beloved Ozark setting.

☐ 🔖 ♡ **Big Lake State Park:** Located in Holt County, this park surrounds a 350-acre oxbow lake, one of the largest natural lakes in Missouri. It's a popular destination for boating, fishing, and birdwatching. Seasonal flooding shapes its wetlands, creating a unique environment for waterfowl and wildlife. Campgrounds and trails make it a relaxing, nature-focused getaway.

☐ 🔖 ♡ **Big Oak Tree State Park:** Near East Prairie, this 1,000-acre park preserves rare bottomland hardwood forest. Towering oaks, cypress, and hickories—some centuries old—dominate the landscape. Elevated boardwalk trails allow visitors to explore wetlands teeming with wildlife. It's a living museum of Missouri's natural heritage and one of the quietest state parks.

☐ 🔖 ♡ **Big Sugar Creek State Park:** Tucked in McDonald County, this 2,000-acre park features rugged Ozark landscapes with steep valleys and clear streams. The park protects a rich mix of plant and animal life, offering opportunities for hiking, nature study, and birdwatching. Its pristine setting makes it a haven for those seeking quiet exploration and biodiversity.

☐ 🔖 ♡ **Bryant Creek State Park:** Established in 2016, this 3,000-acre park in Douglas County protects a wild stretch of Bryant Creek, an Ozark stream with excellent water quality. Visitors can fish, paddle, and hike through oak-hickory forests and limestone bluffs. The undeveloped character of the park offers a wilderness experience rare among Missouri's state parks.

☐ 🔖 ♡ **Castlewood State Park:** Near Ballwin, this 1,800-acre park follows the Meramec River, where towering bluffs overlook wooded valleys and open floodplains. Once a 1920s resort area, today it's a hub for hiking, mountain biking, fishing, and canoeing. Its blend of history and natural beauty make it one of Missouri's most popular recreation areas.

☐ 🔖 ♡ **Crowder State Park:** Situated near Trenton, this 1,900-acre park surrounds a serene lake ideal for fishing, swimming, and paddling. Trails wind through rolling hills and oak woodlands, offering scenic hikes year-round. Developed in the 1930s by the Civilian Conservation Corps, its stone structures still stand as reminders of Missouri's park heritage.

☐ 🔖 ♡ **Cuivre River State Park:** At 6,400 acres, this Troy-area park is one of Missouri's largest. Its forests, prairies, and lakes provide outstanding wildlife habitat and outdoor recreation. Visitors can hike miles of trails, camp, fish, or swim. With its rolling terrain and rustic beauty, the park is often compared to the Ozarks but located closer to St. Louis.

☐ 🔖 ♡ **Current River State Park:** Nestled in Shannon County, this 780-acre park offers direct access to the scenic Current River. Hiking trails, historic stone buildings from a 1930s retreat, and opportunities for fishing and paddling highlight the park. Its quiet, undeveloped setting provides a peaceful escape and a gateway to the Ozark National Scenic Riverways.

☐ 🔖 ♡ **Don Robinson State Park:** Located in Jefferson County, this 800-acre park was donated by a private conservationist in 2012. Sandstone cliffs, box canyons, and glades dominate the rugged landscape. Hiking trails showcase the area's dramatic geology, unique ecosystems, and wildflowers. Its preservation reflects Missouri's modern commitment to expanding public natural spaces.

☐ 🔖 ♡ **Echo Bluff State Park:** Opened in 2016, this 430-acre park in Shannon County centers around its namesake bluff and Sinking Creek. Modern facilities include a lodge, cabins, campground, and picnic areas. Hiking trails and creek access make it ideal for families. Its mix of modern comfort and natural beauty makes it a standout among newer state parks.

MISSOURI

☐ 🔖 ♡ **Elephant Rocks State Park:** In Belleview, this 130-acre park showcases giant granite boulders that resemble a train of circus elephants. The Braille Trail, designed for accessibility, winds among the rocks, allowing visitors of all abilities to enjoy the formations. It's a geologic wonder, a photographer's favorite, and a family-friendly destination for exploration.

☐ 🔖 ♡ **Eleven Point State Park:** In Oregon County, this 4,200-acre park protects riverfront land along the federally designated Eleven Point National Scenic River. It offers opportunities for paddling, fishing, hiking, and primitive camping. With its extensive forests and scenic bluffs, the park provides an immersive wilderness experience in the Missouri Ozarks.

☐ 🔖 ♡ **Finger Lakes State Park:** Near Columbia, this 1,100-acre park is a reclaimed coal mining site transformed into a recreation hub. Lakes formed from mining pits provide boating and fishing opportunities. The park is also a major destination for off-road vehicles, with miles of trails for ATVs and dirt bikes. Hiking, biking, and camping round out the offerings.

☐ 🔖 ♡ **Graham Cave State Park:** Located near Montgomery City, this 370-acre park is home to a limestone cave that preserves evidence of human habitation from over 10,000 years ago. Visitors can explore interpretive trails, hike through woodlands and prairies, and enjoy picnicking along the Loutre River. The park's archaeological significance and natural beauty make it a unique destination.

☐ 🔖 ♡ **Grand Gulf State Park:** Nicknamed the "Little Grand Canyon," this 322-acre park in Oregon County features a collapsed cave system that left behind sheer cliffs and a striking chasm more than 130 feet deep. Trails and overlooks give dramatic views of the gulf, while geologic markers tell the story of its formation. It's a hidden gem for geology lovers and hikers.

☐ 🔖 ♡ **Ha Ha Tonka State Park:** Near Camdenton, this 3,700-acre park blends natural wonders with cultural history. Highlights include castle ruins overlooking the Lake of the Ozarks, a massive natural bridge, sinkholes, caves, and one of Missouri's largest springs. Trails wind through dramatic Ozark terrain, offering scenic views, unique geology, and fascinating history.

☐ 🔖 ♡ **Harry S Truman State Park:** Nestled on a peninsula of Truman Lake in Benton County, this 1,400-acre park is a water recreation haven. Visitors enjoy fishing, swimming, boating, and camping, with picnic areas overlooking the lake. Forested bluffs and open glades offer hiking and wildlife viewing, making it a perfect spot for outdoor fun on Missouri's largest reservoir.

☐ 🔖 ♡ **Hawn State Park:** Located in Ste. Genevieve County, this 5,000-acre park is considered one of Missouri's most beautiful. It features sandstone canyons, clear streams, and rich biodiversity. The popular Whispering Pines Trail loops through pine and oak forests, offering backpacking and day-hiking options. Quiet and scenic, it's a paradise for nature lovers and photographers.

☐ 🔖 ♡ **Johnson's Shut-Ins State Park:** A crown jewel of the Ozarks, this 8,500-acre park in Reynolds County is famous for its natural water slides and rock formations along the East Fork Black River. Visitors swim, climb, and wade among igneous rocks shaped over millennia. Trails, camping, and scenic overlooks make it a family favorite for outdoor adventure.

☐ 🔖 ♡ **Jones-Confluence Point State Park:** Located near St. Charles, this 1,100-acre park marks the meeting of the Missouri and Mississippi rivers. Trails and boardwalks lead to observation areas where visitors can view bald eagles, migratory birds, and river landscapes. Interpretive signs highlight the area's ecological importance and its ties to Lewis and Clark history.

☐ 🔖 ♡ **Katy Trail State Park:** Spanning 239 miles across Missouri, the Katy Trail is the nation's longest developed rail-trail. Stretching from Machens to Clinton, it follows the Missouri River and offers cycling, hiking, and birdwatching through farmland, forests, and river bluffs. Passing through charming towns, it's a premier destination for recreation and heritage tourism.

☐ 🔖 ♡ **Knob Noster State Park:** Located near Whiteman Air Force Base in Johnson County, this nearly 4,000-acre park blends woodlands and tallgrass prairie. Two small lakes provide fishing and canoeing, while trails wind through quiet forests. Built in the 1930s by the Civilian Conservation Corps, its stone structures and rustic setting offer a classic state park experience.

☐ 🔖 ♡ **Lake of the Ozarks State Park:** Missouri's largest state park at over 17,000 acres, this park hugs 85 miles of Lake of the Ozarks shoreline. It offers boating, fishing, hiking, swimming beaches, and two marinas. Trails lead through forests and glades, while campgrounds and cabins provide lodging. Caves, horseback riding, and scenic overlooks round out its diverse attractions.

MISSOURI

☐ 🔖 ♡ **Lake Wappapello State Park:** Located in southeastern Missouri, this 1,800-acre park sits along the shores of Lake Wappapello. It's a popular destination for boating, fishing, and swimming, with scenic campgrounds and picnic sites overlooking the water. Hiking trails wind through Ozark woodlands, offering birdwatching and wildlife opportunities in a peaceful lakeside setting.

☐ 🔖 ♡ **Lewis and Clark State Park:** Situated in Buchanan County near Rushville, this 189-acre park preserves views of Lewis and Clark Lake, named for the explorers who camped nearby in 1804. Visitors enjoy fishing, picnicking, and hiking along the lake's edge. Interpretive displays highlight the expedition's journey, blending history and nature in a compact park.

☐ 🔖 ♡ **Long Branch State Park:** Near Macon, this 1,828-acre park surrounds a 2,400-acre U.S. Army Corps of Engineers lake. Visitors can boat, fish, swim, and camp along its sandy beaches and coves. Trails lead through prairie and forest, offering birdwatching and wildlife sightings. Its expansive waters make it a favorite for summer recreation and family outings.

☐ 🔖 ♡ **Mark Twain State Park:** Located near Florida, Missouri—the boyhood home of Samuel Clemens—this 2,775-acre park lies along Mark Twain Lake. The park features forested bluffs, fishing, hiking, and camping, as well as a nearby museum dedicated to the author. Scenic trails and picnic areas allow visitors to enjoy the landscape that inspired Twain's writings.

☐ 🔖 ♡ **Meramec State Park:** Near Sullivan, this 6,896-acre park along the Meramec River is known for its caves, including Fisher Cave with guided tours. Trails meander through forests and bluffs, while visitors enjoy fishing, boating, and swimming. The park also offers camping and cabins, making it one of Missouri's most popular destinations for family recreation.

☐ 🔖 ♡ **Montauk State Park:** Located at the headwaters of the Current River, this 3,000-acre park is famous for trout fishing in its spring-fed streams. Anglers, hikers, and campers enjoy the park's scenic Ozark setting, while the historic Montauk Mill adds cultural charm. With clear waters and lush forests, it's one of Missouri's premier fishing parks.

☐ 🔖 ♡ **Morris State Park:** A small but geologically unique park in Dunklin County, this 161-acre site protects Crowley's Ridge, a rare landform in the Missouri Bootheel. Trails showcase its steep slopes and diverse plant life. Visitors can hike, picnic, and learn about the ridge's geologic origins, making it a fascinating stop for nature and science enthusiasts.

☐ 🔖 ♡ **Onondaga Cave State Park:** Near Leasburg, this 1,300-acre park features Onondaga Cave, a National Natural Landmark filled with stalactites, stalagmites, and flowstone. Guided cave tours highlight its underground wonders. Above ground, visitors enjoy the Meramec River, camping, and hiking trails through forests and bluffs, making it a versatile park for exploration.

☐ 🔖 ♡ **Pershing State Park:** Located near Brookfield, this 3,600-acre park honors General John J. Pershing, commander of U.S. forces in WWI. It features wetlands, prairies, and forests with excellent birdwatching opportunities. Boardwalks and trails provide access to marshlands rich in wildlife, while camping and fishing round out the park's family-friendly offerings.

☐ 🔖 ♡ **Pomme de Terre State Park:** Spanning two sections along Pomme de Terre Lake, this park offers beaches, boat ramps, and campgrounds with lake views. Fishing, water-skiing, and swimming are popular, while trails and picnic areas provide land-based recreation. Its peaceful setting and aquatic focus make it a popular summer retreat for families.

☐ 🔖 ♡ **Roaring River State Park:** Near Cassville in the Ozarks, this 4,300-acre park is known for its deep valley, limestone cliffs, and spring-fed trout waters. Visitors fish in clear streams, hike seven scenic trails, and camp in forested sites. A hatchery, swimming pool, and rugged landscape make it one of Missouri's most beloved outdoor destinations.

☐ 🔖 ♡ **Rock Bridge Memorial State Park:** Located near Columbia, this 2,273-acre park is famous for its natural rock bridge, caves, and sinkholes. The Devil's Icebox Cave and trails through forests and prairies attract hikers, spelunkers, and nature enthusiasts. Its diverse ecosystems and geologic features make it a fascinating place for exploration and education.

☐ 🔖 ♡ **Route 66 State Park:** Just outside St. Louis, this 419-acre park preserves the history of the "Mother Road." Located on the site of the former town of Times Beach, the park offers a visitor center with Route 66 memorabilia, trails, fishing access, and picnic areas. It's both a cultural landmark and a recreational retreat along the famous highway.

☐ 🔖 ♡ **Sam A. Baker State Park:** Found in the St. Francois Mountains, this 5,323-acre park offers fishing, canoeing, swimming, and hiking. Mudlick Trail leads through rugged terrain to high overlooks. Visitors camp along the St. Francis River or explore forests and glades. CCC-built structures give the park historic charm alongside its natural beauty.

MISSOURI

☐ ▯ ♡ **Saint Francois State Park:** Located near Bonne Terre, this 2,700-acre park offers rolling hills, oak-hickory forests, and the Big River for fishing and swimming. Trails wind through scenic woodlands, while campgrounds and picnic areas make it family-friendly. Wildlife is abundant, and its peaceful setting provides a great retreat into Missouri's natural beauty.

☐ ▯ ♡ **Saint Joe State Park:** Near Park Hills, this 8,238-acre park is one of Missouri's largest off-road vehicle riding areas. Miles of trails for ATVs and dirt bikes attract adventure seekers, while lakes offer fishing, swimming, and boating. Camping, equestrian trails, and wooded hiking paths make it a versatile park for both rugged recreation and family fun.

☐ ▯ ♡ **Stockton State Park:** On a peninsula jutting into Stockton Lake, this 2,175-acre park is known for sailing, fishing, and camping. Its clear waters attract boaters and anglers alike. Trails wind through oak woodlands and glades, and its marina provides easy access to the lake. The park's breezy bluffs make it Missouri's premier sailing destination.

☐ ▯ ♡ **Table Rock State Park:** Situated on the shores of Table Rock Lake near Branson, this 356-acre park is a hub for water recreation. Visitors enjoy fishing, boating, and scuba diving, while trails lead through forested hills. A marina, campgrounds, and picnic areas make it ideal for families. Its proximity to Branson adds cultural attractions nearby.

☐ ▯ ♡ **Taum Sauk Mountain State Park:** Home to Missouri's highest point, this 7,500-acre park in the St. Francois Mountains offers sweeping Ozark views. Mina Sauk Falls, the state's tallest waterfall, highlights its rugged trails. Backpackers can hike the Ozark Trail, while day visitors enjoy picnicking and overlooks. It's a wilderness park with spectacular scenery.

☐ ▯ ♡ **Thousand Hills State Park:** Near Kirksville, this 3,215-acre park features a 703-acre lake for boating, fishing, and swimming. Trails and campgrounds invite extended stays, while preserved Native American petroglyphs connect visitors to the past. The park's mix of cultural heritage and outdoor recreation makes it a regional highlight in northern Missouri.

☐ ▯ ♡ **Trail of Tears State Park:** Located near Jackson, this 3,415-acre park memorializes the forced relocation of Cherokee people along the Trail of Tears. Interpretive exhibits share its tragic history. Visitors can hike bluffs overlooking the Mississippi River, fish, camp, and observe migratory birds. It's a blend of solemn remembrance and natural beauty.

☐ ▯ ♡ **Van Meter State Park:** Found in Saline County, this 1,105-acre park preserves Native American history with the Utz Village site and Old Fort earthworks. Trails lead through forests, wetlands, and prairies, while a cultural center interprets Missouri tribal heritage. Fishing, camping, and hiking combine with history in this unique park.

☐ ▯ ♡ **Wakonda State Park:** In northeast Missouri near La Grange, this 1,054-acre park features six lakes created from old quarry pits, offering fishing, swimming, and boating. Sandy beaches and campgrounds attract families, while trails and wetlands provide birdwatching opportunities. It's a unique park combining reclaimed land with recreational appeal.

☐ ▯ ♡ **Wallace State Park:** Near Cameron, this 502-acre park centers on Lake Allaman, popular for fishing, swimming, and picnicking. Trails wind through quiet forests and rolling hills, offering a peaceful setting for hiking. Campgrounds and picnic shelters provide family amenities. Its small size and tranquil character make it a hidden gem among Missouri's state parks.

☐ ▯ ♡ **Washington State Park:** This 2,147-acre park along the Big River is known for Native American petroglyphs, which are listed on the National Register of Historic Places. Hiking trails explore oak-hickory forests and river bluffs. Swimming, camping, and CCC-built stone structures add to its appeal, making it a park rich in culture and recreation.

☐ ▯ ♡ **Watkins Woolen Mill State Park:** Located near Lawson, this 1,500-acre park preserves a 19th-century textile mill, the only one of its kind in the U.S. with original machinery intact. The park includes a lake for fishing and swimming, camping facilities, and trails. It blends history and outdoor recreation in a National Historic Landmark setting.

☐ ▯ ♡ **Weston Bend State Park:** Overlooking the Missouri River near Weston, this 1,133-acre park offers scenic river views, hiking and biking trails, and a mix of woodlands and farmland. A scenic overlook provides breathtaking vistas, especially in fall. With picnic areas, camping, and proximity to historic Weston, it's a popular getaway close to Kansas City.

MISSOURI

National Parks

  ☐ ☐ ♡ **Gateway Arch National Park:** Located in St. Louis, this park features the iconic Gateway Arch, a symbol of westward expansion. Visitors can ride a tram to the top for sweeping views of the city and Mississippi River, explore the underground museum, and learn about migration, settlement, and the pivotal role St. Louis played in the development of the United States.

 ☐ ☐ ♡ **George Washington Carver National Monument:** Found in Diamond, this site preserves the birthplace and legacy of George Washington Carver, famed scientist and educator. Visitors can tour his childhood home, walk trails through restored prairies, and explore the museum, which highlights his groundbreaking agricultural research and lasting contributions to education and sustainability.

 ☐ ☐ ♡ **Harry S Truman National Historic Site:** In Independence, this historic site protects the longtime home of President Harry S. Truman. Guided tours showcase the modest residence where he lived before, during, and after his presidency. Nearby, the Truman Presidential Library provides exhibits on his leadership, decisions during World War II, and his role in shaping postwar America.

☐ ☐ ♡ **Ozark National Scenic Riverways:** Spanning southern Missouri, this park preserves the free-flowing Current and Jacks Fork Rivers. Known for clear waters, caves, springs, and wooded hills, the area is popular for canoeing, kayaking, fishing, hiking, and camping. It offers a chance to experience the natural beauty of the Ozarks while protecting unique aquatic ecosystems.

 ☐ ☐ ♡ **Ste. Genevieve National Historical Park:** Established in 2020, this site preserves Missouri's oldest European settlement, founded in the 1730s by French colonists along the Mississippi River. Visitors can tour original French Colonial homes, including vertical-log structures, and explore exhibits on French, Native American, and Creole heritage. The park highlights the unique cultural blending that shaped early Missouri history.

 ☐ ☐ ♡ **Ulysses S. Grant National Historic Site:** Located in St. Louis County, this site preserves White Haven, the home of Ulysses S. Grant, Civil War general and 18th U.S. president. Tours highlight his family life, military career, and presidency. The grounds and museum interpret the 19th-century history of slavery, conflict, and the nation's transformation during Grant's era.

 ☐ ☐ ♡ **Wilson's Creek National Battlefield:** Near Republic, this park protects the site of the 1861 Battle of Wilson's Creek, the first major Civil War battle fought west of the Mississippi. Visitors can drive or hike through the preserved battlefield, tour historic structures, and explore the visitor center, which offers exhibits on the battle's significance in shaping the war's course.

State & National Forests

☐ ☐ ♡ **Busiek State Forest:** A 2,700-acre natural area near Springfield, located in Christian County. It features oak-glade savanna ecosystems and supports 18 miles of trails, rustic campsites, a shooting range, and seasonal hunting. Managed for timber, habitat conservation, and public recreation, Busiek blends education with nature immersion.

☐ ☐ ♡ **Mark Twain National Forest:** Spanning 1.5 million acres across southern Missouri, this federal forest protects oak-hickory and pine ecosystems across the Ozark Highlands. It includes the Eleven Point and Current River Corridors, offers extensive hiking, camping, horseback riding, hunting, fishing, and conserves water and wildlife through rugged, wooded landscapes.

MISSOURI

National Scenic Byways & All-American Roads

☐ 🔖 ♡ **Crowley's Ridge Parkway:** A **National Scenic Byway** that follows a rare geological landform stretching from Arkansas into Missouri's Bootheel. The route highlights Civil War battlefields, historic communities, and forested ridges rising above flat delta farmland, offering travelers a unique blend of cultural heritage and striking natural scenery.

☐ 🔖 ♡ **Great River Road:** An **All-American Road** and **National Scenic Byway** tracing the Mississippi River through Missouri. It passes levee towns, blufftop overlooks, wildlife refuges, and historic districts. Rich in culture, history, and commerce, the drive captures the character of river life while providing panoramic views of one of America's great waterways.

☐ 🔖 ♡ **Historic Route 66:** An **All-American Road** and **National Scenic Byway** spanning more than 300 miles across Missouri. The route showcases neon signs, classic diners, vintage motels, and restored service stations, reflecting the nostalgic spirit of America's mid-century highway era while connecting St. Louis to Joplin through small towns and roadside attractions.

State Scenic Byways

☐ 🔖 ♡ **Blue Buck Knob Scenic Byway:** This 24-mile State Scenic Byway winds through the Mark Twain National Forest in the Ozark Highlands. Travelers encounter oak-pine woodlands, rolling ridges, and stream valleys rich in native plants and wildlife. With scenic overlooks, quiet forest roads, and access to hiking and birdwatching, it highlights the tranquil, rugged beauty of southern Missouri.

☐ 🔖 ♡ **Bloomfield Stars & Stripes Historical/Cultural Byway:** Centered in Bloomfield, this route honors the birthplace of the Stars and Stripes military newspaper. It passes historic courthouses, cemeteries, and patriotic landmarks while threading through small towns and farmland. Interpretive signs share stories of soldiers and community resilience, making it a byway steeped in heritage and local pride.

☐ 🔖 ♡ **Cliff Drive Scenic Byway:** Located in Kansas City, this byway follows a winding path along limestone bluffs and wooded parkland within the historic Kessler Park. Drivers and cyclists enjoy sweeping overlooks, shaded curves, and glimpses of vintage homes and city skyline. It offers a rare mix of urban green space and scenic natural beauty right in the heart of the city.

☐ 🔖 ♡ **Little Dixie Highway of the Great River Road:** A **State Scenic Byway** winding through central Missouri's historic "Little Dixie" region along the Missouri River. The route showcases 19th-century architecture, river towns, and fertile farmland once settled by pioneers from the South. With steamboat-era charm, cottonwoods, and scenic bluffs, it highlights the cultural heritage and natural beauty of mid-Missouri's river corridor.

☐ 🔖 ♡ **Old Trails Road Scenic Byway:** This byway traces pioneer routes across the Ozark Plateau, where rolling farmland, wildflower fields, and wooded ridges reflect the landscape early settlers once crossed. Passing through historic small towns with rock-built structures, it provides a nostalgic glimpse into Missouri's frontier past and the enduring spirit of rural communities.

☐ 🔖 ♡ **Ozark Mountain Highroad Scenic Byway:** Stretching for more than 20 miles near Branson, this high-elevation route climbs steep ridges to deliver sweeping vistas of the surrounding Ozark Mountains. Seasonal color, from wildflowers in spring to blazing foliage in fall, makes it a favorite scenic drive. Pull-offs and overlooks allow travelers to pause and enjoy panoramic views.

☐ 🔖 ♡ **Show-Me Santa Fe Trails Scenic Byway:** Following Missouri's portion of the historic Santa Fe Trail, this byway crosses open prairies, farmland, and rolling hills once traversed by wagons and traders. Interpretive markers highlight trading posts, emigrant routes, and early pioneer life. It connects modern travelers to the heritage of westward migration and the state's frontier history

UNITED STATES EDITION

MISSOURI

National Natural Landmarks

 **Big Oak Tree State Park:** Named a National Natural Landmark for its wet-mesic bottomland hardwood forest, this park protects champion trees and an old-growth canopy. Periodic flooding enriches its soils, creating habitat for countless plant and animal species. It offers one of the last, best examples of Missouri's Mississippi Alluvial Plain forests.
GPS: 36.6550, -89.3283

 **Carroll Cave:** This site is a National Natural Landmark for its vast karst system, among the largest in Missouri. Its dendritic cave streams and tributaries reveal subsurface hydrology and cave formation processes. Carroll Cave also supports unique cave-adapted invertebrates and bat colonies, making it an important biological as well as geologic site.
GPS: 37.9718, -92.5072 (approx.)

 **Cupola Pond:** Recognized as a National Natural Landmark for being one of the Ozarks' oldest sinkhole ponds, Cupola Pond illustrates karst processes and long-term ecological succession. Surrounded by upland hardwoods, its waters and margins provide critical habitat for amphibians and rare plant communities tied to aquatic ecosystems.
GPS: 36.8013, -91.1175

 **Golden Prairie:** This National Natural Landmark preserves a fragment of Missouri's historic tallgrass prairie. Never plowed, it hosts rare grasses, colorful wildflowers, pollinators, and ground-nesting birds. Golden Prairie reflects the ecological richness of grasslands that once dominated the Midwest but are now critically endangered.
GPS: 37.3626, -94.1502

 **Grand Gulf State Park:** Known as the "Little Grand Canyon," this collapsed cave system is a National Natural Landmark for its dramatic karst geology. Sheer canyon walls and a natural bridge reveal how underground streams carved and collapsed. Its disappearing stream resurfaces miles away in Arkansas, showcasing the complexity of karst hydrology.
GPS: 36.5243, -91.5439

 **Greer Spring:** Designated a National Natural Landmark as Missouri's second-largest spring, Greer discharges millions of gallons daily into the Eleven Point River. The cool, clear waters create diverse aquatic habitats, while surrounding old-growth forests shelter ferns and wildlife. Its flow and setting highlight the hydrology and ecology of Ozark springs.
GPS: 36.7867, -91.3475

 **Maple Woods Natural Area:** This urban remnant near Kansas City is a National Natural Landmark for preserving a near-virgin hardwood forest. Dominated by sugar maple and hickory, it provides refuge for migratory birds and wildflowers in a heavily developed landscape. The site is both a research asset and a glimpse of Missouri's natural forest heritage.
GPS: 39.2310, -94.5511

 **Maramec Spring:** Listed as a National Natural Landmark for its hydrologic size and cultural history, Maramec Spring is Missouri's fifth-largest. Flowing into the Meramec River, it once powered ironworks and now supports a trout hatchery and park. Its blend of spring geology, industrial ruins, and recreation illustrates the intersection of nature and history.
GPS: 37.9553, -91.5363

 **Mark Twain and Cameron Caves:** Recognized as National Natural Landmarks for their maze cave systems, these caves display intersecting limestone passages and abundant flowstone. Their historical ties to Mark Twain's writings made them famous, while their geological complexity provides valuable insight into karst processes and cave formation.
GPS: 39.6886, -91.3315

 **Marvel Cave:** Designated a National Natural Landmark for its depth and massive chambers, Marvel Cave includes one of the largest entry rooms in the Ozarks. Richly decorated with dripstone formations, it exemplifies spectacular cave geology. Long a destination for exploration and tourism, it remains a natural and cultural showcase of Missouri caves.
GPS: 36.6675, -93.3397

MISSOURI

 ☐ 🔖 ♡ **Onondaga Cave State Park:** Celebrated as a National Natural Landmark for its dense speleothem formations, Onondaga Cave features stalactites, stalagmites, and flowstones of striking variety. This show cave is among the most ornate in Missouri and offers scientists and visitors alike a vivid display of karst geology and underground ecosystems.
GPS: 38.0608, -91.2272

 ☐ 🔖 ♡ **Pickle Springs:** This natural area is a National Natural Landmark for its sandstone box canyons, waterfalls, and relict habitats. Moist, cool microclimates preserve rare Pleistocene-era plant species, making the site a living museum of ancient flora. Its geologic formations and biodiversity highlight the unique ecology of the eastern Ozarks.
GPS: 37.8019, -90.3067

 ☐ 🔖 ♡ **Taberville Prairie Conservation Area:** Protected as a National Natural Landmark for its size and ecological integrity, Taberville Prairie is one of Missouri's largest remaining tallgrass prairies. It harbors native grasses, wildflowers, and diverse wildlife, offering critical insight into a once-dominant ecosystem that now survives only in fragments.
GPS: 38.0400, -93.9788

 ☐ 🔖 ♡ **Tucker Prairie:** A National Natural Landmark for its untouched tallgrass prairie, Tucker represents a transition zone between grassland and oak-hickory forest. The site's diversity of native species and unplowed sod make it invaluable for ecological research, restoration, and long-term study of prairie management and resilience.
GPS: 38.9491, -91.9926

 ☐ 🔖 ♡ **Tumbling Creek Cave:** Named a National Natural Landmark for its exceptional biological diversity, this cave supports more unique fauna than any other west of the Mississippi. Its underground streams and pools shelter rare, endemic species, making it a globally significant site for speleobiology and cave conservation.
GPS: 36.5579, -92.8088

 ☐ 🔖 ♡ **Wegener Woods:** Recognized as a National Natural Landmark for preserving natural forest succession, Wegener Woods transitions from oak-hickory to sugar maple dominance. Undisturbed and rich in biodiversity, it serves as a rare example of an intact old-growth forest ecosystem in Missouri's Ozarks, providing insights into long-term forest change.
GPS: 38.6614, -91.1806

MONTANA

Montana's wild beauty spans soaring mountain peaks, vast prairies, crystal-clear rivers, and remote wilderness. With inspiring state parks, sprawling national forests, iconic national parks, and breathtaking natural landmarks, Big Sky Country promises boundless outdoor adventure amid endless horizons and unspoiled natural majesty.

📅 Peak Season
June–September is Montana's peak season, with warm days, cool nights, and full access to national parks, trails, and mountain passes. Summer is the busiest time for hiking, camping, and wildlife viewing.

📅 Offseason Months
November–April is the offseason for most areas, with snow, cold temperatures, and limited access to high elevations. Winter, however, is peak for skiing and snow sports in resort towns like Big Sky and Whitefish.

🍃 Scenery & Nature Timing
Spring brings snowmelt waterfalls and wildflowers in the valleys. Summer reveals alpine lakes, open trails, and abundant wildlife. Fall paints the mountains with golden larch, while winter covers the landscape in deep snow and clear skies.

✨ Special
Montana features Glacier National Park's towering peaks and turquoise lakes, the geothermal wonders of Yellowstone, and the vast plains of the Missouri River Breaks. Northern lights, alpine glaciers, and immense night skies define its wild beauty.

MONTANA

State Parks

☐ 🔖 ♡ **Ackley Lake State Park:** Near Hobson, this 290-acre park features a reservoir ideal for boating, swimming, and fishing for trout and walleye. The grassy shoreline provides camping and picnicking opportunities, with open skies perfect for stargazing. Its remote setting makes it a peaceful escape for anglers and outdoor lovers in central Montana.

☐ 🔖 ♡ **Anaconda Smelter Stack State Park:** Located in Anaconda, this site protects the 585-foot smelter stack, one of the tallest free-standing brick structures in the world. While closed to direct entry, viewpoints and interpretive signage tell the story of Montana's mining past, copper smelting history, and the community's industrial heritage against a dramatic mountain backdrop.

☐ 🔖 ♡ **Bannack State Park:** Near Dillon, Bannack preserves Montana's best-known ghost town from the 1860s gold rush. Visitors can walk wooden boardwalks past original structures like the schoolhouse, jail, and saloon. Interpretive tours bring history to life, offering a window into frontier life, gold fever, and the struggles of early mining communities in the rugged West.

☐ 🔖 ♡ **Beaverhead Rock State Park:** South of Dillon, this 71-acre park highlights a landmark noted by Sacagawea during the Lewis and Clark Expedition. The massive rock formation rises above the Beaverhead Valley, serving as a navigation point for centuries. Though undeveloped, the site offers history, solitude, and scenic views of ranchlands and distant mountains.

☐ 🔖 ♡ **Beavertail Hill State Park:** Just off I-90 near Clinton, this 65-acre park sits along the Clark Fork River. It features shaded cottonwood groves, a short interpretive trail, and camping options, including rentable tipis. Popular for fishing, rafting access, and picnicking, the park offers a restful stopover amid riparian habitat and striking canyon scenery.

☐ 🔖 ♡ **Big Arm State Park:** A 217-acre unit on Flathead Lake's western shore, Big Arm is known for camping, boating, and swimming in Montana's largest natural freshwater lake. Its open shoreline and hiking trail to a viewpoint offer sweeping vistas across the water to the Mission and Swan mountains. Wildlife sightings include deer, osprey, and occasionally bears.

☐ 🔖 ♡ **Black Sandy State Park:** Located on Hauser Reservoir near Helena, this 43-acre park offers one of the region's most popular campgrounds. Activities include boating, water skiing, fishing, and swimming. The park provides easy access to Helena yet delivers a full outdoor getaway with lakefront sites, cottonwood shade, and abundant birdwatching opportunities.

☐ 🔖 ♡ **Brush Lake State Park:** In northeastern Montana near Plentywood, this 450-acre park centers on a deep, clear, spring-fed lake with white alkali soils. Its unusual chemistry limits vegetation but creates unique scenic beauty. The site supports swimming, non-motorized boating, and wildlife observation, with grassland surroundings ideal for quiet picnics and birdwatching.

☐ 🔖 ♡ **Chief Plenty Coups State Park:** Near Pryor, this cultural site preserves the homestead of Chief Plenty Coups, last traditional chief of the Crow Nation. The park includes his log home, sacred spring, and visitor center with exhibits on Crow history. Trails and picnicking areas provide a reflective setting to learn about Indigenous heritage and resilience.

☐ 🔖 ♡ **Clark's Lookout State Park:** Overlooking Dillon, this 8-acre park commemorates William Clark's 1805 survey point of the Beaverhead River Valley. The elevated viewpoint features interpretive displays and panoramic vistas. Though small, the park offers historical context for the Lewis and Clark Expedition and opportunities for short hikes and quiet reflection.

☐ 🔖 ♡ **Cooney Reservoir State Park:** South of Columbus, this 3,300-acre reservoir park is a hub for boating, water skiing, and year-round fishing for trout and walleye. Its four campgrounds and wide open vistas make it popular with families and recreationists. Surrounded by rolling hills and big sky, the park offers both action and relaxation.

☐ 🔖 ♡ **Council Grove State Park:** West of Missoula, this cottonwood grove marks where the 1855 Hellgate Treaty was signed between the U.S. government and Salish, Pend d'Oreille, and Kootenai tribes. The 187-acre site offers picnic areas, walking trails, and interpretive signs, blending cultural history with riverside scenery along the Clark Fork River.

MONTANA

☐ 🔖 ♡ **Elkhorn State Park:** Near Boulder, this 1,600-acre site preserves remnants of Elkhorn, a historic silver mining town. Visitors can view two restored buildings—the Fraternity Hall and Gillian Hall—against the backdrop of abandoned structures. Surrounding hills offer wildlife habitat and hiking opportunities, combining frontier history with ghost town atmosphere.

☐ 🔖 ♡ **Finley Point State Park:** On Flathead Lake's southern shore, this 28-acre park provides camping, boating, and fishing. Its location at a forested peninsula offers shaded campsites, a boat ramp, and access to excellent waters for kokanee salmon and lake trout. The park is peaceful and scenic, with mountain views across the vast lake.

☐ 🔖 ♡ **First Peoples Buffalo Jump State Park:** Near Ulm, this 1,700-acre park preserves one of North America's largest buffalo jump sites. Plains tribes used the sandstone cliff for communal bison hunts for centuries. The visitor center, trails, and interpretive panels explain the cultural significance, while the sweeping plains offer stunning views of the Missouri River Valley.

☐ 🔖 ♡ **Fish Creek State Park:** Near Alberton, this 5,600-acre park is one of Montana's largest. It offers rugged trails for hiking, mountain biking, and horseback riding through dense forests and along clear creeks. Anglers can fish for trout in pristine waters, while elk, moose, and bears roam the backcountry. With its size, remoteness, and wild beauty, Fish Creek is a premier destination for outdoor adventure and solitude.

☐ 🔖 ♡ **Flathead Lake State Park:** Spread across multiple units—Big Arm, Finley Point, Wayfarers, West Shore, Wild Horse Island, and Yellow Bay—this park surrounds the shores of Flathead Lake, the largest natural freshwater lake west of the Mississippi. Visitors can boat, swim, camp, and hike while enjoying breathtaking views of the Mission and Swan Mountains. Its diversity of sites makes it a cornerstone of Montana recreation.

☐ 🔖 ♡ **Fort Owen State Park:** Located near Stevensville in the Bitterroot Valley, this small but significant park preserves the site of Montana's first permanent white settlement, dating to 1841. Remnants of the original fort remain, and interpretive signs highlight its role as a trading post and mission. Visitors can picnic while enjoying sweeping views of the Sapphire and Bitterroot ranges, reflecting on Montana's early frontier history.

☐ 🔖 ♡ **Frenchtown Pond State Park:** Just outside Missoula, this 41-acre park features a warm, spring-fed pond with a sandy beach and calm waters, making it a favorite for swimming and paddling. Families enjoy its shaded picnic shelters, trails, and easy access. Wildlife like ducks and turtles are common, adding to the appeal. Frenchtown Pond offers an inviting day-use getaway with both relaxation and recreation close to the city.

☐ 🔖 ♡ **Giant Springs State Park:** Near Great Falls, this 4,500-acre park is home to one of the largest freshwater springs in the U.S., releasing over 150 million gallons daily. Visitors can explore scenic riverfront trails, picnic in lush greenery, and tour the fish hatchery. Interpretive signs tell the story of Lewis and Clark, who marveled at the springs in 1805. It's a vibrant, natural oasis rich in history and beauty.

☐ 🔖 ♡ **Granite Ghost Town State Park:** Nestled in the mountains near Philipsburg, this 1,000-acre park preserves the remains of Granite, a once-thriving 1890s silver mining town. Visitors can hike among stone building ruins, old mine structures, and remnants of the bustling past. The park is rugged and remote, offering striking mountain scenery and a tangible sense of history for those who explore its hauntingly beautiful landscape.

☐ 🔖 ♡ **Greycliff Prairie Dog Town State Park:** East of Big Timber, this 98-acre park is dedicated to observing black-tailed prairie dogs in their natural habitat. From viewing platforms, visitors can watch these lively animals socialize, burrow, and bark out alarms. Interpretive panels explain their ecological importance to grassland ecosystems. Surrounded by big-sky vistas, it's an educational and entertaining stop for families and wildlife lovers alike.

☐ 🔖 ♡ **Hell Creek State Park:** On Fort Peck Lake near Jordan, this 337-acre park is a gateway to rugged badlands and world-famous fossil beds. Campers and boaters enjoy access to the vast reservoir, renowned for walleye, pike, and smallmouth bass fishing. Trails and open landscapes invite exploration, while clear night skies make it excellent for stargazing. The park blends recreation with paleontological and geological intrigue.

☐ 🔖 ♡ **Lake Elmo State Park:** Within Billings city limits, this 123-acre park features a 64-acre reservoir for swimming, fishing, kayaking, and ice skating in winter. Its 1.4-mile paved trail circles the lake, and a large dog park adds to its appeal. Wildlife such as pelicans and waterfowl frequent the area. Offering year-round recreation with easy access, Lake Elmo is a beloved urban escape for families and outdoor enthusiasts.

MONTANA

☐ 🔖 ♡ **Lake Mary Ronan State Park:** Tucked in forested terrain near Proctor, this 120-acre park offers a quieter alternative to Flathead Lake. It provides excellent fishing for kokanee salmon and bass, along with camping and boating facilities. Surrounded by pine and fir, the park's trails and lake views invite relaxation and wildlife watching. Its peaceful environment makes it ideal for anglers and those seeking a more secluded retreat.

☐ 🔖 ♡ **Les Mason State Park:** On the eastern shore of Whitefish Lake, this 8-acre park offers a sandy swimming beach, picnic areas, and access for kayaks and canoes. Shaded by trees and framed by scenic mountains, it's perfect for a day of relaxation or water recreation. Just minutes from Whitefish, it provides a peaceful, natural setting and an alternative to busier resort-style lake access nearby.

☐ 🔖 ♡ **Lewis and Clark Caverns State Park:** Montana's first state park, near Whitehall, features spectacular limestone caverns filled with stalactites, stalagmites, and flowstone. Guided tours showcase one of the Northwest's most decorated caves. Above ground, the park offers hiking trails, camping, and abundant wildlife. Combining geology, history, and recreation, it's one of Montana's most popular destinations for adventure and learning.

☐ 🔖 ♡ **Logan State Park:** Situated on Middle Thompson Lake near Libby, this 17-acre park provides shaded campsites, a boat launch, and opportunities for fishing and swimming. Surrounded by forested hills, the park is peaceful and family-friendly, offering birdwatching, picnicking, and hiking. Its location along Highway 2 makes it an inviting stop for travelers and a relaxing getaway for campers in northwest Montana.

☐ 🔖 ♡ **Lone Pine State Park:** Overlooking Kalispell, this 270-acre park provides hiking, biking, and horseback riding trails through ponderosa pine forests leading to stunning views of the Flathead Valley and Glacier National Park peaks. The visitor center offers interpretive displays, and the park hosts programs year-round. Popular for wildlife viewing and photography, Lone Pine combines accessibility with breathtaking scenery.

☐ 🔖 ♡ **Lost Creek State Park:** Near Anaconda, this 502-acre park showcases striking limestone cliffs and colorful rock outcrops that tower 1,200 feet above the valley. A short trail leads to Lost Creek Falls, a 50-foot cascade surrounded by wildflowers in spring. Camping, hiking, and photography are popular, with mountain goats often spotted scaling cliffs. It's a gem for geology, scenery, and outdoor adventure.

☐ 🔖 ♡ **Madison Buffalo Jump State Park:** Near Logan, this 640-acre site preserves a cliff once used by Native tribes to drive bison in communal hunts. Visitors can hike interpretive trails to the jump site, learn about Plains Indian culture, and enjoy sweeping views of the Madison River Valley. The park combines history, archaeology, and natural beauty, offering a reflective and educational outdoor experience.

☐ 🔖 ♡ **Makoshika State Park:** Near Glendive, this 11,000-acre park is Montana's largest, known for its dramatic badlands, fossil discoveries, and striking geological formations. Trails wind through colorful canyons and hoodoos where dinosaurs such as Triceratops and T. rex once roamed. The visitor center offers exhibits, while camping and hiking provide immersive access to this rugged, otherworldly landscape.

☐ 🔖 ♡ **Medicine Rocks State Park:** Near Ekalaka, this 330-acre park features sandstone pillars and hoodoos carved by wind and water into fantastic shapes. Native American petroglyphs adorn the rocks, adding cultural significance. Visitors can hike among the formations, stargaze in its designated Dark Sky Sanctuary, and camp in a peaceful prairie setting. It's a striking blend of history, geology, and solitude.

☐ 🔖 ♡ **Milltown State Park:** Just east of Missoula, this 635-acre park sits at the confluence of the Blackfoot and Clark Fork Rivers. Once the site of a century-old dam, it's now restored to natural beauty with riverfront trails, fishing access, and wildlife habitat. Visitors can picnic, hike, and learn about ecological recovery, making the park both scenic and educational.

☐ 🔖 ♡ **Missouri Headwaters State Park:** Near Three Forks, this 532-acre park marks the confluence of the Jefferson, Madison, and Gallatin Rivers, forming the Missouri River. The site holds deep significance as a Lewis and Clark Expedition landmark. Hiking trails, interpretive exhibits, and camping allow visitors to explore both natural and historical heritage at this iconic riverside landscape.

☐ 🔖 ♡ **Painted Rocks State Park:** Nestled in the Bitterroot Mountains near Darby, this 23-acre park surrounds a scenic reservoir known for fishing, boating, and water skiing. Trails lead through pine forests to striking canyon views, and the park is popular for camping and wildlife viewing. Its colorful lichen-stained cliffs give the area its name, creating a picturesque backdrop for recreation.

MONTANA

☐ ▯ ♡ **Parker Homestead State Park:** Near Three Forks, this tiny half-acre park preserves a log cabin built in the early 1900s. The homestead reflects pioneer life on the Montana frontier, offering visitors a glimpse into the hardships of settlement. With interpretive signage and sweeping views of the Madison Valley, the park is a short but meaningful stop steeped in history.

☐ ▯ ♡ **Pictograph Cave State Park:** Just outside Billings, this 23-acre park protects caves containing ancient rock art, some more than 2,000 years old. Trails lead visitors to view pictographs of animals and human figures, with interpretive signs explaining their significance. The visitor center offers cultural context, making the site both an outdoor hike and a journey into Montana's prehistoric past.

☐ ▯ ♡ **Pirogue Island State Park:** On the Yellowstone River near Miles City, this 269-acre island offers cottonwood groves, hiking trails, and fishing access. A haven for birdwatchers, it hosts herons, bald eagles, and waterfowl. The park is accessible only by boat, providing a peaceful retreat for wildlife viewing and riverside solitude away from busier recreation areas.

☐ ▯ ♡ **Placid Lake State Park:** Near Seeley Lake, this 31-acre park sits on the clear waters of Placid Lake. Known for boating, fishing, and swimming, it also offers shaded campgrounds and picnic areas. The surrounding forested mountains provide habitat for loons and deer, adding to its appeal. Its combination of water recreation and quiet natural setting makes it a family favorite.

☐ ▯ ♡ **Rosebud Battlefield State Park:** Near Busby, this 3,052-acre park preserves the site of the 1876 Battle of the Rosebud, where Lakota and Cheyenne warriors fought U.S. troops. Trails, interpretive signs, and wide-open views of prairie and hills allow visitors to explore the historic landscape. The park offers a reflective atmosphere for learning about Native and U.S. history.

☐ ▯ ♡ **Salmon Lake State Park:** North of Seeley Lake, this 42-acre park is set among forested mountains and centered on a pristine lake. Popular for boating, fishing, and camping, it also offers picnicking and wildlife viewing opportunities. Its calm waters attract loons and osprey, making it a scenic and peaceful spot for outdoor recreation along the Clearwater River chain of lakes.

☐ ▯ ♡ **Sluice Boxes State Park:** Near Belt, this 2,940-acre park features limestone cliffs, canyons, and the scenic Belt Creek. Trails follow an old railroad grade past historic mines and homesteads, offering rugged hiking and history combined. The park is popular for fishing, floating, and photography, with dramatic geology creating an unforgettable backdrop.

☐ ▯ ♡ **Smith River State Park:** This 8,200-acre park spans the legendary Smith River, accessible primarily through a multi-day float trip lottery system. Boaters travel 59 miles of limestone canyons, forests, and secluded campsites. Known for trout fishing, dramatic scenery, and solitude, the river is a bucket-list adventure. The park also preserves important wildlife habitat and cultural sites.

☐ ▯ ♡ **Somers Beach State Park:** Recently added near Somers, this 106-acre park provides rare public access to Flathead Lake's north shore. With wide sandy beaches, wetlands, and mountain views, it's a hub for swimming, paddling, and birdwatching. Still in development, it offers open space and a unique recreational resource close to Kalispell and the Flathead Valley.

☐ ▯ ♡ **Spring Meadow Lake State Park:** In Helena, this 61-acre park centers on a spring-fed lake popular for swimming, fishing, kayaking, and ice skating in winter. Walking trails encircle the lake, while birdwatchers enjoy spotting waterfowl and songbirds. Picnic areas and easy access from downtown make it a family-friendly destination, offering outdoor recreation right at the city's edge.

☐ ▯ ♡ **Thompson Falls State Park:** Located on the Clark Fork River, this 36-acre park is surrounded by pine forests and features shaded campgrounds, trails, and river access. Visitors can fish for trout, enjoy boating, or picnic along the water. Wildlife such as deer and osprey are common. The park's riverside setting and proximity to Thompson Falls make it a scenic, relaxing stop.

☐ ▯ ♡ **Tongue River Reservoir State Park:** Near Decker, this 642-acre park is built around a 12-mile-long reservoir known for fishing, boating, and camping. Walleye, bass, and northern pike draw anglers year-round, while the rolling prairie setting supports deer, antelope, and abundant birdlife. With its large campground and open landscapes, it's a hub for recreation in southeastern Montana.

MONTANA

☐ 🔖 ♡ **Tower Rock State Park:** Near Cascade, this 87-acre park preserves a dramatic 424-foot volcanic rock pillar that served as a landmark for the Lewis and Clark Expedition. Interpretive signs explain its cultural and geological significance, while short trails provide access to viewpoints. Surrounded by river valleys and rugged hills, the park offers history and scenic beauty in one compact site.

☐ 🔖 ♡ **Travelers' Rest State Park:** Near Lolo, this 65-acre park is a National Historic Landmark, marking the only archaeologically verified Lewis and Clark campsite. It also preserves a long-used Native American crossroads. The visitor center and interpretive trails highlight both expedition and tribal history. With its rich cultural significance, it's a must-see blend of heritage and natural scenery.

☐ 🔖 ♡ **Wayfarers State Park:** On Flathead Lake's eastern shore near Bigfork, this 67-acre park offers rocky beaches, swimming areas, and forested campsites. Trails lead to bluffs overlooking the water, providing some of the best sunset views in the valley. With easy lake access and proximity to Bigfork's artsy downtown, Wayfarers is a favorite for both recreation and relaxation.

☐ 🔖 ♡ **West Shore State Park:** Near Lakeside on Flathead Lake, this 129-acre park features rocky shorelines, forested trails, and panoramic views of the Mission and Swan ranges. Camping, boating, swimming, and fishing are popular activities. With its combination of lakefront access, wooded privacy, and mountain scenery, West Shore is a peaceful base for exploring the Flathead region.

☐ 🔖 ♡ **Whitefish Lake State Park:** Just outside Whitefish, this 10-acre park provides swimming access, camping, and a boat ramp on Whitefish Lake. Shaded by pine forests, it offers a quiet escape for fishing, paddling, and picnicking while remaining close to town. Popular for both locals and visitors, the park blends convenient access with classic Montana mountain-lake beauty.

☐ 🔖 ♡ **Wild Horse Island State Park:** Accessible only by boat, this 2,100-acre park in Flathead Lake is famed for its herd of wild horses, along with bighorn sheep, mule deer, and bald eagles. Hiking trails lead across open meadows and forests to stunning lake and mountain views. With its rare wildlife and remote setting, it's a truly unique Montana destination.

☐ 🔖 ♡ **Yellow Bay State Park:** On the eastern shore of Flathead Lake, this 15-acre park is known for its crystal-clear waters, cherry orchards, and quiet camping areas. Swimming, boating, and picnicking are popular activities, while birdwatchers spot waterfowl along the bay. Its intimate, shaded setting makes it one of the lake's most peaceful public access points.

National Parks

☐ 🔖 ♡ **Big Hole National Battlefield:** Located in Montana, this site honors the 1877 Battle of Big Hole, where the Nez Perce Tribe fought U.S. Army troops during their retreat in the Nez Perce War. Visitors can walk the battlefield, view memorials, and explore the visitor center exhibits, gaining insight into the conflict, the Nez Perce people, and the lasting impact of this pivotal event in Native American history.

☐ 🔖 ♡ **Bighorn Canyon National Recreation Area:** Spanning Montana and Wyoming, this vast landscape features striking canyon walls, the winding Bighorn River, and diverse habitats. Visitors can boat through towering cliffs, fish for trout, hike scenic trails, and watch for bighorn sheep, wild horses, and eagles. With its mix of recreation and cultural heritage, the area highlights the dramatic beauty of the Northern Rockies.

MONTANA

 ☐ 🔖 ♡ **Fort Union Trading Post National Historic Site:** On the North Dakota–Montana border, this reconstructed 19th-century fur trading post was once a hub where Assiniboine and other tribes traded with Europeans. Visitors can tour the fort's bastions, warehouse, and trading rooms while learning about the fur trade economy, cultural exchanges, and the vital role Fort Union played in shaping frontier history.

 ☐ 🔖 ♡ **Glacier National Park:** In northwestern Montana, this iconic park protects over a million acres of rugged peaks, alpine meadows, and glacier-carved valleys. Visitors can drive the famed Going-to-the-Sun Road, hike more than 700 miles of trails, and spot grizzly bears, mountain goats, and moose. With pristine lakes and dramatic vistas, it offers one of America's most breathtaking wilderness experiences.

 ☐ 🔖 ♡ **Grant-Kohrs Ranch National Historic Site:** In Deer Lodge, Montana, this site preserves the historic cattle ranch of John Grant and Conrad Kohrs, two pioneers of the open-range cattle industry. Visitors can explore the ranch house, bunkhouses, barns, and working ranch landscape. Guided tours and exhibits highlight 19th-century ranching life and its influence on the growth of the American West.

 ☐ 🔖 ♡ **Little Bighorn Battlefield National Monument:** Near Crow Agency, Montana, this 765-acre site marks the 1876 battle where Lakota, Northern Cheyenne, and Arapaho warriors defeated Custer's 7th Cavalry. Visitors can walk trails across the battlefield, view the Indian Memorial, and reflect at Last Stand Hill. The monument preserves history while honoring both Native and U.S. lives lost in this pivotal clash.

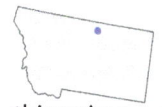 ☐ 🔖 ♡ **Nez Perce National Historical Park:** Spanning Idaho, Montana, Oregon, and Washington, this unique park protects more than 30 sites tied to Nez Perce history and culture. Visitors can explore battlefields, historic villages, and trails, while exhibits and programs highlight the tribe's resilience, the Nez Perce War of 1877, and the enduring traditions of the Nimiipuu people across the Northwest.

 ☐ 🔖 ♡ **Yellowstone National Park:** Established in 1872 across Wyoming, Montana, and Idaho, Yellowstone is the world's first national park. Its geothermal wonders include geysers like Old Faithful, colorful hot springs, and bubbling mud pots. Visitors encounter sweeping valleys, rugged mountains, and abundant wildlife, from roaming bison to wolves and grizzly bears, making Yellowstone a globally iconic wilderness destination.

State & National Forests

☐ 🔖 ♡ **Beaverhead–Deerlodge National Forest:** Spanning 3.3 million acres in southwest Montana, this is the state's largest national forest. It includes rugged mountain ranges, alpine meadows, and wilderness areas like the Anaconda–Pintler and Lee Metcalf. Popular for camping, hiking, horseback riding, and fishing, it also supports abundant wildlife such as elk, deer, moose, and grizzly bears.

☐ 🔖 ♡ **Bitterroot National Forest:** Covering 1.6 million acres along the Idaho–Montana border, this forest features the dramatic Bitterroot Range and Sapphire Mountains. Visitors explore canyons, glacial lakes, and backcountry in the Frank Church–River of No Return Wilderness. The forest offers hiking, horseback riding, fishing, and remote wilderness experiences near Missoula's scenic valleys.

☐ 🔖 ♡ **Clearwater State Forest:** Established in 1925, this 18,000-acre state forest in Missoula County was Montana's first. Managed for sustainable timber harvest, it also protects wildlife habitat and water resources. While public recreation is limited, it provides educational opportunities in forestry, with trails and demonstrations highlighting conservation and fire management practices.

☐ 🔖 ♡ **Custer–Gallatin National Forest:** Stretching over 3 million acres in south-central and southeast Montana, this forest includes six mountain ranges, Yellowstone access points, and Wild and Scenic rivers. It's a haven for camping, hiking, skiing, fishing, and hunting, with vast wilderness ecosystems. Its diverse landscapes, from alpine peaks to prairie grasslands, showcase Montana's natural variety.

MONTANA

☐ 🔖 ♡ **Flathead National Forest:** Encompassing 2.4 million acres west of the Continental Divide, this forest borders Glacier National Park and includes wilderness areas such as the Bob Marshall, Scapegoat, and Great Bear. Known for pristine lakes, dense forests, and abundant wildlife, including grizzlies, it offers over 700 miles of trails, camping, and fishing in breathtaking mountain terrain.

☐ 🔖 ♡ **Helena–Lewis and Clark National Forest:** Covering 2.8 million acres of central Montana, this forest unites rugged mountains, prairie edges, and river valleys. Highlights include Gates of the Mountains near Helena, historic fire lookouts, and wilderness areas. Visitors enjoy hiking, camping, hunting, fishing, and diverse wildlife viewing across this vast and scenic forest system.

☐ 🔖 ♡ **Kootenai National Forest:** Located in Montana's far northwest, this 2.2 million-acre forest includes over half of the Cabinet Mountains Wilderness. Old-growth cedar groves and alpine terrain provide habitat for grizzly bears, wolves, and elk. With rivers, lakes, and scenic drives, visitors can enjoy hiking, camping, and fishing in one of Montana's most diverse and remote forest regions.

☐ 🔖 ♡ **Lolo National Forest:** This 2-million-acre forest surrounds Missoula and stretches west to Idaho. It features lush, moisture-rich forests, hundreds of streams and lakes, and wilderness areas such as Selway–Bitterroot. Recreational opportunities include hiking, boating, fishing, camping, and winter sports. Wildlife like grizzly bears, elk, and mountain goats thrive in its diverse landscapes.

☐ 🔖 ♡ **Stillwater State Forest:** Covering 90,000 acres in Flathead County, this forest was designated in 1925. Managed for timber production, wildlife conservation, and wildfire training, it protects upland conifer ecosystems near the Stillwater River. Limited public access allows for low-impact hiking and educational programs, while its vast forest lands support long-term ecological management.

☐ 🔖 ♡ **Thompson River State Forest:** Spanning nearly 12,000 acres in Sanders County, this state forest was designated in 1925. It protects conifer stands along the Thompson River, serving as habitat for elk, deer, and other wildlife. Managed for sustainable forestry, watershed health, and fire prevention, it offers restricted backcountry recreation while supporting Montana's timber economy.

National Scenic Byways & All-American Roads

☐ 🔖 ♡ **Beartooth Highway:** An **All-American Road** spanning 69 miles on US 212 from Red Lodge, MT, to Yellowstone's northeast entrance in Wyoming. It climbs to 10,947 ft at Beartooth Pass, revealing alpine plateaus, glacial lakes, switchbacks, and panoramic views. Often called "the most beautiful drive in America," it provides access to wilderness, high-country hiking, and Yellowstone National Park.

☐ 🔖 ♡ **St. Regis–Paradise Scenic Byway:** A **National Scenic Byway** running 30 miles along MT 135 in Lolo National Forest, following the Clark Fork River between St. Regis and Paradise. The drive offers lush river canyon scenery, forested slopes, picnic areas, and wildlife viewing. Recognized for its natural beauty, it provides a scenic alternative to I-90 while linking to trailheads, campgrounds, and historic river routes.

State Scenic Byways

☐ 🔖 ♡ **Big Sheep Creek Back Country Byway:** Managed by the BLM, this gravel backcountry route near Dell winds through Big Sheep Creek Canyon and the Tendoy Mountains. Travelers encounter sheer limestone walls, rolling grasslands, and creekside meadows. Popular with 4×4 vehicles, hunters, and wildlife watchers, it offers remote solitude and access to Beaverhead–Deerlodge National Forest.

☐ 🔖 ♡ **Garnet Backcountry Byway:** A U.S. Forest Service Scenic Byway that climbs the Garnet Range between Highway 200 and I-90. This 12-mile gravel road leads to Garnet Ghost Town, one of Montana's best-preserved mining settlements. Along the way, travelers see wildflower meadows, forested ridges, and remnants of historic cabins, making it a blend of frontier heritage and rugged outdoor scenery.

MONTANA

☐ ◻ ♡ **Kings Hill Scenic Byway:** A Montana State Scenic Byway stretching 71 miles along US 89 through the Little Belt Mountains. Rising to 7,385 ft at Kings Hill Pass, it provides access to Showdown ski area, wildflower meadows, campgrounds, and trailheads. With panoramic overlooks of Lewis and Clark National Forest, it links mountain recreation with year-round scenic driving.

☐ ◻ ♡ **Lake Koocanusa Scenic Byway:** Designated by Montana as a State Scenic Byway, this 67-mile drive follows MT 37 along the fjord-like reservoir of Lake Koocanusa. Flanked by the Purcell and Salish Mountains, it features pullouts, marinas, and campgrounds. The route highlights Kootenai National Forest, scenic cliffs, fishing and boating opportunities, and access to the Cabinet Mountains Wilderness.

☐ ◻ ♡ **Missouri Breaks Backcountry Byway:** A BLM Back Country Byway that ventures into the rugged Missouri River Breaks region. The gravel track passes eroded coulees, steep badlands, and prairie benches with dramatic river overlooks. Ideal for 4×4 vehicles, hunters, and history buffs, it provides solitude, sweeping vistas, and connections to landscapes once traversed by the Lewis and Clark Expedition.

☐ ◻ ♡ **Pioneer Mountains Scenic Byway:** A Montana State Scenic Byway extending 49 paved miles through the Beaverhead–Deerlodge National Forest. It rises to 7,800 ft, with access to alpine meadows, granite peaks, trout streams, hot springs, and ghost towns like Coolidge. Open in summer and groomed in winter for snowmobiling, the route blends Montana's natural beauty with mining history.

National Natural Landmarks

☐ ◻ ♡ **Bridger Fossil Area:** Celebrated as a National Natural Landmark, this site preserves Cretaceous fossils including Deinonychus antirrhopus. The remarkable finds offer crucial evidence of raptor evolution, linking dinosaurs to the origins of modern birds and providing paleontologists with a clearer picture of late Mesozoic ecosystems.
GPS: unlisted

 ☐ ◻ ♡ **Bug Creek Fossil Area:** This National Natural Landmark is world-renowned for its small late Cretaceous mammal fossils. The unique strata capture mammalian diversity before the mass extinction, bridging the gap between dinosaurs and early mammals. Its fossil record has helped reshape understanding of mammal evolution in North America.
GPS: 47.68299, -106.219193

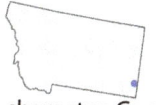 ☐ ◻ ♡ **Capitol Rock:** Designated a National Natural Landmark for its striking geologic character, Capitol Rock is an isolated butte of Tertiary sandstone and volcanic ash. Once part of a vast continuous formation, it now stands as a solitary remnant of erosion, offering a dramatic window into the geologic history of the northern Great Plains.
GPS: 45.59584, -104.120134

☐ ◻ ♡ **Cloverly Formation Site:** As a National Natural Landmark, this fossil-rich unit preserves dinosaurs and vertebrates from the Early Cretaceous. Discoveries here have illuminated ecosystems of 100 million years ago, helping paleontologists trace evolutionary trends in dinosaurs and other vertebrates across ancient North America.
GPS: statewide

 ☐ ◻ ♡ **Glacial Lake Missoula:** This Ice Age lake is a National Natural Landmark for its extraordinary flood features. When ice dams repeatedly burst, massive torrents carved giant ripples, coulees, and scablands across the Northwest. The Missoula Floods remain one of the best-studied examples of catastrophic geologic processes in North America.
GPS: 46.938889, -114.143611

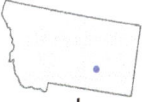 ☐ ◻ ♡ **Hell Creek Fossil Area:** This National Natural Landmark is the type locality of Tyrannosaurus rex and many other dinosaurs. Its late Cretaceous layers capture the final chapter of the dinosaur era and the dawn of the Paleocene, offering scientists one of the most complete records of the great extinction event.
GPS: 46.1500, -107.4800

 ☐ ◻ ♡ **Medicine Lake Site:** Recognized as a National Natural Landmark, Medicine Lake preserves textbook features of continental glaciation, including eskers, kames, and outwash plains. These landforms record the massive ice sheets of the Pleistocene, making the site invaluable for studying the processes and legacy of glacial geology.
GPS: 48.468056, -104.381667

MONTANA

 **Middle Fork Canyon:** This canyon was designated a National Natural Landmark for its rare demonstration of a superposed stream cutting across resistant bedrock. Its steep walls expose deep geologic layers, making it an outstanding example of erosional power and a natural classroom for geomorphology and structural geology.
GPS: 46.131701, -111.109849

 **Red Rock Lakes National Wildlife Refuge:** A National Natural Landmark, this high-mountain valley refuge protects wetlands, meadows, and forested slopes that remain largely unaltered. It provides essential habitat for trumpeter swans and diverse wildlife, preserving an ecological portrait of the Greater Yellowstone region before widespread settlement.
GPS: 44.630278, -111.781389

 **Square Butte:** This iconic formation, named a National Natural Landmark, rises dramatically above the Montana plains. Composed of intrusive igneous rock, it showcases striking examples of columnar jointing and banded volcanic textures. Square Butte is both a geologic wonder and a defining landmark of central Montana's skyline.
GPS: 47.476499, -110.241999

NEBRASKA

Nebraska's landscapes range from towering bluffs and fossil-rich beds to wide-open prairies and scenic rivers. Through its network of state parks, national forests, and striking natural landmarks, Nebraska invites visitors to discover its quiet and surprising beauty, where vast skies, rolling grasslands, and ancient geology meet in harmony.

📅 Peak Season
May–October is Nebraska's peak season, with warm weather, open trails, and colorful prairies. Summer is busiest for camping, river recreation, and scenic drives through the Sandhills and state parks.

📅 Offseason Months
November–April is the offseason, bringing cold temperatures, snow, and lighter travel. Winter offers quiet landscapes and birding opportunities, though outdoor activity slows statewide.

🍃 Scenery & Nature Timing
Spring features migrating cranes and blooming prairies. Summer brings green grasslands and clear skies. Fall offers golden fields and crisp air, while winter highlights frosted plains and peaceful river valleys.

✨ Special
Nebraska showcases the towering sandstone formations of Chimney Rock and Scotts Bluff, the vast dunes of the Sandhills, and the annual sandhill crane migration along the Platte River. Rolling prairies, river bluffs, and open horizons define its natural grandeur.

NEBRASKA

State Parks

☐ 🔖 ♡ **Arbor Lodge State Historical Park**: Located in Nebraska City, Arbor Lodge preserves the legacy of J. Sterling Morton, founder of Arbor Day. The centerpiece is a 52-room neocolonial mansion surrounded by gardens, orchards, and arboretum plantings that celebrate tree culture. Visitors can tour the historic home, stroll landscaped grounds, and learn about the conservation movement born here.

☐ 🔖 ♡ **Ashfall Fossil Beds State Historical Park**: Nestled in northeast Nebraska, Ashfall protects a remarkable Miocene fossil site preserved in volcanic ash. Visitors can see skeletons of rhinos, horses, camels, and other animals in the Hubbard Rhino Barn, where fossils remain in place. The park offers trails, exhibits, and a rare chance to witness an ancient watering hole frozen in time.

☐ 🔖 ♡ **Chadron State Park**: Located in the Pine Ridge Escarpment, Chadron State Park is Nebraska's oldest state park, offering over 970 acres of scenic beauty. Visitors can enjoy hiking, biking, fishing, and horseback riding through the park's varied landscapes. With its rich history and stunning views, Chadron State Park is ideal for outdoor enthusiasts and those seeking solitude in nature.

☐ 🔖 ♡ **Eugene T. Mahoney State Park**: Situated along the Platte River, this park is a popular destination for families and outdoor lovers. The park offers an array of activities such as hiking, fishing, swimming, and wildlife watching. It also features a lodge, cabins, and an observation tower, providing visitors with sweeping views of the Platte River Valley. The park is perfect for a weekend getaway or day trip.

☐ 🔖 ♡ **Fort Robinson State Park**: This historic park was once a military post and is now a destination for history buffs and outdoor adventurers. Located in the Pine Ridge region, Fort Robinson offers hiking, horseback riding, and a chance to explore the old fort and its surrounding landscape. The park also has a rich Native American history and offers wildlife viewing opportunities, making it a unique blend of history and nature.

☐ 🔖 ♡ **Indian Cave State Park**: Located on the Missouri River, Indian Cave State Park is known for its prehistoric petroglyphs and scenic hiking trails. The park features several miles of trails through dense woodlands and along the river, offering picturesque views and opportunities for birdwatching. The cave, which has carvings made by Native Americans, adds historical significance to this natural beauty.

☐ 🔖 ♡ **Niobrara State Park**: Nestled at the confluence of the Missouri and Niobrara Rivers, this park offers stunning views and numerous outdoor activities. Visitors can explore the park's trails, enjoy fishing in the rivers, or relax in one of the park's cabins. Niobrara State Park also features the historic Niobrara River Bridge, which is a prominent landmark in the region.

☐ 🔖 ♡ **Platte River State Park**: Situated along the Platte River, this park offers an array of activities including hiking, fishing, and swimming. The park's highlight is its observation tower, which offers breathtaking views of the surrounding river valley. Platte River State Park is also home to several picnic areas and a spray park, making it a perfect spot for families and outdoor enthusiasts.

☐ 🔖 ♡ **Ponca State Park**: Located in the scenic Missouri River bluffs, Ponca State Park is ideal for those looking to explore nature through hiking, fishing, and camping. The park offers several scenic trails, including the popular Missouri River Trail, and is home to a variety of wildlife. Visitors can also enjoy boating, canoeing, and picnicking in the park's beautiful setting.

☐ 🔖 ♡ **Smith Falls State Park**: Known for Nebraska's tallest waterfall, Smith Falls State Park is a peaceful oasis in the Niobrara River Valley. Visitors can enjoy hiking to the waterfall, fishing in the river, or simply relaxing in the park's scenic surroundings. The park's natural beauty and tranquil atmosphere make it a great destination for outdoor exploration and relaxation.

NEBRASKA

National Parks

 ☐ 🔖 ♡ **Agate Fossil Beds National Monument**: Located in Nebraska's High Plains, this site protects world-renowned Miocene fossil beds where prehistoric horses, rhinos, and other mammals were preserved. Visitors can hike the fossil hills, explore exhibits on paleontology and Lakota culture, and view one of the richest fossil deposits in North America, offering a vivid window into life 20 million years ago.

 ☐ 🔖 ♡ **Homestead National Monument of America**: Near Beatrice, Nebraska, this monument commemorates the 1862 Homestead Act that reshaped the Great Plains. The Heritage Center, trails, and restored tallgrass prairie help visitors understand the challenges faced by pioneers who claimed land. Exhibits highlight the transformation of wilderness into farmland and the Act's profound impact on American history.

 ☐ 🔖 ♡ **Missouri National Recreational River**: Flowing along the Nebraska–South Dakota border, this protected stretch of the Missouri River preserves one of the last relatively free-flowing segments. Visitors enjoy fishing, boating, and hiking amid rugged bluffs and floodplain forests. The river corridor supports abundant wildlife and echoes with the stories of Native peoples, Lewis and Clark, and westward expansion.

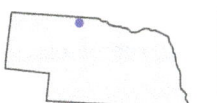 ☐ 🔖 ♡ **Niobrara National Scenic River**: Winding 76 miles through north-central Nebraska, the Niobrara showcases limestone bluffs, waterfalls, and diverse ecosystems that blend prairie, boreal, and hardwood forests. Canoeing and kayaking reveal rich scenery and wildlife including bison, elk, and otters. This National Scenic River offers solitude, outdoor adventure, and a glimpse of one of America's hidden natural treasures.

 ☐ 🔖 ♡ **Scotts Bluff National Monument**: Towering 800 feet above the North Platte Valley, Scotts Bluff was a landmark for Native peoples, emigrants on the Oregon, California, and Mormon Trails, and later railroads. Trails lead to sweeping views from the summit, while exhibits interpret geology, westward migration, and pioneer life. The bluff stands as both a natural wonder and a gateway to the West.

State & National Forests

 ☐ 🔖 ♡ **Nebraska National Forest**: Established in 1908, this 141,864-acre forest is one of the world's largest hand-planted forests, with districts in the Sandhills and Pine Ridge. It features ponderosa pine groves, prairie ecosystems, and the Bessey Nursery, which produces millions of seedlings. Visitors can hike, camp, and explore this living experiment in prairie forestry and ecological restoration.

 ☐ 🔖 ♡ **Samuel R. McKelvie National Forest**: Created in 1971 from the Nebraska Sandhills, this 116,079-acre forest blends planted ponderosa pines with native prairie. It surrounds Merritt Reservoir and provides habitat for deer, elk, and diverse birdlife. Trails and backcountry camping opportunities highlight its quiet, windswept landscapes, while its history reflects ongoing Great Plains forestry and conservation efforts.

National Grasslands

☐ 🔖 ♡ **Oglala National Grassland**: Located in northwestern Nebraska, Oglala National Grassland features mixed-grass prairie, badlands formations, and striking geologic sites like Toadstool Geologic Park. Rich in fossil history and wildlife, the grassland hosts prairie dogs, bighorn sheep, and raptors. Visitors can hike, camp, and explore remnants of prehistoric life and pioneer trails.

NEBRASKA

National Scenic Byways & All-American Roads

☐ ▯ ♡ **Bridges to Buttes Byway**: Traversing U.S. Highway 20 across northern Nebraska, this route connects river valleys, sandstone buttes, and rolling prairie. It showcases diverse landscapes from the Niobrara River Valley to Pine Ridge country. Historic towns, fossil sites, and Native American heritage enrich the drive, offering a deep sense of Nebraska's natural and cultural history.

☐ ▯ ♡ **Gold Rush Byway**: Running along U.S. Highway 385 in western Nebraska, this byway follows routes once traveled by gold seekers heading to the Black Hills. Highlights include the Pine Ridge scenery, Chadron and Crawford's historic sites, and Fort Robinson State Park. The drive immerses travelers in rugged landscapes and stories of frontier adventure.

☐ ▯ ♡ **Lincoln Highway Scenic & Historic Byway**: Following the route of America's first transcontinental highway, this byway spans Nebraska from east to west. Travelers experience historic roadside architecture, small-town main streets, and classic prairie landscapes. Interpretive stops highlight the highway's role in transforming cross-country travel and shaping 20th-century America.

☐ ▯ ♡ **Outlaw Trail Scenic Byway**: Tracing Nebraska Highway 12 along the Missouri River in the state's northeast corner, this byway recalls the haunts of outlaws and frontier legends. Visitors encounter rolling bluffs, river vistas, and historic towns tied to colorful tales of Jesse James and others. The route also provides access to parks, wildlife areas, and rustic byway communities.

☐ ▯ ♡ **Sandhills Journey Scenic Byway**: Stretching along U.S. Highway 83, this route cuts through the heart of the Nebraska Sandhills, one of the world's largest grass-stabilized dune regions. Vast prairies, wildlife, and open skies define the journey, with opportunities for birding, stargazing, and exploring small ranching towns that preserve the traditions of the Great Plains.

State Scenic Byways

☐ ▯ ♡ **Loup Rivers Scenic Byway**: Following Highways 11 and 91 through central Nebraska, this route winds along the Middle Loup, North Loup, and Dismal Rivers. Travelers encounter fertile valleys, historic communities, and sweeping prairie views. The byway showcases agriculture, pioneer heritage, and outdoor opportunities including fishing, canoeing, and wildlife viewing in the river corridors.

☐ ▯ ♡ **Nebraska Highway 2 – Sandhills Scenic Byway**: Traversing nearly 272 miles between Grand Island and Alliance, this byway cuts through the heart of the Sandhills. The landscape of rolling grass-covered dunes, wide skies, and ranching towns offers one of America's most unspoiled prairie regions. Known for birding, stargazing, and photography, it captures the solitude and beauty of the Great Plains.

☐ ▯ ♡ **Native American Scenic Byway (Nebraska segment)**: Crossing the Santee Sioux Reservation in northeast Nebraska, this route honors Native culture and history. Interpretive sites highlight the traditions and struggles of the Santee people, while the drive provides views of the Missouri River bluffs and surrounding prairie. Visitors can explore cultural centers and communities along the way.

☐ ▯ ♡ **Western Trails Scenic & Historic Byway**: Running along U.S. Highway 26 and Nebraska Highway 92, this byway follows the paths of the Oregon, Mormon, California, and Pony Express Trails. Landmarks such as Chimney Rock and Scotts Bluff evoke the westward migration. The route blends pioneer history with dramatic scenery, making it a window into the frontier past of western Nebraska.

☐ ▯ ♡ **Wildflower Byway**: Located in central Nebraska along Highway 70 and connecting roads, this 82-mile loop showcases prairie wildflowers, rolling farmland, and small-town hospitality. Seasonal blooms paint the roadside with vibrant colors, while local museums, historic churches, and parks provide cultural stops. The byway offers a peaceful drive through Nebraska's agricultural heartland.

National Natural Landmarks

 **Ashfall Fossil Beds:** Designated a National Natural Landmark for its extraordinary lagerstätte, Ashfall preserves entire skeletons of rhinos, horses, and camels buried in volcanic ash 12 million years ago. The lifelike poses capture a sudden mass mortality, offering paleontologists a rare glimpse into Miocene ecosystems and the devastating effects of ancient volcanic events.
GPS: 42.440556, -98.148083

 **Dissected Loess Plains:** This National Natural Landmark showcases deep loess deposits eroded into ridges, gullies, and steep canyons. The windblown silt, carried here during the Ice Age, provides scientists with an exceptional record of soil development and erosion. The rugged landscape illustrates the geologic history and natural processes shaping the Great Plains.
GPS: 40.933150, -100.159330

 **Fontenelle Forest:** Recognized as a National Natural Landmark for preserving one of Nebraska's last original hardwood forests, Fontenelle protects oak-hickory uplands, floodplain woods, marshes, and prairies. Its 1,400 acres shelter migratory birds, wildlife, and rare plant species, offering a living window into the pre-settlement ecosystems of eastern Nebraska.
GPS: 41.180000, -95.917778

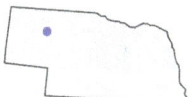 **Nebraska Sand Hills:** The Sand Hills are a National Natural Landmark for being the largest stabilized dune system in the Western Hemisphere, covering nearly 20,000 square miles. Grass-covered dunes and interdunal valleys support a rare mixed-grass prairie ecosystem. The vast region highlights both geologic forces and the ecological resilience of the Great Plains.
GPS: 42.130000, -102.190000

 **Valentine National Wildlife Refuge:** This refuge was named a National Natural Landmark for its outstanding sandhill prairie and wetland habitats. Shaped by ancient dunes and groundwater discharge, the landscape hosts shallow lakes, migratory birds, and diverse wildlife. It remains one of the finest examples of intact Sand Hills ecosystems in the United States.
GPS: 42.493611, -100.572778

NEVADA

Nevada's terrains invite exploration, with fiery red sandstone formations, ancient bristlecone pines, vast desert expanses, and rugged mountains. The state's collection of parks, forests, a stunning national park, and remarkable natural landmarks offers endless adventure in the American West, where stark beauty meets timeless desert solitude.

Peak Season
April–June and September–October are Nevada's peak seasons, offering warm but comfortable temperatures and clear skies. These months are ideal for hiking, desert exploration, and visiting national parks before or after the summer heat.

Offseason Months
November–March is the offseason for most desert regions, bringing cooler days and cold nights. Summer, especially July–August, is extremely hot in southern areas but pleasant in the mountains and northern highlands.

Scenery & Nature Timing
Spring brings desert wildflowers and melting snow in the Sierra Nevada. Summer highlights alpine lakes and cool mountain trails. Fall offers golden aspens in the high country, while winter provides snow in Lake Tahoe and crisp desert vistas.

Special
Nevada features the Black Rock Desert's vast playa, the alpine peaks of the Ruby Mountains, and the red sandstone canyons of Valley of Fire. Lake Tahoe's clarity, Great Basin's bristlecone pines, and seasonal desert blooms showcase its dramatic contrasts.

NEVADA

State Parks

☐ 🔖 ♡ **Beaver Dam State Park:** Nestled in eastern Nevada near the Utah border, Beaver Dam offers a remote escape of canyons, pine-covered plateaus, and streams stocked with trout. Hiking trails wind through dramatic scenery, while wildlife sightings are common. The park's rugged isolation and dark night skies make it a haven for campers, anglers, and nature lovers seeking solitude.

☐ 🔖 ♡ **Berlin–Ichthyosaur State Park:** This unique park blends paleontology and history. It protects the largest known concentration of Ichthyosaur fossils, remnants of giant marine reptiles that swam Nevada's ancient seas. Visitors also explore the preserved ghost town of Berlin, with mine ruins and interpretive displays. The combination of fossils and frontier heritage creates a rare double-layered experience.

☐ 🔖 ♡ **Cathedral Gorge State Park:** Famous for its narrow slot canyons and cathedral-like spires carved from soft bentonite clay, this park offers one of Nevada's most surreal landscapes. Trails weave among dramatic formations perfect for exploration and photography. Once a sacred place for Indigenous peoples, today it provides peaceful picnicking, camping, and awe-inspiring views of sculpted geology.

☐ 🔖 ♡ **Cave Lake State Park:** A high-desert retreat near Ely, this park features a 32-acre reservoir surrounded by aspen and conifers. Fishing for rainbow and brown trout is excellent, while boating and swimming fill summer days. In winter, the frozen lake hosts ice fishing, skating, and snowmobiling. With trails, campgrounds, and wildlife, it's a true year-round outdoor playground.

☐ 🔖 ♡ **Dayton State Park:** Set along the Carson River, Dayton combines natural beauty with Comstock mining history. Visitors find picnic areas, campgrounds, and trails winding past cottonwoods and desert hills. The remains of the 1861 Rock Point Mill recall the silver rush era, when ore from Virginia City was processed here. It's a small but rich site blending Nevada's past and present.

☐ 🔖 ♡ **Echo Canyon State Park:** Surrounded by rainbow-colored cliffs, Echo Canyon is centered on a 65-acre reservoir offering fishing, boating, and swimming. Trails lead into canyons with fascinating rock layers and abundant wildlife. The park also preserves ranching history, with old stone buildings scattered nearby. Its mix of water recreation, geology, and history make it a versatile destination.

☐ 🔖 ♡ **Fort Churchill State Historic Park:** Built in 1861 to guard the Pony Express and settlers along the Carson River, Fort Churchill's adobe ruins stand as reminders of frontier struggles. Visitors can walk through the preserved fort, camp, and hike riparian trails teeming with birds. The park also connects to Buckland Station, offering a deep dive into Nevada's military and pioneer heritage.

☐ 🔖 ♡ **Ice Age Fossils State Park:** One of Nevada's newest parks, located near Las Vegas, it showcases Ice Age paleontology in the Upper Las Vegas Wash. Visitors can hike trails past fossil beds where mammoths, camels, and giant sloths once roamed. Interpretive programs explain the area's scientific significance. It's a fascinating destination combining education, desert scenery, and prehistory.

☐ 🔖 ♡ **Kershaw–Ryan State Park:** An oasis in the desert near Caliente, this park features a spring-fed canyon filled with greenery, wildflowers, and dramatic rock walls. Trails climb to panoramic views, while a shaded lawn and wading pool make it family-friendly. Once a homestead, it was donated in 1936 as a public park. Today it offers peace, history, and natural beauty.

☐ 🔖 ♡ **Lake Tahoe – Nevada State Park:** This large park protects much of Lake Tahoe's Nevada shoreline, offering sandy beaches, forested backcountry, and panoramic views. Units include Sand Harbor, known for swimming and the Shakespeare Festival; Spooner Lake & Backcountry with 50 miles of trails; Cave Rock with its cultural significance; and Van Sickle, linking to California trails.

☐ 🔖 ♡ **Mormon Station State Historic Park:** Located in Genoa, Nevada's first permanent settlement, this park features a replica of the original 1851 trading post. Exhibits highlight pioneer life and the Mormon trail. Shaded picnic grounds provide a peaceful stop at the foot of the Sierra Nevada. Visitors experience the roots of Nevada's settlement and early community building.

☐ 🔖 ♡ **Old Las Vegas Mormon Fort State Historic Park:** In downtown Las Vegas, this adobe fort preserves the site of the valley's first permanent non-Native settlement, built by Mormon missionaries in 1855. A small museum and exhibits tell the story of survival in the harsh desert. It's a rare glimpse into Las Vegas' origins, set amid the city's modern bustle.

NEVADA

☐ 🔖 ♡ **Spring Mountain Ranch State Park:** Once a private retreat for wealthy owners including Howard Hughes, this park preserves historic ranch buildings and expansive lawns under red cliffs. Visitors tour ranch structures, picnic under shade trees, or hike trails into the desert. It offers both cultural history and natural beauty, making it a unique escape from nearby Las Vegas.

☐ 🔖 ♡ **Spring Valley State Park:** Anchored by the Eagle Valley Reservoir, this park blends outdoor recreation with historic ranching remnants. Fishing, camping, and hiking are popular, while old stone buildings recall Nevada's pioneer days. Its peaceful setting, framed by colorful cliffs and open meadows, provides an inviting getaway for both families and history enthusiasts.

☐ 🔖 ♡ **Valley of Fire State Park:** Nevada's oldest and largest state park dazzles with red sandstone formations that blaze in the sun. Petroglyphs carved by Ancestral Puebloans add cultural depth, while hiking trails explore natural arches, slot canyons, and sweeping vistas. A short drive from Las Vegas, it's one of Nevada's most iconic landscapes and a photographer's dream.

☐ 🔖 ♡ **Van Sickle Bi-State Park:** Straddling the Nevada-California border near South Lake Tahoe, this park offers trails that climb quickly to breathtaking views of the lake. Once a private ranch, it now provides easy access to Tahoe's high country. Its unique bi-state management and scenic vistas make it a favorite for hikers seeking Tahoe's beauty without the crowds.

State Recreational Areas

☐ 🔖 ♡ **Big Bend of the Colorado State Recreation Area:** Located near Laughlin on the Colorado River, this recreation area offers boating, fishing, and riverside camping. With sandy beaches, picnic areas, and scenic trails through the Mojave Desert, it's a popular spot for both water recreation and relaxation. The river's beauty and warm climate make it ideal for year-round outdoor fun.

☐ 🔖 ♡ **Lahontan State Recreation Area:** Centered around the 10,000-acre Lahontan Reservoir, this area provides prime opportunities for boating, fishing, water-skiing, and camping. Visitors enjoy sandy beaches and wide-open desert views. Once part of the Newlands Irrigation Project, it blends modern recreation with historic engineering. Its vast waters attract anglers, paddlers, and families alike.

☐ 🔖 ♡ **Rye Patch State Recreation Area:** Spanning a 22-mile-long reservoir on the Humboldt River, this recreation area is popular for boating, fishing, and water-skiing. Campgrounds and picnic sites line the lakeshore, while surrounding desert terrain invites off-road exploration and even gold prospecting. Its expansive waters and rugged landscape offer both adventure and relaxation.

☐ 🔖 ♡ **South Fork State Recreation Area:** Nestled in a scenic valley near Elko, this area surrounds South Fork Reservoir, offering fishing, boating, hunting, and camping. Its blend of meadows, hills, and open water supports abundant wildlife, making it a favorite for birdwatchers and anglers. With both primitive and developed sites, it provides a peaceful outdoor getaway.

☐ 🔖 ♡ **Walker River State Recreation Area:** Encompassing historic ranchlands along 30 miles of the East Walker River, this is one of Nevada's newest recreation areas. It offers fishing, hiking, and camping while preserving cultural landscapes. Visitors can explore river canyons, wildlife habitats, and old ranch sites, enjoying a unique blend of history, solitude, and outdoor adventure.

☐ 🔖 ♡ **Wild Horse State Recreation Area:** Located north of Elko, this area surrounds Wild Horse Reservoir, a high-desert lake renowned for fishing, boating, and winter ice sports. Campgrounds and open meadows invite year-round recreation, while the surrounding mountains offer wildlife viewing. Named for wild horses that roam the area, it captures Nevada's rugged and untamed spirit.

National Parks

 ☐ 🔖 ♡ **Death Valley National Park:** Spanning California and Nevada, Death Valley is the hottest, driest, and lowest place in North America. Its landscapes include salt flats, sand dunes, canyons, and rugged mountains. Visitors explore Badwater Basin, colorful rock formations, and star-filled skies. Despite its harsh environment, the park teems with unique plants, wildlife, and cultural history.

 ☐ 🔖 ♡ **Great Basin National Park:** Nestled in eastern Nevada, this park showcases striking contrasts, from the limestone depths of Lehman Caves to the 13,063-foot summit of Wheeler Peak. Ancient bristlecone pines, alpine lakes, and desert valleys create rich ecosystems to explore. Its remote location offers solitude, abundant wildlife, and some of the darkest night skies in the country.

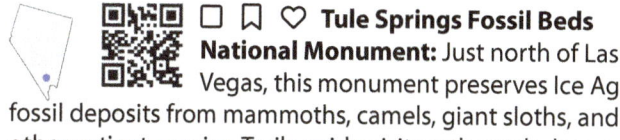

NEVADA

☐ 🔖 ♡ **Lake Mead National Recreation Area:** Straddling Nevada and Arizona, this vast area surrounds Lake Mead and Lake Mohave, reservoirs created by Hoover Dam. Visitors enjoy boating, fishing, swimming, hiking, and camping against a dramatic desert backdrop. With over a million acres, it blends recreation with stunning geology, historic sites, and diverse desert and riparian habitats.

☐ 🔖 ♡ **Tule Springs Fossil Beds National Monument:** Just north of Las Vegas, this monument preserves Ice Age fossil deposits from mammoths, camels, giant sloths, and other extinct species. Trails guide visitors through desert landscapes rich in scientific history. Interpretive signs reveal how these fossils illuminate Nevada's prehistoric past, making it a unique window into ancient ecosystems.

State & National Forests

☐ 🔖 ♡ **Eldorado National Forest:** Spanning the Sierra Nevada of California, about 78 acres extend into Douglas County, Nevada. This small section contains rugged alpine terrain with mixed conifer forests and meadows. Managed by the U.S. Forest Service, it connects Nevada to the greater Sierra ecosystem, offering wilderness character and scenic backcountry at the state line.

☐ 🔖 ♡ **Inyo National Forest:** Largely in California but extending about 60,700 acres into western Nevada, this forest protects Boundary Peak—the state's highest point—and unique bristlecone pine groves. High desert foothills give way to alpine meadows, rugged ridges, and rich biodiversity. Visitors come for hiking, climbing, and exploring one of the most scenic corners of the Sierra–Nevada transition zone.

☐ 🔖 ♡ **Humboldt–Toiyabe National Forest:** Covering over 6.3 million acres, this is the largest National Forest in the lower 48 states, stretching across Nevada and into eastern California. Its landscapes range from desert valleys to alpine peaks, with lakes, canyons, and wildlife habitats. Visitors find endless opportunities for hiking, camping, fishing, horseback riding, and solitude in its vast, remote expanse.

National Scenic Byways & All-American Roads

☐ 🔖 ♡ **City of Las Vegas, Las Vegas Boulevard:** This short byway through downtown showcases the city's vintage neon, historic casinos, and early mid-century architecture. It preserves the classic roadside Americana vibe that defined Las Vegas before the mega-resorts, offering a blend of heritage and nightlife energy. Visitors experience the roots of modern Vegas along this iconic corridor.

☐ 🔖 ♡ **Las Vegas Strip:** Spanning 4.5 miles, this world-famous stretch of Las Vegas Boulevard glitters with neon lights, themed resorts, and nonstop entertainment. Beginning at the "Welcome to Fabulous Las Vegas" sign, the road immerses visitors in a spectacle of nightlife and architecture. It's a destination in itself and one of the most recognizable urban drives worldwide.

☐ 🔖 ♡ **Lake Tahoe – Eastshore Drive:** Stretching 28 miles along U.S. 50 and SR 28, this byway hugs Nevada's shoreline of Lake Tahoe. Towering granite cliffs, alpine forests, and turquoise waters create world-class vistas. Pullouts give access to beaches and trailheads, while year-round recreation opportunities highlight one of the country's most celebrated mountain landscapes.

☐ 🔖 ♡ **Pyramid Lake:** Following NV 447 and 446, this route circles Pyramid Lake, a desert gem and cultural center of the Paiute Tribe. Striking formations like the Stone Mother rise along the shoreline, while vast desert vistas frame turquoise waters. Visitors find world-class trout fishing, tribal heritage sites, and the haunting beauty of Nevada's largest natural lake.

State Scenic Byways

☐ 🔖 ♡ **Angel Lake Road:** This 11-mile byway climbs steeply from Wells into the East Humboldt Range, ending at glacially carved Angel Lake. The drive passes through alpine meadows, forests of aspen and pine, and offers expansive views of the surrounding high desert basin. It's a dramatic ascent that delivers a cool mountain oasis and a striking contrast to the stark lowlands below.

☐ 🔖 ♡ **Baker Road:** Stretching from the Utah border into the small town of Baker, this 11-mile byway leads directly toward Great Basin National Park. The route traverses quiet high-desert valleys framed by distant mountain ridges, creating a sense of solitude. It serves as the gateway to the park and is lined with wide skies, open landscapes, and rural Nevada character.

NEVADA

☐ 🔖 ♡ **Deer Creek Road:** Linking Kyle Canyon and Lee Canyon in the Spring Mountains, this 8-mile route climbs through thick forests of ponderosa pine and aspen. The byway offers cooler air, mountain views, and access to recreation just outside Las Vegas. In autumn the trees blaze with color, while summer brings a shaded escape from the desert heat below.

☐ 🔖 ♡ **Gerlach Road:** A short but scenic 4.5-mile drive near Pyramid Lake, this route offers sweeping views of the desert lake and surrounding ridges. Visitors may spot wild horses roaming along the road while the vast sky dominates the horizon. The byway highlights both the stark beauty of Nevada's high desert and the cultural importance of Pyramid Lake.

☐ 🔖 ♡ **Kyle Canyon Road:** This 13-mile byway climbs from Las Vegas into the Spring Mountains via Kyle Canyon. The road quickly rises into cooler elevations with piñon-juniper forests giving way to tall pines. Along the way are picnic spots, trailheads, and sweeping views, culminating at Mount Charleston, one of Nevada's premier alpine recreation areas.

☐ 🔖 ♡ **Lamoille Canyon Road:** Winding 12 miles into the Ruby Mountains, this byway is often called the "Yosemite of Nevada." Towering cliffs, waterfalls, alpine meadows, and wildflowers line the glacially carved canyon. Trailheads branch into wilderness areas, while roadside pullouts provide stunning views. In fall, golden aspens make it one of the most beautiful drives in the state.

☐ 🔖 ♡ **Lehman Caves Road:** Just over 5 miles long, this byway connects the town of Baker to the entrance of Great Basin National Park. The road leads visitors through open high-desert terrain into the shaded setting of the Lehman Caves area. It offers views of Wheeler Peak and serves as a welcoming approach to one of Nevada's natural treasures.

☐ 🔖 ♡ **Lee Canyon Road:** Stretching 17 miles through the Spring Mountains, this byway climbs from desert lowlands into alpine forests near Mount Charleston. Known for year-round recreation, it offers access to hiking, skiing, and cooler temperatures. The route showcases dramatic elevation change, with sweeping desert views below and snow-capped peaks above.

☐ 🔖 ♡ **Mount Rose Highway:** This 24-mile byway runs between Reno and Lake Tahoe, cresting at nearly 9,000 feet. The road offers expansive views of the Truckee Meadows, Washoe Valley, and the Tahoe Basin. Wildflower meadows, alpine lakes, and rugged ridges make it a striking mountain drive, especially in late summer and autumn when the scenery bursts with color.

☐ 🔖 ♡ **North Shore Road:** Following Nevada State Route 28 along Lake Tahoe's north and east shores, this 16-mile byway delivers quieter lake access than the busy south. Forested overlooks, secluded beaches, and small historic sites line the route. Its combination of tranquil pullouts and sweeping mountain-lake vistas offers a peaceful way to experience Tahoe's beauty.

☐ 🔖 ♡ **Valley of Fire Road:** Cutting through Valley of Fire State Park, this 10-mile byway showcases blazing red sandstone formations, natural arches, and ancient petroglyphs. Pullouts provide access to short trails, picnic areas, and unforgettable views. The shifting colors of the rock at sunrise and sunset make this drive one of Nevada's most photographed scenic experiences.

☐ 🔖 ♡ **US 93 Great Basin Highway:** This 149-mile byway connects Caliente to Great Basin National Park, linking several state parks along the way. The drive traverses open desert basins, rugged mountain ranges, and small historic towns. Scenic views stretch for miles, capturing the wide-open essence of Nevada while guiding travelers to some of its most iconic natural areas.

National Natural Landmarks

 ☐ 🔖 ♡ **Berlin–Ichthyosaur State Park:** This National Natural Landmark preserves both the ghost town of Berlin and one of the world's richest ichthyosaur fossil beds. Massive marine reptiles from the Triassic seas are embedded in limestone here, providing paleontologists with extraordinary evidence of Nevada's ancient ocean life alongside its mining history. *GPS: 38.8747, -117.5897*

 ☐ 🔖 ♡ **Hot Creek Springs & Marsh:** Recognized as a National Natural Landmark for its geothermal wetland, this rare oasis in Hot Creek Valley sustains the endangered White River springfish. Thermal springs and marshes provide life in an otherwise arid landscape, demonstrating the ecological importance of isolated aquatic systems in the Great Basin. *GPS: 38.3791, -115.1511*

UNITED STATES EDITION

NEVADA

 **Lunar Crater:** Designated a National Natural Landmark for its remarkable volcanic geology, Lunar Crater is a maar formed by explosive eruptions. Part of a vast volcanic field, it was used by Apollo astronauts for training. Its preserved features make it an outstanding example of maar volcanism and a unique desert landmark for science and exploration.
GPS: 38.3840, -116.0689

 **Ruby Lake National Wildlife Refuge (Ruby Marsh):** Designated a National Natural Landmark for being one of Nevada's most extensive freshwater marshes, Ruby Lake supports trumpeter swans, sandhill cranes, and countless migratory birds. Its remote setting protects intact wetland ecosystems in stark contrast to the surrounding high desert basin.
GPS: 40.1730, -115.4695

 **Timber Mountain Caldera:** This Miocene-age volcanic structure is a National Natural Landmark for illustrating the immense explosive eruptions that shaped Nevada's interior. The caldera's eroded rim and tuff deposits reveal volcanic processes that influenced the Basin and Range landscape, making it a key site for understanding regional geologic history.
GPS: 38.3494, -115.5003

 **Valley of Fire State Park:** Nevada's oldest state park is also a National Natural Landmark for its blazing Aztec sandstone formations, sculpted arches, and canyons. Petroglyphs carved by Indigenous peoples add cultural depth. The park highlights the geologic artistry of the Mojave Desert and remains one of the state's most scenic natural treasures.
GPS: 36.4367, -114.5262

New Hampshire

New Hampshire is a haven for outdoor enthusiasts, with granite peaks, glacial gorges, ancient bogs, and pristine lakes. Its blend of state parks, the expansive White Mountain National Forest, and remarkable natural landmarks make it an ideal destination for exploration in every season, from vibrant autumn hikes to tranquil snowy retreats.

📅 Peak Season
June–October is New Hampshire's peak season, offering warm weather, mountain access, and stunning fall foliage. Summer draws hikers and lake visitors, while autumn is world-famous for its vibrant colors across the White Mountains.

📅 Offseason Months
November–April is the offseason for general travel, with snow and cold temperatures dominating the mountains. Winter, however, is peak for skiing, snowshoeing, and other snow sports across the state.

🍃 Scenery & Nature Timing
Spring brings rushing waterfalls and greening forests. Summer offers alpine hikes, lake recreation, and wildflowers. Fall transforms the hills with brilliant foliage, while winter blankets peaks and valleys in deep snow.

✨ Special
New Hampshire features Mount Washington's extreme weather, the granite peaks and gorges of the White Mountains, and the clear lakes of the Lakes Region. Fall foliage, ice formations, and rugged alpine summits define its natural drama.

UNITED STATES EDITION

NEW HAMPSHIRE

State Parks

☐ ▢ ♡ **Ahern State Park:** Nestled in Laconia, this 128-acre park offers two miles of undeveloped shoreline on Lake Winnisquam. Visitors can enjoy hiking, mountain biking, fishing, swimming, and picnicking in a quiet, wooded setting. With peaceful trails and scenic water access, Ahern provides a low-key retreat close to town and the heart of the Lakes Region.

☐ ▢ ♡ **Bear Brook State Park:** At over 10,000 acres, Bear Brook is New Hampshire's largest developed state park. It offers camping, fishing, boating, hiking, biking, and horseback riding on a vast trail network. Visitors can also explore historic sites like the Old Allenstown Meeting House and the NH Snowmobile Museum, making it both recreational and educational.

☐ ▢ ♡ **Cardigan Mountain State Park:** Covering 5,655 acres in Orange, the park is centered on Mount Cardigan, whose treeless granite summit provides sweeping views of the White Mountains, Vermont hills, and beyond. Trails range from moderate to steep, making it a popular hiking destination. Its rugged beauty and striking panoramas attract photographers and nature enthusiasts year-round.

☐ ▢ ♡ **Cathedral Ledge State Park:** This 5-acre park in North Conway offers a dramatic 700-foot granite cliff with panoramic views of the Saco River Valley, Mount Washington, and surrounding ranges. Accessible by car or hiking trails, it's also one of the region's premier rock climbing sites. Visitors can picnic, take photos, and enjoy one of the area's most iconic lookouts.

☐ ▢ ♡ **Clough State Park:** Located on the shore of Everett Lake in Weare, this scenic park provides swimming, boating, hiking, picnicking, and fishing opportunities. A sandy beach, boat ramp, and picnic areas make it family-friendly, while wooded trails invite exploration. Its convenient location and lake access make it a popular summer getaway in southern New Hampshire.

☐ ▢ ♡ **Coleman State Park:** Set in northern New Hampshire's Connecticut Lakes Region, this 1,500-acre park near Little Diamond Pond is known for camping, boating, and excellent trout fishing. With direct ATV and snowmobile trail access, it's a hub for outdoor enthusiasts year-round. Its remote setting offers quiet solitude surrounded by forests, ponds, and rugged beauty.

☐ ▢ ♡ **Crawford Notch State Park:** This 5,775-acre White Mountains park is famed for waterfalls, cliffs, and scenic hiking trails. Arethusa Falls, New Hampshire's tallest, is a highlight. Campgrounds, picnic areas, and historic sites like the Willey House draw visitors year-round. It's a gateway to rugged alpine scenery, offering spectacular views and abundant outdoor recreation.

☐ ▢ ♡ **Dixville Notch State Park:** Encompassing 127 acres in northern New Hampshire, this rugged park features jagged cliffs, dramatic waterfalls, and forested trails. Overlooks provide sweeping views of the surrounding mountains and valleys. Its remote location, limited development, and natural beauty make it an ideal destination for hikers, photographers, and those seeking solitude.

☐ ▢ ♡ **Echo Lake State Park:** Situated in Conway, this 118-acre park features a sandy swimming beach on Echo Lake with views of the towering White Horse and Cathedral Ledges. Visitors enjoy kayaking, fishing, picnicking, and hiking trails that connect to surrounding cliffs. Its family-friendly atmosphere and dramatic scenery make it a beloved summer destination.

☐ ▢ ♡ **Ellacoya State Park:** This 82-acre park in Gilford sits along Lake Winnipesaukee and boasts one of the lake's largest sandy beaches. Families enjoy swimming, boating, fishing, and picnicking, while the wide shore offers panoramic views across New England's largest lake. With accessible facilities and a central location, it's a popular Lakes Region destination.

☐ ▢ ♡ **Forest Lake State Park:** Located in Dalton, this 397-acre park is one of the oldest in the system, offering swimming, boating, hiking, and picnicking on the shores of Forest Lake. Its peaceful, undeveloped atmosphere makes it perfect for family outings, wildlife viewing, and quiet recreation. The sandy beach and surrounding forests provide classic New England charm.

☐ ▢ ♡ **Franconia Notch State Park:** Stretching 6,692 acres through a mountain pass, this White Mountains gem is home to waterfalls, lakes, hiking trails, and historic sites. Visitors can ride the Cannon Mountain Aerial Tramway, explore the Flume Gorge, or hike the Appalachian Trail. Its dramatic landscapes and abundant recreation make it one of New Hampshire's most iconic parks.

NEW HAMPSHIRE

Greenfield State Park: Covering 400 acres, this Monadnock Region park features Otter Lake, sandy beaches, and wooded campsites. Visitors can swim, fish, canoe, or hike the park's trail network, which passes through ponds, bogs, and forests. Its variety of habitats and family-friendly amenities make it a peaceful and versatile outdoor destination.

Hampton Beach State Park: Located along the Atlantic Ocean, this 50-acre park offers RV camping, swimming, fishing, and picnicking on one of New England's most popular beaches. Known for its vibrant boardwalk, events, and nightlife, it blends recreation with a lively seaside atmosphere. It's a premier destination for both day-trippers and vacationers.

Jericho Mountain State Park: Spanning 7,430 acres near Berlin, this park is a hub for ATV and trail riding, with connections to over 1,000 miles of routes. It also offers camping, swimming, boating, and hiking in a scenic mountain setting. Year-round recreation, including snowmobiling in winter, makes it a northern New Hampshire adventure hotspot.

Kingston State Park: This 44-acre park on Great Pond in Kingston features a sandy beach, boat rentals, and picnic areas. Families enjoy swimming, fishing, volleyball, and kayaking, while wooded trails provide shady walks. Its convenient location and calm waters make it a popular local spot for day trips and group gatherings in southern New Hampshire.

Lake Francis State Park: Located in Pittsburg's Connecticut Lakes Region, this 38-acre park offers camping, boating, and fishing on scenic Lake Francis. It's popular with anglers seeking trout and salmon, and also provides direct access to ATV and snowmobile trails. Surrounded by forested hills, it's a peaceful northern retreat for year-round recreation.

Lake Tarleton State Park: A 48-acre undeveloped park in Piermont, this property features scenic shoreline along Lake Tarleton. Though primitive, it offers picnicking, paddling, and fishing in a quiet natural setting. With mountain views and calm waters, it's a low-key spot for relaxation and enjoying the Upper Valley's outdoor charm.

Miller State Park: Located in Peterborough on Pack Monadnock Mountain, this park offers an auto road to the summit, picnic areas, and hiking trails. It's popular for birdwatching, especially hawk migrations in fall. Visitors can enjoy sweeping views of Mount Monadnock, the White Mountains, and the Boston skyline on clear days.

Mollidgewock State Park: This 46-acre riverside park in Errol offers camping, fishing, kayaking, and hiking along the Androscoggin River. Known for its peaceful, wooded setting, it provides opportunities to spot moose and other wildlife. Campers enjoy both traditional and remote riverfront sites, making it a favorite for nature lovers and paddlers alike.

Monadnock State Park: Centered on Mount Monadnock in Jaffrey, this park offers over 40 miles of hiking trails, including challenging routes to its bare summit. Considered one of the world's most-climbed mountains, it provides panoramic views of six New England states. Campgrounds and day-use areas make it a premier destination for hikers and outdoor enthusiasts.

Moose Brook State Park: Near Gorham, this 755-acre park features a cold-water brook-fed swimming pool, camping, and hiking trails. Surrounded by the White Mountains, it offers mountain biking and access to nearby attractions. Its forested setting, clear waters, and quiet atmosphere make it a hidden gem for families and outdoor explorers.

Mount Sunapee State Park: In Newbury, this year-round destination includes a sandy beach on Lake Sunapee and trails on Mount Sunapee itself. Summer visitors enjoy swimming, boating, and hiking, while winter brings downhill skiing at Mount Sunapee Resort. Its combination of lakefront relaxation and mountain recreation makes it one of New Hampshire's most versatile parks.

Mount Washington State Park: Situated at the 6,288-foot summit of Mount Washington, this park offers an observation center, museum, and trails with sweeping views of the Northeast. Known for extreme weather, it draws hikers, photographers, and sightseers who can also arrive by cog railway or auto road. It's a must-visit icon of New England.

Northwood Meadows State Park: Located in Northwood, this 675-acre park offers a tranquil pond, multi-use trails, and picnic areas. It's a favorite for hiking, fishing, biking, and wildlife viewing in a quiet forest setting. The park provides year-round recreation and is especially popular in fall when foliage reflects beautifully on the pond.

Odiorne Point State Park: On the rocky seacoast in Rye, this park offers trails through forests, salt marshes, and tidepools, plus sweeping ocean views. It also houses the Seacoast Science Center. Once home to military fortifications, it blends natural beauty with history and education, making it a top destination for families and coastal explorers.

NEW HAMPSHIRE

☐ 🔖 ♡ **Pawtuckaway State Park:** Covering 5,500 acres in Nottingham, this park features a large lake, sandy beaches, and forested hiking trails. Visitors enjoy swimming, boating, fishing, camping, and climbing boulder fields. With wetlands, woodlands, and mountain views, it's one of New Hampshire's most diverse parks, offering something for every outdoor enthusiast.

☐ 🔖 ♡ **Pisgah State Park:** New Hampshire's largest state park at 13,300 acres, Pisgah in Hinsdale protects forests, wetlands, and ponds. It offers extensive trails for hiking, biking, horseback riding, and snowmobiling. Wildlife thrives in its varied habitats, making it a haven for naturalists. Its size and variety provide limitless exploration in a wild, natural setting.

☐ 🔖 ♡ **Rollins State Park:** On the southern slope of Mount Kearsarge in Warner, this park provides picnic areas, hiking trails, and an auto road leading near the summit. Visitors can hike the final half mile to panoramic views of the White Mountains, Monadnock, and beyond. It's a favorite for families and leaf-peepers in autumn.

☐ 🔖 ♡ **Rye Harbor State Park:** This small seaside park in Rye sits on a peninsula at the mouth of Rye Harbor, offering panoramic views of the Atlantic and Isles of Shoals. Visitors enjoy picnicking, fishing from the rocky shore, and watching boats come and go from the harbor. With grassy lawns, picnic tables, and ocean breezes, it provides a peaceful, scenic stop along New Hampshire's short but dramatic coastline.

☐ 🔖 ♡ **Silver Lake State Park:** Located in Hollis, this 80-acre park offers a sandy beach, swimming, and picnicking on the shores of Silver Lake. Popular in summer, it provides clear waters for boating and fishing, as well as shaded areas for family gatherings. Its convenient southern location makes it an easy day trip from Nashua or Massachusetts.

☐ 🔖 ♡ **Umbagog Lake State Park:** Spanning Errol and Cambridge, this 1,360-acre park offers camping, boating, and fishing on the expansive Umbagog Lake, part of a National Wildlife Refuge. It's known for canoeing, kayaking, and abundant wildlife, from moose to bald eagles. Remote campsites accessible only by boat make it a favorite for paddlers seeking solitude.

☐ 🔖 ♡ **Wadleigh State Park:** Situated on Kezar Lake in Sutton, this 43-acre park features a sandy beach, picnic areas, and opportunities for swimming and boating. It's popular for family outings, with calm waters ideal for paddling and fishing. The surrounding hills and small-town charm add to the peaceful setting of this compact but scenic park.

☐ 🔖 ♡ **Weeks State Park:** Situated in Lancaster, this 446-acre park includes the historic home of John Wingate Weeks, with a museum and fire tower. Scenic drives and trails lead to mountain vistas overlooking the Presidential Range. Combining cultural history with outdoor recreation, it's a unique park that honors conservation and offers stunning northern views.

☐ 🔖 ♡ **Wellington State Park:** Located in Bristol, this park boasts the largest freshwater beach in the state, set on the shores of Newfound Lake. It offers swimming, picnicking, boating, and hiking trails. Surrounded by forested hills, it's a summer favorite for families, with clear waters and wide views making it one of New Hampshire's most beautiful lakeside parks.

☐ 🔖 ♡ **White Lake State Park:** In Tamworth, this 1,100-acre park is built around a glacial lake with a sandy beach. Visitors can swim, fish, paddle, or hike trails that circle the lake and pass through forests. It's also known for its preserved glacial features and wildlife viewing. The combination of natural beauty and recreation makes it very popular in summer.

☐ 🔖 ♡ **Winslow State Park:** On the northwest slope of Mount Kearsarge, this park in Wilmot offers picnic areas and hiking trails to the summit. The Winslow Trail climbs steeply, while the Barlow Trail offers a gentler route. From the top, visitors enjoy expansive views of the White Mountains, Monadnock, and even into Vermont, making it a rewarding climb.

NEW HAMPSHIRE

National Parks

☐ ☐ ♡ **Appalachian National Scenic Trail:** Stretching more than 2,190 miles from Georgia to Maine, this legendary trail passes through New Hampshire's White Mountains, where rugged peaks and alpine ridges challenge hikers. Known for sweeping views, diverse ecosystems, and backcountry experiences, the trail offers a premier way to explore the Eastern U.S. on foot.

☐ ☐ ♡ **Saint-Gaudens National Historical Park:** In Cornish, this park preserves the home, studios, and gardens of Augustus Saint-Gaudens, a master sculptor famed for works like the Shaw Memorial and $20 gold coin design. Visitors can tour his residence, view original art, and stroll through landscaped grounds, gaining insight into his influence on American art and culture.

State & National Forests

☐ ☐ ♡ **Annett State Forest:** In Rindge and Sharon, this 1,494-acre forest includes Hubbard Pond and the Annett Wayside Area. Visitors enjoy canoeing, fishing, picnicking, and hiking short interpretive trails. Managed for timber and wildlife, it's a versatile destination that combines recreation with quiet rural beauty in the Monadnock Region.

☐ ☐ ♡ **Belknap Mountain State Forest:** Covering 1,300 acres in the Belknap Range, this forest features the 2,382-foot summit of Belknap Mountain. A fire tower rewards hikers with sweeping views of Lake Winnipesaukee and the surrounding hills. Trails connect to nearby summits, making it a popular outdoor destination for hikers, nature lovers, and birdwatchers.

☐ ☐ ♡ **Chamberlain Reynolds State Forest:** Managed in partnership with the Squam Lakes Association, this 157-acre property in Holderness offers lakeside trails, canoe access, wetlands, and sandy shoreline on Squam Lake. Boardwalks, picnic spots, and wildlife viewing make it a favorite for families and nature enthusiasts in central New Hampshire.

☐ ☐ ♡ **Connecticut Lakes State Forest:** This 1,648-acre tract in Pittsburg preserves the headwaters of the Connecticut River. Visitors can hike, fish, paddle, and watch for moose, loons, and bald eagles. It's a remote destination in the North Country that provides both outdoor recreation and a wilderness experience at New Hampshire's northern tip.

☐ ☐ ♡ **Gile State Forest:** Spanning 6,675 acres in Springfield, this forest includes Gardner Memorial Wayside Park, Butterfield Pond, and woodland trails. Visitors can picnic, hike, and explore quiet forest roads. Managed for timber, habitat, and recreation, it's a large and diverse forest that showcases the balance of conservation and public use.

☐ ☐ ♡ **Hemenway State Forest:** Located in Tamworth, this 2,100-acre forest is home to Big Pines Natural Area, where visitors can see some of the largest white pines in New Hampshire. Trails and boardwalks provide access to these towering trees and to the Swift River. It's a unique natural attraction with ecological and scenic significance.

☐ ☐ ♡ **Hopkinton State Forest:** Near Hopkinton, this accessible woodland provides opportunities for hiking, hunting, and nature study. It's managed for timber and wildlife while offering recreational value to the surrounding community. Its trail system and varied terrain make it a local favorite for low-key outdoor activity.

☐ ☐ ♡ **Kearsarge Mountain State Forest:** Encompassing nearly 3,900 acres across four towns, this forest surrounds Mount Kearsarge and connects to Rollins and Winslow State Parks. Visitors can hike trails to the summit or explore the slopes, enjoying sweeping views. It's both a conservation area and a recreational destination in central New Hampshire.

☐ ☐ ♡ **Nash Stream State Forest:** At 39,000 acres, this is New Hampshire's largest state forest. Located in the North Country, it offers rugged backcountry recreation including hiking, fishing, hunting, snowmobiling, and ATV use. Remote campsites and wildlife viewing opportunities make it a premier destination for those seeking solitude and adventure.

☐ ☐ ♡ **White Mountain National Forest:** Covering nearly 750,000 acres in New Hampshire and Maine, this is the state's only national forest. It includes the Presidential Range, Franconia Ridge, and hundreds of miles of trails including the Appalachian Trail. Visitors enjoy hiking, camping, climbing, skiing, and scenic drives, making it one of New England's crown jewels.

NEW HAMPSHIRE

National Scenic Byways & All-American Roads

☐ ▢ ♡ **Connecticut River Byway:** Following New Hampshire's western border, this byway traces the Connecticut River through rural villages, farmland, and historic mill towns. Travelers enjoy scenic river views, covered bridges, and cultural stops like local museums and artisan shops. It showcases the natural beauty and heritage of the Upper Valley and Great North Woods.

☐ ▢ ♡ **Kancamagus Scenic Byway:** Stretching 34 miles across the White Mountain National Forest, the "Kanc" connects Lincoln and Conway. Famous for fall foliage, it offers overlooks, trailheads, waterfalls, and picnic sites. With no gas stations or towns along its length, it provides an unspoiled mountain drive that captures the wild heart of New Hampshire.

☐ ▢ ♡ **White Mountain Trail:** This 100-mile loop links Franconia Notch, Crawford Notch, and the Kancamagus Highway, circling through the White Mountains' most iconic landscapes. Visitors encounter towering peaks, mountain passes, historic sites, and abundant hiking opportunities. It offers a comprehensive showcase of New Hampshire's alpine scenery and outdoor heritage.

State Scenic Byways

☐ ▢ ♡ **American Independence Byway:** A 21-mile loop through Exeter, Hampton, and Hampton Falls highlighting Revolutionary War and colonial-era history. Stops include Exeter's American Independence Museum, historic homes, and town commons. It blends heritage tourism with small-town charm, linking seacoast villages and offering insights into New Hampshire's role in early America.

☐ ▢ ♡ **Branch River Valley Trail:** Following Route 125 in Wakefield, this short byway connects lakes, wetlands, and small villages in Carroll County. It highlights the Branch River Valley's rural character, historic structures, and scenic water views. The corridor provides access to farm stands, old mills, and the simple beauty of New Hampshire's backroads.

☐ ▢ ♡ **Colonial Byway:** Winding through Amherst, Milford, and Hancock, this route explores quintessential New England villages with town greens, colonial-era homes, and stone walls. Visitors encounter covered bridges, historic inns, and museums. It's a leisurely drive that highlights the region's cultural heritage and preserved 18th- and 19th-century architecture.

☐ ▢ ♡ **Currier & Ives Scenic Byway:** Named for the 19th-century printmakers who captured rural New England scenes, this route runs through Henniker, Hopkinton, Warner, Webster, and Salisbury. It passes farms, historic villages, and covered bridges, with views reminiscent of Currier & Ives' artwork. It celebrates the pastoral and cultural beauty of central New Hampshire.

☐ ▢ ♡ **Great North Woods Byway:** Stretching along Routes 3 and 145 in Pittsburg, Clarksville, and Colebrook, this byway highlights northern New Hampshire's wild character. Visitors see rivers, lakes, and working forests, with chances to spot moose and other wildlife. It also connects travelers to outdoor recreation and the remote Connecticut Lakes Region.

☐ ▢ ♡ **Lakes Region Tour Scenic Byway:** Encircling Lake Winnipesaukee, this 97-mile route links Alton, Gilford, Meredith, Laconia, Wolfeboro, and Center Harbor. It showcases beaches, marinas, resort towns, and sweeping lake views. Visitors enjoy recreation, dining, and cultural stops, making it the definitive drive for exploring New Hampshire's largest and most popular lake.

☐ ▢ ♡ **Monadnock Region Loop:** A state byway highlighting the towns surrounding Mount Monadnock, including Peterborough, Jaffrey, and Dublin. It offers mountain views, historic downtowns, artists' colonies, and access to Monadnock's famous hiking trails. The loop embodies the cultural and scenic richness of southwestern New Hampshire's landscape.

☐ ▢ ♡ **Moose Path Trail:** A 110-mile byway through Lancaster, Northumberland, Stratford, Columbia, and Pittsburg, it follows the Connecticut River and scenic Route 3. Known for frequent moose sightings, it offers rugged beauty, wildlife viewing, and northern forests. It connects to outdoor recreation in the North Country and showcases New Hampshire's wildest roads.

NEW HAMPSHIRE

☐ 🔖 ♡ **Presidential Range Trail:** Passing through Gorham, Randolph, and Jefferson along Route 2, this byway skirts the northern flank of the Presidential Range. Visitors enjoy dramatic views of Mount Washington and surrounding peaks, access to trailheads, and glimpses of the Appalachian Trail. It's a must-drive for White Mountain scenery from the valley floor.

☐ 🔖 ♡ **Seacoast Byway:** Extending from Seabrook through Hampton, Rye, Portsmouth, and New Castle, this coastal drive highlights New Hampshire's short but dramatic shoreline. Visitors see sandy beaches, rocky coasts, historic forts, and Portsmouth's vibrant harbor. It blends maritime heritage with oceanfront scenery, offering a quintessential seacoast experience.

☐ 🔖 ♡ **Upper Valley Scenic Byway:** Running through Lebanon, Hanover, Lyme, and Orford along Route 10, this byway follows the Connecticut River valley. It highlights covered bridges, Dartmouth College, historic town centers, and riverside farmland. The drive blends academic and cultural landmarks with the natural beauty of the Upper Valley corridor.

☐ 🔖 ♡ **Weeks Act Legacy Trail:** This byway commemorates the 1911 Weeks Act, which enabled the creation of national forests. Running through Bethlehem, Twin Mountain, and Lancaster, it highlights White Mountain history, conservation landmarks, and scenic views. Interpretive sites and historic markers tell the story of how the White Mountain National Forest was born.

National Natural Landmarks

☐ 🔖 ♡ **East Inlet Natural Area:** Recognized as a National Natural Landmark for its pristine boreal habitats, this remote northern site preserves black spruce–tamarack bogs and one of the last virgin balsam fir–red spruce forests in New England. Its glaciated terrain provides critical refuge for boreal species in an undisturbed forest–wetland landscape.
GPS: 45.211385, -71.110497

☐ 🔖 ♡ **Floating Island:** Designated a National Natural Landmark for its unusual bog that literally floats on the waters of Umbagog Lake, this peatland supports sphagnum moss, heath shrubs, and rare plants adapted to acidic conditions. Its shifting mat illustrates dynamic peatland processes and offers a rare ecological phenomenon in the Northeast.
GPS: 44.789023, -71.084547

☐ 🔖 ♡ **Franconia Notch:** This dramatic U-shaped valley is a National Natural Landmark for showcasing classic glacial geology in the White Mountains. Features such as Echo Lake and the former Old Man of the Mountain highlight both natural and cultural heritage. The notch provides one of the best-preserved glacial troughs in New England's alpine landscape.
GPS: 44.1707, -71.6881

☐ 🔖 ♡ **Heath Pond Bog:** Celebrated as a National Natural Landmark for exemplifying bog succession, Heath Pond transitions from open water to sphagnum mats to mature black spruce and heath shrubs. Thousands of years of peatland development are visible here, making it an outstanding site for understanding long-term wetland evolution.
GPS: 43.759423, -71.116465

☐ 🔖 ♡ **Madison Boulder:** This massive granite erratic is a National Natural Landmark as the largest known glacial boulder in North America. Measuring 83 feet long and weighing over 5,000 tons, it was carried far from its source by Ice Age glaciers. Its size and placement make it an iconic testament to glacial transport.
GPS: 43.93329, -71.162671

☐ 🔖 ♡ **Mount Monadnock:** Designated a National Natural Landmark for being one of the finest examples of an isolated erosional peak, Monadnock rises 3,165 feet with bare granite summit slopes. Its resistance to weathering left it standing while surrounding rock eroded away. Known as one of the world's most climbed mountains, it embodies monadnock geology.
GPS: 42.860833, -72.108056

☐ 🔖 ♡ **Nancy Brook Virgin Spruce Forest and Scenic Area:** This site is a National Natural Landmark for preserving one of the Northeast's last tracts of virgin red spruce. Waterfalls, narrow ravines, and high-elevation habitat in the White Mountains create unique ecological niches, offering a rare glimpse of old-growth spruce forest dynamics.
GPS: 44.1151136, -71.4133327

☐ 🔖 ♡ **Pondicherry Wildlife Refuge:** Recognized as a National Natural Landmark for its glacial basin ecosystems, Pondicherry contains ponds, marshes, peat bogs, and northern hardwood forest. Rich birdlife and plant diversity thrive here, while views of the Presidential Range from trails and boardwalks make it both biologically and scenically remarkable.
GPS: 44.377846, -71.525937

UNITED STATES EDITION

NEW HAMPSHIRE

☐ ▢ ♡ **Rhododendron Natural Area:** This preserve is a National Natural Landmark for protecting the largest native stand of great laurel rhododendron in central and southern New England. Each July, the dense understory bursts into bloom, creating a rare floral display and conserving a distinctive botanical community in New Hampshire.
GPS: 42.7804, -72.1889

☐ ▢ ♡ **Spruce Hole Bog:** Named a National Natural Landmark for being the last kettle-hole bog in southern New Hampshire, this site formed when glacial ice melted thousands of years ago. Its sphagnum moss mats and bog plants reveal classic peatland succession, offering a compact but invaluable natural archive of glacial history.
GPS: 43.126111, -70.967778

☐ ▢ ♡ **White Lake Pitch Pine:** Recognized as a National Natural Landmark for preserving a rare pitch pine–bear oak forest, this site in White Lake State Park represents fire-adapted ecosystems once widespread in sandy outwash plains. Today, it survives as a vital remnant of New England's pine–oak landscapes.
GPS: 43.8359, -71.2089

New Jersey

New Jersey's landscapes blend cascading waterfalls, whispering Pine Barrens, river valleys, and coastal marshes. With a diverse collection of state parks, national park sites, and fascinating natural landmarks, the Garden State offers scenic escapes throughout the year, from forested trails and sandy shores to vibrant seasonal vistas.

📅 Peak Season
May–October is New Jersey's peak season, bringing warm weather, blooming parks, and busy coastal towns. Summer is the height of the tourism season along the Jersey Shore, while fall draws visitors for mild weather and foliage inland.

📅 Offseason Months
November–April is the offseason, with cold temperatures and quieter beaches. Winter offers peaceful hiking and birdwatching, especially in coastal wetlands, though some areas see snow and ice.

🍃 Scenery & Nature Timing
Spring features cherry blossoms and coastal bird migrations. Summer highlights beaches, forests, and river recreation. Fall showcases colorful hardwoods in the Highlands, while winter brings migrating waterfowl and crisp coastal views.

✨ Special
New Jersey features the Pine Barrens' vast forests and bogs, the Delaware Water Gap's cliffs and waterfalls, and the barrier islands of the Jersey Shore. Seasonal bird migrations at Cape May and brilliant fall colors in the north define its natural character.

NEW JERSEY

State Parks

☐ 🔖 ♡ **Allaire State Park:** Spanning 3,205 acres in Monmouth County, this park preserves Allaire Village, a 19th-century ironworks town, along with the Pine Creek Railroad. Visitors explore historic buildings, ride seasonal trains, and hike diverse trails through forests and along the Manasquan River, making it a mix of history and outdoor recreation.

☐ 🔖 ♡ **Allamuchy Mountain State Park:** Encompassing 9,092 acres across Sussex, Warren, and Morris counties, this rugged park features 14 miles of marked trails for hiking, biking, and horseback riding. The Allamuchy Natural Area protects mature oak forests and abundant wildlife, offering a haven for outdoor enthusiasts in northern New Jersey's highlands.

☐ 🔖 ♡ **Barnegat Lighthouse State Park:** Located on Long Beach Island's northern tip, this 32-acre park features the iconic Barnegat Lighthouse, which visitors can climb for sweeping views. A maritime forest, birdwatching spots, fishing, and the short Maritime Forest Trail make this a compact yet scenic destination blending coastal ecology with maritime heritage.

☐ 🔖 ♡ **Cape May Point State Park:** Covering 244 acres at the southern tip of New Jersey, this park is world-renowned for birdwatching during fall migrations. It features the Cape May Lighthouse, World War II bunkers, trails through wetlands and meadows, and beaches for picnicking and walking. It's a perfect mix of natural beauty and cultural landmarks.

☐ 🔖 ♡ **Cheesequake State Park:** At 1,610 acres in Middlesex County, this park sits at the meeting point of salt marshes, freshwater wetlands, pine barrens, and hardwood forests. Visitors enjoy hiking trails, swimming and canoeing at Hooks Creek Lake, fishing, and nature programs. It's a rare mix of diverse ecosystems in one compact park.

☐ 🔖 ♡ **Corson's Inlet State Park:** A 341-acre preserve on the Jersey Shore between Ocean City and Strathmere, this park protects one of the last undeveloped tracts of coastline. It offers trails through dunes and estuaries, rich birdlife, fishing, and crabbing. The park highlights coastal ecology and provides a quiet alternative to busier beaches.

☐ 🔖 ♡ **Delaware and Raritan Canal State Park:** Stretching 70 miles across central New Jersey, this linear park follows a historic 19th-century canal and towpath. Flat trails are perfect for biking, walking, and jogging while the canal offers canoeing and fishing. Historic bridges, locks, and villages enrich the journey, blending recreation with heritage.

☐ 🔖 ♡ **Double Trouble State Park:** Spanning 8,495 acres in Ocean County, this Pine Barrens park preserves a historic cranberry village and sawmill, offering cultural and natural exploration. Cedar Creek flows through the park, providing canoeing, fishing, and hiking opportunities. Its mix of forested wetlands and heritage sites captures the essence of the Pinelands.

☐ 🔖 ♡ **Farny State Park:** A 4,866-acre preserve in Morris County, Farny protects mature oak forests, swamps, and streams vital for endangered species like the red-shouldered hawk. It offers quiet hiking and birdwatching in an undeveloped setting, serving as an ecological refuge and a key piece of New Jersey's northern highlands conservation lands.

☐ 🔖 ♡ **Fort Mott State Park:** Covering 124 acres in Pennsville, this park preserves 19th-century coastal fortifications built to defend the Delaware River. Visitors walk through massive gun batteries, picnic along the riverbank, and learn about military history. Scenic views of the river and nearby forts across the water complete the experience.

☐ 🔖 ♡ **Hacklebarney State Park:** Encompassing 1,186 acres in Morris County, this park is defined by the Black River's glacial valley. Trails wind past boulder-strewn streams, waterfalls, and forests rich in rare plants like American ginseng. Popular for hiking, fishing, and picnicking, it provides cool wooded scenery and rugged terrain close to suburban New Jersey.

☐ 🔖 ♡ **High Point State Park:** Spanning 16,091 acres in Sussex County, this park is home to New Jersey's highest elevation and its 220-foot granite obelisk monument. Trails traverse forested ridges, lakes, and meadows, with sweeping views of the Kittatinny Mountains and Delaware Water Gap. Swimming, camping, and winter sports make it a year-round destination.

☐ 🔖 ♡ **Hopatcong State Park:** A 163-acre park in Morris County, it provides access to Lake Hopatcong, New Jersey's largest freshwater lake. Popular for boating, fishing, swimming, and picnicking, it also houses the Lake Hopatcong Historical Museum. With scenic views and year-round activities, the park offers both recreational opportunities and insight into the region's resort history.

NEW JERSEY

☐ 🔖 ♡ **Island Beach State Park:** This 3,003-acre barrier island preserve in Ocean County protects one of the last undeveloped shorelines on the Atlantic coast. Visitors enjoy swimming, kayaking, fishing, and birdwatching among dunes, maritime forests, and salt marshes. Its pristine beaches and wildlife habitats, including nesting ospreys, showcase New Jersey's coastal wilderness.

☐ 🔖 ♡ **Kittatinny Valley State Park:** Encompassing 5,656 acres in Sussex County, this park features glacial lakes, limestone outcrops, and fields along the Kittatinny Ridge. Trails support hiking, biking, and horseback riding, while its lakes invite boating and fishing. The park also contains the Aeroflex-Andover Airport and a Forest Fire Service airbase, blending recreation with conservation.

☐ 🔖 ♡ **Liberty State Park:** Located on 1,212 acres in Jersey City, this waterfront park offers unmatched views of the Statue of Liberty, Ellis Island, and Manhattan. Visitors stroll Liberty Walk, visit the "Empty Sky" 9/11 Memorial, explore the Liberty Science Center, or picnic on green lawns. It is both a cultural landmark and a recreational hub for urban New Jersey.

☐ 🔖 ♡ **Long Pond Ironworks State Park:** A 6,911-acre site in Passaic County preserving the ruins of an 18th–19th century ironworking village. Trails lead through forested hills and along the Monksville Reservoir, offering scenic views and heritage interpretation. Visitors explore restored historic structures, hike, and enjoy a park where nature and industrial history meet.

☐ 🔖 ♡ **Monmouth Battlefield State Park:** This 1,818-acre park in Monmouth County preserves the site of the pivotal June 1778 Revolutionary War battle. Features include an interpretive center, historic farmhouses, and open fields where reenactments are held annually. Visitors hike, picnic, and learn about colonial history while enjoying a landscape of meadows and woodlands.

☐ 🔖 ♡ **Parvin State Park:** A 2,092-acre park in Salem County that combines Pine Barrens swamps, hardwood forests, and wetlands. Parvin Lake provides swimming, boating, and fishing, while trails highlight wildflowers and wildlife. The park also carries history as a Civilian Conservation Corps site and World War II internment camp, offering both recreation and cultural depth.

☐ 🔖 ♡ **Pigeon Swamp State Park:** A 1,078-acre natural preserve in Middlesex County, this park protects hardwood forests, wetlands, and ponds once used by nesting passenger pigeons. Managed for conservation and environmental education, it offers quiet hiking, birdwatching, and wildlife observation. Its blend of ecological value and history makes it a rare green refuge in central New Jersey.

☐ 🔖 ♡ **Princeton Battlefield State Park:** Covering 681 acres in Mercer County, this park commemorates the January 1777 Battle of Princeton. Visitors tour the Clarke House, explore preserved battlefield landscapes, and connect with the Revolutionary War through exhibits and walking paths. It's both a historic site and a scenic open space tied to America's independence.

☐ 🔖 ♡ **Rancocas State Park:** This 1,252-acre park in Burlington County protects tidal marshes, forests, and meadows along the North Branch of Rancocas Creek. Trails wind through quiet landscapes ideal for hiking, birdwatching, and wildlife observation. Its wetlands are a vital habitat for migratory birds, making it both a recreational and ecological destination.

☐ 🔖 ♡ **Ringwood State Park:** Encompassing 4,444 acres in Passaic County, this park combines history, horticulture, and recreation. Visitors tour Ringwood Manor and the New Jersey Botanical Garden at Skylands Manor, hike forested trails, or swim and boat at Shepherd Lake. Its mix of cultural landmarks and natural beauty makes it one of New Jersey's most diverse parks.

☐ 🔖 ♡ **Stephens State Park:** An 805-acre park in Warren County, it lines the Musconetcong River and preserves remnants of the historic Morris Canal. Hiking, fishing, and picnicking are popular, with scenic riverbanks and woodland trails providing natural beauty. The park's canal locks and towpaths also highlight New Jersey's industrial heritage within a tranquil setting.

☐ 🔖 ♡ **Swartswood State Park:** Established in 1914 as New Jersey's first state park, this 3,460-acre site in Sussex County is centered on Swartswood and Little Swartswood Lakes, formed by glaciers. Known for boating, fishing, and swimming, it also offers camping and hiking in a serene wooded setting. Its history and scenic waters make it a long-time visitor favorite.

☐ 🔖 ♡ **Voorhees State Park:** A 1,336-acre park in Hunterdon County with trails, campgrounds, and scenic overlooks of Round Valley and Spruce Run Reservoirs. It is home to an observatory with New Jersey's largest publicly accessible telescope, offering stargazing programs. Combining astronomy, hiking, and natural beauty, the park offers unique recreation opportunities.

☐ 🔖 ♡ **Washington Crossing State Park:** Spanning 3,575 acres in Mercer County, this park marks the site where George Washington crossed the Delaware River in 1776. Visitors explore historic buildings, battlefields, and interpretive centers while enjoying hiking, birding, and picnicking. The park blends Revolutionary War history with diverse natural landscapes.

NEW JERSEY

☐ 🔖 ♡ **Washington Rock State Park:** A 52-acre park in Somerset County, it preserves a vantage point George Washington used in 1777 to monitor British troops. Today, visitors enjoy panoramic views, picnic areas, and walking paths. Small but historically significant, it offers insight into Revolutionary strategy and scenic overlooks of central New Jersey.

☐ 🔖 ♡ **Wawayanda State Park:** A vast 34,350-acre preserve spanning Sussex and Passaic counties, this park features 60 miles of trails, including 20 along the Appalachian Trail. Visitors hike Bearfort Mountain, paddle glacial lakes, and explore wetlands teeming with wildlife. Its size, rugged terrain, and natural diversity make it one of New Jersey's most spectacular wild parks.

National Parks

☐ 🔖 ♡ **Appalachian National Scenic Trail:** Stretching over 2,100 miles from Georgia to Maine, this world-famous trail winds through forests, ridgelines, and mountain peaks across the Eastern U.S. In New Jersey, hikers enjoy scenic ridge walks and river views, while the full route offers ecosystems from southern hardwood forests to northern spruce, making it a premier long-distance hiking adventure.

☐ 🔖 ♡ **Delaware Water Gap National Recreation Area:** Spanning New Jersey and Pennsylvania along the Delaware River, this park protects dramatic river valleys, waterfalls, and forested ridges. Visitors hike the Appalachian Trail, paddle quiet waters, camp, or explore cultural sites from colonial settlements to Native American heritage. Its blend of scenery and history makes it a regional gem.

☐ 🔖 ♡ **Gateway National Recreation Area:** Located in New York and New Jersey, this coastal park features beaches, dunes, salt marshes, and bird sanctuaries alongside historic sites. Popular spots include Sandy Hook's seashore and Fort Wadsworth overlooking New York Harbor. Visitors hike, swim, picnic, and explore cultural landmarks like Floyd Bennett Field's Aviation Museum.

☐ 🔖 ♡ **Great Egg Harbor River:** A National Wild and Scenic River in southern New Jersey, it meanders for 129 miles through pine forests, tidal marshes, and historic communities. Known for canoeing, kayaking, and fishing, it also provides critical wildlife habitat. Visitors enjoy tranquil paddling, scenic beauty, and glimpses of cultural heritage tied to the river's historic role.

☐ 🔖 ♡ **Morristown National Historical Park:** Preserving Revolutionary War encampments in Morristown, New Jersey, this park marks where George Washington and the Continental Army endured the harsh winter of 1779–1780. Visitors tour the Ford Mansion headquarters, hike battlefield trails, and explore museums that interpret the struggle, sacrifices, and resilience of America's early military forces.

☐ 🔖 ♡ **New Jersey Pinelands National Reserve:** Established in 1978 as the nation's first National Reserve, this vast 1.1-million-acre landscape spans seven counties and preserves one of North America's most unique ecosystems. Known for sandy soils, dwarf pine forests, cedar swamps, and rare wildlife, it protects both natural and cultural heritage. Visitors explore trails, rivers, historic villages, and the quiet wilderness of the Pine Barrens.

☐ 🔖 ♡ **Paterson Great Falls National Historical Park:** Centered on the 77-foot Great Falls of the Passaic River, this park highlights Paterson's role as America's first planned industrial city. Visitors admire the dramatic falls, walk historic mill sites, and learn how harnessed water power fueled textile, locomotive, and aviation industries that shaped early U.S. manufacturing.

☐ 🔖 ♡ **Statue of Liberty National Monument:** Rising from Liberty Island in New York Harbor, the Statue of Liberty is a global icon of freedom and democracy. Visitors explore the pedestal and crown, learn about its symbolism, and visit Ellis Island's Immigration Museum, which tells the story of millions who entered America seeking new lives and opportunities.

☐ 🔖 ♡ **Thomas Edison National Historical Park:** In West Orange, New Jersey, this site preserves the inventor's home and laboratory where innovations like the phonograph, electric light, and motion picture camera took shape. Visitors step into workshops filled with original equipment, explore Edison's library, and see how his creative vision transformed modern life and technology.

NEW JERSEY

State & National Forests

☐ 🔖 ♡ **Bass River State Forest:** Spanning 23,563 acres in Ocean County, this Pine Barrens forest is centered on Lake Absegami, where visitors swim, fish, boat, and picnic. Trails wind through pine woods and remnants of cranberry bogs, blending recreation with history. With campgrounds and quiet scenery, it's a peaceful gateway into the natural and cultural landscape of the Pinelands.

☐ 🔖 ♡ **Belleplain State Forest:** Covering 21,320 acres in Cape May and Cumberland counties, this forest offers over 40 miles of trails, camping, boating, and fishing. Its pine-oak woodlands and wetlands create rich wildlife habitat, ideal for birdwatching and photography. Popular for year-round recreation, it also preserves unique ecosystems of southern New Jersey's coastal forests.

☐ 🔖 ♡ **Brendan T. Byrne State Forest:** At 37,000 acres, this Pine Barrens forest features long trails, including part of the Batona Trail, and is a sanctuary for the endangered Pine Barrens tree frog. Visitors explore lakes, cedar swamps, and sandy paths while enjoying hiking, camping, and fishing. Its diverse habitats and quiet landscapes make it a premier nature destination.

☐ 🔖 ♡ **Jenny Jump State Forest:** A 4,466-acre forest in Warren County, it's famed for glacial ridges, dense woods, and high vistas from Jenny Jump Mountain. Trails lead to fire towers and overlooks of the Delaware Valley. With campgrounds and rich natural features, it's popular for hiking, stargazing, and connecting with the area's geologic history and scenic views.

☐ 🔖 ♡ **Norvin Green State Forest:** Spanning 4,269 acres in Passaic and Bergen counties, this rugged forest offers miles of trails, many with sweeping vistas of the Wyanokie Wilderness. Wildlife thrives in its varied habitats, and a portion of the Appalachian Trail crosses nearby. It's a top destination for hikers seeking dramatic views, remote woodlands, and natural beauty.

☐ 🔖 ♡ **Penn State Forest:** A 3,366-acre preserve in Burlington County, it centers on Oswego Lake and the Oswego River. Surrounded by Pine Barrens ecosystems of forests and wetlands, it's a haven for birdwatchers, paddlers, and hikers. Picnic spots and quiet trails provide a mix of recreation and solitude, showcasing the unique ecological character of the Pinelands.

☐ 🔖 ♡ **Ramapo Mountain State Forest:** Covering 4,269 acres in Passaic and Bergen counties, this forest features scenic trails and the Ramapo Lake Natural Area. Rolling highlands, mixed hardwood forests, and lakes attract hikers, birdwatchers, and photographers. Its diverse ecosystems make it a prized retreat for those exploring the rugged beauty of northern New Jersey.

☐ 🔖 ♡ **Stokes State Forest:** Spanning 16,025 acres in Sussex County, Stokes offers camping, fishing, and 60 miles of hiking trails, including sections of the Appalachian Trail. Tillman Ravine Natural Area is a highlight, with waterfalls and mossy gorges. Known for fall foliage, lush forests, and wildlife, it provides a peaceful setting for outdoor recreation and discovery.

☐ 🔖 ♡ **Wharton State Forest:** At 115,000 acres, this is New Jersey's largest state forest, covering vast stretches of the Pine Barrens. Visitors enjoy canoeing the Mullica River, camping, and exploring Batsto Village, a preserved 18th-century industrial site. Streams, cedar swamps, and pine forests provide diverse habitats, making it a cornerstone of the Pinelands National Reserve.

☐ 🔖 ♡ **Worthington State Forest:** This 6,421-acre forest in Warren County borders the Delaware Water Gap, offering trails with sweeping ridge and river views. It protects ecosystems from woodlands to fields and wetlands. Popular for camping, hiking, and paddling, it provides access to the Appalachian Trail and highlights one of New Jersey's most scenic natural corridors.

National Scenic Byways & All-American Roads

☐ 🔖 ♡ **Bayshore Heritage Scenic Byway:** Stretching along the Delaware Bay and River through Salem, Cumberland, and Cape May counties, this byway highlights small towns, historic shipyards, lighthouses, and marshlands. Travelers experience the quiet side of coastal New Jersey, with opportunities for birdwatching, seafood sampling, and exploring villages steeped in maritime and agricultural tradition.

☐ 🔖 ♡ **Delaware River Scenic Byway:** Running along Route 29 from Trenton north to Frenchtown, this byway follows the Delaware River's historic corridor. It passes Revolutionary War sites, canal locks, and charming river towns. Scenic overlooks, preserved farmland, and quiet stretches of waterway showcase the cultural and natural richness of the Delaware Valley, blending history with riverside beauty.

NEW JERSEY

☐ ◫ ♡ **Millstone Valley Scenic Byway:** Winding through Somerset County, this byway showcases the Millstone River Valley's Revolutionary War heritage and canal-era history. Stone farmhouses, canal towpaths, and historic districts dot the landscape. With its mix of scenic farmland, preserved open space, and cultural landmarks, the route offers a glimpse into New Jersey's colonial past and rural charm.

☐ ◫ ♡ **Palisades Scenic Byway:** Following the Palisades Interstate Parkway, this byway runs atop dramatic Hudson River cliffs in Bergen County. Visitors stop at overlooks with sweeping views of New York City, the river, and the wooded Palisades. The route connects to picnic areas, hiking trails, and preserved parkland, blending urban proximity with natural grandeur along one of New Jersey's most iconic landscapes.

☐ ◫ ♡ **Pine Barrens Scenic Byway:** Traversing more than 130 miles through the Pinelands National Reserve, this byway highlights dwarf pine forests, cedar swamps, and clear streams. It connects historic villages, cranberry bogs, and cultural landmarks, offering access to hiking, paddling, and wildlife watching. The route immerses travelers in the unique ecological and cultural richness of the Pine Barrens.

☐ ◫ ♡ **Western Highlands Scenic Byway:** Located in Sussex County, this byway winds through New Jersey's rugged Highlands, where mountains, valleys, and forests dominate the landscape. Scenic overlooks reveal panoramic views, while rural roads pass farmland and historic hamlets. Outdoor opportunities like hiking and cycling abound, making it a gateway to the natural beauty of the state's northwestern corner.

State Scenic Byways

☐ ◫ ♡ **Bayshore Heritage Byway:** Winding along the Delaware Bay and River through Cape May, Cumberland, and Salem counties, this byway links historic towns, lighthouses, farms, and marshes. Travelers encounter rich maritime heritage, birding hotspots, seafood hubs, and agricultural landscapes, all framed by serene coastal vistas and quiet rural charm.

☐ ◫ ♡ **Delaware River Scenic Byway:** Following Route 29 from Trenton north to Frenchtown, this scenic road traces the Delaware River's historic edge. Along the way are Revolutionary-era sites, canal remnants, riverside towns, and shaded riverbanks. It blends cultural resonance and natural beauty, inviting leisurely stops for history and river views.

☐ ◫ ♡ **Henry Hudson Drive:** Tucked along the base of the Palisades Cliffs, this short and scenic drive runs under the George Washington Bridge. It provides sweeping views of the Hudson River and NYC skyline, and connects to picnic areas and parkland. Though modest in length, its vistas and connection to the towering cliffs make it uniquely charming.

☐ ◫ ♡ **Millstone Valley Scenic Byway:** Traversing the Millstone River Valley in Somerset County, this historic route threads together canal-era relics, Revolutionary War landmarks, stone farmhouses, and lush farmland. Trails and towpaths meander through villages and preserved open space—offering a glimpse into colonial rural life and natural beauty.

☐ ◫ ♡ **Palisades Scenic Byway:** Tracing the Palisades Interstate Parkway atop New Jersey's Hudson River cliffs, this byway offers dramatic overlook views of Manhattan and the river. Scenic pull-offs, wooded parkland, and hiking access points line the route, merging urban-edge grandeur with serene natural landscapes along one of the state's most iconic drives.

☐ ◫ ♡ **Upper Freehold Historic Farmland Byway:** Stretching across Monmouth County's countryside between Allentown and Walnford, this byway winds past working farms, rolling fields, and historic rural hamlets. It evokes agricultural heritage through scenic country roads lined with barns, farmhouses, and vistas of farmland nostalgia in New Jersey's heartland.

☐ ◫ ♡ **Warren Heritage Scenic Byway:** Traveling along Route 57 through Warren County, this route threads mountain and valley scenery with historic sites tied to the Morris Canal. Along winding roads through riverside and rural scenes, travelers encounter scenic overlook views, preserved farmland, and roots of early state transportation history.

☐ ◫ ♡ **Western Highlands Scenic Byway:** Carving through the rugged Highlands of Sussex County, this byway climbs mountain ridges and drops through forested valleys. Panoramic overlooks reveal sweeping vistas of hills and farmland, while rural roads pass through forest and small communities—highlighting the vibrant, natural character of northwestern New Jersey.

NEW JERSEY

National Natural Landmarks

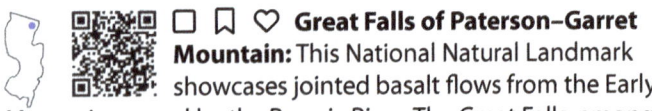 **Great Falls of Paterson–Garret Mountain:** This National Natural Landmark showcases jointed basalt flows from the Early Mesozoic, carved by the Passaic River. The Great Falls, among the largest waterfalls east of the Mississippi by volume, highlight both dramatic geologic history and the role of waterpower in shaping Paterson, one of America's earliest planned industrial cities.
GPS: 40.916189, -74.181597

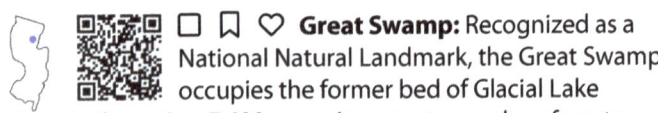 **Great Swamp:** Recognized as a National Natural Landmark, the Great Swamp occupies the former bed of Glacial Lake Passaic. Spanning 7,600 acres, it protects marshes, forests, and meadows shaped by Ice Age retreat. Now a federal wildlife refuge, it provides critical stopover habitat for migratory birds and threatened species in suburban New Jersey.
GPS: 40.708333, -74.466667

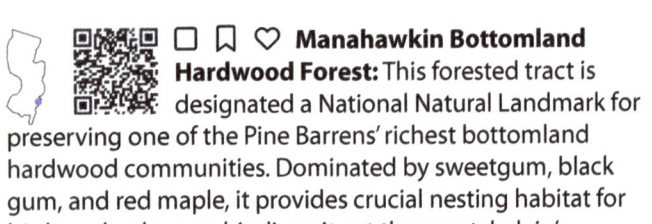 **Manahawkin Bottomland Hardwood Forest:** This forested tract is designated a National Natural Landmark for preserving one of the Pine Barrens' richest bottomland hardwood communities. Dominated by sweetgum, black gum, and red maple, it provides crucial nesting habitat for birds and enhances biodiversity at the coastal plain's ecological edge.
GPS: 39.685591, -74.221745

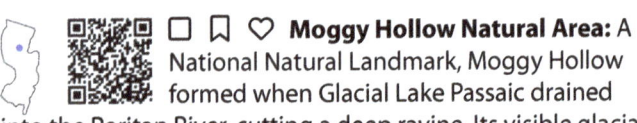 **Moggy Hollow Natural Area:** A National Natural Landmark, Moggy Hollow formed when Glacial Lake Passaic drained into the Raritan River, cutting a deep ravine. Its visible glacial sediments, erratics, and bedrock exposures reveal post-glacial hydrology. Today, the preserve offers a unique glimpse into New Jersey's glacial history.
GPS: 40.67351, -74.614055

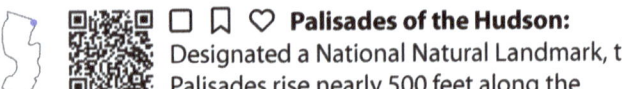 **Palisades of the Hudson:** Designated a National Natural Landmark, the Palisades rise nearly 500 feet along the Hudson River. Their sheer diabase cliffs, formed from lava intrusions 200 million years ago, are celebrated for geological importance, scenic grandeur, and preservation as a natural border shared by New Jersey and New York.
GPS: 40.964507, -73.908591

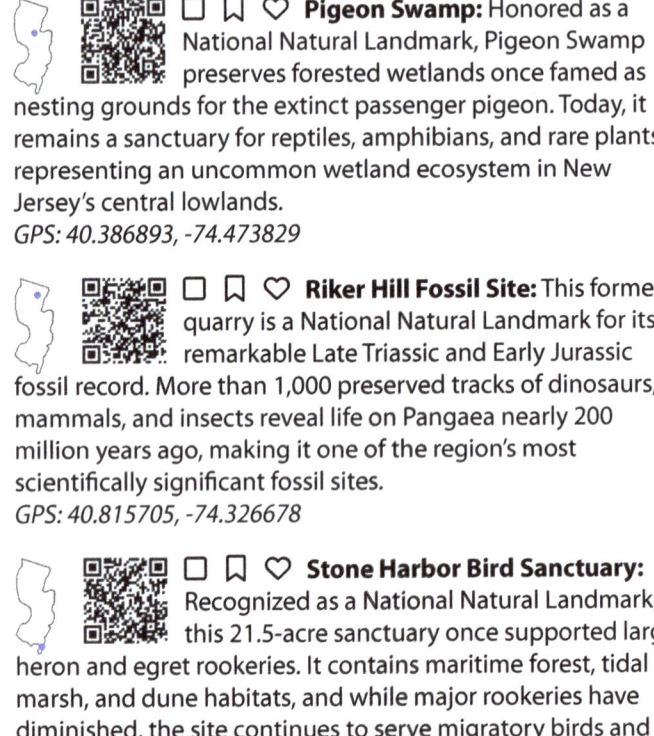 **Pigeon Swamp:** Honored as a National Natural Landmark, Pigeon Swamp preserves forested wetlands once famed as nesting grounds for the extinct passenger pigeon. Today, it remains a sanctuary for reptiles, amphibians, and rare plants, representing an uncommon wetland ecosystem in New Jersey's central lowlands.
GPS: 40.386893, -74.473829

Riker Hill Fossil Site: This former quarry is a National Natural Landmark for its remarkable Late Triassic and Early Jurassic fossil record. More than 1,000 preserved tracks of dinosaurs, mammals, and insects reveal life on Pangaea nearly 200 million years ago, making it one of the region's most scientifically significant fossil sites.
GPS: 40.815705, -74.326678

Stone Harbor Bird Sanctuary: Recognized as a National Natural Landmark, this 21.5-acre sanctuary once supported large heron and egret rookeries. It contains maritime forest, tidal marsh, and dune habitats, and while major rookeries have diminished, the site continues to serve migratory birds and coastal environmental education.
GPS: 39.04164, -74.76879

 **Sunfish Pond:** This glacial tarn atop the Kittatinny Ridge is a National Natural Landmark for its pristine high-elevation lake ecosystem. Nestled in Worthington State Forest, it became nationally known when Justice William O. Douglas cited it in a dissent advocating wilderness preservation, symbolizing the importance of natural spaces.
GPS: 41.003043, -75.073099

 **Troy Meadows:** Designated a National Natural Landmark for its unspoiled freshwater wetlands, Troy Meadows lies in the Passaic River basin. Its marshes, ponds, and meadows provide vital habitat for migratory birds, amphibians, and native wetland plants, representing one of New Jersey's last large natural marsh systems.
GPS: 40.846026, -74.37928

 **William L. Hutcheson Memorial Forest:** This 500-acre site is a National Natural Landmark for protecting one of New Jersey's last virgin old-growth forests. At its heart lies a 65-acre core of untouched oak, hickory, and ash, with trees over 300 years old. Co-managed for education, it remains a living classroom in forest ecology.
GPS: 40.500405, -74.567245

UNITED STATES EDITION

New Mexico

New Mexico's natural wonders include dazzling gypsum dunes, ancient cliff dwellings, expansive deserts, and forested mountains. With its vibrant array of state parks, national forests, iconic national parks, and remarkable natural landmarks, the Land of Enchantment lives up to its name with endless skies, vivid colors, and timeless desert beauty.

📅 Peak Season
March–May and September–October are New Mexico's peak seasons, with mild temperatures, clear skies, and colorful desert landscapes. Spring and fall are ideal for hiking, sightseeing, and exploring national monuments.

📅 Offseason Months
June–August brings extreme heat in southern deserts, though mountain areas stay pleasant. November–February is quieter, with snow in higher elevations and mild days in the valleys and deserts.

🍃 Scenery & Nature Timing
Spring brings desert blooms and clear views. Summer highlights alpine meadows and afternoon monsoon storms. Fall offers golden aspens in the mountains, while winter contrasts snowy peaks with red rock canyons and blue skies.

✨ Special
New Mexico showcases the White Sands' shimmering dunes, the volcanic fields of El Malpaís, and the gypsum caverns of Carlsbad Caverns. The Rio Grande Gorge, Ship Rock, and annual monsoon lightning displays reveal its dramatic desert beauty.

THE ROAMER'S GUIDE

NEW MEXICO

State Parks

☐ 🔖 ♡ **Bluewater Lake State Park:** Nestled in the Zuni Mountains, this park centers on a 1,200-acre reservoir known for trout and tiger muskie fishing. Popular for boating, hiking, and birdwatching, it offers camping under big skies and views of mesas and pine forests. Its blend of water and wilderness makes it a refreshing retreat in western New Mexico.

☐ 🔖 ♡ **Bottomless Lakes State Park:** Near Roswell, this park features vivid green sinkholes called cenotes, once thought bottomless. Lea Lake allows swimming and paddling, while trails circle other lakes for hiking and birdwatching. Stargazing is excellent thanks to dark skies, and geology enthusiasts enjoy the park's striking karst formations and desert setting.

☐ 🔖 ♡ **Brantley Lake State Park:** On the Pecos River near Carlsbad, this 4,000-acre reservoir offers warm-weather recreation with boating, fishing, and lakeside camping. Its desert surroundings create a serene backdrop for hiking, picnics, and wildlife viewing. Brantley provides an oasis of water and outdoor activities in New Mexico's arid southeastern region.

☐ 🔖 ♡ **Caballo Lake State Park:** Spread across 11,500 acres on the Rio Grande, this reservoir attracts boaters, anglers, and birdwatchers. Trails weave through desert hills with views of the Caballo Mountains, while campgrounds line the shore. It's a quieter alternative to nearby Elephant Butte, offering wide waters and a relaxed natural setting.

☐ 🔖 ♡ **Cerrillos Hills State Park:** Off the Turquoise Trail south of Santa Fe, this park blends history with scenery. Trails climb ridges for sweeping views of the Sandia and Ortiz Mountains, while interpretive signs highlight mining ruins from the 19th century. Its high-desert terrain provides peaceful hikes rich in both geology and cultural heritage.

☐ 🔖 ♡ **Cimarron Canyon State Park:** In the Sangre de Cristo Mountains, this 2,000-acre park follows the Cimarron River through a dramatic canyon. Known for trout fishing, it also features trails through forests of spruce and aspen. Visitors find historic sites like the Old Mill, plus campgrounds surrounded by rugged cliffs and alpine beauty.

☐ 🔖 ♡ **City of Rocks State Park:** Between Silver City and Deming, this park showcases volcanic rock pinnacles rising like a natural city skyline. Hiking trails wind among the giant formations, popular with climbers, campers, and stargazers. Its surreal landscape of boulders and open desert creates one of New Mexico's most unique natural attractions.

☐ 🔖 ♡ **Clayton Lake State Park:** In the northeast plains, this reservoir park is renowned for a well-preserved dinosaur trackway. Families can fish, camp, and boat on the 170-acre lake, then explore footprints left by ancient creatures. The combination of paleontology and recreation makes Clayton a rare mix of science and outdoor fun.

☐ 🔖 ♡ **Conchas Lake State Park:** Along the Canadian River, this large 16,400-acre reservoir offers boating, water sports, and quiet fishing coves. Desert vistas surround sandy campgrounds, while trails provide birdwatching and wildlife encounters. Conchas combines big-lake recreation with the peaceful charm of New Mexico's eastern mesas.

☐ 🔖 ♡ **Coyote Creek State Park:** Hidden in a forested valley of the Sangre de Cristos, this small park centers on a stocked trout stream. Campers and anglers enjoy the shaded setting, while hikers explore trails under aspens and evergreens. Its cool mountain environment makes it a refreshing escape in northern New Mexico.

☐ 🔖 ♡ **Eagle Nest Lake State Park:** In the Moreno Valley at 8,300 feet, this 2,400-acre lake offers boating and exceptional fishing for trout and salmon. Wildlife abounds, with elk and eagles often spotted nearby. Campgrounds and trails provide mountain scenery, making it a prime high-altitude retreat in the southern Rockies.

☐ 🔖 ♡ **El Vado Lake State Park:** Tucked near the Rio Chama, this 3,200-acre reservoir provides boating, fishing, and kayaking in a peaceful, less-crowded setting. Campgrounds and hiking trails connect to nearby Heron Lake. Surrounded by forests and mesas, El Vado is prized for quiet recreation and scenic New Mexico landscapes.

NEW MEXICO

☐ 🔖 ♡ **Elephant Butte Lake State Park:** The state's largest park, centered on a 40,000-acre reservoir of the Rio Grande, is a hub for water recreation. Boating, fishing, jet skiing, and swimming dominate summer, while campgrounds line the shore. Desert mountains frame expansive views, creating a lively yet scenic vacation spot.

☐ 🔖 ♡ **Fenton Lake State Park:** In the Jemez Mountains, this small 37-acre lake offers tranquil fishing and camping in a pine forest setting. Families enjoy picnicking by the water, hiking short trails, and spotting abundant wildlife. With its mountain backdrop and intimate feel, Fenton is a beloved weekend getaway.

☐ 🔖 ♡ **Heron Lake State Park:** This 5,900-acre no-wake lake is ideal for paddling and fishing, especially for kokanee salmon and trout. Surrounded by mountains, it features campgrounds, hiking trails, and cross-country skiing in winter. Heron offers quiet beauty and excellent wildlife viewing in a pristine northern New Mexico setting.

☐ 🔖 ♡ **Hyde Memorial State Park:** Just outside Santa Fe in the Sangre de Cristo Mountains, this historic park offers year-round recreation. Visitors hike trails in summer and enjoy cross-country skiing and snowshoeing in winter. Campgrounds and picnic sites sit among ponderosa pines, while scenic views stretch toward the city and surrounding peaks.

☐ 🔖 ♡ **Leasburg Dam State Park:** Along the Rio Grande near Las Cruces, this park combines desert scenery with riparian habitat. Visitors fish in the river, hike trails through cactus-studded terrain, and watch for migratory birds. Interpretive exhibits highlight early irrigation and Mesilla Valley history, making it both a natural and cultural destination.

☐ 🔖 ♡ **Living Desert Zoo & Gardens State Park:** In Carlsbad, this unique park blends a zoo and botanical garden to showcase Chihuahuan Desert life. Trails lead past exhibits of native animals like pronghorn and reptiles, along with desert plants from cacti to agaves. It's an educational experience emphasizing conservation and regional ecology.

☐ 🔖 ♡ **Manzano Mountains State Park:** Nestled on the eastern slopes of the Manzano Mountains, this park offers shaded camping and picnic areas beneath tall ponderosa pines. Trails climb through mixed forests rich with birds and wildlife. Its cooler temperatures and proximity to Albuquerque make it a favorite mountain escape for hikers and campers.

☐ 🔖 ♡ **Mesilla Valley Bosque State Park:** A riverside preserve near Las Cruces, this park protects a section of the Rio Grande bosque. Trails and viewing platforms provide excellent birdwatching, especially during migrations. Cottonwood trees, wetlands, and interpretive programs highlight the importance of this riparian ecosystem for both wildlife and people.

☐ 🔖 ♡ **Morphy Lake State Park:** Tucked high in the Sangre de Cristos, this 37-acre alpine lake offers peaceful fishing and picnicking. Campers enjoy the cool mountain air, while trails wind through spruce and fir forests. Its small size and secluded location make Morphy Lake a quiet retreat for those seeking solitude and natural beauty.

☐ 🔖 ♡ **Navajo Lake State Park:** One of New Mexico's largest reservoirs at 15,000 acres, Navajo Lake is a hub for boating, fishing, and camping. Surrounded by mesas and canyonlands, the park offers trails, marinas, and varied wildlife. It serves as a gateway to the San Juan River, famous for world-class trout fishing.

☐ 🔖 ♡ **Oasis State Park:** Near Portales in eastern New Mexico, this desert park is named for its tree-lined fishing pond and surrounding dunes. Stocked with trout and catfish, it's popular for family outings, picnicking, and birdwatching. Trails explore the sandy landscape, offering a contrast of water and desert habitat in one setting.

☐ 🔖 ♡ **Oliver Lee Memorial State Park:** At the base of the Sacramento Mountains near Alamogordo, this park combines rugged desert scenery with historic ranch remains. Trails lead into Dog Canyon for hiking and wildlife viewing. Campgrounds offer sweeping views, while interpretive exhibits share the story of pioneer rancher Oliver Lee.

☐ 🔖 ♡ **Pancho Villa State Park:** In Columbus near the Mexican border, this park commemorates the 1916 raid led by Pancho Villa. Visitors explore a museum and historic structures, camp under desert skies, and hike trails through wide-open landscapes. The park blends history, culture, and recreation in a unique borderland setting.

☐ 🔖 ♡ **Pecos Canyon State Park:** Along the Pecos River, this newer park protects scenic canyon landscapes ideal for fishing, camping, and hiking. Visitors enjoy the cool waters, lush forests, and rugged rock walls. Wildlife thrives in the riparian corridor, making it a peaceful outdoor destination just east of the Sangre de Cristo Mountains.

NEW MEXICO

☐ 🔖 ♡ **Percha Dam State Park:** Located on the Rio Grande south of Truth or Consequences, this small riverside park centers on a historic diversion dam. Shady cottonwoods make it a prime spot for camping, picnicking, and birdwatching, especially during spring migrations. Its peaceful setting along the river offers a quiet contrast to nearby larger reservoirs.

☐ 🔖 ♡ **Rio Grande Nature Center State Park:** In Albuquerque, this urban park preserves bosque habitat along the Rio Grande. Trails and observation areas wind through wetlands, meadows, and cottonwood groves, providing outstanding birdwatching. An interpretive center highlights river ecology, making it both a recreational escape and an educational resource.

☐ 🔖 ♡ **Rockhound State Park:** Nestled in the Little Florida Mountains near Deming, this park is famous for allowing visitors to collect rocks and minerals. Trails lead through rugged desert hills, popular with geology enthusiasts and hikers alike. Campgrounds provide access to striking landscapes, and dark skies make it excellent for stargazing.

☐ 🔖 ♡ **Santa Rosa Lake State Park:** East of Santa Rosa, this 3,800-acre reservoir draws anglers, boaters, and campers. Surrounded by high plains and mesas, the park offers hiking, birdwatching, and picnicking in a tranquil setting. With wide-open views and quiet waters, it provides a relaxing retreat for outdoor recreation in eastern New Mexico.

☐ 🔖 ♡ **Storrie Lake State Park:** Near Las Vegas, this 1,100-acre lake offers boating, fishing, and camping in a Sangre de Cristo mountain backdrop. Windsurfing and sailing are popular, while campgrounds and picnic areas line the shore. Its proximity to town makes it a convenient escape while still offering wildlife and scenic views.

☐ 🔖 ♡ **Sugarite Canyon State Park:** Just north of Raton on the Colorado border, this canyon park features forests, meadows, and two small lakes. Trails climb to historic coal-mining sites and scenic overlooks. Fishing, hiking, and camping draw visitors, while its high elevation provides cool summer escapes and excellent wildlife viewing.

☐ 🔖 ♡ **Sumner Lake State Park:** On the plains near Fort Sumner, this 4,500-acre reservoir offers fishing, boating, and camping in a wide-open desert landscape. Birdwatchers enjoy spotting waterfowl and eagles, while campgrounds overlook the lake. Its blend of water recreation and quiet high-desert scenery makes it a versatile outdoor destination.

☐ 🔖 ♡ **Ute Lake State Park:** Spanning 8,200 acres along the Canadian River, this long reservoir is ideal for boating, fishing, and watersports. Campgrounds and coves line the shoreline, while trails offer birdwatching and desert vistas. Its vast waters and remote setting make Ute a popular recreation hub in eastern New Mexico.

☐ 🔖 ♡ **Villanueva State Park:** Tucked along the Pecos River in a red sandstone canyon, this small park offers riverside camping, hiking, and picnicking. Trails climb to panoramic views of the canyon walls, while cottonwoods line the water. Its mix of striking scenery and peaceful atmosphere makes it a hidden gem for nature lovers.

National Parks

☐ 🔖 ♡ **Aztec Ruins National Monument:** Preserving a 12th-century Ancestral Puebloan settlement in northwestern New Mexico, this site features the Great House with more than 400 rooms and a reconstructed kiva. Visitors walk through multi-story ruins, learn about ancient trade networks, and experience the ingenuity of a community that thrived over 900 years ago.

☐ 🔖 ♡ **Bandelier National Monument:** Near Los Alamos, this monument protects cliff dwellings and masonry homes built by the Ancestral Puebloans. Trails climb into volcanic tuff caves called cavates and pass through scenic canyons and mesas. Visitors explore archaeological sites, learn about centuries of Native life, and enjoy the rugged beauty of the Jemez Mountains.

NEW MEXICO

 **Capulin Volcano National Monument:** In northeastern New Mexico, this extinct cinder cone rises from the plains as part of the Raton-Clayton Volcanic Field. A road leads nearly to the rim, where trails circle the crater and descend inside. Panoramic views stretch for miles, offering a vivid look at the region's volcanic past.

Carlsbad Caverns National Park: Beneath the Chihuahuan Desert lies a network of more than 100 limestone caves, carved by sulfuric acid over time. Visitors explore the Big Room, one of the world's largest underground chambers, and other spectacular formations. Summer evenings feature the famous bat flight, when thousands of Mexican free-tailed bats emerge.

 **Chaco Culture National Historical Park:** A UNESCO World Heritage Site, Chaco preserves monumental ruins of the Ancestral Puebloans in northwestern New Mexico. Visitors explore great houses, kivas, and roads aligned with astronomical events. The park reveals a sophisticated culture of trade, ceremony, and engineering that flourished between A.D. 850 and 1250.

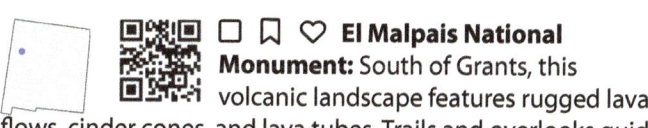 **El Malpais National Monument:** South of Grants, this volcanic landscape features rugged lava flows, cinder cones, and lava tubes. Trails and overlooks guide visitors through terrain formed by ancient eruptions, while sandstone bluffs offer panoramic views. Despite its harsh name, "The Badlands," the monument is rich in geology, ecology, and stark beauty.

 **El Morro National Monument:** Known for Inscription Rock, this site preserves centuries of carvings left by ancestral Puebloans, Spanish explorers, and American settlers. A permanent pool at the base made it a vital stop in the desert. Trails lead to the mesa top for Puebloan ruins and wide vistas, blending culture and scenery.

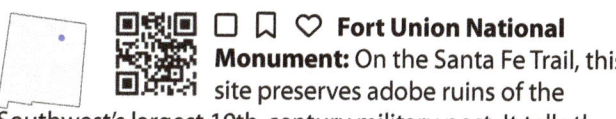 **Fort Union National Monument:** On the Santa Fe Trail, this site preserves adobe ruins of the Southwest's largest 19th-century military post. It tells the story of soldiers, traders, and expansion during the Indian Wars. Trails and exhibits reveal life at this remote fort, standing stark against the high plains landscape of northern New Mexico.

 **Gila Cliff Dwellings National Monument:** Deep in the Gila Wilderness, this monument protects cliff homes built by the Mogollon people around the late 1200s. A short hike leads to caves where families once lived, with rooms carved into the canyon walls. Visitors experience both archaeological history and the wild beauty of the surrounding forests.

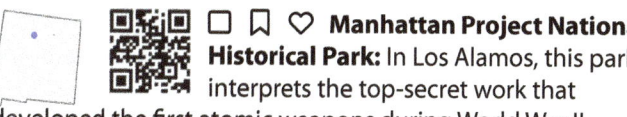 **Manhattan Project National Historical Park:** In Los Alamos, this park interprets the top-secret work that developed the first atomic weapons during World War II. Visitors explore historic sites tied to the Manhattan Project, including laboratories, scientists' homes, and the Bradbury Science Museum, learning about science, secrecy, and the dawn of the nuclear age.

 **Pecos National Historical Park:** East of Santa Fe, this park preserves a large Pueblo village and Spanish mission ruins, reflecting centuries of cultural exchange. Trails guide visitors through adobe walls and into historic battlefields, including Glorieta Pass from the Civil War. It offers both archaeological exploration and sweeping high-desert scenery.

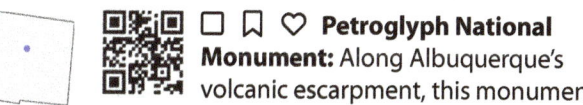 **Petroglyph National Monument:** Along Albuquerque's volcanic escarpment, this monument features more than 20,000 images etched into dark basalt by Native peoples and early settlers. Trails wind among the boulders, where spirals, animals, and symbols tell stories across centuries. The site offers a unique blend of cultural history and accessible desert hiking.

 **Salinas Pueblo Missions National Monument:** Near Mountainair, this site preserves three sets of Pueblo ruins and mission churches from the 1600s. Visitors explore striking adobe and stone walls that reveal the meeting of Native and Spanish cultures. Interpretive trails and exhibits highlight stories of resilience, adaptation, and the region's complex past.

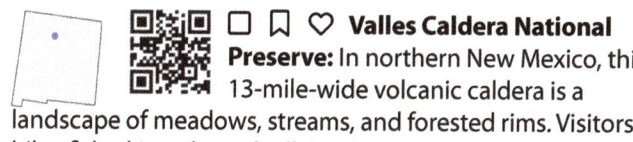 **Valles Caldera National Preserve:** In northern New Mexico, this 13-mile-wide volcanic caldera is a landscape of meadows, streams, and forested rims. Visitors hike, fish, ski, and watch elk herds roaming the vast grass valleys. Hot springs, geothermal features, and high-country trails make it a year-round destination for outdoor adventure and science.

NEW MEXICO

☐ ☐ ♡ **White Sands National Park:** Protecting the world's largest gypsum dune field, this park covers 275 square miles of brilliant white sand. Visitors hike boardwalks or venture into the dunes to sled, picnic, and photograph the surreal landscape. Shaped by wind and sun, the shimmering dunes create one of New Mexico's most iconic natural wonders.

State & National Forests

☐ ☐ ♡ **Carson National Forest:** Encompassing 1.5 million acres from Taos to Moreno Valley, Carson NF spans high-elevation spruce-fir, aspen groves, and Ponderosa pine. It includes five wilderness areas, deep canyon systems, historic pueblos, and Echo Amphitheater—offering hiking, fishing, camping, skiing, and wildlife like elk and bighorn sheep.

☐ ☐ ♡ **Cibola National Forest:** Covering approximately 1.6 million acres across scattered mountain ranges (Sandia, Mt. Taylor, Magdalena, Manzano), Cibola spans elevations from piñon-juniper desert to alpine spruce-fir. It includes four wilderness areas and grasslands, offering hiking, camping, skiing, horseback riding, star-gazing, and habitat for bald eagle and Mexican spotted owl.

☐ ☐ ♡ **Gila National Forest:** One of the largest US National Forests at 2.7 million acres, it contains Gila and Aldo Leopold Wilderness—the first designated wilderness in the US—as well as hot springs and cliff dwellings. With rugged terrain, semi-desert canyons, and high meadows, it offers remote hiking, trout fishing, camping, and habitat for Mexican gray wolves and Gila trout.

☐ ☐ ♡ **Lincoln National Forest:** Spanning 1.1 million acres in southern New Mexico, Lincoln includes the Sacramento, Guadalupe, and Capitan mountain ranges. It ranges from desert scrub to subalpine forests, includes Smokey Bear Ranger District, provides trails, campgrounds, ski areas, wilderness zones, and supports year-round recreation and watershed protection.

☐ ☐ ♡ **Santa Fe National Forest:** Covering about 1.56 million acres in northern New Mexico, this forest spans elevations from 5,300 to 13,100 feet. It includes Jemez, Pecos/Las Vegas, Coyote, and Española Ranger Districts, rich in archaeological sites and wilderness like Pecos. Offers hiking, skiing, camping, fishing, and access to mountain peaks and cultural heritage.

National Grasslands

☐ ☐ ♡ **Kiowa/Rita Blanca National Grasslands**: Spanning northeastern New Mexico, the Oklahoma Panhandle, and parts of Texas, these twin grasslands preserve vast shortgrass prairie and canyon country. Rich in Western history and wildlife, they offer scenic drives, birdwatching, and sites like McNees Crossing and the Santa Fe Trail. A quiet, rugged landscape shaped by wind, time, and resilience.

NEW MEXICO

National Scenic Byways & All-American Roads

☐ ◊ ♡ **El Camino Real National Scenic Byway:** Following the route of the Spanish colonial road between Mexico City and Santa Fe, this byway traces centuries of trade, migration, and cultural exchange along the Rio Grande. Travelers encounter historic missions, pueblos, and desert landscapes that tell the story of how New Mexico connected two continents for over 300 years.

☐ ◊ ♡ **Geronimo Trail National Scenic Byway:** Named for the famed Apache leader, this route links Truth or Consequences to the Black Range and Gila Wilderness. Winding through hot springs, ghost towns, and rugged mountains, it showcases the dramatic landscapes where Apache, Spanish, and Anglo histories collided. Wildlife, geology, and frontier lore enrich every mile.

☐ ◊ ♡ **High Road to Taos National Scenic Byway:** Connecting Santa Fe and Taos through the Sangre de Cristo foothills, this byway passes through Spanish colonial villages, artist communities, and historic churches like Chimayó. Scenic mountain views, weaving valleys, and cultural traditions make the drive both visually stunning and historically rich, blending art and heritage.

☐ ◊ ♡ **Jemez Mountain Trail National Scenic Byway:** Circling through the Jemez Mountains northwest of Albuquerque, this byway features red rock canyons, hot springs, Bandelier cliff dwellings, and the vast Valles Caldera. Pine forests, volcanic formations, and small pueblos line the route. It's a showcase of New Mexico's geologic drama and cultural diversity.

☐ ◊ ♡ **Billy the Kid Trail National Scenic Byway:** Encircling Ruidoso and Lincoln, this byway highlights the storied Old West of Billy the Kid and the Lincoln County War. Historic buildings, museums, and ranching landscapes frame a journey through pine forests and desert valleys. The route blends frontier legend with mountain scenery and cowboy tradition.

☐ ◊ ♡ **Santa Fe Trail National Scenic Byway:** Tracing a portion of the 19th-century trade route between Missouri and Santa Fe, this byway passes wagon ruts, forts, and plains landscapes. Travelers explore Cimarron, Fort Union, and the historic high plains that shaped commerce and expansion. It connects cultural heritage with wide western horizons.

☐ ◊ ♡ **Trail of the Ancients National Scenic Byway:** Linking Aztec Ruins, Chaco Culture, and Canyon of the Ancients, this Four Corners route highlights Ancestral Puebloan heritage and stark desert beauty. Petroglyphs, great houses, and sacred landscapes tell stories of ancient civilizations. The byway combines archaeology, Native traditions, and sweeping canyon country vistas.

☐ ◊ ♡ **Turquoise Trail National Scenic Byway:** Stretching between Albuquerque and Santa Fe, this route winds through old mining towns like Madrid and Cerrillos. Views of the Sandia and Ortiz Mountains frame historic and artistic communities. The trail recalls turquoise mining heritage while offering galleries, roadside charm, and vibrant New Mexico landscapes.

State Scenic Byways

☐ ◊ ♡ **Abo Pass Trail Scenic Byway:** Crossing the Manzano Mountains southeast of Albuquerque, this byway follows a historic route used by Pueblo peoples and later Spanish explorers. Travelers encounter the Salinas Pueblo Missions, red-rock mesas, and desert valleys, blending cultural heritage with sweeping views of New Mexico's high desert landscapes.

☐ ◊ ♡ **Corrales Road Scenic Byway:** Running through the historic village of Corrales along the Rio Grande, this byway highlights a living cultural landscape. Cottonwood bosque, centuries-old adobe homes, and traditional farming fields define the route. It blends natural beauty, Pueblo and Hispanic heritage, and pastoral charm just minutes from Albuquerque.

☐ ◊ ♡ **Enchanted Circle Scenic Byway:** Looping 84 miles around Wheeler Peak, this route connects Taos, Red River, Angel Fire, and Eagle Nest. Travelers pass alpine meadows, mountain lakes, ski resorts, and wildlife-rich forests. The circle captures northern New Mexico's high-altitude beauty, from rugged peaks to vibrant communities with deep cultural traditions.

☐ ◊ ♡ **La Frontera del Llano Scenic Byway:** Stretching across New Mexico's eastern plains near Clayton, this route celebrates ranching heritage and big-sky country. Wide-open grasslands, windmills, and cattle ranches dominate the landscape. The byway highlights the resilience of frontier life and the endless horizons that define the high plains.

NEW MEXICO

☐ 🔖 ♡ **Lake Valley Back Country Byway:** This remote route ventures through desert hills to the ghost town of Lake Valley, once a bustling silver mining center. Visitors find abandoned buildings, mining ruins, and volcanic ridges. The landscape tells the story of boom-and-bust cycles while offering solitude and stark desert beauty far from cities.

☐ 🔖 ♡ **Mesalands Scenic Byway:** Crossing central New Mexico, this byway showcases mesas, badlands, and colorful rock formations shaped by wind and time. Desert valleys and wide horizons dominate the scenery, while small towns highlight local traditions. It's a drive that emphasizes the raw geologic drama of New Mexico's central heartland.

☐ 🔖 ♡ **Narrow Gauge Scenic Byway:** Following the path of historic railroads in northern New Mexico, this route highlights mountain meadows, forested slopes, and remnants of old narrow-gauge lines. Travelers experience sweeping views and a tangible connection to the state's rail and logging heritage while enjoying a quiet, scenic mountain drive.

☐ 🔖 ♡ **Puye Cliffs Scenic Byway:** Leading to the ancestral homes of the Santa Clara Pueblo, this short route ends at the Puye Cliff Dwellings. Volcanic cliffs, cave dwellings, and stone structures carved centuries ago reveal the lives of early Pueblo peoples. The byway combines cultural history with striking mesa and canyon landscapes.

☐ 🔖 ♡ **Sunspot Scenic Byway:** Climbing from Cloudcroft into the Sacramento Mountains, this drive winds through pine forests to the Sunspot Solar Observatory. Overlooks reveal sweeping desert basins thousands of feet below. The route blends high-altitude recreation, astronomy, and science with some of southern New Mexico's most breathtaking vistas.

☐ 🔖 ♡ **Wild Rivers Back Country Scenic Byway:** North of Questa, this byway explores the Rio Grande Gorge where volcanic cliffs tower above a roaring river. Overlooks, trails, and campgrounds highlight geology, wildlife, and traditional use of the land. It's a route of dramatic canyon views and natural power paired with cultural heritage.

National Natural Landmarks

☐ 🔖 ♡ **Bitter Lake Group:** Designated a National Natural Landmark, this system of saline artesian lakes near Roswell harbors rare inland populations of marine algae along with endangered species like the Pecos gambusia and Roswell spring snail. Its unusual hydrology and biodiversity highlight the ecological importance of fragile desert wetlands.
GPS: 33.456047, -104.401621

☐ 🔖 ♡ **Border Hills Structural Zone:** Recognized as a National Natural Landmark, this site is one of the finest U.S. examples of wrench faulting outside the Pacific Coast. The terrain was reshaped by intense lateral tectonic forces, leaving fault lines and deformed rock layers as visible evidence of Earth's shifting crust and the dramatic stress of geologic processes.
GPS: 33.367226, -104.948359

☐ 🔖 ♡ **Bueyeros Shortgrass Plains:** This National Natural Landmark preserves one of the best remnants of the shortgrass prairie ecosystem once spanning the southern Great Plains. Dominated by blue grama and buffalograss, the rolling grasslands support native wildlife and demonstrate the resilience of prairie systems in arid environments.
GPS: 35.97948, -103.68718

☐ 🔖 ♡ **Fort Stanton Cave:** Designated a National Natural Landmark, this extensive cave system is renowned for its starburst selenite crystals, velvet flowstone, and rare helictites. It also contains Snowy River Passage, the world's longest known cave calcite formation, making it a premier site for subterranean geology and cave ecology.
GPS: 33.499099, -105.523798

☐ 🔖 ♡ **Ghost Ranch:** This striking red cliff landscape is a National Natural Landmark and one of North America's most important fossil localities. Vast beds of Triassic Coelophysis skeletons have been unearthed here, revolutionizing understanding of early dinosaurs and making it a world-class site for paleontology.
GPS: 36.329789, -106.474000

☐ 🔖 ♡ **Grants Lava Flow:** A National Natural Landmark within El Malpais National Monument, this basaltic flow is among the youngest and most pristine volcanic features in New Mexico. Its extensive lava fields preserve textbook volcanic structures, offering insight into recent eruptions and the dynamic forces shaping the region.
GPS: 34.888718, -107.993472

NEW MEXICO

Kilbourne Hole: Named a National Natural Landmark, Kilbourne Hole is a classic maar crater formed when magma met groundwater in a violent eruption. Its exposed layers contain rare xenoliths from Earth's mantle, making it a globally significant site for studying volcanic processes and deep Earth geology.
GPS: 31.971944, -106.964722

Mathers Research Natural Area: As a National Natural Landmark, Mathers protects the best-preserved example of shinnery oak–sand prairie ecosystem. Deep sandy soils nurture sprawling oak scrub and rare prairie flora, providing scientists with a living reference point for understanding southern Great Plains ecology.
GPS: 33.476752, -103.827642

Mescalero Sands South Dune: This National Natural Landmark protects one of the Southwest's finest active dune systems. Constantly reshaped by wind, the shifting sands support hardy vegetation and dune-adapted wildlife, making it an outstanding example of modern eolian processes and desert ecology.
GPS: 33.416122, -103.869842

Ship Rock: Rising nearly 1,600 feet above the plain, Ship Rock is a designated National Natural Landmark and a sacred site to the Navajo people. This dramatic volcanic neck, with dikes radiating outward, is one of the best-preserved remnants of explosive volcanic activity in the Four Corners region.
GPS: 36.6875, -108.836389

Torgac Cave: Honored as a National Natural Landmark, Torgac Cave is the type site for Torgac-type helictites, delicate twisted mineral formations found in abundance here. Its large chambers, adorned with rare speleothems, make it a premier cave system for both geological study and conservation.
GPS: 33.862860, -105.079400

Valles Caldera: One of the world's largest volcanic calderas, Valles is recognized as a National Natural Landmark for its immense size and scientific value. Formed 1.25 million years ago, its meadows, forests, and geothermal features preserve an extraordinary record of post-eruption landscapes and ecological recovery.
GPS: 35.900000, -106.533333

New York

New York's outdoor treasures span from the thundering majesty of Niagara Falls to the serene beauty of the Adirondack and Catskill Mountains. Through its vast network of state parks, national park sites, and cherished natural landmarks, the Empire State offers adventures for all seasons, from forest trails to sparkling lakes and misty waterfalls.

📅 Peak Season
May–October is New York's peak season, offering warm weather, green landscapes, and vibrant fall foliage. Summer is busiest in the Adirondacks, Catskills, and Finger Lakes, while autumn draws leaf peepers statewide.

📅 Offseason Months
November–April is the offseason, with cold temperatures and snow across much of the state. Winter, however, is prime for skiing and snowshoeing in the Adirondacks and other mountain regions.

🍃 Scenery & Nature Timing
Spring brings waterfalls at full strength and blooming orchards. Summer highlights hiking, boating, and mountain vistas. Fall peaks with brilliant foliage, while winter offers frozen lakes and snow-covered forests.

✨ Special
New York features the Adirondack High Peaks, the waterfalls of the Finger Lakes, and the dramatic gorges of Watkins Glen. Niagara Falls roars year-round, while Lake Ontario's ice formations and Hudson Valley's fall colors showcase the state's natural grandeur.

NEW YORK

State Parks

☐ 🔖 ♡ **Allan H. Treman State Marine Park:** At the south end of Cayuga Lake in Ithaca, this 91-acre park features one of New York's largest inland marinas with over 400 slips. It offers boating, fishing, birdwatching, and picnicking. Adjacent to bird-rich wetlands, it's a hotspot for water recreation while connecting to the scenic Cayuga Waterfront Trail.

☐ 🔖 ♡ **Allegany State Park:** New York's largest state park at 65,000 acres, Allegany features forested hills, lakes, and two main recreation areas: Red House and Quaker. Visitors enjoy camping, hiking 18 trails, biking, swimming, boating, cross-country skiing, and snowmobiling. Wildlife abounds, with black bear, deer, and wild turkey often spotted amid scenic landscapes of the Allegheny Plateau.

☐ 🔖 ♡ **Battle Island State Park:** Along the Oswego River near Fulton, this 235-acre park offers golfing, picnicking, and fishing. Named after a Revolutionary War skirmish, it's best known for its 18-hole golf course set amid rolling terrain and mature woodlands. The park provides beautiful river views, a clubhouse, and seasonal recreation while honoring its historic setting.

☐ 🔖 ♡ **Bayard Cutting Arboretum State Park:** Located on Long Island's South Shore, this 691-acre park preserves a grand former estate and its English-style landscaped grounds. Visitors stroll trails among rare trees, themed gardens, and along the Connetquot River. The arboretum promotes horticulture, birdwatching, and quiet reflection, offering a peaceful, educational escape in a historic natural setting.

☐ 🔖 ♡ **Bear Mountain State Park:** North of New York City, Bear Mountain offers hiking, picnicking, boating, and a zoo. Its trails connect to the Appalachian Trail and Perkins Memorial Tower provides panoramic Hudson Valley views. The park also features a skating rink, merry-go-round, and swimming pool, making it a year-round favorite for families and outdoor enthusiasts alike.

☐ 🔖 ♡ **Beaver Island State Park:** Located on Grand Island in the Niagara River, this 950-acre park offers golf, beaches, boating, and birdwatching. It has a marina, fishing access, and picnic areas with river views. The golf course, nature trails, and sandy shoreline make it ideal for recreation, while its wetlands provide vital habitat for waterfowl and migratory birds.

☐ 🔖 ♡ **Bethpage State Park:** Famous for its five golf courses, especially the U.S. Open–hosted Black Course, this 1,477-acre Long Island park also offers hiking, biking, cross-country skiing, and picnic areas. Its reputation as a golfing mecca draws players worldwide, while non-golfers enjoy its extensive trails, sports facilities, and scenic open spaces.

☐ 🔖 ♡ **Betty and Wilbur Davis State Park:** A 223-acre hilltop retreat in Otsego County, this park features rolling meadows, ponds, and hardwood forests. Visitors can hike, fish, and cross-country ski, while two furnished cottages with panoramic views provide a secluded getaway. Wildlife watching and quiet trails make it a peaceful, less-crowded state park experience.

☐ 🔖 ♡ **Bond Lake State Park:** Located in Niagara County, this 551-acre park surrounds several small lakes and offers year-round recreation. It features hiking trails, fishing, cross-country skiing, and sledding hills. The park's mix of forests, wetlands, and open spaces provides a scenic setting for birdwatching and seasonal outdoor fun close to the Niagara River corridor.

☐ 🔖 ♡ **Bowman Lake State Park:** In Chenango County, this quiet 967-acre park is known as "a camper's paradise." Surrounded by forests, Bowman Lake offers fishing, swimming, and hiking on peaceful trails. Campgrounds and picnic areas add to its charm, while its tranquil setting, abundant wildlife, and rolling hills make it an inviting escape from busy urban life.

☐ 🔖 ♡ **Brentwood State Park:** This Long Island athletic-focused park spans 52 acres and is dedicated mainly to sports. It features soccer and baseball fields, making it a hub for community recreation. While not a wilderness retreat, it provides an important green space for organized athletics, casual play, and outdoor exercise within Suffolk County's urbanized area.

☐ 🔖 ♡ **Brookhaven State Park:** A 1,638-acre undeveloped preserve in central Long Island, Brookhaven features pine barrens, wetlands, and nature trails. It provides habitat for rare species and connects to the Paumanok Path, offering hiking and birdwatching. With no swimming or camping, it serves as a peaceful natural refuge and conservation area for the region.

NEW YORK

☐ 🔖 ♡ **Buckhorn Island State Park:** On Grand Island near Niagara Falls, this 895-acre park protects wetlands critical for waterfowl and herons. Its hiking and biking trails wind through marshes and woodlands, offering excellent birdwatching. With minimal facilities, it is managed primarily as a nature preserve, balancing recreation with vital habitat conservation.

☐ 🔖 ♡ **Buffalo Harbor State Park:** Opened in 2015, Buffalo Harbor is the city's first state park, revitalizing its Lake Erie waterfront. It offers a sandy beach, playgrounds, boat launches, and fishing piers, with trails and green space for walking and biking. The park connects Buffalo's residents and visitors to the lake with recreation and stunning sunsets.

☐ 🔖 ♡ **Burnham Point State Park:** In Jefferson County's Thousand Islands region, this small 12-acre park on the St. Lawrence River offers camping, boating, and fishing. Its intimate setting features campsites with water views and boat docks, making it a favorite among anglers and boaters exploring the scenic islands and international waterway.

☐ 🔖 ♡ **Buttermilk Falls State Park:** Near Ithaca, this 811-acre park showcases cascading waterfalls along Buttermilk Creek. Trails wind past gorges, woodlands, and meadows, with swimming available at a natural pool beneath the falls. Campgrounds, cabins, and picnic areas make it popular for families, while its scenic cascades draw hikers, photographers, and nature lovers.

☐ 🔖 ♡ **Caleb Smith State Park Preserve:** On Long Island, this 543-acre preserve highlights forests, wetlands, and ponds. Its nature museum, educational programs, and catch-and-release fly fishing stream attract families and schools. With trails through diverse habitats, the park emphasizes conservation and quiet outdoor learning rather than intensive recreation.

☐ 🔖 ♡ **Captree State Park:** Located on Long Island's South Shore, Captree is a popular boating and fishing hub. It provides docking facilities, charter boats, and access to Great South Bay and Fire Island Inlet. The park features picnic areas, a restaurant, and scenic water views, catering to anglers, boaters, and those enjoying coastal recreation.

☐ 🔖 ♡ **Cayuga Lake State Park:** On the Finger Lakes' eastern shore, this 141-acre park offers camping, boating, and fishing. Its swimming beach, playgrounds, and picnic areas make it family-friendly, while cabins and campsites provide overnight stays. The park's views of Cayuga Lake and proximity to wineries make it a favored stop in the Finger Lakes region.

☐ 🔖 ♡ **Cedar Point State Park:** In the Thousand Islands, this 48-acre park sits on the St. Lawrence River. It offers boating, fishing, swimming, and camping, with a marina and picnic facilities. Its riverfront setting makes it ideal for exploring the islands, watching freighters pass, and enjoying water-based recreation in a scenic environment.

☐ 🔖 ♡ **Chenango Valley State Park:** This 1,137-acre park in Broome County is set around glacial lakes and wooded hills. It features camping, fishing, hiking, golf, and swimming. Wildlife is abundant, and birdwatchers enjoy spotting herons and waterfowl. In winter, the park offers cross-country skiing and sledding, making it a four-season retreat for outdoor recreation and relaxation.

☐ 🔖 ♡ **Cherry Plain State Park:** Nestled in Rensselaer County, this 175-acre park features Black River Pond for fishing, boating, and swimming. Its trails connect to the Capital District Wildlife Management Area, offering hiking, biking, and horseback riding. With campgrounds, picnic areas, and diverse wildlife, Cherry Plain provides a peaceful blend of recreation and natural beauty.

☐ 🔖 ♡ **Chimney Bluffs State Park:** Along Lake Ontario in Wayne County, Chimney Bluffs is famed for its dramatic clay spires rising 150 feet above the shoreline. Trails wind through woodlands and along cliffs, offering spectacular views of the lake. The park provides hiking, picnicking, and photography opportunities, showcasing one of the Finger Lakes region's most striking landscapes.

☐ 🔖 ♡ **Chittenango Falls State Park:** This 194-acre park in Madison County highlights a 167-foot waterfall cascading into a gorge. Trails provide access to scenic overlooks and forested habitats, home to rare plants like the endangered Chittenango ovate amber snail. Visitors enjoy picnicking, hiking, and photography while exploring a natural wonder in central New York.

NEW YORK

☐ 🔖 ♡ **Clarence Fahnestock State Park:** Covering 14,000 acres in Putnam and Dutchess Counties, this park features woodlands, lakes, and trails including a stretch of the Appalachian Trail. Visitors camp, swim, fish, hike, and paddle while exploring its varied landscapes. In winter, Fahnestock Winter Park offers cross-country skiing, snowshoeing, and tubing, making it a year-round destination.

☐ 🔖 ♡ **Clark Reservation State Park:** Located near Syracuse, this 377-acre park preserves a glacial plunge basin lake and rugged limestone cliffs. Trails pass through woodlands, wetlands, and meadows rich in flora and fauna. Popular for hiking, birdwatching, and geology study, Clark Reservation provides a peaceful retreat that highlights New York's unique natural history.

☐ 🔖 ♡ **Coles Creek State Park:** On the St. Lawrence River, this 1,800-acre park offers boating, camping, and fishing with scenic waterfront campsites. A marina, playgrounds, and picnic areas make it family-friendly. Its shoreline views and access to international waters make it popular for anglers, boaters, and those seeking a scenic Thousand Islands camping spot.

☐ 🔖 ♡ **Conesus Lake Boat Launch State Park:** Located on Conesus Lake, the westernmost Finger Lake, this small park primarily provides boating and fishing access. Anglers pursue bass, walleye, and perch, while boaters enjoy exploring the scenic lake. Minimal facilities emphasize its role as a gateway for water recreation rather than a developed day-use area.

☐ 🔖 ♡ **Connetquot River State Park Preserve:** A 3,473-acre Long Island preserve, Connetquot protects forests, wetlands, and the river's trout stream. Visitors hike, horseback ride, birdwatch, and enjoy educational programs at the Environmental Center. With rich biodiversity and history as a former sportsmen's club, it is a conservation-focused park prioritizing nature study and quiet recreation.

☐ 🔖 ♡ **Cumberland Bay State Park:** Located near Plattsburgh on Lake Champlain, this 350-acre park features a large sandy beach, camping, and picnicking areas. Its waterfront is ideal for swimming, boating, and fishing, while the nearby Adirondack scenery adds to its appeal. Families enjoy playgrounds and open spaces, making it a summer favorite in the Champlain Valley.

☐ 🔖 ♡ **Darien Lakes State Park:** Near Buffalo, this 1,845-acre park features a 12-acre lake for fishing, boating, and swimming. It offers over 150 campsites, hiking, and equestrian trails. Its rolling woodlands and meadows support diverse wildlife. Popular with families, it provides outdoor fun close to the amusement park region but maintains a quieter, natural atmosphere.

☐ 🔖 ♡ **De Veaux Woods State Park:** Located in Niagara Falls, this 51-acre park preserves old-growth forest and open space for recreation. It offers trails, athletic fields, and picnic areas, as well as educational programs. Its proximity to Whirlpool and Devil's Hole State Parks makes it part of a larger Niagara Gorge recreation and conservation corridor.

☐ 🔖 ♡ **Delta Lake State Park:** In Oneida County, this 720-acre park sits on a peninsula of Delta Reservoir. It offers swimming, boating, camping, and picnicking. Trails wind through woodlands rich in wildlife. Winter recreation includes cross-country skiing and snowmobiling. Its lake views and varied facilities make it a year-round destination for outdoor enthusiasts.

☐ 🔖 ♡ **Devil's Hole State Park:** Overlooking the Niagara River Gorge, this 42-acre park features rugged hiking trails, stairways to the river, and dramatic views of rapids. Fishing is popular, as is photography of the gorge. Its proximity to Whirlpool and Niagara Falls enhances its appeal, offering a wilder, more adventurous counterpoint to nearby attractions.

☐ 🔖 ♡ **Eel Weir State Park:** Near Ogdensburg, this 16-acre park lies between the Oswegatchie River and Black Lake. Small and quiet, it offers camping, fishing, and boating access. Its simple facilities attract anglers and campers seeking a peaceful setting amid northern New York's waterways, providing a rustic alternative to larger Thousand Islands parks.

☐ 🔖 ♡ **Evangola State Park:** On Lake Erie's eastern shore, this 733-acre park is known for its sandy beach backed by unique shale cliffs. It offers swimming, camping, hiking, and sports facilities. The park's natural beauty and diverse programs, from nature walks to family recreation, make it a popular destination near Buffalo throughout summer and beyond.

☐ 🔖 ♡ **Fair Haven Beach State Park:** On Lake Ontario in Cayuga County, this 1,141-acre park boasts a sandy beach, camping, cabins, and trails. Visitors fish, boat, hike, and picnic, enjoying views of bluffs and rolling shoreline. Winter recreation includes ice fishing and sledding. Its large size and facilities make it one of central New York's premier lakefront parks.

NEW YORK

☐ 🔖 ♡ **Fillmore Glen State Park:** South of Auburn, this 941-acre park is famed for its five waterfalls and forested gorge. Trails follow glens with limestone cliffs, while a swimming area, campgrounds, and picnic spots provide recreation. Rich in history, it honors President Millard Fillmore, whose birthplace is nearby, blending natural beauty with cultural heritage.

☐ 🔖 ♡ **Fort Niagara State Park:** At the Niagara River's mouth, this 504-acre park preserves a historic fort dating to the 17th century. Visitors tour buildings, watch reenactments, and learn about military history. The park also offers fishing, picnicking, trails, and views across Lake Ontario. It blends history with outdoor recreation in a scenic setting.

☐ 🔖 ♡ **Gantry Plaza State Park:** In Long Island City, this 12-acre waterfront park offers iconic skyline views of Manhattan. Once an industrial dockyard, it now features restored gantries, fishing piers, gardens, and playgrounds. Visitors enjoy riverside strolls, picnics, and cultural events while taking in dramatic views of the United Nations and Midtown across the East River.

☐ 🔖 ♡ **Gilbert Lake State Park:** Nestled in the Catskills near Oneonta, this 1,584-acre park features wooded hills, a lake for swimming and fishing, and more than 12 miles of hiking trails. Campgrounds and cabins make it a family-friendly retreat. The New York State Civilian Conservation Corps Museum on site preserves history, connecting outdoor recreation with cultural heritage.

☐ 🔖 ♡ **Glimmerglass State Park:** On Otsego Lake near Cooperstown, this 593-acre park offers swimming, camping, and picnicking. Its rolling terrain includes trails for hiking, biking, and winter cross-country skiing. Visitors enjoy boating and fishing on the lake, while history buffs explore nearby Hyde Hall. Scenic lake views and year-round recreation make it a Finger Lakes treasure.

☐ 🔖 ♡ **Golden Hill State Park:** Situated on Lake Ontario in Niagara County, this 510-acre park features camping, fishing, and picnicking. Its highlight is the historic 30 Mile Point Lighthouse, open for tours and overnight stays. Trails, shoreline vistas, and boating access attract visitors seeking both recreation and a glimpse of New York's maritime history.

☐ 🔖 ♡ **Goosepond Mountain State Park:** Located in Orange County, this 1,706-acre undeveloped park offers woodlands, wetlands, and informal trails. Its natural setting is ideal for hiking, horseback riding, and birdwatching. With limited facilities, it serves as a quiet retreat and important wildlife habitat, emphasizing conservation over developed recreation.

☐ 🔖 ♡ **Grass Point State Park:** In the Thousand Islands, this 114-acre park sits on the St. Lawrence River. It features a sandy beach, marina, campsites, and cabins. Boaters, anglers, and swimmers enjoy its waterfront location, while trails and picnic areas provide family recreation. Its scenic setting and river access make it a popular stop for water enthusiasts.

☐ 🔖 ♡ **Green Lakes State Park:** Near Syracuse, this 1,955-acre park is famous for its two glacial meromictic lakes, with striking blue-green waters. Trails circle the lakes and pass through old-growth forest. The park also offers golf, camping, swimming, and boating. Its unique geology, natural beauty, and varied recreation make it one of central New York's premier parks.

☐ 🔖 ♡ **Hamlin Beach State Park:** On Lake Ontario in Monroe County, this 1,287-acre park features a sandy beach, campgrounds, and nature trails. It's popular for swimming, boating, and picnicking, while winter brings cross-country skiing and snowmobiling. The park also preserves remnants of a World War II POW camp, blending recreation with historical interest.

☐ 🔖 ♡ **Harriman State Park:** New York's second-largest state park spans 47,500 acres in Rockland and Orange Counties. It offers more than 200 miles of trails, 31 lakes, and numerous campsites. Visitors hike, camp, boat, and ski amid forested hills and valleys. Adjacent to Bear Mountain, Harriman is a cornerstone of the Hudson Valley's outdoor recreation system.

☐ 🔖 ♡ **Heckscher State Park:** Located on Long Island's south shore, this 1,600-acre park features fields, woodlands, and four miles of shoreline. Known as the "Home of the White-tailed Deer," it offers swimming, picnicking, camping, and trails for hiking and biking. With its beaches, boat launch, and family amenities, it's a favorite coastal recreation spot.

NEW YORK

☐ ◫ ♡ **Hempstead Lake State Park:** Nassau County's largest park spans 737 acres, centered on three freshwater ponds. It offers fishing, hiking, biking, and bridle paths. Facilities include tennis courts, playgrounds, and picnic areas. As a year-round destination, the park also hosts environmental education programs, making it both a recreational and learning resource.

☐ ◫ ♡ **Herbert H. Lehman State Park:** In Westchester County, this 1,000-acre park lies along the Hudson River. It provides ballfields, tennis courts, picnic groves, and walking paths, making it popular for community recreation. Its riverside setting and easy access from New York City make it a valued green space for both families and local organizations.

☐ ◫ ♡ **High Tor State Park:** Perched on cliffs in Rockland County, this 691-acre park offers sweeping views of the Hudson River. Trails lead to the High Tor summit, the highest peak in the area, rewarding hikers with vistas. Limited facilities include picnic areas and a seasonal pool, keeping the park relatively quiet compared to nearby destinations.

☐ ◫ ♡ **Highland Lakes State Park:** This Orange County park spans 3,115 acres of largely undeveloped land. It offers informal trails, fishing ponds, and opportunities for hiking, horseback riding, and birdwatching. With no camping or swimming facilities, the park emphasizes rustic recreation and nature preservation, appealing to those seeking solitude and quiet exploration.

☐ ◫ ♡ **Higley Flow State Park:** In St. Lawrence County, this 1,115-acre park surrounds a reservoir on the Raquette River. It offers camping, swimming, boating, fishing, and hiking. In winter, it's a hub for cross-country skiing and snowmobiling. Its forested setting, water access, and year-round facilities make it a popular choice for outdoor recreation in the North Country.

☐ ◫ ♡ **Hither Hills State Park:** On Long Island's south fork, this 1,755-acre park features oceanfront camping, a sandy beach, and unique "walking dunes." Visitors enjoy swimming, fishing, hiking, and picnicking. Its expansive shoreline, family-friendly campground, and scenic coastal landscapes make it one of Long Island's most popular summer destinations.

☐ ◫ ♡ **Hook Mountain State Park:** Overlooking the Hudson River in Rockland County, this 676-acre park is part of the Palisades Interstate system. It features rugged cliffs, trails, and breathtaking river views. Popular for hiking, birdwatching, and cycling along the Hudson River Greenway, it also serves as a significant natural habitat for migratory raptors.

☐ ◫ ♡ **Hudson River Islands State Park:** Accessible only by boat, this 235-acre park preserves several forested islands between Albany and Hudson. It offers primitive camping, fishing, and paddling. With no developed facilities, it emphasizes low-impact recreation and wildlife habitat, appealing to those seeking a remote experience on the scenic Hudson River.

☐ ◫ ♡ **Irondequoit Bay State Marine Park:** Located in Monroe County near Rochester, this park provides boat access to Irondequoit Bay and Lake Ontario. With a marina, boat launch, and fishing areas, it serves as a hub for water recreation. Visitors enjoy boating, jet skiing, and angling, while nearby facilities connect to the region's vibrant shoreline activities.

☐ ◫ ♡ **James Baird State Park:** This 590-acre park in Dutchess County features rolling hills, an 18-hole golf course, hiking and biking trails, and picnic groves. Sports fields and playgrounds make it family-friendly, while wooded trails provide quiet nature walks. Its central Hudson Valley location makes it a popular destination for both golf and outdoor recreation.

☐ ◫ ♡ **John Boyd Thacher State Park:** Perched atop the Helderberg Escarpment near Albany, this 2,500-acre park offers dramatic views of the Hudson and Mohawk Valleys. Visitors explore 25 miles of trails, including the famed Indian Ladder Trail, which passes limestone cliffs and caves. The park also features a nature center, picnic areas, and winter sports opportunities.

☐ ◫ ♡ **Jones Beach State Park:** Long Island's iconic oceanfront park spans 2,413 acres with six miles of sandy beaches. It offers swimming, fishing, mini-golf, and a boardwalk. The park hosts concerts and events at Northwell Health Theater. Its historic Art Deco architecture, beloved water tower, and expansive recreation areas make it one of New York's most visited parks.

☐ ◫ ♡ **Joseph Davis State Park:** This 388-acre park in Niagara County lies along the lower Niagara River. It offers hiking, cross-country skiing, fishing, and a nature trail with birdwatching stations. Its quiet setting contrasts with nearby Niagara Falls, providing a peaceful retreat with campsites, picnic areas, and recreational access to the scenic river corridor.

NEW YORK

☐ ▢ ♡ **Keewaydin State Park:** On the St. Lawrence River in Jefferson County, this 282-acre park offers camping, boating, and fishing. Facilities include a marina, pool, and tennis courts. Its riverside campsites and easy access to Thousand Islands boating make it a popular summer destination, with opportunities for swimming, picnicking, and enjoying international water views.

☐ ▢ ♡ **Knox Farm State Park:** This 633-acre park in Erie County preserves farmland, pastures, and woodlands once part of a country estate. Visitors explore trails, historic barns, and meadows. The park highlights Western New York's agricultural heritage while providing space for hiking, horseback riding, birdwatching, and seasonal community events in a scenic rural setting.

☐ ▢ ♡ **Kring Point State Park:** Situated in the Thousand Islands near Alexandria Bay, this 61-acre park is surrounded on three sides by the St. Lawrence River. It offers waterfront campsites, boating, fishing, and swimming. Its intimate size and river views create a unique experience for campers and anglers seeking close contact with the water and islands.

☐ ▢ ♡ **Lake Erie State Park:** This 355-acre park in Chautauqua County sits on bluffs overlooking Lake Erie. It offers camping, cabins, and a swimming beach, plus trails for hiking and cross-country skiing. The park is popular for fishing, birdwatching, and watching spectacular sunsets over the lake, making it a year-round retreat in western New York.

☐ ▢ ♡ **Lake George Battlefield State Park:** Located near the southern tip of Lake George, this historic park preserves Revolutionary War and French & Indian War sites. Visitors explore monuments, interpretive displays, and picnic areas. Its scenic grounds provide lake access while honoring New York's military history, making it a blend of cultural and recreational destination.

☐ ▢ ♡ **Lake George Beach State Park (a.k.a. Million Dollar Beach):** This 51-acre park offers one of the largest and most popular swimming beaches on Lake George. It provides lifeguarded swimming, boat launches, and picnic areas. Its sandy shoreline and mountain views make it a summer favorite for families, drawing visitors from across the Adirondack region.

☐ ▢ ♡ **Lake Superior State Park:** In Sullivan County, this 1,410-acre park centers on a large lake offering swimming, boating, and fishing. Managed jointly with the county, it features picnic facilities, campgrounds, and open space for recreation. Surrounded by forested hills, it's a popular Catskills getaway for water-based and family-friendly outdoor activities.

☐ ▢ ♡ **Lake Taghkanic State Park:** Spanning 1,568 acres in Columbia County, this park features a glacial lake surrounded by wooded hills. It offers campgrounds, cabins, and a beach for swimming. Hiking trails, fishing, boating, and winter sports provide year-round recreation. Its peaceful landscapes make it a popular Hudson Valley destination for families and nature lovers.

☐ ▢ ♡ **Lakeside Beach State Park:** Located on Lake Ontario in Orleans County, this 744-acre park offers camping, picnicking, hiking, and disc golf. While swimming is not permitted, visitors enjoy boating and fishing access. Its open fields and lakeshore campsites provide panoramic water views, making it a scenic yet quieter alternative to larger beach parks.

☐ ▢ ♡ **Letchworth State Park:** Nicknamed the "Grand Canyon of the East," this 14,427-acre park in western New York features the Genesee River gorge and three major waterfalls. It offers camping, hiking, hot air ballooning, rafting, and scenic drives. Its dramatic cliffs, forests, and trails make it one of the most spectacular and beloved parks in the state system.

☐ ▢ ♡ **Long Point State Park – Finger Lakes:** Located on the eastern shore of Cayuga Lake, this 297-acre park offers camping, boating, and fishing. A swimming beach, playgrounds, and picnic areas provide family recreation. Its scenic views of the lake and vineyards make it a tranquil Finger Lakes retreat with easy access to nearby wineries and towns.

☐ ▢ ♡ **Long Point State Park – Thousand Islands:** This 23-acre park on Chaumont Bay in Jefferson County provides boating, fishing, and picnicking. With limited facilities and waterfront access, it's a quieter park that emphasizes water recreation and scenic relaxation. Its small size and riverside setting appeal to boaters and anglers seeking a simple getaway.

NEW YORK

Macomb Reservation State Park: Located in Clinton County, this 600-acre park lies along the Salmon River. It offers camping, fishing, swimming, and hiking through forests and wetlands. Trails and picnic areas add to its family-friendly atmosphere. Its mix of river and woodland environments provides excellent opportunities for wildlife observation and outdoor relaxation.

Mary Island State Park: This 13-acre island park in the Thousand Islands is accessible only by boat. It offers camping, fishing, and picnicking in a quiet, wooded setting on the St. Lawrence River. With limited facilities and a secluded atmosphere, it provides a rustic experience for boaters and campers seeking solitude in a scenic island environment.

Max V. Shaul State Park: Nestled in Schoharie County, this 75-acre park offers camping, fishing, hiking, and picnicking. It provides a peaceful alternative to nearby Mine Kill State Park, with wooded campsites and a trout stream. Its small size, family-friendly facilities, and quiet rural setting make it a relaxing gateway to New York's southern Adirondack foothills.

Mine Kill State Park: Located in the Schoharie Valley, this 500-acre park features the dramatic 80-foot Mine Kill Falls on Schoharie Creek. Visitors enjoy hiking, boating, fishing, and a swimming pool. Trails connect to the Long Path, offering extended hikes. The park balances natural beauty with modern recreation, drawing outdoor enthusiasts year-round.

Minnewaska State Park Preserve: Covering 22,275 acres in the Shawangunk Mountains, this preserve boasts waterfalls, sky lakes, and sheer cliffs. It offers hiking, biking, swimming, and rock climbing. Scenic carriage roads and overlooks provide dramatic views of the Hudson Valley. Its diverse ecosystems and rugged beauty make it one of New York's premier natural preserves.

Montauk Downs State Park: On Long Island's South Fork, this 160-acre park is best known for its championship 18-hole golf course designed by Robert Trent Jones. It also offers tennis, swimming, and dining facilities. Surrounded by coastal scenery, the park blends premier recreation with views of Montauk's dunes, beaches, and oceanfront landscapes.

Montauk Point State Park: Located at Long Island's eastern tip, this 862-acre park offers views of the Atlantic Ocean and Montauk Lighthouse. Visitors hike trails, fish, and picnic along rugged shorelines. The park is a major spot for surfcasting and birdwatching, with sweeping coastal panoramas making it a scenic highlight of Long Island's park system.

Moreau Lake State Park: Just outside Saratoga Springs, this 4,600-acre park features a glacial lake surrounded by forests and ridges. It offers swimming, camping, and hiking on more than 20 miles of trails. Winter brings snowshoeing, cross-country skiing, and ice fishing. Its peaceful setting and variety of activities make it a year-round destination.

Newtown Battlefield State Park: This 377-acre park in Chemung County preserves the Revolutionary War battle site of 1779. It offers picnic areas, interpretive programs, and scenic views of the Chemung Valley. Visitors can explore history, walk trails, and reflect at monuments, combining outdoor recreation with an important chapter of American history.

Niagara Falls State Park: Established in 1885, this is the oldest state park in the U.S. Spanning 400 acres, it showcases the American Falls, Bridal Veil Falls, and part of Horseshoe Falls. Visitors enjoy scenic overlooks, the Cave of the Winds, Maid of the Mist, and trails along the Niagara Gorge. It blends natural wonder with cultural significance.

North–South Lake State Park: In the Catskills, this 1,000-acre park is the region's largest campground. It features two connected lakes for swimming, boating, and fishing. Trails lead to historic vistas like Artist's Rock and Kaaterskill Falls. The park combines scenic beauty, rich art history, and abundant recreation, making it a centerpiece of the Catskills.

Nyack Beach State Park: Situated along the Hudson River in Rockland County, this 61-acre park features a riverside path popular for walking, cycling, and birdwatching. Cliffs of the Palisades rise dramatically overhead. With picnic groves and shoreline access, it provides quiet recreation and connects to trails leading into Hook Mountain State Park.

Oquaga Creek State Park: This 1,385-acre park in Broome County offers a 55-acre lake for swimming, fishing, and boating. It features campgrounds, cabins, and trails through wooded hills. Winter brings cross-country skiing and ice fishing. Its tranquil setting in the foothills of the Catskills makes it a year-round destination for outdoor recreation and relaxation.

NEW YORK

☐ 🔖 ♡ **Orient Beach State Park:** Located at the tip of Long Island's North Fork, this 363-acre park boasts a rare maritime forest, saltwater marshes, and a sandy beach. Visitors swim, kayak, fish, and picnic, while birdwatchers spot migratory species. The park is a National Natural Landmark, recognized for its unique coastal habitats and scenic beauty.

☐ 🔖 ♡ **Peebles Island State Park:** At the confluence of the Mohawk and Hudson Rivers, this 190-acre park features wooded trails, river overlooks, and picnic areas. Its historic buildings house park offices and exhibits. Popular for hiking, fishing, and wildlife observation, it provides sweeping views of waterfalls and rapids while highlighting New York's industrial past.

☐ 🔖 ♡ **Pixley Falls State Park:** Located in Oneida County, this 375-acre park is known for its 50-foot waterfall along Lansing Kill. Trails wind through wooded gorges, and picnic areas provide scenic spots to relax. While small, the park offers hiking, fishing, and photography opportunities, drawing visitors seeking a quiet natural retreat in central New York.

☐ 🔖 ♡ **Point Au Roche State Park:** Situated on Lake Champlain north of Plattsburgh, this 860-acre park combines wooded peninsulas, marshes, and shoreline. Trails lead through diverse habitats with rich birdlife. Visitors hike, bike, fish, and picnic while enjoying sweeping views of the lake and Adirondacks. Its natural diversity makes it a gem for wildlife enthusiasts.

☐ 🔖 ♡ **Reservoir State Park:** Located in Lewiston near Niagara Falls, this 132-acre park offers athletic fields, tennis, and basketball courts. Trails and open space provide walking and biking opportunities. Its facilities and easy access make it a community-oriented park, blending recreation with scenic views of the nearby Niagara Power Reservoir.

☐ 🔖 ♡ **Riverbank State Park:** In Harlem, this 28-acre rooftop park is built atop a water treatment plant along the Hudson River. It features athletic fields, an Olympic-size pool, skating rink, cultural theater, and playgrounds. With sweeping city and river views, it serves as a unique urban oasis offering both recreation and community programs in Manhattan.

☐ 🔖 ♡ **Robert H. Treman State Park:** Near Ithaca, this 1,110-acre park is renowned for Enfield Glen, a gorge with 12 waterfalls including 115-foot Lucifer Falls. Trails wind past dramatic cliffs and cascades, while campgrounds and a natural swimming pool offer family recreation. Its rugged scenery and waterfalls make it one of the Finger Lakes' most dramatic parks.

☐ 🔖 ♡ **Robert Moses State Park – Long Island:** This 875-acre park features five miles of Atlantic Ocean beach. Visitors enjoy swimming, surfing, fishing, and picnicking. Boardwalks connect to Fire Island Lighthouse. With fields, playgrounds, and wide sandy shores, it is one of the most popular Long Island beach destinations, drawing millions each summer.

☐ 🔖 ♡ **Robert Moses State Park – Thousand Islands:** Near Massena, this 2,322-acre park on the St. Lawrence River offers camping, boating, fishing, and swimming. It includes the Nicandri Nature Center and trails for hiking and biking. Its riverfront setting, wetlands, and year-round activities make it a family-friendly hub for recreation in northern New York.

☐ 🔖 ♡ **Robert V. Riddell State Park:** Near Oneonta, this 2,163-acre park features forests, meadows, and Schenevus Creek. Trails explore wooded hills, waterfalls, and the historic "Irish Settlement" area. With opportunities for hiking, fishing, and cross-country skiing, it blends cultural history with outdoor recreation, offering a peaceful Catskills gateway.

☐ 🔖 ♡ **Roberto Clemente State Park:** This 25-acre park in the Bronx lies along the Harlem River. It offers ballfields, basketball courts, playgrounds, and a pool complex. Named for baseball legend Roberto Clemente, it provides year-round cultural and recreational programming, serving as a vital community hub for Bronx residents.

☐ 🔖 ♡ **Rock Island Lighthouse State Park:** In the Thousand Islands, this 35-acre park on Rock Island is accessible only by boat. It features a restored 1847 lighthouse, keeper's house museum, and picnic grounds. Visitors enjoy tours, boating, and fishing while learning about maritime history. Its location offers panoramic river views and unique historic charm.

☐ 🔖 ♡ **Rockefeller State Park Preserve:** In Westchester County, this 1,771-acre preserve offers carriage roads, woodlands, meadows, and wetlands. Popular for hiking, horseback riding, and birdwatching, it emphasizes quiet recreation and conservation. The preserve protects diverse habitats while providing scenic landscapes once part of the Rockefeller family estate.

☐ 🔖 ♡ **Rockland Lake State Park:** Located in the Hudson Valley, this 1,133-acre park centers on a glacial lake. It offers a swimming pool, golf courses, fishing, boating, and trails. Historic icehouse sites recall its role in the 19th-century ice industry. With sports facilities and scenic views, it's a popular family recreation hub.

NEW YORK

☐ 🔖 ♡ **Sampson State Park:** On Seneca Lake's eastern shore, this 2,070-acre park occupies a former naval and air force training base. It offers camping, boating, fishing, and a sandy swimming beach. Trails and open space provide hiking and wildlife viewing, while exhibits honor its military history. It's a unique blend of recreation and heritage.

☐ 🔖 ♡ **Sandy Island Beach State Park:** Located on Lake Ontario in Oswego County, this park preserves a stretch of rare freshwater dunes. Visitors swim, picnic, and hike boardwalks that protect fragile habitats. The dunes are part of a National Natural Landmark, making the park a vital site for conservation and a scenic family-friendly beach destination.

☐ 🔖 ♡ **Saratoga Spa State Park:** Famous for its mineral springs, this 2,379-acre park in Saratoga Springs offers historic bathhouses, the Saratoga Performing Arts Center, golf courses, and trails. Visitors can sample spring waters, explore museums, and hike woodlands. It blends cultural heritage, health, and recreation in a setting recognized as a National Historic Landmark.

☐ 🔖 ♡ **Schodack Island State Park:** Along the Hudson River south of Albany, this 1,052-acre park features campsites, picnic areas, and 8 miles of trails. Wetlands support bald eagles and migratory birds. Visitors hike, bike, and fish while enjoying river views. Its location on a long island creates a natural retreat with important ecological value.

☐ 🔖 ♡ **Selkirk Shores State Park:** On Lake Ontario in Oswego County, this 990-acre park features bluffs overlooking the lake. It offers camping, cabins, fishing, boating, and trails. Its location along bird migration routes makes it a hotspot for birdwatching. Scenic shorelines and outdoor recreation make it a summer favorite near Pulaski.

☐ 🔖 ♡ **Seneca Lake State Park:** At the north end of Seneca Lake, this 141-acre park offers a beach, picnic groves, and boating access. A popular sprayground and playgrounds draw families. Trails provide scenic lakefront walks and biking. With fishing, swimming, and easy Finger Lakes access, it's a lively, family-friendly waterfront park.

☐ 🔖 ♡ **Shirley Chisholm State Park:** Opened in 2019 in Brooklyn, this 407-acre park was built on reclaimed land along Jamaica Bay. It features trails, bike paths, and overlooks with sweeping city and bay views. Named for trailblazing congresswoman Shirley Chisholm, it provides urban green space, community programs, and opportunities for outdoor recreation close to NYC.

☐ 🔖 ♡ **Silver Lake State Park:** In Wyoming County, this small park offers a boat launch and fishing access to Silver Lake. With minimal facilities, it primarily supports anglers and boaters while providing scenic views of the surrounding countryside. Its simplicity and quiet lakeside location make it a hidden gem for water recreation.

☐ 🔖 ♡ **Sojourner Truth State Park:** Opened in 2022 in Kingston, this Hudson River waterfront park spans 500 acres of former industrial land. It offers trails, picnic areas, and shoreline access while restoring habitats and connecting communities to nature. Named for abolitionist Sojourner Truth, it combines cultural heritage with outdoor recreation and environmental renewal.

☐ 🔖 ♡ **Sonnenberg Gardens & Mansion State Historic Park:** In Canandaigua, this 50-acre park features a late-19th century mansion and nine themed gardens. Visitors stroll through rose, Japanese, and Italian-style landscapes, explore historic architecture, and enjoy cultural events. It blends horticulture, history, and scenic beauty in the Finger Lakes region.

☐ 🔖 ♡ **Southwick Beach State Park:** On Lake Ontario in Jefferson County, this 464-acre park features a long sandy beach, dunes, and campgrounds. Popular for swimming, picnicking, and birdwatching, it connects to nearby natural areas like Lakeview Wildlife Management Area. Its beach and lake access make it a summer hotspot for families.

☐ 🔖 ♡ **Stony Brook State Park:** In western New York, this 568-acre park is noted for its gorge and three waterfalls. Trails follow rugged terrain past cascades, cliffs, and forests. Visitors enjoy swimming, camping, and picnicking, with scenic geology attracting hikers and photographers. Its dramatic natural features make it a highlight of the Finger Lakes.

NEW YORK

☐ ▢ ♡ **Sunken Meadow State Park:** On Long Island's north shore, this 1,287-acre park features a three-mile beach, boardwalk, and tidal flats. It offers golf, hiking, biking, and horseback riding, plus a popular swimming beach. Scenic bluffs provide panoramic Sound views, making it a versatile park for both recreation and nature exploration.

☐ ▢ ♡ **Taconic State Park – Copake Falls Area:** At the Massachusetts border, this 6,000-acre park offers camping, cabins, and access to Bash Bish Falls, the state's highest waterfall. Trails connect to the Appalachian Trail and Taconic Crest Trail. Visitors enjoy swimming, hiking, and skiing, making it a four-season hub in the Taconic Mountains.

☐ ▢ ♡ **Taconic State Park – Rudd Pond Area:** Near Millerton, this 1,000-acre section of Taconic State Park features a 64-acre pond for swimming, boating, and fishing. Campgrounds and picnic areas are available, while nearby trails connect to the Appalachian and Taconic Crest Trails. Its mix of water recreation and mountain scenery makes it a popular family retreat.

☐ ▢ ♡ **Taughannock Falls State Park:** Located near Ithaca, this 750-acre park features a 215-foot waterfall—taller than Niagara Falls. Trails wind through a dramatic gorge with cliffs nearly 400 feet high. Visitors swim at Cayuga Lake, camp, fish, and picnic. Its iconic falls, scenic overlooks, and lakefront access make it one of the Finger Lakes' most famous parks.

☐ ▢ ♡ **Trail View State Park:** This 400-acre linear park on Long Island links Bethpage and Cold Spring Harbor State Parks. Popular with hikers, bikers, and equestrians, it follows woodlands, meadows, and wetlands. As part of the Nassau–Suffolk Greenbelt Trail, it provides a natural corridor for recreation and wildlife while connecting suburban communities with outdoor spaces.

☐ ▢ ♡ **Two Rivers State Park Recreation Area:** Near Elmira, this 320-acre park offers wooded trails, picnic areas, and scenic overlooks of the Chemung and Susquehanna Valleys. Camping is available at nearby facilities, while visitors enjoy hiking, birdwatching, and fishing. Its peaceful environment and ridge-top views make it a hidden gem in New York's Southern Tier.

☐ ▢ ♡ **Valcour Island State Historic and Primitive Park:** Located on Lake Champlain near Plattsburgh, this 968-acre island park is accessible only by boat. It features primitive camping, hiking, and historic sites, including the Bluff Point Lighthouse and Revolutionary War battle locations. Its wilderness feel, cultural significance, and lake vistas make it a unique destination.

☐ ▢ ♡ **Verona Beach State Park:** On Oneida Lake's eastern shore, this 1,735-acre park offers sandy beaches, boating, and fishing. Trails pass through woodlands, wetlands, and meadows rich in wildlife. Campgrounds, picnic areas, and winter sports make it a year-round destination, combining lakefront fun with natural beauty in central New York.

☐ ▢ ♡ **Walkway Over the Hudson State Historic Park:** Spanning the Hudson River between Poughkeepsie and Highland, this 1.28-mile bridge is the world's longest elevated pedestrian walkway. Converted from a railroad bridge, it offers panoramic river and mountain views. Popular with walkers, cyclists, and events, it connects communities while showcasing the Hudson Valley's beauty.

☐ ▢ ♡ **Wellesley Island State Park:** At 2,636 acres, this Thousand Islands park is one of New York's largest. It offers camping, boating, fishing, and swimming, plus the Minna Anthony Common Nature Center with exhibits and trails. Its varied habitats, including wetlands and forest, support abundant wildlife. Family-friendly facilities and scenic river views make it a standout.

☐ ▢ ♡ **Westcott Beach State Park:** On Lake Ontario near Sackets Harbor, this 318-acre park offers a sandy beach, campgrounds, and picnic areas. Trails wind through rolling meadows and woodlands with lake views. Visitors swim, fish, and hike in summer, while winter activities include cross-country skiing. Its family-friendly atmosphere makes it a north shore favorite.

☐ ▢ ♡ **Whetstone Gulf State Park:** Located on the Tug Hill Plateau, this 2,100-acre park is set around a dramatic gorge three miles long. Trails follow the rim and offer breathtaking views. Campgrounds, picnic areas, and a swimming area add to recreation. Its rugged scenery and quiet setting make it a top spot for hikers and campers.

UNITED STATES EDITION

NEW YORK

☐ 🔖 ♡ **Whirlpool State Park:** Overlooking the Niagara River Whirlpool, this 109-acre park features trails descending into the gorge for close-up views of rapids and cliffs. Visitors hike, picnic, and fish while enjoying dramatic vistas. Its proximity to Niagara Falls makes it a popular but less-crowded destination for experiencing the river's power and beauty.

☐ 🔖 ♡ **Wildwood State Park:** On Long Island's North Shore, this 767-acre park features a beach on Long Island Sound backed by forested bluffs. It offers camping, hiking, picnicking, and fishing. Popular with families, it provides both seaside relaxation and wooded trails. Its scenic shoreline and diverse habitats make it one of Long Island's most visited parks.

☐ 🔖 ♡ **Wilson-Tuscarora State Park:** On Lake Ontario in Niagara County, this 476-acre park features a sandy beach, marina, and nature trails. It offers fishing, boating, swimming, and birdwatching. With open fields, forests, and wetlands, the park combines water-based recreation with habitat preservation, making it a versatile destination for families and outdoor enthusiasts.

☐ 🔖 ♡ **Wonder Lake State Park:** In Putnam County, this 1,145-acre undeveloped park offers more than 8 miles of trails. Its forested hills, wetlands, and namesake lake provide habitat for diverse wildlife. Popular with hikers, birdwatchers, and anglers, the park emphasizes rustic recreation and conservation, offering solitude within easy reach of the New York metro area.

☐ 🔖 ♡ **Woodlawn Beach State Park:** On Lake Erie near Buffalo, this 107-acre park features a sandy swimming beach, picnic facilities, and nature trails through wetlands and dunes. Visitors enjoy volleyball, birdwatching, and sunset views over the lake. Its proximity to the city makes it a convenient getaway, blending natural beauty with family recreation.

National Parks

 ☐ 🔖 ♡ **African Burial Ground National Monument:** In New York City, this site preserves the resting place of more than 15,000 enslaved and free Africans from the colonial era. The visitor center and memorial honor their memory while telling the story of the African-American experience in early New York. It is a moving place of reflection, history, and cultural education.

 ☐ 🔖 ♡ **Appalachian National Scenic Trail:** Stretching over 2,100 miles from Georgia to Maine, the Appalachian Trail crosses New York's Hudson Valley and Connecticut border. Visitors hike forested ridges, wetlands, and scenic overlooks, experiencing a slice of America's most iconic long-distance trail. It offers both casual day hikes and challenging treks through diverse landscapes.

 ☐ 🔖 ♡ **Castle Clinton National Monument:** Located in Battery Park, New York City, this historic fort was built in 1811 for harbor defense. It later served as America's first immigration station, welcoming millions before Ellis Island opened. Today visitors can tour the fort, view exhibits, and learn about its varied history as a theater, aquarium, and landmark.

 ☐ 🔖 ♡ **Eleanor Roosevelt National Historic Site:** In Hyde Park, this site preserves Val-Kill, the home of Eleanor Roosevelt, First Lady and human rights champion. Visitors tour her cottage, learn about her work in civil rights and diplomacy, and gain insight into her independent legacy. The grounds reflect her commitment to social justice and humanitarian causes.

 ☐ 🔖 ♡ **Federal Hall National Memorial:** On Wall Street in New York City, this building marks the site where George Washington took the oath of office as the first U.S. President. Exhibits highlight the nation's founding, early government, and financial beginnings. Visitors walk through the grand rotunda and learn about the history of New York's role in democracy.

 ☐ 🔖 ♡ **Fire Island National Seashore:** Off Long Island's south shore, this park protects barrier beaches, maritime forests, and salt marshes. Visitors enjoy swimming, hiking, birdwatching, and exploring historic sites like the Fire Island Lighthouse. The seashore preserves fragile coastal ecosystems while providing a natural escape just a short distance from New York City.

NEW YORK

 **Fort Stanwix National Monument:** In Rome, New York, this reconstructed fort tells the story of the 1777 siege during the American Revolution. The fort defended the Mohawk Valley and protected settlers from British and allied attacks. Visitors explore the earthworks, barracks, and interpretive programs that bring the Revolutionary War era to life.

 **Gateway National Recreation Area:** Spanning New York and New Jersey, this 27,000-acre urban recreation area includes beaches, marshes, and historic sites. Visitors explore Jamaica Bay Wildlife Refuge, Fort Wadsworth, and Floyd Bennett Field. It blends outdoor recreation with cultural history, offering birdwatching, kayaking, and trails within sight of the city skyline.

 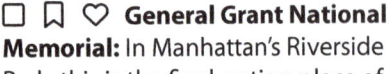 **General Grant National Memorial:** In Manhattan's Riverside Park, this is the final resting place of Ulysses S. Grant, Civil War general and 18th President. The massive granite tomb, the largest mausoleum in North America, honors his leadership. Visitors learn about his life, the war, and Reconstruction while reflecting on his enduring legacy.

 **Governors Island National Monument:** Located in New York Harbor, this site preserves two historic forts: Castle Williams and Fort Jay. Once a strategic military post, the island now welcomes visitors to explore the forts, walk the landscaped grounds, and enjoy panoramic views of Lower Manhattan, the Statue of Liberty, and the harbor.

 **Hamilton Grange National Memorial:** In Harlem, this memorial preserves the relocated home of Alexander Hamilton, Founding Father and the first U.S. Treasury Secretary. Visitors tour the restored house, see period furnishings, and learn about Hamilton's contributions to the nation's government, economy, and political life. It is a personal glimpse into his legacy.

 **Harriet Tubman National Historical Park:** In Auburn, this site honors Harriet Tubman, abolitionist and Underground Railroad leader. Visitors tour her residence, the Home for the Aged, and the church she attended. The park tells the story of her bravery, activism, and lifelong fight for freedom and equality, inspiring generations with her remarkable life.

 **Home of Franklin D. Roosevelt National Historic Site:** In Hyde Park, this estate preserves the lifelong home of FDR, America's 32nd President. Visitors tour Springwood, the library, and museum, learning about his leadership during the Great Depression and World War II. The site reflects both his personal life and public role in shaping the modern presidency.

 **Martin Van Buren National Historic Site:** Located in Kinderhook, this site preserves Lindenwald, the estate of the 8th U.S. President. Visitors tour his home, see period rooms, and learn about his role in shaping American politics during the Jacksonian era. The grounds and exhibits highlight his life, presidency, and influence on the Democratic Party.

 **Sagamore Hill National Historic Site:** In Oyster Bay, this estate was the home of Theodore Roosevelt, 26th U.S. President. Known as the "Summer White House," it preserves his house, furnishings, and grounds. Visitors learn about his family life, political career, and legacy in conservation, diplomacy, and reform while touring this beloved Long Island property.

 **Saint Paul's Church National Historic Site:** In Mount Vernon, this church and burying ground date back to 1665 and played a role in the Revolutionary War. Visitors explore the restored church, historic cemetery, and exhibits on religious freedom and colonial America. Its peaceful grounds honor centuries of local and national history.

 **Saratoga National Historical Park:** Near Stillwater, this park commemorates the 1777 Battle of Saratoga, a decisive American victory and turning point of the Revolution. Visitors tour the battlefield, Saratoga Monument, and Schuyler House. Scenic drives, trails, and reenactments bring to life the story of how this victory changed world history.

 **Statue of Liberty National Monument:** On Liberty Island, this iconic symbol of freedom welcomes millions of visitors each year. Guests can tour the statue, climb to the pedestal or crown, and explore the Ellis Island Immigration Museum. It honors America's immigrant heritage and stands as a global beacon of democracy and hope.

UNITED STATES EDITION

NEW YORK

☐ 🔖 ♡ **Stonewall National Monument:** In Greenwich Village, this site commemorates the 1969 Stonewall Uprising, a catalyst for the modern LGBTQ rights movement. Visitors learn about the events that occurred outside the Stonewall Inn, explore interpretive displays, and reflect on the continuing struggle for equality and human rights in America.

☐ 🔖 ♡ **Theodore Roosevelt Birthplace National Historic Site:** In Manhattan, this site preserves the restored brownstone where Theodore Roosevelt was born in 1858. Visitors tour period rooms, exhibits, and family artifacts to learn about his early life. The site highlights how his childhood shaped the values and character that defined his presidency.

☐ 🔖 ♡ **Theodore Roosevelt Inaugural National Historic Site:** In Buffalo, this site marks where Roosevelt took the oath of office in 1901 after President McKinley's assassination. Visitors explore the historic house, exhibits, and multimedia programs to understand Roosevelt's sudden rise to the presidency and his transformative impact on American politics.

☐ 🔖 ♡ **Vanderbilt Mansion National Historic Site:** In Hyde Park, this Gilded Age estate showcases the opulent home of Frederick W. Vanderbilt. Visitors tour the grand mansion, gardens, and grounds overlooking the Hudson River. The site illustrates the lavish lifestyle of America's wealthy elite while highlighting architectural and cultural history of the late 19th century.

☐ 🔖 ♡ **Women's Rights National Historical Park:** In Seneca Falls, this park commemorates the 1848 Women's Rights Convention. Visitors explore Wesleyan Chapel, homes of key activists, and exhibits that tell the story of the women's suffrage movement. It honors the struggle for equality and highlights the continuing fight for social justice and civil rights.

State & National Forests

☐ 🔖 ♡ **Beaver Creek State Forest:** Spanning 3,484 acres in Madison County, this forest features lowland swamps and forested hills drained by Beaver Creek. With 25 miles of trails, it offers hiking, horseback riding, birdwatching, and picnicking. As part of the Brookfield Trail System, it provides a peaceful retreat with diverse habitats and scenic woodlands.

☐ 🔖 ♡ **California Hill State Forest:** Encompassing 982 acres in Putnam County, this forest is known for rolling hills and scenic woodlands. Visitors hike informal trails, fish in small streams, or enjoy horseback riding. Seasonal hunting is also popular. Its undeveloped character makes it a quiet destination for nature lovers seeking a rustic outdoor experience.

☐ 🔖 ♡ **Clark Hill State Forest:** Covering 2,819 acres in Oneida County, this forest is defined by rugged hills, rocky slopes, and stream valleys. Visitors can hike, birdwatch, or take in panoramic views while exploring its diverse ecosystems. Its peaceful setting and undeveloped lands make it an appealing destination for those seeking solitude in nature.

☐ 🔖 ♡ **Finger Lakes National Forest:** Straddling Seneca and Schuyler Counties, this 16,259-acre expanse is New York's only national forest. It features over 30 miles of trails that wind through gorges, pastures, woodlands, and wetlands. Popular for camping, hiking, horseback riding, and wildlife viewing, it offers an immersive way to explore the scenic Finger Lakes region.

☐ 🔖 ♡ **Hammond Hill State Forest:** Covering 3,618 acres in Tompkins County, this forest features a network of trails for hiking, cross-country skiing, and mountain biking. Its varied terrain and woodlands attract outdoor enthusiasts year-round, especially in winter when snowshoeing and skiing are popular. Wildlife is abundant, adding to its appeal as a natural escape.

☐ 🔖 ♡ **Hand Hollow State Forest:** This 518-acre forest in Columbia County offers a serene environment for hiking, fishing, and birdwatching. Trails and woodland paths lead through lush vegetation and wetlands, supporting diverse wildlife. Its quiet, undeveloped setting makes it a tranquil place for picnics and peaceful walks in nature.

NEW YORK

☐ 🔖 ♡ **Hunts Pond State Forest:** A small, 30-acre site in Chenango County, this forest centers around Hunts Pond, a tranquil spot for fishing, picnicking, and nature walks. The peaceful lake and surrounding woodlands attract wildlife, making it an inviting stop for families and outdoor enthusiasts seeking relaxation in a rustic environment.

☐ 🔖 ♡ **Morgan Hill State Forest:** Spanning 5,284 acres in Onondaga and Cortland Counties, this forest provides opportunities for hiking, camping, hunting, and birdwatching. Its trails connect with the North Country National Scenic Trail, offering extended hiking options. Rolling hills, streams, and dense woodlands make it a scenic destination for year-round recreation.

☐ 🔖 ♡ **Sonyea State Forest:** This 922-acre forest in Livingston County is valued for its tranquility and scenic character. Visitors enjoy hiking, wildlife observation, and picnicking along its quiet trails. The forest's undeveloped nature provides a peaceful experience, making it ideal for those seeking to explore the quieter side of the Finger Lakes landscape.

National Scenic Byways & All-American Roads

☐ 🔖 ♡ **Great Lakes Seaway Trail:** Stretching 454 miles across New York's Great Lakes shoreline, this byway follows Lake Erie, the Niagara River, Lake Ontario, and the St. Lawrence River. It connects cities like Buffalo, Rochester, and Oswego with historic lighthouses, fishing harbors, scenic bluffs, and waterfront parks, offering a journey rich in maritime heritage and natural beauty.

☐ 🔖 ♡ **Lakes to Locks Passage:** Designated an All-American Road, this corridor links Waterford to Rouses Point, following the Hudson River, Champlain Canal, Lake George, and Lake Champlain. It showcases canal history, Adirondack landscapes, and heritage towns. Visitors enjoy boating, cycling, hiking, and cultural attractions along a route that blends natural wonder with historic significance.

☐ 🔖 ♡ **Mohawk Towpath Byway:** Running about 26 miles between Schenectady and Waterford, this byway follows the Mohawk River and Erie Canal, highlighting historic locks, bridges, and canal-era communities. It celebrates early engineering feats and cultural heritage while providing river views, trails, and access points that connect with the larger Lakes to Locks Passage system.

☐ 🔖 ♡ **Palisades Scenic Byway:** This historic parkway travels along the Palisades cliffs above the Hudson River, linking New York City to woodlands and riverfront overlooks. Drivers encounter sweeping views, forested landscapes, and unique parkway design. Its combination of accessible wilderness, natural beauty, and proximity to the metropolis makes it a rare scenic escape near the city.

State Scenic Byways

☐ 🔖 ♡ **Adirondack Trail:** Stretching from Malone to Fonda, this scenic byway traverses the Adirondack Park, showcasing mountain ridges, sparkling lakes, and dense forests. It passes through historic towns, rustic hamlets, and recreational areas, offering a true cross-section of Adirondack beauty. Travelers enjoy outdoor adventures, fall foliage, and a sense of wilderness immersion.

☐ 🔖 ♡ **Black River Trail:** Following the Black River between Rome and Dexter, this byway highlights rapids, wooded gorges, and farmlands. Along the way are historic mill towns, fishing sites, and overlooks rich with birdlife. It provides access to whitewater and outdoor recreation, while offering a scenic corridor through northern landscapes and cultural history.

☐ 🔖 ♡ **Blue Ridge Road Scenic Byway:** A short but dramatic Adirondack drive between North Hudson and Newcomb, this byway rises through rugged terrain with ponds, streams, and mountain ridges. It offers solitude, wilderness views, and access to High Peaks trailheads. Known for its remoteness, it provides a quiet escape into the wild heart of the Adirondacks.

☐ 🔖 ♡ **Bronx River Parkway:** Built as one of America's first parkways, this landscaped route runs from the Bronx into Westchester County, following the river through wooded parklands. Stone bridges, shaded lanes, and natural scenery make it a green corridor amid suburban communities. It remains both a historic roadway and a tranquil urban escape.

NEW YORK

☐ 🔖 ♡ **Catskill Mountains Scenic Byway:** Traveling through four Catskill towns, this route highlights forested peaks, cascading streams, and reservoirs. Historic hamlets, cultural sites, and recreational areas enrich the journey, while panoramic overlooks showcase seasonal color. It celebrates the natural beauty and heritage of the Catskills, offering a balance of culture and wilderness.

☐ 🔖 ♡ **Cayuga Lake Scenic Byway:** Encircling Cayuga Lake in the Finger Lakes, this byway links wineries, farms, and waterfalls with historic villages and state parks. Sweeping lake vistas frame the drive, while travelers enjoy wine trails, birding, and cultural landmarks. It blends scenic beauty with agriculture, creating a classic Finger Lakes experience.

☐ 🔖 ♡ **Central Adirondack Trail:** Crossing the Adirondack interior, this byway passes rivers, mountains, and forested hamlets between Glens Falls and Rome. Visitors encounter rustic towns, historic logging heritage, and plentiful recreation. Seasonal foliage and tranquil waters enhance the journey, making it a quintessential Adirondack drive through varied terrain.

☐ 🔖 ♡ **Dude Ranch Trail Scenic Byway:** This short route in the Hudson Valley recalls the heyday of family dude ranches, passing rolling hills, farmlands, and rustic lodges. It captures nostalgia of cowboy-themed vacations in an eastern setting while still providing pastoral beauty. Travelers find a blend of recreation, heritage, and scenic countryside charm.

☐ 🔖 ♡ **Durham Valley Scenic Byway:** Nestled in Greene County, this byway traverses fertile valleys framed by Catskill ridges. Farms, orchards, and historic churches line the road, while wildflowers and fall foliage add color. It's a peaceful countryside route highlighting rural traditions, scenic open space, and the quiet charm of small towns.

☐ 🔖 ♡ **High Peaks Byway:** Following Route 73, this iconic drive runs between Keene Valley and Lake Placid through towering Adirondack peaks. It offers dramatic mountain vistas, rushing rivers, and trailhead access. Known for fall color and Olympic heritage, the byway provides unforgettable scenery and a gateway to outdoor adventure in New York's highest mountains.

☐ 🔖 ♡ **Historic Parkways of Long Island:** Designed in the early 20th century for leisure motoring, these landscaped parkways link beaches, estates, and preserves. Curving roads, stone bridges, and wooded medians provide timeless beauty. They remain a living example of parkway architecture, blending recreational access with scenic elegance along Long Island's natural landscapes.

☐ 🔖 ♡ **Maple Traditions Scenic Byway:** Winding through central New York, this byway celebrates maple sugaring heritage. Travelers encounter sugar shacks, forested hills, and farmsteads that bring maple culture to life, especially in spring. Small towns and countryside charm enrich the route, blending history, agriculture, and scenic woodland settings in every season.

☐ 🔖 ♡ **Military Trail Scenic Byway:** This corridor through the Mohawk Valley traces historic military routes from colonial times and the Revolution. Rolling farmland, river views, and heritage sites define the drive. Travelers encounter forts, battlegrounds, and quiet villages that preserve New York's role in America's early struggles, framed by pastoral beauty.

☐ 🔖 ♡ **Mountain Cloves Scenic Byway:** This Catskill route winds through dramatic notches, or "cloves," carved by rushing streams. Sheer cliffs, waterfalls, and panoramic overlooks create striking scenery. Travelers encounter mountain villages, trailheads, and rich geology. It captures the rugged grandeur of the Catskills, offering both natural drama and recreational access.

☐ 🔖 ♡ **North Fork Trail Scenic Byway:** Running along Long Island's North Fork, this route highlights vineyards, farms, and coastal heritage. Lighthouses, harbors, and wineries line the drive, with maritime breezes and farmland scenery creating a unique blend. It's a celebrated corridor for food, culture, and nature in one of New York's most distinctive regions.

☐ 🔖 ♡ **Olympic Trail Scenic Byway:** Extending from Lake Champlain to Lake Ontario, this Adirondack route passes through Lake Placid, Saranac Lake, and other Olympic sites. Travelers see ski jumps, lakes, and rugged mountains while exploring the region's sporting legacy. Scenic beauty and cultural history make it one of the state's most celebrated drives.

☐ 🔖 ♡ **Roosevelt–Marcy Trail:** This Adirondack route retraces Theodore Roosevelt's urgent 1901 ride from Mount Marcy to North Creek upon learning of President McKinley's shooting. Passing rivers, forests, and remote hamlets, it combines mountain scenery with a dramatic historical story. It remains a meaningful drive linking natural grandeur with national legacy.

☐ 🔖 ♡ **Route 20 Scenic Byway:** Crossing central New York along one of America's oldest east-west highways, this byway passes farms, villages, and historic inns. Rolling hills, lakes, and cultural landmarks enrich the corridor. With harvest festivals, autumn foliage, and rural charm, it offers a rich cross-section of upstate scenery and heritage.

NEW YORK

☐ ☐ ♡ **Seneca Lake Scenic Byway:** Running along Seneca Lake's shoreline, this byway showcases vineyards, farms, and striking lake vistas. Travelers enjoy wine country scenery, charming villages, and cascading waterfalls nearby. It's a quintessential Finger Lakes drive that blends agriculture, culture, and natural beauty in one of the state's most iconic regions.

☐ ☐ ♡ **Shawangunk Mountains Scenic Byway:** Encircling the Shawangunk Ridge, this byway features cliffs, lakes, and panoramic overlooks. It links trailheads, preserves, and historic communities. Known for dramatic geology, fall color, and outdoor recreation, it offers a scenic journey through one of the Hudson Valley's most striking natural landscapes.

☐ ☐ ♡ **Southern Adirondack Trail:** Traversing the Adirondack foothills, this route highlights forested hills, rivers, and rustic villages. Scenic pull-offs and quiet roads emphasize seasonal beauty and recreational opportunities. It serves as a scenic gateway to the Adirondacks, offering pastoral charm and access to wilderness in a less-traveled region.

☐ ☐ ♡ **Taconic Parkway Scenic Byway:** Designed for graceful motoring, this landscaped parkway runs through the Hudson Valley, linking forests, meadows, and historic estates. Stone bridges, shaded lanes, and sweeping views make it one of New York's most elegant roads. It preserves early parkway ideals while remaining a scenic escape for modern travelers.

☐ ☐ ♡ **Upper Delaware Scenic Byway:** Following the Delaware River along Route 97, this corridor highlights river bends, limestone cliffs, and small towns. It's known for bald eagles, historic bridges, and peaceful river views. With recreation, culture, and seasonal color, it provides a memorable experience in one of New York's most scenic valleys.

☐ ☐ ♡ **WNY Southtowns Scenic Byway:** Traveling through rolling hills and farmland south of Buffalo, this byway highlights small towns, heritage architecture, and rural charm. Visitors enjoy a mix of open landscapes, seasonal color, and cultural sites. It celebrates western New York's agricultural traditions while offering peaceful scenery and community character.

National Natural Landmarks

☐ ☐ ♡ **Albany Pine Bush:** Recognized as a National Natural Landmark, this rare inland pine barrens ecosystem was shaped by glacial sands and fire. It shelters pitch pine–scrub oak communities and over 1,500 species, including the endangered Karner blue butterfly. With trails, research, and education programs, it highlights the ecological and cultural value of fire-adapted landscapes.
GPS: 42.718694, -73.864771

☐ ☐ ♡ **Bear Swamp Preserve:** This 310-acre preserve was named a National Natural Landmark for its mix of swamp, pond, and upland woodland habitats, including a significant population of great laurel. It supports amphibians, reptiles, and diverse birdlife, while offering trails and education programs that showcase the ecology of New York's Catskill foothills.
GPS: 42.474167, -74.059444

☐ ☐ ♡ **Bergen-Byron Swamp:** As the first site in the U.S. to be designated a National Natural Landmark, this 2,000-acre wetland contains marshes, fens, and woodlands. It is home to carnivorous plants, rare orchids, and rich birdlife. Managed by the Bergen Swamp Preservation Society, it remains a premier living laboratory for scientific research and ecological education.
GPS: 43.091389, -78.026667

☐ ☐ ♡ **Big Reed Pond:** This freshwater pond, part of Montauk County Park, earned National Natural Landmark status as one of Long Island's few undeveloped coastal plain pond ecosystems. Surrounded by forest and marsh, it supports fish, amphibians, and diverse birdlife while reflecting the cultural legacy of the Montaukett tribe who once lived here.
GPS: 41.077778, -71.910556

☐ ☐ ♡ **Chazy Fossil Reef:** Recognized as a National Natural Landmark, this site along Lake Champlain preserves the world's oldest known fossil reef, dating back 450 million years. Its Ordovician corals and marine fossils provide unmatched insight into early sea life and evolutionary history, making it a globally significant geologic treasure.
GPS: 44.960000, -73.373000

☐ ☐ ♡ **Deer Lick Nature Sanctuary:** This 398-acre preserve was designated a National Natural Landmark for its old-growth forest and dramatic gorges cut into the Onondaga Escarpment. Towering hemlocks, tulip trees, and red oaks thrive here, while its scenic cliffs and streams sustain diverse wildlife. The sanctuary exemplifies New York's geological and ecological heritage.
GPS: 42.421111, -78.905556

UNITED STATES EDITION

NEW YORK

 ☐ 🔖 ♡ **Dexter Marsh:** A 1,350-acre wetland at Lake Ontario's eastern edge, Dexter Marsh is a National Natural Landmark for its glacially formed marshes, cattail stands, and mudflats. It supports abundant fish, amphibians, and migratory birds, making it vital habitat in the Great Lakes region and a striking example of dynamic shoreline ecology.
GPS: 43.984444, -76.068611

 ☐ 🔖 ♡ **Ellenville Fault-Ice Caves:** This system of fractures within Sam's Point Preserve is recognized as a National Natural Landmark for being the largest open rift in the U.S. The deep crevices trap cold air, forming ice caves that sustain boreal plants far south of their normal range, creating a rare microclimate and a living record of glacial processes.
GPS: 41.671944, -74.347500

 ☐ 🔖 ♡ **Fall Brook Gorge:** Carved into Devonian shale and sandstone, this gorge is a National Natural Landmark for exposing sedimentary layers rich with fossils and ripple marks. The site illustrates ancient environments while providing striking scenery and a natural classroom for geology students, showcasing how water shapes stone over deep time.
GPS: 42.775556, -77.828611

 ☐ 🔖 ♡ **Fossil Coral Reef:** An abandoned limestone quarry near Rochester, this site was designated a National Natural Landmark for preserving a fossilized Middle Devonian coral reef over 375 million years old. Visitors encounter tabulate and rugose corals, crinoids, and brachiopods, making it one of the best windows into prehistoric tropical seas.
GPS: 42.997000, -77.930000

 ☐ 🔖 ♡ **Hart's Woods:** This small preserve outside Rochester was recognized as a National Natural Landmark for its pristine beech-maple climax forest. Ancient sugar maples and American beeches dominate the woodland, which offers rare continuity of pre-settlement ecology in a suburban landscape and provides essential habitat for birds and native plants.
GPS: 43.097778, -77.411944

 ☐ 🔖 ♡ **Hook Mountain and Nyack Beach State Park:** A National Natural Landmark along the Hudson River, this site preserves cliffs and slopes of the Palisades Sill. Its volcanic geology, rare plants, and birdlife make it scientifically valuable, while scenic trails highlight both ecological richness and the dramatic history of ancient lava flows and faulting.
GPS: 41.123889, -73.911944

 ☐ 🔖 ♡ **Iona Island Marsh:** Part of Bear Mountain State Park, this tidal marsh was named a National Natural Landmark for its brackish wetlands and critical role in supporting migratory birds and wintering bald eagles. Once a naval depot, today it serves as a bird sanctuary with uplands, marshes, and sweeping Hudson River views.
GPS: 41.303889, -73.977222

 ☐ 🔖 ♡ **Ironsides Island:** This St. Lawrence River island is a National Natural Landmark for its great blue heron rookery, which hosts over a thousand nesting birds each year. Managed by The Nature Conservancy, its cliffs, forest, and isolation protect fragile wildlife communities, making it a rare sanctuary for colonial waterbirds.
GPS: 44.396111, -75.850556

 ☐ 🔖 ♡ **Lakeview Marsh and Barrier Beach:** Located on Lake Ontario, this 3,461-acre landscape is recognized as a National Natural Landmark for its marshes shielded by a narrow barrier beach. It sustains nesting and migratory waterfowl while showcasing the interplay of dunes, marshes, and lake-driven processes in a coastal wetland system.
GPS: 43.768889, -76.203889

 ☐ 🔖 ♡ **Long Beach, Orient State Park:** This 2.5-mile sand spit at the tip of Long Island is a National Natural Landmark for its barrier beach formation and succession of habitats. Salt marshes, dune grasses, and maritime red cedar forests create a rare ecological gradient that shelters nesting shorebirds and diverse coastal species.
GPS: 41.129444, -72.266389

 ☐ 🔖 ♡ **McLean Bogs:** A National Natural Landmark managed by Cornell University, this acidic kettle bog was formed after glacial retreat. Floating sphagnum mats, carnivorous plants, and rare mosses thrive here, while ongoing ecological research makes it a premier site for understanding bog succession and wetland hydrology in the Northeast.
GPS: 42.548611, -76.266111

NEW YORK

 ☐ 🔖 ♡ **Mendon Ponds Park:** This Monroe County park was designated a National Natural Landmark for its outstanding glacial landforms, including eskers, kettles, and kames. The 2,500-acre park also contains wetlands and a peat bog known as the "Devil's Bathtub," making it a hotspot for birdwatching and ecological study.
GPS: 43.033333, -77.566667

 ☐ 🔖 ♡ **Mianus River Gorge:** Among the first acquisitions by The Nature Conservancy, this preserve is a National Natural Landmark for its climax hemlock forest and clean streams. Located in a heavily developed region, it offers refuge for wildlife, protects old-growth ecosystems, and provides scenic trails along dramatic rock ledges.
GPS: 41.185833, -73.621389

 ☐ 🔖 ♡ **Montezuma Marshes:** This 7,000-acre wetland complex in the Finger Lakes region is a National Natural Landmark for its critical role along the Atlantic Flyway. It supports bald eagles, waterfowl, and swamp forests, while serving as one of New York's best-preserved inland wetland habitats within a National Wildlife Refuge.
GPS: 42.966667, -76.733333

 ☐ 🔖 ♡ **Moss Island:** This tiny island in the Erie Canal is a National Natural Landmark for its remarkable glacial potholes—some of the largest in North America, reaching 50 feet deep. These features were carved by meltwater at the end of the Ice Age, creating a striking geological wonder that also attracts climbers and hikers.
GPS: 43.039722, -74.848333

 ☐ 🔖 ♡ **Moss Lake Bogs:** A sphagnum bog formed within a glacial kettle lake, Moss Lake Bogs was named a National Natural Landmark for its floating peat mats and unique acidic wetland ecology. The site supports carnivorous plants, rare mosses, and wetland wildlife, representing a pristine example of bog succession in western New York.
GPS: 42.398611, -78.184722

 ☐ 🔖 ♡ **Oak Orchard Creek Marsh:** This marshland was designated a National Natural Landmark for its diverse wetland habitats formed by glacial drift blocking the Oak Orchard River. It supports migratory birds, amphibians, and fish while incorporating part of the Niagara Escarpment, making it both a geologic and ecological treasure.
GPS: 43.135000, -78.370833

 ☐ 🔖 ♡ **Palisades of the Hudson:** These towering 350-foot diabase cliffs, formed by volcanic intrusions 200 million years ago, were recognized as a National Natural Landmark for their outstanding geology. The Palisades line the Hudson River with dramatic vertical walls that support raptors, rare plants, and some of the most iconic scenery in the Northeast.
GPS: 40.964444, -73.908611

 ☐ 🔖 ♡ **Petrified Gardens:** Once a private tourist site, this former park was designated a National Natural Landmark for its Cambrian stromatolite fossils—remnants of some of Earth's earliest reef-building organisms. Though now closed, it remains historically significant as an early paleontological discovery site in North America.
GPS: 43.083056, -73.844444

 ☐ 🔖 ♡ **Round Lake:** Found in Green Lakes State Park, Round Lake is a National Natural Landmark because it is a rare meromictic lake whose layers never mix. This unique chemistry preserves undisturbed sediments, providing scientists with centuries of environmental data, while its setting is surrounded by rich mesophytic forest.
GPS: 43.048889, -75.973056

 ☐ 🔖 ♡ **Thompson Pond:** This 507-acre preserve, managed by The Nature Conservancy, earned National Natural Landmark status for its kettle pond and rare calcareous bogs. It is a biodiversity hotspot supporting orchids, ferns, and wetland birds, and serves as the headwaters of Wappinger Creek, connecting hydrology with ecological richness.
GPS: 41.961111, -73.678611

 ☐ 🔖 ♡ **Zurich Bog:** This sphagnum bog, protected by the Bergen Swamp Preservation Society, is a National Natural Landmark for its undisturbed acidic wetland ecosystem. Floating mats, carnivorous plants, and rare mosses make it one of the most intact kettle bogs in the Northeast, serving as a vital site for botanical and ecological research.
GPS: 43.144722, -77.050556

NORTH CAROLINA

North Carolina's landscapes unfold from the towering peaks of Mount Mitchell to the shifting sands of the Outer Banks. With inviting state parks, national forests, iconic national parks, and distinctive natural landmarks, the Tar Heel State offers diverse and breathtaking outdoor experiences.

📅 Peak Season
April–June and September–October are North Carolina's peak seasons, offering mild temperatures, blooming wildflowers, and colorful fall foliage. These months are ideal for hiking, scenic drives, and exploring both mountains and coast.

📅 Offseason Months
November–March is the offseason, with cooler temperatures and snow in the mountains. Summer (July–August) is warm and humid, though coastal areas and higher elevations remain popular for outdoor recreation.

🍃 Scenery & Nature Timing
Spring brings wildflowers and rhododendron blooms in the Blue Ridge Mountains. Summer highlights beaches and lush forests. Fall peaks with vibrant mountain foliage, while winter offers snow-capped peaks and quiet trails.

✨ Special
North Carolina features the Blue Ridge Mountains, Outer Banks barrier islands, and the Great Smoky Mountains' misty ridges. The Linville Gorge, Jockey's Ridge sand dunes, and the rare blue ghost fireflies of the Appalachians showcase its diverse natural wonders.

NORTH CAROLINA

State Parks

☐ 🔖 ♡ **Carolina Beach State Park:** Located in New Hanover County, this 761-acre park is best known for its rare Venus flytrap population and diverse coastal habitats. Visitors explore seven miles of trails through salt marshes, pocosins, and maritime forest, fish along Snow's Cut, or launch boats on the Cape Fear River. With interpretive programs, camping, and unique plant life, it's a coastal treasure for both education and outdoor recreation.

☐ 🔖 ♡ **Carvers Creek State Park:** Spanning 4,530 acres in Cumberland County, this park preserves longleaf pine forests, wetlands, and historic farmland. Its centerpiece is Long Valley Farm, once owned by James Stillman Rockefeller. Trails offer hiking, birdwatching, and access to fishing ponds, while pine savannas support rare wildlife. With cultural history and natural beauty, the park showcases the Sandhills' unique character and ecosystems.

☐ 🔖 ♡ **Chimney Rock State Park:** Rising from Hickory Nut Gorge, this park spans multiple counties and is anchored by the 315-foot Chimney Rock monolith. Hikers climb to sweeping views of Lake Lure and the Blue Ridge Mountains, while trails lead to Hickory Nut Falls and rugged backcountry. The park features rare plant communities, raptors, and scenic overlooks, making it a premier destination for hiking, photography, and outdoor adventure.

☐ 🔖 ♡ **Cliffs of the Neuse State Park:** In Wayne County, this park reveals 90-foot cliffs carved by the Neuse River, displaying layers of ancient sandstone, shale, and clay. Visitors hike five miles of trails, swim in a spring-fed lake, or fish along the riverbank. With campgrounds, picnic shelters, and an educational visitor center, the park offers scenic landscapes, family-friendly recreation, and a glimpse of the coastal plain's natural history.

☐ 🔖 ♡ **Crowders Mountain State Park:** Just west of Charlotte in Gaston County, this park preserves rugged peaks rising above the Piedmont. Crowders Mountain and Kings Pinnacle provide dramatic viewpoints, reached by trails that challenge hikers and climbers. A nine-acre lake allows fishing and canoeing, while diverse wildlife thrives in forests and rocky outcrops. It's a destination for adventure, geology, and quiet escapes into nature.

☐ 🔖 ♡ **Dismal Swamp State Park:** In Camden County, this park safeguards 20,000 acres of the Great Dismal Swamp, a landscape rich in both cultural and ecological history. More than 20 miles of hiking and biking trails traverse cypress swamps, while a canal invites paddling adventures. Wildlife observation abounds with black bears, otters, and migratory birds. The park's visitor center interprets its ties to Native peoples and the Underground Railroad.

☐ 🔖 ♡ **Elk Knob State Park:** Towering in Watauga and Ashe counties, Elk Knob reaches 5,520 feet, offering year-round outdoor adventure. The summit trail provides breathtaking panoramas of the Blue Ridge, while lower trails explore forests rich in wildflowers and wildlife. In winter, the park welcomes snowshoeing and cross-country skiing. Dedicated to conservation, Elk Knob preserves fragile mountain habitats while giving visitors a high-country experience.

☐ 🔖 ♡ **Eno River State Park:** Just minutes from Durham, this park protects 30 miles of riparian corridor along the Eno River. Trails lead past historic mills, swinging bridges, and rushing rapids, with fishing, canoeing, and birdwatching opportunities throughout. The park supports oak-hickory forests and wetlands that host diverse wildlife. With camping, picnic areas, and cultural interpretation, it offers both natural beauty and deep ties to local history.

☐ 🔖 ♡ **Fort Macon State Park:** In Carteret County, this park preserves a restored Civil War–era fort and surrounding coastal habitats on Bogue Banks. Visitors tour casemates, earthworks, and interpretive exhibits, learning about military history from colonial times through World War II. Beyond the fort, the park offers a swimming beach, salt marsh boardwalks, fishing, and picnicking. Its blend of heritage, education, and seaside recreation makes it unique.

☐ 🔖 ♡ **Goose Creek State Park:** Stretching across 1,672 acres along the Pamlico River, this Beaufort County park showcases coastal habitats ranging from cypress swamps to salt marsh. Boardwalks and hiking trails allow exploration, with abundant birdwatching and opportunities for fishing or paddling. Picnic areas, interpretive exhibits, and campgrounds add to its appeal. By protecting estuarine ecosystems, Goose Creek offers both recreation and vital conservation.

NORTH CAROLINA

☐ ▢ ♡ **Gorges State Park:** In Transylvania County, this 8,000-acre park on the Blue Ridge Escarpment is a landscape of steep gorges, plunging waterfalls, and rare plant species. Trails lead to Rainbow and Turtleback Falls, while backcountry camping immerses visitors in remote terrain. Fishing streams, rugged overlooks, and educational programs highlight its biodiversity. Gorges stands out as one of North Carolina's wildest and most scenic state parks.

☐ ▢ ♡ **Grandfather Mountain State Park:** Encompassing high peaks and craggy cliffs, this park spans Avery, Watauga, and Caldwell counties. The Grandfather Trail challenges hikers with ladders, cables, and sheer cliffs, rewarding them with unmatched views. The mountain shelters rare plants and animals, including peregrine falcons. With rugged backcountry and dramatic landscapes, it offers a demanding but spectacular mountain wilderness experience.

☐ ▢ ♡ **Hammocks Beach State Park:** On Onslow County's coast, this park includes Bear Island, a pristine barrier island accessible only by ferry or paddle. Primitive camping, quiet beaches, and tidal salt marshes create a wilderness experience. Visitors fish, swim, kayak, or hike dunes and maritime forests. With nesting sea turtles and shorebirds, Hammocks Beach preserves rare coastal ecosystems and offers a retreat from developed beaches.

☐ ▢ ♡ **Hanging Rock State Park:** Covering nearly 9,000 acres in Stokes County, this park is famed for its quartzite cliffs, cascading waterfalls, and namesake peak. Trails lead to scenic overlooks and mountain ridges, while a lake offers swimming and canoeing. Rock climbing, picnicking, and camping add to its appeal. With abundant wildlife and breathtaking vistas, Hanging Rock is a premier destination for outdoor recreation and adventure.

☐ ▢ ♡ **Haw River State Park:** Situated in Rockingham and Guilford counties, this 1,500-acre park protects wetlands, floodplains, and forests along the Haw River. Trails explore hardwood stands and boardwalks over swamp habitat. Fishing, birdwatching, and wildlife viewing opportunities abound. The Summit Environmental Education Center provides learning programs, making this park a hub for both recreation and conservation-based education in the Piedmont.

☐ ▢ ♡ **Jockey's Ridge State Park:** In Dare County, this Outer Banks landmark preserves the tallest active sand dunes on the East Coast. The ever-shifting landscape is perfect for kite flying, hang gliding, and hiking. Trails traverse dunes, maritime forests, and wetlands, showcasing diverse habitats. Visitors enjoy sunsets over Roanoke Sound and interpretive programs that explain dune dynamics, coastal ecology, and cultural history.

☐ ▢ ♡ **Jones Lake State Park:** This Bladen County park features Jones Lake and nearby Salters Lake, both classic Carolina Bay formations. Trails circle the water, and fishing, swimming, and canoeing invite recreation. Picnic shelters and campgrounds provide family amenities. Surrounded by pocosin wetlands and pine savannas, the park is a living laboratory for unique geology and a peaceful retreat for outdoor relaxation.

☐ ▢ ♡ **Lake James State Park:** Nestled at the edge of the Blue Ridge, this park spans Burke and McDowell counties with a vast reservoir at its heart. Visitors swim at sandy beaches, paddle or motorboat across coves, and fish for bass or walleye. Over 25 miles of trails offer hiking and mountain biking, while campgrounds provide lakeside stays. Lake James blends mountain scenery with aquatic adventure.

☐ ▢ ♡ **Lake Norman State Park:** On North Carolina's largest man-made lake, this Iredell County park offers a 30-mile mountain bike trail, wooded hiking paths, and abundant fishing access. A swim beach and campgrounds make it family-friendly, while picnic areas invite day visits. The lake's 520 miles of shoreline create endless boating opportunities. With diverse recreation, it's a gateway to the Piedmont's biggest reservoir.

☐ ▢ ♡ **Lake Waccamaw State Park:** Columbus County's Lake Waccamaw is the largest natural Carolina Bay lake, with unique limestone-rich waters that support rare aquatic species. The park offers boardwalks, trails through pocosin wetlands, and fishing or paddling access. Campgrounds and picnic areas make it welcoming for families. Its unusual ecology and scenic shoreline provide a one-of-a-kind natural experience in southeastern North Carolina.

NORTH CAROLINA

☐ 🔖 ♡ **Lumber River State Park:** Flowing through Scotland, Hoke, Robeson, and Columbus counties, the Lumber River is a federally designated National Wild and Scenic River. The park protects 115 miles of its blackwater channel, offering canoeing, kayaking, fishing, and camping. Visitors explore swamp forests, sandbars, and wetlands rich in wildlife. With multiple access points, it's an excellent destination for paddling and nature immersion.

☐ 🔖 ♡ **Mayo River State Park:** In Rockingham County, this park preserves the scenic landscape along the Mayo River and its tributaries. Visitors enjoy hiking wooded trails, fishing in quiet pools, and picnicking near the riverbanks. Its undeveloped, peaceful setting highlights rocky outcrops, diverse plant life, and opportunities for birdwatching. With plans for future growth, Mayo River is a tranquil retreat for outdoor exploration.

☐ 🔖 ♡ **Medoc Mountain State Park:** Halifax County's Medoc Mountain is a monadnock rising gently from the Piedmont, its summit just 325 feet yet surrounded by rolling forest. The park's 3,893 acres include 10 miles of hiking trails, campgrounds, and Little Fishing Creek, a favorite for anglers. Known for wildflowers, hardwood forests, and a quiet atmosphere, Medoc Mountain offers a serene blend of natural history and recreation.

☐ 🔖 ♡ **Merchants Millpond State Park:** Located in Gates County, this 3,200-acre park centers around a millpond bordered by cypress swamps draped in Spanish moss. Canoe trails wind through hauntingly beautiful waters, while footpaths explore pine and hardwood forests. Campgrounds and rental canoes make it visitor-friendly, while abundant wildlife—beaver, heron, and owls—highlight the swamp's biodiversity. It's one of North Carolina's most distinctive natural landscapes.

☐ 🔖 ♡ **Morrow Mountain State Park:** In Stanly County, this 5,881-acre park protects the Uwharrie Mountains and the Yadkin/Pee Dee River. Scenic overlooks crown rugged ridges, while trails and campgrounds offer hiking and relaxation. Visitors boat or fish on Lake Tillery, swim in a seasonal pool, and explore cultural history at a reconstructed homestead. Combining mountain vistas with waterways, the park is a beloved Piedmont retreat.

☐ 🔖 ♡ **Mount Mitchell State Park:** Yancey County's Mount Mitchell rises to 6,684 feet, the highest peak east of the Mississippi. This high-elevation park offers breathtaking vistas, a natural museum of spruce-fir forest, and cool summer air. Trails connect to the Black Mountain Crest, while a paved path leads to the summit observation deck. With camping, picnicking, and rare ecology, Mount Mitchell is both a scientific and scenic treasure.

☐ 🔖 ♡ **New River State Park:** Spanning Ashe and Alleghany counties, this park preserves sections of one of the oldest rivers in the world. The New River flows gently, perfect for canoeing, tubing, and fishing. Trails wind through meadows and floodplains, with campgrounds set along its banks. Visitors find wildflowers, pastoral views, and abundant birdlife. The park blends rural charm, ancient geology, and peaceful recreation.

☐ 🔖 ♡ **Pettigrew State Park:** Surrounding 16,600-acre Lake Phelps in Tyrrell and Washington counties, Pettigrew State Park protects one of North Carolina's largest natural lakes. Cypress trees rise from its clear waters, while historic Somerset Place lies nearby. Visitors fish, boat, hike, and camp amid pocosin wetlands and hardwood forests. The park showcases both natural beauty and cultural history in an unspoiled setting.

☐ 🔖 ♡ **Pilot Mountain State Park:** Rising 2,421 feet above the Yadkin Valley, Pilot Mountain's quartzite knob is an unmistakable landmark. Located in Surry and Yadkin counties, the park offers rock climbing, hiking trails, camping, and fishing along the Yadkin River. Scenic overlooks provide sweeping views of the Piedmont and Blue Ridge. A cultural and natural icon, Pilot Mountain is a hub for recreation and inspiration.

☐ 🔖 ♡ **Pisgah View State Park:** Near Asheville in Buncombe County, Pisgah View is a new addition to the state park system, protecting rolling ridges, forests, and farmland near Mount Pisgah. Visitors enjoy scenic views of the Blue Ridge Mountains, hiking trails, picnicking, and abundant wildlife. While still under development, the park promises to provide expanded recreational opportunities and conservation in western North Carolina.

UNITED STATES EDITION

NORTH CAROLINA

☐ ▢ ♡ **Raven Rock State Park:** In Harnett County, this park is named for Raven Rock, a towering 150-foot cliff overlooking the Cape Fear River. Trails lead to scenic river overlooks, waterfalls, and wildflower meadows. Anglers fish along the riverbank, while campgrounds provide overnight adventure. With diverse habitats, geology, and cultural history, Raven Rock blends rugged terrain with peaceful river landscapes.

☐ ▢ ♡ **Rendezvous Mountain State Park:** Nestled in Wilkes County, this park highlights the Brushy Mountains and their role in North Carolina's natural and cultural history. Visitors hike trails through hardwood forests, enjoy picnicking in shaded groves, and watch for wildlife along ridges. Known for its tranquil setting, the park also serves as an educational forest site, offering opportunities for environmental learning alongside recreation.

☐ ▢ ♡ **Singletary Lake State Park:** This Bladen County park surrounds a Carolina Bay lake, one of many mysterious oval depressions of the coastal plain. The park is especially popular for group camping, with cabins, mess halls, and open fields for organized retreats. Hiking trails, canoeing, and fishing opportunities provide outdoor fun. With quiet waters and unique geology, Singletary Lake is a serene and educational destination.

☐ ▢ ♡ **South Mountains State Park:** In Burke County, this 20,000-acre park is the largest in North Carolina's system. Rugged peaks, deep gorges, and waterfalls like High Shoals Falls define the landscape. Over 40 miles of trails support hiking, horseback riding, and mountain biking. Camping, trout streams, and scenic overlooks enhance its wilderness feel. South Mountains delivers adventure and seclusion in a spectacular setting.

☐ ▢ ♡ **Stone Mountain State Park:** In Wilkes and Alleghany counties, this 14,000-acre park centers on a 600-foot granite dome rising above forests and streams. Trails lead to waterfalls, meadows, and the restored Hutchinson Homestead, reflecting the region's cultural past. Rock climbing is a highlight, while trout fishing and camping round out recreation. With dramatic geology and living history, Stone Mountain is a park of many layers.

☐ ▢ ♡ **William B. Umstead State Park:** Between Raleigh and Durham, this 5,599-acre park is an oasis of woodland and lakes amid the Triangle's urban sprawl. Miles of multi-use trails support hiking, biking, and horseback riding, while Big and Little Lakes offer fishing and canoeing. Campgrounds, picnic shelters, and wildlife observation enrich the visitor experience. Umstead provides both escape and connection to nature for city dwellers.

National Parks

☐ ▢ ♡ **Appalachian National Scenic Trail:** Stretching over 2,100 miles from Georgia to Maine, this legendary trail passes through North Carolina's highlands and offers rugged ridges, forested paths, and sweeping views. It provides opportunities for thru-hikes and day trips alike, immersing visitors in diverse ecosystems. As one of America's most iconic long-distance trails, it connects nature, history, and adventure.

☐ ▢ ♡ **Blue Ridge Parkway:** Winding through the Blue Ridge Mountains, this scenic roadway offers breathtaking overlooks, wildflower meadows, and access to trails leading into national forests and the Great Smoky Mountains. Visitors enjoy picnicking, hiking, and wildlife viewing along its 469 miles. Known as "America's Favorite Drive," it blends cultural history with mountain beauty in every season.

☐ ▢ ♡ **Cape Hatteras National Seashore:** Protecting barrier islands along North Carolina's Outer Banks, this seashore features pristine beaches, shifting dunes, and historic lighthouses. Visitors swim, surf, fish, or walk miles of open coastline, highlighted by the famous Cape Hatteras Lighthouse. It preserves coastal ecosystems and maritime heritage, offering both recreation and natural beauty by the Atlantic.

☐ ▢ ♡ **Cape Lookout National Seashore:** Located on the southern Outer Banks, this undeveloped seashore is home to the iconic Cape Lookout Lighthouse and wild Shackleford Banks horses. Accessible mainly by boat, it offers camping, fishing, hiking, and quiet exploration of sandy beaches and salt marshes. Its mix of natural wonder and cultural history makes it a treasured coastal destination.

NORTH CAROLINA

 **Carl Sandburg Home National Historic Site:** In Flat Rock, this site preserves the home of poet, author, and Lincoln biographer Carl Sandburg. Visitors tour the house, walk through historic barns and goat farm, and explore miles of trails. The site reflects Sandburg's literary legacy and his love of nature, offering a cultural and scenic retreat in the Blue Ridge.

 **Fort Raleigh National Historic Site:** On Roanoke Island, this site commemorates the first English settlement attempt in the New World, known as the Lost Colony. Visitors explore exhibits, archaeological remains, and the story of early colonists. The park highlights Native American heritage, early European exploration, and one of America's greatest historical mysteries.

 **Great Smoky Mountains National Park:** Straddling the North Carolina–Tennessee border, this UNESCO World Heritage Site is celebrated for its misty mountains, rich biodiversity, and cultural history. With over 800 miles of trails, visitors hike to waterfalls, ridges, and historic homesteads. Wildlife, scenic drives, and seasonal wildflowers make it the most-visited national park in the U.S.

 **Guilford Courthouse National Military Park:** In Greensboro, this park preserves the site of the 1781 Battle of Guilford Courthouse, a turning point in the Southern campaign of the American Revolution. Visitors walk battlefield trails, view monuments, and learn about the strategies that shaped independence. Its blend of history and nature offers a powerful educational experience.

 **Moores Creek National Battlefield:** Located in Currie, this site marks the 1776 Battle of Moores Creek Bridge, the first significant victory for American patriots in the South. Trails, interpretive exhibits, and preserved earthworks tell the story of the clash between Loyalists and revolutionaries. Visitors explore the grounds and gain insight into a pivotal Revolutionary War event.

 **Wright Brothers National Memorial:** In Kitty Hawk, this memorial honors the first powered flight achieved by Orville and Wilbur Wright in 1903. Visitors see reconstructed camp buildings, a granite monument atop Kill Devil Hill, and exhibits on aviation history. The site celebrates innovation, perseverance, and the moment that launched the modern age of flight.

State & National Forests

 **Bladen Lakes State Forest:** Spanning 33,450 acres in Bladen County, this is North Carolina's largest state forest. Managed for timber, pine straw, and wildlife, it features pocosins, Carolina bays, and sand ridges. Visitors can hike, fish, hunt, ride horses or street-legal vehicles, and stargaze in its remote, open skies. The forest blends conservation with recreation and education.

 **Clemmons Educational State Forest:** This 825-acre forest near Clayton in Johnston and Wake counties is dedicated to teaching forestry and ecology. With self-guided trails, tree ID stations, and interpretive exhibits, it engages visitors of all ages. School groups and families enjoy interactive programs and year-round outdoor learning about woodland ecosystems.

 **Croatan National Forest:** Encompassing 160,000 acres near New Bern, Croatan is one of the only coastal national forests in the East. Its longleaf pine savannas, pocosins, and tidal marshes support diverse wildlife. Visitors hike, paddle, fish, hunt, and camp along sandy beaches. The forest combines coastal ecology with abundant recreation.

 **DuPont State Recreational Forest:** Covering 12,500 acres across Henderson and Transylvania counties, DuPont is famed for its waterfalls—Hooker, High, and Triple—and granite outcrops. With 80+ miles of trails, it's a hotspot for hiking, biking, horseback riding, and fishing. Visitors also enjoy swimming and photography. Its scenery has starred in films like The Hunger Games.

 **Headwaters State Forest:** A rugged 6,730-acre preserve near Brevard, this forest protects the headwaters of the French Broad River. Managed for rare species and watershed conservation, it offers primitive recreation only, including hiking, fishing, and seasonal hunting. With no developed facilities, it provides a wilderness-style experience in a pristine mountain setting.

NORTH CAROLINA

☐ 🔖 ♡ **Holmes Educational State Forest:** This 235-acre site near Hendersonville serves as an outdoor classroom. Interpretive trails with forestry exhibits teach sustainable woodland management and ecology. Hosting school and family programs year-round, it connects people to nature through guided walks, hands-on exhibits, and quiet mountain woodlands.

☐ 🔖 ♡ **Jordan Lake Educational State Forest:** Located in Chatham County near Jordan Lake, this 900-acre site blends recreation with learning. Trails highlight forest ecology, watersheds, and wildlife, while a visitor center provides exhibits and programs. Popular with schools and families, it emphasizes conservation while offering an outdoor classroom experience.

☐ 🔖 ♡ **Mountain Island Educational State Forest:** Spanning 2,000 acres in Gaston and Lincoln counties, this forest emphasizes outdoor education. Visitors, often through scheduled programs, explore interpretive trails focused on forestry, ecology, and conservation. It provides hands-on learning opportunities while protecting woodlands and wildlife along Mountain Island Lake.

☐ 🔖 ♡ **Nantahala National Forest:** At 531,000 acres, this is North Carolina's largest national forest, stretching across the western mountains. It features river gorges, waterfalls, and the Joyce Kilmer–Slickrock Wilderness with old-growth giants. Recreation includes hiking, rafting, camping, and driving scenic byways. Portions of the Appalachian Trail pass through its wild landscapes.

☐ 🔖 ♡ **Pisgah National Forest:** Spanning 512,758 acres in western North Carolina, Pisgah is rich in natural and cultural heritage. Home to the Cradle of Forestry, it features waterfalls like Looking Glass and Sliding Rock, plus extensive hiking and biking trails. Visitors camp, fish, and explore old-growth forests. Its peaks and rivers make it a mountain recreation mecca.

☐ 🔖 ♡ **Turnbull Creek Educational State Forest:** This 890-acre Bladen County site highlights ecology and conservation through self-guided trails and interactive exhibits. School groups and families enjoy learning about forest management, habitats, and wildlife in an engaging outdoor setting. It provides year-round educational opportunities within a living forest laboratory.

☐ 🔖 ♡ **Tuttle Educational State Forest:** A 288-acre site in Caldwell County named for educator Lelia Tuttle, this forest features interpretive trails, forestry exhibits, and hands-on programs. It blends outdoor learning with Appalachian heritage, helping visitors explore forest history, ecology, and conservation while enjoying a peaceful mountain landscape.

☐ 🔖 ♡ **Uwharrie National Forest:** This 50,645-acre forest in south-central North Carolina protects the ancient Uwharrie Mountains. It offers hiking, camping, fishing, and hunting, along with off-highway vehicle trails and historic gold-panning sites. Scenic woodlands and ridges provide year-round recreation while highlighting the state's oldest mountain range.

National Scenic Byways & All-American Roads

☐ 🔖 ♡ **Blue Ridge Parkway:** A 469-mile route linking the Great Smoky Mountains to Shenandoah, the Parkway is famed for its sweeping overlooks, waterfalls, and wildflower meadows. In North Carolina, it provides access to Mount Mitchell, Linville Gorge, and Craggy Gardens. Scenic pull-offs, hiking trails, and picnic areas showcase Appalachian beauty across all four seasons.

☐ 🔖 ♡ **Cherohala Skyway:** Stretching 43 miles from Robbinsville, NC, into Tennessee, this high-elevation roadway climbs through the Cherokee and Nantahala forests. Known for mile-high overlooks, vibrant fall colors, and access to remote hiking trails, it blends rugged wilderness with smooth mountain curves, offering drivers and sightseers a serene Blue Ridge adventure.

☐ 🔖 ♡ **Forest Heritage Scenic Byway:** A 76-mile loop through Pisgah National Forest, this route follows US 276 and NC 215 past Sliding Rock, Looking Glass Falls, and the historic Cradle of Forestry. Winding through dense hardwood forests and mountain valleys, it connects scenic overlooks, trout streams, and cultural landmarks that highlight the region's natural and historic heritage.

☐ 🔖 ♡ **Newfound Gap Road:** This 31-mile drive runs through Great Smoky Mountains National Park, connecting Cherokee, NC, to Gatlinburg, TN. Climbing to 5,046 feet at Newfound Gap, it reveals sweeping views, Appalachian spruce-fir forests, and historic sites. The byway offers access to trailheads, picnic areas, and overlooks, immersing travelers in rich natural beauty.

NORTH CAROLINA

☐ ▯ ♡ **Outer Banks Scenic Byway:** Stretching 131 miles along barrier islands and across ferry routes, this coastal drive showcases lighthouses, marshes, and pristine beaches. Passing through maritime villages like Ocracoke and Hatteras, it reveals seashore ecology, wild horses, and fishing heritage. With sweeping ocean and sound views, it offers an immersive coastal journey.

State Scenic Byways

☐ ▯ ♡ **Alligator River Route:** Stretching through Hyde and Tyrrell counties, this byway passes Lake Mattamuskeet and the Alligator River National Wildlife Refuge. Travelers see vast marshes, cypress stands, and open farmland where black bears, waterfowl, and other wildlife thrive. With fishing villages and sweeping wetlands, the route offers a quiet immersion into coastal ecology and heritage.

☐ ▯ ♡ **Appalachian Medley:** Winding 45 miles through Haywood County, this route threads between Pisgah National Forest and the Great Smoky Mountains. It highlights mountain coves, old farmsteads, and scenic streams. The byway connects to Cold Mountain, historic churches, and outdoor recreation areas, showcasing the cultural roots and rugged natural beauty of western North Carolina.

☐ ▯ ♡ **Averasboro Battlefield Scenic Byway:** Just under five miles, this byway passes the preserved Civil War battlefield where patriots resisted advancing troops in 1865. Markers and exhibits detail the engagement, while peaceful fields and woodlands frame the experience. It blends solemn history with natural scenery, offering visitors reflection on a pivotal moment in the state's past.

☐ ▯ ♡ **Big Horse Creek Scenic Byway:** This 18-mile mountain drive winds through Ashe County near the Virginia border. Narrow country roads follow the curves of Big Horse Creek, passing through woodlands, small farms, and shaded hollows. The route provides a glimpse of rural life and mountain traditions while offering quiet landscapes and serene beauty away from busier highways.

☐ ▯ ♡ **Black Mountain Rag:** Named after a traditional fiddle tune, this 31-mile byway runs from Gerton to Black Mountain. It winds through Hickory Nut Gorge, offering dramatic cliffs, waterfalls, and views of Chimney Rock. The road dips past apple orchards and forested ridges, combining cultural heritage with natural splendor in one of western North Carolina's most scenic drives.

☐ ▯ ♡ **Blue-Gray Scenic Byway:** This 82-mile route in the Coastal Plain traces landscapes once shaped by Civil War campaigns. It passes battle sites, historic cemeteries, and quiet farmland while also offering glimpses of cypress swamps and river valleys. Combining pastoral scenery with reminders of conflict, the byway connects travelers to heritage and nature alike.

☐ ▯ ♡ **Brunswick Town Road:** A short 3-mile route leading to Brunswick Town/Fort Anderson State Historic Site near Southport. Travelers explore colonial-era ruins, earthen fortifications, and riverfront scenery. Interpretive stops reveal the story of an early port town and Civil War defense. Though brief, the drive immerses visitors in both history and the low-country landscape.

☐ ▯ ♡ **Cape Fear Historic Byway:** This 8-mile urban drive loops through downtown Wilmington, connecting the riverfront, colonial homes, and the USS North Carolina Battleship. Brick streets, historic churches, and waterfront parks line the route. It highlights the city's maritime heritage and cultural charm while offering views of the Cape Fear River and its busy port activity.

☐ ▯ ♡ **Clayton Bypass Scenic Byway:** A 10-mile stretch along US 70 near Johnston County, this route blends rural countryside with easy access to the Triangle region. Travelers see rolling farmland, woodlands, and open skies. While short, it provides a relaxing escape into pastoral scenery and serves as a gateway between urban development and traditional Piedmont landscapes.

☐ ▯ ♡ **Colonial Heritage Byway:** A 92-mile journey through the Piedmont, this route traces roads once traveled by settlers and patriots. It winds past historic homes, battle sites, and Quaker meetinghouses, as well as fertile farmland and oak-hickory forests. The byway highlights the state's colonial roots, offering a reflective drive through history and a varied rural landscape.

NORTH CAROLINA

☐ 🔖 ♡ **Crowders Mountain Drive:** This short byway provides access to Crowders Mountain State Park in Gaston County. Passing forested ridges and rolling hills, it offers scenic approaches to the dramatic cliffs of Crowders Mountain and Kings Pinnacle. With recreational access and views of the Piedmont, it links natural beauty to outdoor adventure near Charlotte.

☐ 🔖 ♡ **Devil's Stompin' Ground Road:** A 43-mile drive through Chatham and Lee counties, this route winds past the legendary "Devil's Tramping Ground," a mysterious barren circle tied to folklore. Beyond the legend, the byway reveals hardwood forests, peaceful farms, and small rural towns. It blends storytelling with scenery, making it one of North Carolina's most curious drives.

☐ 🔖 ♡ **Drovers Road:** This 16.5-mile mountain byway recalls historic livestock routes used by settlers. It follows winding roads through Henderson County, passing orchards, ridges, and mountain hollows. Interpretive markers tell the story of the drovers who once guided animals through the Appalachians, combining cultural history with beautiful scenery.

☐ 🔖 ♡ **Edenton-Windsor Loop:** An 87-mile loop through the Albemarle Sound region, connecting the historic port town of Edenton with Windsor. Along the way, travelers encounter cypress-lined rivers, colonial landmarks, and farmlands. The byway reveals the Coastal Plain's rich blend of natural wetlands and deep cultural history, from plantations to Revolutionary War heritage.

☐ 🔖 ♡ **Flint Hill Ramble:** A short 5-mile scenic byway in Randolph County, this route showcases rolling Piedmont hills, shaded woodlands, and quiet farmland. Though brief, it highlights the peaceful rural atmosphere of central North Carolina. Ideal for a slow-paced drive, it offers a glimpse of the region's agricultural landscape and natural charm.

☐ 🔖 ♡ **French Broad Overview:** A 17-mile drive in Madison County that traces the French Broad River. The byway passes through rural farmland, mountain valleys, and riverfront scenery, offering both recreational opportunities and quiet beauty. With fishing access, pastoral views, and historic communities, the route emphasizes the enduring significance of one of the world's oldest rivers.

☐ 🔖 ♡ **Grassy Island Crossing:** A 26-mile byway in Montgomery County, this route winds through Uwharrie National Forest lands and along the Pee Dee River. Travelers pass forested hills, wildlife habitats, and historic farmsteads. With opportunities for hiking, fishing, and exploring cultural landmarks, it provides a window into the unique landscape of the ancient Uwharrie Mountains.

☐ 🔖 ♡ **Green Swamp Byway:** A 53-mile route through Brunswick County, this byway highlights the rare ecology of the Green Swamp. Travelers see longleaf pine savannas, pocosins, and carnivorous plants like Venus flytraps and pitcher plants. The road also connects small farming communities, offering both natural wonder and cultural insight into southeastern North Carolina.

☐ 🔖 ♡ **Hellbender Byway:** A 61-mile mountain drive named for the giant salamander found in nearby streams. Following NC 209 between Lake Junaluska and Hot Springs, it winds through Pisgah National Forest. Tight curves, river crossings, and sweeping mountain views define the journey. It's a favorite for motorcyclists and outdoor enthusiasts seeking a rugged, high-country adventure.

☐ 🔖 ♡ **Historic Albemarle Tour:** Covering more than 100 miles, this byway connects historic sites across northeastern North Carolina. Travelers visit colonial towns, lighthouses, Civil War forts, and maritime museums. The route weaves together rivers, sounds, and estuaries with rich heritage, offering a blend of cultural exploration and coastal scenery through one of the state's oldest regions.

☐ 🔖 ♡ **Indian Heritage Trail:** This eastern Piedmont and Coastal Plain byway highlights the cultural traditions of North Carolina's Native peoples. Passing through Robeson and surrounding counties, it connects Lumbee communities, historic markers, and cultural centers. Alongside heritage, the drive showcases wetlands, pine forests, and farmland, blending stories of resilience with the landscape.

☐ 🔖 ♡ **Ivanhoe Road:** A 12-mile scenic byway in Sampson County that winds through woodlands, farmlands, and the small community of Ivanhoe. It offers a snapshot of rural life and agricultural heritage. Quiet fields, churches, and longleaf pines line the road, creating a peaceful, short drive that reflects the region's simple and enduring countryside character.

☐ 🔖 ♡ **Little Parkway:** A 20-mile stretch of the original scenic route linking Linville to Blowing Rock, this byway predates the Blue Ridge Parkway. Passing Grandfather Mountain, the Linville Viaduct, and mountain resorts, it offers spectacular vistas and historic charm. The road showcases early 20th-century scenic highway design and connects travelers to beloved High Country landmarks.

☐ 🔖 ♡ **Mill Bridge Scenic Byway:** Located in Rowan County, this rural drive passes through rolling farmland, old churches, and homesteads tied to Scotch-Irish settlement. The route highlights the Mill Bridge community's agricultural and cultural heritage. Fields, woodlots, and historic cemeteries frame the landscape, offering a tranquil journey through deep Piedmont roots.

NORTH CAROLINA

☐ 🔖 ♡ **New Hope Road:** This byway winds through Franklin and Nash counties, following gentle Piedmont ridges and farmland. Churches, crossroads communities, and tobacco fields reflect the area's agricultural history. The drive blends pastoral scenery with glimpses of small-town heritage, offering a peaceful escape through the rural heart of central North Carolina.

☐ 🔖 ♡ **Pamlico Scenic Byway:** A 122-mile coastal route skirting the Pamlico River from Washington to Manns Harbor. Travelers see fishing villages, waterfront farmland, and wildlife-rich estuaries. Historic sites and ferry crossings add to the experience. With expansive views of the Pamlico Sound and its tributaries, the byway highlights both natural beauty and maritime culture.

☐ 🔖 ♡ **Peachtree Road:** This 7-mile byway in Cherokee County winds through the southern Appalachians. The road follows valleys dotted with family farms and churches, framed by forested ridges. It reflects the enduring rural heritage of the western mountains while offering travelers quiet mountain views, pastoral charm, and a sense of community rooted in the landscape.

☐ 🔖 ♡ **Perquimans River Byway:** A 12-mile drive in northeastern North Carolina that traces the Perquimans River. Cypress-lined waters, colonial-era towns, and scenic farmland define the route. With historic homes, wildlife viewing, and calm river bends, it blends heritage and natural scenery. The byway provides an intimate look at life along the rivers of the Albemarle region.

☐ 🔖 ♡ **Pisgah Loop Scenic Byway:** A rugged mountain loop through Pisgah National Forest in Burke County. The 47-mile route, partly gravel, traces historic logging roads and forestry experiment sites. Travelers encounter mountain streams, hardwood forests, and panoramic overlooks. It connects to Linville Gorge and highlights both the natural beauty and forest history of the southern Appalachians.

☐ 🔖 ♡ **Pottery Road:** This byway highlights Seagrove, the heart of North Carolina's pottery tradition. Along its 25 miles, visitors discover dozens of potters' studios, historic kilns, and cultural landmarks. Rolling farmland and forests frame the route, but the true draw is the craftsmanship and artistry of generations of potters who define this unique Piedmont heritage.

☐ 🔖 ♡ **Rolling Kansas Byway:** A 33-mile drive across Surry County, this scenic route winds through the foothills of the Blue Ridge. Pastoral valleys, vineyards, and rural communities line the road. Overlooks reveal distant mountains, while historic churches and farms anchor the countryside. The byway highlights the charm of the Yadkin Valley's agricultural and cultural landscapes.

☐ 🔖 ♡ **Sandhills Scenic Drive:** A 65-mile byway through Moore, Richmond, and Montgomery counties. The road reveals longleaf pine savannas, wiregrass landscapes, and the unique ecology of the Sandhills. Small towns, horse farms, and historic sites enrich the journey. With conservation lands and natural areas, it blends rare ecosystems with cultural heritage in a distinct region.

☐ 🔖 ♡ **South Mountain Scenery:** A 33-mile byway through Burke, Cleveland, and Rutherford counties near South Mountains State Park. It winds past forested ridges, trout streams, and small farms. Scenic overlooks and access to hiking trails enhance the experience. The route showcases the quiet beauty of the South Mountains while highlighting outdoor recreation opportunities.

☐ 🔖 ♡ **Upper Yadkin Way:** Following the Yadkin River in Wilkes and Caldwell counties, this route passes fertile valleys, vineyards, and historic communities. With pastoral farmland and wooded ridges, it connects cultural landmarks to natural scenery. Travelers enjoy views of Brushy Mountain foothills, river bends, and rural charm along one of the Piedmont's most storied waterways.

☐ 🔖 ♡ **Whitewater Way:** A 9-mile mountain byway near Cashiers, this route traces the Whitewater River to Whitewater Falls, the highest waterfall east of the Rockies. Dense forests, scenic cascades, and overlooks make it a short but dramatic drive. It offers direct access to hiking trails, picnic areas, and one of the state's most spectacular natural landmarks.

☐ 🔖 ♡ **Yadkin River Valley Byway:** A 65-mile journey through fertile farmland and rolling Piedmont hills. This byway highlights vineyards, historic homesteads, and rural communities shaped by the Yadkin River. With views of the Blue Ridge foothills, it combines natural scenery with agricultural heritage, offering a peaceful yet engaging look at the central North Carolina countryside.

National Natural Landmarks

NORTH CAROLINA

 **Bear Island:** Recognized as a National Natural Landmark for its shifting barrier island system, Bear Island in Hammocks Beach State Park preserves undeveloped beaches, maritime forests, and tidal marshes. This dynamic coastal landscape provides critical habitat for shorebirds and marine life while showcasing the natural processes that shape the Outer Banks.
GPS: 34.631944, -77.145556

 **Goose Creek State Park Natural Area:** Designated a National Natural Landmark for illustrating how rising seas transform coastal plains, Goose Creek preserves tidal wetlands, pocosins, and cypress swamps. Its ecosystems demonstrate ocean transgression and provide a haven for estuarine wildlife, making it a living model of coastal change in North Carolina.
GPS: 35.473611, -76.913889

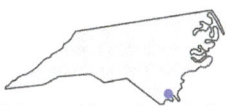 **Green Swamp:** This 15,000-acre preserve was named a National Natural Landmark for its remarkable biodiversity, including longleaf pine savannas and rare carnivorous plants like Venus flytraps and pitcher plants. Its wetland mosaics represent one of the richest natural communities in the Southeast, offering a refuge for unique and endangered species.
GPS: 34.093210, -78.299250

 **Long Hope Creek Spruce Bog:** A National Natural Landmark for its relict boreal community, this spruce bog in the Blue Ridge preserves plant species typically found much farther north. As a remnant of glacial-era conditions, it provides rare ecological insight and supports one of North Carolina's most unusual and fragile ecosystems.
GPS: 36.381101, -81.645663

 **Mount Jefferson State Natural Area:** Recognized as a National Natural Landmark for its outstanding oak-chestnut forest, Mount Jefferson protects one of the Southeast's best remnants of this ecosystem. Its rugged slopes and ridgeline harbor diverse flora, while the summit offers sweeping views and a high-elevation refuge for plants and wildlife.
GPS: 36.400833, -81.462778

 **Mount Mitchell State Park:** At 6,684 feet, Mount Mitchell stands as the highest peak east of the Mississippi. It was designated a National Natural Landmark for its rare spruce-fir forest, a southern outpost of boreal ecosystems normally found in Canada, offering an alpine-like landscape and vital habitat in the Appalachians.
GPS: 35.770278, -82.263333

 **Nags Head Woods and Jockey Ridge:** This paired landmark highlights the sequence of dune formation and ecological succession on the Outer Banks. Nags Head Woods preserves lush maritime forests, while Jockey Ridge boasts the tallest active sand dunes on the East Coast, together representing coastal evolution in striking form.
GPS: 35.961944, -75.634167

 **Orbicular Diorite:** Recognized as a National Natural Landmark for its extreme rarity, this igneous formation displays orb-like patterns of feldspar, hornblende, and pyroxene. Found in only a handful of places worldwide, the North Carolina outcrop is a geological curiosity that illustrates unusual plutonic crystallization.
GPS: 35.853420, -80.410050

 **Piedmont Beech Natural Area:** Within Umstead State Park, this forest was designated a National Natural Landmark for preserving one of the Piedmont's finest near-climax mesophytic communities. Mature beech, oak, and poplar dominate the canopy, creating a living example of the region's original woodland ecology.
GPS: 35.853889, -78.742778

 **Pilot Mountain:** This striking quartzite monadnock, rising abruptly above the Piedmont, was named a National Landmark for its unique geology and ecological significance. Its summit cliffs and slopes host Blue Ridge plant species, while its distinctive profile serves as both a natural landmark and cultural icon.
GPS: 36.340138, -80.474224

NORTH CAROLINA

 ☐ 🔖 ♡ **Salyer's Ridge Natural Area:** Found in Mattamuskeet National Wildlife Refuge, this site is a National Natural Landmark for illustrating forest succession along North Carolina's coast. Once dominated by loblolly pines, it is transitioning naturally into mixed hardwood forest, offering scientists a rare view of coastal woodland regeneration.
GPS: 35.456765, -76.179953

 ☐ 🔖 ♡ **Smith Island:** This barrier island complex, which includes Bald Head Island, was designated a National Natural Landmark for its undisturbed dune fields, salt marshes, and high biodiversity. It remains one of the most pristine island systems on the Atlantic Coast, providing critical nesting grounds for sea turtles and shorebirds.
GPS: 36.541967, -75.908155

 ☐ 🔖 ♡ **Stone Mountain:** A National Natural Landmark for being North Carolina's finest granite dome, Stone Mountain rises dramatically above the surrounding hills. Its exposed rock face, cascading waterfalls, and adjoining woodlands highlight the power of erosion and the beauty of isolated monadnocks in the Southeast.
GPS: 36.393611, -81.043333

UNITED STATES EDITION

North Dakota

North Dakota's rugged beauty spans painted canyons, wide-open prairies, and winding river valleys. With scenic state parks, national forests, national park sites, and distinctive natural landmarks, the state offers a peaceful yet dramatic outdoor experience shaped by vast skies, quiet trails, and timeless Great Plains vistas.

📅 Peak Season
June–September is North Dakota's peak season, with warm weather, open trails, and long daylight hours. These months are best for exploring parks, hiking the badlands, and enjoying scenic byways across the prairie.

📅 Offseason Months
November–April is the offseason, with cold winters, snow, and limited access to some outdoor sites. Spring and fall offer mild weather but fewer visitors, ideal for peaceful exploration.

🍃 Scenery & Nature Timing
Spring brings wildflowers and migrating waterfowl. Summer highlights green prairies and vibrant sunsets. Fall offers golden grasslands and crisp air, while winter transforms the plains into a stark, snow-covered landscape.

✨ Special
North Dakota showcases the painted canyons of Theodore Roosevelt National Park, the rugged Little Missouri Badlands, and the prairie pothole wetlands teeming with birds. Northern lights, rolling grasslands, and eroded buttes reveal its quiet natural majesty.

NORTH DAKOTA

State Parks

☐ 🔖 ♡ **Beaver Lake State Park:** Nestled in Logan County, this 273-acre retreat offers boating, fishing, and camping on tranquil Beaver Lake. Scenic trails wind through meadows and groves, making it perfect for hiking, picnicking, and spotting wildlife. Its quiet, natural setting provides a relaxing escape where visitors can enjoy both outdoor recreation and the peaceful landscapes of south-central North Dakota.

☐ 🔖 ♡ **Cross Ranch State Park:** Located in Oliver County, this 569-acre park protects one of the last free-flowing stretches of the Missouri River. Visitors can canoe, kayak, or fish along its banks, or explore miles of trails through cottonwood forests and prairies. Campsites and cabins provide overnight options, while historic and natural features highlight the rich heritage and beauty of the river valley.

☐ 🔖 ♡ **Fort Abraham Lincoln State Park:** In Morton County, this park combines history with outdoor adventure. It preserves On-A-Slant Indian Village and a reconstructed frontier fort once commanded by Lt. Col. George Custer. Hiking trails cross wooded bluffs with river views, while campsites offer overnight stays. The blend of Native American and military history makes it one of North Dakota's most visited sites.

☐ 🔖 ♡ **Fort Ransom State Park:** Stretching 934 acres in Ransom County's Sheyenne River Valley, this park blends rolling woodlands with cultural history. Visitors can camp along the river, hike through forests, or fish in shaded waters. The historic Sunne Farmstead offers a glimpse of pioneer life. Seasonal events, trails, and scenic overlooks make it a favorite destination for both recreation and heritage exploration.

☐ 🔖 ♡ **Fort Stevenson State Park:** On the shores of Lake Sakakawea in McLean County, this 586-acre park honors its military past with a partial reconstruction of Fort Stevenson. Visitors enjoy boating, sailing, and fishing the vast reservoir, plus exploring an arboretum with diverse trees. Campgrounds, trails, and interpretive displays make it ideal for combining outdoor adventure with regional history and natural beauty.

☐ 🔖 ♡ **Grahams Island State Park:** Found on Devils Lake in Ramsey County, this 959-acre park is a haven for anglers, campers, and boaters. Its shoreline hosts fishing tournaments, while wooded areas offer shaded trails and picnic spots. Cabins and campsites provide overnight stays. The park is a year-round destination, where water recreation meets peaceful escapes in North Dakota's largest natural lake setting.

☐ 🔖 ♡ **Icelandic State Park:** Set around Lake Renwick in Pembina County, this 930-acre park preserves both culture and nature. Visitors explore the Pioneer Heritage Center and restored historic buildings while also hiking trails through the Gunlogson State Nature Preserve. Camping, swimming, and birdwatching round out the experience, making it a unique combination of Icelandic heritage and serene northern landscapes.

☐ 🔖 ♡ **Lake Metigoshe State Park:** At 1,509 acres in Bottineau County, this park straddles the Canadian border in the scenic Turtle Mountains. Lake Metigoshe provides boating, fishing, and swimming, while trails weave through forests for hiking, biking, and winter skiing. Campsites, cabins, and year-round recreation make it one of North Dakota's premier outdoor destinations, offering peaceful retreats in pristine surroundings.

☐ 🔖 ♡ **Lake Sakakawea State Park:** Located in Mercer County, this 740-acre park anchors the southern shore of the massive reservoir. A marina, swimming beach, and campsites make it a hub for water recreation, from sailing to fishing. Trails overlook the sweeping shoreline, offering vistas of North Dakota's largest lake. Wildlife, open skies, and varied recreation ensure a memorable outdoor experience for all ages.

☐ 🔖 ♡ **Lewis and Clark State Park:** Along Lake Sakakawea in Williams County, this 525-acre park recalls the explorers' journey through the region. Visitors enjoy swimming beaches, fishing piers, and a full-service marina. Trails wind through prairies and woodlands, while interpretive sites highlight expedition history. Its blend of water recreation, cultural significance, and scenic lakefront camping makes it a family-friendly destination.

☐ 🔖 ♡ **Little Missouri State Park:** Covering 6,493 rugged acres in Dunn County, this park lies deep in the North Dakota Badlands. Campsites, horseback riding trails, and footpaths reveal dramatic canyons, buttes, and sweeping vistas. Wildlife thrives in the rough terrain, making it ideal for nature photography. Its isolation and beauty attract hikers, riders, and adventurers seeking the state's wildest landscapes.

NORTH DAKOTA

☐ ▭ ♡ **Rough Rider State Park:** This small 63-acre park in Billings County is the starting point for the legendary 144-mile Maah Daah Hey Trail. Visitors come for horseback riding, mountain biking, and hiking in the heart of the Badlands. Despite its modest size, it offers a gateway to one of the nation's most iconic long-distance trails, with stunning views of buttes and canyons.

☐ ▭ ♡ **Turtle River State Park:** Situated in Grand Forks County, this 775-acre wooded park follows the scenic Turtle River. Trails meander through lush forest, offering birdwatching and fishing along the river's bends. Campsites and shelters accommodate overnighters, while a CCC-built lodge recalls the park's New Deal heritage. Its tranquil environment, historic roots, and outdoor amenities make it a popular eastern North Dakota getaway.

National Parks

 ☐ ▭ ♡ **Fort Union Trading Post National Historic Site:** Straddling the North Dakota–Montana border, this reconstructed 19th-century fort was once the Upper Missouri's busiest fur trading post. Here, tribes like the Assiniboine exchanged buffalo robes for goods with traders. Visitors explore historic exhibits, interpreters in period dress, and trails that reveal the region's role in commerce and cultural exchange.

 ☐ ▭ ♡ **Theodore Roosevelt National Park:** Encompassing over 70,000 acres in the Badlands, this park honors the conservation legacy of Theodore Roosevelt, who ranched here in the 1880s. Visitors encounter bison, wild horses, and prairie dogs while exploring rugged canyons, painted buttes, and sweeping overlooks. Scenic drives, hiking trails, and historic ranch sites provide an immersive experience in Roosevelt's beloved western landscape.

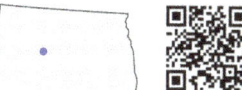 ☐ ▭ ♡ **Knife River Indian Villages National Historic Site:** Near Stanton, this site preserves the remains of Hidatsa and Mandan villages once thriving along the Knife River. Visitors can walk trails to earthlodge depressions, explore a reconstructed lodge, and view museum exhibits detailing indigenous life, agriculture, and trade. The park offers insight into centuries of culture, resilience, and community on the Northern Plains.

State & National Forests

☐ ▭ ♡ **Homen State Forest:** Located in the Turtle Mountains, this 1,200-acre forest features a mix of hardwoods and conifers. It provides a diverse range of habitats for wildlife and offers recreational opportunities such as hiking, cross-country skiing, and wildlife observation. The forest is a peaceful retreat for outdoor enthusiasts seeking a natural, scenic setting.

☐ ▭ ♡ **Sheyenne River State Forest:** Situated in the Sheyenne River Valley, this forest is home to woodlands, prairies, and river ecosystems. Visitors can enjoy hiking, wildlife observation, and picnicking by the river. The park provides a scenic landscape with lush forests and diverse wildlife, making it perfect for a peaceful retreat into nature.

☐ ▭ ♡ **Mouse River State Forest:** Found in north-central North Dakota, this forest encompasses riparian habitats along the Mouse River. It offers hiking trails, birdwatching, and opportunities for fishing in the river. The forest is a serene spot to experience wildlife and the scenic beauty of North Dakota's northern landscapes.

☐ ▭ ♡ **Tetrault Woods State Forest:** Located in the Pembina Hills, this 1,200-acre forest is known for its mature hardwood stands, providing opportunities for hiking, camping, and wildlife observation. Visitors can explore the forest's diverse ecosystems and enjoy the natural beauty of the Pembina Hills, making it a great destination for outdoor recreation.

NORTH DAKOTA

☐ 🔖 ♡ **Turtle Mountain State Forest**: Nestled in the Turtle Mountains, this 4,700-acre forest is known for its diverse ecosystems, including forests, wetlands, and prairies. It offers outdoor activities such as hiking, camping, and wildlife watching. The forest provides a peaceful natural setting with abundant wildlife and a variety of recreational opportunities.

National Grasslands

☐ 🔖 ♡ **Cedar River National Grassland:** Encompassing 6,700 acres in southern North Dakota, this landscape of rolling hills and dry streambeds showcases native prairie habitat. Visitors find quiet hiking routes, birdwatching opportunities, and wildlife such as deer and coyotes. Its wide-open vistas and seasonal wildflowers make it a peaceful retreat for those seeking solitude on the northern plains.

☐ 🔖 ♡ **Grand River National Grassland:** Though primarily in northwestern South Dakota, this grassland stretches near the North Dakota border with a mosaic of prairies, river valleys, and buttes. Wildlife like pronghorn, mule deer, and sharp-tailed grouse thrive here. Visitors enjoy hiking, birding, and exploring historic features such as the Sitting Bull Trail, where cultural and natural history meet.

☐ 🔖 ♡ **Little Missouri National Grassland:** Covering nearly one million acres across western North Dakota, this is the nation's largest national grassland. Rugged Badlands terrain mixes with wide prairies, canyons, and buttes. Visitors hike, camp, and ride horseback through vast open country alive with bison, elk, and raptors. Its dramatic scenery makes it a premier destination for outdoor adventure in the Northern Plains.

☐ 🔖 ♡ **Sheyenne National Grassland:** Southeastern North Dakota is home to the only national grassland in the tallgrass prairie ecosystem. Rolling sandhills, oak savanna, and rare native grasses create critical habitat for wildlife, including greater prairie chickens. Hikers, horseback riders, and photographers enjoy its trails and vistas, making it a treasured reminder of the once-vast tallgrass prairies of the Midwest.

National Scenic Byways & All-American Roads

☐ 🔖 ♡ **Native American Scenic Byway:** Stretching through the Standing Rock Sioux Reservation, this route highlights the deep cultural traditions and history of the Lakota and Dakota people. Travelers encounter tribal landmarks, monuments, and sweeping Missouri River views. Interpretive stops share stories of heritage and resilience, offering a journey through living culture and stunning prairie landscapes.

☐ 🔖 ♡ **Sheyenne River Valley Scenic Byway:** Meandering 63 miles along the Sheyenne River, this byway reveals rolling hills, wooded valleys, and rich farmland shaped by the glacier-fed river. Historic bridges, pioneer settlements, and small towns dot the route, blending natural beauty with cultural heritage. Wildlife sightings and recreational stops make it a scenic passage through eastern North Dakota's heartland.

State Scenic Byways

☐ 🔖 ♡ **Des Lacs National Wildlife Refuge Scenic Backway:** Following a winding gravel road through wetlands and rolling hills, this byway showcases prime waterfowl habitat in the Des Lacs refuge. Birdwatchers and photographers enjoy seasonal migrations of geese, ducks, and swans. Scenic overlooks and interpretive sites highlight the delicate balance of prairie, marsh, and wildlife conservation.

☐ 🔖 ♡ **Killdeer Mountain Four Bears Scenic Byway:** Traversing Badlands buttes, Killdeer Mountains, and the Little Missouri River Valley, this byway links natural splendor with history. It passes Native American sites, the Mandan villages, and areas once roamed by bison herds. Views of rugged canyons and prairie plateaus create a memorable drive through the heart of western North Dakota's cultural and geological heritage.

NORTH DAKOTA

☐ 🔖 ♡ **Old Red Old Ten Scenic Byway:** Once the main highway between Mandan and Dickinson, this route parallels I-94 but winds through charming small towns, rolling farmland, and prairie landscapes. Murals, historic buildings, and local diners provide a nostalgic look at America's classic highway era. Interpretive stops and scenic overlooks give travelers a slower, richer experience of central North Dakota.

☐ 🔖 ♡ **Pembina Gorge Scenic Backway:** Nestled in the northeastern Pembina Hills, this byway explores one of North Dakota's most diverse ecosystems. Forested valleys, wildflower meadows, and riverside cliffs frame a region ideal for hiking, horseback riding, and wildlife viewing. Scenic overlooks reveal sweeping views, while cultural sites tell the story of settlement and natural history in this hidden corner of the state.

☐ 🔖 ♡ **Rendezvous Region Scenic Backway:** Stretching across rolling hills, wooded ravines, and farmland near Cavalier, this route captures both natural and cultural heritage. Visitors explore state parks, pioneer cemeteries, and the Tongue River valley while enjoying hiking, fishing, and birdwatching. Seasonal color changes and historic markers make it a dynamic drive through northeastern North Dakota.

☐ 🔖 ♡ **Sakakawea Scenic Byway:** Skirting the northern shore of Lake Sakakawea, this byway links the Mandan villages, Knife River Indian Villages National Historic Site, and Garrison Dam. Sweeping lake views mix with cultural landmarks that celebrate the legacy of Sacagawea and the Lewis and Clark Expedition. Outdoor recreation blends with history, making it a premier route in central North Dakota.

☐ 🔖 ♡ **Standing Rock National Native American Scenic Byway (State Portion):** Extending from the national byway, North Dakota's state-designated section highlights tribal heritage along the Missouri River. Monuments, cultural centers, and scenic river overlooks offer insight into Lakota and Dakota traditions. The route creates a powerful connection between landscape, culture, and the enduring story of the Standing Rock people.

National Natural Landmarks

☐ 🔖 ♡ **Fischer Lake:** Designated a National Natural Landmark for its classic glacial landforms, Fischer Lake lies within a moraine and pitted outwash plain. Depressions filled by meltwater shaped its basin, while surrounding wetlands host native plants and wildlife. The site preserves a vivid example of how retreating glaciers molded the Northern Plains.
GPS: 47.083268, -99.227339

☐ 🔖 ♡ **Rush Lake:** Recognized as a National Natural Landmark for its pristine prairie pothole ecosystem, Rush Lake is a shallow, undisturbed wetland that provides critical nesting and feeding habitat for migratory waterfowl. As a rare survivor of the once-vast Northern Plains wetlands, it highlights the ecological richness and importance of this habitat type.
GPS: 48.904575, -98.681398

☐ 🔖 ♡ **Sibley Lake:** Named a National Natural Landmark for its unusual saline, alkaline waters, Sibley Lake stands out among prairie wetlands. Its permanent open water supports brine-tolerant aquatic life and attracts migratory birds adapted to unique conditions. The lake illustrates the diversity of wetland ecosystems created by glacial processes.
GPS: 47.520278, -98.345278

☐ 🔖 ♡ **Two Top and Big Top Mesa:** This rugged section of badlands earned National Natural Landmark status for its vividly banded sandstone, siltstone, and clay formations. Wind and water erosion carved the mesas into dramatic shapes, exposing a detailed geologic record and creating one of western North Dakota's most scenic natural landscapes.
GPS: 47.302222, -103.487778

OHIO

Ohio's natural landscapes stretch from forested hills and sandstone gorges to tranquil lakes and winding riverways. With its inviting mix of state parks, national forests, national park units, and notable natural landmarks, Ohio provides year-round outdoor opportunities across its diverse and scenic heartland.

📅 Peak Season
May–October is Ohio's peak season, offering warm weather, lush landscapes, and colorful fall foliage. Summer brings the largest crowds to lakes, parks, and festivals, while autumn is ideal for hiking and scenic drives.

📅 Offseason Months
November–April is the offseason, with cold winters, occasional snow, and lighter visitation. Winter offers quiet trails and frozen waterfalls, though outdoor activities slow across much of the state.

🍃 Scenery & Nature Timing
Spring brings blooming wildflowers and waterfalls at their strongest. Summer highlights lake recreation and shaded forest trails. Fall peaks with bright foliage in October, while winter reveals snow-covered hills and icy rivers.

✨ Special
Ohio features the sandstone cliffs and waterfalls of Hocking Hills, the Lake Erie shoreline and islands, and the Cuyahoga Valley's forested gorges. Glacial plains, underground caverns, and seasonal fall colors define the state's varied natural landscape.

OHIO

State Parks

☐ 🔖 ♡ **A.W. Marion State Park:** Nestled in Pickaway County, this 309-acre park surrounds Hargus Lake and features wooded trails for hiking, mountain biking, and wildlife observation. The lake is popular for fishing and boating, with quiet picnic spots along the shoreline. Its compact size and natural charm make it a favorite for day trips and peaceful outdoor escapes close to Columbus.

☐ 🔖 ♡ **Adams Lake State Park:** Located in Adams County, this small 95-acre park highlights a scenic lake and rolling hills formed by ancient glaciers. Anglers enjoy fishing for bass and catfish, while visitors hike short trails and picnic beneath shade trees. The park's prairie restoration area showcases native grasses and wildflowers, adding ecological diversity to this tranquil retreat.

☐ 🔖 ♡ **Alum Creek State Park:** Spanning nearly 4,630 acres in Delaware County, Alum Creek offers one of Ohio's largest inland beaches, a popular reservoir for boating, and extensive campgrounds. Trails wind through woodlands and meadows, providing year-round recreation from hiking to snowmobiling. Its mix of water sports, wildlife, and natural scenery makes it a premier destination.

☐ 🔖 ♡ **Barkcamp State Park:** In Belmont County's Appalachian foothills, Barkcamp encompasses a 1,005-acre landscape of forest, meadows, and a peaceful lake. Campgrounds, equestrian trails, and hiking paths make it versatile for families and outdoor enthusiasts. Wildlife abounds in the mixed woodlands, and the calm setting provides an inviting escape for boating, swimming, and fishing.

☐ 🔖 ♡ **Beaver Creek State Park:** Set along a scenic creek in Columbiana County, this 2,722-acre park combines outdoor recreation with history. Visitors explore a pioneer village, gristmill, and covered bridge while hiking rugged trails through forests and sandstone gorges. Fishing, picnicking, and photography thrive here, as diverse ecosystems support abundant wildlife and stunning vistas.

☐ 🔖 ♡ **Blue Rock State Park:** Nestled in Muskingum County, this 322-acre park is surrounded by the larger Blue Rock State Forest. Its wooded trails, picnic sites, and quiet lake provide opportunities for fishing, boating, and camping. Known for rugged terrain and natural beauty, it offers peaceful getaways for nature lovers seeking solitude in southeastern Ohio's hills.

☐ 🔖 ♡ **Buck Creek State Park:** Located near Springfield in Clark County, this 4,016-acre park centers on C.J. Brown Reservoir. Boating, sailing, and fishing draw visitors to the expansive lake, while hiking and biking trails extend across woodlands and meadows. Camping facilities and picnic areas make it a year-round destination for families and outdoor recreation.

☐ 🔖 ♡ **Buckeye Lake State Park:** Ohio's oldest state park, located in Fairfield, Licking, and Perry counties, it surrounds a 3,100-acre lake once built as a canal feeder. Today, it's a hub for boating, sailing, and fishing, with shoreline picnic areas and launch ramps. Its historic charm and lively water-based recreation make it a beloved destination statewide.

☐ 🔖 ♡ **Burr Oak State Park:** Spread across Morgan and Athens counties, this 2,593-acre park includes a 664-acre lake tucked within wooded hills. Camping, hiking, and boating are popular, along with stays at its lakeside lodge. With peaceful forested surroundings and abundant wildlife, Burr Oak offers a quiet retreat ideal for relaxation and nature exploration.

☐ 🔖 ♡ **Caesar Creek State Park:** Situated in Warren, Clinton, and Greene counties, this 7,530-acre park boasts a massive reservoir for boating, fishing, and swimming. Fossil-rich limestone outcrops attract amateur paleontologists, while miles of trails welcome hikers, mountain bikers, and horseback riders. Scenic vistas, campgrounds, and beaches make it a premier outdoor destination.

☐ 🔖 ♡ **Catawba Island State Park:** Found on the Lake Erie shore in Ottawa County, this 10-acre park provides boating access, fishing piers, and picnic areas. It's a small but scenic site where visitors enjoy water recreation and views of the islands. Known for its convenience and beautiful setting, it's an ideal stop for Lake Erie explorers.

☐ 🔖 ♡ **Cowan Lake State Park:** In Clinton County, this 1,075-acre park surrounds a picturesque lake ringed by woodlands and wildflowers. Hiking and biking trails wind through the forest, and boating, fishing, and swimming are popular on the water. Campgrounds and picnic spots make it a welcoming destination for families and outdoor enthusiasts alike.

OHIO

☐ 🔖 ♡ **Deer Creek State Park:** Located in Pickaway and Fayette counties, this 2,337-acre park features a wide reservoir, modern lodge, cabins, and campgrounds. Swimming, boating, and fishing are staples on the water, while equestrian, hiking, and biking trails wind through surrounding forests. Its amenities and scenic setting make it ideal for family vacations.

☐ 🔖 ♡ **Delaware State Park:** This 1,686-acre park in Delaware County surrounds a 1,300-acre lake with sandy beaches, boat ramps, and fishing piers. Trails and campgrounds provide year-round recreation, from swimming and wildlife viewing in summer to ice skating and cross-country skiing in winter. Its accessibility and natural charm attract day-trippers and campers alike.

☐ 🔖 ♡ **Dillon State Park:** Nestled in Muskingum County, this 2,285-acre park includes a large reservoir and offers boating, fishing, hiking, and camping. Trails extend through forests and meadows, while winter brings sledding and skiing opportunities. Modern facilities blend with scenic natural landscapes, making Dillon an attractive destination for varied outdoor experiences.

☐ 🔖 ♡ **East Fork State Park:** Spanning 4,870 acres in Clermont County, this park is one of Ohio's largest. It features a vast reservoir popular for boating, swimming, and fishing. Miles of trails invite hikers, equestrians, and mountain bikers, while campgrounds provide overnight stays. Its size and diversity of landscapes make it a premier destination for outdoor recreation.

☐ 🔖 ♡ **East Harbor State Park:** Located along Lake Erie in Ottawa County, this 1,831-acre park offers sandy beaches, boat ramps, and fishing spots. Campgrounds and picnic areas attract families, while nature enthusiasts enjoy hiking through wetlands that harbor abundant birdlife. Its shoreline and wide-open water access make it one of Ohio's most visited parks.

☐ 🔖 ♡ **Findley State Park:** In Lorain County, this 838-acre park is surrounded by agricultural land, offering a peaceful contrast of forest and fields. The 93-acre lake provides boating and fishing, while trails meander through woodlands with diverse flora and fauna. It's a popular spot for camping, hiking, and enjoying quiet natural beauty year-round.

☐ 🔖 ♡ **Forked Run State Park:** Situated in Meigs County near the Ohio River, this 791-acre park offers a 102-acre lake for boating, fishing, and swimming. Trails wind through hilly terrain, and campgrounds provide overnight options. Its scenic location near the Appalachian foothills makes it a serene retreat for outdoor recreation and wildlife watching.

☐ 🔖 ♡ **Geneva State Park:** Located in Ashtabula County on Lake Erie's shore, this 698-acre park is known for its marina, beach, and year-round fishing. Trails pass through wetlands and woodlands, offering birdwatching and nature observation. Its resort-style lodge and proximity to Geneva-on-the-Lake make it ideal for both relaxation and adventure.

☐ 🔖 ♡ **Grand Lake St. Marys State Park:** Spanning 13,500 acres in Mercer and Auglaize counties, this was once the world's largest man-made reservoir. Today, it's a hub for boating, sailing, fishing, and camping. Wetlands provide bird habitat, while hiking and biking trails extend along the shoreline. Its scale makes it a centerpiece of Ohio recreation.

☐ 🔖 ♡ **Great Council State Park:** Opened in 2023 in Greene County, this park honors Shawnee heritage and Ohio's Native American history. Its cultural center highlights the legacy of the Shawnee leader Tecumseh, while surrounding lands provide walking trails and interpretive programs. It's both a natural retreat and an educational experience focused on heritage.

☐ 🔖 ♡ **Great Seal State Park:** Located in Ross County, this rugged 1,862-acre park preserves hills depicted on Ohio's state seal. Hiking and biking trails traverse steep terrain, offering scenic vistas of the Scioto Valley. It's popular for horseback riding and outdoor festivals, combining cultural symbolism with opportunities for active outdoor recreation.

☐ 🔖 ♡ **Guilford Lake State Park:** Found in Columbiana County, this 396-acre park surrounds a tranquil lake popular for fishing, boating, and swimming. Trails and picnic areas provide peaceful escapes, while its compact size makes it a quiet, family-friendly park. Birdwatchers and nature lovers appreciate its calm setting and easy accessibility.

☐ 🔖 ♡ **Headlands Beach State Park:** Located in Lake County, this 120-acre park boasts Ohio's largest natural sand beach. Swimming, sunbathing, and picnicking draw thousands each summer, while nearby Mentor Marsh offers wildlife viewing. Its wide shoreline and views of Fairport Harbor lighthouse make it a favorite for beachgoers and photographers alike.

☐ 🔖 ♡ **Hocking Hills State Park:** Situated in Hocking County, this iconic park is famous for its sandstone cliffs, waterfalls, and gorges. Popular sites include Old Man's Cave, Ash Cave, and Cedar Falls. Miles of hiking trails showcase dramatic scenery, while camping and cabins provide overnight options. It's among Ohio's most visited and beloved natural treasures.

OHIO

☐ 🔖 ♡ **Hueston Woods State Park:** Spanning Preble and Butler counties, this 3,596-acre park offers Acton Lake for boating and fishing, plus extensive forest trails. Camping, golfing, and wildlife programs attract families and groups. The park's lodge and beach add modern amenities, making it one of Ohio's most versatile year-round recreation areas.

☐ 🔖 ♡ **Independence Dam State Park:** Stretching along the Maumee River in Defiance County, this 591-acre park preserves a historic canal era dam. Visitors enjoy boating, kayaking, and fishing on the river, along with picnicking and hiking trails. Its riverside setting offers both recreation and a glimpse into Ohio's transportation heritage.

☐ 🔖 ♡ **Indian Lake State Park:** Located in Logan County, this 800-acre park centers on a 5,800-acre lake once built as a canal feeder. Today it's a hotspot for boating, jet skiing, and fishing, with sandy swimming beaches and modern campgrounds. Birdwatching is excellent here, especially during migratory seasons on the open waters.

☐ 🔖 ♡ **Jackson Lake State Park:** In Jackson County, this 106-acre park features a 242-acre lake with boat ramps and fishing piers. Trails through surrounding woodlands provide opportunities for hiking and wildlife observation. With campgrounds and picnic areas, it offers a quiet, family-friendly destination for relaxation and outdoor activities.

☐ 🔖 ♡ **Jefferson Lake State Park:** Located in Jefferson County, this 962-acre park centers on a 15-acre lake ideal for fishing and boating. Hiking trails wind through peaceful woodlands, offering birdwatching and wildlife observation. With its small size and quiet charm, Jefferson Lake provides a relaxing retreat for campers, anglers, and those seeking tranquility in a natural setting.

☐ 🔖 ♡ **Jesse Owens State Park:** Spanning 5,735 acres in Morgan, Perry, and Noble counties, this park honors the Olympic legend and features reclaimed mining lands transformed into outdoor recreation. Visitors enjoy fishing lakes, hiking trails, and hunting areas, along with historical interpretation. Its vast landscapes and diverse uses make it a unique blend of history and nature.

☐ 🔖 ♡ **John Bryan State Park:** Nestled in Greene County, this 752-acre park is carved by the Little Miami River Gorge, a National Natural Landmark. Dramatic limestone cliffs, waterfalls, and lush forests make it a favorite for hikers, climbers, and nature lovers. Trails connect to Clifton Gorge and Glen Helen, creating one of Ohio's most scenic hiking regions.

☐ 🔖 ♡ **Kelleys Island State Park:** Situated on Lake Erie's Kelleys Island, this 677-acre park offers sandy beaches, hiking trails, and fishing spots. The island is famous for its glacial grooves, one of the largest visible in the world. Accessible by ferry, it's a unique destination combining geology, history, and outdoor recreation in a picturesque island setting.

☐ 🔖 ♡ **Kiser Lake State Park:** Found in Champaign County, this 531-acre park surrounds a 396-acre lake formed by a glacial moraine. Motorized boats are prohibited, preserving its peaceful character for sailing, canoeing, and fishing. Trails wind through wetlands and prairies, while campgrounds provide overnight stays. It's a serene, nature-focused retreat.

☐ 🔖 ♡ **Lake Alma State Park:** Located in Vinton County, this 292-acre park features a 60-acre lake encircled by hiking trails and woodlands. Visitors enjoy boating, swimming, and fishing, with campgrounds and picnic areas nearby. Once developed by the Civilian Conservation Corps, it remains a scenic and historic site perfect for family recreation in southern Ohio.

☐ 🔖 ♡ **Lake Hope State Park:** Nestled within Zaleski State Forest in Vinton County, this 2,983-acre park features a striking lake surrounded by rugged hills and hardwood forests. Rich in iron-mining history, it offers cabins, trails, and abundant wildlife. Its combination of cultural heritage, natural scenery, and outdoor adventure makes it a regional favorite.

☐ 🔖 ♡ **Lake Logan State Park:** Found in Hocking County, this 958-acre park surrounds a 400-acre lake designed for boating, fishing, and swimming. Trails weave through woodlands and meadows, while picnic areas overlook the shoreline. It's a tranquil, family-friendly park that complements nearby Hocking Hills attractions with quieter water-based recreation.

☐ 🔖 ♡ **Lake Loramie State Park:** In Shelby County, this 407-acre park includes a 1,655-acre lake once built as part of the Miami-Erie Canal system. Boating, fishing, and camping are popular, while hiking and biking trails extend through surrounding woods. Its blend of canal history and recreational opportunities makes it a distinctive Ohio destination.

☐ 🔖 ♡ **Lake White State Park:** Located in Pike County, this 92-acre park includes a scenic 333-acre lake. Boating, kayaking, and fishing are highlights, with hiking trails providing views of wooded hillsides. Originally constructed for flood control, it now serves as a peaceful getaway for recreation, picnics, and enjoying the region's natural beauty.

OHIO

☐ 🔖 ♡ **Little Miami Scenic State Park:** Stretching across multiple counties, this 1,050-acre linear park follows the Little Miami River and its nationally designated Scenic Trail. Popular for hiking, cycling, and canoeing, it links communities while preserving natural river corridors. Its blend of recreation and conservation makes it one of Ohio's most unique state parks.

☐ 🔖 ♡ **Madison Lake State Park:** In Madison County, this 106-acre park surrounds a small 106-acre lake known for boating, swimming, and fishing. With picnic areas, campgrounds, and trails, it offers a simple, relaxing environment. Its modest size and accessible location make it a convenient escape for families and day visitors from central Ohio.

☐ 🔖 ♡ **Malabar Farm State Park:** Situated in Richland County, this historic farm was the home of Pulitzer Prize-winning author Louis Bromfield. Visitors can tour his "Big House," explore hiking trails, and view sustainable farming practices. With cultural history, working farmland, and natural beauty, it's a unique mix of heritage tourism and outdoor recreation.

☐ 🔖 ♡ **Mary Jane Thurston State Park:** Located along the Maumee River in Henry County, this 609-acre park provides boat access, fishing, and riverside picnicking. Trails explore wetlands and forests, while campgrounds accommodate overnight visitors. It's a scenic and peaceful spot that blends Ohio's natural beauty with historic ties to Native American and canal-era heritage.

☐ 🔖 ♡ **Maumee Bay State Park:** Situated on Lake Erie in Lucas County, this 1,336-acre park features sandy beaches, wetlands, and a modern lodge. A boardwalk trail offers excellent birdwatching, especially during spring migration. Golf, camping, and fishing add to its appeal, making it one of Ohio's most diverse and popular lakeshore destinations.

☐ 🔖 ♡ **Middle Bass Island State Park:** Located on Lake Erie in Ottawa County, this 124-acre island park offers a marina, boat docks, and waterfront camping. Once home to the Lonz Winery, its historic castle-like structure still stands as a landmark. Visitors enjoy hiking, birdwatching, and fishing, while the island's relaxed pace makes it an inviting retreat accessible only by ferry or private boat.

☐ 🔖 ♡ **Mohican State Park:** Nestled in Ashland County, this 1,110-acre park is known for its scenic Clear Fork Gorge, pine forests, and the Mohican River. Hiking and mountain biking trails explore rugged terrain, while camping and a lodge provide overnight options. Its mix of dramatic landscapes and recreational opportunities makes it a premier outdoor destination.

☐ 🔖 ♡ **Mosquito Lake State Park:** Located in Trumbull County, this 7,850-acre park includes one of Ohio's largest lakes. Boating, sailing, and fishing dominate the waters, while campgrounds, picnic areas, and trails attract families. Birdwatchers find waterfowl and eagles around the marshes, making it a hotspot for both recreation and wildlife observation.

☐ 🔖 ♡ **Mount Gilead State Park:** In Morrow County, this 181-acre park features two small lakes surrounded by wooded hills. Anglers enjoy fishing from the banks, while trails offer short, peaceful hikes. Its intimate scale and tranquil setting make it a family-friendly retreat, especially for visitors seeking a quiet natural escape in central Ohio.

☐ 🔖 ♡ **Nelson-Kennedy Ledges State Park:** Found in Portage County, this 167-acre park is renowned for its striking rock outcroppings, cliffs, and narrow passageways. Short trails lead visitors through formations like "Devil's Icebox" and "Old Maid's Kitchen." With its dramatic geology, it's a unique hiking destination and a favorite among nature photographers.

☐ 🔖 ♡ **North Bass Island State Park:** A remote 593-acre preserve in Lake Erie's Ottawa County, this largely undeveloped island offers primitive camping, hiking, and fishing. With limited access by private boat or charter, it remains one of Ohio's most secluded state parks. Its rugged shorelines, vineyards, and untouched landscapes provide a rare wilderness experience amid the Lake Erie Islands.

☐ 🔖 ♡ **Oak Point State Park:** Ohio's smallest state park at just 1.5 acres, Oak Point sits on South Bass Island in Ottawa County. Despite its size, it provides picnic areas, a small dock, and scenic views of Lake Erie. Often used as a quick stop by boaters, it's valued for its convenience and charm, serving as a tranquil overlook of the islands and a relaxing picnic spot near Put-in-Bay.

☐ 🔖 ♡ **Paint Creek State Park:** Spread across Highland and Ross counties, this 5,652-acre park centers on a 1,190-acre lake popular for boating, fishing, and swimming. Trails cross scenic woodlands and prairies, while campgrounds and picnic areas accommodate families. Its diverse habitats also support birdwatching and wildlife exploration throughout the seasons.

☐ 🔖 ♡ **Pike Lake State Park:** Located in Pike County, this 587-acre park surrounds a small lake nestled in forested hills. Built by the Civilian Conservation Corps, it features historic cabins, campgrounds, and hiking trails. Its cozy scale and rustic atmosphere make it a charming destination for peaceful retreats and family camping trips.

OHIO

☐ 🔖 ♡ **Portage Lakes State Park:** In Summit County, this 411-acre park provides access to eight interconnected lakes totaling over 2,000 acres. Boating, jet skiing, and fishing are popular, with sandy beaches and picnic areas along the shore. Its proximity to Akron makes it a convenient getaway for water recreation and outdoor activities year-round.

☐ 🔖 ♡ **Punderson State Park:** Situated in Geauga County, this 741-acre park includes a natural glacier-formed lake and wooded hills. Visitors enjoy fishing, boating, and hiking, along with winter sports like sledding and cross-country skiing. The Tudor-style lodge and golf course add unique amenities, blending recreation with comfort in a scenic setting.

☐ 🔖 ♡ **Pymatuning State Park:** Straddling the Ohio–Pennsylvania border in Ashtabula County, this 3,512-acre park is centered on a massive reservoir. Known for fishing and boating, it also features campgrounds and hiking trails. Birdwatchers flock here to see waterfowl, while families enjoy swimming beaches, making it a year-round recreation hub.

☐ 🔖 ♡ **Quail Hollow State Park:** Found in Stark County, this 701-acre park includes woodlands, gardens, and meadows surrounding a historic manor house. Trails for hiking, horseback riding, and cross-country skiing wind through diverse habitats. Its mix of cultural heritage and natural beauty makes it an inviting spot for relaxation and exploration.

☐ 🔖 ♡ **Rocky Fork State Park:** Located in Highland County, this 1,142-acre park features a 2,080-acre lake ideal for boating, fishing, and swimming. Beaches, campgrounds, and trails make it a family favorite, while birdwatchers spot herons and eagles along the shoreline. Its expansive waters and amenities attract both locals and travelers.

☐ 🔖 ♡ **Salt Fork State Park:** Ohio's largest state park at 17,229 acres in Guernsey County, Salt Fork offers a vast lake, beaches, campgrounds, and a full-service lodge. Hiking trails, golf, and abundant wildlife make it versatile for all visitors. Its size and variety of activities make it one of Ohio's most popular year-round destinations.

☐ 🔖 ♡ **Scioto Trail State Park:** Nestled in Ross County's Appalachian foothills, this 9,390-acre park blends forested ridges with two small lakes. Trails traverse rugged terrain ideal for hiking and birdwatching, while campgrounds and cabins provide overnight stays. Its seclusion and natural beauty create a peaceful retreat for nature enthusiasts.

☐ 🔖 ♡ **Seneca Lake State Park:** Spread across Guernsey and Noble counties, this 3,550-acre park surrounds Ohio's third-largest inland lake. Boating, sailing, and fishing dominate, with campgrounds, picnic areas, and swimming beaches nearby. Its scenic setting amid rolling hills makes it a popular spot for summer recreation and family vacations.

☐ 🔖 ♡ **Shawnee State Park:** Found in Scioto County, this 1,095-acre park lies within Shawnee State Forest, Ohio's largest. Known as "Ohio's Little Smokies," it features rugged hills, lakes, and scenic overlooks. Visitors hike, boat, camp, or stay at the lodge, enjoying one of the state's most diverse and picturesque natural landscapes.

☐ 🔖 ♡ **Strouds Run State Park:** Located in Athens County, this 2,606-acre park surrounds Dow Lake, a 161-acre reservoir popular for boating, fishing, and swimming. Trails traverse forested hills, offering scenic hikes and wildlife observation. Campgrounds and picnic areas provide family-friendly amenities, while its proximity to Ohio University makes it a popular local escape.

☐ 🔖 ♡ **Sycamore State Park:** Spanning nearly 2,400 acres in Montgomery County, this forested park preserves a mix of woodlands, meadows, and prairies. Miles of hiking, bridle, and biking trails wind through diverse habitats, offering wildlife viewing and quiet exploration. Campgrounds, fishing ponds, and picnic areas make it a versatile destination, while its location near Dayton adds easy accessibility.

☐ 🔖 ♡ **Tappan Lake State Park:** Found in Harrison County, this 2,350-acre park includes a sprawling 2,131-acre lake. Boating, sailing, and fishing are the main draws, along with sandy swimming beaches and shaded picnic spots. Trails through wooded hills provide hiking opportunities. Its lakefront campgrounds make it a beloved destination for summer recreation.

☐ 🔖 ♡ **Tar Hollow State Park:** Nestled in Ross, Hocking, and Vinton counties, this 604-acre park is surrounded by the larger Tar Hollow State Forest. A small lake provides boating and fishing, while rugged trails attract hikers and backpackers. Campgrounds, cabins, and scenic ridges make it an excellent retreat for those seeking rustic outdoor adventure.

☐ 🔖 ♡ **Tinkers Creek State Park:** Located in Portage County, this 370-acre park preserves wetlands and woodlands rich in biodiversity. Birdwatching, fishing, and hiking are popular activities. Its serene landscape, with quiet marshes and wooded trails, provides a peaceful escape for visitors seeking to explore one of northeast Ohio's natural habitats.

OHIO

☐ 🔖 ♡ **Van Buren State Park:** Situated in Hancock County, this 296-acre park features woodlands, prairies, and a 45-acre lake for fishing and boating. Trails wind through restored tallgrass prairies, providing excellent wildlife viewing. Campgrounds, picnic areas, and playgrounds make it a family-friendly destination for day trips and overnight stays.

☐ 🔖 ♡ **West Branch State Park:** In Portage County, this 5,379-acre park centers on the 2,650-acre Michael J. Kirwan Reservoir. Known for boating, sailing, and fishing, it also offers campgrounds, swimming beaches, and extensive hiking and biking trails. Its diverse recreation and modern facilities make it a popular year-round destination.

☐ 🔖 ♡ **Wolf Run State Park:** Located in Noble County, this 1,046-acre park includes a 220-acre lake ideal for boating, fishing, and swimming. Surrounded by forested hills, the park features trails for hiking and horseback riding. Its peaceful campgrounds and wildlife habitats make it a quiet retreat for visitors seeking natural beauty and outdoor activities.

National Parks

 ☐ 🔖 ♡ **Charles Young Buffalo Soldiers National Monument:** Located in Wilberforce, this monument honors Charles Young, the first African American national park superintendent and a decorated Buffalo Soldier officer. Visitors explore his restored home and exhibits that highlight his contributions to the U.S. Army, the national park system, and African American history.

 ☐ 🔖 ♡ **Cuyahoga Valley National Park:** Nestled between Cleveland and Akron, this park features rolling hills, forests, and the winding Cuyahoga River. Visitors hike and cycle the scenic Towpath Trail, enjoy waterfalls like Brandywine Falls, and explore historic sites such as the Boston Mill Visitor Center and the Canal Exploration Center. It's a diverse natural and cultural retreat.

 ☐ 🔖 ♡ **Dayton Aviation Heritage National Historical Park:** Located in Dayton, this park celebrates the Wright Brothers and Paul Laurence Dunbar. Visitors can tour the Wright brothers' bicycle shop, learn at the Wright-Dunbar Interpretive Center, and explore exhibits honoring aviation pioneers. It preserves the stories of innovation, literature, and determination that shaped American history.

 ☐ 🔖 ♡ **First Ladies National Historic Site:** Situated in Canton, this site highlights the lives of America's First Ladies. The Saxton House, once home to Ida Saxton McKinley, and the National First Ladies Library showcase their personal stories and national impact. Visitors gain insight into the changing roles of women in politics, society, and the American presidency.

 ☐ 🔖 ♡ **Hopewell Culture National Historical Park:** Found in Chillicothe, this park preserves ancient earthworks and burial mounds built over 2,000 years ago. These geometric mounds reflect the skill and spiritual life of the Hopewell culture. Trails and exhibits reveal the society's art, trade, and traditions, offering a fascinating glimpse into Native American history.

 ☐ 🔖 ♡ **James A. Garfield National Historic Site:** Located in Mentor, this site preserves the home of the 20th President of the United States. Visitors can tour Garfield's Victorian-era family home, view exhibits on his brief presidency, and learn about his tragic assassination. The site honors both his political career and his lasting legacy in American history.

 ☐ 🔖 ♡ **Perry's Victory and International Peace Memorial:** Standing tall on South Bass Island at Put-in-Bay, this memorial commemorates the Battle of Lake Erie in the War of 1812 and celebrates lasting peace with Canada and Britain. Visitors climb the 352-foot tower for panoramic lake views and explore exhibits detailing the battle's role in U.S. history.

 ☐ 🔖 ♡ **William Howard Taft National Historic Site:** Located in Cincinnati, this site preserves the birthplace and early home of the 27th U.S. President. Guided tours reveal Taft's family life, political career, and unique legacy as the only person to serve as both President and Chief Justice. Exhibits highlight his impact on law, leadership, and national history.

OHIO

State & National Forests

Beaver Creek State Forest: In Columbiana County, this forest blends natural beauty with history. Visitors hike wooded trails, fish along streams, and explore remnants of 19th-century iron furnaces. The Beaver Creek Covered Bridge adds cultural charm, while its peaceful setting makes it ideal for outdoor recreation, wildlife viewing, and learning about Ohio's early industry.

Blue Rock State Forest: Spanning 3,250 acres in Muskingum County, this rugged forest is a sanctuary for diverse wildlife and native plants. Trails wind through wooded ridges and valleys, offering opportunities for hiking, birdwatching, and hunting. Its quiet atmosphere and natural scenery make it a retreat for those seeking solitude and immersion in Ohio's landscapes.

Brush Creek State Forest: Encompassing 13,000 acres in Adams County, Brush Creek is known for its rolling hills, quiet streams, and rich biodiversity. Birdwatching, hiking, and hunting are popular, with forested valleys providing habitats for native plants and wildlife. Its scale and serenity offer nature lovers an excellent escape into southern Ohio's wilderness.

Dean State Forest: Located in Lawrence County, this forest features a mix of open fields and woodlands that support varied habitats. Visitors enjoy hiking, birdwatching, and nature walks in a tranquil environment. Its quiet trails and natural beauty make it an excellent choice for those seeking outdoor recreation away from busier destinations.

Fernwood State Forest: Found in Jefferson County, this peaceful forest is popular for hiking, picnicking, and wildlife observation. Campgrounds nearby allow for extended visits, while trails pass through hardwood stands and rolling hills. Its quiet setting makes it perfect for nature lovers who want to combine recreation with serene outdoor exploration.

Gifford State Forest: Ohio's smallest state forest at just 320 acres, Gifford lies in Athens County. Despite its size, it offers trails that pass through lush woodlands and along quiet streams. Visitors enjoy its peaceful atmosphere and abundant wildlife, making it a charming spot for hiking and reflection in a simple, natural setting.

Harrison State Forest: In Harrison County, this forest offers trails that meander through woodlands and open meadows. Visitors enjoy hiking, wildlife observation, and scenic overlooks. Its diverse ecosystems support a wide range of plant and animal species, making it a rewarding destination for outdoor adventurers and naturalists.

Hocking State Forest: Covering over 3,000 acres in the Hocking Hills region, this forest features dramatic cliffs, waterfalls, and deep gorges. Popular with hikers, rock climbers, and photographers, its trails highlight rugged natural beauty. It provides a wilder counterpart to nearby Hocking Hills State Park, offering more secluded exploration.

Maumee State Forest: Located in Fulton County, this 1,450-acre forest protects woodlands, meadows, and wetlands. Birdwatching and hiking are highlights, with diverse ecosystems supporting migratory species and native wildlife. Its peaceful landscape and well-marked trails make it a quiet outdoor destination for those seeking nature close to Toledo.

Mohican-Memorial State Forest: Stretching across 4,500 acres in Ashland County, this forest surrounds Mohican State Park and features hardwood forests, fishing streams, and hiking trails. The Memorial Forest Shrine honors Ohioans who died in military service. Its mix of recreation and heritage makes it a meaningful and scenic destination.

Perry State Forest: In Perry County, this 8,000-acre forest is known for its rugged trails, popular with off-highway vehicle riders as well as hikers. Its rolling hills and woodlands also support camping and wildlife observation. Visitors enjoy both peaceful natural escapes and adventurous recreation in Ohio's southeastern terrain.

Pike State Forest: Spanning Pike and Highland counties, this 12,084-acre forest features hardwood ridges, valleys, and streams. Hunting, camping, and hiking are popular, with trails winding through dense woodlands. It is home to diverse bird and wildlife species, offering both recreation and excellent nature observation opportunities year-round.

OHIO

☐ 🔖 ♡ **Richland Furnace State Forest:** Found in Vinton County, this forest combines natural beauty with history. Visitors hike trails through woodlands and explore the remains of a 19th-century iron furnace. The mix of cultural heritage and peaceful natural surroundings provides a unique outdoor experience that blends history with exploration.

☐ 🔖 ♡ **Scioto Trail State Forest:** Located in Ross County, this forest covers 9,390 acres of rugged ridges and deep valleys. Trails are ideal for hiking and wildlife observation, with abundant deer and birdlife. Its remote setting offers solitude and striking scenery, making it a haven for nature enthusiasts and backcountry explorers.

☐ 🔖 ♡ **Shade River State Forest:** Situated in Meigs County, this forest features wetlands, streams, and wooded hills. Hiking trails and picnic areas allow visitors to enjoy quiet outdoor recreation. Its diverse habitats support rich plant and animal life, making it an excellent location for birdwatching, nature walks, and peaceful reflection in nature.

☐ 🔖 ♡ **Shawnee State Forest:** Spanning over 64,000 acres in Scioto County, this is Ohio's largest state forest. Nicknamed "Ohio's Little Smokies," it features rugged Appalachian terrain, deep hollows, and diverse wildlife. Hiking, camping, hunting, and horseback riding are popular, with a designated wilderness area providing a rare opportunity for backcountry exploration.

☐ 🔖 ♡ **Sunfish Creek State Forest:** Located in Monroe County, this 637-acre forest is a quiet retreat of steep hills and wooded valleys. Scenic trails follow the creek, offering opportunities for hiking, hunting, and wildlife observation. Its seclusion and natural beauty make it a peaceful spot for those looking to escape into a remote, forested setting.

☐ 🔖 ♡ **Tar Hollow State Forest:** Ohio's third largest state forest, this 16,120-acre property spans Ross, Hocking, and Vinton counties. Rugged hills and dense forests provide opportunities for hiking, camping, hunting, and backpacking. Trails connect with Tar Hollow State Park, creating a vast recreational landscape ideal for outdoor enthusiasts.

☐ 🔖 ♡ **Vinton Furnace State Experimental Forest:** Situated in Vinton County, this forest covers over 12,000 acres and is dedicated to sustainable forestry research. Trails allow visitors to explore unique habitats, old-growth remnants, and wildlife viewing areas. Its blend of active research and public access makes it an educational and recreational destination.

☐ 🔖 ♡ **Wayne National Forest:** Encompassing over 240,000 acres across southeastern Ohio, this is the state's only national forest. It offers more than 300 miles of trails for hiking, horseback riding, and off-road vehicles, plus camping, fishing, and wildlife observation. Its diverse terrain of hills, rivers, and woodlands makes it a premier outdoor destination.

☐ 🔖 ♡ **Yellow Creek State Forest:** Located in Columbiana County, this forest features trails that wind through wooded terrain with streams and small valleys. It's popular for hiking, hunting, and wildlife viewing. The forest's tranquil atmosphere and natural beauty make it a welcome retreat for outdoor recreation in northeastern Ohio.

☐ 🔖 ♡ **Zaleski State Forest:** Spanning over 27,000 acres in Vinton and Athens counties, this is Ohio's second-largest state forest. It offers extensive hiking and backpacking trails, including a 23-mile backpacking loop, as well as camping and hunting. Rich in history and biodiversity, Zaleski is a premier destination for immersive forest exploration.

National Scenic Byways & All-American Roads

☐ 🔖 ♡ **America's Byway: Historic National Road:** Stretching across central Ohio, this route follows the first federally funded highway in the U.S. from the early 1800s. Historic inns, canal towns, and early bridges highlight its role in westward expansion. Visitors can explore charming Main Streets, museums, and scenic countryside along a road that once symbolized America's growth and connection.

☐ 🔖 ♡ **Amish Country Byway:** Winding through Holmes County, this 160-mile byway showcases Ohio's Amish heritage. Visitors encounter horse-drawn buggies, quilt shops, farms, and covered bridges along peaceful country roads. Rolling hills and pastoral landscapes highlight a culture rooted in tradition. It's one of Ohio's most scenic and culturally distinctive drives.

OHIO

☐ 🔖 ♡ **Lake Erie Coastal Ohio Trail:** Extending 293 miles along the Lake Erie shoreline, this All-American Road showcases lighthouses, beaches, and historic port towns. Visitors can explore islands like Put-in-Bay and Kelleys Island, birdwatch at renowned migration hotspots, or tour Marblehead Lighthouse. Its blend of natural beauty, recreation, and maritime heritage makes it a premier Great Lakes journey.

☐ 🔖 ♡ **Lincoln Highway:** As one of America's first coast-to-coast highways, the Lincoln Highway crosses northern Ohio with a mix of small towns, farmland, and historic roadside landmarks. Travelers discover original brick sections, vintage diners, and interpretive sites that recall the rise of automobile travel. It offers a nostalgic journey through the early days of U.S. road culture and history.

☐ 🔖 ♡ **Ohio & Erie Canalway:** Linking Cleveland to New Philadelphia, this byway traces the historic canal corridor that transformed Ohio's economy in the 1800s. Visitors follow the Towpath Trail, explore Cuyahoga Valley National Park, and experience locks, restored villages, and working canal boats. The route blends natural beauty, cultural heritage, and recreation along a storied waterway.

☐ 🔖 ♡ **Ohio River Scenic Byway:** Running across southern Ohio along the mighty river, this byway offers dramatic views, riverfront towns, and echoes of frontier history. From Marietta to Cincinnati, travelers encounter Underground Railroad sites, Native American earthworks, and charming river communities. The route blends history, culture, and scenery while showcasing the Ohio River's central role in the region.

State Scenic Byways

☐ 🔖 ♡ **Archie Griffith Scenic Byway:** Located in Muskingum County, this short byway honors the Ohio State football legend. It winds through rolling countryside and quiet farmland, connecting small communities with a sense of local pride. The route celebrates Ohio's sports heritage while providing a peaceful drive through pastoral landscapes and rural charm.

☐ 🔖 ♡ **Big Darby Plains Scenic Byway:** Stretching through Madison County, this byway highlights one of Ohio's most ecologically significant prairies. Visitors encounter sweeping grasslands, rare plants, and wildlife thriving in restored tallgrass habitats. Scenic farmland, historic barns, and small communities along the route emphasize Ohio's natural and agricultural heritage.

☐ 🔖 ♡ **Byway From River to Lake Scenic Byway:** Stretching from Cleveland to Cincinnati, this byway follows U.S. 42 and connects Lake Erie with the Ohio River. Travelers pass through historic towns, cultural landmarks, and scenic farmland. The route highlights Ohio's role as a transportation corridor while showcasing small-town charm and diverse landscapes along its north–south path.

☐ 🔖 ♡ **Circuit Rider's Heritage Trail Scenic Byway:** Found in southeastern Ohio, this route follows paths once traveled by Methodist circuit riders spreading religion in the early 1800s. It features historic churches, cemeteries, and quiet villages set against rolling Appalachian foothills. The byway blends faith, history, and rugged rural scenery.

☐ 🔖 ♡ **Drovers' Trail Scenic Byway:** In Belmont County, this byway retraces the paths livestock drovers once used to move animals to markets. Historic inns, taverns, and stone bridges recall the commerce of the 1800s. Today, travelers experience rolling hills, farm country, and reminders of Ohio's agricultural and transportation heritage.

☐ 🔖 ♡ **Gateway to Ohio's Erie Canal Scenic Byway:** Running through Tuscarawas County, this byway highlights the history of the Ohio & Erie Canal. Visitors explore restored locks, canal towns, and historic buildings that tell the story of 19th-century trade and settlement. Scenic farmland and waterways frame this cultural and historic drive.

☐ 🔖 ♡ **Hocking Hills Scenic Byway:** This byway winds through Hocking County's sandstone cliffs, waterfalls, and forests. Visitors experience iconic sites like Old Man's Cave and Ash Cave while traveling a route that connects the region's natural wonders. It offers a stunning drive through one of Ohio's most famous and beloved landscapes.

☐ 🔖 ♡ **Johnny Appleseed Historic Byway:** Located in Richland County, this route honors John Chapman, known as Johnny Appleseed, who lived and traveled in the region. The byway features pioneer homesteads, natural areas, and interpretive sites that recall his legacy of conservation and folklore. Rolling hills, woodlands, and farmlands create a scenic backdrop for exploring his story.

☐ 🔖 ♡ **Lake Erie Islands Scenic Byway:** Covering South Bass, Middle Bass, and Kelleys Islands, this byway showcases Ohio's unique island culture. Visitors explore ferry towns, lighthouses, beaches, and historic sites while enjoying views of Lake Erie. With vineyards, glacial grooves, and lively village centers, the route blends geology, recreation, and maritime heritage into a memorable island journey.

☐ 🔖 ♡ **Miami & Erie Canal Scenic Byway:** Stretching across western Ohio, this byway follows the route of the Miami & Erie Canal. Locks, aqueducts, and historic towns recall the canal era that linked Lake Erie with the Ohio River. The drive blends heritage, rural beauty, and glimpses into the state's early transportation system.

OHIO

☐ 🔖 ♡ **Morgan Raider's Trail Scenic Byway:** Tracing the path of Confederate General John Hunt Morgan's 1863 raid, this route winds through southern Ohio. Historical markers and towns highlight Civil War-era events, while scenic hills and farmland provide a backdrop. The byway blends military history with rural Appalachian beauty.

☐ 🔖 ♡ **Muskingum River Parkway and Scenic Byway:** Running along the Muskingum River, this byway showcases a unique hand-operated lock system still in use. Visitors experience riverside towns, boating culture, and natural beauty along wooded banks. The route reflects Ohio's canal heritage and offers one of the most picturesque river drives in the state.

☐ 🔖 ♡ **My Ohio Scenic Byway:** In eastern Ohio, this byway highlights small towns, farmland, and heritage sites that reflect the heart of rural Ohio. It emphasizes community stories, scenic views, and everyday landscapes that define the region. Its charm lies in its authenticity and quiet pace, showcasing the soul of Ohio living.

☐ 🔖 ♡ **Noble County Scenic Byway:** Winding through Appalachian foothills, this route introduces visitors to small villages, historic sites, and coal-mining heritage. Scenic ridges, woodlands, and farmland define the drive, offering a glimpse into Ohio's natural and cultural landscape. It reflects the resilience and character of rural Noble County.

☐ 🔖 ♡ **Old Mill Stream Scenic Byway:** In Hancock County, this byway follows the Blanchard River through parks, farmland, and the city of Findlay. Historic mills, bridges, and riverside communities highlight the area's industrial and cultural past. Today, the route blends natural beauty with heritage, offering a peaceful drive that connects rural landscapes with vibrant local history.

☐ 🔖 ♡ **Paint Valley Scenic Byway:** Located in Ross County, this byway passes through fertile valleys once home to Native American mound-building cultures. Visitors can explore Adena Mansion, earthworks, and rolling farmland. The route blends ancient history, pioneer heritage, and natural beauty in a peaceful countryside setting.

☐ 🔖 ♡ **Presidential Pathways Scenic Byway:** Running through western Ohio, this byway highlights the homes, museums, and birthplaces of eight U.S. presidents from Ohio. Travelers explore towns tied to leaders like William Henry Harrison, Rutherford B. Hayes, and Warren G. Harding. Scenic countryside links these historic sites, reflecting Ohio's unique role in shaping national politics.

☐ 🔖 ♡ **Rails-to-Trails Scenic Byway:** Following a converted rail line, this byway highlights recreational trails in Holmes County. Cyclists, hikers, and Amish buggies share the scenic path through farmland, woodlands, and rural towns. The route offers a unique experience where tradition and outdoor recreation meet in Ohio's countryside.

☐ 🔖 ♡ **Rim of the World Scenic Byway:** Found in southeastern Ohio, this byway follows high ridges overlooking valleys and distant horizons. The route offers sweeping vistas, rugged Appalachian scenery, and quiet backroads. It's a favorite for those seeking a dramatic, panoramic drive through Ohio's hill country.

☐ 🔖 ♡ **Sandusky River Scenic Byway:** Following the Sandusky River through Seneca and Sandusky counties, this byway highlights Ohio's natural and cultural history. Visitors encounter Native American sites, canal heritage, and historic towns set along the winding river. Scenic overlooks, parks, and wildlife areas make it a blend of heritage and outdoor recreation.

☐ 🔖 ♡ **Scenic Scioto Heritage Trail:** Running through Scioto County, this byway follows the Ohio River and into the Appalachian foothills. Visitors explore Native American sites, pioneer landmarks, and Underground Railroad heritage. The route offers dramatic river views, cultural interpretation, and a blend of scenic landscapes and history.

☐ 🔖 ♡ **Shawnee Scenic Byway:** Nestled within Shawnee State Forest in Scioto County, this route explores Ohio's "Little Smokies." Dense woodlands, ridges, and overlooks provide some of the state's most dramatic scenery. Wildlife, hiking trailheads, and cultural sites enhance the drive, making it one of Ohio's most striking natural byways.

☐ 🔖 ♡ **U.S. Grant Memorial Scenic Byway:** Located in southern Ohio, this byway traces the life of Ulysses S. Grant, the Civil War general and U.S. president. Visitors explore his birthplace, boyhood home, and historic sites tied to his legacy. The route passes through rolling hills, small towns, and river valleys, combining military history with rural charm.

☐ 🔖 ♡ **Zane's Trace Scenic Byway:** Following the historic pioneer road built in the 1790s, this byway cuts through central and southeastern Ohio. Small towns, stone bridges, and historic markers recall early settlement and transportation. The route offers a journey through Ohio's frontier history, blending heritage with rolling rural landscapes.

OHIO

☐ 🔖 ♡ **Zoar Valley Scenic Byway:** In Tuscarawas County, this byway centers on Zoar Village, founded by German separatists in 1817. Historic buildings, gardens, and museums interpret the community's cultural heritage. Scenic farmland, wooded hills, and the nearby Tuscarawas River add natural beauty, creating a route that blends living history with quiet countryside landscapes.

National Natural Landmarks

 ☐ 🔖 ♡ **Arthur B. Williams Memorial Woods:** Named a National Natural Landmark for its pristine beech-maple forest, this site preserves a fragment of Ohio's original woodland cover. Protected from logging, it shelters diverse native flora and fauna and offers scientists and visitors a chance to experience the state's ecological past in a landscape increasingly altered by development.
GPS: 41.562282, -81.426792

 ☐ 🔖 ♡ **Blacklick Woods:** Recognized as a National Natural Landmark for its exceptional old-growth beech-maple and swamp forests, this preserve within Columbus Metro Parks is among the least disturbed forests in Ohio's glaciated region. It provides refuge for wildlife, opportunities for environmental education, and a rare glimpse of a mature woodland ecosystem.
GPS: 39.937222, -82.807778

 ☐ 🔖 ♡ **Brown's Lake Bog:** Designated a National Natural Landmark for preserving one of Ohio's few remaining glacial bogs, this acidic wetland supports sphagnum moss, cranberries, pitcher plants, and boreal relict species. It offers a living record of Ohio's glacial heritage and protects a habitat type that has largely disappeared under agricultural conversion.
GPS: 40.6809, -82.0624

 ☐ 🔖 ♡ **Buzzardroost Rock, Lynx Prairie, The Wilderness:** This trio of sites within the Edge of Appalachia Preserve has National Natural Landmark status for its outstanding biodiversity. Rare plants, rugged geology, and nearly 50 years of scientific monitoring make it invaluable for understanding Ohio's ecological and botanical heritage.
GPS: 38.759381, -83.407013

 ☐ 🔖 ♡ **Cedar Bog:** Recognized as a National Natural Landmark for its fen-like wetland system, Cedar Bog hosts orchids, sedges, and carnivorous plants more typical of northern latitudes. Its marl soils and groundwater-fed hydrology create unique conditions that make it one of Ohio's most significant botanical sites.
GPS: 40.059444, -83.795556

 ☐ 🔖 ♡ **Clear Fork Gorge:** This gorge, named a National Natural Landmark for its geologic and ecological value, was carved when glaciers reversed stream flow in the Wisconsinan period. Its Black Hand sandstone walls shelter a rich variety of plants within steep, shaded slopes, illustrating both glacial history and ongoing natural processes.
GPS: 40.610982, -82.286827

 ☐ 🔖 ♡ **Clifton Gorge:** National Natural Landmark designation honors this canyon's outstanding postglacial and interglacial erosional features. The dolomite cliffs and narrow ravines provide a cool microclimate where rare and endangered plants thrive, making it one of Ohio's most scenic and biologically valuable natural preserves.
GPS: 39.793903, -83.831525

 ☐ 🔖 ♡ **Crall Woods:** One of Ohio's finest near-virgin maple-basswood-beech forests, Crall Woods was named a National Natural Landmark for preserving the pre-settlement forest structure of central Ohio. Its old-growth canopy supports wildlife and research, offering a rare glimpse into landscapes that once dominated the region.
GPS: 41.028219, -82.434376

 ☐ 🔖 ♡ **Cranberry Bog:** This unusual floating bog, designated a National Natural Landmark, drifts on a kettle lake and supports boreal plants such as sphagnum moss and cranberries, far south of their usual range. Accessible only by boat, it remains Ohio's only known bog of its kind and a rare ecological treasure.
GPS: 39.931545, -82.468232

OHIO

 ☐ 🔖 ♡ **Dysart Woods:** As one of the last extensive old-growth white oak forests in eastern Ohio, Dysart Woods earned its National Natural Landmark status for its ecological and scientific importance. Some trees exceed 400 years in age, offering rare opportunities to study undisturbed Appalachian hardwood ecosystems.
GPS: 39.9846, -80.9976

 ☐ 🔖 ♡ **Fort Hill State Memorial:** Designated a National Natural Landmark for its mix of geology, ecology, and cultural history, Fort Hill features Silurian to Mississippian bedrock exposures, a natural stone bridge, and a vast tract of old-growth forest. It also protects Hopewell earthworks, blending ancient human and natural heritage.
GPS: 39.1131, -83.4063

 ☐ 🔖 ♡ **Glacial Grooves State Memorial:** This site on Kelleys Island, recognized as a National Natural Landmark, contains the world's largest known glacial grooves carved into limestone. These massive striations were sculpted by Ice Age glaciers and remain one of the clearest illustrations of glacial power anywhere.
GPS: 41.616304, -82.70652

 ☐ 🔖 ♡ **Glen Helen Natural Area:** A National Natural Landmark for its ecological richness, Glen Helen includes travertine waterfalls, diverse woodlands, and abundant wildlife. Created as a living memorial, the preserve supports research, environmental education, and conservation in a biologically significant setting near Yellow Springs.
GPS: 39.804125, -83.881697

 ☐ 🔖 ♡ **Goll Woods:** This site was named a National Natural Landmark for being one of Ohio's best remnants of ancient oak-hickory forest. Some of its massive trees are over 400 years old, and its wildflower-rich understory reflects the primeval forests that once blanketed the Great Black Swamp region.
GPS: 41.554294, -84.361738

☐ 🔖 ♡ **Hazelwood Botanical Preserve:** Designated a National Natural Landmark for its long history of botanical study, Hazelwood protects intact woodland plant communities near Cincinnati. Though not open to the public, it remains vital as a research site managed by the University of Cincinnati for conservation and ecological monitoring.
GPS: 39.263571, -84.354933

 ☐ 🔖 ♡ **Highbanks Natural Area:** Overlooking the Olentangy River, this forested bluff is recognized as a National Natural Landmark for its exposed shale cliffs, ancient terraces, and diverse habitats. Scenic overlooks, rich wildlife, and prehistoric earthworks make it both a natural and cultural treasure.
GPS: 40.143889, -83.028333

 ☐ 🔖 ♡ **Holden Natural Area:** Within the Holden Arboretum, this National Natural Landmark safeguards a broad complex of ravines, wetlands, and mixed forests. Its rich habitats shelter rare plants and wildlife, while also serving as an outdoor laboratory for research on succession, forest ecology, and long-term conservation in northeastern Ohio.
GPS: 41.6114292, -81.3012572

 ☐ 🔖 ♡ **Hueston Woods:** Designated a National Natural Landmark for its pristine beech-maple forest, this site within Hueston Woods State Park has never been logged. Towering trees, spring wildflowers, and a layered understory exemplify the climax communities that once blanketed much of Ohio's pre-settlement landscape.
GPS: 39.5725, -84.741389

 ☐ 🔖 ♡ **Mantua Swamp:** Recognized as a National Natural Landmark for its exceptional wetland diversity, Mantua Swamp contains marshes, swamps, and riparian corridors. These habitats provide refuge for migratory birds, amphibians, and uncommon plants, making it a vital ecological resource in northeastern Ohio.
GPS: 41.280278, -81.211389

 ☐ 🔖 ♡ **Mentor Marsh:** One of Ohio's first National Natural Landmarks, Mentor Marsh preserves an expansive wetland complex along Lake Erie. Its marshes, swamps, and uplands sustain waterfowl and wetland species, while ongoing restoration aims to revive ecosystems once degraded, making it an important site for conservation.
GPS: 41.729164, -81.305492

 ☐ 🔖 ♡ **Serpent Mound Cryptoexplosive Structure:** This Adams County site is designated a National Natural Landmark for its mysterious geologic origins. Believed to mark an ancient buried impact crater, it overlaps with the famous Serpent Mound effigy, blending cultural significance with one of Ohio's most unusual geological features.
GPS: 39.033333, -83.4

UNITED STATES EDITION

OHIO

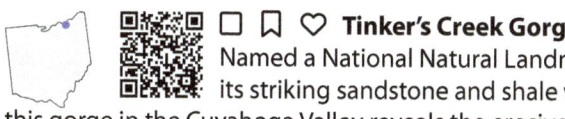 **Tinker's Creek Gorge:** Named a National Natural Landmark for its striking sandstone and shale walls, this gorge in the Cuyahoga Valley reveals the erosive power of Tinker's Creek, a major tributary of the Cuyahoga River. Its rugged cliffs, old-growth forest, and diverse habitats make it both scenic and scientifically valuable.
GPS: 41.365, -81.609722

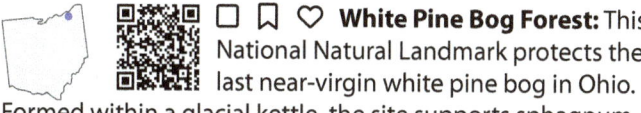 **White Pine Bog Forest:** This National Natural Landmark protects the last near-virgin white pine bog in Ohio. Formed within a glacial kettle, the site supports sphagnum moss, acid-loving plants, and a boreal-style conifer forest. It stands as a rare southern outpost of ecosystems more typical of northern latitudes.
GPS: 41.4240417, -81.1904367

Oklahoma

Oklahoma's diverse landscapes include red rock canyons, rolling prairies, ancient mountains, and scenic rivers. Through its collection of state parks, national forests, national park sites, and fascinating natural landmarks, Oklahoma offers outdoor adventures across its varied terrain, from rugged highlands to peaceful lake shores and open plains.

📅 Peak Season
April–June and September–October are Oklahoma's peak seasons, bringing mild weather, wildflowers, and colorful fall foliage. These months are ideal for hiking, scenic drives, and exploring lakes, mountains, and prairies.

📅 Offseason Months
November–March is the offseason, with cooler weather and lighter crowds. Summer (July–August) is hot and humid, though water recreation and higher elevations remain popular escapes.

🍃 Scenery & Nature Timing
Spring brings wildflowers and green prairies after winter's dormancy. Summer highlights lake recreation and vibrant sunsets. Fall showcases changing foliage, while winter offers clear skies and peaceful landscapes.

✨ Special
Oklahoma features the red sandstone cliffs of the Wichita Mountains, the rolling Tallgrass Prairie Preserve, and the cavern systems of Alabaster Caverns. Dramatic thunderstorms, wind-carved mesas, and sweeping plains capture its dynamic natural beauty.

OKLAHOMA

State Parks

☐ 🔖 ♡ **Alabaster Caverns State Park:** Located near Freedom, this unique park features the world's largest gypsum cave open to the public. Guided tours reveal alabaster, selenite, and rare black alabaster formations. Visitors can also explore wild caves, picnic, and camp in a rugged setting. Its combination of geology, adventure, and natural beauty makes it a rare Oklahoma destination.

☐ 🔖 ♡ **Beavers Bend State Park:** Nestled in the Ouachita Mountains near Broken Bow, this park is among Oklahoma's most popular. It features Broken Bow Lake and the Mountain Fork River for boating and fly fishing. Trails wind through pine and hardwood forests, and cabins and lodges provide overnight stays. It blends outdoor adventure with relaxation in a scenic setting.

☐ 🔖 ♡ **Bernice Area at Grand Lake State Park:** Located in Bernice on Grand Lake O' the Cherokees, this park offers boat ramps, fishing docks, and lakeside trails. Nicknamed the "Crappie Capital of the World," it's especially popular with anglers. The Nature Center highlights local wildlife, while picnic areas and campgrounds provide a relaxed lakefront getaway.

☐ 🔖 ♡ **Black Mesa State Park:** Situated in Oklahoma's far northwest Panhandle, this park showcases mesas, desert-like landscapes, and wildlife habitats. Trails lead to the state's highest point at 4,973 feet. Known for its dark skies, it's a top stargazing destination. The rugged terrain, scenic beauty, and solitude make it a must-see for explorers and nature lovers.

☐ 🔖 ♡ **Boiling Springs State Park:** Near Woodward, this historic park takes its name from a natural "boiling" spring. It features a spring-fed lake, shaded campgrounds, and forested trails. Recreation includes swimming, fishing, golf, and wildlife watching. Developed by the Civilian Conservation Corps, it remains a blend of history, relaxation, and outdoor activity.

☐ 🔖 ♡ **Cherokee Area at Grand Lake State Park:** This Grand Lake access area near Grove offers boating, fishing, and camping along scenic coves. It's popular for family picnics, shoreline exploration, and wildlife observation. Lake views and recreational facilities make it a welcoming spot for water lovers seeking both quiet retreats and active lakefront fun.

☐ 🔖 ♡ **Cherokee Landing State Park:** Located on Fort Gibson Lake in Wagoner County, this park provides opportunities for boating, swimming, and fishing. Trails pass through wooded hillsides, and campgrounds overlook the water. The peaceful setting, abundant wildlife, and scenic lake views make it a favorite for outdoor enthusiasts seeking relaxation and recreation.

☐ 🔖 ♡ **Clayton Lake State Park:** In the Kiamichi Mountains, this 500-acre park centers on an 80-acre lake. Anglers enjoy bass and catfish fishing, while trails lead through forested hills. Visitors can picnic by waterfalls, camp along wooded shores, or paddle in a serene mountain setting. It's an ideal retreat for nature lovers and families.

☐ 🔖 ♡ **Disney Area at Grand Lake State Park:** Found in Disney on the south end of Grand Lake, this area is a hub for boating, swimming, and fishing. Its proximity to the Pensacola Dam makes it unique, with rocky terrain popular for off-road vehicles. Camping, picnic areas, and lake views create a versatile stop for outdoor recreation.

☐ 🔖 ♡ **Fort Cobb State Park:** Located in Caddo County, this park offers boating, skiing, and fishing on Fort Cobb Lake. It also has an 18-hole golf course, campgrounds, and hiking trails. Known for birdwatching and diverse wildlife, the park blends active recreation with peaceful retreats, making it an all-around destination for families and outdoor enthusiasts.

☐ 🔖 ♡ **Foss State Park:** Situated in western Oklahoma near Foss Lake, this park is popular for sailing, water skiing, and fishing. Campgrounds, horse trails, and picnic areas complement the large reservoir. Scenic sunsets and wide-open views create a quintessential western Oklahoma experience, combining water recreation with big-sky landscapes.

☐ 🔖 ♡ **Gloss Mountain State Park:** Near Fairview, this park is famous for its red mesas and gypsum buttes. Cathedral Mountain and other cliffs offer panoramic views, reached via a steep hiking trail. Visitors enjoy photography, wildlife spotting, and exploring rugged terrain. Its striking geology and vistas provide a memorable adventure in northwest Oklahoma.

OKLAHOMA

☐ 🔖 ♡ **Great Plains State Park:** Found in Kiowa County near the Wichita Mountains, this park features Lake Altus-Lugert for boating and fishing. Trails climb rocky hills with views of granite peaks and prairie landscapes. Wildlife includes deer and eagles, while campgrounds and cabins make it a family-friendly retreat surrounded by rugged mountain beauty.

☐ 🔖 ♡ **Great Salt Plains State Park:** Located near Jet, this park is world-famous for its hourglass-shaped selenite crystals, which visitors can dig from designated areas. The salt flats, remnants of an ancient ocean, create a stark and fascinating landscape. Fishing, birdwatching, and camping round out a unique experience blending geology, history, and recreation.

☐ 🔖 ♡ **Greenleaf State Park:** Located near Braggs, this park is known for its forested hills, clear waters, and family-friendly atmosphere. The 930-acre Greenleaf Lake is popular for boating and fishing, while trails wind through woodlands rich in wildlife. Rustic cabins built by the WPA add historic charm. Its natural beauty and diverse recreation make it a beloved getaway.

☐ 🔖 ♡ **Honey Creek Area at Grand Lake State Park:** Situated in Grove, this area provides convenient access to Grand Lake O' the Cherokees. Visitors enjoy fishing, boating, and picnicking along the shoreline, with playgrounds and campgrounds nearby. Its location near marinas and shops makes it a versatile destination for both relaxation and lake-based adventure.

☐ 🔖 ♡ **Hugo Lake State Park:** Found in Choctaw County, this park centers on the scenic 8,000-acre Hugo Lake. It offers boating, fishing, camping, and hiking in a quiet, wooded environment. Cabins and RV sites provide lodging, while birdwatching and wildlife observation enrich the experience. Its peaceful setting makes it a top choice for nature enthusiasts.

☐ 🔖 ♡ **Keystone State Park:** Located near Sand Springs, this park offers access to Keystone Lake, a popular spot for swimming, boating, and fishing. Trails meander through woodlands and meadows, while campgrounds and cabins provide overnight stays. The park's proximity to Tulsa makes it a convenient escape with both relaxation and recreation.

☐ 🔖 ♡ **Lake Eufaula State Park:** On the shores of Oklahoma's largest lake, this park offers boating, fishing, hiking, and camping. Trails lead through wooded hills with abundant wildlife, and the Nature Center provides interactive exhibits. With its mix of natural beauty, diverse activities, and modern facilities, it's a popular destination for outdoor recreation.

☐ 🔖 ♡ **Lake Murray State Park:** Oklahoma's oldest and largest state park, located near Ardmore, spans over 12,500 acres. It offers a wide range of recreation: boating, fishing, hiking, ATV and horseback riding, plus the iconic Tucker Tower Nature Center. Cabins, campgrounds, and a lodge provide overnight options. Its size and diversity make it a premier park.

☐ 🔖 ♡ **Lake Texoma State Park:** Situated on the Oklahoma-Texas border, this park is known for striper bass fishing and water recreation on one of the nation's largest reservoirs. Marinas, campgrounds, and trails provide plenty of activities. With scenic lake views and abundant wildlife, it's a destination that combines sport, relaxation, and family fun.

☐ 🔖 ♡ **Lake Thunderbird State Park:** Located in Norman, this park surrounds the 6,070-acre Lake Thunderbird. It offers boating, swimming, hiking, and equestrian trails, plus two marinas and campgrounds. Birdwatchers flock here for bald eagles and waterfowl. Its location near Oklahoma City makes it a convenient escape for outdoor recreation.

☐ 🔖 ♡ **Lake Wister State Park:** Found in southeastern Oklahoma near the Ouachita Mountains, this park offers boating, swimming, and fishing on Lake Wister. Trails lead through forests and hills, offering opportunities for hiking, wildlife observation, and photography. Campgrounds and cabins make it a scenic, family-friendly retreat year-round.

☐ 🔖 ♡ **Little Blue Area at Grand Lake State Park:** Located near Disney and Afton, this small recreation area on Grand Lake is popular for swimming, fishing, and family picnics. Its shaded sites and creek-fed swimming hole make it a refreshing spot in summer. Simplicity and lakefront charm define this quiet yet beloved area.

☐ 🔖 ♡ **Little Sahara State Park:** Near Waynoka, this 1,600-acre park is famous for its towering sand dunes, some reaching 75 feet high. Off-road vehicle enthusiasts flock here for ATV and dune buggy riding, while others enjoy hiking or sandboarding. Its desert-like landscape offers a thrilling and unusual outdoor experience in Oklahoma.

OKLAHOMA

McGee Creek State Park: Nestled in Atoka County, this park features rugged hills, dense forests, and the scenic McGee Creek Lake. Known for trophy bass fishing, it also offers trails for hiking, biking, and horseback riding. Campgrounds and secluded cabins add to its charm. Its wild and peaceful setting appeals to nature enthusiasts and anglers alike.

Natural Falls State Park: Located near Colcord, this park is home to a stunning 77-foot waterfall that cascades into a grotto. Trails explore forested hills and streams, and camping options include yurts and RV sites. It's popular for photography, hiking, and family outings, offering both scenic beauty and a tranquil natural escape.

Osage Hills State Park: Found near Pawhuska, this park is known for its rolling hills, hardwood forests, and stone structures built by the WPA. Visitors enjoy hiking, camping, and fishing in quiet surroundings rich with wildlife. In autumn, its wooded trails are especially vibrant, making it a top spot for scenic photography and relaxation.

Quartz Mountain State Park: Situated near Altus, this park combines striking granite peaks with a large lake for fishing and boating. Hiking trails climb rugged terrain with panoramic views, while the lodge and amphitheater host cultural programs. Known for its natural beauty and arts events, it's a distinctive blend of recreation and culture.

Raymond Gary State Park: Located in Choctaw County, this cozy park surrounds Raymond Gary Lake, a small but scenic reservoir. It's popular for fishing, boating, and kayaking, with campgrounds and cabins providing overnight stays. Shady picnic areas, a swim beach, and quiet natural beauty make it a peaceful retreat for families and anglers alike.

Robbers Cave State Park: Nestled in the San Bois Mountains near Wilburton, this park is steeped in legend as a former hideout for outlaws Jesse James and Belle Starr. Rugged trails lead to caves and cliffs with sweeping views. Visitors enjoy fishing, boating, horseback riding, and camping. Its mix of history, adventure, and scenery makes it a must-see.

Roman Nose State Park: One of Oklahoma's original seven state parks, Roman Nose is located near Watonga. It features gypsum canyons, natural springs, and lakes for fishing and boating. Activities include golf, hiking, biking, and camping. With historic stone structures built by the Civilian Conservation Corps, it offers both recreation and cultural heritage.

Sardis Lake State Park: Situated in Pushmataha County in the scenic Kiamichi Mountains, this park centers on Sardis Lake. Anglers enjoy bass and catfish fishing, while boaters explore calm waters surrounded by forested hills. Trails, campgrounds, and picnic spots make it a peaceful place for families and nature enthusiasts seeking tranquility.

Sequoyah Bay Area at Grand Lake State Park: Located near Wagoner on Fort Gibson Lake, this park offers marinas, cabins, and RV camping along wooded shoreline. Visitors enjoy boating, fishing, and swimming in a relaxed atmosphere. Its family-friendly facilities and natural setting make it a popular spot for weekend getaways and lake recreation.

Sequoyah State Park: One of Oklahoma's largest and most popular parks, Sequoyah lies on the shores of Fort Gibson Lake. It offers golf, hiking, horse trails, and boating. Lodges, cabins, and campgrounds provide accommodations. With its wide range of facilities, wildlife, and lakefront views, it's a versatile destination for families and groups.

Talimena State Park: Found at the eastern entrance of the Talimena National Scenic Byway near Talihina, this park is a gateway to the Ouachita Mountains. It offers hiking, camping, and picnicking, with access to the Ouachita National Recreation Trail. Known for brilliant fall foliage, it's a starting point for scenic drives and wilderness exploration.

Tenkiller State Park: Located on Lake Tenkiller in eastern Oklahoma, this park is a favorite for scuba diving, boating, and fishing. Clear waters attract divers exploring sunken structures, while trails and campsites offer land-based recreation. Cabins, campgrounds, and a nature center provide amenities, making it a diverse outdoor destination.

OKLAHOMA

☐ 🔖 ♡ **Twin Bridges Area at Grand Lake State Park:** Situated where the Neosho and Spring rivers meet Grand Lake, this park is known for excellent fishing, especially for catfish and paddlefish. Visitors enjoy boating, camping, and wildlife watching in wooded surroundings. Its natural beauty and water access make it a popular spot for anglers and families.

National Parks

☐ 🔖 ♡ **Chickasaw National Recreation Area:** Located in Sulphur, Oklahoma, this park is known for its picturesque springs, lakes, and abundant wildlife. Visitors can enjoy fishing, boating, hiking, and exploring the natural beauty of the area, including the historic Travertine Nature Center and the Platt National Park, which showcases the area's rich cultural history and natural resources.

☐ 🔖 ♡ **Washita Battlefield National Historic Site:** Located in Cheyenne, Oklahoma, this site commemorates the Battle of Washita River, where General George Custer led an attack on a Cheyenne village in 1868. Visitors can learn about the conflict, explore the battlefield, and reflect on its impact on Native American history and the western expansion of the U.S.

☐ 🔖 ♡ **Fort Smith National Historic Site:** Situated in Fort Smith, Arkansas, this site preserves the remains of Fort Smith, a pivotal military post during the Indian Removal and the Civil War. Visitors can explore the historic fort, visit the U.S. District Court (where Judge Isaac Parker served), and learn about the law enforcement efforts of the time.

State & National Forests

☐ 🔖 ♡ **Ouachita National Forest:** Covering more than 1.7 million acres across southeastern Oklahoma and western Arkansas, this is the oldest national forest in the South. Its rugged mountains, pine and hardwood forests, and clear streams provide endless recreation. Visitors hike the 223-mile Ouachita National Recreation Trail, camp in scenic valleys, fish in mountain waters, and enjoy year-round wildlife viewing and adventure.

National Grasslands

☐ 🔖 ♡ **Black Kettle National Grassland:** Spanning over 30,000 acres in western Oklahoma, this grassland preserves rolling prairies, wooded draws, and riparian zones along the Washita River. Known for wildlife like wild turkeys, deer, and migratory birds, it offers hunting, fishing, hiking, and scenic drives. Rich in history, it also contains the Washita Battlefield National Historic Site.

☐ 🔖 ♡ **Kiowa/Rita Blanca National Grasslands:** Stretching across northeastern New Mexico, the Oklahoma Panhandle, and parts of Texas, these sister grasslands feature expansive shortgrass prairie, deep canyons, and historic landmarks. Visitors can explore the Santa Fe Trail, view native wildlife, or hike amid rugged mesas in this serene, windswept High Plains landscape.

OKLAHOMA

☐ 🔖 ♡ **McClellan Creek National Grasslands**: Located in western Oklahoma and the Texas Panhandle, these grasslands preserve a patchwork of prairie, woodlands, and riparian zones. Rich in wildlife and history, the area honors the legacy of Native tribes and early frontier life. Outdoor activities include hiking, fishing, and scenic drives through rolling hills and open skies.

National Scenic Byways & All-American Roads

☐ 🔖 ♡ **Cherokee Hills Byway:** Traversing 84 miles in eastern Oklahoma, this National Scenic Byway showcases the Ozark foothills, Illinois River valley, and the Cherokee Nation capital of Tahlequah. Visitors encounter museums, cultural sites, and reminders of the Trail of Tears, along with forested ridges, rolling hills, and opportunities for outdoor adventure.

☐ 🔖 ♡ **Historic Route 66:** Known nationwide as the Mother Road, Oklahoma's nearly 400-mile stretch is designated an All-American Road. From Quapaw to Erick, it carries travelers past neon signs, diners, motels, and quirky roadside attractions. The route preserves mid-20th-century Americana while tying together small towns, cultural landmarks, and historic highway heritage.

☐ 🔖 ♡ **Talimena Scenic Drive:** Following 54 miles along the crests of the Ouachita Mountains, this National Scenic Byway links Talihina, Oklahoma, with Mena, Arkansas. It features 22 scenic vistas overlooking rugged peaks and forests that blaze with color each fall. Hiking trail connections and old-growth landscapes make it a top destination for nature enthusiasts.

☐ 🔖 ♡ **Wichita Mountains Byway:** Centered on the Wichita Mountains Wildlife Refuge, this National Scenic Byway loops 93 miles through granite peaks, mixed-grass prairie, and cross-timber habitats. Bison, elk, and longhorn cattle roam the landscape, while hiking trails and viewpoints reveal sweeping vistas across ancient geology and a uniquely rugged Oklahoma wilderness.

State Scenic Byways

☐ 🔖 ♡ **Kenton to Keys:** Wind through the Panhandle's high plains from Kenton to Keys, offering layered vistas of mesas, distant mountains, and vast skies. Designated as an Oklahoma State Scenic Byway, this route captures the stark beauty of western landscapes, wildlife sightings, and the region's quiet rural charm—perfect for immersive, wide-open-road exploration.

☐ 🔖 ♡ **Mountain Gateway:** Gateway to the Ouachita's eastern hills, this drive links Talihina to the Talimena Scenic Drive corridor. As an Oklahoma State Scenic Byway, it treats travelers to winding roads through pine-and-oak forests, seasonal wildflowers, and signs of Choctaw heritage, inviting a gentle yet scenic entrance into Little Dixie's mountainous terrain.

☐ 🔖 ♡ **Mountain Pass:** Carving through rugged ridgelines where the Ouachita Mountains rise and fall, this corridor offers elevation, curves, and forested seclusion. Recognized as a State Scenic Byway, it showcases rarely seen overlooks, autumn color, and access to trailheads—and embodies the sense of discovery found in Oklahoma's Little Dixie region.

☐ 🔖 ♡ **Osage Nation Heritage Trail:** Bridging Pawhuska, Pawnee, and other destinations, this route threads through rolling hills, tallgrass prairie, and sites of Osage history. Designated an Oklahoma State Scenic Byway, it traces the legacy of the Osage people—from heritage museums to prairie vistas—combining cultural significance with serene expanses of rural beauty.

OKLAHOMA

National Natural Landmarks

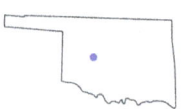 ☐ 🔖 ♡ **Devil's Canyon:** Recognized as a National Natural Landmark for its unusual mix of tallgrass prairie and eastern deciduous forest, this Wichita Mountains canyon forms a rare ecological transition zone. Its cool, moist microclimate sustains oaks, grasses, and ferns uncommon in the surrounding plains, offering both scenic beauty and exceptional biodiversity.
GPS: 35.363333, -98.341667

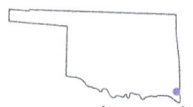 ☐ 🔖 ♡ **McCurtain County Wilderness Area:** Designated a National Natural Landmark for its outstanding xeric oak–pine forest, this 14,000-acre preserve in southeastern Oklahoma protects rugged terrain rich in biodiversity. Managed since 1918, it is one of the oldest wilderness areas in the central U.S., showcasing long-term conservation of native upland ecosystems.
GPS: 34.281971, -94.696655

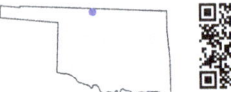 ☐ 🔖 ♡ **Salt Plains National Wildlife Refuge:** This vast refuge holds National Natural Landmark status for its unique salt flat ecosystem. Covering 32,000 acres, it sustains wetlands, hypersaline waters, and crystalline selenite beds. Crucially, it supports 75% of the whooping crane population during migration, making it one of the continent's most important bird habitats.
GPS: 36.750314, -98.224259

OREGON

Oregon's outdoor wonders span rugged coastlines, towering mountains, lush valleys, and high desert plains. With a rich network of state parks, national forests, iconic national parks, and treasured natural landmarks, Oregon inspires exploration in every direction, from misty coastal trails to volcanic peaks and wild river canyons.

📅 Peak Season
June–September is Oregon's peak season, offering warm, dry weather and full access to trails, mountains, and the coast. Summer is ideal for hiking, camping, and exploring national forests and waterfalls.

📅 Offseason Months
November–April is the offseason, bringing rain to western Oregon and snow to the Cascades. Winter offers skiing and storm watching along the coast, though some mountain roads may close.

🍃 Scenery & Nature Timing
Spring brings wildflowers and waterfalls at their peak flow. Summer showcases alpine meadows, volcanoes, and coastal cliffs. Fall adds colorful forests and crisp air, while winter highlights snow-covered peaks and roaring rivers.

✨ Special
Oregon features Crater Lake's deep blue caldera, the volcanic peaks of the Cascades, and the Columbia River Gorge's countless waterfalls. Painted Hills' vivid layers, coastal sea stacks, and ancient lava flows display its striking natural diversity.

THE ROAMER'S GUIDE

OREGON

State Parks

☐ 🔖 ♡ **Ainsworth State Park:** Located in the Columbia River Gorge, this park is surrounded by steep cliffs, lush forests, and waterfalls. It offers shaded picnic areas, access to hiking trails like Angels Rest, and close proximity to historic highway viewpoints. The mix of easy access, natural beauty, and sweeping Gorge scenery makes it a convenient base for exploring one of Oregon's most dramatic landscapes.

☐ 🔖 ♡ **Alfred A. Loeb State Park:** Along the Chetco River near Brookings, this quiet park is known for shaded campsites beneath myrtlewood trees and access to northernmost coastal redwoods. Visitors fish, paddle, or swim in clear waters, hike into lush forests, or stay in cozy cabins. Its combination of rare trees, serene riverside setting, and recreation options makes it a southern Oregon favorite year-round.

☐ 🔖 ♡ **Bald Peak State Park:** High atop the Chehalem Mountains, this park offers sweeping views of the Willamette Valley, Mount Hood, and the Cascades. A broad grassy meadow is ideal for picnicking, kite flying, and photography. Seasonal wildflowers add color, while autumn sunsets paint the sky. Its easy access from wine country and commanding panoramas make it one of Oregon's best scenic overlooks.

☐ 🔖 ♡ **Bates State Park:** In the Blue Mountains at the site of a former sawmill town, this park blends history and outdoor recreation. Trails wind through meadows, forests, and streams once busy with mills, with interpretive signs sharing stories of Oregon's logging past. Wildlife thrives in the surrounding woods, offering visitors both cultural insight and a peaceful retreat in a high-country landscape.

☐ 🔖 ♡ **Beverly Beach State Park:** Located just north of Newport, this popular park combines sandy beach access with a campground tucked beneath spruce and fir. Visitors enjoy clamming, whale watching, and tidepooling, along with shaded trails through coastal forests. Its large family-friendly campground and proximity to iconic Oregon Coast attractions make it a perfect central coast base for adventure.

☐ 🔖 ♡ **Bob Straub State Park:** On a sandy spit near Pacific City, this coastal park offers miles of beach, dunes, and salt marshes. Visitors hike along ocean and riverfront, watch for shorebirds, and picnic among grassy dunes. Horseback riders frequent the beach, while anglers cast into the surf. With sweeping views of Haystack Rock and a rugged, natural feel, it's a peaceful oceanfront destination.

☐ 🔖 ♡ **Bullards Beach State Park:** Near Bandon, this expansive coastal park includes wide sandy beaches, grassy dunes, and access to the historic Coquille River Lighthouse. The large campground supports RVs, tents, and yurts, while equestrian trails and crabbing draws families. Wildlife-rich wetlands and estuaries make it excellent for birdwatching, blending outdoor recreation with historic and scenic coastal charm.

☐ 🔖 ♡ **Cape Arago State Park:** At the southern end of the Cape Arago Highway near Coos Bay, this headland park features rugged cliffs, tidepools, and overlooks of offshore seal and sea lion colonies. Trails wind through spruce forests to rocky beaches rich with marine life. Whale watching, photography, and quiet picnics make it a favorite for experiencing Oregon's dramatic coastal ecosystems.

☐ 🔖 ♡ **Cape Blanco State Park:** Oregon's westernmost state park near Port Orford, it is home to the historic Cape Blanco Lighthouse, built in 1870. Visitors enjoy windswept headlands, secluded beaches, and wooded trails leading to panoramic ocean views. Campgrounds and cabins offer overnight stays. Its history, solitude, and stunning coastal vistas make it one of Oregon's most memorable destinations.

☐ 🔖 ♡ **Cape Lookout State Park:** On the north coast's Three Capes Scenic Route, this park stretches along a narrow headland jutting into the Pacific. Visitors hike through old-growth forest to the cape's tip for sweeping ocean views or descend to miles of sandy shoreline. Campgrounds near the beach make it a year-round favorite for whale watching, tidepooling, and coastal exploration.

☐ 🔖 ♡ **Carl G. Washburne Memorial State Park:** North of Florence, this park combines beach, forest, and creek habitats. Its shaded campground is within walking distance of the beach, while trails connect to Heceta Head Lighthouse and forested ridges. Visitors enjoy birdwatching, beachcombing, and exploring the dunes. The variety of landscapes packed into one area makes it a diverse and scenic coastal stop.

☐ 🔖 ♡ **Casey State Park:** Along the Clackamas River near Estacada, this park is a popular spot for rafting put-ins, fishing, and riverside picnicking. Trails follow riparian habitats rich with birds and wildlife, while shady groves of fir and maple create a relaxing environment. Its combination of river access, wooded scenery, and proximity to Portland makes it an easy and inviting outdoor escape.

UNITED STATES EDITION

OREGON

☐ 🔖 ♡ **Collier Memorial State Park:** Near Chiloquin, this park blends outdoor recreation with history at the Collier Logging Museum, which showcases vintage equipment and Oregon's timber heritage. Visitors camp among pines, fish in Spring Creek, and explore trails winding through forest. Educational exhibits and natural beauty combine here, offering a unique mix of cultural storytelling and Cascade mountain recreation.

☐ 🔖 ♡ **Coquille Myrtle Grove State Park:** On the Coquille River, this small park is shaded by fragrant myrtlewood trees unique to southwestern Oregon. Its riverside picnic areas, trails, and wetlands attract birdwatchers and anglers. The peaceful setting and rare tree groves create a distinctive stop for travelers exploring the Coos Bay area, offering both natural beauty and a sense of quiet seclusion.

☐ 🔖 ♡ **Corbett Memorial State Park:** Overlooking the Columbia River Gorge, this small day-use park features shaded lawns and picnic tables with sweeping views of the Gorge's cliffs and river. Its quiet setting provides a restful stop along the Historic Columbia River Highway. Though modest in size, it offers a scenic and serene place for travelers to pause, picnic, and admire Oregon's grandest landscapes.

☐ 🔖 ♡ **Cottonwood Canyon State Park:** Oregon's second-largest state park at over 8,000 acres, Cottonwood Canyon showcases rugged basalt cliffs, sagebrush hills, and the wild John Day River. Visitors hike or bike along scenic canyon trails, fish for steelhead, or camp beneath star-filled skies. Its dramatic landscapes, rich wildlife, and remote quiet make it a haven for hikers, paddlers, and stargazers alike.

☐ 🔖 ♡ **Detroit Lake State Park:** Nestled in the Cascades, this park surrounds the reservoir of Detroit Lake, a hub for summer recreation. Visitors boat, swim, or fish in sparkling waters framed by forested peaks. Campgrounds accommodate tents and RVs, while nearby trails invite hiking. With a marina, beaches, and scenic views, it is a favorite destination for families seeking mountain adventure.

☐ 🔖 ♡ **Devils Lake State Park:** In Lincoln City, this park surrounds a freshwater lake popular for boating, fishing, and swimming. Trails pass through wetlands and forested areas, providing wildlife watching and quiet walks. Picnic spots and easy lake access make it family-friendly. Its unique setting—steps from the Pacific Ocean—lets visitors experience both coastal and lakeside recreation in one trip.

☐ 🔖 ♡ **Ecola State Park:** Stretching between Cannon Beach and Seaside, Ecola offers some of Oregon's most iconic coastal scenery. Visitors hike forested headlands with sweeping views of Haystack Rock, Tillamook Rock Lighthouse, and rugged cliffs. Beaches provide tidepooling and surfing, while elk and seabirds roam its forests. Its combination of breathtaking views, wildlife, and outdoor adventure make it world-renowned.

☐ 🔖 ♡ **Elijah Bristow State Park:** Just outside Eugene, this expansive park sits along the Middle Fork of the Willamette River. It offers trails for hiking, biking, and horseback riding through forests, meadows, and wetlands teeming with birdlife. Picnic areas and river access make it versatile for families, while its equestrian facilities draw riders. Its diverse habitats provide year-round opportunities for recreation.

☐ 🔖 ♡ **Elk Creek Tunnel Forest State Park:** Near Gold Hill, this small forested park offers quiet trails and shaded picnic spots. Dense stands of Douglas fir and madrone surround the area, providing habitat for birds and wildlife. Visitors enjoy peaceful walks and family picnics in a serene setting. Its simplicity and natural beauty make it an inviting stop for those traveling southern Oregon backroads.

☐ 🔖 ♡ **Ellmaker State Wayside:** Located near Monroe, this park honors pioneer John Ellmaker and provides picnic areas and open lawns along a shaded creek. Trails wind through riparian woodlands, offering birdwatching and quiet reflection. Its rural setting in the Willamette Valley makes it a scenic, peaceful stop for travelers, blending pioneer history with a simple yet charming natural environment.

☐ 🔖 ♡ **Fort Rock State Park:** In central Oregon's high desert, this park preserves a massive volcanic tuff ring rising dramatically from the valley floor. Visitors hike trails through the formation, exploring its unique geology and learning about ancient Native sites. With sweeping desert vistas, striking rock walls, and prehistoric significance, Fort Rock offers a rare glimpse into Oregon's volcanic past.

☐ 🔖 ♡ **Fort Stevens State Park:** Near Astoria at the Columbia River's mouth, this 4,300-acre park blends history and recreation. Visitors explore Civil War-era batteries, bunkers, and the iconic Peter Iredale shipwreck. Beaches, bike trails, and campgrounds make it ideal for extended stays. Its combination of military history, coastal scenery, and abundant outdoor activities makes it one of Oregon's most popular parks.

OREGON

☐ 🔖 ♡ **Geisel Monument State Park:** Near Gold Beach, this small historic park preserves the gravesite of the pioneer Geisel family, who settled in the area in the 1850s. A monument marks the site, while surrounding trees and lawns provide a quiet setting for reflection. Though small, it offers visitors insight into Oregon's pioneer history while serving as a peaceful memorial stop along the coast.

☐ 🔖 ♡ **George W. Joseph State Park:** Situated along the Columbia River Highway, this park is a quiet stop for travelers exploring the Gorge. With shaded lawns, picnic areas, and forested surroundings, it offers a place to rest and take in glimpses of dramatic cliffs and the river. Its peaceful atmosphere and convenient location make it a simple yet scenic roadside retreat.

☐ 🔖 ♡ **Golden and Silver Falls State Park:** Hidden in the Coast Range near Coos Bay, this lush park features two waterfalls plunging more than 100 feet over mossy cliffs. Trails lead through dense maple and alder forests to base and viewpoint overlooks. Wildlife and wildflowers thrive in its rainforest-like environment. Its dramatic waterfalls and secluded setting make it a treasured destination for hikers.

☐ 🔖 ♡ **Guy W. Talbot State Park:** In the Columbia Gorge near Corbett, this park is home to Latourell Falls, a striking waterfall that plunges over columnar basalt. Trails explore mossy forests and lead to stunning Gorge vistas. Shady picnic areas beneath towering maples make it family-friendly. With its iconic waterfall and easy access, it is one of the most scenic stops on the Historic Highway.

☐ 🔖 ♡ **Harris Beach State Park:** On the southern Oregon coast near Brookings, this park is renowned for its offshore sea stacks that form part of the Oregon Islands National Wildlife Refuge. Visitors enjoy sandy beaches, tidepools rich with marine life, and trails with sweeping ocean views. Seals, seabirds, and migrating whales are common sights. Campgrounds and day-use areas make it a top coastal destination.

☐ 🔖 ♡ **Howard Prairie State Park:** In the Cascade foothills near Ashland, this lakeside park is centered on Howard Prairie Lake, stocked with trout and surrounded by forested hills. Visitors boat, fish, and camp while enjoying striking mountain views. Trails and picnic sites create year-round appeal, while the full-service marina and quiet natural setting make it popular with both anglers and families.

☐ 🔖 ♡ **Jackson F. Kimball State Park:** Near Chiloquin, this tranquil park surrounds the headwaters of the Wood River, where icy springs form a crystal-clear stream. Trails explore meadows and pine forests alive with birds and deer, while paddlers and anglers enjoy pristine waters. Rustic campsites enhance its remote charm, making it a peaceful base for exploring southern Oregon's lakes and forests.

☐ 🔖 ♡ **Jasper State Park:** In Springfield's southern Willamette Valley, Jasper Park sits along the Middle Fork Willamette River. It offers shady picnic areas, ball fields, and riverside trails for family recreation. Visitors swim, fish, or walk beneath groves of fir and maple, with abundant opportunities for birdwatching. Its blend of natural beauty and community amenities makes it a popular gathering place year-round.

☐ 🔖 ♡ **Jessie M. Honeyman Memorial State Park:** Just south of Florence, this expansive park is a coastal playground with freshwater lakes surrounded by dunes and forests. Cleawox and Woahink Lakes invite swimming, boating, and fishing, while hiking trails connect to the Oregon Dunes National Recreation Area. With a large campground, yurts, and family-friendly facilities, it's one of Oregon's most popular destinations.

☐ 🔖 ♡ **John B. Yeon State Park:** Located in the Columbia River Gorge, this park provides access to several stunning waterfalls, including Elowah Falls and Upper McCord Creek Falls. Trails climb through moss-covered forests and offer panoramic Gorge views. It's a haven for hikers, photographers, and nature enthusiasts seeking dramatic scenery in a relatively less-crowded corner of the Historic Highway corridor.

☐ 🔖 ♡ **Kam Wah Chung State Park:** In John Day, this historic park preserves an original 19th-century Chinese apothecary and general store run by Ing "Doc" Hay and Lung On. Visitors tour the remarkably intact building, which offers a vivid window into Oregon's Chinese immigrant community. Surrounded by a small park setting, it blends cultural history with quiet reflection in eastern Oregon's high desert.

☐ 🔖 ♡ **L. L. Stub Stewart State Park:** Near Vernonia, this 1,600-acre park is one of Oregon's newest and most versatile destinations. It offers hiking, biking, and horseback riding trails, plus cabins, camping, and disc golf. Its connection to the Banks-Vernonia Trail makes it a hub for cyclists. With forested hills, meadows, and year-round amenities, it attracts families, adventurers, and nature lovers alike.

OREGON

☐ ◫ ♡ **Lake Owyhee State Park:** Tucked into the colorful cliffs of eastern Oregon's Owyhee Reservoir, this park is known for its striking desert canyon scenery. Visitors fish and boat in the long, winding lake while watching for bighorn sheep and raptors. Campgrounds and boat ramps provide access, and its remote beauty makes it a hidden gem for those seeking solitude and dramatic landscapes.

☐ ◫ ♡ **Lewis and Clark State Park:** Just east of Troutdale, this shaded riverside park honors the famous explorers while offering grassy picnic areas and wooded trails. Towering maples and Douglas firs provide cool retreats, while interpretive signs highlight local history. Its convenient location at the western entrance to the Columbia River Gorge makes it a popular family-friendly stop for recreation.

☐ ◫ ♡ **Lowell State Park:** Situated on Dexter Lake near Eugene, this small but inviting day-use park is perfect for boating, fishing, and swimming. Grassy lawns, picnic shelters, and boat ramps offer easy access to the water, while nearby forested hills provide a scenic backdrop. Its blend of convenience and natural charm makes it a favorite warm-weather gathering place for local families.

☐ ◫ ♡ **McVay Rock State Park:** On the southern Oregon coast near Brookings, this small park provides beach access, tidepool exploration, and whale-watching. Picnic areas overlook the Pacific, and offshore rocks host seals and seabirds. Its quiet atmosphere and rugged shoreline make it an excellent stop for travelers seeking a peaceful coastal experience, away from the bustle of larger beaches.

☐ ◫ ♡ **Milo McIver State Park:** Along the Clackamas River near Estacada, this large park offers steelhead fishing, kayaking, and rafting access, plus trails through forested hills and meadows. Equestrian facilities, a disc golf course, and shady picnic areas make it versatile for recreation. Its proximity to Portland, paired with natural beauty and variety, makes it one of Oregon's most popular inland parks.

☐ ◫ ♡ **Molalla River State Park:** At the confluence of the Molalla, Pudding, and Willamette Rivers, this park features wetlands rich with birds, boat ramps, and riverside trails. Visitors spot bald eagles and osprey while fishing or hiking. Picnic shelters and open lawns make it family-friendly. Its diverse ecosystems and river access create a scenic natural escape close to the Willamette Valley's towns.

☐ ◫ ♡ **Mongold State Park:** A day-use area on Detroit Lake, Mongold offers boat ramps, fishing access, and swimming beaches with stunning Cascade Mountain views. Shady picnic sites and grassy lawns make it perfect for families, while the lake's clear waters attract boaters and anglers. Its easy access to campgrounds and scenic surroundings make it a popular recreation hub during summer months.

☐ ◫ ♡ **Munson Creek Falls State Park:** Near Tillamook, this park protects one of Oregon's tallest waterfalls, plunging 319 feet through a lush coastal forest. A short trail winds past towering Sitka spruce and bigleaf maples to a viewpoint near the falls. Seasonal wildflowers and abundant birdlife make it an inviting stop, while its dramatic cascade offers a glimpse of the wild beauty of the Coast Range.

☐ ◫ ♡ **Nehalem Bay State Park:** Situated on a narrow coastal spit, this park offers ocean beaches, bay access, and forested dunes. Campsites, yurts, and trails accommodate hikers, bikers, and horseback riders, while fishing, crabbing, and wildlife viewing are popular. Elk and shorebirds thrive in the area. With both bay and Pacific frontage, it's a versatile coastal destination for year-round recreation.

☐ ◫ ♡ **North Fork Smith River State Park:** Located in the Coast Range, this remote park features rugged terrain, clear streams, and dense forests. Visitors hike riverside paths, fish in pristine waters, or picnic beneath towering evergreens. Its seclusion offers a peaceful retreat from busier destinations, making it a favorite for those who value solitude and immersion in Oregon's natural landscapes.

☐ ◫ ♡ **Oswald West State Park:** On the north coast, this park is famous for Short Sand Beach, a sheltered cove popular with surfers. Trails climb through lush coastal forest to Cape Falcon and Neahkahnie Mountain, offering dramatic views. Old-growth spruce, tidepools, and abundant seabirds highlight its biodiversity. With beaches, forests, and panoramic vistas, it is one of Oregon's most iconic coastal parks.

☐ ◫ ♡ **Pilot Butte State Park:** In Bend, this park is centered on a 480-foot volcanic cinder cone that rises above the city. A road and hiking trail lead to its summit, offering sweeping views of the Cascades, high desert, and town below. Locals and visitors hike for exercise or sunset photography. Its geological significance and panoramic vistas make it one of Oregon's most unique urban parks.

OREGON

☐ 🔖 ♡ **Prineville Reservoir State Park:** In central Oregon's high desert, this park surrounds a large reservoir perfect for boating, fishing, and swimming. Campgrounds accommodate tents, RVs, and cabins, while trails explore surrounding desert hills. Dark skies attract stargazers, and quiet coves provide habitat for wildlife. Its blend of recreation, scenery, and year-round amenities make it a popular inland destination.

☐ 🔖 ♡ **Red Bridge State Park:** In northeast Oregon near the Grande Ronde River, this small park offers shady campsites, picnic areas, and fishing access. Towering cottonwoods and river views create a peaceful atmosphere. Its location along the Blue Mountain Scenic Byway makes it a convenient stop for travelers seeking a quiet riverside retreat with opportunities for wildlife observation and relaxation.

☐ 🔖 ♡ **Rooster Rock State Park:** Set in the Columbia River Gorge, this large park is known for sandy beaches, picnic areas, and river access. Windsurfers, birdwatchers, and hikers flock here, while its trails provide dramatic views of the Gorge. It also hosts one of Oregon's few clothing-optional beaches. Its mix of recreation, natural scenery, and unique culture makes it a popular, diverse destination.

☐ 🔖 ♡ **Sarah Helmick State Park:** Established in 1922 near Monmouth, this was Oregon's first official state park. Nestled along the Luckiamute River, it offers shaded picnic areas, open lawns, and riparian forests. Visitors fish, birdwatch, or enjoy riverside walks. Its historical importance, combined with natural charm, makes it both a cultural landmark and a quiet day-use area in the Willamette Valley.

☐ 🔖 ♡ **Seal Rock State Park:** Just south of Newport, this park is known for offshore rock formations that provide habitat for seals, sea lions, and seabirds. Visitors explore tidepools, stroll sandy beaches, and picnic on grassy bluffs overlooking the Pacific. Its dramatic geology, abundant wildlife, and easy access from Highway 101 make it a favorite stop along the central Oregon coast.

☐ 🔖 ♡ **Shore Acres State Park:** Near Coos Bay, this park sits atop cliffs overlooking the Pacific, once the site of a 1900s estate. Today it features botanical gardens with global plantings, seasonal holiday light displays, and trails to rugged viewpoints. Visitors enjoy whale watching and dramatic surf shows in winter. Its blend of cultivated gardens and wild coastline makes it uniquely memorable.

☐ 🔖 ♡ **Silver Falls State Park:** Oregon's largest state park spans over 9,000 acres in the Cascade foothills. Famous for the "Trail of Ten Falls," it allows hikers to walk behind waterfalls, including 177-foot South Falls. Lush forests, picnic areas, campgrounds, and equestrian trails add to its appeal. Its sheer size, dramatic waterfalls, and natural beauty make it one of Oregon's crown jewels.

☐ 🔖 ♡ **Smith Rock State Park:** In central Oregon near Terrebonne, this world-renowned climbing destination features volcanic cliffs above the Crooked River. Hikers tackle Misery Ridge for sweeping Cascade views, while wildlife watchers spot golden eagles and otters. Camping and trails attract adventurers from around the globe. Its dramatic geology and recreation make it one of Oregon's most iconic parks.

☐ 🔖 ♡ **South Beach State Park:** South of Newport, this large coastal park offers miles of sandy shoreline, hiking and biking trails, and access to Yaquina Bay. A popular campground with yurts, playgrounds, and picnic areas makes it family-friendly. Visitors enjoy kite flying, wildlife watching, and sunsets over the Pacific. Its mix of beaches, forests, and amenities makes it a central coast favorite.

☐ 🔖 ♡ **Starvation Creek State Park:** Located in the Columbia River Gorge, this small but scenic park is home to Starvation Creek Falls, a dramatic cascade beside the Historic Columbia River Highway. Short trails connect to other Gorge paths, weaving through lush forests and mossy cliffs. Visitors enjoy picnicking, photography, and waterfall hikes. Its accessibility and beauty make it a favorite roadside stop.

☐ 🔖 ♡ **Succor Creek State Park:** In Oregon's remote southeastern high desert, this rugged park showcases dramatic canyons, towering rock spires, and colorful wildflowers in spring. It is a popular destination for rockhounding, particularly for Oregon's state rock, the thunderegg. Primitive camping, hiking, and photography attract adventurers seeking solitude. Its dramatic desert landscapes offer a striking contrast to Oregon's forests and coast.

☐ 🔖 ♡ **The Cove Palisades State Park:** In central Oregon near Madras, this park is defined by deep canyons carved by the Deschutes and Crooked Rivers. Lake Billy Chinook provides boating, fishing, and houseboat rentals. Trails like Tam-a-láu climb to panoramic views of cliffs and mesas. With campgrounds, a marina, and dramatic geology, it's a premier destination for water recreation and canyon exploration.

OREGON

☐ 🔖 ♡ **Tolovana Beach State Park:** Situated at the south end of Cannon Beach, this park provides access to wide sandy shores with views of iconic Haystack Rock. Families enjoy picnicking, kite flying, and exploring tidepools rich with sea life. Restrooms, parking, and easy town access make it convenient, while its natural beauty and ocean vistas make it a favorite on Oregon's north coast.

☐ 🔖 ♡ **Tou Velle State Park:** On the Rogue River near Medford, this day-use park is popular for fishing, boating, and swimming. Shady picnic areas and lawns provide space for gatherings, while trails explore riparian forests and wetlands alive with birds and wildlife. Its combination of river access, natural beauty, and family-friendly amenities make it a community favorite in southern Oregon.

☐ 🔖 ♡ **Tryon Creek State Park:** Located in Portland, this 650-acre forested park is the only Oregon state park within a major city. It offers miles of hiking, biking, and equestrian trails winding through lush second-growth forest. A nature center and educational programs engage visitors, while wooden bridges and tranquil streams create a peaceful urban oasis perfect for outdoor exploration year-round.

☐ 🔖 ♡ **Umpqua Lighthouse State Park:** Near Reedsport, this park features the historic Umpqua Lighthouse, built in 1894 and still active today. Visitors tour the lighthouse, camp nearby, or explore trails around Lake Marie and coastal dunes. Whale watching and birding are popular activities. Its mix of maritime history, coastal scenery, and recreational opportunities make it a unique and memorable stop.

☐ 🔖 ♡ **Valley of the Rogue State Park:** Along the Rogue River near Grants Pass, this park combines natural beauty with convenience off I-5. Campgrounds, picnic areas, and trails connect to the Rogue River Greenway, making it ideal for fishing, rafting, or cycling. Shady cottonwoods and scenic river views provide a peaceful backdrop, while its location makes it a perfect stop for travelers.

☐ 🔖 ♡ **Wallowa Lake State Park:** In northeast Oregon near Joseph, this park sits at the base of the Wallowa Mountains, offering stunning alpine scenery. Visitors camp or stay in yurts along the clear glacial lake, fish or boat on its waters, and hike into the Eagle Cap Wilderness. With year-round recreation and breathtaking views, it is considered one of Oregon's most beloved mountain parks.

☐ 🔖 ♡ **Willamette Mission State Park:** North of Salem, this historic park preserves the site of the 1834 Methodist Mission, Oregon's first. Today, it features wetlands, forests, and the nation's largest black cottonwood tree. Trails for hiking, biking, and horseback riding explore diverse habitats. Its blend of history, recreation, and riverside landscapes makes it a unique Willamette Valley destination.

☐ 🔖 ♡ **William M. Tugman State Park:** On the coast near Lakeside, this park sits on Eel Lake, offering swimming, kayaking, and fishing in calm waters. Forested campgrounds, yurts, and trails create opportunities for overnight stays. Birdwatchers enjoy spotting osprey and herons around the lake. Its mix of water recreation and forested setting makes it a peaceful alternative to busier coastal parks.

☐ 🔖 ♡ **Winchuck State Park:** Just north of the California border near Brookings, this park provides beach access and tidepool exploration along a quiet stretch of coast. Visitors picnic on grassy bluffs, walk along sandy shoreline, and watch for whales and seabirds offshore. Its southern location, combined with rugged beauty and solitude, makes it a tranquil introduction to Oregon's coastline.

☐ 🔖 ♡ **Wygant State Park:** In the Columbia River Gorge near Hood River, this undeveloped park preserves rugged forest and canyon terrain. A steep trail climbs from the Historic Highway into old-growth woods, leading to sweeping views of the Gorge. Remote and lightly visited, it appeals to hikers seeking solitude, challenging climbs, and dramatic scenery in one of Oregon's most iconic landscapes.

National Parks

☐ 🔖 ♡ **Crater Lake National Park:** Located in Oregon, Crater Lake is known for its stunning deep blue water, formed within a collapsed volcanic caldera. Visitors can enjoy hiking, scenic drives, and boat tours while exploring the park's geological wonders and pristine landscapes. The Rim Drive offers breathtaking views of the lake and surrounding peaks.

☐ 🔖 ♡ **Fort Vancouver National Historic Site:** Situated in Vancouver, Washington, this historic site preserves the remains of Fort Vancouver, a key center of the fur trade and the Pacific Northwest's first major American settlement. Visitors can explore the reconstructed fort, learn about the fur trade, and discover the region's cultural history.

OREGON

☐ 🔖 ♡ **John Day Fossil Beds National Monument**: Located in Oregon, this monument preserves one of the most significant fossil beds in North America. Visitors can explore colorful rock formations, view ancient fossils, and hike scenic trails to learn about prehistoric life from millions of years ago.

☐ 🔖 ♡ **Lewis and Clark National Historical Park**: Spanning Oregon and Washington, this park commemorates the Lewis and Clark Expedition's journey to the Pacific Ocean. Visitors can explore historic sites, including the Fort Clatsop, and learn about the expedition's challenges, discoveries, and its role in expanding U.S. territory.

☐ 🔖 ♡ **Nez Perce National Historical Park**: Located across Idaho, Montana, and Washington, this park commemorates the Nez Perce Tribe and their resistance to forced relocation during the late 19th century. Visitors can explore historic sites, battlefields, and learn about the cultural and historical significance of the tribe.

☐ 🔖 ♡ **Oregon Caves National Monument and Preserve**: Situated in Southern Oregon, this monument features a stunning marble cave system formed millions of years ago. Visitors can take guided cave tours, explore the surrounding forested landscapes, and enjoy hiking trails that lead through the Oregon Caves Wilderness.

State & National Forests

☐ 🔖 ♡ **Clatsop State Forest**: Located in the northern Oregon Coast Range, this 136,000-acre forest features a mixture of second-growth conifer forests, including Douglas fir, hemlock, and western red cedar. The forest provides a variety of recreational activities, including hiking, camping, wildlife viewing, and fishing in nearby streams. It is an excellent destination for outdoor enthusiasts looking to explore Oregon's coastal ecosystems.

☐ 🔖 ♡ **Deschutes National Forest**: Covering approximately 1.6 million acres in central Oregon, Deschutes National Forest features volcanic landscapes, including the Newberry National Volcanic Monument. The forest offers outdoor activities such as hiking, mountain biking, fishing, and camping, along with beautiful views of snow-capped mountains, high desert terrain, and alpine lakes.

☐ 🔖 ♡ **Elliott State Forest**: Situated in Coos County, this 82,000-acre forest is home to several threatened species, including the northern spotted owl and marbled murrelet. The forest features diverse ecosystems with dense forests, wetlands, and riparian zones. It is an important area for conservation, and visitors can enjoy hiking, birdwatching, and exploring the forest's rich biodiversity.

☐ 🔖 ♡ **Fremont-Winema National Forest**: Spanning over 2.2 million acres in southern Oregon, this forest encompasses a variety of landscapes, from high deserts to lush forests. It is home to numerous lakes, including Upper Klamath Lake, and offers recreational activities such as hiking, boating, and wildlife viewing. The forest is also known for its rich biodiversity and outdoor adventures.

☐ 🔖 ♡ **Gilchrist State Forest**: Found in Klamath County, this 70,000-acre forest is predominantly made up of lodgepole pine and ponderosa pine trees. It offers hiking trails, camping, and wildlife observation. The forest is ideal for those looking to explore the high desert environment and enjoy solitude in a tranquil setting, away from the hustle and bustle of city life.

☐ 🔖 ♡ **Malheur National Forest**: This 1.4 million-acre forest, located in eastern Oregon, is part of the Blue Mountains and features dense forests, open meadows, and wild rivers. It offers various recreational activities such as hiking, fishing, and camping. The forest is a haven for wildlife and provides opportunities for birdwatching and exploring remote wilderness areas.

☐ 🔖 ♡ **Mount Hood National Forest**: Encompassing over 1 million acres in northern Oregon, this forest is home to Mount Hood, the highest peak in the state. Visitors can enjoy skiing, hiking, and mountain biking, along with fishing, camping, and wildlife viewing. The forest is known for its diverse ecosystems, from alpine meadows to old-growth forests.

☐ 🔖 ♡ **Ochoco National Forest**: Spanning over 850,000 acres in central Oregon, this forest is known for its geological features, including rugged ridges, deep canyons, and volcanic peaks. Visitors can hike, camp, and fish in the pristine landscapes, with opportunities to explore remote areas and enjoy breathtaking vistas of Oregon's high desert region.

OREGON

☐ 🔖 ♡ **Rogue River-Siskiyou National Forest**: Covering 1.7 million acres in southern Oregon, this forest is home to the wild and scenic Rogue River. It offers a variety of recreational activities, including hiking, fishing, rafting, and camping. The forest is known for its rich biodiversity, with lush forests, alpine meadows, and rugged mountains providing habitats for wildlife.

☐ 🔖 ♡ **Santiam State Forest**: This 47,000-acre forest in Linn, Marion, and Clackamas counties is home to diverse ecosystems ranging from dense forests to open meadows. The forest offers a wide array of recreational activities, including hiking, horseback riding, and mountain biking. The park also features scenic trails and abundant wildlife, making it a great spot for outdoor exploration.

☐ 🔖 ♡ **Siuslaw National Forest**: Located along the central Oregon coast, this 630,000-acre forest is home to diverse ecosystems, including coastal dunes, tidal marshes, and dense forests. The forest provides numerous opportunities for hiking, camping, beachcombing, and birdwatching, making it a popular destination for outdoor enthusiasts seeking to explore the Oregon coast.

☐ 🔖 ♡ **Sun Pass State Forest**: Situated in Klamath County, this 21,300-acre forest offers a mix of pine and fir trees, along with mountain meadows and year-round creeks. Visitors can enjoy hiking, camping, and wildlife viewing in the rugged terrain. The forest's remote location provides a peaceful environment for those seeking to experience Oregon's high desert landscape.

☐ 🔖 ♡ **Tillamook State Forest**: Located in Washington County, this expansive 364,000-acre forest is known for its rich history, including the Tillamook Burn, a series of wildfires in the 1930s. Visitors can enjoy over 300 miles of hiking, mountain biking, and horseback riding trails. The forest is also home to abundant wildlife and offers picnicking, camping, and fishing opportunities in serene forested settings.

☐ 🔖 ♡ **Umatilla National Forest**: This 1.4 million-acre forest, located in northeastern Oregon, is part of the Blue Mountains and offers a mix of forests, grasslands, and rivers. Visitors can enjoy hiking, fishing, camping, and wildlife observation. The forest's diverse ecosystems provide ample opportunities for outdoor activities and scenic exploration.

☐ 🔖 ♡ **Umpqua National Forest**: Located in southern Oregon, this 983,000-acre forest is known for its temperate rainforests, cascading waterfalls, and wild rivers. The forest offers a range of recreational activities, including hiking, camping, and fishing. Visitors can explore the scenic beauty of the Umpqua River and its surrounding wilderness.

☐ 🔖 ♡ **Wallowa-Whitman National Forest**: This 2.3 million-acre forest in northeastern Oregon is home to the Wallowa Mountains, offering dramatic landscapes, rugged terrain, and abundant wildlife. Visitors can enjoy hiking, fishing, camping, and skiing in the winter. The forest's remote wilderness areas provide a haven for those looking to connect with nature.

☐ 🔖 ♡ **Willamette National Forest**: Spanning approximately 1.7 million acres in western Oregon, this forest is home to a mix of rugged mountains, lush valleys, and ancient forests. Visitors can hike, camp, fish, and ski, with opportunities to explore volcanic landscapes, including the Three Fingered Jack and Mount Jefferson areas.

National Grasslands

☐ 🔖 ♡ **Crooked River National Grassland**: Located in central Oregon, this grassland features sagebrush plains, basalt canyons, and rimrock cliffs carved by the Crooked River. Juniper woodlands and wildflowers add to the scenic beauty, while eagles, mule deer, and coyotes roam the landscape. Popular for hiking, camping, and rock climbing, it offers dramatic views of Oregon's high desert terrain.

OREGON

National Scenic Byways & All-American Roads

☐ ▢ ♡ **Cascade Lakes Scenic Byway:** A high-country drive past shimmering alpine lakes, lava fields, and pine forests south of Bend. Mt. Bachelor and the Deschutes peaks dominate the skyline, while trailheads, campgrounds, and pullouts invite fishing, paddling, and stargazing. The mix of volcanic scenery and outdoor recreation makes this one of Oregon's most memorable mountain routes.

☐ ▢ ♡ **Hells Canyon Scenic Byway:** Encircling the Wallowa Mountains, this route offers dramatic views into North America's deepest gorge. Travelers pass through Joseph, Wallowa Lake, and fertile valleys before reaching overlooks above the Snake River canyon. Rich wildlife, ranching heritage, and rugged peaks combine with Oregon Trail history to create a drive that feels both wild and timeless.

☐ ▢ ♡ **Historic Columbia River Highway:** Built in the early 1900s, this roadway showcases the Columbia Gorge with iconic stone bridges, viaducts, and viewpoints. Visitors hike to waterfalls like Multnomah and Latourell, walk restored trails, and admire sweeping river panoramas. As America's first scenic highway, it blends engineering, landscape architecture, and natural beauty into a national treasure.

☐ ▢ ♡ **McKenzie Pass–Santiam Pass Scenic Byway:** Winding over the central Cascades, this drive highlights stark lava fields, alpine meadows, and cedar-lined rivers. At Dee Wright Observatory, visitors gaze across jagged volcanic peaks, while waterfalls and crystal-clear lakes dot the forested slopes. The contrast of fiery geology and lush greenery creates a uniquely Oregon mountain experience.

☐ ▢ ♡ **Mt. Hood Scenic Byway:** Circling Oregon's highest peak, this route passes through orchards, historic towns, and dense forests before climbing to alpine vistas. Stops include Timberline Lodge, fruit stands in the Hood River Valley, and waterfalls along the old Oregon Trail. Year-round recreation—from skiing to hiking—makes it a showcase of Oregon's natural and cultural heritage.

☐ ▢ ♡ **Outback Scenic Byway:** Stretching through Oregon's remote high desert, this byway reveals vast sagebrush plains, rimrock cliffs, and alkali lakes. Petroglyphs, wildlife refuges, and small frontier towns punctuate the open landscape. Known for its solitude, big skies, and unspoiled beauty, the route offers a journey into Oregon's rugged interior far from the bustle of the coast and cities.

☐ ▢ ♡ **Pacific Coast Scenic Byway:** Running the full length of Oregon's Highway 101, this byway delivers headlands, sea stacks, lighthouses, and windswept dunes. Whale watching, tidepooling, and dramatic sunsets highlight the journey, while historic bridges link coastal towns with endless beaches. It is the quintessential Oregon road trip, blending natural wonder with charming seaside communities.

☐ ▢ ♡ **Rogue–Umpqua Scenic Byway:** Following two of Oregon's wildest rivers, this route connects waterfalls, volcanic cliffs, and dense forests. The Umpqua's cascades and fishing holes give way to the Rogue's famous rapids and scenic gorges. Wildlife, campgrounds, and hiking trails line the way, offering travelers both adventure and quiet moments in spectacular natural surroundings.

☐ ▢ ♡ **Volcanic Legacy Scenic Byway:** Linking Crater Lake to southern Oregon's volcanoes, this route explores calderas, pumice flats, and wetlands alive with birdlife. Visitors marvel at sapphire-blue Crater Lake, then follow the Cascade chain south through forests and lava landscapes. Geology and biodiversity define the drive, offering a vivid portrait of the forces that shaped the Pacific Northwest.

☐ ▢ ♡ **West Cascades Scenic Byway:** Tucked along the western slope of the Cascades, this byway winds through old-growth forests, river canyons, and reservoirs. Frequent waterfalls and trailheads invite exploration, while wildlife and autumn foliage enhance the journey. With a quieter, more intimate feel than major highways, it offers travelers a deep immersion into Oregon's green heart.

State Scenic Byways

☐ ▢ ♡ **Blue Mountain Scenic Byway:** Traversing the rugged Blue Mountains of northeastern Oregon, this route passes through forests, rangeland, and historic ranching towns. Scenic pullouts overlook deep valleys, while elk and deer roam the ridges. With access to campgrounds, hiking trails, and remote vistas, it's a journey into one of Oregon's most unspoiled high-country landscapes.

☐ ▢ ♡ **Cow Creek Back Country Byway:** Following a winding stream through the Klamath Mountains, this route connects the Umpqua Valley to remote forest lands. Steep canyons, historic bridges, and traces of old gold mining camps give it character, while wildlife and quiet picnic sites offer peaceful stops. Its mix of rugged scenery and history creates a memorable southern Oregon backroad.

UNITED STATES EDITION

OREGON

☐ 🔖 ♡ **East Steens Tour Route:** A loop around the eastern side of Steens Mountain, this byway reveals glacial gorges, vast sagebrush basins, and views that stretch for miles. Wild horses roam the uplands, while aspen groves glow in fall. Remote hot springs, small ranching towns, and desert solitude combine to make it a true high-desert adventure.

☐ 🔖 ♡ **Elkhorn Scenic Byway:** Beginning near Baker City, this route circles the Elkhorn Mountains past ghost towns, alpine lakes, and rich mining history. Visitors explore Sumpter's gold dredge, camp in pine forests, and hike to mountain overlooks. The blend of cultural heritage and rugged alpine scenery makes it a classic northeastern Oregon drive.

☐ 🔖 ♡ **Grande Ronde–Blue Mountains Scenic Byway:** Linking La Grande and Elgin, this drive follows the Grande Ronde River through lush valleys before climbing forested ridges. Sweeping vistas, wildlife, and rich tribal and pioneer history line the route. Its combination of fertile farmland and rugged mountain scenery highlights Oregon's eastern contrasts.

☐ 🔖 ♡ **High Desert Discovery Scenic Byway:** Crossing the Hart Mountain region and Warner Valley, this drive immerses travelers in Oregon's most remote landscapes. Seasonal wetlands host migratory birds, while rimrock plateaus and vast sagebrush plains stretch to the horizon. Quiet, expansive, and untamed, it's a byway for those seeking solitude and raw natural beauty.

☐ 🔖 ♡ **Journey Through Time Scenic Byway:** Spanning central Oregon, this byway links fossil beds, ghost towns, and pioneer trails. Travelers explore the John Day Fossil Beds, ochre-colored canyons, and preserved frontier communities. Museums, scenic pullouts, and desert vistas reveal layers of history carved into the landscape, making it both educational and visually striking.

☐ 🔖 ♡ **Marys Peak to Pacific Scenic Byway:** Rising from the Willamette Valley, this route climbs to Marys Peak—the Coast Range's highest point—before winding to the Pacific Ocean. Sweeping views, meadows of wildflowers, and towering forests highlight the summit, while the descent reveals coastal rivers and beaches. It's a compact journey linking valley farmland with ocean horizons.

☐ 🔖 ♡ **McKenzie Pass Scenic Byway:** Climbing into volcanic highlands, this seasonal route showcases lava fields, alpine meadows, and sharp Cascade peaks. The Dee Wright Observatory offers unmatched mountain panoramas, while winding roads reveal ancient forests and sparkling streams. Open only in summer, it's one of Oregon's most dramatic mountain drives.

☐ 🔖 ♡ **North Umpqua Scenic Byway:** Following the wild North Umpqua River, this drive connects Roseburg to Diamond Lake. Waterfalls, hot springs, and legendary fly-fishing runs make it a recreation paradise. Dense forests and canyon walls line the river, while hiking trails climb to overlooks. Its mix of adventure and tranquility defines the southern Cascades.

☐ 🔖 ♡ **Silver Falls Tour Route:** Centered around Silver Falls State Park, this route leads visitors through forested foothills, fertile farmland, and the famous "Trail of Ten Falls." Scenic backroads connect small communities with Oregon's largest state park. The drive combines agricultural landscapes with world-class natural beauty, offering a perfect day trip from the Willamette Valley.

☐ 🔖 ♡ **Trees to Sea Scenic Byway:** Linking Portland's Tualatin Valley to the Pacific, this route climbs through the Coast Range, passing vineyards, farms, and forests before descending to Tillamook Bay. Scenic overlooks, trailheads, and small towns dot the way. It highlights the natural and cultural journey from fertile valley floors to rugged ocean shores.

☐ 🔖 ♡ **Umpqua Scenic Byway:** Beginning near Reedsport, this drive follows the Umpqua River inland through valleys and forests. Salmon runs, historic sites, and charming small towns line the way. The byway showcases the river's role as both a cultural lifeline and a scenic gem, connecting Oregon's coast to its mountainous interior.

☐ 🔖 ♡ **West Cascades Scenic Byway:** Running along the western slope of the Cascades, this route passes waterfalls, reservoirs, and ancient forests. Visitors explore river canyons, hike to mountain lakes, and enjoy vivid autumn foliage. Its quiet beauty and abundance of natural stops make it one of Oregon's most immersive mountain drives.

OREGON

State Scenic Corridors

☐ 🔖 ♡ **Blue Mountain Forest State Scenic Corridor:** Located in Umatilla County along Highway 244, this corridor showcases the beauty of Oregon's Blue Mountains. Dense forests of pine and fir line the roadway, offering a shady, scenic drive through high country. Wildlife is abundant, and picnic areas provide restful stops. Its rugged terrain and sweeping views make it a peaceful, forested gateway to eastern Oregon.

☐ 🔖 ♡ **Booth State Scenic Corridor:** Near Lakeview in south-central Oregon, this corridor preserves a forested landscape donated in honor of Robert Booth, a pioneer lumberman and legislator. Towering pines and open meadows create a classic high-desert forest experience. Travelers find shaded picnic spots and opportunities for wildlife viewing. Its mix of history, natural beauty, and serenity makes it a meaningful stop.

☐ 🔖 ♡ **H. B. Van Duzer Forest State Scenic Corridor:** Stretching for 12 miles along Highway 18 in the Coast Range, this corridor immerses travelers in old-growth Douglas-fir forests. The shaded roadway offers a tranquil, cathedral-like drive through one of Oregon's lush temperate rainforests. Scenic pullouts invite birdwatching and photography. It's a dramatic and memorable approach to the Oregon coast.

☐ 🔖 ♡ **John B. Yeon State Scenic Corridor:** At the western end of the Columbia River Gorge Scenic Highway, this corridor offers access to waterfalls like Elowah Falls and McCord Creek Falls. Trails climb through moss-draped forests and basalt cliffs with sweeping Gorge views. Named after a Portland philanthropist who helped fund the historic highway, it combines cultural legacy with unmatched natural beauty.

☐ 🔖 ♡ **Redmond–Bend Juniper State Scenic Corridor:** Along Highway 97 between Redmond and Bend, this corridor highlights Oregon's high desert with groves of ancient western junipers, sagebrush, and volcanic buttes. Pullouts allow visitors to explore the arid landscape and appreciate its stark beauty. A haven for birdlife and unique vegetation, it preserves the region's desert heritage amid growing urban development.

☐ 🔖 ♡ **Samuel H. Boardman State Scenic Corridor:** Stretching 12 miles along Highway 101 near Brookings, this corridor features dramatic coastal cliffs, sea stacks, and pocket beaches. Scenic viewpoints like Arch Rock and Natural Bridges provide world-class ocean panoramas. Trails lead through Sitka spruce forests to secluded coves. Its wild, rugged coastline makes it one of the crown jewels of Oregon's state park system.

National Natural Landmarks

 ☐ 🔖 ♡ **Crown Point:** Recognized as a National Natural Landmark, this basalt promontory towers 733 feet above the Columbia River, offering sweeping Gorge views. Columnar basalt cliffs reveal volcanic history, while the Vista House—an early 20th-century masterpiece—adds cultural depth, blending geologic and architectural heritage in one iconic site.
GPS: 45.5395, -122.24422

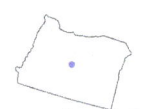 ☐ 🔖 ♡ **Horse Ridge Natural Area:** This Bureau of Land Management site is a National Natural Landmark for preserving high desert ecosystems shaped by volcanic origins. Western juniper woodlands and rugged lava formations dominate the ridge, with bunchgrasses and sagebrush completing the mosaic of central Oregon's arid landscapes.
GPS: 43.924, -121.039

 ☐ 🔖 ♡ **Fort Rock State Monument:** Designated a National Natural Landmark for its dramatic volcanic tuff ring, Fort Rock was formed by explosive magma-water eruptions during the Pleistocene. Rising from an ancient lakebed, it sheltered prehistoric peoples whose artifacts were found nearby, linking geology and archaeology in a singular Oregon landmark.
GPS: 43.372, -121.074

 ☐ 🔖 ♡ **John Day Fossil Beds:** Named a National Natural Landmark for its unparalleled fossil record, this site preserves over 40 million years of Cenozoic plants and mammals in colorful volcanic layers. It remains a world-class destination for paleontology, public education, and understanding the ecological and geologic history of Oregon.
GPS: 44.555833, -119.645278

OREGON

 ☐ 🔖 ♡ **Lawrence Memorial Grassland Preserve:** Honored as a National Natural Landmark for its rare "biscuit and scabland" topography, this preserve highlights Oregon's native prairie ecosystems. Bunchgrasses and wildflowers grow among rocky mounds, offering a living window into interior grasslands that once spread widely across the region.
GPS: 44.950889, -120.7988834

 ☐ 🔖 ♡ **Mount Howard–East Peak:** National Natural Landmark status recognizes this alpine summit for its unique plant life. Overlooking Wallowa Lake, it harbors rare and endemic species adapted to high elevation. Shaped by glaciers and isolation, its fragile grasslands exemplify botanical diversity in Oregon's mountains.
GPS: 45.260987, -117.178778

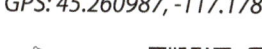
 ☐ 🔖 ♡ **Newberry Crater:** This immense shield volcano is a National Natural Landmark for its 17-square-mile caldera containing lakes, lava flows, and the Big Obsidian Flow. The crater showcases one of the most geologically diverse volcanic systems in the U.S., highlighting rhyolitic eruptions in the Cascade Range.
GPS: 43.689194, -121.254889

 ☐ 🔖 ♡ **Round Top Butte:** This volcanic prominence in southwest Oregon was designated a National Natural Landmark for its intact bunchgrass prairie. Native wildflowers, sagebrush, and sweeping Cascade–Siskiyou views define the site, preserving one of the finest remaining examples of prairie ecosystems in the region.
GPS: 42.5277551, -122.68381

 ☐ 🔖 ♡ **The Island:** This isolated plateau where the Crooked and Deschutes Rivers meet is protected as a National Natural Landmark. Its undisturbed cliffs and juniper-bunchgrass savanna remain untouched by grazing, preserving Oregon's pre-settlement ecology in a rugged, inaccessible natural stronghold.
GPS: 44.558489, -121.277143

 ☐ 🔖 ♡ **Willamette Floodplain:** Within William L. Finley National Wildlife Refuge, this area gained National Natural Landmark recognition for its rare interior valley grassland and wet prairie habitats. It shelters species like Bradshaw's lomatium, supports migrating waterfowl, and represents a once-common ecosystem now largely vanished from the Willamette Valley.
GPS: 44.364, -123.23

 ☐ 🔖 ♡ **Zumwalt Prairie:** Recognized as a National Natural Landmark for being the largest intact bunchgrass prairie in North America, Zumwalt spans over 330,000 acres. Rich biodiversity thrives here, from golden eagles and elk to rare plants, making it a vital stronghold of prairie conservation and ecological heritage.
GPS: 45.54, -117.09

PENNSYLVANIA

Pennsylvania's landscapes reveal forested mountains, rolling farmland, winding rivers, and dramatic waterfalls. With state parks, national forests, national park units, and historic natural landmarks, the Keystone State invites outdoor discovery across all seasons, from misty woodland trails to vibrant autumn vistas and quiet winter retreats.

🗓 Peak Season
May–October is Pennsylvania's peak season, offering warm weather, lush forests, and brilliant fall foliage. Summer is busiest in state parks and lake regions, while autumn attracts travelers for scenic drives and harvest festivals.

🗓 Offseason Months
November–April is the offseason, bringing cold winters and snow in the mountains. Winter offers skiing and quiet trails, while early spring remains cool and less crowded.

🍃 Scenery & Nature Timing
Spring brings blooming forests and rushing waterfalls. Summer highlights lakes, rivers, and green mountain trails. Fall showcases vivid foliage across the Appalachians, while winter provides snowy woods and frozen streams.

✨ Special
Pennsylvania features the forested ridges of the Allegheny Mountains, the gorges and waterfalls of Ricketts Glen, and the karst caves of central Pennsylvania. Autumn color displays, misty valleys, and abundant wildlife define its natural charm.

UNITED STATES EDITION

PENNSYLVANIA

State Parks

☐ 🔖 ♡ **Allegheny Islands State Park:** Located in the Allegheny River near Pittsburgh, this undeveloped park contains several wooded islands accessible only by boat. With no facilities, it offers opportunities for fishing, birdwatching, and exploring quiet natural habitats. Its isolation and pristine environment make it one of Pennsylvania's least-visited and most secluded state parks.

☐ 🔖 ♡ **Archbald Pothole State Park:** In Lackawanna County, this small park is home to a massive glacial pothole over 38 feet deep, formed during the last Ice Age. Short trails and viewing platforms allow visitors to observe this rare geological wonder. It's a unique spot for geology enthusiasts and a quick educational stop for families exploring northeastern Pennsylvania.

☐ 🔖 ♡ **Bald Eagle State Park:** Found in Centre County, this 5,900-acre park is centered on the 1,730-acre Foster Joseph Sayers Reservoir. It offers boating, fishing, and swimming, plus campgrounds and miles of trails with scenic views of Bald Eagle Mountain. Year-round activities make it a favorite for wildlife watchers, anglers, and outdoor adventurers alike.

☐ 🔖 ♡ **Beltzville State Park:** Situated in the southern Poconos, Beltzville boasts a 949-acre lake with a sandy beach, boating, and excellent fishing. Trails wind through woodlands and wetlands, supporting birdlife and seasonal wildflowers. Its accessible facilities, family-friendly atmosphere, and balance of water recreation and hiking make it a popular year-round destination.

☐ 🔖 ♡ **Bendigo State Park:** Nestled in Elk County, Bendigo is a 100-acre day-use park featuring shaded picnic groves, a playground, and open fields. While small, it offers a relaxing and family-friendly setting surrounded by forested hills. The park is known for its peaceful charm, providing an easy escape for visitors seeking a quiet outdoor experience.

☐ 🔖 ♡ **Benjamin Rush State Park:** The only state park within Philadelphia's city limits, this 275-acre green space features community gardens, open meadows, and walking and biking trails. Though still largely undeveloped, it provides an important natural refuge for urban residents. Wildlife observation, hiking, and birdwatching are popular in this urban oasis.

☐ 🔖 ♡ **Big Elk Creek State Park:** One of Pennsylvania's newest parks, this 1,700-acre area in Chester County protects riparian forests, meadows, and farmland along Big Elk Creek. It offers hiking, horseback riding, and wildlife viewing. The park preserves scenic natural corridors in the rapidly developing southeastern corner of the state, ensuring habitat and recreation access.

☐ 🔖 ♡ **Big Pocono State Park:** Spanning 1,300 acres atop Camelback Mountain, this park offers sweeping views of northeastern Pennsylvania and parts of New Jersey and New York. Hiking trails loop through rugged terrain with scenic overlooks, particularly stunning during fall foliage. Picnic areas and wildlife watching make it a rewarding stop for outdoor enthusiasts.

☐ 🔖 ♡ **Big Spring State Park:** A modest day-use site in Fulton County, Big Spring is known for its picnic areas shaded by hemlocks and the ruins of an old iron furnace. Located in a wooded mountain setting, it offers hiking, fishing, and quiet relaxation. Its intimate scale and historic features make it a charming, low-key escape into nature.

☐ 🔖 ♡ **Black Moshannon State Park:** This 3,480-acre park in Centre County is distinguished by its bog ecosystems and the 250-acre Black Moshannon Lake. Its unique wetlands support rare plants and wildlife, making it a biodiversity hotspot. Visitors enjoy hiking, boating, camping, and winter sports, while the tranquil setting appeals to birders and naturalists.

☐ 🔖 ♡ **Blue Knob State Park:** Located on Pennsylvania's second-highest peak, this 6,100-acre park features rugged terrain, forests, and panoramic vistas. Activities include hiking, camping, skiing, and picnicking. Blue Knob's high elevation provides cooler temperatures in summer and excellent snow in winter, making it a year-round destination for outdoor recreation and scenic beauty.

☐ 🔖 ♡ **Buchanan's Birthplace State Park:** This 18.5-acre park in Franklin County preserves the birthplace of James Buchanan, the 15th U.S. President. A large granite pyramid marks the site, surrounded by wooded picnic areas and trails. Visitors can learn about presidential history while enjoying the tranquility of the park's natural setting along Tuscarora Creek.

PENNSYLVANIA

☐ 🔖 ♡ **Bucktail State Park Natural Area**: Stretching 75 miles along Route 120 from Renovo to Emporium, this vast linear park protects rugged forests and the scenic West Branch Susquehanna River Valley. Known for its remote wild character, it provides opportunities for hiking, scenic driving, wildlife viewing, and hunting, while preserving one of Pennsylvania's most unspoiled landscapes.

☐ 🔖 ♡ **Caledonia State Park**: Located in Franklin and Adams Counties along the Appalachian Mountains, this 1,125-acre park offers hiking, camping, fishing, and swimming. Rich in history, it preserves the site of Thaddeus Stevens's ironworks. Its proximity to Gettysburg and connection to the Appalachian Trail make it a favorite destination blending history and recreation.

☐ 🔖 ♡ **Canoe Creek State Park**: A 961-acre park near Hollidaysburg, Canoe Creek includes a 155-acre lake, wetlands, and forests. It is a popular spot for boating, fishing, swimming, and birdwatching, with over 220 bird species recorded. Historic limestone kilns add cultural interest, while trails and picnic areas make it a versatile destination for families and nature lovers.

☐ 🔖 ♡ **Chapman State Park**: Situated in Warren County, this 862-acre park surrounds the 68-acre Chapman Lake, offering swimming, boating, and fishing. Trails connect to Allegheny National Forest, extending hiking opportunities into vast woodlands. The park provides camping, picnicking, and winter activities, making it an inviting, year-round retreat in northwestern Pennsylvania.

☐ 🔖 ♡ **Cherry Springs State Park**: Internationally renowned for stargazing, Cherry Springs in Potter County is a certified International Dark Sky Park. Its remote location and low light pollution provide unmatched night sky views, including the Milky Way. The park also offers camping, hiking, and wildlife observation, combining astronomy with tranquil forest surroundings.

☐ 🔖 ♡ **Clear Creek State Park**: Covering 1,900 acres in Jefferson County, Clear Creek lies within the larger Cook Forest region. It offers camping, hiking, fishing, and canoeing along the Clarion River. Its hemlock-shaded trails and peaceful environment attract wildlife watchers and families alike, while winter brings opportunities for skiing and snowshoeing.

☐ 🔖 ♡ **Codorus State Park**: Located in York County, this 3,500-acre park centers on Lake Marburg, a 1,275-acre reservoir with 26 miles of shoreline. It's popular for boating, fishing, and birdwatching, with bald eagles often seen. Campgrounds, hiking trails, disc golf, and winter ice sports make it a versatile destination for recreation year-round.

☐ 🔖 ♡ **Colonel Denning State Park**: Nestled in Perry County, this 273-acre park offers a quiet escape with hiking, camping, and picnicking. A highlight is the Doubling Gap Trail, which climbs to a scenic overlook of the valley. Centered around a mountain-fed lake, it's known for fishing and cooling off in summer, while its forested ridges provide fall beauty.

☐ 🔖 ♡ **Colton Point State Park**: Perched on the western rim of the Pine Creek Gorge, Colton Point offers stunning vistas of the "Grand Canyon of Pennsylvania." Its rugged landscape features picnic areas, rustic overlooks, and hiking trails along the gorge rim. With waterfalls, wildlife, and dramatic scenery, it's a haven for nature lovers and photographers.

☐ 🔖 ♡ **Cook Forest State Park**: This 8,500-acre park in Clarion County is famed for its old-growth Forest Cathedral, a National Natural Landmark with towering white pines and hemlocks. The Clarion River flows along its edge, providing canoeing, fishing, and tubing. Trails, interpretive programs, and historic CCC-era cabins make it a classic Pennsylvania wilderness destination.

☐ 🔖 ♡ **Cowans Gap State Park**: In Fulton County, this 1,085-acre park offers a 42-acre lake surrounded by mountain ridges. Visitors enjoy swimming, boating, and fishing in summer, plus hiking on trails including a section of the Tuscarora Trail. Winter brings cross-country skiing and ice skating. The park's cabins, campground, and scenery make it a family favorite.

☐ 🔖 ♡ **Delaware Canal State Park**: Stretching 60 miles along the historic Delaware Canal, this linear park preserves lock houses, towpaths, and canal structures. Perfect for hiking, biking, and history exploration, it follows the Delaware River from Easton to Bristol. Fishing, birding, and riverside picnicking add to its appeal, making it rich in history and scenery.

PENNSYLVANIA

☐ ▢ ♡ **Denton Hill State Park:** A 700-acre park in Potter County along scenic Route 6, Denton Hill provides access to hiking, mountain biking, picnicking, and the surrounding Susquehannock State Forest. Though once home to a downhill ski area, it now serves primarily as a rustic base for four-season recreation in the Pennsylvania Wilds, offering trails, forested ridges, and quiet natural escapes.

☐ ▢ ♡ **Elk State Park:** This 3,200-acre park in Cameron and Elk Counties surrounds the George B. Stevenson Reservoir, popular for fishing, boating, and kayaking. Forested hills provide habitat for elk, deer, and bear, offering wildlife viewing opportunities. The park also supports hunting, camping, and hiking, serving as a gateway to the Pennsylvania Wilds.

☐ ▢ ♡ **Erie Bluffs State Park:** Situated along Lake Erie's shoreline, this 587-acre park features high bluffs with sweeping views of the lake. It preserves rare Great Lakes ecosystems, including wetlands, meadows, and old-growth forests. Popular for hiking, birdwatching, and fishing, it provides a quieter alternative to nearby Presque Isle while showcasing natural beauty.

☐ ▢ ♡ **Evansburg State Park:** Spanning 3,300 acres in Montgomery County, Evansburg protects farmland, forests, and Skippack Creek. Trails support hiking, biking, and horseback riding, while anglers enjoy trout fishing. Its mix of cultural landscapes and natural areas provides a glimpse into southeastern Pennsylvania's heritage, offering both quiet recreation and open green space.

☐ ▢ ♡ **Fort Washington State Park:** Just outside Philadelphia, this 493-acre park preserves land used by George Washington's troops in the Revolutionary War. Visitors can explore historic sites, hike wooded trails, and picnic along Wissahickon Creek. The park is also a hotspot for birding, particularly during hawk migration in autumn, combining history and nature.

☐ ▢ ♡ **Fowlers Hollow State Park:** A hidden gem in Perry County, this 104-acre park offers shaded picnic areas, a playground, and access to trout streams. Surrounded by Tuscarora State Forest, it provides a base for hiking, horseback riding, and hunting in the larger region. Its quiet, rustic charm makes it ideal for families seeking peaceful recreation.

☐ ▢ ♡ **Frances Slocum State Park:** Located in Luzerne County, this 1,035-acre park is centered on a 165-acre lake popular for boating, fishing, and swimming. Trails explore forests, wetlands, and meadows that support diverse wildlife. Camping, picnicking, and environmental education programs make it a family-friendly destination in the scenic Wyoming Valley.

☐ ▢ ♡ **French Creek State Park:** Covering 7,730 acres in Berks and Chester Counties, this park is the largest in southeastern Pennsylvania. It features Hopewell and Scotts Run Lakes for boating and fishing, plus miles of hiking and biking trails. Rich forests provide wildlife habitat, while remnants of the iron industry highlight the area's historic past.

☐ ▢ ♡ **Gifford Pinchot State Park:** Located in York County, this 2,338-acre park is centered on Pinchot Lake, a 340-acre reservoir popular for boating, fishing, and swimming. The park offers hiking, camping, and year-round environmental education programs. Named after Pennsylvania's first forester, it combines outdoor recreation with conservation history.

☐ ▢ ♡ **Gouldsboro State Park:** Situated in Monroe and Wayne Counties, this 2,800-acre park includes Gouldsboro Lake, ideal for boating, fishing, and kayaking. Surrounding trails wind through woodlands and wetlands, providing birdwatching and wildlife viewing opportunities. Its calm and natural setting in the Poconos makes it a favored spot for relaxation and outdoor activities.

☐ ▢ ♡ **Greenwood Furnace State Park:** Set in Huntingdon County, this 423-acre park highlights the history of Pennsylvania's iron industry with a preserved furnace stack. Visitors can enjoy swimming and fishing in its small lake, hike trails through nearby ridges, or explore interpretive exhibits. Its blend of history, camping, and scenic landscapes makes it memorable.

☐ ▢ ♡ **Hickory Run State Park:** A 15,990-acre park in the Pocono Mountains, Hickory Run is famous for Boulder Field, a National Natural Landmark. It features over 40 miles of trails, trout streams, and waterfalls, making it a hiker's paradise. Camping, swimming, and winter skiing add to its year-round appeal as a diverse and scenic destination.

PENNSYLVANIA

☐ ▢ ♡ **Hillman State Park**: A 3,600-acre undeveloped park in Washington County, Hillman is managed as a multi-use recreation area. It offers extensive trails for hiking, biking, horseback riding, and hunting. Known for its open fields, forests, and birdwatching opportunities, it provides a rustic, natural retreat not far from the Pittsburgh metropolitan area.

☐ ▢ ♡ **Hills Creek State Park**: Located in Tioga County, this 407-acre park is centered on a 137-acre lake ideal for boating, fishing, and swimming. Trails lead through forests rich in wildlife, offering birdwatching and peaceful hikes. Winter activities include cross-country skiing and ice fishing, making Hills Creek a four-season park in the northern tier.

☐ ▢ ♡ **Hyner Run State Park**: A 180-acre park in Clinton County, Hyner Run offers a family-friendly campground, swimming pool, and picnic areas along its namesake trout stream. Nestled in a valley, it provides access to hiking trails and connects to nearby Hyner View. Its tranquil setting and recreation options make it a popular base in the Wilds.

☐ ▢ ♡ **Hyner View State Park**: Perched high above the West Branch Susquehanna River, this small scenic overlook provides one of the most breathtaking views in Pennsylvania. It is famous as a launch site for hang gliders and a picnic destination for travelers. Though small, it offers unforgettable panoramas of forested ridges and valleys below.

☐ ▢ ♡ **Jacobsburg Environmental Education Center**: Spanning 1,168 acres in Northampton County, Jacobsburg is devoted to outdoor education and conservation. Trails explore forests, streams, and historic sites tied to early American gun-making. Hiking, horseback riding, and birdwatching are popular here, while the center's programs make it a hub for learning about the natural world.

☐ ▢ ♡ **Jennings Environmental Education Center**: Situated in Butler County, Jennings is unique for preserving a prairie ecosystem rare in Pennsylvania. The center offers extensive educational programming, interpretive trails, and exhibits on ecology. Visitors can explore woodlands, wetlands, and wildflower meadows, making it a hub for environmental study and outdoor recreation.

☐ ▢ ♡ **Joseph E. Ibberson Conservation Area**: This 783-acre forest in Dauphin County is dedicated to conservation and education. With limited development, it offers quiet hiking trails, birdwatching, and scenic woodland vistas. Donated by a conservationist to remain undeveloped, the park emphasizes environmental stewardship and provides a peaceful place for reflection in nature.

☐ ▢ ♡ **Keystone State Park**: Found in Westmoreland County, Keystone includes a 78-acre lake with a sandy beach, popular for swimming, boating, and fishing. The park also offers camping, trails, and winter activities. With picnic areas and accessible facilities, it's a family-oriented destination that combines water recreation with wooded landscapes year-round.

☐ ▢ ♡ **Kings Gap Environmental Education Center**: Covering 2,531 acres in Cumberland County, Kings Gap is notable for its historic mansion on a hilltop, extensive gardens, and panoramic valley views. It features over 20 miles of trails and offers programs focused on ecology and history. Its unique blend of culture and scenery makes it a standout park.

☐ ▢ ♡ **Kinzua Bridge State Park**: Located in McKean County, this park preserves the remains of the Kinzua Viaduct, once the world's longest and tallest railroad bridge. Partially destroyed by a tornado, it is now a pedestrian skywalk with glass viewing panels. The park also offers hiking, a visitor center, and spectacular views of the surrounding forested valley.

☐ ▢ ♡ **Kooser State Park**: A 250-acre park in Somerset County, Kooser features a tranquil trout stream and Kooser Lake, popular for fishing and picnicking. Its campground and cozy cabins make it a family-friendly spot for year-round getaways. Trails through hemlock forests provide access to the surrounding Laurel Highlands, offering beauty in all seasons.

☐ ▢ ♡ **Lackawanna State Park**: Located in Lackawanna County, this 1,445-acre park centers on a 198-acre lake. It's a regional favorite for swimming, boating, and fishing. Over 18 miles of trails connect forests, fields, and wetlands, providing year-round opportunities for hiking, biking, and cross-country skiing in a peaceful, scenic Pocono setting.

PENNSYLVANIA

☐ 🔖 ♡ **Laurel Hill State Park**: Nestled in the Laurel Highlands, this 4,000-acre park features Laurel Hill Lake, a popular spot for boating and swimming. Miles of trails wind through hardwood forests, connecting to the Laurel Highlands Hiking Trail. With campgrounds, cabins, and winter activities, it's a four-season destination in a beautiful mountain setting.

☐ 🔖 ♡ **Laurel Mountain State Park**: Once a historic ski area, Laurel Mountain in Westmoreland and Somerset Counties offers downhill skiing in winter and access to nearby Laurel Highlands hiking trails in summer. Though small in acreage, it's significant as part of the region's outdoor recreation heritage, blending mountain vistas with seasonal adventure.

☐ 🔖 ♡ **Laurel Ridge State Park**: Stretching over 13,000 acres across four counties, Laurel Ridge is best known as the route of the 70-mile Laurel Highlands Hiking Trail. Forested ridges and scenic overlooks provide stunning views of valleys below. The park offers year-round hiking, cross-country skiing, and connections to other Laurel Highlands destinations.

☐ 🔖 ♡ **Laurel Summit State Park**: This small, 6-acre park in Somerset County sits high on Laurel Ridge and serves as a picnic area and trailhead. It connects to Forbes State Forest and nearby attractions like Wolf Rocks. Its elevation provides cooler summer temperatures and scenic vistas, making it a pleasant rest stop in the mountains.

☐ 🔖 ♡ **Lehigh Gorge State Park**: Stretching along the Lehigh River, this park is famous for its dramatic gorge, whitewater rafting, and remnants of historic canals and railroads. Trails, including the Delaware & Lehigh Trail, follow the river through waterfalls, cliffs, and dense forest. It's a magnet for hikers, bikers, and water sports enthusiasts.

☐ 🔖 ♡ **Leonard Harrison State Park**: On the eastern rim of Pine Creek Gorge, Leonard Harrison offers sweeping canyon views and access to the popular Turkey Path Trail, which descends to the gorge floor. The park provides camping, picnicking, and educational programs. Its dramatic overlooks make it one of the most visited and photographed parks in the state.

☐ 🔖 ♡ **Linn Run State Park**: A 612-acre park in the Laurel Highlands, Linn Run is known for its mountain streams, waterfalls, and rustic cabins. Hiking trails wind through forested ridges, while fishing and picnicking are popular along Linn Run. Its quiet, wooded setting provides a tranquil getaway and serves as a base for exploring nearby parks.

☐ 🔖 ♡ **Little Buffalo State Park**: Located in Perry County, this 923-acre park is known for Holman Lake, popular for boating and fishing, and its large swimming pool. Historic features include a covered bridge and an old iron furnace. Trails wind through forests and fields, making it a family-friendly destination that blends history, nature, and recreation.

☐ 🔖 ♡ **Little Pine State Park**: Found in Lycoming County, this 2,158-acre park surrounds Little Pine Lake and is a haven for anglers, boaters, and campers. Trails pass through Tiadaghton State Forest, offering hiking and wildlife viewing in a scenic valley. Its remote setting, peaceful waters, and family-oriented facilities make it a year-round favorite.

☐ 🔖 ♡ **Locust Lake State Park**: Located in Schuylkill County, this 1,089-acre park includes a 52-acre lake with sandy beaches, ideal for swimming, boating, and fishing. Trails connect forests and ridges, and camping facilities make it popular for family outings. Its relaxed atmosphere and accessible amenities attract visitors from across eastern Pennsylvania.

☐ 🔖 ♡ **Lyman Run State Park**: Situated in Potter County, this 595-acre park centers on a 45-acre lake stocked with trout. Surrounded by forests and mountains, it provides hiking, camping, boating, and picnicking opportunities. Wildlife is abundant, and the park's remote setting makes it a peaceful place for outdoor exploration and nature immersion.

☐ 🔖 ♡ **McConnells Mill State Park**: In Lawrence County, this 2,546-acre park preserves the rugged Slippery Rock Creek Gorge. Its highlights include a historic gristmill, covered bridge, waterfalls, and trails through steep, rocky terrain. Popular for hiking, rock climbing, and whitewater kayaking, it offers both natural beauty and cultural history in one destination.

☐ 🔖 ♡ **Memorial Lake State Park**: Near Fort Indiantown Gap in Lebanon County, this 230-acre park is centered on an 85-acre lake. It's popular for fishing, boating, and picnicking, with mountain views providing a scenic backdrop. Trails loop around the lake, and the park commemorates military service, blending recreation with a spirit of remembrance.

☐ 🔖 ♡ **Milton State Park**: Unique among Pennsylvania parks, Milton occupies a large island in the Susquehanna River. It offers picnic areas, fishing, and nature trails through floodplain habitats. The park provides a peaceful setting for birdwatching and quiet recreation, serving as a green oasis in central Pennsylvania's river landscape.

PENNSYLVANIA

☐ 🔖 ♡ **Mont Alto State Park**: One of Pennsylvania's oldest state parks, Mont Alto in Franklin County preserves a historic iron furnace and features shaded picnic areas. At just 24 acres, it is small but significant, offering forest access and educational displays. Its legacy as part of the state's conservation history makes it a charming stop.

☐ 🔖 ♡ **Moraine State Park**: Spanning 16,725 acres in Butler County, Moraine is one of Pennsylvania's largest parks and is centered on the 3,225-acre Lake Arthur. Popular for sailing, fishing, swimming, and camping, it also offers hiking, biking, and horseback riding. Its size and variety make it a major recreation hub in western Pennsylvania.

☐ 🔖 ♡ **Mount Pisgah State Park**: In Bradford County, this 1,300-acre park offers panoramic views of the Endless Mountains and Stephen Foster Lake. Fishing, boating, and picnicking are popular, while trails lead to scenic overlooks. Wildlife is abundant, and the park's tranquil hills and valleys provide a quiet retreat in Pennsylvania's northern tier.

☐ 🔖 ♡ **Nescopeck State Park**: Covering 3,550 acres in Luzerne County, this park protects wetlands, forests, and meadows. With over 19 miles of trails, it is ideal for hiking, birdwatching, and environmental education. Nescopeck Creek supports trout fishing, and the park's variety of habitats makes it a hotspot for biodiversity and nature exploration.

☐ 🔖 ♡ **Neshaminy State Park**: Located along the Delaware River in Bucks County, this 339-acre park offers a boat launch, picnic areas, and swimming pools. Trails wind through woodlands and riverfront landscapes. Its proximity to Philadelphia makes it a convenient getaway, while birdwatching and fishing opportunities highlight the park's riverside charm.

☐ 🔖 ♡ **Nockamixon State Park**: Found in Bucks County, this 5,286-acre park features Nockamixon Lake, a 1,450-acre reservoir popular for sailing, boating, and fishing. A marina, cabins, and trails add to its amenities. The park's large size, rolling hills, and water recreation make it a prime destination for both relaxation and adventure.

☐ 🔖 ♡ **Nolde Forest Environmental Education Center**: Near Reading, this 665-acre forest features a historic stone mansion and a network of wooded trails. It specializes in environmental education, offering programs for schools and the public. Its blend of old-growth and reforested areas provides habitat for diverse species, while also serving as a scenic, peaceful retreat.

☐ 🔖 ♡ **Norristown Farm Park**: This 690-acre park preserves historic farmland in Montgomery County, offering a unique mix of meadows, streams, and woodlands. Trails support walking, biking, and birdwatching, while educational programs highlight the area's agricultural heritage. Its open landscapes provide green space in a suburban setting, connecting people to rural traditions.

☐ 🔖 ♡ **Ohiopyle State Park**: Covering more than 20,000 acres in the Laurel Highlands, Ohiopyle is renowned for its waterfalls, rugged landscapes, and whitewater rafting on the Youghiogheny River. Highlights include Cucumber Falls and the Great Allegheny Passage trail. The park is a top destination for outdoor adventure, blending natural beauty with thrilling recreation.

☐ 🔖 ♡ **Oil Creek State Park**: Located in Venango County, this 7,300-acre park preserves the birthplace of the oil industry. Visitors can explore historic oil boom sites, ride the Oil Creek & Titusville Railroad, or hike and bike scenic trails. With waterfalls, streams, and rich history, the park offers a unique blend of industry and nature.

☐ 🔖 ♡ **Ole Bull State Park**: Named after Norwegian violinist Ole Bull, this 132-acre park in Potter County sits along Kettle Creek. It offers camping, hiking, and fishing in a serene, forested valley. Interpretive exhibits highlight Ole Bull's attempt to found a colony nearby, adding cultural history to its scenic wilderness setting.

☐ 🔖 ♡ **Parker Dam State Park**: Nestled in Clearfield County, this 968-acre park is centered on a tranquil lake for swimming, fishing, and boating. Surrounded by forest, it offers trails, camping, and winter recreation. Rustic cabins and historic structures reflect the legacy of the Civilian Conservation Corps, making it both a recreational and historical site.

☐ 🔖 ♡ **Patterson State Park**: Located in Potter County, this 10-acre park provides a rustic picnic area and access to Susquehannock State Forest. With simple facilities, it serves primarily as a gateway for camping, hiking, and snowmobiling in the surrounding wilderness. Its peaceful, no-frills character makes it a practical base for outdoor adventures.

PENNSYLVANIA

☐ 🔖 ♡ **Penn-Roosevelt State Park:** Nestled in Centre County's Rothrock State Forest, this 41-acre park is noted for its remote, forested valley setting. It has historic stonework from the segregated CCC Camp S-63. Camping, picnicking, and hiking on surrounding trails make it a quiet retreat, steeped in both natural beauty and cultural history.

☐ 🔖 ♡ **Pine Grove Furnace State Park:** At the northern tip of the Blue Ridge Mountains, this 696-acre park in Cumberland County preserves iron furnace ruins alongside Laurel and Fuller Lakes. Swimming, camping, and fishing are popular, and it marks the midpoint of the Appalachian Trail. Its mix of history and recreation makes it a unique stop in the state park system.

☐ 🔖 ♡ **Poe Paddy State Park:** At the confluence of Big Poe Creek and Penns Creek in Centre County, Poe Paddy offers camping, picnicking, and trout fishing. The park is popular with hikers and bikers using the nearby rail trail and tunnel. Surrounded by Bald Eagle State Forest, it provides access to rugged terrain and rich outdoor opportunities.

☐ 🔖 ♡ **Poe Valley State Park:** Encompassing 620 acres in Centre County, Poe Valley features a 25-acre lake for swimming, fishing, and boating. Campgrounds and forested trails make it a family destination, while its remote setting ensures a rustic experience. The surrounding Bald Eagle State Forest adds to its appeal as a backcountry getaway.

☐ 🔖 ♡ **Point State Park:** At Pittsburgh's Golden Triangle, this 36-acre urban park sits at the confluence of the Allegheny, Monongahela, and Ohio Rivers. Known for its iconic fountain, it preserves historic Fort Pitt and Fort Duquesne sites. The park is a cultural hub, hosting events and offering green space, trails, and river views in the city's heart.

☐ 🔖 ♡ **Presque Isle State Park:** Pennsylvania's most-visited state park, Presque Isle is a sandy peninsula curving into Lake Erie. Its beaches attract swimmers, while lagoons and trails serve boaters, bikers, and birdwatchers. A critical migratory bird stop, the park also offers fishing, ice activities in winter, and stunning lakefront scenery year-round.

☐ 🔖 ♡ **Prince Gallitzin State Park:** Covering 6,249 acres in Cambria County, this park features Glendale Lake, a 1,635-acre reservoir with 26 miles of shoreline. Popular for boating, fishing, and camping, it also has trails for hiking, biking, and winter activities. Its large size and variety of facilities make it a major regional outdoor destination.

☐ 🔖 ♡ **Promised Land State Park:** Located in the Pocono Mountains, this 3,000-acre park is surrounded by Delaware State Forest. Two lakes provide opportunities for boating, swimming, and fishing, while trails wind through mixed forests. Camping, wildlife watching, and winter skiing make it a four-season favorite, blending rugged wilderness with recreational amenities.

☐ 🔖 ♡ **Prompton State Park:** In Wayne County, this 2,000-acre park surrounds a 290-acre lake. It offers boating, fishing, and over 20 miles of hiking and mountain biking trails. Largely undeveloped, it emphasizes outdoor adventure in a natural setting. Its rugged terrain and peaceful atmosphere attract those seeking less-crowded recreation.

☐ 🔖 ♡ **Prouty Place State Park:** One of Pennsylvania's smallest state parks, this 5-acre site in Potter County is a rustic picnic area and access point to Susquehannock State Forest. With minimal facilities, it offers hunting, fishing, and solitude in a quiet mountain valley. Its simplicity makes it a low-key starting point for outdoor exploration.

☐ 🔖 ♡ **Pymatuning State Park:** Pennsylvania's largest state park spans over 21,000 acres in Crawford County, centered on the 17,000-acre Pymatuning Reservoir. Famous for its "Linesville Spillway" where fish gather in huge numbers, the park offers boating, fishing, camping, and wildlife viewing. Its size and diversity make it one of the state's premier outdoor attractions.

☐ 🔖 ♡ **R. B. Winter State Park:** Formerly called Halfway Lake, this 695-acre park in Union County is centered on a scenic spring-fed lake. Known for swimming, fishing, and picnicking, it's surrounded by Bald Eagle State Forest. Trails lead through rugged woodlands, offering year-round recreation such as hiking, camping, and cross-country skiing.

☐ 🔖 ♡ **Raccoon Creek State Park:** One of Pennsylvania's largest and most popular parks, Raccoon Creek spans 7,572 acres in Beaver County. It features a 101-acre lake, extensive hiking trails, and campgrounds. The park's Wildflower Reserve showcases hundreds of native species, making it a hotspot for nature lovers, families, and outdoor adventurers alike.

PENNSYLVANIA

☐ 🔖 ♡ **Ralph Stover State Park**: In Bucks County, this 45-acre park along Tohickon Creek is popular for hiking, fishing, and picnicking. Its cliffs and gorges attract rock climbers, while High Rocks Vista provides sweeping views. The park's rugged terrain and natural beauty make it a haven for adventurers seeking both scenery and challenge.

☐ 🔖 ♡ **Ravensburg State Park**: A 78-acre park in Clinton County, Ravensburg is nestled in a gorge carved by Rauchtown Creek. It features picnic areas, trout fishing, and shaded trails. Known for its quiet charm, the park is named for the ravens that once nested nearby and offers a peaceful retreat in a forested mountain valley.

☐ 🔖 ♡ **Reeds Gap State Park**: Located in Mifflin County, this 220-acre park lies in a quiet mountain valley. Honey Creek runs through the park, providing fishing opportunities, while open meadows and shaded picnic areas make it family-friendly. Trails connect to Bald Eagle State Forest, offering access to rugged ridges and deeper wilderness exploration.

☐ 🔖 ♡ **Ricketts Glen State Park**: Famous for its 22 named waterfalls, this 13,193-acre park spans Luzerne, Sullivan, and Columbia Counties. The Falls Trail is a highlight, winding through lush forests and cascades. In addition to hiking, it offers camping, boating, and swimming. Its breathtaking natural beauty makes it one of Pennsylvania's crown jewels.

☐ 🔖 ♡ **Ridley Creek State Park**: Covering 2,606 acres in Delaware County, Ridley Creek is a suburban oasis just outside Philadelphia. It features 13 miles of hiking and biking trails, trout fishing, and the historic Hunting Hill Mansion. Meadows, woodlands, and formal gardens make it a unique blend of recreation, history, and natural beauty.

☐ 🔖 ♡ **Ryerson Station State Park**: Found in Greene County, this 1,164-acre park provides camping, hiking, and picnicking in a landscape of rolling hills and streams. Formerly home to a large lake, the park now focuses on trails and natural exploration. Its remote southwestern setting offers solitude, wildlife observation, and a peaceful outdoor experience.

☐ 🔖 ♡ **S. B. Elliott State Park**: This 318-acre park in Clearfield County preserves a historic Civilian Conservation Corps site with rustic pavilions and stone structures. Surrounded by Moshannon State Forest, it offers camping, picnicking, and access to extensive forest trails. Its heritage and quiet setting make it a charming, historically rich park.

☐ 🔖 ♡ **Salt Springs State Park**: A 405-acre park in Susquehanna County, Salt Springs is managed in partnership with a local nonprofit. It preserves old-growth hemlock forests, waterfalls, and gorge trails. Visitors can camp, hike, and birdwatch while learning about conservation. Its wild beauty and grassroots stewardship make it unique among Pennsylvania's parks.

☐ 🔖 ♡ **Samuel S. Lewis State Park**: Overlooking the Susquehanna River in York County, this 85-acre park is known for its sweeping views from Mount Pisgah, open meadows, and kite-flying hill. With picnic areas, short trails, and scenic vistas, it's a popular spot for family outings and gatherings, combining accessibility with natural beauty.

☐ 🔖 ♡ **Sand Bridge State Park**: At just 3 acres, Sand Bridge in Union County is one of Pennsylvania's smallest state parks. It provides shaded picnic areas along Rapid Run, a trout stream flowing through Bald Eagle State Forest. Though modest, it's a popular roadside stop for fishing, picnicking, and relaxation in a peaceful wooded setting.

☐ 🔖 ♡ **Shawnee State Park**: Located in Bedford County, this 3,983-acre park surrounds a 451-acre lake. Visitors can swim at the sandy beach, fish for bass and trout, or boat on its waters. Trails connect to forested ridges and meadows. With camping, picnicking, and year-round activities, Shawnee is a versatile destination for families and adventurers.

☐ 🔖 ♡ **Shikellamy State Park**: At the confluence of the North and West Branches of the Susquehanna River, this 132-acre park features two distinct areas. Packer's Island includes a marina and picnic sites, while Blue Hill offers a scenic overlook. The park is known for boating, fishing, birding, and panoramic views of the river valley.

☐ 🔖 ♡ **Sinnemahoning State Park**: This 1,910-acre park in Cameron and Potter Counties is a wildlife haven, with elk, bear, and bald eagles commonly seen. A reservoir allows boating and fishing, while trails and an education center highlight conservation. Its remote setting in the Wilds provides outstanding opportunities for both recreation and wildlife watching.

PENNSYLVANIA

Sizerville State Park: Straddling Cameron and Potter Counties, this 386-acre park offers camping, hiking, fishing, and swimming. Its nature center interprets the area's logging history and environment. Surrounded by state forests, it's a gateway to wilderness exploration. Hemlock groves and trout streams create a quiet retreat for families and outdoor enthusiasts.

Susquehanna Riverlands State Park: One of Pennsylvania's newest parks, this 1,100-acre area in York County protects woodlands and meadows along the Susquehanna River. It offers trails, wildlife watching, and scenic overlooks. Still being developed, the park emphasizes conservation and public access, ensuring this river corridor remains a natural retreat for generations.

Susquehanna State Park: Nestled in Williamsport, this 20-acre urban park offers boat access to the West Branch Susquehanna River. It's home to the Hiawatha Paddlewheel Riverboat, which offers cruises during warmer months. Fishing, picnicking, and river views make it a unique park that connects visitors to both natural and cultural river heritage.

Susquehannock State Park: Overlooking the Susquehanna River in Lancaster County, this 224-acre park offers dramatic vistas, picnic areas, and hiking trails. Known for Hawk Point Overlook, it's a favorite for birdwatchers, particularly during raptor migrations. Its location on the river bluffs provides both scenic beauty and rich wildlife viewing.

Swatara State Park: Spanning 3,520 acres in Lebanon and Schuylkill Counties, Swatara preserves forested ridges and the scenic Swatara Creek. It offers hiking, biking, fishing, and paddling, with trails connecting to rail-trail systems. The park's rich history includes canal remnants, while its natural diversity provides year-round recreational opportunities.

Tobyhanna State Park: Found in Monroe and Wayne Counties, this 5,440-acre park is centered on Tobyhanna Lake, a 170-acre body of water for boating, fishing, and swimming. Surrounded by forests and wetlands, it offers miles of hiking and biking trails. Campgrounds and picnic areas make it a family favorite, while winter sports add year-round appeal.

Trough Creek State Park: A 541-acre park in Huntingdon County, Trough Creek is carved by Great Trough Creek and features dramatic rock formations. Highlights include Balanced Rock, Rainbow Falls, and Copperas Rocks. Trails, trout fishing, and rustic camping provide a rugged outdoor experience, making it a popular destination for hikers and explorers.

Tuscarora State Park: Located in Schuylkill County, this 1,618-acre park centers on Tuscarora Lake, a 96-acre reservoir popular for boating, fishing, and swimming. A sandy beach, picnic areas, and campgrounds make it family-friendly. Trails connect to nearby Locust Lake State Park, expanding hiking opportunities in Pennsylvania's anthracite coal region.

Tyler State Park: Spanning 1,711 acres in Bucks County, Tyler offers rolling fields, woodlands, and historic farm buildings. Neshaminy Creek winds through the park, supporting fishing and paddling. Over 25 miles of trails are open for hiking, biking, and horseback riding. Its blend of natural beauty and history makes it a suburban recreation treasure.

Upper Pine Bottom State Park: At just 5 acres, this is one of Pennsylvania's smallest parks. Located in Lycoming County along Pine Bottom Run, it serves primarily as a roadside picnic area. Shaded tables, a mountain stream, and access to nearby forestlands make it a simple but scenic stop for travelers passing through the region.

Vosburg Neck State Park: Pennsylvania's newest state park, Vosburg Neck lies in Wyoming County along a sweeping bend of the Susquehanna River. Covering more than 600 acres, it preserves river bluffs, forests, and meadows while offering trails, birdwatching, and boating access. Once a private camp, it now provides public recreation in a serene, ecologically rich landscape of the Endless Mountains.

Warriors Path State Park: Found in Bedford County near Saxton, this 349-acre park is named after a historic Native American trail. It offers picnic areas, hiking trails, and access to Raystown Lake for boating and fishing. Its modest facilities and quiet setting make it ideal for family outings and peaceful reflection in a wooded landscape.

PENNSYLVANIA

☐ 🔖 ♡ **Washington Crossing Historic Park:** Located in Bucks County, this 500-acre park commemorates George Washington's daring 1776 crossing of the Delaware River. Historic buildings, exhibits, and reenactments interpret this pivotal Revolutionary War event. The park also features trails, picnic areas, and scenic river views, blending heritage and outdoor recreation in one of America's most iconic landscapes.

☐ 🔖 ♡ **Whipple Dam State Park:** Located in Huntingdon County, this 256-acre park centers on a 22-acre lake popular for swimming, boating, and fishing. Shaded picnic areas and hiking trails through Rothrock State Forest add to its charm. Winter sports like cross-country skiing also attract visitors, making Whipple Dam a cozy four-season retreat.

☐ 🔖 ♡ **White Clay Creek Preserve**: Situated in Chester County, this 2,072-acre preserve protects rolling hills, woodlands, and the scenic White Clay Creek. Trails are popular for hiking, biking, and horseback riding, while the creek supports fishing and birdwatching. As a cross-state conservation area, it highlights watershed protection and outdoor recreation.

☐ 🔖 ♡ **Worlds End State Park:** In Sullivan County, this 780-acre park lies in a rugged valley of the Loyalsock Creek. Known for dramatic overlooks, waterfalls, and steep trails, it's a favorite for hikers and campers. The park offers swimming, fishing, and seasonal programs. Its wild beauty and remote atmosphere make it one of Pennsylvania's most scenic parks.

☐ 🔖 ♡ **Yellow Creek State Park:** Found in Indiana County, this 2,981-acre park is built around an 800-acre lake. It is popular for boating, fishing, and swimming, with a beach and boat rentals available. Trails circle through forests and fields, offering birdwatching and wildlife viewing. The park's natural diversity makes it a year-round recreational hub.

National Parks

 ☐ 🔖 ♡ **Allegheny Portage Railroad National Historic Site**: Preserving a key transportation route across the Alleghenies, this site in southwestern Pennsylvania tells the story of the 19th-century railroad that connected eastern markets with the western frontier. Visitors can explore Engine House No. 6, hike wooded trails, and learn how this engineering marvel shaped America's early industrial expansion.

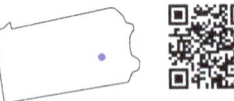 ☐ 🔖 ♡ **Appalachian National Scenic Trail:** Stretching over 2,100 miles from Georgia to Maine, the Appalachian Trail passes through Pennsylvania's ridges and valleys, offering hikers challenging climbs and sweeping views. Known as the "Rocksylvania" section, it provides both rugged experiences and scenic beauty, connecting forests, streams, and small towns along the Eastern U.S. corridor.

 ☐ 🔖 ♡ **Captain John Smith Chesapeake National Historic Trail:** Extending 3,000 miles across the Chesapeake watershed, this water trail follows John Smith's 1607–1609 explorations. In Pennsylvania, it reaches up the Susquehanna River, highlighting native cultures, early settlement history, and rich river ecology. Paddling routes, overlooks, and interpretive stops connect recreation with heritage along this storied waterway.

 ☐ 🔖 ♡ **Delaware Water Gap National Recreation Area:** Along the Delaware River in Pennsylvania and New Jersey, this vast recreation area protects forested mountains, waterfalls, and river valleys. Visitors can hike, camp, paddle, and fish while enjoying cultural history tied to canals and early settlements. Scenic overlooks and diverse wildlife make it a favorite year-round destination.

 ☐ 🔖 ♡ **Edgar Allan Poe National Historic Site:** In Philadelphia, this historic home preserves the legacy of Edgar Allan Poe, where he wrote during the 1830s. Visitors can tour his modest residence, view exhibits on his works, and explore the influence of his time in the city. The site provides an intimate look at America's master of gothic literature.

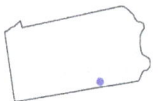 ☐ 🔖 ♡ **Eisenhower National Historic Site**: Located near Gettysburg, this preserved farm was the home of President Dwight D. Eisenhower. Visitors can explore his residence, learn about his military and presidential life, and view personal artifacts. The tranquil setting reflects Eisenhower's retreat from politics, while its historic grounds highlight his role in 20th-century America.

PENNSYLVANIA

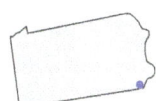 **First State National Historical Park**: Spanning sites in Delaware, this park commemorates the nation's first state and its role in America's founding. Visitors can explore historic New Castle, Dover, and Wilmington, experiencing preserved colonial structures, Revolutionary-era heritage, and cultural landscapes. The park celebrates Delaware's early influence in shaping U.S. independence.

 **Flight 93 National Memorial**: In Shanksville, this memorial honors the passengers and crew of Flight 93, who prevented a terrorist attack on September 11, 2001. Visitors can reflect at the Wall of Names, walk the memorial plaza, and learn the story of courage and sacrifice. The serene setting fosters remembrance and national reflection.

 **Fort Necessity National Battlefield**: Preserving the site of the 1754 Battle of Fort Necessity in Farmington, this park highlights the French and Indian War's first clash involving George Washington. Visitors can tour the reconstructed fort, explore interpretive trails, and discover the conflict's importance in shaping early American and global history.

 **Friendship Hill National Historic Site**: Located near Point Marion, this park preserves the home of Albert Gallatin, a U.S. statesman and Secretary of the Treasury. Visitors can tour his estate, explore the riverside grounds, and learn about his contributions to finance, diplomacy, and expansion. The peaceful setting blends history with scenic landscapes.

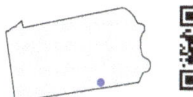 **Gettysburg National Military Park**: This landmark park in Gettysburg preserves the site of the pivotal 1863 Civil War battle. Visitors can tour the battlefield, view monuments, and visit the National Cemetery where Lincoln delivered the Gettysburg Address. The park combines military history, solemn memorials, and expansive landscapes central to U.S. heritage.

 **Hopewell Furnace National Historic Site**: Preserving a 19th-century iron plantation in Elverson, this site interprets early American industry and community life. Visitors can tour the restored furnace, worker homes, and barns, learning about charcoal ironmaking and rural village culture. Trails connect to French Creek State Park, blending history with natural landscapes.

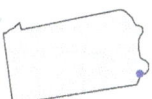 **Independence National Historical Park**: In Philadelphia, this iconic site preserves the Liberty Bell, Independence Hall, and Congress Hall. Here the Declaration of Independence and U.S. Constitution were debated and signed. Visitors can tour historic buildings, explore museums, and learn about America's founding, making it one of the nation's most significant historic parks.

 **Johnstown Flood National Memorial**: Located in Johnstown, this memorial honors the tragic 1889 flood that killed more than 2,200 people. Visitors can explore exhibits detailing the disaster, walk to the remains of the South Fork Dam, and reflect on the human and engineering lessons from one of America's deadliest natural disasters.

 **Middle Delaware National Scenic River**: Flowing between Pennsylvania and New Jersey, this 40-mile section of the Delaware River offers canoeing, kayaking, fishing, and wildlife watching. Protected within the Delaware Water Gap National Recreation Area, it provides scenic vistas, quiet riverbanks, and cultural history tied to early canal and settlement life.

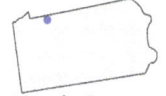 **North Country National Scenic Trail**: Stretching 4,800 miles across eight states, the North Country Trail runs more than 250 miles through northwestern Pennsylvania, including Allegheny National Forest. Its footpaths cross forests, rivers, and historic oil country, offering backpackers rugged terrain, wildlife encounters, and access to some of the state's most remote and scenic landscapes.

 **Potomac Heritage National Scenic Trail**: This 710-mile network links landscapes from Washington, D.C., to western Pennsylvania. In Pennsylvania, segments connect cultural sites and natural areas, offering hiking, biking, and paddling opportunities. The trail highlights river valleys, historic routes, and scenic ridges, blending outdoor adventure with heritage exploration.

 **Steamtown National Historic Site**: In Scranton, this park preserves America's steam railroad heritage. Visitors can see restored locomotives, ride excursion trains, and learn how steam power fueled U.S. transportation and industry. Interactive exhibits and live demonstrations highlight the significance of railroads in shaping commerce, communities, and innovation.

PENNSYLVANIA

☐ 🔖 ♡ **Thaddeus Kosciuszko National Memorial**: The smallest unit of the National Park System preserves the Philadelphia home of Polish engineer Thaddeus Kosciuszko, who aided the American Revolution. Exhibits interpret his life, ideals of liberty, and contributions to military engineering. Despite its size, the site offers a powerful story of freedom and democracy.

☐ 🔖 ♡ **Upper Delaware Scenic and Recreational River**: Protecting 73 miles of the Delaware River on the PA–NY border, this river corridor is known for fishing, boating, and bald eagle viewing. Visitors can explore historic sites like the Roebling Aqueduct while enjoying unspoiled scenery. The river provides both recreation and cultural heritage in a pristine setting.

☐ 🔖 ♡ **Valley Forge National Historical Park**: In Valley Forge, this park preserves the site where George Washington's army endured the winter of 1777–1778. Visitors can tour reconstructed soldier huts, visit the Washington Memorial Chapel, and explore miles of trails. It is both a symbol of American perseverance and a landscape rich in history and beauty.

☐ 🔖 ♡ **Washington–Rochambeau National Historic Trail**: This 680-mile route traces the 1781 march of George Washington's Continental Army and French allies under Rochambeau to victory at Yorktown. In Pennsylvania, the trail passes through Philadelphia and Chester County, with historic sites, interpretive signs, and landscapes that connect visitors to the Revolutionary War's decisive campaign.

State & National Forests

☐ 🔖 ♡ **Allegheny National Forest**: Pennsylvania's only National Forest covers over 513,000 acres in the northwest. It protects hardwood and pine stands, the Kinzua Reservoir, and rich wildlife habitat. Established in 1923, it offers hiking, camping, canoeing, OHV trails, fishing, and hunting. Managed under multiple-use principles, it blends recreation, timber, and watershed conservation.

☐ 🔖 ♡ **Bald Eagle State Forest**: Spanning nearly 194,600 acres across the rugged ridges of central Pennsylvania, this forest features oak–hickory woodlands, mountain streams, and expansive vistas. Popular for hiking, camping, hunting, and fishing, it contains sections of the Mid State and White Mountain Trails. Managed for timber, recreation, and watershed health, it represents classic Ridge and Valley landscapes.

☐ 🔖 ♡ **Buchanan State Forest**: Encompassing 71,700 acres in Bedford, Franklin, and Fulton Counties, this forest is named for President James Buchanan. It features oak-maple-pine ridges, remnants of the historic Pike Road, and quiet hollows. Managed for timber and watershed health, it supports hiking, camping, hunting, and research while conserving Appalachian forest resources.

☐ 🔖 ♡ **Clear Creek State Forest**: Covering 16,700 acres across Clarion and Venango Counties, this mixed hardwood and pine forest protects wildlife habitat and watersheds. Visitors can hike, hunt, and fish while exploring demonstration sites for sustainable forest management. Its varied ecosystems provide opportunities for quiet outdoor recreation and conservation learning.

☐ 🔖 ♡ **Cornplanter State Forest**: At 1,585 acres in Crawford, Forest, and Warren Counties, this small forest honors Seneca leader Cornplanter. It protects riparian woodlands along the Allegheny River and supports hiking, birdwatching, and education through interpretive trails. Focused on watershed conservation, it plays an important role in regional habitat and flood resilience.

☐ 🔖 ♡ **Delaware State Forest**: Spanning 85,100 acres in Pike and Monroe Counties, this forest preserves oak-hickory ridges, wetlands, and river corridors. It offers hiking, hunting, fishing, paddling, and scenic drives. Managed for public recreation and ecological health, it balances human use with watershed protection in the Appalachian foothills.

☐ 🔖 ♡ **Elk State Forest**: Covering 217,000 acres across five counties, Elk State Forest preserves northern hardwood ridges and boreal habitats. It features the scenic Elk Scenic Drive and backpacking along the Quehanna Trail and Bucktail Path. Popular for wildlife viewing, fishing, hunting, snowmobiling, and camping, it safeguards Pennsylvania's wild elk country.

☐ 🔖 ♡ **Forbes State Forest**: A 59,000-acre forest spread across Fayette, Somerset, and Westmoreland Counties. It encompasses the Laurel Ridge Trail and remote highland tracts. Visitors enjoy hiking, camping, hunting, and wildlife observation. Known for its mixed-oak ridges and natural communities, it also supports research and sustainable resource management.

PENNSYLVANIA

☐ 🔖 ♡ **Gallitzin State Forest**: Encompassing 24,370 acres along the Allegheny Front, this forest spans Bedford, Cambria, Indiana, and Somerset Counties. With hardwood ridges and scenic vistas, it includes parts of the Mid-State Trail. Hiking, hunting, and wildlife viewing are popular, while management emphasizes watershed health and rugged upland conservation.

☐ 🔖 ♡ **Loyalsock State Forest**: Covering 114,500 acres in the Endless Mountains, this forest is home to the Loyalsock Trail and High Knob Overlook. Several designated wild areas protect wilderness tracts and pristine streams. Visitors enjoy hiking, camping, hunting, and birding, while its rugged beauty and high-quality waterways highlight conservation priorities.

☐ 🔖 ♡ **Michaux State Forest**: A 85,500-acre tract in southern Pennsylvania's South Mountain region, this forest protects oak-pine ridges and diverse ecosystems. It includes portions of the Appalachian Trail and supports hiking, skiing, hunting, and camping. Known as Pennsylvania's "cradle of forestry," it preserves watersheds and native plant communities.

☐ 🔖 ♡ **Moshannon State Forest**: Spanning 190,000 acres in central Pennsylvania, this forest contains the Quehanna Wild Area and the state's largest contiguous woodland. Trails like the Quehanna Trail offer backpacking, while wetlands provide habitat for rare species. Hunting, fishing, and research highlight its role in both recreation and biodiversity protection.

☐ 🔖 ♡ **Pinchot State Forest**: Named for conservationist Gifford Pinchot, this 54,000-acre forest in northeastern Pennsylvania spans Lackawanna, Luzerne, Wayne, and Wyoming Counties. It protects hardwood ridges and sandstone outcrops while offering hiking, hunting, and birdwatching. Managed for watershed protection and education, it provides a natural haven near urban centers.

☐ 🔖 ♡ **Rothrock State Forest**: Encompassing 97,000 acres across the Ridge and Valley region, Rothrock protects rocky ridges, streams, and forest ecosystems. Popular for hiking, biking, ATV riding, and horseback trails, it also contains research areas and CCC-era stonework. Its landscape blends active recreation, conservation, and sustainable management.

☐ 🔖 ♡ **Sproul State Forest**: Pennsylvania's largest state forest, spanning 305,000 acres in north-central counties. Its rugged wild areas include the Donut Hole and Chuck Keiper Trails, offering challenging backpacking routes. Known for remote hunting, fishing, and wildlife viewing, Sproul represents some of the state's wildest and most biodiverse landscapes.

☐ 🔖 ♡ **Susquehannock State Forest**: Covering 265,000 acres in northern Pennsylvania, this forest includes the Susquehannock Trail System and Hammersley Wild Area. Scenic valleys, streams, and remote ridges attract backpackers, hunters, and anglers. It conserves old-growth remnants and pristine aquatic habitats, making it a vital wilderness resource in the state.

☐ 🔖 ♡ **Tiadaghton State Forest**: At 146,500 acres, this forest preserves Pine Creek Gorge and access to the Pine Creek Rail Trail. Its dramatic ravines and ridges support kayaking, hiking, biking, and hunting. Known as the "Grand Canyon of Pennsylvania," Tiadaghton offers some of the state's most breathtaking outdoor scenery and recreation.

☐ 🔖 ♡ **Tioga State Forest**: A 162,000-acre forest in north-central Pennsylvania, characterized by steep gorges, remote ridges, and diverse hardwood stands. Popular for backpacking along the West Rim Trail, it also supports fishing, camping, and hunting. Conservation efforts protect watershed health, native species, and scenic wildland experiences.

☐ 🔖 ♡ **Tuscarora State Forest**: Spanning 96,000 acres across the Tuscarora Mountain region, this forest preserves hardwood ridges, pine stands, and cool streams. It supports hiking, horseback riding, hunting, and ATV use, while emphasizing water conservation and wildlife habitat. Its rugged terrain offers recreation in a traditional forest setting.

☐ 🔖 ♡ **Weiser State Forest**: A 30,000-acre forest across eastern Pennsylvania, Weiser conserves mixed hardwood forests and riparian corridors. Popular for hiking, fishing, and hunting, it also supports outdoor education and forest restoration. Its proximity to populated areas makes it a key refuge for both recreation and ecological conservation.

PENNSYLVANIA

☐ ◻ ♡ **William Penn State Forest**: Covering 1,683 acres near Valley Forge, this small but important forest preserves hardwood woodlands and natural areas. It includes the Ruth Zimmerman Natural Area and supports hiking, environmental education, and research. As Pennsylvania's only forest in the urban southeast, it balances conservation with suburban access.

National Scenic Byways & All-American Roads

☐ ◻ ♡ **Brandywine Valley Scenic Byway:** Winding through historic Chester and Delaware Counties, this byway showcases rolling farmland, colonial towns, and landmarks tied to the Revolutionary War. Visitors encounter preserved estates, stone bridges, and the landscapes that inspired artists of the Brandywine School, blending cultural heritage with pastoral beauty.

☐ ◻ ♡ **Gateway to the Big Apple Byway:** Crossing into northeastern Pennsylvania, this route connects small river towns and scenic stretches of the Delaware River. It highlights the cultural exchange between rural Pennsylvania and the New York metropolitan region, offering visitors historic architecture, forested hills, and access to outdoor recreation.

☐ ◻ ♡ **Great Lakes Seaway Trail:** Extending into Pennsylvania near Erie, this byway follows Lake Erie's southern shore for stunning waterfront views. It highlights the region's maritime history, lighthouses, and coastal habitats. Scenic pull-offs, birdwatching sites, and cultural attractions link natural beauty with the heritage of the Great Lakes corridor.

☐ ◻ ♡ **Historic National Road:** The first federally funded highway, this byway runs through southwestern Pennsylvania, tracing America's early westward expansion. Historic inns, stone bridges, and towns along the route reveal the 19th-century growth of travel and commerce. Today it offers a journey through rolling farmland, small towns, and preserved historic landscapes.

☐ ◻ ♡ **Journey Through Hallowed Ground Byway:** Extending into south-central Pennsylvania, this byway links Gettysburg with historic sites stretching toward Virginia. It follows a corridor rich in Revolutionary and Civil War heritage, featuring battlefields, monuments, and cultural landmarks. Scenic roads wind through pastoral landscapes that shaped pivotal chapters of American history.

☐ ◻ ♡ **Lake Erie Coastal Pennsylvania Byway:** Running 140 miles along Pennsylvania's Lake Erie shoreline, this All-American Road highlights Presque Isle State Park, working waterfronts, and cultural attractions in Erie. Travelers enjoy sandy beaches, lighthouses, and bird habitats while experiencing the dynamic mix of natural beauty and maritime heritage along the Great Lakes coast.

☐ ◻ ♡ **Longhouse National Scenic Byway:** Nestled within Allegheny National Forest, this loop road offers sweeping views of the Allegheny Reservoir and lush hardwood forests. Scenic overlooks, waterfalls, and wildlife provide year-round appeal. The route highlights the forest's conservation history and recreational opportunities, from hiking to boating, in northwestern Pennsylvania.

☐ ◻ ♡ **National Forest Scenic Byway – Allegheny Forest Loop:** Crossing the Allegheny National Forest, this byway explores rolling hills, river valleys, and remote woodlands. Visitors discover oil heritage sites, rustic towns, and access to outdoor activities such as camping, kayaking, and hiking. The drive showcases Pennsylvania's only national forest and its diverse ecosystems.

☐ ◻ ♡ **Seaway Trail – Pennsylvania Segment:** Covering Pennsylvania's short but scenic stretch of the larger Seaway Trail, this route offers lake vistas, historic lighthouses, and cultural sites in and around Erie. As part of a multistate All-American Road, it connects Pennsylvania to the broader Great Lakes travel corridor, emphasizing both natural and cultural heritage.

☐ ◻ ♡ **Susquehanna River Valley Scenic Byway:** Following the curves of the Susquehanna River in central Pennsylvania, this byway links historic river towns, farmland, and rolling ridges. Visitors encounter covered bridges, colonial heritage sites, and abundant wildlife along the waterway. The route emphasizes the Susquehanna's role in shaping the region's history and culture.

PENNSYLVANIA

State Scenic Byways

☐ ▯ ♡ **Blue Route Scenic Byway (I-476):** This byway winds through Delaware and Montgomery Counties, linking the Schuylkill and Delaware Rivers. Scenic overlooks, rolling hills, and wooded stretches contrast with suburban surroundings, while historic towns and cultural attractions highlight the corridor's importance as both a modern connector and a scenic drive.

☐ ▯ ♡ **Brandywine Valley Scenic Byway:** Following quiet country roads in Chester and Delaware Counties, this route showcases the pastoral landscapes of the Brandywine River Valley. Visitors encounter Revolutionary War landmarks, charming villages, and the cultural legacy of the Brandywine School of artists, blending history, art, and rural beauty in a classic Pennsylvania setting.

☐ ▯ ♡ **Bucktail Trail Scenic Byway:** Extending 75 miles along PA Route 120 from Lock Haven to Emporium, this byway traces the remote West Branch Susquehanna River valley. Known for rugged mountains, forested ridges, and abundant wildlife—including the famed elk herd—it highlights Pennsylvania's wilderness heritage and offers a quintessential backcountry drive.

☐ ▯ ♡ **Conestoga Ridge Scenic Byway:** Winding through Lancaster County, this byway traverses farmland, covered bridges, and Amish communities. Rolling fields and quiet lanes reveal the agricultural traditions of the Pennsylvania Dutch, while historic towns like Ephrata and Blue Ball provide cultural landmarks. It's a route rich in heritage and pastoral charm.

☐ ▯ ♡ **Delaware River Valley Scenic Byway:** This route follows the Delaware River's winding course, connecting historic towns, farms, and river overlooks. Covered bridges, Revolutionary War sites, and cultural festivals enrich the experience, while the scenic river corridor provides habitat for wildlife. It blends natural beauty with the deep history of Pennsylvania's eastern borderlands.

☐ ▯ ♡ **Dutch Country Roads Scenic Byway:** Located in central Pennsylvania, this byway highlights the heart of Amish and Mennonite country. Visitors encounter horse-drawn buggies, fertile farmland, and traditional homesteads, while stopping at farmers' markets and craft shops. The route showcases a way of life that continues to shape the culture and landscape of the region.

☐ ▯ ♡ **Falls to Falls Scenic Byway:** Stretching from Bushkill Falls to Dingmans Falls in the Pocono Mountains, this byway highlights dramatic waterfalls, hemlock forests, and steep ridges. Scenic pull-offs and trailheads give access to cascading waters, while surrounding small towns offer cultural and historic charm. It's a journey through some of Pennsylvania's most iconic natural wonders.

☐ ▯ ♡ **Journey Through Hallowed Ground Scenic Byway:** Passing through Adams County near Gettysburg, this state-designated route connects Revolutionary and Civil War sites with pastoral farmland. It is part of a larger multistate corridor that celebrates America's heritage, offering access to battlefields, monuments, and scenic countryside tied to the nation's founding and preservation.

☐ ▯ ♡ **Lincoln Highway Heritage Corridor Scenic Byway:** Tracing the historic Lincoln Highway (U.S. Route 30), this byway runs through southern Pennsylvania. Roadside architecture, vintage diners, and quirky attractions preserve the feel of early motoring. Combined with mountain vistas, farmland, and historic towns, it celebrates America's first coast-to-coast highway and its cultural legacy.

☐ ▯ ♡ **National Road Heritage Corridor Scenic Byway:** Running through southwestern Pennsylvania, this corridor follows America's first federally funded highway. Historic stone bridges, taverns, and small towns tell the story of westward expansion and frontier life. Scenic farmland and rolling ridges enrich the journey, connecting heritage tourism with Pennsylvania's rural beauty.

☐ ▯ ♡ **Schuylkill River Scenic Byway:** Following the Schuylkill River through Philadelphia and into Schuylkill, Berks, and Montgomery Counties, this byway highlights industrial heritage, Revolutionary War sites, and restored canal paths. Cultural attractions, river towns, and natural landscapes tell the story of a region where industry, history, and recreation converge.

☐ ▯ ♡ **State Route 6 Scenic Byway:** Spanning the northern tier of Pennsylvania, this classic route showcases small towns, rolling farmland, and forested highlands. Known as one of America's great "long drives," it connects the Endless Mountains to the Allegheny National Forest, offering access to historic sites, parks, and breathtaking overlooks.

☐ ▯ ♡ **U.S. Route 202 Parkway Scenic Byway:** This suburban parkway in Bucks and Montgomery Counties features landscaped medians, bike paths, and wooded buffers. It provides a green, scenic travel corridor while preserving open space and offering recreational trails alongside the roadway. The parkway blends transportation with conservation and visual appeal.

PENNSYLVANIA

National Natural Landmarks

 ☐ 🔖 ♡ **Bear Meadows Natural Area:** Hidden in a high mountain basin, Bear Meadows is a bog that has preserved layers of peat and pollen for thousands of years. These records make it an invaluable site for studying long-term climate patterns and plant succession. Its poor drainage supports unique boreal vegetation, while the surrounding ridges isolate and protect this unusual ecosystem in central Pennsylvania.
GPS: 40.72917, −77.76389

 ☐ 🔖 ♡ **Box Huckleberry Site:** This 10-acre natural area is home to one of the most remarkable plant colonies in North America—a clonal box huckleberry thought to be more than 1,000 years old. The site offers a rare chance to observe an ancient organism that reproduces vegetatively rather than by seed, providing insight into longevity, genetic persistence, and the resilience of relict plant communities.
GPS: 40.406111, -77.173889

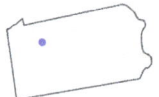 ☐ 🔖 ♡ **Cook Forest State Park:** Known for its majestic stands of Eastern white pine and hemlock, Cook Forest protects trees that date back to the mid-1600s. The towering canopy makes it one of the finest old-growth forests in the Northeast. Within its 8,500 acres, visitors find trails, wildlife habitat, and scenic river overlooks that preserve a living example of Pennsylvania's original woodland landscape.
GPS: 41.323611, -79.163889

 ☐ 🔖 ♡ **Ferncliff Peninsula Natural Area:** Enclosed by a great bend of the Youghiogheny River, this 100-acre peninsula shelters a forest shaped by its isolation. Rich soils and unique hydrology support plant species not found in surrounding areas. Over centuries, the peninsula has developed into a distinct late-successional forest, offering a fascinating look at natural ecological processes and riparian diversity.
GPS: 39.867555, -79.498229

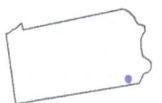 ☐ 🔖 ♡ **Ferncliff Wildflower and Wildlife Preserve:** This lush preserve is celebrated for its mesophytic forest, where shaded ravines and cool, moist valleys nurture an abundance of native wildflowers. The habitat also supports songbirds, amphibians, and small mammals. By protecting such diverse species, the site illustrates the importance of conserving small forested landscapes in maintaining biodiversity.
GPS: 39.782590, -76.242740

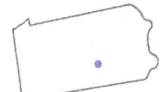 ☐ 🔖 ♡ **Florence Jones Reineman Wildlife Sanctuary:** Covering more than 3,100 acres, this sanctuary preserves a wide array of ecosystems, from hardwood forests and wetlands to meadows and ridgelines. Its unbroken habitat is crucial for wildlife such as black bear, bobcat, and migratory birds. Beyond recreation, the site functions as an outdoor laboratory, supporting conservation research and ecological education.
GPS: 40.266667, -77.266667

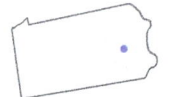 ☐ 🔖 ♡ **Hawk Mountain Sanctuary:** Perched along the Kittatinny Ridge, Hawk Mountain is one of the world's premier raptor migration watchpoints. Tens of thousands of hawks, falcons, and eagles pass overhead each fall. The sanctuary also protects a rich ridge-top ecosystem and serves as a center for bird research, environmental education, and international conservation, drawing visitors from across the globe.
GPS: 40.640833, -75.992222

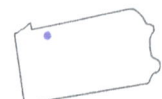 ☐ 🔖 ♡ **Hearts Content Scenic Area:** A rare remnant of Pennsylvania's original forest, this 120-acre grove features massive white pines and hemlocks rising above a lush understory. Many trees are over 200 years old, creating a cathedral-like atmosphere. The old-growth woodland offers both a refuge for diverse wildlife and a living classroom for understanding pre-settlement forest conditions in the Northeast.
GPS: 41.691000, -79.254000

PENNSYLVANIA

 **Hemlocks Natural Area:** Within Tuscarora State Forest lies one of the finest stands of old-growth eastern hemlock in Pennsylvania. Towering trees form a dense canopy that shades the understory, creating a cool, moist habitat for mosses, ferns, and salamanders. The largely untouched setting provides a rare glimpse into the forest ecosystems that once dominated large portions of the Appalachian landscape.
GPS: 40.238418, -77.641379

 **Hickory Run Boulder Field:** This remarkable 16.5-acre boulder field was formed during the last Ice Age when freeze-thaw cycles fractured sandstone and shifted massive blocks downslope. The treeless expanse creates an otherworldly landscape, with boulders stretching as far as the eye can see. Now preserved in Hickory Run State Park, it remains one of the most dramatic periglacial features in the Northeast.
GPS: 41.036111, -75.683889

 **John Heinz National Wildlife Refuge at Tinicum:** Situated in urban Philadelphia, this 350-acre tidal marsh is the largest remaining freshwater wetland in the city. Once heavily threatened by development, it now serves as a critical refuge for migratory birds, amphibians, and fish. Trails and boardwalks give the public access to a thriving ecosystem that illustrates the importance of urban conservation.
GPS: 39.885866, -75.262356

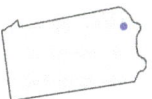 **Lake Lacawac:** A pristine glacial lake covering 52 acres, Lacawac remains one of the southernmost unpolluted examples of its kind in the U.S. Encircled by hemlock and hardwood forests, it preserves intact limnological processes and provides habitat for fish, amphibians, and migratory birds. The lake is part of a research station, contributing long-term ecological studies of freshwater ecosystems.
GPS: 41.382289, -75.292078

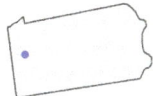 **McConnells Mill State Park:** A 2,500-acre park defined by a rugged gorge carved by Slippery Rock Creek. Sheer cliffs, waterfalls, and old-growth forest line the ravine, creating habitats for a wide variety of species. Alongside these natural wonders, visitors can explore a historic gristmill and covered bridge, blending Pennsylvania's natural and cultural history into one striking destination.
GPS: 40.926667, -80.190000

 **Monroe Border Fault:** Found along the Delaware River, this geological boundary exposes rock layers of multiple ages that reveal evidence of tectonic movement. The site demonstrates how faulting shaped the Appalachian landscape. Today, scenic trails follow ridges and river valleys where geology and ecology intersect, making the area both a scientific resource and a recreational destination.
GPS: 40.579756, -75.197556

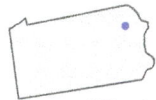 **Nay Aug Park Gorge and Waterfall:** Within Scranton's city limits, this gorge showcases sheer cliffs, dense woodland, and a cascading waterfall. Despite its urban setting, the gorge maintains remarkable natural beauty and biodiversity. Trails and a pedestrian bridge provide access, while the site serves as a rare example of an intact natural gorge thriving in the heart of a bustling community.
GPS: 41.401389, -75.642778

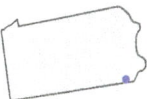 **Nottingham Park Serpentine Barrens:** Stretching over 650 acres, this site protects one of the largest serpentine barrens in the eastern United States. Nutrient-poor, rocky soils give rise to unusual grassland-like vegetation, where rare plants adapted to harsh conditions flourish. The landscape resembles open prairie dotted with scrub and wildflowers, offering a glimpse of a unique ecological community.
GPS: 39.740507, -76.039112

 **Pine Creek Gorge:** Carved by glacial meltwater, this dramatic canyon is often called the "Grand Canyon of Pennsylvania." Nearly 50 miles long and more than 1,000 feet deep in places, it offers breathtaking views, extensive trails, and remarkable biodiversity. The gorge highlights the combined power of glaciers and rivers in shaping landscapes, while surrounding forests provide critical wildlife habitat.
GPS: 41.271667, -77.326944

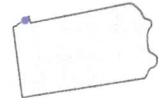 **Presque Isle State Park:** A sandy, crescent-shaped peninsula extending into Lake Erie, Presque Isle was created by wave-driven deposition. Its 3,112 acres include beaches, marshes, lagoons, and woodlands, making it a vital stopover for migratory birds. As one of Pennsylvania's most visited parks, it blends recreation with conservation, offering year-round outdoor opportunities amid rich biodiversity.
GPS: 42.163056, -80.100833

PENNSYLVANIA

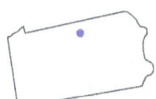 **Reynolds Spring and Algerine Swamp Bogs:** These two remote bogs preserve over 1,300 acres of peatland ecosystems surrounded by oak and pine forest. Their acidic soils, sphagnum mats, and unusual plant assemblages provide habitat for rare species. The sites are also valuable research areas, helping scientists study peatland ecology, carbon storage, and the ecological importance of wetlands.
GPS: 41.550902, -77.497481

 **Snyder Middleswarth Natural Area:** Covering 500 acres, this natural area preserves a mix of old-growth hemlock, white pine, and oak within a narrow valley. A mountain stream winds through the site, supporting rich plant and animal life. Its undisturbed woodland serves as both a refuge for wildlife and a living reminder of the forests that once dominated central Pennsylvania.
GPS: 40.810000, -77.283056

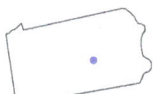 **Susquehanna Water Gaps:** North of Harrisburg, the Susquehanna River slices through five parallel Appalachian ridges, forming dramatic water gaps. These geologic features reveal millions of years of river erosion and mountain uplift. Today the gaps offer panoramic views, important wildlife corridors, and striking examples of how rivers carve through resistant rock over immense spans of time.
GPS: 40.520918, -76.978867

 **Tamarack Swamp:** This acidic kettle pond bog in northwestern Pennsylvania harbors tamarack trees, sphagnum moss, and carnivorous plants rarely found this far south. Formed during the last glaciation, the swamp preserves a relict boreal ecosystem. Its fragile wetland community provides habitat for amphibians and birds, while also offering a valuable window into glacial and peatland ecology.
GPS: 41.989000, -79.555000

 **Tannersville Cranberry Bog:** Among the southernmost boreal bogs in the eastern U.S., this 1,000-acre fen formed in a glacial kettle. Its floating sphagnum mats support orchids, pitcher plants, and other northern species unusual at this latitude. Boardwalks allow visitors to explore without damaging the delicate ecosystem, while the preserve offers educational programs about wetland ecology and conservation.
GPS: 41.040000, -75.305000

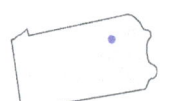 **The Glens Natural Area:** Located in Ricketts Glen State Park, this 2,845-acre tract features old-growth forest and more than 20 named waterfalls cascading through a rugged gorge. Towering hemlocks, oaks, and maples dominate the canopy, while trails allow visitors to experience its scenic beauty. The Glens also serve as an outstanding site for studying forest ecology and watershed dynamics.
GPS: 41.326111, -76.279444

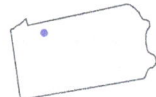 **Tionesta Scenic and Research Natural Areas:** Together these adjoining tracts encompass more than 4,100 acres of old-growth forest on the Allegheny Plateau. Towering hemlocks, maples, and oaks dominate the canopy, providing habitat for bears, fishers, and countless songbirds. The area functions as both a recreational treasure and a research site, preserving one of the state's largest old-growth remnants.
GPS: 41.645000, -78.941000

 **Titus and Wattsburg Bogs:** Located near Lake Erie, this 125-acre peatland features acidic pools, floating mats, and boreal species such as pitcher plants and cranberries. The bogs preserve glacially formed wetland habitat that is increasingly rare in Pennsylvania. They serve as important breeding grounds for amphibians and migratory birds, while also highlighting the ecological importance of northern bogs.
GPS: 41.943388, -79.763107

 **Wissahickon Valley:** This forested gorge along Wissahickon Creek offers waterfalls, stone bridges, and more than 50 miles of trails within northwest Philadelphia. Its wooded slopes preserve a diverse urban ecosystem, while historic mills and bridges tell the story of human use along the stream. Today it remains a vital green refuge, blending cultural history with the conservation of natural landscapes.
GPS: 40.016056, -75.205744

UNITED STATES EDITION

RHODE ISLAND

Rhode Island's coastal charm is reflected in its sandy beaches, rocky shorelines, salt marshes, and wooded trails. With a welcoming collection of state parks, coastal reserves, and notable natural landmarks, the Ocean State offers scenic outdoor escapes close to home, where sea breezes, lighthouses, and forest paths meet in harmony.

📅 Peak Season
June–September is Rhode Island's peak season, with warm weather and bustling coastal towns. Summer brings beachgoers, sailing, and festivals along Narragansett Bay and the Atlantic shore.

📅 Offseason Months
November–April is the offseason, with cooler temperatures and quieter beaches. Winter offers peaceful seaside scenery and birdwatching, though some attractions reduce hours.

🍃 Scenery & Nature Timing
Spring brings blooming coastal gardens and migratory shorebirds. Summer highlights sandy beaches and rocky coves. Fall offers mild weather and colorful foliage inland, while winter provides crisp ocean views and calm coastal walks.

✨ Special
Rhode Island features Narragansett Bay's intricate coastline, the cliffs of Newport's Ocean Drive, and the barrier beaches of Block Island. Powerful tides, sea fog, and coastal storms shape its ever-changing natural landscape.

RHODE ISLAND

State Parks

☐ 🔖 ♡ **Beavertail State Park**: Located at the southern tip of Conanicut Island in Jamestown, this park is renowned for dramatic ocean vistas, rocky shores, and the historic Beavertail Lighthouse. Visitors can enjoy hiking, fishing, picnicking, and exploring tide pools. Interpretive programs highlight marine ecology and the park's coastal defense history, making it a scenic and educational destination.

☐ 🔖 ♡ **Brenton Point State Park**: Situated along Newport's Ocean Drive, Brenton Point offers sweeping views where Narragansett Bay meets the Atlantic. Once a grand estate, the park now features open fields, seaside trails, and picnic spots perfect for kite flying, birdwatching, and fishing. The Portuguese Discovery Monument adds cultural depth to this spectacular coastal setting.

☐ 🔖 ♡ **Burlingame State Park**: Located in the southwestern part of the state, Burlingame State Park offers a blend of woodlands and freshwater lakes, including Watchaug Pond. It's a popular spot for fishing, boating, hiking, and camping. Visitors can explore its scenic trails, enjoy picnicking, or unwind by the lake in this peaceful natural setting.

☐ 🔖 ♡ **Colt State Park**: Situated in Bristol along the scenic Narragansett Bay, Colt State Park offers beautiful views, picnic areas, and walking paths. The park's open fields, waterfront, and historic features make it a great location for hiking, cycling, and enjoying outdoor events. It's also a popular spot for weddings and gatherings with its picturesque landscapes.

☐ 🔖 ♡ **Fishermen's Memorial State Park**: Located in Narragansett, this park offers camping facilities, picnicking areas, and easy access to the beach. The park is near Point Judith Pond, ideal for fishing, swimming, and boating. It's a family-friendly park that provides a great spot for outdoor recreation and waterfront activities.

☐ 🔖 ♡ **Fort Adams State Park**: Located at the entrance to Newport Harbor, Fort Adams State Park is famous for its historic fortifications and stunning harbor views. Visitors can explore the fort, hike along its trails, picnic on the waterfront, and participate in various recreational activities. The park also hosts the annual Newport Jazz Festival and other events.

☐ 🔖 ♡ **Fort Wetherill State Park**: Perched on high granite cliffs in Jamestown, Fort Wetherill combines panoramic bay views with military history. The former coastal defense site features old fortifications, hiking trails, and picnic areas. It's also a premier scuba diving and fishing destination, offering rich marine life and dramatic underwater landscapes for adventurous visitors.

☐ 🔖 ♡ **Goddard Memorial State Park**: Situated in Warwick, Goddard Memorial State Park is known for its expansive grounds and scenic views of Greenwich Cove. It offers a variety of outdoor activities, including picnicking, hiking, horseback riding, and golfing. The park's peaceful atmosphere and historic features make it a great place to relax and enjoy nature.

☐ 🔖 ♡ **Haines Memorial State Park**: Located in Barrington, Haines Memorial State Park features scenic views of Narragansett Bay and a peaceful environment for outdoor recreation. Visitors can enjoy walking along the park's trails, have a picnic, or take in views of the bay, making it an ideal spot for a quiet day of relaxation by the water.

☐ 🔖 ♡ **Lincoln Woods State Park**: Located in Lincoln, this park features a 100-acre freshwater pond, popular for fishing, swimming, and boating. Visitors can enjoy hiking, picnicking, and cross-country skiing in the winter. With its scenic woodlands and open fields, it's a versatile park for year-round outdoor recreation.

☐ 🔖 ♡ **Pulaski State Park and Recreational Area**: Nestled in Glocester within the George Washington Management Area, Pulaski State Park offers a mix of forested trails, ponds, and open spaces for recreation. Popular for swimming at Peck Pond, the park also provides fishing, canoeing, hiking, and picnicking. With its family-friendly facilities and quiet woodland setting, it's a classic Rhode Island outdoor escape.

☐ 🔖 ♡ **Rocky Point State Park**: Located in Warwick, this park is a former amusement park turned into a natural space for outdoor activities. Visitors can hike along its scenic trails, enjoy a picnic by the water, or take in beautiful views of Narragansett Bay. The park offers a peaceful retreat with remnants of its amusement park history, making it a unique spot.

RHODE ISLAND

☐ 🔖 ♡ **Snake Den State Park**: Spanning over 700 acres in Johnston, Snake Den remains largely undeveloped, offering woodlands, fields, and trails for walking and nature observation. The park includes historic Dame Farm, showcasing traditional agriculture. With its quiet, rustic setting, Snake Den provides a glimpse into Rhode Island's natural and cultural heritage away from busier parks.

National Parks

☐ 🔖 ♡ **Blackstone River Valley National Historical Park**: Spanning Rhode Island and Massachusetts, this park preserves the birthplace of America's Industrial Revolution. Visitors can tour historic textile mills, walk canal paths, and learn how the Blackstone River powered 19th-century innovation. Interpretive sites and exhibits showcase the region's lasting impact on U.S. industry and culture.

☐ 🔖 ♡ **Roger Williams National Memorial**: Located in downtown Providence, this memorial honors Roger Williams, founder of Rhode Island and advocate of religious freedom. The landscaped grounds and visitor center highlight his legacy of liberty and tolerance, offering exhibits, programs, and a tranquil green space where visitors can reflect on Williams' role in shaping American democracy.

State & National Forests

☐ 🔖 ♡ **George Washington Memorial State Forest**: Established in 1932 near Chepachet, this 4,000-acre forest anchors the George Washington Management Area. It features hardwoods, pine groves, and a 100-acre primitive campground. Managed for wildlife habitat, forestry, and recreation, it offers hiking, fishing, hunting, and camping in a rustic, scenic setting.

☐ 🔖 ♡ **Wickaboxet State Forest**: Located in Kent County, this upland forest covers hardwood and pine stands interlaced with streams and ridges. Overseen by RIDEM, it's managed for habitat, forestry, and public enjoyment. Visitors can explore its quiet trails for hiking and birdwatching, or take part in seasonal hunting in a serene, natural setting.

National Scenic Byways & All-American Roads

☐ 🔖 ♡ **Ocean Drive:** A famed 10-mile loop around Newport, Ocean Drive blends dramatic Atlantic coastline, historic mansions, and sweeping vistas of Narragansett Bay. Visitors enjoy beaches, sailing views, and open parkland. Highlights include Brenton Point State Park, rocky shores, and breathtaking sunsets, making it one of New England's most iconic coastal drives.

☐ 🔖 ♡ **Revolutionary Heritage Byway:** Running through historic Bristol, this byway showcases colonial architecture, waterfront parks, and the nation's oldest continuous Fourth of July celebration site. The route links museums, churches, and tree-lined streets with Narragansett Bay views, offering travelers an intimate journey through Rhode Island's Revolutionary-era legacy.

State Scenic Byways

☐ 🔖 ♡ **Ten Mile River Greenway Scenic Byway:** This 3-mile greenway in East Providence follows the Ten Mile River through woodlands, wetlands, and historic landscapes. The paved path connects Slater Park to Kimberly Rock fields, offering river views, bridges, and birdlife. Cyclists and walkers can explore a peaceful stretch of Rhode Island that links recreation with industrial history in a quiet, scenic setting.

☐ 🔖 ♡ **Woonasquatucket River Greenway Scenic Byway:** Beginning in downtown Providence, this greenway extends along the Woonasquatucket River through parks, historic mills, and restored natural areas toward Johnston. The route highlights cultural landmarks, public art, and wildlife habitats. Travelers experience a unique blend of urban vitality and natural beauty while following one of the state's revitalized waterways.

RHODE ISLAND

National Natural Landmarks

Ell Pond: Tucked between rugged granitic monadnocks, this glacial kettle hole is encircled by a swamp of red maple and Atlantic white cedar. Its steep terrain creates a striking contrast of wetland and dry upland habitats, supporting both hydrophytic and xeric plants. This unusual overlap of ecosystems makes Ell Pond a botanically rich site and a natural laboratory for ecological study.
GPS: 41.505331, -71.782908

SOUTH CAROLINA

South Carolina's natural beauty ranges from Blue Ridge Mountain peaks and rushing waterfalls to coastal wetlands and sun-drenched beaches. Through its inviting state parks, national forests, national park sites, and remarkable natural landmarks, South Carolina offers rich outdoor experiences.

📅 Peak Season
March–May and September–November are South Carolina's peak seasons, offering warm, comfortable weather and blooming or colorful landscapes. These months are ideal for exploring beaches, gardens, and mountain trails.

📅 Offseason Months
June–August brings high heat and humidity, though beaches remain popular. December–February is cooler and quieter, with mild coastal temperatures and occasional mountain snow.

🍃 Scenery & Nature Timing
Spring brings azaleas, dogwoods, and lush greenery. Summer highlights beaches, cypress swamps, and boating. Fall offers vivid mountain foliage, while winter provides mild hiking conditions and migratory bird activity along the coast.

✨ Special
South Carolina features the Blue Ridge foothills, the blackwater swamps of Congaree National Park, and the barrier islands of the Lowcountry. The shifting dunes of Hunting Island, ancient maritime forests, and phosphorescent tidal waters reveal its diverse natural beauty.

SOUTH CAROLINA

State Parks

☐ 🔖 ♡ **Aiken State Park:** Nestled along the Edisto River, Aiken State Park is a peaceful retreat of wetlands, forests, and scenic waterways. Visitors can paddle the river, fish its quiet banks, or explore shady trails teeming with wildlife. Picnic areas invite families to linger, while the park's natural beauty offers a serene escape from daily life, making it a favorite spot for outdoor enthusiasts in South Carolina.

☐ 🔖 ♡ **Andrew Jackson State Park:** This Lancaster County park honors President Andrew Jackson, who was born nearby. A museum highlights his life and times, while scenic trails, a fishing lake, and picnic grounds create opportunities for relaxation and recreation. History buffs enjoy the cultural exhibits, and families appreciate the combination of heritage, outdoor activities, and tranquil settings in one inviting destination.

☐ 🔖 ♡ **Baker Creek State Park:** Stretching along Lake Thurmond, Baker Creek State Park offers fishing, boating, camping, and miles of forested hiking trails. Its lakeside setting draws visitors for kayaking or quiet shoreline walks, while the wooded interior provides birdwatching and wildlife spotting opportunities. Popular with families and outdoor adventurers alike, it's an ideal year-round destination for relaxation and recreation.

☐ 🔖 ♡ **Barnwell State Park:** Built by the CCC in the 1930s, this Barnwell County park is home to three peaceful lakes that invite fishing, paddling, and lakeside picnics. Surrounded by pine and hardwood forests, it provides a quiet escape into nature. Trails wind through woodlands rich with wildlife, offering visitors a chance to slow down, explore, and enjoy a nostalgic glimpse into South Carolina's conservation history.

☐ 🔖 ♡ **Caesars Head State Park:** Perched high in the Blue Ridge Mountains, Caesars Head offers breathtaking panoramic views and rugged hiking trails. It anchors the Mountain Bridge Wilderness, with paths leading to waterfalls, overlooks, and wildlife habitats. Known for raptor migrations, it's a top birdwatching site. The park's dramatic cliffs and sweeping vistas make it one of the most iconic outdoor destinations in South Carolina.

☐ 🔖 ♡ **Calhoun Falls State Park:** Nestled on the shores of Lake Russell, this park blends water recreation with scenic relaxation. Visitors can boat, fish, or camp along wooded peninsulas with stunning lake views. Trails invite exploration of the shoreline, while playgrounds and picnic spots cater to families. With its peaceful setting and variety of activities, Calhoun Falls is a beloved retreat for all ages year-round.

☐ 🔖 ♡ **Cheraw State Park:** One of South Carolina's oldest parks, Cheraw sits along the Great Pee Dee River and features diverse habitats for hiking, fishing, and wildlife watching. It is home to an 18-hole championship golf course and a large lake for boating. The park's blend of recreation and scenic beauty makes it a unique destination, offering both outdoor adventure and quiet riverfront relaxation in a historic setting.

☐ 🔖 ♡ **Chester State Park:** Centered around a 160-acre lake, this Chester County park offers fishing, boating, and kayaking in a scenic woodland setting. Trails loop through forests rich with wildlife, while picnic shelters provide gathering spots for families. With its peaceful atmosphere, abundant natural beauty, and convenient amenities, the park is an ideal location for outdoor enthusiasts seeking both recreation and quiet relaxation.

☐ 🔖 ♡ **Colleton State Park:** Small but scenic, Colleton lies along the Edisto River and is a favorite for canoeing, kayaking, and fishing. Towering trees shade trails and picnic areas, while wildlife thrives in the park's wetlands and forests. A gateway to the Edisto River Canoe Trail, it's a hub for paddlers exploring South Carolina's longest free-flowing blackwater river, offering a serene place for nature appreciation and adventure.

☐ 🔖 ♡ **Croft State Park:** Once a World War II Army training base, this 7,000-acre Spartanburg County park is now a haven for recreation. It features over 20 miles of trails for hiking, biking, and horseback riding, plus lakes for fishing and boating. Diverse landscapes—from rolling hills to hardwood forests—support abundant wildlife. With its rich history and variety of activities, Croft is one of the state's largest and most versatile parks.

☐ 🔖 ♡ **Devils Fork State Park:** Nestled on Lake Jocassee in the Blue Ridge foothills, Devils Fork is prized for its crystal-clear waters, mountain scenery, and hidden waterfalls. Visitors enjoy boating, fishing, swimming, and diving in one of the state's most pristine lakes. Campsites and villas provide overnight stays, while trails wind through forests and wildflower meadows. Its beauty makes it a jewel of the South Carolina park system.

UNITED STATES EDITION

SOUTH CAROLINA

☐ 🔖 ♡ **Dreher Island State Park:** Spread across three islands on Lake Murray, Dreher Island offers boating, fishing, and camping in a picturesque setting. The park's trails lead through forests and along shorelines, perfect for hiking or birdwatching. Anglers prize the lake for bass fishing, while families enjoy picnics and swimming. With scenic lake views and ample space for recreation, it's a popular destination for water and land lovers alike.

☐ 🔖 ♡ **Edisto Beach State Park:** A coastal gem, Edisto Beach offers access to sandy beaches, maritime forests, and salt marshes along the Atlantic. The park is known for its biodiversity, with birdwatching, fishing, and crabbing opportunities. Trails weave through forests and marshlands, providing glimpses of native plants and wildlife. With campsites near the ocean and a relaxed seaside atmosphere, it's a favorite destination for families and nature enthusiasts.

☐ 🔖 ♡ **Givhans Ferry State Park:** Along the winding Edisto River, Givhans Ferry offers canoeing, fishing, and camping in a serene setting. Trails lead through hardwood forests rich with wildlife, while sandy banks provide peaceful river views. It's a quieter alternative to busier parks, perfect for paddlers and birdwatchers seeking tranquility. The park's CCC-built structures also add historic charm, blending natural beauty with South Carolina's cultural heritage.

☐ 🔖 ♡ **Goodale State Park:** Located near Camden, Goodale features a 30-acre lake ideal for fishing, kayaking, and canoeing. Its peaceful surroundings include cypress trees, wetlands, and shaded picnic areas, offering visitors both recreation and relaxation. Trails loop through woodlands filled with wildlife, creating a natural escape close to town. Known for its quiet charm and accessible amenities, it's a hidden gem for families and outdoor enthusiasts.

☐ 🔖 ♡ **Hamilton Branch State Park:** On a wooded peninsula of Lake Thurmond, Hamilton Branch offers boating, fishing, and camping with stunning water views. Spacious sites stretch along the shoreline, providing easy lake access. Visitors enjoy hiking, picnicking, and wildlife watching in a peaceful, forested setting. Its combination of recreation and scenery makes it a favorite for families, anglers, and outdoor enthusiasts year-round.

☐ 🔖 ♡ **Hickory Knob State Resort Park:** South Carolina's only resort state park, Hickory Knob sits on Lake Thurmond and blends recreation with comfort. Amenities include an 18-hole golf course, lodge, cabins, and a restaurant. Guests can hike, fish, or boat while enjoying resort-style lodging. The park's mix of lakeside relaxation, wooded trails, and full-service accommodations makes it a unique destination for both leisure and adventure.

☐ 🔖 ♡ **Hunting Island State Park:** This barrier island is one of South Carolina's most popular parks, known for five miles of unspoiled beaches, marshes, and maritime forest. Visitors explore nature trails, camp near the ocean, or climb the historic lighthouse for sweeping Atlantic views. Wildlife abounds, from seabirds to deer. Its natural beauty and coastal charm make it a top destination for relaxation, photography, and family vacations.

☐ 🔖 ♡ **Huntington Beach State Park:** A premier coastal destination, this park combines beaches, salt marshes, and freshwater lagoons with rich wildlife. Birdwatchers flock here to see migratory species, while history lovers tour Atalaya Castle, the Moorish-style home of Archer and Anna Hyatt Huntington. With trails, fishing, and camping, the park offers a blend of natural wonders and cultural intrigue along South Carolina's scenic coast.

☐ 🔖 ♡ **Jones Gap State Park:** Set in the Blue Ridge Mountains, Jones Gap features rugged trails, cascading waterfalls, and the clear Middle Saluda River. It offers some of the state's best hiking, with paths linking to Caesars Head in the Mountain Bridge Wilderness. Anglers enjoy trout fishing, while naturalists explore pristine habitats. Remote and breathtaking, the park attracts hikers and adventurers seeking dramatic scenery and solitude.

☐ 🔖 ♡ **Keowee-Toxaway State Park:** Nestled on Lake Keowee in the foothills of the Blue Ridge, this park is prized for its clear waters and mountain views. Boating, fishing, and kayaking are popular, while hiking trails showcase wildflowers and scenic overlooks. Campsites and cabins invite overnight stays. Its mix of lakefront recreation and upland beauty makes it a favorite for nature lovers exploring South Carolina's Upstate region.

SOUTH CAROLINA

☐ 🔖 ♡ **Kings Mountain State Park:** Adjacent to the historic battlefield, this park offers a rich mix of history and recreation. Visitors explore a living history farm, hike or horseback ride on miles of trails, and fish in two lakes. Camping and picnicking are popular among families. With cultural heritage, scenic woodlands, and ties to Revolutionary War history, it provides both educational experiences and outdoor enjoyment.

☐ 🔖 ♡ **Lake Greenwood State Park:** On the shores of Lake Greenwood, this park offers boating, fishing, and picnicking amid peaceful scenery. Campers enjoy lakefront sites, while trails wind through woodlands filled with wildlife. Known for hosting the annual Festival of Flowers Triathlon, it's a hub for recreation and community events. With its balance of natural beauty and family-friendly amenities, the park is a versatile year-round destination.

☐ 🔖 ♡ **Lake Hartwell State Park:** Stretching along the South Carolina–Georgia border, this park provides access to Lake Hartwell, one of the Southeast's largest reservoirs. Visitors enjoy boating, fishing, and swimming, while campsites and cabins offer overnight stays. Trails and picnic areas provide land-based recreation. With scenic lake views and abundant wildlife, it's a gateway to outdoor adventure and a popular base for exploring the Upstate.

☐ 🔖 ♡ **Lake Warren State Park:** Located in Hampton County, this park centers around a 200-acre lake ideal for fishing and boating. Surrounded by woodlands, it offers hiking trails, wildlife viewing, and picnic spots. Its quiet atmosphere makes it a peaceful getaway, far from crowds. Families enjoy playgrounds and open space, while anglers prize its waters. A charming retreat, it highlights South Carolina's rural beauty and relaxed pace.

☐ 🔖 ♡ **Lake Wateree State Park:** A favorite for boating and fishing, Lake Wateree State Park provides access to one of the state's largest reservoirs. Campsites and picnic areas line the scenic shoreline, offering families plenty of space for relaxation. Trails lead through surrounding forests rich with wildlife. With water recreation and woodland charm, the park is ideal for those seeking a blend of activity and tranquility in nature.

☐ 🔖 ♡ **Landsford Canal State Park:** Preserving a historic 19th-century canal on the Catawba River, this park combines cultural heritage with natural wonders. Each spring, its shoals bloom with one of the world's largest populations of rocky shoals spider lilies, drawing nature lovers from afar. Trails follow the canal's remains and riverbanks, providing scenic walks and wildlife observation. It's a destination where history and wild beauty converge.

☐ 🔖 ♡ **Lee State Park:** Built by the CCC during the Great Depression, Lee State Park protects hardwood bottomlands along the Lynches River. Visitors enjoy fishing, horseback riding, and hiking through diverse habitats, while artesian wells offer cool drinking water. The park is also home to rich wildlife and birdlife. Combining history, recreation, and ecological diversity, it remains a peaceful, family-friendly destination in the Sandhills region.

☐ 🔖 ♡ **Little Pee Dee State Park:** Along the quiet Little Pee Dee River, this park provides opportunities for fishing, canoeing, and camping. Its centerpiece is Lake Norton, surrounded by pine forests and cypress trees. Trails and picnic areas invite relaxation, while birdwatchers enjoy spotting diverse species. Known for its tranquility and natural beauty, it's a hidden gem offering simple outdoor pleasures in a peaceful, rural setting.

☐ 🔖 ♡ **May Forest State Park:** A small urban retreat in Charleston, May Forest offers walking trails, shaded woodlands, and wildlife observation close to the city. It provides a peaceful green space for locals seeking a quiet escape from urban life. With its forested landscapes and accessible amenities, the park is ideal for nature walks, picnics, or simply enjoying the outdoors without leaving the metropolitan area.

☐ 🔖 ♡ **Myrtle Beach State Park:** Set along one of America's busiest coastlines, this park preserves a stretch of maritime forest and sandy beach. Families enjoy swimming, fishing from the pier, or exploring nature trails through shaded woodlands. Campsites lie just steps from the ocean, creating a rare mix of seclusion and convenience. It's a beloved destination for vacations, offering both natural beauty and classic seaside recreation.

SOUTH CAROLINA

☐ 🔖 ♡ **Oconee State Park:** Nestled in the Blue Ridge Mountains, Oconee State Park blends rugged scenery with family-friendly amenities. Visitors hike trails to waterfalls, fish in the clear park lake, or camp beneath tall pines. Rustic cabins built by the CCC add charm and history. With mountain views, cool streams, and easy access to nearby Sumter National Forest, it's a gateway to outdoor adventure in South Carolina's Upstate.

☐ 🔖 ♡ **Paris Mountain State Park:** Just minutes from Greenville, this historic park offers trails for hiking and biking, plus a lake for swimming, fishing, and paddling. Once a city reservoir, it now provides wooded escapes and scenic views for locals and visitors alike. Its mix of outdoor recreation, picnic spots, and convenient access makes it a popular destination, offering both quick getaways and deeper exploration of nature.

☐ 🔖 ♡ **Poinsett State Park:** In the High Hills of Santee, Poinsett features diverse ecosystems where mountain hardwoods meet coastal wetlands. Visitors hike and bike through forests, fish in the lake, or explore scenic streams. Rich in history, the park showcases CCC craftsmanship in stone bridges and shelters. Its unique blend of habitats and cultural features make it a fascinating destination for naturalists and outdoor explorers alike.

☐ 🔖 ♡ **Sadlers Creek State Park:** Located on a wooded peninsula in Lake Hartwell, this park offers boating, fishing, camping, and hiking with wide water views. Trails wind through shady forests, while campsites provide lake access for anglers and swimmers. Wildlife is abundant, from deer to waterfowl. Known for its peaceful setting and family-friendly facilities, it's an inviting spot for relaxation and outdoor recreation on the Upstate's largest lake.

☐ 🔖 ♡ **Santee State Park:** Situated on Lake Marion, one of South Carolina's largest lakes, this park is a hub for boating, fishing, and camping. Visitors can rent unique over-the-water cabins, hike scenic trails, or watch abundant birdlife along the shoreline. Its combination of modern facilities and natural beauty draws anglers, families, and vacationers alike, making it one of the most popular recreational destinations in the state.

☐ 🔖 ♡ **Sesquicentennial State Park:** Known locally as "Sesqui," this Columbia park is a favorite green space for families. A 30-acre lake provides fishing, canoeing, and kayaking, while miles of trails are popular for hiking, biking, and jogging. Picnic shelters, playgrounds, and open fields make it ideal for gatherings. With its natural scenery in an urban setting, it offers a quiet, accessible retreat just minutes from the state capital.

☐ 🔖 ♡ **Table Rock State Park:** Dominated by its namesake granite monolith, this iconic Blue Ridge park offers some of South Carolina's most challenging and rewarding hikes. Trails climb to sweeping mountain vistas and cascade past waterfalls. Visitors also enjoy fishing, camping, and swimming in the clear park lake. With CCC-built cabins and picnic shelters, it blends rugged beauty, rich history, and modern amenities for a complete mountain getaway.

☐ 🔖 ♡ **Woods Bay State Park:** Located near Olanta, this 1,590-acre park preserves one of the last large Carolina bays—mysterious, oval wetlands unique to the Atlantic Coastal Plain. Visitors can explore a boardwalk through cypress-tupelo swamps, hike trails through sandhills and bogs, and enjoy birdwatching with over 100 species recorded. Alligators, carnivorous plants, and diverse habitats make it a fascinating natural retreat.

National Parks

 ☐ 🔖 ♡ **Charles Pinckney National Historic Site:** Near Mount Pleasant, this site preserves part of the plantation of Charles Pinckney, a signer of the U.S. Constitution and influential statesman. Visitors explore the historic house, walk shaded trails, and learn about his political career, plantation life, and the enslaved people who lived here. It offers insight into the early foundations of American democracy.

 ☐ 🔖 ♡ **Congaree National Park:** South Carolina's only national park protects one of the largest intact old-growth bottomland hardwood forests in the U.S. Visitors paddle through swampy waterways, hike boardwalks beneath towering champion trees, and witness incredible biodiversity. The park teems with wildlife and offers a glimpse into rare ecosystems, making it a must-visit destination for outdoor enthusiasts and nature lovers.

SOUTH CAROLINA

 ☐ 🔖 ♡ **Cowpens National Battlefield:** In Gaffney, this battlefield marks a decisive 1781 Revolutionary War victory that turned the tide in the South. Visitors can walk the fields where Daniel Morgan's troops defeated the British, tour the visitor center, and follow interpretive trails. Blending history with scenic landscapes, the site brings to life a key moment in America's fight for independence.

 ☐ 🔖 ♡ **Fort Sumter and Fort Moultrie National Historical Park:** In Charleston Harbor, this park preserves two forts tied to America's military past. Fort Sumter is famed as the site where the Civil War began, while Fort Moultrie chronicles 171 years of coastal defense history. Visitors reach Sumter by boat, explore exhibits, and learn how these strongholds shaped pivotal chapters of U.S. history.

 ☐ 🔖 ♡ **Kings Mountain National Military Park:** Near Blacksburg, this park honors the 1780 Patriot victory at Kings Mountain, often called a turning point of the Revolutionary War. A trail loops around the battlefield, with monuments marking key spots. Visitors learn about the fierce clash that weakened British control in the South, making this site both a solemn memorial and a scenic hiking destination.

 ☐ 🔖 ♡ **Ninety-Six National Historic Site:** Preserving a Revolutionary War battlefield in Greenwood County, Ninety-Six recalls the 1781 siege of Fort Ninety-Six, one of the war's longest. Trails lead past earthworks, reconstructed defenses, and interpretive exhibits. Visitors discover how this small backcountry town played an outsized role in America's fight for independence and the struggle for control of the South.

 ☐ 🔖 ♡ **Reconstruction Era National Historical Park:** Located in Beaufort, this park highlights the transformative years following the Civil War. Visitors can explore historic sites like the Penn Center, among the first schools for freed slaves, and learn about political, social, and cultural change during this era. It provides powerful insight into the challenges and progress of rebuilding the nation after emancipation.

State & National Forests

☐ 🔖 ♡ **Francis Marion National Forest:** Located near Charleston, this 258,000-acre coastal forest features cypress-tupelo swamps, pine ridges, and Carolina bays. It includes seaside trails, canoe and paddle access, nine rifle ranges, four OHV trails, campgrounds, mountain biking, hunting, and fishing—reflecting diverse ecosystems from salt marsh to upland pine.

☐ 🔖 ♡ **Harbison State Forest:** A 2,177-acre urban woodland next to the Broad River near Columbia. One of the largest greenspaces inside an eastern U.S. city, it combines pine-hardwood woodlands with open meadows. Managed for public access, education, sustainable timber, and wildlife habitat; includes trails, ponds, and birdwatching.

☐ 🔖 ♡ **Manchester State Forest:** Spanning 28,675 acres in Clarendon and Sumter counties, Manchester protects oak-pine woods along the Wateree River region. Established in 1949, it supports sustainable timber, wildlife habitat, and recreation—including the High Hills of Santee Passage of the Palmetto Trail (11.4 miles), hunting, fishing, horseback riding, and hiking.

☐ 🔖 ♡ **Poe Creek State Forest:** A 6,200-acre mixed hardwood and pine tract in Pickens County's foothills. Managed by SC Forestry Commission for watershed protection, wildlife habitat, sustainable timber, and fire control. Provides low-impact recreation like hiking, wildlife viewing, and seasonal hunting in the Upstate's upland woodlands.

☐ 🔖 ♡ **Sand Hills State Forest:** A 15,800-acre inland longleaf pine plantation and working forest in Chesterfield County. Managed by SC Forestry Commission, it features sandhill ridges, restored wiregrass ecosystems, timber production, prescribed burning, greatly improved habitat for red-cockaded woodpeckers, and offers hunting, hiking, and birdwatching trails.

☐ 🔖 ♡ **Sumter National Forest:** Covering about 370,900 acres across central and western SC, Sumter spans Enoree, Long Cane, and Andrew Pickens districts. Preserves Appalachian foothills, wild rivers (Chattooga, Chauga), waterfalls, and mountain ridges. Offers hiking, biking, OHV, horseback riding, hunting, fishing, canoeing, and national wilderness areas.

SOUTH CAROLINA

☐ 🔖 ♡ **Wee Tee State Forest:** Located in Georgetown County, this 12,000-acre bottomland hardwood and pine area protects floodplain and wetland habitats along the Waccamaw River. Managed for sustainable forestry, water-quality protection, and habitat. It offers hunting, birding, and fishing in a serene Lowcountry riverine landscape.

National Scenic Byways & All-American Roads

☐ 🔖 ♡ **Ashley River Road:** Shaded by live oaks draped in Spanish moss, this corridor along SC-61 threads the historic Ashley River plantation district near Charleston. The drive links landmark sites like Drayton Hall, Magnolia, and Middleton Place, with views of marsh, rice-field remnants, and blackwater creeks. It's a compact route where Lowcountry scenery and layered colonial and Gullah Geechee history meet.

☐ 🔖 ♡ **Cherokee Foothills Scenic Highway:** Tracing the old Cherokee path beneath the Blue Ridge escarpment, SC-11 sweeps past peach orchards, lakes, and gateway parks such as Table Rock, Caesars Head, and Oconee. Pull-offs reveal waterfalls and granite domes; side roads lead to trout streams and the Chattooga Wild & Scenic River. Small towns, farm stands, and Revolutionary War sites add texture to this classic mountain-edge drive.

☐ 🔖 ♡ **Edisto Island National Scenic Byway:** Following SC-174 across tidal creeks and salt marsh to the Atlantic, this route showcases barrier-island life at an unhurried pace. Maritime forests of live oak and palmetto frame views of shrimp docks, historic churches, and roadside produce stands. It culminates at wide, quiet sands in Edisto Beach State Park, where dolphins cruise offshore and shorebirds work the flats—pure Lowcountry from river to sea.

☐ 🔖 ♡ **Savannah River Scenic Byway:** Winding through the state's western tier near the Georgia line, this route skirts lakes Hartwell, Russell, and Thurmond while shadowing the Savannah River. Expect pine ridges, quiet coves, mill towns, and turnoffs into Revolutionary War history. Anglers, paddlers, and birders find plentiful stops; scenic overlooks and small museums tell the story of the border country's forests, waterways, and communities.

State Scenic Byways

☐ 🔖 ♡ **Bohicket Road Scenic Highway:** Lined with centuries-old live oaks draped in Spanish moss, this corridor runs between Johns and Kiawah Islands. The shaded avenue evokes the romance of the Lowcountry while passing tidal marshes and historic churches. It is one of the most photographed roads in South Carolina, offering both cultural heritage and natural beauty on a short but memorable drive.

☐ 🔖 ♡ **Cowpens Battlefield Scenic Byway:** This byway leads to Cowpens National Battlefield, site of a pivotal Revolutionary War victory in 1781. Rolling pastures and wooded hills surround the route, creating a landscape similar to what Patriot and British troops once marched through. Visitors find interpretive stops, trails, and sweeping views that blend history with rural tranquility.

☐ 🔖 ♡ **Edisto Beach Scenic Highway:** Following SC-174, this route crosses tidal creeks and salt marshes to reach Edisto Island and its unspoiled beaches. Maritime forests and small rural communities provide a glimpse of coastal life untouched by heavy development. The highway ends at Edisto Beach State Park, where broad sands and abundant wildlife highlight the quiet charm of the Lowcountry coast.

☐ 🔖 ♡ **Falling Waters Scenic Byway:** Running along SC-107 through Oconee County, this mountain road climbs into Sumter National Forest and toward the North Carolina border. Visitors encounter high-elevation forests, waterfall trails, and scenic overlooks with far-reaching views. Known for brilliant fall colors and tranquil mountain settings, it offers one of the Upstate's most dramatic drives.

☐ 🔖 ♡ **Fort Johnson Road Scenic Highway:** Located on James Island near Charleston Harbor, this byway passes historic Fort Johnson, where the first Civil War shot was fired. Marsh views, old live oaks, and waterfront glimpses accompany the drive. It provides a mix of coastal scenery and historical resonance, offering travelers a short but significant connection to Charleston's past.

☐ 🔖 ♡ **Hilton Head Scenic Highway:** Approaching Hilton Head Island along US-278, this byway showcases sweeping marshes, tidal rivers, and broad Lowcountry horizons. The drive builds anticipation for reaching one of the state's premier resort islands. Along the corridor, travelers glimpse pine forests, creeks, and cultural reminders of the Gullah community that has long shaped the region.

SOUTH CAROLINA

☐ ▢ ♡ **Hilton Head Island Scenic Highway:** Once on Hilton Head, this designated route links shaded maritime forests, residential enclaves, and resort areas with preserved natural spaces. Bike paths and causeways highlight the island's integration of nature and development. With stops at beaches, cultural landmarks, and marsh overlooks, the byway offers a balanced portrait of island life.

☐ ▢ ♡ **Long Point Road Scenic Highway:** Near Mount Pleasant, this short byway meanders through forest, creeks, and marshy landscapes before connecting to plantations and historic sites. Quiet and lesser known, it highlights the subtler scenery of the Lowcountry, where waterways and wooded corridors create a peaceful transition between town and countryside.

☐ ▢ ♡ **Mathis Ferry Road Scenic Highway:** Winding along the Cooper River near Mount Pleasant, this shaded corridor is framed by ancient oaks and views of tidal marsh. The byway preserves a sense of Old South character within a rapidly growing region. Historic homes, churches, and cultural markers line the road, offering a glimpse into Charleston's heritage as well as natural beauty.

☐ ▢ ♡ **May River Scenic Byway:** Stretching along SC-46 between Hardeeville and Bluffton, this route is celebrated for live oak canopies, historic churches, and marsh vistas. The byway captures the essence of the Lowcountry, with roadside produce stands and access to Bluffton's riverfront. It reflects a landscape where small-town charm and coastal ecology coexist gracefully.

☐ ▢ ♡ **McTeer Bridge and Causeways Scenic Highway:** Crossing into Beaufort County, this byway traverses the McTeer Bridge and surrounding causeways, revealing sweeping views of salt marshes, tidal creeks, and distant islands. The blend of water and sky creates a classic coastal panorama. It highlights both natural splendor and the region's unique geography shaped by rivers and inlets.

☐ ▢ ♡ **Old Sheldon Church Road Scenic Byway:** Near Yemassee, this atmospheric drive leads through oak-shaded lanes to the ruins of Old Sheldon Church. Burned during the Revolutionary and Civil Wars, the roofless brick columns now stand as solemn reminders of history. Surrounded by forest and farmland, the route combines haunting beauty with quiet rural scenery.

☐ ▢ ♡ **Plantersville Scenic Byway:** This Pee Dee region route winds past fields, churches, and plantation sites tied to rice culture and Gullah heritage. The byway offers glimpses of cypress swamps, moss-draped oaks, and traditional rural communities. Interpretive markers highlight the region's agricultural legacy, while today's quiet landscapes invite reflection on centuries of history.

☐ ▢ ♡ **Riverland Drive Scenic Highway:** On James Island, this byway skirts the Stono River and marshes, with shady oaks forming a green tunnel overhead. The corridor combines natural scenery with a lived-in Lowcountry character—waterfront homes, docks, and churches dotting the roadside. It's a tranquil reminder of Charleston's river-bound setting.

☐ ▢ ♡ **SC 170 Scenic Highway:** Running through Beaufort County, this byway links tidal marshes, rivers, and maritime forests between Okatie and Beaufort. It provides expansive views of waterways and wetlands, along with access to fishing spots and nature preserves. Travelers see the Lowcountry's landscape at its most open, with broad horizons and abundant wildlife.

☐ ▢ ♡ **US 21 Scenic Highway:** This corridor runs from Beaufort inland through farmlands, pine forests, and historic communities. Once part of a major coastal route, today it reveals the quieter side of South Carolina's countryside. Along the way, travelers pass churches, fields, and small towns, with views that reflect the enduring rhythm of the rural Lowcountry.

☐ ▢ ♡ **Western York Scenic Byway:** Located north of Rock Hill, this byway rolls through the Piedmont's patchwork of farmland, forests, and small communities. Scenic ridges, historic churches, and Revolutionary War sites highlight the region's past. It is a drive that connects South Carolina's heritage with the quiet beauty of its western uplands.

UNITED STATES EDITION

SOUTH CAROLINA

National Natural Landmarks

 ☐ 🔖 ♡ **Congaree River Swamp:** Standing as one of the nation's great floodplain forests, this site was named a National Natural Landmark for containing the largest tract of old-growth cypress–gum swamp and bottomland hardwood in the United States. Its towering trees, intact hydrology, and rich biodiversity illustrate the primeval wetlands of the Southeast.
GPS: 33.7833, -80.7833

 ☐ 🔖 ♡ **Flat Creek Natural Area and 40 Acre Rock:** Atop South Carolina's Piedmont, this landmark was designated a National Natural Landmark for showcasing the largest undisturbed granitic flat-rock outcrop in the region. Its thin soils host rare lichens, mosses, and specialized plants, while the massive Flat Creek Dike underscores its geological importance.
GPS: 34.6689, -80.5272

 ☐ 🔖 ♡ **Francis Beidler Forest:** Deep in the coastal plain, this forest received National Natural Landmark recognition for preserving one of the country's largest remaining virgin stands of bald cypress and tupelo gum. With centuries-old trees and five distinct community types, it exemplifies the ecological richness of southern swamplands.
GPS: 33.2333, -80.35

 ☐ 🔖 ♡ **John de la Howe Forest:** In the Piedmont, this forest earned National Natural Landmark status for being a rare, long-protected oak–pine woodland. Shielded from fire and logging since 1797, it demonstrates natural forest succession over centuries and offers one of the few intact glimpses of historic upland forest.
GPS: 33.9333, -82.4

 ☐ 🔖 ♡ **St. Phillips Island:** Off South Carolina's coast, this barrier island was designated a National Natural Landmark because of its undisturbed dune ridges, maritime forest, and salt marshes. Largely free from development, it preserves a near-pristine Atlantic ecosystem that is increasingly rare along the seaboard.
GPS: 32.2833, -80.6167

 ☐ 🔖 ♡ **Stevens Creek Natural Area:** Along the Savannah River, this site gained National Natural Landmark status for protecting a Pleistocene relict ecosystem. Here, cool ravines and unique microclimates support an extraordinary mix of northern and southern plant species, making it one of the state's most botanically diverse natural landscapes.
GPS: 33.8442, -82.2242

SOUTH DAKOTA

South Dakota's dramatic landscapes include granite spires, rolling plains, deep canyons, and ancient caves. With state parks, expansive national forests, iconic national parks, and unique natural landmarks, the state delivers awe-inspiring outdoor adventures amid wide skies, sacred lands, and timeless natural beauty.

Peak Season
June–September is South Dakota's peak season, with warm weather, open parks, and long days ideal for sightseeing. Summer draws visitors to the Black Hills, Badlands, and scenic byways across the prairies.

Offseason Months
November–April is the offseason, with cold weather, snow, and lighter visitation. Spring and fall offer mild temperatures and fewer crowds, perfect for quiet outdoor exploration.

Scenery & Nature Timing
Spring brings wildflowers and active wildlife across the plains. Summer highlights green hills, open trails, and warm evenings. Fall colors the forests and grasslands, while winter adds snow to the rugged western landscapes.

Special
South Dakota showcases the eroded spires of Badlands National Park, the granite peaks and caves of the Black Hills, and the mighty Missouri River. The annual bison roundup at Custer State Park, prairie storms, and wide open skies define its wild spirit.

SOUTH DAKOTA

State Parks

☐ 🔖 ♡ **Bear Butte State Park**: Known for its historical and cultural significance to Native American tribes, Bear Butte offers scenic hiking trails leading to the top of the butte, where visitors are rewarded with panoramic views of the surrounding plains. The park also serves as a peaceful space for reflection, making it a popular destination for hikers, spiritual seekers, and nature enthusiasts.

☐ 🔖 ♡ **Custer State Park**: One of South Dakota's most famous parks, Custer State Park is known for its wildlife, including a herd of bison. The park offers hiking, fishing, boating, and scenic drives. Visitors can explore the picturesque Black Hills, enjoy picnicking, or take the Needles Highway to see its unique rock formations.

☐ 🔖 ♡ **Fisher Grove State Park**: Located along the James River, Fisher Grove offers fishing, hiking, and picnicking in a serene environment. This small park is perfect for a quiet retreat, with its large trees and grassy areas providing shade and comfort for visitors. Its historical connection to early settler Frank I. Fisher adds a cultural touch to its natural beauty.

☐ 🔖 ♡ **Fort Sisseton Historic State Park**: This park preserves the remains of a 19th-century military fort, offering a glimpse into South Dakota's frontier history. Visitors can explore historical exhibits, enjoy reenactments, and hike along trails through the park. With its beautiful setting and rich history, it's a must-visit for history buffs and outdoor enthusiasts alike.

☐ 🔖 ♡ **Good Earth State Park at Blood Run**: Established in 2013, this park preserves one of the oldest sites of human habitation in the U.S., once home to Native American trading villages. Overlooking the Big Sioux River near Sioux Falls, it offers scenic hiking trails through woodlands and prairies. Interpretive exhibits highlight its cultural history, blending nature, archaeology, and education.

☐ 🔖 ♡ **Hartford Beach State Park**: Situated along Big Stone Lake, Hartford Beach offers a range of activities, including swimming, fishing, and camping. The park's scenic beauty and peaceful environment make it a great spot for picnics and relaxation. With its access to the lake, it's a favorite for water sports and outdoor recreation throughout the year.

☐ 🔖 ♡ **Lake Herman State Park**: Located near Madison, this 100-acre park is centered around Lake Herman, offering excellent opportunities for fishing and boating. The park also has hiking trails, camping areas, and picnicking spots. It's an ideal location for outdoor activities, with its serene environment and abundant wildlife, making it perfect for nature lovers and families.

☐ 🔖 ♡ **Newton Hills State Park**: Nestled in the eastern part of the state, Newton Hills offers hiking, picnicking, and camping in a scenic woodland setting. The park's rolling hills provide excellent views of the surrounding landscape, and the park's location near Sioux Falls makes it a convenient retreat for both locals and visitors.

☐ 🔖 ♡ **Oakwood Lakes State Park**: This park, situated among eight connected lakes, offers a variety of activities, including fishing, swimming, and hiking. The park's picturesque lakes provide opportunities for picnicking and camping, while its scenic surroundings make it perfect for wildlife observation and leisurely walks, making it an ideal destination for outdoor enthusiasts.

☐ 🔖 ♡ **Palisades State Park**: This park, near Sioux Falls, is known for its dramatic Sioux Quartzite cliffs that rise above the Split Rock Creek. Visitors can hike, picnic, and fish in the park's tranquil environment. The park's picturesque landscapes and the creek's deep gorges make it a favorite for those seeking outdoor beauty and adventure.

☐ 🔖 ♡ **Roy Lake State Park**: Located in northeastern South Dakota, Roy Lake is known for excellent fishing, boating, and swimming opportunities. The park features campgrounds, cabins, and a resort, making it a favorite family destination. Surrounded by wooded landscapes and clear waters, it offers trails, birdwatching, and peaceful settings ideal for relaxation and outdoor recreation year-round.

☐ 🔖 ♡ **Sica Hollow State Park**: Located in the northeastern part of the state, Sica Hollow is known for its unique topography, deep ravines, and dense forests. The park offers hiking and wildlife watching, with an emphasis on its peaceful, remote setting. It's also a place of historical significance, with Native American connections and local legends.

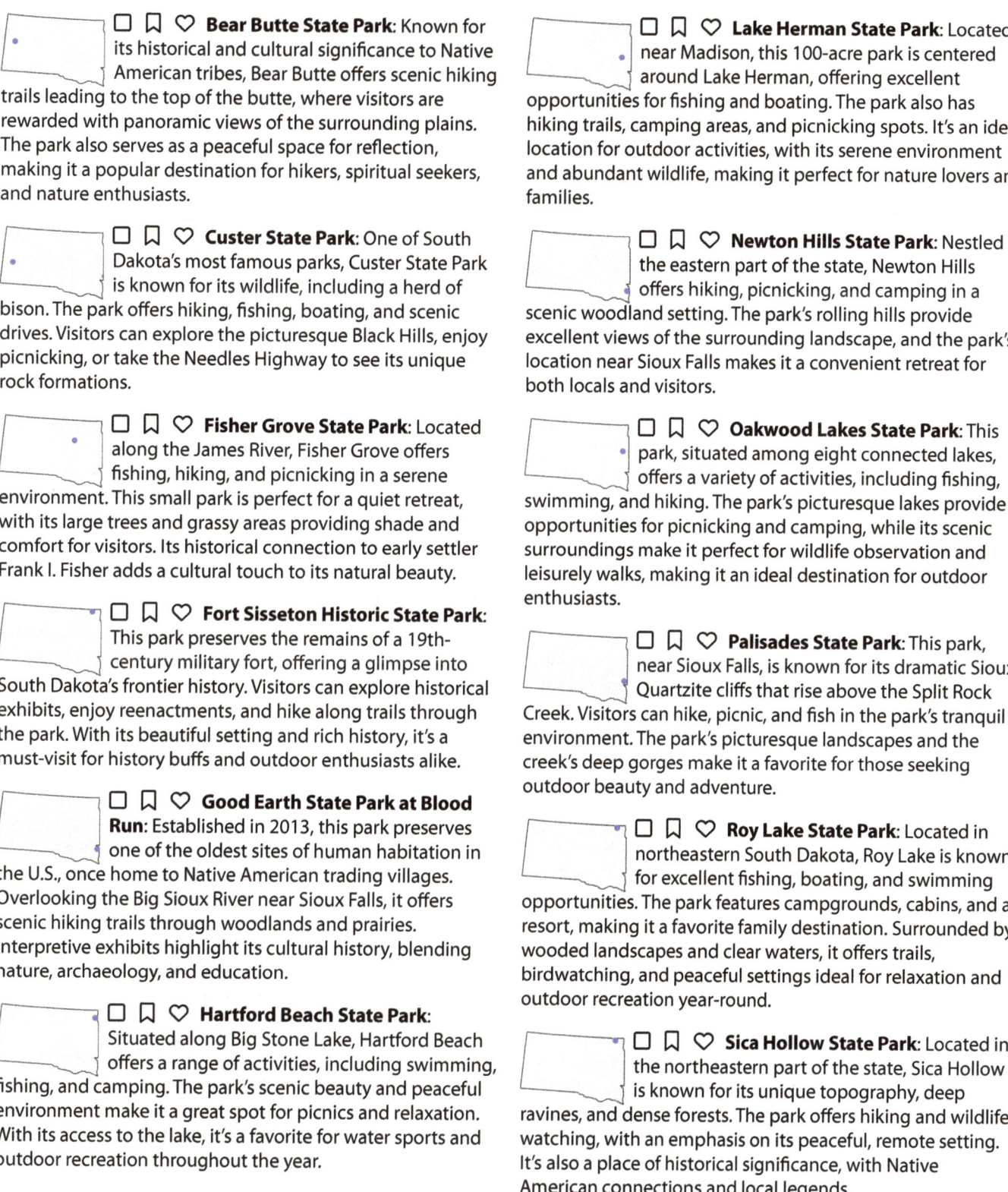

SOUTH DAKOTA

☐ 🔖 ♡ **Union Grove State Park**: Located in the southeastern part of the state, this park is ideal for fishing, hiking, and picnicking. It's known for its beautiful wooded landscapes and tranquil atmosphere, making it a great spot for relaxation and outdoor activities. The park's lake is perfect for fishing or simply enjoying a peaceful day outdoors.

State Recreational Areas

☐ 🔖 ♡ **Angostura Recreation Area**: Located on Angostura Reservoir, this popular recreation area offers fishing, boating, and picnicking opportunities. The scenic surroundings of the reservoir make it a perfect spot for water sports and relaxing by the water. The park's diverse landscape provides great hiking and wildlife watching opportunities, making it a year-round destination for outdoor enthusiasts.

☐ 🔖 ♡ **Big Sioux Recreation Area**: This park, located near Sioux Falls, is popular for hiking, picnicking, and camping. The Big Sioux River offers fishing and canoeing opportunities, while the park's scenic trails and diverse ecosystems provide a great environment for wildlife watching and outdoor relaxation just a short drive from the city.

☐ 🔖 ♡ **Burke Lake Recreation Area**: Situated near the town of Burke, this small recreation area is perfect for fishing, picnicking, and enjoying the outdoors. The peaceful setting around the lake provides a relaxing environment for visitors, whether they are camping, walking the nature trails, or simply enjoying the views. The area is ideal for a quiet day of outdoor activities with family or friends.

☐ 🔖 ♡ **Buryanek Recreation Area**: Located along the Missouri River, Buryanek Recreation Area offers fishing, boating, and camping opportunities. Its proximity to the river makes it a great spot for water activities, while the surrounding nature provides excellent hiking and wildlife observation. It's a wonderful destination for visitors seeking a quiet retreat or outdoor adventures by the river.

☐ 🔖 ♡ **Chief White Crane Recreation Area**: This area along the Missouri River offers fishing, picnicking, and hiking opportunities. It's a popular spot for water-based activities like boating and fishing, and its natural surroundings provide a peaceful escape for visitors. Whether exploring the river or enjoying the park's tranquil environment, Chief White Crane is ideal for outdoor enthusiasts.

☐ 🔖 ♡ **Cow Creek Recreation Area**: Cow Creek is a small, peaceful park offering fishing and picnicking. Located along the Missouri River, this recreation area is perfect for those seeking a relaxing outdoor experience. Visitors can enjoy quiet moments by the creek or explore the surrounding nature. Its calm, serene atmosphere makes it a perfect spot for nature lovers and outdoor relaxation.

☐ 🔖 ♡ **Farm Island Recreation Area**: Located near Pierre, this area offers camping and boating along the Missouri River. With beautiful river views, it's a popular spot for fishing, swimming, and picnicking. The surrounding wooded area provides hiking opportunities and a tranquil setting for outdoor activities. Whether boating on the river or relaxing by the shore, Farm Island is a favorite for visitors.

☐ 🔖 ♡ **Indian Creek Recreation Area**: This small, peaceful park offers fishing and picnicking opportunities along the Missouri River. The park's calm setting is perfect for those looking to enjoy a quiet day in nature, with plenty of space for relaxation and outdoor activities. Its location along the river also provides great birdwatching and wildlife observation opportunities.

☐ 🔖 ♡ **Lake Alvin Recreation Area**: Located near Sioux Falls, this park features a small lake ideal for swimming, fishing, and picnicking. The park also offers hiking trails that wind through scenic woodlands, making it a great spot for outdoor recreation. Whether swimming in the lake, hiking the trails, or just relaxing by the water, Lake Alvin provides a peaceful outdoor experience.

☐ 🔖 ♡ **Lake Andes Recreation Area**: Located near the town of Lake Andes, this park is popular for fishing, boating, and picnicking. The park features a serene lake surrounded by grassy plains, providing a peaceful environment for outdoor recreation. It's a great spot for families to enjoy fishing or a leisurely day by the water.

SOUTH DAKOTA

☐ 🔖 ♡ **Lake Cochrane Recreation Area:** Known for its fishing and birdwatching opportunities, Lake Cochrane is a peaceful location for nature lovers. Visitors can fish in the lake, observe local wildlife, or enjoy a quiet day by the water. The park's natural beauty and serenity make it an excellent place for outdoor activities and relaxation in the southeastern part of South Dakota.

☐ 🔖 ♡ **Lake Hiddenwood Recreation Area:** A quiet, serene park offering fishing and picnicking along the shores of Lake Hiddenwood. The park's natural beauty and peaceful atmosphere provide an ideal environment for relaxation and outdoor activities. Whether fishing, hiking, or just unwinding by the water, visitors can enjoy the tranquility of this hidden gem in South Dakota.

☐ 🔖 ♡ **Lake Louise Recreation Area:** Located in a beautiful wooded area, Lake Louise offers fishing, swimming, and hiking opportunities. The park's peaceful setting makes it perfect for picnicking and outdoor relaxation. Visitors can enjoy the scenic beauty of the area while spending the day by the lake or exploring the park's wooded trails.

☐ 🔖 ♡ **Lake Poinsett Recreation Area:** A popular spot for water sports, fishing, and camping, Lake Poinsett offers beautiful lakeside views and ample recreational opportunities. Visitors can enjoy picnicking, swimming, boating, and hiking, making it an ideal location for families and outdoor adventurers looking to experience nature on the water.

☐ 🔖 ♡ **Lake Thompson Recreation Area:** This recreation area offers fishing, picnicking, and camping opportunities along the shores of Lake Thompson. The park's tranquil environment provides a peaceful escape, with plenty of space for outdoor activities. Visitors can relax by the lake, enjoy a picnic, or take a peaceful walk along the water's edge.

☐ 🔖 ♡ **Lake Vermillion Recreation Area:** This park, located near the city of Canistota, offers boating, fishing, and hiking. Its namesake, Lake Vermillion, is perfect for water-based activities, while the surrounding forested hills provide a tranquil setting for camping and outdoor recreation in a scenic part of southeastern South Dakota.

☐ 🔖 ♡ **Lewis and Clark Recreation Area:** Situated along the Missouri River, this park offers a variety of outdoor activities, including boating, fishing, hiking, and wildlife watching. It's a popular spot for camping, with scenic views of the river and nearby bluffs. The park is also steeped in history, named after the famous explorers Lewis and Clark.

☐ 🔖 ♡ **Little Moreau Recreation Area:** This peaceful area provides fishing and picnicking opportunities. Located in a serene environment, Little Moreau is perfect for those looking to enjoy a quiet outdoor retreat. The surrounding woodlands and waters create a beautiful backdrop for a relaxing day of outdoor activities, including fishing, birdwatching, and enjoying the natural beauty of South Dakota.

☐ 🔖 ♡ **Llewellyn Johns Recreation Area:** Located on Shadehill Reservoir, this recreation area is ideal for fishing, camping, and enjoying the outdoors. Visitors can fish in the reservoir, take a boat out, or hike the nearby trails. The park provides a tranquil setting to relax by the water, making it a great destination for nature lovers and those looking to escape into the wilderness.

☐ 🔖 ♡ **Mina Lake Recreation Area:** Set along the peaceful Mina Lake, this area offers excellent fishing, swimming, and picnicking opportunities. The park's scenic beauty, with its quiet waters and surrounding nature, creates a peaceful environment for visitors to enjoy a relaxing day outdoors. It's perfect for families looking for a fun day on the lake or a quiet retreat.

☐ 🔖 ♡ **North Point Recreation Area:** Situated along the Missouri River, this area offers fishing, hiking, and picnicking. With beautiful river views and a peaceful atmosphere, it's a perfect spot for relaxing or enjoying the outdoors. Visitors can explore the park's trails, fish in the river, or simply unwind by the water, taking in the natural beauty of the landscape.

☐ 🔖 ♡ **North Wheeler Recreation Area:** A small, serene park offering fishing and picnicking opportunities, North Wheeler is ideal for those seeking a quiet outdoor escape. Visitors can enjoy a peaceful day by the river, fish, and enjoy the natural surroundings. The calm atmosphere of the park makes it perfect for unwinding and spending time in nature.

☐ 🔖 ♡ **Oahe Downstream Recreation Area:** Located near Pierre, this park offers camping, fishing, and boating along the Missouri River. The scenic beauty of the river and its surroundings makes it a great spot for outdoor activities. Visitors can fish, enjoy water sports, or relax by the river, making it a perfect destination for a peaceful outdoor retreat.

SOUTH DAKOTA

☐ 🔖 ♡ **Okobojo Point Recreation Area**: Located on Lake Oahe, Okobojo Point offers camping, fishing, and hiking opportunities. The recreation area is known for its scenic beauty, with access to the lake for water activities and panoramic views of the surrounding area. It's a great place for visitors to relax, enjoy the outdoors, and partake in various recreational activities.

☐ 🔖 ♡ **Pease Creek Recreation Area**: A small area offering fishing and picnicking, Pease Creek is a peaceful spot for visitors seeking solitude and outdoor recreation. Located near a creek, it's ideal for relaxing by the water, fishing, and enjoying the quiet surroundings. The park is perfect for those who enjoy being surrounded by nature and away from the crowds.

☐ 🔖 ♡ **Pelican Lake Recreation Area**: Known for its excellent fishing and birdwatching opportunities, Pelican Lake is a serene location for outdoor enthusiasts. Visitors can fish in the lake, hike the nearby trails, or enjoy a picnic by the water. The area offers beautiful views and a tranquil setting, making it a great spot for nature lovers and those seeking relaxation.

☐ 🔖 ♡ **Pickerel Lake Recreation Area**: Located near the town of Webster, Pickerel Lake offers great fishing, boating, and hiking opportunities. The lake is perfect for water activities, while the surrounding nature provides a peaceful environment for picnicking and relaxing. The area is ideal for outdoor enthusiasts looking to enjoy a day in nature.

☐ 🔖 ♡ **Pierson Ranch Recreation Area**: This recreation area near Yankton offers camping, fishing, and picnicking along the Missouri River. With its scenic views and abundant wildlife, it's a great spot for outdoor activities such as hiking and boating. Visitors can relax by the river, fish, or take in the natural beauty surrounding the area.

☐ 🔖 ♡ **Platte Creek Recreation Area**: A small area offering fishing and picnicking, Platte Creek provides a peaceful environment for those looking to spend a quiet day outdoors. Visitors can enjoy the beauty of the creek, fish, or simply relax in the serene surroundings. The park's tranquil atmosphere makes it a perfect retreat for nature lovers.

☐ 🔖 ♡ **Randall Creek Recreation Area** : Located on the Missouri River, Randall Creek offers fishing, picnicking, and camping. Its scenic riverfront location provides plenty of opportunities for water-based recreation and outdoor relaxation. The peaceful environment and beautiful views make it an ideal spot for enjoying a day in nature, fishing, or simply unwinding by the river.

☐ 🔖 ♡ **Revheim Bay Recreation Area**: A small area located on Lake Oahe, Revheim Bay offers fishing, picnicking, and hiking opportunities. It's a peaceful spot to enjoy the lake's beauty, fish, or relax by the water. The park's tranquil atmosphere and scenic surroundings make it a great choice for visitors seeking a quiet outdoor experience.

☐ 🔖 ♡ **Richmond Lake Recreation Area**: This park features a lake for fishing and swimming, with picnicking areas and hiking trails. Located near Aberdeen, it's an excellent spot for outdoor recreation. The park offers a range of activities, from relaxing by the lake to exploring the natural beauty of the surrounding area. It's a perfect destination for families and nature lovers.

☐ 🔖 ♡ **Rocky Point Recreation Area**: Located on Belle Fourche Reservoir, this area offers fishing, boating, and camping opportunities. Visitors can enjoy the water, hike the trails, or relax by the reservoir. With its peaceful setting and abundant outdoor activities, Rocky Point is a popular spot for those seeking a day of recreation in a serene environment.

☐ 🔖 ♡ **Sandy Shore Recreation Area**: This small area offers swimming, picnicking, and fishing opportunities. Located near the Missouri River, it provides a relaxing environment for visitors to enjoy the outdoors and the peaceful beauty of the river. Sandy Shore is a quiet spot for families and outdoor enthusiasts looking to spend a day by the water.

☐ 🔖 ♡ **Shadehill Recreation Area**: Located on Shadehill Reservoir, this area offers fishing, boating, and camping. The park's picturesque setting provides a perfect environment for outdoor activities, with opportunities for hiking, birdwatching, and relaxation by the water. Shadehill is ideal for those seeking a tranquil escape in nature.

SOUTH DAKOTA

☐ 🔖 ♡ **Sheps Canyon Recreation Area:** Near Custer State Park, Sheps Canyon offers camping and hiking opportunities with scenic views of the surrounding Black Hills. The area provides a peaceful environment for outdoor activities, including picnicking and wildlife observation. It's a great spot for visitors looking to explore the natural beauty of the Black Hills.

☐ 🔖 ♡ **Snake Creek Recreation Area:** Located along the Missouri River, Snake Creek offers fishing and picnicking opportunities. The park is ideal for those seeking a quiet escape with a scenic view of the river. Its tranquil atmosphere makes it perfect for relaxation and outdoor activities like fishing, hiking, and nature observation.

☐ 🔖 ♡ **Spring Creek Recreation Area:** This small area offers fishing, picnicking, and peaceful relaxation by the Missouri River. It's a perfect spot for visitors seeking a quiet day in nature. Whether enjoying the calm waters, fishing, or simply relaxing, Spring Creek offers a serene escape for outdoor enthusiasts.

☐ 🔖 ♡ **Swan Creek Recreation Area:** Located along the Missouri River, Swan Creek offers fishing and picnicking opportunities in a peaceful setting. Its tranquil environment makes it an ideal destination for visitors looking to unwind and enjoy nature. The scenic river views and nearby trails make this a great spot for outdoor relaxation.

☐ 🔖 ♡ **West Whitlock Recreation Area:** Nestled on the shores of Lake Oahe, this park is a favorite for anglers chasing walleye and families seeking lakeside recreation. It features a modern campground, boat ramps, and picnic areas with wide prairie views. A reconstructed Arikara earth lodge connects visitors to the region's Native American heritage, blending cultural history with outdoor adventure.

National Parks

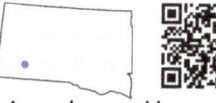 ☐ 🔖 ♡ **Badlands National Park:** Known for its dramatic landscape of eroded buttes, pinnacles, and layered rock formations, Badlands offers hiking, scenic drives, and wildlife like bison and prairie dogs. Panoramic overlooks reveal colorful geology shaped by time and weather, making it one of South Dakota's most awe-inspiring natural treasures for exploration and photography.

 ☐ 🔖 ♡ **Jewel Cave National Monument:** Home to one of the world's longest caves, Jewel Cave features dazzling calcite crystals and intricate passageways. Guided tours lead visitors through chambers filled with rare formations, offering a glimpse into the underground world. Above ground, trails and exhibits highlight the area's unique geology and history of cave exploration.

 ☐ 🔖 ♡ **Minuteman Missile National Historic Site:** Preserving the history of the Cold War, this site tells the story of the Minuteman missile system and America's strategy of nuclear deterrence. Visitors can tour the Delta-09 missile silo and Delta-01 launch control facility, gaining a rare, firsthand look at the technology and tension of this pivotal era in U.S. history.

 ☐ 🔖 ♡ **Missouri National Recreational River:** Flowing through South Dakota and Nebraska, this protected stretch of the Missouri River offers canoeing, kayaking, and fishing along its scenic banks. Hiking trails and overlooks provide access to unaltered river habitats, while interpretive sites highlight its role in westward expansion and the cultural history of the Great Plains.

 ☐ 🔖 ♡ **Mount Rushmore National Memorial:** Carved into granite in the Black Hills, this iconic memorial honors George Washington, Thomas Jefferson, Theodore Roosevelt, and Abraham Lincoln. Visitors can walk the Presidential Trail, explore exhibits on its creation, and take in stunning views of the monument, which symbolizes democracy, leadership, and American ideals.

 ☐ 🔖 ♡ **Wind Cave National Park:** Known for its vast underground maze, Wind Cave features unique boxwork formations found in few other caves worldwide. Guided tours explore its complex passageways, while above ground, visitors can hike prairie and forest trails, spot bison and elk, and experience the blend of geology, wildlife, and natural beauty unique to this park.

SOUTH DAKOTA

State & National Forests

☐ ☐ ♡ **Black Hills National Forest:** Spanning about 1.25 million acres across western South Dakota and northeastern Wyoming, this forest protects pine-covered hills, granite outcrops, 11 reservoirs, 30 campgrounds, and over 350 miles of trails including the Centennial and Mickelson Trails. It offers camping, hiking, OHV riding, fishing, rock climbing, wildlife viewing (elk, mountain goats, bears), and historic CCC-built facilities.

☐ ☐ ♡ **Custer National Forest:** Covering ~1.19 million acres in Montana, with eastern "island" units in northwestern South Dakota, this forest protects ponderosa pine ridges and grassland mosaics. Offers hiking, camping, hunting, fishing, and unique ecosystems like the Sioux Ranger District, with scenic byways such as the Beartooth Highway extending access into South Dakota.

National Grasslands

☐ ☐ ♡ **Buffalo Gap National Grassland:** Stretching across southwestern South Dakota, Buffalo Gap National Grassland surrounds Badlands National Park and showcases mixed-grass prairie, rugged buttes, and fossil-rich soils. It supports bison, prairie dogs, and raptors, offering solitude, stargazing, and hiking amid iconic Great Plains scenery shaped by wind and time.

☐ ☐ ♡ **Grand River National Grassland:** Spanning rolling prairies in northwestern South Dakota, this 155,000-acre grassland is rich in wildlife, from sharp-tailed grouse to pronghorn. Once farmland, it was restored after the Dust Bowl and now offers hunting, birdwatching, hiking, and camping. Visitors can explore scenic buttes, open rangelands, and the nearby Shadehill Reservoir for fishing and boating.

☐ ☐ ♡ **Fort Pierre National Grassland:** Located in central South Dakota, Fort Pierre National Grassland features rolling prairie, ephemeral wetlands, and historic grazing lands. Home to sharp-tailed grouse, coyotes, and burrowing owls, it's a prime spot for birdwatching and hunting. Once traveled by Native nations and pioneers, the land now supports both wildlife and sustainable cattle grazing.

National Scenic Byways & All-American Roads

☐ ☐ ♡ **Native American Scenic Byway:** Stretching across Sioux tribal lands along the Missouri River, this byway links cultural sites, memorials, and sacred landscapes of the Crow Creek, Lower Brule, Cheyenne River, and Standing Rock reservations. Travelers experience sweeping plains, river bluffs, and interpretive centers that honor Lakota heritage, offering a journey rich in history and living culture.

☐ ☐ ♡ **Peter Norbeck Scenic Byway:** A looping drive through the Black Hills, this route winds past Mount Rushmore, Crazy Horse, and through Custer State Park. Famous for its pigtail bridges, granite tunnels framing mountain views, and towering spires along Needles Highway, it blends natural beauty with remarkable engineering. Wildlife, forests, and dramatic rock formations make every mile unforgettable.

State Scenic Byways

☐ ☐ ♡ **Badlands Loop Scenic Byway:** Winding through Badlands National Park via SD 240, this 40-mile loop showcases stark, layered formations and expansive prairies. Scenic overlooks punctuate the drive, offering vantage points to view dramatic rock spires, sweeping vistas, and roaming bighorn sheep. It's a captivating blend of geologic wonder and solitude, perfect for wilderness discovery.

☐ ☐ ♡ **Skyline Drive Scenic Byway:** Perched atop Rapid City, this 2-mile drive offers sweeping views over the city and surrounding plains. Along rocky ridges you'll pass quirky icons like the Depression-era dinosaur sculptures of Dinosaur Park and the storied Hangman's Tree. It leads to trailheads and overlooks in the Skyline Wilderness Area—a short but scenic urban escape.

SOUTH DAKOTA

☐ 🔖 ♡ **Spearfish Canyon Scenic Byway:** Traveling north from Spearfish along US 14A, this deep gorge drive carves through towering limestone cliffs, waterfalls, and lush forest. The road traces an old railbed, offering scenic pull-offs, historic sites, and access to trails and relic hydroelectric plant remains. It's a beautiful fusion of geology, history, and dense woodland charm.

☐ 🔖 ♡ **Wildlife Loop Road Scenic Byway:** Circling through Custer State Park, this 18-mile gravel-paved route winds past rolling prairies and ponderosa forests. Keep an eye out for free-roaming bison, elk, deer, prairie dogs, and burros in their native habitat. Lookouts and trails along the way invite wildlife viewing and immersive solitude in one of South Dakota's wildest state parks.

National Natural Landmarks

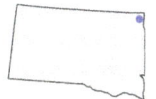 ☐ 🔖 ♡ **Ancient River Warren Channel:** This immense Ice Age channel became a National Natural Landmark for its role in draining glacial Lake Agassiz, one of the largest lakes in Earth's history. Though now dry, its deep trough and broad floodplain reveal the colossal meltwater flows that reshaped the Upper Midwest and remain etched into the landscape.
GPS: 45.6199, -96.8613

 ☐ 🔖 ♡ **Cathedral Spires and Limber Pine Natural Area:** Celebrated as a National Natural Landmark for both its geology and botany, this Black Hills site features joint-controlled granite spires and a rare stand of limber pine. Together they form a dramatic landscape where weathering and elevation create one of South Dakota's most distinctive natural communities.
GPS: 43.8411, -103.5444

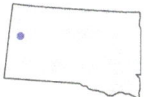 ☐ 🔖 ♡ **Bear Butte:** Designated a National Natural Landmark for its geological and cultural importance, Bear Butte is a solitary igneous intrusion rising above the plains. It illustrates volcanic activity in the Black Hills region while also serving as a sacred site for Plains Indian tribes, blending spiritual heritage with striking natural prominence.
GPS: 44.4758, -103.4269

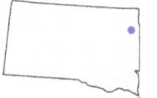 ☐ 🔖 ♡ **Cottonwood Slough–Dry Run:** This wetland complex achieved National Natural Landmark recognition for being a pristine example of the prairie pothole region. Undisturbed marshes, lakes, and streams maintain their natural hydrology, offering vital habitat for migratory birds, aquatic plants, and native species dependent on intact wetlands.
GPS: 44.9571, -97.1935

 ☐ 🔖 ♡ **Bijou Hills:** These erosional remnants of soft shale and clay capped by sandstone and quartzite stand as a National Natural Landmark for their representation of South Dakota's geologic past. Their rugged slopes support native prairie vegetation and highlight the interplay of resistant and erodible rock in shaping distinctive topography.
GPS: 43.5178, -99.1472

 ☐ 🔖 ♡ **Fort Randall Eagle Roost:** Wintering bald and golden eagles gather here in large numbers, making this site a National Natural Landmark of avian importance. With open water, abundant prey, and tall roosting perches along the Missouri River, it remains a critical habitat on the central migration corridor for these iconic raptors.
GPS: 43.055717, -98.550233

 ☐ 🔖 ♡ **Buffalo Slough:** Recognized as a National Natural Landmark for preserving an intact prairie pothole system, Buffalo Slough provides rare refuge for migratory waterfowl, amphibians, and prairie wildlife. Its emergent wetlands, bluestem prairie, and natural hydrology showcase the biological richness once common across the Great Plains.
GPS: 43.8743, -96.9390

 ☐ 🔖 ♡ **Lake Thompson:** Named a National Natural Landmark for its size and ecological integrity, Lake Thompson is one of South Dakota's largest natural lakes. Its extensive marshes and shallow waters provide nesting and migratory habitat for waterfowl, preserving the natural wetland systems that once covered the prairie landscape.
GPS: 44.2850, -97.4619

SOUTH DAKOTA

☐ 🔖 ♡ **Red Lake:** As one of the last large prairie pothole lakes left undisturbed, Red Lake earned National Natural Landmark status for preserving a critical wetland ecosystem. Its shallow waters and surrounding marshes are havens for breeding waterfowl, amphibians, and aquatic plants, exemplifying the ecological richness of prairie wetlands.
GPS: 43.7264, -99.2252

☐ 🔖 ♡ **Sica Hollow:** This richly forested tract became a National Natural Landmark for its combination of unique soils, colorful streambeds, and glacial landforms. Long tied to Native American legends, the hollow illustrates unusual chemical processes in its waters while providing a biologically diverse haven within northeastern South Dakota.
GPS: 45.7419, -97.2425

☐ 🔖 ♡ **Snake Butte:** Designated a National Natural Landmark for its exceptional mineralogy, Snake Butte preserves one of only two known natural sand calcite deposit formations in the world. This small outcrop holds scientific significance for understanding rare geologic processes and stands as a unique feature of the Great Plains.
GPS: 43.4350, -101.9003

☐ 🔖 ♡ **The Castles:** These flat-topped buttes rise dramatically above the surrounding prairie, earning National Natural Landmark status for their illustration of erosional processes shaping the northern Great Plains. Their vertical walls provide habitat for raptors and prairie wildlife, while also serving as a striking visual reminder of geologic time.
GPS: 45.5276, -103.1710

☐ 🔖 ♡ **The Mammoth Site:** This world-renowned paleontological dig site was designated a National Natural Landmark for preserving the remains of more than 60 Ice Age mammoths. The prehistoric sinkhole offers unmatched scientific insight into Pleistocene megafauna and their sudden mass death, making it one of America's most significant fossil deposits.
GPS: 43.4247, -103.4831

TENNESSEE

Tennessee's scenic beauty stretches from the forested peaks of the Smokies to winding rivers and fertile valleys. With a vibrant mix of state parks, national forests, beloved national parks, and fascinating natural landmarks, Tennessee offers outdoor experiences rich in both beauty and heritage.

📅 Peak Season
April–June and September–October are Tennessee's peak seasons, with mild temperatures, wildflowers, and colorful fall foliage. These months are ideal for hiking, scenic drives, and visiting mountain and river regions.

📅 Offseason Months
November–March is the offseason, bringing cooler weather and occasional snow in the mountains. Summer (July–August) is hot and humid, though waterfalls and forest trails offer refreshing escapes.

🍃 Scenery & Nature Timing
Spring brings blooming dogwoods and rhododendrons in the Smokies. Summer highlights waterfalls, rivers, and green forests. Fall transforms mountain slopes with brilliant color, while winter reveals clear views and quiet trails.

✨ Special
Tennessee features the misty peaks of Great Smoky Mountains National Park, the deep gorges of Fall Creek Falls, and the underground wonders of The Lost Sea and Ruby Falls. Synchronous fireflies, limestone caves, and roaring waterfalls showcase its natural marvels.

TENNESSEE

State Parks

☐ 🔖 ♡ **Bicentennial Capitol Mall State Park:** Located in downtown Nashville, this 19-acre park preserves Tennessee's history with a granite state map, Pathway of History, WWII memorial, and a 200-foot granite fountain. It offers a peaceful green space amid the city and serves as an outdoor classroom for state heritage, making it a unique mix of urban park and historic monument.

☐ 🔖 ♡ **Big Cypress Tree State Park:** Nestled in Weakley County, this 330-acre park protects wetlands once dominated by a massive 132-foot bald cypress lost to lightning in 1976. It now serves as a sanctuary for birdwatchers and nature lovers with boardwalks through cypress swamp, educational exhibits, and serene natural settings showcasing Tennessee's wetland ecosystems.

☐ 🔖 ♡ **Big Hill Pond State Park:** Covering 4,138 acres in McNairy County, this rugged park features wetlands, bottomland forests, and Big Hill Pond itself. Visitors enjoy hiking, fishing, boating, and birding. A 70-foot observation tower offers panoramic views of the surrounding forest, making the park a great destination for outdoor adventurers and wildlife enthusiasts alike.

☐ 🔖 ♡ **Big Ridge State Park:** A 3,687-acre wooded retreat in Union County, this park highlights Norris Lake's shoreline, a 45-acre lake, and remnants of 18th-century settlements. Trails range from easy strolls to challenging backcountry routes. With fishing, camping, and swimming, Big Ridge blends history, nature, and recreation in the foothills of the Appalachian Ridge-and-Valley region.

☐ 🔖 ♡ **Bledsoe Creek State Park:** On Old Hickory Lake in Sumner County, this 169-acre park was once a Native American hunting ground. Today, it offers scenic lake views, 6 miles of trails, fishing, boating, and campsites. Visitors find abundant wildlife, including migrating waterfowl, making the park a peaceful haven for birdwatchers, hikers, and history enthusiasts.

☐ 🔖 ♡ **Booker T. Washington State Park:** Situated on Chickamauga Lake in Hamilton County, this 353-acre park is named for the famed African American educator. It offers hiking, fishing, boating, and picnicking with views of the Tennessee River. The park also interprets Washington's legacy and provides a family-friendly retreat blending history with recreation.

☐ 🔖 ♡ **Burgess Falls State Park:** Located in Putnam and White counties, this 350-acre park is famed for its waterfalls on the Falling Water River. The highlight is a 136-foot cascade plunging into a gorge. Short but steep trails lead to overlooks, making it a favorite for photographers and hikers seeking dramatic natural beauty in Tennessee's Highland Rim.

☐ 🔖 ♡ **Cedars of Lebanon State Park:** Covering 900 acres within a larger state forest, this Wilson County park protects rare cedar glades found almost nowhere else. Trails wind through limestone outcrops, caves, and wildflower meadows. The park also features camping, picnicking, and a golf course, offering recreation alongside protection of globally significant plant communities.

☐ 🔖 ♡ **Chickasaw State Park:** In Chester County, this 1,400-acre park offers a 54-acre lake for boating and fishing, plus 14 miles of trails through hardwood forest. Named for the Chickasaw people, the park is popular for horseback riding, camping, and picnicking. Its serene setting and diverse facilities make it a family-friendly destination for outdoor recreation.

☐ 🔖 ♡ **Cordell Hull Birthplace State Park:** A 55-acre park in Pickett County honoring the Nobel Peace Prize–winning U.S. Secretary of State who authored the United Nations charter. Visitors can tour Hull's restored log cabin, interpretive center, and a museum of artifacts. Hiking trails and picnic areas provide a peaceful blend of history and nature.

☐ 🔖 ♡ **Cove Lake State Park:** At the base of Cumberland Mountains in Campbell County, this 673-acre park surrounds a 210-acre lake. Known for birding, fishing, and picnicking, the park has trails linking to Cumberland Trail State Park. Its scenic views of Cross Mountain and Devil's Racetrack ridge make it a popular spot for both locals and travelers.

☐ 🔖 ♡ **Cumberland Mountain State Park:** Established in the 1930s by the New Deal, this 1,720-acre park in Cumberland County showcases Crab Orchard sandstone structures built by the CCC. Centered around Byrd Lake, it offers boating, fishing, hiking, and camping. With historic bridges, cabins, and trails, the park preserves history while serving as a vibrant recreation hub.

TENNESSEE

☐ 🔖 ♡ **Cummins Falls State Park:** A rugged 282-acre park in Jackson County, home to Tennessee's eighth-largest waterfall at 75 feet. Visitors hike down to the gorge and swim in natural pools below the falls. Ranked among America's top swimming holes, the park combines challenging hikes with breathtaking scenery, drawing adventurers and photographers year-round.

☐ 🔖 ♡ **David Crockett Birthplace State Park:** On the Nolichucky River in Greene County, this 105-acre park commemorates the frontier hero's 1786 birthplace. Features include a replica cabin, museum, and interpretive programs. Campgrounds, picnic areas, and riverside trails blend history with outdoor recreation, allowing visitors to experience the early life of Tennessee's iconic pioneer.

☐ 🔖 ♡ **David Crockett State Park:** Spanning 1,319 acres in Lawrence County, this park honors the legendary frontiersman with museums and reconstructed mills. Its 40-acre Lake Lindsey provides boating, fishing, and paddle sports, while miles of trails offer hiking and biking. Visitors enjoy a mix of heritage, nature, and recreation in the park's wooded setting.

☐ 🔖 ♡ **Dunbar Cave State Park:** A 144-acre park in Clarksville featuring a large limestone cave with evidence of Mississippian-era cave art. Guided tours highlight ancient pictographs and geologic features. Above ground, trails loop through forest and wetlands around Swan Lake. The park blends archaeology, history, and nature in one of Middle Tennessee's most unique cultural landscapes.

☐ 🔖 ♡ **Edgar Evins State Park:** Located on Center Hill Lake in DeKalb County, this 6,000-acre park offers boating, fishing, and hiking along rugged terrain. The park features a marina, cabins, and unique platform campsites. Trails wind through hardwood forests rich with wildlife, making it an ideal destination for outdoor enthusiasts and families seeking both adventure and comfort.

☐ 🔖 ♡ **Fall Creek Falls State Park:** Tennessee's largest and most visited park spans 29,800 acres across Van Buren and Bledsoe counties. Famous for Fall Creek Falls, the state's tallest waterfall at 256 feet, the park offers canyons, gorges, caves, and streams. Visitors enjoy extensive hiking, biking, camping, and a nature center, making it a premier destination in the Southeast.

☐ 🔖 ♡ **Fiery Gizzard State Park:** Showcases one of the Southeast's most iconic wild places. Now a standalone state park spanning rugged woodlands and creek gorges in Grundy and Marion counties, it's famed for the challenging, scenic Fiery Gizzard Trail with sweeping overlooks, waterfalls, boulder fields and lush forest. A must-visit for hikers and nature lovers seeking adventure and beauty.

☐ 🔖 ♡ **Fort Loudoun State Historic Park:** In Monroe County, this 1,200-acre park preserves the site of an 18th-century British fort built during the French and Indian War. Reconstructed fort walls and barracks allow visitors to step back in time, with living history events and reenactments. Hiking trails, boating access, and exhibits combine colonial history with scenic natural settings.

☐ 🔖 ♡ **Fort Pillow State Historic Park:** Located on the Mississippi River bluffs in Lauderdale County, this 1,642-acre park preserves a Civil War battlefield. Interpretive trails, a museum, and earthworks tell the story of the 1864 battle. With forested hills, wildlife, and scenic river overlooks, the park offers both solemn history and peaceful outdoor recreation.

☐ 🔖 ♡ **Frozen Head State Park:** A rugged 24,000-acre park in Morgan County, known for challenging hikes and wild backcountry. Named for its 3,324-foot peak often snowcapped in winter, the park includes 50 miles of trails, cascading streams, and remote campsites. Its wilderness character and rich biodiversity attract serious hikers and nature lovers seeking solitude and adventure.

☐ 🔖 ♡ **Harpeth River State Park:** Stretching along 40 miles of river in Middle Tennessee, this linear park preserves archaeological sites, scenic bluffs, and historic structures like Montgomery Bell's tunnel. Popular for kayaking, canoeing, fishing, and hiking, the park offers a peaceful natural escape near Nashville with a blend of history, geology, and recreation.

☐ 🔖 ♡ **Harrison Bay State Park:** Covering 1,200 acres on Chickamauga Lake in Hamilton County, this was Tennessee's first state park. It offers boating, fishing, camping, and hiking, plus an 18-hole golf course. Named for a submerged Cherokee village, the park provides abundant birdwatching and wildlife opportunities while preserving Cherokee and early settler history.

TENNESSEE

☐ 🔖 ♡ **Head of the Crow State Park:** A rugged Tennessee landscape of caves, springs, sinkholes, hardwood forest, and the stunning Sewanee Natural Bridge. Visitors come for peaceful hiking, geology, wildlife watching, and photography. With scenic overlooks, karst formations, and rare species, it offers a quiet, immersive escape for nature lovers and explorers.

☐ 🔖 ♡ **Henry Horton State Park:** Built on the estate of former governor Henry Horton, this 1,140-acre park in Marshall County features the scenic Duck River. Popular for fishing, paddling, and birdwatching, the park also has trails, a golf course, and cabins. Its river access, recreation amenities, and rich natural setting make it a versatile outdoor destination.

☐ 🔖 ♡ **Hiwassee/Ocoee Scenic River State Park:** Tennessee's first scenic river park protects stretches of the Hiwassee and Ocoee rivers. Known for whitewater rafting, trout fishing, and paddling, it also offers campgrounds and trails. The park provides public access to world-class waterways while preserving riparian ecosystems and historic sites tied to Cherokee removal and early settlements.

☐ 🔖 ♡ **Indian Mountain State Park:** Located in Campbell County on reclaimed strip-mined land, this 213-acre park demonstrates successful land restoration. It offers a 33-acre lake for fishing and paddling, campgrounds, and nature trails. The park's setting amid the Cumberland Mountains makes it a peaceful retreat and a prime example of conservation through reclamation.

☐ 🔖 ♡ **Johnsonville State Historic Park:** Situated on Kentucky Lake in Humphreys County, this 1,075-acre park commemorates the Civil War Battle of Johnsonville. Visitors can explore earthworks, interpretive trails, and a museum on the Union supply depot. With lake access, fishing, and wildlife viewing, the park blends military history with outdoor recreation and scenic river vistas.

☐ 🔖 ♡ **Justin P. Wilson Cumberland Trail State Park:** A linear state park spanning over 300 miles of trail across the Cumberland Plateau. Still under development, it will eventually stretch from Chickamauga Creek to the Cumberland Gap. The trail highlights waterfalls, gorges, and sandstone bluffs, offering challenging hikes and connecting communities across eastern Tennessee.

☐ 🔖 ♡ **Long Hunter State Park:** Located on J. Percy Priest Lake near Nashville, this 2,600-acre park offers diverse recreation, from boating and fishing to 25 miles of hiking trails. Highlights include the Volunteer Trail, Sellars Farm archaeological site, and a designated wildflower area. Its mix of cultural history and natural beauty makes it a favorite day-use park.

☐ 🔖 ♡ **Meeman-Shelby Forest State Park:** Covering 12,539 acres along the Mississippi River north of Memphis, this is one of Tennessee's largest parks. It features bottomland hardwood forests, lakes, and 20 miles of trails. Camping, boating, and abundant wildlife, including bald eagles, make it a popular destination for nature lovers and outdoor recreation in West Tennessee.

☐ 🔖 ♡ **Middle Fork Bottoms State Park:** Tennessee's newest park (2024), located in Madison County, preserves over 1,000 acres of wetlands and farmland along the South Fork Forked Deer River. It's designed as a conservation and recreation hub, featuring walking trails, fishing areas, and wildlife viewing. The park emphasizes ecological restoration and outdoor education in a rich natural setting.

☐ 🔖 ♡ **Montgomery Bell State Park:** Spanning 3,850 acres in Dickson County, this park was once the hub of Tennessee's iron industry. Today, it features three lakes, 20 miles of trails, and camping areas. Visitors enjoy boating, fishing, and golfing, as well as historic sites tied to the Cumberland Presbyterian Church. It's a versatile park blending history, recreation, and nature.

☐ 🔖 ♡ **Mousetail Landing State Park:** Along the Tennessee River in Perry County, this 1,247-acre park got its name from a Civil War tannery fire that drove mice to the riverbank. It offers camping, hiking, and boating with a 90-acre lake and scenic overlooks. The park's rugged trails and historic roots make it a hidden gem for outdoor adventurers.

☐ 🔖 ♡ **Natchez Trace State Park:** Covering nearly 48,000 acres across four counties, this park offers extensive recreation on Pin Oak, Cub, and Browns Lakes. It features horseback riding trails, camping, fishing, and hiking. The park also preserves history tied to the Natchez Trace trail. With its size and diversity, it's one of Tennessee's premier outdoor destinations.

TENNESSEE

☐ ▢ ♡ **Nathan Bedford Forrest State Park:** Located on Kentucky Lake in Benton County, this 2,587-acre park honors the Confederate general while interpreting Civil War history. It features Pilot Knob, the highest point on the Tennessee River, with panoramic views. Visitors can hike, camp, fish, and explore the Tennessee River Folklife Museum, blending history and recreation.

☐ ▢ ♡ **Norris Dam State Park:** Established in 1933 around TVA's first dam, this Anderson County park covers 4,000 acres along Norris Lake. It offers hiking, biking, camping, and water sports. The CCC-built cabins and historic structures showcase early TVA history. With rich cultural heritage and abundant outdoor activities, it's a cornerstone of Tennessee's state park system.

☐ ▢ ♡ **North Chickamauga Creek Gorge State Park:** Protecting 7,000 acres near Chattanooga, this rugged park features gorges, waterfalls, and sandstone bluffs. Popular with hikers, paddlers, and climbers, it offers backcountry trails and stunning views. The park is a vital conservation area and gateway to the Cumberland Trail, providing wilderness adventures close to the city.

☐ ▢ ♡ **Old Stone Fort State Archaeological Park:** In Coffee County, this 875-acre park preserves a 2,000-year-old Native American ceremonial enclosure. Interpretive trails explain the site's cultural significance, while waterfalls and rivers provide scenic beauty. The park combines archaeology, history, and recreation, with a museum, picnicking areas, and hiking paths along the Duck and Little Duck rivers.

☐ ▢ ♡ **Panther Creek State Park:** Overlooking Cherokee Lake in Hamblen County, this 1,444-acre park offers 17 hiking trails, 8 horseback trails, and an observation point with panoramic lake views. Popular for fishing, boating, and camping, it also has disc golf and playgrounds. The park blends outdoor adventure with family-friendly amenities in a scenic mountain-lake setting.

☐ ▢ ♡ **Paris Landing State Park:** On the western shore of Kentucky Lake in Henry County, this 841-acre park offers boating, fishing, golfing, and camping. A modern lodge and marina make it a hub for water recreation. Its location on a major reservoir draws anglers, boaters, and families seeking both relaxation and resort-style amenities in a natural lakeside environment.

☐ ▢ ♡ **Pickett CCC Memorial State Park:** Dedicated to the Civilian Conservation Corps, this 19,200-acre park in Pickett County features unique rock formations, caves, and natural bridges. The CCC-built cabins and structures are still in use. Visitors enjoy astronomy programs in Tennessee's first dark-sky park, alongside hiking, paddling, and historic interpretation. It honors both nature and heritage.

☐ ▢ ♡ **Pickwick Landing State Park:** A 1,400-acre park on Pickwick Lake in Hardin County, it offers a golf course, cabins, campgrounds, and a marina. The lake draws boaters, anglers, and swimmers, while trails and picnic areas round out the experience. The park's resort lodge makes it one of the state's most developed parks for recreation and relaxation.

☐ ▢ ♡ **Pinson Mounds State Archaeological Park:** This 1,200-acre park in Madison County preserves the largest Native American Middle Woodland period mound group in the Southeast. It includes at least 15 mounds, with the tallest rising 72 feet. A museum interprets the culture, while trails and boardwalks allow visitors to explore. It's a cultural treasure and outdoor classroom.

☐ ▢ ♡ **Port Royal State Park:** A 30-acre historic park in Montgomery County preserving a 19th-century tobacco inspection station and remnants of the Trail of Tears. Visitors can explore hiking trails, picnic, and learn about early Tennessee trade routes. Small but significant, the park interprets both Native American history and the state's river commerce heritage.

☐ ▢ ♡ **Radnor Lake State Park & Natural Area:** Located in Nashville, this 1,368-acre park protects a biologically rich ecosystem with 7 miles of hiking trails. It's a day-use only natural area, famous for its wildlife, including otters, herons, and deer. Educational programs and scenic trails make it a haven for birdwatchers and conservationists just minutes from downtown.

☐ ▢ ♡ **Red Clay State Park:** This 263-acre historic park in Bradley County preserves the last seat of Cherokee national government before the Trail of Tears. Visitors explore replicas of council houses, the Eternal Flame of the Cherokee Nation, and Blue Hole Spring. Hiking trails and interpretive exhibits connect guests with the site's cultural significance and natural beauty.

TENNESSEE

Reelfoot Lake State Park: Created by a series of New Madrid earthquakes in 1811–12, Reelfoot Lake covers 15,000 acres of cypress swamp. The park features bald eagle viewing, fishing, boating, and wetlands exploration. Boardwalks, canoe trails, and interpretive programs highlight its unique ecosystem, making it a premier birding and wildlife destination in West Tennessee.

Roan Mountain State Park: Nestled at the base of Roan Mountain in Carter County, this 2,000-acre park is famous for its rhododendron gardens and access to the Appalachian Trail. It offers cabins, campgrounds, trout streams, and hiking trails. With spectacular mountain scenery, it's a year-round destination for wildflower enthusiasts, hikers, and naturalists.

Rock Island State Park: Located at the confluence of the Caney Fork, Collins, and Rocky rivers, this 883-acre park in Warren and White counties is known for Great Falls and limestone gorges. Trails, swimming areas, and kayaking opportunities attract outdoor adventurers. Its striking geology and cascading waterfalls make it a photographer's dream.

Rocky Fork State Park: A 2,076-acre park in Unicoi County, protecting part of the Southern Appalachian Highlands. Known for rugged trails, mountain streams, and rich biodiversity, it offers trout fishing, backcountry hiking, and panoramic overlooks. This relatively new park preserves wilderness character while offering access to some of East Tennessee's most pristine landscapes.

Savage Gulf State Park: Established in 2022, this 19,000-acre park preserves one of the largest wilderness areas on the Cumberland Plateau. Known for waterfalls, deep gorges, and sandstone cliffs, it offers over 60 miles of hiking trails. Previously part of South Cumberland, it's now a standalone park highlighting Tennessee's rugged and wild natural heritage.

Scott's Gulf Wilderness State Park: Created in 2025, this 9,000-acre park protects a wild section of the Caney Fork River in White County. With waterfalls, caves, and gorges, it offers challenging backcountry hiking and primitive camping. The park emphasizes preservation and wilderness recreation, adding to Tennessee's growing network of rugged natural areas.

Seven Islands State Birding Park: Spanning 416 acres along the French Broad River in Knox County, this park is dedicated to bird conservation, with over 200 species documented. Visitors enjoy meadows, wetlands, and riverside trails ideal for birdwatching, hiking, and photography. It's a unique park focused on wildlife observation and environmental education.

Sgt. Alvin C. York State Historic Park: Honoring the World War I hero, this Fentress County park preserves York's home, farm, and gristmill. Visitors learn about his life through tours, exhibits, and living history programs. Hiking trails and the Wolf River setting add natural beauty, making it both a cultural landmark and a peaceful retreat.

South Cumberland State Park: Encompassing over 30,000 acres across several counties, this park protects gorges, waterfalls, and sandstone cliffs. Popular destinations include Fiery Gizzard and Savage Gulf (now a separate park). With extensive trails, backcountry camping, and stunning vistas, it's a premier destination for hikers and rock climbers in Tennessee.

Standing Stone State Park: Located in Overton County, this 1,000-acre park features Standing Stone Lake, surrounded by wooded hills. It offers fishing, boating, hiking, and camping, with CCC-built cabins and a lodge. Known for the National Rolley Hole Marble Tournament, the park combines recreation, history, and cultural traditions in a scenic Highland Rim setting.

Sycamore Shoals State Historic Area: Situated in Elizabethton, this park commemorates significant Revolutionary War-era events, including the muster of the Overmountain Men. Features include a replica fort, interpretive trails, and a visitor center. The park blends history and natural beauty, serving as a cultural heritage site and community gathering place.

T. O. Fuller State Park: One of the first state parks in the U.S. open to African Americans, this 1,138-acre park near Memphis honors Dr. Thomas O. Fuller. It features hiking trails, camping, and sports facilities. Archaeological work at Chucalissa Village highlights Native American history, making it both a recreational and educational destination.

TENNESSEE

 ☐ 🔖 ♡ **Tims Ford State Park:** A 3,546-acre park in Franklin County along Tims Ford Lake, known for fishing, boating, and camping. It offers cabins, a marina, golf course, and hiking trails. The lake's deep, clear waters attract anglers, while its wooded shoreline provides a scenic setting for relaxation, family outings, and water-based recreation.

 ☐ 🔖 ♡ **Warriors' Path State Park:** Located on Boone Lake near Kingsport, this 950-acre park offers boating, fishing, and hiking. Named after a Cherokee war trail, it features a nationally recognized accessible playground and golf course. Its mix of history, recreation, and inclusivity makes it a standout family-friendly park in Northeast Tennessee.

National Parks

 ☐ 🔖 ♡ **Andrew Johnson National Historic Site:** In Greeneville, this site honors the 17th U.S. President with his tailor shop, two homes, and the Andrew Johnson National Cemetery. Visitors can trace Johnson's rise from humble beginnings to the White House, gaining insight into his presidency and complex role in the Reconstruction Era following the Civil War.

 ☐ 🔖 ♡ **Appalachian National Scenic Trail:** Stretching over 2,100 miles from Georgia to Maine, the Appalachian Trail is one of the world's most iconic long-distance hikes. It passes through rugged mountains, forests, and scenic ridges. Offering a mix of solitude and challenge, the trail invites adventurers to explore the diverse landscapes of the Eastern United States.

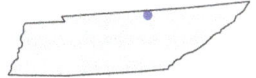 ☐ 🔖 ♡ **Big South Fork National River and Recreation Area:** Straddling Tennessee and Kentucky, this park preserves gorges, sandstone bluffs, and the wild Big South Fork River. Outdoor enthusiasts can hike, ride horseback, paddle, or fish while exploring its rugged beauty. The area also protects historic homesteads, mining sites, and the cultural heritage of Appalachian settlers.

 ☐ 🔖 ♡ **Chickamauga and Chattanooga National Military Park:** Spanning Georgia and Tennessee, this was the first U.S. national military park, commemorating key Civil War battles. Visitors can tour battlefields, monuments, and lookouts, including Missionary Ridge and Lookout Mountain. The park interprets the Union's victories here, which helped secure control of Chattanooga, a vital rail hub.

 ☐ 🔖 ♡ **Cumberland Gap National Historical Park:** Crossing Tennessee, Kentucky, and Virginia, this park preserves the famed mountain pass once called the "Gateway to the West." Trails lead to scenic overlooks, caves, and historic sites. Visitors learn how this corridor enabled pioneer migration and symbolized America's early westward expansion through the Appalachian frontier.

 ☐ 🔖 ♡ **Fort Donelson National Battlefield:** Located in Dover, Tennessee, this site marks a decisive Union victory in February 1862. Visitors can walk the preserved earthworks, tour the river batteries, and reflect at the national cemetery. The victory opened the Cumberland River to Union control, boosting Ulysses S. Grant's reputation and shifting the war's momentum.

 ☐ 🔖 ♡ **Great Smoky Mountains National Park:** Straddling Tennessee and North Carolina, this is America's most visited national park, famed for its misty ridges, wildflowers, and wildlife. More than 800 miles of trails lead to waterfalls, historic cabins, and sweeping views. With unmatched biodiversity and scenic drives like Newfound Gap, it's a natural treasure.

 ☐ 🔖 ♡ **Manhattan Project National Historical Park:** Preserving World War II history, this multi-site park interprets the top-secret project that created the atomic bomb. Tennessee's Oak Ridge unit highlights laboratories, reactors, and worker housing tied to the effort. Together with sites in New Mexico and Washington, it tells the story of science, secrecy, and global change.

TENNESSEE

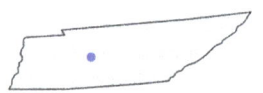 ☐ ☐ ♡ **Natchez Trace National Scenic Trail:** Running through Mississippi, Alabama, and Tennessee, this trail parallels parts of the historic Natchez Trace. Once traveled by Native Americans, traders, and settlers, it now offers peaceful footpaths through forests and farmland. Hikers enjoy scenic beauty, wildlife, and glimpses of a route central to America's early history.

 ☐ ☐ ♡ **Natchez Trace Parkway:** Extending 444 miles from Natchez, Mississippi, to Nashville, Tennessee, this scenic road follows the path of the historic Natchez Trace. Visitors can stop at overlooks, historic inns, and cultural landmarks while enjoying recreational trails. The parkway provides both a tranquil drive and a journey through centuries of Southern history.

 ☐ ☐ ♡ **Obed Wild and Scenic River:** In East Tennessee, the Obed protects 45 miles of free-flowing river across rugged gorges and sandstone bluffs. It's a paradise for paddlers, climbers, anglers, and hikers seeking solitude and dramatic scenery. Preserved for its unspoiled character, the Obed offers challenging rapids, sheer cliffs, and star-filled night skies.

 ☐ ☐ ♡ **Shiloh National Military Park:** Preserving one of the Civil War's bloodiest battles, this park in Hardin County, Tennessee, tells the story of the April 1862 clash that cost over 23,000 casualties. Visitors explore preserved fields, historic sites, and the Shiloh National Cemetery. Museums and interpretive trails connect the land to its wartime legacy.

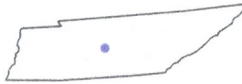 ☐ ☐ ♡ **Stones River National Battlefield:** Located in Murfreesboro, this site commemorates the pivotal 1862–63 battle. With one of the highest casualty rates of the war, it became a rallying symbol for the Union. Visitors can explore monuments, preserved earthworks, and the Stones River National Cemetery, reflecting on sacrifice and strategy in the Western Theater.

State & National Forests

 ☐ ☐ ♡ **Bledsoe State Forest:** A ~1,090-acre woodland on the Cumberland Plateau in Bledsoe County, managed for sustainable forestry, habitat, and watershed health. Featuring pine-hardwood stands, scenic bluffs, and seasonal hunting, it serves as a working forest while offering opportunities for wildlife observation, hiking, and forestry demonstrations in Tennessee's mid-Appalachian region.

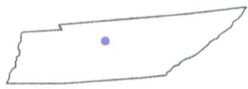 ☐ ☐ ♡ **Cedars of Lebanon State Forest:** Encompassing ~9,420 acres in Wilson County, this forest preserves globally rare cedar glades with unique limestone barrens and wildflower communities. Managed for conservation and research, it offers hiking, birding, and hunting while educating visitors about glade ecology. Its rocky terrain and biodiversity make it one of Tennessee's most distinctive forests.

 ☐ ☐ ♡ **Cheatham State Forest:** Spanning ~20,000 acres across Cheatham and Davidson counties, this is Tennessee's largest state forest. It provides hiking, horseback riding, hunting, and wildlife viewing amid oak-hickory uplands and river bottoms. Managed for timber and watershed health, it balances recreation with resource conservation just outside Nashville's urban edge.

 ☐ ☐ ♡ **Cherokee National Forest:** Tennessee's only national forest, stretching ~655,600 acres along the Appalachian Mountains in East Tennessee. Split by Great Smoky Mountains National Park, it offers wilderness areas, the Appalachian Trail, scenic byways, and abundant wildlife. Visitors enjoy camping, fishing, hiking, and paddling in a landscape rich with biodiversity and cultural history.

TENNESSEE

Chickasaw State Forest: A ~1,400-acre pine-hardwood tract in Hardeman County, managed for timber, erosion control, and wildlife conservation. With primitive roads and trails, it provides opportunities for hiking, hunting, and forestry research. Its location in West Tennessee's Highland Rim highlights reforestation and land stewardship in a formerly depleted landscape.

Chuck Swan State Forest: Spanning ~24,700 acres in Union and Campbell counties along Norris Lake, this forest preserves rugged Cumberland Mountain terrain. Managed jointly by the Division of Forestry and TVA, it emphasizes watershed protection, sustainable timber, and wildlife habitat. Primitive roads, hiking, and hunting offer recreation in a remote, scenic setting.

Franklin State Forest: Covering ~7,600 acres in Marion County on the Cumberland Plateau, this forest is managed for sustainable timber, wildlife, and watershed health. Visitors enjoy quiet hiking, hunting, and wildlife viewing in oak-pine woodlands. Its undeveloped, rugged character provides a natural retreat and demonstration of conservation forestry practices.

John Tully State Forest: A ~4,200-acre bottomland hardwood forest in Lauderdale County along the Mississippi River. Managed for sustainable timber and wetland restoration, it offers birdwatching, hunting, and forestry education. Its mix of cypress, oak, and wetland habitats makes it an important conservation site in Tennessee's northwestern lowlands.

Lewis State Forest: A ~1,000-acre forest in Lewis County showcasing upland hardwood and pine management. Used as a demonstration forest for forestry practices and resource stewardship, it supports wildlife habitat and watershed protection. Public uses include hiking and hunting in a compact but valuable woodland representative of Middle Tennessee ecosystems.

Lone Mountain State Forest: Encompassing ~23,000 acres in Morgan County, this large forest lies atop a high Cumberland Plateau ridge. Known for its rugged terrain, mixed hardwoods, and pine stands, it offers hunting, hiking, and primitive recreation. Managed for watershed health, sustainable timber, and habitat, it is a vital conservation area in East Tennessee.

Martha Sundquist State Forest: A ~6,000-acre forest in Cocke County bordering Cherokee National Forest. Once owned by Champion International, it is managed for forest restoration, timber, and wildlife. Visitors enjoy hiking, hunting, and quiet exploration of oak-pine uplands. Its location in the Appalachian foothills makes it a valuable conservation resource.

Natchez Trace State Forest: Spanning ~25,000 acres in Henderson County, adjacent to Natchez Trace State Park, this is one of Tennessee's largest state forests. Managed for sustainable forestry, watershed protection, and wildlife, it offers hunting, hiking, and education programs. Its upland pine-hardwood forests showcase large-scale restoration and conservation in West Tennessee.

Pickett State Forest: Covering ~19,000 acres in Pickett County, this forest complements the adjacent state park. It protects sandstone bluffs, caves, and mixed forests on the Cumberland Plateau. Managed for timber and wildlife, it provides hunting, hiking, and primitive camping. The forest also supports watershed health and outdoor education opportunities.

Prentice Cooper State Forest: A ~25,000-acre forest in Marion County atop the Cumberland Plateau, known for oak-hickory woodlands, sandstone cliffs, and scenic overlooks of the Tennessee River Gorge. Popular for hiking, hunting, and rock climbing, it balances recreation with forestry management and watershed conservation near Chattanooga.

Scott State Forest: Spanning ~4,000 acres in Scott County, this rugged upland forest features oak and pine woodlands in the Cumberland Mountains. Managed for sustainable timber, habitat, and watershed health, it is used for forestry research and education. Hunting and primitive recreation are allowed, highlighting its role as a working demonstration forest.

Standing Stone State Forest: An ~8,600-acre hardwood and pine forest in Overton County's Highland Rim. Managed for timber, wildlife, and watershed resources, it complements the nearby state park. With ridge-top trails, hunting, and scenic overlooks, the forest demonstrates sustainable management while preserving natural beauty in north-central Tennessee.

TENNESSEE

☐ 🔖 ♡ **Stewart State Forest:** Covering ~4,000 acres in Stewart County, this forest lies in the Cumberland River floodplain. Managed for timber, habitat restoration, and wetland protection, it offers hunting, hiking, and birdwatching. Its bottomland hardwoods and wetlands provide important wildlife habitat while supporting research in floodplain conservation.

National Scenic Byways & All-American Roads

☐ 🔖 ♡ **Cherohala Skyway:** This 43-mile mountain drive links Tellico Plains, Tennessee, to Robbinsville, North Carolina. It winds through the Cherokee and Nantahala national forests, offering sweeping vistas, crisp mountain air, and access to hiking and picnic areas. Travelers experience high-elevation ridgelines and some of the most spectacular scenery in the Southern Appalachians.

☐ 🔖 ♡ **Cumberland Historic Byway:** Traversing more than 150 miles across the northern Cumberland Plateau, this route connects Cumberland Gap to the Cumberland River. It highlights rugged geology, lush forests, and pioneer heritage. Visitors encounter small towns, historic sites, and recreational areas that tell the story of Tennessee's frontier past amid dramatic natural beauty.

☐ 🔖 ♡ **East Tennessee Crossing Byway:** Following the paths of the Cherokee Warrior's Trail and the historic Wilderness Road, this 83-mile corridor crosses Clinch Mountain and links the Great Smoky Mountains and Cumberland Gap. It blends history and scenery, with rolling valleys, mountain ridges, and echoes of centuries of migration through the Appalachian frontier.

☐ 🔖 ♡ **Great River Road:** Tracing the Mississippi River along Tennessee's western edge, this legendary byway links historic towns, scenic overlooks, and cultural landmarks. Visitors encounter wetlands, interpretive centers, and panoramic views of the river. The route highlights the heritage, commerce, and natural beauty of America's iconic waterway and its riverfront communities.

☐ 🔖 ♡ **Natchez Trace Parkway:** Stretching 444 miles from Natchez, Mississippi, to Nashville, Tennessee, this scenic parkway follows an ancient travel route. In Tennessee, it offers forested landscapes, wildlife viewing, and stops at historic inns and trail segments. It provides a tranquil journey blending nature, culture, and history along one of America's oldest pathways.

☐ 🔖 ♡ **Newfound Gap Road:** Crossing 31 miles of Great Smoky Mountains National Park, this route links Gatlinburg, Tennessee, with Cherokee, North Carolina. It climbs to 5,046 feet at Newfound Gap, offering overlooks, picnic areas, and Appalachian Trail access. The drive showcases dramatic elevation changes, biodiversity, and some of the park's most iconic vistas.

☐ 🔖 ♡ **Norris Freeway:** Running from Rocky Top to Halls, this byway highlights the Tennessee Valley Authority's first major hydroelectric project at Norris Dam. Travelers see rolling farmland, lake views, and historic CCC-built structures. It interprets early 20th-century engineering achievements while providing a scenic, leisurely drive through East Tennessee landscapes.

☐ 🔖 ♡ **Woodlands Trace:** Stretching through Land Between the Lakes, this quiet route passes wooded ridges, wildlife-rich corridors, and recreational sites. Visitors encounter overlooks, picnic areas, and trails that showcase the natural heritage of Tennessee and Kentucky. It provides a peaceful escape into forests and waterways, emphasizing ecological richness and scenic beauty.

State Scenic Byways

☐ 🔖 ♡ **Foothills Parkway:** Stretching along the northern edge of the Smoky Mountains, this parkway provides dramatic vistas across valleys, ridges, and distant peaks. Multiple overlooks and the Look Rock observation tower invite travelers to pause and take in sweeping views. With gentle curves and seasonal color, it is one of Tennessee's most scenic mountain drives.

☐ 🔖 ♡ **Great Smoky Mountains Byway:** Acting as a gateway to the national park, this route offers winding mountain roads, forested tunnels, and scenic pull-offs. It highlights rushing streams, wildlife habitats, and cultural landmarks of the Smokies. With each season bringing new beauty, the drive captures the essence of the state's most famous mountain landscape.

TENNESSEE

☐ 🔖 ♡ **Ocoee Scenic:** Following the Ocoee River Gorge through Cherokee National Forest, this corridor blends history and adventure. It traces the Old Copper Road and passes whitewater rapids, cliffs, and forested ridges. Recreation areas and trails provide access to the rugged terrain, making the drive a showcase of Tennessee's wild and untamed eastern mountains.

☐ 🔖 ♡ **Sequatchie Valley Scenic:** Running the length of one of Tennessee's most distinctive valleys, this route is framed by mountain ridges and dotted with farms and small towns. The valley's geology and cultural history come alive along the road, where travelers experience pastoral beauty, quiet landscapes, and the rural traditions that define the region.

☐ 🔖 ♡ **Tennessee River Trail:** Meandering along the Tennessee River, this route reveals a landscape shaped by water and time. Scenic bluffs, historic towns, and wildlife-rich shorelines line the drive. With opportunities for boating, fishing, and cultural exploration, the trail blends natural beauty with heritage, offering a journey through the heart of river country.

☐ 🔖 ♡ **Walton Road:** Once a key pioneer route across the Cumberland Plateau, this historic trail has been reborn as a scenic drive through wooded uplands and rolling ridges. Travelers follow the path settlers once used to reach the West, experiencing a mix of history and landscape. The road embodies Tennessee's frontier spirit while offering timeless beauty.

National Natural Landmarks

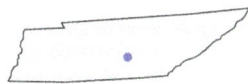 ☐ 🔖 ♡ **Arnold Engineering Development Center Natural Areas:** Designated a National Natural Landmark for preserving one of Tennessee's rarest swamp ecosystems, this site contains virgin forest and undisturbed marshland. It offers a critical refuge for wetland plants and wildlife while serving as an invaluable living laboratory for ecological and hydrological research.
GPS: 35.4978045, -86.0746915 (county wide)

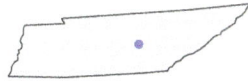 ☐ 🔖 ♡ **Big Bone Cave:** Famous as the discovery site of giant ground sloth remains, this limestone cavern was recognized as a National Natural Landmark for its paleontological and archaeological value. In addition to Ice Age fossils, it preserves evidence of early saltpeter mining, showcasing both natural and cultural history within its chambers.
GPS: 35.7726, -85.5570

 ☐ 🔖 ♡ **Cedar Glades:** Tennessee's cedar glades became National Natural Landmarks for their rare plant life and distinctive geology. Shallow limestone soils support unique species found nowhere else, thriving in open, sunlit spaces between forested lands. These habitats are among the most botanically significant ecosystems in the Southeast.
GPS: 36.0737, -86.3115

 ☐ 🔖 ♡ **Conley Hole:** Recognized as a National Natural Landmark for its dramatic vertical descent, Conley Hole is one of the deepest and most impressive pit caves in the United States. Its depth, form, and surrounding karst features vividly demonstrate the processes that shape limestone landscapes over geologic time.
GPS: 35.2000, -85.8200 (approximate)

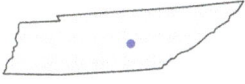 ☐ 🔖 ♡ **Cumberland Caverns:** Stretching more than 27 miles, this vast cave system holds National Natural Landmark status for its extraordinary karst features. Visitors encounter underground waterfalls, expansive chambers, and rare mineral formations, making it both one of America's longest caves and a premier showcase of subterranean geology.
GPS: 35.6692, -85.6808

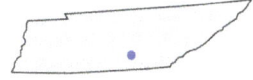 ☐ 🔖 ♡ **Dick Cove:** This near-virgin forest earned its National Natural Landmark status as one of Tennessee's best surviving old-growth woodlands. Its mature hardwoods and intact understory host diverse species in a natural setting, offering scientists and conservationists a valuable reference point for pre-settlement forests.
GPS: 35.2278, -85.9554

TENNESSEE

 **Grassy Cove Karst Area:** A National Natural Landmark for its outstanding karst geology, Grassy Cove is a massive enclosed valley filled with sinkholes, caves, and underground streams. It illustrates the processes of limestone dissolution and groundwater movement, offering a living example of how karst landscapes evolve.
GPS: 35.8568, -84.9264

 **May Prairie:** As Tennessee's largest surviving prairie remnant, May Prairie gained National Natural Landmark designation for its unique plant communities. Its open grasslands harbor rare wildflowers and grasses uncommon in the Southeast, providing a striking ecological contrast to the surrounding forests.
GPS: 35.4502, -86.0223

 **McAnulty's Woods:** This old forest, honored as a National Natural Landmark, protects the last known stand of upland hardwoods from the Mississippi Embayment region. The site's undisturbed character preserves a rare ecological community, offering insight into Tennessee's original woodland diversity.
GPS: 35.251944, -88.988167 (approximate)

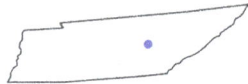 **Piney Falls:** Awarded National Natural Landmark status for its mix of natural features, Piney Falls combines towering waterfalls with an old-growth mesophytic forest. The deep gorge harbors intact plant and animal communities, making it one of Tennessee's most biologically valuable protected sites.
GPS: 35.7276749, -84.8559883

 **Reelfoot Lake:** Born of the massive New Madrid earthquakes of 1811–1812, Reelfoot Lake was designated a National Natural Landmark for its geological origin and ecological importance. Its bald cypress swamps, bottomland forests, and wetlands support exceptional biodiversity, making it one of the Mississippi Valley's richest natural areas.
GPS: 36.3889, -89.3889

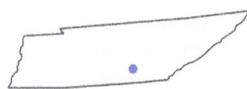 **Savage Gulf:** This deep sandstone gorge, spanning thousands of acres, was recognized as a National Natural Landmark for its pristine old-growth forests and diverse plant life. With sheer cliffs, waterfalls, and rugged terrain, Savage Gulf represents one of the most unspoiled forested canyons in the eastern United States.
GPS: 35.2590, -85.7890

 **The Lost Sea:** This cavern, home to America's largest underground lake, was named a National Natural Landmark for its remarkable hydrology and geological features. Beyond the vast lake, the cave preserves rare speleothems and traces of saltpeter mining, making it both a natural wonder and a cultural archive.
GPS: 35.5356, -84.4311

UNITED STATES EDITION

TEXAS

Texas's vast and varied landscapes include rugged canyons, sprawling deserts, towering pine forests, and sun-drenched coastlines. Through its extensive state parks, national forests, iconic national parks, and distinctive natural landmarks, Texas invites exploration on a grand scale.

🗓 Peak Season
March–May and October–November are Texas's peak seasons, offering mild temperatures and colorful landscapes. Spring brings wildflowers and ideal hiking weather, while fall provides clear skies and comfortable warmth.

🗓 Offseason Months
June–September is the offseason across much of the state due to high heat, though the Gulf Coast and Hill Country rivers remain popular. December–February is cooler and quieter, with mild weather in southern regions.

🍃 Scenery & Nature Timing
Spring explodes with bluebonnets and wildflowers across the Hill Country. Summer highlights beaches, rivers, and desert sunsets. Fall offers golden prairies and crisp mountain air, while winter brings migrating birds and clear desert nights.

✨ Special
Texas showcases the desert peaks of Big Bend, the limestone caverns of the Hill Country, and the coastal wetlands of Padre Island. Palo Duro Canyon, Enchanted Rock, and vast spring wildflower blooms reveal the state's dramatic natural variety.

THE ROAMER'S GUIDE

TEXAS

State Parks

☐ 🔖 ♡ **Abilene State Park:** Nestled in the hills of Taylor County, Abilene State Park offers shady campsites, hiking trails, and fishing in Lake Abilene. Visitors enjoy picnicking under large oak and elm trees, swimming in the historic pool, and observing wildlife. It's a peaceful retreat where families can connect with nature and enjoy a slower pace near the city of Abilene.

☐ 🔖 ♡ **Atlanta State Park:** Situated on Wright Patman Lake in East Texas, Atlanta State Park is a 1,475-acre haven for boating, fishing, and swimming. Visitors enjoy shaded campsites beneath towering pines, scenic hiking trails, and birdwatching opportunities. The park's quiet woodlands and lakeside setting make it an ideal escape for family camping, water recreation, and outdoor relaxation.

☐ 🔖 ♡ **Balmorhea State Park:** Famous for its spring-fed swimming pool, Balmorhea in Reeves County is a desert oasis where visitors can swim, snorkel, and scuba dive in crystal-clear water. The San Solomon Springs pumps millions of gallons daily, supporting fish and turtles. Desert mountains frame this unique retreat, offering picnic areas, camping, and a refreshing experience unmatched in Texas.

☐ 🔖 ♡ **Bastrop State Park:** Located in the Lost Pines of Central Texas, Bastrop State Park blends history and nature. Civilian Conservation Corps cabins, trails, and picnic areas remain among loblolly pines recovering from wildfire. A small lake offers fishing, and campsites welcome visitors. The park provides a tranquil space to hike, bike, or camp while reflecting on Texas' conservation history.

☐ 🔖 ♡ **Bentsen-Rio Grande Valley State Park:** This 800-acre park in the Rio Grande Valley is world-renowned for birdwatching, with more than 350 recorded species. As part of the World Birding Center, it features tram tours, observation decks, and hiking or biking trails. Visitors immerse themselves in subtropical habitats while spotting rare migratory birds in one of Texas' premier wildlife destinations.

☐ 🔖 ♡ **Big Bend Ranch State Park:** Spanning over 300,000 acres, Big Bend Ranch is Texas' largest state park. Rugged desert canyons, scenic drives, and remote trails invite exploration. Outdoor enthusiasts hike, bike, paddle, or ride horseback through its dramatic landscapes. Night skies rival anywhere on Earth, making it a top stargazing spot. Its sheer size offers solitude and wild adventure.

☐ 🔖 ♡ **Big Spring State Park:** Overlooking the West Texas city of Big Spring, this park offers dramatic vistas from a 200-foot bluff. Visitors enjoy scenic drives, hiking trails, and picnicking areas with panoramic views. The rugged limestone terrain provides habitat for desert plants and wildlife. With easy access to town, it blends outdoor recreation with natural beauty in a desert setting.

☐ 🔖 ♡ **Blanco State Park:** Set along the Blanco River, this small park in the Hill Country is perfect for swimming, tubing, or fishing. Shady picnic areas and campgrounds welcome visitors seeking relaxation. Cypress trees line the riverbanks, and hiking trails wind through gentle terrain. It's a family-friendly destination offering easy access to water recreation right in the town of Blanco.

☐ 🔖 ♡ **Bonham State Park:** Just northeast of Dallas, this 261-acre park centers on a 65-acre lake. Canoeing, kayaking, fishing, and swimming attract visitors, while trails wind through woodlands and grasslands. Historic CCC structures dot the landscape, adding cultural value. The park provides a peaceful getaway for families seeking boating, hiking, and camping amid a quiet natural setting.

☐ 🔖 ♡ **Brazos Bend State Park:** Known for its alligators and wetlands, Brazos Bend near Houston offers more than 37 miles of trails for hiking, biking, and horseback riding. The George Observatory allows stargazing, while lakes provide fishing and birdwatching. Boardwalks and viewing platforms help visitors explore diverse ecosystems safely, making it a favorite for nature lovers and families.

☐ 🔖 ♡ **Buescher State Park:** Neighboring Bastrop, Buescher features pine woodlands and a scenic 30-acre lake. Fishing, canoeing, and hiking draw visitors to this quieter gem. Shaded campgrounds, CCC-built shelters, and tranquil trails provide a relaxed alternative to busier parks. The forested setting makes it a peaceful retreat for wildlife watching, camping, or simply enjoying nature's quiet beauty.

☐ 🔖 ♡ **Caddo Lake State Park:** Famous for its cypress trees draped in Spanish moss, Caddo Lake State Park offers a bayou experience unlike any other in Texas. Visitors explore paddling trails by canoe or kayak, fish from piers, or hike through wooded terrain. The swamp-like environment supports diverse wildlife, making it a prime destination for photographers, birdwatchers, and nature enthusiasts.

TEXAS

☐ 🔖 ♡ **Caprock Canyons State Park and Trailway:** In the Texas Panhandle, Caprock Canyons is home to the Texas State Bison Herd. Red rock canyons, dramatic cliffs, and 90 miles of trails attract hikers, bikers, and horseback riders. The abandoned railroad trail offers unique scenery, while bison roam freely. It's a rugged, adventurous landscape showcasing Texas' wild, untamed natural beauty.

☐ 🔖 ♡ **Cedar Hill State Park:** Just minutes from Dallas, Cedar Hill offers quick access to Joe Pool Lake for boating, swimming, and fishing. Campsites sit among wooded hills, while more than 1,000 acres provide hiking and biking trails. It's a convenient urban escape, combining outdoor recreation with city proximity, making it popular for day trips and family weekends alike.

☐ 🔖 ♡ **Choke Canyon State Park:** Centered on Choke Canyon Reservoir, this South Texas park offers excellent fishing, boating, and birdwatching. Wildlife includes deer, javelina, and numerous migratory birds. Visitors camp near the lake, hike trails, or picnic under mesquite trees. Its blend of water recreation and wildlife habitat makes it a favorite for anglers and nature lovers.

☐ 🔖 ♡ **Cleburne State Park:** Anchored by the spring-fed Cedar Lake, Cleburne offers fishing, swimming, and no-wake boating. Miles of hiking and biking trails wind through limestone hills and cedar forests. Campgrounds and shaded picnic areas make it inviting for families. The park's natural beauty and accessible facilities provide a peaceful outdoor experience close to the Dallas-Fort Worth area.

☐ 🔖 ♡ **Colorado Bend State Park:** A rugged Hill Country destination, Colorado Bend offers 35 miles of hiking and biking trails, spelunking in caves, and guided tours to 70-foot Gorman Falls. The Colorado River provides fishing and paddling. Primitive camping adds adventure, while diverse habitats attract wildlife. It's a challenging yet rewarding park for explorers seeking wild Texas landscapes.

☐ 🔖 ♡ **Cooper Lake State Park:** Split into two units—Doctors Creek and South Sulphur—this park surrounds a large reservoir. Fishing, boating, and swimming are major draws, with sandy beaches for families. Trails wind through woodlands, offering wildlife viewing and birdwatching. Spacious campgrounds, equestrian facilities, and quiet lakeside settings make it versatile for outdoor recreation.

☐ 🔖 ♡ **Copper Breaks State Park:** Known for its International Dark Sky designation, Copper Breaks offers stargazing, rugged hiking trails, and fishing lakes in North Texas. Red-rock mesas and juniper-covered hills create striking scenery. Wildlife ranges from longhorn cattle to prairie birds. Remote and quiet, the park is a favorite for astronomy enthusiasts, campers, and those seeking solitude.

☐ 🔖 ♡ **Daingerfield State Park:** East Texas woodlands surround a serene 80-acre lake at Daingerfield. Visitors enjoy swimming, paddle boating, and fishing in a picturesque setting. Trails wind through pine and hardwood forests, vibrant with wildflowers in spring. CCC-built cabins and picnic areas add historic charm. The peaceful atmosphere makes it perfect for relaxation, family gatherings, and nature appreciation.

☐ 🔖 ♡ **Davis Mountains State Park:** Nestled in far West Texas, this park offers rugged mountain scenery with miles of hiking, biking, and equestrian trails. Scenic Skyline Drive provides sweeping views, while camping includes both modern sites and historic CCC-built cabins. Wildlife like javelina and deer roam the area, and dark skies make it a superb destination for stargazing.

☐ 🔖 ♡ **Dinosaur Valley State Park:** Famous for preserved dinosaur tracks in the Paluxy River, this park in Glen Rose offers a prehistoric adventure. Visitors wade the riverbed to view tracks, hike wooded trails, or swim and picnic along the river. With camping, fishing, and educational exhibits, it's both a natural wonder and family-friendly learning experience in Texas' Hill Country.

☐ 🔖 ♡ **Eisenhower State Park:** Perched on bluffs above Lake Texoma, this park offers boating, fishing, and swimming in a massive reservoir. Trails wind through wooded areas rich in wildflowers and wildlife. Campsites include lakeside views, and sandy coves provide easy water access. The park blends recreation and relaxation in a scenic setting honoring President Dwight D. Eisenhower.

☐ 🔖 ♡ **Estero Llano Grande State Park:** Part of the World Birding Center in the Rio Grande Valley, this park features wetlands, woodlands, and prairies. Boardwalks and trails let visitors observe diverse wildlife, including rare migratory birds. With picnic areas, guided programs, and accessible trails, it's a premier destination for birdwatchers and nature enthusiasts exploring subtropical Texas habitats.

TEXAS

☐ 🔖 ♡ **Falcon State Park:** Located on Falcon Reservoir along the Rio Grande, this park offers top-notch fishing for bass and catfish. Visitors camp under mesquite and cactus, hike desert trails, or watch diverse bird species. Its vast lake is perfect for boating and water sports, while quiet coves provide tranquil settings for picnicking and stargazing under expansive South Texas skies.

☐ 🔖 ♡ **Fort Boggy State Park:** A small but charming park in Leon County, Fort Boggy features a 15-acre lake ideal for fishing, kayaking, and swimming. Shaded trails loop through pine and hardwood forests, offering wildlife observation and birding opportunities. Campsites and picnic areas make it a convenient family getaway, balancing water recreation with peaceful East Texas woodlands.

☐ 🔖 ♡ **Fort Leaton State Historic Site:** At the gateway to Big Bend Ranch, Fort Leaton preserves an adobe fortress from 1848. Visitors explore historic rooms and exhibits while learning about frontier trade and cultural exchanges along the Rio Grande. Picnic areas and scenic views add outdoor charm. It's both a cultural landmark and a relaxing stop for history enthusiasts.

☐ 🔖 ♡ **Fort Parker State Park:** Anchored by a 750-acre lake, this park in Limestone County offers boating, fishing, and swimming. Hikers and bikers enjoy shaded trails through forests and prairies. Historic sites tell the story of the Texas frontier, while CCC-built facilities provide rustic charm. With abundant wildlife and water recreation, it's a versatile spot for family outings.

☐ 🔖 ♡ **Fort Richardson State Park & Historic Site:** Combining history and nature, this park showcases preserved frontier military buildings from the 1860s. Trails connect the fort to Lost Creek Reservoir for hiking, biking, and horseback riding. Visitors camp, fish, and explore both the historic site and surrounding natural landscapes, making it a unique Texas experience.

☐ 🔖 ♡ **Galveston Island State Park:** Stretching from beach to bay, Galveston Island offers swimming, fishing, kayaking, and birdwatching along the Gulf Coast. Trails cross dunes and wetlands, providing diverse habitats for wildlife. Campsites accommodate tents and RVs, with stunning sunrise and sunset views. It's a rare coastal park that lets visitors explore both seaside and bayside ecosystems.

☐ 🔖 ♡ **Garner State Park:** A Hill Country favorite, Garner sits along the crystal-clear Frio River, offering tubing, swimming, and fishing. Trails climb scenic limestone hills, while summer evenings feature jukebox dances that have become tradition. With campgrounds, cabins, and rental paddleboats, Garner is one of Texas' most popular parks, drawing families for fun on the river since the 1940s.

☐ 🔖 ♡ **Goliad State Park & Historic Site:** This park blends history and nature along the San Antonio River. Visitors explore Mission Espíritu Santo, a restored Spanish mission built in 1749, or enjoy camping, fishing, and hiking. The park commemorates Texas' independence era while providing river access, shaded picnic areas, and opportunities for birdwatching in a culturally rich setting.

☐ 🔖 ♡ **Goose Island State Park:** Famous for the "Big Tree," a massive live oak centuries old, this coastal park offers fishing piers, boat ramps, and campsites on Aransas Bay. Birdwatchers spot whooping cranes in winter, while anglers reel in redfish and trout. With oak motts, salt marshes, and bayside breezes, Goose Island is a diverse mix of history, nature, and recreation.

☐ 🔖 ♡ **Guadalupe River State Park:** Flowing through the Hill Country, this park offers tubing, kayaking, and fishing along a scenic stretch of river. Campgrounds and picnic sites dot the shoreline, while trails explore limestone bluffs, woodlands, and meadows. Wildlife abounds, from deer to songbirds, and swimming holes invite cooling dips, making it a classic Texas outdoor destination.

☐ 🔖 ♡ **Hueco Tanks State Historic Site:** Renowned for ancient pictographs and world-class rock climbing, Hueco Tanks near El Paso preserves cultural history and desert landscapes. Visitors join guided tours to view rock art, hike rugged trails, or boulder on granite formations. Its mix of archaeology, recreation, and unique desert ecology makes it an unforgettable Texas park experience.

☐ 🔖 ♡ **Huntsville State Park:** Nestled in the Pineywoods, this 2,000-acre park features Lake Raven for fishing, canoeing, and swimming. Trails wind through loblolly pines and hardwoods, home to deer, alligators, and abundant birdlife. Campsites, cabins, and picnic areas provide lodging and relaxation. Close to Houston, it's a convenient destination for camping, hiking, and enjoying East Texas nature.

TEXAS

☐ 🔖 ♡ **Inks Lake State Park:** Located in Burnet County, Inks Lake offers year-round water activities on a constant-level reservoir. Swimming, boating, and fishing are popular, while hiking trails wind through granite outcrops and shady woodlands. Campsites and cabins provide lakeside lodging. Its mix of water recreation, scenery, and accessibility makes it a Hill Country favorite.

☐ 🔖 ♡ **Kickapoo Cavern State Park:** On the western Edwards Plateau, Kickapoo Cavern features over 20 known caves, with guided tours into its namesake cavern. Trails cross rugged canyons and woodlands rich with wildlife like bats, deer, and birds. Primitive camping enhances the remote experience, while nightly bat flights in summer add a dramatic natural spectacle.

☐ 🔖 ♡ **Lake Arrowhead State Park:** Near Wichita Falls, this 524-acre park offers fishing and boating on a large reservoir, along with equestrian and hiking trails. Prairie landscapes support buffalo and prairie dog colonies. Visitors enjoy camping, birdwatching, and water recreation, making it an accessible escape blending North Texas prairie ecology with outdoor fun.

☐ 🔖 ♡ **Lake Bob Sandlin State Park:** Nestled in East Texas, this park features a reservoir popular for fishing, boating, and swimming. Shady trails meander through pine and hardwood forests, while campsites and screened shelters offer cozy stays. Wildlife, including deer and waterfowl, abounds. It's a peaceful lakeside retreat perfect for family camping and water recreation.

☐ 🔖 ♡ **Lake Brownwood State Park:** Built by the CCC, this park features stone structures, shaded campsites, and lake access for fishing, boating, and swimming. Trails wind through oak woodlands, offering birdwatching and wildlife viewing. Its historic charm and recreational opportunities make it a balanced destination for nature exploration and cultural appreciation.

☐ 🔖 ♡ **Lake Casa Blanca International State Park:** Located near Laredo, this 371-acre park centers on a reservoir for boating, fishing, swimming, and water skiing. Trails and picnic areas provide family fun, while camping offers overnight stays. Its international border location makes it unique, drawing visitors for outdoor recreation and cross-cultural connections.

☐ 🔖 ♡ **Lake Colorado City State Park:** Built around a reservoir in West Texas, this park features fishing, swimming, and kayaking opportunities. Trails loop through semi-arid landscapes of mesquite and prickly pear, with excellent birdwatching. Campgrounds and group facilities make it suitable for gatherings, offering both relaxation and recreation in a rugged desert setting.

☐ 🔖 ♡ **Lake Corpus Christi State Park:** Featuring a 21,000-acre reservoir, this park offers boating, fishing, and swimming near Corpus Christi. Visitors camp lakeside, hike trails, and picnic under shade trees. The CCC's stonework adds historic character. It's a popular South Texas getaway where water recreation, wildlife, and history converge.

☐ 🔖 ♡ **Lake Livingston State Park:** This East Texas park provides access to one of the state's largest reservoirs. Boating, fishing, and swimming dominate, while trails explore pineywoods habitats. Campgrounds, cabins, and equestrian facilities serve families and groups. Abundant wildlife, from bald eagles to deer, make it a versatile destination for water recreation and nature appreciation.

☐ 🔖 ♡ **Lake Mineral Wells State Park:** Known for its rock-climbing area at Penitentiary Hollow, this North Texas park offers hiking, biking, and equestrian trails along with lake fishing and swimming. Historic features include CCC structures. With varied terrain and recreational options, it's a popular park for adventurers and families seeking both thrills and relaxation.

☐ 🔖 ♡ **Lake Somerville State Park:** Surrounding Lake Somerville, this park includes two main units—Birch Creek and Nails Creek—linked by a 13-mile trailway. Visitors enjoy boating, fishing, horseback riding, and camping. Trails cross prairies and woodlands rich in wildlife. With water access and diverse activities, it's a Central Texas hub for recreation.

☐ 🔖 ♡ **Lake Tawakoni State Park:** Situated on a 37,000-acre reservoir, this park features sandy swimming beaches, fishing piers, and boating access. Trails loop through oak woodlands and prairies, offering wildlife viewing and birdwatching. Campgrounds accommodate tents and RVs, making it a family-friendly getaway with plenty of water-based activities and scenic natural beauty.

TEXAS

☐ 🔖 ♡ **Lake Whitney State Park:** Perched on limestone bluffs, this park offers stunning views of Lake Whitney, a large North Texas reservoir. Visitors enjoy swimming, boating, fishing, and hiking through rolling woodlands. Campsites and picnic areas provide comfort, while wildlife observation adds interest. Its dramatic lake setting makes it a prime recreation spot.

☐ 🔖 ♡ **Lockhart State Park:** A unique park combining natural beauty with recreation, Lockhart features a 9-hole golf course, hiking trails, and a creek for fishing. Shady campgrounds and CCC-built stone structures add character. Located in the "Barbecue Capital of Texas," it's an ideal stop for combining outdoor fun with cultural experiences nearby.

☐ 🔖 ♡ **Longhorn Cavern State Park:** Known for its dramatic underground passages, Longhorn Cavern offers guided tours through sculpted limestone caves. Above ground, visitors enjoy hiking trails and historic CCC buildings. The park blends geology, history, and recreation, making it a fascinating destination for those interested in natural wonders and Texas heritage.

☐ 🔖 ♡ **Lost Creek Reservoir State Trailway:** This 10-mile rail-trail connects Fort Richardson State Park to Lake Jacksboro, offering hiking, biking, and horseback riding. Traversing prairies, woodlands, and creek crossings, it provides scenic variety and opportunities for wildlife viewing. It's a linear park that highlights outdoor exploration and connects historic and natural landmarks.

☐ 🔖 ♡ **Lyndon B. Johnson State Park & Historic Site:** Celebrating the life and legacy of the 36th U.S. president, this park preserves rural Texas history with exhibits, longhorn herds, and a working farm. Trails, picnic areas, and river access add outdoor enjoyment. Visitors can explore history while experiencing the natural beauty of the Hill Country.

☐ 🔖 ♡ **Martin Creek Lake State Park:** Located in East Texas, this park offers fishing and boating on a reservoir with warm waters. Shaded trails meander through pine forests, while campsites and cabins provide lodging. Birdwatching, swimming, and wildlife observation round out activities. Its quiet lake setting is ideal for relaxation and outdoor recreation.

☐ 🔖 ♡ **Martin Dies Jr. State Park:** At the confluence of the Angelina and Neches Rivers, this park features bottomland forests and access to B.A. Steinhagen Lake. Canoeing, kayaking, and fishing are popular, while trails and boardwalks lead through wetlands. Campsites and picnic areas make it inviting for families. It's a watery, wooded escape rich in wildlife.

☐ 🔖 ♡ **McKinney Falls State Park:** Located in Austin, this park features Onion Creek cascading over limestone ledges, creating scenic waterfalls and swimming holes. Visitors enjoy hiking and biking trails through wooded areas, picnicking under large trees, and exploring historic homesteads. With easy city access, it's a popular urban escape blending recreation with natural beauty.

☐ 🔖 ♡ **Meridian State Park:** Nestled in Bosque County's Hill Country limestone hills, Meridian State Park surrounds a serene 72-acre lake built by the Civilian Conservation Corps in the 1930s. Visitors can swim, paddle, or fish (no license required), explore over 5 miles of trails with limestone overlooks, picnic by the water, camp in cabins or sites, and spot rare golden-cheeked warblers nesting nearby.

☐ 🔖 ♡ **Mission Tejas State Park:** In East Texas, this small but historic park commemorates Spain's first mission in the region. Trails wind through pine and hardwood forests, and a reconstructed log cabin offers a glimpse of frontier life. Visitors camp, hike, and fish in a quiet setting, enjoying a blend of cultural history and tranquil natural landscapes.

☐ 🔖 ♡ **Monahans Sandhills State Park:** Vast dunes stretch for miles in this desert park, where visitors sandboard, hike, or ride horses across shifting landscapes. Campsites offer overnight stays under starry skies, while wildlife such as roadrunners and jackrabbits inhabit the area. The park provides a unique Texas experience, resembling a miniature Sahara in West Texas.

☐ 🔖 ♡ **Mother Neff State Park:** Texas' first state park, founded in 1921, Mother Neff offers hiking trails through woodlands and along the Leon River. CCC-built facilities remain, providing rustic charm. Birdwatchers and families enjoy its quiet setting, shaded picnic areas, and natural beauty. As the birthplace of the park system, it carries both historical and recreational significance.

☐ 🔖 ♡ **Mustang Island State Park:** Along the Gulf Coast, Mustang Island offers five miles of sandy beaches for swimming, fishing, and camping. Paddling trails wind through coastal marshes, attracting kayakers and birdwatchers. Visitors camp steps from the surf, enjoy kite flying, or simply relax by the water. It's a quintessential Texas beach park with abundant wildlife.

TEXAS

☐ 🔖 ♡ **Old Tunnel State Park:** A former railroad tunnel turned bat haven, this tiny park near Fredericksburg is famous for summer bat emergences. Visitors watch millions of Mexican free-tailed bats soar at dusk, while trails explore Hill Country landscapes. The park emphasizes wildlife conservation and offers a unique natural spectacle tied to Texas' ecological diversity.

☐ 🔖 ♡ **Palmetto State Park:** Located along the San Marcos River, Palmetto features lush vegetation unusual for Central Texas, including dwarf palmettos in swampy habitats. Visitors canoe, fish, and swim in the river or hike trails through tropical-like scenery. CCC-built pavilions add historic charm. Its unique ecosystem makes it a fascinating blend of Texas and Gulf Coast nature.

☐ 🔖 ♡ **Palo Duro Canyon State Park:** Known as the "Grand Canyon of Texas," this Panhandle park showcases colorful cliffs and dramatic rock formations. Hiking, biking, and horseback trails crisscross the canyon, while camping provides overnight stays in a breathtaking setting. Visitors enjoy scenic drives, amphitheater shows, and unrivaled stargazing in this iconic natural wonder.

☐ 🔖 ♡ **Palo Pinto Mountains State Park:** Encompassing 4,800 acres of rugged hills, canyons, and Tucker Lake, this developing park lies west of Fort Worth in the Western Cross Timbers. Once open, it will feature trails for hiking, biking, and horseback riding, plus fishing, paddling, camping, birding, and stargazing. Its diverse habitats and scenic views promise a premier North Texas outdoor destination.

☐ 🔖 ♡ **Pedernales Falls State Park:** Centered on the Pedernales River, this park offers cascading limestone falls, swimming holes, and sandy beaches. Miles of trails welcome hikers, bikers, and equestrians, while birdwatchers spot golden-cheeked warblers. Camping and picnicking areas make it family-friendly. Its striking scenery and flowing waters make it one of the Hill Country's most beloved parks.

☐ 🔖 ♡ **Purtis Creek State Park:** A hidden gem in East Texas, Purtis Creek offers a quiet 355-acre lake popular for catch-and-release bass fishing. Trails wind through post oak and pine woodlands, while campsites provide restful stays. Kayaking, birding, and picnicking add to the activities. The park's peaceful waters and shaded forests make it an ideal retreat.

☐ 🔖 ♡ **Resaca de la Palma State Park:** Part of the World Birding Center, this park preserves one of the largest tracts of native habitat in the Rio Grande Valley. Trails and tram tours help visitors explore wetlands and woodlands teeming with migratory birds. With picnic areas and quiet observation decks, it's a premier destination for birdwatchers and naturalists.

☐ 🔖 ♡ **San Angelo State Park:** This 7,500-acre park on O.C. Fisher Reservoir features camping, fishing, and boating alongside miles of multi-use trails. Visitors encounter the official Texas longhorn herd and even fossilized Permian trackways. With diverse wildlife and recreation, it's a fascinating blend of natural and cultural history in West Texas.

☐ 🔖 ♡ **San Jacinto Battleground State Historic Site:** Preserving the site of the pivotal 1836 battle for Texas independence, this park features the towering San Jacinto Monument, a museum, and trails. Visitors learn history while exploring marshes and the Houston Ship Channel. It's a blend of heritage and nature that highlights Texas' struggle for independence.

☐ 🔖 ♡ **Sea Rim State Park:** On the Gulf Coast near Port Arthur, this park offers 5 miles of sandy beach and 4,000 acres of marshland. Visitors swim, fish, and paddle coastal waters, or explore boardwalk trails through wetlands. Primitive beachfront campsites let guests sleep near the surf. It's a wild, less-developed alternative to Texas' busier beaches.

☐ 🔖 ♡ **Seminole Canyon State Park & Historic Site:** Overlooking the Rio Grande, this park preserves ancient rock art dating back thousands of years. Visitors hike canyons and cliffs, join tours to see pictographs, or camp amid desert terrain. The park offers both cultural heritage and rugged recreation, making it a significant archaeological and outdoor destination.

☐ 🔖 ♡ **Sheldon Lake State Park & Environmental Learning Center:** Near Houston, this park focuses on wetland education and urban outdoor recreation. Visitors fish in the lake, hike trails, and explore boardwalks over marshes. Observation towers provide skyline views, while environmental programs teach conservation. It's a family-friendly introduction to nature within city limits.

☐ 🔖 ♡ **South Llano River State Park:** Flowing through the Hill Country, this park features tubing, kayaking, and swimming along the South Llano River. Trails explore woodlands home to wild turkeys and deer, while campgrounds provide riverside stays. Its combination of water recreation, dark skies, and wildlife makes it a peaceful outdoor destination.

TEXAS

☐ 🔖 ♡ **Stephen F. Austin State Park:** Located west of Houston along the Brazos River, this park celebrates Texas history while offering outdoor recreation. Shady campsites, hiking trails, and picnic areas line the river, where birdwatchers spot migratory species. Floodplain woodlands provide habitat for diverse wildlife. It's a relaxing destination blending history and natural beauty.

☐ 🔖 ♡ **Tyler State Park:** Nestled in East Texas pine forests, this 985-acre park features a spring-fed 64-acre lake for fishing, swimming, and boating. Visitors hike trails winding through tall trees and wildflowers, picnic under shaded pavilions, and camp in cabins or tent sites. With its tranquil waters and lush woodlands, it's a popular family destination year-round.

☐ 🔖 ♡ **Village Creek State Park:** Located near Beaumont, this park protects a free-flowing stream in the Pineywoods. Visitors paddle canoes and kayaks along Village Creek, hike trails through cypress swamps, or fish from its sandy banks. With abundant wildlife, camping, and quiet settings, it offers a unique East Texas river experience and is perfect for nature immersion.

☐ 🔖 ♡ **Washington-on-the-Brazos State Historic Site:** Known as the "Birthplace of Texas," this park preserves the site where the Texas Declaration of Independence was signed in 1836. Visitors explore historic buildings, museums, and trails along the Brazos River. It's a destination rich in heritage, blending outdoor relaxation with cultural education.

☐ 🔖 ♡ **Wyler Aerial Tramway State Park:** Situated in El Paso, this park once offered a scenic tram ride to Ranger Peak, giving panoramic views of the Franklin Mountains and surrounding desert. Although the tramway is currently closed, the park remains a symbol of West Texas' unique landscapes and is undergoing plans for future revitalization.

State Natural Areas

☐ 🔖 ♡ **Devil's Sinkhole State Natural Area:** In Edwards County, this 1,860-acre preserve protects a massive vertical cavern nearly 400 feet deep. Home to millions of Mexican free-tailed bats, it offers spectacular summer evening emergences. Guided tours, a bat-viewing platform, exhibits, and picnic areas make it a premier spot for wildlife watching and Hill Country geology.

☐ 🔖 ♡ **Devils River State Natural Area:** Covering 37,000 acres in Val Verde County, this rugged preserve protects one of Texas' wildest rivers. Clear spring-fed waters invite paddling, fishing, and swimming, but entry is limited and primitive. Visitors explore canyons, desert plateaus, and wildlife habitats while camping under dark skies in one of the state's most remote, pristine backcountry areas.

☐ 🔖 ♡ **Government Canyon State Natural Area:** Just outside San Antonio, this 12,000-acre area protects rugged canyons, grasslands, and forests while offering over 40 miles of hiking and biking trails. It shelters endangered birds like the golden-cheeked warbler. A visitor center, guided hikes, and picnic areas enhance the experience, making it a unique balance of recreation and conservation.

☐ 🔖 ♡ **Hill Country State Natural Area:** This 5,400-acre Bandera County preserve offers back-to-basics adventure with multiuse trails for hiking, biking, and horseback riding. Primitive campsites dot rugged canyons, plateaus, and creek bottoms. Known for solitude, stargazing, and natural beauty, it provides a rustic escape for those seeking quiet reflection and outdoor challenge in the Hill Country.

☐ 🔖 ♡ **Honey Creek State Natural Area:** In Comal County, this 2,300-acre site preserves a pristine spring-fed creek, limestone bluffs, and diverse habitats. Accessible only on guided tours, it highlights conservation, water quality, and endangered species. The experience combines education with scenic beauty, offering a rare glimpse into an untouched section of the Texas Hill Country.

☐ 🔖 ♡ **Lost Maples State Natural Area:** In Bandera and Real counties, this 2,900-acre preserve is renowned for fall foliage of Uvalde bigtooth maples. Trails lead to canyons, springs, and scenic overlooks. Visitors hike, camp, birdwatch, and fish in a setting rich with wildlife, including rare golden-cheeked warblers. It's a beloved Hill Country destination for nature and seasonal color.

National Parks

 **Alibates Flint Quarries National Monument:** Near Amarillo, this site preserves ancient quarries where Native Americans mined colorful flint for tools over 13,000 years. Guided tours reveal quarry pits, petroglyphs, and stories of prehistoric cultures. Visitors learn about ancient craftsmanship and the site's importance in early trade networks across North America.

 **Amistad National Recreation Area:** Along the Rio Grande near Del Rio, Amistad Reservoir offers clear waters for boating, fishing, scuba diving, and swimming. Rugged canyons and desert landscapes surround the lake, while prehistoric rock art sites tell stories of early peoples. Campgrounds and trails make it a hub for both recreation and cultural exploration.

 **Big Bend National Park:** Covering over 800,000 acres along the Rio Grande, Big Bend is Texas' crown jewel of desert, mountain, and river landscapes. Visitors hike Chisos Mountains trails, float canyons carved by the river, and stargaze under some of the darkest skies in the U.S. Its vast biodiversity and sweeping views make it one of America's great wilderness parks.

  **Big Thicket National Preserve:** In Southeast Texas, Big Thicket protects nine ecosystems, from pine forests to bayous. Designated a UNESCO Biosphere Reserve, it harbors remarkable biodiversity, including carnivorous plants and migratory birds. Visitors paddle quiet waterways, hike over 40 miles of trails, and immerse themselves in one of the most diverse natural regions in the U.S.

 **Chamizal National Memorial:** In El Paso, this memorial commemorates the peaceful resolution of a century-long boundary dispute between the U.S. and Mexico. Visitors explore cultural exhibits, art galleries, and outdoor performance spaces. It's both a reminder of diplomacy and a vibrant cultural hub celebrating the shared heritage of borderland communities.

 **Fort Davis National Historic Site:** Preserving one of the best-surviving frontier forts, this site showcases the 1854–1891 post that protected travelers and settlers. Restored buildings and museum exhibits interpret the lives of Buffalo Soldiers, officers, and families. Scenic trails connect to the surrounding Davis Mountains, blending frontier history with rugged landscapes.

 **Guadalupe Mountains National Park:** In West Texas, this park protects the state's highest peak, Guadalupe Peak, rising 8,751 feet. Trails climb through canyons, desert, and pine forests, while limestone cliffs reveal ancient fossil reefs. Visitors explore striking landscapes, rich wildlife, and rugged backcountry, making it a premier hiking and wilderness destination.

 **Lake Meredith National Recreation Area:** Near Amarillo, Lake Meredith offers boating, fishing, camping, and water sports in the Texas Panhandle. Surrounded by colorful cliffs and prairie, it's also home to archaeological sites reflecting thousands of years of human history. Visitors enjoy trails, scenic overlooks, and wildlife viewing in this High Plains reservoir park.

 **Lyndon B. Johnson National Historical Park:** In Stonewall and Johnson City, this park preserves the life and legacy of the 36th U.S. President. Visitors tour the LBJ Ranch, known as the "Texas White House," along with his boyhood home and family cemetery. Exhibits interpret Johnson's Great Society programs and contributions to American civil rights.

  Padre Island National Seashore: Protecting 66 miles of undeveloped barrier island, Padre Island offers pristine beaches, dunes, and lagoons along the Gulf Coast. It provides critical nesting habitat for Kemp's ridley sea turtles and is a top spot for birdwatching. Visitors swim, camp, fish, and enjoy the wild beauty of one of America's longest natural seashores.

 **Palo Alto Battlefield National Historical Park:** In Brownsville, this park preserves the site of the first battle of the U.S.-Mexican War in 1846. Trails and exhibits interpret the conflict and its impact on Texas and the nation. Visitors walk the battlefield, explore the visitor center, and reflect on this pivotal moment in North American history.

  Rio Grande Wild and Scenic River: Flowing through Big Bend country, this protected stretch of river highlights the dramatic canyons and desert landscapes of the U.S.-Mexico border. Paddlers navigate Santa Elena, Mariscal, and Boquillas canyons, while rugged backcountry offers solitude. It protects both natural beauty and cultural history tied to the Rio Grande.

TEXAS

☐ 🔖 ♡ **San Antonio Missions National Historical Park:** Preserving four Spanish colonial missions—Concepción, San José, San Juan, and Espada—this UNESCO World Heritage Site tells the story of early Texas. Visitors tour historic churches, grounds, and acequias while learning about Spanish and Indigenous heritage. Trails and bike paths link the missions across the San Antonio River valley.

☐ 🔖 ♡ **Waco Mammoth National Monument:** This site preserves the nation's only recorded nursery herd of Ice Age Columbian mammoths. Excavated fossils remain in situ beneath a protective shelter, allowing visitors to view them up close. Exhibits and guided tours interpret the lives of mammoths and other prehistoric creatures that once roamed Central Texas.

State & National Forests

☐ 🔖 ♡ **Angelina National Forest:** Spanning ~154,000 acres of the East Texas Pineywoods, Angelina protects loblolly, longleaf, and shortleaf pine forests. It provides habitat for bald eagles and endangered red-cockaded woodpeckers. Visitors enjoy Ratcliff Lake, wilderness areas like Upland Island, hiking trails, camping, hunting, and fishing in a landscape managed for both conservation and recreation.

☐ 🔖 ♡ **Davy Crockett National Forest:** Established in 1936, this ~160,600-acre forest preserves mixed pine-hardwood ecosystems of East Texas. Centered around Ratcliff Lake, it offers camping, hiking, equestrian and OHV trails, hunting, and fishing. Managed for timber, water, and wildlife, it is home to deer, turkey, and songbirds, making it a multi-use landscape blending recreation and conservation.

☐ 🔖 ♡ **E.O. Siecke State Forest:** Texas' first state forest, established in 1923, covers 1,722 acres in Jasper County. Managed by Texas A&M Forest Service, it serves as a living laboratory for forestry research and education. The forest demonstrates sustainable practices, supports diverse plant and animal life, and provides opportunities for hiking, wildlife observation, and environmental learning.

☐ 🔖 ♡ **I.D. Fairchild State Forest:** This 2,760-acre forest in Cherokee County is Texas' largest state forest, managed for research, conservation, and recreation. Its pine-hardwood stands support wildlife like songbirds and deer. Trails allow hiking, biking, and horseback riding, while educational programs highlight sustainable forestry. It's a working forest that also welcomes the public to explore.

☐ 🔖 ♡ **Kirby State Forest:** Covering 626 acres in Tyler County, Kirby was donated in 1929 by lumberman John Henry Kirby. It's managed primarily for demonstration forestry and wildlife conservation. Though not developed for recreation like larger parks, it provides research opportunities and limited access for education, illustrating the importance of forest management in East Texas.

☐ 🔖 ♡ **Little River State Forest:** Located in San Augustine County, this 2,209-acre forest emphasizes sustainable timber production and wildlife habitat. Managed by Texas A&M Forest Service, it is used for forestry demonstrations, research, and public education. While access is limited, it plays an important role in conserving East Texas pine ecosystems and showcasing stewardship practices.

☐ 🔖 ♡ **Sabine National Forest:** Encompassing ~160,900 acres along the Texas–Louisiana border, Sabine protects longleaf and loblolly pine forests and features the Indian Mounds Wilderness. Toledo Bend Reservoir offers fishing, boating, and camping, while trails wind through diverse habitats. Established in 1936, it balances recreation, timber, and habitat management in a scenic borderland setting.

☐ 🔖 ♡ **Sam Houston National Forest:** Stretching over ~163,000 acres north of Houston, this forest features lakes Conroe and Livingston, the 129-mile Lone Star Hiking Trail, and habitats for red-cockaded woodpeckers. Popular for camping, hiking, hunting, and fishing, it also supports OHV and equestrian trails. Managed for multiple uses, it is a major outdoor destination near urban Texas.

☐ 🔖 ♡ **W. Goodrich Jones State Forest:** Located near The Woodlands, this 1,722-acre urban forest serves as a research and education site. Managed by Texas A&M Forest Service, it conserves loblolly pine habitat and supports endangered red-cockaded woodpeckers. Visitors enjoy hiking, biking, horseback riding, and educational programs, making it a vital green space for both conservation and public learning.

TEXAS

National Grasslands

 ☐ 🔖 ♡ **Kiowa/Rita Blanca National Grasslands**: This two-unit grassland complex spans northeastern New Mexico, the Oklahoma Panhandle, and northwest Texas. Featuring shortgrass prairie, canyons, mesas, and historic routes like the Santa Fe Trail, it offers quiet landscapes ideal for hiking, wildlife viewing, and exploring remnants of ranching and pioneer life on the High Plains.

☐ 🔖 ♡ **Lyndon B. Johnson/Caddo National Grasslands**: Located in north Texas, these two separate units protect pockets of restored tallgrass prairie, oak woodlands, and lakes. The Lyndon B. Johnson unit features hiking trails and fishing at Lake Crockett, while the Caddo unit offers rich bird habitat and camping areas. Together, they preserve rare prairie ecosystems within a forested setting.

National Natural Landmarks

  ☐ 🔖 ♡ **Cave Without a Name:** This active limestone cavern is designated a National Natural Landmark for its dazzling speleothems—delicate soda straws, draperies, and towering columns. Still forming today through mineral-rich water, it is one of the nation's finest living caves, valued for both its beauty and its ongoing geologic processes.
GPS: 29.8792, -98.6419

 ☐ 🔖 ♡ **Lost Maples State Natural Area:** Celebrated as a National Natural Landmark for safeguarding a rare stand of Uvalde bigtooth maples, this preserve shelters relict plant species from cooler past climates. Its limestone canyons and woodlands highlight both botanical rarity and striking seasonal color displays that are unmatched in Texas.
GPS: 29.8078, -99.5708

  ☐ 🔖 ♡ **Fort Worth Nature Center and Refuge:** Recognized as a National Natural Landmark for preserving a large remnant of the Cross Timbers, this refuge blends oak-hickory woodlands with prairie and wetland ecosystems. Its intact landscape illustrates how these habitats once mingled across Texas and provides an important sanctuary for native biodiversity.
GPS: 32.8433, -97.4772

 ☐ 🔖 ♡ **Natural Bridge Caverns:** The largest show cave in Texas, this site is a National Natural Landmark due to its multilevel passages and unusual speleothems, including rare "fried egg" formations and delicate helictites. Its features provide a textbook example of phreatic cave development and underground mineral deposition.
GPS: 29.6922, -98.3428

 ☐ 🔖 ♡ **High Plains Natural Area:** Designated a National Natural Landmark for protecting one of the best remaining climax shortgrass prairies of the Great Plains, this tract within Buffalo Lake National Wildlife Refuge retains its natural plant communities. Native grasses, wildflowers, and prairie wildlife flourish in this rare, undisturbed grassland ecosystem.
GPS: 34.9194, -102.1111

 ☐ 🔖 ♡ **Odessa Meteor Crater:** Designated a National Natural Landmark for being one of the best-preserved small impact craters in the U.S., this 550-foot-wide site was formed roughly 63,500 years ago. The crater's structure and scattered meteorite fragments make it an important location for the study of planetary impact processes.
GPS: 31.7569, -102.4792

 ☐ 🔖 ♡ **Longhorn Cavern:** This unique cave system earned National Natural Landmark status because it formed underwater during the phreatic stage, carving smooth passages and vast chambers. Flowstone, columns, and striking mineral features remain well preserved, making it an outstanding record of karst processes in Texas's Hill Country.
GPS: 30.6844, -98.3508

 ☐ 🔖 ♡ **Palo Duro Canyon State Park:** Known as the "Grand Canyon of Texas," this immense gorge is a National Natural Landmark because of its dramatic erosional landforms and multicolored sedimentary layers. Stretching over 120 miles, it reveals millions of years of geologic history and provides unmatched scenery in the southern Plains.
GPS: 34.9847, -101.7019

TEXAS

☐ 🔖 ♡ **Santa Ana National Wildlife Refuge:** This subtropical forest along the Rio Grande was named a National Natural Landmark for preserving one of the last intact lowland forests of its kind in the U.S. Its rich plant communities and strategic location make it a critical stopover for migratory birds and a biodiversity treasure.
GPS: 26.0853, -98.1344

UNITED STATES EDITION

UTAH

Utah's natural wonders range from towering sandstone arches and sculpted canyons to alpine lakes and high desert plateaus. With its collection of state parks, national forests, world-famous national parks, and unforgettable natural landmarks, Utah is a paradise for adventurers.

📅 Peak Season
April–June and September–October are Utah's peak seasons, with mild temperatures, clear skies, and vivid desert colors. These months are ideal for hiking, photography, and exploring the state's national parks.

📅 Offseason Months
November–March is the offseason in most desert areas, bringing cold nights and occasional snow. Winter is peak for skiing in the Wasatch Range, while summer heat limits mid-day desert travel.

🍃 Scenery & Nature Timing
Spring brings desert wildflowers and snow-capped red rock vistas. Summer offers alpine meadows and high-elevation hikes. Fall highlights golden aspens and crisp air, while winter transforms red cliffs and arches with snow.

✨ Special
Utah features the red rock arches of Arches National Park, the hoodoos of Bryce Canyon, and the vast canyons of Zion. The Great Salt Lake's shimmering shores, Canyonlands' mesas, and desert monsoon storms showcase its stunning natural drama.

UTAH

State Parks

☐ 🔖 ♡ **Anasazi State Park Museum:** Located in Boulder, this park preserves the site of one of the largest Ancestral Puebloan villages in Utah, occupied from A.D. 1160–1235. Visitors explore a museum with artifacts, a life-size replica dwelling, and interpretive programs that reveal the daily life of ancient peoples. Trails, exhibits, and hands-on displays bring history alive.

☐ 🔖 ♡ **Antelope Island State Park:** The largest island in the Great Salt Lake offers sweeping views and abundant wildlife, including bison, pronghorn, and bighorn sheep. Popular for hiking, cycling, horseback riding, and photography, the park also features beaches, camping, and stargazing in its dark-sky setting. It's a mix of natural beauty and wildlife habitat.

☐ 🔖 ♡ **Bear Lake State Park:** Famous for its turquoise waters, Bear Lake straddles the Utah-Idaho border. The Utah side features multiple units for boating, fishing, sailing, and swimming. The "Caribbean of the Rockies" is popular for year-round recreation, from water sports in summer to ice fishing and snowmobiling in winter. Sandy beaches and scenic vistas draw families.

☐ 🔖 ♡ **Camp Floyd State Park Museum:** Near Fairfield, this site interprets the short-lived U.S. Army presence during the Utah War of 1858–1861. Visitors can tour historic buildings, explore exhibits on the army camp, and learn about the Pony Express and Stagecoach Inn. The park highlights the military, pioneer, and communication history of Utah's frontier days.

☐ 🔖 ♡ **Coral Pink Sand Dunes State Park:** Situated near Kanab, the park features rolling dunes of vibrant pink sand created by wind and erosion of Navajo sandstone. It's a hotspot for ATV riders, sandboarders, and photographers, with hiking trails offering unique desert views. The constantly shifting dunes provide a playground for adventure and discovery.

☐ 🔖 ♡ **Dead Horse Point State Park:** Overlooking a dramatic bend of the Colorado River, this park offers some of the most photographed views in Utah. Hiking trails wind along canyon rims, and a visitor center interprets geology and history. Its International Dark Sky status makes it superb for stargazing. Camping and biking trails extend the outdoor experience.

☐ 🔖 ♡ **Deer Creek State Park:** Nestled at the base of Mount Timpanogos, Deer Creek Reservoir is a popular spot for water sports. Visitors enjoy boating, fishing, windsurfing, and swimming, with marinas and camping facilities available. Scenic views of the Wasatch Mountains complement hiking and picnicking, making it a convenient getaway near Heber Valley.

☐ 🔖 ♡ **East Canyon State Park:** Centered on East Canyon Reservoir, this park offers fishing, boating, and camping opportunities in the mountains east of Salt Lake City. The canyon played a role in pioneer travel, including the Donner Party and Mormon pioneers. Today, it blends outdoor recreation with history, featuring trails, RV sites, and year-round activities.

☐ 🔖 ♡ **Echo State Park:** This newer park encompasses Echo Reservoir in Summit County. It provides a quieter setting for boating, fishing, paddleboarding, and camping. With mountain backdrops and calm waters, it appeals to families and anglers seeking relaxation. Its proximity to Park City makes it an easy escape for day trips or extended recreation.

☐ 🔖 ♡ **Edge of the Cedars State Park Museum:** Located in Blanding, the park protects a Puebloan village dating back to A.D. 825–1125. The museum showcases one of the largest collections of Ancestral Puebloan pottery and artifacts in the region. Visitors can explore the ruins, climb into a kiva, and learn about cultural traditions of the Four Corners area.

☐ 🔖 ♡ **Escalante Petrified Forest State Park:** Near the town of Escalante, this park features a reservoir for boating and fishing, alongside trails lined with colorful petrified wood. The Petrified Forest Trail offers a chance to see ancient fossilized trees, while Wide Hollow Reservoir provides recreation. It's a unique mix of geology, water, and desert scenery.

☐ 🔖 ♡ **Fred Hayes State Park at Starvation:** Near Duchesne, this park surrounds Starvation Reservoir. It offers boating, fishing, camping, and sandy beaches. Renamed in honor of longtime Utah State Parks director Fred Hayes, the park draws water enthusiasts and anglers chasing walleye, bass, and trout. Trails and scenic views add to its appeal year-round.

UTAH

☐ 🔖 ♡ **Fremont Indian State Park and Museum:** Situated in Clear Creek Canyon, this park preserves the largest known Fremont culture village. Visitors explore trails leading to petroglyphs and pictographs while the museum displays artifacts and interpretive exhibits. Camping, hiking, and ATV trails make it both a cultural and recreational hub in central Utah.

☐ 🔖 ♡ **Frontier Homestead State Park Museum:** In Cedar City, this heritage park highlights pioneer history, including iron mining, blacksmithing, and agriculture. Historic structures, horse-drawn vehicles, and hands-on exhibits showcase life from the mid-1800s to early 1900s. The site connects visitors with the struggles and creativity of Utah's early settlers.

☐ 🔖 ♡ **Goblin Valley State Park:** Known for its whimsical hoodoo formations, Goblin Valley invites exploration of surreal landscapes that resemble stone goblins. Hiking, camping, and canyoneering are popular activities, with nearby slot canyons adding adventure. Its otherworldly scenery has made it a favorite filming location and a family-friendly outdoor playground.

☐ 🔖 ♡ **Goosenecks State Park:** Overlooking a series of dramatic meanders of the San Juan River, this small park offers one of the best examples of entrenched river meanders in the world. Scenic overlooks provide breathtaking views, and campsites on the rim offer quiet solitude. It's a photographer's dream, especially at sunrise and sunset.

☐ 🔖 ♡ **Great Salt Lake State Park:** Located near Saltair, this park gives visitors access to the iconic Great Salt Lake. It features a marina for sailing and boating, picnic areas, and trails with birdwatching opportunities. Interpretive displays explain the lake's unique ecosystem. Sunsets over the water are a highlight, drawing photographers and day-trippers alike.

☐ 🔖 ♡ **Green River State Park:** Situated along the Green River, this park features a shady campground, nine-hole golf course, and boat ramp. It serves as a popular launch site for river trips through Labyrinth and Stillwater Canyons. Cottonwoods provide a relaxing environment for camping, fishing, and picnicking, making it an oasis in the desert.

☐ 🔖 ♡ **Gunlock State Park:** Surrounding Gunlock Reservoir in southern Utah, this park is a quiet retreat for boating, fishing, and swimming. When water levels are high, waterfalls spill dramatically over nearby red rock, creating a seasonal spectacle. The park offers camping and scenic desert surroundings, popular with locals and visitors seeking a peaceful escape.

☐ 🔖 ♡ **Historic Union Pacific Rail Trail State Park:** Stretching 28 miles from Park City to Echo Reservoir, this converted rail line is ideal for hiking, biking, horseback riding, and cross-country skiing. The trail passes through mountains, wetlands, and rural towns, offering scenic views and a glimpse into Utah's railroading past. It's a year-round recreational corridor.

☐ 🔖 ♡ **Huntington State Park:** A warm-water oasis in Emery County, this park features a reservoir surrounded by sandy beaches and campgrounds. Popular for fishing, boating, and swimming, it's also a hub for birdwatching and picnicking. With a relaxed atmosphere and small-town charm, it's a family-friendly destination in central Utah's desert landscape.

☐ 🔖 ♡ **Hyrum State Park:** Nestled in Cache Valley, this 450-acre reservoir park provides opportunities for boating, swimming, fishing, and camping. The surrounding foothills make for scenic picnicking and wildlife watching. In winter, it's a popular spot for ice fishing. Its combination of water recreation and mountain scenery draws locals and visitors alike.

☐ 🔖 ♡ **Jordanelle State Park:** Near Heber City, Jordanelle surrounds a large reservoir with marinas, campgrounds, and day-use areas. Popular for boating, wakeboarding, and paddle sports, it also offers trails for hiking and biking. Its proximity to the Wasatch Mountains and Park City makes it an easily accessible year-round recreation hub.

☐ 🔖 ♡ **Kodachrome Basin State Park:** Named for its striking multicolored sandstone spires, Kodachrome Basin features over 60 unique monolithic chimneys. Hiking, camping, and horseback riding immerse visitors in its vibrant desert scenery. The park's geology and dark skies provide both daytime and nighttime beauty, making it a photographer's paradise.

☐ 🔖 ♡ **Lost Creek State Park:** One of Utah's newest parks, this area surrounds Lost Creek Reservoir in Morgan County. Known for its trophy trout fishing, it offers boating, camping, and quiet desert mountain scenery. Less crowded than many parks, it appeals to anglers and families seeking relaxation in a peaceful, undeveloped setting.

☐ 🔖 ♡ **Millsite State Park:** Adjacent to Ferron Canyon, Millsite Reservoir provides a backdrop of sandstone cliffs and green valleys. Visitors enjoy boating, swimming, and fishing, along with access to a nearby golf course. The park also serves as a gateway to ATV trails and the Manti-La Sal National Forest, blending recreation with stunning scenery.

UTAH

☐ 🔖 ♡ **Otter Creek State Park:** A secluded gem in south-central Utah, this reservoir park is prized for excellent fishing—especially rainbow trout. Campgrounds, boating, and birdwatching add to its appeal. The surrounding mountains create a peaceful environment, and its location along migratory flyways makes it popular among wildlife enthusiasts.

☐ 🔖 ♡ **Palisade State Park:** Nestled in Sanpete County, this park centers on a small reservoir popular for fishing, canoeing, and paddleboarding. It also boasts a golf course, campgrounds, and trails. With cool mountain air and scenic surroundings, Palisade offers a quiet, family-friendly getaway rich in outdoor opportunities.

☐ 🔖 ♡ **Piute State Park:** A remote reservoir setting, Piute State Park is a favorite among anglers, boaters, and campers. Surrounded by high desert landscapes, it offers solitude and opportunities to explore nearby ATV trails. With fewer facilities, it appeals to those seeking a rugged outdoor experience and peaceful fishing waters.

☐ 🔖 ♡ **Quail Creek State Park:** Located near St. George, Quail Creek Reservoir provides some of the warmest waters in Utah. It's popular for boating, kayaking, and fishing for bass and trout. With red rock cliffs and desert views, the park offers camping and picnicking, making it a year-round water recreation hotspot in southern Utah.

☐ 🔖 ♡ **Red Fleet State Park:** Famous for its striking red sandstone cliffs and dinosaur trackway, this park north of Vernal features a reservoir for boating, swimming, and paddleboarding. Visitors can hike the Dinosaur Trackway Trail to see 200-million-year-old tracks. Its blend of paleontology, water sports, and red rock scenery is unforgettable.

☐ 🔖 ♡ **Rockport State Park:** Surrounding Rockport Reservoir in Summit County, this park provides fishing, boating, and water sports opportunities. Campgrounds, day-use areas, and winter ice fishing make it a versatile destination. The mountain setting and reservoir views create a peaceful escape close to the Wasatch Front.

☐ 🔖 ♡ **Sand Hollow State Park:** One of Utah's most popular state parks, Sand Hollow combines a warm-water reservoir with massive red sand dunes. Visitors enjoy boating, fishing, swimming, and extensive off-road trails for ATVs. Its desert landscape, camping facilities, and year-round recreation make it a premier destination in Washington County.

☐ 🔖 ♡ **Scofield State Park:** High in the Manti-La Sal Mountains, Scofield surrounds a cool-water reservoir popular for trout fishing. Boating, camping, and hiking draw visitors in summer, while winter brings ice fishing and snowmobiling. Its alpine setting and peaceful environment make it a year-round retreat in central Utah.

☐ 🔖 ♡ **Snow Canyon State Park:** Near St. George, Snow Canyon showcases dramatic red and white Navajo sandstone, lava tubes, and extinct cinder cones. Hiking, rock climbing, and photography highlight the park's diverse geology. As a designated Dark Sky Park, it offers stellar night skies. Its landscapes rival nearby national parks.

☐ 🔖 ♡ **Steinaker State Park:** Just north of Vernal, Steinaker Reservoir offers warm-water fishing, boating, swimming, and camping. Set against the backdrop of the Uinta Mountains, it provides opportunities for hiking, wildlife viewing, and picnicking. Its combination of water recreation and desert scenery makes it a local favorite.

☐ 🔖 ♡ **Territorial Statehouse State Park Museum:** Located in Fillmore, this museum preserves Utah's first territorial capitol building. Exhibits detail pioneer politics, history, and daily life. The grounds feature pioneer-era artifacts, gardens, and historic furnishings. It's both a cultural landmark and a quiet park-like setting for exploring Utah's early governance.

☐ 🔖 ♡ **This Is The Place Heritage Park:** Overlooking Salt Lake City, this living history park commemorates the Mormon pioneers' 1847 arrival. Visitors can explore historic buildings, ride heritage trains, and learn about Utah's diverse cultural past. Costumed interpreters, Native heritage exhibits, and hands-on activities make it both educational and family-friendly.

☐ 🔖 ♡ **Utah Field House of Natural History State Park Museum:** Located in Vernal, this park museum interprets the paleontological richness of the Uinta Basin. Life-size dinosaur replicas, interactive exhibits, and a fossil garden showcase Utah's prehistoric life. Visitors gain insight into geologic history while exploring both indoor galleries and outdoor displays.

☐ 🔖 ♡ **Utah Lake State Park:** At the heart of Utah Valley, this park offers access to Utah Lake, the state's largest freshwater body. Popular for boating, sailing, fishing, and birdwatching, it also has campgrounds and picnic areas. With the Wasatch Mountains as a backdrop, it provides year-round recreation for families and outdoor enthusiasts.

UTAH

☐ 🔖 ♡ **Utahraptor State Park:** Established in 2021 near Moab, this is Utah's newest state park, protecting striking red rock landscapes and dinosaur fossil sites. It honors Utahraptor, the state dinosaur, discovered nearby. Hiking, biking, and camping complement paleontological exploration. A new visitor center opened in 2025, expanding interpretation and amenities.

☐ 🔖 ♡ **Wasatch Mountain State Park:** Nestled in the Wasatch Mountains near Midway, this expansive park offers golf courses, campgrounds, and trails for hiking, biking, horseback riding, and winter sports. Wildlife abounds in its alpine valleys. Year-round recreation and scenic drives, including Guardsman Pass, make it a cornerstone of Utah's park system.

☐ 🔖 ♡ **Willard Bay State Park:** North of Ogden, this freshwater reservoir on the Great Salt Lake's floodplain is popular for boating, swimming, and fishing. Sandy beaches, campgrounds, and picnic areas make it family-friendly. The park is also a haven for birdwatching, especially during migrations, offering a mix of water recreation and wildlife observation.

☐ 🔖 ♡ **Yuba State Park:** Located along I-15, Yuba Reservoir attracts visitors for boating, fishing, and camping. Known for warm waters and long sandy beaches, it's a favorite for watersports, including waterskiing and wakeboarding. Campgrounds, trails, and nearby rock formations like the "Painted Rocks" add to its appeal as a central Utah getaway.

National Parks

 ☐ 🔖 ♡ **Arches National Park:** Renowned for over 2,000 natural sandstone arches, this park near Moab showcases sculpted red rock landscapes shaped by time and erosion. Visitors hike to landmarks like Delicate Arch, Landscape Arch, and Double Arch, explore desert trails, and enjoy world-class photography and stargazing in one of Utah's most iconic destinations.

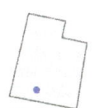 ☐ 🔖 ♡ **Bryce Canyon National Park:** Famous for its colorful amphitheaters filled with towering hoodoos, Bryce Canyon offers views unlike anywhere else. Visitors marvel from overlooks such as Inspiration Point and Sunset Point or hike into the labyrinth of spires. The park also boasts abundant wildlife, crisp mountain air, and dazzling dark night skies.

 ☐ 🔖 ♡ **Canyonlands National Park:** Vast and rugged, Canyonlands protects a dramatic landscape of deep canyons, mesas, and buttes carved by the Colorado and Green Rivers. Divided into districts—Island in the Sky, The Needles, The Maze, and the rivers—the park offers hiking, rafting, biking, and stargazing in a remote, awe-inspiring desert setting.

 ☐ 🔖 ♡ **Capitol Reef National Park:** Centered on the Waterpocket Fold, a 100-mile wrinkle in Earth's crust, Capitol Reef blends geology and history. Visitors explore colorful cliffs, natural arches, and the Fruita Historic District, where orchards still thrive. Scenic drives, hikes, and petroglyphs offer a glimpse into Utah's natural and cultural heritage.

 ☐ 🔖 ♡ **Cedar Breaks National Monument:** At 10,000 feet, Cedar Breaks reveals a giant natural amphitheater of orange, red, and purple hoodoos. Wildflower meadows, bristlecone pines, and alpine trails add to its high-mountain beauty. Designated as a Dark Sky Park, it's also one of the best places in Utah to experience clear, star-filled night skies.

 ☐ 🔖 ♡ **Dinosaur National Monument:** Straddling Utah and Colorado, this monument preserves one of the richest Jurassic fossil beds in the world. Visitors explore the Quarry Exhibit Hall, where dinosaur bones are still embedded in rock walls, and enjoy hiking, rafting, and stunning canyon scenery along the Green and Yampa Rivers.

 ☐ 🔖 ♡ **Glen Canyon National Recreation Area:** Encompassing Lake Powell and the canyons of the Colorado Plateau, Glen Canyon offers endless adventure. Boating, kayaking, and fishing on the lake are popular, while hiking reveals slot canyons and desert vistas. The area also preserves archaeological sites and stories of human history in this dramatic landscape.

 ☐ 🔖 ♡ **Golden Spike National Historical Park:** At Promontory Summit in 1869, the nation's first transcontinental railroad was completed. This park commemorates the driving of the Golden Spike with exhibits, replica steam locomotives, and reenactments. Visitors learn about the monumental achievement that united the U.S. and transformed commerce and travel.

UTAH

☐ 🔖 ♡ **Hovenweep National Monument:** Scattered across the Utah-Colorado border, Hovenweep preserves striking stone towers and dwellings built by the Ancestral Puebloans. Visitors hike trails connecting ancient villages, explore canyon overlooks, and gain insight into the ingenuity of the people who lived here nearly 1,000 years ago in a rugged desert setting.

☐ 🔖 ♡ **Natural Bridges National Monument:** Home to three immense natural stone bridges—Sipapu, Kachina, and Owachomo—this monument highlights the power of water shaping desert rock. Visitors hike loop trails, enjoy scenic overlooks, and stargaze in one of the world's first certified International Dark Sky Parks, where the Milky Way blazes overhead.

☐ 🔖 ♡ **Rainbow Bridge National Monument:** Accessible by boat from Lake Powell or by challenging hikes, Rainbow Bridge is one of the world's largest natural bridges. This graceful sandstone span rises 290 feet and holds sacred significance for Native American tribes. Visitors marvel at its size and serenity amid stunning canyon scenery.

☐ 🔖 ♡ **Timpanogos Cave National Monument:** Nestled in American Fork Canyon, this monument protects a cave system filled with delicate formations like stalactites, stalagmites, and helictites. Reached via a steep mountain trail, guided tours showcase its underground wonders. Visitors also enjoy sweeping canyon views and insights into Utah's geologic past.

☐ 🔖 ♡ **Zion National Park:** Utah's first national park dazzles with soaring sandstone cliffs, deep canyons, and diverse landscapes. Famous hikes like Angels Landing and The Narrows draw adventurers, while scenic drives and overlooks offer unforgettable views. From desert mesas to lush riverbanks, Zion is a crown jewel of the American Southwest.

State & National Forests

☐ 🔖 ♡ **Ashley National Forest:** Spanning 1.38 million acres in northeastern Utah and southwestern Wyoming, this vast forest includes alpine peaks, canyons, and the High Uintas Wilderness. Flaming Gorge National Recreation Area offers boating, fishing, and scenic overlooks. Wildlife like elk, moose, mountain goats, and bald eagles thrive here, making it a premier destination for recreation and exploration.

☐ 🔖 ♡ **Dixie National Forest:** Utah's largest forest at 1.89 million acres, Dixie stretches across southern Utah from red rock deserts to alpine plateaus. Bordering Bryce Canyon and Capitol Reef, it offers diverse scenery and outdoor recreation. Visitors enjoy scenic drives, lakes, trails, camping, OHV riding, and horseback exploration. Its contrasting landscapes showcase Utah's rich natural beauty.

☐ 🔖 ♡ **Fishlake National Forest:** Encompassing 1.46 million acres in central Utah, this forest is home to Fish Lake, the state's largest mountain lake. With meadows, volcanic plateaus, and aspen groves, it shelters elk, deer, mountain goats, and black bears. It also contains Pando, the world's largest living organism, and offers fishing, hiking, camping, and year-round mountain recreation.

☐ 🔖 ♡ **Manti–La Sal National Forest:** Covering 1.27 million acres in central and southeastern Utah, this forest spans the Wasatch Plateau, Abajo Mountains, and La Sal Mountains. It protects rivers, archaeological sites, and alpine ecosystems. Popular with campers, hikers, bikers, and skiers, it also offers scenic drives and stunning vistas, blending cultural history with mountain wilderness.

☐ 🔖 ♡ **Uinta–Wasatch–Cache National Forest:** Spanning 2.2 million acres across northern Utah, Wyoming, and Idaho, this is the state's most-visited forest. It includes alpine lakes, seven wilderness areas, ski resorts, and peaks like Mount Timpanogos. Offering hiking, skiing, fishing, and camping, it balances accessible recreation near Salt Lake City with remote backcountry escapes.

UNITED STATES EDITION

UTAH

National Scenic Byways & All-American Roads

☐ ▢ ♡ **Dinosaur Diamond Prehistoric Highway:** Looping through eastern Utah and western Colorado, this byway strings together fossil sites, red-rock river canyons, and dinosaur lore. Drive cliff-hugging SR-128 along the Colorado River, visit Dinosaur National Monument's Quarry, find rock art and Jurassic bone beds, and explore towns like Vernal, Moab, and Fruita. Rafting, hiking, and overlooks reveal 150 million years of deep time.

☐ ▢ ♡ **Flaming Gorge–Uintas National Scenic Byway:** From Vernal to Manila, the route climbs the Uinta Mountains to panoramic overlooks of Flaming Gorge Reservoir. Watch for bighorn sheep, peer into Red Canyon, and fish the Green River below the dam. Forested plateaus, tilted rock layers, and brilliant night skies make this a classic for boating, camping, and geology lovers—all framed by dramatic cliffs and deep water.

☐ ▢ ♡ **Logan Canyon Scenic Byway:** Following the Logan River to Bear Lake, the drive shifts from limestone narrows and shady cottonwoods to high meadows and turquoise-lake vistas. Hike to the Jardine Juniper or Tony Grove, watch fall colors blaze across maples and aspens, and explore caves, campgrounds, and picnic sites. Winter brings snow sports, while summer offers cool canyon breezes and plentiful wildlife.

☐ ▢ ♡ **Nebo Loop Scenic Byway:** Winding between Payson and Nephi, this high-country route skirts 11,928-foot Mount Nebo with wide pullouts, crimson rock at Devil's Kitchen, and sweeping views over Utah Valley. Aspen and maple groves explode with color in September, while trailheads lead to alpine ridges and quiet lakes. The road closes for snow; late spring through fall is the prime season to go.

☐ ▢ ♡ **Scenic Byway 12 (All-American Road):** Linking Bryce Canyon and Capitol Reef, this "Journey Through Time" crosses the Grand Staircase–Escalante and Boulder Mountain, with razor-edge ridges like the Hogback, slot-canyon trailheads, and heritage towns including Tropic, Escalante, Boulder, and Torrey. Expect constant transitions—petrified dunes, slickrock, ponderosa forests—and dark-sky nights that rival the day's vistas.

☐ ▢ ♡ **Scenic Byway 143 – Utah's Patchwork Parkway:** Crossing high plateaus between Parowan and Panguitch, SR-143 passes Brian Head, Panguitch Lake, and the rim of Cedar Breaks National Monument. Named for quilts pioneers laid over snow to travel in winter, the byway blends volcanic fields, wildflower meadows, and fiery fall colors. Fishing, hiking, and ski-area access make it a four-season gateway between I-15 and US-89.

☐ ▢ ♡ **The Energy Loop: Huntington/Eccles Canyons Scenic Byway:** Climbing the Wasatch Plateau, this loop links coal-mining heritage with big scenery—Huntington and Eccles Canyons, Electric Lake, Scofield Reservoir, and sweeping overlooks into the San Rafael country. Interpretive stops share stories of energy towns and engineers, while campgrounds, OHV routes, fishing, and autumn foliage reward unhurried exploration across forested highlands.

☐ ▢ ♡ **Trail of the Ancients:** Threading through Utah's Four Corners country and into Colorado, the route connects Monument Valley, Valley of the Gods, Natural Bridges and Hovenweep, plus museums and rock art near Blanding. Drive the Moki Dugway's dramatic grades, walk past thousand-year-old towers, and explore canyonlands where Ancestral Puebloan culture flourished. Remote roads, big skies, and deep time define the journey.

☐ ▢ ♡ **Zion Scenic Byway:** Following SR-9 from La Verkin through Springdale to the park's east entrance, this corridor forms the gateway to Zion National Park. Pass soaring cliffs and the 1930s Zion–Mt. Carmel Tunnel, with trailheads, pullouts, and Virgin River views along the way. The route links small towns with iconic canyon scenery and delivers four-season access to hikes, shuttles, and unforgettable park overlooks.

UTAH

State Scenic Byways

☐ 🔖 ♡ **Alpine Loop Scenic Byway:** Winding through American Fork and Provo Canyons, SR-92 climbs above 9,000 feet into alpine forests and meadows. Towering limestone cliffs, summer wildflowers, and blazing autumn foliage make it a visual highlight. Pullouts and picnic areas offer mountain views, while trailheads lead into the high peaks of the Wasatch.

☐ 🔖 ♡ **Bear Lake Scenic Byway:** Following SR-30 along Bear Lake's west shore, this route reveals the lake's famous turquoise waters, nicknamed the "Caribbean of the Rockies." The drive offers sweeping views of the lake and mountains, with easy access to sandy beaches, boating, and water recreation. Garden City's lakeside charm and summer raspberry treats complete the experience.

☐ 🔖 ♡ **Beaver Canyon Scenic Byway:** Starting in the town of Beaver, this byway climbs deep into the Tushar Mountains. Lush forests, meadows, and high-elevation streams line the road, with opportunities for fishing, camping, and hiking. Fall brings spectacular color in the aspens, while winter snow blankets the peaks. It's a quiet, less-traveled high-country retreat.

☐ 🔖 ♡ **Bicentennial–Trail of the Ancients Scenic Byway:** Connecting Hanksville, Natural Bridges, and Blanding, this byway threads through red-rock desert and mesas rich with archaeological sites. Petroglyphs, Ancestral Puebloan ruins, and interpretive pullouts reveal cultural history. The drive blends sweeping vistas, sandstone canyons, and access to lesser-known Four Corners landscapes.

☐ 🔖 ♡ **Big Cottonwood Canyon Scenic Byway:** From Salt Lake Valley into the Wasatch, SR-190 follows the Big Cottonwood Creek past sheer canyon walls, alpine lakes, and dense forests. Popular for hiking, climbing, and skiing at Brighton, the drive showcases dramatic rock formations and seasonal wildflowers. In fall, the canyon becomes a corridor of vibrant colors.

☐ 🔖 ♡ **Brian Head–Panguitch Lake Scenic Byway:** Rising from Parowan, the route climbs to Brian Head Peak before descending to Panguitch Lake. The byway crosses volcanic plateaus, forests of fir and aspen, and open meadows. In summer, anglers flock to Panguitch Lake, while winter brings snow sports. High-elevation overlooks provide expansive southern Utah views.

☐ 🔖 ♡ **Capitol Reef Country Scenic Byway:** Extending across SR-72 and SR-95, this drive links small towns with Capitol Reef's rugged cliffs and canyons. Scenic viewpoints highlight colorful sandstone formations, historic orchards, and Fremont culture sites. The byway blends natural wonder with cultural heritage, offering a gateway into one of Utah's most diverse landscapes.

☐ 🔖 ♡ **Cedar Breaks Scenic Byway:** This short but dramatic route leads to the rim of Cedar Breaks National Monument, where a natural amphitheater of orange and red hoodoos spreads below. Meadows filled with summer wildflowers and bristlecone pines line the high plateau. Overlooks and trailheads provide access to some of Utah's most stunning alpine scenery.

☐ 🔖 ♡ **Dead Horse Mesa Scenic Byway:** Climbing from Moab toward Dead Horse Point, this byway traverses red-rock desert, canyons, and high plateaus. Pullouts reveal sweeping views of the Colorado River and sculpted canyonlands. The route ends at Dead Horse Point State Park, one of Utah's most iconic overlooks, with hiking trails and breathtaking desert sunsets.

☐ 🔖 ♡ **Energy Loop – Huntington/Eccles Scenic Byway (State Route Sections):** The state-designated portions climb through high alpine forests and connect small mountain communities with reservoirs like Electric Lake and Scofield. Interpretive sites highlight coal mining, geology, and pioneer settlement. The loop blends forested plateaus, lakeside recreation, and sweeping vistas over the Wasatch Plateau.

☐ 🔖 ♡ **Fishlake Scenic Byway:** This mountain road highlights Fish Lake, Utah's largest natural mountain lake and home to the immense Pando aspen clone. The drive passes through meadows, spruce-fir forests, and volcanic plateaus. Campgrounds, fishing spots, and hiking trails line the way, offering a cool alpine retreat surrounded by wildlife and natural beauty.

☐ 🔖 ♡ **Indian Canyon Scenic Byway:** Connecting Duchesne to Helper along US-191, this route climbs through layered cliffs, pinyon-juniper forests, and sweeping canyons. Interpretive pullouts tell the story of ancient peoples, coal mining, and geology. Scenic overlooks provide far-reaching views, while wildlife like deer and elk often appear along the forested stretches.

UTAH

☐ ▯ ♡ **Mirror Lake Scenic Byway:** Winding through the western Uintas from Kamas to Evanston, WY, this high-elevation drive reaches 10,687-foot Bald Mountain Pass. Dozens of lakes dot the landscape, including Mirror Lake itself. Visitors enjoy fishing, camping, hiking, and autumn colors in alpine valleys. Snow closes the road in winter, making summer and fall prime seasons.

☐ ▯ ♡ **Monte Cristo Scenic Byway:** SR-39 climbs east of Ogden into the Monte Cristo Range. The route offers sweeping views, mountain meadows, and roadside trailheads. In summer, wildflowers blanket the highlands; in fall, aspens glow gold. Campgrounds, ATV routes, and wildlife sightings make it a quiet but rewarding drive through northern Utah's mountains.

☐ ▯ ♡ **Ogden River Scenic Byway:** Following SR-39 up Ogden Canyon, the drive traces the river past sheer canyon walls, resorts, and historic sites. It opens into Pineview Reservoir, a hub for boating, fishing, and picnicking. Continuing upward, the road provides access to trails and campgrounds in the Wasatch-Cache National Forest, blending water and mountain scenery.

☐ ▯ ♡ **Provo Canyon Scenic Byway:** US-189 follows the Provo River past Bridal Veil Falls, Deer Creek Reservoir, and steep canyon cliffs. Recreational areas line the route, with fishing, rafting, hiking, and picnicking opportunities. Scenic pullouts provide mountain vistas, while the byway connects Utah Valley with Heber Valley and the Alpine Loop.

☐ ▯ ♡ **Silver Reef Scenic Byway:** Near St. George, this short drive highlights the ghost town of Silver Reef, where 19th-century miners extracted silver from sandstone. Historic buildings, interpretive exhibits, and red-rock backdrops reveal a blend of natural and cultural history. The byway connects desert landscapes with the preserved mining heritage of southern Utah.

☐ ▯ ♡ **South Fork Scenic Byway:** Branching from the Ogden River corridor, this drive ascends South Fork Canyon into forested mountain terrain. Campgrounds and picnic areas line the route, while trails provide access to alpine lakes and wildlife habitat. The peaceful canyon environment makes it a favorite for locals seeking a quiet getaway in the Wasatch.

☐ ▯ ♡ **Thistle to Soldier Summit Scenic Byway:** Following US-6 through Spanish Fork Canyon, this byway climbs past the ghost town of Thistle and through rugged canyon country. Interpretive signs recall the 1983 landslide that buried the town. The drive continues to Soldier Summit, offering railroad history, mountain scenery, and connections to central Utah.

☐ ▯ ♡ **Trappers Loop Scenic Byway:** Connecting Mountain Green and Huntsville, SR-167 winds over forested slopes with wide vistas of the Wasatch Mountains. Scenic pullouts overlook Pineview Reservoir and Snowbasin Resort. Popular year-round, the road provides access to skiing in winter, hiking and cycling in summer, and brilliant fall foliage across the high ridges.

☐ ▯ ♡ **Upper Colorado Scenic Byway (State Portion):** From Cisco to Moab along SR-128, the state-designated section follows the Colorado River through towering red-rock cliffs. The drive hugs the water's edge with frequent pullouts for rafting, photography, and camping. Dramatic canyon walls and arches create one of Utah's most striking desert corridors.

☐ ▯ ♡ **White Mountain Scenic Byway:** Near Vernal, this lesser-known route climbs into the highlands overlooking Flaming Gorge. The drive passes through forests, meadows, and overlooks with views of Red Canyon and the surrounding plateaus. Wildlife, including deer and elk, are common, and the route provides a quieter alternative to the main recreation areas.

UTAH

National Natural Landmarks

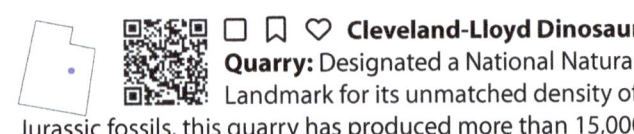 **Cleveland-Lloyd Dinosaur Quarry:** Designated a National Natural Landmark for its unmatched density of Jurassic fossils, this quarry has produced more than 15,000 bones, mostly from carnivorous dinosaurs such as Allosaurus. Believed to have been a predator trap, the site offers rare insights into dinosaur behavior, ecosystem dynamics, and fossil preservation.
GPS: 39.3228, -110.6895

 **Joshua Tree Natural Area:** Recognized as a National Natural Landmark for hosting the northernmost stand of Joshua trees, this desert site marks a rare ecological transition between the Mojave Desert and Colorado Plateau. The yucca woodlands, along with desert-adapted flora and fauna, highlight species persisting at the edges of their range.
GPS: 37.025913, -113.904427

 **Little Rockies:** This area achieved National Natural Landmark status because it is the classic site where geologists first studied laccoliths—igneous intrusions that bulge and uplift overlying rock layers. Exposing sills, dikes, and plugs, the formations here provide key evidence for understanding how magma shapes mountain landscapes.
GPS: 37.77443, -110.56348

 **Neffs Canyon Caves:** These alpine karst caves in the Wasatch Mountains were named a National Natural Landmark for demonstrating the unusual process of stream piracy, where surface water is diverted underground. Their hydrology and geology make them rare scientific windows into the interaction between alpine streams and cave systems.
GPS: 40.676161, -111.775073

VERMONT

Vermont's timeless landscapes feature forested mountains, winding rivers, tranquil lakes, and pastoral valleys. With its inviting state parks, national forests, scenic trails, and cherished natural landmarks, the Green Mountain State is an ideal destination for outdoor lovers seeking beauty, serenity, and adventure in every season.

📅 Peak Season
June–October is Vermont's peak season, offering warm weather, green mountains, and brilliant fall foliage. Summer draws hikers and lake visitors, while autumn brings world-famous leaf color across the hills and valleys.

📅 Offseason Months
November–April is the offseason for general travel, with cold temperatures and snow. Winter, however, is peak for skiing, snowshoeing, and other mountain recreation throughout the Green Mountains.

🍃 Scenery & Nature Timing
Spring brings maple sugaring and budding forests. Summer highlights mountain trails, waterfalls, and wildflowers. Fall transforms the landscape with vibrant color, while winter blankets the state in deep snow and frozen beauty.

✨ Special
Vermont features the forested Green Mountains, Lake Champlain's glacial waters, and Quechee Gorge's striking cliffs. Autumn foliage, misty valleys, and covered bridges set among rolling hills create its timeless natural charm.

VERMONT

State Parks

☐ 🔖 ♡ **Alburgh Dunes State Park:** On Lake Champlain, this 625-acre park features one of Vermont's largest sandy beaches, formed by unique inland dunes. Visitors enjoy swimming, sunbathing, and picnicking along the shore while exploring dune habitats that support rare plants and wildlife. Its natural beauty and peaceful atmosphere make it a favorite family destination.

☐ 🔖 ♡ **Allis State Park:** Set on a hilltop in Brookfield, this 625-acre park provides scenic trails, a restored fire tower with sweeping views, and quiet woodlands for hiking and picnicking. Known for its tranquility, it offers visitors a chance to connect with nature while exploring Vermont's rolling hills and enjoying a peaceful retreat.

☐ 🔖 ♡ **Big Deer State Park:** Located in Groton State Forest, this cozy campground is surrounded by woodlands, wetlands, and wildlife. It offers access to hiking trails, birdwatching, and peaceful picnics in a quiet setting. Its intimate scale and natural charm make it a great option for visitors seeking a low-key, rustic experience.

☐ 🔖 ♡ **Bomoseen State Park:** Vermont's largest lake anchors this 3,526-acre park in Castleton, featuring a sandy beach, campground, and wooded trails. Visitors enjoy boating, fishing, and swimming, with opportunities to explore the Taconic Mountains and marshlands nearby. It's a well-rounded destination for both water recreation and forest adventures.

☐ 🔖 ♡ **Boulder Beach State Park:** Found on Lake Groton, this 80-acre day-use park features a broad sandy swimming beach, shaded picnic areas, and calm waters ideal for families. Surrounded by forested hills, it's a relaxing place for swimming, sunbathing, and enjoying the outdoors, with access to trails and nearby campgrounds.

☐ 🔖 ♡ **Branbury State Park:** Nestled between Lake Dunmore and the Moosalamoo mountains, this 69-acre park offers a sandy beach, swimming, and picnic areas. Hiking trails connect to the adjacent national recreation area, while forests and lake views provide a scenic backdrop. Its mix of water access and mountain terrain makes it a favorite stop.

☐ 🔖 ♡ **Brighton State Park:** Located in the Northeast Kingdom, this 1,400-acre park surrounds Spectacle Pond with campgrounds, trails, and rich wildlife habitat. Visitors can fish, hike, or enjoy peaceful water views while exploring northern Vermont's rugged forests. Its quiet charm and remote setting make it ideal for those seeking solitude.

☐ 🔖 ♡ **Burton Island State Park:** Accessible only by boat from St. Albans Bay, this 253-acre island offers car-free camping, hiking, and shoreline exploration. With scenic trails, lake views, and a marina, it's a haven for paddlers and outdoor lovers. Its remote yet welcoming atmosphere makes it a unique Vermont destination.

☐ 🔖 ♡ **Button Bay State Park:** Overlooking Lake Champlain in Ferrisburgh, this 253-acre park features a swimming pool, shoreline trails, and open fields for picnics. Visitors enjoy fishing, boating, and relaxing by the water with views of the Adirondacks. Its accessible amenities and lakeside setting make it popular for families and groups.

☐ 🔖 ♡ **Camel's Hump State Park:** Encompassing over 20,000 acres, this wilderness park protects Vermont's iconic Camel's Hump peak. Rugged trails lead to the alpine summit, offering sweeping views of the Green Mountains, Lake Champlain, and beyond. With rich habitats and challenging terrain, it's one of the state's premier backcountry destinations.

☐ 🔖 ♡ **Camp Plymouth State Park:** On Echo Lake in Ludlow, this 295-acre park features wooded campsites, picnic areas, and a sandy beach. Visitors enjoy swimming, boating, and fishing in a mountain-framed setting, while hiking trails provide forest exploration. Its mix of water access and peaceful woodland makes it a versatile retreat.

☐ 🔖 ♡ **Coolidge State Park:** Located in Plymouth, this 1,300-acre park offers one of Vermont's classic camping experiences. Overlooks provide views of the Green Mountains, while trails wind through forests rich in wildlife. Its rustic layout and connection to the Calvin Coolidge Historic Site nearby add cultural depth to its natural beauty.

☐ 🔖 ♡ **Crystal Lake State Park:** In Barton, this 16-acre day-use park features a wide sandy beach, picnic areas, and clear mountain waters perfect for swimming. Surrounded by forested hills, it offers boating and fishing opportunities along with family-friendly amenities. Its tranquil setting makes it one of northern Vermont's most scenic lake parks.

☐ 🔖 ♡ **D.A.R. State Park:** Situated on Lake Champlain in Addison, this 95-acre park provides open fields, picnic areas, and shady woodlands. It's known for birdwatching, shoreline access, and views of the Adirondacks. With a relaxed atmosphere and easy trails, it's a peaceful spot for gatherings, family outings, or quiet reflection.

VERMONT

☐ 🔖 ♡ **Elmore State Park:** At the base of Mount Elmore, this 700-acre park features a sandy beach, wooded trails, and a historic fire tower hike. Campgrounds and lakefront access make it ideal for families seeking swimming, boating, and hiking opportunities. Its blend of water, mountain, and forest offers a full outdoor experience.

☐ 🔖 ♡ **Emerald Lake State Park:** Nestled in Dorset, this 430-acre park centers on the calm waters of Emerald Lake. It offers a beach, fishing, boating, and wooded campsites. Surrounded by forested hills, it's popular for hiking and paddling, providing a scenic and tranquil place to enjoy southern Vermont's natural beauty.

☐ 🔖 ♡ **Fort Dummer State Park:** Near Brattleboro, this 217-acre park honors Vermont's first permanent European settlement. It features wooded campsites, trails, and abundant wildlife along the Connecticut River Valley. Visitors enjoy birdwatching, hiking, and history, making it a quiet spot that blends cultural heritage with outdoor recreation.

☐ 🔖 ♡ **Gifford Woods State Park:** Situated in Killington, this 40-acre park is famous for its old-growth forest. Campgrounds and trails connect to the Appalachian and Long Trails, making it a hub for hikers. Birdwatching and fall foliage are highlights, while its compact size preserves a rare pocket of ancient Vermont woodland.

☐ 🔖 ♡ **Grand Isle State Park:** Vermont's most visited campground, this 226-acre park sits on Lake Champlain's shoreline. It offers swimming, boating, and picnic areas with Adirondack views. Families enjoy its open fields, wooded campsites, and nature programs. As a central hub in the Champlain Islands, it's perfect for summer recreation.

☐ 🔖 ♡ **Green River Reservoir State Park:** Covering 5,500 acres in Hyde Park, this remote park is popular with paddlers. Its undeveloped shoreline stretches for miles, with only canoe or kayak access to campsites. Visitors enjoy fishing, birdwatching, and hiking in a peaceful, wild setting. The quiet reservoir and surrounding forest provide one of Vermont's most secluded outdoor experiences.

☐ 🔖 ♡ **Half Moon Pond State Park:** Tucked in the Taconic Mountains near Hubbardton, this 1,000-acre park surrounds a tranquil pond. The rustic campground offers a quiet retreat for swimming, fishing, and paddling. Trails connect to nearby Bomoseen State Park, giving hikers access to forests and ridges. Its remote, wooded setting makes it ideal for nature lovers seeking solitude.

☐ 🔖 ♡ **Hazen's Notch State Park:** Found in Westfield, this 307-acre park protects a scenic mountain pass in northern Vermont. Known for diverse wildlife and striking views, it offers hiking, picnicking, and access to the Long Trail. With rugged terrain, dense forests, and abundant birdlife, it's a quiet destination for exploration and natural beauty.

☐ 🔖 ♡ **Jamaica State Park:** Encompassing 772 acres along the West River, this park features hiking trails, campsites, and access to Hamilton Falls, one of Vermont's tallest waterfalls. The river corridor is popular for fishing, swimming, and tubing. Surrounded by lush forests, it's a favorite for families, hikers, and those seeking scenic river landscapes.

☐ 🔖 ♡ **Kettle Pond State Park:** Located in Marshfield's Groton State Forest, this 1,000-acre park surrounds a glacial kettle pond. Campsites are only accessible by foot, canoe, or kayak, creating a true back-to-nature experience. With hiking trails, paddling opportunities, and peaceful surroundings, it offers a rustic retreat into Vermont's wilderness.

☐ 🔖 ♡ **Kill Kare State Park:** On Lake Champlain near St. Albans, this 17-acre day-use park occupies a historic summer camp peninsula. With open lawns, picnic areas, and swimming access, it's a relaxing family spot. It also serves as the ferry launch for Burton Island. Its scenic lakefront views and historic charm make it a unique destination.

☐ 🔖 ♡ **Kingsland Bay State Park:** In Ferrisburgh, this 264-acre park lies along a sheltered bay of Lake Champlain. Visitors enjoy picnicking, birdwatching, and hiking in a peaceful landscape with wooded trails and shoreline views. Its natural beauty and quiet charm provide a low-key escape with lake access and scenic vistas.

☐ 🔖 ♡ **Knight Island State Park:** Accessible only by boat, this 125-acre island park in North Hero offers primitive camping and shoreline hiking. With limited development, it preserves a rugged, wilderness-like atmosphere. Visitors enjoy kayaking, fishing, and birdwatching while surrounded by Lake Champlain's expansive views and tranquil waters.

☐ 🔖 ♡ **Knight Point State Park:** At the southern tip of North Hero Island, this 54-acre park offers a sandy beach, shaded picnic areas, and easy lake access. With panoramic views of Lake Champlain and a relaxed setting, it's popular for swimming, sunbathing, and family outings. Trails wind through open meadows and wooded shoreline.

VERMONT

☐ 🔖 ♡ **Lake Carmi State Park:** This 482-acre park in Franklin encompasses Vermont's fourth-largest natural lake. It features campgrounds, a sandy beach, and boat access for fishing or paddling. With forested trails and wetlands supporting diverse wildlife, it's both a recreational hub and a destination for quiet nature appreciation.

☐ 🔖 ♡ **Lake Shaftsbury State Park:** Found in Shaftsbury, this 84-acre park centers on a small lake with a sandy beach, picnic areas, and wooded trails. A quiet day-use and camping destination, it's popular for swimming, paddling, and fishing. Its intimate scale and peaceful setting make it perfect for family visits and relaxation.

☐ 🔖 ♡ **Lake St. Catherine State Park:** In Poultney, this 117-acre park offers a beach, campground, and wooded picnic areas on the shores of Lake St. Catherine. Popular for swimming, boating, and fishing, it's a favorite family destination. Its mix of water recreation and forested landscapes makes it a versatile and scenic retreat.

☐ 🔖 ♡ **Little River State Park:** Covering 850 acres along Waterbury Reservoir, this park combines history and recreation. It offers hiking trails through abandoned 19th-century farmsteads, as well as camping, fishing, and swimming. Surrounded by Green Mountain scenery, it's a top spot for both outdoor adventure and cultural discovery.

☐ 🔖 ♡ **Lowell Lake State Park:** A 356-acre day-use park in Londonderry, it offers a quiet shoreline trail circling the lake, perfect for hiking, birdwatching, and paddling. With picnic areas and undeveloped forest, it provides a serene, low-impact recreation area. Its tranquil waters and scenic beauty make it a hidden gem in southern Vermont.

☐ 🔖 ♡ **Maidstone State Park:** One of Vermont's most remote parks, this 475-acre site in Essex County sits on a glacial lake surrounded by forested mountains. Campgrounds, fishing, and hiking make it ideal for nature enthusiasts. Its quiet setting and northern location in the Northeast Kingdom provide a true wilderness experience.

☐ 🔖 ♡ **Molly Stark State Park:** Located in Wilmington, this 148-acre park sits along the Molly Stark Scenic Byway. It offers hiking trails to Mt. Olga's summit for panoramic views, plus camping and picnicking in wooded surroundings. Its combination of accessible hiking and forest setting makes it popular for families and travelers alike.

☐ 🔖 ♡ **Molly's Falls Pond State Park:** Spanning over 1,000 acres in Cabot, this park surrounds a reservoir with opportunities for fishing, paddling, and picnicking. Hiking trails and scenic viewpoints make it attractive to nature enthusiasts. Its mix of water access and undeveloped forest ensures a peaceful setting for recreation and relaxation.

☐ 🔖 ♡ **Mount Ascutney State Park:** Encompassing over 3,100 acres, this park highlights the rugged slopes of Mount Ascutney. Trails ascend to the summit, offering sweeping views of the Connecticut River Valley. With camping, picnicking, and abundant wildlife, it's a top destination for hikers and those seeking mountain adventures.

☐ 🔖 ♡ **Mount Philo State Park:** Vermont's oldest state park, established in 1924, covers 237 acres in Charlotte. Trails climb to a summit overlooking Lake Champlain and the Adirondacks. Visitors enjoy hiking, picnicking, and wildlife watching in a setting known for its sweeping vistas and historical significance as the first park in the system.

☐ 🔖 ♡ **Muckross State Park:** Near Springfield, this 200-acre undeveloped park offers hiking trails, streams, and forests perfect for quiet exploration. With limited facilities, it emphasizes a natural, rustic experience. Visitors enjoy wildlife viewing, peaceful walks, and immersion in unspoiled woodland landscapes, making it a retreat for those seeking solitude.

☐ 🔖 ♡ **New Discovery State Park:** In Groton State Forest, this 700-acre park offers camping, hiking, and access to Kettle Pond and other nearby sites. Visitors enjoy trails through forests and hills, fishing in quiet waters, and family-friendly camping. Its location makes it a hub for exploring the wider Groton recreation area.

☐ 🔖 ♡ **Niquette Bay State Park:** Located in Colchester, this 584-acre park offers hiking trails to scenic overlooks of Lake Champlain. With a rocky beach, forested hills, and abundant wildlife, it's popular for swimming, fishing, and picnicking. Its peaceful setting combines lakeside relaxation with woodland exploration.

☐ 🔖 ♡ **North Hero State Park:** Situated on Lake Champlain's island shoreline, this 399-acre park offers camping, picnicking, and lake access for fishing, swimming, and boating. With open fields, shaded groves, and mountain views, it's a spacious and scenic destination for family recreation and outdoor relaxation.

VERMONT

☐ 🔖 ♡ **Quechee State Park:** This 611-acre park in Hartford is home to Vermont's famous Quechee Gorge, often called the state's "Grand Canyon." Trails and overlooks provide dramatic views, while campgrounds and picnic areas invite extended visits. With river access and forested surroundings, it's a highlight for sightseeing and outdoor adventure.

☐ 🔖 ♡ **Ricker Pond State Park:** Part of Groton State Forest, this 95-acre park centers on Ricker Pond, with campsites and lean-tos along the shore. Visitors can fish, paddle, and swim in calm waters or explore nearby trails. Its scenic lakeside setting and quiet environment make it a peaceful family camping destination.

☐ 🔖 ♡ **Sand Bar State Park:** At the southern end of Lake Champlain's causeway, this 15-acre park features one of Vermont's most popular beaches. Its shallow waters make it perfect for swimming with children, while picnic areas and open views create a relaxing day-use setting. It's a summertime favorite for families.

☐ 🔖 ♡ **Sentinel Rock State Park:** Located in Westmore, this 356-acre day-use park centers on a massive glacial boulder known as Sentinel Rock. Visitors can hike a short interpretive trail to the rock, which offers panoramic views of Lake Willoughby, Mount Pisgah, and Mount Hor. The park protects open meadows and forested slopes, providing wildlife habitat and a peaceful setting for picnicking and nature walks.

☐ 🔖 ♡ **Seyon Lodge State Park:** Unique among Vermont parks, this 39-acre site features a historic lodge on Noyes Pond in Groton State Forest. Popular for weddings, retreats, and group stays, it offers fly-fishing, hiking, and birdwatching in a tranquil, forested landscape. Its blend of natural beauty and rustic comfort makes it special.

☐ 🔖 ♡ **Silver Lake State Park:** Located in Barnard, this 35-acre park features a sandy beach, swimming area, and shady picnic spots along Silver Lake. Visitors enjoy boating, fishing, and camping with views of surrounding hills. Its small size and welcoming environment make it ideal for families and day trips.

☐ 🔖 ♡ **Smugglers' Notch State Park:** In Stowe, this 1,000-acre park sits at the base of a dramatic mountain pass. Popular for hiking, rock climbing, and sightseeing, it offers access to rugged trails and striking cliffs. Its narrow roadway and scenic beauty reflect its history as a smuggling route and outdoor destination.

☐ 🔖 ♡ **Stillwater State Park:** On Lake Groton, this 57-acre park offers waterfront campsites, boating, and family-friendly recreation. Its campground, beach, and forested surroundings make it a relaxing place to swim, paddle, and hike. With quiet waters and accessible facilities, it's one of Groton State Forest's most popular camping parks.

☐ 🔖 ♡ **Sweet Pond State Park:** A 100-acre day-use park in Guilford, it features a scenic pond ringed by forest trails. Visitors enjoy paddling, fishing, and wildlife observation in a peaceful setting. With its quiet waters and simple facilities, it's an excellent retreat for relaxation and low-key recreation in southern Vermont.

☐ 🔖 ♡ **Taconic Mountains Ramble State Park:** This 204-acre park in Hubbardton highlights rugged terrain, meadows, and Japanese gardens set against the Taconic Mountains. Hiking trails climb ridges with sweeping views, while open fields support wildlife and birdwatching. It offers a unique blend of cultural features and wild landscapes.

☐ 🔖 ♡ **Thetford Hill State Park:** Located in Thetford, this 262-acre park offers wooded trails, open meadows, and scenic overlooks. Once a Civilian Conservation Corps site, it's popular for hiking, birding, and quiet exploration. Its history and natural setting combine to make it a peaceful, under-the-radar destination.

☐ 🔖 ♡ **Townshend State Park:** Nestled at the foot of Bald Mountain, this 41-acre park provides camping, picnicking, and hiking in a quiet West River valley setting. Trails connect to mountain ridges, while shaded sites create a rustic atmosphere. Its mix of river access and forested terrain makes it appealing for campers.

☐ 🔖 ♡ **Underhill State Park:** At the base of Mount Mansfield, Vermont's highest peak, this 2,000-acre park offers challenging trails to the summit. Hikers enjoy sweeping views of the Green Mountains and beyond. With camping and access to alpine terrain, it's a premier destination for adventure in the northern mountains.

☐ 🔖 ♡ **Waterbury Center State Park:** On Waterbury Reservoir, this 90-acre day-use park features a sandy beach, accessible trails, and picnic areas. Popular for kayaking, swimming, and fishing, it's family-friendly and scenic. Its location near Stowe and the Green Mountains makes it a convenient stop for summer recreation.

☐ 🔖 ♡ **Wilgus State Park:** Located on the Connecticut River in Weathersfield, this 100-acre park offers riverside campsites, canoe access, and hiking trails. Paddlers and anglers find it ideal for exploring the scenic river corridor. With peaceful wooded sites and water views, it's a quiet retreat in southern Vermont.

VERMONT

☐ ◻ ♡ **Woodford State Park:** In the Green Mountains near Bennington, this 400-acre park includes Adams Reservoir and high-elevation forest. Campgrounds, hiking trails, and cool mountain air make it ideal for summer camping. With paddling, fishing, and quiet woodlands, it provides a refreshing outdoor escape in southern Vermont.

☐ ◻ ♡ **Woods Island State Park:** Accessible only by boat, this 125-acre island in Lake Champlain offers primitive camping and hiking. Visitors enjoy paddling, fishing, and birdwatching along rocky shores and forested trails. Its undeveloped character and remote setting create a rare wilderness experience close to the Champlain Islands.

National Parks

☐ ◻ ♡ **Appalachian National Scenic Trail:** Stretching more than 2,100 miles from Georgia to Maine, the Appalachian Trail crosses Vermont's Green Mountains as part of its route. Known for rugged ridges, hardwood forests, and sweeping vistas, it offers hikers a chance to experience wilderness and challenge themselves on one of America's most iconic long-distance footpaths.

☐ ◻ ♡ **Marsh-Billings-Rockefeller National Historical Park:** In Woodstock, this park honors conservation pioneers George Perkins Marsh and the Rockefeller family. Visitors explore a historic mansion, formal gardens, and forest trails that highlight sustainable land management. As the only U.S. national park dedicated to conservation history, it blends cultural heritage with outdoor beauty.

State & National Forests

☐ ◻ ♡ **Aitken State Forest:** Near Mendon, this 918-acre forest of hardwood and softwood slopes supports wildlife and watershed protection. Trails and woods roads provide hiking, hunting, and skiing. Its proximity to Pico and Killington offers a quiet retreat where visitors can explore upland forests and enjoy mountain scenery in every season.

☐ ◻ ♡ **Arlington State Forest:** A small tract in the Batten Kill valley, this forest preserves river corridors and mixed woods. Anglers, hikers, and birdwatchers appreciate its quiet setting, while hunters use it seasonally. Though modest in size, it contributes to the conservation of Vermont's historic trout waters and provides accessible outdoor recreation.

☐ ◻ ♡ **Baker Pond State Forest:** Spanning 626 acres in Brookfield, this forest encircles a serene pond where visitors paddle, fish, and watch for loons. Trails and woods roads meander through mixed hardwoods and wetlands rich in wildlife. Its pond-centered ecosystem provides a scenic and tranquil retreat for nature lovers and families alike.

☐ ◻ ♡ **Black Turn Brook State Forest:** Located in Norton, this 1,500-acre forest offers rugged backcountry terrain of spruce–fir and hardwood ridges. Moose, bear, and boreal birds thrive here. Hunters, hikers, and snowshoers explore old woods roads and brook corridors, enjoying the solitude and wild character of Vermont's Northeast Kingdom.

☐ ◻ ♡ **Boyer State Forest:** In Berlin, this forest offers hiking, mountain biking, and cross-country skiing close to Montpelier. Its wetlands and upland woods support beaver, deer, and diverse songbirds. Visitors find a convenient yet peaceful landscape that balances recreation with conservation in a community-friendly setting.

☐ ◻ ♡ **Bradley Hill State Forest:** A 500-acre tract in Chelsea, this forest blends hardwood ridges, wetlands, and steep slopes. Managed for habitat and watershed protection, it also supports hunting, birding, and hiking. Visitors enjoy quiet trails and seasonal color in a forest that demonstrates sustainable multi-use management in central Vermont.

☐ ◻ ♡ **Calvin Coolidge State Forest:** Vermont's largest state forest spans over 20,000 acres in Windsor and Rutland counties. It includes CCC-era sites, overlooks, and a web of trails for hiking, skiing, hunting, and snowmobiling. Surrounding Coolidge State Park, it combines cultural history with vast Green Mountain landscapes and abundant wildlife.

☐ ◻ ♡ **Cambridge State Forest:** Encompassing about 1,000 acres, this forest preserves upland hardwoods and protects watershed lands above the Lamoille Valley. Visitors enjoy dispersed recreation such as hiking, hunting, and skiing. Its undeveloped character provides habitat for bear, deer, and songbirds, offering a quiet Green Mountain foothill experience.

VERMONT

☐ 🔖 ♡ **C.C. Putnam State Forest:** Covering 13,633 acres in the Worcester Range, this forest features rugged peaks like Mount Hunger and White Rock. Trails climb steep slopes to panoramic views, while dense woods support moose and black bear. It is managed for habitat, timber, and recreation, offering classic Green Mountain backcountry adventure.

☐ 🔖 ♡ **Camel's Hump State Forest:** Protecting 2,323 acres on the slopes of Vermont's iconic peak, this forest is a gateway to the Long Trail and rugged backcountry. It safeguards alpine ecosystems and montane spruce–fir while providing challenging hikes with sweeping vistas. A conservation stronghold, it balances recreation with ecological preservation.

☐ 🔖 ♡ **Crossett Hill State Forest:** A 1,500-acre tract in Duxbury, this forest protects high-elevation watersheds and habitats for moose, bear, and migratory birds. Visitors hike and hunt along old woods roads in a quiet setting with little development. Its conservation focus ensures clean water and wildlife corridors in central Vermont.

☐ 🔖 ♡ **Dorand State Forest:** Situated in Windham County, this forest contains hardwood ridges, hemlock groves, and headwater streams. It provides habitat for deer and songbirds while supporting hiking, hunting, and seasonal skiing. Its quiet woodlands contribute to watershed protection and showcase southern Vermont's forested hills.

☐ 🔖 ♡ **Downer State Forest:** This 4,000-acre forest in Sharon and Thetford features diverse hardwood stands and varied terrain. Woods roads and trails offer hiking, hunting, and cross-country skiing. Managed for timber, wildlife, and recreation, it provides habitat while supporting sustainable forestry and a broad range of public uses.

☐ 🔖 ♡ **Glebe Mountain State Forest:** In Londonderry, this forest protects high-elevation woodlands on the slopes of Glebe Mountain. It safeguards watersheds and provides habitat for moose, bear, and raptors. Hunting, hiking, and backcountry skiing are possible here. With rugged terrain and undeveloped character, it emphasizes conservation and dispersed recreation.

☐ 🔖 ♡ **Granville Gulf Reservation State Forest:** Stretching through a dramatic mountain pass along VT Route 100, this 1,171-acre reservation preserves Moss Glen Falls, old-growth stands, and cool ravines. Visitors stop for waterfalls, wildflowers, and roadside viewpoints, or hike into misty spruce–fir woods. It's a scenic highlight of the Green Mountains.

☐ 🔖 ♡ **Green Mountain National Forest:** Vermont's only national forest spans nearly 400,000 acres across the spine of the Green Mountains. It hosts the Long Trail and Appalachian Trail, wilderness areas, ski resorts, and campgrounds. From hiking and paddling to skiing and hunting, it is the state's premier multi-use forestland and ecological treasure.

☐ 🔖 ♡ **Groton State Forest:** Covering over 26,000 acres, Groton is a recreation hub with lakes, ponds, campgrounds, and a rich trail network. It includes seven state parks and diverse ecosystems from bogs to hardwood ridges. Families, hikers, and paddlers enjoy its varied landscapes, making it one of Vermont's most popular forest destinations.

☐ 🔖 ♡ **Hapgood State Forest:** Centered near Bromley Mountain in Peru, this forest protects upland hardwoods and watersheds while supporting skiing, hiking, and hunting. Wildlife such as bear and deer thrive in its varied cover. It offers dispersed outdoor opportunities and conservation values, linking recreation to the Green Mountain landscape.

☐ 🔖 ♡ **Hazens Notch State Forest:** Encompassing rugged terrain in Montgomery and Westfield, this forest surrounds a dramatic mountain pass. Visitors hike Long Trail segments, watch for moose and hawks, and enjoy striking views. It combines conservation with outdoor adventure, offering a scenic and wild landscape in Vermont's Northeast Kingdom.

☐ 🔖 ♡ **Jay State Forest:** In Orleans County near the Canadian border, this high-elevation forest protects ridges, wetlands, and cold spruce–fir habitat. The Long Trail crosses its slopes, providing rugged hiking and striking views. Moose, black bear, and boreal birds thrive here, while visitors enjoy hiking, skiing, and snowshoeing in a true northern wilderness setting.

☐ 🔖 ♡ **Jim Jeffords State Forest:** Established in 2016 near Shrewsbury, this 1,349-acre forest honors Vermont's late U.S. Senator. It preserves hardwood ridges, trout streams, and wildlife corridors. Hunters, hikers, and snowmobilers find trails and old woods roads here. Managed for habitat, sustainable forestry, and recreation, it links conservation with Vermont's working landscape.

☐ 🔖 ♡ **Jones State Forest (L.R. Jones):** Known for Spruce Mountain, this 642-acre forest near Plainfield leads hikers to a historic fire tower with sweeping views of central Vermont. Dense spruce stands, vernal pools, and abundant wildlife enrich the climb. It's a small but beloved forest, balancing rugged recreation with conservation of old montane habitats.

VERMONT

☐ 🔖 ♡ **Les Newell State Forest:** A vast 7,000-acre tract in Rochester and Hancock, this forest features ridges, valleys, and diverse hardwoods. It provides habitat for moose, bear, and migratory birds while supporting hiking, hunting, and snowmobiling. With large blocks of conserved land, it represents central Vermont's wild backcountry at scale.

☐ 🔖 ♡ **Long Trail State Forest:** Encompassing over 9,000 acres along Vermont's iconic Long Trail, this forest protects ridgelines, alpine zones, and rugged backcountry. Backpackers and day hikers enjoy its challenging terrain and sweeping views. It safeguards critical ecosystems while offering premier wilderness hiking across the Green Mountains.

☐ 🔖 ♡ **Lord State Forest:** A smaller but scenic tract, Lord preserves upland hardwoods and streams in southern Vermont. Visitors explore woods roads for hiking, birding, and hunting. Its undeveloped character emphasizes watershed protection and wildlife habitat, providing a quiet natural space that supports both conservation and dispersed recreation.

☐ 🔖 ♡ **Lower Clarendon Gorge State Forest:** Located near Rutland, this forest preserves steep cliffs and cascades carved by the Mill River. Trails and footbridges give access to dramatic gorge views and swimming holes. It protects a geologically significant corridor while offering hikers and families a striking natural landmark in the Green Mountains.

☐ 🔖 ♡ **Lyndon State Forest:** A compact forest near Lyndonville, it provides woodland habitat and watershed benefits while serving the local community. Visitors enjoy seasonal hiking, hunting, and birdwatching. Its modest size belies its importance as a green buffer in Vermont's Northeast Kingdom, conserving natural resources close to town.

☐ 🔖 ♡ **Mathewson State Forest:** Situated in Orange County, this forest features rolling hills, streams, and a mix of hardwoods. It supports wildlife such as deer and songbirds, and provides trails for hunting, hiking, and skiing. Its conservation role emphasizes watershed health and habitat while offering dispersed, low-key recreation opportunities.

☐ 🔖 ♡ **Mollie Beattie State Forest:** Named for the former U.S. Fish & Wildlife Service director, this Northeast Kingdom forest preserves remote wetlands and mixed woods. Moose, loons, and boreal birds thrive in its quiet terrain. Visitors find opportunities for hunting, paddling nearby waters, and backcountry hiking in a landscape of wild beauty.

☐ 🔖 ♡ **Morse Brook State Forest:** Near Bristol, this 2,500-acre forest protects headwater streams and upland hardwood ridges. It provides habitat for black bear, deer, and songbirds, while supporting hiking, skiing, and hunting on primitive woods roads. Its undeveloped character offers solitude and a backcountry feel in central Vermont.

☐ 🔖 ♡ **Mount Carmel State Forest:** A rugged tract in southern Vermont, this forest contains steep slopes, hardwood ridges, and brook valleys. It provides habitat for wildlife while protecting water resources. Hikers and hunters value its quiet woodlands, which showcase Vermont's tradition of conserving high-elevation forestland for public use.

☐ 🔖 ♡ **Mount Cushman State Forest:** This mountain forest preserves upland ecosystems and headwater streams in central Vermont. Visitors enjoy dispersed recreation such as hiking, snowshoeing, and hunting. Its steep terrain supports moose and bear while safeguarding watersheds. With little development, it emphasizes conservation and wilderness character.

☐ 🔖 ♡ **Mount Mansfield State Forest:** Vermont's largest state forest spans 44,000+ acres, encompassing the state's tallest peak and alpine tundra. Trails include the Long Trail, leading hikers to panoramic ridges and waterfalls. It offers skiing, climbing, hunting, and camping, while safeguarding rare ecosystems and some of Vermont's most iconic landscapes.

☐ 🔖 ♡ **Mount Tabor State Forest:** In Rutland County, this forest protects hardwood ridges, trout streams, and wildlife corridors. Hunters, hikers, and snowmobilers explore its network of woods roads. Managed for conservation and sustainable forestry, it provides habitat for moose and bear while offering quiet backcountry recreation.

☐ 🔖 ♡ **Okemo State Forest:** Encompassing over 7,000 acres around Ludlow, this forest includes the slopes of Okemo Mountain. Visitors enjoy hiking, hunting, and snowmobiling, while skiing dominates in winter. Its mix of recreation, conservation, and working forest management reflects Vermont's approach to blending outdoor tourism with habitat protection.

☐ 🔖 ♡ **Proctor-Piper State Forest:** Located in Cavendish, this forest offers woodland trails and old roads for hiking, hunting, and wildlife viewing. Its hardwood ridges support deer, bear, and songbirds, while streams contribute to watershed protection. Modest in size but rich in resources, it provides a quiet corner for recreation.

VERMONT

☐ 🔖 ♡ **Putnam State Forest:** Not to be confused with C.C. Putnam, this forest protects uplands and streams in central Vermont. Its wooded slopes support diverse wildlife and dispersed recreation. Hikers and hunters find access along old roads, while its management emphasizes conservation of headwaters and habitat corridors.

☐ 🔖 ♡ **Roxbury State Forest:** Covering over 5,500 acres in Roxbury and Warren, this forest protects ridgelines, streams, and a wide variety of wildlife. Visitors hike, hunt, and ski across its rugged Green Mountain terrain. Managed for timber, habitat, and recreation, it represents a classic Vermont multi-use forest with both wild and working values.

☐ 🔖 ♡ **Rupert State Forest:** Nestled in the Taconic Mountains of southwestern Vermont, this forest conserves upland hardwoods, streams, and wildlife corridors. Hunters and hikers explore old woods roads, while birdwatchers enjoy seasonal migrations. Its rugged ridges and quiet valleys provide a backcountry feel, balancing conservation with dispersed recreation.

☐ 🔖 ♡ **South Duxbury State Forest:** A mid-sized tract in Washington County, this forest protects headwaters and hardwood slopes above the Winooski River. With limited development, it emphasizes watershed health and wildlife habitat. Hunters, skiers, and hikers use its woods roads, while its undeveloped nature offers solitude near central Vermont towns.

☐ 🔖 ♡ **Thetford Hill State Forest:** Surrounding Thetford Academy, this 262-acre forest is a model of community forestry. Trails weave through hardwoods and meadows, supporting hiking, cross-country skiing, and outdoor education. It protects wildlife corridors and scenic ridges while serving as a local outdoor classroom and recreation resource.

☐ 🔖 ♡ **Townshend State Forest:** Located along the West River valley, this forest encompasses Bald Mountain's lower slopes. Trails lead to overlooks with expansive views, while shaded woods support deer and songbirds. Hunters and hikers enjoy its varied terrain. Combined with the nearby state park, it offers camping, nature study, and cultural history.

☐ 🔖 ♡ **Victory State Forest:** Covering 16,000 acres in Essex County, this is one of Vermont's largest state forests. It protects remote boreal habitats of spruce–fir and wetlands, home to moose, black bear, and rare birds. Hunters, skiers, and snowmobilers traverse its wild landscape, making it a Northeast Kingdom stronghold for wilderness recreation.

☐ 🔖 ♡ **Washington State Forest:** A compact forest in central Vermont, this tract preserves upland hardwoods and headwater streams. Hunters and hikers use its old woods roads, while birdwatchers enjoy seasonal flocks in its ridges and valleys. It provides habitat connectivity and watershed benefits while supporting quiet, low-impact recreation.

☐ 🔖 ♡ **West Rutland State Forest:** Situated near the Taconic Range, this small forest protects ridges, wetlands, and wildlife habitat. Hunters and hikers find quiet trails through hardwood stands, while birders enjoy open views. Its proximity to the town of West Rutland makes it an important conservation area and local recreation space.

☐ 🔖 ♡ **William C. Putnam State Forest:** This large northern tract preserves rugged ridges, streams, and hardwood forests in the Worcester Range. Moose, bear, and raptors thrive here. Trails provide access to remote summits and viewpoints. Its size and wildness make it an important conservation anchor, balancing forestry with wilderness adventure.

☐ 🔖 ♡ **Williams River State Forest:** Following the Williams River in Chester, this forest protects riparian corridors and steep wooded hillsides. Visitors enjoy fishing, hunting, and hiking along old roads. Its role in safeguarding streams and wildlife habitat makes it valuable for both recreation and watershed protection in southern Vermont.

☐ 🔖 ♡ **Willoughby State Forest:** Encompassing 7,600 acres in Westmore, this forest includes dramatic cliffs on Mount Pisgah and Mount Hor overlooking Lake Willoughby. Trails climb to panoramic vistas, and peregrine falcons nest on sheer rock faces. Hikers, climbers, and wildlife enthusiasts enjoy its unique mix of geology, ecology, and recreation.

☐ 🔖 ♡ **Woodford State Forest:** At nearly 4,000 acres near Bennington, this high-elevation forest surrounds Adams Reservoir. Campgrounds and trails connect to cool spruce–fir woods, where moose and songbirds thrive. Hunting, fishing, cross-country skiing, and camping make it a year-round destination. Its rugged terrain ensures a refreshing mountain retreat.

VERMONT

National Scenic Byways & All-American Roads

☐ ◫ ♡ **Lake Champlain Byway:** Stretching along the eastern shore of Lake Champlain from Addison County through the Champlain Islands, this route highlights Vermont's rich lakefront heritage. Travelers enjoy sweeping views of the Adirondacks, historic villages, apple orchards, and abundant birdlife. It blends recreation, culture, and natural beauty across one of Vermont's most scenic corridors.

☐ ◫ ♡ **Molly Stark Byway:** Crossing southern Vermont along Route 9 from Brattleboro to Bennington, this corridor traverses the Green Mountains with historic towns, covered bridges, and cultural sites tied to Revolutionary War heroine Molly Stark. Visitors encounter hiking trails, farm stands, and panoramic overlooks, making it a blend of history and mountain scenery.

☐ ◫ ♡ **Stone Valley Byway:** Running north–south along the western flank of the Green Mountains, this byway follows the Taconic Range and the Poultney River Valley. It highlights Vermont's slate quarrying heritage, farm landscapes, and small historic towns. Scenic vistas, outdoor recreation, and cultural landmarks define this unique Green Mountain corridor.

☐ ◫ ♡ **The Crossroad of Vermont Byway:** Following U.S. Route 4 across central Vermont, this byway links White River Junction to Fair Haven. It traverses river valleys, forested ridges, and villages shaped by commerce and travel. Visitors enjoy covered bridges, farmsteads, and mountain views, experiencing a historic east–west travel route across the state.

☐ ◫ ♡ **The Green Mountain Byway:** Anchored by Stowe and Waterbury, this route winds through valleys framed by Mount Mansfield and the Worcester Range. Scenic farmland, historic villages, and access to iconic outdoor recreation areas make it a premier destination. It highlights the heart of Vermont's Green Mountains, where culture and landscape merge beautifully.

☐ ◫ ♡ **The Mad River Byway:** This byway traces the Mad River Valley, showcasing mountain scenery, family farms, and the lively towns of Warren and Waitsfield. Known for covered bridges, ski resorts, and artisan culture, it provides a quintessential Vermont experience. Visitors find year-round recreation paired with striking Green Mountain backdrops and rural charm.

☐ ◫ ♡ **The Northeast Kingdom Byway:** Extending from St. Johnsbury to Newport and Derby Line, this corridor travels through Vermont's wildest region. It offers views of forested hills, glacial lakes, and pastoral valleys dotted with farmsteads. Wildlife watching, hiking, and cultural stops reveal the rugged beauty and heritage of Vermont's Northeast Kingdom.

☐ ◫ ♡ **The Scenic Route 100 Byway:** Spanning nearly the entire length of Vermont, Route 100 is one of New England's most celebrated drives. It passes ski areas, waterfalls, mountain valleys, and historic villages. The byway showcases the Green Mountains at their finest, with opportunities for outdoor adventure, fall foliage viewing, and year-round recreation.

State Scenic Byways

☐ ◫ ♡ **Connecticut River Byway:** Following Vermont's eastern edge along the Connecticut River, this byway highlights fertile valleys, covered bridges, and historic river towns. Travelers enjoy farm landscapes, fishing spots, and scenic overlooks across to New Hampshire's White Mountains. It captures the heritage of the river as a trade route and cultural corridor.

☐ ◫ ♡ **Shires of Vermont Byway:** Linking Bennington and Manchester through the valleys of southwestern Vermont, this route showcases historic districts, colonial architecture, and mountain vistas. Visitors find cultural attractions like museums and theaters alongside farmstands and artisan shops. It celebrates the "shire towns" that anchor Vermont's southern counties.

☐ ◫ ♡ **Silvio O. Conte National Fish and Wildlife Refuge Byway (Nulhegan Basin):** This remote byway in the Northeast Kingdom winds through boreal forest and wetlands within the Nulhegan Basin division of the Conte Refuge. Wildlife enthusiasts come for moose, loons, and migratory birds. Its wild scenery and conservation lands emphasize Vermont's northernmost natural heritage.

☐ ◫ ♡ **Skyline Drive (Mount Equinox):** A privately operated toll road recognized as a state byway, Skyline Drive ascends to the summit of Mount Equinox. Visitors enjoy sweeping views of the Taconic Range, Adirondacks, and Green Mountains. Its scenic switchbacks and high-elevation landscapes make it a unique Vermont driving experience.

VERMONT

☐ 🔖 ♡ **Stone Valley Byway (State sections):** Beyond the federally designated corridor, Vermont also recognizes additional stretches as part of its scenic byway network. These areas highlight slate quarries, farm valleys, and small villages. The route connects communities through the Taconic Range, extending the cultural and natural story of the region.

☐ 🔖 ♡ **William Jarvis Byway:** Honoring the diplomat who brought the first merino sheep to Vermont, this byway passes through Weathersfield and surrounding farmland. Rolling hills, pastoral fields, and historic homes tell the story of Vermont's agricultural legacy. Travelers encounter a quiet, rural landscape where sheep once shaped the state's economy.

National Natural Landmarks

 ☐ 🔖 ♡ **Barton River Marsh:** This shallow wetland was designated a National Natural Landmark as one of New England's finest freshwater marshes. Its intact hydrology and diverse plant communities sustain marsh birds, amphibians, and migratory waterfowl, making it an outstanding example of large, healthy wetland ecosystems in the Northeast.
GPS: 44.856917, -72.204000

 ☐ 🔖 ♡ **Fisher-Scott Memorial Pines:** National Natural Landmark recognition was given to this old-growth stand of towering white pines, some centuries old. It preserves the structure and species mix of Vermont's original pine forests, minimally altered by human activity, and offers critical habitat for birds, mammals, and understory plants.
GPS: 43.1031197, -73.138458

 ☐ 🔖 ♡ **Battell Biological Preserve:** Recognized as a National Natural Landmark for its pristine climax forest, this site preserves mature northern hardwoods with undisturbed soils and a full complement of native flora and fauna. The preserve provides a living reference for what Vermont's forests looked like before logging and development transformed the region.
GPS: 44.0038, -73.1226

 ☐ 🔖 ♡ **Franklin Bog:** Designated a National Natural Landmark for its intact sphagnum-heath bog community, this acidic wetland supports boreal plants, insects, and carnivorous species more common to northern climates. Its deep peat deposits preserve ecological history, offering a rare scientific record of Vermont's colder, post-glacial environments.
GPS: 44.9565567, -72.8790105

 ☐ 🔖 ♡ **Camel's Hump:** National Natural Landmark status was given to Camel's Hump for supporting Vermont's second-largest alpine tundra zone. Its rugged summit ridge harbors rare arctic-alpine plants, shaped by harsh winds and cold. The mountain remains a vital research site for monitoring climate change impacts on fragile high-elevation ecosystems.
GPS: 44.3195, -72.8863

 ☐ 🔖 ♡ **Gifford Woods:** This site was designated a National Natural Landmark for its exemplary old-growth northern hardwood forest. Dominated by sugar maple, beech, and hemlock, the woods shelter ferns, fungi, spring ephemerals, and nesting birds. It provides a living picture of Vermont's pre-settlement forest communities.
GPS: 43.6762, -72.8109

 ☐ 🔖 ♡ **Chazy Fossil Reef:** Celebrated as the world's oldest known biologically diverse fossil reef, this site in the Champlain Valley was named a National Natural Landmark for its extraordinary Ordovician fossils. Ancient corals, trilobites, and other marine life provide unparalleled evidence of early reef ecosystems more than 450 million years old.
GPS: 44.8528, -73.3400

 ☐ 🔖 ♡ **Lake Willoughby Natural Area:** Recognized as a National Natural Landmark for its striking glacial origins, Lake Willoughby lies in a classic U-shaped valley flanked by cliffs. Vermont's deepest lake harbors clear cold waters, alpine plants, and rare aquatic life, making it one of the best-preserved glacial landscapes in New England.
GPS: 44.7519, -72.0628

 ☐ 🔖 ♡ **Cornwall Marsh:** Cornwall Marsh earned National Natural Landmark designation as Vermont's largest continuous red maple swamp. Its peat soils, seasonal flooding, and swamp hardwoods provide essential breeding grounds for wetland birds, mammals, and amphibians, making it an outstanding example of northern swamp ecology.
GPS: 43.9159, -73.1863

 ☐ 🔖 ♡ **Little Otter Creek Marsh:** Little Otter Creek was named a National Natural Landmark as Vermont's most important large marshland. With cattail stands, open water, and wet meadows, it sustains migratory birds, aquatic mammals, and amphibians. Its biodiversity and intact wetland functions make it regionally significant.
GPS: 44.226263, -73.324316

VERMONT

 ☐ 🔖 ♡ **Molly Bog:** This high-elevation bog became a National Natural Landmark for its specialized boreal plant communities and early-stage bog succession. With black spruce, sphagnum moss, and carnivorous plants, it reflects acidic, nutrient-poor conditions and serves as a valuable site for monitoring bog ecology and climate effects.
GPS: 44.499200, -72.642400

  ☐ 🔖 ♡ **Mount Mansfield:** Vermont's highest summit was designated a National Natural Landmark for its rare arctic-alpine tundra and virgin spruce–fir forest. The ridgeline harbors plants found nowhere else in the Northeast, shaped by severe alpine weather. It remains a critical natural laboratory for studying fragile high-mountain ecosystems.
GPS: 44.5439, -72.8143

UNITED STATES EDITION

VIRGINIA

Virginia's diverse beauty stretches from the Blue Ridge Mountains and cascading waterfalls to coastal marshes and barrier islands. Through its network of state parks, national forests, national park units, and inspiring natural landmarks, Virginia offers outdoor experiences steeped in history and natural wonder.

📅 Peak Season
April–June and September–October are Virginia's peak seasons, offering mild temperatures, blooming landscapes, and colorful fall foliage. These months are ideal for hiking, scenic drives, and exploring the mountains and coast.

📅 Offseason Months
November–March is the offseason, with cooler temperatures and fewer visitors. Winter offers peaceful hiking and mountain vistas, while summer can be hot and humid, especially in eastern regions.

🍃 Scenery & Nature Timing
Spring brings wildflowers and dogwood blooms along the Blue Ridge. Summer highlights beaches, forests, and waterfalls. Fall peaks with brilliant foliage across the Appalachians, while winter offers clear skies and quiet natural beauty.

✨ Special
Virginia showcases the Blue Ridge Parkway's sweeping vistas, the caverns of Shenandoah Valley, and Great Dismal Swamp's mysterious wetlands. Natural Bridge, rolling Piedmont hills, and cascading waterfalls reveal its rich geological diversity.

VIRGINIA

State Parks

☐ 🔖 ♡ **Bear Creek Lake State Park:** Tucked in Cumberland State Forest, this 326-acre park centers on a 40-acre lake for fishing, swimming, and boating. Trails loop through hardwoods and pines, while cabins, campgrounds, and picnic shelters provide family fun. It's a peaceful retreat where forested hillsides and quiet waters create a welcoming outdoor getaway.

☐ 🔖 ♡ **Belle Isle State Park:** Stretching along the Rappahannock River, Belle Isle protects wetlands, fields, and forests with seven miles of shoreline. Kayakers and anglers flock here, while trails and birding opportunities draw nature lovers. Its mix of ecosystems supports bald eagles, osprey, and herons, making it a quiet, scenic haven for both outdoor recreation and wildlife viewing.

☐ 🔖 ♡ **Caledon State Park:** Once part of a colonial estate, Caledon preserves Potomac River shoreline and old-growth forests known for bald eagles. Trails wind through marshes and woods, offering solitude and wildlife watching. With its rich habitats, guided tours, and picnic areas, the park is a sanctuary for birders, photographers, and anyone seeking quiet natural beauty.

☐ 🔖 ♡ **Chippokes State Park:** Over 400 years of farming history come alive at this James River plantation. Visitors can tour the 19th-century mansion, explore gardens and a farm museum, then hike woodland trails or camp along the river. Chippokes blends agricultural heritage with outdoor recreation, offering one of Virginia's most unique history-meets-nature experiences.

☐ 🔖 ♡ **Claytor Lake State Park:** This 472-acre park fronts a 4,500-acre lake, drawing boaters, anglers, and swimmers to its sandy beaches and marina. Cabins and campgrounds offer lodging, while trails provide hiking and biking through forested hills. With panoramic lake views and abundant recreation, it's a favorite destination for family-friendly summer fun.

☐ 🔖 ♡ **Clinch River State Park:** Virginia's first blueway park protects sections of the biologically rich Clinch River. Paddlers, anglers, and hikers enjoy its calm waters and forested banks, home to rare mussels and fish species. As one of the most biodiverse waterways in North America, the park balances outdoor adventure with conservation in a quiet mountain setting.

☐ 🔖 ♡ **Culpeper Battlefields State Park:** This multi-unit park preserves key Civil War sites including Brandy Station and Cedar Mountain. Visitors follow interpretive trails, monuments, and rolling fields once scarred by battle. With hiking paths, wildlife habitats, and educational programs, the park invites reflection on history while exploring Virginia's rural landscapes.

☐ 🔖 ♡ **Douthat State Park:** A classic mountain retreat built by the Civilian Conservation Corps in 1936, Douthat features a 50-acre lake and over 40 miles of trails. Fishing, swimming, and boating highlight the lake, while cabins and campgrounds provide lodging. Its scenic valleys and wooded ridges make it a beloved spot for year-round outdoor adventure.

☐ 🔖 ♡ **Fairy Stone State Park:** This park is famed for staurolite crystals known as "fairy stones," found in surrounding hills. A 168-acre lake provides swimming, fishing, and boating, while trails wind through 4,700 acres of forest. Families enjoy its campgrounds, cabins, and picnic shelters, making it both a place of legend and a hub of recreation.

☐ 🔖 ♡ **False Cape State Park:** Among Virginia's most remote parks, False Cape sits between Back Bay and the Atlantic, accessible only by foot, bike, or boat. Six miles of wild beach, dunes, and maritime forest support abundant wildlife. Primitive camping, paddling, and hiking here offer rare solitude and an authentic coastal wilderness experience.

☐ 🔖 ♡ **First Landing State Park:** Site of the 1607 English settlers' landing, this 2,888-acre park offers Chesapeake Bay beaches, cypress swamps, and 20 miles of trails. Visitors enjoy swimming, boating, and birding alongside colonial history. With cabins, campsites, and rich biodiversity, it's Virginia's most-visited park and a mix of heritage and natural beauty.

☐ 🔖 ♡ **Grayson Highlands State Park:** High in the Blue Ridge, this 4,500-acre park is renowned for wild ponies, rhododendron-covered slopes, and alpine meadows. Trails link to the Appalachian Trail, offering rugged hikes with sweeping vistas. Camping, trout streams, and scenic overlooks make it a premier mountain destination filled with rare highland scenery.

VIRGINIA

☐ 🔖 ♡ **High Bridge Trail State Park:** Following a converted rail line, this 31-mile trail features the spectacular High Bridge, soaring 125 feet above the Appomattox River. Ideal for hiking, biking, or horseback riding, it connects towns and Civil War history. Panoramic views from the bridge highlight one of Virginia's signature recreational trails.

☐ 🔖 ♡ **Holliday Lake State Park:** Surrounded by Appomattox-Buckingham State Forest, this 255-acre park offers a lake for swimming, fishing, and boating. Hiking trails wind through hardwood forest rich with wildlife, while picnic shelters and campgrounds make it family-friendly. Quiet, wooded, and accessible, it's a favorite for simple outdoor relaxation.

☐ 🔖 ♡ **Hungry Mother State Park:** One of Virginia's original six state parks, Hungry Mother combines a mountain lake, sandy beach, and wooded ridges. Trails and campgrounds make it popular with hikers, swimmers, and boaters. Rooted in Appalachian legend, its cabins, scenic beauty, and family amenities create a timeless escape in the mountains of Southwest Virginia.

☐ 🔖 ♡ **James River State Park:** With three miles of river frontage, this 1,500-acre park offers canoeing, kayaking, and fishing along the historic James. Meadows, forests, and bluffs provide trails for hiking and biking, while cabins and campgrounds extend the stay. Its mix of recreation and pastoral scenery makes it a versatile destination for families.

☐ 🔖 ♡ **Kiptopeke State Park:** On the Eastern Shore, Kiptopeke provides Chesapeake Bay beaches, fishing piers, boat launches, and unique overnight stays like yurts and RV sites. Trails explore coastal forest and bird habitat, especially during migrations. With broad views of the bay and abundant recreation, it's a vibrant coastal getaway.

☐ 🔖 ♡ **Lake Anna State Park:** Once a gold-mining site, this park now anchors recreation on Lake Anna. With over 15 miles of trails, sandy beaches, and boating access, it's a top spot for swimming and fishing. Mining exhibits highlight history, while cabins, campsites, and picnic areas support families seeking lake-centered fun.

☐ 🔖 ♡ **Leesylvania State Park:** Rich in history and nature, this Potomac River park offers fishing piers, boat launches, hiking trails, and picnic shelters. Visitors explore Civil War earthworks and plantation remnants while enjoying river views. Close to Washington, D.C., it blends outdoor recreation with cultural heritage in a convenient, family-friendly setting.

☐ 🔖 ♡ **Machicomoco State Park:** Opened in 2021, this York River park honors Virginia's Indigenous peoples through interpretive exhibits and programs. Visitors paddle, fish, or hike scenic trails along the water, then camp in modern sites or yurts. Its combination of cultural storytelling and riverside beauty makes it a truly unique addition to Virginia's park system.

☐ 🔖 ♡ **Mason Neck State Park:** Located on the tidal Potomac, Mason Neck is a sanctuary for bald eagles, herons, and ospreys. Trails and boardwalks wind through forests, marshes, and wetlands, offering birding and hiking opportunities. With picnic areas and paddling access, it's a prime destination for nature lovers just outside the bustle of Northern Virginia.

☐ 🔖 ♡ **Mayo River State Park:** Spanning Virginia's share of the Mayo River, this park provides trails, picnic spots, and scenic river overlooks. The river corridor shelters diverse wildlife and quiet wooded habitats, making it ideal for hiking, photography, and family outings. Its peaceful setting highlights the natural charm of southern Virginia's rolling Piedmont landscape.

☐ 🔖 ♡ **Middle Peninsula State Park:** Situated on Mobjack Bay, this park protects coastal habitats, wetlands, and quiet forests. Though currently closed to general recreation, it remains important for conservation and shoreline access. Its natural beauty, birdlife, and potential for low-impact exploration mark it as a significant but limited-access state park.

☐ 🔖 ♡ **Natural Bridge State Park:** Anchored by a 215-foot limestone arch, this park showcases one of Virginia's most iconic landmarks. Trails follow Cedar Creek beneath the bridge, past caves and natural springs, while overlooks frame sweeping valley views. With a visitor center and historic ties, it blends geology, history, and outdoor exploration in a striking setting.

VIRGINIA

☐ 🔖 ♡ **Natural Tunnel State Park:** This park is centered on an 850-foot tunnel carved through a mountain, once dubbed the "Eighth Wonder of the World." Hiking trails lead to overlooks and forested ridges, while a chairlift descends to the tunnel floor. Camping, picnics, and interpretive programs make it a fascinating mix of geology and recreation.

☐ 🔖 ♡ **New River Trail State Park:** A 57-mile rail trail paralleling the New River, this linear park is ideal for biking, hiking, and horseback riding. It passes through tunnels, over trestle bridges, and along river bluffs. With fishing access and campgrounds, the park highlights scenic river landscapes and cultural history across Southwest Virginia.

☐ 🔖 ♡ **Occoneechee State Park:** Bordering Buggs Island Lake, Virginia's largest reservoir, this park is a favorite for boating, fishing, and swimming. Trails explore hardwood forests, meadows, and lakefront coves. With cabins, campgrounds, and equestrian facilities, it blends water recreation with wildlife viewing in a quiet southern Virginia setting.

☐ 🔖 ♡ **Pocahontas State Park:** Just outside Richmond, this 8,000-acre park is Virginia's largest. Visitors enjoy over 90 miles of trails, three lakes, and interpretive exhibits about coal mining history. Popular for mountain biking, hiking, and camping, it's a year-round outdoor hub with diverse ecosystems and abundant opportunities for families and adventurers alike.

☐ 🔖 ♡ **Powhatan State Park:** Stretching along the James River, Powhatan offers boat launches, fishing, and riverside trails through meadows and forests. Campsites and picnic shelters support family visits, while its quiet woodlands attract birdwatchers and hikers. The park's balance of water access and pastoral landscapes makes it a peaceful retreat near Richmond.

☐ 🔖 ♡ **Sailor's Creek Battlefield State Park:** This historic site preserves the battleground of April 6, 1865, one of the Civil War's final major conflicts. Trails, exhibits, and monuments interpret the battle and its role in ending the war. Visitors can hike fields, view historic structures, and reflect on a pivotal moment in American history.

☐ 🔖 ♡ **Seven Bends State Park:** Nestled in the Shenandoah Valley, this park offers river access, scenic trails, and mountain vistas. Visitors fish, paddle, and hike along the North Fork of the Shenandoah River. With wooded ridges, meadows, and wildlife habitats, it provides both quiet outdoor escapes and opportunities for community recreation near Woodstock.

☐ 🔖 ♡ **Shenandoah River State Park:** Officially named for Delegate Andy Guest, this park stretches along five miles of riverfront. Canoeing, fishing, and tubing are popular, while trails climb to overlooks with sweeping views of Massanutten Mountain. With campgrounds and cabins, it's a year-round spot for water recreation, hiking, and Appalachian beauty.

☐ 🔖 ♡ **Shot Tower Historical State Park:** Centered on a stone tower built in the 1800s to manufacture lead shot, this small park blends industrial history with natural scenery along the New River. Visitors learn about the tower's construction, hike short trails, and picnic in forested surroundings. It's a unique mix of history and quiet outdoor space.

☐ 🔖 ♡ **Sky Meadows State Park:** Located in the Blue Ridge foothills, Sky Meadows combines open meadows, forested ridges, and historic farm buildings. With the Appalachian Trail crossing through, it's popular for hiking, birdwatching, and stargazing events. Its pastoral landscapes and mountain views make it a favorite for photographers and outdoor enthusiasts alike.

☐ 🔖 ♡ **Smith Mountain Lake State Park:** Covering 1,248 acres on Virginia's largest lake, this park offers sandy beaches, boat ramps, and fishing piers. Trails explore wooded hillsides and lakeshore coves, while cabins and campsites provide overnight stays. It's a summer destination for water sports, relaxation, and mountain-lake scenery in central Virginia.

☐ 🔖 ♡ **Southwest Virginia Museum Historical State Park:** Housed in a stone mansion in Big Stone Gap, this museum interprets the region's coal, railroad, and cultural history. Exhibits highlight Appalachian heritage, while gardens and grounds host events. As both museum and park, it preserves artifacts, stories, and landscapes central to Virginia's mountain past.

UNITED STATES EDITION

VIRGINIA

☐ ◽ ♡ **Staunton River Battlefield State Park:** This Civil War site preserves the Battle of Staunton River Bridge. Visitors walk trails past earthworks, view historic structures, and explore exhibits about local history. Blending natural beauty with cultural significance, the park provides a peaceful place for reflection, learning, and quiet exploration.

☐ ◽ ♡ **Staunton River State Park:** Set on a peninsula where the Dan and Staunton rivers meet, this 2,400-acre park offers water recreation, trails, and a pool. It is also an International Dark Sky Park, drawing stargazers from afar. Cabins, camping, and fishing make it a versatile destination for families and astronomy lovers alike.

☐ ◽ ♡ **Sweet Run State Park:** One of Virginia's newest, Sweet Run protects forests, streams, and meadows in Loudoun County. Trails invite hiking and birdwatching, while picnic areas and quiet overlooks create a serene retreat. With a focus on conservation and simple recreation, it's an emerging gem for residents of Northern Virginia and beyond.

☐ ◽ ♡ **Twin Lakes State Park:** Built around Prince Edward and Goodwin lakes, this park offers boating, swimming, and fishing in a family-friendly setting. Trails wind through forests and connect to Civil Rights history at nearby sites. With cabins, camping, and picnic shelters, it's both a recreational hub and a reflection of Virginia's diverse heritage.

☐ ◽ ♡ **Westmoreland State Park:** Stretching along the Potomac River's Northern Neck, this park offers dramatic cliffs, fossil hunting, and sweeping river views. Visitors enjoy boating, fishing, hiking, and swimming at its beach. With cabins, campgrounds, and rich natural habitats, it's a classic Virginia destination combining geology, history, and family recreation.

☐ ◽ ♡ **Widewater State Park:** Located on a peninsula between Aquia Creek and the Potomac, Widewater features wetlands, forests, and riverside access. Kayakers and anglers enjoy its quiet waterways, while trails and overlooks invite birdwatching and nature walks. With picnic shelters and simple facilities, it provides peaceful outdoor escapes in Northern Virginia.

☐ ◽ ♡ **Wilderness Road State Park:** At Cumberland Gap, this park traces Daniel Boone's Wilderness Road, gateway to the frontier. Visitors explore hiking trails, restored 18th-century Martin's Station, and scenic mountain landscapes. With living history programs, camping, and heritage interpretation, it blends Appalachian history and outdoor adventure in a memorable setting.

☐ ◽ ♡ **York River State Park:** Stretching along Taskinas Creek and the York River, this park protects marshes, forests, and estuaries rich in wildlife. Trails and boardwalks offer birding and hiking, while fishing and boating attract water enthusiasts. With archaeological sites and interpretive exhibits, it combines natural beauty with cultural discovery on Virginia's coast.

National Parks

 ☐ ◽ ♡ **Appalachian National Scenic Trail:** Extending over 2,100 miles from Georgia to Maine, the Appalachian Trail winds through forests, ridges, and valleys across the Eastern U.S. In Virginia, hikers enjoy more miles of the trail than any other state, with sweeping mountain vistas and diverse ecosystems. It's both a physical challenge and a natural sanctuary for outdoor exploration.

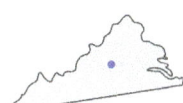 ☐ ◽ ♡ **Appomattox Court House National Historical Park:** In Appomattox, Virginia, this park preserves the site of General Robert E. Lee's 1865 surrender to General Ulysses S. Grant, ending the Civil War. Visitors can tour the restored courthouse and village, view historic exhibits, and walk grounds where a nation's healing began, reflecting on one of the most pivotal moments in U.S. history.

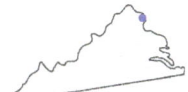 ☐ ◽ ♡ **Arlington House, The Robert E. Lee Memorial:** Overlooking Washington, D.C., in Arlington National Cemetery, this site preserves the home of Confederate General Robert E. Lee. Visitors explore the Greek Revival mansion, view exhibits on Lee's life and legacy, and take in sweeping views of the capital. The memorial serves as both a historic house and a place of reflection.

 ☐ ◽ ♡ **Assateague Island National Seashore:** Shared by Virginia and Maryland, this seashore features wild horses roaming windswept beaches, salt marshes, and dunes. Visitors swim, fish, camp, and hike along the island's shifting landscapes. Assateague is celebrated for its natural beauty and for protecting fragile coastal ecosystems while showcasing the iconic Assateague ponies.

VIRGINIA

 **Blue Ridge Parkway:** Linking Shenandoah and Great Smoky Mountains National Parks, this 469-mile scenic drive winds through Virginia and North Carolina. Known for panoramic overlooks, wildflower meadows, and historic trails, it's ideal for road trips, hiking, and picnicking. The Parkway offers unforgettable views of the Blue Ridge Mountains in every season.

 **Booker T. Washington National Monument:** In Hardy, Virginia, this park preserves the birthplace of Booker T. Washington, an influential educator and leader. Visitors explore the reconstructed 19th-century farm, exhibits on Washington's life, and trails through rolling fields. The site honors his journey from enslavement to becoming a pioneering voice for education and civil rights.

 **Cedar Creek and Belle Grove National Historical Park:** Located in Middletown, Virginia, this park commemorates the 1864 Battle of Cedar Creek and preserves the Belle Grove Plantation. Visitors can tour battlefields, explore historic buildings, and learn about the Civil War's impact on the Shenandoah Valley. The park blends military history with cultural heritage and scenic views.

 **Colonial National Historical Park:** This park links Jamestown, the first permanent English settlement in America, with Yorktown, the site of the Revolution's last major battle. Visitors explore battlefields, colonial towns, and Cape Henry Memorial. It preserves the birthplace of English America and the struggle for independence, framing centuries of Virginia history.

 **Cumberland Gap National Historical Park:** Spanning Virginia, Kentucky, and Tennessee, this park preserves the mountain pass that once served as a gateway for westward expansion. Visitors hike to overlooks with sweeping views, explore caves, and tour historic sites. The Cumberland Gap remains a symbol of frontier exploration and the resilience of early settlers.

 **Fort Monroe National Monument:** Located in Hampton, Virginia, this massive coastal fort—once called the "Gibraltar of the Chesapeake"—played key roles from the War of 1812 to the Civil War. It was where enslaved people sought freedom under "Contraband of War" status in 1861. Visitors explore casemates, ramparts, and museums, reflecting its layered military and African American history.

 **Fredericksburg and Spotsylvania National Military Park:** This park preserves battlefields of Fredericksburg, Chancellorsville, Wilderness, and Spotsylvania Court House—sites of immense Civil War bloodshed. Visitors walk trails, see preserved earthworks, and explore exhibits detailing the human cost of war. It's the second-largest military park in the nation, honoring sacrifice and history.

 **George Washington Birthplace National Monument:** On Virginia's Northern Neck, this park preserves the plantation where George Washington was born. Visitors tour a reconstructed colonial farm, family cemetery, and trails along the Potomac River. Exhibits highlight Washington's upbringing, offering insight into the formative years of the nation's first president.

 **George Washington Memorial Parkway:** Designed as a scenic drive along the Potomac, this parkway links historic landmarks like Mount Vernon, Arlington House, and Great Falls Park. Visitors enjoy access to trails, picnic areas, and overlooks. The route honors Washington's legacy while preserving riverfront landscapes and providing a green corridor through Virginia and D.C.

 **Harpers Ferry National Historical Park:** Where the Potomac and Shenandoah meet, this park spans Virginia, Maryland, and West Virginia. It preserves the site of John Brown's 1859 raid, a flashpoint before the Civil War. Visitors explore the restored town, historic buildings, and scenic trails, discovering its role in abolition, industry, and American history.

 **Maggie L. Walker National Historic Site:** In Richmond, Virginia, this site preserves the home of Maggie L. Walker, the first African American woman to charter and lead a bank. Tours of her house, along with exhibits, showcase her leadership in business, education, and civil rights. The park celebrates her pioneering impact on the African American community.

 **Manassas National Battlefield Park:** This park preserves the sites of the First and Second Battles of Bull Run, fought near Manassas, Virginia. Visitors tour battlefields, monuments, and a museum detailing the Civil War's opening clashes. Walking trails and historic landscapes help bring to life the significance of these conflicts in shaping the war's early course.

UNITED STATES EDITION

VIRGINIA

 **Petersburg National Battlefield:** South of Richmond, this park interprets the nine-month siege of Petersburg, a decisive campaign that led to the Confederacy's collapse. Visitors explore miles of earthworks, trenches, and battle sites, along with exhibits on soldiers' daily lives. The battlefield highlights the endurance and toll of the Civil War's final months.

 **Potomac Heritage National Scenic Trail:** This evolving trail network follows the Potomac River through Virginia, Maryland, Pennsylvania, and D.C. Visitors hike, bike, or paddle across varied landscapes, from forested paths to urban walkways. The trail links natural beauty with historic sites, creating a living corridor that celebrates both culture and environment.

 **Prince William Forest Park:** Covering more than 15,000 acres near Washington, D.C., this forested park offers a tranquil retreat of streams, trails, and woodlands. Visitors camp, hike, bike, and explore cabins once used by New Deal programs. As the largest green space in the D.C. metro area, it's a haven for outdoor recreation and wildlife.

 **Richmond National Battlefield Park:** This park preserves multiple Civil War sites in and around Richmond, including battlefields, fortifications, and the Tredegar Iron Works. Visitors tour historic landscapes and learn about the Confederate capital's central role in the war. Trails, exhibits, and preserved earthworks connect natural scenery with powerful history.

 **Shenandoah National Park:** Stretching along Virginia's Blue Ridge Mountains, this park offers Skyline Drive, 200,000 acres of wilderness, and over 200 miles of the Appalachian Trail. Visitors hike to waterfalls, overlooks, and rocky summits while encountering deer, bears, and diverse flora. Shenandoah is a premier destination for mountain scenery and outdoor adventure.

 **Wolf Trap National Park for the Performing Arts:** Located in Vienna, Virginia, this park is the only national park dedicated to live performance. Visitors enjoy concerts, opera, dance, and theater at the Filene Center and smaller venues, all set within rolling meadows and forest. It's a cultural landmark blending the arts with natural surroundings.

State & National Forests

Appomattox-Buckingham State Forest: Virginia's largest state forest spans over 19,000 acres of oak-hickory and pine woodlands in central Virginia. It features the Carter-Taylor multi-use trail and offers hiking, biking, horseback riding, hunting, and fishing. Managed for sustainable timber, watershed protection, and wildlife habitat, it demonstrates multiple-use forest management at scale.

Channels State Forest: Encompassing 4,836 acres in Washington and Russell counties, this forest safeguards the famous sandstone slot canyons of the Channels Natural Area Preserve. Managed for geology-forward conservation, it supports passive recreation such as hiking and horseback riding while showcasing unique Appalachian ecosystems in a rugged mountain landscape.

Charlotte State Forest: Covering nearly 5,700 acres in Charlotte County, this forest protects Piedmont woodlands of oak and pine. Managed for timber, wildlife, and watershed conservation, it provides hiking and hunting opportunities. Its role as a working forest highlights sustainable forestry practices while serving as a green corridor among rural farmlands.

Chesterfield State Forest: At 440 acres, Chesterfield is Virginia's smallest state forest, located near Richmond. It conserves pine and hardwood stands while offering trails for hiking, environmental education, and school field trips. Managed for forestry demonstration, habitat, and water protection, it is a model of conservation in an urban-border setting.

Chilton Woods State Forest: This compact 397-acre forest in Lancaster County protects pine-hardwood uplands near the Chesapeake Bay. It is managed for sustainable timber, wildlife habitat, and watershed benefits. Visitors enjoy seasonal hunting, hiking, and birdwatching. Its small size makes it an accessible site for forestry demonstration and conservation education.

Conway Robinson State Forest: Spanning 444 acres in Prince William County, this oak-hickory woodland offers hiking, biking, and horseback riding. It is managed as a living classroom for forestry, watershed, and wildlife conservation. As one of Northern Virginia's last large forested tracts, it balances suburban growth with environmental education and public recreation.

VIRGINIA

☐ 🔖 ♡ **Crawfords State Forest:** This 264-acre Coastal Plain forest in New Kent County conserves upland hardwoods typical of Virginia's Tidewater. Managed for sustainable forestry, watershed protection, and wildlife habitat, it provides low-impact walking trails and serves as an educational resource for forestry demonstration in a rapidly developing region.

☐ 🔖 ♡ **Cumberland State Forest:** Virginia's second-largest state forest covers 16,154 acres of oak-pine ridges and bottomlands in Cumberland County. It borders Bear Creek Lake State Park and offers hiking, fishing, hunting, and camping. Managed for timber, wildlife, and watershed protection, it's a prime example of multiple-use forest management in central Virginia.

☐ 🔖 ♡ **Devil's Backbone State Forest:** Located in Shenandoah County, this 705-acre high-ridge forest protects oak-hickory hilltops and native ecosystems. Managed for demonstration forestry and conservation, it allows hunting and low-impact recreation. Its ridge-top setting offers scenic views while serving as a model of mountain-forest stewardship in Virginia's Valley region.

☐ 🔖 ♡ **Dragon Run State Forest:** Covering 9,563 acres in King & Queen County, this forest conserves one of the Chesapeake Bay's most pristine tributaries. It features bottomland hardwoods, pine, and wetlands supporting high biodiversity. Hunting, fishing, and low-impact recreation are allowed. Managed for timber, wildlife, and water quality, it protects a unique tidal ecosystem.

☐ 🔖 ♡ **First Mountain State Forest:** A 573-acre property in Rockingham County near Harrisonburg, this forest preserves upland hardwoods and pine stands in the Shenandoah Valley. It supports timber management, wildlife habitat, and watershed protection. With short trails and hunting access, it's a small but significant public resource in a rapidly growing region.

☐ 🔖 ♡ **George Washington & Jefferson National Forests:** Together spanning 1.8 million acres, this national forest complex covers much of western Virginia and extends into adjacent states. It protects mountains, old-growth forests, wilderness areas, and a vast trail network including the Appalachian Trail. Visitors enjoy hiking, camping, fishing, hunting, biking, and scenic driving.

☐ 🔖 ♡ **Hawks State Forest:** This 121-acre site in Carroll County serves as a forestry demonstration and environmental education area. Managed for habitat, timber, and watershed protection, it offers passive recreation such as hiking and birdwatching. Though small, it contributes to conservation in Virginia's Blue Ridge foothills and supports outdoor learning.

☐ 🔖 ♡ **Holliday Lake State Forest:** At 2,565 acres in Appomattox and Buckingham counties, this forest borders the state park of the same name. It features mixed hardwood-pine uplands, supports wildlife, and offers opportunities for hiking, hunting, and forestry education. Managed for timber and watershed protection, it provides an accessible natural area in central Virginia.

☐ 🔖 ♡ **Lesesne State Forest:** A 422-acre forest in Nelson County, Lesesne protects oak-hardwood slopes along the eastern Blue Ridge. Managed for wildlife, timber, and watershed conservation, it supports low-impact hiking and serves as a demonstration site for sustainable forestry practices in a scenic mountain-valley transition zone.

☐ 🔖 ♡ **Matthews State Forest:** This 566-acre property in Grayson County adjoins Jefferson National Forest lands. It is managed for forest research, wildlife conservation, and watershed protection. With small trails and educational programs, Matthews highlights the role of forestry science in sustaining Appalachian upland ecosystems and rural communities.

☐ 🔖 ♡ **Moore's Creek State Forest:** Located in Rockbridge County, this 2,353-acre forest conserves hardwood ridges and mixed wood stands. Managed for timber, water quality, and wildlife habitat, it has minimal public access. The site is used for research, forestry demonstration, and watershed management, illustrating sustainable land stewardship in the Ridge and Valley region.

☐ 🔖 ♡ **Niday Place State Forest:** A 265-acre tract in Craig County, Niday Place serves as a demonstration forest for watershed protection, wildlife habitat, and timber management. Visitors can enjoy limited hiking and hunting. With its Appalachian setting near the national forest, it provides hands-on forestry education and conservation in a mountain environment.

VIRGINIA

☐ ▢ ♡ **Northampton State Forest:** Spanning 582 acres on Virginia's Eastern Shore, this forest is primarily loblolly pine managed for research, timber, and conservation. It supports water quality and wildlife habitat while offering limited public access. As a coastal resource, it demonstrates pine management practices important to Virginia's timber industry.

☐ ▢ ♡ **Old Flat State Forest:** A 320-acre high-elevation site in Grayson County, Old Flat conserves mountain hardwood ecosystems and headwater streams. Managed for watershed protection, wildlife habitat, and forestry demonstration, it allows limited hiking and passive recreation. Its location atop the Blue Ridge makes it an important conservation area.

☐ ▢ ♡ **Paul State Forest:** This 173-acre property in Rockingham County preserves oak-dominated hardwoods. Managed for wildlife, timber, and watershed values, it provides seasonal hunting and passive hiking. As a field site for education and demonstration forestry, Paul State Forest helps showcase sustainable land management practices in the Shenandoah Valley.

☐ ▢ ♡ **Prince Edward-Gallion State Forest:** Encompassing 6,491 acres, this was Virginia's first state forest and includes the state nursery. Its oak-pine terrain supports hiking, hunting, and education. Managed for timber, wildlife, and watershed conservation, it remains a flagship demonstration site for forestry practices in the Piedmont region.

☐ ▢ ♡ **Sandy Point State Forest:** This 2,074-acre property in King William County conserves bottomland hardwoods, loblolly pine, and tidal creeks. Managed for water quality, timber, and wildlife, it allows hunting, fishing, and limited trails. Its ecological value lies in protecting wetlands and showcasing lowland forest management in the Coastal Plain.

☐ ▢ ♡ **Whitney State Forest:** Just 148 acres in Fauquier County, Whitney is one of Virginia's smallest state forests. It offers short interpretive trails, seasonal hunting, and serves as a site for environmental education. Managed for timber, wildlife, and watershed health, it provides accessible green space near Northern Virginia's suburban communities.

☐ ▢ ♡ **Zoar State Forest:** This 378-acre woodland in King William County protects oak-pine forests once part of an early 20th-century estate. Managed for timber, water quality, and habitat, it features short hiking trails and hunting access. As a demonstration site, Zoar showcases integrated forest resource management in Virginia's coastal region.

National Scenic Byways & All-American Roads

☐ ▢ ♡ **Blue Ridge Parkway:** A 469-mile ribbon of road along the Blue Ridge crest, linking Shenandoah and Great Smoky Mountains national parks. In Virginia, it offers sweeping overlooks, seasonal wildflowers, trailheads, and landmarks like Mabry Mill. Designed for leisurely travel, it pairs mountain vistas with abundant hiking, picnicking, and wildlife viewing.

☐ ▢ ♡ **Colonial Parkway:** This 23-mile parkway connects Jamestown, Williamsburg, and Yorktown in a historic corridor. Built with low bridges and natural stone, it hugs riverbanks and woodlands to preserve a colonial atmosphere. Pull-offs, trails, and interpretive stops invite exploration of Tidewater history amid scenic shorelines and protected landscapes.

☐ ▢ ♡ **George Washington Memorial Parkway:** A ceremonial greenway along the Potomac, this route links Mount Vernon, Alexandria, Arlington Memorial Bridge, and Great Falls Park. Designed as a scenic entry to the capital, it provides river overlooks, trails, and historic access while buffering the corridor with forests and meadows for a tranquil drive near the city.

☐ ▢ ♡ **Journey Through Hallowed Ground Byway:** Stretching from Gettysburg to Monticello, this multi-state corridor runs through northern and central Virginia. It features battlefields, presidential homes, and early towns framed by Blue Ridge views. Visitors encounter museums, historic squares, and rural landscapes that tell stories of the Revolution, Civil War, and democracy's evolution.

VIRGINIA

☐ 🔖 ♡ **Skyline Drive:** Running 105 miles along the crest of the Blue Ridge in Shenandoah National Park, Skyline Drive offers 75+ overlooks, trailheads to waterfalls and rocky peaks, and abundant wildlife. Built for scenic pauses, it's famed for spring wildflowers and fall color. Waysides, picnic spots, and visitor centers make it a premier mountain driving experience.

State Scenic Byways

☐ 🔖 ♡ **Big Walker Mountain Scenic Byway:** This mountain route in southwest Virginia climbs winding ridges with overlooks of the Appalachian highlands. It highlights Big Walker Lookout, a historic observation tower, and passes through hardwood forests rich with wildlife. Seasonal blooms, fall color, and sweeping vistas make it a favorite for photographers and road-trippers.

☐ 🔖 ♡ **Colonial National Historical Parkway Scenic Extension (State Segment):** Distinct from the federally designated Colonial Parkway, Virginia's state-recognized scenic portions connect rural roads between historic towns and farmlands. They frame colonial-era architecture, riverside farmland, and Tidewater landscapes, providing quieter drives that complement the larger historic corridor.

☐ 🔖 ♡ **Crooked Road Scenic Byway:** This southwestern route celebrates Virginia's musical heritage, linking communities central to bluegrass and country music. Travelers encounter heritage music venues, rolling farmland, and Appalachian mountain scenery. Festivals, jam sessions, and historic stops make it both a scenic drive and a cultural immersion in mountain traditions.

☐ 🔖 ♡ **George Washington Heritage Scenic Byway:** A state-recognized corridor tracing Washington's early life in Virginia. The route passes historic plantations, colonial settlements, and rural landscapes. Interpretive stops highlight Washington's upbringing, while farmland and riverside views preserve the Tidewater character that shaped the nation's first president.

☐ 🔖 ♡ **Highland Scenic Byway:** Traversing the Allegheny Highlands, this state byway winds through high ridges, valleys, and pastoral landscapes. It passes small mountain communities, historic churches, and farms surrounded by rugged scenery. Seasonal wildflowers and autumn foliage add color to the rolling, open-ridge drive across Virginia's western mountains.

☐ 🔖 ♡ **Nelson Scenic Loop:** A 50-mile drive through Nelson County, this loop climbs into the Blue Ridge and back down through river valleys. It features orchards, vineyards, waterfalls, and trailheads into the George Washington National Forest. With mountain vistas, historic sites, and farmsteads, it captures the county's mix of natural beauty and heritage.

☐ 🔖 ♡ **Old Dominion Scenic Byway:** A designated state corridor highlighting Virginia's Piedmont farmland and historic towns. Visitors enjoy rolling hills, Civil War sites, wineries, and preserved architecture. The route emphasizes the state's cultural identity, connecting working landscapes with landmarks that tell stories of settlement, conflict, and rural life.

☐ 🔖 ♡ **Route 5 Scenic Byway:** Following the James River between Richmond and Williamsburg, this corridor features preserved plantations, historic churches, and pastoral river views. The route is lined with centuries-old estates such as Shirley and Berkeley, offering a living museum of Virginia's colonial and antebellum heritage along a peaceful, tree-shaded drive.

☐ 🔖 ♡ **Skyline Wine Trail Scenic Byway:** This byway meanders through northern Virginia's wine country, offering views of the Blue Ridge foothills and Shenandoah Valley. Vineyards, orchards, and charming small towns line the route, with plenty of tasting rooms and farm markets. It blends agricultural tourism with scenic driving through rolling countryside.

☐ 🔖 ♡ **Smithfield Scenic Byway:** Running through Isle of Wight County, this byway showcases Smithfield's historic waterfront and colonial-era architecture. The drive highlights farmland, marshes, and views of the Pagan River. Interpretive stops tell the story of Virginia's early trade economy, while modern shops and museums add cultural variety.

☐ 🔖 ♡ **Stonewall Jackson Scenic Byway:** A 90-mile state route through the Shenandoah Valley and Blue Ridge foothills. It traces landscapes tied to Civil War campaigns, with historic markers, small towns, and mountain vistas. Farms, churches, and valleys provide a window into both Virginia's wartime heritage and its enduring rural culture.

UNITED STATES EDITION

VIRGINIA

☐ 🔖 ♡ **Swift Run Gap Scenic Byway:** This drive climbs into the Blue Ridge at Swift Run Gap, linking farmland valleys with wooded ridges. Views open onto Shenandoah's rolling landscapes, while access roads connect to hiking and recreation. Seasonal color enhances its appeal, and interpretive pull-offs highlight the gap's role in regional travel history.

☐ 🔖 ♡ **U.S. Route 11 Valley Pike Scenic Byway:** Following the Shenandoah Valley, this route parallels the Blue Ridge and Alleghenies. It runs through historic towns like Lexington and Staunton, Civil War sites, and farmland landscapes. Known as the "Valley Pike," it reflects the region's cultural and military past while offering mountain and pastoral views.

National Natural Landmarks

 ☐ 🔖 ♡ **Butler Cave–Breathing Cave:** Named a National Natural Landmark for its outstanding karst features, this vast cave system includes a 40-foot underground waterfall, a hidden lake, and immense crystal-lined chambers. It also contains a natural bridge and one of Virginia's largest cave rooms, making it a premier site for speleological study and preservation.
GPS: 38.210655, -79.620752 (approximate)

 ☐ 🔖 ♡ **Great Dismal Swamp:** Once part of a million-acre wetland, the Great Dismal Swamp was designated a National Natural Landmark for preserving vital bald cypress swamps, Atlantic white cedar stands, and marshes. It remains a sanctuary for black bears, migratory birds, and rare amphibians, safeguarding one of the last extensive coastal wetlands in the eastern U.S.
GPS: 36.6409, -76.4518

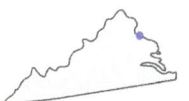 ☐ 🔖 ♡ **Caledon Natural Area:** Caledon earned National Natural Landmark status for protecting a virgin upland hardwood forest along the Potomac River. Towering oaks and tulip poplars dominate this rare, undisturbed woodland, which also serves as a major nesting area for bald eagles. Its ecological integrity makes it one of the Mid-Atlantic's most valuable forest preserves.
GPS: 38.3525, -77.1328

 ☐ 🔖 ♡ **Luray Caverns:** This celebrated cavern system holds National Natural Landmark designation for its extraordinary formations, including mirrored pools, stalactites, and massive columns. Its most iconic feature, the Great Stalacpipe Organ, adds cultural significance. The site exemplifies Virginia's karst heritage and stands as one of the most spectacular caves in the nation.
GPS: 38.6643, -78.4838

 ☐ 🔖 ♡ **Charles C. Steirly Natural Area:** This swamp forest, honored as a National Natural Landmark, is among the few remaining untouched stands of bald cypress and water tupelo in the eastern United States. Its primeval wetland character and rich biodiversity preserve a living fragment of the once-vast lowland ecosystems of southeastern Virginia.
GPS: 37.0508, -76.9811

 ☐ 🔖 ♡ **Montpelier Forest:** National Natural Landmark status was granted to Montpelier Forest for its undisturbed Piedmont hardwood community. Located on the estate of President James Madison, it protects a thriving woodland of tulip poplar, oak, and spicebush, offering a rare look at pre-settlement forest conditions in the Virginia Piedmont.
GPS: 38.2197, -78.1694

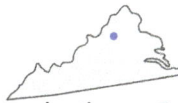 ☐ 🔖 ♡ **Grand Caverns:** Recognized as a National Natural Landmark for its exceptional speleothems, Grand Caverns is famed for rare shield formations found in only a handful of caves worldwide. Stalactites, stalagmites, and draperies fill its chambers. Opened in 1806, it is both geologically significant and historically notable as America's oldest show cave.
GPS: 38.2603, -78.8353

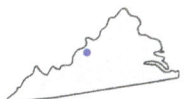 ☐ 🔖 ♡ **Rich Hole:** Rich Hole is a National Natural Landmark recognized for its southern Appalachian cove hardwood forest, one of the most pristine in the eastern U.S. Towering tulip trees and maples dominate the secluded gorge, where centuries of protection have preserved a rich and intact plant community. It remains a vital example of natural mountain ecosystems.
GPS: 37.8714, -79.6383

VIRGINIA

 **Seashore Natural Area:** Designated a National Natural Landmark for its barrier island ecosystems, this site preserves dune ridges, maritime forests, and freshwater swales along Virginia's Atlantic coast. Its parallel vegetation zones illustrate coastal succession and protect rare plants and animals, making it a critical refuge and ecological teaching site.
GPS: 36.9061, -76.0153

 **Virginia Coast Reserve:** Honored as a National Natural Landmark, this barrier island-lagoon complex on Virginia's Eastern Shore remains one of the largest intact coastal systems on the Atlantic seaboard. Its undeveloped islands, tidal marshes, and mudflats provide essential habitat for shorebirds and support vital research on coastal resilience and ecology.
GPS: 37.4163, -75.6890

UNITED STATES EDITION

WASHINGTON

Washington's landscapes include snow-capped volcanoes, lush rainforests, rugged coastlines, and fertile valleys. With its rich tapestry of state parks, national forests, iconic national parks, and remarkable natural landmarks, the Evergreen State invites exploration in every season.

📅 Peak Season
June–September is Washington's peak season, offering warm, dry weather and full access to national parks, trails, and coastlines. Summer is ideal for hiking, camping, and exploring the mountains and islands.

📅 Offseason Months
November–April is the offseason, bringing rain to western Washington and snow to the Cascades. Winter is popular for skiing and snowshoeing, while spring starts the wildflower and waterfall season.

🍃 Scenery & Nature Timing
Spring brings waterfalls, wildflowers, and greening forests. Summer highlights alpine meadows, volcano views, and coastal tidepools. Fall adds golden larches in the mountains, while winter covers peaks and forests in snow.

✨ Special
Washington features Mount Rainier's glaciers, the volcanic landscapes of Mount St. Helens, and Olympic National Park's temperate rainforests. The San Juan Islands' orca sightings, alpine wildflower meadows, and mossy old-growth forests showcase its dramatic natural diversity.

WASHINGTON

State Parks

☐ 🔖 ♡ **Alta Lake State Park:** Set in Okanogan County, this 181-acre park offers camping, fishing, and swimming along a mile-long lake framed by steep cliffs. Trails lead into forested hillsides, and the park is popular for boating, kayaking, and family picnics. Its sunny climate makes it a reliable summer retreat in north-central Washington.

☐ 🔖 ♡ **Anderson Lake State Park:** This 496-acre park in Jefferson County centers on Anderson Lake, a tranquil freshwater body surrounded by forest. Activities include hiking, horseback riding, fishing, and birdwatching. The park is noted for its quiet trails and diverse wetlands that support abundant wildlife. Motorboats are prohibited, keeping the setting peaceful.

☐ 🔖 ♡ **Battle Ground Lake State Park:** A volcanic crater lake in Clark County forms the centerpiece of this 280-acre park. It's a favorite for swimming, fishing, and non-motorized boating. Trails circle through dense forest, and campsites provide overnight stays. The unique geology and accessibility from Vancouver make it one of southwest Washington's most beloved family parks.

☐ 🔖 ♡ **Bay View State Park:** This 66-acre park in Skagit County offers shoreline access to Padilla Bay and sweeping views of the North Cascades. Campsites and picnic areas sit beside tidal flats, where birdwatchers can spot migratory species. With its sandy beach, shallow waters, and calm setting, it's an ideal spot for family outings, kayaking, and relaxed coastal recreation.

☐ 🔖 ♡ **Beacon Rock State Park:** Rising dramatically above the Columbia River Gorge, Beacon Rock anchors this 4,460-acre park in Skamania County. The trail to its summit offers sweeping views of the river and surrounding cliffs. Beyond the iconic hike, visitors enjoy camping, climbing, horseback riding, and exploring waterfalls and deep forest canyons in one of Washington's signature landscapes.

☐ 🔖 ♡ **Belfair State Park:** A Hood Canal favorite, this 94-acre park in Mason County features tidal flats, estuaries, and saltwater beaches. Popular for clamming, crabbing, and birdwatching, it also offers camping and picnic areas shaded by alders and maples. Trails wind through wetlands that teem with waterfowl, making it a blend of recreation and nature study.

☐ 🔖 ♡ **Birch Bay State Park:** Along Whatcom County's coastline, this 664-acre park fronts a wide sandy beach ideal for shellfish harvesting, tidepooling, and swimming. Families flock here in summer to enjoy warm shallows and spectacular sunsets over the Strait of Georgia. Trails and campsites lie under forest canopy, offering a balance of beach fun and wooded retreat.

☐ 🔖 ♡ **Bogachiel State Park:** Nestled in the Olympic Peninsula near Forks, this 127-acre park offers a lush rainforest setting along the Bogachiel River. Towering evergreens, thick ferns, and moss-draped maples create an immersive natural atmosphere. Campers, anglers, and hikers find it an accessible base to explore the Olympic National Park while enjoying a quieter environment.

☐ 🔖 ♡ **Bottle Beach State Park:** A 75-acre site on Grays Harbor, this park preserves vital estuarine habitat. Its tidal flats and salt marshes attract thousands of shorebirds during migration, making it a premier birdwatching location. A boardwalk trail provides access to viewing areas, and visitors can picnic or learn about the region's ecology in a tranquil coastal setting.

☐ 🔖 ♡ **Bridgeport State Park:** Overlooking Rufus Woods Lake on the Columbia River, this 748-acre park offers a semi-arid landscape of sagebrush, basalt cliffs, and irrigated lawns. Campgrounds and picnic shelters draw families, while anglers pursue trout and walleye. With boating access, hiking trails, and sunny weather, it provides an oasis of recreation in north-central Washington.

☐ 🔖 ♡ **Bridle Trails State Park:** This 489-acre King County park is famous for its 28 miles of equestrian trails winding through Douglas fir and western hemlock forests. Horses have right of way, making it a haven for riders. Hikers and joggers also enjoy the shaded paths. Located near urban areas, it preserves a green sanctuary where wildlife and recreation coexist.

☐ 🔖 ♡ **Brooks Memorial State Park:** In Klickitat County along U.S. 97, this 700-acre park spans pine forests and grasslands with hiking trails that climb into the Simcoe Mountains. Campgrounds and group facilities host visitors, while its nature trail and interpretive programs highlight ecology. Its location offers views of Mount Adams and access to quiet eastern Washington scenery.

UNITED STATES EDITION

WASHINGTON

☐ 🔖 ♡ **Cama Beach Historical State Park:** On Camano Island, this 486-acre park preserves a 1930s fishing resort. Visitors can stay in restored waterfront cabins, stroll the beach, or learn traditional crafts at the Center for Wooden Boats. Trails connect to neighboring Camano Island State Park. It blends recreation, heritage, and stunning Puget Sound views in a unique setting.

☐ 🔖 ♡ **Camano Island State Park:** A 244-acre Island County park, it features rocky beaches, forested trails, and campsites overlooking Saratoga Passage. Boating, fishing, and crabbing are popular, while hiking loops showcase coastal forests and shoreline views. The park's compact size and variety of activities make it a family-friendly escape just north of Seattle.

☐ 🔖 ♡ **Cape Disappointment State Park:** At the mouth of the Columbia River, this 2,023-acre park combines history and dramatic scenery. Two lighthouses, coastal headlands, and the Lewis & Clark Interpretive Center tell stories of exploration and shipwrecks. Visitors hike oceanfront trails, comb beaches, or camp in ocean-view sites. It's one of Washington's most iconic coastal parks.

☐ 🔖 ♡ **Columbia Hills State Park:** This 3,338-acre Klickitat County park protects sweeping hillsides along the Columbia River Gorge. Famous for spring wildflower displays and Native American petroglyphs, it also offers rock climbing, fishing, and camping. Trails climb to panoramic views of Mount Hood and the Gorge, blending cultural heritage with outdoor recreation.

☐ 🔖 ♡ **Columbia Plateau State Park Trail:** Stretching 130 miles along a former rail line, this 4,109-acre linear park crosses basalt canyons, channeled scablands, and farmlands. Sections are open to hikers, cyclists, and horseback riders. Wildlife abounds, with opportunities to spot hawks, owls, and deer. It connects travelers to the geological and cultural history of eastern Washington.

☐ 🔖 ♡ **Conconully State Park:** Nestled in Okanogan County, this 97-acre park features shady lawns beside Conconully Reservoir and State Park Lake. Visitors enjoy boating, fishing, and camping with mountain views. Established in 1910, it is one of Washington's oldest state parks. Its small-town setting and historic features create a relaxed atmosphere.

☐ 🔖 ♡ **Crawford State Park:** Known for Gardner Cave, this 49-acre Pend Oreille County park offers guided tours through a 2,000-foot limestone cavern filled with stalactites and stalagmites. Surrounded by forest, it also provides picnicking and wildlife viewing. Its unique geology makes it one of Washington's most intriguing hidden gems in the far northeast.

☐ 🔖 ♡ **Curlew Lake State Park:** This 123-acre Ferry County park surrounds a scenic mountain lake rich in rainbow trout and bass. Families camp along the shoreline, swim at the beach, and hike short forested trails. Wildlife includes ospreys and deer. Its mix of water recreation and tranquility makes it a favorite in northeastern Washington.

☐ 🔖 ♡ **Daroga State Park:** Located on the Columbia River north of Wenatchee, this 127-acre park offers lawns, beaches, and campsites along a reservoir. Once an orchard, it now provides boating, swimming, and picnicking opportunities. Trails and views of the river make it a relaxing getaway. It's especially popular with families seeking sunny weather.

☐ 🔖 ♡ **Dash Point State Park:** Near Federal Way, this 461-acre park offers Puget Sound beaches, forested trails, and camping close to urban centers. Its sandy shore is popular for skimboarding and swimming. Trails wind through ravines and wetlands, hosting birdlife like herons. It's a convenient spot where Seattle-Tacoma residents can enjoy both forest and saltwater.

☐ 🔖 ♡ **Deception Pass State Park:** Spanning 4,134 acres between Whidbey and Fidalgo Islands, this is Washington's most-visited park. Famous for its dramatic bridge and rugged coastline, it offers beaches, tidepools, forests, and over 30 miles of trails. Campgrounds, boating, and wildlife viewing complete the experience. It epitomizes Pacific Northwest natural beauty.

☐ 🔖 ♡ **Dosewallips State Park:** This 425-acre Jefferson County park sits at the meeting of river, forest, and Hood Canal shoreline. Campsites range from forested to beachfront. Visitors enjoy clamming, hiking, and watching elk graze nearby. Its mix of saltwater and freshwater habitats supports diverse wildlife, making it a versatile destination for outdoor enthusiasts.

WASHINGTON

☐ 🔖 ♡ **Doug's Beach State Park:** A 379-acre Klickitat County site on the Columbia River, it's world-renowned for windsurfing and kiteboarding thanks to steady Gorge winds. Day-use facilities support picnicking and water access. Scenic basalt cliffs frame the area, making it a spectacular yet specialized park catering to water-sports adventurers.

☐ 🔖 ♡ **Federation Forest State Park:** This 574-acre old-growth forest preserve in King County showcases towering Douglas firs and interpretive trails. The park protects natural ecosystems along the White River and features a visitor center with educational displays. It's a peaceful spot for nature study, picnicking, and quiet hikes in the shadow of Mount Rainier.

☐ 🔖 ♡ **Fields Spring State Park:** Covering 792 acres in Asotin County, this Blue Mountains park offers year-round recreation. Trails traverse meadows and forests with views of Idaho and Oregon. In winter, visitors enjoy cross-country skiing and snowshoeing. Its campground and group lodge make it a popular retreat for outdoor programs and mountain getaways.

☐ 🔖 ♡ **Flaming Geyser State Park:** Located on the Green River in King County, this 480-acre park once featured a methane-fed "geyser" flame, now mostly dormant. It remains popular for rafting, tubing, fishing, and picnicking. Trails explore forest and riverbank habitats. Its unusual history and riverfront activities make it a unique day-use destination near Seattle.

☐ 🔖 ♡ **Fort Casey Historical State Park:** On Whidbey Island, this 999-acre park preserves a coastal defense fort from the early 1900s. Massive concrete gun emplacements overlook Admiralty Inlet, and a lighthouse adds historic charm. Visitors explore bunkers, hike bluff trails, and camp near the beach. Its combination of history and scenery makes it unforgettable.

☐ 🔖 ♡ **Fort Columbia State Park:** Perched above the Columbia River in Pacific County, this 593-acre park preserves a coastal artillery post built in the late 1800s. Visitors explore historic batteries, barracks, and trails through forested bluffs. With panoramic river views, picnic areas, and a link to regional military history, it's both scenic and educational.

☐ 🔖 ♡ **Fort Ebey State Park:** On Whidbey Island, this 651-acre park features World War II bunkers overlooking the Strait of Juan de Fuca. Hikers enjoy 25 miles of trails through forests and along bluff-top vistas. The park also offers camping, paragliding, and beach access, making it a popular spot for both history buffs and outdoor adventurers.

☐ 🔖 ♡ **Fort Flagler Historical State Park:** Located on Marrowstone Island, this 784-acre park preserves another coastal defense fort from the "Triangle of Fire." Concrete batteries, a military museum, and scenic beaches invite exploration. Campgrounds and trails provide recreational opportunities, while the park's setting offers views of Puget Sound and Mount Baker.

☐ 🔖 ♡ **Fort Simcoe State Park:** In Yakima County, this 200-acre park preserves a mid-1800s military fort established during Indian conflicts. Original buildings, officers' quarters, and interpretive exhibits highlight the site's role in frontier history. Shaded lawns and picnic areas beneath oaks create a serene contrast to the fort's turbulent past.

☐ 🔖 ♡ **Fort Townsend Historical State Park:** Near Port Townsend, this 367-acre park combines military history with forested trails. The site once held a 19th-century Army post, and remnants blend with woodland paths, campsites, and shoreline access. Visitors enjoy a mix of heritage and natural exploration on the Quimper Peninsula.

☐ 🔖 ♡ **Fort Worden Historical State Park:** Spanning 434 acres, this Port Townsend park preserves one of Washington's best-known forts, complete with bunkers, batteries, and museums. It also hosts festivals, conferences, and workshops. The park's sandy beaches and bluff trails overlook the Strait of Juan de Fuca, making it a cultural and recreational hub.

☐ 🔖 ♡ **Ginkgo Petrified Forest State Park:** Near Vantage, this 7,470-acre park protects one of the world's most diverse fossil forests. Petrified wood, Ice Age flood-carved landscapes, and Columbia River views make it remarkable. The interpretive center showcases geology and archaeology, while trails and campgrounds connect visitors to both science and scenery.

☐ 🔖 ♡ **Goldendale Observatory State Park:** In Klickitat County, this 85-acre heritage park is dedicated to public astronomy. It features a state-of-the-art observatory with powerful telescopes and educational programs. By day, visitors picnic and hike the grounds; at night, they marvel at planets, stars, and galaxies under dark rural skies.

☐ 🔖 ♡ **Grayland Beach State Park:** This 581-acre park in Grays Harbor County features wide sandy beaches backed by dunes and forests. Visitors enjoy camping, clam digging, beachcombing, and kite flying. Its year-round campground and oceanfront setting make it a top destination for coastal recreation, with plenty of space for solitude or family fun.

WASHINGTON

☐ 🔖 ♡ **Griffiths-Priday State Park:** At the mouth of the Copalis River, this 364-acre park offers quiet access to saltwater beaches, dunes, and estuaries. Known for birdwatching and fishing, it provides a less crowded alternative to busier coastal parks. Picnic areas and trails create opportunities to explore natural habitats shaped by tides and shifting sands.

☐ 🔖 ♡ **Ike Kinswa State Park:** Located on Mayfield Lake in Lewis County, this 421-acre park offers camping, boating, and fishing in a wooded setting. Trails wind through forests along the lake's edge. Once a homestead area, it's now a favorite for water recreation with convenient access to Mount St. Helens and the Cowlitz River Valley.

☐ 🔖 ♡ **Illahee State Park:** This 82-acre Kitsap County park lies on Puget Sound, featuring a dock, boat ramp, and wooded campground. Its beach is popular for shellfish harvesting and diving. Trails connect forested uplands to shoreline picnic areas. The park's proximity to Bremerton makes it a convenient escape into marine and forest habitats.

☐ 🔖 ♡ **Jarrell Cove State Park:** A small, 67-acre marine and land park on Harstine Island, it offers moorage, camping, and wooded trails. Visitors kayak quiet inlets, fish, or watch wildlife such as seals and herons. Its sheltered coves make it especially appealing for boaters seeking a tranquil Puget Sound stopover.

☐ 🔖 ♡ **Joemma Beach State Park:** On Key Peninsula, this 122-acre park fronts Puget Sound with 3,000 feet of shoreline. A pier, boat ramp, and campsites support fishing, crabbing, and boating. Inland trails pass through forest, and its relative seclusion offers a quieter experience than larger regional parks.

☐ 🔖 ♡ **Joseph Whidbey State Park:** On Whidbey Island's west coast, this 112-acre park provides beach access, hiking trails, and picnic sites with sweeping views of the Strait of Juan de Fuca. Named after a member of Captain Vancouver's expedition, it's a day-use destination popular for beachcombing, birdwatching, and enjoying sunsets.

☐ 🔖 ♡ **Kanaskat-Palmer State Park:** Nestled along the Green River in King County, this 320-acre park offers camping, hiking, rafting, and fishing. Rapids draw whitewater enthusiasts, while calmer stretches invite families. Forested trails lead to scenic overlooks, making it a convenient wilderness retreat near the Seattle-Tacoma area.

☐ 🔖 ♡ **Kitsap Memorial State Park:** Overlooking Hood Canal, this 63-acre park is known for weddings and gatherings thanks to its scenic lawns and event facilities. It also provides camping, beach access, and fishing. Forested uplands and shoreline habitats make it a relaxing destination with both natural beauty and amenities for special occasions.

☐ 🔖 ♡ **Kopachuck State Park:** This 280-acre park near Gig Harbor features saltwater shoreline, wooded trails, and views of Puget Sound islands. It's popular for kayaking, clamming, and family picnics. Sunset views are especially striking, and low tide reveals sandbars leading to nearby Cutts Island, accessible for adventurous explorers.

☐ 🔖 ♡ **Lake Chelan State Park:** On the lake's south shore, this 139-acre park is a hub for water recreation. Campgrounds, docks, and swimming beaches attract boaters and families. With sunshine, mountain views, and easy access to Lake Chelan's 50-mile fjord-like waters, it's one of Washington's most popular vacation spots.

☐ 🔖 ♡ **Lake Easton State Park:** Situated in Kittitas County along I-90, this 516-acre park includes a mountain lake bordered by forest. It offers camping, fishing, hiking, and winter snow play. The Yakima River and Palouse to Cascades Trail connect nearby. Its alpine setting and year-round access make it a versatile stop in the Cascades.

☐ 🔖 ♡ **Lake Sammamish State Park:** This 530-acre urban park in Issaquah provides two lakefront beaches, boat launches, and wetlands rich in wildlife. Families flock to picnic, swim, and kayak, while trails connect to regional greenways. Its balance of water recreation and habitat preservation makes it a valuable natural escape near Seattle.

☐ 🔖 ♡ **Lake Sylvia State Park:** Nestled in Grays Harbor County, this 252-acre park surrounds a quiet reservoir once formed by a logging dam. Shaded campgrounds, fishing docks, and forested trails invite relaxation. Interpretive signs highlight its logging history, while its family-friendly beach and peaceful setting make it a small but charming retreat.

☐ 🔖 ♡ **Lake Wenatchee State Park:** On the eastern slopes of the Cascades, this 489-acre park spans sandy beaches, forests, and alpine lake views. Visitors swim, boat, and windsurf in summer, then ski and snowshoe in winter. Trails connect to the surrounding wilderness, making it a four-season gateway to the mountains.

WASHINGTON

☐ 🔖 ♡ **Larrabee State Park:** Washington's first state park, established in 1915, covers 2,748 acres south of Bellingham. It features forested trails, freshwater lakes, and saltwater beaches on Samish Bay. Rock climbing, boating, and camping are popular, while Chuckanut Drive provides scenic access. Its mix of land and marine features makes it iconic.

☐ 🔖 ♡ **Leadbetter Point State Park:** At the northern tip of Long Beach Peninsula, this 1,615-acre park protects dunes, marshes, and forests. Birdwatching is exceptional, with migratory waterfowl and shorebirds common. Trails weave between Pacific Ocean and Willapa Bay. It's a prime spot for solitude and wildlife in a wild coastal setting.

☐ 🔖 ♡ **Lewis and Clark State Park:** This 621-acre park in Lewis County preserves one of the state's largest lowland old-growth forests. Trails wind beneath Douglas fir and western red cedar, while meadows offer group camping and recreation. It's both a historic and natural treasure, named for the famous explorers but known for its rare forest habitat.

☐ 🔖 ♡ **Lime Kiln Point State Park:** Located on San Juan Island, this 42-acre day-use park is famous for whale watching. A lighthouse, interpretive center, and shoreline trails provide views of orcas and marine life in the Salish Sea. Its blend of education, recreation, and natural spectacle makes it one of the most celebrated coastal parks.

☐ 🔖 ♡ **Lincoln Rock State Park:** On the Columbia River near Wenatchee, this 80-acre park is named after a basalt formation resembling Abraham Lincoln's profile. Campgrounds, boat launches, and sports courts make it family-friendly, while trails and river access appeal to hikers and boaters. Its sunny location provides year-round recreation.

☐ 🔖 ♡ **Lyons Ferry State Park:** At the confluence of the Snake and Palouse Rivers, this 168-acre park offers boating, fishing, and swimming in eastern Washington's dry landscape. A marina and group areas support gatherings. Its location near Palouse Falls makes it a convenient base for exploring both rivers and dramatic canyon country.

☐ 🔖 ♡ **Manchester State Park:** Once a U.S. Navy torpedo warehouse, this 111-acre Kitsap County park combines history with forested shoreline. Visitors explore military structures, camp in wooded sites, and picnic by Rich Passage. Its waterfront views of ferries and naval vessels make it both scenic and historically intriguing.

☐ 🔖 ♡ **Maryhill State Park:** On the Columbia River in Klickitat County, this 99-acre park offers lawns, beaches, and river access beneath basalt cliffs. It's popular for boating, windsurfing, and camping. Nearby attractions include Maryhill Museum of Art and Stonehenge replica, making the park a cultural and recreational hub.

☐ 🔖 ♡ **Millersylvania State Park:** South of Olympia, this 903-acre park features Deep Lake, old-growth cedar and fir, and a large campground. Built by the CCC in the 1930s, its stone shelters and trails remain in use. Swimming, boating, and hiking draw families, while its history and natural beauty make it a classic state park.

☐ 🔖 ♡ **Moran State Park:** The largest in the San Juans, this 5,424-acre Orcas Island park includes five lakes, over 30 miles of trails, and the summit of Mount Constitution. Campgrounds and picnic areas provide access to kayaking, fishing, and hiking. From the 2,409-foot summit tower, visitors enjoy unmatched views of the islands and beyond.

☐ 🔖 ♡ **Mount Pilchuck State Park:** This 1,903-acre Snohomish County park is centered around the rugged 5,324-foot Mount Pilchuck. The 3-mile trail to the fire lookout offers sweeping views of the Cascades and Puget Sound. Popular with hikers, it provides challenging terrain and alpine scenery, though weather can shift quickly at high elevation.

☐ 🔖 ♡ **Mount Spokane State Park:** Washington's largest state park spans 12,293 acres in the Selkirk Mountains. It offers year-round activities, including hiking, biking, horseback riding, skiing, and snowshoeing. Mount Spokane Ski & Snowboard Park operates within it. With dense forests, meadows, and peaks, it's a cornerstone of eastern Washington recreation.

☐ 🔖 ♡ **Nisqually State Park:** A 1,300-acre park in development near Eatonville, it preserves prairies, wetlands, and forest along the Nisqually River. Plans include trails, interpretive facilities, and habitat restoration. Though still evolving, it represents Washington's next generation of parks, blending cultural heritage with ecological protection.

☐ 🔖 ♡ **Nolte State Park:** This 117-acre King County park surrounds Deep Lake, a former resort site. Visitors fish for trout, swim from a small beach, and circle the lake on a mile-long trail. Picnic shelters and forested groves make it a pleasant day-use destination, offering a quick nature escape from nearby urban centers.

WASHINGTON

☐ 🔖 ♡ **Obstruction Pass State Park:** A 76-acre San Juan Island park, it offers waterfront campsites, tidepools, and a half-mile sandy beach—the longest in the islands. Trails pass through madrona and fir forest, leading to scenic coastal overlooks. Its rustic campsites accessible by foot or boat make it a favorite for adventurous visitors.

☐ 🔖 ♡ **Ocean City State Park:** Just north of Ocean Shores, this 170-acre coastal park features dunes, beach access, and a large campground. Visitors enjoy clamming, kite flying, and birdwatching in the adjacent wetlands. It's a family-friendly base for beach vacations, with easy access to both the Pacific surf and town amenities.

☐ 🔖 ♡ **Olallie State Park:** A 2,336-acre park along the Snoqualmie River, it is known for Twin Falls and rushing cascades. Trails range from riverside walks to backcountry hikes connecting to the Iron Horse Trail. Rock climbing and mountain biking are popular. Its proximity to Seattle makes it one of the most accessible mountain parks.

☐ 🔖 ♡ **Olmstead Place Historical State Park:** This 221-acre Kittitas County park preserves a pioneer homestead from the 1870s. Visitors tour historic farm buildings, gardens, and equipment that reflect early agricultural life. Trails, picnic areas, and open fields provide a peaceful backdrop, while interpretive programs highlight farming heritage and rural traditions.

☐ 🔖 ♡ **Pacific Beach State Park:** This 17-acre park in Grays Harbor County offers direct access to a wide sandy beach on the Pacific Ocean. Popular for kite flying, clamming, and surf fishing, it also has a small campground near the dunes. Its compact size and oceanfront setting make it a cozy base for coastal exploration.

☐ 🔖 ♡ **Pacific Pines State Park:** A 10-acre day-use park on Long Beach Peninsula, it provides beach access through groves of shore pines. Its quiet, uncrowded stretch of sand is ideal for walks, picnics, and clam digging. The park's simplicity and serenity appeal to those seeking solitude and natural coastal beauty away from larger parks.

☐ 🔖 ♡ **Palouse Falls State Park Heritage Site:** This 94-acre park showcases the dramatic 198-foot Palouse Falls, carved by Ice Age floods. Overlooks provide breathtaking views, while interpretive signs explain geology and cultural history. Camping and picnicking areas make it a destination, though rugged terrain highlights the untamed power of the eastern Washington landscape.

☐ 🔖 ♡ **Paradise Point State Park:** In Clark County, this 101-acre park offers access to the East Fork of the Lewis River and a popular swimming hole. Its campground and picnic shelters attract families, while trails explore riparian forests. Close to Interstate 5, it provides a quick natural getaway and riverside recreation near Vancouver.

☐ 🔖 ♡ **Peace Arch Historical State Park:** Straddling the U.S.-Canada border near Blaine, this 30-acre park features the Peace Arch monument, celebrating peace between nations. Formal gardens, lawns, and picnic areas host cultural events. With views of Boundary Bay and international significance, it blends history, diplomacy, and recreation in a unique setting.

☐ 🔖 ♡ **Pearrygin Lake State Park:** Near Winthrop in Okanogan County, this 1,186-acre park surrounds a large alpine lake. Boating, fishing, swimming, and camping are top activities, with trails offering scenic views of the Methow Valley. Its sunny climate and family-friendly amenities make it one of Washington's premier inland lake destinations.

☐ 🔖 ♡ **Penrose Point State Park:** This 165-acre Pierce County park extends into Case Inlet with two miles of shoreline. Clam digging, crabbing, and tidepooling are popular, while forested trails wind through cedar and fir groves. Its scenic campsites and beaches make it a favorite for families seeking both saltwater fun and wooded relaxation.

☐ 🔖 ♡ **Peshastin Pinnacles State Park:** A 34-acre park near Cashmere, it features sandstone spires rising above orchards and vineyards. Rock climbers tackle its routes, while trails provide views of the Wenatchee River Valley. Spring wildflowers brighten the arid landscape. Its unique geology and recreation draw both climbers and hikers to this desert-like oasis.

☐ 🔖 ♡ **Potholes State Park:** Located in Grant County, this 773-acre park surrounds a reservoir formed by Ice Age floods. It's a haven for fishing, boating, and birdwatching, with diverse habitats ranging from wetlands to sand dunes. Campsites and picnic areas provide family-friendly access to this striking and ecologically rich landscape.

☐ 🔖 ♡ **Potlatch State Park:** A 57-acre park on Hood Canal in Mason County, it offers camping, clamming, and oyster harvesting along its tidal shoreline. The forested uplands include picnic areas and trails. With both saltwater recreation and a peaceful wooded setting, it's a well-loved destination for shellfish enthusiasts and campers.

WASHINGTON

☐ 🔖 ♡ **Rainbow Falls State Park:** This 139-acre Lewis County park features a scenic waterfall on the Chehalis River. Trails wind through old-growth forests of Douglas fir and western red cedar, while campsites offer overnight stays. Once a CCC project, its historic structures and natural charm make it a beloved local destination.

☐ 🔖 ♡ **Rasar State Park:** On the Skagit River, this 180-acre park combines forest, riverfront, and meadow habitats. Campgrounds, cabins, and picnic areas welcome families, while trails provide access to salmon spawning areas and wildlife viewing. Its quiet natural beauty makes it a restful spot in the Skagit Valley.

☐ 🔖 ♡ **Reed Island State Park:** This 427-acre island in the Columbia River is accessible only by boat. Primitive camping, beaches, and hiking appeal to paddlers and boaters seeking seclusion. Its sandy shores and forested interior provide a wilderness-like escape, despite being close to Vancouver and Portland.

☐ 🔖 ♡ **Riverside State Park:** Spokane's largest state park spans 14,000 acres along the Spokane and Little Spokane Rivers. Activities include camping, hiking, rafting, and horseback riding. Historical sites like the Bowl and Pitcher rock formation and Civilian Conservation Corps structures add interest. It's a major hub of recreation in eastern Washington.

☐ 🔖 ♡ **Rockport State Park:** This 632-acre park in Skagit County preserves one of Washington's finest remaining old-growth forests. Trails wind beneath towering Douglas firs and mossy understory, offering a true rainforest experience. Educational programs emphasize forest ecology, while its tranquility and giant trees inspire awe in visitors.

☐ 🔖 ♡ **Sacajawea Historical State Park:** At the confluence of the Snake and Columbia Rivers, this 267-acre park highlights Lewis and Clark Expedition history. Interpretive exhibits, a museum, and shaded picnic areas enrich the experience. Its riverfront trails and cultural significance make it both a recreational and historical landmark.

☐ 🔖 ♡ **Saint Edward State Park:** This 326-acre park in King County preserves a former Catholic seminary surrounded by forest. The historic Art Deco building now houses a lodge, while trails descend to Lake Washington's shoreline. It combines heritage, natural landscapes, and urban accessibility, offering a unique retreat near Seattle.

☐ 🔖 ♡ **Saltwater State Park:** Between Seattle and Tacoma, this 137-acre park fronts Puget Sound with a sandy beach and underwater marine sanctuary. Popular for scuba diving, picnicking, and swimming, it also features forested trails. Its central location and accessible shoreline make it one of Puget Sound's busiest and most beloved parks.

☐ 🔖 ♡ **Scenic Beach State Park:** Overlooking Hood Canal in Kitsap County, this 121-acre park features stunning Olympic Mountain views. Its shoreline is perfect for beachcombing, crabbing, and picnicking, while gardens and event spaces make it a popular wedding venue. Trails through forests complement the breathtaking water vistas.

☐ 🔖 ♡ **Schafer State Park:** This 122-acre park on the Satsop River in Mason County offers shady campgrounds, grassy meadows, and river access for fishing and swimming. Once donated by the Schafer family, it preserves both natural beauty and local logging history. Trails wind through second-growth forests, while CCC structures add heritage. Families, anglers, and picnickers enjoy its quiet rural charm.

☐ 🔖 ♡ **Seaquest State Park:** A 505-acre forested park in Cowlitz County, Seaquest sits across from the Mount St. Helens Visitor Center. It offers camping, hiking trails, and wetlands with a mile-long boardwalk that's perfect for birdwatching. Its location near Silver Lake makes it a family base for exploring the volcano, blending recreation with education about the eruption's history and landscape.

☐ 🔖 ♡ **Sequim Bay State Park:** Nestled along a sheltered inlet on the Olympic Peninsula, this 92-acre marine park offers camping, boating, and fishing opportunities. Forested trails connect to the Olympic Discovery Trail, while shoreline access supports clamming and crabbing. Its quiet setting, wildlife, and easy access to both Sequim and Port Angeles make it a favored stop for coastal recreation and camping.

☐ 🔖 ♡ **Shine Tidelands State Park:** This 249-acre Jefferson County park lies on the eastern shore of Hood Canal, offering sweeping saltwater vistas. Wide tidal flats support shellfish harvesting, while beaches attract birdwatchers and walkers. Picnic areas and shoreline trails provide simple amenities, but its main draw is its natural setting, where marine and estuarine habitats create a haven for wildlife.

WASHINGTON

☐ 🔖 ♡ **South Whidbey State Park:** Covering 381 acres of forest and shoreline, this Whidbey Island park protects some of the last old-growth stands in the region. Trails wind beneath massive Douglas firs and red cedars, leading to bluffs overlooking Puget Sound. Though its campground is closed, day-use visitors enjoy hiking, picnicking, wildlife watching, and experiencing the island's serene natural heritage.

☐ 🔖 ♡ **Spencer Spit State Park:** This 200-acre Lopez Island park is centered on a sandy spit reaching into the Salish Sea. Campsites are tucked into the forest near the beach, where kayaking, crabbing, and tidepooling are popular. The mix of shoreline, wetlands, and historic cabin sites offers variety. Its location in the San Juan Islands makes it a favorite destination for boaters and campers.

☐ 🔖 ♡ **Squak Mountain State Park:** Part of the "Issaquah Alps," this 1,545-acre park offers miles of hiking and equestrian trails through dense forests. Near urban areas yet quiet and undeveloped, it provides habitat for birds, deer, and black bears. Trails climb to summits with forested viewpoints, giving residents a close-to-home wilderness experience just east of Seattle in King County.

☐ 🔖 ♡ **Squilchuck State Park:** Situated south of Wenatchee, this 249-acre park offers camping, group lodges, and forested trails at the base of Mission Ridge. In summer, it's a hub for hiking and mountain biking, while winter brings snowshoeing and sledding. Surrounded by ponderosa pine, the park offers a year-round mountain retreat, blending recreation and rustic tranquility.

☐ 🔖 ♡ **Steamboat Rock State Park:** A 3,522-acre park on Banks Lake, it features the massive basalt monolith Steamboat Rock rising 800 feet above the water. Trails lead to its summit for panoramic views of the Coulee. Campgrounds, beaches, and boat launches make it a recreation hub for fishing, boating, and swimming. Its dramatic landscape and diverse activities attract visitors statewide.

☐ 🔖 ♡ **Steptoe Battlefield State Park Heritage Site:** Near Rosalia, this 3-acre park commemorates the 1858 battle between U.S. Army forces and Native tribes. Interpretive panels explain the conflict's context, and the grassy setting invites reflection. Though small, it preserves an important part of Washington's frontier history, providing a quiet memorial to a turbulent chapter of cultural encounters.

☐ 🔖 ♡ **Steptoe Butte State Park:** This 150-acre park in Whitman County offers one of Washington's most iconic viewpoints. A road spirals to the 3,612-foot summit of Steptoe Butte, where 360-degree views reveal the rolling Palouse farmland. Photographers come for sunrise and sunset scenes, while hikers and sightseers marvel at the geologic prominence created by ancient quartzite uplift.

☐ 🔖 ♡ **Sun Lakes–Dry Falls State Park:** Spanning 4,027 acres in Grant County, this park showcases Dry Falls, a 3.5-mile-wide cliff once the world's largest waterfall during Ice Age floods. Today, lakes and campgrounds occupy the basin, offering boating, fishing, and hiking. Trails and viewpoints highlight the geology. It's both a natural wonder and recreation hub in central Washington.

☐ 🔖 ♡ **Tolmie State Park:** This 154-acre park on Puget Sound north of Olympia combines forest, saltwater shoreline, and wetlands. It offers clamming, crabbing, and scuba diving at an underwater artificial reef. Trails lead through second-growth forests to the beach, while picnic shelters and tidepools attract families. Its mix of habitats makes it a versatile destination for outdoor exploration.

☐ 🔖 ♡ **Triton Cove State Park:** A compact 30-acre park on Hood Canal, it serves primarily as a boat launch and day-use site. Visitors enjoy fishing, crabbing, and access to marine waters. Lawns and picnic areas provide space for relaxing with mountain views. Though small, it's an important access point for boaters and a scenic stop along the canal.

☐ 🔖 ♡ **Twanoh State Park:** On Hood Canal, this 188-acre park features warm, shallow waters ideal for swimming, kayaking, and shellfish harvesting. Its CCC-built stone structures from the 1930s add historic character. Forested trails climb into surrounding hills, while the beach and campground host families year-round. It's one of Washington's sunniest and most popular saltwater parks.

☐ 🔖 ♡ **Twenty-Five Mile Creek State Park:** On Lake Chelan's south shore, this 232-acre park is a gateway to the remote upper lake and surrounding wilderness. It offers a marina, boat launches, campgrounds, and hiking opportunities. Steep mountains frame the lake, creating a dramatic backdrop for recreation. Boaters especially prize it as a base for longer lake adventures.

WASHINGTON

☐ ◻ ♡ **Twin Harbors State Park:** This 172-acre park south of Westport features forested dunes and long stretches of Pacific Ocean beach. Campgrounds accommodate tents and RVs, while beachcombing, clamming, and kite flying are favorite activities. Its windswept, oceanfront character makes it a classic Washington coastal camping destination for families and groups.

☐ ◻ ♡ **Wallace Falls State Park:** Located in Snohomish County, this 1,380-acre park is known for its spectacular series of waterfalls, including a 265-foot main drop. The popular Woody Trail leads hikers through forest to viewpoints of the falls. Campgrounds, cabins, and views of Mount Index enhance its appeal. It's a premier Cascades hiking destination.

☐ ◻ ♡ **Wenatchee Confluence State Park:** At the meeting of the Columbia and Wenatchee Rivers, this 197-acre park offers campgrounds, sports fields, and a swimming lagoon. Trails link to the Apple Capital Loop, while wetlands host herons, eagles, and other wildlife. Its unique setting blends urban park amenities with natural river habitat, serving as both community hub and refuge.

☐ ◻ ♡ **Westport Light State Park:** Adjacent to Washington's tallest lighthouse, Grays Harbor Light, this coastal park features beaches, dunes, and seaside trails. Visitors picnic, beachcomb, and birdwatch, while surfers take advantage of the Pacific waves. Its mix of maritime history and recreation makes it a highlight of the southern coast.

☐ ◻ ♡ **Willie Keil's Grave State Park Heritage Site:** At just 0.34 acres, this is one of Washington's smallest parks, preserving the grave of Willie Keil, the "Pickled Pioneer." His unusual journey west in a whiskey-filled coffin is part of Oregon Trail lore. Today, the site near Menlo offers interpretive signage and quiet reflection on pioneer perseverance and frontier history.

☐ ◻ ♡ **Yakima Sportsman State Park:** A 266-acre park along the Yakima River, it was created by local sportsmen in 1940 to protect riparian habitat. Visitors camp, fish for trout, or birdwatch in wetlands frequented by herons and songbirds. Trails and lawns provide recreation within city limits, making it a rare and vital green space in central Washington's arid landscape.

National Parks

☐ ◻ ♡ **Ebey's Landing National Historical Reserve:** On Whidbey Island, this reserve protects a rare blend of farmland, shoreline, prairies, and historic structures that reflect early Euro-American settlement. Scenic trails cross bluffs with sweeping Salish Sea views, while interpretive sites share stories of pioneers, Coast Salish people, and the enduring cultural landscape.

☐ ◻ ♡ **Fort Vancouver National Historic Site:** Located in Vancouver, this park preserves the reconstructed 19th-century Hudson's Bay Company fort, once a center of the fur trade and cultural exchange. Visitors tour historic buildings, gardens, and blacksmith shops, explore stories of early settlers and Native peoples, and see how this post shaped the Pacific Northwest's growth.

☐ ◻ ♡ **Ice Age Floods National Geologic Trail:** Spanning parts of Washington, Oregon, Idaho, and Montana, this trail links landscapes shaped by cataclysmic Ice Age floods more than 13,000 years ago. Visitors explore coulees, dry falls, and scablands that reveal one of Earth's greatest geological events. Museums, overlooks, and interpretive sites connect the science and cultural history of these floods.

☐ ◻ ♡ **Klondike Gold Rush National Historical Park:** In Seattle's historic Pioneer Square, this site tells the story of the 1897–98 rush to Canada's Yukon Territory. Exhibits highlight the hardships and hopes of prospectors, the role Seattle played as a supply hub, and the transformative impact on the region. Visitors walk through restored buildings and learn about this dramatic migration.

☐ ◻ ♡ **Lake Chelan National Recreation Area:** Reached only by boat, plane, or trail, this 62,000-acre area surrounds the upper end of Lake Chelan and the remote Stehekin Valley. Visitors explore alpine lakes, waterfalls, and rugged peaks, hike into the North Cascades, and discover a community accessible only through wilderness travel. It's a place of seclusion and pristine beauty.

☐ ◻ ♡ **Lake Roosevelt National Recreation Area:** Stretching 130 miles along the Columbia River behind Grand Coulee Dam, this vast area preserves reservoirs, canyons, and cultural sites. Visitors camp, boat, and fish for walleye and trout, while also exploring Fort Spokane and Kettle Falls. Its landscapes mix recreation with layered histories of tribes, settlers, and modern power generation.

WASHINGTON

☐ ◩ ♡ **Lewis and Clark National Historical Park:** Spanning Oregon and Washington, this park commemorates the Corps of Discovery's 1805–06 winter at Fort Clatsop and their journey to the Pacific. Trails, museums, and reconstructed structures highlight their struggles, discoveries, and contact with Native tribes. It's a vivid window into one of America's most famous expeditions.

☐ ◩ ♡ **Manhattan Project National Historical Park:** This multi-state park preserves sites from the top-secret World War II project that created the atomic bomb. In Hanford, Washington, visitors explore the B Reactor, the world's first full-scale plutonium reactor, and learn about science, industry, and ethics. Together with sites in New Mexico and Tennessee, it tells a story that reshaped global history.

☐ ◩ ♡ **Mount Rainier National Park:** Dominated by 14,410-foot Mount Rainier, this park protects glaciers, old-growth forests, and alpine meadows. Visitors hike over 260 miles of trails, climb to icy peaks, and camp in subalpine wilderness. Wildlife like marmots and elk thrive here. Its beauty and challenges make it a crown jewel of Washington's landscapes and recreation.

☐ ◩ ♡ **Nez Perce National Historical Park:** Spanning Washington, Idaho, Oregon, and Montana, this park preserves 38 sites tied to the Nez Perce Tribe. Visitors learn about centuries of cultural traditions, explore battlefields and sacred landscapes, and understand the Nez Perce resistance to forced relocation. Museums, trails, and historic markers tell stories of resilience and heritage.

☐ ◩ ♡ **North Cascades National Park:** This 500,000-acre wilderness is famed for jagged peaks, over 300 glaciers, and deep valleys. Trails range from rugged alpine routes to accessible lakeshores. Campers, climbers, and nature lovers encounter diverse ecosystems, from lush temperate rainforests to wildflower-filled meadows. Remote and untamed, it's often called the "American Alps."

☐ ◩ ♡ **Olympic National Park:** Encompassing nearly a million acres, this park protects three distinct ecosystems: glacier-capped peaks, lush temperate rainforests, and wild Pacific coastline. Visitors hike to waterfalls, explore tide pools, and camp beneath giant cedars. From Roosevelt elk to sea otters, its biodiversity and landscapes make it a UNESCO World Heritage Site.

☐ ◩ ♡ **Pacific Crest National Scenic Trail:** Stretching 2,650 miles from Mexico to Canada, the PCT traverses Washington's Cascade Range on its northernmost leg. Hikers pass alpine lakes, volcanic peaks, and wildflower meadows while navigating rugged backcountry. As a National Scenic Trail, it offers long-distance adventure and a showcase of the state's wilderness heritage.

☐ ◩ ♡ **Ross Lake National Recreation Area:** Surrounding the Skagit River and Ross Lake, this area provides gateways into the North Cascades. Visitors boat, fish, and camp along remote lakeshores while dramatic mountains rise overhead. With rugged backcountry trails and access to Diablo and Gorge Lakes, it serves as both recreation hub and wilderness corridor.

☐ ◩ ♡ **San Juan Island National Historical Park:** This park preserves sites tied to the 1859 "Pig War" boundary dispute between the U.S. and Britain. At American Camp and English Camp, visitors tour historic structures, hike coastal bluffs, and see sweeping views of the Salish Sea. Bald eagles and orcas add natural spectacle to this island's layered history.

☐ ◩ ♡ **Whitman Mission National Historic Site:** Near Walla Walla, this site commemorates the 1836 mission of Marcus and Narcissa Whitman, who sought to aid westward emigrants. It tells of the Oregon Trail, the Whitmans' tragic 1847 massacre, and the cultural clashes between settlers and the Cayuse Tribe. Trails, a museum, and reconstructed mission grounds invite reflection.

State & National Forests

☐ ◩ ♡ **Ahtanum State Forest:** This ~20,000-acre forest in Yakima County is managed by Washington DNR. It preserves ponderosa pine and Douglas-fir ecosystems while supporting sustainable timber, wildlife, and watershed protection. Popular for hiking, horseback riding, mountain biking, and seasonal hunting, it also serves as a demonstration area for forest stewardship in Central Washington.

☐ ◩ ♡ **Blanchard State Forest:** Located in Skagit County near Bellingham, this ~4,800-acre working forest balances timber harvest with recreation and conservation. Managed by Washington DNR, it protects coastal forests of Douglas-fir, western red cedar, and hemlock. Popular trails like Oyster Dome provide hiking, biking, and birdwatching with sweeping views of the San Juan Islands.

WASHINGTON

☐ 🔖 ♡ **Capitol State Forest:** Spanning ~110,000 acres across Thurston and Grays Harbor counties, this is the most visited state forest in Washington. Managed for sustainable timber, wildlife, and habitat, it offers extensive hiking, biking, horseback, and OHV trail systems, along with hunting and camping. Its proximity to Olympia makes it a hub for both recreation and education.

☐ 🔖 ♡ **Colville National Forest:** Encompassing ~1.5 million acres in northeast Washington, this forest covers parts of the Selkirk, Cabinet, and Okanogan Mountains. It includes old-growth stands, alpine lakes, and wilderness areas rich in wildlife like caribou and grizzly bears. Popular activities include hiking, camping, fishing, hunting, OHV use, and winter sports across diverse terrain.

☐ 🔖 ♡ **Elbe Hills–Tahoma State Forest:** Together covering ~12,000 acres in Pierce and Lewis counties, these two adjacent forests form a DNR-managed working landscape near Mount Rainier. They support sustainable timber harvest, watershed protection, and wildlife habitat. Visitors explore gravel roads and trails for hiking, horseback riding, and dispersed recreation with views of volcanic foothills.

☐ 🔖 ♡ **Gifford Pinchot National Forest:** Spanning ~1.32 million acres from Mount Rainier to the Columbia River, this forest protects volcanic landscapes, glaciers, and wilderness areas. It also contains Mount St. Helens National Volcanic Monument. Visitors hike, climb, camp, fish, and ski here, exploring waterfalls, old-growth forests, and the dramatic Cascade mountain environment.

☐ 🔖 ♡ **Green Mountain–Tahuya State Forest:** This ~7,600-acre working forest on the Kitsap Peninsula is managed for timber, water, and wildlife while offering recreation. Popular with hikers, equestrians, and mountain bikers, it also supports OHV use and hunting. Trails pass through conifer and hardwood forests, while ridges provide views of Hood Canal and the Olympics.

☐ 🔖 ♡ **Little Pend Oreille State Forest:** The only state forest in northeastern Washington, it covers ~120,000 acres in Stevens and Pend Oreille counties. It features dry pine-oak woodlands, riparian corridors, and diverse wildlife including elk and moose. DNR manages it for timber, watershed, and habitat, while recreation includes hiking, horseback riding, camping, and hunting.

☐ 🔖 ♡ **Loomis State Forest:** Covering more than 120,000 acres in north-central Okanogan County, this forest protects one of the largest roadless areas managed by Washington DNR. Its dry pine forests, rugged ridges, and alpine meadows provide habitat for lynx, wolves, and other sensitive wildlife. Recreation includes hiking, horseback riding, hunting, and dispersed camping in a wild, largely undeveloped landscape.

☐ 🔖 ♡ **Loup Loup State Forest:** Nestled near Loup Loup Pass between Twisp and Okanogan, this ~10,000-acre DNR-managed forest blends timber production with watershed and habitat protection. Ponderosa pine and mixed conifer stands cover its ridges and valleys, supporting wildlife such as deer and black bear. Visitors enjoy hunting, hiking, camping, and snow recreation, with scenic mountain access in north-central Washington.

☐ 🔖 ♡ **Mount Baker–Snoqualmie National Forest:** Stretching ~1.7 million acres along the west slope of the Cascades, this forest includes Glacier Peak, Mount Baker, and hundreds of glaciers. It contains 1,500 miles of trails including the Pacific Crest Trail. Popular for hiking, skiing, climbing, camping, and scenic drives, it's one of the most accessible forests from Seattle.

☐ 🔖 ♡ **Okanogan–Wenatchee National Forest:** Washington's largest national forest at ~4 million acres, it stretches nearly the length of the eastern Cascades. Habitats range from sagebrush steppe to alpine tundra, with wild rivers and wilderness areas throughout. Over 1,200 miles of trails support hiking, hunting, fishing, camping, and climbing, making it a year-round recreation destination.

☐ 🔖 ♡ **Olympic National Forest:** Surrounding Olympic National Park, this ~628,000-acre forest spans rugged peaks, temperate rainforests, and wild coastlines on the Olympic Peninsula. Managed for both conservation and recreation, it offers trails through old-growth, alpine lakes, and wilderness areas, plus opportunities for camping, fishing, and wildlife watching. Its diverse habitats complement the park, creating a vast mosaic of public lands.

☐ 🔖 ♡ **Tiger Mountain State Forest:** Covering ~13,700 acres east of Issaquah, this DNR-managed working forest is a model for sustainable timber production. It also provides extensive trails for hiking, biking, horseback riding, and paragliding. With proximity to Seattle, it is a heavily used recreation area and an outdoor classroom for urban forestry education.

WASHINGTON

☐ 🔖 ♡ **Umatilla National Forest (WA unit):** While primarily in Oregon, ~600,000 acres of this 1.4 million-acre forest extend into Washington's Blue Mountains. It protects mixed conifer forests, rivers, and grasslands that support elk, bighorn sheep, and other wildlife. Recreation includes hiking, camping, hunting, fishing, and winter sports in rugged, remote terrain.

☐ 🔖 ♡ **Yacolt Burn State Forest:** Encompassing ~90,000 acres in Clark and Skamania counties, this forest regenerated after the 1902 Yacolt Burn wildfire. Today it's managed for timber, habitat, and recreation, with extensive trails for hiking, horseback riding, mountain biking, and OHV use. It serves as a living landscape of recovery and sustainable management.

National Scenic Byways & All-American Roads

☐ 🔖 ♡ **Cascade Loop Scenic Byway:** A 440-mile circuit that links Puget Sound, Skagit Valley, the North Cascades, Lake Chelan, and the Columbia River. Travelers cross alpine passes, wind through orchard country, and explore desert cliffs. Quaint towns, abundant wildlife, and recreation year-round make this a signature journey through Washington's most varied landscapes.

☐ 🔖 ♡ **Chinook Scenic Byway:** Climbing from lush valleys near Enumclaw over 5,430-foot Chinook Pass into the Naches Valley, this route delivers constant views of Mount Rainier. Alpine lakes, waterfalls, and wildflower meadows line the road, with historic trailheads and picnic spots along the way. Designated an **All-American Road**, it captures the drama of the Cascade high country.

☐ 🔖 ♡ **Coulee Corridor Scenic Byway:** Journey through the Channeled Scablands, where Ice Age floods carved towering basalt cliffs and left chains of desert lakes. Highlights include Dry Falls, wildlife refuges, and sweeping desert panoramas. Visitors hike, boat, birdwatch, and stargaze in a landscape that feels both otherworldly and inviting, revealing the power of ancient natural forces.

☐ 🔖 ♡ **International Selkirk Loop:** Encircling the Selkirk Mountains across Washington, Idaho, and British Columbia, this international byway showcases pristine rivers, glacial lakes, and forested peaks. Washington's portion includes historic towns, refuges, and overlooks perfect for wildlife spotting. Recognized as an **All-American Road**, it blends cultural charm with sweeping wilderness scenery.

☐ 🔖 ♡ **Mountains to Sound Greenway:** Stretching along I-90 from Seattle's waterfront across Snoqualmie Pass to the Columbia Plateau, this corridor highlights conservation and community. Stops include waterfalls, forest trails, alpine lakes, ski areas, and historic railroads. It tells a story of balance between urban vibrancy and wilderness access, linking Puget Sound to Washington's dry side.

☐ 🔖 ♡ **Stevens Pass Greenway:** Following the Skykomish River into the Cascades, this byway ascends misty valleys to high peaks before dropping into Wenatchee's orchard country. Waterfalls, tunnels, trail networks, and railroad history line the way. The route reveals Washington's dramatic climatic transition, from temperate rainforest to the sunny interior, in a single day's drive.

☐ 🔖 ♡ **Strait of Juan de Fuca Highway:** Running along Washington's far northwest coast, this byway offers sweeping views of the Pacific Ocean and Strait of Juan de Fuca. Rugged headlands, tribal heritage sites, lighthouses, and fishing villages highlight the route. Visitors can spot whales, explore tidepools, and hike rainforest headlands where ocean and mountains meet.

☐ 🔖 ♡ **White Pass Scenic Byway:** Linking I-5 to Yakima, this route travels through valleys framed by Mount Rainier, Mount Adams, and Mount St. Helens. Lakes, waterfalls, and campgrounds provide four-season recreation, from fishing to skiing. Scenic overlooks reveal volcanic peaks and broad forests, making it a memorable gateway to Washington's South Cascades.

State Scenic Byways

☐ 🔖 ♡ **Cape Flattery Tribal Scenic Byway:** A 12-mile journey on the Makah Reservation that leads to the northwestern-most tip of the continental U.S. The road winds through coastal forests before reaching overlooks above rugged sea cliffs and Tatoosh Island. It blends cultural heritage and natural wonder, connecting travelers to sacred Makah lands and the edge of the Pacific Ocean.

☐ 🔖 ♡ **Cascade Valleys Scenic Byway:** This 30-mile corridor follows the Sammamish and Snoqualmie Rivers from Woodinville to North Bend. Wineries, farms, and forested foothills line the route, with the Cascades rising dramatically ahead. Charming small towns provide rest stops along a path that links Puget Sound communities with the region's alpine wilderness and outdoor adventures.

WASHINGTON

☐ 🔖 ♡ **Chuckanut Drive Scenic Byway:** A short but dramatic 21-mile cliffside highway between Burlington and Bellingham. Forests hug sandstone bluffs above Samish Bay, with pullouts offering sweeping marine views. The route provides access to trails, state parks, and shoreline beaches, making it a perfect blend of coastal scenery, wildlife, and northwest charm.

☐ 🔖 ♡ **Columbia River Gorge Scenic Byway:** An 80-mile drive along SR 14 on the Washington side of the Columbia River. Towering basalt cliffs, waterfalls, and wide river views dominate the landscape, while orchards and small towns offer culture and hospitality. Trails, overlooks, and history enrich the drive through this world-class river canyon.

☐ 🔖 ♡ **Cranberry Coast Scenic Byway:** A 48-mile coastal route between Raymond and Aberdeen showcasing tidal flats, cranberry bogs, and windswept beaches. Wildlife thrives in the estuaries, while roadside stands and rural communities highlight the area's heritage. It's a quiet, scenic path where industry, culture, and natural beauty intersect along the Pacific shoreline.

☐ 🔖 ♡ **Hidden Coast Scenic Byway:** This 41-mile byway along SR 109 runs from Hoquiam to Taholah, paralleling the Pacific Ocean and coastal dunes. Small fishing villages and tribal lands give the route cultural depth, while beaches, tidepools, and wildlife offer recreation. A quieter, more contemplative alternative to the busier Olympic Peninsula highways.

☐ 🔖 ♡ **Lewis and Clark Trail Scenic Byway:** Stretching 572 miles across Washington, this byway traces the Corps of Discovery's journey from the Pacific Coast to the Idaho border. It passes forts, interpretive sites, and wide-open plateaus that reveal the expedition's challenges. Visitors experience history intertwined with river valleys, rolling prairies, and dramatic landscapes.

☐ 🔖 ♡ **Mount Baker Scenic Byway:** A 58-mile drive on SR 542 from Bellingham to Artist Point, climbing into the North Cascades. It winds through forests, waterfalls, and alpine meadows before ending at panoramic views of Mount Baker and Mount Shuksan. With year-round recreation from hiking to skiing, it's one of Washington's premier mountain routes.

☐ 🔖 ♡ **North Cascades Scenic Byway:** Covering 140 miles across SR 20 from Sedro-Woolley to Twisp, this is Washington's most rugged mountain highway. Jagged peaks, glacier-fed rivers, and turquoise lakes line the route. Trailheads, overlooks, and small towns provide access points, creating a drive that captures the wild essence of the North Cascades.

☐ 🔖 ♡ **North Pend Oreille Scenic Byway:** A 27-mile corridor along SR 31 from Tiger to the Canadian border. The road passes through forested valleys, quiet farmland, and the Pend Oreille River. Wildlife refuges, historic rail sites, and peaceful communities make it a tranquil and scenic northern drive into Washington's remote corner.

☐ 🔖 ♡ **Okanogan Trails Scenic Byway:** This 83-mile journey from Pateros to the Canadian border follows the Okanogan River through a blend of orchards, vineyards, and grasslands. Desert-like hills frame the landscape, while the Methow Valley adds alpine character. Wildlife viewing, small towns, and agricultural heritage define this eastern Washington drive.

☐ 🔖 ♡ **Pacific Coast Scenic Byway:** A 350-mile loop around the Olympic Peninsula via US 101. Visitors encounter wild Pacific beaches, lush rainforests, rivers, and towering mountains. Lighthouses, fishing towns, and countless trailheads provide variety. The route offers one of Washington's most immersive experiences, combining shoreline wilderness with cultural heritage.

☐ 🔖 ♡ **Palouse Scenic Byway:** Spanning 208 miles across Whitman County, this byway showcases the Palouse's rolling farmland and rural charm. Golden wheat fields, striking basalt outcrops, and historic towns create a picturesque journey. Scenic overlooks and backroads reveal a landscape shaped by agriculture, offering a peaceful, quintessentially eastern Washington experience.

☐ 🔖 ♡ **San Juan Islands Scenic Byway:** Covering about 120 miles of ferry routes and island roads across Orcas, Lopez, and San Juan Islands. The journey blends marine crossings with drives through forests, farmlands, and waterfront towns. Visitors enjoy views of the Salish Sea, opportunities to spot whales, and a unique island-hopping adventure.

☐ 🔖 ♡ **Sherman Pass Scenic Byway:** A 35-mile mountain crossing on SR 20 through the Kettle River Range, rising to Washington's highest maintained pass at 5,575 feet. Dense forests, alpine meadows, and historic markers define the route. It's a remote, scenic drive that rewards travelers with sweeping views and access to quiet backcountry.

☐ 🔖 ♡ **Spirit Lake Memorial Highway:** A 52-mile drive along SR 504 from Castle Rock to Johnston Ridge Observatory. The route climbs into landscapes reshaped by the 1980 eruption of Mount St. Helens, where forests regenerate and interpretive sites tell the story of destruction and renewal. Sweeping views of the volcano and valleys dominate the journey.

WASHINGTON

☐ 🔖 ♡ **Swiftwater Corridor Scenic Byway:** A 42-mile drive through Kittitas County along forested hillsides and river valleys. It connects Ellensburg with the Cascades, passing through rugged terrain and rural communities. Scenic pullouts, trail access, and historic features highlight the area's blend of recreation, natural beauty, and small-town character.

☐ 🔖 ♡ **Whidbey Scenic Isle Way:** A 54-mile route looping around Whidbey Island on SR 20 and SR 525. It features farmland, seaside bluffs, and forested shorelines with views across Puget Sound. Small towns, historic forts, and wildlife refuges line the way, offering a drive that mixes maritime heritage with island scenery.

☐ 🔖 ♡ **Yakama Scenic Byway:** A 76-mile corridor along US 97 through the Yakama Nation Reservation. The route spans desert hills, river valleys, and broad plateaus framed by Mount Adams. Interpretive sites highlight Yakama cultural heritage, while wildlife and sweeping vistas make it a powerful blend of landscape and tradition.

☐ 🔖 ♡ **Yakima River Canyon Scenic Byway:** An 18-mile stretch of SR 821 between Selah and Ellensburg. Sheer basalt cliffs tower above the river, where eagles soar and bighorn sheep graze. The winding road passes fishing spots, hiking trails, and picnic areas, creating a scenic gorge experience in central Washington's desert landscape.

National Natural Landmarks

 ☐ 🔖 ♡ **Boulder Park and McNeil Canyon Haystack Rocks:** Recognized as a National Natural Landmark for showcasing some of the finest glacial erratics in the U.S., these massive boulders were carried from their origins and deposited across the Columbia Plateau by Ice Age glaciers. Scattered dramatically across the landscape, they serve as striking evidence of glacial transport and power.
GPS: 47.8786, -119.8017

 ☐ 🔖 ♡ **Davis Canyon:** Honored as a National Natural Landmark, this canyon preserves one of the last undisturbed antelope bitterbrush–Idaho fescue shrub-steppe ecosystems on the Columbia Plateau. The rolling, semi-arid hills provide a living snapshot of a landscape once widespread in eastern Washington but now largely converted to agriculture.
GPS: 48.2438, -119.7518

 ☐ 🔖 ♡ **Drumheller Channels:** Designated a National Natural Landmark for its dramatic scabland terrain, this labyrinth of mesas, buttes, and dry channels was carved by cataclysmic Ice Age floods. It remains one of the most spectacular examples of flood-carved topography in the Columbia Basin, showcasing the raw force of glacial outburst events.
GPS: 46.9750, -119.1964

 ☐ 🔖 ♡ **Ginkgo Petrified Forest:** This National Natural Landmark protects thousands of petrified logs preserved by ancient lava flows. With an unusually diverse array of tree species fossilized in stone, the site is one of the world's most significant paleobotanical localities, offering an irreplaceable record of Washington's prehistoric forests.
GPS: 46.9489, -120.0028

 ☐ 🔖 ♡ **Grand Coulee:** Recognized as a National Natural Landmark for its immense size and geological importance, Grand Coulee is a steep-walled canyon sculpted by Ice Age floods. One of the largest features of its kind in North America, it dramatically illustrates the erosive power of glacial outburst floods that reshaped the Columbia Basin.
GPS: 47.7667, -119.2167

 ☐ 🔖 ♡ **Mima Mounds:** This prairie landscape, protected as a National Natural Landmark, contains thousands of small, evenly spaced earthen mounds whose origins remain debated. Whether formed by seismic activity, frost, or burrowing animals, the Mima Mounds represent one of the most mysterious and best-preserved landform puzzles in North America.
GPS: 46.8900, -123.0500

 ☐ 🔖 ♡ **Nisqually Delta:** Celebrated as a National Natural Landmark for its intact estuarine ecosystem, the Nisqually Delta features tidal flats, marshes, and freshwater wetlands at the southern end of Puget Sound. It provides vital migratory bird habitat and stands as a nationally important example of delta restoration and conservation.
GPS: 47.1086, -122.7031

WASHINGTON

 **Point of Arches:** Part of Olympic National Park, this rugged coastal stretch is designated a National Natural Landmark for its sea stacks, arches, and tide pools. Constantly sculpted by Pacific Ocean waves, it represents one of the most dramatic examples of marine erosion and intertidal ecosystems on the Washington coast.
GPS: 48.2465, -124.7002

 **Sims Corner Eskers and Kames:** Named a National Natural Landmark for its outstanding glacial features, this area preserves ridges of sediment (eskers) and rounded hills (kames) deposited by retreating ice. These landforms provide a clear geologic record of the processes that shaped the Columbia Plateau during the Pleistocene.
GPS: 47.8250, -119.3667

 **Steptoe and Kamiak Buttes:** These ancient granite peaks rise above the basalt plains of eastern Washington and are protected as National Natural Landmarks. They act as ecological "islands," supporting forests, meadows, and unique biodiversity, while also offering insight into the region's pre-volcanic geologic history.
GPS: 47.0325, -117.2986

 **The Great Gravel Bar of Moses Coulee:** Designated a National Natural Landmark for being a textbook example of a pendent river bar, this massive gravel deposit formed during Ice Age flooding. Its size and composition reveal the extraordinary hydraulic energy of glacial meltwater events that once thundered through Moses Coulee.
GPS: 47.4583, -119.8000

 **Umtanum Ridge Water Gap:** This striking landmark, recognized as a National Natural Landmark, demonstrates the interplay between tectonic uplift and river erosion. The Yakima River carved through folded basalt to create a dramatic water gap, making it an outstanding site to study structural geology and fluvial dynamics.
GPS: 46.8500, -120.5444

 **Wallula Gap:** Designated a National Natural Landmark for its role in Ice Age flood history, Wallula Gap is a deep basalt gorge where glacial outburst waters once surged. Its cliffs and constricted channel created a flood bottleneck, leaving behind some of the region's most dramatic erosional landforms.
GPS: 46.0444, -118.9467

 **Withrow Moraine and Jameson Lake Drumlin Field:** Recognized as a National Natural Landmark for preserving some of the best terminal moraine and drumlin features in the Columbia Plateau. This landscape of ridges and streamlined hills records the southern reach of the Pleistocene ice sheet, offering a clear picture of glacial advance and retreat.
GPS: 47.6875, -119.6247

UNITED STATES EDITION

WEST VIRGINIA

West Virginia's wild beauty shines through misty mountains, rushing rivers, deep gorges, and forested hollows. Through its array of state parks, national forests, national park units, and breathtaking natural landmarks, the Mountain State is a haven for outdoor adventure, where rugged trails and scenic rivers reveal untamed Appalachian splendor.

📅 Peak Season
May–October is West Virginia's peak season, with warm weather, wildflowers, and colorful fall foliage. These months are ideal for hiking, whitewater rafting, and exploring mountain trails and state parks.

📅 Offseason Months
November–April is the offseason, with cold winters and snow in higher elevations. Winter offers skiing and quiet scenic beauty, while early spring remains cool and less crowded.

🍃 Scenery & Nature Timing
Spring brings blooming rhododendrons and rushing rivers. Summer highlights lush forests and mountain adventures. Fall transforms the hills with vivid color, while winter provides snowy ridges and clear mountain views.

✨ Special
West Virginia features the rugged New River Gorge, the highlands of Spruce Knob and Dolly Sods, and the cavern systems of Seneca Rocks. Misty valleys, cascading waterfalls, and forest-cloaked ridges define its wild, unspoiled landscape.

WEST VIRGINIA

State Parks

☐ 🔖 ♡ **Audra State Park:** Nestled along the Middle Fork River in Barbour and Upshur Counties, this 355-acre park is famous for its boardwalk through a stunning hemlock and rhododendron forest. Visitors enjoy camping, hiking, fishing, and swimming in the clear, fast-flowing river. Its sandstone outcrops and shady trails make it a favorite for photographers and families seeking natural beauty.

☐ 🔖 ♡ **Babcock State Park:** Located in Fayette County, this 4,127-acre park is best known for the Glade Creek Grist Mill, a working replica and one of the most photographed landmarks in WV. With 20 miles of trails, fishing streams, cabins, and scenic overlooks, the park offers outdoor recreation surrounded by Appalachian hardwood forest. It's a quintessential mountain retreat.

☐ 🔖 ♡ **Beartown State Park:** Set atop Droop Mountain near Hillsboro, Beartown State Park spans 110 acres of striking rock formations, deep crevices, and moss-covered boulders. Boardwalks guide visitors through the sandstone maze, revealing hidden views and cool shaded passages. Its peaceful, forested setting makes it a favorite for nature walks, photography, and quiet outdoor exploration.

☐ 🔖 ♡ **Beech Fork State Park:** Spanning over 3,000 acres near Huntington, this park features Beech Fork Lake, ideal for boating, kayaking, and fishing. The park's campgrounds accommodate both RVs and tents, with hiking and biking trails weaving through forested ridges. Wildlife watchers enjoy spotting deer, waterfowl, and songbirds. It's a top choice for water-based recreation close to the city.

☐ 🔖 ♡ **Berkeley Springs State Park:** Located in the town of Berkeley Springs, this unique park centers on mineral springs used since colonial times for their healing qualities. It features historic Roman bathhouses, a modern spa, and George Washington's famed bath site. Visitors enjoy warm spring-fed pools, a museum, and shaded grounds, making it a rare blend of history, wellness, and recreation.

☐ 🔖 ♡ **Blackwater Falls State Park:** Famous for its amber-colored, 57-foot waterfall, this park near Davis is one of WV's crown jewels. Overlook platforms and hiking trails showcase the dramatic falls and the surrounding Blackwater Canyon. Year-round recreation includes cross-country skiing, sledding, hiking, and fishing. The lodge and cabins make it a four-season destination.

☐ 🔖 ♡ **Blennerhassett Island Historical State Park:** Accessible only by boat from Parkersburg, this island park preserves 18th-century history with its grand Blennerhassett Mansion replica, museum, and horse-drawn carriage tours. Visitors explore hiking paths, picnicking areas, and interpretive programs that recount Aaron Burr's controversial 1800s dealings. The Ohio River setting adds to the charm.

☐ 🔖 ♡ **Bluestone State Park:** Situated on the shores of Bluestone Lake in Summers County, this 2,100-acre park offers cabins, boating, fishing, and scenic camping. Trails wind through forested hills rich with wildlife, while the lake is popular for bass fishing and water sports. Its peaceful setting near Pipestem makes it a haven for relaxation and nature exploration.

☐ 🔖 ♡ **Cacapon Resort State Park:** In Morgan County, this 6,000-acre park features a lodge, golf course, lake, and miles of trails. Cacapon Mountain provides scenic overlooks and hiking challenges. The lake invites swimming, fishing, and paddle boating in summer. The resort setting balances outdoor adventure with comfort, making it a versatile retreat for families and groups.

☐ 🔖 ♡ **Camp Creek State Park:** Located in Mercer County, this 6,000-acre park blends with Camp Creek State Forest to offer miles of hiking, biking, and horse trails. The park is noted for its beautiful waterfalls, shaded picnic spots, and quiet campgrounds. Anglers enjoy fishing in Camp Creek's trout-stocked waters. It's an outdoor escape with both rugged and family-friendly appeal.

☐ 🔖 ♡ **Canaan Valley Resort State Park:** This park in Tucker County sits in a high mountain valley known for diverse wildlife and rare plant species. Winter sports like skiing, snowboarding, and tubing draw visitors, while warmer months bring hiking, biking, golf, and scenic chairlift rides. The lodge, cabins, and conference center make it a year-round mountain resort.

☐ 🔖 ♡ **Cass Scenic Railroad State Park:** A living history park, Cass features an 11-mile heritage railroad powered by Shay steam locomotives. The ride ascends to Bald Knob, WV's second-highest peak, offering sweeping views. Visitors can explore the historic logging town, museum, and company houses available for overnight stays. It's a blend of industrial history and natural beauty.

WEST VIRGINIA

☐ 🔖 ♡ **Cathedral State Park:** This 133-acre park in Preston County protects WV's last stand of ancient hemlock forest, with trees up to 90 feet tall and 21 feet in circumference. Its peaceful trails showcase a rich understory of ferns, wildflowers, and rhododendron. The park is small but ecologically significant, offering a quiet sanctuary of old-growth forest.

☐ 🔖 ♡ **Chief Logan State Park:** Spanning 4,000 acres in Logan County, this park is a hub for cultural and recreational activities. Visitors find hiking trails, campgrounds, and a lodge, as well as an outdoor amphitheater hosting plays and concerts. The park also features a museum and wildlife exhibit. Its mix of heritage and outdoor adventure makes it unique.

☐ 🔖 ♡ **Droop Mountain Battlefield State Park:** A Civil War battlefield preserved in Pocahontas County, this park offers scenic views, a museum, and interpretive signs detailing the 1863 battle. Trails wind past trenches and historic sites, while picnicking areas provide mountain vistas. The annual reenactments and educational programs keep history alive in a serene setting.

☐ 🔖 ♡ **Fairfax Stone State Park:** One of the smallest WV state parks, it marks the historic boundary of the 1746 survey determining the Fairfax land grant. The stone monument is historically significant, though the park itself is under 2 acres. Its remote setting in Grant County makes it a quick stop for history buffs exploring the Allegheny Highlands.

☐ 🔖 ♡ **Hawks Nest State Park:** Overlooking the New River Gorge, this park in Fayette County is known for its breathtaking views, aerial tramway, and access to whitewater rafting. Visitors enjoy trails, a lodge, and a museum highlighting the region's history. The dramatic cliffs and river overlook make it one of the state's most photographed scenic spots.

☐ 🔖 ♡ **Holly River State Park:** Covering nearly 8,300 acres in Webster County, it is WV's second-largest state park. Visitors find waterfalls, lush forests, cabins, and campgrounds. Miles of trails showcase mountain streams, wildflowers, and wildlife. Its remote location offers solitude, making it a hiker's paradise and a peaceful escape for nature lovers.

☐ 🔖 ♡ **Little Beaver State Park:** This 562-acre park in Raleigh County centers around a 18-acre lake popular for fishing, kayaking, and swimming. Trails wind through quiet woods, and a modern campground accommodates families and RVs. Picnic shelters and playgrounds make it a family-friendly spot. The park offers both relaxation and easy outdoor adventure near Beckley.

☐ 🔖 ♡ **Lost River State Park:** Nestled in Hardy County's mountains, this 3,700-acre park offers 26 rustic cabins, hiking trails to Cranny Crow overlook, horseback riding, swimming, and archery. The historic Lighthorse Harry Lee Cabin connects visitors to the 1800s. Its mix of outdoor recreation, history, and scenic views makes it a peaceful retreat in the Eastern Panhandle.

☐ 🔖 ♡ **Moncove Lake State Park:** Located in Monroe County, this park surrounds a 144-acre lake that's great for fishing, boating, and birding. The campground, picnic areas, and trails provide a peaceful retreat. The area is known for its abundant birdlife, particularly during migrations. It's a quiet, scenic park ideal for nature observation and relaxation.

☐ 🔖 ♡ **North Bend State Park:** Nestled in Ritchie County, this park features North Bend Lake, ideal for boating and fishing, plus access to the 72-mile North Bend Rail Trail. With a lodge, cabins, and campgrounds, it's popular for hiking, biking, and birdwatching. Its combination of water recreation, scenic trails, and amenities makes it a hub for outdoor adventure.

☐ 🔖 ♡ **Pinnacle Rock State Park:** Known for its towering sandstone formation rising 3,100 feet above sea level, this small park in Mercer County offers scenic overlooks and picnicking. Trails wind around Pinnacle Rock, providing panoramic views of rugged Appalachian terrain. It's a favorite stop along U.S. Route 52 for travelers seeking dramatic mountain scenery.

☐ 🔖 ♡ **Pipestem Resort State Park:** Overlooking the Bluestone Gorge in Summers County, this 4,000-acre park blends outdoor adventure with resort comfort. Visitors can ride the aerial tram, golf, hike, fish, or go horseback riding. Two lodges, cabins, and camping offer year-round stays. Stunning views of the gorge make Pipestem one of WV's premier destinations.

☐ 🔖 ♡ **Prickett's Fort State Park:** Located in Marion County, this reconstructed 18th-century frontier fort brings colonial history to life with costumed interpreters, demonstrations, and a museum. Trails connect to the Mon River Rail Trail, while picnic areas and fishing add to outdoor fun. The park blends living history with recreation in a scenic riverside setting.

☐ 🔖 ♡ **Stonewall Resort State Park:** Surrounding Stonewall Jackson Lake in Lewis County, this 1,900-acre park combines outdoor recreation with modern luxury. Guests enjoy boating, fishing, hiking, and golf, plus a full-service resort with spa, lodge, and dining. It's a unique blend of lake adventure and upscale amenities in a tranquil setting.

WEST VIRGINIA

☐ 🔖 ♡ **Tomlinson Run State Park:** The northernmost state park in WV, located in Hancock County, it offers a lake, campground, and cabins. Visitors enjoy swimming, fishing, paddle boating, and hiking trails through wooded hills. Playgrounds, picnic shelters, and an array of family-friendly amenities make it a popular park near the Ohio River Valley.

☐ 🔖 ♡ **Tu-Endie-Wei State Park:** At the confluence of the Ohio and Kanawha Rivers in Point Pleasant, this 4-acre park commemorates the 1774 Battle of Point Pleasant. An 84-foot granite monument and the historic Mansion House museum highlight its significance. Visitors enjoy riverside scenery, quiet walks, and insights into West Virginia's early frontier and Revolutionary-era history.

☐ 🔖 ♡ **Twin Falls Resort State Park:** In Wyoming County, this 4,000-acre park is known for its two scenic waterfalls, miles of hiking and biking trails, and an 18-hole golf course. Visitors can stay at the lodge, cabins, or campground. The park also features a pioneer farm museum that offers a glimpse into 19th-century Appalachian life.

☐ 🔖 ♡ **Tygart Lake State Park:** Centered on a 1,750-acre lake in Taylor County, this park is popular for boating, swimming, and fishing. Trails wind along the lake's wooded shoreline, and a lodge, cabins, and campground provide year-round accommodations. The lake's clear waters and scenic hillsides create a relaxing setting for both water sports and nature exploration.

☐ 🔖 ♡ **Valley Falls State Park:** Located in Marion and Taylor Counties, this 1,145-acre park is renowned for its four cascading waterfalls on the Tygart Valley River. Visitors enjoy hiking, fishing, and picnicking while taking in dramatic river scenery. Trails through forested hills add to its appeal, making it one of the state's most photogenic parks.

☐ 🔖 ♡ **Watoga State Park:** WV's largest state park, spanning over 10,000 acres in Pocahontas County, features lakes, streams, and 40 miles of trails. Cabins and campgrounds provide lodging, while Beaver Creek Lake offers fishing and boating. Dense forests and abundant wildlife make it a premier destination for outdoor lovers seeking solitude and variety.

☐ 🔖 ♡ **Watters Smith Memorial State Park:** Covering 532 acres in Harrison County, this park preserves pioneer history with restored log cabins, barns, and a museum highlighting rural life from 1796 onward. Hiking and biking trails wind through forests and fields, while picnic shelters welcome gatherings. It offers both recreation and education in a scenic, heritage-rich setting.

National Parks

 ☐ 🔖 ♡ **Appalachian National Scenic Trail:** Stretching over 2,190 miles from Georgia to Maine, the Appalachian Trail is the longest hiking-only footpath in the world. Passing through 14 states, including a portion of West Virginia, it offers sweeping mountain vistas, forested ridges, and diverse ecosystems. The trail provides hikers with both scenic beauty and a challenging outdoor adventure.

 ☐ 🔖 ♡ **Bluestone National Scenic River:** Flowing through southern West Virginia, this 10.5-mile section of the Bluestone River protects steep gorges, rugged cliffs, and rich forests. Visitors enjoy hiking the Bluestone Turnpike Trail, canoeing, and fishing for smallmouth bass in its clear waters. The remote setting makes it a quiet haven for those seeking both solitude and natural beauty.

 ☐ 🔖 ♡ **Chesapeake & Ohio Canal National Historical Park:** Following the Potomac River for 184.5 miles, this park preserves the historic C&O Canal, once vital for commerce in the 1800s. Visitors walk or bike the towpath, explore restored lockhouses, and learn about canal engineering and history. Stretching into Maryland, DC, and West Virginia, it's a mix of culture, history, and riverside recreation.

 ☐ 🔖 ♡ **Gauley River National Recreation Area:** Known worldwide for extreme whitewater, this park in central West Virginia protects 25 miles of the Gauley River and 6 miles of the Meadow River. The rapids range from Class III to V, drawing expert kayakers and rafters each fall. Beyond rafting, visitors can fish, hike, and camp while enjoying the rugged mountain scenery and wildlife.

UNITED STATES EDITION

WEST VIRGINIA

☐ 🔖 ♡ **Harpers Ferry National Historical Park:** At the meeting of the Potomac and Shenandoah Rivers, this park blends natural beauty with deep history. It preserves the site of John Brown's raid, key Civil War battles, and early civil rights milestones. Visitors can tour historic buildings, hike scenic trails to Jefferson Rock, and explore a town where history and landscape converge.

☐ 🔖 ♡ **New River Gorge National Park & Preserve:** America's newest national park, this 70,000-acre preserve in southern West Virginia showcases the dramatic New River Gorge and its iconic steel arch bridge. Visitors hike along rim trails, climb sandstone cliffs, paddle whitewater rapids, or fish the ancient river. Lush forests, scenic drives, and historic mining sites make it a year-round destination.

State & National Forests

☐ 🔖 ♡ **Cabwaylingo State Forest:** Spanning 8,123 acres in Wayne County, this rugged forest is named from Cabell, Wayne, Lincoln, and Mingo counties. Its mixed hardwood and pine woodlands feature multi-use trails for hiking, biking, and horseback riding. Managed by the WV Division of Forestry, it supports sustainable timber, wildlife habitat, watershed protection, and recreation year-round.

☐ 🔖 ♡ **Calvin Price State Forest:** Covering 9,000 acres in Pocahontas and Greenbrier Counties, this forest honors conservationist Calvin W. Price. Dominated by upland hardwoods and pines, it remains largely undeveloped, offering quiet spaces for hiking, hunting, and wildlife observation. Managed for forestry and watershed protection, it highlights the balance between resource use and conservation.

☐ 🔖 ♡ **Camp Creek State Forest:** Encompassing 6,000 acres in Mercer County, this forest is known for waterfalls, trout streams, and 35 miles of trails for hiking, biking, fishing, and horseback riding. Partnered with Camp Creek State Park, it provides both recreation and conservation. It is actively managed for sustainable timber, wildlife, and water quality protection in southern West Virginia.

☐ 🔖 ♡ **Coopers Rock State Forest:** Near Morgantown, this 12,747-acre forest is one of WV's most-visited. It's famous for its dramatic Cheat River Canyon overlooks and over 50 miles of hiking and biking trails. Managed for forestry, wildlife, and watershed protection, it also offers climbing, picnicking, and camping. Its rugged cliffs and expansive views make it a year-round favorite.

☐ 🔖 ♡ **George Washington & Jefferson National Forests:** Though mostly in Virginia, this 1.8 million-acre system extends into eastern WV's highlands, including Hardy and Pendleton Counties. It preserves old-growth stands, cold-water streams, and Appalachian Trail sections. Visitors enjoy hiking, hunting, fishing, and camping in remote terrain managed for both recreation and forest health.

☐ 🔖 ♡ **Greenbrier State Forest:** A 5,100-acre forest in Greenbrier County, it combines sustainable timber harvests with outdoor recreation. Visitors find cabins, campgrounds, and trails for hiking, biking, and horseback riding. With wooded ridges and peaceful valleys, it provides a balance of recreation, forestry, and watershed protection while remaining a quiet alternative to larger parks.

☐ 🔖 ♡ **Kanawha State Forest:** Just outside Charleston in Kanawha County, this 9,300-acre forest is a favorite for hiking, biking, and birdwatching. With over 25 miles of trails, campgrounds, picnic areas, and an outdoor shooting range, it combines rugged mountain terrain with accessible recreation. Known for spring wildflowers and fall foliage, it serves as an outdoor retreat near the capital city.

☐ 🔖 ♡ **Kumbrabow State Forest:** Set atop Rich Mountain in Randolph County, this 9,474-acre forest lies above 3,000 feet, making it the highest state forest in WV. It protects high-elevation hardwoods and spruce-fir habitats, while offering trails, camping, and hunting. Managed for watershed health, logging, and wildlife, it provides visitors with cool summers and expansive mountain views.

☐ 🔖 ♡ **Monongahela National Forest:** Covering over 921,000 acres across 10 eastern WV counties, this vast forest includes Dolly Sods, Spruce Knob, and eight wilderness areas. It protects rugged mountains, bogs, and diverse ecosystems, offering hiking, camping, fishing, and hunting. As one of America's most biologically varied forests, it anchors West Virginia's outdoor recreation and conservation.

☐ 🔖 ♡ **Panther State Forest:** West Virginia's southernmost state forest, spanning 7,810 acres in McDowell County, offers a quiet retreat in the Appalachian highlands. Facilities include a seasonal pool, picnic shelters, and a small campground. Its wooded ridges and valleys provide opportunities for hiking, hunting, and wildlife viewing, making it a secluded destination for nature lovers in the state's coalfield region.

WEST VIRGINIA

☐ 🔖 ♡ **Seneca State Forest:** The oldest and largest state forest in WV, spanning 12,884 acres in Pocahontas County, it adjoins the Monongahela National Forest. Known for historic fire towers, cabins, and deep woodlands, it demonstrates sustainable forestry in action. With camping, fishing, hunting, and trails, it offers both outdoor adventure and a living history of conservation.

National Scenic Byways & All-American Roads

☐ 🔖 ♡ **Coal Heritage Trail:** Winding through southern coal country, this byway threads company towns, tipples, rail corridors, and steep mountain hollows that powered America's industrial age. Explore miners' memorials, museums, and historic depots; trace rivers carved beside rail lines; and see camps, company stores, and reclaimed landscapes that reveal the culture, grit, and innovation of West Virginia's coalfields.

☐ 🔖 ♡ **Highland Scenic Highway:** A 43-mile ridge-top drive across Monongahela National Forest on WV 39/150, with four developed overlooks and long views over spruce-topped summits and high Allegheny bogs. Stop for short walks to Falls of Hills Creek, boardwalks at Cranberry Glades, and quiet picnic spots above trout streams. Sparse development, dark skies, and sweeping vistas make it a classic mountain cruise.

☐ 🔖 ♡ **Historic National Road (West Virginia):** An **All-American Road** segment centered on Wheeling, where the nation's first federally funded highway crossed the Ohio River. Roll past 19th-century inns, tollhouses, and the landmark suspension bridge, then into brick streets and market districts that chart two centuries of travel and trade. Short in miles but rich in layers of transportation and frontier history.

☐ 🔖 ♡ **Midland Trail:** Following US-60 from Kenova to White Sulphur Springs, this cross-state route pairs river-city heritage with rugged gorge scenery. Drive from the Capitol in Charleston through Malden and Kanawha Falls, climb to Gauley and New River overlooks near Hawks Nest, and continue past ironworks, stone arches, and mountain towns. Antiquing, roadside diners, and trailheads dot the corridor.

☐ 🔖 ♡ **Staunton–Parkersburg Turnpike:** A 19th-century mountain turnpike turned byway linking Shenandoah valleys to the Ohio River. Trace Civil War routes over Rich Mountain and through Beverly, pass covered bridges and farm clearings, and connect with forest backroads and excursion rail. Waypoints reveal frontier travel, timber and rail booms, and quiet hamlets tucked among high Allegheny ridges.

☐ 🔖 ♡ **Washington Heritage Trail:** A 136-mile loop through the Eastern Panhandle that follows George Washington's footsteps across Berkeley, Jefferson, and Morgan counties. Visit warm springs in Berkeley Springs, Washington family homesites, canal and railroad towns, and preserved Main Streets in Shepherdstown, Harpers Ferry area communities, and beyond. Scenic river bends, orchards, and Blue Ridge views frame the drive.

State Scenic Byways

☐ 🔖 ♡ **Byway of the Coal:** Traversing Boone, Logan, and Mingo counties, this route follows winding valleys where coal once dominated life. It passes miners' memorials, historic tipples, murals, and company towns that preserve coalfield culture. Scenic hollows and forested ridges frame communities that tell the story of labor, industry, and Appalachian resilience across southern West Virginia.

☐ 🔖 ♡ **East Ridge Byway:** Running along high ridges near the Kentucky line, this byway offers expansive views into the Tug Fork Valley. The drive connects small, remote towns, forested slopes, and sites shaped by timber and coal. Quiet hollows, mountain vistas, and rustic scenery reflect the rugged beauty of the southwest corner of the state and its strong frontier traditions.

☐ 🔖 ♡ **Guyandotte Scenic Byway:** Following the Guyandotte River through Cabell, Lincoln, and Logan counties, this corridor highlights rolling valleys, small river towns, and wooded hills. Travelers see historic bridges, churches, and remnants of early rail and timber operations. Today, the byway offers a blend of cultural heritage and Appalachian scenery along one of the state's historic waterways.

WEST VIRGINIA

☐ 🔖 ♡ **Indian Creek–Greenbrier Valley Byway:** Stretching through Monroe and Greenbrier counties, this route showcases pastoral farmlands, karst landscapes, and limestone outcrops. Covered bridges, historic villages, and spring-fed creeks highlight the agricultural heritage of the region. Broad meadows framed by mountains create a peaceful, scenic drive rich in Appalachian charm and rural traditions.

☐ 🔖 ♡ **Paint Creek Scenic Byway:** A narrow, winding corridor paralleling Paint Creek through Kanawha and Fayette counties. Once home to coal camps, it now reveals waterfalls, fishing holes, and lush forest scenery. Stone walls, historic remnants, and interpretive stops tell the story of coal heritage while today's travelers find quiet beauty along the shaded creekside road.

☐ 🔖 ♡ **Seneca Trail:** Following part of US-219 through the Greenbrier Valley northward, this byway traces Native American pathways and early pioneer routes. It passes historic farms, Civil War sites, and charming small towns. With sweeping mountain views, cultural landmarks, and ties to centuries of travel, it remains a living corridor through eastern West Virginia's landscapes.

National Natural Landmarks

 ☐ 🔖 ♡ **Bear Rocks and Allegheny Front Preserve:** Recognized as a National Natural Landmark, Bear Rocks crowns the Allegheny Front with sweeping heath barrens, wind-swept spruce, and expansive mountain views. This high-elevation plateau harbors boreal species usually found much farther north, making it both a scenic treasure and an ecological refuge.
GPS: 39.0666, -79.3013

 ☐ 🔖 ♡ **Big Run Bog:** Named a National Natural Landmark for its rare high-altitude spruce bog, this Monongahela National Forest site preserves boreal plants such as sphagnum moss, cotton grass, and stunted black spruce. Its acidic waters and fragile wetland community represent one of the most unique and delicate ecosystems in West Virginia.
GPS: 39.1191, -79.5860 (approximate)

 ☐ 🔖 ♡ **Blister Run Swamp:** This unusual balsam fir swamp, designated a National Natural Landmark, preserves a relict ecosystem tied to colder Pleistocene climates. The fir trees and bog vegetation are typically found far to the north, making the site an important outpost for biodiversity and a reminder of the region's glacial past.
GPS: 38.6037, -79.8547

 ☐ 🔖 ♡ **Canaan Valley:** Honored as a National Natural Landmark, Canaan Valley is the largest high-elevation valley in the central and southern Appalachians. Its wetlands, sedge meadows, and spruce forests provide essential habitat for rare boreal species and serve as a refuge for cold-adapted wildlife in the state's rugged highlands.
GPS: 39.1267, -79.3781

 ☐ 🔖 ♡ **Cathedral State Park:** Designated a National Natural Landmark for its exceptional virgin hemlock forest, this 133-acre preserve shelters trees more than 300 years old. Towering over 90 feet, these hemlocks and their shaded understory reveal what much of the region's forest looked like before logging altered the landscape.
GPS: 39.3267, -79.5381

 ☐ 🔖 ♡ **Cranberry Glades Botanical Area:** Recognized as a National Natural Landmark, Cranberry Glades protects five acidic bogs that resemble arctic tundra. Carnivorous plants, cranberries, and sphagnum moss dominate this striking landscape, which represents one of the southernmost boreal bog ecosystems in North America.
GPS: 38.2031, -80.2664

 ☐ 🔖 ♡ **Cranesville Swamp Nature Sanctuary:** This frost-pocket wetland was named a National Natural Landmark for preserving boreal plants such as tamarack and bog rosemary. It is a living remnant of colder climates, hosting species normally found in Canada, and continues to serve as an important site for research and conservation.
GPS: 39.5314, -79.4819

 ☐ 🔖 ♡ **Fisher Spring Run Bog:** Designated a National Natural Landmark, this isolated spruce bog in Monongahela National Forest harbors rare wetland flora and amphibians. Its mossy, waterlogged soils and boreal plant community are relics of the Ice Age, making it a fragile and ecologically significant site.
GPS: 39.0143, -79.3351 (approximate)

WEST VIRGINIA

Gaudineer Scenic Area: Named a National Natural Landmark for its 50-acre stand of virgin red spruce, this old-growth forest escaped logging due to a surveying error. Towering spruce trees and their cool, shaded understory sustain unique mountain wildlife and preserve a rare example of original Appalachian forest.
GPS: 38.6281, -79.8425

Germany Valley Karst Area: This scenic limestone valley earned National Natural Landmark status for its textbook karst terrain of caves, sinkholes, and underground streams. It supports unique cave fauna and provides an outstanding example of how soluble rock landscapes evolve through erosion and water flow.
GPS: 38.7650, -79.3900

Greenville Saltpeter Cave: Recognized as a National Natural Landmark, this extensive cave system was historically mined for saltpeter and today shelters bats and cave-adapted species. Its long corridors and striking formations make it both a site of natural beauty and scientific interest.
GPS: 37.5457, -80.6755 (approximate)

Ice Mountain: Awarded National Natural Landmark status for its rare ice vents, this talus slope creates cold-air seeps that support arctic plants far south of their range. Twinflower and other boreal species persist here in a microclimate that has fascinated scientists and inspired conservation efforts.
GPS: 39.3633, -78.4669

Lost World Caverns: This subterranean wonder earned National Natural Landmark designation for its dramatic limestone formations. Visitors descend into a 120-foot-deep chamber to see pedestal stalagmites, soda straws, and other striking features, making it an important showcase of West Virginia's karst geology.
GPS: 37.8326, -80.4469

Organ Cave System: Named a National Natural Landmark, Organ Cave is West Virginia's largest cave system, with more than 45 miles of mapped passages. Historic saltpeter mining and a diverse bat population add cultural and ecological value to this geologic marvel.
GPS: 37.7181, -80.4369

Shavers Mountain Spruce-Hemlock Stand: This forest remnant, recognized as a National Natural Landmark, preserves old-growth red spruce and hemlock within Monongahela National Forest. It provides critical habitat for rare Appalachian species, including the endangered Cheat Mountain salamander.
GPS: 38.6700, -79.8200 (approximate)

Sinnett-Thorn Mountain Cave System: Honored as a National Natural Landmark, this complex limestone cave network contains vertical pits, underground streams, and extensive passages. Its depth, structure, and hydrology make it one of the most geologically significant cave systems in the region.
GPS: not listed

WISCONSIN

Wisconsin's natural landscapes blend forested bluffs, winding rivers, sparkling lakes, and rolling prairies. With its extensive collection of state parks, national forests, national park units, and treasured natural landmarks, Wisconsin offers outdoor exploration across every corner of the state.

📅 Peak Season
May–October is Wisconsin's peak season, offering mild temperatures, lake recreation, and brilliant fall foliage. Summer is busiest for boating and festivals, while autumn draws visitors for scenic drives and colorful forests.

📅 Offseason Months
November–April is the offseason, bringing cold weather and snow across much of the state. Winter is popular for skiing, snowmobiling, and ice fishing, though overall tourism is quieter.

🍃 Scenery & Nature Timing
Spring brings greening forests and blooming wildflowers. Summer highlights the Great Lakes' beaches, inland lakes, and waterfalls. Fall delivers vivid color across the Northwoods, while winter creates frozen lakes and snow-covered pines.

✨ Special
Wisconsin features the sandstone sea caves of the Apostle Islands, the glacial formations of Kettle Moraine, and the cliffs of Door County. Waterfalls, northern lights, and driftless hills carved by ancient rivers showcase its striking natural beauty.

WISCONSIN

State Parks

☐ 🔖 ♡ **Amnicon Falls State Park:** Located in Douglas County, this scenic park highlights a series of waterfalls and rapids along the Amnicon River. Visitors cross a historic covered bridge to explore multiple cascades, hike short trails, and enjoy picnic spots by the river. It's a family-friendly park offering camping, swimming, and a close-up view of Wisconsin's glacially shaped landscapes.

☐ 🔖 ♡ **Aztalan State Park:** In Jefferson County, this park preserves the remains of a 1,000-year-old Mississippian village with earthen platform mounds and reconstructed stockades. Visitors learn about Native American history through interpretive trails and exhibits. The Crawfish River adds fishing and wildlife viewing opportunities, making it a rare blend of cultural heritage and outdoor recreation.

☐ 🔖 ♡ **Belmont Mound State Park:** A day-use park in Lafayette County, it surrounds a 400-foot hill offering quiet hiking and picnicking opportunities. The wooded mound once featured a popular observation tower and provides scenic views of the Driftless Area. The nearby historic village of Belmont, Wisconsin's first territorial capital, adds historical context to this small but significant park.

☐ 🔖 ♡ **Big Bay State Park:** On Madeline Island in Lake Superior, this park features 4 miles of sandy beach, dramatic sandstone cliffs, and a coastal lagoon. Visitors enjoy swimming, kayaking, hiking, and camping on the island's north shore. Accessible by ferry from Bayfield, it's a unique blend of wilderness and water recreation in Wisconsin's only Lake Superior island state park.

☐ 🔖 ♡ **Big Foot Beach State Park:** Situated on Lake Geneva, this 271-acre park offers a swimming beach, shady picnic areas, and five miles of hiking trails. The campground provides access to fishing and boating on the lake. Its convenient location near the resort town makes it one of southern Wisconsin's most visited parks, combining recreation with lakeside relaxation.

☐ 🔖 ♡ **Blue Mound State Park:** Located in Iowa County, this park protects Wisconsin's highest point, offering panoramic views from twin observation towers. Visitors enjoy hiking, mountain biking, cross-country skiing, and camping. The Driftless Area landscape features rugged hills and valleys, while the park's swimming pool and picnic areas make it a favorite for year-round family outings.

☐ 🔖 ♡ **Brunet Island State Park:** In Chippewa County, this park sits at the confluence of the Chippewa and Fisher Rivers. Small islands linked by footbridges create a unique setting for camping, hiking, and canoeing. Wildlife abounds, with frequent sightings of deer, waterfowl, and eagles. It's a peaceful retreat where rivers and forest blend for quiet outdoor recreation.

☐ 🔖 ♡ **Buckhorn State Park:** Spanning a peninsula on Castle Rock Lake in Juneau County, this park offers swimming beaches, boat launches, and miles of hiking trails. It's popular for camping, fishing, and paddling in sheltered coves. Known for its wildlife observation opportunities, including sandhill cranes and waterfowl, the park is a tranquil spot for families and nature lovers.

☐ 🔖 ♡ **Copper Culture State Park:** Located in Oconto, this small park preserves the Copper Culture burial site, one of North America's oldest known cemeteries dating back over 5,000 years. Visitors can tour a museum with Native copper artifacts, walk interpretive trails, and picnic on the grounds. Though day-use only, it provides a rare glimpse into ancient history within a natural riverside setting.

☐ 🔖 ♡ **Copper Falls State Park:** Located in Ashland County, this park is known for its striking waterfalls, including Copper and Brownstone Falls, carved into ancient lava flows. Trails follow the Bad River Gorge through scenic forests and geologic formations. Camping, fishing, and picnicking round out the experience, making it one of Wisconsin's most iconic and photographed state parks.

☐ 🔖 ♡ **Council Grounds State Park:** On the banks of the Wisconsin River near Merrill, this park blends history and recreation. Once a gathering site for Native Americans, it now offers boating, fishing, hiking, and camping. The park's historic CCC-era stone structures, sandy beach, and picnic areas highlight its role as both a cultural site and a riverside retreat.

☐ 🔖 ♡ **Devil's Lake State Park:** Wisconsin's largest and most visited park, located in Sauk County, it surrounds a 360-acre lake nestled between towering quartzite bluffs. Over 29 miles of trails showcase dramatic overlooks and talus slopes. Popular for hiking, rock climbing, swimming, and camping, it offers year-round adventure in the heart of the Baraboo Hills.

WISCONSIN

☐ 🔖 ♡ **Governor Dodge State Park:** Spanning 5,000 acres in the Driftless Area of Iowa County, this park features steep hills, deep valleys, sandstone cliffs, and two lakes. Visitors enjoy boating, fishing, hiking, and camping. Stephens Falls, a picturesque waterfall, is a highlight. Its diverse terrain and rich history make it one of Wisconsin's most scenic and versatile parks.

☐ 🔖 ♡ **Governor Nelson State Park:** Located on Lake Mendota in Dane County, this day-use park offers beaches, hiking trails, picnic areas, and a boat launch. It's popular for swimming, fishing, and birdwatching, with views of the Madison skyline. Named for former Governor Gaylord Nelson, founder of Earth Day, the park honors conservation while offering modern outdoor recreation.

☐ 🔖 ♡ **Governor Thompson State Park:** One of Wisconsin's newest state parks, located in Marinette County, it features 2,800 acres of forest and 6.5 miles of shoreline along Caldron Falls Flowage. Visitors enjoy boating, camping, hiking, and wildlife viewing. Its undeveloped feel and connection to Peshtigo River State Forest provide a mix of solitude and recreation in the Northwoods.

☐ 🔖 ♡ **Harrington Beach State Park:** In Ozaukee County along Lake Michigan, this park features a mile-long sandy beach, wooded trails, a quarry lake, and camping. Birdwatchers flock here during migration seasons, and the park's Astronomy Center offers public stargazing events. Its mix of shoreline scenery and inland forests makes it a top destination just north of Milwaukee.

☐ 🔖 ♡ **Hartman Creek State Park:** Located in Waupaca County, this park spans glacial lakes and rolling forests. It's known for hiking, biking, horseback riding, and camping, plus excellent fishing and paddling on Chain O'Lakes. The park's Ice Age National Scenic Trail segment highlights its geologic past. It's a year-round recreation spot blending quiet lakeshores with wooded trails.

☐ 🔖 ♡ **Heritage Hill State Park:** Situated in Green Bay, this living history park interprets Wisconsin's past with historic buildings, costumed reenactors, and cultural exhibits. While primarily educational, it is managed as a state park. Visitors experience life from different eras, including Native American, fur trade, and pioneer periods, alongside picnicking and special events in a historic setting.

☐ 🔖 ♡ **High Cliff State Park:** Overlooking Lake Winnebago in Calumet County, this park features limestone cliffs, effigy mounds, and scenic trails. Popular for boating, swimming, and hiking, it offers panoramic views of Wisconsin's largest inland lake. Visitors explore historic lime kilns and quarry ruins while enjoying campgrounds, picnic areas, and year-round recreation opportunities.

☐ 🔖 ♡ **Interstate State Park:** Straddling the Wisconsin–Minnesota border on the St. Croix River, this park features glacial potholes and dramatic cliffs. Hiking trails, camping, boating, and rock climbing are popular. Its geology, shaped by ancient lava flows and Ice Age floods, makes it a natural wonder. As Wisconsin's oldest state park, it offers history and outdoor adventure together.

☐ 🔖 ♡ **Kinnickinnic State Park:** Located at the confluence of the Kinnickinnic and St. Croix Rivers in Pierce County, this park offers sandy beaches, scenic bluffs, and quiet trails. Visitors enjoy swimming, fishing, and birdwatching, with excellent opportunities to spot bald eagles. Its mix of riverside recreation and wooded hikes makes it a favorite in western Wisconsin.

☐ 🔖 ♡ **Kohler-Andrae State Park:** Situated along Lake Michigan in Sheboygan County, this park is known for its dunes, beaches, and boardwalks through rare sand ecosystems. Visitors swim, fish, hike, and camp while exploring prairies and woodlands. It's a top birdwatching site and features an accessible cordwalk, blending recreation with conservation along Wisconsin's coast.

☐ 🔖 ♡ **Lake Kegonsa State Park:** Found in Dane County, this park sits on the shores of Lake Kegonsa, offering swimming, boating, and fishing. Trails wind through woodlands and prairies, while the sandy beach and picnic areas make it a family favorite. The campground provides overnight stays, and the park is just minutes from Madison, offering a quick nature getaway.

☐ 🔖 ♡ **Lake Wissota State Park:** Located in Chippewa County, this park overlooks Lake Wissota, offering fishing, boating, swimming, and camping. Miles of trails weave through forests and prairies, providing hiking, biking, and horseback riding opportunities. Wildlife watchers enjoy spotting deer and waterfowl. Its lake-centered recreation makes it a popular stop in the Chippewa Valley.

WISCONSIN

☐ 🔖 ♡ **Lakeshore State Park:** Set in downtown Milwaukee on Lake Michigan, this urban park offers trails, fishing, and wildflower prairies with skyline views. Its lagoon is used for kayaking and canoeing, while a paved trail connects to the city's lakefront. It's a unique mix of natural restoration and metropolitan setting, showcasing Wisconsin's only urban state park.

☐ 🔖 ♡ **Lizard Mound State Park:** In Washington County, this park preserves one of the Midwest's best collections of effigy mounds built by Native Americans 800–1,200 years ago. Trails lead past animal-shaped burial mounds amid quiet woodlands. It offers history, culture, and nature together, making it a sacred and educational site in Wisconsin's state park system.

☐ 🔖 ♡ **Merrick State Park:** Located along the Mississippi River in Buffalo County, this park is a haven for boating and fishing. Backwaters, channels, and islands provide excellent canoeing and birdwatching opportunities. Campgrounds sit right on the water, making it a favorite for anglers and wildlife enthusiasts exploring the Upper Mississippi River Valley.

☐ 🔖 ♡ **Mill Bluff State Park:** In Juneau and Monroe Counties, this park showcases dramatic sandstone bluffs rising from the landscape, remnants of ancient glacial Lake Wisconsin. Hiking trails lead to scenic overlooks, and picnicking areas provide quiet rest stops. Its striking formations make it a distinctive part of the Ice Age National Scientific Reserve.

☐ 🔖 ♡ **Mirror Lake State Park:** Near Wisconsin Dells, this park is known for its calm, cliff-lined lake, perfect for paddling, swimming, and fishing. Trails wind through forested hills, offering hiking and cross-country skiing. With campgrounds, picnic areas, and sandstone cliffs, it's a popular year-round destination for both relaxation and recreation in a scenic setting.

☐ 🔖 ♡ **Natural Bridge State Park:** Found in Sauk County, this park protects Wisconsin's largest natural sandstone arch, spanning 35 feet. It also preserves a rock shelter used by Native Americans thousands of years ago. Hiking trails and picnic areas allow visitors to explore both geology and history in a quiet, educational park within the Driftless Area.

☐ 🔖 ♡ **Nelson Dewey State Park:** Overlooking the Mississippi River in Grant County, this park is named after Wisconsin's first governor. It features trails with sweeping river views, campgrounds, and picnicking spots. The nearby Stonefield Historic Site complements the park, making it a blend of natural beauty and state heritage in Wisconsin's southwest corner.

☐ 🔖 ♡ **New Glarus Woods State Park:** A smaller park in Green County, it connects to the Sugar River State Trail and offers wooded hiking paths, camping, and wildlife viewing. Its rolling hills and oak savannas provide a quiet, natural escape near the town of New Glarus. It's a family-friendly park perfect for biking, camping, and stargazing.

☐ 🔖 ♡ **Newport State Park:** Wisconsin's only formally designated wilderness park, located in Door County along Lake Michigan. It features 30 miles of hiking trails, backpack camping sites, and dark-sky stargazing. With rugged shoreline and deep forests, it offers solitude and primitive recreation for hikers, campers, and astronomy enthusiasts seeking a wilder experience.

☐ 🔖 ♡ **Peninsula State Park:** The crown jewel of Door County, this 3,776-acre park offers sandy beaches, a golf course, miles of bike and hiking trails, and campgrounds. Eagle Bluff Lighthouse and dramatic shoreline cliffs add history and scenery. It's one of Wisconsin's most visited parks, combining rich amenities with some of the state's finest natural landscapes.

☐ 🔖 ♡ **Perrot State Park:** Situated in Trempealeau County, this park highlights bluffs rising above the Mississippi River. Brady's Bluff offers sweeping views, while trails pass through hardwood forests and wetlands. Visitors enjoy camping, boating, and birdwatching, especially during migrations. Its mix of river scenery and hiking opportunities makes it a Mississippi Valley favorite.

☐ 🔖 ♡ **Potawatomi State Park:** Located in Door County, this park sits at the eastern terminus of the Ice Age National Scenic Trail. Visitors enjoy camping, hiking, fishing, and boating on Sturgeon Bay. Scenic limestone cliffs and panoramic overlooks provide stunning views of Green Bay. It's a perfect blend of recreation, history, and natural beauty.

☐ 🔖 ♡ **Rib Mountain State Park:** Centered on one of the world's oldest geological formations, this park in Marathon County features rugged quartzite outcrops and scenic overlooks. Granite Peak Ski Area offers downhill skiing in winter, while trails, picnicking, and a tower provide year-round recreation. The mountain's prominence makes it one of Wisconsin's most distinctive parks.

WISCONSIN

☐ 🔖 ♡ **Richard Bong State Recreation Area:** In Kenosha County, this large recreation area provides diverse opportunities, including hiking, biking, horseback riding, ATV trails, and camping. Its open fields, prairies, and wetlands attract birdwatchers and outdoor enthusiasts. Named after World War II flying ace Richard Bong, it's a multipurpose park supporting both active and passive recreation.

☐ 🔖 ♡ **Roche-a-Cri State Park:** Located in Adams County, this park is known for Roche-a-Cri Mound, a sandstone bluff rising 300 feet above the surrounding landscape. Visitors can climb a stairway to the top for sweeping views, hike trails through woodlands and prairies, and view ancient Native American petroglyphs. It's a blend of cultural history, geology, and outdoor recreation.

☐ 🔖 ♡ **Rock Island State Park:** Accessible only by ferry from Door County, this park offers pristine beaches, hiking trails, and camping in a remote island setting. Visitors can explore the historic Pottawatomie Lighthouse, one of the oldest on Lake Michigan. With no vehicles allowed, it provides a wilderness-like experience of quiet seclusion and stunning natural scenery.

☐ 🔖 ♡ **Rocky Arbor State Park:** Near Wisconsin Dells, this small wooded park is named for its sandstone cliffs and shady groves. It offers camping, hiking trails, and picnicking just minutes from the Dells' attractions. Visitors enjoy its peaceful atmosphere, short interpretive trails, and opportunities to observe wildlife in a sheltered forest setting.

☐ 🔖 ♡ **Straight Lake State Park:** Situated in Polk County, this 2,780-acre park protects glacial lakes, hardwood forests, and wetlands along the Ice Age National Scenic Trail. With primitive camping, hiking, fishing, and paddling, it offers a quiet wilderness feel. Its rugged landscape of eskers, kettles, and moraines showcases Wisconsin's glacial heritage while providing a peaceful escape in the Northwoods.

☐ 🔖 ♡ **Tower Hill State Park:** Situated in Iowa County near Spring Green, this park preserves the site of a 19th-century shot tower once used for manufacturing lead ammunition. Trails lead to restored historic structures and scenic overlooks of the Wisconsin River Valley. Today it offers hiking, picnicking, and camping while interpreting Wisconsin's early industrial history.

☐ 🔖 ♡ **Whitefish Dunes State Park:** Located in Door County along Lake Michigan, this park protects the state's largest sand dune complex. Trails wind through dunes, forests, and wetlands, while the beach offers swimming and scenic views. Archaeological sites highlight early Native American villages. It's a mix of natural beauty, recreation, and cultural heritage along the shoreline.

☐ 🔖 ♡ **Wildcat Mountain State Park:** Found in Vernon County, this park overlooks the Kickapoo River Valley and is known for its rugged terrain and panoramic vistas. Visitors enjoy hiking, horseback riding, and camping in a Driftless Area setting of steep hills and sandstone bluffs. Canoeing and kayaking are popular on the nearby Kickapoo River.

☐ 🔖 ♡ **Willow River State Park:** In St. Croix County, this popular park features Willow Falls, a stunning multi-tiered waterfall set in a gorge. Trails lead to overlooks and riverbanks, while campgrounds, picnic areas, and swimming beaches provide family recreation. Its dramatic scenery and diverse activities make it one of Wisconsin's most visited parks.

☐ 🔖 ♡ **Wyalusing State Park:** Overlooking the confluence of the Wisconsin and Mississippi Rivers, this Grant County park spans 2,700 acres of river bluffs, Native American burial mounds, and forests. Trails lead to panoramic overlooks, while camping and canoeing are popular. It's also an International Dark Sky Park, offering exceptional stargazing opportunities.

☐ 🔖 ♡ **Yellowstone Lake State Park:** Situated in Lafayette County, this park centers on a 450-acre reservoir known for boating, fishing, and swimming. Trails loop through prairies and woodlands, while campgrounds provide overnight stays. The lake attracts birdwatchers and anglers alike, making it a peaceful recreation destination in Wisconsin's southwest corner.

WISCONSIN

National Parks

☐ 🔖 ♡ **Apostle Islands National Lakeshore:** Protecting 21 islands and shoreline along Lake Superior in northern Wisconsin, this park is famous for its sandstone sea caves, historic lighthouses, and pristine beaches. Visitors enjoy kayaking, sailing, hiking, and camping. The islands provide rich wildlife habitat and a cultural landscape showcasing centuries of maritime history.

☐ 🔖 ♡ **Ice Age National Scenic Trail:** Winding for over 1,000 miles entirely within Wisconsin, this long-distance trail follows the edge of the last continental glacier. It highlights kettle lakes, moraines, and drumlins formed by Ice Age forces. Hikers explore prairies, forests, and small towns along the route. Segments are popular for day hikes, backpacking, and learning about glacial geology.

☐ 🔖 ♡ **North Country National Scenic Trail:** Stretching 4,800 miles across 8 states, this trail includes nearly 220 miles in northern Wisconsin. It traverses forests, rivers, and glacial landscapes, offering backpacking and day hiking opportunities. Wisconsin's section passes through Chequamegon National Forest and connects remote wilderness areas with local communities.

☐ 🔖 ♡ **Saint Croix National Scenic Riverway:** Spanning the Saint Croix and Namekagon Rivers across Wisconsin and Minnesota, this 200-mile waterway preserves one of the Midwest's last free-flowing rivers. Visitors canoe, kayak, and fish while enjoying scenic bluffs, wooded shores, and abundant wildlife. Campsites and trails along the rivers offer quiet outdoor escapes.

State & National Forests

☐ 🔖 ♡ **Black River State Forest:** Encompassing about 67,000 acres in Jackson County, this forest protects pine and hardwood stands along the Black River. Established in 1957, it offers camping, hiking, hunting, fishing, birdwatching, and extensive ATV and snowmobile trails. Managed by the Wisconsin DNR, it balances sustainable timber harvests with outdoor recreation and wildlife habitat.

☐ 🔖 ♡ **Brule River State Forest:** Covering over 40,000 acres in Douglas County, this forest follows the Bois Brule River, famous for trout fishing and canoeing. Established in 1907, it includes Cedar Island Lodge, once a "Summer White House." Today, visitors enjoy hiking, skiing, wildlife viewing, and paddling, while the forest also serves as a center for conservation education.

☐ 🔖 ♡ **Chequamegon–Nicolet National Forest:** Wisconsin's only national forest, it spans 1.5 million acres across northern counties. Created in 1998 by merging two forests, it features hardwoods, pines, wetlands, and more than 2,000 lakes. Nine wilderness areas provide backcountry experiences, while camping, hiking, fishing, hunting, and ATV use make it a recreation hub managed by the U.S. Forest Service.

☐ 🔖 ♡ **Coulee Experimental State Forest:** A 3,000-acre research forest in La Crosse County, established in 1960 to study forestry and watersheds in the Driftless Area. Its steep bluffs and valleys protect oak and maple forests along Dutch Creek. Public access is limited, though visitors can hike and view wildlife. It remains a working demonstration site for sustainable land management.

☐ 🔖 ♡ **Flambeau River State Forest:** Spanning over 90,000 acres in Sawyer and Price Counties, this forest was established in 1930 along the Flambeau River corridor. It conserves northern hardwoods and pine while offering camping, canoeing, fishing, hunting, hiking, and skiing. Managed for timber, water, and wildlife, it showcases the balance of recreation and resource stewardship.

☐ 🔖 ♡ **Governor Knowles State Forest:** Nearly 20,000 acres along the St. Croix River in Burnett and Polk Counties form this wilderness buffer. Established in 1970, it protects river scenery and water quality. Hiking trails, canoeing, hunting, and birdwatching opportunities abound, with rustic campsites available. Its management focuses on preserving natural values near the National Scenic Riverway.

☐ 🔖 ♡ **Havenwoods State Forest:** A 237-acre urban forest and environmental education center in Milwaukee, established in 1979. It preserves floodplain woodlands along Lincoln Creek and provides trails, wildlife observation, birdwatching, and outdoor classrooms. Havenwoods offers a unique blend of community forestry, nature study, and green space within Wisconsin's largest city.

WISCONSIN

☐ 🔖 ♡ **Kettle Moraine State Forest:** Spanning roughly 56,000 acres in southeastern Wisconsin, this forest showcases glacial landforms like kettles, eskers, and kames. It's divided into Northern, Southern, Pike Lake, Lapham Peak, and Loew Lake units. Popular for camping, hiking, biking, skiing, horseback riding, and water recreation, it's one of the state's best-known outdoor destinations.

☐ 🔖 ♡ **Northern Highland–American Legion State Forest:** Wisconsin's largest state forest, covering over 223,000 acres in Vilas, Oneida, and Iron Counties. Established in 1925, it protects a landscape of lakes, rivers, and northern forests. Visitors enjoy fishing, boating, snowmobiling, camping, hunting, and hiking. It remains both a working timber forest and a premier year-round recreation area.

☐ 🔖 ♡ **Peshtigo River State Forest:** Created in 2001, this 9,200-acre forest spans Marinette and Oconto Counties along the Peshtigo River. It conserves wetlands, pine, and hardwood forests while offering riverfront camping, hiking, fishing, hunting, and paddling. Managed for wildlife habitat and watershed health, it provides a mix of recreation and conservation in the Northwoods.

☐ 🔖 ♡ **Point Beach State Forest:** This 2,900-acre forest lies along Lake Michigan in Manitowoc County, established in 1938. It preserves sand dunes, pine-oak woodlands, and lakeshore habitat. Visitors enjoy camping, hiking, picnicking, and birdwatching, with the Rawley Point Lighthouse as a highlight. It offers a unique combination of coastal scenery and forest recreation.

National Scenic Byways & All-American Roads

☐ 🔖 ♡ **Door County Coastal Byway:** A 66-mile loop on Highways 42 and 57, this route circles the Door Peninsula with dramatic Niagara Escarpment bluffs, lighthouses, and harbor villages. Visitors enjoy orchards, galleries, and beaches, while access to state parks like Peninsula and Newport highlights the mix of culture, shoreline, and outdoor recreation that defines Door County.

☐ 🔖 ♡ **Great River Road:** Following the Mississippi River for 250 miles through 33 river towns, this nationally designated route showcases towering bluffs, backwaters, and sweeping overlooks. Travelers can stop at wildlife refuges, historic sites, and small riverfront communities. It's a celebrated drive where river heritage, natural beauty, and Midwest charm come together.

☐ 🔖 ♡ **Wisconsin Lake Superior Scenic Byway:** Stretching 70 miles along Highway 13 around the Bayfield Peninsula, this byway features sandy beaches, boreal forests, and rocky shoreline vistas of Lake Superior. Visitors explore Apostle Islands National Lakeshore, lighthouses, orchards, and fishing villages. The drive blends stunning water views with cultural history and Northwoods solitude.

State Scenic Byways

☐ 🔖 ♡ **Lower Wisconsin River Road Scenic Byway:** This 100-mile route follows Highway 60 from Lodi to Prairie du Chien, tracing the Lower Wisconsin State Riverway. Sandbars, river bluffs, and bottomland forests frame the drive, with canoe launches, fishing spots, and wildlife watching. Small river towns provide cultural stops, while the byway offers a slower pace through a largely undeveloped river valley.

☐ 🔖 ♡ **Nicolet–Wolf River Scenic Byway:** A 145-mile loop through the Chequamegon–Nicolet National Forest, this drive highlights the Wolf River's whitewater rapids, dense pine and hardwood forests, and glacial lakes. Rustic campgrounds, waterfalls, and trailheads line the route. Visitors enjoy paddling, fishing, and hiking, with year-round opportunities for wildlife observation in the Northwoods.

☐ 🔖 ♡ **Wisconsin Lake Superior Scenic Byway:** A 70-mile drive along Highway 13 on the Bayfield Peninsula, it skirts beaches, forests, and cliffs on Lake Superior's south shore. Fishing villages, orchards, and views of the Apostle Islands provide cultural and scenic richness. The route connects shoreline recreation with heritage sites, making it a showcase of northern Wisconsin.

☐ 🔖 ♡ **Wisconsin River Scenic Byway:** Spanning 100 miles from Merrill to Necedah along Highways 107 and 78, this byway follows the Wisconsin River through forests, farmlands, and small towns. Visitors encounter hydroelectric dams, fishing spots, and trail systems that reflect the river's historic and economic importance. Scenic overlooks and public lands highlight its natural beauty.

WISCONSIN

National Natural Landmarks

 **Abraham's Woods:** Recognized as a National Natural Landmark, this small preserve holds a remnant of climax maple–basswood forest once widespread across southern Wisconsin. Undisturbed soils, mature hardwoods, and a diverse understory make it a living laboratory for studying forest succession, biodiversity, and the pre-settlement landscape.
GPS: 42.6828, -89.4839

 **Avoca River-Bottom Prairie:** Designated a National Natural Landmark for its size and integrity, Avoca Prairie is the largest intact tallgrass remnant in Wisconsin. Seasonal flooding enriches its soils, sustaining native grasses, rare wildflowers, migratory birds, and prairie wildlife. It reflects the natural richness of the once-vast Midwestern prairies.
GPS: 43.2008, -90.3047

 **Baraboo Range:** This billion-year-old quartzite uplift, honored as a National Natural Landmark, offers a dramatic record of ancient mountain building and erosion. Rugged ridges and cliffs shelter rare plants and unique communities, making it a prime site for geologic study and a refuge of ecological diversity within southern Wisconsin.
GPS: 43.4250, -89.6556

 **Bose Lake Hemlock Hardwoods:** Named a National Natural Landmark for its untouched eastern hemlock stands, this tract in Chequamegon–Nicolet National Forest preserves towering trees and rich wildlife habitat. It provides an invaluable glimpse into Wisconsin's pre-logging forests, maintaining both ecological integrity and scientific research value.
GPS: 45.9322, -88.9719

 **Cave of the Mounds:** Recognized as a National Natural Landmark, this living limestone cave displays spectacular stalactites, stalagmites, and flowstone formed over millions of years. Still actively developing, its formations and geology illustrate subterranean processes, making it one of the Midwest's most celebrated natural showcases.
GPS: 43.0181, -89.8161

 **Cedarburg Bog:** Designated a National Natural Landmark for its size and diversity, Cedarburg Bog is the largest intact bog in southeastern Wisconsin. Glacial lakes, sedge meadows, and tamarack swamp create a rich wetland mosaic that supports rare plants, wildlife, and long-term research on peatland ecology.
GPS: 43.3872, -88.0075

 **Chippewa River Bottoms:** Honored as a National Natural Landmark, this extensive forest contains the largest remaining tract of bottomland hardwoods in Wisconsin. Dominated by silver maple and cottonwood, it reflects the once-vast floodplain forests along glacial rivers, providing critical habitat for migratory birds and fish.
GPS: 44.4123, -91.9923

 **Chiwaukee Prairie:** This coastal remnant earned National Natural Landmark status as one of the finest wet-mesic prairies on Lake Michigan. Hosting over 400 plant species, including orchids and blazing stars, it preserves a rare community type and offers an outstanding example of pre-settlement prairie biodiversity.
GPS: 42.5550, -88.8167

 **Finnerud Forest Scientific Area:** Recognized as a National Natural Landmark for its conifer diversity, this tract safeguards old-growth jack pine, white pine, and spruce in northern Wisconsin. Minimal disturbance makes it a model for studying natural succession and forest ecology in a landscape shaped by fire and glaciation.
GPS: 45.8581, -89.7481

 **Flambeau River Hemlock-Hardwood Forest:** This forest, designated a National Natural Landmark, holds the state's largest old-growth conifer–hardwood tract. Eastern hemlock and sugar maple dominate, preserving the structure and character of pre-logging forests while providing critical habitat for wildlife in northern Wisconsin.
GPS: 45.7483, -90.7642

WISCONSIN

 ☐ 🔖 ♡ **Kakagon Sloughs:** Recognized as a National Natural Landmark for its pristine wetland ecosystem, Kakagon Sloughs near Lake Superior preserve wild rice beds, aquatic vegetation, and vital fish spawning grounds. The marshes sustain migratory birds and waterfowl while reflecting centuries of ecological and cultural importance to the Ojibwe people.
GPS: 46.6622, -90.7411

 ☐ 🔖 ♡ **Kickapoo River Natural Area:** This Driftless Area site, designated a National Natural Landmark, showcases steep sandstone bluffs, meandering streams, and diverse plant communities. Shaped by erosion rather than glaciation, it offers a window into unique geology and a haven for wildlife in southwestern Wisconsin.
GPS: 43.8981, -90.4575

 ☐ 🔖 ♡ **Moquah Barrens Research Natural Area:** Honored as a National Natural Landmark, this tract within Chequamegon National Forest preserves rare pine barrens and scrub oak savannas. The fire-dependent ecosystem supports sharp-tailed grouse, rare butterflies, and prairie flora, offering invaluable research opportunities on restoration and management.
GPS: 46.6264, -91.2500

 ☐ 🔖 ♡ **Point Beach Ridges:** This site earned National Natural Landmark status for its striking series of beach ridges and swales formed by fluctuating levels of Lake Michigan. The alternating sandy rises and wet depressions host diverse habitats, including rare dune and wetland plants.
GPS: 44.2136, -87.5153

 ☐ 🔖 ♡ **Spruce Lake Bog:** As one of Wisconsin's best-preserved bog ecosystems, this National Natural Landmark includes floating mats of sphagnum moss, black spruce, and Labrador tea. Its acidic, nutrient-poor environment supports rare northern plants and insects, serving as an excellent example of bog succession and ecology.
GPS: 43.6706, -88.2011

 ☐ 🔖 ♡ **Summerton Bog:** This botanically rich wetland, designated a National Natural Landmark, harbors orchids, pitcher plants, and glacial relicts within its intact bog ecosystem. Amphibians and wetland birds thrive in its acidic pools, making it an outstanding site for both biodiversity and long-term ecological study.
GPS: 43.7508, -89.5231

 ☐ 🔖 ♡ **The Ridges Sanctuary:** Designated a National Natural Landmark for its unique ridge-and-swale complex, this Door County preserve protects boreal forests, wetlands, and one of the Midwest's richest orchid populations. The sequence of parallel ridges formed by Lake Michigan waves provides both scenic beauty and ecological diversity.
GPS: 45.0728, -87.1186

 ☐ 🔖 ♡ **Wyalusing Hardwood Forest:** Recognized as a National Natural Landmark for its old-growth qualities, this forest lies near the confluence of the Wisconsin and Mississippi rivers. Deep valleys, mesic hardwoods, and ancient trees support diverse wildlife, offering one of the finest surviving examples of presettlement forest.
GPS: 42.9797, -91.1086

Wyoming's legendary landscapes span towering mountain ranges, vast high plains, dramatic geysers, and deep canyons. With its inspiring array of state parks, sprawling national forests, world-renowned national parks, and iconic natural landmarks, Wyoming promises boundless adventure and awe.

Peak Season
June–September is Wyoming's peak season, offering warm days, cool nights, and full access to national parks and mountain trails. Summer is ideal for hiking, wildlife viewing, and scenic drives across open landscapes.

Offseason Months
November–April is the offseason, with snow, cold temperatures, and limited access to many high-elevation areas. Winter, however, is peak for skiing, snowmobiling, and serene park exploration.

Scenery & Nature Timing
Spring brings thawing rivers and wildlife migrations. Summer highlights alpine meadows, lakes, and open trails. Fall glows with golden aspens and rutting elk, while winter transforms mountains and geysers under blankets of snow.

Special
Wyoming features Yellowstone's geysers and hot springs, the peaks of Grand Teton National Park, and the vast plains of the Wind River Range. Glacial valleys, geothermal wonders, and vivid night skies reveal its untamed natural beauty.

WYOMING

State Parks

☐ 🔖 ♡ **Ayres Natural Bridge Park:** Located west of Douglas in Converse County, this free county-managed park features one of the few natural bridges in the U.S. with a stream running beneath it. Once a landmark for Oregon Trail travelers, it offers picnic areas, trails, fishing, and camping. Though not a state park, it's a scenic hidden gem combining geology, history, and relaxation along LaPrele Creek.

☐ 🔖 ♡ **Bear River State Park:** Located near Evanston, this park is a convenient stop off I-80, featuring scenic trails along the Bear River. It's home to captive herds of bison and elk, and offers picnic areas, wildlife viewing, and year-round recreation. Visitors can hike or bike the river trails and enjoy a peaceful introduction to Wyoming's natural beauty.

☐ 🔖 ♡ **Boysen State Park:** Situated on Boysen Reservoir in Hot Springs County, this park is a hub for fishing, boating, and camping. Surrounded by the Wind River Mountains and high desert terrain, it provides opportunities for hiking, birdwatching, and water recreation. Its vast shoreline makes it a favorite for families and outdoor enthusiasts seeking adventure.

☐ 🔖 ♡ **Buffalo Bill State Park:** Nestled along the Shoshone River near Cody, this park surrounds Buffalo Bill Reservoir, created by the historic Buffalo Bill Dam. Visitors enjoy camping, boating, and fishing while taking in panoramic views of nearby mountains. Trails and picnic areas offer chances to explore, and wildlife is frequently seen in this scenic setting.

☐ 🔖 ♡ **Curt Gowdy State Park:** Between Cheyenne and Laramie, this park is known for its extensive trail system, perfect for hiking, biking, and horseback riding. Crystal and North Crow reservoirs provide boating, fishing, and paddling opportunities. With granite outcrops, rolling hills, and well-designed facilities, it's one of Wyoming's most popular recreation destinations.

☐ 🔖 ♡ **Edness K. Wilkins State Park:** Just outside Casper, this park offers a peaceful retreat along the North Platte River. It features shaded picnic areas, easy walking trails, and access for fishing and birdwatching. Its cottonwood groves and riparian habitat support diverse wildlife, making it a quiet escape for day-use visitors and nature lovers.

☐ 🔖 ♡ **Glendo State Park:** Centered around Glendo Reservoir, this park is one of Wyoming's top spots for water recreation. Visitors enjoy boating, fishing, and swimming, along with miles of hiking and biking trails. With campgrounds, sandy beaches, and scenic overlooks, Glendo combines outdoor adventure with family-friendly amenities for year-round enjoyment.

☐ 🔖 ♡ **Guernsey State Park:** Located in Platte County, this park highlights Guernsey Reservoir and the Oregon Trail. It offers camping, boating, fishing, and swimming, plus historic CCC-built structures like stone buildings and walls. Trails and interpretive sites showcase both natural beauty and cultural heritage, making it a unique destination for history and recreation.

☐ 🔖 ♡ **Hawk Springs State Recreation Area:** South of Torrington, this small reservoir park is popular with anglers and birdwatchers. Visitors can fish for walleye and catfish, boat across calm waters, or camp at shaded sites. Its wetlands attract migratory birds, making it a quiet and scenic stop for wildlife observation and outdoor relaxation on the plains.

☐ 🔖 ♡ **Hot Springs State Park:** In Thermopolis, this park is renowned for its natural mineral hot springs and the State Bath House, where visitors can soak for free. The park features terraces of colorful mineral deposits, trails along the Bighorn River, and a herd of bison. It combines recreation, geology, and wellness in a striking landscape.

☐ 🔖 ♡ **Keyhole State Park:** Near Moorcroft and the Black Hills, this park surrounds Keyhole Reservoir, offering boating, swimming, and excellent fishing. Its campgrounds, trails, and picnic spots provide a peaceful setting with views of pine-covered hills. Wildlife like deer and bald eagles are common, making it a top spot for both recreation and relaxation.

☐ 🔖 ♡ **Legend Rock State Petroglyph Site:** Northwest of Thermopolis, this state-managed site preserves over 300 petroglyphs carved by Indigenous peoples over thousands of years. The sandstone cliff panels display intricate figures and symbols, offering a glimpse into ancient cultures of the region. Visitors explore interpretive trails and viewing areas that highlight the cultural and archaeological significance.

WYOMING

☐ 🔖 ♡ **Medicine Lodge Archaeological Site:** Near Hyattville in the Bighorn Mountains foothills, this park protects a sandstone cliff with over 10,000 years of human history preserved in petroglyphs and pictographs. Archaeological digs reveal layers of Indigenous habitation. Visitors enjoy shaded campgrounds, trails, and interpretive exhibits that connect natural beauty with deep cultural heritage.

☐ 🔖 ♡ **Seminoe State Park:** North of Sinclair, this park spans the Seminoe Mountains and features Seminoe Reservoir, a destination for trophy trout fishing and boating. Rugged hills, sandy beaches, and wide open vistas create a dramatic setting. Campgrounds, trails, and access to the nearby Miracle Mile of the North Platte River add to its appeal.

☐ 🔖 ♡ **Sinks Canyon State Park:** Near Lander, this park showcases the Popo Agie River's mysterious "sinks," where the water vanishes into limestone caves before reemerging downstream. Visitors explore hiking trails through forests and canyons, fish in mountain streams, and enjoy rock climbing. The park blends geology, outdoor recreation, and stunning Wind River scenery.

National Parks

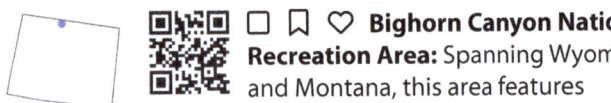 ☐ 🔖 ♡ **Bighorn Canyon National Recreation Area:** Spanning Wyoming and Montana, this area features towering cliffs, the winding Bighorn River, and breathtaking canyon views. Visitors can boat, fish, hike, and spot wildlife like bighorn sheep and eagles. Rugged terrain, dramatic geology, and sweeping vistas make it one of the region's most striking outdoor destinations.

 ☐ 🔖 ♡ **Devils Tower National Monument:** Rising dramatically above the prairie in northeast Wyoming, Devils Tower is a volcanic butte sacred to many Native tribes. Visitors can hike the Tower Trail, climb its sheer walls, or learn its cultural stories at the visitor center. Its striking form and spiritual significance make it an unforgettable landmark.

 ☐ 🔖 ♡ **Fort Laramie National Historic Site:** Once a vital 19th-century trading post and military outpost, Fort Laramie played a key role in the Oregon, California, and Mormon Trails. Today, visitors can tour preserved buildings, explore museum exhibits, and learn about frontier life, westward expansion, and Native American history at this historic site.

 ☐ 🔖 ♡ **Fossil Butte National Monument:** Near Kemmerer, this site preserves one of the world's richest fossil beds, offering a glimpse into a 50-million-year-old ecosystem. Visitors can view fossil exhibits of ancient fish, reptiles, and plants, hike scenic trails, and discover the prehistoric story of Fossil Lake amid rolling sagebrush hills.

 ☐ 🔖 ♡ **Grand Teton National Park:** Famed for the jagged peaks of the Teton Range, this park offers alpine lakes, wildlife-rich valleys, and wildflower meadows. Visitors enjoy hiking, climbing, boating, and scenic drives, with views of the Grand Teton towering above. It's a destination of rugged beauty and iconic Western landscapes.

 ☐ 🔖 ♡ **John D. Rockefeller Jr. Memorial Parkway:** This scenic 27-mile corridor links Grand Teton and Yellowstone National Parks. Following forested valleys and mountain ridges, the parkway offers access to hiking, camping, and wildlife viewing. It provides a seamless transition between two of America's most celebrated wilderness areas.

 ☐ 🔖 ♡ **Yellowstone National Park:** Established in 1872 as the world's first national park, Yellowstone spans Wyoming, Montana, and Idaho. It's known for geysers like Old Faithful, hot springs, and the Grand Canyon of the Yellowstone. Visitors explore its vast trails, abundant wildlife, and geothermal wonders in an unparalleled natural setting.

WYOMING

State & National Forests

☐ ▢ ♡ **Ashley National Forest:** Spanning 1.38 million acres in Utah and southwestern Wyoming, this forest includes part of Flaming Gorge National Recreation Area. Its Wyoming section in Sweetwater County features high plateaus, alpine lakes, and rugged canyons. Visitors enjoy hiking, fishing, boating, and wildlife viewing, with opportunities to spot elk, bighorn sheep, and raptors.

☐ ▢ ♡ **Bighorn National Forest:** Covering 1.11 million acres in north-central Wyoming, the Bighorns are known for glacier-carved valleys, alpine meadows, and forested mountains. The forest includes the Cloud Peak Wilderness and 1,200 miles of trails. Visitors can hike, camp, fish trout-filled streams, or drive scenic byways while spotting moose, elk, and deer.

☐ ▢ ♡ **Black Hills National Forest:** Encompassing 1.2 million acres across South Dakota and northeastern Wyoming, this forest features pine-covered hills, granite spires, and mixed grasslands. The Wyoming portion offers camping, hiking, rock climbing, and winter sports. Wildlife ranges from elk to bald eagles, making it a diverse outdoor destination with striking scenery.

☐ ▢ ♡ **Bridger–Teton National Forest:** At 3.4 million acres, this is one of the largest national forests in the U.S., located in western Wyoming adjacent to Yellowstone and Grand Teton. It protects alpine valleys, glacial lakes, and 1.2 million acres of wilderness. With over 3,000 miles of trails, visitors enjoy hiking, climbing, skiing, fishing, and abundant wildlife.

☐ ▢ ♡ **Caribou–Targhee National Forest:** Spanning 2.63 million acres in Idaho, Utah, and Wyoming, this forest borders Yellowstone and Grand Teton. The Wyoming portion protects montane pine forests and habitats for moose, elk, and wolves. Visitors can hike, fish, camp, and take in dramatic views of the Teton Range, with easy access to nearby national parks.

☐ ▢ ♡ **Medicine Bow–Routt National Forest:** Covering 2.22 million acres in Wyoming and Colorado, this forest includes the Snowy Range and Thunder Basin National Grassland. Its Wyoming lands feature alpine lakes, granite peaks, and dense conifer forests. Popular activities include hiking, skiing, camping, and fishing, with rich wildlife ranging from marmots to moose.

☐ ▢ ♡ **Shoshone National Forest:** The nation's first national forest, established in 1891, Shoshone spans 2.47 million acres in northwestern Wyoming. Home to rugged peaks, glaciers, and eight wilderness areas, it offers over 500 lakes and extensive trails. Visitors enjoy camping, fishing, climbing, and exploring scenic drives like the Beartooth and Chief Joseph highways.

☐ ▢ ♡ **Uinta–Wasatch–Cache National Forest:** While mostly in Utah, this forest extends into Wyoming's southwest corner. It conserves alpine meadows, subalpine forests, and mountain streams, supporting diverse wildlife. Visitors can hike, bike, fish, and camp in a less-traveled setting. Its Wyoming portion is small but offers access to scenic high-country terrain.

National Grasslands

☐ ▢ ♡ **Thunder Basin National Grassland:** Located in northeastern Wyoming between the Black Hills and Bighorn Mountains, this 547,000-acre grassland showcases rolling prairies, sagebrush steppe, and rugged badlands. It supports elk, pronghorn, raptors, and sage-grouse, while also providing grazing and energy resources. Visitors enjoy solitude, birding, and scenic drives under vast open skies.

WYOMING

National Scenic Byways & All-American Roads

☐ ▯ ♡ **Beartooth Highway:** This 68-mile route climbs above 10,000 feet between Red Lodge, Montana, and Yellowstone's northeast entrance. Known for alpine tundra, wildflower meadows, and glacier-carved lakes, it showcases dramatic mountain scenery. Sweeping switchbacks and high plateaus make it one of the most spectacular drives in North America.

☐ ▯ ♡ **Big Horn Scenic Byway:** Crossing the Bighorn Mountains on US 14 between Shell and Dayton, this drive features deep canyons, alpine meadows, and panoramic overlooks. Highlights include Shell Falls and access to the Cloud Peak Wilderness. Visitors experience striking geology, diverse forests, and abundant wildlife in north-central Wyoming.

☐ ▯ ♡ **Bridger Valley Historic Byway:** This 20-mile loop in southwestern Wyoming follows paths of the Oregon, California, and Mormon Trails. Passing through Fort Bridger and small ranching towns, it interprets the westward migration. Historic trail ruts, frontier structures, and interpretive stops reveal the daily lives of emigrants and early settlers.

☐ ▯ ♡ **Buffalo Bill Cody Scenic Byway:** Extending west from Cody through Shoshone Canyon and the Absaroka Mountains to Yellowstone's east entrance, this byway honors Buffalo Bill's legacy. Travelers encounter dramatic cliffs, rushing rivers, and historic lodges built for early park visitors. Wildlife sightings often include bighorn sheep, elk, and bears.

☐ ▯ ♡ **Cheyenne Frontier Days Historic Trails Byway:** Located around Cheyenne, this route highlights the area's western heritage and links to the world-famous rodeo. It features the historic Union Pacific Depot, rodeo grounds, and trail corridors once used by pioneers. Interpretive stops connect visitors to cowboy culture and Wyoming's frontier traditions.

☐ ▯ ♡ **Cloud Peak Skyway:** Traversing US 16 between Ten Sleep and Buffalo, this byway climbs into the Bighorn Mountains, offering views of alpine lakes, high meadows, and rugged granite peaks. Named for 13,167-foot Cloud Peak, it provides access to wilderness trailheads, wildlife viewing, and striking vistas of north-central Wyoming's high country.

☐ ▯ ♡ **Medicine Wheel Passage:** Following US 14A over the northern Bighorn Mountains, this route provides access to the sacred Medicine Wheel National Historic Landmark. The drive features alpine tundra, broad valleys, and sweeping overlooks stretching to the Big Horn Basin and Pryor Mountains. It blends Native heritage with high-elevation scenery.

☐ ▯ ♡ **Snowy Range Scenic Byway:** Crossing the Medicine Bow Mountains on Highway 130 west of Laramie, this route passes crystalline lakes, subalpine forests, and jagged granite peaks. At over 10,000 feet, it offers dramatic views of Medicine Bow Peak. Summer visitors enjoy hiking, fishing, and wildflowers in this high-alpine landscape.

State Scenic Byways

☐ ▯ ♡ **Black Hills Scenic Byway:** Traversing northeastern Wyoming along Highway 85 near Sundance, this byway showcases ponderosa pine forests, open grasslands, and rugged outcrops of the western Black Hills. It highlights the transition from prairie to forest and provides access to recreation areas, hiking trails, and wildlife viewing in a quiet corner of the state.

☐ ▯ ♡ **Bridger Scenic Byway:** Running south from Interstate 80 near Fort Bridger, this route climbs into the Uinta Mountains and scenic high country of southwestern Wyoming. It passes forested slopes, alpine meadows, and rushing streams. Visitors encounter historic sites tied to trappers and pioneers while enjoying panoramic views of mountain landscapes.

☐ ▯ ♡ **Flaming Gorge–Green River Basin Scenic Byway:** Beginning in Green River, this byway travels south through high desert plateaus and the Flaming Gorge region. It showcases colorful cliffs, deep canyons, and overlooks of the Green River. Interpretive pullouts reveal geology, paleontology, and history, while recreational access includes fishing, boating, and camping.

☐ ▯ ♡ **Oregon Trail Historic Byway:** Following Highway 26 in central Wyoming, this route traces one of the most storied pioneer paths. Travelers see original wagon ruts, historic markers, and interpretive sites that tell the story of emigrants heading west. Scenic river valleys and wide-open plains combine natural beauty with rich cultural heritage.

WYOMING

☐ 🔖 ♡ **Red Gulch–Alkali Scenic Backway:** Near Greybull, this gravel route offers striking views of red sandstone badlands and arid basins. The highlight is the Red Gulch Dinosaur Tracksite, where visitors can walk among 167-million-year-old fossilized footprints. The drive combines paleontology, rugged scenery, and off-the-beaten-path adventure.

☐ 🔖 ♡ **Star Valley Scenic Byway:** Running along US 89 through western Wyoming near the Idaho border, this byway winds through lush valleys framed by the Salt River and Wyoming ranges. Small farming communities, historic sites, and access to fishing and hiking make it both a cultural and natural showcase of this picturesque valley corridor.

National Natural Landmarks

 ☐ 🔖 ♡ **Como Bluff:** Famous worldwide for its late Jurassic fossil beds, Como Bluff was central to the 19th-century "Bone Wars" and helped establish North America's dinosaur record. Species like Allosaurus and Diplodocus were first uncovered here, making it a cornerstone of paleontology and a National Natural Landmark of global scientific importance.
GPS: 41.8814, -106.0762

 ☐ 🔖 ♡ **The Big Hollow:** Recognized as one of the largest wind-eroded deflation basins in North America, The Big Hollow spans thousands of acres in the Laramie Basin. Persistent Ice Age winds scoured away sediments, leaving a vast depression that illustrates large-scale aeolian processes in a cold desert environment rarely seen elsewhere.
GPS: 41.3132, -105.7213

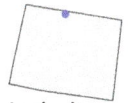 ☐ 🔖 ♡ **Crooked Creek Natural Area:** This fossil-rich site preserves rare Early Cretaceous vertebrate remains, including some of the continent's oldest known mammals. The exposures provide a unique window into ecosystems over 100 million years old, offering researchers invaluable evidence of early mammalian evolution alongside dinosaurs.
GPS: 44.958524, -108.291169 (approximate)

 ☐ 🔖 ♡ **Two Ocean Pass:** A hydrologic wonder on the Continental Divide, Two Ocean Pass marks the point where North Two Ocean Creek splits into two channels—Pacific Creek and Atlantic Creek—sending water to both oceans. This "parting of the waters" is one of the world's rarest natural drainage phenomena.
GPS: 44.0429, -110.1750

 ☐ 🔖 ♡ **Red Canyon:** Designated for both geological and cultural significance, Red Canyon showcases vivid Triassic redbeds carved into cliffs and slopes, along with layers of sandstone, limestone, and shale. Archaeological discoveries reveal human occupation dating back 10,000 years, blending geologic history with ancient human heritage.
GPS: 42.6721, -108.6582

 ☐ 🔖 ♡ **Sand Creek:** This dramatic site along the Wyoming–Colorado border is renowned for textbook examples of cross-bedded sandstone and topple blocks, where massive slabs of rock have shifted or overturned. It provides an exceptional natural laboratory for studying sedimentary processes and slope instability in rugged terrain.
GPS: 40.9969, -105.7706

About the Publisher

Roamwell Press is an independent travel and heritage publisher dedicated to inspiring exploration of The World's natural and cultural landscapes. From national parks and forests to small-town landmarks and scenic byways, our mission is to help readers experience the wonder of every place—responsibly, curiously, and with respect for the land and its stories.

Visit us online at www.roamwellpress.com For updates, digital resources, and information on future editions of The Roamer's Guide series.

Corrections and Errata

We strive for accuracy in every edition. If you discover an error, omission, or change in park information (such as hours, closures, or coordinates), please let us know.

Submit corrections at www.roamwellpress.com or email roamwellpress@gmail.com with the subject line Errata Submission.

Each verified correction will be reviewed for inclusion in subsequent printings and digital updates.

Copyright & Edition Information

© 2025 Roamwell Press. All rights reserved.
No part of this publication may be reproduced or transmitted in any form or by any means—electronic, mechanical, photocopying, or otherwise—without prior written permission from the publisher.

Printed in the United States of America.

First Edition. ISBN: 979-8-218-78084-5

Connect With Us

Follow Roamwell Press on social media for news, destination highlights, and behind-the-scenes updates at https://www.facebook.com/RoamwellPress/

All inquiries: roamwellpress@gmail.com

A Note to Readers

Every effort has been made to ensure the information contained in this guide is accurate as of the publication date. However, park conditions, operating hours, and designations may change. Always confirm details with official park or forest agencies before traveling. Your feedback helps keep this guide accurate and valuable for future explorers—thank you.

www.ingramcontent.com/pod-product-compliance
Lightning Source LLC
Chambersburg PA
CBHW080539030426
42337CB00024B/4795